AMERICAN
ORNITHOLOGICAL BIBLIOGRAPHY

Introduction by
Keir B. Sterling

ARNO PRESS
A New York Times Company
New York, N. Y. • 1974

Reprint Edition 1974 by Arno Press Inc.

Reprinted from a copy in the University
of Illinois Library

NATURAL SCIENCES IN AMERICA
ISBN for complete set: 0-405-05700-8
See last pages of this volume for titles.

Manufactured in the United States of America

Library of Congress Cataloging in Publication Data

Coues, Elliott, 1842-1899.
    American ornithological bibliography.

    (Natural sciences in America)
    Consists of the 2d and 3d installments of American
ornithological bibliography reprinted from the 1870-80
ed. issued by the U. S. Govt. Print. Off.
    Originally published in the U. S. Geological and
Geographical Survey of the Territories. Bulletin,
v. 5, 2, p. 239-330 and no. 4, p. 521-1066.
    1. Birds--North America--Bibliography. I. Title.
II. Series.
Z5334.N65C68 1974   016.5982'973   73-17794
ISBN 0-405-05704-0

CONTENTS

INTRODUCTION

Elliott Coues' *Ornithological Bibliography* represents the most outstanding work of its kind undertaken during the nineteenth century. Twentieth century American bibliographers have consistently acknowledged their debt to this singularly perceptive and able physician-naturalist, whom many consider to have been equalled in his time only by Audubon and Baird. His accomplishments are even more outstanding when one considers that he completed this work while shuttling from one army post to another as an assistant surgeon.

Born in 1842, Coues received his A.B. (1861) and M.D. (1863) from Columbian College in Washington, D. C., now George Washington University. He also received the honorary degrees of M.A. (1862) and Ph.D. (1869) from his alma mater. During his eighteen-year military career Coues managed to write a host of papers, notes, reviews and monographs on various aspects of ornithology and mammalogy, chiefly centering upon the United States and Canada. These numbered several hundred in all, and a selection of his major works and shorter pieces is included elsewhere in this *Natural Sciences in America* series.

While fulfilling his military duties, Coues found time to make extensive collections of animal specimens. He also did considerable research as surgeon and naturalist for the U.S. Northern Boundary Commission (1873-1876) and as secretary naturalist to the United States Geological and Geographical Survey of the Territories under Dr. Ferdinand V. Hayden (1876-1880). He served for a time as professor of anatomy at his alma mater both during and after his military career (1877-1886). Though he made an impressive start upon a projected multi-volumed study of North American mammals, and was responsible for other significant writings in this field between 1868 and 1877, his major contributions lay in the field of ornithology.

Beginning with his *Key to North American Birds* (1872), which went through four other editions, his forceful, literate, and eminently readable style made classics of *Birds of the Northwest* (1874) and the *Birds of the Colorado Valley* (1878). A founder of the American Ornithologists Union (1883), he served as its president and also as associate editor of its journal, *The Auk* (1884-1888), as he had previously done for its predecessor publication, the *Bulletin of the Nuttall Ornithological Club* (1876-1883). In the late 1890's, he founded and for a time edited a minor ornithological periodical, *The Osprey*. He was a member of the committee which prepared the A.O.U.'s first *Check List of American Birds* (1886) and the nomenclatural code this publication introduced.

The matter of nomenclature brought out a strong trait in Coues which was to have a considerable effect upon his career: a penchant for quarrelling. He at first resisted the tendency begun by Baird toward using "so many needless and burdensome generic names," and avoided them in the first edition of his *Key*. He soon fell in, however, with the "prevailing custom," as his sometime collaborator, J. A. Allen, later revealed, and thereafter engaged in fierce debates with colleagues on major and minor questions of nomenclature.

His pugnaciousness was manifested in the decade-long "Sparrow War" which he carried on with Thomas Mayo Brewer (1814-1880), a Boston physician and journalist who also enjoyed a considerable reputation as an ornithologist. Coues became convinced by 1874 that the introduction of the English Sparrow in the 1850's and later had been a zoological disaster. Brewer and others were equally certain that Coues was irresponsibly maligning an important exotic addition to our fauna. By the time of his death, Coues' judgement had been sustained, but the contest left permanent scars upon his reputation, both professionally and as a person.

His resignation from the Army came in 1881, when he realized that continued service would interfere with his scientific interests. From then on, he maintained an active ornithological career, and moved into other areas as well. Between 1884 and 1891, he served as editor for *The Century Dictionary,* with responsibility for some forty thousand definitions in the fields of general zoology, biology, and comparative anatomy. About this time, in an unexpected departure from his previous interests, Coues became a student of psychical research and theosophy, which ended when he failed to become president of the American Section of the Theosophical Society and denounced the organization as "Mme. Blavatsky's famous hoax."

Fortunately for the cause of history and science, he returned, in his final decade, to edit fifteen volumes of various journals, diaries, and other materials. All of the manuscripts dealt with early travel in the American west, and he shepherded them through the publication process. Among others, he took Biddle's famous *History of the Expedition of Lewis and Clark,* and edited it, adding much valuable data concerning wildlife observed and specimens brought back by the expedition. Coues did take some unwarranted liberties with the original text, but the venture is still considered an important piece of work.

Coues was nothing if not grandiose in his concepts of the scientific work he wished to accomplish. One of his major projects was no less than a "Universal Bibliography of Ornithology," intended to cover the entire world literature on the subject. This plan stemmed from Coues' consuming passion for compilation. He was an indefatigable list maker, a kind of scientific housekeeper, determined to bring order out of the ferment of recent discoveries, and saw this as one important tool in the process.

For several years in the late 1870's, he devoted his efforts to the "Universal Bibliography," but illness intervened. In 1880, Coues later related,

". . . my machinery for doing the work broke down, and I found myself amidst the debris of the great plan I had projected or partially accomplished, with many thousand manuscript titles on hand and no prospect of their ever seeing the light . . . I think I never did anything else in my life which brought me such hearty praise 'in mouths of widest censure' — immediate and almost universal recognition, at home and abroad, from ornithologists who knew that bibliography was a necessary nuisance and a horrible drudgery that no mere drudge could perform. It takes a sort of inspired idiot to be a good bibliographer, and his inspiration is as dangerous a gift as the appetite of the gambler or dipsomaniac — it grows with what it feeds upon, and finally possesses its victim like any other invincible vice. Perhaps it was lucky for me that I was forcibly divorced from my bibliographical mania; at any rate years have cured me of the habit, and I shall never again be spellbound in that way."

He finally published only the three installments dealing with American ornithology (all reprinted in this series), the first of which had appeared as an appendix to the *Birds of the Colorado Valley,* and a fourth installment having to do with British Birds. Coues remarked in 1897 that he regarded the North American portion of the work as incomplete but also the most important:

> "This raises another question, which may be put in this way: Where is the man who will undertake to bring my North American Bibliography up-to-date? . . . Among the requisite qualifications may be reckoned more zeal than discretion, youth, health, strength, staying power, unlimited time at command, and access to the foci of ornithological literature in some large eastern city. All my material, both published, shall be at the service of any such individual, with such opportunities, and any such appetite for bibliographical immortality; I will even throw my blessing into the bargain. What do I hear in answer to this advertisement: Wanted — A competent bibliographer of North American ornithology?"

No one came forward in the remaining two years of Coues' life. No attempt at a project of this scope has been made in the years since, and in this century most bibliographies have been confined to the contents of single libraries or collections.

The second and third installments of the *Ornithological Bibliography* reprinted in this volume originally appeared in 1879 and 1880. The second listed faunal works and papers having to do with Latin America and the West Indies, the third included titles covering avian systematics and also publications dealing with "particular species, genera, or families." While Coues considered all three American installments as incomplete "published proof sheets," his work was highly accurate and remarkably complete for the period covered (late sixteenth century to the late 1870's), and the annotations he provided have proved invaluable to ornithologists and historians of science.

Coues' death at 57 in 1899 followed strenuous travels in the southwest in connection with one of his editing projects. Surprisingly, no full-length biography has yet been written, though one by Profs. Paul Russell Cutright and Michael Brodhead is in progress. Previously, the most satisfactory accounts have been the "Biographical Memoir of Elliott Coues" by J. A. Allen, in the *National Academy of Sciences Biographical Memoirs,* vol. IV (1909), 395-446, and Edgar Erskine Hume's very useful sketch in his *Ornithologists of the United States Army Medical Corps* (Baltimore, Johns Hopkins University Press, 1942), 52-89. Coues' role in late nineteenth century ornithology and early conservation efforts in this country are mentioned in Peter Mathiessen's well-written *Wildlife in America* (New York, Viking, 1959), 152-181. For a perceptive view of Coues' personality as an ornithologist, see Michael Brodhead's "Elliott Coues and the Sparrow War," *New England Quarterly* (September, 1971), 420-432.

Essentially, it was fortunate both for Coues and for the American science of ornithology that a man of his talents came along exactly at the time he did. His insatiable curiosity, his peculiar ability to lavish thousands of hours on projects other men would consider beyond them, and his real desire to be of service to his fellow ornithologists produced in the end a monument to scientific bibliography which has not since been superseded.

January, 1974   Keir B. Sterling
                                 Tarrytown, N. Y.

Art. XVII.—Second Instalment of American Ornithological Bibliography.

Art. XVII.—Second Instalment of American Ornithological Bibliography.

By Dr. Elliott Coues, U. S. A.

Part First of the "Birds of the Colorado Valley", etc., contains a Bibliographical Appendix (pp. 567–784, or [1]–[218]), which consists of a "List of Faunal Publications relating to North American Ornithology", being the first instalment of a Universal Bibliography of Ornithology upon which the author of that work is still engaged.

The present article may be considered to continue the subject, as it gives the titles of "Faunal Publications" relating to the Ornithology of the rest of America.

The former piece of work has been received with great favor by ornithologists, whose kind expressions of interest assure him that his bibliographical material is welcome.

This further instalment of the work is constructed upon the same principles as the other, and with the same great pains to secure good results. Though of course much less extensive, containing only about 700 titles, it is scarcely less complete, and no less accurate, than the North American portion. The compiler takes this occasion to renew the request that those who are interested in the matter will point out defects which may be detected in any portion of the work now printed.

To those who may not be informed of the general plan of the whole Bibliography, he may explain that it is modelled after the "Zoological Record", and that the titles given in this second instalment are only those which an editor of the "Record" would have brought under the head of "Neotropical Region"—all general and miscellaneous works, and all those upon particular species, genera, or families of birds, being excluded.

1648. MARCGRAVE, G. Historia Natvralis | Brasiliae, | Auspicio et Beneficio | Illustriss. I. Mavritii Com. Nassav | illivs Provincjæ et Maris summi Praefecti Adornata | In qua | Non tantum Plantæ et Animalia, sed et In- | digenarum morbi, ingenia et mores describuntur et | Iconibus supra quingentas illustrantur. | Lvgdvn. Batavorvm, | Apud Franciscum Hackium, et | Amstelodami, | Apud Lud. Elzevirium. 1648. | [*Or*,]

Gulielmi Pisonis, M. D. | Lugduno-Batavi, | De | Medicina Brasiliensi | Libri Qvatvor: | I. De Aëre, Aquis, & Locis. | II. De Morbis Endemiis. | III. De Venenatis & Antidotis. | IV. De Facultatibus Simplicium. | Et | GeorgI MarcgravI de Liebstad, | Misnici Germani, | Historiæ Rervm Na-

1648. MARCGRAVE, G.—Continued.

tvralivm | Brasiliæ, | Libri Octo : | Quorum | Tres priores agunt de Plantis. | Quartus de Piscibus. | Quintus de Avibus. | Sextus de Quadrupedibus & Serpentibus. | Septimus de Insectis. | Octavus de ipsa Regione, & illius Incolis. | Cvm | Appendice de Tapuyis, et Chilensibvs. | Ioannes De Laet, | Antwerpianus, | In ordinem digessit & Annotationes addidit, & varia ab Auctore | Omissa supplevit & illustravit. |

Above titles covering both Piso and Marcgrave; latter also separately subtitled in nearly identical words, omitting the Piso part of the title. 1 vol. folio. Engraved title to both, 1 l. ; plain title to both, 1 l. ; Piso to Prince William, 2 ll. ; Piso to the reader, 1 l. ; Piso's contents, 1 l. ; Piso's text, pp. 1–122; Piso's index, 1 l.—Marcgrave's subtitle, 1 l. ; Marcgrave's dedication, 1 l. ; De Laet to the reader, 1 l. ; Marcgrave's contents and errata, 1 l. ; Marcgrave's text, pp. 1–292; Appendix, p. 293; Index, ½ + 3 ll. Unnumbered cuts in text of both authors.

The *fifth* book of Marcgrave's part of this work treats of birds in fifteen chapters, as follows :—

Georgi Marcgravi Historiæ Naturalis Brasiliæ Liber Quintus. Qui agit de Avibus, in Quo sunt Icones quatuor supra quinquaginta, et Annotationes octo, pp. 190–220, Cap. I.–XV.—I, p. 190, Nhanduguacu, Iacana (fig.), variæ ejus species, Curicaca (fig.). II, p. 192, Tijepiranga (fig.), Iacapu, Iambu, Gallina africana (fig.), Guirangeima, Iupujuba (fig.), Sayacu, Ani (fig.), Guira guainumbi (fig.). III, p. 194, Jaguacati (fig.), Mitu (fig.), Mituporanga (fig.), Ibijau (2 figg.). IV, p. 196, Guainumbi variæ species (fig.). V, p. 198, Iacupema (fig.), Iacamacaij (fig.), Iacurutu (fig.), Soco (fig.), Matuitui (fig.). VI, p. 200, Iabiru (fig.), Iabiru guacu (fig.), Manucodiata. VII, p. 201, Guirapunga utraque (2 figg.), Guiraquerea (fig.), Jacamaciri (fig.), Cariama (fig.) VIII, p. 203, Guara (fig.), Urutaurana (fig.), Maguari, Guarauna (fig.), Ajaia, Picui pinima, Pica cureba, Tuidara, Guacuguacu, Tapera. IX, p. 205, Psittacorum majorum & minorum variæ species. Tui vulgo Perroquet. Araracanga (fig.), etc. X, p. 207, Ipecu (fig.), Urubu (fig.), Tamatia utraque (2 figg.), Guirajemoja (fig.), Gurraru nheengeta (fig.). XI, p. 209, Cocoi Ardeae species (fig.) ; alia species, Guiratinga, Ardeola (fig.), Iacarini, Guiratirica, Guiranheengatu. XII, p. 211, Curucui (fig.), Caracara (fig.), Tijeguacu (fig.), Teitei, Guiragiracu beraba (fig.), Guiracocreba, Guiraperea, Iapacani, Cabure, Andira aca. XIII, p. 213, Macucagua (fig.), Columbæ silvestris species, Anas sylvestris, Urubitinga (fig.), Mareca utraque, Tiieguacu paroara (fig.), Tangara utraque (fig.). XIV, p. 215, Anhima (fig.), Pitangua guacu (fig.), Atingacu camucu (fig.), Guira acangatara (fig.). XV, Matuitui (fig.), Aracari, Tucana, Anhinga (fig.), Ipecati apoa (fig.), Pullus gallinaceus monstrosus (quadrupes, fig.).

The figures are monstrous, reminding us of those of Gesner, for example, though many of the marked species are recognizable. The text, however, is minutely descriptive, and most of the species are identifiable.

This is a celebrated work, standing in much the same ornithological relation to South America that its virtual contemporary, Hernandez's, bears to Mexico. We have here the first description and primary basis of many species. Linnæus and other early species-makers cite Marcgrave freely, and he remains, in fact, quotable to-day. The reader will not fail to note that he has here the vernacular derivation of many names with which he is familiar in their quasi-Latin and even English rehabilitation, but the etymology of which would not necessarily be obvious to a classicist. Compare with the above the following, for example : *Nandou, Pyranga, Guira, Guiraca, Ani, Mitu, Mituporanga, Jacamar, Nacurutu, Jabiru, Cariama, Ajaja, Cœrcba, Maguari, Guarauna, Tapera, Aracanga, Ararauna, Urubu, Nengeta, Cocoi, Carasara, Urubitinga, Tangara, Tanagra, Pitangus, Aracari, Tucana, Toucan,* etc.

For an elaborate commentary on this work, see 1820 and 1824, LICHTENSTEIN, H.

1658. ROCHEFORT, C. DE. Histoire | naturelle et morale | des | Iles antilles | de l'Amerique. | Enrichie de plusieurs belles figures des Raretez les plus | considerables qui y sont décrites. | Avec vn Vocabulaire Caraïbe. | [Dessin.] | A Roterdam, | Chez Arnould Leers, | — | M. DC. LVIII. 1 vol. 8vo or sm. 4to. Eng. title, 8 prel. pp. incl. regular title, pp. 1–527, 6 ll. (contents).

Chapitre Quinziéme, pp. 147–167, a fig. on p. 152, and a page of figs. on p. 166. " Des oiseaux les plus considerables des Antilles ", des Fregates, des Fauves, des Aigrettes. etc., du Grand Gosier, des Poules d'eau, des Flammans (= *Platalea*), de l'Hirondelle, de plusieurs Oiseaux de terre, des Arras, des Canides, des Perroquets, des Perriques du tremble, du Passereau, de l'Aigle de l'Orinoco, du Mansreny, du Colibry.—This is the orig. ed.

1666. ROCHEFORT, C. DE. The History of the Caribby-Islands, viz. Barbades, [etc.] In two Books. The First containing the Natural the Second the Moral History, of these islands. Illustrated, [etc.] Rendered into English by John Davis of Kidwelly. London. 1666. 4to. pp. 3?6, 4 pll.
Not seen: title from Sabin's *Bibl. Amer.* Orig. ed. 1658, *q. v.*

1667. [STUBBES, DR. —.] Observations Made by a Curious and Learned Person, sailing from England, to the Caribe-Islands. < *Philos. Trans.*, ii, 1667, pp. 493–500.

1667. WARREN, G. Impartial Description of Surinam, . . . with a History of several strange Beasts, Birds, etc. 1667.
Not seen. [See beyond, ADDENDA, 1745.]

1668. STUBBES, DR. —. An Enlargement of the Observations, formerly publisht, Numb. 27, made and generously imparted by that Learn'd and Inquisitive Physitian, Dr. Stubbes. < *Philos. Trans.*, iii, 1668, pp. 699–709.
Allusions to a few birds.

1681. [ROCHEFORT, C. DE.] Histoire | Naturelle et Morale | des | Iles Antilles | de l'Amerique, | Enrichie d'un grand nombre de belles Figures en taille douce, | qui | representent au naturelles Places, & les Raretez les plus | considerables qui y sont décrites. | Avec un Vocabulaire Caraïbe. | Derniere Edition. | Reveuë & augmentée par l'Autheur d'un Recit de l'Estat present des | celebres Colonies de la Virginie, de Marie-Land, de la Caroline, du | nouveau Duché d'York, de Penn-Sylvania, & de la nouvelle An- | gleterre, situées dans l'Amerique septentrionale, & qui rele- | vent de la Couronne du Roy de la grand' Bretagne. | Tiré fidelement des memoires des habitans des mêmes Colonies, | en faveur de ceus, qui auroyent le dessein de s'y | transporter pour s'y établir. [Par César de Rochefort.] | [Vignette.] | A Rotterdam, | Chez Reinier Leers, | — | M. DC. LXXXI. 1 vol. Sm. 4to. Eng. title, plain title, both backed blank, and 16 more unpaged ll., pp. 1–583, and 13 unpaged pp.; then follow pp. 1–43, with a separate title, backed blank; many plates and other illustrations.
Orig. ed. 1658, *q. v.* Chap. XV, pp. 163–182, "Des oiseaus les plus considerables des Antilles"; cut on p. 168, and page full of cuts p. 182.

1682. NIEUHOF, J. Joan Nieuhofs Gedenkwaerdige Zee en Lantreize door de Voornaemste Landschappen van West en Oostindien. Amsterdam. 1682. Folio.
Not seen. "The second part, beginning at p. 29, contains a cut representing several birds and a bat, with text descriptive of these and numerous other Brazilian birds. The figures are very good, much better than Marcgrave's; the names are vernacular."—J. A. ALLEN, *in epist.* [See beyond, ADDENDA.]

1703. OLIVER, W. A Letter from Dr. William Oliver to the Publisher, giving his Remarks in a late Journey into Denmark and Holland. < *Philos. Trans.*, xxiii, 1703, pp. 1400–1410.
Contains an account of a curious bird seen in Amsterdam from "Carthagena in America", described as "Vultur Americanus minor Carthagenæ Corpore eleganti & plumis admodum Concinne variegatis".

1707-25. SLOANE, H. A | Voyage | To the Islands | Madera, Barbados, Nieves, S. Christophers | and | Jamaica, | with the | Natural History | of the | Herbs and Trees, Four-footed Beasts, Fishes, | Birds, Insects, Reptiles, &c. | Of the last of those Islands; | To which is prefix'd An | Introduction, | Wherein is an Account of the | Inhabitants, Air, Waters, Diseases, Trade, &c | of that Place, with some Relations concerning the Neigh- | bouring Continent, and Islands of America. | — | Illustrated with | The Figures of the Things describ'd, | which have not been heretofore engraved; | In large Copper-Plates as big as the Life. | — | By Hans Sloane, M. D. | Fellow of the College of Physicians and Secretary | of the Royal-Society. | — | In Two Volumes. Vol. I [II]. | — | Many shall run to and fro, and Knowledge shall be increased. Dan. xii. 4 | — | London: | Printed by B. M. for the Author, 1707 [1725]. 2 vols. Folio

1707–25. SLOANE, H.—Continued.

    Vol. I, 1707, 8 p. ll., pp. i–cliv, 1–264, pll. i–iv (i being a map), 1–156. Vol. II, 1725, 2 p. ll. (title and dedication), pp. i–xviii, 1–499, pll. v–xi, 157–274.

    There are some literal discrepancies in the titles of the two vols.: in the second the author appears as "Sir Hans Sloane, Bar^t.", and the last line is simply "Printed for the author. 1725."—Vol. II, Book VI, Part II, pp. 293–325, "Of the Birds of Jamaica", pll. 254–272.—Chap. I, Of Land Birds, 54 spp. Chap. II, Of Birds which Wade, or Frequent Watery Places, 17 spp. Chap. III, Of Water-Fowl, or such as are web-footed and Swim, 11 spp.; in all, 82 spp. The plates are very coarse and poor; some of them are as ludicrous as anything in Gesner, for example. The ornithology of this work has no intrinsic value, but derives some importance from the fact that here are the original descriptions of various birds upon which Linnæan species rest wholly or in part. Sloane's pages and plates were constantly cited by writers of the century, as Catesby, Edwards, Brisson, Linnæus, etc., and are sometimes referred to still.

1724. LABAT, —. Nouveau Voyage aux Iles de l'Amérique. 1724.

    Not seen: said to contain natural history illustrations. [See ADDENDA, beyond.]

1729. WAFER, L. A New | Voyage | and | Description | of the | Isthmus of America. | Giving an Account of the | Author's Abode there, | The Form and Make of the Country, the Coasts, | Hills, Rivers, &c. Woods, Soil, Weather, &c. Trees, | Fruit, Beasts, Birds, Fish, &c. | The Indian Inhabitants, their Features, Complexion, | &c. their Manners, Customs, Employments, | Marriages, Feasts, Hunting, Computation, | Language, &c. | With Remarkable Occurrences in the South-Sea and | elsewhere. | — | By Lionel Wafer. | — | The Third Edition. | — | To which are added, | The Natural History of those Parts, | By a Fellow of the Royal Society: | and | Davis's Expedition to the Gold Mines, in 1702. | Illustrated with several Copper-Plates. | — | London, | Printed for James and John Knapton, at the | Crown in St. Paul's Church-Yard. M DCC XXIX.

    Contained in vol. III of the series called "A Collection of Voyages", etc., 4 vols., London, 1729, being pp. 263–463 + 9, maps, plates.

    "The Birds, and Flying Insects", pp. 334–339, consists of an account of sundry species by the author.

    "An Additional Account of several Beasts, Birds, Fishes, Reptiles, &c, . . . Communicated by a Member of the Royal Society", Chap. II. Of the Birds, pp. 402–410. A formal account of no fewer than 118 spp., very curtly described under English names applied wholly at random.

1749. CONDAMINE, C. M. DE LA. Relation abrégée d'un Voyage fait dans l'intérieur de l'Amérique méridionale, depuis la Côte de la Mer du Sud, jusques aux Côtes du Brésil & de la Guiane, en descendant la rivière des Amazones. < *Mém. de l'Acad. Roy. des Sci. pour l'année* 1745, 1749, pp. 391–492, pll. viii, ix.

    Notes sur les oiseaux, pp. 471–474.

1750. HUGHES, G. The | Natural History | of | Barbados. | — | In Ten Books. | — | By the Reverend | Mr. Griffith Hughes, A. M. | Rector of St. Lucy's Parish, in the said Island, and F. R. S. | — | [Vignette.] | — | London: | Printed for the Author; | And sold by most Booksellers in Great Britain and Ireland. MDCCL. 1 vol. Folio. 8 p. ll. (title, dedication, subscribers, etc.), pp. i–viii (preface, errata), 1–314, + 11 ll. (explanatory notes, index, addenda), pll. 1–29, folded map, and head- and tail-pieces.

    Book III, pp. 69–79, Of Birds. A few species are very lightly treated, though it is stated that "An Inspection into the Structure, Nature and Qualities of every Species will convince us, that every Individual is stamped with Marks of infinite Wisdom".

1756. BROWNE, PATRICK. The | Civil and Natural | History | of | Jamaica. | In Three Parts. | Containing, | I. An accurate Description of that Island, its Situation and Soil; | with a brief Account of its former and present State, Government, | Revenues, Produce, and Trade. | II. A History of the natural Productions, including the various Sorts | of native Fossils; perfect and imperfect Vegetables; Quadrupedes, | Birds, Fishes, Reptiles and Insects; with their Properties and Uses | in Mechanics, Diet, and Physic. | III. An Account of the Nature of Climates in General, and their | different Effects upon the human Body; with a Detail of the | Diseases arising from this Source, particularly within the Tropics. | In Three Dissertations. | The Whole illustrated with

1756. BROWNE, PATRICK.—Continued.

Fifty Copper-Plates: | In which the most curious Productions are represented of the natural Size, and | delineated immediately from the Objects. | — | By Patrick Browne, M. D. | — | London: | Printed for the Author; and sold by T. Osborne, and J. Shipton, | in Gray's-Inn. MDCCLVI. 1 vol. Folio. 4 p. ll. (two titles, dedication, and list of subscribers), pp. v–viii (preface), 1–503, + 1 l., pl. i, map, pll. 1–49.

Chap. IV, Of Birds, pp. 466–483, none of the plates. § 1. Of the smaller frugivorous and granivorous birds with short and pointed conic bills, etc.: *Hirundo* 4, *Loxia* 1, *Fringilla* 5, *Motacilla* 1. § 2. Of the smaller granivorous and vermivorous birds with conic and moderately slender lengthened bills, etc.: *Columba* 10, *Teta* 1, *Turdus* 2. § 3. Of birds of the larger granivorous tribe with thick, conic, and moderately arched bills, proportioned limbs, and divided claws: *Pavo* 1, *Crax* 1, *Meleagris* 1, *Gallus* 4, *Tetrao* 1. § 4. Of birds that have strong crooked bills and open claws, whose digits are generally furnished with strong arched nails: *Falco* 3, *Vultur* 1, *Psittacus* 11, *Strix* 2. § 5. Of birds that have large straight bills, of a length nearly equal to the middle digits, and moderately flatted above: *Corvus* 1, *Crotophagus* 1, *Picus* 1, *Baristus* 1. § 6. Of birds that have long slender bills that arch and taper very moderately to the top: *Polytmus* 4, *Todus* 1, *Oriolus* 1, *Cuculus* 1, *Merops* 1, *Xanthornus* 2. § 7. Of birds whose bills are of a length with or longer than the middle digits, having long legs, partly naked thighs, and divided claws, and living chiefly in watery places, though they do not swim: *Tringa* 2, *Numenius* 1, *Ardea* 7. § 8. Of water-fowls, or birds that pass a considerable part of their time upon the water: *Fulica* 4, *Colymbus* 1, *Phœnicopterus* 1, *Pelecanus* 1, *Cygnus* 2, *Anas* 6, *Anœthetus* 2, *Larus* 4, *Sterna* 3, *Alcyon* 2. Under such classification the number of species indicated by the figures given are treated, with numbered generic, but no specific names, with Latin diagnoses, some little synonymy, both Latin and vernacular, and miscellaneous observations. It was a considerable ornithological treatise in its time, freely cited by Brisson, Linnæus, Edwards, and others; and some of these descriptions, like Sloane's, are the bases of species.—This is the orig. ed.; there is another, 1789.

1769. [BANCROFT, E.] An | Essay | on the | Natural History | of | Guiana, | In South America. | Containing | A Description of many Curious Productions | in the Animal and Vegitable Systems | of that Country. | Together with an Account of | The Religion, Manners, and Customs | of several Tribes of its Indian Inhabitants. | Insterspersed with | A Variety of Literary and Medical Observations. | In Several Letters | from | A Gentleman of the Medical Faculty [E. Bancroft], | During his Residence in that Country. | — | —Ad res pulcherrimas ex tenebris ad lucem erutas alieno | labore deducimur. | Seneca, De brevitate vitæ, cap. xiv. | — | London, | Printed for T. Becket and P. A. De Hondt | in the Strand. MDCCLXIX. 1 vol. 16mo. Frontisp. (2-headed snake), 2 p. ll. (title and dedication), pp. i–iv, 1–402, + 3 ll. (contents and advts.).

This anonymous work, by Dr. E. Bancroft, contains, pp. 152–185, "the Description of Birds inhabiting the aerial regions of Guiana, which, for the variety, vivacity and lustre of colours that adorn their plumage, are no where excelled".—There is a German version of same date.

1769. BANCROFT, E. Naturgeschichte | von | Guiana | in | Süd-Amerika. | worinn | von der natürlichen Beschaffenheit und den vor- | nehmsten Naturproducten des Landes, ingleichen der Re- | ligion, Sitten und Gebräuchen verschiedener Stämme | der wilden Landes-Einwohner, Nachricht | ertheilet wird. | — | In vier Briefen. | Von | Eduard Bancroft, Esq. | — | Aus dem Englischen. | — | [Quotation from Seneca.] | — | Frankfurt und Leipzig, | bey J. Dodsley und Compagnie, 1769. 1 vol. 16mo. Frontispiece (2-headed snake), pp. i–x, 1 l., pp. 1–248, 1 l.

Vögel, pp. 91–112. In dieser Ausgabe, die Arten die bereits in den Schriften des Herrn Linné, oder von andern Schriftstellern beschrieben worden sind, sind mit den unter den Text gesetzten linnäischen Trivialnamen, oder Benennung anderer Schriftsteller kennbarer gemacht worden.—Vergl. die Originalausgabe, 1769.

1775. SONNINI DE MANONCOUR, C. N. S. Observation sur les Coqs et Poules de l'Amérique méridionale. < *Journ. de Physique*, vi, 1775, pp. 128, 129.

Not seen: title from Carus and Engelmann.—The article doubtless refers to *Cracidæ* or *Tinamidæ*.

1775. SONNINI DE MANONCOUR, C. N. S. Observation sur les Mareils ou Faisans de la Guiana. < *Journ. de Physique*, v, 1775, pp. 345–350.

Not seen: title from Carus and Engelmann.—*Tinamidæ? Cracidæ?*

1776. ANON. [Molina, G. I.] Compendio della Storia geografica, naturale e civile del regno del Chili. Bologna. 1776. 8vo. 10 pll.

Not seen. Giebel, doubtless from Engelmann, gives such an edition as of "Molina"; but the first recognized edition is of 1782, *q. v.* See also Molina at 1808 and 1810. I do not know what this is, or what it may contain. Some clue to it may be given in the preface of the English version of 1808, where the American translator says:—"Through the politeness of a gentleman of his acquaintance, the translator has also been furnished with an anonymous compendium of the history of Chili, printed in Bologna in 1776, from which the supplementary notes to this volume are taken."

In respect to this anonymous compend, here is what Molina himself says in his preface to the original edition of the "Saggio", 1782—it is tacit admission of its authorship—"Le storie, o piuttosto le relazioni stampate, oltre ai quattro Poemi, che corono impressi sulla guerra Araucana, . . . *ed un Compendio anonimo, che si pubblicò in lingua Italiana nel* 1776., il quale in certo modo dà una notizia più compiuta del Chili di quella, che danno le altre opere stampate, particolamente intorno alla Geografia, *e alla storia Naturale.* Nulladimeno come questo Compendio è anche troppo ristretto, così io ho creduto di fare un servigio non inutile agli amatori delle cose Americàne, presentando loro un ragguaglio più disteso e più circo-stanziato de' prodotti, e de' successi più notabili dello stesso Paese."

1776. CLAYTON, W. An Account of the Falkland Islands. < *Philos. Trans.*, lxvi, pt. i, 1776, pp. 99–108.

Considerable account of Penguins, Geese, and other birds, pp. 103–105.

1782. MOLINA, G. I. Saggio | sulla Storia Naturale | del | Chili | del Signor Abate | Giovanni Ignazio | Molina. | [Vignette.] | In Bologna MDCCLXXXII. | — | Nella Stamperia di S. Tommaso d'Aquino. | Con licenza de' Superiori. 1 vol. 16mo (sigs. A 1, 1 l.; A 2, 1 l.; A 3, 1 l.; A 4, 5 ll.). pp. 368, map opp. p. 17. >Libro IV. Vermi, Insetti, Rettili, Pesci, Uccelli, o Quadrupedi del Chili, pp. 196–367.

This is the *editio princeps* of the celebrated work. There are numerous later editions in various languages, which see below: German, Leipzig, 1786; Spanish, Madrid, 1788; French, Paris, 1789; American, Middletown, Conn., 1808; English, London, 1809; Italian again, Bologna, 1810. See especially 1808 and 1810. Consult also 1776, ANON. See *Trans. Linn. Soc.*, vii, p. 225; *Oken's Isis*, ix, 1833, p. 824; *Rev. Zoologique*, 1840, p. 147. See also Philippi's Comentario, *Anal. Univ. Chile*, xxix, 1867, pp. 788–795.

Molina is famous in the annals of South American ornithology. Being a binomenclator after the most approved fashion of the time, he is citable as authority for species, and most of those he describes are new, antedating Gmelin (1788) and Latham (*Ind. Orn.*, 1790). The ornithological matter consists, first, of a general treatise on the birds of Chili, pp. 232–268; second, of a synopsis, pp. 343–345, in which the species receive formal Latin diagnoses in the Linnæan manner (Catalogo delle nuove specie descritte in questo Saggio ordinate secondo il Sistema Linneano). The general text of the former is accompanied also by Latin diagnoses of the species treated in footnotes. As this edition is not very generally accessible, I give the names of the species treated, with the pages on which each occurs. All are new except-ing the three marked "Linn."

Anas regia, pp. 234, 344; *A. coscoroba*, pp. 234, 344; *A. melancoripha*, pp. 234, 344; *Ardea erytrocephala*, pp. 235, 344; *A. galatea*, pp. 235, 344; *A. cyanocephala*, pp. 235, 344; *A. thula,* pp. 235, 344; *Columba melanoptera*, pp. 236, 345; *Picus lignarius*, pp. 236, 343; *P. pitius*, pp. 236, 343; *Diomedea chilensis*, pp. 238–344; *D. chilocnsis*, pp. 239, 344; *Pelecanus thagus*, pp. 240, 344; *Anas hybrida*, pp. 241, 344; *Phœnicopterus chilensis*, pp. 242, 344; *Tantalus pillus*, pp. 243, 344; *Trochilus minimus* ("Linn."), p. 246; *T. cyanocephalus*, pp. 247, 343; *T. galeritus*, pp. 247, 343; *Fringilla barbata*, pp. 247, 345; *F. diuca*, pp. 249, 345; *Turdus thilius*, pp. 250, 345; *T. thenca*, pp. 250, 345; *Turdus curœus*, pp. 252, 345; *Sturnus loyca*, pp. 254, 345; *Phytotoma* (gen. nov.) *rara*, pp. 254, 345; *Psittacus cyanalysios*, pp. 256, 343; *P. chorœus*, pp. 257, 343; *P. jaguilma*, pp. 257, 343; *Parra chilensis*, pp. 258, 344; *Otis chilensis*, pp. 250, 344; *Struthio rea* (Linn.), p. 261; *Strix cunicularia*, pp. 263, 343; *Falco tharus*, pp. 264, 343; *Vulcur* [sic] *jota*, p. 265, 343; *Vultur gryphus* (Linn.), p. 266.

The following is a complete and exact transcript of the systematic catalogue, pp. 343–345, giving the names and diagnoses of all Molina's new species:—

AVES.

Accipitres.

Vultur *Jota* niger, remigibus fuscis, rostro cineraceo.

Falco *Tharus* cera, pedibusque luteis, corpore albo-nigrescente, vertice cristato.

Strix *Cunicularia* capite lævi, corpore supra fusco, subtus albo, pedibus tuberculatis pilosis.

1782. MOLINA, G. I.—Continued.

Picæ.

Psittacus *Jaguilma* macrourus viridis, remigibus apice fuscis, orbitis fulvis.

Psittacus *Cyanalysios* brachyurus luteo-virens, collare cæruleo, uropygio rubro.

Psittacus *Choræus* brachyurus viridis, subtus cinereus, orbitis incarnatis.

Picus *Lignarius* pileo coccineo, corpore albo, cæruleoque vittato.

Picus *Pitius* cauda brevi, corpore fusco maculis ovalibus albis guttato.

Trochilus *Cyanocephalus* rectirostris capite, remigibus, rectricibusque cæruleis, abdomine rubro.

Trochilus *Galeritus* curvirostris viridi-aureus, remigibus, rectricibusque fuscis, crista purpurea.

Anseres.

Anas *Melancorypha* rostro semicylindrico rubro, capite nigro, corpore albo.

Anas *Hybrida* rostro semicylindrico, cera rubra, cauda acutiuscula.

Anas *Regia* caruncula compressa frontali, corpore cæruleo subtus fusco, collari albo.

Anas *Coscoroba* rostro extremo dilatato, rotundato, corpore albo.

Diomedea *Chilensis* alis impennibus, pedibus compedibus tridactylis, digitis omnibus connexis.

Diomedea *Chiloensis* alis impennibus, pedibus compedibus tetradactylis palmatis, corpore lanuginoso cinereo.

Pelecanus *Thagus* cauda rotundata, rostro serrato, gula saccata.

Grallæ.

Phænicopterus *Chilensis* ruber, remigibus albis.

Ardea *Erythrocephala* crista dependente rubra corpore albo.

Ardea *Galatea* occipite subcristato, corpore lacteolo, rostro luteo, pedibus coccineis.

Ardea *Cyanocephala* vertice cristato cæruleo, remigibus nigris albo marginatis.

Ardea *Thula* occipite cristato concolore, corpore albo.

Tantalus *Pillus* facie, rostro, pedibusque fuscis, corpore albo, remigibus rectricibusque nigris.

Parra *Chilensis* unguibus modicis, pedibus fuscis, occipite subcristato.

Otis *Chilensis* capite, juguloque lævi, corpore albo, vertice tectricibusque cinereis, remigibus primor. nigris.

Passeres.

Columba *Melanoptera* cauda cuneata, corpore cærulescente, remigibus nigris.

Sturnus *Loyca* fusco, alboque maculatus, pectore coccineo.

Turdus *Thilius* ater, axillis luteis, cauda cuneata.

Turdus *Thenca* fusco-cinereus, subtus pallido-cinereus, remigibus rectricibusque apice albis.

Turdus *Curæus* ater nitens, rostro substriato, cauda cuneata.

Fringilla *Barbata* lutea, alis viridibus, nigro rubroque maculatis, gula barbata.

Fringilla *Diuca* cærulea, gula alba.

Phytotoma (*gen. nov.*) Rostrum conicum, rectum, serratum.

 1. Phytotoma *Rara.* Nares ovatæ.
          Lingua brevis obtusa.

1783. MOLINA, G. I. Essai sur l'Histoire Naturelle de Chili. Paris. 1783. 8vo.

 Not seen: title of this French version from Ag. & Strickl., *Bibl.*—Orig. ed. 1782, *q. v.* There is another French ed., 1789, *q. v.*

1784. DOBRIZHOFFER, M. Historia de Abiponibus, Equestri, Bellicosaque Paraquariæ Natione, locupletata copiosis Barbararum Gentium, Urbium, Fluminum, Terrarum, Amphibiorum, Insectorum, Serpentium præcipuorum, Piscium, Avium, Arborum, Plantarum, aliorumque ejusdem Provinciæ Proprietatum Observationibus; Authore Martino Dobrizhoffer, Presbytero, et per Annos duodeviginti Paraquariæ Missionario. Vienna, 1784.

 The *editio princeps*, not seen by me. There is a German translation, Vienna, 1784, and a later English version, London, 1822, *q. v.*

1785. SONNINI DE MANONCOUR, C. N. S. Du Sasa, Oiseau de la Guyane. < *Journ. de Physique*, xxvii, 1785, pp. 222–224.—*Licht. und Voigt's Magaz.*, (3), iv, 1787, pp. 45–50 (über den Sasa, einen Vogel aus Guiana).

 Not seen: titles of both these articles from Carus and Engelmann. The "Sasa" is *Opisthocomus cristatus.* Giebel makes "du Sasa" a part of Sonnini's name.

1786. FAHLBERG, S. Slutet, af Samlingar til Natural-Historien öfver Ön St. Barthelemi i Vestindien. < *Kongl. Vetensk.-Acad. Nyt Handl.*, vii, 1786, pp. 248–254.

 Chiefly botanical; a few birds given on p. 253.

1786. MOLINA, G. I. Versuch | einer | Naturgeschichte | von | Chili. | — | Von |
Abbé J. Ignatz Molina. | Aus dem Italiänischen übersetzt | von | J. D. Brandis,
| Doctor der Arzneywissenschaft. | — | Mit einer Landcharte. | — | Mit
Churfürstl. Sächsischer Freyheit. | — | Leipzig, | bey Friedrich Gotthold
Jacobäer 1786. 1 vol. 16mo (sigs. *1, 1 l.; *2, 1 l.; *3, 1 l.; *4, 1 l.; *5, 4 ll.).
9 p. ll., pp. 1–328, map.

See the orig. ed., 1782. In this German version, the birds are at pp. 205-238, 304-306.

1788. MOLINA, G. I. Compendio | de la Historia Geografica, | Natural y Civil | del
Reyno de Chile, | escrito en Italiano | por el Abate Don Juan | Ignacio Molina. |
Primera [Segunda] Parte, | que abraza la Historia Geografica | y Natural, |
traducida en Español | Por Don Domingo Joseph | de Arquellada Mendoza,
Individuo de la | Real Academia de Buenas Letras de Sevilla, y Maestrante |
de Ronda. | En Madrid | por Don Antonio de Sancha. | Año M. DCC.
LXXXVIII. | Se hallará en su Libreria en la Aduana vieja. 2 vols. sm. 4to
shape, 16mo type-bed (sigs. *1, 1 l.; *2, 4 ll.; **2, 4 ll., etc.). Vol. I, pp. i–xx,
1–418, 1 map.

See the orig. ed., 1782. Only the first vol. is here cited; the second has a different title,
though beginning similarly, relates to the civil history of Chili, translated and augmented by
various notes by Nicolas de la Cruz y Bahamonde, and dates 1795; has portrait of Molina
and several maps.

In this Spanish version, the bird-matter is in Part or Vol. I, as above cited, pp. 257-301,
390-393.

1789. BROWNE, PATRICK. Civil and Natural History of Jamaica. London. 1789. Fol.

Not seen: said to contain a Linnæan index. It is the 2d ed. See the orig. ed., 1756.

1789. MOLINA, G. I. Essai | sur | L'Histoire Naturelle | du Chili, | Par M. l'Abbé
Molina; | Traduit de l'Italien, & enrichi de notes, | Par M. Gruvel, D. M. | — |
A Paris, | Chez Née de la Rochelle, Libraire, rue du | Hurepoix, près du pont
Saint-Michel, n°. 13. | — | M. DCC. LXXXIX. | Avec Approbation et Privilège
du Roi. 1 vol. 16mo. (sigs. a 1, 1 l.; a 2, 1 l.; a 3, 1 l.; a 4, 5 ll.). pp. i–xvj,
1–352, no map.

See the orig. ed., 1782. In this French version, the bird-matter is at pp. 211-249, 321-324.
The translator makes a separate head ("§ XXXV. Oiseaux. Gùnùn en Chilien.") for the
birds, and introduces Molina's binomials into the general text, in brackets.

1792. RICHARD, L. C., *and* BERNARD, J. P. Catalogue des Oiseaux envoyés de Cayenne par Le Blond. < *Actes Soc. Hist. Nat. Paris,* i, 1792, pp. 116–119.

Not seen: title from Carus and Engelmann, *Bibl.*

1794. WEST, H. Beyträge | zur | Beschreibung | von | St. Croix. | — | Nebst einer |
kurzen Uebersicht | der benachbarten Inseln, | St. Thomas, St. Jean, Tortola,
Spanishtown | und Krabbeneyland | von | Hans West, | Rector am Westin-
dischen Schulinstitut. | — | Aus dem Dänischen, | mit Verbesserungen und
Vermehrungen des Verfassers. | — | Kopenhagen, 1794. | Bey C. G. Proft,
Sohn und Compagnie. 1 vol. 16mo. 2 p. ll., pp. 1–274.

Orig. ed. 1793, [*q. v.,* beyond, ADDENDA.] *Ardea coerulea* and *Fulica chloropus,* p. 243.

1802-05. AZARA, F. DE. Apuntamientos | para la Historia Natural | De Los Pá-
xaros | del Paragüay | y Rio de la Plata, | escritos | Por Don Felix de Azara. |
Tomo Primero [Segundo, Tercero]. | Madrid MDCCCII [MDCCCV]. | en la
imprenta de la viuda de Ibarra. | Con licencia. 3 vols. very small 4to (type-
bed size of a 12mo). Vol. I, 1802, 1 p. l., pp. i–xx, 1–534 + 1 l. Vol. II, 1805,
1 p. l., pp. i–viii, 1–562 + 1 l. Vol. III, 1805, 1 p. l., pp. i–vi, 1–479 + 1 l.

Editio princeps—scarce, and seldom actually consulted, though constantly quoted. Sonnini's
French translation, Paris, 1809, is oftener handled. Azara describes 418 species, all unfortunately under Spanish names only, as many of them are here published for the first time, and
form the original basis of many binomial names later bestowed by Vieillot, Temminck, Lichtenstein, and others, to which, in the nature of the case, much uncertainty and no little confusion
attaches in many instances. Hartlaub has published an invaluable Systematic Index (Bre-
men, 1847) to Azara, identifying the species as far as possible, with a concordance of *ed.
princ.* and *ed. Sonnini,* and a considerable synonymy. From the latter I quote the following,
referring to the learned and accurate commentator himself for further particulars:—

"Nur Wenigen ist Azara's berühmtes Werk über die Vögel Paraguay's in der spanischen

1802–05. AZARA, F. DE.—Continued.

1802 bis 1805 zu Madrid erschienenen Originalausgabe bekannt. Erst durch Sonnini's sehr verdienstliche Uebersetzung wurde dasselbe für die Wissenschaft im weiteren Umfange zugänglich. In dieser Uebersetzung sind die oft etwas verworren aneinandergefügten Originalbeschreibungen zweckmässig in Formen, Maasse und Färbung gesondert, und des Verfassers Bekanntschaft mit den Vögeln Gujana's erhöht den Werth des critischen Theils desselben. Das erste Werk, in welchem Azara'sche Vögel systematische Benennungen erhalten, ist, wenn wir nicht irren, Temminck's ,,Histoire naturelle des Pigeons et des Gallinacées". Bald darauf versuchte Vieillot in dem 1816 bis 1819 bei Déterville herausgekommenen ,,Dictionnaire d'histoire naturelle" dieselben sämmtlich den dazumal aufgestellten Gattungen einzuverleiben und den seiner Ansicht nach zuvor unbeschriebenen wissenschaftliche Namen zu geben; ein Versuch, dessen mehr als zweifelhafter Erfolg namentlich dem Umstande beizumessen ist, das Vieillot diese Vögel nur nach Beschreibungen kannte, mithin sowohl hinsichtlich ihrer systematischen Stellung als auch ihrer Artselbständigkeit in zahlreiche Irrthümer verfallen musste. Unbenannt blieben von ihm nur wenige Arten, welche er nicht mit genügender Sicherheit in dieser oder jener Gattung unter bringen zu können glaubte. Für einzelne schuf er neue Genera, so Alectrurus für den ,,Gallito" und Steganopus für den ,,Chorlito del tarso comprimido". In den drei die Ornithologie umfassenden Theilen des ,,Tableau encyclopédique et méthodique des trois règnes de la nature" findet sich Vieillot's Nomenclatur der ,,Páxaros" mit geringen Abänderungen reproducirt. Gleichzeitig mit letztgenanntem Buche, also 1823, erschien Lichtenstein's ,,Verzeichniss der Doubletten des zoologischen Museums der Königl. Universität zu Berlin", ein Werkchen, welchem die Wissenschaft zum Theil aus dem Grunde einen dauernden Werth zugestanden hat, weil es die erste umfassendere critische Benutzung und Berücksichtigung der ,,Páxaros" enthält. Unter 120 darin aufgeführten brasilianischen vom Verfasser mit Arten Azara's für identisch erklärten Vögeln befinden sich etwa 50, welche, da derselbe das ,,Dictionnaire d'histoire naturelle" noch nicht kannte, von ihm systematische Benennungen erhalten, die denn freilich mit wenig Ausnahmen durch die früheren Vieillot's in den Rang von Synonymen zurückgedrängt werden. Eine sehr angemessene Würdigung finden Azara's Arbeiten in des Prinzen von Neuwied trefflichen ,,Beiträgen zur Naturgeschichte Brasitiens". Etwa 150 Vögelarten Paraguay's glaubt derselbe für mit von ihm beobachteten gleichartig halten zu dürfen, und häufig findet er Gelegenheit des spanischen Naturforschers Bemerkungen über Lebensweise mit seinen eigenen zusammenzustellen und zu bestätigen."

1807. HUMBOLDT, A. v. Über die Chinawälder in Südamerika. < *Mag. Gesell. Naturf. Freunde zu Berlin*, i, 1807, pp. 57–68.

Behandelt Vögel, p. 59.

1808. MOLINA, G. I. The | Geographical, | Natural and Civil History | of | Chili. | — | By Abbe Don J. Ignatius Molina. | — | Illustrated by a half-sheet map of the country. | — | With notes | from the Spanish and French versions, | and | an appendix, | containing copious extracts from the Araucana | of Don Alonzo de Ercilla. | — | Translated from the original Italian, | by an American gentleman [A. Alsop]. | — | In two volumes. | Vol. I [II]. | — | Middletown, (Conn[ecticut, U. S.].) | Printed for I. Riley, | — | 1808. 2 vols. 8vo size, 4to by sigs., 4 ll. to a sig. Vol. I, 4 p. ll., pp. i–xii, 1–271, 1 l., map. Vol. II, 1 p. l., pp. i–viii, 1 blank l., 1–306, 1 unpaged p., 1 blank l.; (Appendix), pp. i–iv, 5–68.

See the original edition, 1782. In this, the earliest English version I know of, the bird-matter is in vol. I, chap. IV, sect. V, pp. 162–188, with the original Latin diagnoses at pp. 240–242; see also p. 268. *Phytotoma* here becomes "Phitotoma". As in some other versions, the footnotes of the original are here dispensed with, and the technical names are inserted in the text in parentheses.

"The author of the present work, Don Juan Ignatius [*i. e.* Giovanni Ignazio] Molina, was a native of Chili, distinguished for his literary acquirements, and particularly his knowledge of natural history, large collections in which he had made during his residence in that country. On the dissolution of the celebrated order of the Jesuits, of which he was a member, he shared the general fate of that community, in being expelled from the territories of Spain, and was at the same time deprived not only of his collections in natural history, but also of his manuscripts. The most important of the latter relative to Chili, he had, however, the good fortune to regain by accident some time after his residence in Bologna, in Italy, whither he had gone on his arrival in Europe. Furnished with these materials, he applied himself to writing the History of that country, which was published at two different periods; the first part, comprising the Natural History, in the year 1787 [qu. 1782], and the second, for reasons mentioned in his preface, not until some years after."

1809. AZARA, F. DE. Voyages | dans | l'Amérique Méridionale, | par Don Félix de
Azara, | Commissaire et Commandant des limites Espagnoles de Paraguay |
depuis 1781 jusqu'en 1801; | Contenant la description géographique, politique
et civile du | Paraguay et de la rivière de La Plata; l'histoire de la décou- |
verte et de la conquête de ces contrées; des détails nom- | breux sur leur his-
toire naturelle, et sur les peuples sauvages | qui les habitent; le récit des
moyens employés par les | Jésuites pour assujétir et civiliser les indigènes,
etc. | Publiés d'après les manuscrits de l'auteur, |`avec une notice sur sa vie
et ses écrits, | Par C. A. Walckenaer; | enrichis de notes par G. Cuvier, | Sec-
rétaire perpétuel de la classe des Sciences Physiques de l'Institut, etc. | Suivis
de l'histoire naturelle des Oiseaux du Paraguay et de La Plata, par | le même
auteur, traduite, d'après l'original espagnol, et augmentée | d'un grand nombre
de notes, par M. Sonnini ; | Accompagnés d'un atlas de vingt-cinq planches. |
Tome Premier [-Quatrième]. | — | Paris, | Dentu, Imprimeur-Libraire, | Rue
du Pont-de-Lodi, n° 3. | 1809. 4 vols. small 8vo, and large 4to atlas. Vols.
I, II, no ornithology. Vol. III, 2 p. ll., pp. i, ii, 1–479. Vol. IV, 2 p. ll., pp.
1–380. Atlas, 4to, same date and imprint, titled Voyages | dans | L'Amérique
méridionale, | par Don Félix de Azara. | — | Collection de planches. 2 ll. of
text, pll. xxv, of which xxii–xxv are of birds.

<small>In this French version by Sonnini, much better known than the original, Azara's Apunta-
mientos para la historia natural de los Páxaros de Paraguay, etc., are contained in the third and
fourth volumes ; four birds are figured in the atlas. Sonnini's translation is considered "meri-
torious", but has its short-comings. See especially Hartlaub's *Systematischer Index*, 1847.</small>

1809. MOLINA, G. I. The | Geographical, | Natural, and Civil | History of Chili. |
Translated from the original Italian of | the Abbe Don J. Ignatius Mo-
lina. | — | To which are added, | Notes | from the Spanish and French ver-
sions, | and | two Appendixes, | by the English editor; | [etc., 5 lines.] | — |
In two volumes. | — | Vol. I [II]. | — | [London:] printed for Longman,
Hurst, Rees, and Orme. | Paternoster-row. | — | 1809. 2 vols. 8vo. Vol. I,
pp. i–xx, 1–321+1½ ll. advt., map. Vol. II, pp. i–xii, 1–385+1½ ll. advt.

<small>See the original edition, 1782. This is apparently reprinted from the Middletown (Conn.) ed.
of 1808, q. v., with which it is substantially identical in the ornithological matter. Birds: Vol.
I, Chap. IV, sect. V, pp. 191–222, and pp. 282–284; see also p. 317. But the English editor (as
I may state for others than ornithologists) has added occasional notes over the initials E. E.,
and subjoined a further elucidation of the language of the Araucanos, from Falkner's Patagonia, besides adding the two appendixes mentioned in the title.</small>

1810. LEDRU, A.-P. Voyage aux Iles de Ténériffe, la Trinité, Saint Thomas, Sainte-
Croix et Porto-Ricco, . . . &c. Par Andre-Pierre Ledru . . . &c. Paris.
1810. 2 vols. 16mo. [See complete title beyond, ADDENDA.]

<small>Not seen: cited from *Ibis*, 1859, pp. 374, 375. M. Ledru was one of the naturalists (with
Maugé) of the expedition commanded by Captain Baudin in 1796–98. His work contains (vol.
II, pp. 36 et seq.) an "Essai sur l'histoire naturelle des îles danoises", by M. Sonnini, in which
ornithology is represented by a variety of matter, some of it wild.</small>

1810. MOLINA, G. I. Saggio | sulla Storia Naturale del Chili | di | Gio: Ignazio Mo-
lina | Seconda Edizione | accresciuta e arricchita di una nuova carta geogra-
fica | e del ritratto dell' autore. | ,, Hic vir assiduum, atque alienis mensibus
aestas, | ,, Bis gravidae pecudes, bis pomis utilis arbos . . . . | ,, Haec eadem
argenti rivos, aerisque metalla | ,, Ostendit venis, atque auro plurima fluxit |
Virg. Georg. lib. 2. | Bologna 1810. | — | Tipografia de' fratelli Masi e comp. |
1 vol. Large 4to. Title, backed blank, frontisp. (portrait of Molina), dedication
2 ll., preface pp.)(i)(-)(v)(, p. vi blank ; pp.)(1)(-)(306)(; 1 ll. errata ; map.

<small>The second *Italian* edition (original edition, 1782) ; but there had meanwhile been sundry
others, in Spanish, French, German, and English, qq. vv. Respecting the present, the author
says in the preface:—"Il Saggio sulla Storia naturale del Regno del Chili venuto alla luce
nell' anno 1782 non era altro che un succinto Compendio delle Osservazioni da me fatte cerca
gli Esseri appartenenti ai tre Regni della Natura, che si ritrovano in quel Paese. . . . Tutti
le Nazioni colte dell' Europa lo vollero tradotto nelle loro lingue. L'edizione originale fu ben
presto smaltita. Parecchi dilettanti di storia naturale, che non potevano più provvedersene,
s'accordarono a farne una ristampa, e mi significarono il desiderio che avevan di arricchirla di
un appendice, so io fossi in grado di somministrar loro i materiali necessarj."</small>

1810. MOLINA, G. I.—Continued.

In this late edition, the ornithology occupies § xiii – § xvii, pp. 197–226. It is entirely re-modelled, largely rewritten, and much augmented. While all the earlier versions of "Molina" are substantially the same as the original of 1782, the present is therefore quite a different thing, and should be gingerly touched, by any one unfamiliar with the original, in any matter relating to nomenclature, or authority for species. The Latin diagnoses and the footnotes of the original have all disappeared, and with them has gone Molina as an original authority; he is here like another person or editor compiling from and enlarging upon "Molina". The following names occur here:—

Anas regia "Frez.", *A. picta* "Lath.", *A. coscoroba* "Diz. Chil.", *A. hybris* "Diz. Chil.", p. 198. *A. dispar, A. magellanica* "Lath.", *A. melancorypha* "Bougainv.", *Pelecanus thagus* "Diz. Chil.", p. 199. *P. carunculatus* "Lath.", *P. cristatus* "Lath.", p. 200. *P. magellanicus* "Lath.", *Aptenodytes maxima, patagonica* "Lath.", p. 201. *A. cyanocephala, papua* "Lath.", *A. saltatrix, chrysocome* "Lath.", *A. præcincta, magellanica* "Lath.", *A. chiloensis* "Diz. Chil.", *A. chilensis* "Lath.", p. 202. *Phoenicopterus chilensis* "Oval. Stor.", p. 203. *Tantalus pillus* "Diz. Chil.", *Ardea cyanocephala,* p. 204. *A. erythrocephala* "Vid.", *A. galatea, A. alba, ligthula* "Diz. Chil.", *Parra chilensis* "Diz. Chil. Oval.", p. 205. *Fringilla barbata* "Diz. Chil. Ov.", p. 209. *F. diuca* "Diz. Chil.", p. 210. *Turdus thilius* "Diz. Chil.", *T. curæus* "Diz. Chil.", p. 211. *T. militaris* "Lath.", p. 212. *T. thenca* "Diz. Chil.", p. 213. *Phytotoma rara* "gen. nov. Vid." [!], p. 214. *Picus pileatus* [!], *P. lineatus, al. lignarius, P. pitius,* p. 215. *Psittacus cyanolysios, P. choraeus,* p. 216. *P. jahuilma, Columba turtur* [!], *C. melanoptera, C. passerina,* p. 217. *Tetrao perdix* [!], *Strix cunicularia,* p. 218. *Otis chilensis* "Diz. Chil.", p. 219. *Struthio rhea* "Linn. Diz. Chil. Oval.", *Vultur iota* "Diz. Chil.", p. 220. *Falco tharus* "Diz. Chil.", p. 221. *F. calquin* "Diz. Chil.", *Vultur gryphus* "Linn.", p. 223.

1814–26. LICHTENSTEIN, H. Die Werke von Marcgrave und Piso über die Naturge-schichte Brasiliens u. s. w. < *Abhandl. Berlin. Akad.* (Phys. Kl.), 18^{14}⁄$_{15}$, pp. 201–222; 18^{16}⁄$_{17}$, pp. 155–178; 18^{20}⁄$_{21}$, pp. 237–257, 267–288; 1826, pp. 49–66.

It appears from Carus and Engelmann, that Lichtenstein's commentary on Piso and Marcgrave originally appeared in instalments in *Abhandl. Berlin. Akad.* during several years; but I cannot now lay hands on the *Abhandlungen.* I give beyond, 1820 and 1824, titles taken from *Isis,* of what I suppose to be substantially the same thing, as far as the birds are concerned; the whole commentary, as above cited, relating also to other animals.

1819. ANON. [Notice of Spix and Martius's Brazilian Birds.] < *Isis,* Jahrg. iii, 1819, pp. 1346–1350.

1820. LICHTENSTEIN, H. Marcgrave's und Piso's Berichte über die Brasilischen Thiere, erläutert aus den wiederaufgefundenen Original-Abbildungen. < *Oken's Isis,* Jahrg. iv, 1820, *Litter. Anzeig.,* pp. 635–652. (Vorgelesen in der Berliner Akademie 17. April 1817.)

An important commentary on the work, identifying the names and descriptions of these authors, as far as the birds are concerned.—See preceding title; also, 1824, same author.

1820. MAXIMILIAN, PRINZ ZU WIED-NEUWIED. Reise des Prinzen Maximilian von Wied-Neuwied. Gedrängter Auszug aus dem ersten Theile desselben. Frank-furth bei Brönner. 4. < *Oken's Isis,* Jahrg. iv, 1820, *Litter. Anzeig.,* pp. 809–832, 965–990.

1820. SCHREIBERS, C. v. Nachrichten von den kaiserl. österreichischen Naturforschern in Brasilien und den Resultaten ihrer Betriebsamkeit, vom Hof-Naturalien-cabinets-Direktor C. v. Schreibers. Brünn bey Tratzler 1820. 8. 191 nebst 1 Abb. v. Rio Janeiro und einem Plan der Stadt < *Oken's Isis,* Jahrg. iv, 1820, pp. 289–309.

Vergleiche 1823, SCHREIBERS, C. v.

1820–21. MAXIMILIAN, PRINZ ZU WIED-NEUWIED. Reise | nach | Brasilien | in den Jahren 1815 bis 1817 | von Maximilian | Prinz zu Wied-Neuwied. | — | Mit zwei und zwanzig Kupfern, | neunzehn Vignetten und drei Karten. | — | Erster [zweyter] Band. | — | Frankfurt a. M. 1820 [1821]. | Gedruckt und ver-legt bei Heinrich Ludwig Brönner. 2 vols. Gr. 4to. Vol. I, 1820, pp. xxxvi, 380, 3 ll. Vol. II, 1821, pp. xviii, 346.

1821–22. MAXIMILIEN, PRINCE DE WIED-NEUWIED. Voyage | au Brésil, | dans les années 1815, 1816 et 1817, | par S. A. S. Maximilien, | Prince de Wied-Neu-wied; | traduit de l'Allemand | par J. B. B. Eyriès. | Ouvrage enrichi d'un

1821-22. MAXIMILIEN, PRINCE DE WIED-NEUWIED.—Continued.

superbe atlas, composé de 41 planches | gravées en taille-douce, et de trois cartes. | — | Tome Premier [Second, Troisième]. | — | Paris, | Arthur Bertrand, Libraire, | Rue Hautefeuille, nᵒ 23. | 1821 [1821, 1822]. | H. Baillière, 219, Regent street, London. 3 vols. 8vo. Vol. I, 1821, pp. xvj, 399. Vol. II, 1821, 2 p. ll., pp. iii, 400. Vol. III, 1822, 2 p. ll., pp. iii, 384, 3 maps.

1822. DOBRIZHOFFER, M. An | Account | of | the Abipones, | An Equestrian People | of | Paraguay. | — | From the Latin of Martin Dobrizhoffer, | eighteen years a missionary in that country. | — | In three volumes. | Vol. I[-III]. | — | London: | John Murray, Albemarle street. | 1822. 3 vols. 8vo.

Orig. ed. Latin, Vienna, 1784 ; ed. alt. Germ., ibid., 1784.—This English translation is anonymous, said to be by Sara Coleridge. Vol. I contains, pp. 308-333, accounts of sundry birds of Paraguay, of no special consequence.

1822. MAXIMILIAN, PRINZ ZU WIED-NEUWIED. Reise nach Brasilien in den Jahren 1815-17, von Maximilian, Prinz zu Wied-Neuwied. 2ter Band. Frankfurt a. M. bei Brönner, 1821. 4. 345. mit 8 Kupf. in 4. und 8 in Fol. nebst 1 Charte. < *Oken's Isis*, Jahrg. vi, 1822, *Litter. Anzeig.*, pp. 249-262, 265-280.

1822. SAINT-HILAIRE, AUGUSTE DE. Aperçu d'un Voyage dans l'intérieur du Brésil, La province Cisplatine et les Missions dites du Paraguay. < *Mém. du Mus. d'Hist. Nat.*, ix, 1822, pp. 307-380.

Note sur la *Cariama*, p. 323; *Oriolus aurantius* Valenc., p. 324.

1822. THUNBERG, C. P. Piprae novae species descriptae. < *Mém de l'Acad. St.-Pétersb. for* 1817-1818, viii, 1822, pp. 282-287, pll. vii, viii.

PP. caudata (pl. 7, f. 1),forficata (pl. 7, f. 2), lineata (pl. 8, f. 1), cyanea (pl. 8, f. 2), viridis (pl. 8, f. 3), virens, pusilla (pl. 8, f. 4), fasciata, frontalis, cephaleucos, flavogaster, brunnea, atra—nec omnes Pipræ generis sunt.

1823. ANON. Brasilianisches Museum in Wien. < *Oken's Isis*, Jahrg. vii, 1823, Beylage No. 9.

Remarks upon the specimens contained, with notes on the birds *passim*.

1823. SCHREIBERS, C. v. Nachrichten von den kaiserl. österreichischen Naturforschern in Brasilien und den Resultaten ihrer Betriebsamkeit. < *Oken's Isis*, Jahrg. vii, 1823, pp. 714-724.

Aus Amtsrelationen der k. k. Gesandschaft und aus den Berichten der Naturforscher an Herrn v. Schreibers, und nach Untersuchung der eingesendeten Gegenstände u. s. w. (Brünn, bey Tratzler, Hft. 2, 1822, 8°, SS. 114.)—Unter den Vögeln, von 61 verschiedenen Arten, befinden sich 2 Geyer, 23 Papageyen, 69 Singvögel, 25 Tauben, 2 Hühner u. s. w.—Vergl. 1820, SCHREIBERS, C. v.

1823. SCHREIBERS, C. v. Nachrichten von den kayserl. österreichischen Naturforschern in Brasilien den Resultaten ihrer Betriebsamkeit. < *Oken's Isis*, Jahrg. vii, 1823, pp. 1042-1065.

Aus Amtsrelationen der k. k. Gesandschaft und aus den Berichten der Naturforscher. Von Hrn. von Schreibers und nach Untersuchung der eingesendeten Gegenstände u. s. w. (Brünn, bey Tratzler, Heft 2, 1822, 8°, SS. 114.)—Vögel, pp. 1061-1063.—Vergl. 1820, SCHREIBERS, C. v.

1823-31. SPIX, J. B. V., *and* MARTIUS, C. F. E. Reise in Brasilien auf Befehl Sr. Majestät Maximilian Joseph I, Königs von Baiern in den Jahren 1817 bis 1820 gemacht und beschrieben von Dr. Joh. Bapt. von Spix, und Dr. Carl. Frieder. Phil. von Martius. München, 1823[-1831]. 3 Thle. 4to.

[See beyond, ADDENDA.]

1824. DESM . . ST [DESMAREST, A. G.] Abbildungen zur Naturgeschichte Brasiliens . . . par le prince Maximilien . . . < *Féruss. Bull.*, 2ᵉ sect., ii, 1824, p. 191.

1824. F[ÉRUSSAC, — DE ?] Abbildungen zur Naturgeschichte Brasiliens. . . . . < *Féruss. Bull.*, 2ᵉ sect., iii, 1824, pp. 221, 222.

1824. LICHTENSTEIN, H. Die Werke von Marcgrave und Piso, über die Naturgeschichte Brasiliens, erläutert aus den wieder aufgefundenen Original-Abbildungen von Lichtenstein. < *Oken's Isis*, Jahrg. viii, 1824, *Litter. Anzeig.*, pp. 57-74.

Aus d. *Abhandl. Berl. Akad.*—Vergl. auch 1820, LICHTENSTEIN. H.

1824-25. SPIX, J. B. v. "Avium species novae, quas in itinere per Brasiliam annis 1817-20 collegit et descripsit. 2 vols. Folio. Monachii, 1824-25. Vol. I, 1824, pp. 90, pll. 104. Vol. II, 1825, pp. 85, pll. 118."
> Not seen,—as I specially regret to say in this case.

1825. ANON. Beyträge zur Nat. Gesch. v. Brasilien von M. Prinzen zu Wied. Weimar, Landes-Industrie-Comptoir. 1825, 8. B. I. 612 mit 3 Kpfrt. < *Oken's Isis*, Jahrg. ix, 1825, pp. 1335-1340.
> Vögel, pp. 1337, 1338.

1825. BONAPARTE, C. [L.] Descriptions of ten species of South American Birds. < *Journ. Acad. Nat. Sci. Phila.*, iv, 1825, pp. 370-387.
> *Monasa fusca* Bp., *Picus rubricollis* var. ?, *Dendrocolaptes angustirostris*, *Fringilla flaveola*, *Tanagra flava*, *Muscicapa violenta* Bp., *Muscicapa taenioptera* Bp., *Muscicapa pullata* Bp., *Caprimulgus semitorquatus*, *Rallus nigricans*.

1825. BONAPARTE, C. [L.] Notes to the paper entitled Descriptions of ten species of South American Birds. < *Journ. Acad. Nat. Sci. Phila.*, v, 1825, pp. 137-140.
> *Picus rubricollis* and 3 spp. of *Rallus. R. melanurus* Bp., p. 139.—Also separate, pp. 4.

1825. LESSON, [R.] P. Remarques sur quelques Oiseaux de la province de Rio-de-Janeiro et des environs de Monte-Vidéo; . . . par MM. Quoy et Gaimard. . . . < *Féruss. Bull.*, 2ᵉ sect., vi, 1825, p. 93.
> Extrait des *Annales des Sci. Nat.*, t. iv, Avril 1825, pp. 474-481, *q. v.*

1825. LESSON, R. P. Description de dix espèces d'oiseaux de l'Amérique méridionale . . . ; par Ch. Bonaparte. . . . < *Féruss. Bull.*, 2ᵉ sect., vi, 1825, pp. 412, 413.
> *Journ. Phila. Acad.*, iv, No. 12, Mai 1825, pp. 370-387, *q. v.*

1825. QUOY, J. R. C., *and* GAIMARD, J. P. Remarques sur quelques Oiseaux de la province de Rio-de-Janeiro et des environs de Montévidéo; sur leurs mœurs et leur distribution géographique. < *Ann. des Sci. Nat.*, iv, 1825, pp. 474-481.

1825. SPIX, J. B. v., *and* MARTIUS, C. F. P. Musical Thrush [?] of Brazil. < *Edinb. Philos. Journ.*, xii, 1825, pp. 186, 187.
> From 'Travels in Brazil'.

1825. SUCH, G. Descriptions of some hitherto uncharacterized Brazilian Birds. < *Zool. Journ.*, ii, 1825, pp. 110-117, pl. 4.
> *Galbula ceycoides*, p. 112; *Gubernetes* (g. n., p. 114) *cunninghami*, p. 114, pl. 4; *Dendrocolaptes crassirostris*, *D. fortirostris*, p. 115; *Ardea fasciata*, p. 117.

1825-33. MAXIMILIAN, PRINZ ZU WIED-NEUWIED. Beiträge zur Naturgeschichte von Brasilien, . . . Weimar. 1825-33. 4 vols. 8vo.
> This is the date of the whole work: see vols. III, IV, cited beyond, 1830-33.

1826. GARNOT, P. Remarques sur la Zoologie des îles Malouines, faites pendant le Voyage autour du monde de la Corvette la Coquille, exécuté en 1822, 1823, 1824 et 1825. < *Ann. des Sci. Nat.*, vii, 1826, pp. 39-59.
> *Sylvia macloviana*, p. 44; *Certhia antarctica*, p. 45; *Charadrius pyrocephalus*, *Tringa urvillii*, p. 46; *Haematopus leucopodus*, p. 47; *Podiceps occipitalis*, p. 50; *Procellaria lessonii*, p. 54; *Anser antarcticus*, p. 58, spp. nn.—Observations sur le *Chionis*.

1826. LESS[ON, R. P.] Description de quelques oiseaux du Brésil jusqu'à présent mal caractérisés, par George Such. . . . < *Féruss. Bull.*, 2ᵉ sect., vii, 1826, pp. 246, 247.
> *Zool. Journ.*, ii, No. 5, 1825, pp. 110-117.

1826-27. SCOULER, J. Account of a Voyage to Madeira, Brazil, Juan Fernandez, and the Gallapagos Islands, performed in 1824 and 1825, with a view of examining their Natural History, &c. < *Edinb. Journ. Sci.*, v, 1826, pp. 195-214; vi, 1827, pp. 51-73, 228-236.
> Containing cursory remarks on birds, especially *Procellariidæ*.

1827. [EDITORIAL.] [Note on Mr. W. S. MacLeay's "Remarks on the comparative anatomy of certain Birds of Cuba" (in Trans. Linn. Soc. ?).] < *Philos. Mag.*, i, 1827, p. 65.

1827. GARNOT, P. Notice respecting the Zoology of the Falkland Islands. < *Edinb. Journ. Sci.*, vi, 1827, pp. 321-325.
> Translated from *Ann. Sc. Nat.*, vii, 1826, pp. 39-59. A summary of the ornithological features occupies most of the article.

1827. L[UROTH], S. G. Remarques sur la zoologie des îles Malouines, . . . ; par M. Garnot. . . . < *Féruss. Bull.*, 2ᵉ sect., x, 1827, pp. 127–129.

Ann. des Sc. Nat., Janv. 1826, pp. 39–59.

1827-28. KING, P. P. Extracts from a letter addressed by Capt. Philip Parker King, R. N., F. R. S. and L. S., to N. A. Vigors, Esq., on the Animals of the Straits of Magellan. < *Zool. Journ.*, iii, 1827, pp. 422–432; iv, 1828, pp. 91–105, pl. suppl. 29.

I. *Haliæetus erythronotus*, p. 424; *Strix rufipes*, p. 426; *S. nana*, p. 427; *Sylvia dorsalis*, p. 428; *S. obscura*, p. 429; *Picus magellanicus*, p. 430; *Mellisuga kingii* Vig., p. 432, spp. nn.— Annotations throughout by Mr. Vigors. II. *Columba meridionalis*, p. 92; *Scolopax magellanicus*, p. 93; *Rhynchœa occidentalis*, *Rallus setosus*, p. 94; *Rallus antarcticus*, *Fulica chloropoides*, p. 95; *F. gallinuloides*, *Charadrius rubecola*, p. 96; *Anas rafflesii*, p. 97, pl. suppl. 29; *Anas specularis*, *A. specularioides*, p. 98; *A. creccoides*, p. 99; *Oidemia patachonica*, p. 100; *Podiceps, leucopterus*, *Phalacrocorax niger*, p. 101; *P. atriceps*, p. 102; *P. cirriger*, *Larus haematorhynchus*, p. 103, spp. nn.

1828. ANON. Avium species novae, quas in itinere per Brasiliam annis 1817–1820 collegit et descripsit Dr. J. B. de Spix. Tabulæ lithographicæ 118 a M. M. Schmid sculptæ. Monachii 1825. 4. maj. < *Oken's Isis*, Bd. xxi, 1828, pp. 88–92.

Inhaltsverzeichniss der Tafeln, Vögel, pp. 89–92.

1828. LESSON, [R. P.] Extrait d'une lettre adressée à M. Vigors par le capitaine King, sur les productions animales du détroit de Magellan. . . . < *Féruss. Bull.*, 2ᵉ sect., xv, 1828, pp. 150, 151.

Zool. Journ., No. 11, 1827, pp. 422–432, and No. 13, 1828, pp. 91–105.

1828. LESSON, [R. P.] Notes à ajouter au mémoire intitulé : Description de dix espèces d'Oiseaux américains; par Charles Bonaparte. . . . < *Féruss. Bull.*; 2ᵉ sect., xiii, 1828, pp. 240, 241.

Journ. Phila. Acad., v, pp. 137–140: voyez *Féruss. Bull.*, vi, 1825, pp. 412, 413.

1828. VIGORS, N. A. On some species of Birds from Cuba. < *Zool. Journ.*, iii, 1828, pp. 432–448.

Treats of 45 spp. *Accipiter fringilloides*, p. 434; *Falco sparverioides*, p. 436; *Pyrrhula collaris*, p. 440; *Colaptes fernandinæ*, p. 445; *Columba inornata*, p. 446, spp. nn.—The above is a sub-title of Art. XLVI, "Sketches in Ornithology," etc.

1829. ANON. Notices Zoologiques communiquées par le Dr. Poeppig, pendant son voyage dans le Chili. . . . < *Féruss. Bull.*, 2ᵉ sect., xix, 1829, pp. 95–104.

Extrait de *Fror. Notizen*, No. 529, juillet 1829.

1829. ANON. Abbildungen zur Naturgeschichte Brasiliens, herausgegeben von Maximilian, Prinzen von Wied. Weimar, Industrie-Comptoir. Lief. xii. 28. Fol. ill. < *Oken's Isis*, Bd. xxii, 1829, pp. 74, 75.

1829. BECKLIMICHEW, A. Notice sur deux nouvelles espèces d'oiseaux du Brésil. < *Nouv. Mém. Soc. Imp. Nat. de Moscou*, i, 1829, pp. 375–390.

Not seen: title from *Roy. Soc. Cat.*

1829. FÉRUSSAC, — DE. Voyage de M. Alcide d'Orbigny dans le sud de l'Amérique méridionale. < *Féruss. Bull.*, 2ᵉ sect., xix, 1829, pp. 212–222.

1830. [FISCHER, G.] [Note sur les Oiseaux envoyés par M. Coffrane de Bahia en Amérique.] < *Bull. Soc. Imp. Nat. Moscou*, ii, 1829, p. 10.

1830. KING, P. P. Ueber die Thiere an der Magellans-Strasse. < *Oken's Isis*, Bd. xxiii, 1830, pp. 1181–1183, 1234–1236.

Aus dem *Zool. Jour.*, 1827, pp. 422–432, und 1828, pp. 91–105. Vergl. 1827–28, KING, P. P.

1830. KING, P. P. [Characters of New Genera and Species of Birds from the Straits of Magellan.] < *P. Z. S.*, i, 1830, pp. 14–16, 29, 30.

Turdus magellenicus, *Psittacara leptorhyncha*, *Picus melanocephalus*, p. 14; *Hylactes* (n. g.) *tarnii*, *Columba fitzroyii*, *Cygnus anatoïdes*, *Anser inornatus*, *Micropterus patachonicus*, *Anas chiloensis*, *A. fretensis*, p. 15; *Synallaxis anthoides*, *Dendrocolaptes albogularis*, *Trochilus fernandensis*, *T. stokesii*, *Phalacrocorax imperialis*, *P. sarmientonus*, *P. erythrops*, p. 30.

1830. MACLEAY, W. S. Bemerkungen über die vergleichende Anatomie verschiedener Vögel aus Cuba, mit Rücksicht auf ihren Platz im System. < *Oken's Isis*, Bd. xxiii, 1830, pp. 895–898.

Auszug aus den „*Trans. Linn. Soc. Lond.*, xvi, p. 149, tb. 1–15" (?).

183-? D'ORBIGNY, A.   Extrait de deux Lettres à M. de Férussac, de Buenos-Ayres le 30 Oct. 1828 et de Rio Negro le 18 Févr. 1829, sur l'Histoire Naturelle de ces Contrées.   < *Féruss. Bull.*, xix, p. 212.
> Not seen: title from Ag. & Strickl. *Bibl.*

1830. SUCH, G.   Einige unbestimmte brasilische Vögel.   < *Oken's Isis*, Bd. xxiii, 1830, pp. 843, 844.
> Auszug aus dem *Zool. Jour.*, ii, 1825, pp. 110-117, *q. v.*

1830. VIGORS, N. A.   Ueber einige Vögel aus Cuba.   < *Oken's Isis*, Bd. xxiii, 1830, pp. 1165-1168.
> *Zool. Journal*, No. xi, p. 432.

1830-33. MAXIMILIAN, PRINZ ZU WIED.   Beiträge | zur | Naturgeschichte | von | Brasilien, | von | Maximilian, Prinzen zu Wied. | — | III. [IV.] Band. | Erste [Zweite] Abtheilung. [. . . .] | — | Weimar, | [. . .] 1830 [-1833]. 8vo. Vol. III, Erste Abth., 1830, 2 p. ll., pp. 1-636; Zweite Abth., 1831, pp. xii, 637-1278 + 1 l., mit einer Tafel (figg. 1-7).   Vol. IV, Erste Abth., 1832, 2 p. ll., pp. 1-442; Zweite Abth., 1833, pp. viii, 443-946, mit 2 Tafeln (figg. 1-10, 1-5).
> The secondary title of this work is:—Verzeichniss | der | Amphibien, Säugethiere und Vögel, | welche | auf einer Reise zwischen dem 13ten und dem 23sten | Grade südlicher Breite | im östlichen Brasilien | beobachtet wurden.—As above indicated, Birds occupy the 3d and the 4th Band, each of 2 Abtheilungen; in all, 4 vols., the pagination of the two portions of each Band being continuous. Some 450 spp. or more are systematically treated, the text being chiefly descriptive, but also including general matter, and some little criticism and synonymy. The author's new species appear to have been already described in his 'Reise', or elsewhere, and many of them were figured by Temminck in the Planches Coloriées. The three copper-plates represent some anatomical subjects, bills, and feet.—Whole work, 1825-33.

1831. KING, P. P.   [On the distinctive characters of several species of Birds from the Straits of Magellan.]   < *Philos. Mag.*, ix, 1831, pp. 226, 227.
> *Synallaxis anthöides, Dendrocolaptes albo-gularis,* p. 226; *Trochilus fernandensis, T. stokesii, Phalacrocorax imperialis, P. sarmientonus, P. erythrops,* p. 227. From *P. Z. S.,* Jan. 25, 1831.

1831. VIGORS, N. A.   [Remarks on the exhibition of several new species of birds from the Straits of Magellan.]   < *Philos. Mag.*, ix, 1831, pp. 64-66.
> From *P. Z. S.,* Dec. 14, 1830. Being those collected by P. P. King, and described from his MSS.

1832. GARNOT, [P.]   Ueber die Zoologie der Malwinen zwischen 52 und 53° S. B. und 56—60° W. L., östlich von Patagonien.   < *Oken's Isis,* Bd. xxv, 1832, pp. 180-184.
> Auszug aus *Annales des Sciences,* t. vii, 1826, p. 39.   (Lesson und D'Urville, *Voy. Coquille.*)

1832. MAXIMILIAN, PRINZ ZU WIED.   Beyträge zur Naturgeschichte von Brasilien von Maximilian, Prinzen zu Wied. Weimar, Ind. Compt. Bd. 3.   Abth. 1. 30. 8. 636; Abth. 2. 31. 637—1278.   < *Oken's Isis,* Bd. xxv, 1832, pp. 56-60.
> Auszug, SS. 55 u. folg.   Vögel, pp. 57-60.

1832. VIGORS, N. A.   [Characters of New Species of Birds collected by Mr. Cuming in Chili and Mexico.]   < *P. Z. S.,* ii, 1832, pp. 3, 4.
> *Capito aurifrons, Xanthornus chrysocarpus, Aglaïa chilensis,* p. 3; *Picus aurocapillus, Coccothrauste chrysopeplus, Ortyx spilogaster,* p. 4.

1834. GEOFFROY ST. HILAIRE, ISID., *and* DE BLAINVILLE, H. M. D.   Rapport sur les résultats scientifiques du voyage de M. Alcide D'Orbigny dans l' Amérique du sud, pendant les années 1826, 1827, 1828, 1829, 1830, 1831, 1832 et 1833.   < *Nouv. Ann. du Mus.,* iii, 1834, pp. 84-115.
> Quant aux oiseaux . . . etc., pp. 92 et seq.

1834. GOULD, J.   Sur des Oiseaux de l'Amérique Méridionale.   < *L'Institut,* ii, 1834, No. 64, p. 252.
> Not seen: title from Carus and Engelmann, *Bibl.*

1834. HEARNE, J.   [Note on Birds of Hayti.]   < *P. Z. S.,* ii, 1834, p. 25.

1834. HEARNE. J.   [Letter accompanying a Present of several Living Animals from the Island of Hayti.]   < *P. Z. S.,* ii, 1834, p. 110.

1834. KING, P. P.   Vögel von Magellanstrasse.   <*Oken's Isis,* Bd. xxvii, 1834, pp. 818, 819.
  Auszug aus *Philos. Mag.*, ix, 1831, pp. 226, 227.

1834. VIGORS, N. A.   Ueber Kings Vögel von der Magellanstrasse.   <*Oken's Isis,* Bd. xxvii, 1834, pp. 815, 816.
  Aus *Philos. Mag.*, ix, 1831, pp. 64–66.

1834–41. SWAINSON, W.   Ornithological Drawings: a Selection of Birds of Brazil and Mexico.   London.   Pub. in seven parts, 1834–41.   8vo.   78 pll.
  Not seen: others quote a literally very different title. [See beyond, ADDENDA.]

1835. HEARNE, J.   [Notice of a Collection of Bird-skins, 16 spp., formed by him in Hayti.]   < *P. Z. S.*, iii, 1835, p. 105.

1835. VIGORS, N. A.   [Thiere von Cuming von Vigors bestimmt.]   < *Oken's Isis,* Bd. xxviii, 1835, pp. 365, 366.
  Aus Chili und Mexico. Auszug aus *P. Z. S.*, 1832 pp. 3, 4, *q. v.*

1835-44-47. D'ORBIGNY, A.   Voyage | dans | L'Amérique Méridionale | (le Brésil, la République Orientale de l'Uruguay, la République | Argentine, la Patagonie, la République du Chili, la République de Bolivia, | la République du Pérou), | exécuté pendant les années 1826, 1827, 1828, 1829, 1830, 1831, 1832 et 1833, | par | Alcide d'Orbigny, | Chevalier de l'Ordre royale de la Légion d'Honneur, Officier de la Légion d'Honneur de la République | Bolivienne, Président de la Société Géologique de France et Membre de plusieurs Académies | et Sociétés savantes nationales et étrangères. | Ouvrage dédié au Roi, | et publié sous les auspices de M. le Ministre de l'Instruction publique | (commencé sous le ministère de M. Guizot). | — | Tome Quatrième. | 3.ᵉ Partie : Oiseaux. | — | Paris, | chez P. Bertrand, éditeur, | Libraire de la Société géologique de France, | rue Saint-André-des-Arcs, 38. | Strasbourg, | chez V.ᵉ Levrault, rue de Juifs, 33. | — | 1835-1844.   Very large 4to.   3 p. ll. (titles, each backed blank), pp. i–iij (advts.), pp. 1–395, with col'd folded map.—Also, Atlas Zoologique, being Vol. IX of the series, Oiseaux, 4to, pll. 1–6, 6 bis, 7–66 (= 67), 1847.

  The above title is that of Part 3 of Vol. IV, being the Birds, separately paged from the rest of the volume, and furnished with 3 title-pages. The composition of the whole work is: Tomes I, II, and III, Partie 1, Partie Historique. Tome III, Partie 2, Géographie; Partie 3, Géologie. Tome IV, Partie 1, Homme Américain; Partie 2, Mammifères; Partie 3, OISEAUX; Tome V, Partie 1, Reptiles; Partie 2, Poissons; Partie 3, Mollusques; Partie 4, Polypiers; Partie 5, Foraminifères. Tome VI, Partie 1, Crustacés; Partie 2, Insectes. Tome VII, Parties 1 et 2, Cryptogames; Partie 3, Palmiers. Tome VIII, ATLAS Historique, Géographique, Géologique, Paléontologique et Botanique. Tome IX, ATLAS Zoologique, comprenant les Mammifères, les OISEAUX, etc.
  The date of the ornithological text is 1833-44, as per title-page; that of the ornithological atlas is ostensibly 1847, but the plates are cited in the text. The Atlas Zoologique forms the IX. and last vol. of the series. It has no text except the title-page, which corresponds closely, but is not identical with that of the text above cited, the author having added more titles after his name, and another change being of course to | — | Tome Neuvième. | Atlas | Zoologique | (Mammifères, Oiseaux, Reptiles, Poissons, Mollusques, Polypiers, Foraminifères, Crustacés et Insectes.) |
  The sixty-seven plates of birds of the atlas are as follows:—Pl. 1, f. 1, 2, *Carthartes urubu,* tête et œuf; f. 3, 4, *C. aura,* tête et œuf; f. 5, *Polyborus vulgaris,* œuf. Pl. 2, f. 1, 2, *Phalcobœnus montanus,* ad. et jun.; f. 3, 4, œufs de *Polyborus chimango.* Pl. 3, f. 1 ♂, 2 ♀, *Butea tricolor.* Pl. 4, f. 1, *Tamnophilus* [sic] *aspersiventer;* f. 2, *T. schistaceus.* Pl. 5, f. 1, *T. fuliginosus* [by error for *schistaceus*]; f. 2, *T. aterrimus.* Pl. 6, f. 1, *T. fresnayanus;* f. 2, *Conopophaga nigro-cincta.* Pl. 6 bis , f. 1, 2, *Myothera* [sic] *analis;* f. 2, *M. nigro-maculatus.* Pl. 7, f. 1–2, *Rhinomya lanceolata;* f. 3, 4, *Megalonix* [sic] *rufo-gularis.* Pl. 8, f. 1, *M. ruficeps;* f. 2, *M. albicollis.* Pl. 9, f. 1, *Turdus fuscater;* f. 2, *T. chiguanaco.* Pl. 10, f. 1, œuf de *T. rufiventris ;* f. 2, 2 a, *Orpheus calandria;* f. 3, *O. thenca.* Pl. 11, f. 1, *O. dorsalis;* f. 2, *O. patagonicus.* Pl. 12, f. 1, *Donacobius albolineatus;* f. 2, *Sylvia leucoblephora.* Pl. 13, f. 1, *Hylophilus ruficeps ;* f. 2, *Dacnis flaviventer* [sic]. Pl. 14, f. 1, 2, *Synallaxis dorso-maculata;* f. 3, 4, *S. maluroïdes.* Pl. 15, f. 1, *S. torquata;* f. 2, *S. bitorquata.* Pl. 16, f. 1, *S. striaticeps;* f. 2, *S. albiceps.* Pl. 17, f. 1, *S. fuliginiceps;* f. 2, *S. humicola.* Pl. 18, f. 1, *Sylvia concolor;* f. 2, *Nemosia sordida.* Pl. 19, f. 1, *Tachyphonus versicolor;* f. 2, *T. capitatus.* Pl. 20, f. 1 ♂, 2 ♀, *T. luctuosus.* Pl. 21, f. 1, *T. flavinucha;* f. 2, 3, *Euphonia serrirostris.* Pl. 22, f. 1, *E. laniirostris;* f. 2, *E.*

1835–44–47. D'ORBIGNY, A.—Continued.

ruficeps; f. 3, œuf de *Embernagra platensis;* f. 4, œuf de *Aglaya* [sic] *episcopus.* Pl. 23, f. 1, *Tanagra montana;* f. 2, *T. cyanocephala.* Pl. 24, f. 1, *T. scrankii* [sic]; f. 2, *T. yeni.* Pl. 25, f. 1, *T. cyanicollis* [sic]; f. 2, *T. igniventris.* Pl. 26, f. 1, *Ramphocelus atro-sericeus;* f. 2, *Pyranga albicollis.* Pl. 27, f. 1, *Embernagra torquata;* f. 2, *E. rufinucha.* Pl. 28, f. 1, *Saltator rufiventris;* f. 2, *S. si·nalis;* f. 3, œuf de *S. aurantiirostris;* f. 4, œuf de *S. cœrulescens.* Pl. 29, f. 1, *Phylotoma rutila;* f. 2, *P. angustirostris.* Pl. 30, f. 1, *Pipra fasciata;* f. 2, *Ampelis viridis.* Pl. 31, f. 1, *A. rubro-cristata;* f. 2, 3, 4, *Pachyrhynchus marginatus.* Pl. 32, f. 1, 2, *Tyrannus tuberculifer;* f. 3, 4, *T. rufiventris.* Pl. 33, f. 1, 2, *Todirostrum ecaudatum;* f. 3, 4, *T. margaritaceiventer* [sic]. Pl. 34, f. 1, 2, *Muscipeta cinnamomea* [= *vieillotii* of the text, p. 321]; f. 3, 4, *Setophaga brunneiceps.* Pl. 35, f. 1, *S. verticalis;* f. 2, *Muscicapa striaticollis.* Pl. 36, f. 1, *Alecturus* [= *Arundinicola* of text, p. 335] *flaviventris;* f. 2, *Culicivora* [= *Setophaga* of the text, p. 330] *budytoides.* Pl. 37, f. 1, *C. reguloides;* f. 2, *Fluvicola rufipectoralis.* Pl. 38, f. 1, *F. leucophrys;* f. 2, *F. œnanthoides.* Pl. 39, f. 1, *Muscigralla brevicauca* [sic]; f. 2, *Pepoaza variegata;* f. 3, œuf de *Tyrannus sulphuratus;* f. 4, œuf de *Pepoaza polyglotta.* Pl. 40, f. 1, *Muscisaxicola mentalis;* f. 2, *M. rufivertex.* Pl. 41, f. 1, *M. striaticeps;* f. 2, *M. maculirostris.* Pl. 42, f. 1, *Cypselus montivagus;* f. 2, *C. andecolus;* f. 3, œuf de *Caprimulgus nacunda.* Pl. 43, f. 1, *Certhilauda cunicularia;* f. 2, *C. tenuirostris;* f. 3, œuf de *Passerina flava;* f. 4, œuf de *P. nigriceps.* Pl. 44, f. 1, *Certhilauda maritima;* f. 2, *Embernagra luteocephala;* f. 3, œuf de *Tyrannus savanha* [sic]; f. 4, œuf de *Fluvicola icterophrys.* Pl. 45, f. 1, *Emberiza hypochondria;* f. 2, *E. carbonaria;* f. 3, œuf de *Muscicapa icterophrys;* f. 4, œuf de *Loxia cucultata* [sic]. Pl. 46, f. 1, *Emberiza speculifera;* f. 2, *E. fulviceps.* Pl. 47, f. 1, *Emberiza griseocristata;* f. 2, *E. atriceps;* f. 3, œuf de l'*E. matutina;* f. 4, œuf de l'*E. gubernatrix.* Pl. 48, f. 1, *Linaria analis;* f. 2, *Carduelis atratus;* f. 3, œuf de *C. tristis;* f. 4, œuf de *Icterus virescens.* Pl. 49, f. 1 ♂ 2 ♀, *Pitylus aureoventris;* f. 3, œuf de *Tyrannus sulphuratus;* f. 4, œuf de *Cassicus solitarius.* Pl. 50, f. 1, *Pyrrhula bicolor;* f. 2, *P. glauco-cœrulea;* f. 3, œuf de *Icterus pyrrhopterus;* f. 4, œuf de *Fringilla cucullata.* Pl. 51, f 1, *Cassicus yuracares;* f. 2, *C. atrovirens;* f. 3, œuf de *Tyrannus melancholicus;* f. 4, œuf de *Pepoaza rixosa.* Pl. 52, f. 1, *Cassicus chrysonotus;* f. 2, 3, *Icterus maxillaris;* f. 4, œuf de *I. brevirostris;* f. 5, œuf de *I. flavus.* Pl. 53, f. 1, *Garrulus viridicyanus* [sic]; f. 2, *Dendrocolaptes procurvus* [= *D. lafresnayanus* in text]; f. 3, œuf de *Garrulus chrysops;* f. 4, œuf de *G. cyanomelas.* Pl. 54, f. 1, *Dendrocolaptes atrirostris;* f. 2, *Anabates squammiger;* f. 3, œuf de *Tyrannus melancholicus;* f. 4, œuf de *Saltator cœrulescens.* Pl. 55, f. 1, *Anumbius unirufus;* f. 2, nid de *Furnarius rufus;* f. 3, *Anabates gutturalis.* Pl. 56, f. 1, *Uppucerthia montana;* f. 2, *U. andœcola;* f. 3, œuf de *Furnarius rufus;* f. 4, œuf de *Anumbius striaticeps.* Pl. 57, f. 1, *Uppucerthia vulgaris;* f. 2, *U. nigro-fumosa;* f. 3, œuf de *Fluvicola bicolor;* f. 4, œuf de *Pepoaza polyglotta.* Pl. 58, f. 1, 2, œuf de *Serrirostrum carbonarium;* f. 3, *S. sittoides.* Pl. 59, f. 1, *Conirostrum cinereum;* f. 2, *Orthorhynchus smaragdinicollis.* Pl. 60, f. 1, *O. pamela;* f. 2, *O. amethysticollis.* Pl. 61, f. 1, *O. estella;* f. 2, *O. adela.* Pl. 62, *Colaptes rupicola;* f. 2, *Picus cactorum.* Pl. 63, f. 1, *P. atriventris;* f. 2, *P. canicapillus.* Pl. 64, f. 1, *P. puncticeps;* f. 2, *Picumnus albosquamatus.* Pl. 65, f. 1, *P. fumigatus;* f. 2, *P. nigriceps.* Pl. 66, f. 1, *Trogon antisianus;* f. 2, *Aulacorhynchus cœruleicinctus.*

This treatise with its many beautiful plates takes a conspicuous place among the few great works on South American ornithology, and d'Orbigny is to be named with such leaders as Azara and Molina of earlier times, Lafresnaye, Hartlaub, Tschudi, and the Prinz von Wied of his own period, and Burmeister, Pelzeln, Cabanis, Sclater, Salvin, Lawrence, and others, who have subsequently made the history of South American ornithology what it is. It is a comprehensive systematic treatise on some three or four hundred species, introduced and interspersed with general considerations of the avifauna of South America and the classification and geographical distribution of the birds, treating the families, genera, and species in detail—the latter with synonymy, description, and critical and field-notes. A colored map of the comparative zones of latitude and altitude illustrates the geographical distribution of the avifauna. It is an expensive work, not generally accessible in its entirety; but the ornithological portion is found separate, with or without the atlas.

The new species discovered on this Expedition appear to have been earlier described by the author and the Baron de Lafresnaye, in Guérin-Ménéville's *Magasin de Zoologie*, or elsewhere. The following may be here new, being those for which no earlier reference is given:— *Thamnophilus schistaceus*, p. 170; *Myrmothera menetriesii*, p. 184; *Thryothorus modulator*, p. 230; *Synallaxis maluroides*, *S. troglodytoides*, p. 238; *S. maximiliani*, p. 247; *S. patagonica*, p. 249; genus *Anumbius*, p. 251; *Embernagra olivascens*, p. 285; *Saltator azarae*, p. 287; *Tyrannus rufescens*, p. 308; *Todirostrum ecaudatum*, p. 316; *Muscipeta guillemini*, p. 319; *M. vieillotii*, p. 321; *M. ralloides*, p. 322; genus *Muscicapara*, p. 325; *M. gaimardi*, p. 326; *M. boliviana*, p. 328; genus *Arundinicola*, p. 335; genus *Suiriri* [!!!], p. 337; genus *Pepoaza*, p. 346; *P. andecola*, p. 351; *Dendrocolaptes lafresnayanus*, p. 308; *Colaptes rupicola*, p. 377; *Picus cactorum*, *P. atriventris*, p. 278; *P. canipileus*, *P. puncticeps*, p. 379; *P. fumigatus*, *P. nigriceps*, *Picumnus albosquamatus*, p. 380; *Aulacorhynchus cœruleo-cinctus*, p. 382.

1836. KITTLITZ, [F. H. v.] Ueber einige Vögel von Chili, [u. s. w.] < *Oken's Isis*, Bd. xxix, 1836, pp. 347–351.

Auszüge aus *Mém. Acad. Imp. des Sciences de Pétersbourg*, tome i, 1831, p. 174.

1836. MARTIN, R. M.   History | of the | West Indies: | comprising | . . . . [the rest of the title differs in the two vols.] By R. Montgomery Martin, F. S. S. | [Seal.] | Vol. I. [II.] | — | London: | Whittaker & Co. Ave Maria Lane. | — | MDCCCXXXVI. | 2 vols. 16mo? [half-sheets—8 ll. to a sig.]. Vol. I, pp. xxxvi, 308; Vol. II, pp. viii, 350.
　　Slightly ornithological in some places—as at I, pp. 83, 84; II, pp. 83-94.

1836. MORITZ, C.   Notizen zur Fauna der Insel Puertorico. <*Arch. f. Naturg.*, ii, (1), 1836, pp. 373-392.
　　Ornithologisch *passim.*

1836. TAYLOR, R. C.   Notes on Natural Objects observed while staying in Cuba. <*Loudon's Mag. Nat. Hist.*, ix, 1836, pp. 449-457.
　　Narrative, partly ornithological.

1837. BONAPARTE, C. L.   [Notices and Descriptions of new or interesting Birds from Mexico and South America.] <*P. Z. S.*, v, 1837, pp. 108-122.
　　I, on birds from Mexico, 35 spp.; II, from Guatemala, 39 spp.; III, from Brazil near Peru, 20 spp.—*Centurus subelegans*, p. 109; *Icterus parisorum*, p. 110; *Cardinalis sinuatus*, p. 111; *Tyrannus divaricata, Pipra elegantissima*, p. 112; *P. linearis*, p. 113; *Centurus Santa Cruzi*, p. 116; *Euphonia hirundinacea, Arremon giganteus, Icteria velasquezii*, p. 117; *Sylvicola decurtata, Turdus grayi*, p. 118; *Scolopacinns* (g. n.) *rufiventris*, p. 119; *Micropogon flavicolle, Asthenurus rufiventris, Guiracamagnirostris, Spizaversicolor*, p. 120; *Tanagra darwinii, Aglaia nigrocincta, Rhamphocelus icteronotus*, p. 121; *Agalaia schrankii, Pipra scrutata*, p. 122, spp. nn.

1837. BREDOW, — v.   Auszüge aus den Schreiben des reisenden Naturforschers C. Moritz in Süd-Amerika. <*Arch. f. Naturg.*, 1837, (1), pp. 408-414.
　　Ornithologisch *passim.*

1837. GOULD, J.   [Characters of three New Neotropical Birds.] <*P. Z. S.*, v, 1837, pp. 79, 80.
　　Corvus nobilis, Ortyx guttata, p. 79; *Thamnophilus fuliginosus*, p. 80.

1837. L'HERMINIER, DR. —.   Anatomie verschiedener Vögel aus Südamerica. <*Oken's Isis*, Bd. xxx, 1837, pp. 847, 848.
　　Auszüge aus der Zeitschrift: *L'Institut*, 1837, Nr. 220.

1837. LESSON, R. P.   Neue Vögel. <*Oken's Isis*, Bd. xxx, 1837, pp. 714, 715.
　　Auszüge aus der Zeitschrift: *L'Institut*, ii, 1834, 316. 10 Arten: *Megalonyx medius, Phytotoma molinæ, Pyrgita peruviensis*, p. 714; *Pithylus* [sic] *olivaceus, P. luteus, Dolichonyx griseus, Fringilla erythrorhyncha, Ada commersonii, Vermivora elegans, Troglodytes hornensis*, p. 715.

1837. D'ORBIGNY, A.   Mémoire sur la distribution géographique des Oiseaux Passereaux, dans l'Amérique méridionale. <*Compt. Rend. de l'Acad. Sci.*, v, 1837, pp. 496-498.
　　Division des régions de l'Amérique méridionale en trois zones suivant leur distance à l'équateur.—Considération des espèces sous le rapport de la température des lieux qu'elles habitent.

1837. D'ORBIGNY, A.   Observations on the Raptores of South America. <*Mag. of Zool. and Bot.*, i, 1837, pp. 347-359.
　　Trans. from *Voy. Amér. Mérid.* Of very general character, but with special reference to their distribution in zones of latitude and to their habits.

1837. ——   Beyträge zur Naturgeschichte von Brasilien von Maximilian, Prinzen zu Wied. Weimar, Indust. Compt. iv. 1. 32. 8. 442. <*Oken's Isis*, Bd. xxx, 1837, pp. 97, 98.

1837. ——   Beyträge zur Naturgeschichte von Brasilien von Max. Prinzen zu Wied. Weimar. Industrie Comptoir. vi. 2. 1833. 8. 443-946. 2 Tafeln. <*Oken's Isis*, Bd. xxx, 1837, pp. 177-179.

1837-38. D'ORBIGNY, A., *and* LAFRESNAYE, F. DE.   Synopsis Avium in itinere per Americam meridionalem collectarum. <*Magas. de Zool.*, vii, 1837, pp. ——— ; viii, 1838, pp. ———. [88 + 34 pp.. with pll.]
　　Not seen: defective title from Giebel.

1838. BONAPARTE, C. L.   Catalogo di Uccelli Messicani e Peruviani. <*Nuovi Ann. Sci. Nat. Bologna*, ii, 1838, pp. 340-348, 401-416.
　　This paper appears to be very similar to, if not a mere version of, that in *P. Z. S.*, 1837, *q. v.*

1838. LAFRESNAYE, [F.] DE, *and* D'ORBIGNY, [A.] Notice sur quelques oiseaux de Carthagène et de la partie du Mexique la plus voisine, rapportés par M. Ferdinand de Candé, officier de la Marine royale. < *Rev. Zool.*, i, 1838, pp. 164–166.

17 espèces.—*Embernagra albinucha, Pipra pareolides, Synnalaxis* [sic] *candei,* p. 165; *Tamatia gularis,* p. 166, spp. nn.

1838. D'ORBIGNY, A. Rapport sur un Mémoire de M. Alcide D'Orbigny, intitulé: Sur la distribution géographique des oiseaux passereaux dans l'Amérique méridionale. < *Compt. Rend. de l'Acad. Sci.*, vi, 1838, pp. 190–194.

1839. GOULD, J. [Polyborus gallapagoensis von Darwin, u. s. w.] < *Oken's Isis,* Bd. xxxii, 1839, pp. 139, 140.

P. Z. S. London, 1837.

1839. LAFRESNAYE, F. DE. Quelques oiseaux nouveaux de la collection de M. Charles Brelay, à Bordeaux. < *Rev. Zool.*, ii, 1839, pp. 97–100.

Pyranga sanguinolenta, Embernagra brunnei-nucha, E. pyrgitoïdes, p. 97; *Pachyrhynchus aglaiæ, Myadestes* [sic] *obscurus,* p. 98; *Thriothorus guttulatus, Pyrrhula cinnamomea,* p. 99; *Dendrocolaptes affinis, Uncirostrum brelayi,* p. 100. Toutes les espèces sont du Mexique.

1839. D'ORBIGNY, A. Histoire | Physique, Politique et Naturelle | de | L'Ile De Cuba | par M. Ramon de la Sagra, Directeur du Jardin Botanique de la Havane, | Correspondant de l'Institut Royal de France, etc. | — | > Ornithologie, | par Alcide D'Orbigny. | [Dessin.] | Paris, | Arthur Bertrand, éditeur, | Libraire de la Société de Géographie | et de la Société Royale des Antiquaires du Nord, | Rue Hautfeuille, 23. | — | 1839. 8vo, paper, forming part (with the mammals) of one vol. of the series, separately paged, pp. xxxi, 336. Folio atlas of pll. i–xix, xix bis, xx–xxi.

A standard work, to be used in connection with Vigor's earlier and Gundlach's and others' later treatises on the same subject. The Introduction, pp. vii–xxxi, is a résumé, from which it appears there were known 129 Cuban spp., of 33 families—14 South American, 49 North American, 26 American, 8 Arctogæan, 5 Neotropico-Arctogæan, and 27 Cuban and Antillian. The main text treats of those species seriatim, systematically, and is synonymical, descriptive, and general. French, Latin, and Spanish indexes follow. The plates are published separately; they are as follows:—Pl. 1, *Falco sparverioides.* 2, *Otus siguapa* D'Orb. 3, *Noctua siju* O'Orb. 4, *Turdus rubripes.* 5, *Turdus minor.* 6, *Sciurus* [sic] *sulfurascens.* 7, *Turdus carolinensis.* 8, *Sylvia palmarum.* 9, *Sylvia caerulescens.* 10, *Sylvia maritima.* 11, *Tanagra zena.* 12, *Tyrannus caudifasciatus* D'Orb. 13, *Tyrannus magnirostris* D'Orb. 14, *Tyrannus matutinus.* 15, *Passerina olivacea.* 16, *Linaria caniceps* D'Orb. 17, *Pyrrhula nigra.* 18, *Quiscalus barytus.* 19, *Q. atroviolaceus* D'Orb. 19 bis, *Xanthornus dominicensis.* 20, *Icterus humeralis.* 21, f. 1, *Orthorhynchus colubris;* f. 2, *O. ricordi.* 22, *Todus multicolor.* 23, *Colaptes superciliaris.* 24, *Colaptes fernandinæ.* 25, f. 1, *Saurothera merlini* D'Orb.; f. 2, 3, *Crotophaga ani.* 26, *Trogon temnurus.* 27, *Columba portoricensis.* 28, *C. inornata.* 29, *Phœnicopterus americanus.* 30, *Aix sponsa.* 31, f. 1, *Totanus flavipes,* egg; f. 2, *Parra jacana,* egg; f. 3, *Aramus guarauna;* f. 5, *Rallus longirostris* (head).

1839. D'ORBIGNY, A. Naturhistorische Schilderung des nördlichen Patagonien. < *Arch. f. Naturg.*, 1839, (1), pp. 47–61.

Aus dessen *Voy. dans l'Amér. Mérid.* Grössten Theils ornithologischen Inhalts.

1839. D'ORBIGNY, A. Ueber die geographische Verbreitung und die Lebensweise der südamerikanischen Singvögel. < *Arch. f. Naturg.*, 1839, (1) pp. 235–251.

Mitgetheilt aus dessen *Reise,* SS. 141–158.

1839. D'ORBIGNY, A. Voyage dans l'Amérique méridionale, par A. D'Orbigny. Paris, Levrault, I. 1834. 672. II. 1836. 4. < *Oken's Isis,* Bd. xxxii, 1839, pp. 406–435.

Verzeichniss der Vögel, pp. 408, 410, 411. Auszüge, pp. 414–435.

1839. VIGORS, N. A. [Observations upon a Collection of Birds from the West Coast of South America.] < *P. Z. S.*, vii, 1839, p. 115.

1840. BOISSONNEAU, [A.] Oiseaux nouveaux ou peu connus de Santa-Fé de Bogota. < *Rev. Zool.*, iii, 1840, pp. 2–8.

Ampelis nattererii, p. 2; *A. rufocristata, A. riefferii, Tanagra constantii,* p. 3; *T. vassorii, T. riefferii, Uncirostrum La Fresnayii,* p. 4; *U. d'Orbignyi,* p. 5; *Ornismia* [sic] *bonarpartei* [sic], *O. torquata, O. paradiscea,* p. 6; *O. guerinii,* p. 7; *Trochilus La Fresnayi,* p. 8.

1840. BOISSONNEAU, [A.]   Oiseaux nouveaux de Santa-Fé de Bogota.   < *Rev. Zool.*, iii, 1840, pp. 66–71.

Tanagra eximia, p. 66; *T. tœniata, T. labradorides, T. assimilis*, p. 67; *T. albofrenatus, T. pallidinucha*, p. 68; *T. schistaceus, T. semirufus*, p. 69; *Pteroglossus albivitta, Quiscalus subalaris, Setophaga ornata*, p. 70; *Tyrannula fumigata*, p. 71.

1840. BONAPARTE, C. L.   Catalogue d'Oiseaux du Mexique et du Pérou.   < *Rev. Zool.*, iii, 1840, pp. 19, 20.

This is not the article itself, but merely an editorial notice of Bp.'s new genus *Scolopacinus*. See *P. Z. S.* 1837.

1840. FRASER, L.   [On some New Species of Birds from Bogota in the Collection of the Earl of Derby.]   < *P. Z. S.*, viii, 1840, pp. 59, 60.

Turdus gigas, Psittacus chalcopterus, p. 59; *Picus elegans*, p. 60.

1840. LAFRESNAYE, [F.] DE.   Oiseaux nouveaux de Santa-Fé de Bogota.   < *Rev. Zool.*, iii, 1840, pp. 101–106.

Uncirostrum cyaneum, Conirostrum sitticolor, p. 102; *Merulaxis senilis, M. griseicollis, M. squamiger*, p. 103; *M. analis, Anabates Boissonneautii*, p. 104; *Limnornis unirufus, L. canifrons*, p. 105.

1840. LAFRESNAYE, F. DE.   Nouvelles espèces d'oiseaux tuées et rapportées par M. Léclancher, chirurgien de la marine, embarqué sur la Vénus, dans son dernier voyage de circumnavigation.   < *Rev. Zool.*, iii, 1840, pp. 259–261.

Turdus rufopalliatus, p. 259; *Passerina leclancheri*, p. 260, spp. nn.

1840. LESSON, R. P.   Oiseaux nouveaux.   < *Rev. Zool.*, iii, 1840, p. 1.

Melias corallirhynchus, Ramphocelus affinis.

1840. SCHOMBURGK, R. H.   A Description | of | British Guiana, | Geographical and Statistical: | exhibiting | its resources and capabilities, | together with | the present and future condition and prospects | of the colony. | By | Robert H. Schomburgk, Esq. | London: | Simpkin, Marshall, and Co., | Stationers' Hall Court. | 1840.   1 vol. 8vo.   2 p. ll., map, pp. 155.

In this little tract (by no means to be taken for Schomburgk's great work on Guiana) there occurs, under head of "Animal Kingdom", some remarks on birds, pp. 37, 38.

1841. BRIDGES, T.   [Notes on various Birds (19 spp.) and Mammals from Chile.]   < *P. Z. S.*, ix, 1841, pp. 93–95.

1841. GOULD, J. The | Zoology | of | the Voyage of H. M. S. Beagle, | under the command of Captain Fitzroy, R. N., | during the years | 1832 to 1836. | Published with the approval of | the Lords Commissioners of her Majesty's Treasury. | Edited and Superintended by | Charles Darwin, Esq., M. A. F. R. S. Sec. G. S. | Naturalist to the Expedition. | — | Part III. | Birds, | by | John Gould, Esq., F. L. S. | — | London: | Published by Smith, Elder and Co. 65, Cornhill. | MDCCCXLI.   4to.   4 p. ll., pp. ii, 156, 4 ll., pll. col'd 50.

The technical matter of the work was prepared by Gould, with assistance from G. R. Gray; but the general text is Darwin's. Most of the new species collected on the voyage appear to have been before described. The following names occur without citation of previous authority, most of which, doubtless, if not all, are new:—*Craxirex*, p. 22; *Strix punctatissima* (Gray), p. 34; *Progne modesta*, p. 39; *Hirundo frontalis*, p. 40; *Pyrocephalus*, p. 44; *P. parvirostris*, p. 44; *P. obscurus, P. nanus*, p. 45; *P. dubius*, p. 46; *Myiobius* (Gray), p. 46; *M. auriceps*, p. 47; *M. magnirostris, M. parvirostris*, p. 48; *Serpophaga, S. albocoronata*, p. 49; *Pachyrhamphus* (Gray), *P. albescens*, p. 50; *P. minimus*, p. 51; *Lichenops erythropterus*, p. 52; *Fluvicola azaræ*, p. 53; *Agriornis, A. striatus*, p. 56; *A. micropterus*, p. 57; *Opetiorhynchus lanceolatus*, p. 68; *Eremobius, E. phœnicurus*, p. 69; *Synallaxis major*, p. 76; *S. rufogularis*, p. 77; *S. flavigularis, S. brunnea*, p. 78; *Limnornis, L. rectirostris*, p. 80; *L. curvirostris*, p. 81; *Dendrodramus, D. leucosternus*, p. 82; *Muscisaxicola brunnea*, p. 84; *Sylvicola aureola*, p. 86; *Pyrrhalauda nigriceps*, p. 87; *Spermophila nigrogularis, Crithagra? brevirostris*, p. 88; *Ammodramus longicaudatus*, p. 90; *A. xanthornus*, p. 90; *Zonotrichia canicapilla*, p. 91; *Z. strigiceps*, p. 92; *Fringilla formosa*, p. 93; *Chlorospiza? xanthogramma* (Gray), p. 96; *Emberozoides poliocephala* (Gray), p. 98; *Geospiza magnirostris. G. strenua*, p. 100; *G. fortis, G. nebulosa, G. fuliginosa*, p. 101; *G. dentirostris, G. parvula*, p. 102; *G. dubia, Camarhynchus psittaculus, C. crassirostris*, p. 103; *Cactornis scandens*, p. 104; *C. assimilis*, p. 105; *Certhidea olivacea*, p. 106; *Zenaida galapagoensis*, p. 115; *Squatarola fusca*, p. 126; *Totanus fuliginosus*, p. 130; *Porphyrio simplex*, p. 133; *Larus fuliginosus*, p. 141. (*Cinclodus* and *Rhinocrypta* are proposed, apparently newly, by Gray, on one of the unpaged leaves.) Most of the birds of the volume are South American. An appendix, by T. C. Eyton, gives some anatomical details respecting 12 spp. The plates are as follows:—

1841. GOULD, J.—Continued.

Pl. 1, *Milvago albogularis* ; 2, *Craxirex galapagoensis* ; 3, *Otus galapagoensis* ; 4. *Strix punctatissima;* 5, *Progne modesta* ; 6, *Pyrocephalus parvirostris* ; 7, *P. nanus;* 8, *Tyrannula magnirostris;* 9, *Lichenops erythropterus* ; 10, *Fluvicola azaræ*; 11, *Xolmis variegata* (marked *Tænioptera v.*) ; 12, *Agriornis micropterus* ; 13, *A. leucurus* ; 14, *Pachyrhamphus albescens* ; 15, *P. minimus* ; 16, *Mimus trifasciatus;* 17, *M. melanotis;* 18, *M. parvulus;* 19, *Uppucerthia dumetoria;* 20, *Opetiorhynchus nigrofremosus* (marked *O. lanceolatus*) ; 21. *Eremobius phœnicurus;* 22, *Anumbius acuticaudus* (marked *Synallaxis major*) ; 23, *Synallaxis rufogularis;* 24, *S. flavogularis;* 25, *Limnornis curvirostris;* 26. *L. rectirostris;* 27. *Dendrodramusleucosternus;* 28, *Sylvicola aureola* ; 29. *Ammodramus longicaudatus;* 30, *A. manimbe* (marked *A. xanthornus*); 31, *Passer jagoensis;* 32, *Chlorospiza melanodera* ; 33, *C. xanthogramma* ; 34, *Aglaia striata* (marked *Tanagra darwini*) ; 35, *Pipilo personata* ; 36, *Geospiza magnirostris* ; 37, *G. strenua* ; 38, *G.fortis* ; 39, *G. parvula* ; 40, *Camarhynchus psittaculus;* 41, *C. crassirostris* ; 42, *Cactornis scandens* ; 43, *C. assimilis* ; 44, *Certhidea olivacea* ; 45. *Xanthornus flaviceps* ; 46, *Zenaida galapagoensis* ; 47, *Rhea darwinii* ; 48, *Zapornia notata* ; 49, *Z. spilonota* ; 50, *Anser melanopterus.*

1841. HILL, R. [Letter relating to the Nests of Birds of Jamaica.] < *P. Z. S.,* ix, 1841, pp. 69, 70.

1842. HILL, R. [On the Nests of Jamaican Birds.] < *Ann. Mag. Nat. Hist.,* ix, 1842, pp. 145–147.

From *P. Z. S.,* Sept. 14, 1841, pp. 69, 70.

1842. LAFRESNAYE, [F.] DE. Description de quelques oiseaux nouveaux de Colombie. < *Rev. Zool.,* v, 1842, pp. 301, 302.

Catamblyrhynchus (g. n.) *diadema, Conirostrum albifrons,* p. 301; *C. coeruleifrons,* p. 302.

1842. LAFRESNAYE, [F.] DE. Oiseaux nouveaux de Colombie. < *Rev. Zool.,* v, 1842, pp. 332–336.

Grallaria ruficapilla, p. 333; *G. nana,* p. 334; *Copurus leuconotus, Arremon atropileus,* p. 335; *Tachyphonus victorinæ,* p. 336. Coup-d'œil sur 9 esp. de *Grallaria.*

1842. LESSON, R. P. Notes sur les Oiseaux nouveaux ou peu connus rapportés de la Mer du Sud, par M. Adolphe Lesson. < *Rev. Zool.,* v, 1842, pp. 135, 136.

Megalonyx nanus, Parra cordifera, Arara erythrofrons, Psittacus auropalliatus, P. chrysopogon, P. eburnirostrum, p. 135; *Trogon capistratum,* p. 136, spp. nn.

1842. LESSON, R. P. Species avium novæ aut minùs cognitæ: auctore R. P. Lesson, in itinere A. Lessonio collectæ. < *Rev. Zool.,* v, 1842, pp. 174, 175.

Crypticus apiaster, Momotus Lessonii, Penelope albiventer, Pipra fastuosa, Picolaptes capistrata. Pitylus lazulus, p. 174; *Tanagra diaconus, T. affinis, Ornismya cinnamomea, Ortyx leucopogon,* p. 175.

1843. CABOT, S., JR. [*Corvus vociferus,* p. 155; *Oriolus musicus,* p. 155; *Momotus yucatacensis,* p. 156, spp. nn. from Yucatan.] < *Proc. Bost. Soc. Nat. Hist.,* i, 1843, pp. 155, 156.

1843. FRASER, L. [On the Collection of South American Birds brought to England by Mr. Bridges.] < *P. Z. S.,* xi, 1843, pp. 108–121.

Numerous species fully annotated by the collector, constituting an approximate list of Chilian birds.

1843. HARTLAUB, G. Description de quatre espèces d'oiseaux de la Nouvelle-Grenade. < *Rev. Zool.,* vi, 1843, pp. 289, 290.

Vireo versicolor, Myiobius diadema, M. pyrrhopterus, Todirostrum granadense, p. 289.

1843. LAFRESNAYE, F. DE. Quelques oiseaux nouveaux ou peu connus de Colombie. < *Rev. Zool.,* vi, 1843, pp. 68–70.

Ampelis atureopectus, p. 68; *Tanagra olivicyanea, T. argentea, T. nigroviridis,* p. 69, spp. nn.

1843. LAFRESNAYE, F. de. Description de deux Oiseaux de Colombie. < *Rev. Zool.,* vi, 1843, pp. 131–133.

Merulaxis orthonyx, p. 131; *Tangara albocristatus,* p. 132.

1843. LAFRESNAYE, F. de. Oiseaux nouveaux de Colombie. < *Rev. Zool.,* vi, 1843, pp. 290, 292.

Tanagra atricapilla, T. aurulenta, Cassicus uropygialis, Synnalaxis [sic] *striaticollis, S. unirufus, S. fuliginosus, S. brachyurus, S. gularis,* p. 290; *S. cinnamomeus, Muscicapa cinnamomeiventris, M. fuscocapilla, M. ruficeps, Pachyrhynchus squamatus, Fringilla analis, Spermophila luctuosa, S. olivaceoflava, Querula fuscocinerea,* p. 291; *Carduelis colombianus, Setophaga nigrocincta,* p. 292.

1843. TSCHUDI, J. J. v. Diagnosen einiger neuer peruanischer Vögel. <*Arch. f. Naturg.*, 1843, (1), pp. 385–390.

Ampelis elegans, A. cincta, Columba gracilis, C. meloda, p. 385; *C. frenata, Penelope rufi-ventris, P. adspersa*, p. 386; *Thinocorus ingæ, Crypturus kleei, Odontophorus speciosus, Oedicnemus superciliaris*, p. 387; *Charadrius winterfeldtii, C. resplendens, Crex facialis, C. femoralis*, p. 388; *Larus modestus, Fulica ardesiaca, Sterna acutirostris, S. exilis*, p. 389; *Dysporus varic. gatus, Anser montana, Anas leucogenis*, p. 390, 22 spp.; die ausführlichen Beschreibungen und Abbildungen dieser Vögel in dem ornithologischen Theile, Fauna Peruana.

1844. ABBOTT, S. L. [Remarks on Exhibition of some Birds from Surinam.] <*Proc. Bost. Soc. Nat. Hist.*, i, 1844, p. 171.

1844. CABOT, S., JR. Descriptions and Habits of Some of the Birds of Yucatan. <*Journ. Bost. Soc. Nat. Hist.*, iv, pt. iv, 1844, pp. 460–467. (Read Nov. 1, 1843.)

Ortyx nigrogularis Gould. *Falco percontator*, p. 462; *Corvus vociferus*, p. 464; *Oriolus musicus*, p. 465; *Momotus yucatacensis* [sic], p. 466, spp. nn.

1844. HARTLAUB, [G.] Description de sept Oiseaux nouveaux de Guatemala. <*Rev. Zool.*, vii, 1844, pp. 214–216.

Picus guatemalensis, Turdus (Merula) rufitorques, Tyrannus (Milvulus) monachus, p. 214; *Conirostrum superciliosum, Garrulus (Cyanocorax) melanocyaneus, Geococcyx affinis*, p. 215; suivie de la synonymie de *G. viaticus*.

1844. HILL, R. [Letter accompanied by a donation of two Birds' Skins from Jamaica.] <*P. Z. S.*, xii, 1844, p. 1.

1844. LAFRESNAYE, [F.] DE. Observations ornithologiques [sur divers Oiseaux de la Nouvelle-Grenade]. <*Rev. Zool.*, vii, 1844, pp. 78–80.

Muscicapa fuscocapilla Lafr. = *Myiobus diademata* Hartl., *Myiobius pyrrhopterus* Hartl. = *Muscipeta cinnamomea* d'Orb. et Lafres., *Setophaga nigrocincta* Lafr. = *S. canadensis* auct.

1844. LAFRESNAYE, [F.] DE. Nouvelles espèces d'oiseaux de Colombie. <*Rev. Zool.*, vii, 1844, pp. 80–83.

Dendrocolaptes perrotii, Tyrannula ardosiaca, p. 80; *Hylophilus leucophrys, Chætura brunni-torques, Setoph aga flaveola*, p. 81; *Thamnophilus albicans, T. multistriatus, T. brevirostris*, p. 82; *T. shistaceus* [sic], *T. aspersiventer*, p. 83.

1844. LAFRESNAYE, F. DE. Description de quelques Oiseaux de la Guadeloupe. <*Rev. Zool.*, vii, 1844, pp. 167–169.

Saltator guadelupensis, Turdus montanus, T. L'Herminieri, p. 167; avec des détails sur la *Procellaria diabolica* L'Herm.

1844. LESSON, R. P. Oiseaux nouveaux. <*Rev. Zool.*, vii, 1844, pp. 433–437.

Picolaptes cinnamomeus, Ornismya feliciana, p. 433; *Troglodytes murinus*, p. 434; *Arremon abeillei, Tiaris cruentus*, p. 435; *Pendulinus californicus*, p. 436.

1844. TSCHUDI, J. J. VON. Avium conspectus quae in Republica Peruana reperiuntur et pleraeque observatae vel collectae sunt in itinere a Dr. I. I. de Tschudi. <*Arch. f. Naturg.*, 1844, (1), pp. 262–317.

Spp. 357 enumeratio, descriptionibus specierum et generum quorundam novorum, necnon synonymis multis, adjectis: genera nova proposita sunt a Cabanis, qui ad constituendam hanc enumerationem observationes varias communicavit.—*Polyborus taeniurus, Hypomorphnus*, p. 263; *Circaetus solitarius*, p. 264; *Climacocercus*, p. 265; *Circus poliopterus, Noctua melanota*, p. 266; *Caprimulgus ocellatus, C. decussatus, C. pruinosus* (Licht., Mus. Berol.), p. 268; *C. climacocercus*, p. 269; *Ampelis rufaxilla, Ptilogonys leucotis, P. griseiventer*, p. 270; *Pipra chloromeros, P. coeruleo-capilla*, p. 271; *Scaphorhynchus chrysocephalus, Tyrannus cinchoneti* (Licht., M. B.), *Myiarchus*, p. 272; *M. atropurpureus* (Licht., Mus. Ber.), *Euscarthmus pileatus, E. rufipes*, p. 273; *Elaenia modesta, E. brevirostris, E. viridiflava*, p. 274; *Mionectes, M. poliocephalus, Leptopogon, L. superciliaris*, p. 275; *L. cinereus, Setophaga melanocephala, S. chrysogaster, Ptyonura albifrons*, p. 276; *Ochthites*, p. 277; *Thamnophilus luctuosus, T. olivaceus, T. axillaris, Pithys leucophrys*, p. 278; *Corythopis torquata, Cinclus leucocephalus, Chamaeza olivacea*, p. 279; *Turdus serranus, Mimus longicaudatus*, p. 280; *Cillurus, C. palliatus, Pteroptochus femoralis*, p. 281; *P. acutirostris, Cyphorhinus, C. thoracicus, Troglodytes audax, T. leucophrys*, p. 282; *Myiodioctes coronatus, M. tristriatus*, p. 283; *Hylophilus frontalis, H. olivaceus, Procnopis*, p. 285; *P. atrocoerulea, P. argentea, Callospiza pulchra, C. xanthocephala*, p. 285; *C. calliparaea* (Licht., Mus. Berol.), *Tanagra frugilegus*, p. 286; *T. analis, Phaenisoma ardens*, p. 287; *Saltator elegans*, p. 288; *Arremon frontalis, Phrygilus*, p. 289; *P. plebejus, P. rusticus* (Licht., M. B.), *Sporophila, S. luctuosa* (Licht., M. B.), p. 291; *Diglossa melanops, Anabates auritus* (Licht., M. B.), p. 294; *A. montanus, A. ochrolaemus, A. melanorhynchus, Dendrocolaptes chunchotambo*, p. 295; *D. validus, Trochilus apicalis* (L., M. B.), p. 296; *T. phoeo-*

1844. TSCHUDI, J. J. VON.—Continued.
   pygus (L., M. B.), *T. leucogaster*, p. 297; *T. opacus* (L., M. B.), *T. insectivorus*, *T. otero*, p. 298;
   Trogon heliothrix, *Lypornix ruficapilla*, p. 300; *Capito glaucogularis*, p. 301; *Picus haemato-*
   gaster, p. 302; *Psittacus mercenarius*, p. 303; *P. tumultuosus*, *Conurus mitratus*, *O. rupicola*,
   C. sitophagus, p. 304; *Columba melancholica*, *Odontophorus pachyrhynchus*, p. 306; *Crypturus*
   atro-capillus, p. 307; *Larus serranus*, p. 314; *Anas puna* (Licht., M. B.), p. 315, genn. et spp. nn.

1845. CABOT, S., JR.   Further accounts of some of the Birds of Yucatan.   *< Journ. Bost.*
   Soc. Nat. Hist., v, pt. i, 1845, pp. 90–93, pl. xii.   (Read Jan. 3, 1844.)
   Pyrrhula raptor, p. 90, pl. xii; *Picus dubius*, p. 91; *Picus parvus*, *P. yucatanensis*, p. 92,
   spp. nn.

1845. CABOT, S., JR.   [On Himantopus nigrocollis and Anhinga carolinensis from
   Surinam.]   *< Proc. Bost. Soc. Nat. Hist.*, ii, 1845, p. 46.

1845. DES MURS, O.   Description de quelques espèces nouvélles d'Oiseaux.   *< Rev.*
   Zool., viii, 1845, pp. 207–209.
   Psittacus amazonicus, *Ortyx perrotiana*, *Galbalcyrhynchus* (g. n.) *leucotis*, p. 207.   Avec une
   note sur *Falco isidori.*

1845. FRASER, L.   [On Chilian Birds.]   *< Ann. Mag. Nat. Hist.*, xv, 1845, pp. 430, 431.
   From *P. Z. S.*, October 8, 1844.

1845. FRASER, L.   [Exhibition of two Birds from Chili.]   *< P. Z. S.*, xiii, 1845, p. 1.

1845. LAFRESNAYE, [F.] DE.   Oiseaux nouveaux rapportés par M. Léclancher, chirurgien de l'expédition de la corvette la Favorite.   *· < Rev. Zool.*, viii, 1845, pp.
   93, 94.
   Scissirostrum (g. n.) *pagei*, p. 93; *Pericrocotus cinereus*, *Dicæum leclancherii*, p. 94.

1845. LAFRESNAYE, F. DE.   Description de quelques oiseaux nouveaux.   *< Rev.*
   Zool., viii, 1845, pp. 337–342.
   Thriothorus fasciato-ventris, *T. rufalbus*, p. 337; *T. leucotis*, *T. maculipectus*, *T. striatulus*,
   p. 338; *Campylorhynchus rufinucha*, *C. brevirostris*, *C. megalopterus*, p. 339; *Thamnophilus*
   immaculatus, p. 340; *Myioturdus fuscater*, *Tyrannula icterophrys*, *Tyrannulus nigrocapillus*,
   Hylophilus semibrunneus, p. 341; *H. flavipes*, p. 342.

1845. TSCHUDI, J. J. V.   Nachträgliche Bemerkungen zu meinem Conspectus Avium
   etc. [op. cit. 1844, (1), pp. 262–317].   *< Arch. f. Naturg.*, 1845, (1), pp. 360–366.
   Cyclarhis ochrocephala, *C. poliocephala*, p. 362, spp. nn.

1845. ——— Histoire physique, politique et naturelle de l'Ile de Cuba, par Ramon
   de la Sagra, Director du Jardin de Botanique de la Havane.   Paris chez A.
   Bertrand.   *< Oken's Isis*, Bd. xxxviii, 1845, pp. 196–218.
   Vögel, pp. 200–202.   Bearbeitet von A. d'Orbigny.

1845. ——— Voyage en l'Amérique meridionale, exécuté pendant 1826–1833. par
   Alcide d'Orbigny.   Strasbourg chez Levrault.   *< Oken's Isis*, Bd. xxxviii,
   1845, pp. 588–600.

1845–46. TSCHUDI, J. J. v., *and* CABANIS, J.   Untersuchungen | über die | Fauna Peru-
   ana | von J. J. von Tschudi, | Doctor der Philosophie, Medecin und Chirurgie,
   Mitglied der kaiserlich leopoldinisch-carolinischen Academie | der Naturfor-
   scher etc. etc. etc. | — | St. Gallen. | Druck und Verlag von Scheitlin und
   Zollikofer. | 1844–1846.   1 vol.   Large 4to.   > Ornithologie | bearbeitet von |
   Dr. J. J. von Tschudi | mit Anmerkungen | von | J. Cabanis, | Adjunkt am
   zoologischen Museum in Berlin. | — | 1845 und 1846.   1 p. l., pp. 1–316, pll.
   col'd i–xxxvi.
   Contains a systematic synonymatic conspectus of Peruvian birds (cf. *Arch. f. Naturg.*, x,
   1844, p. 262; xi, 1845, p. 360), followed by a general systematic account of the Peruvian avifauna, descriptive, critical, and biographical.   The new species appear to have been mostly
   described already, as the "Conspectus" (*Arch. für Naturg.*, l. c.) is quoted in the present
   volume.
   Turdus swainsonii Cab., p. 187; *Procnias viridis* Cab., p. 197; *Sycalis chloris* Cab., p. 216;
   Conurus frontatus Cab., p. 272, spp. nn.—Pl. I, *Hypomorphnus unicinctus* (pl. marked *Polyborus*
   taeniurus).   II, *Circaetus solitarius*.   III, *Circus poliopterus*.   IV, *Noctua melanonota*.   V,
   f. 1, *Caprimulgus decussatus;* f. 2, *C. ocellatus.*   VI, f. 1, *C. climacocercus;* f. 2, *C. pruinosus.*
   VII, f. 1, *Ampelis rufaxilla;* f. 2. *Ptilogonys leucotis.*   VIII, f. 1, *Scaphorhynchus chrysocepha-*
   lus; f. 2. *Tyrannus cinconeti.*   IX, f. 1, *Euscarthmus pileatus;* f. 2, *Elaenia viridiflava.*   X,
   f. 1. *Mionectes poliocephalus;* f. 2. *Leptopogon superciliaris.*   XI, f. 1, *Thamnophilus olivaceus;*

1845–46. TSCHUDI, J. J. V., *and* CABANIS, J.—Continued.

f. 2, *Lithys leucophrys.* XII, f. 1, *Setophaga melanocephala;* f. 2, *Ptyonura albifrons.* XIII, f. 1, *Hylophilus frontalis;* f. 2, *Procnopis atrocoerulea.* XIV, f. 1, *Myiodioctes tristriatus;* f. 2, *Procnopis argentea.* XV, f. 1, *Cinclus leucocephalus;* f. 2, *Mimus longicaudatus.* XVI, f. 1, *Cyphorhinus thoracicus;* f. 2. *Cillurus palliatus.* XVII, f. 1, *Tanagra frugilegus;* f. 2, *Callispiza xanthocephala.* XVIII, f. 1, *Tanagra analis,* f. 2; *Callospiza pulchra.* XIX, *Phrygilus plebeius;* f. 2, *Arremon frontalis.* XX, f. 1, *Anabates montanus;* f. 2, *A. ochrolaemus.* XXI, f. 1, *A. melanorhynchus;* f. 2, *Dendrocolaptes validus.* XXII, f. 1, *D. chunchotambo;* f. 2, *Trochilus leucogaster.* XXIII, f. 1, *T. insectivorus;* f. 2, *T. otero.* XXIV, f. 1, *Lypornix ruficapilla;* f. 2, *Capito glaucogularis.* XXV, *Picus haematogaster.* XXVI, f. 1, *Conurus rupicola;* f. 2, *C. mitratus.* XXVII, *Psittacus mercenarius.* XXVIII, *Columba frenata.* XXIX, *C. meloda.* XXX, *C. gracilis.* XXXI, *Penelope rufiventris.* XXXII, *Crypturus kleei.* XXXIII, *Odontophorus speciosus.* XXXIV, *Charadrius winterfeldtii.* XXXV, *Larus modestus.* XXXVI, *Merganetta leucogenys.*

1846. BRIDGES, T. [Letter addressed to G. R. Waterhouse, Esq., containing notices of Bolivian Mammals and Birds.] <*P. Z. S.,* xiv, 1846, pp. 7–10.

1846. LAFRESNAYE, [F.] DE. Sur quelques nouvelles espèces d'oiseaux de Colombie. <*Rev. Zool.,* ix, 1846 pp. 206–209.

Tachyphonus brevipes, p. 206; *Tyrannula rufipectus, Spermophila olivaceoflava,* p. 207; *Dendrocolaptes albolineatus,* p. 208.

1846. LAFRESNAYE, F. DE. Sur quelques oiseaux nouveaux de l'embouchure de l'Orénoque. <*Rev. Zool.,* ix, 1846, pp. 273–277.

Nemosia nigrogenis, p. 273; *Saltator orenocensis,* p. 274; *Coracina granadensis, C. orenocensis,* p. 277.

1846. LAFRESNAYE, F. DE. Quelques nouvelles espèces d'oiseaux de la Jamaïque. <*Rev. Zool.,* ix, 1846, pp. 320–322.

Tachyphonus rufo-gularis, Pachyrhynchus aterrimus, p. 320; *Piaya cinnamomeiventris, Pionus vinaceicollis, Columbigallina versicolor,* p. 321. Voir *R. Z.,* 1847, pp. 64, 80–83.

1846. MAXIMILIAN, PRINCE DE NEUWIED. Note rectificative sur quelques oiseaux du Brésil. <*Rev. Zool.,* ix, 1846, pp. 162–164.

1846. —— Untersuchungen über die Fauna peruviana auf einer Reise in Peru von D. J J. von Tschudi. St. Gallen bey Scheitlin. Lief. vi. 1846. S. 189. 244. ·Taf. 6. ill. <*Oken's Isis,* Bd. xxxix, 1846, pp. 312, 313.

1846–47. JARDINE, W. Horæ Zoologicæ:—No. VIII. Ornithology of the Island of Tobago. <*Ann. Mag. Nat. Hist.,* xviii, 1846, pp. 114–121; xix, 1847, pp. 78–83; xx, 1847, pp. 328–334, 370–378.

Acanthylis brachyura, p. 120.

1847. BRIDGES, T. Notes in addition to former [P. Z. S. 1843, p. 108, and 1846, p. 9] Papers on South American Ornithology. <*P. Z. S.,* xv, 1847, pp. 28–30.

Miscellaneous notes on a few species.

1847. BRIDGES, T. Notes in addition to former [P. Z. S., 1843, p. 108; 1846, p. 9] Papers on South American Ornithology. <*Ann. Mag. Nat. Hist.,* xix, 1847, pp. 419–421.

From *P. Z. S.,* Mar. 23, 1847, pp. 28–30.

1847. DENNY, W. A few remarks on the Geographical Distribution of Birds in the West Indies. <*P. Z. S.,* xv, 1847, pp. 36–41.

I. 45 spp. land-birds common to Jamaica, Cuba, and United States. II. 7 spp. land-birds observed in Terra Firma, but unknown in North America. III. 60 spp. peculiar to the West Indies. With numerous water-birds of general dispersion. The list is obviously defective and very inaccurate, having no authority whatever.

1847. GARDNER, G. Notes of Birds in Brazil. <*Zoologist,* v, 1847, p. 1637.

1847. GAY, C. Historia | fisica y politica | de Chile | segun documentos adquiridos en esta republica | durante doce años de residencia en ella | y publicada | bajo los auspicios del supremo Gobierno | por Claudio Gay | Ciudadano Chileno, | individuo de varias sociedades cientificas nacionales y estrangeras, | caballero de la legion de honor. | Zoologia. | — | Tomo primero. | [Blazon.] | Paris | en casa del autor. | Chile | en el Museo de Historia Natural de Santiago. | — | MDCCCXLVII | 8vo. pp. 496. >Aves, pp. 183–496. Atlas, folio.

1847. GAY, C.—Continued.

Gay was little of an ornithologist, and his work passes for no more than it is worth. The text consists of a diagnosis and description of each species and group, with a slight synonymy and miscellaneous matter, chiefly relating to habits. Birds are divided into Rapaces, Pajarillos, Trepadoras, Palomas, Gallinaceas, Zancudas, and Nadadoras. *Ulula fasciata*, p. 252; *Sylviorthorhynchus* (g. n., p. 315) *desmurii*, p. 316; *Chlorospiza aldunatei*, p. 356; *Zenaida souleyetiana*, p. 380; *Peristera auriculata*, p. 381; *Nothura punctulata*, p. 391; *Squatarola urvillii*, p. 401, spp. nn. Cf. *Edinb. New Philos. Jour.*, n. s., iii, 1856, pp. 335–338.

1847. GOSSE, P. H. The | Birds of Jamaica. | By | Philip Henry Gosse ; | assisted by Richard Hill, Esq., of Spanish-town. | London : | John Van Voorst, Paternoster Row. | M.DCCC.XLVII. 1 vol. 8vo. 1 p. l., pp. x, 447, and 1 l. of advts. (A separately-titled vol. of 52 colored plates attends this work. See 1849.)

Nearly 200 spp. Text almost entirely biographical and "entirely from original investigation" of the author and R. Hill, "whose notes *pervade* this volume". . . "An observer is hardly competent to determine what circumstance is trivial and what is important; many a recorded *fact* in science has lost half its value from the omission of some attendant circumstance, which the observer either did not notice, or thought irrelevant."—(Gosse, p. iv.)

The new species are :—*Ephialtes grammicus*, p. 19; *Nyctibius pallidus*, p. 49; *Tachornis phœnicobia*, p. 58; *Hirundo pœciloma*, p. 64 (lege *pœcilona*); *H. euchrysea*, p. 68; *Mellisuga humilis*, p. 127; *Sylvicola eoa*, p. 158; *S. pannosa*, p. 162; *S. pharetra*, p. 163; *Myiobius pallidus*, p. 166; *M. tristis*, p. 167; *M. stolidus*, p. 168; *Spermophila anoxantha*, p. 247; *S. adoxa*, p. 253; *Pyrrhula robinsonii*, p. 259; *Geotrygon sylvatica*, p. 316; *Egretta nivea*, p. 334; *E. ruficollis*, p. 338; *Rallus concolor*, p. 369; *Anas maxima*, p. 399; *Cyanopterus inornatus*, p. 402; *Erismatura ortygoides* "Hill", p. 406.

1847. GOSSE, P. H. Extracts from the 'Birds of Jamaica, by Philip Henry Gosse.' *< Zoologist*, v, 1847, pp. 1808–1820.

1847. HARTLAUB, G. Systematischer Index | zu | Don Felix de Azara's | Apuntamientos para la historia natural | de los Páxaros | del | Paraguay y Rio de la Plata. | — | Von | Dr. G. Hartlaub. | — | Bremen, | Druck von C. Schünemann. | 1847. 1 vol. sm. 4to. pp. i–vi, 1–29.

Important commentary on Azara. See 1802–05, AZARA.

1847. HARTLAUB, [G.] [Note sur quelques espèces nouvelles d'oiseaux de la Jamaïque, R. Z. 1846, pp. 320–322.] *< Rev. Zool.*, x, 1847, p. 64.

1847. HARTLAUB, [G.] [Sur quelques oiseaux de la Jamaïque recemment décrits par M. de Lafresnaye.] *< Rev. Zool.*, x, 1847, pp. 271, 272.

1847. LAFRESNAYE, [F.] DE. Quelques oiseaux nouveaux ou rares rapportés par M. Delattre, de Bolivie, de la Nouvelle-Grenade, et de Panama. *< Rev. Zool.*, x, 1847, pp. 67–79.

27 esp.—*Grallaria monticola*, p. 68; *Tyrannula frontalis*, p. 70; *Tanagra palpebrosa*, *Aglaia wilsoni*, p. 71; *A. fanny*, *Tachyphonus delattrii*, *Arremon aurantiirostris*, p. 72; *Saltator striatipectus*, *S. maculipectus*, p. 73; *Coccoborus cyanoïdes*, p. 74; *Linaria analoïdes*, *L. inornata*, *Geositta peruviana*, p. 75; *Dendroplex picirostris*, p. 76; *Picumnus granadensis*, p. 78; *Malacoptila panamensis*, p. 79, spp. nn.

1847. LAFRESNAYE, [F.] DE. Réponse de M. de Lafresnaye aux Observations du docteur Hartlaub, du dernier numéro de la Revue Zoologique. *< Rev. Zool.*, x, 1847, pp. 80–83.

1847. LAFRESNAYE, F. DE. Mélanges ornithologiques sur l'espèce de Ramphocèle à plumage variable, rapporté de la Nouvelle-Grenade par M. Delattre ; et sur le Cassicus uropigyalis [sic]. *< Rev. Zool.*, x, 1847, pp. 215–218.

Ramphocelus varians, sp. n., p. 216; *Cassicus uropigyalis* (sive *curvirostris*, sp. n. supp.), p. 218.

1847. LAFRESNAYE, [F.] DE. Réponse de M. de Lafresnaye à la notice de M. le Dr Hartlaub, de l'avant-dernier numéro de cette Revue. *< Rev. Zool.*, x, 1847, pp. 350–352.

1847. SCHOMBURGK, R. H. The History of Barbadoes, . . . London. 1847. Roy. 8vo.

Not seen.—Cf. *P. Z. S.*, 1871, p. 267. [See beyond, ADDENDA.]

1847. TSCHUDI, J. J. v. Animal Life in the Peruvian Forests. *< Zoologist*, v, 1847, pp. 1716–1728.

1847. TSCHUDI, J. J. v. Animals of the Puna of Peru. *< Zoologist*, v, 1847, pp. 1758–1763.

1847. TSCHUDI, J. J. v. Zoology of Valparaiso. < *Zoologist*, v, 1847, pp. 1763, 1764.

1847. TSCHUDI, J. J. v. Zoology of Chiloe. < *Zoologist*, v, 1847, p. 1764.

1847. TSCHUDI, J. J. v. Animals in the Bay of Callao. < *Zoologist*, v, 1847, pp. 1764–1766.

> This and the four preceding papers are extracted from " Travels in Peru ".

1847. YARRELL, W. Descriptions of the Eggs of some [about 30] of the Birds of Chile. < *P. Z. S.*, xv, 1847, pp. 51–55.

1847. ——— Untersuchungen über die Fauna peruana auf einer Reise während 1838–42, von Dr. J. J. Tschudi. St. Gallen bey Scheitlin. Heft vii–xii, 1846. Kl. Folio. S. 33–316. und 80. und 35 Tafeln ill. < *Oken's Isis*, Bd. xl, 1847, pp. 703–705.

1847–48. HARTLAUB, G. Ueber den heutigen Zustand unserer Kenntnisse von West-indiens Ornithologie. < *Oken's Isis*, Bd. xl, 1847, pp. 604–615; Bd. xli, 1848, pp. 401–409.

> An important résumé of the subject.

1848. CABANIS, J. Reisen in | Britisch-Guiana | in den Jahren 1840–1844. | Im Auf-trag S^r· Majestät des Königs von Preussen | ausgeführt von | Richard Schom-burgk. | — | Nebst einer Fauna und Flora Guiana's nach Vorlagen | von | Johannes Müller, Ehrenberg, Erichson, Klotzsch, Troschel, | Cabanis und andern. | — | Mit Abbildungen und einer Karte von Britisch-Guiana | aufge-nommen von | Sir Robert Schomburgk. | Erster [zweiter, dritter] Theil. | — | Leipzig, | Verlagsbuchhandlung von J. J. Weber. 1847 [1848, 1848]. 3 vols. Sm. 4to, shape of a large 8vo. Vol. I, 1847, map, pp. i–viii, i–x, 1–470, maps and pll. Vol. II, 1848, pp. i–xiv, 1–530, 1 l., pll. Vol. III, 1848, with special title: Versuch | einer | Fauna und Flora | von | Britisch-Guiana. | Nach Vor-lagen | von | Johannes Müller, Ehrenberg, | Erichson, | Klotzsch, Troschel, | Cabanis und andern. | Systematisch bearbeitet | von | Richard Schomburgk. | — | Leipzig, | Verlagsbuchhandlung von J. J. Weber. | 1848. pp. i–viii, 531–1260, 1 l. > Vögel, bearbeitet von J. Cabanis, pp. 662–765.

> The third volume, as just indicated, has a special title, by which it is sometimes cited apart from the rest, giving the impression that it is a different work.
>
> Schomburgk's Guiana becomes a very important work in South American ornithology, from the number of new genera and species described by Cabanis in his elaborate presentation of the subject. Various touchings of birds, by Schomburgk himself, occur through the other volumes ; but Cabanis's article is the formal presentation of the ornithological affair. It is a systematic synopsis, with synonymy, description, and much critical comment by Cabanis, and miscellaneous matter by Schomburgk. According to Schomburgk's opening paragraphs :
>
> "Meine Vögelsammlung enthält 424 Arten, also noch 6 Arten mehr, als in der Einleitung zur Fauna angegeben sind : *Oscines* 83, darunter 12 neue ; *Clamatores* 93, darunter 11 neue ; *Strisores* 36, darunter 3 neue ; *Scansores* 77, darunter 2 neue ; *Raptatores* 43, darunter 1 neue ; *Gyratores* 6 ; *Rasores* 15, darunter 1 neue ; *Grallatores* 55, darunter 1 neue ; *Natatores* 16. Im Ganzen 31 neue Arten.
>
> "Bei der systematischen Anordnung ist das neuaufgestellte System des Herrn CABANIS zu Grunde gelegt worden, was hoffentlich um so willkommener geheissen werden wird, als dies jedenfalls unter allen bisher aufgestellten, das erste ist, welches den Anforderungen, die man an ein natürliches System zu stellen berechtigt ist, wirklich entspricht."
>
> Vergl. Ornithologische Notizen von Cabanis in : *Archiv für Naturgeschichte*, Bd. i, 1847, SS. — — — ; und besonders abgedruckt.
>
> *Turdus gymnophthalmus*, p. 665 ; *T. phaeopygus*, genus *Basileuterus*, p. 666 ; *Setophaga cas-taneocapilla*, p. 667 ; *Euphona minuta*, p. 671 ; *Troglodytes rufulus*, p. 672 ; *Thryothorus al-bipectus*, p. 673 ; *Diglossa major*, *Saltator olivascens*, p. 676 ; *Arremon personatus*, *Coccoborus ater*, p. 678 ; *Sporophila castaneiventris*, *Sycalis minor*, p. 679 ; *Molothrus atronitens*, *Lamprop-sar* (g. n.) *guianensis*, p. 682 ; *Chalcophanes minor*, *? Cyanocorax hyacinthinus* ("Natt."), p. 683 ; *Conopophaga angustirostris*, p. 685 ; *Dasycephala uropygialis*, p. 686 ; *Anabates pyrrhodes*, *Premnocopus* (g. n.) *undulatus*, p. 689 ; *Copurus poecilonotus*, p. 702 ; *Campylopterus hypery-thrus*, p. 709 ; *Caprimulgus nigrescens*, p. 710 ; *? Nyctibius rufus*, p. 711 ; *Coccygus helviventris*, p. 714 ; *Psittacula modesta*, p. 727 ; *Buteo abbreviatus* ("Licht. Mus. Berol."), p. 739 ; *Trachy-pelmus* (g. n.) *subcristatus*, p. 749 ; *Crex schomburgkii* descr. orig. Theil ii, p. 245, spp. nn. Other genera of Cabanis's here new, or lately new, are *Geothlypis*, p. 666 ; *Phoenicosoma* (for *Phoenisoma*), *Pogonothraupis*, p. 669 ; *Arbelorhina*, p. 675 ; *Calyphtrophorus* [sic], p. 678 ; *Pyr-rhocorax*, p. 713 ; *Monasta* (for *Monasa*), p. 719 ; *Ortygarchus*, p. 759.

1848. [CABOT, S., JR.?] Incidents of Travel | in Yucatan. | By John L. Stephens, | Author of "Incidents of Travel in Egypt, Arabia, Petræa, and the | Holy Land," "Incidents of Travel in Central America," etc. | Illustrated by 120 engravings. | In two Volumes. ⫣ Vol. I [II]. New York : | Published by Harper & Brothers | for Henry Bill. | 1848. 2 vols. 8vo. Vol. I, pp. i–xii, 9–459, 54 engravings. Vol. II, pp. i–xvi, 9–478, 70 engravings. >Vol. II, Appendix, Memorandum for the Ornithology of Yucatan, pp. 469–476.

> I find no indication of the authorship of this "Memorandum", but am under the impression that it is by Dr. Samuel Cabot, jr. It consists of a brief general essay on the subject, concluded with a list of "Birds observed in Yucatan during the winter of 1841, '2, between the months of October and June, which are also found in the United States, and have been figured and described by Wilson, Audubon, Bonaparte, and Nuttall", pp. 475, 476. Both volumes also contain cursory bird-matter by the author.

1848. CASTELNAU, [F. DE]. Considérations sur l'ornithologie de l'Amérique tropicale. <*Arch. des Sc. Phys. et Nat.*, viii, 1848, p. 72.

> *Compt. Rend.* du 6 Mars 1848.

1848. CASTELNAU, F. DE. Considérations générales sur l'ornithologie de l'Amérique tropicale. <*Compt. Rend. de l'Acad. Sci.*, xxvi, 1848, pp. 306, 307.

1848. CASTELNAU, [F.] DE. Considérations générales sur l'ornithologie de l'Amérique tropicale. <*Rev. Zool.*, xi, 1848, pp. 89, 90.

1848. DUBUS, [B.] Ueber einige neue Vögel aus Amerika. <*Oken's Isis*, Bd. xli, 1848, p. 959.

> *Bull. Acad. Bruxelles,* 1848, p. 347. (I cannot get this. See next title.)

1848. LAFRESNAYE, F. DE. Description de quelques oiseaux nouveaux de Caracas (province de Venezuela) et de Bogota. <*Rev. Zool,,* xi, 1848, pp. 2–12.

> *Merula olivatra,* p. 2 ; *M. atro-sericea,* p. 3 ; *Turdus nudigenis,* p. 4 ; *T. minimus, Scaphorhynchus chrysocephalus,* p. 5 ; *Tyrannula cineracea,* p. 7 ; *Setophaga albidiadema,* p. 8 ; *Conirostrum atro-cyaneum,* p. 9 ; *Tachyphonus canigularis,* p. 11 ; *T. albitempora,* p. 12.

1848. LAFRESNAYE, F. DE. Sur le genre Psittacula et sur quelques nouvelles espèces d'oiseaux de Colombie et du Mexique. <*Rev. Zool.*, xi, 1848, pp. 170–176.

> *Ps. conspicillata, Ps. viridissima,* p. 172 ; *Tachyphonus ruficeps,* p. 173 ; *Muscicapa vieillotioïdes,* p. 174 ; *Pipilo rufipileus,* p. 176, spp. nn.

1848. LAFRESNAYE, [F.] DE. [Reconnaissance d'une notice, extraite des bulletins de l'Académie royale de Belgique, de quinze nouvelles espèces d'oiseaux d'Amérique, décrites par M. le vicomte Dubus.] <*Rev. Zool.*, xi, 1848, pp. 239–249.

> *Morphnus mexicanus,* p. 239 ; *Ischnosceles niger,* p. 241 ; *Cyanocorax nanus, C. unicolor, C. violaceus,* p. 243 ; *Tityra albitorques,* p. 244 ; *Sylvia tæniata, Pyranga cucullata, Pitylus poliogaster,* p. 245 ; *Pipilo torquatus,* p. 246 ; *Carduelis notata, Arremon ophthalmicus,* p. 247 ; *Monasa unitorques,* p. 248 ; *M. inornata, Prionites carinatus,* p. 249 ; en suite de chaque description des observations qu'elles lui ont suggérées.

1848. POEY, D. A. Catalogo metodico de las Aves de la isla de Cuba. <*Mem. Real. Soc. Econom. de la Habana,* Nov. 1848.

> Not seen : title from Giebel.

1849. CORNALIA, E. Vertebratorum Synopsis in Museo Mediolanense extantium quæ per Novem Orbem Caietanus Osculati collegit annis 1846–47–48. Speciebus novis vel minus cognitis adjectis, necnon descriptionibus atque iconibus illustratis, curante. Mediolani. 1849. 4to. pp. 15, 1 pl.

> Not seen.—Cf. *Nuov. Ann. Sc. Nat. Bologna,* 3d ser., iii, 1851, pp. 349–351.

1849. DEVILLE, E. Description de quelques Mammifères et Oiseaux nouveaux de l'Amérique méridionale. <*Rev. et Mag. Zool.*, i, 1849, pp. 55–58.

> *Jacamerops isidori, Galbula chalcocephala,* p. 55 ; *G. cyanescens, Bucco lanceolata, Oncorhynchus castelncaui,* p. 56 ; *Cassicus oseryi,* p. 57.

1849. GOSSE, P. H. Illustrations | of the | Birds of Jamaica. | By | Philip Henry Gosse. | — | London : | John Van Voorst, 1, Paternoster Row. | 1849. Large 8vo, 1 vol. 3 pp. text (title, advt., and contents), 52 col'd pll.

　　Bull. v, 2——8

1849. GOSSE, P. H.—Continued.

The plates, 52 in number, representing 51 spp., drawn and engraved by the author, printed by Reeve, Benham & Reeve, form the only published part of a series designed to illustrate all the species noticed in the *Birds of Jamaica;* their numbers are consequently, not continuous, though usually arranged consecutively. They represent, among others, Gosse's new species, and include some not in the *Birds of Jamaica,* and are as follows (references to pages being to the *Birds of Jamaica,* 1848, *q. v.*):—

Pl. II, *Buteo borealis,* p. 11. IV, *Ephialtes grammicus* Gosse, p. 19. VI, *Nyctibius jamaicensis,* p. 41. VII, *N. pallidus* Gosse, p. 49. VIII, *Acanthylis collaris?,* p. 51. IX, *Tachornis phœnicobia* Gosse, with nest, p. 58. X, *Cypselus niger,* p. 63. XII, *Hirundo euchrysea* Gosse, p. 68. XIV, *Todus viridis,* p. 72. XVI, *Certhiola flaveola,* p. 84. XVII, *C. maritima* [ex Wils. = *tigrina* Gm.], p. 87. XVIII, *Lampornis mango,* p. 88. XIX, *Trochilus polytmus,* ♂, and XX, the same, ♀, and nest, p. 104. XXI, *Mellisuga humilis,* ♂, ♀, nest, p. 127. XXII, *Trochilus Maria* "Hill" (*Ann. N. H.,* 1849; not in *B. Jam.*). XXIII, *Merula leucogenys,* p. 136. XXIV, *M. jamaicensis,* p. 142. XXVIII, *Seirus noveboracensis,* p. 151. XXXII, *Sylvicola pensilis,* p. 156. XXXIV, *S. eoa* Gosse, p. 158. XXXVII, *S. pannosa* Gosse, p. 162. XXXVIII, *S. pharetra* Gosse, p. 163. XL, *Myiobius pallidus* Gosse, p. 166. XLI, *M. tristis* Gosse, p. 167. XLII, *M. stolidus* Gosse, p. 168. XLIV, *Tyrannus caudifasciatus,* p. 177. XLV, *Elania cotta* Gosse (*Ann. Nat. Hist.,* 1849; not in *B. Jam.*). LII, *Corvus jamaicensis,* p. 209. LIII, *Quiscalus crassirostris,* p. 217. LVI, *Tanagra nigrocephala,* p. 231 ("*T. zena*"). LVIII, *Tanagrella ruficollis,* ♂, ♀, p. 236. LIX, *Euphonia jamaica,* ♂, ♀, p. 238. LX, *Coturniculus tixicrus* Gosse, p. 242. LXI, *Crithagra brasiliensis,* p. 245. LXII, *Spermophila anoxantha* Gosse, p. 247 (p. "242", err. on pl.). LXIV, *S. bicolor,* p. 252. LXV, *S. adoxa* Gosse, p. 253. LXVI, *Pyrrhula violacea,* p. 254. LXVII, *P. robinsonii,* Gosse, p. 259. LXXIV, *Piaya pluvialis,* p. 277. LXXXIV, *Geotrygon sylvatica* Gosse, p. 316. LXXXV, *Zenaida? plumbea* Gosse, MSS., ref. to p. 324. XC, *Egretta nivea* Gosse, p. 334. XCIII, *E. ruficollis* Gosse, p. 338. CII, *Rallus concolor* Gosse, p. 369. CIV, *Ortygometra minuta,* p. 372. CVIII, *Himantopus nigricollis,* p. 386. CX, *Anas maxima* Gosse, p. 399. CXI, *Cyanopterus inornatus* Gosse, p. "209". CXIII, *Erismatura ortygoides,* p. 406. CXX, *Podiceps dominicus,* p. 440.

1849. GOSSE, P. H. Descriptions of two new Birds from Jamaica. <*Ann. Mag. Nat. Hist.,* (2), iii, 1849, pp. 257–259.

Elania [sic] *cotta,* p. 257; *Trochilus maria,* p. 258.

1849. HARTLAUB, G. Description de deux nouvelles espèces d'Oiseaux de Caraccas. < *Rev. et Mag. de Zool.,* i, 1849, pp. 274, 275.

Conurus erythrochlorus, p. 274 (voir op. cit., ii, 1850, p. 158); *Icterus melanopterus,* p. 275.

1849. HARTLAUB, G. Description de deux nouvelles espèces d'Oiseaux de Venezuela. < *Rev. et Mag. de Zool.,* i, 1849, pp. 275, 276.

Ampelis formosa, p. 275; *Turdus vulpinus,* p. 276.

1849. [JARDINE, W.] Ornithology of Quito. <*Jard. Contrib. Orn.,* 1849, pp. 41–45, 66.

Chiefly relating to zones of elevation. A following paper under the same title describes certain *Trochilidæ;* you will find it under head of *Trochilidæ,* in the "systematic" portion of my Bibliography, if this is ever published.

1849. LAFRESNAYE, [F.] DE. Faune du Pérou, du docteur Tschudi, partie ornithologique; par M. J. Cabanis, conservateur du Muséum de Berlin. < *Rev. et Mag. de Zool.,* i, 1849, pp. 97–108, 232–247.

Critique de cet ouvrage.

1850. LEMBEYE, J. Aves | de la Isla de Cuba, | por | Juan Lembeye. | — | Habana. | Imprenta del Tiempo, | Calle de Aguiar num. 45 | — | 1850. 1 vol. 4to. pp. 136, 2 ll., pll. 20.

Text synonymatic, descriptive, and general, treating of 86 spp.; 3 others given in a Suplemento. Contains also a compiled nominal list of 222 spp. arranged after d'Orbigny.— *Vireo gundlachii,* p. 29, pl. 5, f. 1; *Muscicapa elizabeth,* p. 39, pl. 5, f. 3; *Hirundo coronata* "Mus. Berol.", p. 45; *Cypselus iradii,* p. 50, pl. 7, f. 4; *Agelaius assimilis* Gundl. MSS., p. 64; *Anabates fernandinæ,* p. 66, pl. 5, f. 2; *Orthorhynchus helenæ* Gundl. MSS., p. 70, pl. 10, f. 2; *Ardea cubensis* Gundl. MSS., p. 84, pl. 13, f. 1; *A. brunescens* Gundl. MSS., p. 84, pl. 12; *Hemipalama minor* Gundl. MSS., p. 97, pl. 13, f. 1, spp. nn.

1850. MITCHELL, D. W. [Notice of Lord Harris's collection from Trinidad.] < *P. Z. S.,* xviii, 1850, pp. 99, 100.

1850. STRICKLAND, H. E. [Descriptions of four species of birds from the Peruvian Andes.] < *Jard. Contrib. Orn.,* 1850, pp. 47–50.

Monasa flavirostris, p. 47; *Todirostrum chrysocrotaphum, Euphonia bicolor,* p. 48, spp. nn., the other being *Tachyphonus rufiventer* (Spix).

1850. WALLACE, A. R.   Journey to explore the Natural History of the Amazon River. <*Ann. Mag. Nat. Hist.*, (2), vi, 1850, pp. 494–496.
Field-notes on several birds.

1851. BONYAN, G. R.   Notes on the Raptorial Birds of British Guiana. <*P. Z. S.*, xix, 1851, pp. 53–61.
Field-observations on a large number of species, mostly given only under English names.

1851. DEVILLE, E.   Note sur quatre espèces nouvelles d'oiseaux provenant de l'expédition de M. Castelnau; le Conurus Weddellii, C. jugularis, C. Luciani et Cultrides Pucheranii. <*Rev. et Mag. de Zool.*, iii, 1851, pp. 209–213.

1851. GOSSE, P. H.   A | Naturalist's Sojourn | in | Jamaica. | By | Philip Henry Gosse, A. L. S., &c. | Assisted by Richard Hill, Esq., Cor. M. Z. S. Lond., | Mem. Counc. Roy. Soc. Agric. of Jamaica. | [Quotation.] | London: | Longman, Brown, Green, and Longmans. | 1851. 1 vol.   Sm. 12mo.   pp. iii–xxxiv, 1–508, pll. i–viii.
Birds and flowers, pp. 166–177, in the author's well-known delightful style.

1851–52. GOSSE, P. H.   Singing Birds and Sweet Flowers in Jamaica. <*Edinb. New Philos. Journ.*, lii, 1852, pp. 31–33, 268–271.
Extract from "A Naturalist's Sojourn in Jamaica", p. 170.—Controverting the flippant dogma that in tropical countries, where birds and flowers are of brilliant colors, the former are songless and the latter without fragrance.

1852. ARBOLEYA, J. G. DE.   Manual | de la | Isla de Cuba. | Compendio | de su Historia, Geografia, Estadistica y Administracion. | Su autor | D. José G. de Arboleya. | — | Con 5 planos y 30 láminas. | — | Havana: 1852. | Imprenta del Gobierno y Capitania General por S. M.   1 vol.   18mo.   pp. 1–382 + 1 l., maps, plates.
"En punto á aves tiene la Isla excelente y abundante caza. Hé aquí una lista alfabetica de las principales", pp. 165–167, 2 lám.

1852. DEVILLE, E.   Observations faites en Amérique sur les mœurs de différentes espèces d'Oiseaux-Mouches, suivies de quelques notes anatomiques et de mœurs sur l'Hoazin, le Caurale et le Savacou. <*Rev. et Mag. de Zool.*, iv, 1852, pp. 208, 226, pl. 9.
Ornismyia, dix esp. *Opisthocomus* (pl. 9). *Eurypyga helias. Cancroma cochlearia.*

1852. GUNDLACH, J.   Description of five new Species of Birds, and other Ornithological notes of Cuban Species. Read before the Boston Society of Natural History, March 3d, 1852. <*Journ. Bost. Soc. Nat. Hist.*, vi, pt. iii, 1852, pp. 313–319.
Muscicapa sagræ, p. 313; *M. lembeyei*, p. 314; *Orpheus saturninus* Licht., *Columba caniceps*, p. 315; notes on 13 other spp.

1852. [JARDINE, W.]   Ornithology of the Island of Tobago. <*Jard. Contrib. Orn.*, 1852, pp. 63–68, 81–88.
Merely a general sketch of the subject.

1852. [JARDINE, W.]   Descriptions of some [lately] New Species of Birds from the Parisian Collections. <*Jard. Contrib. Orn.*, 1852, pp. 129–132, pll. xcvi–c.
Just before published by P. L. Sclater in *Rev. et Mag. Zool.*, iv, 1852, pp. 8, 9, *q. v.;* descr. here quoted and figg. given. *Cotinga porphyrolæma* Deville & Scl., pl. xcvi; *Arremon mysticalis* Scl., pl. xcix; *Pipilopsis flavigularis* Scl., pl. xcviii; *Pipraeidea albiventris* Scl., pl. c, f. 2; *P. isidorei* Scl., pl. c, f. 1; *P. flavicapilla* Scl., pl. xcvii, f. 2; *P. pyrocephala*, pl. xcvii, f. 1.

1852. KNOX, J. P.   An Historical Account of St. Thomas, W. I., with notices of St. Croix and St. John's. By John P. Knox. New York: 1852.
Not seen: said to contain (pp. 220 et seq.) a slight sketch of the ornithology of St. Thomas, largely copied from Ledru's 'Voyage'.

1852. MOSQUERA, T. C. DE.   Memoria sobre la Geografia fisica y politica de la Nueva Granada. New York. 1852. 8vo.
Not seen: title from Giebel. See the American ed., 1853.

1852. SCLATER, P. L.   Ornithological Observations.   IX.—On the Birds from Yucatan described by Dr. Cabot in the Journal of the Boston Natural History Society [vols. iv, v].   < *Jard. Contrib. Orn.*, 1852, p. 96.
　Mr. Cassin's identifications of 9 spp., only one of which is allowed to stand.

1852. SCLATER, P. L.   Description de six Oiseaux nouveaux appartenant à la collection du Muséum d'histoire naturelle de Paris.   < *Rev. et Mag. de Zoologie*, iv, 1852, pp. 8, 9.
　Arremon mysticalis [sic], *Pipilopsis flavigularis, Fipraidea albiventris*, p. 8; *Pipra isidorei, P. flavicapilla, P. pyrocephala*, p. 9.

1852. SEEMANN, B.   Notes on the Zoology of the Isthmus of Panama.   < *Zoologist*, x, 1852, pp. 3313–3320.
　Only a slight paragraph on birds, p. 3315.

1852. WILLIAMS, J. J.   The | Isthmus | of | Tehuantepec | . . . . | New York : | D. Appleton & Company, 200 Broadway. | M DCCC LII.   1 vol.   8vo.   pp. 295.
　Cursory allusion to a few spp. of birds at pp. 208–210.

1853. BONYAN, G. R.   Notes on the Raptorial Birds of British Guiana.   < *Ann. Mag. Nat. Hist.*, (2), xi, 1853, pp. 138–146.
　From *P. Z. S.*, xix, 1851, pp. 53–61.

1853. BURMEISTER, H.   Ueber die Eier und Nester einiger brasilianischer Vögel.   < *J. f. O.*, 1853, i, pp. 161–177.
　Treats of 17 spp., exclusive of the *Trochilidæ* mentioned, with extended descriptions of nests and eggs.

1853. MOSQUERA, T. C. DE.   Memoir | on the | Physical and Political Geography | of | New Granada. | Dedicated to the American Geographical and Sta- | tistical Society of New York. | By General T. C. de Mosquera, | [etc., 5 lines.] | Translated from the Spanish by | Theodore Dwight. | New York : | Published by T. Dwight, 116 Broadway. | 1853.   1 vol.   8vo.   pp. 105, map.
　I have not seen the original, 1852. In this version, under head of "Animals", occurs a nominal (Spanish and Latin) list of a few birds, not well determined, pp. 35–37. It is of no consequence.

1853. ROSENSCHÖLD, E. M. AF.   Bref från D:r E. Munck af Rosenschöld i Paraguay.   < *Öfvers. Kongl. Vetensk.-Akad. Förhandl. för år* 1852, 1853, pp. 174–176.

1853. SCLATER, P. L.   Description de deux nouvelles espèces d'Oiseaux.   < *Rev. et Mag. de Zool.*, v, 1853, p. 480.
　Dacnis pulcherrima, Formicivora ornata.

1853. WALLACE, A. R.   A | Narrative of Travels | on the | Amazon and Rio Negro, | with an account | of the | Native Tribes, | and observations on the Climate, Geology, and Natural | History of the Amazon Valley. | By Alfred R. Wallace. | With a Map and Illustrations. | London : | Reeve and Co., Henrietta Street, Covent Garden. | 1853.   1 vol. 8vo.   pp. viii, 542, with 18 pp. of advts., map, folding table, col'd frontisp., pll. vii, and other illust.
　Chap. XVI, Observations on the Zoology of the Amazon District, pp. 446–475; B. Birds, pp. 461–463: only mention of a few of the most interesting and beautiful. Cf. *Nat. Hist. Rev.*, i, 1854, pp. 117–121.

1854. ROSENSCHÖLD, E. M. AF.   Bref från Paraguay.   < *Öfvers. Kongl. Vetensk.-Akad. Förhandl. för år* 1853, 1854, pp. 102–114.

1854. SCLATER, P. L.   On two [lately] new species of South American Birds.   < *Ann. Mag. Nat. Hist.*, (2), xiv, 1854, p. 158.
　Culicivora boliviana, Pipra flavo-tincta. From *P. Z. S.*, Feb. 24, 1852.

1854. SCLATER, P. L.   List of a Collection of Birds received by Mr. Gould, from the Province of Quijos in the Republic of Ecuador.   < *P. Z. S.*, lxxii, 1854, pp. 109–115, pll. (Aves) lxvi, lxvii.
　69 spp., with critical annotation and synonymy and descriptions of some of them. *Galbula chalcothorax*, p. 110; *Tyrannula phœnicura*, p. 113, pl. lxvi, f. 1; *Arremon spectabilis*, p. 114, pl. lxvii, spp. nn.

1854. WALLACE, A. R.   Habits of Birds.   *<Ann. Mag. Nat. Hist.*,(2), xiii, 1854, pp. 74, 75.

> Editorial excerpt from his 'Travels on the Amazon and Rio Negro', 1853, *q. v.*

[1854-56.] DESCOURTILZ, J. T.   Ornithologie Brésilienne | ou | Histoire des Oiseaux du Brésil, | remarquables par leur plumage, leur chant ou leurs habitudes. | Par le Dr. J. T. Descourtilz, | Membre de la Société Linnéenne de Paris et de la Société auxiliaire de l'industrie de Rio de Janeiro. | [Dessin.] | Rio de Janeiro: | Éditeur, Thomas Reeves. | [1854-56.]   1 vol. gr. fol. (publ. par livr. i–iv).   pp. 42, pll. lithochr. 48.

> Contient les descriptions et les figures de 164 espèces diverses d'oiseaux du Brésil, accompagnées de quelques courts renseignements sur leurs habitudes, etc.   On cite une traduction Anglais sous le nom de "Brazilian Ornithology, or a History of the Birds of Brazil".

1855. BERNSÉE, F.   [Extract from a letter relating to various birds of the East Falkland Island.]   *<Proc. Acad. Nat. Sci. Phila.*, vii, 1855, pp. 287, 288.

> Relates to *Bernicla*, 3 spp. ; *Hœmatopus*, 2 spp. ; and *Chionis alba.*

1855. BOECK, E. v.   Vorläufige Bemerkungen über die Ornis der Provinz Valdivia, in der Republik Chile.   *< Naumannia*, 1855, pp. 494-513.

1855. CASSIN, J.   The | U. S. Naval Astronomical Expedition | to | the Southern Hemisphere, | during | the years 1849-'50-'51-'52. | Lieut. J. M. Gilliss, Superintendent. | .... | Vol. II.   Washington.   MDCCCLV.   >Appendix F.   Birds.   By John Cassin.   pp. 172-206, pll. (col'd) xiv–xxviii.

> Systematic account, with miscellaneous field-notes, of 119 spp. of (chiefly? entirely?) South American birds. Pl. xiv, *Falco nigriceps;* xv, *Psaracolius* [sic] *curæus;* xvi, f. 1, *Agelaius thilius;* p. 2, *Sturnella militaris;* xvii, *Chrysomitris marginalis;* xviii, f. 1, *Calliste cyanicollis;* f. 2, *C. larvata;* xix, f. 1, *C. gyroloides;* f. 2, *C. desmarestii;* xx, f. 1, *Euphonia rufiventris;* f. 2, *Chlorophonia occipitalis;* xxi, f. 1, *Ericornis melanura;* f. 2, *Scytalopus fuscus;* xxii, *Psittacus ochrocephalus;* xxiii, *Branta antarctica;* xxiv, *Bernicla magellanica;* xxv, *Anas melanocephala;* xxvi, *Querq. creccoides;* xxvii, *Fuligula metopias;* xxviii, *Phalacrocorax brasilianus.*

1855. DES MURS, P. O.   Oiseaux nouveaux ou rare recueillis dans l'Amérique du Sud, par F. de Castelnau, etc.   Paris, 1855.   4to.   20 pll.

> Not seen: title from a bookseller's catalogue. Compare 1856, same author.

1855. GOULD, J.   Descriptions of Eight New Species of Birds from South America.   *<P. Z. S.*, xxiii, 1855, pp. 67-70, pl. (Aves) lxxxiii.

> *Campylorhynchus hyposticus, Chamœza nobilis, Formicarius nigrifrons,* p. 68 ; *F. erythropterus, Schistochlamys speculiger, Thamnophilus corvinus, T. melanurus* (pl.), p. 69 ; *T. hyperythrus,* p. 70.

1855. GOULD, J.   Descriptions of Eight [lately] New Species of Birds from South America.   *<Ann. Mag. Nat. Hist.*, (2), xv, 1855, pp. 343-346.

> *Campylorhynchus hyposticus,* p. 343 ; *Chamœza nobilis, Formicarius nigrifrons,* p. 344; *F. erythropterus, Schistochlamys speculigera, Thamnophilus corvinus, T. melanurus,* p. 345; *T. hyperythrus,* p. 346.—From *P. Z. S.*, 1855, pp. 67-70, pl. lxxxiii.

1855. GOULD, J.   [Remarks on Exhibition of a portion of a collection of Birds formed by Mr. Hauxwell in the neighbourhood of the River Ucayali.]   *<P. Z. S.*, xxiii, 1855, pp. 77, 78.

1855. JARDINE, W.   Contributions to Ornithology.   I. Professor W. Jameson's Collections from the Eastern Cordillera of Ecuador.   *<Edinb. New Philos. Journ.*, new ser., ii, 1855, pp. 113-119.

> Letters from W. Jameson. Field-notes on 10 spp. *Tanagara* [sic] *notabilis, Saltator arremonops,* p. 119, spp. "nn."

1855. PHILIPPI, R. A.   Ueber einige Vögel Chile's.   Briefliche Mittheilung an den Herausgeber.   *<Arch. f. Naturg.*, 1855, (1), pp. 9-14.

> Behandelt vier Arten—*Phoenicopterus andinus,* sp. n., p. 12 ; *Ardea cocoi, Xanthornus cayennensis, Circus macropterus.*

1855. SCLATER, P. L.   List of a Collection of Birds received by Mr. Gould, from the Province of Quijos in the Republic of Ecuador.   *<Ann. Mag. Nat. Hist.*, (2), xvi, 1855, pp. 279-285.

> From *P. Z. S.*, May 9, 1854, pp. 109-113, pll., *q. v.*

1855. SCLATER, P. L. Descriptions of some New Species of Birds from Santa Fé di Bogota. < *P. Z. S.*, xxiii, 1855, pp. 109, 110, pll. (Aves) xcix–cii.

    Nemosia albigularis, pl. xcix; *Pyriglena ellisiana*, pl. c; *Anthus bogotensis*, pl. ci, p. 109; *Otocorys peregrina*, pl. cii, p. 110.

1855. SCLATER, P. L. On the Birds received in collections from Sante Fé di Bogota. < *P. Z. S.*, xxiii, 1855, pp. 131–164, pll. (Aves) ciii, civ.

    435 spp. briefly annotated. *Heterocnemis* (g. n.) *marginata*, p. 145; *Todirostrum gracilipes*, p. 149; *Calliste inornata* "Gould", p. 158, spp. nn.; pl. ciii, *Vireolanius icterophrys* Bp.; pl. civ, *Ampelion cinctus* (Tsch.).

1855–57. GUNDLACH, J., *and* CABANIS, J. Dr. J. Gundlach's Beiträge zur Ornithologie Cuba's. Nach Mittheilungen des Reisenden an Hr. Bez.-Dir. Sezekorn in Cassel; von Letzterem zusammengestellt. Mit Zusätzen und Anmerkungen geordnet vom Herausgeber. < *J. f. O.*, ii, 1854 (Extrah. 1855), pp. lxxvii–lxxxvii; iii, 1855, pp. 465–480; iv, 1856, pp. 1–16, 97–112, 337–352, 417–432; v, 1857, pp. 225–242.

    An important review of the subject. This is the first of numerous articles upon Cuban birds, wholly or in part by Dr. Gundlach; it is chiefly to be regretted that in the beginning insufficient attention to precision of identification resulted in too many "additions and corrections". The present series constitutes a systematic synopsis of Cuban birds, the technicalities by Cabanis, the field-notes by Gundlach. *Hypomorphnus gundlachii*, p. lxxx; *Phyllomanes barbatulus*, p. 467; *Mimus gundlachii*, p. 470; *Teretistris*, p. 475; *Melittarchus*, p. 478; *Contopus*, p. 479; *Blacicus*, p. 480; *Aulanax*, p. 1; *Chordediles minor*, p. 5; *Corvus minutus* Gundl., p. 97; *Geotrygon caniceps* Gundl., p. 110; *Perissura*, p. 111; *Ocniscus*, p. 343; *Tryngites*, p. 418; *Notherhodius holostictus*, p. 426; *Limnopardalus*, p. 428; *Creciscus*, p. 428, are new genn. or spp., all but 2 by Cabanis; 251 spp. in all are treated. See especially *J. f O.*, ix, 1861, pp. 401–416; x, 1862, pp. 81–96, 177–191.

1856. BURMEISTER, H. Systematische Uebersicht | der Thiere Brasiliens, | welche | während einer Reise durch die Provinzen von Rio de | Janeiro und Minas geraës | zusammelt oder beobachtet | wurden | von | Dr. Hermann Burmeister, | o ö Prof. d. Zoologie und Direct. d. zool. Mus. der Universität zu Halle. | Zweiter Theil. | Vögel (Aves). | Erste [Zweite] Hälfte. | Berlin. 1856. | Druck und Verlag von Georg Reimer. 2 vols. 8vo. Vol. I, pp. x, 526 + 2. Vol. II, pp. xiv, 466.

    Ornithology occupies the 2d and 3d vols. of this work (1st vol., Mammals, Berlin, 1854). It is an extensive and elaborate general treatise upon the subject.

1856. BURMEISTER, H. Erläuterungen zur Fauna Brasiliens, enthaltend Abbildungen und ausführliche Beschreibungen neuer oder ungenügend bekannter Thier-Arten. Von Dr. Herm. Burmeister. Berlin. 1856. Folio.

    Not seen.

1856. DES MURS, P. O. Expédition dans les parties centrales de l'Amérique du Sud, de Rio Janeiro à Lima et de Lima au Para, etc. Par Fr. de Castelnau. Oiseaux, par P. O. Desmurs. 1856. 4to.

    Not seen: title from Giebel. Compare 1855, same author.

1856. GOULD, J. Descriptions of Eight New Species of Birds from South America. < *Ann. Mag. Nat. Hist.*, (2), xvii, 1856, pp. 428–431.

    From *P. Z. S.*, April 10, 1855.

1856. JARDINE, W. Contributions to Ornithology. No. II., Professor W. Jameson's Collections from the Eastern Cordillera of Ecuador continued.—Expedition from Quito to the Mountain Cayambe. < *Edinb. New Philos. Journ.*, new ser., iii, 1856, pp. 90–92, pl. iv.

    Collector's notes of the locality. Writer's remarks on *Tetragonops ramphastinus* (pl. iv) and other birds.—*Arremon leucopterus*, n. s., p. 92.

1856. KINAHAN, [R. J.] Letter from Dr. Kinahan, dated Callao, August, 1855. < *Nat. Hist. Rev.* (*Pr. Soc.*), iii, 1856, pp. 24–26.

    Referring, among other things, to birds, especially Albatrosses.

1856. LAWRENCE, G. N. Descriptions of New Species of Birds of the Genera Chordeiles, Swainson, and Polioptila, Sclater. < *Ann. Lyc. Nat. Hist. New York*, vi, 1856, pp. 165–169.

    Chordeiles gundlachii, p. 165; *C. texensis*, p. 167; *Polioptila melanura*, p. 168.

1856. PELZELN, A. V. Ueber neue u. wenig bekannte Arten der kais. ornithologischen Sammlung nebst Auszügen aus J. Natterers handschriftlichen Katalog über die von ihm in Brasilien gesammelten Species der Familien Trogonidae und Alcedinidae. < *Sitz.-Berichte Königl. Akad. Wiss. Wien*, xx, 1856, pp. 492 - —.
Not seen.

1856. RAIMONDI, A. Mémoire sur le huano des îles de Chincha et les oiseaux qui le produisent. < *Comp. Rend. de l'Acad. Sci. Paris*, xlii, 1856, pp. 735–738.

1856. RAIMONDI, A. [Résumé d'un mémoire sur le huano des îles de Chincha et les oiseaux qui le produisent.] < *Rev. et Mag. de Zool.*, viii, 1856, pp. 190, 191.

1856. SCLATER, P. L. Descriptions of some [lately] New Species of Birds from Santa Fé di Bogota. < *Ann. Mag. Nat. Hist.*, (2), xviii, 1856, pp. 60, 61.
From *P. Z. S.*, June 26, 1855, pp. 109, 110.

1856. SCLATER, P. L. On two [lately] new species of Birds from Santa Fé di Bogota. <*Ann. Mag. Nat. Hist.*, (2), xviii, 1856, pp. 186, 187.
From *P. Z. S.*, July 24, 1855, pp. 131–164.

1856. SCLATER, P. L. Descriptions of eight new species of Birds from South America. <*Ann. Mag. Nat. Hist.*, (2), xviii, 1856, pp. 466–470.
Synallaxis castanea, p. 466; *Diglossopsis* (g. n.) *cærulescens*, p. 467; *Diglossa indigotica* (J. & E. Verr. MS.), p. 467; *Anabates infuscatus*, A. *lineaticeps*, *Myiadestes venezuelensis*, p. 468; *Pipreola melanolæma, Chiroxiphia regina*, p. 469.

1856. SCLATER, P. L. On some additional Species of Birds received in collections from Bogota. < *P. Z. S.*, xxiv, 1856, pp. 25–31, pll. (Aves) cxvi–cxix.
Synallaxis elegans, p. 25; S. *mæsta*, p. 26; *Anabates erythropterus*, p. 27; *Margarornis brunnescens*, p. 27, pl. cxvi; *Ochthoëca fumicolor*, p. 28, pl. cxvii; *Euscarthmus agilis*, p. 28, pl. cxviii; *Pipra coracina*, p. 29; *Conopophaga cucullata*, p. 29, pl. cxix; *Chlorospingus xanthophrys, C. lichtensteini*, p. 30; *Gallinago nobilis, Rallus semiplumbeus*, p. 31, spp. nn.

1856. SCLATER, P. L. List of Mammals and Birds collected by Mr. Bridges in the vicinity of the town of David in the Province of Chiriqui in the State of Panama. < *P. Z. S.*, xxiv, 1856, pp. 138–143.
Of birds, 46 spp.—*Thamnophilus bridgesi*, p. 141; *Geotrygon chiriquensis*, p. 143, spp. nn.

1857. BONAPARTE, C. L. Catalogue méthodique accompagné de notes des Oiseaux recueillis à Cayenne par M. E. Desplanches, chirurgien de la marine impériale, pendant la première campagne de l'aviso à vapeur, la Rapide, années 1854–1856. < *Bull. Soc. Linn. Normandie*, ii, 1857, pp. 29–40.
Of this piece I have not seen the original, but a MS. copy made by S. F. Baird, Nov. 21–26, 1863. It is an annotated list of 130 spp., a few of which are described, the rest merely given by name. *Planchesia* Bp. (type *Muscicapa fuliginosa* Gm., *fusca* Bodd.; P. E. 574, f. 1), p. 36, g. n.

1857. GOULD, J. Description of a [lately] new Trogon and a [lately] new Odontophorus. <*Ann. Mag. Nat. Hist.*, (2), xix, 1857, pp. 110, 111.
From *P. Z. S.*, May 13, 1856.

1857. HARTLAUB, G. Zur Ornithologie Südamerika's. < *J. f. O.*, 1857, v, pp. 36–50.
Burmeister's Thiere Bras.; Cassin's Birds of Gilliss' U. S. Naval Astron. Exped.; Des Murs' Castelnau's Voy. and Sclater's B. of Bogotá in *P. Z. S.*, 1855. In some measure a review of the works quoted, but rather a systematic summary of their results.

1857. JARDINE, W. Contributions to Ornithology. No. IV. < *Edinb. New Philos. Journ.*, new ser., v, 1857, pp. 255–257.
Brief notes on 5 spp. from Quito.

1857. PHILIPPI, R. A. Ueber einige Chilenische Vögel und Fische. < *Arch. f. Naturg.*, 1857, (1), pp. 262–272.
Rallus salinasi, p. 262; *Upucerthia atacamensis*, p. 263; *Totanus chilensis*, p. 264; *Culicivora fernandeziana*, p. 265.

1857. SALLÉ, A. Liste des Oiseaux rapportés et observés dans la République Dominicaine (ancienne partie Espagnole de l'Ile St. Domingue ou d'Haiti), pendant son voyage de 1849 à 1851. (Communicated by Philip Lutley Sclater.) <*P. Z. S.*, xxv, 1857, pp. 230–237.
61 spp., with field-notes; and critical comment by the communicator.

1857. SCLATER, P. L. On some additional Species of Birds received in collections from Bogota. <*Ann. Mag. Nat. Hist.*, (2), xix, 1857, pp. 85–92.
   From *P. Z. S.*, Feb. 26, 1856, pp. 25–31.

1857. SCLATER, P. L. On a [lately] new Genus of Birds from Mexico. <*Ann. Mag. Nat. Hist.*, (2), xx, 1857, p. 470.
   From *P. Z. S.*, July 14, 1857.

1857. SCLATER, P. L. On two [lately] new Species of Birds from Bogota. <*Ann. Mag. Nat. Hist.*, (2), xx, 1857, p. 472.
   From *P. Z. S.*, Jan. 27, 1857.

1857. SCLATER, P. L. Further Additions to the List of Birds received in Collections from Bogota. <*P. Z. S.*, xxv, 1857, pp. 15–20.
   52 spp., shortly annotated. *Anabates striaticollis, Sclerurus brunneus*, p. 17, spp. nn.

1857. SCLATER, P. L. On a Collection of Birds transmitted by Mr. H. W. Bates from the Upper Amazon. <*P. Z. S.*, xxv, 1857, pp. 261–268.
   79 spp., with annotation. *Eubucco aurantiicollis*, p. 267, sp. n., and synopsis of 7 spp. of that section of the genus *Bucco*. See 1863, and 1864, BATES, H. W.

1857. SCLATER, P. L. Descriptions of Eleven New Species of Birds from Tropical America. <*P. Z. S.*, xxv, 1857, pp. 271–277, pl. (Aves) cxxx.
   Campylorhynchus pardus, p. 271; *C. striaticollis*, p. 272; *Anabazenops guttulatus*, p. 272, pl. cxxx; *Synallaxis multostriata, Turdus fulviventris* Verr. MS., *T. ignobilis*, p. 273; *Cinclus leuconotus, Tyrannus atrifrons*, p. 274; *Melanoptila* (g. n.) *glabrirostris*, p. 275, woodcc.; *Lipaugus rufescens*, p. 276; *Tinamus castaneus*, p. 277.—Note that *Tyrannus atrifrons* Scl. = *Saurophaga bairdii* Gamb. = *Tyrannus bairdi* Scl.

1857. TAYLOR, W. J. Investigation on the Rock Guano from the Islands of the Caribbean Sea. <*Proc. Acad. Nat. Sci. Phila.*, ix, 1857, pp. 91–100.
   Chemical analyses, etc.

1857. THIENEMANN, F. A. L. Ueber die von Dr. Gundlach eingesendeten Eier und Nester cubanischer Vögel. <*J. f. O.*, v, 1857, pp. 145–159.
   Systematic description of the eggs, and in many cases of the nests, of 49 spp.

1858. BURMEISTER, H. Zur Fauna von Süd-America; Briefliches aus Mendoza. <*J. f. O.*, 1858, vi, pp. 152–162.

1858. DE VERTEUIL, L. A. A. Trinidad : | Its Geography, | Natural Resources, Administration, Present | Condition, and Prospects. | By | L. A. A. De Verteuil, M. D. P. | — | [Quotation, 3 lines.] | — | London : | Ward and Lock, 158, Fleet street. | — | 1858. 1 vol. 8vo. pp. i–xii, 1–508.
   Chapter III, Natural History, p. 100; Birds, by the author, pp. 118–126.—Appendix: An Essay on the Ornithology of Trinidad, by Antoine Léotaud, M. D. P., pp. 423–439, giving considerable information on the subject.

1858. GUNDLACH, J. Notes on some Cuban Birds, with Descriptions of three New Species. <*Ann. Lyc. Nat. Hist. New York*, vi, 1858, pp. 267–275. (Read June 29, 1857.)
   Colaptes chrysocaulosus, Culicivora lembeyi, p. 273; *Teretistris fornsi*, p. 275, spp. nn.

1858. LAWRENCE, G. N. Observations of the Preceding Paper [*i. e.*, Notes on some Cuban Birds, with Descriptions of three New Species, by Gundlach]. <*Ann. Lyc. Nat. Hist. New York*, vi, 1858, pp. 275–277. (Read June 29, 1857.)

1858. SCLATER, P. L. Description of a [lately] new genus and some [lately] new species of American Birds. <*Ann. Mag. Nat. Hist.*, (3), i, 1858, pp. 239, 240.
   From *P. Z. S.*, 1857.

1858. SCLATER, P. L. Descriptions of Eleven [lately] New Species of Birds from Tropical America. <*Ann. Mag. Nat. Hist.*, (3), i, 1858, pp. 302–308, figg.
   From *P. Z. S.*, Dec. 8, 1857, pp. 271–277.

1858. SCLATER, P. L. On [lately] new Species of Birds from the Rio Napo, in the Republic of Ecuador. <*Ann Mag. Nat. Hist.*, (3), ii, 1858, pp. 144–150.
   From *P. Z. S.*, Jan. 26, 1858.

1858. SCLATER, P. L. On [lately] new Species of Birds from the Rio Napo, in the Republic of Ecuador. <*Ann. Mag. Nat. Hist.*, (3), ii, 1858, p. 235.
   From *P. Z. S.*, Jan. 26, 1858, pp. 50–77.

1858. SCLATER, P. L.   Notes on a Collection of Birds received by M. Verreaux of Paris from the Rio Napo in the Republic of Ecuador. < *P. Z. S.*, xxvi, 1858, pp. 59–77, pl. (Aves) cxxxii.

174 spp.—*Anabates melanopezus*, p. 61; *Anabates pulvericolor, Synallaxis brunneicaudalis*, p. 62; *S. albigularis*, p. 63 ; *Malacocichla maculata*, p. 64; *Thamnophilus œthiops, T. capitalis*, p. 65; *Dysithamnus leucostictus, D. semicinereus*, p. 66; *Heterocnemis albigularis*, p. 67; *Conopophaga torrida, Grallaria flavirostris, G. fulviventris*, p. 68; *Agathopus* (n. g.) *micropterus*, p. 69; *Todirostrum picatum Cyclorhynchus æquinoctialis*, p. 70; *Platyrhynchus coronatus* "Verr.", *Elænia luteiventris*, p. 71; *Creurgops* (n. g.) *verticalis* Verr., pl. cxxxii, f. 2; *Euchætes* (n. g., "Verr.") *coccineus* "Verr.", p. 73, pl. cxxxii, f. 1; *Celeus verreauxi* "Malh.", p. 74, spp. nn.

1858. SCLATER, P. L.   List of Birds [39 spp.] collected by Geo. Cavendish Taylor, Esq., in the Republic of Honduras. < *P. Z. S.*, xxvi, 1858, pp. 356–360.

1858. SCLATER, P. L.   Characters of Five New Species of [Central and South] American Birds. < *P. Z. S.*, xxvi, 1858, pp. 446–449.

Euchlornis frontalis, p. 446; *Turdus leucauchen, Geothlypis speciosa*, p. 447; *Cyclorhis flavipectus, Cinclodus bifasciatus*, p. 448.

1858. SCLATER, P. L.   List of Birds collected by Mr. Louis Fraser, at Cuenca, Gualaquiza and Zamora, in the Republic of Ecuador. < *P. Z. S.*, xxvi, 1858, pp. 449–461, pl. (Aves) cxlv.

87 spp., with critical and field-notes.—*Conirostrum fraseri*, p. 452; *Phrygilus ocularis*, p. 454, pl. cxlv; *Synallaxis antesiensis*, p. 457; *Tyrannulus chrysops*, p. 458.

1858. SCLATER, P. L.   On the Birds collected by Mr. Fraser in the vicinity of Riobamba, in the Republic of Ecuador. < *P. Z. S.*, xxvi, 1858, pp. 549–556, pl. (Aves) cxlvi.

59 spp., with collector's and author's notes.—*Troglodytes solstitialis*, p. 550; *Catamenia homochroa*, p. 552; *Agriornis solitaria*, p. 553; *Elainia griseigularis*, pl. cxlvi, f. 1; *E. stictoptera*, pl. cxlvi, f. 2, p. 554, spp. nn.

1859. CASSIN, J.   La Plata, | the Argentine Confederation, | and Paraguay. | Being a Narrative of the Exploration of the Tributaries of the | River La Plata and Adjacent Countries during the years | 1853, '54, '55, and '56, | under the orders of the United States Government. | By Thomas J. Page, U. S. N., | Commander of the Expedition. | With Map and Numerous Engravings. | New York: Harper & Brothers, Publishers, | Franklin Square. | 1859. 1 vol. 8vo. pp. i–xxii, 23–632, map and engs. >App. J. Notes on the Birds collected by the La Plata Expedition. By John Cassin. pp. 599–602.

Merely a list of the species collected, with a slight commentary of general character.

1859. EDITORIAL.   [Letter from Mr. Fraser at Nanegal, Pichincha, relating to various birds.] < *Ibis*, i, 1859, pp. 208.

1859. EDITORIAL.   [Correspondence from Mr. Fraser, in Ecuador.] < *Ibis*, i, 1859, pp. 332, 333.

1859. EDITORIAL.   [Correspondence from O. Salvin, en route to Guatemala.] < *Ibis*, i, 1859, pp. 333, 334.

1859. EDITORIAL.   [Annotated extracts of letters from Fraser, at Quito and Babahoyo, June and July.] < *Ibis*, i, 1859, pp. 462–464.

1859. EDITORIAL.   [Extracts from a letter of O. Salvin, en route to, and in, Guatemala.] < *Ibis*, i, 1859, pp. 466–469.

1859. GOULD, J.   List of Birds from the Falkland Islands, with Descriptions of the Eggs of some of the Species, from specimens collected principally by Captain C. C. Abbott, of the Falkland Islands Detachment. < *P. Z. S.*, xxvii, 1859, pp. 93–98.

38 spp.—*Gavia roseiventris*, p. 97, sp. n.

1859. GUNDLACH, J.   Ornithologisches aus Briefen von Cuba. < *J. f. O.*, 1859, vii, pp. 294–299, 347–351.

Desultory notes on various species, in continuation of his previous more formal papers on the same subject in the same journal.

1859. MOORE, T. J. List of Mammals and Birds collected by Mr. Joseph Leyland in Honduras, Belize, and Guatemala. < *P. Z. S.*, xxvii, 1859, pp. 50–65, pll. (Aves) cl, cli.

> 125 spp. of birds, with brief field-notes.—*Ortyx leylandi*, p. 62, sp. n.

1859. NEWTON, A., *and* NEWTON, E. Observations on the Birds of St. Croix, West Indies, made, between February 20th and August 6th 1857 by Alfred Newton, and, between March 4th and September 28th 1858 by Edward Newton. (Part I [–IV].) < *Ibis*, i, 1859, pp. 59–69, 138–150, 252–264, 365–379, pll. i, xii.

> Opens with sketch of the locality; finishes with sketch of the literature of the subject. Critical, descriptive, and field-notes on 64 spp., some of which are queried or left undetermined, and many bibliographical references. Woodcut of trachea of *Dendrocygna arborea*. Eight spp. of eggs figured on pl. xii. *Gymnoglaux nudipes*, pl. i.

1859. OSBURN, W. Notes on the Birds of Jamaica. < *Zoologist*, xvii, 1859, pp. 6368–6373.

> "Contains graphic pictures of Jamaican Ornithology."

1859. OSBURN, W. Notes on the Bats and Birds of Jamaica. < *Zoologist*, xvii, 1859, pp. 6587–6594.

1859. OSBURN, W. Notes on the Mountain Birds of Jamaica. < *Zoologist*, xvii, 1859, pp. 6658–6665.

1859. OSBURN, W. Notes on the Mountain Birds of Jamaica. < *Zoologist*, xvii, 1859, pp. 6709–6721.

1859. OSBURN, W. Notes on the Mountain Birds of Jamaica. < *Zoologist*, xvii, 1859, pp. 6753–6761.

> These notes continued in same journal for 1860. *q. v.*

1859. SAGRA, RAMON DE LA. Énumération des espèces zoologiques et botaniques de l'ile de Cuba utiles à acclimer dans autres régions analogues du globe. < *Bull. Soc. Acclim.*, vi, 1859, pp. 169–184.

> Oiseaux, pp. 178–181.

1859. SCLATER, P. L. Characters of Five [lately] New Species of American Birds. < *Ann. Mag. Nat. Hist.*, (3), iii, 1859, pp. 443–446.

> From *P. Z. S.*, Nov. 9, 1858, pp. 446–449.

1859. SCLATER, P. L. List of the First Collection of Birds made by Mr. Louis Fraser at Pallatanga, Ecuador, with Notes and Descriptions of New Species. < *P. Z. S.*, xxvii, 1859, pp. 135–147, pl. (Aves) cliv.

> 102 spp.—*Vireo josephæ*, p. 137, pl. cliv; *Nemosia ornata*, p. 138; *Anabates subularis, A. temporalis, Dysithamnus unicolor*, p. 141; *Formicivora caloptera, Pachyrhamphus homochrous, Cephalopterus penduliger*, p. 142, spp. nn.

1859. SCLATER, P. L. On some new or little-known Birds from the Rio Napo. < *P. Z. S.*, xxvii, 1859, pp. 440, 441.

> 9 spp.—*Buarremon castaneiceps, Grallaria nuchalis*, p. 441, spp. nn.

1859. SCLATER, P. L., *and* SALVIN, O. On the Ornithology of Central America. Part I [–III]. < *Ibis*, i, 1859, pp. 1–22, 117–138, 213–234, pll. iv, v.

> Sketch of literature of the subject; 382 spp. with field-notes, mainly from Mr. Salvin's personal observations, and some synonymy. *Cistothorus elegans*, p. 8; *Cœreba lucida*, p. 14: *Xiphocolaptes elegans*, p. 118; *Sayornis aquatica*, p. 119; *Empidonax albigularis*, p. 122; *Elainia vilissima*, p. 122, pl. 4, f. 1; *E. placens*, p. 123, pl. 4, f. 2. Various eggs figured at pl. 5. Several species are left undetermined. Cf. *Ibis*, 1866, pp. 188–206.

1860. BREWER, T. M. [List of the Birds of Cuba, compiled from two lists furnished by Dr. Gundlach, of Havana.] < *Proc. Boston Soc. Nat. Hist.*, vii, 1860, pp. 305–308.

> Nominal list of 250 spp.

1860. BRYANT, H. [Notes on two Birds from Bogota.] < *Proc. Boston Soc. Nat. Hist.*, vii, 1860, pp. 226, 227.

> *Turdus minimus* Lafr.; *Vireo bogotensis*, sp. n., p. 227.

1860. BURMEISTER, H. Systematisches Verzeichniss der in den La Plata-Staaten beobachteten Vögelarten. < *J. f. O.*, viii, 1860, pp. 241–268.

> 261 spp.; the list shortly annotated and with a few references.

1860. CASSIN, J. Catalogue of Birds collected during a survey of a route for a Ship Canal across, the Isthmus of Darien, by order of the Government of the United States, made by Lieut. N. Michler, of the U. S. Topographical Engineers, with notes and descriptions of new species. < *Proc. Acad. Nat. Sci. Phila.*, xii, 1860, pp. 132–144, 188–197.

144 spp.—*Monasa pallescens*, p. 134 (with synop. of 6 spp. of *Monasa*); *Celeus mentalis*, p. 137; *Orthogonys olivaceus*, *Pittasoma* (g. n.) *michleri*, p. 189; *Dendroica vieillotii*, p. 192 (with synop. of 5 allied spp.), spp. nn.

1860. CASSIN, J. Catalogue of Birds from the Island of St. Thomas, West Indies, collected and presented to the Academy of Natural Sciences by Mr. Robert Swift. With Notes. < *Proc. Acad. Nat. Sci. Phila.*, xii, 1860, pp. 374–379.

27 spp., annotated.

1860. EDITORIAL. [Notice of Mr. Fraser's Movements and Operations.] < *Ibis*, ii, 1860, pp. 192, 193.

1860. FRAUENFELD, G. v. Ueber den Aufenthalt in Valparaiso und die Ausflüge daselbst, während der Weltfahrt der k. k. Fregatte Novara. < *Verh. (Abhandl.) k. k. zool.-bot. Ges. Wien*, x, 1860, pp. 635.

Grössten Theils ornithologischen Inhalts.

1860. GERMAIN, M. F. Notes upon the Mode and Place of Nidification of some [69 spp.] of the Birds of Chili. < *Proc. Boston Soc. Nat. Hist.*, vii, 1860, pp. 308–316.

1860. GODET, T. L. Bermuda : | its History, Geology, Climate, Products, | Agriculture, Commerce, and Government | from the earliest period to the present time; | with hints to invalids. | By Theodore L. Godet, M. D. | London : | Smith, Elder and Co., 65, Cornhill. | — | M.DCCC.LX. 1 vol. 8vo. > Chap. XIII, pp. 193–198.

Treats of a very few spp., with running commentary.

1860. LAWRENCE, G. N. Description of a New Species of Bird of the Genus Phaeton, also of a New Species of Humming Bird of the Genus Heliopaedica. < *Ann. Lyc. Nat. Hist. New York*, vii, 1860, pp. 142–145.

Ph. flavo-aurantius, p. 142; *H. castaneocauda*, p. 145.

1860. LAWRENCE, G. N. Notes on some Cuban Birds, with Descriptions of New Species. < *Ann. Lyc. Nat. Hist. New York*, vii, 1860, pp. 247–275.

27 spp. critically treated; many observations of Dr. J. Gundlach's. *Accipiter gundlachi*, p. 252; *Antrostomus cubanensis*, p. 260, spp. nn.

1860. LAWRENCE, G. N. Descriptions of New Species of Birds of the Genera Myiarchus and Phlogopsis. < *Ann. Lyc. Nat. Hist. New York*, vii, 1860, pp. 284–286.

M. Panamensis, p. 284; *Ph. McLeannani*, p. 285.

1860. OSBURN, W. Notes on the Mountain Birds of Jamaica. < *Zoologist*, xviii, 1860, pp. 6833–6841.

1860. OSBURN, W. Notes on the Mountain Birds of Jamaica. < *Zoologist*, xviii, 1860, pp. 6873–6880.

1860. OSBURN, W. Notes on the Mountain Birds of Jamaica. < *Zoologist*, xviii, 1860, pp. 6925–6934.

Continued from same journal for 1859, *q. v.*

1860. PHILIPPI, R. A. Ueber zwei vermuthlich neue Chilenischen Enten und über Fringilla barbata Mol. < *Arch. f. Naturg.*, 1860, (1), pp. 24–28.

Anas iopareia, p. 24. *Erismatura vittata*, p. 26. Synonymik von *Chrysomitris barbata*.

1860. PHILIPPI, R. A., *and* LANDBECK, L. Beschreibung zweier neuen Chilenischen Vögel aus den Geschlechtern Procellaria und Caprimulgus. < *Arch. f. Naturg.*, 1860, (1), pp. 279–284.

Caprimulgus andinus, p. 279; *Thalassidroma segethi*, p. 282.

1860. SALVIN, O. [Editorial Extracts from Letters from Dueñas, Guatemala, Aug. 30 and Oct. 25, 1859.] < *Ibis*, ii, 1860, pp. 99–101.

1860. SALVIN, O. [Letters from Vera Paz, relating to various Birds, with a comparative list of the Trochilidæ of Dueñas and Coban.] < *Ibis*, ii, 1860, pp. 193–197.

1860. SALVIN, O., *and* SCLATER, P. L. Contributions to the Ornithology of Guatemala. < *Ibis*, ii, 1860, pp. 28–45, pl. iii, pp. 272–278, 396–402, pl. xiii.

80 + 39 + 52 = 171 spp. The first article contains species not mentioned in the authors' paper on the same subject in *Ibis*, vol. i, 1859, with the whole of Salvin's field-notes on his first collection; the second, 39 more new to the fauna of the country; the third, 52 more, both with Salvin's field-notes. *Thryothorus pleurostictus*, p. 30; *Elainia subpagana*, p. 36; *Malacoptila veraepacis*, p. 40; *Chrysotis guatemalæ* "Hartl.", p. 46, spp. nn. The pll. represent *Chætura rutila* and *Pionus haematotis*. Cf. *Ibis*, 1866, pp. 188–206.

1860. SCLATER, P. L. Descriptions of [lately] New Species of Birds collected by Mr. Louis Fraser at Pallatanga, Ecuador. < *Ann. Mag. Nat. Hist.*, (3), v, 1860, pp. 427–430.

From *P. Z. S.*, April 12, 1859, pp. 135–147, *q. v.*

1860. SCLATER, P. L. On two [lately] new Birds from the Rio Napo. < *Ann. Mag. Nat. Hist.*, (3), v, 1860, p. 498.

From *P. Z. S.*, Nov. 22, 1859, pp. 440, 441, *q. v.*

1860. SCLATER, P. L. On the Eggs of Two Raptorial Birds from the Falkland Islands. < *Ibis*, ii, 1860, pp. 24–28, pl. i.

Pl. i, fig. 1, *Milvago australis;* fig. 2, *Cathartes* sp., wrongly identified as *Milvago australis;* fig. 3, *Buteo erythronotus.*

1860. SCLATER, P. L. List of Additional Species of Birds collected by Mr. Louis Fraser at Pallatanga, Ecuador; with Notes and Descriptions of New Species. < *P. Z. S.*, xxviii, 1860, pp. 63–73.

64 spp.—*Thryothorus mystacalis*, p. 64; *Grallaria erythrops, G. regulus*, p. 66; *Myiarchus nigriceps, Platyrhynchus albogularis, Eupsilostoma pusillum*, p. 68; *Tyrannulus flavidifrons, T. cinereiceps*, p. 69, spp. nn.

1860. SCLATER, P. L. List of Birds collected by Mr. Fraser in the vicinity of Quito, and during excursions to Pichincha and Chimborazo; with Notes and Descriptions of New Species. < *P. Z. S.*, xxviii, 1860, pp. 73–83, pl. (Aves) clix.

52 spp.—*Thryothorus eophrys*, p. 74; *Oreomanes* (n. g.) *fraseri*, p. 75, fig. pl. clix; *Cinclodes excelsior, C. albidiventris*, p. 77; *Agriornis andecola*, p. 78; *Attagis chimborazensis*, p. 82, spp. nn.

1860. SCLATER, P. L. List of Birds collected by Mr. Fraser in Ecuador, at Nanegal, Calacali, Perucho, and Puellaro; with Notes and Descriptions of New Species. < *P. Z. S.*, xxviii, 1860, pp. 83–97, pl. (Aves) clx.

130 spp.—*Thryothorus nigricapillus, Basileuterus semicervinus*, p. 84; *Oryzoborus æthiops*, p. 88; *Pipreola jucunda*, p. 89; *Pipra deliciosa*, p. 90, figg.; *Masius coronulatus*, p. 91; *Cyclorhynchus fulvipectus*, p. 92; *Myiobius villosus*, p. 93, spp. nn.

1860. SCLATER, P. L. [Announcement of the arrival of some Mammals and Birds from British Honduras.] < *P. Z. S.*, xxviii, 1860, p. 206.

1860. SCLATER, P. L. List of Birds collected by Mr. Fraser at Babahoyo in Ecuador, with Descriptions of New Species. < *P. Z. S.*, xxviii, 1860, pp. 272–290, pl. (Aves) cxliv.

134 spp.—*Geothlypis semiflava*, p. 273; *Cyclorhis virenticeps* (pl. cxliv). *Saltator flavidicollis*, p. 272; *Embernagra chrysomus*, p. 275; *Spermophila ophthalmica, Oryzoborus occidentalis*. *Cassiculus flavicrissus*, p. 276; *Xiphorhynchus thoracicus*, p. 277; *X. pusillus* (ex Nova Granada), p. 278; *Formicivora consobrina, Cercomacra maculosa, Pachyramphus spodiurus*, p. 279; *Attila torridus, Fluvicola atripennis*, p. 280; *Megarhynchus chrysogaster. Tyrannus niveigularis, Myiarchus phæocephalus*, p. 281; *Cyclorhynchus subbrunneus, Muscivora occidentalis*, p. 282; *Bucco leucocrissus*, p. 284; *Dryocopus fuscipennis*, p. 286, spp. nn.

1860. SCLATER, P. L. List of Birds collected by Mr. Fraser at Esmeraldas, Ecuador, with Descriptions of New Species. < *P. Z. S.*, xxviii, 1860, pp. 291–298.

93 spp.—*Cyphorinus phæocephalus*, p. 291, sp. n.

1860. SCLATER, P. L. Catalogue of Birds of the Falkland Islands. < *P. Z. S.*, xxviii, 1860, pp. 382–391, pl. (Aves) clxxiii. (Cf. op. cit., 1861, p. 45; 1864, p. 73.)

57 spp., with brief field-notes. *Chloephaga rubidiceps*, p. 387, pl. clxxiii, sp. n.

1860. SCLATER, P. L. Characters of Ten New Species of American Birds. <*P. Z. S.*, xxviii, 1860, pp. 461–467.

Campylorhynchus nigriceps, p. 461; *C. gularis, Vireo modestus*, p. 462; *Vireosylvia cobanensis*, p. 463; *Myiobius flavicans, M. pulcher, M. crypterythrus*, p. 464; *M. cryptoxanthus*, p. 465; *Heteropelma amazonum, H. flavicapillum*, p. 466. The article includes synopses of the species of *Myiobius* and *Heteropelma*.

1860. SCLATER, P. L., *and* SALVIN, O. Characters of Eleven [lately] New Species of Birds discovered by Osbert Salvin in Guatemala. <*Ann. Mag. Nat. Hist.*, (3), vi, 1860, pp. 215–217.

From *P. Z. S.*, May 22, 1860, pp. 298–301.

1860. SCLATER, P. L., *and* SALVIN, O. Characters of Eleven New Species of Birds discovered by Osbert Salvin in Guatemala. <*P. Z. S.*, xxviii, 1860, pp. 298–301.

Polioptila albiloris, Dendrœca chrysoparia, p. 298; *Hylophilus cinereiceps, Glyphorhynchus pectoralis, Thamnistes anabatinus, Platyrhynchus cancrominus*, p. 299; *Tyrannulus semiflavus, Heteropelma verœpacis, Lipaugus holerythrus, Pionus hœmatotis, Corethrura rubra*, p. 300.

1860. TAYLOR, G. C. On Birds collected or observed in the Republic of Honduras, with a short Account of a Journey across that country from the Pacific to the Atlantic Ocean. <*Ibis*, ii, 1860, pp. 10–24, 110–122, 222–228, 311–317.

Description of the region and field-notes on 96 spp.

1861. ABBOTT, C. C. [Field-] Notes on the Birds [66 spp.] of the Falkland Islands. <*Ibis*, iii, 1861, pp. 149–167.

Cf. *P. Z. S.*, 1860, p. 382, and Feb. 12, 1861, p. 45; also, *Ibis*, 1860, p. 336.

1861. ALBRECHT, R. Zur Ornithologie Cuba's. Nach Geo. N. Lawrence und J. Gundlach mitgetheilt. <*J. f. O.*, 1861, ix, pp. 198–215.

Ann. Lyc. Nat. Hist. N. Y., passim, 1855-60. 28 spp.

1861. BOLLE, C. Guano-Gewinnung auf den Chincha-Inseln. <*J. f. O.*, ix, 1861, pp. 387–390.

Aus *Cuzco und Lima* von Clements Markham, London, 1856.

1861. BURMEISTER, H. Reise durch die La Plata-Staaten, mit besonderer Rücksicht auf die physische Beschaffenheit und den Culturzustand der Argentinischen Republik. Ausgeführt in den Jahren 1857–61. Zweiter Band. Halle. 1861.

Not seen. Said to contain lists of mammals, birds, etc. Cf. *Ibis*, 1863, pp. 357, 358; *J.f. O.*, viii, 1860, pp. 241–268.

1861. EDITORIAL. [Notes on some birds of the Falkland Islands.] <*Ibis*, iii, 1861, p. 312.

1861. GUNDLACH, J. Tabellarische Uebersicht aller bisher auf Cuba beobachteten Vögel. <*J. f. O.*, 1861, ix, pp. 321–349.

With tabular statement of periods of migration and breeding, comparative abundance or scarcity, and general geographical distribution, in seven categories. 249 spp.

1861. LAWRENCE, G. N. Descriptions of three new new species of Birds [from Middle America]. <*Ann. Lyc. Nat. Hist. New York*, vii, 1861, pp. 303–305.

Grallaria perspicillata, p. 303; *Polioptila superciliaris*, p. 304; *Chlorostilbon nitens*, p. 305.

1861. OWEN, ROBERT. On the Nesting of some Guatemalan Birds. With remarks by Osbert Salvin, . . . <*Ibis*, iii, 1861, pp. 58–69, pl. ii.

23 spp. Field-notes; desc. of nests and eggs by O. Salvin; 5 spp. eggs figured on pl. ii.

1861. PHILIPPI, [R. A.], *and* LANDBECK, [L.] Descripcion. De algunas especies nuevas de pájaros [chilenos]. <*Anal. Univ. Chile*, xviii, 1861, pp. 731–734.

Upucerthia albiventris, p. 731; *Larus frobenii*, p. 732; *L. cinereo caudatus*, p. 733.—These three species are also described in *Arch. für Naturg.* of same year.

1861. PHILIPPI, [R. A.], *and* LANDBE[C]K, [L.] Descripcion de unas nueve especies de pájaros peruanos del Museo Nacional. <*Anal. Univ. Chile*, xix, Nov., 1861, pp. 609–622.

Synallaxis striata, p. 609; *Chlorospiza erythronota*, p. 610; *Pitylus albociliaris*, p. 611; *Sterna lorata*, p. 612; *S. Trobeni* [sic!], p. 613 (commonly quoted *frobeeni* or *frobeni*) ("fué muerta en setiembre de 1851 por el finado Trobén"); *S. comata*, p. 614; *Leistes albipes*, p. 616; *Recurvirostra andina*, p. 618; *Dasycephala albicauda*, p. 618.—Cuatro especies del jénero *Pepoaza* d'Orb.,—*livida, andecola, montana, maritima.*—Noticias sobre el modo de vivir de las dos especies chilenas de *Dasycephala*.

1861. PHILIPPI, R. A., *and* LANDBECK, L.   Neue Wirbelthiere von Chile.   <*Arch. f. Naturg.*, (1), 1861, pp. 289–301.

> B. Aves: *Upucerthia albiventris*, p. 290; *Larus frobenii*, p. 292; *L. cinereo-caudatus*, p. 293.

1861. SALLÉ, A.   Liste d'Oiseaux | a vendre | provenant des chasses faites en Amérique | par M. Auguste Sallé, | Rue Guy-de-la-Brosse, 13, a Paris. | Paris, mars 1861 | 8vo pamph.   pp. 7.

> Ces oiseaux sont en peaux bien préparées; ils ont été mentionnés par Bonaparte dans les *Compt. Rend.*, et ils ont aussi fourni la matière de plusieurs articles publiés par Sclater dans les *P. Z. S.*, 1856, '57, '58, '59 et '60.   Ils proviennent du Mexique, de l'ile de St. Domingue, de la Vénézuela et de l'Amérique du Nord.

1861. SALVIN, O.   A List of [28] Species to be added to the Ornithology of Central America.   <*Ibis*, iii, 1861, pp. 351–357.

> Cf. same author's and P. L. Sclater's several articles on same subject in same journal, previous numbers.   Cf. *Ibis*, 1866, pp. 188–206.

1861. SALVIN, O.   Descriptions of three new species of Birds from Guatemala.   <*P. Z. S.*, xxxix, 1861, pp. 202, 203.

> *Cyphorinus philomela, Embernagra chloronota*, p. 202; *Aphantochroa roberti*, p. 203.

1861. SALVIN, O.   Descriptions of three [lately] new species of Birds from Guatemala.   <*Ann. Mag. Nat. Hist.*, (3), viii, 1861, pp. 334, 335.

> From *P. Z. S.*, May 14, 1861, pp. 202, 203, *q. v.*

1861. SCLATER, P. L.   Characters of Eight [lately] New Species of American Birds.   <*Ann. Mag. Nat. Hist.*, (3), vii, 1861, pp. 327–330.

> From *P. Z. S.*, Dec. 11, 1860.

1861. SCLATER, P. L.   Additions and Corrections to the List of the Birds of the Falkland Islands [in *P. Z. S.*, 1860, pp. 382–391].   <*P. Z. S.*, xxxix, 1861, pp. 45–47. (See *P. Z. S.*, 1864, p. 73.)

> 11 spp.   List of 8 spp. of Falkland *Spheniscidæ*.

1861. SCLATER, P. L.   List of a Collection of Birds made by the late Mr. Osburn in Jamaica, with notes.   <*P. Z. S.*, xxxix, 1861, pp. 69–82, pl. xiv and woodcc.

> 92 spp.—*Laletes osburni*, g. sp. n., p. 72, pl. xiv, f. 2; *Siphonorhis*, g. n., p. 77; *Elainia fallax*, sp. n., p. 76.

1861–62. GUNDLACH, J.   Zusätze und Berichtigungen zu den „Beiträgen zur Ornithologie Cuba's".   (In den früheren Jahrgängen dieses Journals.)   <*J. f. O.*, ix, 1861, pp. 401–416; x, 1862, pp. 81–96, 177–191.

> Reviews a large number of his species, mainly upon information acquired through Baird, Cassin and Lawrence's *Birds of North America*.   In using Dr. Gundlach's work, it is essential to consult this article in connection with the previous ones.   See 1855–57, GUNDLACH, J.

1861–62. SCLATER, P. L.   Catalogue | of | a Collection | of | American Birds | belonging to | Philip Lutley Sclater, M. A., Ph. D., F. R. S., | Fellow of Corpus Christi College, Oxford; | Secretary to the Zoological Society of London; | Editor of "The Ibis." | [Vignette.   Motto.] | London: | N. Trübner and Co., Paternoster Row. | [1861,] 1862.   1 vol. 8vo.   pp. xvi, 338, with or without pll. xx.

> The collection consisted of about 4,100 specimens of 2,170 species of American *Passeres, Fissirostres*, and *Scansores*, 386 being type-specimens.   The text consists of a copious synonymy, with enumeration of specimens of each species by locality whence procured, and some little running commentary in footnotes.
>
> *Phœnicothraupis erythrolœma* Bp. ?, p. 83; *Tachyphonus cristatellus*, p. 86; *Paroaria cervicalis*, p. 108; *Chrysomitris uropygialis*, p. 125; *Icterus xanthornus*, p. 131; *Quiscalus æquatorialis*, p. 140; *Q. assimilis*, p. 141; *Glyphorhynchus major*, p. 161; *Thamnophilus strenuus*, p. 173; *Pachyrhamphus cinereiventris*, p. 242; *P. dorsalis*, p. 243; *Momotus swainsoni*, p. 261; *Bucco napensis*, p. 269; *Chelidoptera brasiliensis*, p. 275; *Chloronerpes malherbii*, p. 338; *Conurus propinquus*, p. 346, are spp. nn. indicated in footnotes.   *Hyetornis*, g. n., p. 321. and probably some other generic names, are here used for the first time without particular notice of the fact. A list of the author's publications from 1850 to 1861 inclusive, 165 in number, is appended.
>
> The completed vol. dates 1862. but some copies of the sheets were distributed as printed; date of printing is on each signature, according to which the first twelve (to p. 192) appeared in 1861, the rest in 1862.   The book is found with or without the plates: perfect copies, with the plates, are scarce.   These are as follows:—Pl. I, *Turdus pinicola*.   II, *Cinclus leucoitotus*. III, *Campylorhynchus jocosus*.   IV, *Thryothorus pleurostictus*.   V, *Hylophilus ochracceiceps*.

1861–62. SCLATER, P. L.—Continued.

VI, *Diglossa indigotica.* VII, *Dacnis egregia.* VIII, *D. pulcherrima.* IX, *Calliste cyanotis.* X, *Chlorospingus castaneicollis.* XI, *Embernagra chrysoma.* XII, *Sclerurus mexicanus.* XIII, *Synallaxis castanea.* XIV, *Anabazenops subalaris.* XV, *Myrmotherula ornata.* XVI, *Formicivora boucardi.* XVII, *Platyrhynchus coronatus.* XVIII, f. 1, *Oncostoma cinereigulare;* f. 2, *Todirostrum schistaceiceps.* XIX, *Masius coronulatus.* XX, *Chiroxiphia regina.*

1861–63. LAWRENCE, G. N. Catalogue of a Collection of Birds, made in New Grenada, by James McLeannan, Esq., of New York, with Notes and Descriptions of New Species. Part I. < *Ann. Lyc. Nat. Hist. New York*, vii, 1861, pp. 288–302 (Jan., 1861); Part II, pp. 315–334 (June, 1861); Part III, pp. 461–479 (Feb., 1862); Part IV, viii, pp. 1–13 (May, 1863).

I. *Leucopternis semiplumbeus,* p. 288; *Chlorostilbon assimilis,* p. 292; *Pachyramphus cinnamomeus,* p. 295; *Tachyphonus cassinii,* p. 297; *Capito maculicoronatus,* p. 300; *Corethrura albigularis,* p. 302. II. *Thryothorus galbraithii,* p. 320; *Th. castaneus,* p. 321; *Hylophilus pusillus,* p. 323; *H. aurantiifrons,* p. 324; *H. viridiflavus,* p. 324; *Myiarchus brunneiceps,* p. 327. III. *Syrnium lineatum,* p. 462; *Trogon concinnus,* p. 463; *Dacnis venusta,* p. 464; *Automolus pallidigularis,* p. 465; *Dendrocincla olivacea,* p. 466; *Dendrornis lachrymosus,* p. 467; *Myrmetherula fulviventris,* p. 468; *Ramphoccænus semitorquatus,* p. 469; *Myrmeciza ferruginea,* p. 470; *Turdus obsoletus,* p. 470; *Attila sclateri,* p. 470; *Empidonax griseigularis,* p. 471; *Leptopogon flavovirens,* p. 472; *Psittovius subcœruleus,* p. 475; *Pionius coccinicollaris,* p. 475; *Chloronerpes callopterus,* p. 476. IV. *Petrochelidon albilinea,* p. 2; *Cyphorinus lawrencii* Scl. MS., p. 5; *Pithys bicolor,* p. 6; *Rhynchocyclus flavo-olivaceus,* p. 8; *Lipaugus albogriseus,* p. 9; *Spermophila semicollaris,* p. 10; *Spermophila schistacea,* p. 10, spp. nn. 415 spp. (as numbered, but some of the Nos. duplicated) treated, with various critical notes, besides the descriptions of new species. The reception of collections at different times causes the several lists to be successive additions, and gives occasion for some rectifications in later lists of earlier identifications. The sequence of the species is systematic in each of the four lists, but not continuously so throughout the whole.

1861–69. CABANIS, J. Uebersicht der im Berliner Museum befindlichen Vögel von Costa Rica. < *J. f. O.*, viii, 1860, pp. 321–336 (pub. Jan., 1861), 401–416 (pub. May, 1861); ix, 1861, pp. 1–11, 81–96, 241–256; x, 1862, pp. 161–176, 321–336; xvii, 1869, pp. 204–213.

None published till Jan., 1861, though the first two portions appear in the Nos. for Sept.–Nov., 1860. Based on the investigations of Drs. v. Frantzius, Hoffmann, and Ellendorf. This important systematic review of Costa Rican birds is full of critical matter, and gives many new generic and specific names, as follows:—

Pezopetes, p. 415; *Amaurospiza,* p. 3; *Callispiza* (pro *Calliste*), p. 87; *Acrocompsa,* p. 88; *Panterpe,* p. 164; *Ceophloeus,* p. 176, gen. nn.

[Jan., 1861] *Catharus frantzii, Turdus plebejus,* p. 323; *T. nigrescens,* p. 324; *Rhimamphus ruficeps,* p. 326; *Compsothlypis gutturalis,* p. 329; *Trigliphidia callophrys,* p. 331; *Phonasca luteicapilla,* p. 332; *P. gracilis,* p. 333; *P. humilis,* p. 334; *P. gnatho,* p. 335; *P. saturata,* p. 336. [May, 1861] *Polioptila —— (not named), p. 401; *Ptilogonys caudatus,* p. 402; *Cyclorhis subflavescens,* p. 405; *Troglodytes intermedius,* p. 407; *Thryothorus modestus,* p. 409; *Diglossa plumbea,* p. 411; *Melozone leucotis,* p. 413; *Pezopetes capitalis,* p. 415. [1861] *Amaurospiza concolor,* p. 3 (*Cyanospiza minor,* p. 4); *Sporophila leucopsis, S. ochropyga* (Licht., Mus. Ber.), p. 5; *S. hoffmanni,* p. 6 (*Lampropsar warczwiczi,* p. 83); *Phoenicothraupis fuscicauda,* p. 86; *Callispiza frantzii,* p. 87; *Atticora cyanophœa,* p. 92; *Myrmornis hoffmanni,* p. 95; *Thamnophilus punctatus,* p. 241; *Thripobrotus compressus,* p. 243; *Myiarchus nigricapillus,* p. 250. [1862] *Hemithylaca hoffmannii,* p. 163; *Panterpe insignis,* p. 164; *Chlorolampis salvini,* p. 164; *Malacoptila costaricensis,* p. 172; *Trogon tenellus,* p. 173; *Chloronerpes uropygialis,* p. 321; *Centurus hoffmannii,* p. 322 (*C. polygrammicus,* p. 326); *Ramphastos approximans,* p. 333, spp. nn. Synopsis of 6 spp. of *Pyrrhocorax,* 4 spp. of *Chloronerpes,* 10 spp. of *Centurus,* and various less formal special criticisms.

[1869] This portion treats of 8 spp. of *Glaucidium* and of various *Raptatores* and other birds. *Asturina polionota,* p. 208; *Ortalida frantzii,* p. 211; *Crypturus modestus,* p. 212, spp. nn.

1862. ALBRECHT, R. Zur Ornithologie von Jamaica. Nach Osburn, Sclater und Gosse zusammengestellt. < *J. f. O.*, x, 1862, pp. 192–207.

Compilation from the sources named. 191 spp.

1862. EDITORIAL. [O. Salvin's and F. Godman's Operations in Guatemala.] < *Ibis*, iv, 1862, p. 195.

1862. LAWRENCE, G. N. Descriptions of Six New Species of Birds [of Middle America], of the Families Charadridæ [sic], Trochilidæ, and Caprimulgidæ. < *Ann. Lyc. Nat. Hist. New York*, vii, 1862, pp. 455–460.

Aegialitis tenuirostris, p. 455; *Thalurania luciæ,* p. 456; *Chlorostilbon insularis,* p. 457; *Trochilus aurigularis,* p. 458; *Sapphironia luminosa,* p. 458; *Stenopsis maculicaudus,* p. 459.

1862. LAWRENCE, G. N.   Descriptions of Six New Species of Birds from the Isthmus of Panama.   < *Ibis*, iv, 1862, pp. 10–13.

Heleodytes albo-brunneus, p. 10; *Pitangus albovittatus, Myozetetes granadensis*, p. 11; *Todirostrum olivaceum, Tyranniscus parvus, Tyrannulus brunneicapillus*, p. 12.

1862. SALLÉ, A., *and* PARZUDAKI, E.   Nº 2.   Avril 1862. | Catalogue | des | Oiseaux du Mexique | composant | les collections de M. A. Sallé, | Rue Guy-de-la-Brosse, 13, a Paris, | et | de M. E. Parzudaki, Rue du Bouloi, 2. | — | [Paris: Impr. de Mme. Ve. Bouchard-Huzard, Rue de l'Éperon, 5.   1862.]   8vo. pp. 7.

Ces oiseaux sont en peaux bien préparées et ont été mentionnés par Bonaparte dans les *Comptes Rendus* de l'Institut; ils ont aussi fourni la matière de plusieurs notices publiés par Sclater dans les *P. Z. S.*, 1856–1860.

1862. SALVIN, O.   [Letter on Birds from Dueñas, Guatemala.] < *Ibis*, iv, 1862, p. 96.

1862. SCLATER, P. L.   On some Birds recently Collected by M. Boucard in Southern Mexico.   < *P. Z. S.*, xxx, 1862, pp. 18–20, pl. iii.

16 spp.—*Harporhynchus ocellatus*, p. 18, pl. iii, sp. n.

1862. SCLATER, P. L.   Characters of Nine New Species of Birds received in collections from Bogota.   < *P. Z. S.*, xxx. 1862, pp. 109–112, pl. xi.

Turdus ephippialis, p. 109; *Hylophilus ferruyineifrons, Chlorospingus oleagineus, Philydor panerythrus*, p. 110; *Leptopogon erythrops, L. pœcilotis, Myiobius bellus*, p. 111; *Empidochanes pœcilurus, Urochroma stictoptera* (pl. xi), p. 112.

1862. SCLATER, P. L.   Characters of Nine [lately] New Species of Birds received in collections from Bogota.   < *Ann. Mag. Nat. Hist.*, (3), x, 1862, pp. 309–313.

From *P. Z. S.*, March 25, 1862, pp. 109–112, *q. v.*

1862–63. NATTERER, J., *ed.* PELZELN, A. v.   Handschriftliche Notizen [über die Cathartidæ und Falconidæ Brasiliens].   < *Verh. (Abh.) k.-k. zool.-bot. Ges. Wien*, xii, 1862, pp. 171–192; xiii, 1863, pp. 631–636.

Notizen über 25 Arten der hier besprochenen Gruppen, als Anhang zu Pelzelns ,,Die Geier und Falken der Kaiserl. Ornith. Sammlung", tomm. citt. pp. 123–192, 585–636.

1863. [BAIRD, S. F.]   List of the described Birds of Mexico, Central America, and the West Indies not in the collection of the Smithsonian Institution.   January 1, 1863.   8vo, double column, pp. 6.

Names only.

1863. BATES, H. W.   The Naturalist on the River Amazons; a record of adventures, habits of animals, sketches of Brazilian and Indian life, and aspects of Nature under the Equator during eleven years of travel.   By Henry Walter Bates. London.   Murray, 1863.   2 vols.   8vo. figg.

Orig. ed., not seen: see 2d ed., 1864.   Numerous ornithological passages, and some of the woodcuts.   Mr. Bates's collection of birds, upwards of 400 species, is said to have been dispersed with only imperfect record (*P. Z. S.*, 1857, pp. 261–268, *q. v.*) of names, dates, or localities.   Cf. *Ibis*, 1863, pp. 462, 463; *Nat. Hist. Rev.*, 2d ser., iii, 1863, pp. 385–389; *Zoologist*, xxi, 1863, pp. 8537–8554.

1863. EDITOR.   The Naturalist on the Amazons. < *Nat. Hist. Rev.*, 2d ser., iii, 1863, pp. 385–389.

Editorial review of H. W. Bates's work.

1863. LAWRENCE, G. N.   Descriptions of Eight New Species of Birds from the Isthmus of Panama. < *Ibis*, v, 1863, pp. 181–184.

Cotyle uropygialis, Dendrornis nana, Formicivora virgata, Myrmelastes corvinus, Myiozetetes marginatus, Myiobius atricaudus, Platyrhynchus superciliaris, Celeus squamatus.

1863. LAWRENCE, G. N.   Descriptions of New Species of Birds of the Families Vireonidæ and Rallidæ.   < *Proc. Acad. Nat. Sci. Phila.*, xv, 1863, pp. 106, 107.

Vireo atripennis, Corethrura guatemalensis, p. 106; *Aramides axillaris*, p. 107.

1863. NEWMAN, E.   Notices of New Books. < *Zoologist*, xxi, 1863, pp. 8537–8554.

Extended notice of Bates's "The Naturalist on the River Amazons".

1863. PELZELN, A. v.   Ueber vier von Natterer in Brasilien gesammelte noch unbeschriebene Vögelarten.   < *Verh. k.-k. zool.-bot. Gesellsch. Wien*, xiii, Oct. 10, 1863, pp. 1125–1128.

Syrnium superciliare, p. 1125; *Strix superciliaris, Tinamus guttatus*, p. 1126; *T. erythropus* p. 1127.

1863. PHILIPPI, R. A., *and* LANDBECK, L. Beiträge zur Fauna von Peru. < *Arch. f. Naturg.*, —, 1863, pp. 118 - —.

> *Synallaxis striata; Chlorospiza erythronota; Pitylus albociliaris; Sterna lorata; S. frobeenii; S. comata; Leistes albipes; Recurvirostra andina; Dasycephala (Agriornis) albicauda.*—Cf. *Ibis*, 1864, pp. 120, 121.   (Seen, but transcript defective; volume missing from set when wanted for revision.)

1863. SALVIN, O. [Letter on his operations in Guatemala; suggests name of sancti jeromæ for a perhaps new Panyptila.] < *Ibis*, v, 1863, p. 239.

1863. SALVIN, O. Descriptions of Thirteen New Species of Birds discovered in Central America by Frederick Godman and Osbert Salvin. < *P. Z. S.*, xxxi, 1863, pp. 186–192, pll. (Aves) xxiii, xxiv, woodc.

> *Thryothorus petenicus, Dendrœca niveiventris* (pl. xxiv, f. 2), p. 187; *Cardellina versicolor* (pl. xxiv, f. 1), *Vireo pallens, V. ochraceus, V. semiflavus*, p. 188; *Petrochelidon littorea, Spizella pinetorum, Ammodromus petenicus, Junco alticola*, p. 189; *Chrysomitris atriceps, Elaënia arenarum, Panyptila sancti hieronymi* (pl. xxiii), p. 190 (cf. *Ibis*, 1863, p. 239).

1863–64. MARCH, W. T. Notes on the Birds of Jamaica. With Remarks by S. F. Baird. < *Proc. Acad. Nat. Sci. Phila.*, xv, 1863, pp. 150–154, 283–304; xvi, 1864, pp. 62–72.

> An extended commentary on the habits, etc., of numerous species, with some technic by S. F. Baird. *Mimus hillii*, p. 291, sp. n. Cf. *Ibis*, 1864, p. 404.

1864. BATES, H. W. The | Naturalist on the River | Amazons. | A record of adventures, habits of animals, sketches of | Brazilian and Indian Life, and aspects of nature under | the Equator, during eleven years of travel. | By Henry Walter Bates. | [Cut.] | Pelopæus Wasp building nest. | Second Edition. | With map and illustrations. | London : | John Murray, Albemarle street. | 1864. | [The Right of Translation is reserved.] ¦ 1 vol. 16mo. pp. iii–xii, 1–466, map, pll., and cuts (40 illusts. in all).

> Orig. ed. 1863, *q. v.* This work is pleasantly ornithological here and there throughout, and includes figures of several birds. Chap. XII, pp. 388–426, Animals of the neighbourhood of Ega. Birds, pp. 402–412; especially full on *Rhamphastidæ*.

1864. CASSIN, J. Notes on some Species of Birds from South America. < *Proc. Acad. Nat. Sci. Phila.*, xvi, 1864, pp. 286–288, pll. i–iv.

> Critical; 7 spp.—Pl. I, f. 1, *Calliste laviniæ*; f. 2, *C. hannahiæ*, sp. n., p. 287. Pl. II, *Orthogonys olivaceus*. Pl. III, *Pittasoma michleri*. Pl. IV, *Monasa pallescens*.

1864. LANDBECK, L. Contribuciones a la Ornitolojía de Chile. < *Anales de la Universidad de Chile*, tom. xxiv, No. 4, April, 1864, pp. 336–348.

> The original Spanish version of the paper by the author and Dr. Philippi in the *Archiv für Naturgeschichte*, 1864, (1), pp. 41–54 (cf. *Zool. Rec.*, ii, p. 81), and of the paper in the same periodical, 1864, (1), pp. 55–62, by the author alone (cf. *Zool. Rec.*, ii, p. 80).—*Dendroica atricapilla* Ldb., p. 336; *Arundinicola citreola* Ldb., p. 338; *Chlorospiza plumbea* Ph. & L., p. 341; *Sycalis aureiventris* Ph. & L., p. 342, spp. nn. Sobre los Azores chilenos, p. 345; *Accipiter chilensis* Ph. & L., p. 346, sp. n.

1864. LANDBECK, L. Beiträge zur Ornithologie Chiles. < *Arch. f. Naturg.*, 1864, (1), pp. 55–62. (Cf. *Arch. f. Nat.*, (1), 1864, pp. 41–54; 1865, pp. 56–106; 1866, pp. 121–132.)

> *Dendroica atricapilla*, p. 56; *Arundinicola citreola*, p. 58.

1864. LAWRENCE, G. N. Descriptions of New Species of Birds [of Central and South America] of the Families Tanagridæ, Cuculidæ, and Trochilidæ, with a Note on Panterpe insignis. < *Ann. Lyc. Nat. Hist. New York*, viii, 1864, pp. 41–46.

> *Saltator fulviventris*, p. 41; *Tachyphonus tibialis*, p. 41; *T. napensis*, p. 42; *Coccyzus julieni*, p. 42; *Urochroa leucura*, p. 43; *Urosticte ruficrissa*, p. 44; *Ramphomicron olivaceus*, p. 44.

1864. LAWRENCE, G. N. Catalogue of Birds collected at the Island of Sombrero, W. I., with Observations by A. A. Julien. < *Ann. Lyc. Nat. Hist. New York*, viii, 1864, pp. 92–106.

> 34 spp., of which only 12 are land-birds; among them are *Vireosylvia atripennis* and *Coccyzus julieni*; collector's field-notes; *Vireosylvia virginalis*, sp. n. prob., p. 97.

1854. LAWRENCE, G. N.   Descriptions of New Species of Birds of the Families Caere-
bidæ, Tanagridæ, Icteridæ, and Scolopacidæ.   < *Proc. Acad. Nat. Sci. Phila.*,
xvi, 1864, pp. 106–108.

> *Dacnis ultramarina, Saltator intermedius*, p. 106; *Cassicus vitellinus, Ereunetes occidentalis*,
> p. 107; all but the last from Isthmus of Panama, the *Ereunetes* being from North America.

1864. PHILIPPI, R. A., *and* LANDBECK, L.   Contribuciones a la ornitolojía de Chile.
< *Anales Univ. Chile*, xxv, Set. de 1864, pp. 408–439.

> 1. *Pteroptochus castaneus*, sp. n., p. 408.—2. De las Alondras Chilenas, pp. 409–418. *Certhi-
> lauda frobeni*, p. 411; *C. isabellina*, p. 412; *Geobamon fasciatus*, p. 415, spp. nn.—3. De las
> Muscisaxicolas Sud-Americanas, pp. 418–439. *Muscisaxicola cinerea*, p. 422; *M. rubricapilla*,
> p. 429; *M. flavivertex*, p. 434; *M. nigrifrons*, p. 436, spp. nn.—This paper reappears in *Arch.
> f. Naturg.*, 1865, *q. v.*

1864. PHILIPPI, R. A., *and* LANDBECK, L.   Beiträge zur Ornithologie Chiles.   < *Arch.
f. Naturg.*, 1864, (1), pp. 41–54. (Cf. *Arch. f. Nat.*, (1), 1864, pp. 55–62; 1865,
pp. 56–106; 1866, pp. 121–132.)

> *Accipiter chilensis*, p. 43; *Chlorospiza plumbea*, p. 47; *Sycalis auriventris*, p. 49.

1864. SALVIN, O.   A Fortnight amongst the Sea-birds of British Honduras.   < *Ibis*,
vi, 1864, pp. 372–387.

> Treating of numerous spp. in form of continuous narrative.

1864. SALVIN, O.   Descriptions of Seventeen New Species of Birds from Costa Rica.
< *P. Z. S.*, xxxii, 1864, pp. 579–586, pll. xxxv–xxxvi.

> *Catharus gracilirostris, Thryothorus albogularis, T. thoracicus, Myiadestes melanops* (pl.
> xxxv), p. 580; *Lanio leucothorax, Chlorospingus pileatus*, p. 581; *Embernagra superciliosa,
> Myrmeciza læmosticta, Grallaria dives*, p. 582; *Myiobius capitalis, Piprites griseiceps, Carpo-
> dectes* (g. n.) *nitidus* (pl. xxxvi), p. 583; *Oreopyra hemileuca, O. calolœma*, p. 584; *Chalybura
> melanorrhoa*, p. 585; *Selasphorus flammula, Odontophorus melanotis*, p. 586. The author is
> acquainted with about 300 species of Costa Rican birds, about 65 of which have been described
> as new, which have not been found beyond the limits of Costa Rica, even in the adjoining
> province of Veragua.

1864. SCLATER, P. L.   On some Additions to the List of the Birds of the Falkland
Islands.   < *P. Z. S.*, xxxii, 1864, p. 73.

> Two species, obtained by Captain Packe, are added to the lists previously drawn up by Dr.
> Sclater (*P. Z. S.*, 1860, pp. 382–391; 1861, pp. 45–47, *q. v.*). These are *Egretta leuce* and *Prion
> turtur*. The author adds, from the "Ibis" (1861, p. 312), rectifications of the names of two
> others, viz: *Nycticorax obscurus* for *N. gardeni*, and *Larus glaucotis* for *L. roseiventris*.

1864. SCLATER, P. L.   Descriptions of Seven New Species of Birds discovered by the
late Dr. John Natterer in Brazil.   < *P. Z. S.*, xxxii, 1864, pp. 605–611, pll.
xxxvii–xxxix, woodcc.

> *Granatellus pelzelni*, p. 606, pl. xxxvii, f. 1, with synopsis of 3 spp.; *Tanagra olivina* Natt.,
> *Spermophila pileata* (Natt.), p. 607, with synopsis of 8 spp.; *Poospiza oxyrhyncha* (Natt.), p.
> 608; *Hypocnemis flavescens* (Natt.), *Pteroptochus thoracicus* (pl. xxxiii), p. 609, woodcc. on p.
> 610; *Pipra nattereri*, p. 611, pl. xxxix.

1864. SCLATER, P. L., *and* SALVIN, O.   Notes on a Collection of Birds from the
Isthmus of Panama.   < *P. Z. S.*, xxxii, 1864, pp. 342–373, pl. xxx.

> Two hundred and seventy-two species are included in this list, to which is prefixed a con-
> cise notice of previous papers treating of the same subject. Four new species are described.
> namely, *Cassiculus microrhynchus, Myrmeciza immaculata, Camptostoma flaviventre*, and
> *Conurus ocularis*, while of all those enumerated a very full synonymy is given, correcting a
> great many former errors. One species, *Eucometis cassini*, is figured.

1864. TAYLOR, E. C.   Five Months in the West Indies.   < *Ibis*, vi, 1864, pp. 73–97,
157–173.

> Part I, pp. 73–97, Trinidad and Venezuela; sketch of region; 141 spp.; *Tyrannus rostratus*
> Scl., sp. n.   Part II, pp. 157–173, Martinique, Dominica, and Porto Rico; same treatment of
> subject; 48 spp.; *Certhiola dominicana*, p. 167; *Pitangus taylori* "Scl.", p. 169, spp. nn. Cf.
> *Ibis*, 1864, p. 405.

1865. CASSIN, J.   On some Conirostral Birds from Costa Rica in the Collection of the
Smithsonian Institution.   < *Proc. Acad. Nat. Sci. Phila.*, xvii, 1865, pp. 169–172.

> 22 spp.—*Fringillidæ* + *Tanagridæ*. *Arremon rufidorsalis, Buarremon crassirostris*, p. 170;
> *Euphonia anneæ*, p. 172, spp. nn.

1865. LAWRENCE, G. N. Descriptions of New Species of Birds [of Central and South America] of the Families Tanagridæ, Dendrocolaptidæ, Formicaridæ, Tyrannidæ, and Trochilidæ. < *Ann. Lyc. Nat. Hist. New York*, viii, 1865, pp. 126–135.

 Buarremon ocai, p. 126; *Philydor rufobrunneus*, p. 127; *Anabazenops lineatus*, p. 127; *Margarornis rubiginosa, M. guttata*, p. 128; *M. brunneicauda* (proband.), p. 130; *Dysithamnus striaticeps*, p. 130; *D. rufiventris*, p. 131; *Myrmotherula albigula*, p. 131; *Myrmeciza stictoptera*, p. 132; *Empidonax flavescens*, p. 133; *Contopus lugubris, Eupherusa niveicauda*, p. 134.

1865. LAWRENCE, G. N. Descriptions of Six New Species of Birds from Central America. < *Ann. Lyc. Nat. Hist. New York*, viii, 1865, pp. 171–174.

 Spermophila hicksi, S. badiiventris, S. fortipes, Formicivora schisticolor, Elainea frantzii, and *Mitrephorus aurantiiventris*.

1865. LAWRENCE, G. N. List of Birds from near David, Chiriqui, New Grenada, collected for the Smithsonian Institution, Washington, by Mr. Fred. Hicks, with Descriptions of New Species. < *Ann. Lyc. Nat. Hist. New York*, viii, 1865, pp. 174–178.

 Spermophila collaris, p. 176; *Elainea chiriquensis*, p. 176; *E. semiflava*, p. 177, spp. nn.—39 spp.

1865. LAWRENCE, G. N. Catalogue of a Collection of Birds in the Museum of the Smithsonian Institution, made by Mr. H. E. Holland at Greytown, Nicaragua, with Descriptions of New Species. < *Ann. Lyc. Nat. Hist. New York*, viii, 1865, pp. 178–184.

 Thryothorus brunneus, p. 178; *Synallaxis nigrifumosa*, p. 180; *Thamnophilus hollandi*, p. 180, spp. nn. 61 spp.

1865. LAWRENCE, G. N. Descriptions of new species of Birds of the Families Paridæ, Vireonidæ, Tyrannidæ, and Trochilidæ, with a note on Myiarchus Panamensis. < *Proc. Acad. Nat. Sci. Phila.*, xvii, 1865, pp. 37–39.

 Polioptila plumbiceps, Hylophilus acuticaudus, p. 37; *Myiarchus venezuelensis, Chalybura aeneicauda*, p. 38; *C. carnioli, Panychlora parvirostris*, p. 39—the last two from Costa Rica, the others from Venezuela.

1865. LAWRENCE, G. N. Descriptions of four new Species of Birds from the Isthmus of Panama, New Grenada. < *Proc. Acad. Nat. Sci. Phila.*, xvii, 1865, pp. 106–108.

 Tachyphonus rubrifrons, Anthus (Notiocorys) parvus, p. 106; *Thamnophilus nigricristatus*, p. 107; *Geotrygon albiventer*, p. 108.

1865. LEYBOLD, F. Cuatro especies nuevas de pájaros, descubiertos en la pendiente oriental de la cordillera que separa a la provincia de Santiago de la de Mendoza. < *Anales Univ. Chile*, tomo xxvi, Junio de 1865, pp. 712–718.

 Synallaxis crissirostris Landb., p. 713; *Myarchus* (sic) *fasciatus* Landb., p. 714; *Sporofila* (sic) *rufirostri* (sic) [lege *Sporophila rufirostris*] Landb., p. 716; *Phrygilus ornatus* Landb., p. 717.

1865. PHILIPPI, R. A., *and* LANDBECK, L. Beiträge zur Ornithologie von Chile. < *Arch. für Naturg.*, 1865, (1), pp. 56–106. (Vergl. *Arch.*, 1864, (1), pp. 41–54, 55–62; 1866, pp. 121–132.)

 Enthaltend: *Pteroptochos castaneus*, p. 56; Die Lerchen Chiles, pp. 58–73; *Certhilauda cunicularia* Lafr., *C. froberi*, p. 62; *C. isabellina*, p. 63; *Geobamon fasciata*, p. 68; *Certhilauda nigrofasciata*. Monographie der südamerikanischen Muscisaxicolinen, pp. 74–106; *M. albifrons, M. cinerea*, p. 80; *M. maculirostris, M. mentalis, M. rubricapilla*, p. 90; *M. rufiventris, M. flavivertex*, p. 98; *M. nigrifrons*, p. 101; *M. striaticeps, M. frontalis, M. capistrata ; M. brunnea, M. flavinucha, M. albilora, M. albimentum*—15 Arten.—Cf. Cab., *J.f. O.*, 1860, p. 249, note; Scl., *Ibis*, 1865, p. 59.
 This paper continues one of similar title by Landbeck in same *Archiv*, 1864, pp. 55–62, *q. v.*; which latter continues one by Philippi and Landbeck, in same *Archiv*, 1864, pp. 41–54, *q. v.*; both these papers of 1864 also appearing in Spanish in *Anal. Univ. Chile*, xxiv, 1864, pp. 336–348, *q. v.*, under LANDBECK, L. It is continued in same *Archiv*, 1866, pp. 121–132, *q. v.*
 The original Spanish version of this paper is in *Anales Univ. Chile*, xxv, 1864, pp. 408–439.

1865. SALVIN, O. The Sea-birds and Waders of the Pacific Coast of Guatemala. < *Ibis*, 2d ser., i, 1865, pp. 187–199.

 Narrative; running commentary on numerous spp.

1865-66. GUNDLACH, J.   Revista y Catálogo de las Aves Cubanas.   < *Poey's Reper-*
torio Físico-Nat. Isla Cuba, tomo i, 1865-66, pp. 165-180 (entrega 7, Octubre
1865), 221-242 (ent. 8, 9, Noviembre, Diciembre, 1865), 281-302 (entregas 10,
11, Enero, Febrero, 1866), 347-363 (ent. 12, 13, Abril, Junio, 1866), 384-403
(ent. 14, Agosto 1866); Indice de las Aves Cubanas, pp. 414, 415.

Hasta ahora se conocen 257 especies en estado silvestre en esta isla; 119 especies que tam-
bien pertenecen á la América Setentrional; á la América Meridional, 8; á las dos Américas,
55; á la América Setentrional y á la Europa, 8; á las dos Américas y á la Europa, 9; otras
Antillas, 18; no en otras tierras, 40 (lámina de la distribucion geográfica á la página 168).

La clasificacion es la que se ha usado en el catálogo publicado por el autor en *J.f. O.,* Jahrg.
ix, Nr. 53, 1861, SS. 321-349.

Apendice, pp. 396-402. Catálogo de las Aves introducidas, 4 esp. Cat. de las Aves obser-
vadas en el campo, pero probablemente huidas de jaulas, 6 esp. Cat. de las Aves indicadas
como pertenecientes á la Ornitol. cubana, pero equivocadas con otras que en efecto se encuentran, 87 esp. Cat. de las Aves indicadas como pertenecientes á la Orn. Cub., pero indudable-
mente por error, 39 esp. Correcciones de erratas esenciales, p. 403.

Sketch of general character of the avifauna; table of geographical distribution of species.
Of 257 species found feral in the island, 40 are peculiar to it, and 119, or more than half the
remainder, are common to North America, 8 to South America. Extracts ᶜᵒᵐ a letter of
Dr. Gundlach relating to Cuban ornithology are also printed in *Journ. f. Orn.,* 1866, pp. 352-
354. Cf. *Ibis,* 1867, pp. 377, 378.

1866. BAIRD, S. F.   [On dates of original publication of various spp. nn. of Philippi
and Landbeck's as between Anales Univ. Chile and Arch. f. Naturg.]   < *Ibis,*
2d ser., ii, 1866, pp. 424, 425.

1866. BENVENUTI, E.   Descrizione di quattro nuove specie della famiglia dei Trochilidi provenienti della Nuova Granata e di una nuova specie di Dendroica
del Brasile con l'aggiunta di una nota riguardante la Fauna Toscana.
< *Annali R. Mus. di Fisica e Storia Nat. di Firenze per il* 1865, nuova serie, i, 1866,
pp. 197-209.

Polytmus (Campylopterus) ceciliae, p. 202; *Mellisuga (Panaplites) judith,* p. 203; *M. (Cynanthus) salvadorii,* p. 204; *M. (Eriocnemis) ridolfii,* p. 205; *Dendroica picciolii,* p. 207.

1866. BRYANT, H.   H. Bryant, Vögel von Porto Rico.   < *J. f. O.,* xiv, 1866, pp. 181-191.
From *Proc. Bost. Soc. N. H.,* Jan., 1866, pp. 248-257.

1866. BRYANT, H.   A List of Birds from Porto Rico presented to the Smithsonian
Institution, by Messrs. Robert Swift and George Latimer, with descriptions
of new Species or Varieties.   < *Proc. Bost. Soc. Nat. Hist.,* x, Jan., 1866, pp.
248-257.

41 spp.—*Tyrannus antillarum,* p. 249; *Todus hypochondriacus,* p. 250; *Mimus polyglottus*
var. *portoricensis,* p. 251; *Certhiola flaveola* var. *portoricensis, Vireo latimeri* (descr. nulla);
Spindalis portoricensis, p. 252; *Fringilla zena* var. *portoricensis, Icterus dominicensis* var.
portoricensis, p. 254; *Saurothera vieillotii* var. *rufescens,* p. 256. Cf. *Ibis,* 1867, pp. 129, 130.

1866. GUNDLACH, J.   Briefliches von Cuba.   < *J. f. O.,* xiv, 1866, pp. 352-354.
Desultory remarks on a few species.

1866. GUYON, —.   Des animaux disparus de la Martinique et de la Guadeloupe
depuis notre établissement dans ces iles.   < *Comptes Rendus de l'Acad. Sci.
Paris,* lxiii, 8 Oct. 1866, pp. 589-593.
Not seen: title from *Zool. Rec.*

1866. LAWRENCE, G. N.   Characters of Seven New Species of Birds from Central and
South America, with a Note on Thaumatias chionurus.   < *Ann. Lyc. Nat. Hist.
New York,* viii, 1866, pp. 344-350.

Campylorhynchus brevipennis, p. 344; *Automolus rufescens,* p. 345; *Grallaria gigantea,* p.
345; *Grallaricula costaricensis,* p. 346; *Phæthornis cassinii,* p. 347; *Eupherusa cupreiceps,* p.
348; *Geotrygon veraguensis,* p. 349.

1866. LAWRENCE, G. N.   Descriptions of Six New Species of Birds of the Families
Hirundinidæ, Formicaridæ, Tyrannidæ, and Trochilidæ.   < *Ann. Lyc. Nat.
Hist. New York,* viii, 1866, pp. 400-405.

Hirundo æquitorialis, p. 400 (Ecuador); *Thamnophilus leucopygus,* p. 401 (Panama); *Empidonax pectoralis,* p. 402 (Panama); *Heliodoxa henryi,* p. 402 (Costa Rica); *Thaumatias viridicaudus,* p. 404 (Buenaventura); *Amazilia (Pyrrophæna) graysoni,* p. 404 (Tres Marias Islands).

1866. LÉOTAUD, A.　Oiseaux | de | L'Ile de la Trinidad, | (Antilles), | par A. Léotaud, | Docteur en Médecine de la Faculté de Paris; membre correspondant de la | Société de Médecine de Gand. | — | Ouvrage publié par souscription nationale | — | Port d'Espagne: | Chronicle Publishing Office. | — | 1866.　1 vol. 8vo.　2 p. ll., pp. i–xx, 1 l., 1–560, 1 l., i–viii, i–iv.

A systematic treatise on 294 + 3 species, with synonymy, description, and general remark. Geographical categories are given at pp. ix–xiii.　*Cymindis pucherani*, p. 40; *Dendrocolaptes altirostris*, p. 166; *Empidonax cabanisi*, p. 232; *Tachyphonus albispecularis*, p. 303, spp. nn.

The author appears to have labored under the usual disadvantages of those who work away from centres of learning, and his work has a somewhat amateurish air; but it is most creditable to him, considering what difficulties he had to contend with, and becomes a standard work on the special subject.

"L'ornithologie de la Trinidad frappe tout d'abord par le grand nombre d'espèces, 294 [297] qui la composent; . . .

"Ce qui frappe ensuite dans l'ornithologie de la Trinidad c'est qu'elle relève presqu'entièrement de l'Amérique Méridionale.　En effet en jetant un coup d'œil sur les tableaux qui précèdent, . . . on ne trouve pour total que 95 espèces communes à l'une ou à plusieurs des localités désignées dans ces tableaux.　Il reste donc déjà, par ce seul fait, 199 espèces propres exclusivement à la Trinidad et par conséquent à l'Amérique Méridionale. . . . Il en resterait 274 propres à la Trinidad et à l'Amérique du Sud.

"Un troisième fait non moins intéressant ressort de la limite qu'atteignent, dans les Antilles, les oiseaux migrateurs partis soit du Sud soit du Nord."

Cf. especially *Ibis*, 1867, pp. 104–108, for critique on the work.

1866. LEYBOLD, F.　Beschreibung von vier neuen Vogelarten aus der Argentinischen Provinz Mendoza.　<*J. f. O.*, xiii, 1865, pp. 401–406.　(Pub. 1866.)

Synallaxis crassirostris, p. 401; *Myiarchus fasciatus*, p. 402; *Sporophila rufirostris*, p. 404; *Phrygilus ornatus*, p. 405.　Described by Herr L. Landbeck.　See 1865, LEYBOLD, F.

1866. PHILIPPI, R. A., *and* LANDBECK, L.　Beiträge zur Fauna Chiles.　<*Arch. f. Naturg.*, 1866, (1), pp. 121–132.

Pteroptochos castaneus, p. 121; *Sterna luctuosa*, sp. n., p.126; *Synallaxis masafucræ* (sic—lege *masafueræ*), sp. n., p. 127; *Numenius microrhynchus*, sp. n., p. 129.

This concludes a series of papers by one of, or both, these authors, of same or similar title, in same *Archiv*, 1864, pp. 41–54, 55–64; 1865, pp. 56–106.

1866. SALVIN, O.　A further Contribution to the Ornithology of Guatemala.　<*Ibis*, 2d ser., ii, 1866, pp. 188–206.

81 spp., briefly annotated.　The paper continues under a subheading "Corrections to the former Papers on the Ornithology of Central Guatemala"—which must not be overlooked in using them.　The papers referred to are in *Ibis*, i, 1859; ii, 1860; iii, 1861.　*Chamæospiza torquata* S. & S., *Ibis*, 1860, 274, is *Pyrgisoma leucote*.

1866. SALVIN, O.　Descriptions of Eight New Species of Birds from Veragua.　<*P. Z. S.*, xxxiv, 1866, pp. 67–76, pll. vii, viii.

Catharus griseiceps, p. 68, with synopsis of 10 spp.; *Microcerculus luscinia*, p. 69, with synopsis of 5 spp.; *Euphonia rufivertex*, p. 71, pl. vii; *Buarremon mesoxanthus*, *Philydor fuscipennis*, *Dysithamnus puncticeps*, p. 72; *Formicarius rufipectus*, p. 73, pl. viii, with synopsis of 7 spp.; *Trogon clathratus*, p. 75.

1866. SCLATER, P. L.　On the Birds of the Vicinity of Lima, Peru.　With Notes on their habits; by Prof. W. Nation, of Lima, C. M. Z. S.　[Part I.]　<*P. Z. S.*, xxxiv, 1866, pp. 96–100, pl. xi.

23 spp.—*Geositta crassirostris*, p. 98; *Myiobius nationi*, p. 99, pl. xi, f. 1, spp. nn.　The other figure of the same plate represents *M. pulcher*.—Continued, *P. Z. S.*, 1867, pp. 340–344.

1866. SCLATER, P. L., *and* SALVIN, O.　Catalogue of Birds collected by Mr. E. Bartlett on the River Ucayali, Eastern Peru, with Notes and Descriptions.　<*P. Z. S.*, xxxiv, 1866, pp. 175–201, pl. xviii.

The collection contained about 700 specimens, of 252 spp.—*Leucippus chlorocercus* "Gould", p. 194; *Thaumatias bartletti* Gould, p. 194; *Hypocnemis melanura*, p. 186; *H. hemileuca*, p. 187; *Synallaxis terricolor*, p. 183; *S. vulpecula*, p. 184; *Metopothrix* (g. n.) *aurantiacus*, p. 190, pl. xviii; *Serpophaga hypoleuca*, p. 188; *Spermophila ocellata*, p. 181; *Muscisaxicola fluviatilis*, p. 187; *Furnarius torridus*, p. 183, spp. nn.

1866. SCLATER, P. L., *and* SALVIN, O.　On some Additions to the Catalogue of Birds collected by Mr. E. Bartlett on the River Ucayali.　<*P. Z. S.*, xxxiv, 1866, pp. 566, 567.

20 species in addition to those of the former list are noticed; none new.

1866-69. Sclater, P. L., and Salvin, O. Exotic Ornithology, | containing | Figures and Descriptions of New or Rare Species | of | American Birds, | by | Philip Lutley Sclater, M. A., Ph. D., F. R. S., | Secretary to the Zoological Society of London, | late Fellow of Corpus Christi College, Oxford; | and | Osbert Salvin, M. A., F. L. S., F. Z. S. | — | London : | Bernard Quaritch, 15 Piccadilly. | [1866 to] 1869. 1 vol. Folio. pp. i–vi, 1–204, pll. i–c. (Published in 13 parts.)

Exact dates of publication are :—Part I, pll. i–viii, Oct. 1, 1866. II, pll. ix–xvi, Feb. 1, 1867. III, pll. xvii–xxiv, May 1, 1867. IV, pll. xxv–xxxii, Aug. 1, 1867. V, pll. xxxiii–xl, Jan. 1, 1868. VI, pll. xli–xlviii, Apr. 1, 1868. VII, pll. xlix–lvi, July 1, 1868. VIII, pll. lvii–lxiv, Aug. 1, 1868. IX, pll. lxv–lxxii, Dec. 1, 1868. X, pll. lxxiii–lxxx, Jan. 1, 1869. XI, pll. lxxxi–lxxxviii, June 1, 1869. XII, pll. lxxxix–xcvi, Aug. 1, 1869. XIII, pll. xcvii–c, Nov. 1, 1869. The last part contains permanent title, preface, contents, and errata (pp. i–vi), and index (pp. 201–204). The temporary cover-title is a little different from the permanent one.

Cf. *Ibis*, 1867, pp. 123, 372; 1868, pp. 335–337; 1869, pp. 109, 110; 1870, 262–264; *Zool. Rec.*, iii, p. 48; iv, p. 51; v, p. 38; vi, p. 60.

The plates are all by Mr. Smit; they are very beautiful. The whole number of species figured is 104, referred to 51 genera. In most cases, a systematic list of the other American species of the same genus is appended to the final illustration of each, thereby enlarging the scope and greatly increasing the value of the work. Each of the species is systematically treated with synonymy, diagnosis, and critical and biographical matter. The authors are the highest authorities in neotropical ornithology, and this work is a monument of erudition, industry, and artistic excellence.

Pl. 1, *Lipaugus unirufus.* Pl. 2, *L. subalaris.* Pl. 3, *L. rufescens.* Pl. 4, *Furnarius torridus.* Pl. 5. *Xipholena atropurpurea.* Pl. 6, *Ptilogonys caudatus.* Pl. 7, *Vireolanius melitophrys.* Pl. 8, *V. pulchellus.*—Pl. 9, *Phlogopsis macleannani.* Pl. 10, *Cinclocerthia ruficauda.* Pl. 11, *C. macrorhyncha.* Pl. 12, *C. gutturalis.* Pl. 13, *Accipiter ventralis.* Pl. 14, *A. chionogaster.* Pl. 15, *Rupicola sanguinolenta.* Pl. 16 *Porzana rubra.*—Pl. 17, *Accipiter erythrocnemis.* Pl. 18, *A. castanilius.* Pl. 19, *Cichlopsis leucogonys.* Pl. 20, *Nyctibius bracteatus.* Pl. 21, *Cyphorinus lawrencii.* Pl. 22. *C. phæocephalus.* Pl. 23, f. 1, *Thryothorus solstitialis;* f. 2, *T. brunneicollis.* Pl. 24, *Icterus pustulatus.*—Pl. 25, *Myiadestes obscurus.* Pl. 26, *M. unicolor.* Pl. 27, *M. ralloides.* Pl. 28, *M. elizabethæ.* Pl. 29, *Hylactes castaneus.* Pl. 30, *Oedicnemus superciliaris.* Pl. 31, *Lanio aurantius.* Pl. 32, *L. leucothorax.* Pl. 33, *Tachyphonus phoeniceus.* Pl. 34, *T. delattrii.* Pl. 35, *Xiphocolaptes emigrans.* Pl. 36, *X. major.* Pl. 37, *Accipiter chilensis.*—Pl. 38, *Leucopternis superciliaris.* Pl. 39, *Geotrygon "chiriquensis"* (= *albifacies,* see *Exot. Ornith.,* viii, 1868, p. 123). Pl. 40, *G. bourcieri.*—Pl. 41, f. 1, *Chlorophonia frontalis;* f. 2, *C. longipennis.* Pl. 42, *C. occipitalis.* Pl. 43, *Melanotis hypoleucus.* Pl. 44, *Tinamus robustus.* Pl. 45, *Crypturus sallcei* (lege *sallæi*). Pl. 46, *C. boucardi.* Pl. 47, *C. meserythrus.* Pl. 48, *Tigrisoma cabanisi.*—Pl. 49, *Leucopternis palliata.* Pl. 50, *Scops flammeola.* Pl. 51, *S. barbarus.* Pl. 52, *Chætura semicollaris.* Pl. 53, *Porzana hauxwelli.* pl 54, *P. melanophæa.* Pl. 55, *P. albigularis.* Pl. 56, *P. leucopyrrha.*—Pl. 57, *Fulica ardesiaca.* Pl. 58, *F. armillata.* Pl. 59, *F. leucopyga.* Pl. 60, *F. leucoptera.* Pl. 61, *Leucopternis semiplumbea.* Pl. 62, *Geotrygon chiriquensis* (verus; vide suprà). Pl. 63, *Cardinalis phoeniceus.* Pl. 64, f. 1, *Pyrgisoma rubricatum;* f. 2, *P. leucote.*—Pl. 65, f. 1, *P. cabanisi;* f. 2, *P. kieneri.* Pl. 66, *Oxyrhamphus frater.* Pl. 67, *Thyrorhina schomburgki.* Pl. 68, *Chlorophonia calophrys.* Pl. 69, *Accipiter bicolor.* Pl. 70, *Turdus gigas.* Pl. 71, *T. albicollis.* Pl. 72, *T. leucomelas.*—Pl. 73, *T. crotopezus.* Pl. 74, *T. albiventris.* Pl. 75, *T. phæopygus.* Pl. 76, *T. gymnophthalmus.* Pl. 77, *Bucco striolatus.* Pl. 78, *Porzana castaneiceps.* Pl. 79, *Attagis chimborazensis.* Pl. 80, *Formicivora strigilata.*—Pl. 81. *Conurus hoffmanni.* Pl. 82, *Rallus antarcticus.* Pl. 83, *R. semiplumbeus.* Pl. 84, *Pitylus humeralis.* Pl. 85, *Accipiter guttatus.* Pl. 86, *Ampelion arcuatus.* Pl. 87, *Asturina nattereri.* Pl. 88, *A. ruficauda.*—Pl. 89, *A. pucherani.* Pl. 90, *A. plagiata.* Pl. 91, *Botaurus pennatus.* Pl. 92, *Tigrisoma fasciatum.* Pl. 93, *Thripadectes flammulatus.* Pl. 94, *Icterus abeillii.* Pl. 95, *Centropelma micropterum.* Pl. 96, *Centrites oreas.*—Pl. 97, *Gallinago imperialis.* Pl. 98, *G. nobilis.* Pl. 99, *Querquedula puna.* Pl. 100, *Merganetta turneri.*

1867. Bryant, H. A List of the Birds of St. Domingo, with Descriptions of some New Species or Varieties. < *Proc. Boston Soc. Nat. Hist. for* Dec. 5, 1866, xi, pub. 1867, pp. 89–98.

79 spp., in part annotated. *Tyrannula stolida* var. *dominicensis,* p. 90 ; *T. carribœa* var. *hispaniolensis. Mimus polyglottus* var. *dominicus, Chrysomitris dominicensis,* p. 93, fig. p. 94, spp. nn. *Kalochelidon,* p. 95, gen. n. Cf. *Ibis,* 1868, p. 229.

1867. Lawrence, G. N. Descriptions of New Species of American Birds. < *Ann. Lyc. Nat. Hist. New York,* viii, 1867, pp. 466–482.

Euphonia purpurea, p. 466; *Buarremon flavovirens,* p. 467; *Pytilus* (*Caryothraustes*) *humeralis,* p. 467; *Philydor virgatus,* p. 468; *Thamnophilus tenuifasciatus,* p. 468; *Thamnophilus nigres-*

1867. LAWRENCE, G. N.—Continued.

cens, p. 469; *Myiodynastes superciliaris,* p. 470; *Aglœactis olivaceocauda,* p. 470; *Heliomaster spectabilis,* p. 472; *Passerculus guttatus,* p. 473; *Zonotrichia melanotis,* p. 473; *Coturniculus mexicanus,* p. 474; *Hadrostomus albiventris,* p. 475; *Ortyx graysoni,* p. 476; *Saltator plumbiceps* Bd. MS., p. 477; *Pheucticus tibialis* Bd. MS., p. 478; *Spermophila atriceps* Bd. MS., p. 479; *Pyrgisoma xantusii* Bd. MS., p. 480; *Dendrornis mentalis* Bd. MS., p. 481. Cf. *Ibis,* 1868, pp. 114, 115.

1867. LAWRENCE, G. N. Notes on certain Birds from New Grenada, with descriptions of New Species. < *Proc. Acad. Nat. Sci. Phila.,* xix, 1867, pp. 94, 95.

Tachyphonus propinquus, Phœnicothraupis vinacea, Leptoptila cassini, p. 94, spp. nn. Cf. *Ibis,* 1868, p. 230.

1867. LAWRENCE, G. N. Descriptions of Five New Species of Central American Birds. < *Proc. Acad. Nat. Sci. Phila.,* xix, 1867, pp. 232-234.

Glaucis œneus, Eupherusa nigriventris, p. 232; *Thaumatias luciœ, Dromococcyx rufigularis,* p. 233; *Aramides albiventris,* p. 234. Cf. *Ibis,* 1868, pp. 114 and 485.

1867. PHILIPPI, R. A. Comentario crítico sobre los animales descritos por Molina. < *Anales Univ. Chile,* xxix, Oct.. 1867, pp. 775-802.

"Vienen ahora las 'aves'", pp. 788-795, Nos. 104-170.

1867. SALVIN, O. On some Collections of Birds from Veragua. < *P. Z. S.,* xxxv, 1867, pp. 129-161, pl. (Aves) xiv.

220 spp., less 4. Avifaunal characters of the region. Pl. xiv, *Buarremon crassirostris.—Chamœpetes unicolor,* p. 159; *Odontophorus leucolœmus,* p. 161, spp. nn.

1867. SCLATER, P. L. Remarks on Dr. Léotaud's 'Birds of Trinidad.' < *Ibis,* 2d ser., iii, 1867, pp. 104-108.

Criticism of the work as a whole, and of names of various species in particular.

1867. SCLATER, P. L. [Extracts from letters received from Mr. E. Bartlett, relating to Peruvian Birds.] < *P. Z. S.,* xxxv, 1867, p. 2.

1867. SCLATER, P. L. Notes on the Birds of Chili. < *P. Z. S.,* xxxv, 1867, pp. 319-340.

Abstract of bibliography. Running commentary on the birds, under heads of the several families; nominal list of 209 species. The article is the most complete summary of the subject extant. It has special reference to the species described by Philippi and Landbeck. Cf. *Naumannia,* 1853, pp. 207-222; *Zool. Rec.,* ii, pp. 80, 81, and iii, p. 64.

1867. SCLATER, P. L. On the Birds of the Vicinity of Lima, Peru. With Notes on their Habits; by Prof. Nation, of Lima.—(Part II.) < *P. Z. S.,* xxxv, 1867, pp. 340-344, pll. xx, xxi.

Continued from *P. Z. S.,* 1866, p. 100.—12 spp.—*Poospiza bonapartii,* p. 341, pl. xx; *Porzana erythrops,* p. 343, pl. xxi, spp. nn.—Continued, *P. Z. S.,* 1869, pp. 146-148.

1867. SCLATER, P. L., *and* SALVIN, O. List of Birds collected on the Blewfields River, Mosquito Coast, by Mr. Henry Wickham. < *P. Z. S.,* xxxv, 1867, pp. 278-280.

39 spp.; none new.

1867. SCLATER, P. L., *and* SALVIN, O. List of Birds collected by Mr. Wallace on the Lower Amazons and Rio Negro. < *P. Z. S.,* xxxv, 1867, pp. 566-596, pll. xxix, xxx.

282 spp., annotated; with several synopses of different groups, and summary comparisons of local faunas. *Hylophilus rubrifrons,* p. 569, pl. xxx, f. 1; *H. semicinereus,* p. 570, pl. xxx, f. 2; *Heteropelma wallacii,* p. 579. Pl. xxix is *Turdus phaeopygus.*

1867. SCLATER, P. L., *and* SALVIN, O. Catalogue of Birds collected by Mr. E. Bartlett on the River Huallaga, Eastern Peru, with Notes and Descriptions of New Species. < *P. Z. S.,* xxxv, 1867, pp. 748-759, pl. xxxiv.

Tabular list of 205 spp., followed by critical commentary on many of them. *Dendrocolaptes radiolatus* Scl. MS., p. 755; *Thamnophilus murinus* Natt. MS., *Myrmotherula cinereiventris* Scl. MS., p. 756; *Chœtura brachycerca* (pl. xxxiv), *Celeus citreopygius* Bp. MS., p. 758, spp. nn.

1867. SCLATER, P. L., *and* SALVIN, O. List of Birds collected at Pebas, Upper Amazon, by Mr. John Hauxwell, with Notes and Descriptions of New Species. < *P. Z. S.,* xxxv, 1867, pp. 977-981, pl. xlv.

135 spp. *Oryzoborus melas,* p. 979; *Percnostola fortis,* p. 980, pl. xlv, and fig. xylog.; *Tyranniscus gracilipes, Porzana fasciata,* p. 981, spp. nn.

1867. SCLATER, P. L., *and* SALVIN, O.   On Peruvian Birds collected by Mr. H. Whitely.—Part I. $< P. Z. S.$, xxxv, 1867, pp. 982–991, pl. xlvi.

58 spp., annotated—Continued, *P. Z. S.*, 1868, pp. 173–178.

1867–69. EULER, C.   Beiträge zur Naturgeschichte der Vögel Brasiliens. $< J. f. O.$,
xv, 1867, pp. 177–198, 217–233, 399–420 ; xvi, 1868, pp. 182–194; xvii, 1869, pp.
241–255.

Cf. *Zool. Rec.*, 1867, p. 68; 1868, p. 55; 1869, p. 49.

1868. ANON.   A strange [apparently fabulous] Bird. $< Zoologist$, 2d ser., iii, 1868,
p. 1295.

From a Copiapo (Chili) paper.

1868. BELL, A. S.   [Allusions to some of the] Wild-fowl of Jamaica. $< Zoologist$, 2d
ser., iii, 1868, p. 1483.

1868. BURMEISTER, H.   Contributions to the Ornithology of the Argentine Republic
and Adjacent Lands.   Part I. $< P. Z. S.$, xxxvi, 1868, pp. 633–636.

Since the publication of the author's "Systematisches Verzeichniss der in den La Plata-
Staaten beobachteten Vögelarten" (*Journ. für Orn.*, 1860, pp. 241–268), and his "Reise durch
die La-Plata-Staaten" (1861), he lived five years in Buenos Ayres, and, in studying the ornithology of the district, observed some new species, three of which (*Cymindis boliviensis*, p.
633; *Pachyrhamphus albinucha*, p. 635; *Synallaxis sulphurifera*, p. 636) are now described, and
notes on 11 others are given.—Title and part of the comment from *Zool. Rec.*

1868. COPE, E. D.   The Birds of Palestine and Panama compared. $< American Nat-
uralist$, ii, No. 7, Sept., 1868, pp. 351–359.

Founded on the researches of Messrs. Tristram, Sclater, and Salvin.

1868. CUNNINGHAM, R. O.   [Letters on South American Ornithology.] $< Ibis$, 2d ser.,
iv, 1868, pp. 122–129, 486–495.

His first letter gives a general account of the birds met with on his voyage to Patagonia.
His second letter describes briefly the localities visited, mentioning their chief ornithological features.   (Another letter follows, *Ibis*, 1869, pp. 232–234.)

1868. GIEBEL, C.   Einige neue und wenig bekannte argentinische Vögel. $< Zeitschr.
für die gesammten Naturwissenschaften$, 1868, pp. 11–17.

Notes on 4 species, 2 of which, *Furnarius tricolor* "Burm.", p. 11, and *Campylorhynchus
pallidus* "Burm.", p. 13, appear to be described as new.—Not seen.

1868. PHILIPPI, R. A.   Catálogo de las aves chilenas existentes en el Museo Nacional
de Santiago, formado por su director don Rodulfo Armando Philippi.
$< Anal. Univ. Chile$, tomo xxxi, nº 2º, Agosto de 1868, pp. 241–335.

Prólogo, p. 241. Catálogo, pp. 242–292, el órden i la nomenclatura adoptada en la obra de Gay;
229 especies; las especies descritas como chilenas que faltan en el Museo con la seña † (89).—
Aves chilenas descritas en la obra de Gay que faltan en el Museo ó que deben borrarse, pp.
292–294, 86 esp.—Aves chilenas no descritas en la obra de Gay, pero existentes en el Museo,
pp. 295–298, 55 esp.—El cuadro siguientes, pp. 298–319, indica cuales de las aves chilenas se
hallan aun en los paises limítrofos i otros paises, i cuales son peculiares a la República Chi-
lena.—Apendices: I, pp. 319, 320, Lista de algunos pájaros peruanos en el Museo. II, p. 320,
Pájaros nuevos mendocinos descritos por Landbeck. III, pp. 320–335, Observaciones críticas
sobre algunas especies chilenas mencionas por diversos autores: 1. Hartl., *Naum.*, p. 220 i
siguientes; 2. Beit. zur Zool. gesammelt auf einer Reise um die Welt von Dr. F. I. F. Meyen,
vierte Abth.; 3. Burmeister, Reise durch die La Plata-Staaten; 4. Bibra, Viaje; 5. T. R. Peale,
U. S. Exploring Expedition; 6. Tschudi, Beit. zur geogr. Verbreit. der Meeresvögel u. s. w.;
7. Hombron i Jacquinot; 8. Cassin, U. S. Naval Astron. Exped.; 9. Sclater, Notes on the
Birds of Chile, *P. Z. S.*, March 25, 1867, p. 319 i sig.

"Quedarian, pues, solo 193, nuestro catálogo de las especies chilenas existentes en el Museo abraza 229 especies ó si se quiere eliminar . . . siempre 224, i faltan al Museo una docena
de aves de alta mar, que conocemos ser chilenas, de modo que el número de las aves chilenas
se elevaria a unas 236 o 240."

1868. PHILIPPI, R. A.   [Letter relating to certain Birds of Chili.] $< P. Z. S.$, xxxvi,
1868, pp. 531, 532.

Contains a few corrections of previous paper (*P. Z. S.*, 1867, pp. 319, 320, notes), the principal one referring to two species of *Anatidæ*.

1868. SALVADORI, T. Intorno ad alcuni Uccelli di Costa Rica. < *Atti della R. Accad. delle Sci. di Torino*, iv, Dec., 1868, pp. 170–185, pl.

23 spp.; none new. *Urospatha*, g. n., p. 179. The plate represents *Pheucticus tibialis*. Cf. *Zool. Rec.*, iv, p. 107; *Ibis*, 1869, pp. 222, 223.

1868. SCLATER, P. L. [Report on Lecompte's Expedition to the Falkland Islands.] < *P. Z. S.*, 1868, p. 526.

1868. SCLATER, P. L., *and* SALVIN, O. List of Birds collected in the Straits of Magellan by Dr. Cunningham, with remarks on the Patagonian Avifauna. < *Ibis*, 2d ser., iv, 1868, pp. 183–189.

Briefly bibliographical. List of Patagonian *Passeres* (30 spp.); 61 specimens, referable to 44 spp.—Continued, *Ibis*, 1869, pp. 283–286.

1868. SCLATER, P. L., *and* SALVIN, O. Descriptions of New Species of Birds of the Families Dendrocolaptidæ, Strigidæ, and Columbidæ. < *P. Z. S.*, xxxvi, 1868, pp. 53–60, pl. v, woodc.

Dendrocincla ruficeps, p. 54; *Dendrocolaptes puncticollis*, p. 54, pl. v, woodc.; synopses of these genera; *Syrnium fulvescens*, p. 58; *Scops barbarus*, p. 56, woodc.; synopsis of 7 spp. of *Scops*; *Leptoptila plumbeiceps*, *L. cerviniventris*, p. 59, with synopsis of 8 spp. of the genus.

1868. SCLATER, P. L., *and* SALVIN, O. List of Birds collected at Conchitas, Argentine Republic, by Mr. William H. Hudson. < *P. Z. S.*, xxxvi, 1868, pp. 137–146.

96 spp. briefly annotated; 14 additional to those of Burmeister's 'Reise', q. v., 1856.

1868. SCLATER, P. L., *and* SALVIN, O. On Venezuelan Birds collected by Mr. A. Goering.—Part I. < *P. Z. S.*, xxxvi, 1868, pp. 165–172, pl. xiii, woodc.

126 spp., in tabular form showing geographical distribution, and critical commentary on some of them. *Basileuterus griseiceps*, p. 170, *Euscarthmus impiger*, p. 171, woodc. pl. xiii, f. 1; *Sublegatus* (g. n.) *glaber*, p. 171, pl. xiii, f. 2, woodc., p. 172, spp. nn.

1868. SCLATER, P. L., *and* SALVIN, O. On Peruvian Birds collected by Mr. H. Whitely. Part II. < *P. Z. S.*, xxxvi, 1868, pp. 173–178, woodcc.

Continued from *P. Z. S.*, 1867, pp. 982–991.—A list of a collection made in the Tambo Valley, including 28 spp., none of which are new; but valuable critical notes are appended, and woodcuts of the heads of 2 spp., belonging to *Tanagridæ* (?) and *Rallidæ* (*Fulica chilensis*), are introduced.—Continued, *P. Z. S.*, 1868, pp. 568–570.

1868. SCLATER, P. L., *and* SALVIN, O. Descriptions of New or Little-known American Birds of the Families Fringillidæ, Oxyrhamphidæ, Bucconidæ, and Strigidæ. < *P. Z. S.*, xxxvi, 1868, pp. 322–329, pl. xxix.

Peucæa notosticta, sp. n., p. 322, with list of 5 spp. *Zonotrichia quinquestriata*, p. 323, sp. n. List of 5 spp. of *Pyrgisoma*. *Oxyrhamphus frater*, p. 326, sp. n. *Monasa grandior*, p. 327, sp. n. *Gymnoglaux lawrencii*, p. 328, pl. xxix, with synonymy of 2 spp. of this genus.

1868. SCLATER, P. L., *and* SALVIN, O. Descriptions of Four New Species of Birds from Veragua. < *P. Z. S.*, xxxvi, 1868, pp. 388–390.

Pyranga testacea, p. 388; *Chlorospingus hypophæus*, *Leptotriccus superciliaris*, *Eupherusa egregia*, p. 389.

1868. SCLATER, P. L., *and* SALVIN, O. On Peruvian Birds collected by Mr. H. Whitely. Part III. < *P. Z. S.*, xxxvi, 1868, pp. 568–570.

Continued from *P. Z. S.*, 1868, pp. 173–178.—A list of a small collection of 11 spp. made near Arequipa; with a nominal list of 83 spp. procured by Mr. Whitely in Western Peru.—Continued, *P. Z. S.*, 1869, pp. 151–159.

1868. SCLATER, P. L., *and* SALVIN, O. On Venezuelan Birds collected by Mr. A. Goering.—Part II. < *P. Z. S.*, xxxvi, 1868, pp. 626–632.

Nominal list of 99 spp., with commentary on 13 of them. *Myiarchus erythrocercus*, p. 631; *Heteropelma stenorhynchum*, p. 632, spp. nn.

1868–69. LAWRENCE, G. N. A Catalogue of the Birds found in Costa Rica. < *Ann. Lyc. Nat. Hist. New York*, ix, 1868, pp. 86–149 (pp. 86–141, Apr., 1868; pp. 141 bis–149, Feb., 1869).

Based upon the collections received by the Smithsonian Institution, supplemented by information received from other sources, and includes notices of 474 spp. of land-birds, of which 12 (belonging to *Trogonidæ*, *Formicariidæ*, *Dendrocolaptidæ*, *Tyrannidæ*, *Mniotiltidæ*, *Tanagridæ*, *Columbidæ*, and *Tinamidæ*) are described as new, while a thirteenth (*Trochilidæ*) may be so. In the introductory remarks, the author gives a summary of previous writings

1868–69. LAWRENCE, G. N.—Continued.

on Costa Rican ornithology, and three lists, the first two of species noted from Chiriqui and Veragua, respectively, which may be found in Costa Rica, and the third of northern species obtained in Panama, but not yet observed in the country of which the paper treats. The remainder of the paper is devoted to the catalogue, which, in the great majority of cases, gives only the name of the species and of the locality where it has been obtained. (Cf. *Ibis*, 1869, pp. 110, 222, and especially O. Salvin, *Ibis*, 1869, pp. 310–319, for extended and elaborate criticism.)—(Above paragraph mostly from *Zool. Rec.*, 1868, p. 55.)

Basileuterus melanotis, p. 95; Phœnicothraupis carmioli, p. 100; Synallaxis rufigenis, p. 105; Myrmotherula modesta, p. 108; Mionectes olivaceus, p. 111; Rhynchocyclus grissimentalis, p. 112; Trogon bairdii, p. 119; Chloroenas subvinacea, p. 135; Geotrygon costaricensis, C. cœruleiceps, p. 136; Leptoptila riottei, p. 137; Tinamus frantzii, p. 140; Pogonotriccus? zeledoni, p. 144, spp. nn. 511 spp. Much critical commentary.

1868–70. PELZELN, A. v. Zur | Ornithologie | Brasiliens. | Resultate von Johann Natterers Reisen | in den Jahren 1817 bis 1835. | Dargestellt | von | August von Pelzeln, | Custos am k. k. zoologischen Cabinete in Wien, Mitglied der kais. Leopold. | Carol. Academie der Naturforscher, Ehrenmitglied der British Ornithologist's | Union u. s. w. | — | Wien. | Druck und Verlag von A. Pichler's Witwe & Sohn. | 1871 [*i. e.* 1868–1870]. 1 vol. 8vo. 4 p. ll., pp. i–lx, 1–462, 9 ll. (Zusätze und Index), 2 maps.

Published in 4 parts, at different dates, as follows: I. Abth., 1868, map, 3 p. ll., pp. i–lx, 1–68. II. Abth., 1869, pp. 69–188. III. Abth., 1870, pp. 189–390. IV. Abth., "1871" [*i. e.* 1870], pp. 391–462, 9 ll., general title-page, map.—The date of the concluding part is ostensibly in question; for the date on the cover-title of the part itself is 1871, but the back of the general title-page of the work gives it as 1870, and a note on the cover-title of Part III announces: ,, Die vierte (Schluss-) Abtheilung erscheint Anfangs des Jahres 1870.'' The actual date is 1870.

Inhalt:—ABTH. I, 1868. Vorwort, 2 p. ll. Itinerarium von Natterer's Reisen in Brasilien, von 1817 bis 1835, pp. i–xx. Tabellarische Uebersicht der von Natterer in Brasilien gesammelten Arten nach ihrer Verbreitung in den wichtigsten Faunaengebieten, pp. xxi–lix (1238 spp.). *Accipitres* und *Passeres Fissirostres* et *Tenuirostres*, pp. 1–49 (78 + 99 + 177 = 354 spp.), Beschreibung neuer oder wenig gekannter Arten, pp. 49–68. *Stenopsis candicans* N., p. 49 ; *S. langsdorffi* P., p. 52 ; *S. platura* N., p. 53 (Diagnosen dieser drei Arten finden sich in den *P. Z. S.*, 1866, pp. 588, 589) ; *Antrostomus cortapau* N., p. 53 ; *Chaetura sclateri* P., p. 56 ; *Thalurania iolaemus* N., p. 57 ; *Cephalolepis beskii* P., p. 58 ; *Sittasomus stictolaemus* P., p. 59 ; *Dendrocincla longicauda* N., *D. minor* P., p. 60 ; *Dendrocolaptes pallascens* P., p. 61 ; *D. concolor* P., p. 62 ; *Picolaptes fuscicapillus* P., *Dendrornis elegans* P., p. 63 ; *Dendroplex similis* N., p. 64 ; *Cyphorinus (Microcerculus) cinctus* N., p. 65 ; *Thryothorus minor* P., p. 66 ; *Odontorhynchus* (Pelz., g. n.) *cinereus* N., p. 67.—ABTH. II, 1869. *Passeres Dentirostres*, pp. 69–136 (371 spp.). Beschreibung neuer oder wenig gekannter Arten, pp. 136–188. *Hylophilus hypoxanthus* P., p. 136 ; *Basileuterus leucophrys* N., *Cyclorhis wiedii* P., p. 137 ; *Thamnophilus unduliger* N., p. 139 ; *T. borbae* N., p. 140 ; *T. tschudii* P., *T. moestus* P., p. 141 ; *T. cinereoniger* P., p. 143 ; *T. sticturus* P., p. 144 ; *T. cinereiceps* P., *T. cinereinucha* P., p. 145 ; *T. stictocephalus* P., *T. punctuliger* P., p. 146 ; *T. polionotus* P., *T. saturninus* P., p. 147 ; *T. incertus* P., *Dysithamnus* P., p. 149 ; *Herpsilochmus atricapillus* N., *H. longirostris* N., p. 150 ; *H. dorsimaculatus* N., p. 151 ; *Myrmotherula assimilis* N., p. 152 ; *M. luctuosa* (Temm. msc.), *M. longipennis* P., p. 153 ; *Formicivora melanogaster* N., p. 154 ; *F. leucophthalma* P., *F. ruficauda* N., p. 155 ; *F. bicolor* N., p. 156 ; *Terenura melanoleuca* N., *Rhamphocaenus collaris* N., p. 157 ; *Cercomacra approximans* P., *C. ruficauda* P., p. 158 ; *Percnostola minor* P., p. 159 ; *P. leucostigma* (Natt. et Lafres. msc.), p. 160 ; *Sclerurus rufigularis* N., *Heterocnemis albiventris* P., p. 161 ; *Myrmecisa* [sic] *squamosa* N., p. 162 ; *Hypocnemis flavescens* (N.) Scl., p. 163 ; *H. maculicauda* P., p. 164 ; *H. margaritifera* P., p. 165 ; *Pithys cristata* N., p. 166 ; *P. griseiventris* P., *Phlogopsis erythroptera* (Gould), p. 167 ; *Grallaria imperator* N., *Attila validus* P., p. 169 ; *A. rufigularis* P., p. 170 ; *A. phoenicurus* N., p. 171 ; *Todirostrum guttatum* P., p. 172 ; *Euscarthmus zosterops* P., *E. latirostris* P., *E. senex* P., p. 173 ; *E. inornatus* P., *Hapalocercus rufomarginatus* P., p. 174 ; *Phyllomyias subviridis* N., p. 175 ; *P. lividus* (Temm. msc.), *Elainea spectabilis* P., p. 176 ; *E. cristata* P., *E. albivertex* P., p. 177 ; *E. parvirostis* [sic—lege *-rostris*] P., p. 178 ; *E. elegans* P., *E. ruficeps* P., p. 179 ; *E. littoralis* N., *E. cinerea* P., p. 180 ; *Rhynchocyclus assimilis* P., *Pitangus parvus* P., *Empidochanes poecilocercus* P., p. 181 ; *Myiarchus cantans* P., *M. tricolor* N., p. 182 ; *M. gracilirostris* P., *Tityra (Erator) leucura* N., p. 183 ; *Lipaugus virussù* N., p. 184 ; *Heteropelma rufum* N., *H. chrysocephalum* P., p. 185 ; *Heterocercus flavivertex* P., *Pipra opalizans* P., p. 186 ; *P. virescens* P., p. 187.—ABTH. III, 1870. *Passeres Conirostres, Scansores, Columbae, Gallinae, Struthiones, Grallae, Anseres*, pp. 189–326. Beschreibung neuer oder wenig gekannter Arten, pp. 326–344. *Leistes erythrothorax* N., p. 326 ; *Euphona ochrascens* P., *Tachyphonus nattereri* P., p. 328 ; *Oryzoborus? fringilloides* P.,

1868–70. PELZELN, A. V.—Continued.

p. 329; *Spermophila superciliaris* N., p. 330; *S. caboclinho* N., *S. melanops* N., p. 331; *S. mela-nogaster* N., *Haplospiza ? crassirostris* N., p. 332; *Sycalis citrina* N., p. 333; *Picumnus auri-frons* N., *P. borbae* P., p. 334; *P. leucogaster* N., *P. fuscus* N., p. 335; *Peristera cyanopis* N., p. 336; *Leptoptila reichenbachii* P., *Penelope ochrogaster* N., p. 337; *P. boliviana* "Reich.", p. 339; *P. pileata* "Licht.", p. 340; *P. nigricapilla* "Gray", p. 341; *Crax pinima* N., p. 341; *C. mikani* P., p. 343. Betrachtungen über die ornithologische Fauna Brasiliens, pp. 344–390.— ABTH. IV, 1870. Fundorte der Vögel Brasiliens nach den hauptsächlichen Quellen, pp. 391–462; Summa der in Brasilien beobachteten Arten, 1680.—Zusätze.—Index.

The work also includes a disquisition on the faunal divisions of Brazil as determined from its *Ornis*. Four subregions are laid down, and mapped, with tabular exhibits of their characteristic species. These are termed the Columbian, Amazonian, South Brazilian, and Chileno-Patagonian. The summary list of 1,680 Brazilian species is compiled from various sources, as Maximilian, Spix, Burmeister, and Wallace.

Cf. *Zeitschr. f. d. ges. Naturw.*, 1867, p. 537; *Ibis*, 1868, pp. 226, 227; 1869, pp. 113–117; 1870, pp. 272–274; *Zool. Gart.*, 1868, p. 40; *Zool. Rec.*, v, pp. 55, 56; vi, p. 51.

"John Natterer has been called a model traveller, and the most energetic and successful ornithological collector that ever lived. He explored Brazil from 1817 to 1835, securing 12,293 bird-skins, beautifully prepared and fully labelled, representing about 1,200 spp., besides registering various additional items of information. He died in his prime, on his return to Europe, leaving his collection, almost untouched, in the Imperial Cabinet of Zoology at Vienna. For nearly thirty years little was done to render his labors available in the cause of science, though instances of 'Natt. MSS.' were of not infrequent occurrence in different quarters. Upon the accession of Pelzeln to the charge of the collection, he began to work upon the material, and publish the results, with selections from Natterer's MSS. His numerous papers, which were received with favor, may be considered preliminary to the present work, which undertakes a complete exposition of Natterer's labors and results."

1869. BISHOP, N. H. The Pampas and Andes. | — | A | Thousand Miles' Walk | across | South America. | By | Nathaniel H. Bishop. | — | With an Introduction | by | Edward A. Samuels, Esq., | author of "Ornithology and Oölogy of New England," | etc., etc. | — | Boston : | Lee & Shepard. | 1869. 1 vol. 8vo. 1 p. l., pp. 310.

Slightly ornithological *passim.*

1869. CUNNINGHAM, R. O. [Letter on Birds seen in the Straits of Magellan.] < *Ibis*, 2d ser., v, 1869, pp. 232–234.

Two earlier letters appeared in *Ibis*, 1868, pp. 122–129, 486–495.

1869. FRANTZIUS, A. V. Ueber die geographische Verbreitung der Vögel Costaricas und deren Lebensweise. < *J. f. O.*, xvii, 1869, pp. 195–204, 289–318, 361–379.

The natural and proper complement of Cabanis's technical articles upon the same avifauna in *J. f. O.*, 1861–69, *q. v.* 518 spp. known to him as Costa Rican, with occasional notes on them. The paper has special reference to Lawrence's *Catalogue*, 1868–69, *q. v.* Cf. Salvin, *Ibis*, 1870, pp. 107–116.

1869. GOERING, A. Excursion a algunas cuevas hasta ahora no esploradas (al sureste de Caripe). < *Vargasia*, No. 5, 1869, pp. 124–128.

Contains an account of *Steatornis caripensis*. (Cf. *Ibis*, 1870, p. 522.)

1869. HABEL, *Dr.* —. [Exhibition of some Birds from the Galapagos Islands.] < *P. Z. S.*, xxxvii, 1869, p. 433.

The collection contained about 70 spp., some supposed to be new, but no particulars are given. Cf. *Comptes Rendus*, lxix, pp. 273–277; *P. Z. S.*, May, 1870, pp. 322–327.

1869. LAWRENCE, G. N. List of a Collection of Birds from Northern Yucatan. < *Ann. Lyc. Nat. Hist. New York*, ix, 1869, pp. 198–210.

103 spp.—*Contopus schottii*, p. 202; *Zenaidura yucatanensis*, p. 207, spp. nn. Cf. *Ibis*, 1870, p. 280; *Zool. Rec.*, 1869, p. 50.

1869. LAWRENCE, G. N. Catalogue of Birds from Puna Island, Gulf of Guayaquil, in the Museum of the Smithsonian Institution, collected by J. F. Reeve, Esq. < *Ann. Lyc. Nat. Hist. New York*, ix, 1869, pp. 234–238.

Turdus reevei, p. 234; *Thryothorus superciliaris*, p. 235; *Empidonax griseipectus*, p. 236; *Contopus punensis*, p. 237, spp. nn.—21 spp. Cf. *Ibis*, 1870, p. 281.

1869. LAWRENCE, G. N.   Characters of some New South American Birds, with Notes on other rare or little known species.   < *Ann. Lyc. Nat. Hist. New York*, ix, 1869, pp. 265–275.

> *Turdus hauxwelli*, p. 265; *Ochthoëca rufomarginatus, Mecocerculus uropygialis*, p. 266; *Pogonotriccus plumbeiceps, Myiozetetes rufipennis*, p. 267; *M. inornatus*, p. 268; *Lesbia ortoni*, p. 269; *Accipiter nigroplumbeus*, p. 270, spp. nn.   Cf. *Ibis*, 1870, p. 281.

1869. LAWRENCE, G. N.   Description of Seven New Species of American Birds from various localities, with a note on Zonotrichia melanotis.   < *Proc. Acad. Nat. Sci. Phila.*, xx, 1868 [pub. 1869], pp. 359–362.

> *Dendrœca capitalis*, p. 359; *Tachyphonus atricapillus*, p. 359; *Quiscalus fortirostris*, p. 360; *Thamnophilus virgatus*, p. 361; *Pipra* (?) *cinnamomea*, p. 361; *Rhynchocyclus marginatus*, p. 361; *Harpagus fasciatus*, p. 361.   Cf. *Ibis*, 1870, p. 280.

1869. ROGERS, H.   Natural-History Notes from Rio.   < *Zoologist*, 2d ser., iv, 1869, pp. 1923, 1925.

1869. SALVIN, O.   Notes on Mr. Lawrence's List of Costa-Rica Birds [in Ann. Lyc. Nat. Hist. N. Y., ix, pp. 86–149].   < *Ibis*, 2d ser., v, 1869, pp. 310–319.

> A detailed critical commentary.   Makes 13 different determinations, expunges 14 spp., and adds 13 others—40 changes in 474 spp.   This article relates only to the first portion of Mr. Lawrence's catalogue, the Land Birds.—Continued in *Ibis*, 1870, pp. 107–116, *q. v.*

1869. SCLATER, P. L.   On the Birds of the Vicinity of Lima, Peru.   With Notes on their Habits; by Prof. W. Nation, of Lima.   (Part III.)   < *P. Z. S.*, xxxvii, 1869, pp. 146–148, pl. xii.

> Continued from *P. Z. S.*, 1867, p. 344.—13 spp.   The pl. represents *Neorhynchus* (g. n.) *nasesus* (lettered *maseus* on the pl.).—Continued, *P. Z. S.*, 1871, pp. 496–498.

1869. SCLATER, P. L., *and* SALVIN, O.   Second [cf. Ibis, 1868, p. 183] List of Birds collected, during the Survey of the Straits of Magellan, by Dr. Cunningham.   < *Ibis*, 2d ser., v, 1869, pp. 283–286.

> 33 spp.   Note on *Zonotrichia canicopilla* and synonymatic and diagnostic notice of *Phrygilus gayi* and *P. aldunatii.*—Continued, *Ibis*, 1870, pp. 499–504.

1869. SCLATER, P. L., *and* SALVIN, O.   On Peruvian Birds collected by Mr. Whitely.   Part IV.   < *P. Z. S.*, xxxvii, 1869, pp. 151–158, pl. xiii.

> Cf. *P. Z. S.*, 1867, p. 982; 1868, pp. 173, 568.   46 spp.   *Saltator laticlavius*, p. 151; *Poospiza cœsar*, p. 152, pl. xii; *Agriornis insolens*, p. 153; *Centrites oreas*, p. 154, spp. nn.   Critical and field-notes.—Continued, *P. Z. S.*, 1869, pp. 596–601.

1869. SCLATER, P. L., *and* SALVIN, O.   Second List of Birds collected at Conchitas, Argentine Republic, by Mr. William H. Hudson; together with some notes upon another Collection from the same locality.   < *P. Z. S.*, xxxvii, 1869, pp. 158–162.

> Cf. *P. Z. S.*, 1868, p. 137.   14 spp. in one coll., 10 in the other; with critical notes.

1869. SCLATER, P. L., *and* SALVIN, O.   On Venezuelan Birds collected by Mr. A. Goering.   Part III.   < *P. Z. S.*, xxxvii, 1869, pp. 250–254, pl. xviii.

> Cf. *P. Z. S.*, 1868, pp. 165, 626.   Sketch of locality; nominal list of 56 spp., with notes on 9 of them.   *Brachygalba goeringi*, p. 253, pl. xviii, sp. n.—Continued, *P. Z. S.*, 1870, pp. 779–788.

1869. SCLATER, P. L., *and* SALVIN, O.   Descriptions of Six New Species of American Birds of the Families Tanagridæ, Dendrocolaptidæ, Formicariidæ, Tyrannidæ, and Scolopacidæ.   < *P. Z. S.*, xxxvii, 1869, pp. 416–420, pl. xxviii.

> *Calliste florida*, p. 416, pl. xxviii; *Synallaxis arequipæ, Gymnocichla chiroleuca*, p. 417; *Grallaria princeps*, p. 418 (with list of 6 spp.) ; *Contopus ochraceus, Gallinago imperialis*, p. 419.

1869. SCLATER, P. L., *and* SALVIN, O.   On two new Birds collected by Mr. E. Bartlett in Eastern Peru.   < *P. Z. S.*, xxxvii, 1869, pp. 437–439, pl. xxx.

> *Neopipo* (g. n.) *rubicunda*, p. 438, pl. xxx, f. 3; *Euphonia chrysopasta*, p. 438, pl. xxx, figg. 1, 2.

1869. SCLATER, P. L., *and* SALVIN, O.   On Peruvian Birds collected by Mr. Whitely.— Part V.   < *P. Z. S.*, xxxvii, 1869, pp. 596–601.

> Continued from *P. Z. S.*, 1869, pp. 151–158.—42 spp. from Cosnipata, 4 annotated; about 57 from Tinta, 13 of which are annotated as additional to former lists.   *Ochthoeca polionota*, p. 599; *Merganetta turneri*, p. 600, spp. nn.

1869. SCLATER, P. L., *and* SALVIN, O.   Third List of Birds collected at Conchitas, Argentine Republic,.by Mr. William H. Hudson.   <*P. Z. S.*, xxxvii, 1869, pp. 631–636.

  Cf. *P. Z. S.*, 1868, p. 137 ; 1869, p. 158.   92 spp., with remarks on 34 of them.

1869. STERNBERG, C.   Notizen aus der Vogelwelt von Buenos-Ayres.   <*J. f. O.*, xvii, 1869, pp. 174–193, 257–278.

  Lebensweise—35 spp.

1869? SUNDEVALL, C. J.   Foglarne på ön S:t Barthelemy, efter de af Dr. A. von Goës hemsända samlingarna bestämde af Carl J. Sundevall.   < *Öfvers. Konigl. Vetensk.-Akad. Förh.*, 1869, pp. 579–591.

  47 spp.   Some new "Stirpes" are indicated.—Compare 1870?, same author.

1869? SUNDEVALL, C. J.   Foglarne på ön Portorico, efter Hr Hjalmarsons insamlingar framställda af Carl J. Sundevall.   < *Öfvers. Konigl. Vetensk.-Akad. Förh.*, 1869, pp. 593–603.

  90 species.—Compare 1870?, same author.

1870. ERNST, A.   Apuntes para la fauna ornitologica de Venezuela.   < *Vargasia*, núm. 7, 1870, pp. 195–198, con una lámina.

  Estracto de las publicaciones de P. L. Sclater y O. Salvin sobre las colecciones de pájaros venezolanos hechas por Antonio Goering ; *Proc. Zool. Soc.* 27 de Febrero (p. 165) y 10 de Diciembre (p. 626) de 1868, y 22 de Abril (p. 250) de 1869.   Lám., *Brachygalba goeringi, Sublegatus glaber, Euscarthmus impiger.*

1870. FINSCH, O.   On a Collection of Birds from the Island of Trinidad.   < *P. Z. S.* xxxviii, 1870, pp. 552–589.

  115 spp., critically annotated.   The article includes local synonymy and review of previous labors (especially Léotaud's) upon the same subject.   *Spermophila lessoni*, sp. renom., p. 582.   About 350 spp. are known to occur in Trinidad.

1870. HOLTZ, LUDWIG.   Beschreibung südamerikanischer Vögel-Eier.   < *J. f. O.*, xviii, 1870, pp. 1–24, pl. i.

  Supplementary to C. Sternberg's articles on Birds of Buenos Ayres in *J.f. O.*, 1869, pp. 174–193, 257–278.   Eggs of 46 spp. described.   Those of *Molobrus sericeus* (fig. 1) and *M. badius* (fig. 2) figured, as well as those of *Opisthocomus cristatus* (fig. 3).

1870. HUDSON, W. H.   [First Letter on the Ornithology of Buenos Ayres.]   < *P. Z. S.*, xxxviii, 1870, pp. 87–89.

  The beginning of a series of 12 letters, giving miscellaneous information upon the subject.

1870. HUDSON, W. H.   [Second Letter on the Ornithology of Buenos Ayres.]   < *P. Z. S.*, xxxviii, 1870, pp. 112–114.

1870. HUDSON, W. H.   [Third Letter on the Ornithology of Buenos Ayres.]   < *P. Z. S.*, xxxviii, 1870, pp. 158–160.

1870. HUDSON, W. H.   [Fourth Letter on the Ornithology of Buenos Ayres.]   < *P. Z. S.*, xxxviii, 1870, pp. 332–334.

1870. HUDSON, W. H.   [Fifth Letter on the Ornithology of Buenos Ayres.]   < *P. Z. S.*, xxxviii, 1870, pp. 545–547.

1870. HUDSON, W. H.   [Sixth Letter on the Ornithology of Buenos Ayres.]   < *P. Z. S.*, xxxviii, 1870, pp. 548–550.

1870. HUDSON, W. H.   [Seventh Letter on the Ornithology of Buenos Ayres.]   < *P. Z. S.*, xxxviii, 1870, pp. 671–673.

1870. HUDSON, W. H.   [Eighth Letter on the Ornithology of Buenos Ayres.]   < *P. Z. S.*, xxxviii, 1870, pp. 748–750.

1870. HUDSON, W. H.   [Ninth Letter on the Ornithology of Buenos Ayres.]   < *P. Z. S.*, xxxviii, 1870, pp. 798–802.

  For Letters 10–12 see 1871, same author.

1870. NEWTON, A.   Additional Note on the Nests and Eggs collected by Dr. Cunningham.   < *Ibis*, 2d ser., vi, 1870, pp. 501–504.

  The nests or eggs of 15 spp. of South American birds are described.

1870. REINHARDT, J. Bidrag til Kundskab om Fuglefaunaen i Brasiliens Campos.
< *Vidensk. Meddel. Naturhist. Foren. Kjöbenhavn*, 1870, pp. 1–124, 315–457, pl. viii.

Elaenia lundi, p. 344, pl. 8, f. 1; Myiopatis superciliaris (Lund), p. 346, pl. 8, f. 2, spp. nn.

1870. REINHARDT, J. Bidrag til Kundskab om Fuglefaunaen i Brasiliens Campos.
Kjöbenhavn. 1870. 8vo. pp. 1–267, pl. viii.

Based on collections of the author and P. W. Lund in 1833–35, in the Brazilian Provinces of
São Paulo, Goyaz, and Minas Geraes. Annotated list of 393 spp. Elainia lundii, p. 154, pl.
viii, and Myiopatis superciliaris, p. 156, pl. viii, spp. nn.—Cf. Journ. de Zool., i, 1872, pp.75–77.

1870. SALVIN, O. Additional Notes on Mr. Lawrence's List of Costa-Rica Birds.
< *Ibis*, 2d ser., vi, 1870, pp. 107–116.

Continued from Ibis, 1869, pp. 310–319, q. v.—Adds 19 spp. to Lawrence's List. Contains
much criticism, and includes a synonymatic synopsis of three species of Capito, important
as showing that the opposite sexes of each had generally been rated as different species.

1870. SALVIN, O. On some Collections of Birds from Veragua.—Part II. < *P. Z. S.*,
xxxviii, 1870, pp. 175–219, pl. xvii (map).

Cf. P. Z. S., 1867, pp. 129–161, which gave 216 spp. In this paper are 216 more, making the
whole avifauna 432.—Thryothorus semibadius, p. 181; Empidonax atriceps, p. 198; Chiroma-
chœris aurantiaća, p. 200; Antrostomus saturatus, p. 203; Chœtura fumosa, p. 204; Lophornis
adorabilis, p. 207; Selasphorus torridus, p. 208; S. ardens, p. 209; Chloronerpes simplex, p. 212;
Melanerpes chrysauchen, p. 213, spp. nn. The paper gives a general summary of the avifauna,
and much critical matter on the characters and distribution of the species.

1870. SCLATER, P. L. On some new or little-known Birds from the Rio Paraná.
< *P. Z. S.*, xxxviii, 1870, pp. 57, 58, pl. iii, with cut.

Various species mentioned. Cnipolegus cincreus, sp. n., p. 58, woodc.; Coraphistera alaudina, p. 57, pl. iii.

1870. SCLATER, P. L. Notices of some new or little-known Species of South-American
Birds. < *P. Z. S.*, xxxviii, 1870, pp. 328–330.

Philydor consobrinus, p. 328; Melanerpes pulcher, p. 330, spp. nn.—Synopsis of 2 spp. of
Chœtura: Chœtura brachycerca, p. 329; Thryothorus rufiventer "Natt.", p. 328.

1870. SCLATER, P. L., *and* SALVIN, O. Third [cf. Ibis, 1869, p. 283] List of Birds
collected, during the Survey of the Straits of Magellan, by Dr. Cunningham.
With additional Note by A. Newton. < *Ibis*, 1870, 2d ser., vi, pp. 499–504.

33 spp., with notes on 3 of them. The article includes "Additional note on the Nests and
Eggs collected by Mr. Cunningham. By the Editor" (A. Newton). 15 spp. are described.

1870. SCLATER, P. L., *and* SALVIN, O. Characters of new Species of Birds collected by
Dr. Habel in the Galapagos Islands. < *P. Z. S.*, xxxviii, 1870, pp. 322–327, woodc.

Certhidea fusca, p. 324, fig. 1; Camarhynchus variegatus, p. 324, fig. 2; C. habeli, p. 325, fig.
3; C. prosthemelas, p. 325, fig. 4; Cactornis abingdoni, p. 326, fig. 5; Cactornis pallida, p. 327,
fig. 6; Nycticorax pauper, p. 327, spp. nn. List of 37 spp. collected.

1870. SCLATER, P. L., *and* SALVIN, O. On Venezuelan Birds collected by Mr. A. Goering. Part IV. < *P. Z. S.*, xxxviii, 1870, pp. 779–788, pll. xlvi, xlvii.

Continued from P. Z. S., 1869, pp. 250–254.—Nominal list of 106 spp., with notes on many
of them. Setophaga albifrons, Diglossa gloriosa (pl. xlvi, f. 1), Chlorospingus goeringi (pl.
xlvi, f. 2), p. 784; Buarremon meridæ, p. 785; Grallaria griseonucha, Ochthoëca superciliosa,
p. 786; O. nigrita, Conurus rhodocephalus, p. 787; Urochroma delectissima, pl. xlvii, p. 788,
spp. nn.

1870. SCLATER, P. L., *and* SALVIN, O. On Birds collected by Mr. George M. Whitely
on the Coast of Honduras. < *P. Z. S.*, xxxviii, 1870, pp. 835–839.

135 spp., a few of which are annotated.

1870. SCLATER, P. L., *and* SALVIN, O. Descriptions of five new Species of Birds from the
United States of Columbia. < *P. Z. S.*, xxxviii, 1870, pp. 840–844, pl. liii.

Pheucticus uropygialis, Synallaxis vyatti, p. 840; Tyranniscus leucogonys, pl. liii, f. 1; T.
improbus, f. 2; T. griseiceps, f. 3, p. 841; Trogon chionurus, p. 843. Synopsis of 9 spp. of the
genus Tyranniscus.

1870? SUNDEVALL, C. J. Foglarne på ön S:t Barthelemy, efter de af Dr A. von
Goës hemsände samlingarna bestamde af Carl J. Sundevall. < *Öfvers. Konigl.
Vetensk.-Akad. Förhandl. för år* 1869, 1870?, pp. 579–591.

Treating 47 spp. at greater or less length, after a notice of the general subject.—Diagnosis
of 3 spp. of the genus Phaëthon.—Compare 1869 ?, same author.

1870? SUNDEVALL, C. J. Foglarne på ön Portorico, efter Hr Hjalmarsons insamlingar framställda af Carl J. Sundevall. < *Öfvers. Konigl. Vetensk.-Akad.
Förhandl. för år* 1869, 1870 ?, pp. 593–604.

> Treats of upward of 100 spp. Interspersed with the notes on the collection are many
> critical observations in the author's well-known quiet and pithy style.—Compare 1869 ?, same
> author.

1871. BELLO Y ESPINOSA, —. Zoologische Notizen aus Puerto Rico von Herrn Bello y
Espinosa daselbst. Nach dem Spanischen frei bearbeitet von Herrn E. von
Martens in Berlin. <*Der Zoolog. Garten*, 1871, pp. 348–351.

> Von der Classe der Vögel sind 64 Arten bekannt.

1871. CUNNINGHAM, R. O. Notes on | the Natural History | of the | Strait of Magel-
lan | and West Coast of Patagonia | made during the voyage of H. M. S.
'Nassau' | in the years 1866, 67, 68, & 1869 | By | Robert O. Cunningham, |
M. D., F. L. S., etc. | Naturalist to the Expedition | With Map and Illustrations
| Edinburgh | Edmonston and Douglas | 1871 | All rights reserved   1 vol.
16mo. pp. i–xviii, 1–517, 22 illust., some colored.

> Ornithological matter *passim*. Previous publication of much of the author's material is
> found in *Ibis*, 1868, p. 183; 1869, p. 283; and 1870, p. 499; and in his letters to the same journal,
> *qq. vv. suprà*.—Fig. 6, head of Steamer Duck (*Micropterus*).

1871. CUNNINGHAM, R. O. On the Terrestrial and Marine Fauna of the Strait of
Magellan and Western Patagonia. < *Rep. Brit. Ass. Adv. Sci. for* 1870, 1871,
(*Misc. Comm.*), p. 114.

> Mere allusions to a few birds.

1871. HAMILTON, J. F. Notes on Birds from the Province of Saõ Paulo, Brazil.
< *Ibis*, 3d ser., i, 1871, pp. 301–309.

> Field-notes on 45 spp. observed in the spring of 1869.

1871. HUDSON, W. H. [Tenth Letter on the Ornithology of Buenos Ayres.] < *P. Z.
S.*, xxxix, 1871, pp. 4–7.

> For Letters 1–9, see 1870, same author.

1871. HUDSON, W. H. [Eleventh Letter on the Ornithology of Buenos Ayres.] < *P.
Z. S.*, xxxix, 1871, pp. 258–262.

1871. HUDSON, W. H. [Twelfth Letter on the Ornithology of Buenos Ayres.] < *P.
Z. S.*, xxxix, 1871, pp. 326–329.

1871. JULIET, C. Esploracion científica practicada por órden del Supremo Gobierno
i segun las instrucciones del doctor don R. A. Philippi, . . . <*Anales Univ.
Chile*, tomo xli, ent. de julio 1871, pp. 81–168, pll.

> A few birds are mentioned here and there in running narrative. The illustrations do not
> relate to birds.

1871. LAWRENCE, G. N. Descriptions of New Species of Birds from Mexico, Central
America, and South America, with a Note on Rallus longirostris. <*Ann. Lyc.
Nat. Hist. N. Y.*, x, 1871, pp. 1–21.

> *Harporhynchus graysoni* Baird, MS., p. 1; *Cistothorus aequatorialis*, p. 3; *Troglodytes insu-
> laris* Bd. MS., p. 3; *Parula insularis*, p. 4; *Haemophila sumichrasti*, p. 6; *Pipilo carmani*, p. 7;
> *Attila cinnamomeus*, p. 8; *Todirostrum superciliaris*, p. 9; *Elainea macilvainii*, p. 10; *Empi-
> donax fulvipectus, Trogon eximius*, p. 11; *Chlorostilbon caribœus*, p. 13; *Conurus holochlorus*
> var. *brevipes* Bd. MS., p. 14; *Leptoptila bonapartii*, p. 15; *Zenaidura graysoni* Bd. MS., p. 17;
> *Vireosylvia magister* Bd. MS., p. 20. Interesting field-notes of Col. A. J. Grayson's accompany
> several of the species. The note on *Rallus longirostris* states that with this species *R. crassi-
> rostris* Lawr. from Bahia agrees, it being apparently different from *R. crepitans* Gm.

1871. LAWRENCE, G. N. Descriptions of three New Species of American Birds, with a
Note on Eugenes spectabilis < *Ann. Lyc. Nat. Hist. N. Y.*, x, 1871, pp. 137–140.

> *Mimus nigriloris*, p. 137 (Mexico); *Buarremon sordidus*, p. 138 (Bogotá); *Serpophaga grisea*,
> p. 139 (Costa Rica). Distinctness of *E. spectabilis* reiterated.

1871. ORTON, J. Contributions to the Natural History of the Valley of Quito.—No. I.
< *Amer. Nat.*, v, No. 10, Oct., 1871, pp. 619–626.

> Birds, pp. 623–626.—Annotated list of 184 spp., 38 of which are believed to be confined to
> the valley; followed by general remarks on geographical distribution.

1871. ORTON, J.   Notes on some Birds in the Museum of Vassar College.   < *Amer. Nat.*, iv, No. 12, Feb., 1871, pp. 711–717.

Observations on 50 or more spp., the greater part of the notes relating to neotropical birds. At time of writing, Vassar College contained nearly 1,200 spp., of which about 700 were N. and 60C S. American; among them several type-specimens, and others of interest as the originals of Audubon's plates.

1871. ORTON, J.   On the Condors and Humming-birds of the Equatorial Andes.   < *Ann. Mag. Nat. Hist.*, (4), viii, 1871, pp. 185–192.

1871. ORTON, J.   The Vultures and Humming Birds of Tropical America.   < *Canad. Nat. & Quart. Journ.*, n. s., v, 1871, pp. 357–360.

Abstract of his paper in *Amer. Nat.*

1871. SCLATER, P. L.   On the Land-birds of Juan Fernandez.   < *Ibis*, 3d ser., i, 1871, pp. 178–183, pl. vii.

Sketch of the islands; 6 spp., with comment. Pl. vii, f. 1, *Anæretes fernandezianus;* f. 2, *Oxyurus masafueræ.*

1871. SCLATER, P. L.   The Birds of the Lesser Antilles.   < *Nature*, iv, 1871, pp. 473– —.

Not seen.

1871. SCLATER, P. L.   [Extracts from Correspondence with Mr. G. W. des Vœux concerning the expediency of introducing Secretarius reptilivorus or Dacelo gigas for destruction of the Rat-tailed Serpent of Santa Lucia (Trigonocephalus lanceolatus).]   < *P. Z. S.*, xxxix, 1871, pp. 2–4.

1871. SCLATER, P. L.   On the Birds of the Island of Santa Lucia, West Indies.   < *P. Z. S.*, xxxix, 1871, pp. 263–273, pl. xxi.

Summary of Antillean avifauna; 25 spp., variously annotated. *Icterus laudabilis*, pl. xxi, p. 270.

1871. SCLATER, P. L.   On the Birds of the Vicinity of Lima, Peru.   . . .   With Notes on their Habits; by Prof. W. Nation, of Lima, C. M. Z. S.—Part IV.   < *P. Z. S.*, xxxix, 1871, pp. 496–498, fig.

Continued from *P. Z. S.*, 1869, p. 148.–5 spp. *Euscarthmus fulviceps*, p. 497, fig., sp. n.

1871. SCLATER, P. L.   Remarks on a Collection of Birds from Oyapok [Cayenne].   < *P. Z. S.*, xxxix, 1871, pp. 749, 750.

Ochthoëca murina, p. 749; *Heteropelma igniceps*, p. 750, spp. nn. Synopsis of 16 + 3 spp. of *Ochthoëca.*

1871. SUNDEVALL, C. J.   On Birds from the Galapagos Islands.   < *P. Z. S.*, xxxix, 1871, pp. 124–130.

A list of 26 spp., of which two are new (*Ardea plumbea*, pp. 125, 127–129, and *Spheniscus mendiculus*, pp. 129, 130; also a new variety of *Ardea violacea*), obtained by the Swedish 'Eugenie' expedition in 1852. Remarks on the species allied to some of those recorded are added. Some are noticed from the Galapagos for the first time.

1871. WYATT, C. W.   Notes on some of the Birds of the United States of Columbia.   < *Ibis*, i, 1871, 3d ser., pp. 113–131, pl. v (map), 319–335, 373–384.

Extended account of the region and route; field-notes on 210 spp.; map of author's journey.

1871–74. GUNDLACH, J.   Neue Beiträge zur Ornithologie Cubas.   < *J. f. O.*, xix, 1871, pp. 265–295, 353–378; xx, 1872, pp. 401–432; xxii, 1874, pp. 113–166, 286–303.

There are literal discrepancies in the titles of the successive instalments. The first part is wholly occupied with a review of what has been done on the subject, from Macleay (1827) to the author himself (1865-66). The second begins The Revised List of Cuban Birds.

1872. ANON.   Zoology of the Galapagos.   < *Pop. Sci. Monthly*, Sept., 1872, pp. 633–635.

Various allusions to the birds.

1872. EDITORS.   New Galapagos Birds.   < *Am. Nat.*, vi, 1872, p. 38.

Notice of Scl. & Salv., *P. Z. S.*, May, 1870, on Dr. Habel's discoveries.

1872. HUDSON, W. H.   On the Birds of the Rio Negro of Patagonia.   With Notes by P. L. Sclater.   < *P. Z. S.*, xl, 1872, pp. 534–550, fig., pl. xxxi.

Field-notes on 23 spp., technical names of most of which are supplied by Dr. Sclater, who appends a nominal list of 48 spp. of the region, 7 of them peculiar to it.—*Cnipolegus hudsoni*, Scl., p. 541, pl. 31, sp. n.

1872. LANDBECK, L.   Sobre algunos pájaros chilenos.   <*Anales Univ. Chile*, xli, Aug., 1872, pp. 515–519.

Sterna trudeaui, Conurus cyanolyseos, i *Sterna galericulata.*

1872. LAWRENCE, G. N.   Descriptions of New Species of Birds of the Genera Icterus and Synallaxis.   <*Ann. Lyc. Nat. Hist. N. Y.*, x, 1872, pp. 184–186.

Icterus formosus, p. 184 (Tehuantepec) ; *Synallaxis maculata,* p. 186 (Tumbe, Peru).

1872. LAYARD, E. L.   [Letter relating to birds seen during a voyage from England to Pará.]   <*Ibis*, 3d ser., ii, 1872, pp. 336–338.

1872. [SALVIN, O.]   [Notice of E. L. Layard's departure for Pará, South America.] *Ibis*, 3d ser., ii, 1872, p. 208.

1872. SALVIN, O.   Notes on the Birds of Nicaragua, based upon a Collection made at Chontales by Mr. Thomas Belt.   <*Ibis*, 3d ser., ii, 1872, pp. 311–323.

130 specimens of 73 spp.   Sketch of history of the subject ; general characters of the avifauna of the region.

1872. [SALVIN, O.]   [Notice of G. A. Maack's researches in the vicinity of Panamá.] <*Ibis*, 3d ser., ii, 1872, pp. 339, 340.

1872. SEMPER, J. E.   Observations on the Birds of St. Lucia.   With Notes by P. L. Sclater.   <*P. Z. S.*, xl, 1872, pp. 647–653.

Cf. *P. Z. S.*, 1871, p. 263.   Notes on 25 spp. contained in the former list, and on 6 additional ones.

1872. SPERLING, R. M.   [Letter.]   <*Ibis*, 3d ser., ii, 1872, pp. 74–79.

Refers to various South American birds and some *Procellariidæ.*

1873. CABANIS, J.   [Neue peruanische Vögel des Herrn C. Jelski.]   <*J. f. O.*, 1873, pp. 64–68.

Hylophilus flaviventris, Dacnis modesta, p. 64 ; *Hypocnemis subflava, Thamnistes rufescens, Lochmias obscurata,* p. 65 ; *Phylydor subflavescens, Ipoborus (Automolus) stictoptilus,* p. 66 ; *Sclerurus olivaceus, Euscarthmus rufigularis, Phyllomyias cinereicapillus,* p. 67 ; *Capsiempis orbitalis, Hadrostomus audax,* p. 68, spp. nn.

1873. CABANIS, J.   [Neue Vögel des Berliner Museums, von C. Jelski in Peru entdeckt.]   <*J. f. O.*, 1873, pp. 315–320, pl. iv, f. 3 ; 1874, pl. ii.

Turdus gigantodes, p. 315 ; *Basileuterus diachlorus, Myiothlypis striaticeps, Iridornis jelskii,* p. 316 (pl. ii, f. 1, Jahrg. 1874) ; *Poecilothraupis ignicrissa, Presbys peruanus,* p. 317 ; *Diglossa pectoralis, Chlorospingus (Hemispingus) auricularis, Hypsibamon andicolus,* p. 318, pl. iv, f. 3 ; *Cillurus rivularis, Synallaxis humilis, S. albicapilla, Schizoeaca palpebralis,* p. 319 (pl. ii, fig. 2, Jahrg. 1874) ; *Mitrephorus ochraceiventris,* p. 320.

1873. LAYARD, E. L.   [Letter on Birds observed on a Voyage from Pará to England.] <*Ibis*, 3d ser., iii, 1873, pp. 331, 332.

1873. LAYARD, E. L.   Notes on Birds observed at Para.   . . .   With Descriptions of two new Species.   By P. L. Sclater.   <*Ibis*, 3d ser., iii, 1873, pp. 374–396, pll. xiv, xv.

List of 120 spp., quite fully annotated.   *Picolaptes layardi,* p. 386, pl. xiv ; *Thamnophilus simplex,* p. 387, pl. xv, spp. nn.

1873. LEE, W. B.   Ornithological Notes [on 33 spp.] from the Argentine Republic. <*Ibis*, 3d ser., iii, 1873, pp. 129–138.

1873. LEYBOLD, F.   Escursion a las Pampas Argentinas.   Hojas de mi diario.   Por Frederico Leybold.   Santiago.   1873.   8vo.   pp. 108, map.

Not seen.—Many notes on the birds observed or obtained.   *Columbina aurisquamata,* p. 38 ; *Conurus glaucifrons,* p. 38, spp. nn.

1873. MATHEW, G. F.   Natural-History [Ornithological] Notes from Coquimbo. <*Zoologist*, 2d ser., viii, 1873, pp. 3578, 3579.

1873. PELZELN, A. v.   Verzeichniss einer an Dr. L. W. Schaufuss gelangten Sendung Vögel aus Neu-Freiburg in Brasilien.   <*Nunquam Otiosus*, 1873, pp. 291, 292.

Not seen.

1873. SALVIN, O.   [Letter off St. Domingo, noting various Birds observed en route.] <*Ibis*, 3d ser., iii, 1873, pp. 333, 334.

Bull. v, 2——10

1873. SALVIN, O. [Letter relating to some Guatemalan Birds.] <*Ibis*, 3d ser., iii, 1873, pp. 428, 429.

1873. SCLATER, P. L. Additions to the List of Birds of Nicaragua. <*Ibis*, 3d ser., iii, 1873, pp. 372, 373.

Adding 17 spp. to the list given in *Ibis*, 1872, pp. 311–323.

1873. SCLATER, P. L. [Note on Sclater and Salvin's 'Nomenclator Avium Neotropicalium'.] <*P. Z. S.*, 1873, pp. 554, 555.

Gives the classification to be adopted in the work. Eliminates *Turdus subcinereus* and *Cnipolegus* sp. from the American avifauna.

1873. SCLATER, P. L. [Descriptions of two new species of Birds from the State of Antioquia, Columbia.] <*P. Z. S.*, 1873, pp. 728, 729.

Chlorochrysea nitidissima, p. 728; *Grallaria ruficeps*, p. 729.

1873. SCLATER, P. L. On Peruvian Birds collected by Mr. Whitely. Part VII. <*P. Z. S.*, 1873, pp. 779–784.

39 spp., with notes on some of them. *Thryophilus fulvus, Todirostrum pulchellum*, p. 781; *Tyranniscus viridissimus, Myiobius aureiventris*, p. 782; *Grallaria erythroleuca*, p. 783, spp. nn.

1873. SCLATER, P. L., *and* SALVIN, O. Nomenclator | Avium Neotropicalium | sive | avium | quæ in regione neotropica hucusque repertæ sunt | nomina systematice disposita adjecta sua cuique | speciei patria accedunt generum et | specierum novarum diagnoses. | Auctoribus | Philippo Lutley Sclater A. M. Phil. Doct. | Soc. Reg. Lond. Socio | Soc. Zool. Lond. Secretario. | Et Osberto Salvin A. M. | Soc. Reg. Lond. Socio. | — | [Icon.] | Londini : | — | MDCCCLXXIII. 1 vol. Fol. pp. viii, 163.

Avium omnium e regione Neotropica hucusque auctoribus obviarum tenet Nomenclator, secundum systema quo in opere adhuc inedito, sed jam per multos annos elaborato, cujus titulus "Index Avium Americanorum" usi sunt. Species asterisco nototæ neque in ornithotheca P. L. S. neque in Museo Salvino-Godmannico asservantur, sed in aliis locis auctoribus obviæ sunt.

Expositio ordinum classis avium in hoc opere usitatorum, adjecto in quoque ordine specierum numero. A. *Carinatae*. (I. *Aegithognathæ*.) 1. *Passeres*, 1976. 2. *Cypseli*, 444. 3. *Pici*, 116. (II. *Desmognathæ*.) 4. *Coccyges*, 214. 5. *Psittaci*, 142. 6. *Striges*, 37. 7. *Accipitres*, 114. 8. *Steganopodes*, 17. 9. *Herodiones*, 44. 10. *Anseres*, 64. (III. *Schizognathæ*.) 11. *Columbæ*, 66. 12. *Gallinæ*, 90. 13. *Opisthocomi*, 1. 14. *Grues*, 57. 15. *Limicolæ*, 73. 16. *Gaviæ*, 53. 17. *Pygopodes*, 9. 18. *Impennes*, 9. (IV. *Dromæognathæ*.) 19. *Crypturi*, 36.—B. *Ratitæ*. 20. *Apteryges*, 0. *Struthiones*, 3. Summa specierum Avium Neotropicalium, 3565.

Appendix, pp. 155-163, continens diagnoses generum et specierum, quorum nominibus in hoc opere pro prima vice usi sunt:—

P. 155: *Uropsila*, p. 7; *Phlogothraupis*, p. 21; *Porphyrospiza*, p. 30; *Clibanornis*, p. 61; *Microbates*, p. 72; *Nesoceleus*, p. 101. P. 156: *Gymnopelia*, p. 133; *Nothoprocta*, p. 153; *Calodromas*, p. 156; *Basileuterus leucopygius*, p. 10; *Hylophilus muscicapinus*, p. 12; *Cyclorhis albiventris*, p. 13. P. 157: *Chlorophanes purpurascens*, p. 16; *Euphonia chalcopasta*, p. 18; *Chlorospingus semifuscus*, p. 24; *Arremon wuchereri*, p. 25; *Haplospiza uniformis*, p. 29. P. 158: *Cnipolegus pusillus*, p. 43; *Euscarthmus wuchereri*, p. 45; *Serpophaga subflava*, p. 47; *S. pœcilocerca*, p. 47. P. 159: *Phyllomyias platyrhyncha*, p. 48; *Lipaugus immundus*, p. 57; *Casiornis fusca*, p. 57; *Furnarius agnatus*, p. 61. P. 160: *Philidor erythronotus*, p. 66; *Margarornis stellata*, p. 67; *Picolaptes puncticeps*, p. 69; *Thamnophilus tristis*, p. 69; *Myrmotherula pyrrhonota*, p. 72. P. 161: *Microbates torquatus*, p. 72; *Cercomacra carbonaria*, p. 73; *Rhinocrypta fusca*, p. 76; *Dendrocygna discolor*, p. 129. P. 162: *Querquedula andium*, p. 129; *Leptoptila rufinucha*, p. 134; *Odontophorus hypospodius*, p. 138; *Psophia napensis*, p. 141; *Tinamus ruficeps*, p. 152. P. 163: *Nothoprocta curvirostris*, p. 153.

1873. SCLATER, P. L., *and* SALVIN, O. On Peruvian Birds collected by Mr. Whitely. Part VI. <*P. Z. S.*, 1873, pp. 184-187, pl. xxi.

Pl. xxi, *Tanagra olivina*. List of 80 spp.; comment on 7 of them. *Hapalocercus acutipennis*, p. 187, sp. n. (Continued, *P. Z. S.*, 1873, p. 779, by Sclater alone.)

1873. SCLATER, P. L., *and* SALVIN, O. On the Birds of Eastern Peru. With Notes on the habits of the Birds, by Edward Bartlett. <*P. Z. S.*, 1873, pp. 252-311, pll. xxv, (map) xxvi.

Important: contains a summary of nearly all that is accurately known of the birds of the region; complete list of previous papers, 7 in number, on the same subject; general geographical considerations; subdivisions of the Amazonian Fauna. 473 spp., of which 108 are peculiar to the Upper Amazonian Fauna. *Pithys lunulata*, p. 276, pl. xxvi; *Rhynchocyclus viridiceps*, p. 280, spp. nn.

1873. SCLATER, P. L., *and* SALVIN, O.   On some Venezuelan Birds collected by Mr. James M. Spence. $<$ *P. Z. S.*, 1873, pp. 511, 512.

    8 spp.—*Lochmias sororia*, p. 511, *Crypturus cerviniventris*, p. 512, spp. n.

1873–74. BERLEPSCH, H.   Zur Ornithologie der Provinz Santa Catharina, Süd-Brasilien. $<$ *J. f. O.*, 1873, pp. 225–293; 1874, pp. 241–284.

    118 Arten, gut bearbeitet, namentlich in Bezug auf geographische Verbreitung.

1874. CABANIS, J.   Uebersicht der von Herrn Carl Euler im District Cantagallo, Provinz Rio de Janeiro, gesammelten Vögel. $<$ *J. f. O.*, 1874, pp. 81–90, 225–231.

    Sporophila euleri, sp. n., p. 84; *Ceratotriccus*, g. n., p. 87.   See 1867–69, EULER, C.

1874. CABANIS, J.   [Neue peruanische Vögel des Herrn Jelski.] $<$ *J. f. O.*, 1874, pp. 97–100.

    Turdus nigriceps Jelski, *Urolampra eupogon*, p. 97; *Coprotretes jelskii, Euscarthmus pyrrhops, Mecocerculus taeniopterus*, p. 98; *Hemipipo tschudii, Metallura jelskii*, p. 100.

1874. GOLZ, —.   [Notiz über die Guanolager Peru's.] $<$ *J. f. O.*, 1874, pp. 343, 344.

1874. GUNDLACH, J.   Beitrag zur Ornithologie der Insel Portorico. $<$ *J. f. O.*, 1874, pp. 304–315.

    116 spp.

1874. JULIET, C.   Informe del ayudante de la comission esploradora de Chiloé i Llanquihue, don Carlos Juliet. $<$ *Anales Univ. Chile*, tomo xlv, 1ª secc., Deciembre 1874, pp. 661–734.

    A few birds are mentioned here and there in running narrative.

1874. LANDBECK, L.   Zur Ornithologie Chiles. $<$ *Arch. f. Naturg.*, 1874, (1), pp. 112–116.

    Behandelt *Sterna trudeaui, S. galericulata, Conurus cyanolyseos* und *C. patagonus*.

1874. LAWRENCE, G. N.   Descriptions of Six Supposed New Species of American Birds. $<$ *Ann. Lyc. Nat. Hist. N. Y.*, x, 1874, pp. 395–399.

    Chlorospingus brunneus, p. 395 (Costa Rica); *C. axillaris*, p. 395 (Costa Rica); *Buarremon atricapillus*, p. 396 (Bogota?); *Phonipara fumosa*, p. 396 (Trinidad); *Cyanospiza rositæ*, p. 397 (Tehuantepec, Mex.); *Thripadectes virgaticeps*, p. 398 (Quito, Ecuador).

1874. LAWRENCE, G. N.   Descriptions of Two New Species of Birds of the Families Tanagridæ and Tyrannidæ. $<$ *Ann. Lyc. Nat. Hist. N. Y.*, xi, 1874, pp. 70–72.

    Phaenicothraupis cristata, p. 70 (Bogota); *Myiarchus flammulatus*, p. 71 (Tehuantepec).

1874. LAWRENCE, G. N.   Descriptions of Four New Species of Birds from Costa Rica. $<$ *Ann. Lyc. Nat. Hist. N. Y.*, xi, 1874, pp. 88–91.

    Cyanocitta argentigula, p. 88; *Stenopsis albicauda*, p. 89; *Geotrygon rufiventris, Porzana cinereiceps*, p. 90.

1874. PELZELN, A. v.   Ueber eine Sendung von Vögeln aus Ecuador. $<$ *Verh. (Abh.) k.-k. zool.-bot. Ges. Wien*, xxiv, 1874, pp. 171–174.

    Die Sendung von circa 30 Arten enthält in der That Objecte von vielem Interesse, darunter einige Arten welche bisher noch nicht aus Ecuador bekannt waren.

1874. REED, E. C.   Remarks on the Birds of Juan Fernandez and Mas-a-fuera. $<$ *Ibis*, 3d ser., iv, 1874, pp. 81–84.

    In the former island, 6 spp. of land-birds; in the latter, 5.   Cf. Sclater, *Ibis*, 1871, pp. 178–183, on the same subject.

1874. SCLATER, P. L.   News of Mr. Salvin [*i. e.*, a letter from O. Salvin, on certain Guatemalan birds]. $<$ *Ibis*, 3d ser., iv, 1874, pp. 99–100.

1874. SCLATER, P. L.   [Notice of Mr. Jelski's Collections in Western Peru.] $<$ *Ibis*, 3d ser., iv, 1874, p. 100.

1874. SCLATER, P. L.   On a small Collection of Birds from Barbadoes, West Indies. $<$ *P. Z. S.*, xlii, 1874, pp. 174, 175.

    Nine species.

1874. SCLATER, P. L., *and* SALVIN, O.   On Peruvian Birds collected by Mr. Whitely. Part VIII. $<$ *P. Z. S.*, 1874, pp. 677–680, pl. lxxxiv.

    List of 32 spp., and notes on 9 of them.   Synopsis of 6 spp. of *Northoprocta; N. taczanowskii*, p. 679, pl. lxxxiv, sp. n.

1874. TACZANOWSKI, L.   Description des Oiseaux nouveaux du Pérou central.   < *P. Z. S.*, xlii, 1874, pp. 129–140, pll. xix, xx, xxi.

> *Cistothorus graminicola, * Thryothorus cantator, p. 130; *Dacnis xanthophthalma, Dacnidea (g. n.) leucogastra* (pl. xix, f. 2), p. 131; *Microspingus (n. g.) trifasciatus* (pl. xix, f. 1), *Chlorospingus cinereocephalus, *Spermophila simplex, p. 132; *Sycalis raimondii, *Ochthœca thoracica, p. 133; *Muscisaxicola rufipennis, *Leptopogon auritus, p. 134; Pogonotriccus ophthalmicus, Doliornis (g. n.) sclateri (pl. xx), *Corythopis humivagans, *Herpsilochmus motacilloides, p. 136; Myrmotherula atrogularis, *Thripadectes scrutator, p. 137; *Scytalopus sylvestris, Thalurania jelskii, *Helianthea dichroura, p. 138; Metallura hedvigæ (pl. xxi, f. 2), *Eriocnemis sapphiropygia, p. 139; Lampraster (n. g.) branickii, pl. xxi, f. 1, p. 140, spp. nn.; those marked with an asterisk being from C. Jelski's MS. Cf. *J.f. O.*, 1873, pp. 64–68, 315–320; 1874, pp. 97–100.

1874. TACZANOWSKI, L.   Liste des Oiseaux recueillis par M. Constantin Jelski dans la partie centrale du Pérou Occidental.   <*P. Z. S.*, Nov. 3, 1874, pp. 501–565, pll. lxiv, lxv.

> Most of the new Peruvian birds discovered by Jelski had been described by Cabanis in *J.f. O.*, 1873, and by Taczanowski in *P. Z. S.*, 1874, when the latter drew up the present important article, giving a complete list of the 490 species secured by the intrepid and indefatigable traveller during the three years he passed in exploring the narrow but interesting region comprised between Lima, Huanta, Monterico, Farma, and Junin, which is situated in the Cordilleras, and therefore presents a marvellously rich avifauna, composed of species living from torrid regions to the line of perpetual snow. The following 19 species are here described as new:—*Anthus brevirostris, A. calcaratus*, p. 507; *Conirostrum cyaneum*, p. 512; *Buarremon mystacalis*, p. 515; *B. tricolor*, p. 516; *Chlorospingus chrysogaster*, p. 517; *Spermophila obscura*, p. 519; *Pipilo mystacalis*, p. 521; *Geositta saxicolina*, p. 524; *Upucerthia serrana*, p. 525; *Anabazenops cabanisi*, p. 528; *Ochthodiœta signatus*, p. 532; *Rhyncocyclus peruvianus*, p. 537; *Myiobius superciliosus*, p. 538; *Empidonax andinus*, p. 539; *Leucippus pallidus*, p. 542; *Hypoxanthus brevirostris*, p. 546; *Gallinago andina*, p. 561; *Nothoprocta branickii*, p. 563.— Pl. xliv, *Turdus nigriceps*. Pl. xlv, *Buarremon tricolor*.—The text is chiefly descriptive, biographical, and critical.

1875. DUBUS, A.   Descriptions de Quelques Oiseaux Nouveaux.   < *Bull. Acad. Roy. Belg.*, 2d ser., xl, No. 12, Dec., 1875, pp. 13–17.

> *Cyanocitta yucatanica*, p. 13, Yucatan; *Icterus virescens*, p. 15, Mexico; *I. xanthornus* var. *a. dubusii*, p. 16, Panama; *I. xanthornus* var. *marginalis*, p. 17, Panama.—Not seen.

1875. LAWRENCE, G. N.   Descriptions of five new Species of American Birds.   <*Ibis*, 3d ser., v, July, 1875, pp. 383–387, pl. ix.

> *Chlorospingus? speculiferus*, p. 383, pl. ix, f. 1; *C. nigrifrons*, p. 384; *Serpophaga leucura*, p. 384, pl. ix, f. 2; *Orchilus atricapillus*, p. 385; *Empidonax nanus*, p. 386.

1875. PELZELN, A. V.   On some Birds from Spanish Guiana collected by Herr Münzberg.   <*Ibis*, 3d ser., v, July, 1875, pp. 329–332.

> 24 spp.; among them *Machetes pugnax! Heleodytes bicolor*, p. 330, sp. n.

1875. PHILIPPI, R. A.   Escursion al cajon de los Cipreses en la hacienda de Cauquenes (Rancagua).   < *Anales Univ. Chile*, tomo xlvii, 1ª secc., 1875, pp. 651–670.

> La Fauna del Valle, p. 670.—*Conurus cyanolysios, Attagis gayana*.

1875. SALVIN, O.   Additional [cf. Ibis, 1871, p. 178; 1874, p. 81] Notes on the Birds of the Islands of Masafuera and Juan Fernandez.   < *Ibis*, 3d ser., v, July, 1875, pp. 370–377.

> *Buteo exsul*, p. 371; *Œstrelata externa*, p. 373, spp. nn. Letter from E. Oustalet on type of *Puffinus sericeus* Less. List of 17 known species of the two islands.

1875. SCLATER, P. L., *and* SALVIN, O.   On Venezuelan Birds collected by Mr. A. Goering.   Part V.   <*P. Z. S.*, Mar. 16, 1875, pp. 234–238, pl. xxxv.

> List of 42 + 33 spp., with notes on 7 of them. *Buarremon castaneifrons*, p. 235, pl. xxxv, f. 1; *Chlorospingus chrysophrys*, p. 235; *Chloronerpes xanthochlorus*, p. 238, spp. nn. Pl. xxxv, f. 2, *Buarremon taczanowskii*.

1875. SCLATER, P. L., *and* SALVIN, O.   Description of two new Species of Birds from the State of Antioquia, U. S. C.   <*P. Z. S.*, Nov. 2, 1875, pp. 541–542.

> *Catharus phœopleurus*, p. 541; *Automolus holostictis*, p. 542.

1876. ALLEN, J. A.   Exploration of Lake Titicaca, by Alexander Agassiz and S. W. Garman.   III. List of Mammals and Birds.   By J. A. Allen, with Field-Notes by Mr. Garman.   < *Bull. Mus. Comp. Zoöl.*, iii, No. 15, July, 1876, pp. 349–359.

> An annotated l'st of 69 spp. of birds, pp. 353–359. *FalcineRus ridgwayi, Gallinula garmani*, spp. nn. Cf. *Ibis*, 4th ser., i, 1877, pp. 119, 120.

1876. A[LLEN], J. A.   Description of new species of American Birds.   < *Bull. Nutt. Ornith. Club*, i, No. 2, July, 1876, p. 47.

Notice of two recent papers by G. N. Lawrence in *Ann. Lyc. N. Y.* and *Ibis*.

1876. BROWN, C. B.   Canoe and Camp Life in British Guiana.   By C. Barrington Brown, Assoc. R. S. M., late Government Surveyor in British Guiana.   London: Stanford. 1876. 1 vol. 8vo.

Not seen: cited from *Ibis*, 1877, p. 239, where favorably noticed. It is said to be replete with natural history notes, many of which relate to birds, and among which are some of novelty or other special interest.

1876. DURNFORD, H.   Ornithological Notes from the Neighbourhood of Buenos Ayres.   < *Ibis*, 3d ser., vi, April, 1876, pp. 157–166.

1876. [HOTCHKISS, TRUMAN.]   South American Game Birds.   < *Scientific American* of Sept. 3, 1876.

Reprinted in *Forest and Stream*, vii, Oct. 12, 1876, p. 148.

1876. NAPP, R.   Argentine Republic. Buenos Ayres. 1876. 8vo. pp. 560, 5 maps.

Not seen.

1876. ORTON, J.   The Andes and the Amazon; or across the Continent of South America.   By James Orton, A. M.   Third edition, revised and enlarged, containing notes of a second journey across the continent from Para to Lima and Lake Titicaca.   New York: 1876. 8vo.

Not seen; nor do I know the date of the original or 2d edition. Cf. *Ibis*, 1877, p. 373.

1876. PELZELN, A. V.   Ueber eine weitere Sendung von Vögeln aus Ecuador.   < *Verh. (Abh.) d. k.-k. zool.-bot. Gesellsch. zu Wien*, Dec. 6, 1876, pp. 765–772.

Ein ausführliches Verzeichniss der Arten, theilweise mit Anmerkungen versehen. Cf. *Ibis*, 1877, p. 383.

1876. SALVIN, O.   On some new Species of Birds from Western Ecuador.   < *Ibis*, 3d ser., vi, 1876, pp. 493–496, pl. xiv.

Euscarthmus ocularis, p. 493; *Formicivora speciosa*, p. 494; *Capito squamatus*, p. 494, pl. xiv; *Pionopsitta pyrrhops*, p. 495; *Leucopternis occidentalis*, p. 496.

1876. SALVIN, O.   On the Avifauna of the Galapagos Archipelago.   < *Trans. Zool. Soc. Lond.*, vol. ix, pt. ix, May, 1876, art. x, pp. 447–510, pll. lxxxiv-lxxxix, many woodcc.

This important paper contains:—Introductory remarks, physical and historical, including Dr. Habel's account of his visit (cf. *P. Z. S.*, 1870, pp. 322–327), p. 447. Short account of the literature of the subject, p. 461. List of the birds, with remarks on their relationships with those of other countries, *a*, as to species, *b*, as to genera, *c*, as to families, p. 463. Summary of the birds of each island, p. 466. On the variation of the species in certain genera (*Geospiza, Cactornis, Camarhynchus*), and consequent difficulty of defining them, p. 469. Account of each species, with synonymy, description, distribution, biography, and general remarks, p. 471. Conclusions, p. 509.

Families 20; genera 39, of which 27 are wide-ranging; species 57, of which 38, or more than 66 per cent., are peculiar to the islands; 21 water-birds, 36 land-birds. Pl. lxxxiv, map of the Archipelago; lxxxv, *Camarhynchus variegatus*; lxxxvi, *C. habeli*; lxxxvii, *Larus fuliginosus*; lxxxviii, ff. 1, 2, *Œstrelata phæopygia*, sp. n., p. 507; f. 2, *Procellaria tethys*; lxxxix, *Spheniscus mendiculus*. Also, heads, etc., of the species of *Geospiza, Cactornis*, and *Camarhynchus* figured in the numerous woodcuts. Dr. Habel's field-notes *passim*; his new species were previously described by S. & S., *P. Z. S.*, 1870, pp. 322–327, *q. v.*

Original date of *Creagrus* Bp., 1853; also pub. in 1854 in separates of a paper in *Rev. Zool.*, Jan., 1855.

1876. SCLATER, P. L.   On some additional Species of Birds from St. Lucia, West Indies.   < *P. Z. S.*, Jan. 4, 1876, pp. 13, 14, pl. ii.

Cf. *P. Z. S.*, 1871, p. 263, and 1872, p. 647.—List of 8 spp. *Thryothorus mesoleucus, Leucopeza* (g. n.) *semperi* (pl. ii), p. 14, spp. nn.

1876. SCLATER, P. L., *and* SALVIN, O.   On Peruvian Birds collected by Mr. Whitely.—Part IX.   < *P. Z. S.*, Jan. 4, 1876, pp. 15–19, pl. iii.

List of 65 spp., with remarks on 9 of them. *Thamnophilus melanchrous*, p. 18, pl. iii; *Columba albipennis*, p. 18, spp. nn.

1876. SCLATER, P. L., *and* SALVIN, O.   Descriptions of new Birds obtained by Mr. C. Buckley in Bolivia.   <*P. Z. S.*, Feb. 1, 1876, pp. 253, 254.

    Diglossa glauca, p. 253; *Buarremon melanops*, p. 253; *Leptopogon tristis*, p. 254; *Hypoxanthus atriceps*, p. 254.

1876. SCLATER, P. L., *and* SALVIN, O.   On new Species of Bolivian Birds.   <*P. Z. S.*, Apr. 4, 1876, pp. 352–358, pll. xxx–xxxiii, woodcc.

    Catharus mentalis, Basileuterus euophrys, p. 352; *Malacothraupis* (g. n.) *dentata* (pl. xxxi), fig. on p. 353, *Calliste punctulata*, p. 353; *C. fulvicervix* (pl. xxx, f. 1), *C. argyrofenges* (pl. xxx, f. 2), *Chlorospingus calophrys, Cyanocorax nigriceps, Ochthodiæta fuscorufus*, p. 354; *Ochthæca pulchella, Anæretes flavirostris, Lathria uropygialis* (pl. xxxii, fig. on p. 356), p. 355; *Grallaria erythrotis, Thamnophilus subfasciatus* (pl. xxxiii), *Asturina saturata*, p. 357.

1877. ALLEN, J. A.   List of Birds collected by Mr. Charles Linden, near Santarem, Brazil.   <*Bull. Essex Inst.*, viii, No. 8, 1876, pp. 78–83.   (Pub. Feb., 1877.)

    Annotated list of 128 spp.; *Coccygus lindeni*, sp. n.

1877. DURNFORD, H.   Notes on some Birds observed in the Chuput Valley, Patagonia, and in the neighbouring District.   <*Ibis*, 4th ser., i, 1877, pp. 27–46.

    Extended field-notes on about 62 spp.

1877. DURNFORD, H.   Notes on the Birds of the Province of Buenos Ayres.   <*Ibis*, 4th ser., i, 1877, pp. 166–203, pl. iii.

    Excellent field-notes on 144 spp., with some little editorial criticism.   *Porzana spiloptera* "Burm. MS.", p. 194, pl. iii, sp. n.

1877. EDITORS.   Allen's 'Birds of Lake Titicaca.'   <*Ibis*, 4th ser., i, 1877, pp. 119, 120.

    Review of that paper.

1877. EDITORS.   Brown's Travels in British Guiana.   <*Ibis*, 4th ser., i, 1877, p. 237.

    Notice of the work of that name.

1877. EDITORS.   Pelzeln on Birds from Ecuador.   <*Ibis*, 4th ser., i, 1877, p. 383.

    A notice of the paper in *Verh.* (*Abh.*) *zool.-bot. Gesch. zu Wien*, 1876, pp. 765–772.

1877. EDITORS.   Roraima and its mysteries.   <*Ibis*, 4th ser., i, 1877, pp. 399, 400.

    À propos of C. B. Brown's work on British Guiana, 1876, *q. v.*   The article is chiefly an extract from the London *Spectator*, date unknown to me.

1877. ERNST, A.   Estudios | sobre la | Flora y Fauna | de Venezuela | por | A. Ernst. | — | Caracas | Imprenta federal | . . . | 1877.   4°.   2 p. ll., pp. 211–330.

    Catálogo sistemático de las especies de Aves que han sido observadas hasta ahora en los Estados Unidos de Venezuela, pp. 293–316.   315 géneros y 556 especies.—Publicado en el *Primer Annuario Estadístico*, Caracas, 1877.

1877. LAWRENCE, G. N.   Descriptions of New Species of Birds from the Island of Dominica.   <*Ann. N. Y. Acad. Sci.*, i, Oct., 1877, pp. 46–49.

    Thryothorus rufescens, Dendrœca plumbea, Myiarchus oberi, spp. nn.   Cf. *Bull. Nutt. Ornith. Club*, iv, Jan., 1879, pp. 48, 49.

1877. LAWRENCE, G. N.   A Provisional List of the Birds Procured and Noticed by Mr. Fred. A. Ober in the Island of Dominica.   <*Forest and Stream*, ix, Dec. 6, 1877, p. 345.

    Provisional list of 56 spp., anticipating the final paper in *Proc. U. S. Nat. Mus.*, 1878, *q. v.*

1877. REED, E. C.   Apuntes de la Zoologia de la Hacienda de Cauquenes, Provincia de Colchagua [Chile], por Edwyn C. Reed.   Santiago de Chile.   1877.   8vo.

    Not seen.   Cf. *Ibis*, Oct., 1878, pp. 485, 486.

1877. SCLATER, P. L., *and* SALVIN, O.   Descriptions of eight new Species of South-American Birds.   <*P. Z. S.*, Jan. 2, 1877, pp. 18–22, pl. i.

    Euphonia finschi (Demerara), *Pheucticas crissalis* (Ecuador), *Ochthoeca leucometopa* (Western Peru), p. 19; *O. arenacea* (Columbia), *Chloronerpes dignus* (Columbia) (pl. i), p. 20; *Celeus subflavus* (Bahia), *Chamæpelia buckleyi* (Santa Rita, Rep. Æquat.), p. 21; *Crax erythrognatha*, p. 22.

1877. SCLATER, P. L., *and* SALVIN, O. Descriptions of six new Species of South-American Birds. < *P. Z. S.*, June 5, 1877, pp. 521-523, pl. lii.

Basileuterus castaneiceps, Euphonia insignis (pl. lii, f. 1), *Chlorospingus phœocephalus* (pl. lii, f. 2), p. 521; *Todirostrum rufigene, Lathria cryptolopha, Fuligula nationi*, p. 522, from collections made in Peru and Ecuador.

1877. SHARPE, R. B. Account of the Zoological Collection made during the visit of H. M. S. 'Petrel' to the Galapagos Islands. Communicated by Dr. Albert Günther, . . . < *P. Z. S.*, Feb. 6, 1877, pp. 64-93.

I. BIRDS. By R. Bowdler Sharpe, pp. 65, 66, 4 spp.; *Mimus parvulus, Dendrœca aureola, Geospiza fuliginosa, Pyrocephalus nanus.*

1877. TACZANOWSKI, L. Liste des Oiseaux recueillis au nord du Pérou occidental par MM. Jelski et Stolzmann. < *P. Z. S.*, 1877, pp. 319 - —, pl. xxxvi.

Not seen. (Part ii of this volume missing from my set.)

1877. TACZANOWSKI, L. Supplément à la Liste des Oiseaux recueillis au nord du Pérou occidental par MM. Jelski et Stolzmann. < *P. Z. S.*, Nov. 6, 1877, pp. 744-754.

Un séjour prolongé aux environs de Tumbez ayant procuré aux voyageurs plusieurs espèces qui n'étaient pas fournies dans les envois précédents (voir tome cit. pp. 319 - —), ces oiseaux sont ici indiqués, au nombre de 31; ce qui joint à 72 esp. de la liste précédente, fait en tout 103 espèces des environs de Tumbez qui n'étaient pas trouvées dans le Pérou central par M. Jelski.—*Penelope albipennis*, p. 746; *Rallus cypereti* Stolzm. MS., p. 747, spp. nn.

1878. BISHOP, N. H. Notes on the Illustrations in Don Juan Lembeye's "Birds of the Island of Cuba." < *Forest and Stream*, x, July 25, 1878, p. 482.

Very unfavorable to the author here criticised.

1878. BOUCARD, A. On Birds collected in Costa Rica. < *P. Z. S.*, Jan. 15, 1878, pp. 37-71, pl. iv.

This interesting paper gives notes, both field and critical, upon 258 spp. collected by the author himself during the five months spent in the country, with headquarters at San José, the capital. This is just half the total recorded number of Costa Rican birds, 520. Many varieties were secured, though only one novelty, as the ground had already been well worked over by several explorers, as set forth in the papers of Lawrence, Salvin, Cabanis, and others.—*Zonotrichia vulcani*, p. 57, pl. iv, sp. n.

1878. CABANIS, J. Ueber eine Sammlung von Vögeln der Argentinischen Republik. < *J. f. O.*, Apr., 1878, pp. 194-199.

Da dieser Jahrgang gerade gebunden wurde, war es mir nicht möglich denselben einzusehen.

1878. DURNFORD, H. Notes on the Birds of the Province of Buenos Ayres. < *Ibis*, 4th ser., ii, 1878, pp. 58-69.

Not seen. (This volume of the *Ibis* is at the binder's.)

1878. DURNFORD, H. Notes on the Birds of Central Patagonia. < *Ibis*, 4th ser., ii, No. 8, Oct., 1878, pp. 389-406.

Not seen. (This volume of the *Ibis* is at the binder's.)

1878. [GRINNELL, G. B.] New Birds from the West Indies. < *Forest and Stream*, x, July 25, 1878, p. 483.

Comments upon recent collections by Fred. A. Ober.

1878. [GRINNELL, G. B.] Four New Birds from the West Indies. < *Forest and Stream*, xi, Aug. 8, 1878, p. 2.

Notice of F. A. Ober's collections.

1878. [GRINNELL, G. B.] Birds of Dominica and St. Vincent. < *Forest and Stream*, xi, Nov. 21, 1878, p. 320.

Notice of George N. Lawrence's catalogues of F. Ober's ornithological collections in the West Indies.

1878. [GRINNELL, G. B.] Frederick A. Ober ("Fred Beverly.") < *Forest and Stream*, xi, Nov. 21, 1878, p. 327.

Portrait and brief biographical notice.

1878. GUNDLACH, J. Neue Beiträge zur Ornithologie der Insel Portorico. < *J. f. O.*, Apr., 1878, pp. 157–194.

Dieses Buch befindet sich beim Buchbinder und ist mir deshalb nicht zugänglich.

1878. LAWRENCE, G. N. Descriptions of Seven New Species of Birds from the Island of St. Vincent, West Indies. < *Ann. N. Y. Acad. Sci.*, i, No. 5, June, 1878, pp. 147–153.

Turdus nigrirostris, Myiadestes sibilans, Thryothorus musicus, Certhiola atrata, C. saccharina, Leucopeza bishopi, Calliste versicolor. Cf. *Ibis*, Oct., 1878, p. 468; *Bull. Nutt. Ornith. Club*, iv, 1879, pp. 48, 49.

1878. LAWRENCE, G. N. Descriptions of Supposed New Species of Birds from the Islands of Grenada and Dominica, West Indies. < *Ann. N. Y. Acad. Sci.*, i, July, 1878, pp. 160–163.

Turdus caribœus (Grenada), *Thryothorus grenadensis* (Grenada), *Blacicus brunneicapillus* (Dominica), *Quiscalus luminosus* (Grenada). Cf. *Bull. Nutt. Ornith. Club*, iv, Jan., 1879, pp. 48, 49.

1878. LAWRENCE, G. N. Catalogue of the Birds of Dominica from Collections made for the Smithsonian Institution by Frederick A. Ober, together with his Notes and Observations. < *Proc. U. S. Nat. Mus.*, vol. i, 1878, (pub. July, 1878), pp. 48–69.

Fully annotated list of 59 spp.; collector's field-notes and sketch of the locality; author's critical commentary. *Vireosylvia calidris* var. *dominicana*, p. 55; *Strix flammea* var. *nigrescens*, p. 64, varr. nn. Cf. *Bull. Nutt. Ornith. Club*, iv, Jan., 1879, pp. 48, 49.

1878. LAWRENCE, G. N. Catalogue of the Birds of St. Vincent, from Collections made by Mr. Fred. A. Ober, under the Direction of the Smithsonian Institution, with his Notes thereon. < *Proc. U. S. Nat. Mus.*, vol. i, 1878, (pub. Oct., 1878), pp. 185–198.

Treats of 59 spp., 3 undetermined, with collector's field-notes and sketch of the island; author's critical commentary on several of the species. Seven new species of this collection were described just previously, in *Ann. N. Y. Acad. Sci.*, 1878, *q. v.* Cf. *Bull. Nutt. Ornith. Club*, iv, 1879 pp. 48, 49.

1878. LAWRENCE, G. N. Catalogue of the Birds of Antigua and Barbuda, from Collections made for the Smithsonian Institution, by Mr. Fred A. Ober, with his Observations. < *Proc. U. S. Nat. Mus.*, vol. i, 1878, (pub. Dec., 1878), pp. 232–242.

From Antigua, 42 spp.; from Barbuda, 39 spp.; both lists fully annotated by Mr. Ober, with his field-notes. *Speotyto amaura*, p. 234, sp. n.

1878. PELZELN, A. V. Weitere Sendungen von Vögeln aus Ecuador. < *Verh. (Abh.) d. k.-k. zool.-bot. Gesellsch. zu Wien*, —, 1878, pp. 15–20.

Nicht selbst gesehen: Titel aus Ridgway's MS. citirt. Unter den beschriebenen interessanten Arten befinden sich *Urochroa bougueri, Urosticte ruficrissa, Bourcieria insectivora* und *Cyanocitta pulchra. Chlorochrysa sodiroi* sp. n. = *C. phœnicotis* ♀; cf. *Ibis*, 1878, pp. 478, 479.

1878. SCLATER, P. L., *and* SALVIN, O. On the Collection of Birds made by Prof. Steere in South America. < *P. Z. S.*, Feb. 5, 1878, pp. 135–142, pll. (Aves) xi–xiii, woodcc.

Prof. Steere collected about 911 bird-skins, from Pará to Callao, belonging to about 362 spp., 22 of which furnish the occasion for remark in this paper. Among them is *Xema sabinii!*— *Myiarchus semirufus* (pl. xi), p. 138; *Furnarius pileatus*, p. 139; *Capito steerii* (pl. xii), p. 140; *Crypturus transfasciatus* (pl. xiii), p. 141, spp. nn.

1878. SCLATER, P. L., *and* SALVIN, O. Reports on the Collections of Birds made during the voyage of H. M. S. 'Challenger.'—No. IX. On the Birds of Antarctic America. < *P. Z. S.*, Apr. 16, 1878, pp. 431–438.

Report on 41 spp. collected on the voyage from Juan Fernandez, along the coast of Patagonia, to the Falklands. It is little more than a list of the specimens, with collector's notes, though some technic occurs.

1878. SCLATER, P. L., *and* SALVIN, O. Descriptions of three new Species of Birds from Ecuador. < *P. Z. S.*, Apr. 16, 1878, pp. 438–440, pll. (Aves) xxvii, xxviii.

Buarremon leucopis, Neomorphus radiolosus, pl. xxvii, *Aramides calopterus*, pl. xxviii, p. 439.

1878. SPENCE, J. M.   The Land of Bolivar, or War, Peace, and Adventure in the Republic of Venezuela.   With maps and illustrations.   . . .   London: Sampson Low & Co.   1878.   2 vols.   8vo.

Not seen: contains a catalogue of birds, reprinted from *P. Z. S.*, 1873, pp. 511, 512.

1879. A[LLEN], J. A.   Lawrence and Ober on the Birds of Dominica and St. Vincent. < *Bull. Nutt. Ornith. Club*, iv, No. 1, Jan., 1879, pp. 48, 49.

Notices of five of G. N. Lawrence's recent papers on F. A. Ober's collections in the Lesser Antilles, in *Ann. N. Y. Acad.* and *Proc. Nat. Mus.*

1879. LAWRENCE, G. N.   Catalogue of the Birds of Grenada, from a Collection made by Mr. Fred. A. Ober for the Smithsonian Institution, including others seen by him, but not obtained.   < *Proc. U. S. Nat. Mus.*, vol. i, 1878, (pub. Feb., 1879), pp. 265–278.

Grenada, one of the Lesser Antillian Islands, about 12° N., 18½ miles long by 7½ broad.   Mr. Ober's general remarks on the island, and his field-notes in the body of the article.   Treats of 54 spp., represented in the collection by 66 specimens.   *Vireosylvia calidris* var. *dominicana*, p. 268; *Strix flammea* var. *nigrescens*, p. 273, varr. nn.?

1879. LAWRENCE, G. N.   Catalogue of the Birds collected in Martinique by Mr. Fred. A. Ober for the Smithsonian Institution.   < *Proc. U. S. Nat. Mus.*, vol. i, 1878, (pub. Mar. 10, 1879), pp. 349–360.

Sketch of Martinique by Mr. Ober, and his copious field-notes throughout the list of 40 spp.   Important note on *Dendrœca rufigula* Baird, p. 353, and on *Quiscalus inflexirostris* Swains., p. 356.   *Myiarchus sclateri*, p. 357, sp. n.

1879. LAWRENCE, G. N.   Catalogue of a Collection of Birds obtained in Guadeloupe for the Smithsonian Institution, by Mr. Fred. A. Ober.   < *Proc. U. S. Nat. Mus.*, vol. i, 1878, (pub. Apr. 22, 1879), pp. 449–462.

Of the same characters as previous papers of this series.   Mr. Ober collected in Guadeloupe in August and September, 1878, sending in 132 specimens, and noting 45 spp.

1879. LAWRENCE, G. N.   A General Catalogue of the Birds noted from the Islands of the Lesser Antilles visited by Mr. Fred. A. Ober; with a Table showing their Distribution and those found in the United States.   < *Proc. U. S. Nat. Mus.*, vol. i, 1878, (pub. 1879), pp. 486–488.

A *résumé* of the preceding catalogues in tabular form.   All these papers of Mr. Lawrence's are also published separately, same pagination, with cover and new title-page.

ADDENDA.

I continue with a few titles acquired during the impression of the preceding pages.

1625. DE LAET, J.   Nieuwe Wereldt | ofte | Beschrijvinghe | van | West-Indien, | wt veelerhande Schriften ende Aen-teekeningen | van verscheyden Natien by eenversamelt | Door Ioannes de Laet, | Ende met Noodighe Kaerten en Tafels voorsien. | Tot Leyden, | In de Druckerye van Isaack Elzevier. | Anno 1625. | Met Privilege der Ho. Mo. Heeren Staten Generael, voor 12 Jaren. | Folio. pp. (2), xxii, 526, maps.

Not seen: title from Sabin's *Bibl.*   See ed. of 1630.

1630. DE LAET, J.   Beschrijvinghe | van | West-Indien | door Ioannes de Laet. | Tweede Druck: | In ontallijcke plaetsen ver- | betert, vermeerdert, met eenige nieuwe Caerten, beelden van | verscheyden dieren ende | planten verciert. | Tot Leyden, bij de Elzeviers.   A°. 1630. | Met Priuilegie.   1 vol.   Folio. 14 p. ll., incl. half-title, eng. title, dedication, privilege, introduction, contents, list of (14) maps, and errata, pp. 1–622, 9 ll. (index), maps and other illustrations.

Orig. ed. 1625.   This is the only edition of the famous work I have seen; I cite several others from Sabin's *Bibl.*

1633. DE LAET, J.   Novvs Orbis | seu | Descriptionis | Indiæ Occidentalis—Libri XVIII. | Authore | Ioanne de Laet Antverp. | Novis Tabulis Geographicis et variis | Animantium, Plantarum Fructuumque | Iconibus illustrati. | Cvm Privilegio. | Lvgd. Batav. apud Elsevirios. Aº. 1633. 1 vol. Folio. 16 p. ll. incl. half-title, eng. title, and list of (14) maps, pp. 1–690, 9 ll. (index).

1640. DE LAET, J.   L'Histoire | dv | Nouveau Monde | ou | description | des Indes Occidentales, | Contenant dix-huict Liures, | Par le Sieur Iean de Laet, d'Anuers; | Enrichi de nouuelles Tables Geographiques & Figures des | Animaux, Plantes & Fruicts. | [Dessin.] | A Leyde, | Chez Bonauenture & Abraham Elseuiers, Imprimeurs | ordinaires de l'Vniuersité. | — | cIↃ IↃc XL. 1 vol. Folio. 14 p. ll., pp. 1–632, 6 ll., 14 maps.

"This French translation of Laet contains many materials not found in the original Dutch, . . . This work is full of the most excellent and curious details of the natural history, . . ."

1682. NIEUHOF, J.   Johan Nieuhofs | Gedenkweerdige | Brasiliaense | Zee- en Lant- | Reize. | Behelzende | Al het geen op dezelve is voorgevallen. | Beneffens | Een bondige beschrijving van gantsch | Neerlants Brasil, | Zoo van lantschappen, steden, dieren, gewassen, als | draghten, zeden en godsdienst der inwoonders: | En inzonderheit | Een wijtloopig verhael der merkwaardigste voorvallen | en geschiedenissen, die zich, geduurende zijn negenjarigh | verblijf in Brasil, in d'oorlogen en opstant der Portugesen | tegen d' onzen, zich sedert het jaer 1640. tot 1649. | hebben toegedragen. | Doorgaens verciert met verscheide afbeeldingen, na 't leven aldaer getekent. | [Afbeeld.] | t' Amsterdam, | — | Voor de Weduwe van Jacob van Meurs, op de Keizers-gracht. 1682. 1 vol. Folio. Eng. title, illum. title, dedication, arms, privilege, introduction, each one leaf; pp. 1–308, 2 ll. (directions to binder, and index); 44 engravings.

See what is said anteà, p. 241. In addition to this, there is on p. 281 a heading "Indiaense en Javaense vogels en viervoetige dieren"; under which descriptions of various East Indian and particularly Javan birds run to p. 288, including two engravings on which the Dodo and various other birds are figured.

The above is the full printed title. The work is scarcely citable in the present connection, being of a more general character.

1724. [LABAT, Père J. B.]   Nouveau | Voyage | [du Père Jean Baptiste Labat] | aux Isles | de l'Amerique. | Contenant | L'Histoire Naturelle de ces Pays, | l'Origine, les Mœurs, la Religion & le Gouvernement des | Habitans anciens & modernes: | Les Guerres & les Evenemens singuliers qui y sont arrivez pendant | le long séjour que l'Auteur y a fait: | le Commerce et les Manufactures | qui y sont établies, & les moyens de les augmenter. | Ouvrage enrichi d'un grand nombre de Cartes, Plans, & Figures en Taille-douce. | Tome premier [second]. | [Vignette.] | A la Haye, | Chez ⟨ P. Husson.   T. Johnson. ⟩ ⟨ J. Van Duren. R. Alberts. ⟩ P. Gosse & C. Le Vier. | M. DCC. xxiv. 2 vols. 4to. Vol. I, 3 p. ll., pp. j–viij, 1–360, 2 ll., 47 maps and plates. Vol. II, 4 p. ll., pp. 1–520, 9 ll., many maps and plates.

There are many editions. Sabin's Bibl. gives the following, besides the above:—Paris, 6 vols., 12mo. 1722.—La Haye, 6 vols., 12mo, 1724.—Paris, 8 vols., 12mo, 1742; augmented.—Paris, 8vo, 1831; abridged.—Dutch, Amsterdam, 4 vols., 4to, 1725.—Latin, Nürnberg, 7 vols., 12mo, 1782–88.

The celebrated work is very full on the Natural History of the West Indies, and ornithology comes in for its share of treatment; but the copious details are so scattered through the volumes that formal citation of the bird-matter becomes inconvenient.

1745. WARREN, G.   Impartial Description of Surinam, &c.

The date of the original is said to be 1667. The only shape in which I have handled it is as a part of Vol. II of Osborne's "A Collection of Voyages and Travels", etc., folio, London, 1745, where it is given with a half-title-page as follows:—An impartial | Description | of | Surinam | upon the | Continent of Guinea | in | America. | With a | History of several strange

1745. WARREN, G.—Continued.

Beasts, Birds, Fishes, Serpents, In- | sects, and Customs of that Colony, &c. | Worthy the Perusal of all, from the Experience of | George Warren, Gent. | pp. 919-931. Chap. IV. Of the Birds; p. 924, a column of remarks, of no consequence.

1765. FERMIN, P. Histoire | Naturelle | de la | Hollande Equinoxiale: | ou | Description | des Animaux, Plantes, Fruits, et autres | Curiosite's Naturelles, qui se trouvent | dans la colonie de | Surinam; | avec Leurs Noms différents, tant François, que Latins, | Hollandois, Indiens & Négre-Anglois. | Par | Philippe Fermin, | Docteur en Medicine. | [Vignette.] A Amsterdam, | Chez M. Magérus, Libraire. MDCCLXV. 1 vol. 8vo. pp. i-xii, 1-240, 1 l.

Seconde Partie, Des Oiseaux, Poissons, et Testacées, pp. 57-108, where a few birds, fishes, and mollusks are given in alphabetical order, mixed together, with slight descriptions, or definitions of the names, of each.

1782. [PALLAS, P. S.] Beschreibung zweyer südamerikanischer merkwürdiger Vögel. < *Neue Nordische Beyträge*, iii, 1782, pp. 1-7, pl. i.

1. Der kleine schwarze Kukuk aus Surinam (*Cuculus tenebrosus*), p. 2, pl. i, f. 1. 2. Der allerkleinste Specht oder Wendehals, aus Südamerika (*Picus minutissimus*), p. 5, pl. i, f. 2.

1793. WEST, H. Bidrag | til | beskrivelse | over Ste Croix | med en | kort Udsigt | over | St. Thomas, St. Jean, Tortola, | Spanishtown og Crabeneiland. | Af | H. West, | Rector ved det vestindiske Skole-Institut. | — | Kiöbenhavn, 1793. . | Trykt hos Frederik Wilhelm Thiele. 1 vol. 16mo. 3 p. ll., 1-364, folded sheet opp. p. 204.

This is the *ed. princ.;* there is another, German, Kopenhagen, 1794. The only bird-matter consists of a list of 2 spp., on p. 317—*Ardea coerulea* and *Fulica chloropus* (= *Gallinula galeata*).

1810. LEDRU, A.-P. Voyage | aux Iles | de Ténériffe, | La Trinité, Saint-Thomas, | Sainte-Croix et Porto-Ricco, | exécuté par ordre du Gouvernement Français, | Depuis le 30 Septembre 1796 jusqu'au 7 Juin 1798, sous la | Direction du Capitaine Baudin, pour faire des Recherches | et des Collections relatives à l'Histoire Naturelle; | contenant | Des Observations sur le Climat, le Sol, la | Population, | l'Agriculture, les Productions de ces Iles, le Caractère, les | Mœurs et le Commerce de leurs Habitants. | Par André-Pierre Ledru, | [etc., trois lignes.] | Ouvrage accompagné de notes et d'additions, | par M. Sonnini. | Avec une très-belle Carte gravée par J. B. Tardieu, d'après Lopez. | Tome premier [second]. | A Paris, | Chez Arthur Bertrand, Libraire, rue Haute feuille, no 23. | — | 1810. 2 vols. 16mo. Vol. I, 2 p. ll., pp. i-xlviij, 1-315, 1 l. Vol. II, 2 p. ll., pp. 1-324, 1 l., map.

Vol. I, Chap. XIII, Essai sur l'histoire naturelle de l'île de Ténériffe, pp. 176 et seq. Oiseaux, pp. 177-185, par l'auteur. Notes sur les animaux dont il est question dans le chapitre précédent, par Sonnini, pp. 219-231. Note sur le Pélecan, par Sonnini, pp. 245, 246. Chap. XVI, Notice sur l'île de la Trinité, par l'auteur, pp. 247 et seq. Oiseaux, pp. 258-261. Notes sur l'histoire, et particulièrement sur l'histoire naturelle de l'île de la Trinité, par Sonnini, pp. 267 et seq. Oiseaux, pp. 296-307.—Vol. II, Chap. XIX, Essai sur l'histoire naturelle des îles danoises, pp. 36 et seq. Oiseaux, pp. 38, 39. Chap. XXVIII, Histoire naturelle de Porto-Ricco, pp. 194 et seq. Oiseaux, pp. 199-209. Addition à l'histoire naturelle de Porto-Ricco, par Sonnini, pp. 255 et seq. Oiseaux, pp. 256-274.

1811. HUMBOLDT, A. v. Recueil d'Observations de Zoologie. 1811.

Not seen; said to contain a few brief notices of the birds of Colombia.

1811-12. LEDRU, A.-P. Reise nach den Inseln Ténériffa, Trinidad, St. Thomas, St. Cruz, und Porto-Rico, . . . Aus dem Französischen, mit Bemerkungen über Colonialwaaren von E. A. W. Zimmermann. Leipzig, 1811-12. 2 vols. 8vo.

Not seen: title from Sabin's *Bibl.*

1823-31. SPIX, J. B. v., *and* MARTIUS, C. F. P. v. Reise | in | Brasilien | auf Befehl Sr. Majestät | Maximilian Joseph I. | Königs von Baiern | in den Jahren 1817 bis 1820 gemacht und beschrieben | von | Dr. Joh. Bapt. von Spix, | [etc., 3 Zeilen,] | und Dr. Carl Friedr. Phil. von Martius, | [etc., 3 Zeilen.] | Erster

1823-31. SPIX, J. B. v., *and* MARTIUS, C. F. P. v.—Continued.

[-dritter] Theil. | — | München, 1823 [1828, 1831]. . . . 3 vols. 4to.—
Erster Theil, München, 1823, gedruckt bei M. Lindauer, 4 p. ll., pp. i-x, 1–412.
Zweiter Theil, bearbeitet und herausgegchen von Dr. C. F. P. von Martius,
München, 1828, gedruckt bei I. J. Leutner, pp. i-viii, 413–884, 1 l.   Dritter
Theil, bearb. u. herausg. von Dr. C. F. P. von Martius, München, 1831, bei
dem Verfasser, Leipzig, in Comm. bei Friedr. Fleischer, pp. i-viii, 885–1388,
geographischer Anhang, 1 p. l., pp. 1–40, und Karte vom Amazonenstrome.

> The copy examined contains no formal presentation of the ornithology, and only one map.
> There is an English translation of a portion of the work, 1824, *q. v.* The natural history
> is said to be contained in a special appendix to Theil III, and to be also found separate under
> the title „Die Pflanzen und Thiere des tropischen America" u. s. w., München, 1831, gr.4to
> mit 4 Taf. in-folio.

1824. SPIX, J. B. v., *and* MARTIUS, C. F. P. v.   Travels | in | Brazil, | in the years |
1817-1820. | Undertaken by command of | His Majesty the King of Bavaria. |
By | Dr. Joh. Bapt. von Spix, | and Dr. C. F. Phil. von Martius, | [etc., 3
lines.] | — | Volume the first [second]. | — | London: | printed for | Long-
man, Hurst, Rees, Orme, Brown, and Green, | Paternoster-row. | 1824.   2 vols.
in 1.   8vo.   Vol. I, pp. iii-xxii, 1–327, 4 pll.   Vol. II, pp. iii-x, 1–298, 5 pll.

> This is an English translation of *portions* of Spix and Martius's *Reise*, not of the whole
> work, which was not completed until 1831. It does not contain the natural history proper of
> the work, which is in the concluding part of the German work; only giving some little bird-
> matter incidentally, here and there. (See this Bibliography, *anteà*, p. 250, at date of 1823-31.)

1831. WAGNER, J. A.   Beiträge | zur | Kenntniss der warmblütigen Wirbelthiere |
Amerika's. | Von | Professor Dr. Johann Andreas Wagner. | [n. d., n. p.
Kempten, 1831.] 1 vol.   4to.   pp. 94, pll. v.

> Diese mit Halbtitel versehene Broschüre enthält : Osteographische Beiträge zur Kenntniss
> einiger südamerikanischen Vögel. I. *Crypturus variegatus*, pp. 56–66, pl. iii, f. 1–6. II. *Dicho-*
> *lophus cristatus*, pp. 66–72, pl. iii, f. 7–11. III. *Psophia crepitans*, pp. 72–77, pl. iv, f. 1–4.
> IV. *Mycteria americana*, pp. 77–83, pl. iv, f. 5–7.

1831-35. KITTLITZ, F. H. v.   Über einige Vögel von Chili, beobachtet im März und
Anfang April 1827.   < *Mém. présentés à l'Acad. Imp. des Sci. de St.-Pétersb. par*
divers Savans Étrang., i, 1831, pp. 173–194, pll. — ?; ii, 1835, pp. 465–472, pll.
1–5.   (Auch als Separat-Abdruck erschienen.)

> I. 1831.—*Phytotoma silens*, p. 175; *Pteroptochos rubecula*, p. 179; *P. albicollis*, p. 180; *P.*
> *megapodius*, p. 182; *Troglodytes paradoxus*, p. 184; *Synnalaxis* [sic] *humicola*, p. 185; *S.*
> *aegithaloides*, p. 187; *Opetiorynchos* [sic] *rupestris*, p. 188; *Muscicapa parulus*, p. 190; *M.*
> *pyrope*, p. 191; *Fringilla diuca* (Mol.), p. 192; *Crypturus perdicarius*, p. 193. (Title calls for
> 12 colored plates; no plates found in copy examined.)
> II. 1835.—13, *Tamnophilus* [sic] *lividus*, p. 465, pl. 1; 14, *Sturnus aterrimus*, p. 467, pl. 2;
> 15, *Alauda fissirostris*, p. 468, pl. 3; 16, *Fringilla arvensis*, p. 470, pl. 4; 17, *Anas chalcoptera*,
> pl. 471, pl. 5 (lettered *chalcontera*).
> *Obs.* This reference is often misquoted as if it were to the regular *Mém. de l'Acad. St.-*
> *Pétersb.*

1833. SCHREIBER, [C. v.]   Collectanea ad Faunam Braziliæ.

> Not seen. "M. Schreiber of Vienna commenced, in 1833, the 'Collectanea ad Faunam Bra-
> ziliæ', but only one number of that work was ever published."

1834. LESSON, R. P.   Sur quelques Oiseaux du Chili.   < *L'Institut*, ii, 1834, No. 72,
p. 316.   (Soc. des Sc. et Arts de Rochefort.)

> Not seen: title from Carus and Engelmann.

1834-41. SWAINSON, W.   The | Ornithological | Drawings | of | William Swainson |
Esq., A. C. G. | [etc., 4 lines.] | — | Part 5 [mut. mut.]. | The Birds of Brazil.
| — | London: | Baldwin & Cradock. | Treuttel. Würtz & Richter Paris, &
Strasbourgh. | Oliver & Boyd, Edinburgh Robinson's Liverpool. | Robᵗ.
Havell, 77, Oxford Stᵗ.   Price 7/.   Cold. 10/6.   Double Plates 15/. | [n. d.
"1834-1841."]   8vo.   Engr. cover-title and 62 ("78") colored plates.   "Pub.
in 7 parts."

> The piece handled consists of 62 colored plates, without any text, there being only the en-
> graved cover-title above transcribed. It is not dated; but there is pencilled in msc. of T. N.

1834–41. SWAINSON, W.—Continued.

Gill a date, "1834–1841"; and the same hand notes on the fly-leaf "Part 6 wanting", leaving it open to infer that there are several lots or "Parts". The number of Part "5" is also written, not printed; so that probably the same engraved title covers other parts. The dates above cited are presumed to be those of publication of the whole series. The plates are as follows; I do not know that these 62 (some cite "78") are all of them:—Pl. 1, *I[cterus] hæmorrhous.* 2, *C[assicus] affinis.* 3, *C. icteronotus.* 4, *C. nigerrimus.* 5, Blueheaded Tanager, "*A.*" *cyanocephala.* 6, *A. citrinella.* 7, *A. cuculata.* 8, *A. cyanoptera.* 9, Long-billed Puff Bird, "*T[amatia?]*" *somnolenta.* 10, *T. leucotis.* 11, *T. maculata.* 12, *T. leucops.* 13, *T[roglo-dytes] æquinoctialis.* 14, *T. carinatus.* 15, *T. nititans.* 16, *Thryothorus striolatus.* 17, Black-masked Tanager, *R[hampho . . . ?] gularis.* 18, *R. coccineus.* 19, same, ♀. 20, *R. atro-cocci-neus.* 21, *T[rochilus] cristatus.* 22, *T. delalandii.* 23, *P[ipra] galeata.* 24, *Calyptura cristata.* 25, *P[ipra] strigilata.* 26, *Pepra* [sic] *manacus.* 27, Mango Hummingbird, young. 28, *L[am-pornis] mango.* 29, *T[rochilus] auritus.* 30, *T. moschitus.* 31, Black-backed Tanager, "*A.*" *melanotus* Sw. 32, *C[assicus] cristatus.* 33, *Lochmias squamulata* Sw. 34, *Lypornix striata.* 35, *L. rubicula.* 36, *L. tenebrosa.* 37, *T[anagra] cana* Sw. 38, *T. olivascens* Licht. 39, *T. epis-copus.* 40, *T. mornata* [sic—lege *inornata*]. 41, *T. cœlestes.* 42, *T. ornata.* 43, Black-backed Tanager, "*A.*" *melanotis* [sic—lege *melanonotus*]. 44, *Pipra pareola.* 45, *P. caudata.* 46, *Ty-rannula superciliosa.* 47, *T. megacephala.* 48, *T. modesta.* 49, *T. caniceps.* 50, *Tyrannus circumcinctus.* 51, *Megalophus regius.* 52, same. 53, *Tyrannula ferruginea.* 54, *T. curtipes.* 55, *Platyurus corniculatus.* 56, same, ♀. 57, *P. affinis.* 58, *Cyclarius* [sic] *guianensis.* 59, *Thamnophilus nævius.* 60, *T. bicolor.* 61, *Trogon auratus.* 62, same, ♀. The complete series is said to consist of 78 plates, published in 7 parts. Other titles of the same thing in current quotation are: "Ornithological Drawings, being figures of the rarer and most interesting Birds of Brazil"; and "A selection of the Birds of Brazil and Mexico."

1836. KITTLITZ, F. H. v. Cinq nouvelles espèces d'Oiseaux du Chili. < *L'Institut,* iv, No. 190, 1836, p. 442.

Not seen: title from Carus and Engelmann. Compare 1831–35, same author. See, also, *Isis,* 1836, pp. 347–351.

1843. GOUDOT, J. Observations sur l'organisation et les habitudes du coq de roche péruvien (Pipra peruviana, Lath.), et du caurale (Ardea helias, Lin.). < *Guér. Mag. de Zool.,* 2e sér., 1843, Ois., pp. 1–4, pll. 37, 38.

Pl. 37, œuf du *Rupicola peruviana;* pl. 38, œuf de l'*Eurypyga phalenoïdes.*

1848. SCHOMBURGK, R. H. The | History of Barbadoes; | comprising | a geographical and statistical | description of the Island; | a sketch of the | historical events since the settlement; | and an account of its | geology and natural productions. | By | Sir Robert H. Schomburgk, Ph. D., [etc., 6 lines.] | [Seal.] | London: | Longman, Brown, Green and Longmans. | 1848. 1 vol. Roy. 8vo. pp. i–xxii, 1–722, frontisp., eng. title, 7 other plates, 13 woodcc., folding sheet opp. p. 686.

Part III, Chap. V, Animated Nature as developed in the Barbadoes, ... Birds, pp. 680–682; an inconsiderable list, preceded by a few general observations.

1863. PHILIPPI, R. A., *and* **LANDBECK, L.** Beschreibung einer neuen Ente und einer neuen Seeschwalbe. < *Arch. f. Naturg.,* —, 1863, pp. 202 – —.

Not seen.—*Querquedula angustirostris, Sterna atrofasciata,* aus Südamerika.

1866. [GUYON, —.] Ueber die Thiere, die auf den Inseln Martinique und Guade-loupe seit der Besitznahme durch die Franzosen verschwunden sind. < *Aus der Natur,* xxxviii, oder n. F. xxvi, 1866, pp. 730–733.

Auszug aus den *Compt. Rend.,* lxiii, 1866, pp. 589–593.

INDEX.

A.—AUTHORS.

[NOTE.—With catch-titles. Chronological arrangement under each head. Joint-authorships under leading name. Figures refer to dates under which titles are alphabetized: double dates are found in the Bibliography at end of series of single dates; thus, 1877–78 at end of 1877. Anonymous, pseudonymous, editorial, and initial titles mostly omitted.]

ABBOTT, C. C.
Notes on Birds of the Falkland Islands, 1860, 1861.

ABBOTT, S. L.
Remarks on Birds from Surinam, 1844.

ALBRECHT.
Zur Ornithologie Cuba's, 1861.
Zur Ornithologie von Jamaica, 1862.

ALLEN.
Exploration of Lake Titicaca, 1876.
Review of Lawrence's Papers, 1876.
Birds collected by Linden in Brazil, 1877.

ARBOLEYA.
Manual de la Isla de Cuba, 1852.

AZARA.
Apuntamientos, 1802–05, 1809.

BAIRD.
List of Birds of Mexico, Central and South America not in Smithsonian Institution, 1863.
Dates of Publication of Anales Univ. Chile and Arch. f. Naturg., 1866.

BANCROFT.
Natural History of Guiana, 1769, 1769.

BATES.
Naturalist on the Amazon, 1863, 1864.

BECKLEMICHEW.
Deux Oiseaux Nouveaux du Brésil, 1829.

BELL.
Wildfowl of Jamaica, 1868.

BELLO Y ESPINOSA.
Zoologische Notizen aus Porto Rico, 1871.

BENVENUTI.
Descrizione di quattro Trochilidi e di una Dendroeca, 1866.

BERLEPSCH.
Zur Ornith. der Provinz Sta. Catharina, 1873–74.

BERNSÉE.
On Birds of the East Falklands, 1855.

BISHOP.
The Pampas and Andes, 1869.
Notes on Lembeye's 'Birds', 1878.

BOECK.
Über die Ornis der Provinz Valdivia, 1855.

BOISSONNEAU.
Oiseaux Nouveaux de Santa-Fé de Bogota, 1840, 1840.

BOLLE.
Guano-Gewinnung auf den Chincha-Inseln, 1861.

BONAPARTE.
Descriptions of Ten South American Birds, 1825.
Notes to former paper, 1825.
Catalogue Méthodique des Oiseaux recueillis à Cayenne par Desplanches, 1857.
Notices and Descriptions of Birds from Mexico and South America, 1837.
Catalogo di Uccelli Messicani e Peruviani, 1838.
Catalogue d'Oiseaux du Mexique et du Pérou, 1840.

BONYAN.
On Raptorial Birds of British Guiana, 1851, 1853.

BOUCARD.
On Birds collected in Costa Rica, 1878.

BREDOW.
Auszüge aus den Schreiben des reisenden C. Moritz in Süd-Amerika, 1837.

BREWER.
List of Birds of Cuba, 1859.

BRIDGES.
Notes on Birds from Chile, 1841.
Notice of Bolivian Birds, 1846.
Additional Notes on South American Ornithology, 1847, 1847.

BROWN, C. B.
Canoe and Camp Life in British Guiana, 1876.

BROWNE, P.
Jamaica, 1756, 1789.
BRYANT.
On Two Birds from Bogota, 1859.
Vögel von Porto Rico, 1866.
List of Birds from Porto Rico presented by Swift and Latimer, 1866.
List of the Birds of St. Domingo, 1867.
BURMEISTER.
Ueber die Eier und Nester einiger brasilianischer Vögel, 1853.
Systematische Uebersicht der Thiere Brasiliens, 1856.
Erläuterungen zur Fauna Bras., 1856.
Briefliches aus Mendoza, 1858.
Systematisches Verz. der in den La Plata Staaten beobachteten Vögel, 1860.
Reise durch die La Plata Staaten, 1861.
Contrib. to the Ornithology of the Argentine Republic, 1868.
CABANIS.
Tschudi's Fauna Peruana, 1845–46.
Schomburgk's Reisen in Britisch Guiana, 1848.
Uebersicht der im Berliner Mus. befindlichen Vögel von Costa Rica, 1861–69.
Neue peruanische Vögel Jelski's, 1873, 1873.
Uebers. der von Euler in Cantagallo, Rio de Janeiro, ges. Vögel, 1874.
Neue peruanische Vögel Jelski's, 1874.
Sammlung von Vögeln der Argentinischen Republik, 1878.
CABOT.
New Birds from Yucatan, 1843.
Descr. and Habits of some Birds of Yucatan, 1844.
Further Accounts of Birds of Yucatan, 1845.
Himantopus nigricollis and Anhinga carolinensis, 1845.
Stephens's Incidents of Travel in Yucatan, 1848.
CASSIN.
Gilliss's U. S. Naval Astron. Exped., 1855.
Cat. of Birds collected by Swift in St. Thomas, 1860.
Page's La Plata, etc., 1859.
Catalogue of Birds collected during survey for a Ship Canal across Isthmus of Darien, 1860.
Catalogue of Birds from St. Thomas, 1860.
Notes on some Birds of South America, 1864.

CASSIN.—Continued.
On some Conirostral Birds from Costa Rica, 1865.
CASTELNAU.
Considérations sur l'Ornith. de l'Amér. tropicale, 1848, 1848, 1848.
CLAYTON.
Account of the Falkland Islands, 1776.
CONDAMINE.
Voyage dans l'Amérique mérid., 1749.
CORNALIA.
Vertebratorum Synopsis, etc., 1849.
COPE.
Birds of Palestine and Panama, 1868.
CUNNINGHAM.
Letters on South American Ornithology, 1868.
Letters on Birds of Straits of Magellan, 1869.
Notes on the Nat. Hist. of Straits of Magellan and Patagonia, 1870.
Fauna of the Strait of Magellan, 1871.
DE LAET.
Nieuwe Wereldt, 1625, (p. 305).
Beschrijvinghe van West-Indien, 1625, (p. 305).
Novvs Orbis, 1633, (p. 306).
L'Histoire dv Nouv. Monde, 1640, (p. 306).
DES MURS.
Quelques espèces nouvelles d'Oiseaux, 1845.
Ois. nouv. ou rares de l'Amér. du Sud, 1855 or 1856.
Expéd. de M. Castelnau, 1856.
DENNY.
Geographical Distribution of West Indian Birds, 1847.
DESCOURTILZ.
Ornithologie Brasilienne, 1854–56.
DE VERTEUIL.
Trinidad, 1858.
DEVILLE.
Ois. nouv. de l'Amér. mérid., 1849.
Quatre Ois. nouv. provenant de l'Expéd. de M. Castelnau, 1851.
Observations faites en Amérique, etc., 1852.
DOBRIZHOFFER.
Historia de Abiponibus, 1784, 1822.
DUBUS.
Ueber einige neue Vögel aus Amerika, 1848.
Quelques Ois. nouveaux, 1875.
DURNFORD.
Notes from Buenos Ayres, 1876.

DURNFORD.—Continued.

Birds observed in the Chuput Valley, 1877.

Birds of the Province of Buenos Ayres, 1877, 1878.

Birds of Central Patagonia, 1878.

ERNST.

Apuntos para la fauna ornitológica de Venezuela, 1870.

Flora y Fauna de Venezuela, 1877.

EULER.

Beob. zur Naturg. der Vögel Brasiliens, 1867–69.

FAHLBERG.

Til Natural-Historien öfver ön St. Barthelemi, 1786.

FERMIN.

Hist. Nat. de la Hollande Equinoxiale, 1765, (p. 307).

FÉRUSSAC.

Voyage de M. A. d'Orbigny, 1829.

FINSCH.

Collection of Birds from Trinidad, 1870.

FISCHER.

Sur les Oiseaux envoyés par M. Coffrane de Bahia, 1830.

FRANTZIUS.

Ueber die geogr. Verbreitung der Vögel Costarica's, 1869.

FRASER.

New Birds from Bogota, 1840.

Bridges's South American Birds, 1843.

On Chilian Birds, 1845, 1845.

FRAUENFELD.

Ueber den Aufenthalt in Valparaiso, 1860.

GARDNER.

Notes of Birds in Brazil, 1847.

GARNOT.

Remarques sur la Zoologie des Isles Malouines, 1826.

Notice of the Zoology of the Falklands, 1827.

Ueber die Zoologie der Malvinen, 1832.

GAY.

Historia de Chile, 1847.

GERMAIN.

Notes on Nidification of some Birds of Chili, 1860.

GIEBEL.

Einige neue argentinische Vögel, 1868.

GODET.

Bermuda; its History, etc., 1860.

GOERING.

Excursion a algunas cuevas, 1869.

GOLZ.

Ueber die Guanolager Peru's, 1874.

GOSSE.

The Birds of Jamaica, 1847.

Extracts from Birds of Jamaica, 1847.

Two new Birds from Jamaica, 1849.

Illustr. of the Birds of Jamaica, 1849.

Naturalist's Sojourn in Jamaica, 1851.

Singing Birds in Jamaica, 1851–52.

GOUDOT.

Sur le Coq de roche et le Caurale, 1843, (p. 309).

GOULD.

Sur des Oiseaux d'Amérique méridionale, 1834.

Polyborus gallapagoensis u. s. w., 1839.

Zoology of Voyage of the Beagle, 1841.

Exhibition of a collection by Hauxwell near the River Ucayali, 1855.

Eight new species from South America, 1855, 1855, 1856.

New Trogon and Odontophorus, 1857.

List of Birds from the Falklands, 1859.

[GRINNELL.]

Four papers on Lawrence's papers on Ober's Birds from West Indies, 1878.

GUNDLACH.

Five new Cuban Birds, 1852.

Notes on Cuban Birds, with three new species, 1858.

Ornithologisches aus Cuba, 1859.

Tabellarische Uebersicht aller bisher auf Cuba beobachteten Vögel, 1861.

Zusätze u. Berichtigungen zu seinen Beitr. Ornith. Cuba's, 1861–62.

Revista y Catálogo de las Aves Cubanas, 1865–66.

Briefliches von Cuba, 1866.

Neue Beit. zur Ornith. Cubas, 1871–74.

Beitrag zur Ornith. der Insel Portorico, 1874.

Neue Beiträge zur Ornith. Portorico, 1878.

GUNDLACH and CABANIS.

Beiträge zur Ornith. Cuba's, 1855–57.

GUYON.

Animaux disparus de la Martinique et de la Guadeloupe, 1866.

HABEL.

Exhibition of Birds from the Galapágoes, 1869.

HAMILTON.

Notes on Birds from São Paulo, Brazil, 1871.

HARTLAUB.

Quatre espèces d'Oiseaux de la N. Grenade, 1843.

Sept Oiseaux nouv. de Guatemala, 1844.

Index zu Azara's Apuntamientos, 1847.

Sur quelques Ois. nouv. de Jamaïque, 1847, 1847.

Deux Ois. nouv. de Caracas, 1849.

Deux Ois. nouv. de Vénézuéla, 1849.

Zur Ornithologie Süd-Amerika's, 1857.

HEARNE.

Note on Birds of Hayti, 1834.

Letter accompanying Animals from Hayti, 1834.

Notice of a Collection from Hayti, 1835.

L'HERMINIER.

Anatomie verschiedener Vögel aus Süd-America, 1837.

HILL.

Nests of Jamaican Birds, 1841, 1842.

Two Birds' skins from Jamaica, 1844.

HOLTZ.

Beschreibungen südamerikanischer Vögeleier, 1870.

HOTCHKISS.

South American Game Birds, 1876.

HUDSON.

Twelve Letters on the Ornithology of Buenos Ayres, 1870–71.

Birds of the Rio Negro of Patagonia, 1872.

HUGHES.

Barbadoes, 1750.

HUMBOLDT.

Ueber die Chinawälder in Südamerika, 1807.

Recueil des Observations, 1811, (p. 307).

JARDINE.

Ornithology of Tobago, 1846–47.

Ornithology of Quito, 1849.

New Birds from the Parisian Collections, 1852.

Ornithology of Tobago, 1852.

Jameson's Collections from Ecuador, 1855, 1856.

Notes on five species from Quito, 1857.

JULIET.

Esploracion científica, 1871.

Esploracion de Chiloe, 1874.

KINAHAN.

Letter from Callao, 1856.

KING.

Letter on Animals of Magellan's Straits, 1827–28.

KING.—Continued.

New Genera and Species of Birds from Straits of Magellan, 1830.

Ueber die Thiere an der Magellans-Strasse, 1830.

Distinctive Characters of Birds from Straits of Magellan, 1831.

Vögel von Magellans-Strasse, 1834.

KITTLITZ.

Ueber einige Vögel von Chile, 1831–35, (p. 308).

Cinq. Ois. nouv. du Chile, 1836, (p. 309).

Ueber einige Vögel von Chili, 1836.

KNOX.

Account of St. Thomas, 1852.

LABAT.

Nouveau Voyage, 1724, (p. 306).

LAFRESNAYE.

Quelques Oiseaux nouveaux de M. Charles Brelay, 1839.

Ois. nouv. de Santa-Fé de Bogota, 1840.

Ois. nouv. rapportés par Léclancher 1840.

Ois. nouv. de Colombie, 1842, 1842, 1844, 1846.

Ois. de Colombie, 1843, 1843, 1843, 1844.

Sur divers Oiseaux de la Nouvelle-Grenade, 1844.

Quelques Ois. de la Guadeloupe, 1844.

Ois. nouv. rapportés par M. Léclancher, 1845.

Descr. de quelques Ois. nouv., 1845.

Ois. nouv. de l'Orénoque, 1846.

Ois. nouv. de la Jamaïque, 1846.

Quelques Ois. nouv. rapportés par M. Delattre, 1847.

Réponse aux Obs. du Docteur Hartlaub, 1847, 1847.

Mélanges Ornithologiques, 1847.

Recomaissance d'une notice de quinze Oiseaux nouveaux décrits par M. Dubus, 1848.

Ois. nouv. de Caracas et de Bogota, 1848.

Sur Psittacula et sur quelques Ois. nouv. de Colombie et du Mexique, 1848.

Faune du Pérou, du Dr. Tschudi, 1849.

LAFRESNAYE and D'ORBIGNY.

Notice sur quelques Oiseaux de Carthagène et d'une partie du Mexique, 1838.

LANDBECK.

Contribuciones a la Ornitolojía de Chile, 1864.

Beiträge zur Ornithologie Chiles, 1864, 1864, 1865, 1866.

LANDBECK.—Continued.
  Sobre algunos Pájaros Chilenos, 1873.
  Zur Ornithologie Chiles, 1874.
LAWRENCE.
  New species of Polioptila and Chordei-
    les, 1856.
  On Gundlach's Notes on Cuban Birds,
    1858.
  New Phaeton and new Heliopaedica,
    1860.
  Notes on some Cuban Birds, 1860.
  New Myiarchus and new Phlogopsis,
    1860.
  Three new Birds from Middle America,
    1861.
  Catalogue of a Collection of New Grena-
    da Birds made by McLeannan, 1861–63.
  Six new species of Charadriidæ, Trochi-
    lidæ, and Caprimulgidæ, 1862.
  Six new Birds from Isthmus of Panama,
    1862.
  Eight new Birds from Panama, 1863.
  New Vireonidæ and Rallidæ, 1863.
  New species of Tanagridæ, Cuculidæ,
    and Trochilidæ, 1864.
  New species of Cærebidæ, Tanagridæ,
    Icteridæ, and Scolopacidæ, 1864.
  Catalogue of Birds from Sombrero, col-
    lected by Julien, 1864.
  New Cærebidæ, Tanagridæ, Icteridæ,
    and Scolopacidæ, 1864.
  New Tanagridæ, Dendrocolaptidæ, For-
    micaridæ, Tyrannidæ, Trochilidæ,
    1865.
  Six new Birds from Central America,
    1865.
  List of Birds from near David, Chiriqui,
    New Grenada, collected by Hicks, 1865.
  Catalogue of Birds collected by Holland
    at Greytown, Nicaragua, 1865.
  New species of Paridæ, Vireonidæ, Tyran-
    nidæ, and Trochilidæ, 1865.
  Four new Birds from Isthmus of Pana-
    ma, 1865.
  Seven new Birds from Central and South
    America, 1866.
  Six new species of Hirundinidæ, Formi-
    caridæ, Tyrannidæ, and Trochilidæ,
    1866.
  New species of American Birds, 1867.
  Notes on certain Birds from New Grena-
    da, 1867.
  Five new Central American Birds, 1867.
  Catalogue of the Birds of Costa Rica,
    1868–69.

LAWRENCE.—Continued.
  List of Birds from Northern Yucatan,
    1869.
  Catalogue of Birds from Puna Island,
    collected by Reeve, 1869.
  Characters of some new South American
    Birds, 1869.
  Seven new species of American Birds,
    1869.
  New Birds from Mexico and Central and
    South America, 1871.
  Three new species of American Birds,
    1871.
  New species of Icterus and Synallaxis,
    1872.
  Six supposed new American Birds, 1874.
  Two new Tanagridæ and Tyrannidæ,
    1874.
  Four new Birds from Costa Rica, 1874.
  Five new American Birds, 1875.
  New Birds from Dominica, 1877.
  Provisional list of Ober's Birds from
    Dominica, 1877.
  Seven new Birds from St. Vincent, 1878.
  New Birds from Grenada and Dominica,
    1878.
  Catalogue of Ober's Birds from Domin-
    ica, 1878.
  Catalogue of Ober's Birds from St. Vin-
    cent, 1878.
  Catalogue of Ober's Birds from Antigua
    and Barbuda, 1878.
  Catalogue of Ober's Birds from Grenada,
    1879.
  Catalogue of Ober's Birds from Marti-
    nique, 1879.
  Catalogue of Ober's Birds from Guade-
    loupe, 1879.
  General Catalogue of Ober's Birds from
    the Lesser Antilles, 1879.
LAYARD.
  Voyage from England to Pará, 1872, 1873.
  On Birds observed at Pará, 1873.
LEDRU.
  Voyage, 1810, 1811–12, (p. 307).
LEE.
  Ornithological Notes from the Argen-
    tine Republic, 1873.
LEMBEYE.
  Aves de la Isla de Cuba, 1849.
LÉOTAUD.
  Oiseaux de l'Île de Trinidad, 1866.
LESSON.
  Remarques sur quelques Oiseaux de Rio
    de Janeiro, 1825.

LESSON.—Continued.
Descriptions de dix espèces, etc., par Bonaparte, 1825.
Descriptions de nouveaux Oiseaux du Brésil, par Such, 1826.
Extrait d'une lettre du Capitaine King, 1828.
Notes à ajouter aux "Descriptions de dix espèces d'Oiseaux," par Bonaparte, 1825.
Sur quelques Ois.du Chile, 1834, (p. 308).
Neue Vögel, 1837.
Oiseaux nouveaux, 1840.
Sur les Oiseaux nouveaux rapportés par A. Lesson, 1842.
Species avium novæ A. Lessonio collectæ, 1842.
Oiseaux nouveaux, 1844.

LEYBOLD.
Cuatro especies nuevas de Pájaros, 1865.
Beschr. vier neuer Vögelarten aus Mendoza, 1866.
Escursion a las Pampas Argentinas,1873.

LICHTENSTEIN.
Die Werke von Marcgrave und Piso, 1814–26, 1820, 1824.

MACLEAY.
Ueber die vergl. Anatomie verschiedener Vögel aus Cuba, 1830.

MARCGRAVE.
Historia Naturalis Brasiliæ, 1648.

MARCH.
Notes on the Birds of Jamaica, 1863–64, 1864.

MARTEN, R. M.
History of the West Indies, 1836.

MATHEW.
Notes from Coquimbo, 1873.

MAXIMILIAN.
Reise, 1820, 1820–21, 1821–22, 1822.
Beiträge zur Naturgeschichte von Brasilien, 1830–33, 1832.
Note rectificative sur quelques Ois. du Brésil, 1846.

MITCHELL.
Lord Harris's collection from Trinidad, 1849.

MOLINA.
Chili, 1776?, 1782, 1783, 1786, 1788, 1789, 1808, 1809, 1810.

MOORE.
Birds collected by Leyland in Honduras, Belize, and Guatemala, 1809.

MORITZ.
Notizen zur Fauna der Insel Puertorico, 1836.

MOSQUERA.
Memoria sobre la Geografia de la Nueva Granada, 1852, 1853.

NAPP.
Argentine Republic, 1876.

NATTERER, *ed.* PELZELN.
Handschriftliche Notizen, 1862–63.

NEWMAN.
Notice of Bates's Naturalist on the Amazons, 1863.

NEWTON, A.
Additional Note on Nests and Eggs collected by Cunningham, 1870.

NEWTON, A., *and* NEWTON, E.
Observations on the Birds of St. Croix, 1859.

NIEUHOF.
Gedenkweerdige Brasiliaense Reeze, 1682, (p. 306).
West en Oosteindien, 1689.

OLIVER.
Letter from, 1703.

D'ORBIGNY.
Lettres à M. Férussac, 183–.
Voyage dans l'Amérique Méridionale, 1835–44–47.
Sur la Distribution Géographique des Oiseaux Passereaux de l'Amérique Mérid., 1837.
Observations on the Raptores of South America, 1837.
Rapport sur un Mémoire, etc., 1838.
Ueber die geographische Verbreitung der Südamerikanischen Singvögel, 1839.
Histoire de l'Ile de Cuba par Ramon de la Sagra, 1839.
Schilderung des nördlichen Patagonien, 1839.

D'ORBIGNY *and* LAFRESNAYE.
Synopsis Avium, 1837–38. [Vide notam, infra.*]

*Dele titulum, anteà, p. 256; stet—

1837–38. D'ORBIGNY, A., *and* LAFRESNAYE, F. DE. Synopsis Avium ab Alcide d'Orbigny, in ejus per Americam meridionalem itinere, collectarum et ab ipso viatore necnon A [sic] de Lafresnaye in ordine redactarum. <*Guér. Mag. de Zool.*,

ORTON.

Contrib. to Nat. Hist. of the Valley of Quito, 1871.

Notes on Birds in Museum of Vassar College, 1871.

Condors and Hummingbirds of Andes, 1871, 1871.

Andes and the Amazon, 1876.

OSBURN.

Notes on the Birds of Jamaica (eight papers), 1859, 1860.

OWEN, ROB.

Nesting of some Guatemalan Birds, 1861.

PALLAS.

Beschr. zweyer südamerik. Vögel, 1782, (p. 307).

PELZELN.

Ueber neue u. wenig bekannte Arten der Familien Trogonidae und Alcedinidae, 1856.

PELZELN.—Continued.

Ueber vier von Natterer in Brasilien gesammelte neue Vögelarten, 1863.

Zur Ornithologie Brasiliens. Resultate von Natterers Reisen, 1868–70.

Verz. einer an Schaufuss gelangten Sendung aus Brasilien, 1873.

Sendung von Vögeln aus Ecuador, 1874.

Birds collected by Münzberg in Guiana, 1875.

Weitere Sendung von Vögeln aus Ecuador, 1876, 1878.

PHILIPPI.

Ueber einige Vögel Chilc's, 1855.

Ueber einige Chilenische Vögel, 1857.

Zwei neue Chilenische Enten und über Fringilla barbata Mol., 1860.

Comentario sobre Molina, 1867.

Letter on Birds of Chili, 1868.

Catálogo de las Aves Chilenas, 1868.

1837–38. D'ORBIGNY, A., *and* LAFRESNAYE, F. DE.—Continued.

7e année, 1837, Classe II., pp. 1–88, pll. lxxvii–lxxix; 8e année, 1838, Classe II., pp. 1–34.

Species novæ aut nuper a d'Orbigny ipso editæ :—*Ibycter gymnocephalus, Phalcoboenas montanus,* p. 2; *Buteo tricolor,* p. 6; *B. unicolor,* p. 7; *Tamnophilus* [sic] *fuliginosus, T. aspersiventer,* p. 10; *T. atropileus, T. maculatus, T. aterrimus,* p. 11; *T. rufater, T. affinis,* p. 12; *T. lafresnayanus, Conopophaga ardesiaca, C. nigro-cincta,* p. 13; *Merularis* [sic] *analis, M. nigromaculata,* p. 14; *Megalonyx ruficeps,* p. 15; *T. fuscater, T. chiguanco,* p. 16; *T. olivaceus, ? Orpheus calandria,* p. 17; *O. dorsalis, ? O. tricaudatus,* p. 18; *O. patagonicus, Donacobius albo vittatus,* p. 19; *Sylvia ruficeps, S. concolor,* p. 20; *Dacnis flaviventer, D. analis, Synallaxis dorso maculata,* p. 21; *S. maluroides, S. troglodytoides, S. striaticeps,* p. 22; *S. albiceps, S. fuliginiceps,* p. 23; *S. leucocephala, S. bitorquata,* p. 24; *S. torquata, Troglodytes pallida, T. tecellata* [sic], p. 25; *T. guarayana,* p. 26; *Anthus furcatus, A. rufescens,* p. 27; *Nemosia sordida, Tachyphonus versicolor,* p. 28; *T. flavinucha, T. luctuosus, ? T. capitatus,* p. 29; *Euphonia laniirostris, E. serrirostris, E. ruficeps,* p. 30; *Aglaia yeni,* p. 31; *A. montana, A. igniventris, A. cyanocephala,* p. 32; *A. cyanicollis, Pyranga albicollis,* p. 33; *Ramphocelus atro sericeus, Embernagra torquata,* p. 34; *E. rufi-nucha, Saltator rufiventris,* p. 35; *S. similis,* p. 36; *Phytotoma angustirostris,* p. 37; *Pipra fasciata,* p. 38; *Ampelis rubro-cristata,* p. 39; *A. viridis,* p. 40; *Tyrannus tuberculifer, T. fumigatus,* p. 43; *T. rufescens* (Sw.?), p. 44; *T. rufiventris,* p. 45; *T. aurantio atrocristatus,* p. 45; *? Todirostrum margaritacei venter,* p. 46; *T. ecaudatum, Muscipeta albiceps,* p. 47; *M. obscura, M. bimaculata,* p. 48; *M. brevirostris, M. cinnamomea,* p. 49; *Setophaga brunneiceps, S. verticalis,* p. 50; *Muscicapa striaticollis, M. bivittata,* p. 51; *M. elegans, M. angustirostris,* p. 52; *M. leucophrys, M. stramineo-ventris,* p. 53; *M. olivacea,* p. 54; *Culicivora budytoides,* p. 56; *C. reguloides,* p. 57; *Fluvicola nigerrima,* p. 59; *F. leucophrys, F. rufi-pectoralis, F. oenanthoides,* p. 60; *Muscigralla* (g. n. ?) *brevicauda, Pepoaza* (g. n. ?), p. 61; *P. murina, P. variegata,* p. 63; *P. montana.* p. 64; *P. maritima,* p. 65; *Muscisaxicola* (g. n.?), p. 65; *M. rufivertex, M. mentalis, M. maculirostris, M. striaticeps,* p. 66; *Hirundo patagonica, H. andecola,* p. 69; *Cypselus montivagus, C. andecolus,* p. 70; *Certhilauda maritima, C. tenuirostris,* p. 72; *Emberiza lutea, E. luteo-cephala,* p. 74; *E. uropigyalis* [sic], *E. olivascens,* p. 75; *E. atriceps,* p. 76; *E. fulviceps,* p. 77; *E. speculifera,* p. 78; *E. griseo-cristata, E. unicolor, E. carbonaria,* p. 79; *E. hypochondria,* p. 80; *E. obscura,* p. 81; *E. torquata,* p. 82; *Carduelis atratus, Linaria analis,* p. 83; *Pitylus aureoventris,* p. 84; *Pyrrhula glauco-cœrulea,* p. 85; *P. bicolor,* p. 86; *P. cinerea, P. nigro-rufa,* p. 87; *P. alaudina,* p. 88.

1838. *Cassicus atro-virens,* p. 1; *C. yuracares,* p. 2; *C. chrysonotus,* p. 3; *Icterus maxillaris,* p. 6; *I. brevirostris,* p. 7; *Garrulus viridi-cyanus* [sic!], p. 9; *Dendrocolaptes atrirostris,* p. 12; *Anabates squaniger, A. gutturatus,* p. 14; *A. ruficaudatus, A. certhioides, A. gutturalis,* p. 15; *A. unirufus,* p. 16; *Anumbius* (g. n.) *anothoides,* p. 17; *A. striaticollis,* p. 18; *A. striaticeps,* p. 19; *Uppucerthia* [sic] (*Oppetiorhynchos* [sic]) *dumetorum* "Is. Geoff. et d'Orb. Mus. Paris", p. 20; *U. andæcola,* p. 21; *U. montana, U. vulgaris,* p. 22; *U. nigrofumosa,* p. 23; *Serrirostrum* (g. n., p. 24) *carbonarum, S. sittoides, Conirostrum* (g. n.) *cinereum,* p. 25; *Ornismya glaucopoides,* p. 27; *O. aureo-ventris,* p. 28; *O. pamela* "d'Orb.", p. 29; *O. smaragdihicollis, O. amethysticollis,* p. 31; *Trochilus estella* "d'Orb.", p. 32; *T. adela* "d'Orb.", p. 33.

PHILIPPI.—Continued.
Escursion al Cajon de los Cipreses, 1875.
PHILIPPI *and* LANDBECK.
Beschreibung zweier neuen Chilenischen Vögel aus den Geschlechtern Procellaria und Caprimulgus, 1860.
Descripcion de unas nueve especies de Pájaros Peruanos, 1861.
Descripcion de algunas especies nuevas de Pájaros Chilenos, 1861.
Neue Wirbelthiere von Chile, 1861.
Beiträge zur Fauna von Peru, 1863.
Beschr. einer neuen Ente und Seeschwalbe, 1863, (p. 309).
Contribuciones a la ornitolojía de Chile, 1864.
Beiträge zur Ornithologie Chiles, 1864.
Beiträge zur Ornith. von Chile, 1865, 1866.
POEY.
Catálogo metódico de las aves de Cuba, 1848.
QUOY *and* GAIMARD.
Sur quelques Oiseaux de la province de Rio-de-Janeiro, etc., 1825.
RAIMONDI.
Sur le huano des Iles de Chincha, 1856, 1856.
REED.
Birds of Juan Fernandez and Mas-a-fuera, 1874.
Apuntes de la Zoologia de Chile, 1877.
REINHARDT.
Fuglefaunaen i Brasiliens Campos, 1870, 1870.
RICHARD *and* BERNARD.
Catalogue des Oiseaux envoyés de Cayenne, 1792.
ROCHEFORT.
Histoire des Iles Antilles, 1658, 1666, 1681.
ROGERS.
Natural History Notes from Rio, 1869.
ROSENSCHÖLD.
Bref från Paraguay, 1853, 1854.
SAGRA, RAMON DE LA.
Enumération des espèces, etc., de Cuba, 1859.
(*See, also,* D'ORBIGNY.)
ST. HILAIRE, A. DE.
Aperçu d'un Voyage dans le Brésil, 1822.
SALLÉ.
Liste des Oiseaux rapportés dans la République Dominicaine, 1857.

SALLÉ.—Continued.
Liste d'Oiseaux à vendre, 1861.
SALLÉ *and* PARZUDAKI.
Liste d'Oiseaux à vendre, 1862.
SALVADORI.
Uccelli di Costa Rica, 1868.
SALVIN.
Letters from Dueñas, Guatemala, 1860.
Letters from Vera Paz, Guatemala, 1860.
Three new Birds from Guatemala, 1861, 1861.
List of Species to be added to the Ornithology of Central America, 1861.
Letter from Dueñas, Guatemala, 1862.
Fortnight amongst Sea Birds of Honduras, 1864.
Seventeen new Birds from Costa Rica, 1864.
Letter from Guatemala, 1864.
Thirteen new Birds discovered by Salvin and Godman in Central America, 1864.
Sea Birds and Waders of Pacific Coast of Guatemala, 1865.
Further Contributions to Ornithology of Guatemala, 1866.
Eight new Birds from Veragua, 1866.
On some Birds from Veragua, 1867.
Notes on Lawrence's Costa Rican List, 1869.
Additional Notes on Lawrence's Costa Rican List, 1870.
On some Collections of Birds from Veragua, 1870.
Layard's Departure for Pará, 1872.
Notes on Belt's Birds from Chontales, Nicaragua, 1872.
Maack's Researches in Panama, 1872.
Letter off St. Domingo, 1873.
Letter on some Guatemalan Birds, 1873.
Additional Notes on Birds of Juan Fernandez and Mas-a-fuera, 1875.
Avifauna of the Galapagoes, 1876.
New Birds from Western Ecuador, 1876.
SALVIN *and* SCLATER.
Contrib. to the Ornithology of Guatemala, 1860.
SCLATER.
On Birds from Yucatan described by Cabot, 1852.
Description de six Ois. nouv. appartenant aux collections en Paris, 1852.
Descr. de deux nouvelles espèces d'Oiseaux, 1853.
On two [lately] new species of South American Birds, 1854.

SCLATER.—Continued.

List of a Collection received by Gould from Quijos in Ecuador, 1854, 1855.

New species from Santa Fé di Bogota, 1855.

On Birds received in Collections from Santa Fé di Bogota, 1855.

Additional Species in Collections from Bogota, 1856.

Birds collected by Bridges at Davis in Chiriqui in Panama, 1856.

Some new species from Santa Fé di Bogota, 1856.

Two new species from Santa Fé di Bogota, 1856.

Eight new species from South America, 1856.

Further Additions to the List of Birds from Bogota, 1857.

Additional Birds received from Bogota, 1857.

Collection transmitted by Bates from Upper Amazon, 1857.

Eleven new species from Tropical America, 1857.

New genus from Mexico, 1857.

Two new species from Bogota, 1857.

Notes on a Collection received by Verreaux from Rio Napo in Ecuador, 1858.

Birds collected by Taylor in Honduras, 1858.

New Birds from the Rio Napo in Ecuador, 1858, 1858.

New genus and some new species of American Birds, 1858.

Five new species of American Birds, 1858, 1859.

Birds collected by Fraser at Cuenca, etc., in Ecuador, 1858.

Birds collected by Fraser at Riobamba, in Ecuador, 1858.

First collections made by Fraser at Pallatanga, Ecuador, 1859.

New or little-known Birds from the Rio Napo, 1859.

Eggs of two Raptores from the Falklands, 1860.

List of additional Birds collected by Fraser at Pallatanga, etc., 1860.

List of Birds collected by Fraser at Quito, etc., 1860.

List of Birds collected by Fraser at Nanegal, etc., 1860.

Arrival of Birds from British Honduras, 1860.

SCLATER.—Continued.

List of Birds collected by Fraser at Babahoyo, etc., 1860.

List of Birds collected by Fraser at Esmeralda, 1860.

Catalogue of Birds of the Falklands, 1860.

New Birds collected by Fraser at Pallatanga, 1860.

Ten new species of American Birds, 1860.

Two new Birds from the Rio Napo, 1860.

Eight new species of American Birds, 1861.

Additions and corrections to List of Birds of the Falklands, 1861.

Collection of Birds made by Osburn in Jamaica, 1861.

Catalogue of a collection of American Birds, 1861–62.

Birds collected by Boucard in Southern Mexico, 1862.

Nine new Birds from Bogota, 1862, 1862.

Additions to List of Birds of the Falklands, 1864.

Seven new Birds discovered by Natterer in Brazil, 1864.

On Birds of the vicinity of Lima, with notes by Nation, 1866, 1867, 1869, 1871.

Letters from E. Bartlett, 1867.

Remarks on Léotaud's Ois. Trinidad, 1867.

Notes on the Birds of Chili, 1867.

Lecompte's Expedition to the Falklands, 1868.

New Birds from the Rio Paraná, 1870.

Notices of some new Birds of South America, 1870.

The Birds of the Lesser Antilles, 1871.

Land Birds of Juan Fernandez, 1871.

Correspondence with C. W. des Vœux, 1871.

Birds of the Islands of Santa Lucia, 1871.

Collection of Birds from Oyapok, 1871.

Additions to List of Nicaraguan Birds, 1873.

Note on the 'Nomenclator Avium Neotropicalium', 1873.

Two new Birds from Antioquia, 1873.

Peruvian Birds collected by Whitely, 1873. (For eight other lists, *see* SCLATER *and* SALVIN.)

News of Mr. Salvin, 1874.

Notice of Jelski's Collections, 1874.

Collection of Birds from Barbadoes, 1874.

SCLATER.—Continued.
Additional Birds from St. Lucia, 1876.
SCLATER *and* SALVIN.
On the Ornithology of Central America, 1859.
Eleven new Birds from Guatemala, 1860, 1860.
Notes on a Collection of Birds from Isthmus of Panama, 1864.
Catalogue of Birds collected by Bartlett on the Ucayali, 1866.
Additions to Catalogue of Birds collected by Bartlett on the Ucayali, 1866.
Exotic Ornithology, 1866–69.
Birds collected by Cunningham in Straits of Magellan, 1868, 1869, 1870.
Venezuelan Birds collected by Goering, 1868, 1868, 1869, 1870, 1875.
Birds collected at Conchitas by Hudson, 1868, 1869, 1869.
New Species of Fringillidæ, Oxyrhamphidæ, Bucconidæ, and Strigidæ, 1868.
Four new Birds from Veragua, 1868.
New Species of Dendrocolaptidæ, Strigidæ, and Columbidæ, 1868.
Birds collected on the Blewfields River by Wickham, 1867.
Birds collected by Wallace on the Amazon, 1867.
Birds collected by Bartlett on the Huallaga, 1867.
Birds collected by Hauxwell at Pebas, 1867.
Peruvian Birds collected by Whitely, 1867, 1868, 1868, 1869, 1869, 1873, 1874, 1876. (For one of these lists, *see* SCLATER.)
Six new Species of Tanagridæ, Dendrocolaptidæ, Formicariidæ, Tyrannidæ, and Scolopacidæ, 1869.
Two new Birds collected by Bartlett in Eastern Peru, 1869.
New Birds collected by Habel in the Galapagoes, 1870.
Birds collected by Whitely in Honduras, 1870.
Five new Birds from Columbia, 1870.
Nomenclator Avium Neotropicalium, 1873.
Birds of Eastern Peru, with Notes by Bartlett, 1873.
Venezuelan Birds collected by Spence, 1873.
Two new Birds from Antioquia, 1875.

SCLATER *and* SALVIN.—Continued.
New Birds obtained by Buckley in Bolivia, 1876.
New Species of Bolivian Birds, 1876.
Eight new Species of South American Birds, 1877.
Six new Species of South American Birds, 1877.
Collection made by Steere in South America, 1878.
Report on Birds of H. M. S. 'Challenger', 1878.
Three new Birds from Ecuador, 1878.
SCHOMBURGK.
Description of British Guiana, 1840.
History of Barbadoes, 1847.
Reisen in Britisch Guiana, 1848.
History of Barbadoes, 1848, (p. 308).
SCHREIBER.
Nachrichten, 1820, 1823, 1823.
Collectanea ad Faunam Brasiliae, 1833, (p. 308).
SCOULER.
Voyage to Madeira, Brazil, etc., 1826.
SEEMANN.
Notes on the Zoology of Panama, 1852.
SEMPER.
On the Birds of St. Lucia, 1872.
SHARPE.
Collections made by H. M. S. 'Petrel', 1877.
SLOANE.
Voyage, 1707–25.
SONNINI DE MANONCOUR.
Sur les Coqs et Poules de l'Amérique méridionale, 1775.
Sur les Marails ou Faisans de la Guiane, 1775.
Du Sasa, 1785.
SPENCE.
The Land of Bolivar, 1878.
SPERLING.
Letter on South American Birds, 1872.
SPIX.
Avium species novæ, 1825–26.
SPIX *and* MARTIUS.
Musical Thrush [?] of Brazil, 1825.
Reise in Brasilien, 1823–31, (p. 307).
Travels in Brazil, 1824, (p. 308).
STERNBERG.
Notizen aus der Vogelwelt von Buenos Ayres, 1869.
STRICKLAND.
Four Birds from the Peruvian Andes, 1849.

STUBBES.
Observations on the Caribe-Islands, 1667, 1668.
SUCH.
Descriptions of new Brazilian Birds, 1825.
Einige unbestimmte brasilische Vögel, 1830.
SUNDEVALL.
Foglarne på ön S:t Barthelemy, 1869 or 1870.
Foglarne på ön Portorico, 1869 or 1870.
On Birds from the Galapagoes, 1871.
SWAINSON.
Birds of Brazil, 1834–41, (p. 309).
TACZANOWSKI.
Oiseaux nouveaux du Pérou, 1874.
Liste d'Ois. recueillis par Jelski dans le Pérou, 1874.
Ois. recueillis au nord du Pérou par Jelski et Stolzman, 1877.
Supplément à la même, 1877.
TAYLOR, E. C.
Five months in the West Indies, 1864.
TAYLOR, G. C.
Birds collected or observed in Honduras, 1860.
TAYLOR, R. C.
Natural Objects observed in Cuba, 1836.
TAYLOR, W. J.
Rock Guano from the Caribbean Islands, 1857.
THIENEMANN.
Ueber Eier und Nester Cubanischer Vögel, 1857.
THUNBERG.
Pipræ species novæ descriptæ, 1822.
TSCHUDI.
Diagnosen einiger neuer peruanischer Vögel, 1843.
Avium conspectus quæ in Republica Peruana reperiuntur, etc., 1844.
Nachträgliche Bemerkungen zu seinem Conspectus Avium, 1845.

TSCHUDI.—Continued.
Five papers on Birds of Peru and Chili, 1847, 1847, 1847, 1847, 1847.
TSCHUDI and CABANIS.
Fauna Peruana, 1845–46.
VIGORS.
On some Birds from Cuba, 1828.
Ueber einige Vögel aus Cuba, 1830.
Exhibition of Birds from Magellan Straits, 1831.
New Birds collected by Cuming in Chili and Mexico, 1832.
Ueber Kings Vögel von der Magellanstrasse, 1834.
Thiere von Cuming, 1835.
On a. Collection of Birds from the West Coast of South America, 1839.
WAFER.
New Vogage, 1729.
WAGNER.
Beit. zur Kennt. der warmblütigen Wirbelth. Amer., 1831, (p. 308).
WALLACE.
Journey to the Amazon River, 1850.
A Narrative of Travels on the Amazon, 1853.
Habits of Birds, 1854.
WARREN.
Description of Surinam, 1667, 1745, (p. 306).
WEST.
Bidrag til beskrivelse over St. Croix, 1793, (p. 307).
Beiträge zur Beschreibung von St. Croix, 1794.
WILLIAMS.
The Isthmus of Tehuantepec, 1852.
WYATT.
Birds of the U. S. of Colombia, 1871.
YARRELL.
Descriptions of Eggs of Chilian Birds, 1847.

B.—LOCALITIES.

[NOTE.—In the nature of the case some of the titles can scarcely be indexed here, and anonymous, pseudonymous, and ephemeral titles are mostly omitted, the intention being mainly to give a ready clue to the Faunal Lists, etc., of the leading geographical areas of Neotropical America. The few *Mexican* titles here given are only those that should have come in the Nearctic list given on a previous occasion. Articles relating to Central and South America at large are grouped together under the first head following. "West Indies" is given; but see also the several islands composing them.]

AMERICA (*neotropica*).

Condamine. Relation d'un Voyage, 1749.

Sonnini. Sur les Coqs et Poules de l'Amérique du Sud, 1775.

Sonnini. Du Sasa, 1785.

Pallas. Zwey südamerikanische Vögel, 1782, (p. 307).

Humboldt. Ueber die Chinawälder, 1807.

Thunberg. Pipræ species novæ, 1822.

Bonaparte. Ten species of Birds, 1825.

Bonaparte. Note to ten species of Birds, 1825.

Scouler. Account of a Voyage, 1826.

Férussac. Voyage de M. A. d'Orbigny, 1829.

d'Orbigny. Lettres à M. de Férussac, 183-.

Wagner. Beiträge zur Kenntniss der Wirbelthiere, 1831, (p. 308).

Vigors. New Birds collected by Cuming in Chile and Mexico, 1832, 1835.

Gould. Sur des Oiseaux, 1834.

Bonaparte. New Birds from Mexico and South America, 1837.

Bredow. Auszüge aus den Schreiben von C. Moritz, 1837.

d'Orbigny. Voyage, 1835-44-47.

Bonaparte. Notices and Descriptions of new Birds from Mexico and South America, 1837.

Gould. Characters of three new Birds, 1837.

L'Herminier. Anatomie verschiedener Vögel aus, 1837.

Lesson. Neue Vögel aus, 1837.

d'Orbigny. Distrib. Géograph. des Passereaux de, 1837.

Bonaparte. Catalogi di Uccelli Messicani e Peruviani, 1838.

d'Orbigny. Obs. on the Raptores of, 1837, 1838, 1839.

d'Orbigny and Lafresnaye. Synopsis Avium, 1837-38.

Lafresnaye and d'Orbigny. Notice sur quelques Oiseaux de Carthagène et du Mexique, 1838.

AMERICA (*neotropica*).—Continued.

Vigors. Obs. on a Collection from West Coast of America, 1839.

Lafresnaye. Oiseaux nouveaux tués par Léclancher, 1840.

Lesson. Oiseaux nouveaux, 1840.

Gould. Zoology of the Voyage of the Beagle, 1841.

Lesson. Sur les Ois. nouv. de la Mer du Sud, 1842.

Lesson. Species avium novæ aut minùs cognitæ, 1842.

Fraser. On Bridges's Collection of Birds, 1843.

Lesson. Ois. nouveaux, 1844.

Des Murs. Quelques espèces nouvelles d'Oiseaux, 1845.

Lafresnaye. Ois. nouveaux rapportés par Léclancher, 1845.

Lafresnaye. Quelques Ois. nouveaux, 1845.

Bridges. Notes in addition to former papers on Ornithology, 1847, 1847.

Lafresnaye. Quelques Ois. nouv. rapportés par Delattre de Bolivie, de la Nouv. Grenade et de Panama, 1847, 1847.

Castelnau. Considérations de l'Ornithologie, 1848.

Dubus. Ueber einige Vögel, 1848, 1848, 1848.

Lafresnaye. Reconnaissance de quinze Ois. nouv. décrits par Dubus, 1848.

Lafresnaye. Quelques Ois. nouv. de Caracas et de Bogota, 1848.

Lafresnaye. Quelques Ois. nouv. de Colombie et du Mexique, 1848.

Cornalia. Vertebratorum Synopsis, 1849.

Deville. Descr. de quelques Ois nouv., 1849.

Deville. Quatre Ois. nouv. de l'expédition de M. Castelnau, 1851.

Deville. Observations faites en Amérique, 1852.

AMERICA (*neotropica*).—Continued.

Jardine. New Birds from the Parisian Collections, 1852.

Sclater. Six Ois. nouv., 1852.

Sclater. Deux nouvelles esp. d'Oiseaux, 1853, 1854.

Cassin. Gilliss's U. S. Astron. Exped., 1855.

Des Murs. Ois. nouv. ou rares recueillis, 1855.

Gould. Eight new species of Birds, 1855, 1855.

Des Murs. Expédition de M. Castlenau dans les parties centrales, 1856.

Gould. Eight new species of Birds, 1856.

Lawrence. New species of Chordeiles and Polioptila, 1856.

Sclater. Eight new species of Birds, 1856.

Gould. New Trogon and Odontophorus, 1857.

Hartlaub. Zur Ornithologie, 1857.

Sclater. Eleven new Birds from Tropical America, 1857, 1858.

Sclater. New genus and some new species, 1858.

Sclater. Five new species from Central and, 1858, 1859.

Cassin. La Plata, the Argentine Republic, and Paraguay, 1859.

Moore. List of Birds collected by Leyland in Honduras, Belize, and Guatemala, 1859.

Sclater and Salvin. On the Ornithology of, 1859.

Sclater. Ten new species of American Birds, 1860.

Lawrence. New Phaeton and Heliopaedica, 1860.

Lawrence. New Myiarchus and Phlogopsis, 1860.

Lawrence. Three new Birds from Central America, 1861.

Sclater. Eight new species of American Birds, 1861.

Lawrence. New Charadriidæ, Trochilidæ, and Caprimulgidæ, 1862.

Sclater. Cat. of a Collection of American Birds, 1861–62.

Lawrence. New Vireonidæ and Rallidæ, 1863.

Salvin. Thirteen new Birds discovered by Godman and Salvin in Central America, 1863.

AMERICA (*neotropica*).—Continued.

Cassin. Notes on some Birds, 1864.

Lawrence. New Tanagridæ, Cuculidæ, and Trochilidæ, 1864.

Lawrence. New Cærebidæ, Tanagridæ, Icteridæ, and Scolopacidæ, 1864.

Lawrence. New Tanagridæ, Dendrocolaptidæ, Formicaridæ, Tyrannidæ, and Trochilidæ, 1865.

Lawrence. Six new Birds from Central America, 1865.

Lawrence. New Paridæ, Vireonidæ, Tyrannidæ, and Trochilidæ, 1865.

Lawrence. Seven new Birds, 1866.

Lawrence. Six new species of Hirundinidæ, Formicaridæ, Tyrannidæ, and Trochilidæ, 1866.

Sclater and Salvin. Exotic Ornithology, 1866–69.

Lawrence. New Species of American Birds, 1867.

Lawrence. Five new Birds of Central America, 1867.

Sclater and Salvin. New Fringillidæ, Oxyrhamphidæ, Bucconidæ, and Strigidæ, 1868.

Sclater and Salvin. New Dendrocolaptidæ, Strigidæ, and Columbidæ, 1868.

Bishop. The Pampas and Andes, 1869.

Sclater and Salvin. New Tanagridæ, Dendrocolaptidæ, Formicariidæ, Tyrannidæ, and Scolopacidæ, 1869.

Lawrence. New Birds, 1869.

Lawrence. Seven new Birds, 1869.

Holtz. Besch. südamerikanischer Vögel-Eier, 1870.

Sclater. New or little-known species of Birds, 1870.

Lawrence. New Birds from Mexico, Central and South America, 1871.

Lawrence. Three new species of American Birds, 1871.

Orton. Birds in Museum of Vassar College, 1871.

Orton. Vultures and Humming-birds of Tropical America, 1871.

Lawrence. New Species of Icterus and Synallaxis, 1872.

Sclater. Note on Nomenclator, 1873.

Sclater and Salvin. Nomenclator Avium Neotropicalium, 1873.

Lawrence. Six supposed new American Birds, 1874.

Lawrence. Two new Tanagridæ and Tyrannidæ, 1874

AMERICA (*neotropica*).—Continued.

Dubus.   Quelques Ois. nouveaux, 1875.

Lawrence.   Five new American Birds, 1875.

Orton.   Andes and Amazon, 1876.

Sclater and Salvin.   Eight new South American Birds, 1877.

Sclater and Salvin.   Six new South American Birds, 1877.

Sclater and Salvin.   On Steere's Collection, 1878.

Sclater and Salvin.   On the Challenger's Collection, 1878.

ARGENTINE REPUBLIC.

Burmeister.   Briefliches aus Mendoza, 1858.

Burmeister.   Systematisches Verz. der in den La Plata Staaten beobachteten Vögel, 1860.

Burmeister.   Reise durch die La Plata Staaten, 1861.

Leybold.   Beschreib. vier neuer Arten aus Mendoza, 1866.

Burmeister.   Contributions to the Ornithology of the, 1868.

Giebel.   Einige neue Vögel von, 1868.

Sclater and Salvin.   Birds collected by Hudson at Conchitas, 1868.

Sclater and Salvin.   Second list of Birds collected by Hudson at Conchitas, 1869.

Sclater and Salvin.   Third list of Birds collected by Hudson at Conchitas, 1869.

Sternberg.   Notizen aus der Vogelwelt von Buenos Ayres, 1869.

Sclater.   New Birds from the Rio Parana, 1870.

Hudson.   Letters on the Ornithology of Buenos Ayres, 1870–71.

Lee.   Notes from the, 1873.

Leybold.   Escursion a las Pampas, 1873.

Durnford.   Ornith. Notes from Buenos Ayres, 1876.

Napp.   Argentine Republic, 1876.

Durnford.   Notes on the Birds of Buenos Ayres, 1877.

Cabanis.   Eine Sammlung von Vögeln aus, 1878.

BARBADOES.

Hughes.   Natural History of, 1750.

Schomburgk.   History of, 1847, 1848, (p. 308).

Sclater.   Small collection of Birds from, 1874.

BERMUDA.

Godet.   Its History, etc., 1860.

BOLIVIA.

Bridges.   Notices of Mammals and Birds of, 1846.

Sclater and Salvin.   New Birds obtained by Buckley in, 1876.

Sclater and Salvin.   New Species of Bolivian Birds, 1876.

BRAZIL.

Marcgrave.   Historia Naturalis Brasiliæ, 1648.

Nieuhof.   Brasiliaense Reize, 1682, (p. 306).

Lichtenstein.   Die Werke von Piso und Marcgrave, 1814–26, 1820, 1824.

Schreiber.   Nachrichten, 1820, 1823, 1823.

Maximilian.   Reise, 1820, 1820–21, 1821–22, 1822.

St. Hilaire.   Aperçu d'un Voyage en, 1822.

Maximilian.   Beiträge zur Naturgeschichte von, 1825–33, 1830–33, 1832.

Spix and Martius.   Reise, 1823–31, (p. 307); 1824, (p. 308).

Spix.   Avium species novae, 1824–25.

Becklemichew.   Sur deux nouvelles Oiseaux du, 1829.

Fischer.   Ois. envoyés par Coffrane de Bahia, 1829.

Quoy and Gaimard.   Remarques sur quelques Oiseaux de, 1825.

Spix and Martius.   Musical thrush [?] of, 1825.

Such.   New Birds of, 1825, 1830.

Schreiber.   Collectanea, 1833, (p. 308).

Swainson.   Ornithological Drawings, 1834–41, (p. 308).

Maxim.   Note rectificative sur des Ois. du, 1846.

Gardner.   Notes of Birds in, 1847.

Wallace.   Journey to explore the Amazon, 1850.

Burmeister.   Ueber Eier und Nester einiger Vögel von, 1853.

Wallace.   Narrative of travels on the Amazon and Rio Negro, 1853.

Wallace..   Habits of Birds of, 1854.

Burmeister.   Systematische Uebersicht der Thiere Brasiliens, 1856.

Burmeister.   Erläuterungen zur Fauna Brasiliens, 1856.

Descourtilz.   Ornithologie Brasilienne, 1854–56.

BRAZIL.—Continued.

Pelzeln. Arten der Familien Trogonidæ und Alcedinidæ aus, 1856.

Sclater. Birds transmitted by Bates from the Upper Amazon, 1857.

Pelzeln. Ueber vier von Natterer gesammelte neue Vögel von, 1862.

Bates. Naturalist on the Amazon, 1863, 1864.

Sclater. Seven new Birds discovered by Natterer in, 1864.

Sclater and Salvin. Birds collected by Wallace on the Lower Amazons, 1867.

Euler. Zur Naturgeschichte der Vögel von, 1867–69.

Pelzeln. Zur Ornithologie Brasiliens, 1868–70.

Rogers. Natural History Notes from Rio, 1869.

Reinhardt. Bidrag til Kundskab om Fuglefaunaen i Brasiliens Campos, 1870, 1870.

Hamilton. Birds from São Paulo, 1871.

Salvin. Notice of Layard's Departure for Pará, 1872.

Layard. Letters on Birds seen on voyage to Pará, 1872, 1873.

Layard. Notes on Birds observed at Pará, 1873.

Pelzeln. Verz. einer Sendung aus Neufreiburg, 1873.

Berlepsch. Zur Ornithologie Santa Catharina's, 1873–74.

Cabanis. Uebersicht der von Euler in Cantagallo ges. Vögel, 1874.

Allen. Birds collected by Linden near Santarem, 1877.

BUENOS AYRES.   *See* ARGENTINE REPUBLIC.

CAYENNE.   *See* GUIANA.

CHILE.

Molina. Storia Naturali, 1776, 1782, 1783, 1786, 1788, 1789, 1808, 1809.

Lesson. Sur quelques Oiseaux de, 1834, (p. 308).

Kittlitz. Cinq nouv. esp. d'Oiseaux de, 1836, (p. 309).

Kittlitz. Ueber einige Vögel von, 1836.

Bridges. Various Birds from, 1841.

Fraser. On Birds of, 1845.

Fraser. Exhibition of two Birds of, 1845.

Gay. Historia de, 1847.

Philippi. Ueber einige Vögel Chile's, 1855.

CHILE.—Continued.

Boeck. Bemerk. über die Ornis der Provinz Valdivia, 1855.

Philippi. Ueber einige Chilenische Vögel, 1857.

Frauenfeld. Ueber den Aufenthalt in Valparaiso, 1860.

Germain. On Nidification of some Birds of, 1860.

Philippi. Ueber zwei neue Enten und Fringilla barbata, 1860.

Philippi and Landbeck. Zwei neue Arten Procellaria und Caprimulgus, 1860.

Philippi and Landbeck. Algunas especies nuevas de Pájaros de, 1861.

Philippi and Landbeck. Neue Wirbelthiere von, 1861.

Philippi. Neue Ente und Seeschwalbe, 1863, (p. 309).

Landbeck. Contribuciones a la Ornitolojía de, 1864.

Landbeck. Beiträge zur Ornithologie von, 1864.

Philippi and Landbeck. Beiträge zur Ornith. von, 1864, 1865, 1866.

Sclater. Notes on the Birds of, 1867.

Philippi. Letter on certain Birds of, 1868.

Philippi. Catálogo de las Aves existentes en el Museo de Santiago, 1868.

Sclater. On the Land Birds of Juan Fernandez, 1871.

Landbeck. Sobre algunos Pájaros Chilenos, 1872.

Mathew. Notes from Coquimbo, 1873.

Juliet. Comission Esploradora de Chiloe, 1874.

Landbeck. Zur Ornith. Chiles, 1874.

Reed. Remarks on Birds of Juan Fernandez, 1874.

Salvin. Additional Notes on Birds of Juan Fernandez, 1874.

Philippi. Escursion al Cajon de los Cipreses, 1875.

Reed. Apuntes de la Zoologia de Cauquenas, 1877.

COLOMBIA.   *See* NEW GRANADA.

COSTA RICA.

Cabanis. Uebersicht der im Berliner Mus. befind. Vögel von, 1861–69.

Cassin. Conirostral Birds from, 1865.

Salvin. Seventeen new Birds from, 1864.

COSTA RICA.—Continued.

Salvadori. Intorno ad alcuni Uccelli di, 1868.

Lawrence. Catalogue of Birds found in, 1868–69.

Frantzius. Ueber d. geogr. Verbreitung der Vögel von, 1869.

Salvin. Notes on Lawrence's List, 1869.

Salvin. Additional Notes on Lawrence's List, 1870.

Lawrence. Four new Birds from, 1874.

Boucard. On Birds collected in, 1878.

CUBA.

Vigors. On some Birds of, 1828, 1830.

Taylor, R. C. Notes on Natural Objects observed in, 1836.

d'Orbigny. Ramon de la Sagra's Histoire, 1839.

Yarrell. Description of Eggs of Birds of, 1847.

Poey. Catálogo metódico de las Aves de la Isla de, 1848.

Lembeye. Aves de la Isla de, 1850.

Gundlach. Five new Birds of, etc., 1852.

Arboleya. Manual de la Isla de, 1852.

Gundlach and Cabanis. Beiträge zur Ornithologie Cuba's, 1855–57.

Thienemann. Ueber Eier und Nester Cubanischer Vögel, 1857.

Gundlach. Notes on Birds of . . . and descr. of three new species, 1858.

Lawrence. Obs. on Gundlach's paper, 1858.

Gundlach. Ornithologisches aus Briefen von, 1859.

Ramon de la Sagra. Énumération des espèces zoologiques de l'île de, 1859.

Brewer. Compiled List of Birds of, 1860.

Lawrence. Notes on some Cuban Birds, 1860.

Albrecht. Zur Ornithologie von, 1861.

Gundlach. Tabell. Uebers. aller bisher auf . . . beobachteten Vögel, 1861.

Gundlach. Zusätze und Bericht. zu den Beiträgen zur Ornith. von, 1861–62.

Gundlach. Revista y Catálogo de las Aves de, 1865–66.

Gundlach. Neue Beit. zur Ornith. Cubas, 1871–74.

Bishop. Notes on Lembeye's 'Birds' of, 1878.

DOMINICA.

Lawrence. New Birds from, 1877.

Lawrence. Provisional List of Ober's Birds from, 1877.

DOMINICA.—Continued.

Lawrence. Catalogue of Ober's Birds from, 1878.

ECUADOR.

Jardine. Ornithology of Quito, 1849.

Jardine. Five Birds from Quito, 1857.

Sclater. Collection of Birds received by Gould from Quijos in, 1854, 1855.

Jardine. Jameson's Collections from Eastern Cordillera of, 1855, 1856.

Sclater. Notes on Birds received by Verreaux from the Rio Napo, 1858, 1858.

Sclater. New Birds from the Rio Napo, 1858.

Sclater. List of Birds collected by Fraser in, 1858, 1858.

Sclater. On New or Little-known Birds from the Rio Napo, 1859.

Sclater. Two New Birds from the Rio Napo, 1860.

Sclater. Birds collected by Fraser at Babahoyo, 1860.

Sclater. Birds collected by Fraser at Esmeraldas, 1860.

Sclater. Birds collected by Fraser at Pallatanga, 1860.

Sclater. Additional Birds collected by Fraser at Pallatanga, 1860.

Sclater. Birds collected by Fraser at Quito, 1860.

Sclater. Birds collected by Fraser at Nanegal, etc., 1860.

Sclater and Salvin. Birds collected by Hauxwell, at Pebas, on the Upper Amazon, 1867.

Lawrence. Catalogue of Birds from Puna Island, 1869.

Orton. Contrib. to Nat. Hist. of Valley of Quito, 1871.

Pelzeln. Sendung von Vögeln aus, 1874.

Salvin. New Birds from Western, 1876.

Pelzeln. Weitere Sendung von Vögeln aus, 1876.

Pelzeln. Weitere Sendung von Vögeln aus, 1878.

Sclater and Salvin. Three new Birds from, 1878.

FALKLAND ISLANDS.

Clayton. An account of the, 1776.

Garnot. Sur la Zoologie des Iles Malouines, 1826, 1827, 1832.

Bernsée. On Various Birds of East, 1855.

Gould. List of Birds from, 1859.

FALKLAND ISLANDS.—Continued.
Sclater. Eggs of Two Raptorial Birds of, 1860.
Sclater. Catalogue of the Birds of, 1860.
Abbott. Field-notes on Birds of, 1861.
Sclater. Add. and Corr. to the List of Birds of, 1861.
Sclater. Addition to List of Birds of, 1864.

GALAPAGOES.
Habel. Exhibition of Birds from the, 1869.
Sclater and Salvin. New Birds collected by Habel in the, 1870.
Sclater. On Birds from the, 1871.
Anon. Zoology of the, 1872.
Editors. New Galapagoes Birds, 1872.
Salvin. On the Avifauna of the, 1876.
Sharpe. Zoological Collections of H. M. S. 'Petrel', 1877.

GRENADA.
Lawrence. Catalogue of Ober's Birds of, 1879.

GUADELOUPE.
Lafresnaye. Quelques Ois. de la, 1844.
Lawrence. Catalogue of Ober's Birds of, 1879.

GUATEMALA.
Hartlaub. Sept Ois. nouv. de, 1844.
Salvin. Letters from Dueñas, 1860.
Salvin. Letters from Vera Paz, 1860.
Salvin and Sclater. Contrib. to the Ornithology of, 1860.
Sclater and Salvin. Eleven new Birds discovered by Salvin in, 1860, 1860.
Salvin. Three new Birds from, 1861, 1861.
Salvin. Twenty-eight species to be added to Ornithology of, 1861.
Owen. Nesting of some Birds of, 1861.
Salvin. Letter from Dueñas, 1862.
[*Sclater.*] Salvin and Godman's operations in, 1862.
Salvin. Letter from, 1863.
Salvin. Sea Birds and Waders of Pacific Coast of, 1865.
Salvin. Another Contrib. to Ornith. of, 1866.
Salvin. Letter on some Birds of, 1873.
Sclater. Letter from Salvin on Birds of, 1874.

GUIANA.
Warren. Description of Surinam, 1745, (p. 306).

GUIANA.—Continued.
Fermin. Hist. Nat. de la Hollande Equinox., 1765, (p. 307).
Bancroft. Essay on the Natural History of, 1769, 1769.
Sonnini. Observations sur les Marails ou Faisans de la, 1775.
Richard and Bernard. Cat. des Ois. envoyés de Cayenne, 1792.
Schomburgk. Description of British, 1840.
Abbott. Exhibition of Birds from Surinam, 1844.
Cabanis. Schomburgk's Reisen in Britisch, 1848.
Bonyan. Raptorial Birds of British, 1851.
Bonyan. On Raptorial Birds of British, 1853.
Bonaparte. Cat. des Ois. recueillis par Desplanches à Cayenne, 1857.
Sclater. Birds from Oyapok, 1871.
Pelzeln. Birds collected by Münzberg in Spanish, 1875.
Brown, C. B. Canoe and Camp Life in British, 1876.

HAYTI.
Hearne. Note on Birds of, 1834.
Hearne. Present of Living Animals from, 1834.
Hearne. Collection of Birds formed in, 1835.
Sallé. Oiseaux rapportés dans la République Dominicaine, 1857.
Bryant. List of the Birds of, 1867.
Salvin. Letter off, 1873.

HONDURAS.
Sclater. List of Birds collected by Taylor in, 1858.
Sclater. Arrival of Birds from British, 1860.
Taylor, G. C. Birds collected or observed in, 1860.
Salvin. Fortnight among Sea Birds of, 1864.
Sclater and Salvin. Birds collected by Whitely on the Coast of, 1870.

JAMAICA.
Sloane. Voyage to, 1707–25.
Browne. Civil and Natural History of, 1756, 1789.
Hill. On Nests of Birds of, 1841, 1842.
Hill. Two Bird-skins from, 1844.
Lafresnaye. Quelques Ois. nouv. de la, 1846.

JAMAICA.—Continued.

Gosse. The Birds of, 1847.

Gosse. Extracts from the Birds of, 1847.

Hartlaub. Sur quelques Ois. nouv. de la, 1847, 1847.

Lafresnaye. Réponse à M. Hartlaub sur quelques Ois. de la, 1847, 1847.

Gosse. Two new Birds from, 1849.

Gosse. Illustrations of the Birds of, 1849.

Gosse. Naturalist's Sojourn in, 1851.

Gosse. Singing Birds in, 1851.

Osburn. Notes on the Birds of (several papers), 1859, 1860.

Osburn. Notes on Mountain Birds of, 1860.

Sclater. Birds collected by Osburn in, 1861.

Albrecht. Zur Ornith. von, 1862.

March. Notes on the Birds of, 1863–64.

Bell. Wildfowl of, 1868.

MARTINIQUE.

Lawrence. Catalogue of Ober's Birds of, 1879.

MEXICO.

Lafresnaye. Quelques Ois. nouv. de la collection de M. Brelay, 1839.

Williams. The Isthmus of Tehuantepec, 1852.

Sclater. Birds collected by Boucard in Southern, 1862.

NEW GRANADA.

Humboldt. Recueil d'observations, 1811, (p. 307).

Boissonneau. Oiseaux nouveaux de Santa-Fé de Bogota, 1840, 1840.

Fraser. New Species from Bogota in Collection of Lord Derby, 1840.

Lafresnaye. Ois. nouv. de Santa-Fé de Bogota, 1840.

Lafresnaye. Quelques Ois. nouv. de la Colombie, 1842, 1842, 1843, 1843, 1844, 1846.

Hartlaub. Quatre Ois. de la, 1843.

Lafresnaye. Sur divers Ois. de la, 1844.

Seemann. Notes on the Zoology of the Isthmus of Panama, 1852.

Mosquera. Memoria sobre la geografia de la, 1852, 1853.

Sclater. New Birds from Santa Fé de Bogota, 1855.

Sclater. On Birds received from Santa Fé de Bogota, 1855.

Sclater. Additional new Birds from Bogota, 1856.

NEW GRANADA.—Continued.

Sclater. New Species of Birds from Bogota, 1856.

Sclater. Two new Species of Birds from Bogota, 1856.

Sclater. Birds collected by Bridges at David, Chiriqui, 1856.

Sclater. Further additions of List of Birds from Bogota, 1857.

Sclater. Additional Birds received from Bogota, 1857.

Sclater. Two new Species from Bogota, 1857.

Bryant. On Two Birds from Bogota, 1860.

Cassin. Catalogue of Birds collected on the Isthmus of Darien by Michler, 1860.

Sclater. Nine new Birds from Bogota, 1862, 1862.

Lawrence. Catalogue of a Collection made by McLeannan in, 1861–63.

Lawrence. Six new Birds from Isthmus of Panama, 1862.

Lawrence. Eight new Birds from Isthmus of Panama, 1863.

Benvenuti. Descrizione di quattro nuove specie, etc., 1866.

Sclater and Salvin. Notes on a collection of Birds from Isthmus of Panama, 1864.

Lawrence. List of Birds collected by Hicks near David, Chiriqui, 1865.

Lawrence. Four new Birds from Isthmus of Panama, 1865.

Lawrence. Notes on certain Birds from, 1867.

Cope. Birds of Palestine and, 1868.

Sclater and Salvin. Five new Birds from the U. S. of Colombia, 1870.

Wyatt. Notes on Birds of the U. S. of Colombia, 1871.

Salvin. Maack's Researches in Panama, 1872.

Sclater. Two new Birds from Antioquia, 1873.

Sclater and Salvin. Two new Birds from Antioquia, 1875.

NICARAGUA.

Lawrence. Catalogue of Collection made by Holland at Greytown, 1865.

Sclater and Salvin. Birds collected by Wickham on Blewfields River, 1867.

Salvin. Notes on Belt's Chontales Birds of, 1872.

NICARAGUA.—Continued.
  Sclater. Additions to List of Birds of,
    1873.
PANAMA. *See* NEW GRANADA.
PARAGUAY.
  Dobrizhoffer. Historia de Abiponibus,
    1784, 1822.
  Azara. Apuntamientos para la Histo-
    ria Natural, 1802–05, 1809.
  Hartlaub. Index zu Azara's Apunta-
    mientos, 1847.
  Rosenschöld. Bref från, 1853, 1854.
PATAGONIA.
  King. Letter on Animals of Straits of
    Magellan, 1827–28, 1828, 1830.
  King. New genera and species from
    Straits of Magellan, 1829, 1831, 1834.
  Vigors. Remarks on several new Birds
    from Straits of Magellan, 1831, 1834.
  d'Orbigny. Naturh. Schilderung des
    nördlichen, 1839.
  Sclater and Salvin. Birds collected by
    Cunningham in Straits of Magellan,
    1868.
  Cunningham. Letter on Birds of Straits
    of Magellan, 1869.
  Sclater and Salvin. Second List of Birds
    collected by Cunningham in Straits
    of Magellan, 1869.
  Cunningham. Nat. Hist. of Straits of
    Magellan and west coast of, 1870.
  Newton, A. Additional Note on Nests
    and Eggs collected by Cunningham,
    1870.
  Sclater and Salvin. Third List of Birds
    collected by Cunningham in the
    Straits of Magellan, 1870.
  Cunningham. Fauna of the Straits of
    Magellan and Western, 1871.
  Hudson. On Birds of the Rio Negro,
    1872.
  Durnford. Birds observed in Chuput
    Valley, 1877.
  Durnford. Notes on the Birds of Cen-
    tral, 1878.
PERU.
  Tschudi. Diagnosen einiger neuer peru-
    anischer Vögel, 1843.
  Tschudi. Avium Conspectus quæ in
    Repub. Peruana reperiuntur, 1844.
  Tschudi. Nachträgliche Bemerkungen
    zu seinem Conspectus, 1845.
  Tschudi and Cabanis. Fauna Peruana,
    1845–46.
  Tschudi. Five papers on animal life
    in . . . and Chili, 1847.

PERU.—Continued.
  Lafresnaye. Faune du Pérou du Dr.
    Tschudi, 1849.
  Strickland. Four species of Birds from
    Andes of, 1850.
  Kinahan. Letter from Callao, 1856.
  Bolle. Guano auf den Chincha-Inseln,
    1861.
  Raimondi. Huano des îles de Chincha,
    1856, 1856.
  Sclater. On the Birds of the Vicinity
    of Lima, 1866.
  Sclater and Salvin. Birds collected by
    Bartlett on the Ucayali, 1866.
  Sclater and Salvin. Additions to Birds
    collected by Bartlett on the Ucayali,
    1866.
  Sclater and Salvin. Birds collected by
    Bartlett on the Huallaga, 1867.
  Sclater. On Birds of the vicinity of
    Lima, 1867.
  Sclater. Extracts from Bartlett's let-
    ters, 1867.
  Sclater and Salvin. On Peruvian Birds
    collected by Whitely, 1867, 1868, 1868,
    1869, 1869, 1873, 1874, 1876.
  Sclater. Birds of the vicinity of Lima,
    1869.
  Sclater and Salvin. Two new Birds
    collected by Bartlett in Eastern,
    1869.
  Sclater. On Birds of the vicinity of
    Lima, 1871.
  Sclater. Peruvian Birds collected by
    Whitely, Part VII, 1873.
  Sclater and Salvin. Bartlett's Birds of
    Eastern, 1873.
  Cabanis. Neue peruanische Vögel Jels-
    ki's, 1873, 1873, 1874.
  Sclater. Notice of Jelski's Collections
    in, 1874.
  Taczanowski. Oiseaux nouveaux du,
    1874.
  Taczanowski. Oiseaux recueillis par
    Jelski dans, 1874.
  Golz. Ueber die Guanolager, 1874.
  Allen. Exploration of Lake Titicaca,
    1876.
  Taczanowski. Liste des Ois. recueillis
    par Jelski et Stolzmann, 1877.
  Taczanowski. Supplement à la même,
    1877.
PORTO RICO.
  Moritz. Notizen zur Fauna der Insel,
    1836.
  Bryant. Vögel von, 1866.

PORTO RICO.—Continued.

Bryant. List of Birds collected by Swift and Latimer in, 1866.

Sundevall. Foglarne på ön, 1869 *or* 1870.

Bello y Espinosa. Zoologische Notizen aus, 1871.

Gundlach. Beitrag zur Ornith. der Insel, 1874.

Gundlach. Neue Beiträge zur Ornith. der Insel, 1878.

ST. BARTHOLOMEW.

Fahlberg. Slutet, af Samlingar til Natural-Historien, 1786.

Sundevall. Foglarne på ön, 1869 *or* 1870.

ST. CROIX.

West. Beyträge zur Beschreibung von, 1794.

Newton, A., and Newton, E. Observations on the Birds of, 1859.

ST. DOMINGO. *See* HAYTI.

ST. LUCIA.

Sclater. Correspondence with des Vœux, 1871.

Sclater. On the Birds of, 1871.

Sclater. On Birds of the Island of, 1871.

Semper. Observations on the Birds of, 1872.

Sclater. Additional Birds from, 1876.

ST. THOMAS.

Knox. Historical Account of, 1852.

Cassin. Catalogue of Birds from, 1860.

ST. VINCENT.

Lawrence. Seven new Birds from the Island of, 1878.

Lawrence. Catalogue of Ober's Birds from, 1878.

SOMBRERO.

Lawrence. Birds collected by Julien in, 1864.

SURINAM. *See* GUIANA.

TOBAGO.

Jardine. Ornithology of the Island of, 1852.

TRINIDAD.

Mitchell. Notice of Lord Harris's Collection, 1850.

De Verteuil. Trinidad, 1858.

Léotaud. Ois. de l'Ile de la, 1866.

Sclater. On Léotaud's Birds of, 1867.

Finsch. On Coll. of Birds from, 1870.

VENEZUELA.

Lafresnaye. Ois. nouv. de l'Orénoco, 1846.

Sclater and Salvin. Birds collected by Goering in, 1868, 1868, 1869, 1870, 1875.

Sclater and Salvin. On Birds collected by Spence in, 1873.

Ernst. Apuntos para la fauna ornithológica de, 1870.

Ernst. Estudios sobre la Flora y Fauna de, 1877.

Spence. The Land of Bolivar, 1878.

Hartlaub. Deux Ois. nouv. de Caracas, 1849.

Hartlaub. Deux Ois. nouv. de Vénézuéla, 1849.

VERAGUA.

Salvin. Eight new Birds from, 1866.

Salvin. On some Collections of Birds from, 1867.

Sclater and Salvin. Four new Birds from, 1868.

Salvin. On some Collections of Birds from, 1870.

WEST INDIES. (*See, also, the several Islands.*)

De Laet. Beschrijvinghe van, 1625, 1630, 1633, 1640, (pp. 305, 306).

Labat. Voyage, 1724, (p. 306).

West. Bidrag til beskrivelse over St. Croix, etc., 1793, (p. 307).

Rochefort. Histoire des Iles Antilles, 1658, 1660, 1681.

Stubbes. Observations on the Caribe Islands, 1667, 1668.

Ledru. Voyage, 1810, 1811–12, (p. 307).

Taylor, E. C. Five months in the, 1864.

Guyon. Thiere die auf Martinique und Guadeloupe verschwunden sind, 1866, (p. 309).

Guyon. Des animaux disparus de la Martinique et de la Guadeloupe, 1866.

Hill. History of, 1836.

Denny. On Geographical Distrib. of Birds of the, 1847.

Hartlaub.. Ueber den heutigen Zustand unserer Kenntniss von Westindiens Ornithologie, 1847–48.

Taylor. Guano from Caribbean Islands, 1857.

Sclater. The Birds of the Lesser Antilles, 1871.

Lawrence. New Birds from Grenada and Dominica, 1878.

Art. XXVI.—Third Instalment of American Ornithological Bibliography.

Art. XXVI.—Third Instalment of American Ornithological Bibliography.

By Dr. Elliott Coues, U. S. A.

The Appendix to the Birds of the Colorado Valley (pp. 567[1]–784[218]), which gives the titles of "Faunal Publications" relating to North America, is to be considered as the *first* instalment of this work.

The *second* instalment occupies pp. 239–330 of this Bulletin, this Vol., No. 2, and similarly gives the titles of "Faunal Publications", being those relating to the rest of America.

These two instalments represent all that I am at present prepared to publish of titles of this kind, *i. e.*, in "regional" Ornithology.

This present, *third* instalment consists of an entirely different set of titles, namely, those belonging to the "systematic" department of the whole Bibliography.

In this department come the titles of all publications treating of particular species, genera, or families of Birds, sytematically arranged *by Families*, in chronological order under each family, with alphabetization of authors' names under each date. The lot of titles herewith presented, however, are only those that relate to *American* species. Of those families which are exclusively American, as, for example, *Mniotiltidæ, Icteridæ, Tanagridæ, Trochilidæ*, etc., I give, of course, all the titles in my possession; but of those families which are more cosmopolitan, as the *Turdidæ* or *Fringillidæ*, I select only the titles relating to American species; and of extra-limital families no titles whatever are given. Such is the ostensible scope of the present instalment; but I actually give many titles relating to extra-limital species, when the close relationship of such species makes it desirable, or when the insertion of a few such additional titles enables me to present all those that I possess of certain families.

The three instalments together represent a nearly complete Bibliography of Ornithology so far as *America* is concerned. They are published in this manner in advance of the whole work for several reasons— among others, both to render immediately available certain departments of the Bibliography which are practically completed, and to invite criticism and suggestions for the bettering of the work. I am satisfied that, if I can come anywhere near the standard I have set for myself, I shall have done a very useful thing; and I beg those who are interested in the accomplishment of this undertaking to inform me of any defects they may perceive. In only one particular would I deprecate criticism at present—and this is respecting the *arrangement* of the titles; for the scheme of the work cannot be fairly appreciated until the whole is published, including the several contemplated Indexes.

The portions of the Bibliography now before the public suffice for an estimate of its plan and purpose; but I may add that nothing has yet appeared of several other important departments, such as those of "General and Miscellaneous" publications, of publications in "Anatomy and Physiology", of publications relating to "Birds in Domestication or Captivity", etc. It is not my intention, however, to print any more of the work at present, the *American* departments being the only ones sufficiently perfected to warrant their leaving my hands. But meanwhile I am making manuscript for the rest as rapidly and as continuously as possible.

NOTA BENE: It being absolutely necessary, in this part of the work, to have some fixed standard (no matter what one) for the grouping of species and genera into families, and for the sequence of the families, I have adopted as most convenient the arrangement of *Gray's* HAND-LIST, as far as the *Passeres* are concerned—the limitations of the families in other orders being sufficiently nearly agreed upon by ornithologists. *For Passerine families, then, the titles have been assorted strictly and exactly according to the composition and sequence of those groups in the work just mentioned.*

Hirundinidæ.

[Here only titles additional to those given in "Birds of the Colorado Valley", pp. 378–389, 396–401, *q. v.*]

1769. LAXMANN, E. Hirundo daurica, area temporali rubra, Uropygio luteo rufescente. < *Köngl. Svensk. Vetensk.-Acad. Handl.*, XXX, 1769, pp. 209–213, pl. vii.

1774. WHITE, G. Account of the House Martin, or Martlet. < *Philos. Trans.*, lxiv, pt. i, 1774, pp. 196–201.

Habits of *Chelidon urbica*.

This celebrated memoir is curiously misquoted in Carus and Engelmann. *Bibl. Zool.*, ii, 1861, p. 1375, as if referring to the mammal *Mustela foina*, known as the "Marten". Gill and Coues perpetuate the blunder in *Monogrs. N. A. Rodentia*, 1877. App., p. 1005, by transcription of the title into their *Bibl. of N. A. Mammals.* Coues exaggerated it in his *Fur-bearing Animals*, 1877, p. 77, by making out *Mustela foina* to have been instituted by Gilbert White, as above! The funny mistake is shown up by Alston, *P. Z. S.*, 1879, p. 469. The title is correctly cited by Coues in *Birds Colorado Valley*, 1878, p. 396; as it is also by Giebel, *Thes. Orn.*, p. 145.—It is hard to teach some people to verify quotations!

On the same page of Carus and Engelmann, 6 lines higher up, occurs a no less singular mistake: John Hunter's account of the "Free Martin" (a local name for cattle with a certain malformation) being cited as if relating to some species of *Mustela*. Again, on p. 1345, same work, a paper on the anatomy "of a *male* Otter", *Lutræ maris* (in the genitive), is allocated with *Enhydris*, as if it were *Lutræ maris*, "of a *Sea* Otter".

1789. CARLSON, G. V. Anmärkningar om Svalor. < *Kongl. Vetensk.-Acad. Nyt Handl.*, x, 1789, pp. 315–317.

1809. REEVE, H.   An | Essay | on | the Torpidity | of | Animals. | By Henry Reeve, M. D. | Member of the Royal College of Physicians of | London, and Fellow of the Linnæan Society. | — | [Quotation.] | — | London : | Printed for Long-man, Hurst, Rees, and Orme, | Paternoster Row, | by Richard Taylor & Co. Shoe Lane. | — | 1809.   1 vol.   8vo.   pp. iii–viii, 1–152.

P. 39.   "Here a curious question arises respecting the disappearance of birds." And the author goes on to discuss the alleged hibernation of Swallows.   Cf. *Philos. Mag.*, xxxv, 1810, p. 241.

1813. FORSTER, T.   Observations | on the | Brvmal Retreat | of the Swallow. | — | To which is annexed | a copiovs Index | to many passages relating to this bird, | in the works of ancient and modern authors. | — | By | Thomas Forster, F. L. S. | Author of | "Researches about atmospheric Phaenomena," etc. | — | Third edition, corrected and enlarged. | — | London : | Printed by J. Moyes, Greville Street, Hatton Garden ; | for Thomas Underwood, 32, Fleet Street, | and 40 West Smithfield. | — | 1813.   8vo.   pp. i–xiv, 1–46.

See other editions, of 1814 and 1817.

1814. FORSTER, T.   Observations | on the | brvmal retreat | of the | Swallow. | — | To which is annexed | a copiovs index | to many passages relating to this bird, | in the works of ancient and modern authors. | — | By Thomas Forster, F. L. S. | Author of [etc.] | — | Fourth Edition, corrected and enlarged. | [This Edition is not published separately.] | 1814.   < *The Pamphleteer,* iv, 1814, pp. 431–462.

This and two others are the only editions I have been able to lay hands on, of this rather notable paper ; as stated in the title, the present edition is not issued separately.   I give eds. of 1813 and 1817, and find another quoted of 1817. In the present, the author alludes to three earlier editions. The treatise in its present shape seems to be materially modified, with a new preface ; besides which, it consists of the original (?) preface, pp. 433–438, observations, etc., 439–454, appendix, 455–459, giving first and latest appearance of Swallows near London for several years ; and of index, 460–462, of passages relating to history of the Swallow in various works, ancient and modern, and the names of Swallows in many different languages. (He derives Swallow, as usual, from A. S. *swelgan*, to swallow, and says the Greek "is supposed to have come either from χεῖλη δονεῖν *quod scil.* labia agitet, vel quod χεῖλεσιν ᾄδει labiis canit" —in which he differs from other authority.   The latin supposititious derivation, ab *hœrendo*, from the adhesive nests, seems to me very far-fetched.)   Cf. *Birds Col. Vall.,* i, 1878, pp. 369–371.

1816? ANON.   The | Swallows : | or, | Observations & Reflections | upon | Their Late Assemblage | at Rotherham, | and their | subsequent departure. | — | [Quo-tation, 4 lines.] | — | Albion Press : | Printed and Sold by T. Crookes, Rother-ham ; | sold also by [etc. 3 lines].   [n. d. 1816?]   1 vol.   16mo.   pp. i–viii, 9–38.

Anonymous : preface dated Clifton Cottage, Dec. 1815.—A sermon by a clergyman to his parishioners, on the wisdom and goodness of God as illustrated by the habits of *Hirundinidæ.*

1817. FORSTER, T.   Observations | on the | Brvmal Retreat | of the | Swallow ; | with | a copiovs reference | to passages relating | to this subject, | in differ-ent authors. | — | By Thomas Forster, F. L. S. | [etc.] | — | Fifth Edition. | — | London : | Printed by J. Moyes, Greville Street ; | for Thomas and George Underwood, | 32, Fleet street. | — | 1817.   8vo.   pp. i–xiv, 1–46.

Substantially the same as, if not identical with, the 4th ed., published in *The Pamphleteer,* iv, 1814, pp. 431–462, *q. v.*

"I do not mean to say that swallows may not have occasionally been found under water ; for it is well known that they have ; . . . but I should certainly attribute their being found in such situations to mere accident ; . . . they have sometimes been taken out of the water, in winter, in a torpid state, . . . they have likewise been found concealed in the crevices of rocks, in holes in old decayed trees, in old ruined towers, and under the thatch of houses."

1823? STEINMÜLLER, J. R.   [Sur l'Hirundo rupestris.]   < *Neue Alpina,* i, p. 530.

Not seen.

1824. AUDUBON, J. J.   [Note on the Hirundo fulva.]   < *Ann. Lyc. Nat. Hist. N. Y.,* i, pt. 1, 1824, pp. 163–166.

Forms part of the article by DeWitt Clinton, *loc. cit., q. v.*

1824. DEFRANCE, —.   Notice sur le vol des hirondelles de cheminée.   < *Féruss. Bull.*, 2e sect., i, 1824, p. 183.

1825. L[ESSON], [R.] P.   Faits et observations relatives à la résidence permanente des Hirondelles dans les États-Unis; par John Audubon.   < *Féruss. Bull.*, 2e sect., vii, 1825, p. 109.
    Résumé des *Ann. Lyc. Nat. Hist.*, i, 1824, pp. 166-168.

1826. LESS[ON, R. P.]   Sur l'Hirundo fulva de Vieillot, avec quelques remarques sur les oiseaux de ce genre; par Dewitt Clinton. . . .   < *Féruss. Bull.*, 2e sect., ix, 1826, pp. 232, 233.
    Extrait des *Ann. Lyc. Nat. Hist. N. Y.*, i, 1824, pp. 156-166.

1828. ANON.   Faits concernant l'hibernation de l'Hirondelle de cheminée (Hirundo rustica); par le Rév. Colin Smith . . .   < *Féruss Bull.*, 2e sect., xiv, 1828, pp. 117, 118.
    Précis, tiré du *Edinb. New Philos. Journ.*, juillet-sept., 1827, pp. 231-234.

1830. ANON.   Tableau sur l'arrivée et le départ des hirondelles de la Grande-Bretagne; par W. F. Bree. . . .   < *Féruss. Bull.*, 2e sect., xxii, 1830, pp. 118, 119.
    Extrait de *Loudon's Mag. Nat. Hist.*, ii, mars, 1829, pp. 16-20.

1830. "PHILOCHELIDON."   On the wanton Destruction of Swallows.   < *Loudon's Mag. Nat. Hist.*, iii, 1830, pp. 35-38.

1831. "G. M."   The Swallow and the Stoat.   < *Loudon's Mag. Nat. Hist.*, iv, 1831, p. 146.
    Attack by *Hirundo rustica* upon a Stoat.

1832. BREE, W. T.   Effects of the Swallow Tick (Hippobosca Hirundinis L.) on the Swallow Tribe (Hirundines.)   < *Loudon's Mag. Nat. Hist.*, v, 1832, p. 677.

1832. "J. D[ENSON ?]."   Intrepidity of the Swallow [Hirundo rustica].   < *Loudon's Mag. Nat. Hist.*, v, 1832, p. 84.

1833. "J. C."   Swallow (Hirundo rustica) [in confinement].   < *Loudon's Mag. Nat. Hist.*, vi, 1833, pp. 270, 271.

1835. CHAMBERLAIN, R. D.   A Swallow accidentally fettered into the Nest in which it had been reared, and hence detained from accompanying other Swallows in their Departure in Autumn from Britain: one of its Parents had stayed to attend it.   < *Loudon's Mag. Nat. Hist.*, viii, 1835, p. 513.

1835. MORRIS, B. R.   Birds of the Swallow Kind: Means conducive to the keeping of them alive in Britain through the Winter.   < *Loudon's Mag. Nat. Hist.*, viii. 1835, p. 572.

1835. MORRIS, B. R.   Earliest and Latest Dates of seeing the Swallow in Britain.   < *Loudon's Mag. Nat. Hist.*, viii, 1835, p. 572.
    A model article—shorter than its title!

1836. TULK, A.   Swallows, an extended String is used as a perch by certain.   < *Loudon's Mag. Nat. Hist.*, ix, 1836, p. 107.

1845. HARDY, J.   Superstition respecting the Martin (Hirundo urbica).   < *Zoologist*, 1845, p. 870.

1845. HORNE, C.   Do Swallows eat the Honey-bee ?   < *Zoologist*, iii, 1845, p. 1137.

1846. CLIBBORN, B.   Ornithological Note.   [On Cotyle riparia?]   < *Zoologist*, iv, 1846, pp. 1368, 1369.

1846. THIENEMANN, F. A. L.   Meine Schwalbe.   < *Rhea*, i, 1846, pp. 98-103.
    Aus dem Leben.

1846. TURNER, W.   Anecdote of confidence in the Swallow.   < *Zoologist*, iv, 1846, p. 1551.

1848. HUSSEY, A.   Swallows, and a Plea on their Behalf.   < *Zoologist*, vi, 1848, p. 2303.

1849. STRICKLAND, H. E. Hirundo albigularis [n. sp.]. < *Jard. Contrib. Orn.*, 1849, p. 17, pl. xv.

1850. ALLAN, W. Anecdote of Martins (Hirundo [Chelidon] urbica). < *Zoologist,* viii, 1850, pp. 2824, 2825.

1850. [SUNDEVALL, C. J.] Svalornas hibernation. < *Öfvers. Kongl. Vetensk.-Akad. Förhandl. för år* 1849, 1850, pp. 181–185.

1850. WAKEFIELD, R. On the Cruelty of Swallow Shooting. < *Zoologist*, viii, 1850, p. 2952.

1851. [ASCHAN, N. N.] Om svalans hibernation. < *Öfvers. Kongl. Vetensk.-Akad. Förhandl. för år* 1850, 1851, pp. 6, 7.

1851. [GRILL, G.] Om svalans hibernation. < *Öfvers. Kongl. Vetensk.-Akad. Förhandl. för år* 1850, 1851, pp. 7, 8.

1851. HARPER, J. O. Death of Martins [Chelidon urbica] and Swallows [Hirundo rustica, in Norwich]. < *Zoologist*, ix, 1851, p. 2988.

1851. [JARDINE, W.] Birds of Western Africa. < *Jard. Contrib. Orn.*, 1851, p. 141.
Consisting only of a description of *Hirundo gordoni*, sp. n.

1851. MATTHEWS, A. Display of Parental Affection by Martins [Chelidon urbica]. < *Zoologist*, ix, 1851, pp. 3173, 3174.

1851. [SUNDEVALL, C. J.] Om svalans hibernation. < *Öfvers. Kongl. Vetensk.-Akad. Förhandl. för år* 1850, 1851, pp. 8–11.

1852. HARRIS, G. Anecdote of the House Martin, (Hirundo [Chelidon] urbica). < *Zoologist*, x, 1852, pp. 3512, 3513.

1853. CASSIN, J. Catalogue | of the | Hirundinidæ | in the Collection of | the Academy of Natural Sciences | of Philadelphia. < Published with the *Proc. Acad. Nat. Sci. Phila.*, vol. vi; dated July 1, 1853; not paged; also, separately, 8vo, one signature, 8 foll.

1853. RODD, E. H. Supposed Occurrence of the Rufous Swallow (Hirundo rufula) near Penzance. < *Zoologist*, xi, 1853, p. 3753.

1854. MOORE, F. Notice of a New Indian Swallow [Delichon (g. n.) nipalensis Hodgs.]. < *P. Z. S.*, xxii, 1854, p. 104, pl. (Aves) lxiii.

1854. SUNDEVALL, C. J. Om Svalans hibernation. < *Öfvers. Kongl. Vetensk.-Akad. Förhandl. för år* 1853, 1854, pp. 135–140.

1855. BRIGGS, J. J. Note on the destruction of Swallows, &c., by the severity of the weather [in Derbyshire, Engl., May, 1855]. < *Zoologist*, xiii, 1855, pp. 4808, 4809.

1855. LOWE, E. J. Singular Mortality amongst the Swallow Tribe. < *Canad. Journ.*, iii, 1855, p. 388.

1855. MOORE, F. Notice of a [lately] New Indian Swallow. < *Ann. Mag. Nat. Hist.*, 2d ser., xvi, pp. 225, 226.
From *P. Z. S.*. Apr. 25, 1854, p. 104, pl. (Aves) 63 (*Delichon nipalensis* Hodgs.).

1856. ASCHNER, T. [Ueber eine weisse Schwalbe.] < *Verh. zool.-bot. Ver. Wien*, vi, 1856, p. 76.

1856. HADFIELD, H. W. Anecdote of Swallows. < *Zoologist*, xiv, 1856, p. 5204.

1856. HELLMANN, A. Beitrag zur Ptilographie und Anatomie der Hirundo rustica. < *J. f. O.*, iv, 1856, pp. 360–370.

1858. GOULD, J. Descriptions of Two New Species of the Family Hirundinidæ. < *P. Z. S.*, xxvi, July 13, 1858, pp. 355, 356.
Atticora pileata, p. 355; *Chelidon cashmeriensis*, p. 356.

1859. GOULD, J. Descriptions of Two [lately] New Species of the Family Hirundinidæ. < *Ann. Mag. Nat. Hist.*, 3d ser., iii, 1859, p. 77.
From *P. Z. S.*. July 13, 1858, pp. 355, 356, *q. v.*

1860. HADFIELD, H.   Note on the Barn Swallow of Jamaica (Hirundo americana).
     < Zoologist, xviii, 1860, pp. 6975, 6976.

1861. FRAUENFELD, G. V.   Dritter Beitrag zur Fauna Dalmatiens, nebst einer orni-
     thologischen Notiz.   *< Verh. (Abhandl.) k.-k. zool.-bot. Ges. Wien*, xi, 1861, pp.
     97–110.
       Ornithologische Notiz über *Hirundo [Chelidon] urbica*, pp. 108–110, fig.

1862. ANDRAEA, V.   Sinologisch-zoologische Notizen.   *< Zool. Gart.*, iii, 1862, pp.
     178–180.
       No. III. Die Schwalben (*Hirundinidæ*).—Gedicht.

1863. GURNEY, J. H.   [Note on Hirundo monteiri.]   *< Ibis*, v, 1863, pp. 116, 117.

1863. MOGGRIDGE, M. W.   [On the habits of Hirundo rupestris.]   *< Ibis*, v, 1863,
     pp. 233–235.

1863. SAVILLE, S. P.   A Swallow turning Pirate.   *< Zoologist*, xxi, 1863, p. 8824.

1865. DEVIS, C. W.   Note on the Swallow['s mode of feeding on wing].   *< Zoologist*,
     xxiii, 1865, p. 9729.

1866. GURNEY, J. H., JR.   [Occurrence of Hirundo riocouri at Teesmouth, July 6,
     1866.]   *< Ibis*, 2d ser., ii, 1866, p. 423.
       Afterward ascertained to have been *H. rustica*: cf. *Ibis*, 1875, p. 519.

1866. LAWRENCE, G. N.   Descriptions of Six New Species of Birds of the Families
     Hirundinidæ, Formicaridæ, Tyrannidæ, and Trochilidæ.   *< Ann. Lyc. Nat.
     Hist. New York*, viii, 1866, pp. 400–405.
       Hirundo æquitorialis, p. 400 (Ecuador).

1866. LEBOUR, G. A.   Swallow Stones.   *< Zoologist*, 2d ser., i, 1866, p. 523.
       "Calcareous opercula of some species of Turbo" found in Swallows' nests, and their use as
     'eye-stones'.

1866. STEVENSON, H.   Effects of Cold on the House Martin [Chelidon urbica].   *< Zo-
     ologist*, 2d ser., i, 1866, pp. 269, 270.

1867. CLARK-KENNEDY, A.   Swallows [Hirundo rustica] and Martins [Chelidon
     urbica] dying from Cold.   *< Zoologist*, 2d ser., ii, p. 1015.

1867. HARTING, J. E.   An Inquiry into the Nature and Properties of the Swallow-stone
     and Swallow's-herb.   *< Zoologist*, 2d ser., ii, 1867, pp. 744–747.

1867. LONGFELLOW, [H. W.]   Swallow-stones (see Zool. S. S. 523).   *< Zoologist*, 2d
     ser., ii, 1867, p. 561.
       Quotation from 'Evangeline'.

1867. MOOR, E. C.   Swallows [Hirundo rustica] and Martins [Chelidon urbica] picked
     up dead at Aldeburgh.   *< Zoologist*, 2d ser., ii, 1867, p. 990.

1869. HUGHES, D. D.   Sagacity of the Purple Martin [Progne subis].   *< Am. Nat.*
     iii, 1869, p. 554.

1869. SHARPE, R. B.   [On Hirundo nigrita as type of a new genus, Waldenia.]
     Ibis, 2d ser., v, 1869, p. 461.

1870. ANON.   Der moderne Bau des Nestes unserer Hausschwalbe [Chelidon urbica].
     < Aus der Natur, lii, oder n. F., xl, 1870, pp. 413–415.

1870. ANON.   Unsere Schwalben.   *< Aus der Natur*, liii, oder n. F., xli, 1870, pp.
     566, 567.
       Ueber den Bau des Nestes.

1870. MATHEW, M. A.   Swallow taking a Fly from a Horse.   *< Zoologist*, 2d ser., v,
     1870, p. 2307.

1870. POUCHET, A.   Transformation des nids de l'hirondelle de fenêtre (Hirundo [Cheli-
     don] urbica Lin.)   *< Compt. Rend.*, lxx, 7 mars 1870, pp. 492–496.
       Cf. *Birds of the Colorado Valley*, i, 1878, p. 450.

1870. SHARPE, R. B.   On the Hirundinidæ of the Ethiopian Region.   *< P. Z. S.*, May
     12, 1870, pp. 286–322.
       38 species and 7 genera are treated very fully under two subfamilies. *Psalidoprocninæ*, 1
     gen., 4 spp., and *Hirundininæ*, 6 genn., 34 spp.   Characters, synonymy, distribution, are pre-
     sented, with some account of habits and much criticism.   *Atticora obscura* Temm. is identi-

1870. SHARPE, R. B.—Continued.

fled with *Psalidoprocne holomelæna,* juv., and *Hirundo alfredi* (*Zool. Rec.*, v, p. 81) with *Petrochelidon spilodera* (Sund., *Öf. Sv. Ak.*, 1850, p. 10β). A table of the geographical distribution is added, in which an attempt is made to divide the region naturally into five subregions—the Abyssinian, Mozambican, Cape, Guinean, and Madagascarian.

1871. HUDSON, W. H.   [Twelfth Letter on the Ornithology of Buenos Ayres.] < *P. Z. S.*, 1871, pp. 326–329.

Treats of the *Hirundinidæ* of that country.

1872. WHITAKER, J., JR.   Swallows roosting on Rushes.   < *Zoologist,* 2d ser., vii, 1872, p. 3314.

1873. "L. W. L."   Rambling Martins.   < *Forest and Stream,* i, Nov. 6, 1873, p. 198.

1873. SCHACHT, H.   Ein ornithologisches Räthsel.   < *Zool. Gart.*, xiv, 1873, pp. 235, 236.

1874. ANON.   [Nesting of Swallows.]   < *Am. Sportsman,* iv, 1874, p. 390.

1874. CAREY, C. B.   Song of the Swallow.   < *Zoologist,* 2d ser., ix, 1874, pp. 4156, 4157.

1874. CORBIN, G. B.   Swallows roosting on Rushes.   < *Zoologist,* 2d sér., ix, 1874, p. 4035.

1874. "TRANSIT."   [Instance of co-operation in nest-building among Swallows.] < *Forest and Stream,* ii, April 2, 1874, p. 123.

1875. GURNEY, J. H.   [The supposed Hirundo "savigni" shot at Teesmouth, Durham, (cf. Ibis, 1866, 423), was really H. rustica.]   < *Ibis,* 3d ser., v, 1875, p. 519.

1875. HATCH, T. E.   Instinct and Reason.   < *Rod and Gun,* vi, Sept. 25, 1875, p. 388.

Sagacity of Barn Swallows.

1875. INGERSOLL, E.   The Biography of a Bird [Cotyle riparia].   < *Pop. Sci. Monthly,* July, 1875, pp. 315–320, 1 illust.

1875. INGERSOLL, E.   The Biography of a Bird [Cotyle riparia].   < *Rod and Gun,* vii, Nov. 6, 1875, p. 91.

From *Popular Science Monthly* for July, 1875, pp. 315-320.

1876. COUES, E.   Notable Change of Habit of the Bank Swallow [i. e., of Stelgidopteryx serripennis].   < *Am. Nat.*, x, No. 6, 1876, pp. 372, 373.

Erroneous information from R. Haymond; the species being *Stelgidopteryx serripennis.*

1876. COUES, E.   Peculiar Nesting-Site of the Bank Swallow [i. e., of Stelgidopteryx serripennis].   < *Bull. Nutt. Ornith. Club,* i, No. 4, Nov., 1876, p. 96.

"Cotyle riparia", *fide* R. Haymond; afterward proved to be *Stelgidopteryx serripennis.*

1876. HAYMOND, R.   Note on the Bank Swallow [*i. e.*, Stelgidopteryx serripennis]. < *Field and Forest,* i, No. 11, Apr., 1876, p. 88.

1876. RIDGWAY, R.   "The Bank Swallow" [Stelgidopteryx serripennis] again. < *Am. Nat.*, x, No. 8, 1876, pp. 493, 494.

Correction of error in *tom. cit.*, p. 372.

1876. STERLING, E.   Birds' Nests.   < *Rod and Gun,* viii, July 8, 1876, p. 233.

Breeding habits of *Hirundinidæ* along Lake Erie.

1876. VAN FLEET, W.   Notes on the [habits of the] Rough-winged Swallow (Hirundo [Stelgidopteryx] serripennis), in Pennsylvania.   < *Bull. Nutt. Ornith. Club,* i, No. 1, 1876, pp. 9–11.

1877. COUES, E.   Letters on Ornithology.   No. 11.—Swallows [Hirundinidæ].   < *The Chicago Field,* Jan. 6, 1877, p. 331, figg. 2.

An imaginative piece, with figg. of heads of *Tachycineta bicolor* and *Petrochelidon lunifrons.*

1877. COUES, E.   To the Swallow.   < *Am. Sportsman,* Feb. 3, 1877.

Reprinted from *The Chicago Field,* Jan. 6, 1877, without the cuts.

1877. [SCOTT, W. E. D.]   Do Birds Hybernate?   < *The Country,* i, Nov. 24, 1877, p. 55.   See pp. 133, 165.

Asking further information concerning a paragraph quoted from the *Popular Science Monthly,* alleging hibernation of Swallows in Michigan.

1878. [ABBOTT, L. S.] Hibernation of Birds. < *The Country,* i, Jan. 19, 1878, p.
165. See pp. 55, 133, 181.
Invalidating the evidence of hibernation of Swallows given *tom. cit.,* p. 55.

1878. ANON. Curious, If True. < *Forest and Stream,* x, June 20, 1878, p. 379.
Account of a horseman attacked and injured by troops of Swallows in Virginia.—Copied
from Springfield (Mass.) *Union,* June 10, 1878.

1878. ANON. The Purple Martin. (Progne Purpuria.) < *Journ. of Sci.* (Toledo, Ohio),
n. s., i, No. 6, Sept., 1878, cut.
Popular account, with a figure.

1878. ANON. Bank Swallow [Cotyle riparia]—natural size. < *Journ. of Sci.* (Toledo,
Ohio), n. s., i, No. 6, Sept., 1878, suppl. sheet, fig., no text.

1878. ANON. The Barn Sparrow [sic]. (Hirundo Horreorum.) <*Journ. of Sci.* (Toledo, Ohio), 2d ser., i, No. 9, Dec., 1878, cut.
Popular biography, with a figure.

1878. COUES, E. The Eave, Cliff, or Crescent Swallow (Petrochelidon lunifrons).
< *Bull. Nutt. Ornith. Club,* iii, No. 3, July, 1878, pp. 105–112.
Biographical sketch, "by permission, from advance sheets of the 'Birds of the Colorado
Valley', vol. i."

1878. [INGERSOLL, E.] Hibernation of Birds, again. < *The Country,* i, Jan. 5, 1878,
p. 133. See pp. 55, 165.
Critical notice of alleged torpidity of Swallows in Maine and Michigan.

1878. SMITH, EVERETT. Notes on the Hibernation of Birds. < *The Country,* i, Jan.
26, 1878, p. 181. See pp. 55, 133, 165.

1878. TROTTER, S. Description of a Hybrid (Hirundo horreori-lunifrons) between two
North American Swallows. < *Bull. Nutt. Ornith. Club,* iii, No. 3, July, 1878,
pp. 135, 136.
The first instance of hybridity in this family reported in this country. The specimen has
since been examined by E. Coues. J. A. Allen, and others, who agree that there is no question that it is a hybrid between *Hirundo horreorum* and *Petrochelidon lunifrons.*

1879. ANON. Rough winged Swallow (Hirundo serripennis.) < *Journ. of Sci.* (Toledo, Ohio), 2d ser., i, No. 10, Jan., 1879, cut.
Popular biography, with a figure.

1879. ANON. Migrations of Swallows. < *The Chicago Field,* xii, No. 13, Nov. 8, 1879,
p. 199.
Touching also on their alleged hibernation.

1879. BOARDMAN, G. A. Interesting Note on Albinism [in Hirundo horreorum].
< *Forest and Stream,* xiii, Aug. 7, 1879, p. 525.
With a note on melanism in *Turdus migratorius.*

1879. BRYANT, WALTER E. Cliff-swallows [Petrochelidon lunifrons] and their Parasites. < *Science News,* i, No. 9, Mar. 1, 1879, p. 144.

1879. STANNIS, J. A. The Rough-winged Swallow [Stelgidopteryx serripennis] in
Connecticut. < *Bull. Nutt. Ornith. Club,* iv, No. 2, Apr., 1879, p. 119.

1879. [WILLARD, S. L.] [Laying of Cotyle riparia in nest of Ceryle alcyon.] < *The
Oölogist,* iv, No. 11, June, 1879, p. 86.

Cœrebidæ.

1838. BONAPARTE, C. L.   Di un Uccello messicano fin ad ora non conosciuto [Agrilo-
rhinus sittaceus]. $<$ *Nuov. Ann. delle Scienze Nat. Bologna*, i, 1838, pp. 407, 408.
  Not seen: title from Carus and Engelmann.

1840. FRASER, L.   [On some new Species of the Genus Agrilorhinus.] $<$ *P. Z. S.*,
viii, Feb. 25, 1840, pp. 22, 23.
  A. bonapartei, A. humeralis, A. olivaceus, p. 22; *A. personatus,* p. 23.

1840. FRASER, L.   [On some lately new Species of Agrilorhinus.] $<$ *Annals of Nat.
Hist.*, vi, 1840, pp. 304–306.
  From *P. Z. S.*, Feb. 25, 1840, pp. 22, 23, *q. v.*

1843. LAFRESNAYE. [F.] DE.   G. Conirostre.   Conirostrum.   D'Orb. et Lafr. $<$ *Guér.
Mag. de Zool.*, 2ᵉ sér., année 1843, Oiseaux, pp. 1–4, pl. 35.
  Pl. 35, *C. albifrons,* Lafr., *R. Z.*, 1842, p. 301.—En suite, une liste descriptive des cinq espèces
dont à sa connaissance se compose ce petit groupe de Guitguits.

1846. LAFRESNAYE, F. DE.   Essai d'une monographie du genre Diglossa, Wagler,
G.-B. [sic] Gray, Gen. of birds, p. 23. $<$ *Revue Zoologique*, ix, 1846, pp.
317–320.
  11 espèces.—*D. similis, D. mystacalis, D. brunneiventris* (Des Murs), p. 318; *D. aterrima,*
p. 319, spp. nn.

1847. HARTLAUB, G.   Notice sur une nouvelle espèce du genre Cæreba [nitida], Vieillot. $<$ *Revue Zoologique*, x, 1847, p. 84.

1850. STRICKLAND, H. E.   Cæreba nitida, Hartlaub. $<$ *Jard. Contrib. Orn.*, 1850, p.
147, pl. lxvi.

1851. SCLATER, P. L.   IV.—On the genus Dacnis, Cuvier, with description of a new
Species. $<$ *Jard. Contrib. Orn.*, 1851, pp. 105–110.
  6 spp. systematically treated.   *D. cœrebicolor,* p. 106, sp. n.

1851. STRICKLAND, H. E.   On an hitherto unnamed species of Dacnis [melanotis].
$<$ *Jard. Contrib. Orn.*, 1851, pp. 15, 16.
  With synonymy of this and *D. cayana.*

1852. GIRAUD, J. P., JR.   Description of a new Species of Helinai [sic;—H. brevipennis].
$<$ *Ann. Lyc. Nat. Hist. New York*, v, 1852, p. 40, pl. iii, fig. 1.
  Read Oct. 8, 1850.—(It is a species of *Dacnis,* near *speciosa* Max.)

1852. SCLATER, P. L.   X.—On certain species of Dacnis. $<$ *Jard. Contrib. Orn.*, 1852,
pp. 101, 102, pl. xciii.
  D. speciosa Maxim., pl. xciii, fig. 1; *D. plumbea* (Lath.).   The second fig. of the pl. is *D.
cœrebicolor* (Scl.).

1854. SCLATER, P. L.   On two New Species of Dacnis, and on the General Arrange-
ment of the Genus. $<$ *P. Z. S.*, xxii, Nov. 28, 1854, pp. 251, 252.
  Dacnis hartlaubi. D. egregia, p. 251, spp. nn.   List of 9 spp. of the genus.   (See especially
Ibis, 1863, pp. 311–317.)

1856. SCLATER, P. L.   On two New Species of Dacnis, and on the General Arrangement of the Genus. $<$ *Ann. Mag. Nat. Hist.*, 2d ser., xvii, 1856, pp. 62, 63.
  From *P. Z. S.*, Nov. 28, 1854, pp. 251, 252, *q. v.*

1860. [ANON.]   [Notiz über Arbelorhina cærulea Cab.] $<$ *Zool. Gart.*, i, 1860, p. 144.

1863. SCLATER, P. L.   Synopsis of the known Species of Dacnis. $<$ *Ibis*, v, 1863, pp.
311–317, pl. vii.
  12 spp.—A general account of the genus, including synonymy, diagnosis, and habitat of the
species; none new.   The plate represents *D. venusta* Lawr.   (Cf. *Cont. Orn.*, 1851, p. 106 *et seq.;*
P. Z. S., 1854, pp. 251, 252.)   *D. hartlaubi* Scl., *P. Z. S.*, 1854, p. 251, is a *Calliste.*

1864. CASSIN, J.   Notes of an Examination of the Birds of the Subfamily Coerebinæ.
$<$ *Proc. Acad. Nat. Sci. Phila.*, xvi, 1864, pp. 265–275.
  7 genn. (with numerous subgenn.), 44 spp.—*Cyanodacnis,* p. 268; *Polidacnis,* p. 269; *Eudac-
nis, Ateleodacnis,* p. 270; *Hemidacnis,* p. 271; *Tephrodiglossa,* p. 273; *Pyrrhodiglossa, Cyano-
diglossa, Melanodiglossa,* p. 274, subgenn. nn.   *Chlorophanes cærulescens, C. melanops,* p. 269,
subspp. nn.   The matter is descriptive and critical, with some synonymy.

1864. LAWRENCE, G. N.   Descriptions of New Species of Birds of the Families Caere-
bidæ, Tanagridæ, Icteridæ, and Scolopacidæ.   < *Proc. Acad. Nat. Sci. Phila.*,
xvi, 1864, pp. 106–108.
Dacnis ultramarina, p. 106.

1870. SUNDEVALL, C. J.   Öfversigt af slägtet Certhiola.   < *Öfvers. Kongl. Vetensk.-
Akad. Förhandl. för år* 1869, 1870, pp. 619–625.
I. Speculo alarum albo ornatæ. *a*) Uropygio pure flavo. 1. *flaveola*, 2.? *bairdii*, 3. S:ti
Thomæ, 4. ex Minas Geraes, 5. *luteola*, 6. *major*, 7. *columbiana*, 8. *minor*. *b*) Plaga uropy-
gii virescente, indefinita. 9. *bartholemica*, 10. *portoricensis*, 11. *mexicana*, 12. *peruviana*. II.
Speculo alari nullo. *a*) Plaga uropygii virescente, indefinita. 13. ex insula S:t Croix, 14.
dominicana, 15. *chloropyga*, 16.? *guianensis*, 17. *majuscula*, 18. *albigula*, 19.? *bahamensis*. *b*)
Plaga uropygii lata, definita, pure flava. 20. *minima*.

1871. FINSCH, O.   Monographie der Gattung Certhiola.   < *Verh. (Abh.) k.-k. zool.-bot.
Ges. Wien*, xxi, 1871, pp. 739–790, pl. iv.
This is a very complete and workmanlike monograph, in which, after general considerations
and an account of the genus, the ten species recognized by the author are treated at full
length, with copious synonymy, description, and criticism. Finsch recognizes *CC. bahamensis,
flaveola, portoricensis, bartholemica, luteola, clusiae* (v. Würt., sp. n.), *mexicana, chloropyga, dominicana, martinicana*, as valid, with *C. minor* Bp., *Muscicapa melanoxantha* Sparrm., and
Certhia trochlea Sparrm., as dubious, and adds a note on *Certhiola caboti* Bd. MS. A map
shows the geographical distribution of the species.

1871. [SAUSSURE, H. DE.]   Les Diglosas [Cœrebidæ].   < *La Naturaleza*, ii, 1871, pp.
28, 29.
Sobre las costumbres.

1873. BERLEPSCH, H.   [Arten des Genus Dacnis.]   < *J. f. O.*, 1873, pp. 68–70.
5 subgenn., 12 spp.

1873. CABANIS, J.   [Ueber Xenodacnis parina, gen. sp. n., des Berliner Museums, von
C. Jelski in Peru entdeckt.]   < *J. f. O.*, 1873, pp. 311, 312, pl. iv, f. 1, 2.

1875. SCLATER, P. L.   Synopsis of the Species of the Subfamily Diglossinæ.   < *Ibis*,
3d ser., v, 1875, pp. 204–221, pll. iv, v.
Chars., syns., hab., and criticism of 15 spp. *Diglossa*, 1 sp. *Diglossopsis*. Pl. iv, *Diglossa pectoralis;* pl. v, *D. albilateralis* ♂ ♀.

1878. ANON.   Poaching Birds.   < *The Country*, ii, June 1, 1878, p. 89.
Ingenuity of *Certhiolæ*, etc., in procuring food. From *Nature*.

Anabatidæ.

[The genus *Sitta* is ranged in this family by Gray, and I give all the titles I possess relating to it.]

1819–21? LICHTENSTEIN, H.   Ueber die Gattung Dendrocolaptes.   <*Abhandl. Berlin.*
Akad., 1818–19, Phys. Klasse, pp. 197–210; 1820–21, pp. 258–266, pll.
I have not seen this, the original edition of the memoir, which, however, reappears in a
manner in *Isis*, 1824, pp. 615–619, *q. v.*

1824. LICHTENSTEIN, H.   [Ueber die Gattung Dendrocolaptes.]   <*Oken's Isis*, Jahrg.
viii, 1824, pp, 613–619.
Auszug aus *Abh. k. Acad. Wiss. Berlin* für die Jahre 1818 und 1819, pp. 197–210.   In dem
Bande für 1820 und 1821 lieferte der Verfasser eine Fortsetzung.   *D. decumanus, squamatus,*
bivittatus, erythacus, spp. nn.—Der Verfasser ordnet nun 18 Arten, mit Synonymik, Diagnostik und Lokale.

1829. BREE, W. T.   Nuthatch.   <*Loudon's Mag. Nat. Hist.*, ii, 1829, p. 243, fig. 69.
On the habits of *Sitta europœa*.

1829. "H. S."   On the Manners of the Nuthatch [Sitta europæa].   By H. S.   With
a Note by W. Swainson, F. R. S., &c.   <*Loudon's Mag. Nat. Hist.*, i, 1829, pp.
328–330, figg. 162, 163.

1831. BREE, W. T.   The Nuthatch [Sitta europæa] in the Neighbourhood of Bedford.
<*Loudon's Mag. Nat. Hist.*, iv, 1831, p. 275.

1831. WHITE, W. H.   The Nuthatch (Sitta europæa.)   <*Loudon's Mag. Nat. Hist.*, iv,
1831, pp. 465, 466.
Habits and nidification.

1832. "J. D[ENSON?]."   The Nuthatch, Sitta europæa, L.   <*Loudon's Mag. Nat. Hist.*,
v, 1832, p. 591.

1832. LAFRESNAYE, F. DE.   Anabate.   Anabates.   Temm.   <*Guér. Mag. de Zool.*, 2e
année, 1832, classe ii, notice viii, pl. 8.
Anabates aradoïdes, pl. viii, sp. n.

1832. NEWMAN, E.   The Nuthatch (Sitta europæa L.) is resident throughout the Year
[in various parts of England].   <*Loudon's Mag. Nat. Hist.*, v, 1832, p. 488,
fig. 97, with notes by "J. D[enson?].", pp. 488, 489, and "J. M.", p. 489.

1833. LAFRESNAYE, F. DE.   Sur le Fourmilier a long Bec.   Cuv. Gal. du Muséum.
<*Guér. Mag. de Zool.*, 3e année, 1833, classe ii, notice x, pl. x.
Myothera longirostris Cuv. = *Thamnophilus caudacutus* V. = *Myothera caudacuta* Lafr.,
pl. 10.   (The species belongs to the genus *Sclerurus*.)

1833. LAFRESNAYE, F. DE.   Picucule.   Dendrocolaptes. Herm.   P. rubigineux.   D. ru-
biginosus.   De Lafresnaye.   <*Guér. Mag. de Zool.*, 3e année, 1833, classe ii,
notice xvi, pl. xvi.

1833. LAFRESNAYE, F. DE.   Picucule.   Dendrocolaptes. Herm.   P. a bec en coin.   D.
cuneatus.   Licht.   Catal. p. 17.   <*Guér. Mag. de Zool.*, 3e année, 1833, classe ii,
notice xvii, pl. xvii.

1837. S[ELBY], P. J.   Sitta europea [in Cornwall].   <*Mag. of Zool. and Bot.*, i, 1837,
p. 103.

1838. SIEMUSZOWA-PIETRUSKI, S. K. V.   Nutzen der Spechtmeise (Sitta europæa),
durch die Vertilgung der Borkenkäfer beobachtet . . .   <*Arch. f. Naturg.*,
1838, (1), p. 48.

1842. LAFRESNAYE, [F.] DE.   G. Acanthisitte.   Acanthisitta.   De Lafr.   <*Guér. Mag.*
de Zool., 2e sér., année 1842, Oiseaux, pp. 1, 2, pl. 27.
Acanthisitta g. n. = *Acanthisa* (*tenuirostris*), *Rev. Zool.*, 1841, p. 242.

1843. ATKINSON, J. C.   Note on the Habits of the Nuthatch [Sitta europæa].   <*Zo-*
ologist, i, 1843, pp. 213–215.

1843. LAFRESNAYE, [F.] DE.   G. Picucule.   Dendrocolaptes. Cuvier.   P. a taches tri-
angulaires.   D. triangularis. De Lafr., Rev. Zool., 1842, p. 134.   *< Guér. Mag.
de Zool.*, 2ᵉ sér., année 1843, Oiseaux, pp. 1, 2, pl. 32.

1843. ROSS, H. J.   [Occurrence of Sitta europæa at Kaipariah.]   *< P. Z. S.*, xi, 184?,
p. 122.

1844. LAFRESNAYE, [F.] DE.   G. Dendrocolaptes.   D. Perrotii. Lafresnaye.   *< Guér.
Mag. de Zool.*, 2ᵉ sér., année 1844, Oiseaux, pp. 1, 2, pl. 54.
Rev. Zool., 1844, p. 80.

1846. MOSLEY, O.   Remarks on the Nuthatch [Sitta europæa].   *< Zoologist*, iv, 1846.
pp. 1498, 1499.

1847. LAFRESNAYE, F. DE.   [Notice du genre Dendrocolaptes, à propos de la monographie dont il nous donne l'avertissement.]   *< Revue Zoologique*, x, 1847,
pp. 209-211.

1849. LAFRESNAYE, F. DE.   Monographie du genre Dendrocolaptes.   *< Rev. et Mag.
Zool.*, i, 1849, pp. 328-331.
Ici seulement l'aperçu général du sujet.   Voir *op. cit.*, ii, 1850, et iii, 1851.

1850. [JARDINE, W.]   Synallaxis flammulatus, Jard. [n. sp.]   *< Jard. Contrib. Orn.*,
1850, p. 82, pl. lvi.

1850-51. LAFRESNAYE, F. DE.   Essai d'une monographie du genre Picucule (Buffon),
Dendrocolaptes (Hermann, Illiger), devenu aujourd'hui la sous-famille Den-
drocolaptinæ (Gray, Genera of birds), de la famille Certhiadæ de Swains.
< Rev. et Mag. Zool., ii, 1850, pp. 95-104, 145-154, 275-285, 369-388, 417-426,
588-598; iii, 1851, pp. 145-147, pl. 4, 317-329, 465-470, 590, 591.
Dendrocolaptes, 6 esp.   *D. simpliciceps*, p. 100; *D. devillei*, p. 102, spp. nn.—*Picolaptes*, 11 esp.
P. lineaticeps, p. 277, sp. n.—*Xiphorhynchus*, 5 esp.   *X. procurvoides*, p. 376, sp. n.—*Nasica*, 14
esp.   *N. guttatoides*, p. 387; *N. beauperthuysii*, p. 419; *N. dorbignyanus*, p. 420, spp. nn.?—*Sittasomus*, 4 esp.   *S. amazonus*, p. 590, sp. n.?—*Glyphorhynchus*, 1 esp.—*Dendroplex*, 2 esp.—*Dendrocolaptes temminckii*, p. 145, pl. 4.—*Dendrocops*, 11 esp.   *D. tyranninus*, p. 328; *D. meru-
loides*, p. 467, spp. nn.—*Dendrexetastes*, 1 esp.

1851. EYTON, T. C.   Description of some New Species and a New Genus of Dendrocolaptinæ.   *< Jard. Contrib. Orn.*, 1851, pp. 75-77.
Dendrocolaptes multistrigatus, Picolaptes validirostris, p. 75; *P. atripes, Dendrexetastes* (g. n.)
capitoides, p. 76.

1851. EYTON, T. C.   Descriptions of two New Species of Synalaxis [sic].   *< Jard.
Contrib. Orn.*, 1851, p. 159, pl. lxxxi*.
S. olivacens [sic], *S. modestus.*

1852. EYTON, T. C.   Remarks on Dendrocolaptinæ, with descriptions of Two New
Genera and Species.   *< Jard. Contrib. Orn.*, 1852, pp. 21-26.
Drymornis, Dendrornis, p. 23, genn. nn.   *Dendrocops olivaceus.* p. 25; *Picolaptes notatus*,
p. 26, spp. nn.

1853. LAFRESNAYE, F. DE.   Mélanges Ornithologiques.   *< Rer. et Mag. de Zool.*, v.
Nov., 1853, pp. 490-493.
Sur l'*Anabates squamiger*, type d'un nouveau genre *Anabasitta*, p. 492.

1853. SCLATER, P. L.   On a new species of Dendrocolaptes [eytoni].   *< P. Z. S.*, xxi,
1853, pp. 68, 69, pl. (Aves) lvii.

1855. SCLATER, P. L.   On a [lately] new species of Dendrocolaptes [eytoni].   *< Ann.
Mag. Nat. Hist.*, 2d ser., xv, 1855, pp. 223, 224.
From *P. Z. S.*, 1853, pp. 68, 69.

1856. SCLATER, P. L.   On some New or Imperfectly-known Species of Synallaxis.
< P. Z. S., xxiv, 1856, pp. 97-99.
3 spp.   *S. spixi, S. caniceps*, p. 98, spp. nn.   The third sp. is *S. ruficapilla* V.

1857. ANTINORI, O.   Einige Bemerkungen über das Nest von Sitta syriaca.   *< Naumannia*, vii, 1857, pp. 429-431.

1857. HADFIELD, H. W.   Note on the European Nuthatch (Sitta europæa).   *< Zoologist*, xv, 1857, pp. 5684, 5685.

1857. SCLATER, P. L.   On some New or Imperfectly-known Species of Synallaxis.
<Ann. Mag. Nat. Hist., 2d ser., xix, 1857, pp. 179–181.
From P. Z. S., April 22, 1856, pp. 97–99, q. v.

1857. SCLATER, P. L.   Further Additions to the List of Birds received in Collections
from Bogota.   < P. Z. S., xxv, 1857, pp. 15–20.
The article is a briefly annotated list of 52 spp., among which two new Anabatidæ are
described, namely, Anabates striaticollis and Sclerurus brunneus, p. 17.

1857. SCLATER, P. L.   On two [lately] new Species of Birds from Bogota.   < Ann
Mag. Nat. Hist., 2d ser., xx, 1857, p. 472.
Anabates striaticollis, Sclerurus brunneus, the descriptions of which are here extracted
from a paper of wider scope in P. Z. S., Jan. 27, 1857, pp. 15–20.

1859. PELZELN, A. V.   Ueber neue Arten der Gattungen Synallaxis, Anabates und
Xenops in der Kaiserlichen ornithologischen Sammlung, nebst Auszügen aus
J. Natterer's nachgelassenen Notizen über die von ihm in Brasilien gesam-
melten Arten der Furnarinæ und Synallaxinæ.   <Sitzungsber. der Wien. Akad.,
math.-nat. Classe, xxxiv, 1859, pp. 99–134.
Not seen.

1859. SCLATER, P. L.   On some New Species of Synallaxis, and on the Geographical
Distribution of the Genus.   <P. Z. S., xxvii, 1859, pp. 191–197.
S. pudica, S. stictothorax, S. scutata, p. 191, spp. nn. List of 41 spp., with localities, and men-
tion of 18 others.

1859. SCLATER, P. L.   On a [lately] new species of Synallaxis [antisiensis] from the
Republic of Ecuador.   <Ann. Mag. Nat. Hist., 3d ser., iii, 1859, p. 448.
From P. Z. S., Nov. 9, 1858, p. 457, where the species is named among others in a paper of
more extended scope.

1860. HEINE, F.   Beschreibung eines neuen Riesen-Baumhackers (Xiphocolaptes
[fortis] Less.).   <J. f. O., viii, 1860, pp. 185, 186.

1860. REINHARDT, J.   Notits om Slægten Malacurus Rchb. og de dertil hörende Arter.
<Vidensk. Meddel. Naturhist. Foren. Kjöbenharn 1859, 1860, pp. 103–105.
M. rufifrons (Ill.), M. obsoletus, sp. n., p. 105, M. striaticeps (d'Orb. et Lafr.) og M. ruber
(Vieill.).

1860. SCLATER, P. L.   On some [lately] New Species of Synallaxis.   <Ann. Mag. Nat.
Hist., 3d ser., v, 1860, p. 332.
From P. Z. S., May 10, 1859, pp. 191–197, q. v.

1861. KRÜPER, T.   Ueber Sitta syriaca in Griechenland.   <J. f. O., ix, 1861, pp.
129–132.

1863. NEWTON, A.   On a New Bird from the Island of Madagascar [Hypherpes (n.
g.) corallirostris].   <P. Z. S., xxxi, 1863, p. 85, pl. xiii.

1864. PHILIPPI, R. A., and LANDBECK, L.   De las Alondras [sc. Anabatidæ] Chilenas.
< Anal. Univ. Chile, xxv, Set. de 1864, pp. 409–418.
A subtitle of a paper of more extended scope.—Six species are treated, among which Certhilauda frobeni, p. 411; C. isabellina, p. 412; and Geobamon fasciatus, p. 415, are described as
new. The matter reappears in a German version in Arch. f. Naturg., 1865, Bd. i, pp. 58–73, q. v.

1865. LAWRENCE, G. N.   Descriptions of New Species of Birds of the Families Tanagridæ, Dendrocolaptidæ, Formicaridæ, Tyrannidæ, and Trochilidæ.   < Ann.
Lyc. Nat. Hist. New York, viii, 1865, pp. 126–135.
The Dendrocolaptidæ=Anabatidæ here described are Philydor rufobrunneus, p. 127; Anabazenops lineatus, p. 127; Margarornis rubiginosa, M. guttata, p. 128; M. brunneicauda (proband.), p. 130.

1865. PHILIPPI, R. A., and LANDBECK, L.   Die Lerchen [sc. Anabatidæ] Chiles.
<Arch. f. Naturg., 1865, Bd. i, pp. 58–73.
A subtitle of a paper having a more extended scope.—The birds treated are not Larks, or
Alaudidæ, to which they have some superficial resemblance, but Anabatidæ of Gray's arrangement. They are six in number, namely: Geositta cunicularia (V.) Bp., Certhilauda frobeni P. & L., p. 62; C. isabellina P. & L., p. 63; Geobamon rufipennis Burm., G. fasciata P.
& L., p. 68; Certhilauda nigrofasciata Lafr. Cf. Zool. Rec. for 1865, pp. 102, 103.—The article
originally appeared in Spanish in Anal. Univ. Chile, xxv, 1864, pp. 409–418, q. v.

1865. SCLATER, P. L. Notes on Krüper's Nuthatch and on the other known Species of the Genus Sitta. <*Ibis*, 2d ser., i, 1865, pp. 306–311, pl. vii.

> 12 spp., with critical, descriptive, and geographical annotation. The pl. represents *S. krueperi* (cf. *P. Z. S.*, 1864, p. 433). *S. aculeata* Cass. is disallowed.

1866. SCLATER, P. L. Note on the Genus Geobates of Swainson. <*P. Z. S.*, Apr. 24, 1866, pp. 204, 205, pl. xxi.

> The only known species, *Anthus pœcilopterus* Max., *Beitr.*, ii, p. 633, which = *Geobates brevicauda* Sw., *An. in Menag.*, 1838, p. 322, is described and figured, with extracts from Natterer's MS. concerning it, under the name of *Geobates pœcilopterus*. *Geobamon rufipennis* Burm. (*J. f. O.*, 1860, p. 465) "seems to be somewhat allied".

1867. MOOR, A. C. Nesting of the Nuthatch [Sitta europæa]. <*Zoologist*, 2d ser., ii, 1867, pp. 559, 560.

1868. CLIFTON, *Lord*. Nuthatch in Ireland [Sitta europæa]. <*Zoologist*, 2d ser., iii, 1868, p. 1134.

1868. SCLATER, P. L., *and* SALVIN, O. Descriptions of New Species of Birds of the Families Dendrocolaptidæ, Strigidæ, and Columbidæ. <*P. Z. S.*, xxxvi, 1868, pp. 53–60, pl. v, woodcc.

> *Dendrocincla ruficeps*, p. 54; *Dendrocolaptes puncticollis*, p. 54, pl. v, woodc. ꞉ synopses of these genera.

1868. SCLATER, P. L., *and* SALVIN, O. Descriptions of New or Little-known American, Birds of the Families Fringillidæ, Oxyrhamphidæ, Bucconidæ, and Strigidæ. <*P. Z. S.*, xxxvi, 1868, pp. 322–329.

> *Oxyrhamphus frater*, p. 326, sp. n.

1869. SCLATER, P. L. On Two new Species of Synallaxinæ. <*P. Z. S.*, xxxvii, 1869, pp. 636, 637, pl. xlix.

> *Synallaxis curtata*, p. 636, pl. fig. 1; *Leptasthenura andicola*, p. 636, pl. fig. 2.

1869. SCLATER, P. L., *and* SALVIN, O. Descriptions of Six New Species of American Birds of the Families Tanagridæ, Dendrocolaptidæ, Formicariidæ, Tyrannidæ, and Scolopacidæ. <*P. Z. S.*, xxxvii, 1869, pp. 416–420, pl. xxviii.

> *Synallaxis arequipæ*, p. 417.

1870. GURNEY, J. H. Nest of a Nuthatch [Sitta europæa]. <*Zoologist*, 2d ser., v, 1870, p. 2224.

1871. BOND, F. Singular nesting of the Nuthatch [Sitta europæa] at East Grinstead, Sussex. <*Zoologist*, 2d ser., vi, 1871, pp. 2850, 2851.

1871. SCLATER, P. L. Remarks on some Species of Dendrocolaptidæ in the Collection of the Smithsonian Institution. <*P. Z. S.*, xxxix, 1871, pp. 85, 86.

> Critical observations on *Synallaxis candæi*, *Anabates ochrolæmus*, *A. montanus* (both of which are referred to *Philydor*), and *Dendrocolaptes chuncotambo* (= *Dendrornis ocellata*).

1872. LAWRENCE, G. N. Descriptions of New Species of Birds of the Genera Icterus and Synallaxis. <*Ann. Lyc. Nat. Hist. N. Y.*, x, 1872, pp. 184–186.

> The Anabatoid is *S. maculata*, p. 186, from Tumbe, Peru.

1872. MEYER, R. Ueber den Nestbau des Kleibers oder der Spechtmeise. (Sitta caesia Wolf.). <*Zool. Gart.*, xiii, 1872, pp. 238–241.

1874. SCLATER, P. L. On the Species of the Genus Synallaxis of the Family Dendrocolaptidæ. <*P. Z. S.*, xlii, 1874, pp. 2–28, pll. ii, iii, iv.

> Very full. Bibliographical summary. Synonymy, diagnosis, and criticism. 58 spp. +4 spp. doubtful, in 2 sections, rectric. 10 or 12.—*S. hypospodia*, *S. subpudica*, p. 10; *S. hudsoni*, p. 25, spp. nn.—Pl. ii, f. 1, *S. stictothorax*; f. 2, *S. scutata*. Pl. iii, f. 1, *S. kollari*; f. 2, *S. candæi*. Pl. iv, f. 1, *S. subcristata*; f. 2, *S. hyposticta*.

1874. SCLATER, P. L. Descriptions of three new Species of the Genus Synallaxis. <*P. Z. S.*, xlii, 1874, pp. 445–447, pl. lviii.

> *S. pudibunda*, p. 445, pl. lviii, f. 1; *S. graminicola* Jelski, MS., p. 446, pl. f. 2; *S. virgata* Jelski, MS., p. 446.

1876. COUES, E.   Letters on Ornithology.   No. 8.—Nuthatches [Sitta].   < *The Chicago Field*, Dec. 16, 1876, figg. 2.
> General account of the North American species, with figg. of the heads of *S. carolinensis* and of *S. pygmæa.*

1878. HARDY, MANLY.   Nesting Habits of the Red-bellied Nuthatch [Sitta canadensis].   < *Bull. Nutt. Ornith. Club,* iii, No. 4, Oct., 1878, p. 196.
> Good original observations on a subject none too well known before.

1879. DOWSE, W. B.   The White-bellied Nuthatch [Sitta carolinensis] concealing Food.   < *Bull. Nutt. Ornith. Club,* iv, No. 1, Jan., 1879, p. 61.

1879. [WILLARD, S. L.]   [Field] Notes on Sitta canadensis.   < *The Oölogist,* v, No. 2, Aug., 1879, p. 15.

1879. [WILLARD, S. L.]   Nest of the White-bellied Nuthatch (Sitta carolinensis). < *The Oölogist,* iv, No. 9, Apr., 1879, p. 65.

Certhiidæ.

1782. Götz, G. F.   Beytrag zur Naturgeschichte des Mauerspechts.   Certhia [Ticho-
droma] muraria Linn.   < *Der Naturforscher*, xvii, 1782, pp. 40–44.

1805. Bartram, W.   Description of an American species of Certhia, or Creeper.
< *Philadelphia Med. Phys. Journ.*, i, 1805, (pt. 2), pp. 103–106.
Not seen: title from *Roy. Soc. Cat.*

1831. White, W. H.   The Tree Creeper (Certhia familiaris).   < *Loudon's Mag. Nat.
Hist.*, iv, 1831, pp. 473, 474.

1832. Bree, W. T.   The Tree Creeper (Certhia familiaris L.) a Winter Resident [in
England].   < *Loudon's Mag. Nat. Hist.*, v, 1832, p. 489, with note by "J. D.",
pp. 489, 490.

1832. "M. P."   The Creeper (Certhia familiaris L.) [resident in Great Britain].   < *Loudon's Mag. Nat. Hist.*, v, 1832, p. 738.

1832. Newman, E.   The Creeper (Certhia familiaris.)   < *Loudon's Mag. Nat. Hist.*, v,
1832, p. 204.

1832. "T, G."   The Creeper (Certhia familiaris) resident, not migratory, in Lancashire.   < *Loudon's Mag. Nat. Hist.*, v, 1832, p. 204.

1832. "T. G."   The Creeper (Certhia familiaris L.) it is, and not the Nuthatch (Sitta
europæa L.), which associates with the Titmouse in winter, in Lancashire.
< *Loudon's Mag. Nat. Hist.*, v, 1832, pp. 737, 738.

1832. Turner, H.   The Creeper (Certhia familiaris.)   < *Loudon's Mag. Nat. Hist.*, v,
1832, p. 204, with note by "J. D.", pp. 204, 205.

1847. Gray, G. R.   On two new Genera of Certhinæ.   < *P. Z. S.*, xv, 1847, pp. 6, 7.
Caulodromus gracei, gen. sp. n., p. 6, Darjeeling.   *Salpornis*, g. n., p. 7, type *Certhia spilonota* Franklin, *P. Z. S.*, 1831, 121, Behar.

1847. Gray, G. R.   On two [lately] new Genera of Certhinæ.   < *Ann. Mag. Nat. Hist.*,
xix, 1847, pp. 351–353.
From *P. Z. S.*, Feb. 23, 1847, pp. 6, 7, q. v.

1852.   Bailly, [J. B.]   Notice supplémentaire sur le Grimpereau Costa [Certhia
costæ].   < *Bull. Soc. Hist. Nat. Savoie*, janv. 1852, pp. — - —.
Pas vue moi-même.

1852. Gerbe, Z.   Notice sur la Certhia Costæ, Bailly, (Grimpereau Costa).   < *Rev.
et Mag. de Zool.*, 2e sér., iv, avril, 1852, pp. 162–172, pl. 8.
Sous-titre de ses Mélanges Zoologiques, l. c. pp. 161–174 et suiv.   L'auteur constate que cette
espèce est réellement distincte de la *C. familiaris*.   La planche, de sept figures, donne les
caractères des deux espèces.

1855. König-Warthausen, R. v.   Zur Naturgeschichte des Mauerläufers, Tichodroma
muraria Illig.   < *J. f. O.*, iii, 1855, pp. 43–45.

1855. Sundevall, C. J.   Notiz über Certhia Costae.   < *J. f. O.*, iii, 1855, pp. 60, 61.

1856. Brehm, [C. L.]   [Ueber die Baumläufer (Certhia).]   < *Naumannia*, vi, 1856,
pp. 356–362.

1857. Brehm, C. L.   Einige Bemerkungen über die europäischen Baumläufer, Certhia L.   < *Allgem. deutsche naturh. Zeitung*, n. F., Bd. iii, 1857, pp. 99–106.
Nicht mir zugänglich: Titel aus Carus und Engelmann.

1860. Alston, E. R.   Attachment of the Creeper (Certhia familiaris) to its Nest and
Eggs.   < *Zoologist*, xviii, 1860, p. 6891.

1862. Brunton, T.   Nesting of the Tree Creeper [Certhia familiaris].   < *Zoologist*,
xx, 1862, p. 8162.

1863. Bridger, C.   Nests of the Creeper [Certhia familiaris].   < *Zoologist*, xxi, 1863,
p. 8720.

1864. CRICHTON, A. W.   Habits of the Creeper [Certhia familiaris].   <*Zoologist*, xxii, 1864, p. 9111.

1865. GIRTANNER, A.   [Notizen über Tichodroma phœnicoptera.]   < *Verh. St. Gallen. Naturf. Gesell.*, 1865, pp. 63, 64.
Nicht mir selbst zugänglich.

1865. GIRTANNER, A.   [Mauerläufer (Tichodroma phœnicoptera) in Gefangenschaft.]   <*Zool. Gart.*, vi, 1865, pp. 72, 73.

1865. HAMLIN, C. E.   On a Habit of Certhia americana supposed to have been hitherto unnoticed by Authors.   <*Proc. Boston Soc. Nat. Hist.*, x, Dec., 1865, p. 80.
Dropping down on wing to reascend by creeping—a well-known and characteristic trait.

1867. GOULD, J.   On the Australian Genus Climacteris, with a Description of a New Species.   <*P. Z. S.*, xxxv, 1867, pp. 975–977.
List of 7 spp. (*scandens, rufa, erythrops, melanota, melanura, leucophœa,* and *pyrrhonota* (sp. n. p. 976)), with remarks on habits and geographical distribution.

1868. GIRTANNER, A.   [Einiges über die Fortpflanzungsgeschichte der Mauerläufer (Tichodroma muraria).]   <*Zool. Gart.*, ix, 1868, pp. 110, 111.

1869. GIRTANNER, A.   Ueber den Alpen-Mauerläufer, Tichodroma phœnicoptera, . . . <*Zool. Gart.*, x, 1869, pp. 317–319.
Further notes; cf. *op. cit.*, vi, p. 72 ; ix, 1863, p. 110.

1873. BROOKS, W. E.   Notes on the Certhiinæ of India.   < *Journ. Asiatic Soc. Bengal*, xlii, pt. 2, 1873, pp. 255–257.
Treats of 5 spp.   *C. himalayana, C. hodgsoni, C. nipalensis, C. stoliczkœ,* sp. n., p. 256, *C. mandellii*, sp. n., p. 256.

1874. BARRINGTON, R. M.   Peculiar Position in Feet of Certhia familiaris.   <*Zoologist*, 2d ser., ix, 1874, p. 3998.

1875. [SALVIN, O.]   [Note of Discovery of ten MS. letters of White of Selbourne, 1790–1793.]   < *Ibis*, 3d ser., v, 1875, pp. 521, 522.
A letter shows that *Tichodroma muraria* once occurred in Norfolk, and the editor enlarges on the subject.   *Cf.* Merrett, *Pinax*, 1667, p. 177.

1876. COUES, E.   Letters on Ornithology.   No. 2.—The American Tree-Creeper [Certhia familiaris].   < *The Chicago Field*, Aug. 12, 1876, fig.
Biography of the bird, with a figure, from advance sheets of *Birds of the Colorado Valley.*

1879. BAGG, E.   Nesting of Certhia familiaris.   < *Bull. Nutt. Ornith. Club*, iv, No. 3, July, 1879, p. 183.

1879. BREWER, T. M.   The American Brown Creeper [Certhia familiaris].   <*Bull. Nutt. Ornith. Club*, iv, No. 2, Apr., 1879, pp. 87–90.
Chiefly relating to the nidification of the species, compiled from various sources.

1879. BREWSTER, W.   Breeding Habits of the American Brown Creeper (Certhia familiaris americana).   < *Bull. Nutt. Ornith. Club*, iv, No. 4, Oct., 1879, pp. 199–209.
A well-written account, from original observations ; decidedly the best article upon the subject we have.

1879. [WILLARD, S. L.]   Habits of Young Brown Creepers [Certhia familiaris].   < *The Oölogist*, v, No. 1, July, 1879, p. 8.

1879. [WILLARD, S. L.]   Habits of young Brown Creepers [Certhia familiaris].   < *The Temperance Vidette* (Texas newspaper), Sept. 20, 1879.

Pteroptochidæ.

1832. GEOFFROY ST.-HILAIRE, ISID.   Rhinomie.   Rhinomya. Is. Geoff. $<$ *Guér. Mag. de Zool.*, 2e sér., année 1832, classe ii, Oiseaux, notice iii, pl. iii.
> *Rhinòmya lanceolata* d'Orb. et Isid. Geoffr., gen. sp. n.

1836. GOULD, J.   [Scytalopus (g. n.) fuscus, S. albogularis, spp. nn.] $<$ *P. Z. S.*, Aug. 9, 1836, pp. 89, 90.
> The genus and species are established in an untitled paper, which also describes certain *Troglodytidæ*.

1837. GOULD, J.   [On Scytalopus.] $<$ *Lond. and Edinb. Philos. Journ.*, x, 1837, p. 295.
> From *P. Z. S.*, Aug. 9, 1836, pp. 89, 90, *q. v.*

1838. GOULD, J.   [Ueber die Gattung Scytalopus.] $<$ *Oken's Isis*, Bd. xxxi, 1838, pp. 199, 200.
> Aus den *P. Z. S.*, 1836, pp. 89, 90, *q. v.*

1841. LESSON, R. P.   Revision des Espèces d'Oiseaux du Genre Megalonyx. $<$ *Actes Soc. Linn. de Bordeaux*, xii, 1841, pp. 187–197.
> Pas vu moi-même: le titre tiré de la *Bibl.* de Carus & Engel.

1842. GEOFFROY ST.-HILAIRE, ISID.   [Rhinomya lanceolata.] $<$ *Oken's Isis*, Bd. xxxv, 1842, p. 51.
> Aus *Guér. Mag. de Zool.*, Bd. ii, 1832.

1844. LAFRESNAYE, [F.] DE.   G. Merulaxis. Lesson.   (Fam. Formicaridæ.—S.-Fam. Rhinominæ.) $<$ *Guér. Mag. de Zool.*, 2e sér., année 1844, Oiseaux,, pp. 1–6, pl. 53.
> Pl. 53, *Merulaxis orthonyx* Lafr., *R. Z.*, 1843, p. 131.

1851. [JARDINE, W.]   Scytalopus, Gould, 1836. $<$ *Jard. Contrib. Orn.*, 1851, pp. 115–118, pll. lxxvi–lxxviii.
> Descriptions of, and remarks on, 4 spp.   Pl. lxxvi, f. 1, *S. undulatus;* f. 2, *S. albiventris.* Pl. lxxvii, *S. fuscus.*   Pl. lxxviii, *S. albogularis.*

1851. LAFRESNAYE, [F.] DE.   Observations on the Genus Scytalopus. $<$ *Jard. Contrib. Orn.*, 1851, pp. 145–150.
> 17 spp.,,referred to the genus *Merulaxis* Less.   *M. fuscoides*, p. 149, sp. n.

1857. LANDBECK, L.   Pteroptochos albifrons n. sp. $<$ *Arch. f. Naturg.*, 1857, (1), pp. 273–275.

1864. PHILIPPI, R. A., *and* LANDBECK, L.   [Pteroptochus castaneus, sp. n.] $<$ *Anal. Univ. Chile*, xxv., Sept., 1864, p. 408.
> A separate sub-head of a paper of much more extended scope.

1865. PHILIPPI, R. A., *and* LANDBECK, L.   [Pteroptochos castaneus.] $<$ *Arch. f. Naturg.*, 1861, (1), p. 56.
> A separate sub-head of a paper of much more extended scope.   The orig. descr. is in *Anal. Univ. Chile*, xxv, 1864, p. 408.

1874. SCLATER, P. L.   On the Neotropical Species of the Family Pteroptochidæ. $<$ *Ibis*, 3d ser., iv, 1874, pp. 189–206, pl. viii.
> History of the group in brief; systematic, synonymatic, diagnostic synopsis, with comment, of 19 spp., referred to 8 genera; tabular view of their distribution.   The pl. represents *Rhinocrypta fulva*.

Troglodytidæ.

1832. "T. G." Materials composing the Nest of the common Brown Wren (Anorthura communis Rennie). < *Loudon's Mag. Nat. Hist.*, v, 1832, pp. 738–740, with note by "J. D.", pp. 740,741.

1833. GARDINER, W. The Materials of the Nest of the Common Wren (Troglodytes vulgaris). < *Loudon's Mag. Nat. Hist.*, vi, 1833, p. 523.

1833. JENNINGS, J. Structure of the Nest of the Common Brown Wren [Anorthura communis]. < *Loudon's Mag. Nat. Hist.*, vi, 1833, pp. 172,173.

1835. LAFRESNAYE, F. DE. Sur le genre Grimpic (Picolaptes, Lesson.) < *Guér. Mag. de Zool.*, 5e sér., année 1835, classe ii, notices xlvi, xlvii, pll. xlvi, xlvii.
  P. scolopaceus (Spix), pl. 46. *P. brunneicapillus*, sp. n., pl. 47.

1835. "S. D. W." A Nest of the Wren (Anorthùra) built within that of the Chimney Swallow. < *Loudon's Mag. Nat. Hist.*, viii, 1835, pp. 617,618.

1836. AUDUBON, J. J. Ueber das Vorkommen der nordamerikanischen Schlüpfer (Troglodytes). < *Arch. f. Naturg.*, ii, (1), 1836, p. 312.
  7 spp. aus dessen *Ornith. Biogr.*, ii, p. 452.

1836. GOULD, J. [Exhibition of Birds allied to the European Wren, with characters of new species.] < *P. Z. S.*, iv, 1836, pp. 88–90.
  Troglodytes magellanicus, p. 88; *T. leucogastra*, *T. guttatus*, p. 89; *Scytalopus* (g. n.) *fuscus*, p. 89; *S. albogularis*, p. 90, spp. nn. (See *Pteroptochidæ*, 1836, 1837, 1838.)

1838. GOULD, J. Ueber verschiedene Zaunkönige (Wren) [Troglodytidæ und Pteroptochidæ]. < *Oken's Isis*, Bd. xxxi, 1838, pp. 199,200.
  Auszug aus *Proc. Zool. Soc. Lond.*, iv, 1836, pp. 88–90, *q. v.*

1844. HASLAM, S. H. Anecdote of the Common Wren [Troglodytes europæus]. < *Zoologist*, ii, 1844, p. 564.

1846. LAFRESNAYE, F. DE. Mélanges ornithologiques. < *Revue Zoologique*, ix, 1846, pp. 91–94.
  Sur le genre *Campylorhynchus* de Spix (1824), *Picolaptes* Lesson (1830).—*C. zonatoides*, p. 92; *C. pallescens*, *C. unicolor*, p. 93, spp. nn.; avec une liste de 11 espèces de ce genre.

1846. LAFRESNAYE, F. DE. Description d'une nouvelle espèce de Campylorhynche [Campylorhynchus unicoloroïdes] de la Bolivie. < *Revue Zoologique*, ix, 1846, pp. 316, 317.

1847. CABOT, S., JR. [Troglodytes albinucha, sp. n.] < *Proc. Bost. Soc. Nat. Hist.*, ii, Nov. 17, 1847, pp. 258,259.
  This is the orig. descr. of the species, not formally titled, but simply given at conclusion of a paper the full title of which will be found under *Laridæ*. (See 1848, CABOT, S., JR., *bis*.)

1847. GARNIER, —. [Nid du Troglodyte vulgaire contenant sept petits encore sans plumes, le 16 Décembre 1846.] < *Compt. Rend. de l'Acad. Sci. Paris*, xxiv, 1847, p. 79.

1847. GARNIER, —. Nidification du troglodyte (Troglodyta vulgaris) en hiver. < *Arch. des Sci. Phys. et Nat.*, iv, 1847, p. 222.
  Extrait des *Comptes Rendus de l'Acad. Sci. Paris*, 18 janvier 1847.

1848. CABOT, S., JR. Troglodytes albinucha, a new species of Wren. < *Am. Journ. Sci.*, 2d ser., vi, 1848, p. 137.
  Here given as a sub-head of a more extended title, from *Proc. Bost. Soc. Nat. Hist.*, ii, Nov. 17, 1847, pp. 257–259; but it is properly citable as a separate article, as it was in the original.

1848. CABOT, S., JR. A Comparison between Sterna Cantiaca, Gm., of Europe, and Sterna Acuflavida, Nobis, hitherto considered identical with S. cantiaca, and a description of a new species of Wren [Troglodytes albinucha]. < *Ann. Mag. Nat. Hist.*, 2d ser., ii, 1848, pp. 364,365.
  From *Proc. Boston Soc. Nat. Hist.*, ii, Nov. 17, 1847, pp. 257–259.—The editor here combines two originally distinct articles in one formally titled paper.

1850. [KIRTLAND, J. P.] A Rare Bird [Thryothorus ludovicianus, in Ohio]. < *The Family Visitor*, i, No. 52, p. 412.

1851. BREE, C. R. Nesting of the Wren (Troglodytes vulgaris). < *Zoologist*, ix, 1851. pp. 3146, 3147.

1851. NORMAN, A. M. Nesting of the Wren (Troglodytes vulgaris). < *Zoologist*, ix, 1851, pp. 3207, 3208.

1852. BOENIGK, O. v. [Troglodytes parvulus nistend.`] < *Naumannia*, ii, Heft iii, 1852, pp. 81–84.

1852. SCHACH, F. [Fortpflanzung von Troglodytes domestica.] < *Naumannia*, ii, Heft ii, 1852, p. 123.

1854. TOBIAS, R. Beiträge zur Fortpflanzungsgeschichte des Zaunkönigs, Troglodytes parvulus, Koch. < *J. f. O.*, ii, 1854, pp. 281–284.

1856. SCLATER, P. L. Characters of an apparently undescribed bird belonging to the genus Campylorhynchus [humilis], of Spix, with remarks upon other Species of the same group. < *Proc. Acad. Nat. Sci. Phila.*, viii, 1856, pp. 263–265.
  Synopsis of 13 spp.

1856. SCLATER, P. L. Note on Buglodytes albicilius, Bp. < *P. Z. S.*, xxiv, 1856, p. 97.
  Identified with *Furnarius griseus* Sw., *An. in Menag.*, p. 325, which is the type of *Heleodytes* Cab.

1857. BEALE, S. C. T. Note on the Common Wren [Troglodytes vulgaris]. < *Zoologist*, xv, 1857, p. 5516.

1857. SCLATER, P. L. Note on Buglodytes albicilius, Bp. < *Ann. Mag. Nat. Hist.*, 2d ser., xix, 1857, p. 179.
  From *P. Z. S.*, April 22, 1856, p. 97, *q. v.*

1857. SMITH, R. B. Nesting of the Wren [Troglodytes vulgaris]. < *Zoologist*, xv, 1857, p. 5791.

1861. FISCHER, J. C. H. Der faröische Zaunkönig, Troglodytes borealis, n. sp. < *J. f. O.*, ix, 1861, pp. 14–16, Taf. "i" (*i. e.* ii).
  Die Tafel stellt den Vogel mit seinen Eiern dar. Fig. 2, Eier von *T. europæus.*

1861. FISCHER, J. C. H. Ueber den faröischen Zaunkönig, Troglodytes borealis. < *J. f. O.*, ix, 1861, pp. 431–433, Taf. ii (irrthümlich mit "i" bezeichnet).

1862. BROCKHOLES, J. F. Food of the Wren [Anorthura troglodytes]. < *Zoologist*, xx, 1862, p. 7935.

1862. DOUBLEDAY, H. Food of the Wren [Anorthura troglodytes]. < *Zoologist*, xx, 1862, p. 7881.

1862. DOUBLEDAY, H. Food of the Wren [Anorthura troglodytes]. < *Zoologist*, xx, 1862, p. 7999.

1862. SAVILLE, S. P. Further Notes on the Common Wren [Anorthura troglodytes]. < *Zoologist*, xx, 1862, pp. 7999, 8000.

1862. TRINTHAMMER, W. H. Ein Curiosum in Betreff einer Nistweise [Anorthura troglodytes]. < *J. f. O.*, x, 1862, pp. 223, 224.

1865. BROWN, W. Wren's [Anorthura troglodytes] Nest. < *Zoologist*, xxiii, 1865, p. 9466.

1865. NEAVE, E. Early Wren's [Anorthura troglodytes] Nest [27 Dec.]. < *Zoologist*, xxiii, 1865, p. 9539.

1869. HILL, M. S. The House Wren. < *Am. Nat.*, iii, 1869, 49.
  Note on the mischievousness of *Troglodytes aëdon* [= *domestica* Bartr.].

1869. MURTON, J. Pugnacity of the Wren [Anorthura troglodytes]. < *Zoologist*, 2d ser., iv, 1869, pp. 1644, 1645.

1869. SCLATER, P. L. Description of a new Species of Mexican Wren [Thryothorus nisorius]. < *P. Z. S.*, xxxvii, 1869, pp. 591, 592, pl. xlv.

1870. CORDEAUX, J.   Common Wren [Anorthura troglodytes] at Spurn Point.   *< Zoologist*, 2d ser., v, 1870, p. 2407.

1870. MCLAUGHLIN, W. J.   House Wrens.   *< Am. Nat.*, iii, 1870, p. 614.
Note on the nidification of *Troglodytes aëdon* [= *domestica* Bartr.].

1871. TUCK, J. G.   Wren's [Anorthura troglodytes] Nest on a Pulpit.   *< Zoologist*, 2d ser., vi, 1871, p. 2641.

1872. GIZYCKI, —.   [Troglodytes parvulus im Käfig nistend.]   *< J. f. O.*, xx, 1872, p. 317.

1873. T[RIPPE], T. M.   Occurrence of the Rock Wren [Salpinctes obsoletus] in Iowa.   *< Am. Nat.*, vii, 1873, p. 566.

1871. LAWRENCE, G. N.   Descriptions of New Species of Birds of the Families Troglodytidæ and Tyrannidæ.   *< Proc. Acad. Nat. Sci. Phila.*, 1871, pp. 233–236.
The Troglodyte here described is *Catherpes sumichrasti*, p. 233, from Vera Cruz, Mexico.

1874. ANON.   Value of the Wren.   *< Am. Sportsman*, iii, 1874, p. 250.

1874. WALDEN, *Lord*.   [Proposes for Troglodytes punctatus Blyth nec Brehm, the name of T. formosus.]   *< Ibis*, 3d ser., iv, 1874, p. 91.

1875. RIDGWAY, R.   Description of a New Wren [Thryothorus ludovicianus var. miamensis] from Eastern Florida.   *< Am. Nat.*, ix, No. 8, Aug.. 1875, pp. 469, 470.

1875. SWINHOE, R.   [On the identity of Troglodytes alascensis Baird with T. fumigatus Temm.]   *< Ibis*, 3d ser., v, 1875, pp. 143, 144.

1876. ABBOTT, C. C.   Bewick's Wren (Thryothorus Bewicki).   *< Am. Nat.*, x, No. 4, 1876, pp. 237, 238.
Note of its considerable numbers in New Jersey.

1876. COOPER, J. G.   Nesting Habits of the Californian House Wren (Troglodytes aëdon var. parkmanni).   *< Bull. Nutt. Ornith. Club*, i, No. iv, Nov., 1876, pp. 79–81.

1876. COUES, E.   [Bewick's Wren, Thryothorus bewicki, breeding in Virginia.]   *< Am. Nat.*, x, No. 1, 1876, p. 48.

1876. COUES. E.   Tarsal Envelope in Campylorhynchus and allied genera.   *< Bull. Nutt. Ornith. Club*, i, No. 2, July, 1876, pp. 50, 51.
Verifying the statements of S. F. Baird (*Rev. Am. Birds*, 1864, p. 109) respecting the tarsal envelope of *Salpinctes*, and extending observations to *Campylorhynchus*, finding that in the latter "the lateral plates, but especially the outer one, are broken up into a series of conspicuous scutella; and that *Catherpes* shows a tendency, not so fully expressed, to similar division of the tarsal envelope". In the tarsus of a species of *Thamnophilus*, a typical Formicarian, "the plates are divided behind, and the general structure is substantially the same as in *Salpinctes*". The question of the systematic position of these genera is thus raised. "These points may not suffice for the summary dismissal of the genera under consideration from the *Troglodytidæ*, but they go to show that their position in that family is not assured."

1876. COUES, E.   Letters on Ornithology.   No. 5.—Marsh Wrens [Cistothorus stellaris and Telmatodytes palustris].   *< The Chicago Field*, Nov. 18, 1876, figg. 2.
Popular biographical notices of these two species, with figures of their heads.

1876. MINOT, H. D.   The Great Carolina Wren [Thryothorus ludovicianus] in Massachusetts.   *< Bull. Nutt. Ornith. Club*, i, No. 3, Sept., 1876, p. 76.

1877. ALLEN, J. A.   Nest and Eggs of the Alaskan Wren [Anorthura troglodytes alascensis].   *< Bull. Nutt. Ornith. Club*, ii, No. 3, July, 1877, p. 82.

1877. DURY, C.   Fecundity of the Carolina Wren (Thryothorus ludovicianus).   *< Bull. Nutt. Ornith. Club*, ii, No. 2, Apr., 1877, p. 50.

1877. FRAZER, A. W.   Persistency at Nest-Building in a House Wren [Troglodytes domestica Bartr.].   *< Bull. Nutt. Ornith. Club*, ii, No. 3, July, 1877, p. 78.

1877. [SCOTT, W. E. D.]   Notes on Habits of the Long-billed Marsh Wrens [Telmatodytes palustris].   *< The Country*, i, Nov. 17, 1877, p. 43.

1878. BREWER, T. M.   The Carolina Wren [Thryothorus ludovicianus] in Massachu-
      setts.   <Bull. Nutt. Ornith. Club, iii, No. 4, Oct., 1878, p. 193.

1878. KING, F. H.   The Winter Wren [Anorthura troglodytes hyemalis] breeding in
      Southern New York.   <Bull. Nutt. Ornith. Club, iii, No. 4, Oct., 1878, pp. 194,
      195.

1878. RIDGWAY, R.   Description of a new Wren [Thryothorus felix, β. lawrencii]
      from the Tres Marias Islands.   <Bull. Nutt. Ornith. Club, iii, No. 1, Jan.,
      1878, pp. 10, 11.

1879. BICKNELL, E. P.   The Carolina Wren [Thryothorus ludovicianus] breeding in
      New York.   <Bull. Nutt. Ornith. Club, iv, No. 3, July, 1879, pp. 183, 184.

1879. DEANE, R.   Breeding of the Winter Wren [Anorthura troglodytes hyemalis] at
      Houlton, M[ain]e.   <Bull. Nutt. Ornith. Club, iv, No. 1, 1879, pp. 37-39.
      Three cases fully described.

1879. DEANE, R.   The Great Carolina Wren [Thryothorus ludovicianus] breeding on
      Long Island, N. Y.   <Bull. Nutt. Ornith. Club, iv, No. 3, July, 1879, p. 184.

1879. PURDIE, H. A.   The Great Carolina Wren [Thryothorus ludovicianus] in Con-
      necticut.   <Bull. Nutt. Ornith. Club, iv, No. 1, Jan., 1879, p. 61.

Lusciniidæ.

[Includes *Saxicola, Sialia,* and *Regulus.*]

1834. COUCH, J. The Habits of the Wheatear (Motacilla [Saxicola] Œnanthe). <*Loudon's Mag. Nat. Hist.*, vii, 1834, pp. 466, 467.

1846. REECE, G. Singular variety of the Wheatear (Motacilla [Saxicola] Œnanthe). <*Zoologist*, iv, 1846, p. 1496.

1848. HUSSEY, A. Note on the Wheatears (Sylvia [Saxicola] Œnanthe). <*Zoologist*, vi, 1848, p. 2298.

1849. THORNCROFT, T. Arrival of the Wheatear (Sylvia [Saxicola] Œnanthe) at Brighton. <*Zoologist*, vii, 1849, p. 2412.

1850. GURNEY, J. H. Note on a [albinotic] Variety of the Wheatear (Sylvia [Saxicola] Œnanthe). <*Zoologist*, viii, 1850, p. 2923.

1850. [KIRTLAND, J. P.] The Blue Bird [Sialia sialis]. <*The Family Visitor*, i, No. 7, 1850, p. 55.
Popular account.

1858. GOULD, J. [Exhibition of a specimen of the American Regulus calendula shot on Loch Lomondside by Dr. Dewar.] <*P. Z. S.*, xxvi, 1858, p. 290.

1862. COUPER, W. Occurrence of the Stone Chat (Saxicola œnanthe, Bechst.) at Beauport, near Quebec. <*Canad. Nat. & Geol.*, vii, 1862, p. 319.

1862. MORE, A. G. Early Arrival of the Wheatear [Saxicola œnanthe, Mar. 7, in Bembridge]. <*Zoologist*, xx, 1862, p. 7998.

1863. SAVILLE, S. P. A Word for the Stonechat [Saxicola œnanthe]. <*Zoologist*, xxi, 1863, p. 8819.

1863. SAXBY, H. Two Wheatears [Saxicola œnanthe] Nests together. <*Zoologist*, xxi, 1863, pp. 8719, 8720.

1864. DUTTON, J. Wheatear [Saxicola œnanthe] near Eastbourne in March. <*Zoologist*, xxii, 1864, p. 9041.

1864. HARTING, J. E. Wheatears [Saxicola œnanthe] in March. <*Zoologist*, xxii, 1864, p. 9108.

1864. HARVIE-BROWN, J. A. Early Appearance of the Wheatear [Saxicola œnanthe]. <*Zoologist*, xxii, 1864, p. 9108.

1864. PAMPLIN, W. Wheatears [Saxicola œnanthe] in March [in North Wales]. <*Zoologist*, xxii, 1864, p. 9041.

1865. GUNN, T. E. The Stonechat [Saxicola œnanthe] and Winchat [S. rubetra] Winter Residents in Norfolk. <*Zoologist*, xxiii, 1865, pp. 9455, 9456.

1869. FISH, W. C. The Blue-bird [Sialia sialis]. <*Am. Nat.*, ii, 1868, pp. 667, 668.
Dates of its appearance on the coast of Massachusetts.

1869. HALDEMAN, S. S. Citation of Authorities. <*Am. Nat.*, iii, 1869, p. 159.
Claims the name *Sialia sialis*, usually accredited to S. F. Baird.

1869. INGERSOLL, E. Variation in Bluebirds' [Sialia sialis] Eggs. <*Am. Nat.*, iii, 1869, pp. 391, 392.
White eggs of this species.

1869. WONFOR, T. W. Variety of the Wheatear [Saxicola œnanthe]. <*Zoologist*, 2d ser., iv, 1869, p. 1918.

1870. ALLEN, J. A. The Ruby-crowned Kinglet [Regulus calendula]. <*Am. Nat.*, iv, 1870, p. 54.
  With reference to possession of scarlet on the crown by ♀ of this species.

1870. COUES, E. The Ruby-crowned Wren [Regulus calendula]. <*Am. Nat.*, iv, 1870, p. 316.
  Replies to J. A. Allen (*tom. cit.*, 54) that this species ♀ is "ruby-crowned" like the ♂.

1870. DALL, W. H. The Ruby Crowned Kinglet [Regulus calendula]. <*Am. Nat.*, iv, 1870, pp. 376, 377.
  Note on *Regulus calendula* ♂, and on certain *Anatinæ.*

1870. GATCOMBE, J. Early Appearance of the Wheatear [Saxicola œnanthe]. <*Zoologist*, 2d ser., v, 1870, p. 2100.

1871. TRISTRAM, H. B. Notes on Sylviads. <*Ann. Mag. Nat. Hist.*, 4th ser., viii, 1871, pp. 28, 29.
  Treats of 4 spp.—*Phyllopneuste major*, p. 29, sp. n.

1871. TRISTRAM, H. B. [Critical notes on certain Sylviidæ.] <*Ibis*, 3d ser., i, 1871, pp. 109, 110.
  Phyllopneuste schwartzi Radde = *P. viridanus* Blyth = *Abrornis tenuiceps* Hodgs.—*P. eversmanni* Midd. = *P. sylvicultrix* Swinh., which latter stands, unless, as is probable, it = *P. borealis* Blas.—*P. eversmanni* Bp. is totally distinct, and = *icterina* Eversm.—Of three species confounded under the name of *P. fuscatus* Blyth, one = *P. siberica* Midd.; another is *P. maackii* Schr.; the third is not determined.

1874. ABBOTT, C. C. The Kinglets [Regulus] of New Jersey. <*Am. Nat.*, viii, 1874, pp. 364, 365.
  Field-notes on *Regulus setrapa* and *R. calendula.*

1874. BREWER, T. M. The Kinglets [Regulus] in New Jersey. <*Am. Nat.*, viii, 1874, pp. 502–503.
  Controversial; ref. to C. C. Abbott, *tom. cit.*, 364.

1874. BLANFORD, W. T., *and* DRESSER, H. E. Monograph of the Genus Saxicola, Bechstein. <*P. Z. S.*, xlii, 1874, pp. 213–241, pll. xxxvi–xxxix, woodcc.
  A very timely and desirable article. The genus includes *Dromolæa* and *Campicola.* 69 current spp. reduced to 37. *S. griseiceps*, p. 233, pl. xxxvii, f. 3; *S. diluta*, p. 234, pl. xxxix, f. 1, spp. nn. A nearly complete synonymy, representing numerous important rectifications, with full description and habitat of all the spp. Pl. 36, f. 1, *S. bottæ*; f. 2, *S. heuglini*; pl. xxxvii, f. 1, 2, *S. leucomelæna*; pl. xxxviii, f. 1, *S. pollux*; f. 2, *S. castor*; pl. xxxix, f. 2, *S. schlegeli.*

1876. GILLMAN, H. The Bluebird [Sialia sialis] feeding on Ampelopsis. <*Am. Nat.*, x, No. 9, 1876, p. 556.

1876. INGERSOLL, E. Our present Knowledge of the Nidification of the American Kinglets [Regulus]. <*Bull. Nutt. Ornith. Club*, i, No. iv, Nov., 1876, pp. 77–79.

1877. CLIFTON, —. [Letter on the two distinct races of Saxicola œnanthe found in England.] <*Ibis*, 4th ser., i, Apr., 1877, pp. 256, 257.

1877. COLLETT, R. On Phylloscopus borealis and its Occurrence in Norway. <*P. Z. S.*, 1877, pp. 43–47.

1877. [COUES, E.] The Song that the Bluebird [Sialia sialis] sings. <*Harper's New Monthly Mag.*, May, 1877, p. 891.
  Poem. Reprinted in *The Country*, Dec. 1, 1877, and elsewhere.

1877. INGERSOLL, E. Our present Knowledge of the Nidification of the American Kinglets [Regulus]. <*Forest and Stream*, viii, Feb. 22, 1877, p. 33.
  Reprinted from *Bull. Nutt. Ornith. Club*, i, No. 4, Nov., 1876, pp. 77–79.

1877. [INGERSOLL, E.] Our present Knowledge of the Nidification of the American Kinglets [Regulus]. <*Oölogist*, ii, No. 11, 1877, pp. 75, 76.
  From *Bull. Nutt. Ornith. Club*, i, No. 4, Nov., 1876, pp. 77–79.

1877. MEEHAN, T. The Bluebird [Sialia sialis] and Holly berries. <*Proc. Phila. Acad. Nat. Sci.*, 1877, p. 129.

1877. SEEBOHM, H.   On the Phylloscopi or Willow-Warblers.   <*Ibis*, 4th ser., i, Jan., 1877, pp. 66–108.

> This is an important monography, treating of 32 spp. in due form, with copious synonymy, full description, geographical distribution, and critical comment.—These species are divided into the following sections: *Acanthopneuste* with 13 spp.; *Phylloscopus* proper with 15 spp., and *Reguloides* with 5 spp.; each of the former two subgenera being further analyzed into species of two groups, by pattern of coloration.—The American *Phyllopneuste kennicottii* Baird is referred to *Phylloscopus borealis* (Blas. = *eversmanni* Midd. nec Bp.).—*Phylloscopus gaetkei*, p. 92, sp. n. (=*major* Tristr. 1871, nec Forst. 1817).

1877. "VERD MONT ABROAD."   Blue Birds [Sialia sialis].—New Haven [Conn.], Dec. 19th.   <*Forest and Stream*, ix, Dec. 27, 1877, p. 397.

1878. EARLE, C. F.   Sialia [sialis]: The story of a [captive] bluebird.   <*Forest and Stream*, xi, Nov. 28, 1878, p. 339.

1878. [SCOTT, W. E. D.]   Blue-Birds [Sialia sialis].   <*The Country*, i, March 16, 1878, p. 292.

1879. BREWER, T. M.   Nest and Eggs of the Golden Crowned Kinglet (Regulus satrapa).   <*Bull. Nutt. Ornith. Club*, iv, No. 2, Apr., 1879, pp. 96–99.

> Description of eggs from "an unknown nest", inferred to belong to this species, found by H. Merrill near Bangor, Me.; argument with the author of "Birds of the Colorado Valley" respecting general character of the nest; attention called by J. C. Merrill to the overlooked illustration of the egg in *J. f. O.*, 1856, p. 33, pl. 1, f. 8; attention called by J. A. Allen to overlooked account of nest in Minot's *B. New Engl.*, p. 56.

1879. BRYANT, W. E.   The Arctic Bluebird [Sialia arctica] near San Francisco.   <*Science News*, i, No. 9, Mar. 1, 1879, p. 144.

1879. MORRIS, R. H.   A white Bluebird [Sialia sialis].   <*Forest and Stream*, xiii, Sept. 4, 1879, p. 605.

1879. "OBSERVER."   A strange nesting place [of Sialia sialis—in a cannon].   <*Forest and Stream*, xii, July 17, 1879, p. 464.

Paridæ.

1845. HARRIS, E.   Description of a new species of Parus [septentrionalis] from the Upper Missouri.   <*Proc. Acad. Nat. Sci. Phila.*, ii, 1845, pp. 300, 301.

1846. HARRIS, E.   Description of a [lately] new species of Parus [septentrionalis] from the Upper Missouri.   <*Ann. Mag. Nat. Hist.*, xvii, 1846, pp. 452–454.
From *Proc. Acad. Phila.*, ii, 1845, pp. 300, 301.

1850. BONAPARTE, C. L.   Sur deux espèces nouvelles de Paridæ.   <*Compt. Rend. de. l'Acad. Sci.*, xxxi, Sept., 1850, pp. 478, 479.

Psaltriparus (g. n.) *personatus* (Western.), *Lophophanes wollweberi* (Western.), p. 478.   *Callacanthis*, g. n., (type *Carduelis burtoni* Gould), p. 479.   Voyez t. c., p. 539.

1850. CASSIN, J.   Descriptions of new species of Birds of the genera Parus, Linn.; . . .   <*Proc. Acad. Nat. Sci. Phila.*, v, Oct., 1850, pp. 103 — —, pll. i, ii.

The article is of much more extended scope than *Paridæ*, and I give the full title elsewhere; but here occur the original descriptions of *Parus annexus* [=*Lophophanes wollweberi*], p. 103, pl. i, and of *Parus* [*Lophophanes*] *atricristatus*, p. 103, pl. ii.

1851. WESTERMAN, G. F.   Beschrijving van twee nieuwe Soorten van Meezen.   <*Bijdrag tot de Dierk.*, i. Deel, derde Aflevering, 1851, pp. 15, 16, met eene Plaat.

I. *Parus* (*Lophophanes*) *wollweberi*, p. 15, met eene Afbeelding; habitat in Mexico.   II. *Psaltria personata*, p. 16, met eene Afbeelding van het Wijfje en Mannetje; habitat in Mexico, (= *Parus melanotis* Hartl., *R. Z.*, 1844, 216).

1852. LAWRENCE, G. N.   Descriptions of new species of Birds of the genera Conirostrum [ornatum], . . .   <*Ann. Lyc. Nat. Hist. N. Y.*, v, 1852, pp. 112–117, pl. v.   (Read Apr. 28, 1851.)

Here occurs, in a paper of wider scope, the orig. descr. of *Conirostrum ornatum*, p. 112, pl. v, f. 1, = *Aegithalus flaviceps* Sund.= *Paroides f.* sive *Auriparus f.* Baird.   The title will be found in full in the North American part of this Bibliography.

1855. SCLATER, P. L.   On the Genus Culicivora of Swainson, and its component Species.   <*P. Z. S.*, Jan. 9, 1855, pp. 11, 12.

Culicivora Sw., *Zool. Journ.* 1827, type *Muscicapa stenura* Temm., also embraces *M. cærulea* Wils., thus including birds of different families.   Cabanis separated them, rightly, but left *Culicivora* for *M. cærulea*, proposing *Hapalura* for *M. stenura*.   But *Hapalura* is thus strictly synonymous with *Culicivora*, and a new name is required for the genus of which *cærulea* is typical.   Hence *Polioptila*, g. n., p. 11.—The author treats of four spp. of the genus, *PP. cærulea, dumicola, leucogastra*, and *bilineata*.

1856. FATIO-BEAUMONT, J. "S. [*i. e.* G.]"   Bemerkungen über die Gruppe der Grau-Meisen.   Mésanges grises—Pari cinerei.   <*Naumannia*, vi, 1856, pp. 160–163.
P. borealis, P. atricapillus; P. alpestris, sp. n., p. 161.

1856. LAWRENCE, G. N.   Descriptions of New Species of Birds of the Genera Chordeiles, Swainson, and Polioptila, Sclater.   <*Ann. Lyc. Nat. Hist. New York*, vi, 1856, pp. 165–169.
Polioptila melanura, p. 168.

1856. SCLATER, P. L.   On the Genus Culicivora of Swainson, and its component Species.   <*Ann. Mag. Nat. Hist.*, xvii, 1856, pp. 68–70.
Not seen: from *P. Z. S.*, 1865, pp. 11, 12, q. v.

1856. SCLATER, P. L.   Note on Psaltria flaviceps, a third American Species of the Parine Genus Psaltria.   <*P. Z. S.*, xxiv, 1856, pp. 37, 38.

The bird which had been described by Sundevall as *Aegithalus flaviceps* (Foglar från Nord-östra Afrika, *Öfvers. K. Vet. Ac. Förh.*, vii, 1850, p. 129) is here referred to the genus *Psaltria*; and the *Conirostrum ornatum* of Lawrence (*Ann. Lyc. N. Y.*, v, 1851, p. 112, pl. 5, f. 1) is shown to be synonymous therewith.

1857. SCLATER, P. L.   Note on Psaltria flaviceps, a third American Species of the Parine Genus Psaltria.   <*Ann. Mag. Nat. Hist.*, 2d ser., xix, 1857, pp. 92, 93.
From *P. Z. S.*, March 11, 1856, pp. 37, 38, q. v.

1857. SCLATER, P. L.   On Parus meridionalis and some other species mentioned in the Catalogue of Birds collected by M. Sallé in Southern Mexico.   *<P. Z. S.*, xxv, 1857, pp. 81, 82.
  Maintaining the distinctness of the species named from *P. atricapillus.*

1865. BRYANT, H.   Description of a New Variety of Parus [hudsonicus var. littoralis] from Yarmouth, Nova Scotia.   *<Proc Boston Soc. Nat. Hist.*, ix, 1865, pp. 368, 369.

1865. LAWRENCE, G. N.   Descriptions of new species of Birds of the Families Paridæ, Vireonidæ, Tyrannidæ, and Trochilidæ, with a note on Myiarchus Panamensis.   *< Proc. Acad. Nat. Sci. Phila.*, xvii, 1865, pp. 37–39.
  Polioptila plumbiceps, p. 37; from Venezuela.

1867. TRIPPE, T. M.   The Chickadee [Parus atricapillus].   *<Am. Nat.*, i, 1867, pp. 584–587.
  Biographical, with special reference to the nesting and eggs.

1875. WILDER, HARVEY.   The Chickadees [Parus atricapillus].   *<St. Nicholas Mag.*, ii, 1875, pp. 79–81, one illust.
  Popular account.

1876. COLES, C. E.   The Blue-gray Gnatcatcher.   (Polioptila cœrulea.)   *< The Oölogist*, ii, No. 4, —, 1876, p. 31.

1876. COUES, E.   Letters on Ornithology.   No. 3.—The Blue-gray Gnatcatcher [Polioptila cœrulea].   *< The Chicago Field*, Aug. 26, 1876, figure.
  Biography of the bird, from advance sheets of *Birds of the Colorado Valley*, with an original figure.

1876. COUES, E.   Letters on Ornithology.   No. 10.—Titmice, Tomtits or Chicadees [Paridæ].   *< The Chicago Field*, Dec. 30, 1876, figg. 2.
  Popular account of North American species, with figg. of the heads of *Parus montanus* and of *Lophophanes bicolor.*

1878. BELDING, L.   Nesting-Habits of Parus montanus.   *<Bull. Nutt. Ornith. Club*, iii, No. 2, Apr., 1878, pp. 102, 103.

1878. BREWER, T. M.   The Blue-gray Gnatcatcher (Polioptila cærulea) in Massachusetts.   *< Bull. Nutt. Ornith. Club*, iii, No. 3, July, 1878, pp. 146, 147.
  Being the second known instance of its occurrence in that State, the first having been recorded in *op. tom. cit.*, p. 45.

1878. COOPER, W. A.   Notes on the breeding habits of Hutton's Vireo (Vireo huttoni) and the Gray Titmouse (Lophophanes inornatus), with a description of their Nests and Eggs.   *<Bull. Nutt. Ornith. Club*, iii, No. 2, Apr., 1878, pp. 68, 69.

1878. DEANE, R.   The Blue-gray Gnatcatcher (Polioptila cœrulea) in Massachusetts.   *< Bull. Nutt. Ornith. Club*, iii, No. 1, Jan., 1878, p. 45.

1879. [ALDRICH, C.]   The Chickadee [Parus atricapillus].   *<Hamilton Freeman* (newspaper of Webster City, Iowa), of Feb. 26, 1879.
  Popular account of habits.

1879. HENSHAW, H. W.   Nest and Eggs of the Gray Titmouse (Lophophanes inornatus).   *<Bull. Nutt. Ornith. Club*, iv, No. 3, July, 1879, pp. 182, 183.

1879. INGERSOLL, [E.]   Nest and Eggs of the Tufted Titmouse [Lophophanes bicolor].   *< The Oölogist*, v, No. 2, Aug., 1879, p. 10.
  Quoted from his *Nests and Eggs of American Birds,* Part II, p. 44.

1879. INGERSOLL, E.   Nest and Eggs of the Blue-gray Gnatcatcher [Polioptila cœrulea].   *< The Oölogist*, iv, No. 11, June, 1879, p. 86.
  Quoted from his *Nests and Eggs of American Birds,* Part II, p. 41.

1879. LANGDON, F. W.   Albinism in the Tufted Titmouse [Lophophanes bicolor].   *<Bull. Nutt. Ornith. Club*, iv, No. 2, Apr., 1879, p. 116.

Chamæidæ.

1847. GAMBEL, W.   Chamæa, new genus of Birds allied to Parus. $<$ *Am. Journ. Sci.*, iv, Sept., 1847, p. 286.

> This, though the first special title on the subject, does not cover the original description of *Chamæa*, g. n., which occurs in a paper entitled "Remarks on the Birds observed in Upper California", *Proc. Phila. Acad.*, iii, Feb., 1847, p. 154.   The genus also ·reappears in a translation of this paper, ,,Ueber die in Oberkalifornien beobachteten Vögel", in *Arch. f. Naturg.*, 1848, Bd. i, p. 102.   The species, *C. fasciata*, was first described as *Parus fasciatus* in *Proc. Phila. Acad.*, ii, Aug., 1845, p. 265; and was figured in *Journ. Phila. Acad.*, 2d ser., i, pt. i, Dec., 1847, p. 34, pl. viii, f. 3.

1847. GAMBEL, W.   Chamæa, a new genus of Birds allied to Parus. $<$ *Ann. Mag. Nat. Hist.*, xx, 1847, pp. 441, 442.

> From *Am. Journ. Sci.*, iv, Sept. 1847 p. 286.

Mniotiltidæ.

1818. RAFINESQUE, C. S.   Further Account of Discoveries in Natural History, in the Western States, . . .   *<Amer. Monthly Mag.*, iv, 1818, pp. 39–42.

  No other bird-matter than *Rimamphus citrinus*, g. sp. n., p. 41, (*Cf.* Hartl., *R. Z.* viii, 1845, p. 343; Baird, B. N. A., 1858, p. 264.   See also *Journ. de Phys.*, lxxxviii 1819, p. 418, where the genus and species reappears, along with *Helmitheros migratorius*, g. sp. n.)

1840. TOWNSEND, J. K.   Description of a New Species of Sylvia [tolmœi], from the Columbia River.   *<Journ. Acad. Nat. Sci. Phila.*, viii, 1839, pp. 149, 150.   (Read Apr. 2, 1839; vol. not pub. till 1840.)

1840. TOWNSEND, J. K.   Note on Sylvia Tolmœi.   *<Journ. Acad. Nat. Sci. Phila.*, viii, 1839, p. 159.   (Read Sept. 10, 1839; vol. pub. 1840.)

  Claims priority for the name over that of *S. macgillivrayi* Aud., *Orn. Biog.*, v. 1839, p. 75; but actual priority of publication is with the latter. (See Baird, *B. N. A.*, 1858, p. 245.)

1842. LEIB, G. C.   [Note on Parus leucotis, Giraud.]   *<Proc. Acad. Nat. Sci. Phila.*, i, 1842, p. 140.

  Identified as *Setofaga* (sic) *rubra*.   The bird is the *Cardellina (Ergaticus) rubra* of late authors.

1842. STORER, D. H.   [Note on Sylvia formosa.]   *<Proc. Bost. Soc. Nat. Hist.*, i, 1842, p. 55.

1844. MCCULLOCH, T.   On the importance of habit as a guide to accuracy in Systematical arrangement, illustrated in the instance of the Sylvia petechia [Dendrœca palmarum Baird] of Wilson, and all subsequent writers.   *<Journ. Bost. Soc. Nat. Hist.*, iv, pt. iv, 1844, pp. 406–410.

  Taking habit as his guide, makes the bird out to be a *Seiurus*.   The article is in effect an argument *against* the importance of habit as a guide to classification, unless checked by investigation of physical characters.

1845. CABOT, S., JR.   [Occurrence of Silvia agilis at Brookline, Mass.]   *<Proc. Bost. Soc. Nat. Hist.*, ii, 1845, 63.

1845. HARTLAUB, G.   Notes ornithologiques.   *<Revue Zoologique*, viii, 1845, pp. 342, 343.

  1. Sous la description de *Rimamphus citrinus* de Rafinesque (*Am. Month. Mag.*, iv, 1818, p. 41; *Journ. de Phys.*, lxxxviii, 1819, p. 418) l'auteur croit reconnaître la *Motacilla* [*Dendrœca*] *œstiva* des auteurs; et par conséquent le genre *Rhimamphus* serait identique avec *Sylvicola*, Sw., 1827.—2. *Helmitheros migratorius* Raf. (loc. cit) est déclaré par Rafinesque même comme identique avec la *Sylvia vermivora* de Latham, pour laquelle Swainson et Audubon ont créé les genres *Vermivora* (1827) et *Helinaia* (1839) : et l'auteur croit devoir réclamer la priorité en faveur de Rafinesque.

1852. BAIRD, S. F.   Description of a new Species of Sylvicola [kirtlandi].   *<Ann. Lyc. Nat. Hist. New York*, v, 1852, pp. 217, 218, pl. vi.

1855. BRYANT, H.   [Notice of the occurrence in Massachusetts, in January, of Sylvicola coronata and S. parus.]   *<Proc. Bost. Soc. Nat. Hist.*, v, 1855, p. 142.

1855. GUNDLACH, J.   Description of a New Species of Bird of the Genus Sylvicola [pityophila] Swainson.   *<Ann. Lyc. Nat. Hist. New York*, vi, 1855, pp. 160, 161.

1856. BREWER, T. M.   [Observations on a nest of the Nashville Warbler (Vermivora rubricapilla) discovered by Mr. George Wells, at Lynn, Mass.   With remarks on nests and eggs of other New England Sylvicolidæ.]   *<Proc. Bost. Soc. Nat. Hist.*, vi, 1856, pp. 4–6.

1859. BREWER, T. M.   [On the Distribution and Habits of the Summer Yellow-bird, Dendrœca œstiva.]   *<Proc. Bost. Soc. Nat. Hist.*, vii, 1859, pp. 21, 22.

  With special reference to the building of "two-story" nests by this species, to obviate incubation of egg of *Molothrus pecoris*.

1860. [KIRKPATRICK, J.] Kirtland's Warbler [Dendrœca kirtlandi]. < *Ohio Farmer* (newspaper), vol. ix, No. 23, June 9, 1860, p. 179.

A specimen of this rare bird was shot a short time ago, near the "old river bed", Cleveland, by Mr. Durby, of University Heights. It was identified by R. K. Winslow, preserved and mounted by him, and proved to be a female. Until now there was but one specimen of this bird known, that obtained by Dr. Kirtland, now in the collection of the Smithsonian Institution at Washington. It was first described by Baird in the *Annals of the New York Lyceum* (1852), and afterward in Cassin's *Illustrations*. The present specimen is more lead-colored on the upper parts than Cassin's figure. Mr. Winslow informs us that Wm. Case, Esq., once shot a specimen, but it was so badly injured as to be unfit for preserving.

1861. VENNOR, H. G.   A short review of the Sylviadæ or Wood-Warblers found in the vicinity of Montreal. < *Canad. Nat. and Geol.*, vi, Oct., 1861, pp. 349–362.

Descriptions, compiled, and some accounts of habits.

1865. SCLATER, P. L.   Note on two rare Species of the American genus Dendrœca. < *Ibis*, 2d ser., i, 1865, pp. 87–89, and p. 237.

Critical remarks on 4 closely allied species—*D. virens, occidentalis, townsendi,* and *chrysoparia,* with a synonymatic and diagnostic list of them. *D. niveiventris* Salv., *P. Z. S.*, 1863, p. 187, pl. xxiv, f. 2, is referred to *occidentalis*. Cf. *tom. cit.*, p. 237, for correction of an error respecting *D. chrysoparia*.

1865. SCLATER, P. L.   On a New Species of the Genus Basileuterus of Cabanis, with a Synopsis of the known Species of the Genus. < *P. Z. S.*, xxxiii, 1865, pp. 282–286, pll. ix, x.

Diagnostic and synonymatic list of 15 spp., exclusive of *Myiothlypis nigricristata* and *Euthlypis lachrymosa*. *B. mesoleucus*, p. 286, pl. ix, f. 1, sp. n.   Pl. ix, fig. 2, *B. cinereicollis;* pl. x, f. 1, *B. semicervinus;* pl. x, f. 2, *B. uropygialis*.

1866. BENVENUTI, E.   [Descrizione di una nuova specie di Dendroica (picciolii) del Brasile.] < *Annali R. Mus. Fisica e Storia Nat. di Firenze per il 1865*, nuova serie, i, 1865, p. 207.

The description occurs in an article of wider scope, describing four new *Trochilidæ*, with a note on Birds of Tuscany. The full title is given elsewhere.

1867. BREWER, T. M.   [Remarks on the Wood-Warblers (Dendrœcæ) of North America.] < *Proc. Bost. Soc. Nat. Hist.*, xi, 1867, pp. 139, 140.

1868. TRIPPE, T. M.   The Warblers [Sylvicolidæ]. < *Am. Nat.*, ii, 1868, pp. 169–183.

Biographical notes on various North American species.

1869. BOARDMAN, G. A.   Tennessee Warbler [Helminthophaga peregrina]. < *Am. Nat.*, iii, 1869, p. 222.

Very common at Milltown, Maine.

1869. JACKSON, T. H.   The Worm-eating Warbler [Helmitherus vermivorus]. < *Am. Nat.*, iii, 1869, p. 556.

Note on the nest and eggs.

1869. PURDIE, H. A.   [Notice of the Capture of Helminthophaga peregrina in Newton, Mass.] < *Proc. Bost. Soc. Nat. Hist.*, xiii, 1869, p. 93.

1869. PURDIE, H. A.   Tennessee Warbler [Helminthophaga peregrina]. < *Am. Nat.*, iii, 1869, p. 31.

Note on its geographical distribution.

1869. PURDIE, H. A.   Golden-winged Warbler [Helminthophaga chrysoptera]. < *Am. Nat.*, iii, 1869, p. 497.

On its local distribution and breeding.

1869. TRIPPE, T. M.   The Tennessee Warbler [Helminthophaga peregrina]. < *Am. Nat.*, iii, 1869, p. 496.

On its local distribution.

1870. SUNDEVALL, C. J.   Öfversigt af fogelslägtet Dendrœca. < *Öfvers. Kongl. Vetensk.-Akad. Förhandl. för år 1869*, 1870, pp. 605–618.

Div. I. Flavovirides. 1. aestiva. 2. petechia, a) bartholemica, b) cruzianca, c) barbadensis, d) cubana, e) jamaicensis, f) gallapagensis, g) peruviana, h) aequatoralis? i) panamensis?, var. nn. 3? eoa. II. Stigmatopterae: 4. olivacea. 5. caerulescens. III. Albifasciatae. 6. nigrescens.

1870. SUNDEVALL, C. J.—Continued.

7. *townsendi.* 8. *chrysopareia.* 9. *occidentalis.* 10. *virens.* 11. *blackburniæ.* 12. *graciae.* 13. *dominica.* 14. *pityophila.* 15. *icterocephala.* 16. *pinus.* 17? *montana.* 18. *coronata.* 19. *auduboni.* 20. *castanea.* 21. *striata.* 22. *caerulea.* 23. *adelaidæ.* 24. *maculosa.* IV. *Acutirostres.* 25. *discolor.* 26. *palmarum.* 27. *tigrina.*—Necnon, auctori ignotae, 28. *pharetra.* 29. *kirtlandi.* 30. *carbonata.*—Adjectis descriptionibus, synonymis, locis, observationibusque.

1872. BREWER, T. M. [On the appearance of Oporornis agilis in Massachusetts.] < *Proc. Boston Soc. Nat. Hist.*, xv, 1872, pp. 3, 4.

1872. BREWER, T. M. [Note of the breeding of Dendrœca coronata in Maine.] <*Proc. Boston Soc. Nat. Hist.*, xv, 1872, p. 4.

1872. BREWER, T. M. [On the abundance of Dendrœca castanea in Wisconsin and Massachusetts in 1872.] < *Proc. Boston Soc. Nat. Hist.*, xv, 1872, pp. 192, 193.

1872. BREWER. T. M. [On the movements of Dendrœca castanea.] < *Ibis*, 3d ser., ii, 1872, p. 334.

1872. COUES, E. Nest and Eggs of Helminthophaga luciæ. < *Am. Nat.*, vi, 1872, p. 493.

Discovered by C. Bendire in Arizona; *cf.* Coues, *B. C. V.*, 1878, p. 221.

1872. RIDGWAY, R. On the Occurrence of Setophaga picta in Arizona. < *Am. Nat.*, vi, 1872, p. 436.

1872. SALVIN, O. Remarks on the Mniotiltine Genus Geothlypis. < *Ibis*, 3d ser., ii, 1872, pp. 147–152.

General commentary: differentiation of 8 spp.; details of their geographical distribution and migration.—*G. chiriquensis*, p. 148, new form of *G. œquinonctialis.*

1874. BREWSTER, W. A New Species of North American Warbler [Helminthophaga leucobronchialis]. < *Am. Sportsman*, v, Oct. 17, 1874, p. 33.

1874. HERRICK, H. Description of a new species of Helminthophaga [lawrencii]. < *Proc. Phila. Acad. Nat. Sci.*, 1874, p. 220, pl. 15.

1874. "SIGMA PHI." A bird not to be imposed upon. < *Forest and Stream*, iii, Sept. 10, 1874, p. 68.

Device of *Dendrœca œstiva* to escape infliction of the egg of *Molothrus ater.*

1874. STARK, A. C. The Chestnut-sided Warbler [Dendrœca pennsylvanica]. < *Am. Nat.*, viii, 1874, p. 756.

Breeding in West Virginia.

1875. ALLEN, J. A. Influence of Elevation and Latitude upon the Distribution of Species. < *Am. Nat.*, ix, No. 3, Mar., 1875, pp. 181, 182.

With special reference to *Dendrœca pennsylvanica.*

1875. BREWSTER, W. Habits of the Mourning Warbler (Geothlypis philadelphia). < *Rod and Gun*, vi, Apr. 24, 1875, p. 50.

Observations made in Maine: read before *Nutt. Ornith. Club*, April 3, 1875.

1875. FINSCH, O. Notes on Phænicomanes iora, Sharpe, and Abrornis atricapilla, Blyth. < *P. Z. S.*, Dec. 7, 1875, pp. 640, 641.

The "*Abrornis*" described from "China" (*Ibis.* 1870, p. 169) is no other than the North American *Myiodioctes pusillus* (Wils.).

1875. FISHER, A. K. Oporornis formosus breeding in Eastern New York. < *Am. Nat.*, ix, No. 10, Oct., 1875, p. 573.

1875. JORDAN, D. S. Dendroica dominica in Indiana. < *Am. Nat.*, ix, No. 5, May, 1875, p. 313.

With note on *Siurus ludovicianus* in Wisconsin.

1875. MINOT, H. D. Nesting of the Prairie Warbler [Dendrœca discolor] in New Hampshire. < *Am. Nat.*, ix, No. 9, Sept., 1875, p. 520.

1875. RIDGWAY, R. Nesting of the Worm-eating Warbler [Helmitherus vermivorus]. < *Field and Forest*, i, No. 2, July, 1875, pp. 10–12.

1875. W[ILLARD], S. L. Eggs and Nest of Black-Throated Green Warbler [Dendrœca virens.] < *Oölogist*, i, 1875, pp. 2, 3.

1875. [WILLARD, S. L.].   Warblers' [Sylvicolidæ] Nests.   < Oölogist, i, 1875, p. 35.

1875. [WILLARD, S. L.].   The Yellow Warbler [Dendrœca æstiva] and its Enemy [Molothrus ater].   < Oölogist, i, 1875, p. 43.

1876. BREWSTER, W.   Description of a [lately] new species of Helminthophaga [leucobronchialis].   < Bull. Nutt. Ornith. Club, i, No. 1, Apr., 1876, pp. 172, pl. 1.
    The first notice of this species was in the American Sportsman, v, Oct. 17, 1874, pp. 33.

1876. BREWSTER, W.   Capture of the Orange-crowned Warbler [Helminthophaga celata] in Massachusetts.   < Bull. Nutt. Ornith. Club, i, No. iv, Nov., 1876, pp. 94, 95.

1876. ERNEST, H.   Warblers of the Western Reserve [Ohio].   < Forest and Stream, vi, June 15, 1876, p. 300.
    Thirty-one species, with remarks.

1876. JONES, C. M.   On the breeding of the Black-throated Blue Warbler (Dendrœca cærulescens) in Connecticut.   < Bull. Nutt. Ornith. Club, i, No. 1, 1876, pp. 11–13.

1876. RIDGWAY, R.   Notes on the Genus Helminthophaga.   < Ibis, 3d ser., vi, Apr., 1876, pp. 166–171.
    Critical discrimination of 10 spp. of the genus, with geographical distribution, and remarks on H. lawrencii and H. leucobronchialis. The former is suggested as possibly a hybrid between pinus and chrysoptera.

1876. RIDGWAY, R.   On Geographical Variation in Dendrœca palmarum.   < Bull. Nutt. Ornith. Club, i, No. iv, Nov., 1876, pp. 81–87.
    D. palmarum subsp. n. hypochrysea, p. 84. The two supposed subspecies are very fully described.

1876. SALVIN, O.   Dendrœca chrysoparia.   (The Yellow-cheeked Warbler.)   < Rowley's Ornith. Misc., part iii, Jan., 1876, pp. 181–184, plate.
    Complete history of the species to date, with a beautiful colored plate of 3 figures. Cf. Purdie, Bull. Nutt. Ornith. Club, 1878, p. 60, and Coues, ibid.

1876. WARREN, J.   Nesting of the Golden-winged Warbler (Helminthophaga chrysoptera), in Massachusetts.   < Bull. Nutt. Ornith. Club, i, No. 1, 1876, pp. 6–8.

1877. BREWER, T. M.   [Letter on the Nest and Eggs of Dendrœca auduboni.]   < Ibis, 4th ser., i, July, 1877, pp. 394, 395.
    Fully describing specimens from Summit County, Colorado.

1877. BREWSTER, W.   The Black-and-Yellow Warbler (Dendrœca maculosa).   < Bull. Nutt. Ornith. Club, ii, No. 1, Jan., 1877, pp. 1–7.
    Full account of habits.

1877. BREWSTER, W.   The Yellow-throated Warbler (Dendrœca dominica).   < Bull. Nutt. Ornith. Club, ii, No. 4, Oct., 1877, pp. 102–106.
    Very full account of its habits, with special reference to its breeding. Cf. op. cit., 1878, p. 43.

1877. BOUDWIN, G.   Yellow-pool [i. e., poll] wood-warbler (Dendrœca æstiva).   < Forest and Stream, viii, Apr. 5, 1877, p. 129.
    Habits as observed at Philadelphia.

1877. COUES, E.   Letters on Ornithology.   No. 16 [bis]—The American Warblers.—Family Sylvicolidæ.   < The Chicago Field, Dec. 15, 1877, p. 284, fig.
    Popular account, with fig. of Dendrœca virens.

1877. FRAZAR, A. M.   Audubon's Warbler [Dendrœca auduboni] in Massachusetts.   < Bull. Nutt. Ornith. Club, ii, No. 1, Jan., 1877, p. 27.

1877. HERRICK, H.   Capture of a second specimen of Helminthophaga lawrencei.   < Bull. Nutt. Ornith. Club, ii, No. 1, Jan., 1877, pp. 19, 20.

1877. MAYNARD, C. J.   Nesting Habits of the Worm-eating Warbler (Helmintherus vermivorus).   < Oölogist, iii, No. 3, 1877, pp. 19, 20.

1877. NUTTER, F. H.   Red-Bellied Nut-Hatch (Sitta Canadensis) nesting on the Ground (?).   < Am. Nat., xi, No. 9, 1877, pp. 565, 566.
    Afterward shown to be probably Myiodioctes canadensis.

1877. SMITH, G. STUART.　Nesting of the Maryland Yellow-throat [Geothlypis trichas].　< *Oölogist*, iii, No. 10, p. 77; fig. in No. 11, p. 87.

1877. TROTTER, S.　Capture of a Second Specimen of Helminthophaga leucobronchialis.　< *Bull. Nutt. Ornith. Club*, ii, No. 3, July, 1877, pp. 79, 80.

1877. TROTTER, S.　On Helminthophaga leucobronchialis (Brewster).　< *Proc. Phila. Acad. Nat. Sci.*, 1877, p. 292.
　　Discovery of a third specimen, longtime in the Mus. Acad. Phila.

1878. BREWSTER, W.　Note on Dendrœca dominica.　< *Bull. Nutt. Ornith. Club*, iii, No. 1, Jan., 1878. p. 43.
　　Correction of Brewster, *op. cit.*, Oct., 1876, pp. 102–106.

1878. BREWSTER, W.　The White-Throated Warbler (Helminthophaga leucobronchialis) in Connecticut.　< *Bull. Nutt. Ornith. Club*, iii, No. 2, Apr., 1878, p. 99.

1878. BREWSTER, W.　The Prothonotary Warbler (Protonotaria citrea).　< *Bull. Nutt. Ornith. Club*, iii, No. 4, Oct., 1878, pp. 153–162.
　　An extended biographical sketch, well-written, interesting, and perfectly reliable.

1878. BREWSTER, W.　Capture of a Fifth Specimen of the White-throated Warbler (Helminthophaga leucobronchialis).　< *Bull. Nutt. Ornith. Club*, iii, No. 4, Oct., 1878, pp. 199, 200.
　　At Suffolk, Conn., July 3, 1875, by E. I. Shores.

1878. BUEL, J. A.　[Capture of Kirtland's warbler (Dendrœca kirtlandi) at Cleveland, Ohio.]　< *The Country*, ii, June 1, 1878, p. 89.

1878. COLLINS, W. L.　Tragic Fate of a Summer Warbler [Dendrœca æstiva].　< *Bull. Nutt. Ornith. Club*, iii, No. 4, Oct., 1878, p. 197.
　　Noosed and killed by a thread from her unfinished nest.

1878. COUES, E.　Nest and Eggs of Helminthophaga pinus.　< *Bull. Nutt. Ornith. Club*, iii, No. 4, Oct., 1878, p. 194.
　　Notes on two nests secured by S. N. Rhoads near West Chester, Pa.

1878. DEANE, R.　The Blue-winged Yellow Warbler (Helminthophaga pinus) in Massachusetts.　< *Bull. Nutt. Ornith. Club*, iii, No. 4, Oct., 1878, p. 188.
　　The second record of its occurrence in the State, where it had recently been denied by T. M. Brewer, though long since recorded as a Massachusetts bird, and the original specimen preserved (cf. *Proc. Bost. Soc.*, vi, p. 386).

1878. [ERNST, H.]　Another Kirtland Warbler [Dendrœca kirtlandi].　< *Forest and Stream*, x, June 20, 1878, p. 379.
　　Supposed "third instance" (really about the eighth) of its capture in U. S.; this time near Cleveland, Ohio. See above, 1878, BUEL, J. A.

1878. FISHER, A. K.　The Kentucky Warbler (Oporornis formosus) at Sing Sing, N. Y.　< *Bull. Nutt. Ornith. Club*, iii, No. 4, Oct., 1878, pp. 191, 192.
　　"There must have been at least sixteen individuals here, and undoubtedly four nests."

1878. INGERSOLL, E.　Nesting Habits of the Black-and-White Creeper (Mniotilta varia).　< *Oölogist*, iv, No. 1, Mar., 1878, pp. 1, 2.

1878. MURDOCH, J.　Report of the Second Capture of the Orange-crowned Warbler (Helminthophaga celata) in New Hampshire.　< *Bull. Nutt. Ornith. Club*, iii, No. 2, Apr., 1878, pp. 96, 97.

1878. NUTTER, F. H.　Nesting Habits of the Canada Flycatcher [Myiodioctes canadensis (?)].　< *Amer. Nat.*, xii, No. 6, June, 1878, p. 397.
　　Referring to a set of eggs formerly (*op. cit.*, xi, p. 565) referred to "*Sitta canadensis?*" now doubtfully identified as above.

1878. PURDIE, H. A.　Capture of the Yellow-throated Warbler [Dendrœca dominica] in Massachusetts, and Notes on other Rare Massachusetts Birds.　< *Bull. Nutt. Ornith. Club*, iii, No. 3, July, 1878, p. 146.
　　The remainder of the paragraph speaks of *Rallus elegans* and *Anser hyperboreus* in the same State.

Bull. v, 4——3

1878. SALVIN, O. A Synopsis of the Genus Setophaga. < *Ibis*, 4th ser., ii, No. 7, July, 1878, pp. 302–321, pll. vii, viii.

> A carefully-wrought article, giving synonymy, diagnosis, habitat, and criticism of 15 spp.
>
> The genus reads *Setophaga* Sw., 1827 = *Sylvania* Nutt., 1832 nec 1840; with *Euthlypis* Cab., 1850, as a subgenus, based on *E. lachrymosa*, and *Myioborus* Baird, 1865, as a subgenus, covering 13 spp. (all the rest except *S. ruticilla*).
>
> The species recognized are *S. ruticilla*, *S. (M.) picta, miniata, aurantiaca, verticalis, melanocephala, brunneiceps, castaneocapilla, chrysops* (sp. n., p. 314, pl. vii, f. 2 = *flaveola* Kaup nec Lafr.), *ornata, ruficoronata* (pl. vii, f. 1), *bairdi*, sp. n., p. 317, pl. viii, f. 1 = *ruficoronata* Scl. Salv. Bd. nec Kaup), *albifrons* (pl. viii, f. 2), *torquata*, and *S. (E.) lacrymosa.*—Note on *Setophaga multicolor* Bp.

1878. TROTTER, S. A Third Specimen of Helminthophaga leucobronchialis. < *Bull. Nutt. Ornith. Club*, iii, No. 1, Jan., 1878, pp. 44, 45.

> See Trotter, *Pr. Phila. Acad.*, 1877, p. 292.

1879. ALLEN, J. A. Nest and Eggs of the Cerulean Warbler [Dendrœca cœrulea]. < *Bull. Nutt. Ornith. Club*, iv, No. 1, Jan., 1879, pp. 25–27.

> Fully describing three nests and eggs of this species, heretofore not satisfactorily known, Audubon's account being "evidently erroneous in nearly every particular", and the only other one, Brewer's, being very discrepant.

1879. BREWER, T. M. The Eggs of the Redstart (Setophaga ruticilla). < *Bull. Nutt. Ornith. Club*, iv, No. 2, Apr., 1879, p. 118.

1879. CORY, C. B. Capture of Kirtland's Warbler (Dendrœca kirtlandi) in the Bahama Islands. < *Bull. Nutt. Ornith. Club*, iv, No. 2, Apr., 1879, p. 118.

1879. C[OUES], E. [Note on the fourth known specimen of Dendrœca chrysoparia.] < *Bull. Nutt. Ornith. Club*, iv, No. 1, Jan., 1879, p. 60.

1879. COUES, E. Note on Dendrœca townsendi. < *Bull. Nutt. Ornith. Club*, iv, No. 2, Apr., 1879, p. 117.

> Observations on habits, by W. A. Cooper.

1879. DEANE, R. Occurrence of the Western Variety of the Yellow Red-poll Warbler [Dendrœca palmarum hypochrysea] in Massachusetts. < *Bull. Nutt. Ornith. Club*, iv, No. 1, Jan. 1879, p. 60.

> Correction, *tom. cit.*, p. 186.

1879. DEANE, R. Additional Capture of the Cœrulean Warbler [Dendrœca cœrulea] in New England. < *Bull. Nutt. Ornith. Club*, iv, No. 3, July, 1879, p. 185.

1879. DEANE, R. Correction [respecting Dendrœca palmarum hypochrysea, this Bull., iv, p. 60]. < *Bull. Nutt. Ornith Club*, iv, No. 3, July, 1879, p. 186.

1879. FISHER, A. K. Helminthophaga leucobronchialis in New York. < *Bull. Nutt. Ornith. Club*, iv, No. 4, Oct., 1879, p. 234.

1879. GIBBS, M. A New Bird [Helminthophaga gunnii]. < *Daily Morning Democrat* (Grand Rapids, Mich.), xvi, No. 224, June 1, 1879.

> Taken in Ottawa County, Mich., May 25, 1879; subsequently identified with *H. leucobronchialis*; cf. *Bull. Nutt. Club*, iv, 1879, pp. 185 and 232.

1879. JEFFRIES, J. A. The Yellow-rumped Warbler (Dendrœca coronata) wintering in Swampscott, Mass. < *Bull. Nutt. Ornith. Club*, iv, No. 2, Apr., 1879, p. 118.

1879. KEPPEL, R. J. Nesting Habits of the American Redstart. (Setophaga-ruticilla.) < *The Journ. of Sci.* (Toledo, Ohio), 2d ser., ii, No. 7, Sept., 1879.

1879. LANGDON, F. W. Nesting of the Kentucky Warbler (Oporornis formosa) in Ohio. < *Bull. Nutt. Ornith. Club*, iv, No. 4, Oct., 1879, pp. 236, 237.

> With full description of the nest and eggs.

1879. NEWTON, [A.] [Remarks on Exhibition of rare Sylvicolidæ from Jamaica.] < *P. Z. S.*, June 17, 1879, pp. 552, 553.

> *Dendrœca pharetra* Gosse, and *Helinaia swainsoni* Aud.!—According to Agassiz the name of the latter genus should be written *Helonœa*.

1879. NICHOL[A]S, GEO. LAWRENCE. Migration of Some Warblers Through Summit, N. J., During the Last Spring. < *Forest and Stream*, xii, July 17, 1879, p. 464.

> Notes on arrivals and departures of 18 spp.

1879. PURDIE, H. A.   Record of Additional Specimens of the White-throated Warbler (Helminthophaga leucobronchialis).   < *Bull. Nutt. Ornith. Club*, iv, No. 3, July, 1879, pp. 184, 185.

Three, in addition to five before known, with presumptive identification of *H. gunnii* Gibbs (*Daily Democrat*, newspaper of Grand Rapids, Mich., June 1, 1879) as still another.

1879. PURDIE, H. A.   Another Kirtland's Warbler (Dendrœca kirtlandi).   < *Bull. Nutt. Ornith. Club*, iv, No. 3, July, 1879, pp. 185, 186.

Making the ninth known specimen, all of which are here recorded.

1879. RATHBUN, S. F., *and* WRIGHT, F. S.   Hooded Warbler [Myiodioctes mitratus] in Western New York.   < *Bull. Nutt. Ornith. Club*, iv, No. 2, Apr., 1879, pp. 116, 117.

1879. RHOADS, S. N.   Helminthophaga pinus, Oporornis formosa, and Mniotilta varia breeding in Pennsylvania.   < *Bull. Nutt. Ornith. Club*, iv, No. 4, Oct., 1879, pp. 234, 235.

1879. RIDGWAY, R.   Note on Helminthophaga gunnii, Gibbs.   < *Bull. Nutt. Ornith. Club*, iv, No. 4, Oct., 1879, pp. 233, 234.

Its identification with *H. leucobranchialis*, upon examination of the type-specimen.

1879. TROTTER, S.   Some Light on the History of a Rare Bird [Helminthophaga leucobronchialis].   < *Bull. Nutt. Ornith. Club*, iv, No. 1, Jan., 1879, p. 59.

Note of the third specimen known, being one shot by J. G. Bell, at Rockland, N. Y., so long ago as 1832.

1879. WHEATON, J. M.   Kirtland's Warbler [Dendrœca kirtlandi] again in Ohio.   < *Bull. Nutt. Ornith. Club*, iv, No. 1, Jan., 1879, p. 58.

Record of two specimens, and perhaps of a third, additional to those before known.

Motacillidæ.

1814. NILSSON, S.   Analecta Ornithologica.   Pars I.   Motacillas Scanenses sistens. Præs. Sv. Nilsson, Resp. A. A. Retzius, Lundensis. Lundae 1814. 4to.   pp. 16.—Resp. C. G. Retzius, Lundens. cont. pp. 17–30, m. tabb. 2.
  Non mihi obvia.—Pars II., vide sub *Charadriidis*, hujusce bibliographiæ.

1827. FABER, F.   [Anthus rupestris.]   < *Tidssk. for Naturvid.*, No. 13, 1827, p. 58.
  Not seen.   *Cf. Isis*, 1827, p. 1028; *Féruss. Bull.*, xv, 1828, p. 392.

1827. FABER, F.   Ueber Anthus rupestris.   < *Oken's Isis*, Bd. xx, 1827, pp. 1028, 1029.
  Nebst Nachtrag von Heinr. Lichtenstein, p. 1029.

1827. TRAILL, [T. S.]   Tit-Lark [Anthus pratensis] caught at Sea.   < *Edinb. New Philos. Journ.*, ii, 1827, p. 393.

1828. FABER, [F.]   Sur l'Anthus rupestris, nouvelle espèce ; par M. Faber. . . < *Féruss. Bull.*, 2e sect., xv, 1828, p. 392.
  Tidssk. for Naturvid., 1827, No. 13, p. 58; *Isis*, 1827, p. 1028.

1828. GLOGER, C. W. L.   Wegen Anthus rupestris und A. aquaticus.   < *Oken's Isis*, Bd. xxi, 1828, p. 693, 694
  Vergl. *Isis*, 1827, s. 597, folg. Nebst Nachtrag von Heinr. Lichtenstein.

1831. GOURCY-DROITAUMONT, F. (*Graf von*).   Etwas über das verschiedene Farbenkleid der Motacilla Feldegg Michahelles, oder der in Dalmatien vorkommenden Motacilla melanocephala Lichtenstein, von Felix, Grafen von Gourcy-Droitaumont, eingesandt von Brehm.   < *Oken's Isis*, Bd. xxiv, 1831, pp. 701–705.
  Nebst Nachschrift von C. L. Brehm.

1831. MICHAHELLES, *Dr.* —.   Nachträgliche Bemerkung zu Motacilla Feldegg mihi. *Oken's Isis*, Bd. xxiv, 1831, p. 403.

1832. GOULD, J.   [On a New Species of Wagtail, Motacilla neglecta.]   < *P. Z. S.*, ii, 1832, pp. 129, 130.

1832. "ORNIS."   The Pipit Lark distinct from the Meadow Pipit, or Titlark.   < *Loudon's Mag. Nat. Hist.*, v, 1832, pp. 287, 288.

1832. "SCOLOPAX RUSTICOLA."   The Spring, or Yellow, Wagtail (Motacilla [Budytes] flava).   < *Loudon's Mag. Nat. Hist.*, v, 1832, p. 288.

1832. "SCOLOPAX RUSTICOLA."   The Pied Wagtail (Motacilla lotor Rennie, M. alba Linn.).   < *Loudon's Mag. Nat. Hist.*, v, 1832, pp. 288, 289.

1834. BOIE, J. F.   Anthus Richardi.   < *Oken's Isis*, Bd. xxvii, 1834, pp. 385, 386.

1834. "T. G."   On the Habits and Note of the Grey Wagtail [Motacilla boarula], and on the Note of the Spring Wagtail [Budytes flava].   < *Loudon's Mag. Nat. Hist.*, vii, 1834, pp. 577–579.

1835. GOULD, [J.]   Viele Exemplare von 2 Vögeln, die unter dem Namen Motacilla flava verwechselt wurden.   < *Oken's Isis*, Bd. xxxviii, 1835, p. 432.
  Motacilla neglecta.   Cf. P. Z. S., 1832, p. 129.

1836. HOY, J. D.   A Notice of the Fact of the Capture of an Individual of the Grey-headed Yellow Wagtail (Motacilla neglecta Gould), at Stoke Nayland, Suffolk.   < *Loudon's Mag. Nat. Hist.*, ix, 1836, p. 352.

1837. EDITORIAL.   Motacilla neglecta Gould [in Suffolk].   < *Mag. of Zool. and Bot.*, i, 1837, p. 200.

1837. GOULD, J.   [Motacilla leucopsis, sp. n. from India.]   < *P. Z. S.*, v, 1837, p. 78.

1837. GOULD, J.   [Remarks on the Common British Wagtail (Motacilla yarrelli, sp. n.).]   < *P. Z. S.*, v, 1837, pp. 73, 74, 78.

1837. GOULD, J.   Observations on some Species of the Genus Motacilla of Linnæus.
      < Charlesw. Mag. Nat. Hist., i, 1837, pp. 459–461.
      Discrimination of *MM. flava, yarrelli,* and *lugubris.*

1837. HANCOCK, A.   Motacilla neglecta [in England].   *< Mag. of Zool. and Bot.*, i, 1837,
      p. 491.

1841. MUMMERY, S.   Anthus Richardi [in England].   *< Ann. Mag. Nat. Hist.*, vi,
      1841, p. 398.

1841. YARRELL, W.   [Exhibition of a British Specimen of Motacilla alba.]   *< P.Z. S.*,
      ix, 1841, pp. 46, 47.

1841. YARRELL, W.   Motacilla alba of Linnæus.   *< Ann. Mag. Nat. Hist.*, vii, 1841, p.
      350.

1842. MUMMERY, S.   Anthus Richardi [in the Isle of Thanet].   *< Ann. Mag. Nat.
      Hist.*, viii, 1842, p. 396.

1843. ATKINSON, J. C.   Observations on previous [*Zool.*, i, 136 and 230] notes on the
      Grey Wagtail [Motacilla boarula].   *< Zoologist*, i, 1843, pp. 358–360.

1843. GREENWOOD, A.   Note on the occurrence of Richard's Pipit [Anthus richardi]
      in Cornwall.   *< Zoologist*, i, 1843, p. 190.

1843. HEPPENSTALL, J.   Note on the Grey Wagtail [Motacilla boarula].   *< Zoologist,*
      i, 1843, p. 140.

1843. HOLLAND, A.   Enquiry respecting a Wagtail [Motacilla boarula.   With note
      in answer by H. Doubleday].   *< Zoologist*, i, 1843, pp. 136, 137.

1843. KNOX, A. E.   Note on the Pied Wagtail [Motacilla yarrelli].   *< Zoologist*, i,
      1843, p. 190.

1843. NICHOLSON, C.   Note on the Grey Wagtail [Motacilla boarula].   *< Zoologist*, i,
      1843, pp. 230–233.

1843. TRATHAN, J. J.   Note on the appearance of the Continental White Wagtail
      (Motacilla alba) at Falmouth.   *< Zoologist*, i, 1843, p. 188.

1844. ANON.   Note on a singular locality for a Wagtail's Nest.   *< Zoologist*, ii, 1844,
      p. 726.

1844. BOND, F.   Note on Anthus petrosus (Montagu).   *< Zoologist*, ii, 1844, p. 447.

1844. BRIGGS, J. J.   Remarks upon [the habits of] the Tree Pipit [Anthus arboreus].
      < Zoologist, ii, 1844, p. 658.

1844. CORNISH, J.   Notes on the Habits of the Wagtail [Motacilla yarrelli].   *< Zoolo-
      gist*, ii, 1844, pp. 566–568.

1844. HARDY, J.   Note on a singular habit of the Grey Wagtail [Motacilla boarula].
      < Zoologist, ii, 1844, p. 568.

1844. HORE, W. S.   Note on Richard's Pipit [Anthus richardi].   *< Zoologist*, ii, 1844,
      p. 496.

1844. JERDON, A.   Note on [the habits of] Wagtails [Motacilla yarrelli, M. boarula].
      < Zoologist, ii, 1844, p. 764.

1844. SLADEN, E. H. M.   Note on the Grey Wagtail (Motacilla boarula).   *< Zoologist*,
      ii, 1844, p. 763.

1844. TRATHAN, J. J.   Correction of a previous [*Zool.*, 188] note on the Pied Wagtail
      [Motacilla yarrelli].   *< Zoologist*, ii, 1844, p. 452.

1845. DEBY, J.   Habits of the White Wagtail (Motacilla alba, Lin.).   *< Zoologist*, iii,
      1845, pp. 940, 941.

1845. SUNDEVALL, [C. J.]   Varietet af Motacilla alba [M. yarrelli].   *< Öfvers. Kongl.
      Vetensk.-Akad.Förhandl. för år* 1844, 1845, pp. 161, 162.

1845. WEBSTER, T.   Occurrence of Anthus aquaticus at Fleetwood.   *< Zoologist*, iii,
      1845, p. 1023

1846. BOLD, T. J.   Occurrence of Richard's Pipit [Anthus richardi] near Newcastle.   *< Zoologist*, iv, 1846, pp. 1210, 1211.

1846. FRERE, H. T.   Occurrence of Anthus arboreus in February [at Aylsham].   *< Zoologist*, iv, 1846, p. 1210.

1846. PLOMLEY, F.   Frequent occurrence of the White Wagtail [Motacilla alba] in Kent.   *< Zoologist*, iv, 1846, p. 1497.

1848. RODD, E. H.   Occurrence of the White Wagtail (Motacilla alba) near Penzance.   *< Zoologist*, vi, 1848, p. 2143.

1848. RODD, E. H.   Frequent Occurrence of the Continental White Wagtail [Motacilla alba] near Penzance.   *< Zoologist*, vi, 1848, pp. 2143, 2144.

1848. RODD, E. H.   Occurrence of the Gray-headed Wagtail (Motacilla neglecta) near Penzance.   *< Zoologist*, vi, 1848, p. 2144.

1848. WEBB, J. S.   Occurrence of the White Wagtail (Motacilla alba) near York.   *< Zoologist*, vi, 1848, p. 2229.

1849. THIENEMANN, F. A. L.   Über einige Arten des Geschlechts Pieper, Anthus. Bechst.   *< Rhea*, Heft ii, 1849, pp. 171–175.
    Anthus pensylvanicus, A. cervinus, A. richardi betreffend.

1849. THORNCROFT, T.   Early Arrival of the Tree Pipit (Anthus arboreus) [at Shoreham].   *< Zoologist*, vii, 1849, p. 2415.

1850. RODD, E. H.   Note on the Pied Wagtail (Motacilla Yarrellii).   *< Zoologist*, viii, 1850, p. 2651.

1851. ELLMAN, J. B.   Occurrence of the Gray-headed Wagtail (Motacilla neglecta) at Eastbourne, Sussex.   *< Zoologist*, ix, 1851, p. 3145.

1851. RODD, E. H.   Occurrence of Richard's Pipit (Anthus Richardi) at the Scilly Isles.   *< Zoologist*, ix, 1851, p. 3300.

1851. SMITH, J.   Occurrence of the Gray-headed Wagtail (Motacilla neglecta) at Great Yarmouth.   *< Zoologist*, ix, 1851, p. 3174.

1851. ZANDER, H. D. F.   Einiges über die Abänderungen der Motacilla alba, L. und des Budytes flavus, Cuv.   *< Naumannia*, i, Heft iii, 1851, pp. 9–21.
    Kritisches; Beschreibungen.—Für Bemerkungen und Zusätze, vergl. Naum., Heft iv, 1854, pp. 24–30.

1852. RODD, E. H.   Occurrence of the Continental White Wagtail [Motacilla alba] near Penzance.   *< Zoologist*, x, 1852, p. 3453.

1852. STRICKLAND, H. E.   VIII.—On Parus ignotus, Gm.   *< Jard. Contrib. Orn.*, 1852, pp. 44–45.
    Identified by Sundevall with *Anthus pratensis.*

1853. BORRER, W., JR.   Occurrence of the Continental White Wagtail (Motacilla alba, Linn.) in Sussex.   *< Zoologist*, xi, 1853, p. 3908.

1853. LANFOSSI, P.   Sulla motacilla alba ed altre affini.   *< Bianconi's Repert. Ital. Stor. Nat.*, i, 1853, pp. 1, 2, No. 1.
    From *Comment. dell' Ateneo di Brescia*, 1848–50, p. 148.—Latin transl. of the title and article follows.

1853. RODD, E. H.   Occurrence of the Gray-headed Wagtail (Motacilla neglecta) near Penzance.   *< Zoologist*, xi, 1853, p. 3919.

1854. BALDAMUS, E.   Bemerkungen und Zusätze [an Zander's Artikel über die europäischen Pieper, Anthus, in Naum., iii, 1851, pp. 9–21].   *< Naumannia*, Heft iv, 1854, pp. 24–30.

1854. BORRER, W., JR.   Occurrence of the Continental White Wagtail (Motacilla alba) in Sussex.   *< Zoologist*, xii, 1854, p. 4408.

1854. GURNEY, J. H.   Note on the occurrence of the Gray-headed Wagtail (Motacilla neglecta) at Lowestoft.   *< Zoologist*, xii, 1854, p. 4440.

1854. ZANDER, H. [D. F.] Ueber die europäischen Pieper [Anthus]. (Beil. nr. 8. zum Protokol d. siebensten ornith.-versamml. zu Halberstadt.) < *Naumannia*, Heft iv, 1854, pp. 1–24.
8 Arten, monographisch bearbeitet.

1854. ZANDER, H. [D. F.] Kurze Uebersicht der europäischen Pieper, Anthus Bechst. (Anhang x. zu Berichte über die vii. Jahresversammlung der deutschen Ornithologen-Gesellschaft.) < *J. f. O.*, i, 1853, Extraheft (1854), pp. 60–65.
Behandelt 8 Arten, nebst Synonymik, Kritik, Beschreibungen und geogr. Verbreitung.

1856. BREHM, [C. L.] [Ueber die Pieper (Anthus).] < *Naumannia*, vi, 1856, pp. 337–349.

1857. BREHM, [C.] L. Die Mauser und die daraus hervorgehende Verfärbung der Bach- und Schafstelzen. < *J. f. O.*, v, 1857, pp. 25–35.
Treats very fully of the various plumages of *Motacilla alba* and *Budytes flava*.

1857. CARTER, S. Abundance of Wagtails [Motacilla yarrelli, in England]. < *Zoologist*, xv, 1857, p. 5517.

1857. GLOGER, C. W. L. Anfrage, betreffend Anthus aquaticus var. rupestris. < *Naumannia*, vii, 1857, Hft. ii, pp. 74–76.

1857. GOSTLING, W. Wagtail's Nest in a Scarlet Geranium. < *Zoologist*, xv, 1857, pp. 5789, 5790.

1857. HADFIELD, H. W. Great abundance of the Pied Wagtail (Motacilla Yarrellii), &c. < *Zoologist*, xv, 1857, p. 5363.

1857. JÄCKEL, J. [Anthus pratensis mit zwei Köpfen.] < *Naumannia*, vii, 1857, p. 190.
Fide *Sev. Weinhart*, ann. 1693.

1857. KÄSERMANN, C. Einige Beobachtungen über Anthus aquaticus. < *Naumannia*, vii, 1857, pp. 138–140.

1857. SMURTHWAITE, H. Change of Plumage in Motacilla alba. < *Zoologist*, xv, 1857, p. 5592.

1858. GOULD, J. [Exhibition of British specimens of Motacilla flava, Ray, and note from Mr. Thirtle of Lowestoft, on its occurrence in that part of England.] < *P. Z. S.*, xxvi, 1858, pp. 77, 78.

1858. GOULD, J. [Remarks on Exhibition of British specimens of Motacilla flava.] < *Ann. Mag. Nat. Hist.*, 3d ser., i, 1858, pp. 441, 442.
From *P. Z. S.*, Feb. 9, 1858, pp. 77, 78.

1858. JÄGER, C. Motacilla sulphurea Bechst. < *Naumannia*, viii, 1858, p. 507.

1858. SMURTHWAITE, H. Motacilla [Anthus] campestris and M. boarula. < *Zoologist*, xvi, 1858, p. 6239.

1858. ZANDER, H. [D. F.] Die zweifelhaften Arten der europäischen Motacillen. < *Naumannia*, viii, 1858, pp. 238–243.

1859. PÄSSLER, W. Die Species-Dignität des Anthus cervinus. < *J. f. O.*, vii, 1859, pp. 464–469.
Elaborately discussed.

1861. CAVAFY, J. [Letter on the occurrence of Budytes cinereocapillus at Kafr Dowar, near Alexandria.] < *Ibis*, iii, 1861, p. 210.

1862. BOLLE, C. Anthus Berthelotii, eine neue Pieperart. < *J. f. O.*, x, 1862, pp. 357–360.

1862. BOLLE, C. Sur l'Anthus des Canaries reconnu comme espèce nouvelle et nommé Anthus berthelotii. < *Ibis*, iv, 1862, pp. 343–348, pl. xii.
Synonymie, description et biographie.

1863. HARCOURT, E. V. [Letter on Anthus berthelotii, Bolle.] < *Ibis*, v, 1863, pp. 230–233.

1863. KERR, J. A Note on Pipits [Anthus]. < *Zoologist*, xxi, 1863, p. 8822.

1863. RANSON, J. Singular Nesting Place of the Pied Wagtail [Motacilla yarrelli]. *< Zoologist*, xxi, 1863, pp. 8844, 8845.

1863. ROWLEY, G. D. Notice of the Occurrence of the Tawny Pipit (Anthus rufescens) in Great Britain. *< Ibis*, v, 1863, pp. 37–39.

1863. SAXBY, H. L. Gray Wagtail (Motacilla boarula) an Autumn Visitor to Shetland. *< Zoologist*, xxi, 1863, pp. 8819, 8820.

1864. PRATT, J. Water Pipit [Anthus aquaticus] near Brighton. *< Zoologist*, xxii, 1864, pp. 9279, 9280.
    With contrasted characters of *A. spinoletta* and *A. aquaticus.*

1864. ROWLEY, G. D. Anthus campestris or A. rufescens at Brighton. *< Zoologist*, xxii, 1864, pp. 9327, 9328.

1864. SCHWAITZER, F. Motacilla sulphurea Bechst. in der Provinz Posen. *< J. f. O.*, xii, 1864, p. 143.

1864. STEVENSON, H. Rock Pipit [Anthus rupestris] in Norfolk. *< Zoologist*, xxii, 1864, p. 9109.
    Cf. particularly *Ibis*, 1865, pp. 237, 238.

1865. ALTUM, B. Unsere Bachstelzen. *< J. f. O.*, xiii, 1865, pp. 245–248.
    Zur Lebensweise von *Motacilla alba, M. boarula, Budytes flava.*

1865. GOULD, J. [Anthus "spinoletta" (?) at Brighton, England.] *< Ibis*, 2d ser., i, 1865, pp. 114–116.
    Cf. particularly *Ibis*, 1865, pp. 237, 238.

1865. MATHEWS, G. F. Richard's Pipit [Anthus richardi] at Braunton Burrows. *< Zoologist*, xxiii, 1865, p. 9456.

1865. [NEWTON, A.] [On species of Anthus killed in England; cf. Ibis, 1865, p. 116; Zool., p. 9109.] *< Ibis*, 2d ser., i, 1865, pp. 237, 238.

1865. ROWLEY, G. D. Richard's Pipit [Anthus richardi] at Brighton. *< Zoologist*, xxiii, 1865, pp. 9466, 9467.

1865. SCLATER, P. L. [Remarks on Exhibition of a specimen of Anthus spinoletta, from the collection of the Bishop of Oxford.] *< P. Z. S.*, xxxiii, 1865, p. 60.

1866. BOULTON, W. W. Richard's Pipit [Anthus richardi] in Ceylon. *< Zoologist*, 2d ser., i, 1866, p. 32.

1866. MACHIN, W. Richard's Pipit [Anthus richardi] obtained in Leadenhall Market. *< Zoologist*, 2d ser., i, 1866, p. 269.

1866. WHARTON, C. B. [Motacilla sulphurea breeding in North Wales; cf. Ibis, 1865, 123; and Yarr. B. B., i, 434.] *< Ibis*, 2d ser., ii, 1866, pp. 323, 324.

1867. BOND, F. Water Pipit [Anthus aquaticus] at Brighton. *< Zoologist*, 2d ser., ii, 1867, p. 792.

1867. BREE, C. R. Habits of the Rock Pipit [Anthus rupestris]. *< Zoologist*, 2d ser., ii, 1867, p. 792.

1867. DOBRÉE, N. F. Pied Wagtails [Motacilla yarrelli] near Hornsea in January. *< Zoologist*, 2d ser., ii, 1867, p. 634.

1867. GUNN, T. E. Grayheaded Wagtail [Motacilla neglecta] near Norwich. *< Zoologist*, 2d ser., ii, 1867, p. 824.

1867. RANSON, J. Pied Wagtail [Motacilla yarrelli] wintering in North Yorkshire. *< Zoologist*, 2d ser., ii, 1867, p. 875.

1867. SHORTO, J., JR. Pied Wagtails [Motacilla yarrelli] in January. *< Zoologist*, 2d ser., ii, 1867, p. 704.

1867. STEVENSON, H. The Rock Pipit [Anthus rupestris] in Norfolk. *< Zoologist*, 2d ser., ii, 1867, p. 876.

1867. WEST, E. Does the Yellow Wagtail [Budytes flava] always Migrate. *< Zoologist*, 2d ser., ii, 1867, p. 705.

1867. WHARTON, C. B.   Rock Pipit [Anthus rupestris] inland.   < *Zoologist*, 2d ser., ii, 1867, p. 558.

1868. GATCOMBE, J.   Vinous-breasted Pipit [Anthus spinoletta] near Plymouth.   < *Zoologist*, 2d ser., iii, 1868, p. 1254.

1868. GORDON, C.   Richard's Pipit [Anthus richardi] at Dover.   < *Zoologist*, 2d ser., iii, 1868, p. 1458.

1868. RODD, E. H.   The Tawny Pipit and Richard's Pipit at Scilly.   < *Zoologist*, 2d ser., iii, 1868, p. 1458.

1868. ROWLEY, G. D.   Richard's Pipit at Brighton: The Tawny Pipit.   < *Zoologist*, 2d ser., iii, 1868, p. 1479.

1869. ANON.   Ray's Wagtail [Budytes rayi] at Scilly.   < *Zoologist*, 2d ser., iv, 1869, p. 1847.

1869. MATHEW, G. F.   Richard's Pipit [Anthus richardi] near Barnstable.   < *Zoologist*, 2d ser., iv, 1869, p. 1561.

1869. ROWLEY, G. D.   [Exhibition of some British-killed Pipits (Anthus aquaticus and A. obscurus)].   < *P. Z. S.*, xxxvii, 1869, p. 249.

1869. ROWLEY, G. D.   The Water and Rock Pipits.   < *Zoologist*, 2d ser., iv, 1869, pp. 1682, 1683.

1869. WONFOR, T. W.   Richard's Pipit [Anthus Richardi] at Brighton.   < *Zoologist*, 2d ser., iv, 1869, p. 1513.

1869. WONFOR, T. W.   Dwarf Meadow Pipit.   < *Zoologist*, 2d ser., iv, 1869, p. 1561.

1869. WONFOR, T. W.   Richard's Pipit [Anthus richardi].   < *Zoologist*, 2d ser., iv, 1869, p. 1683.

1869. WONFOR, T. W.   Meadow Pipit.   < *Zoologist*, 2d ser., iv, 1869, p. 1683.

1869. WONFOR, T. W.   Tawny Pipit near Brighton.   < *Zoologist*, 2d ser., iv, 1869, p. 1918.

1870. BOYNTON, T.   The Pennsylvania Pipit [Anthus ludovicianus], &c., at Bridlington.   < *Zoologist*, 2d ser., v, 1870, pp. 2021, 2022.

1870. BREE, C. R.   Anthus ludovicianus vel Anthus rufescens?   < *Zoologist*, 2d ser., v, 1870, pp. 2100, 2101.
  Contends for its being the former.

1870. GURNEY, J. H., JR.   Grayheaded Wagtail [Motacilla neglecta] at Gateshead.   < *Zoologist*, 2d ser., v, 1870, pp. 2382, 2383.

1870. HARRIS, J. W.   Wagtail in pure White Plumage.   < *Zoologist*, 2d ser., v, 1870, p. 2100.

1870. REEKS, H.   The Pipit ["Anthus ludovicianus"= A. campestris] shot at Bridlington.   < *Zoologist*, 2d ser., v, 1870, pp. 2067, 2068.

1870. RICKARDS, M. S. C.   Vinous-breasted Pipit on the Banks of Severn.   < *Zoologist*, 2d ser., v, 1870, p. 2222.

1870. RICKARDS, M. S. C.   Grayheaded Wagtail [Motacilla neglecta] near Clifton.   < *Zoologist*, 2d ser., v, 1870, p. 2306.

1870. RICKARDS, M. S. C.   Grayheaded Wagtails [Motacilla neglecta] near Clevedon.   < *Zoologist*, 2d ser., v, 1870, p. 2222.

1870. STEVENSON, H.   Richard's Pipit [Anthus richardi, near Yarmouth].   < *Zoologist*, 2d ser., v, 1870, pp. 2066, 2067.

1870. SWINHOE, R.   On the Pied Wagtails of China, Part I [II].   < *P. Z. S.*, xxxviii, 1870, pp. 120–124, woodc.; pp. 129, 130.
  A synopsis, with descriptions and figures of the head, of the China species of *Motacilla*, 7 in number; 3 (*M. felix*, p. 121, *M. francisi*, p. 123, and *M. frontata*, p. 129) being new, and a race of the first-named being described as var. *sechuensis*.

1870. WALDEN, *Lord*.   [Letter relating to Indian Motacillæ.]   < *Ibis*, 2d ser., vi, 1870, pp. 293, 294.

1870. WATSON, J.   Grayheaded Wagtail [Motacilla neglecta] breeding near Gateshead.   < Zoologist, 2d ser., v, 1870, pp. 2343, 2344.

1870. WATSON, J.   Nesting of Motacilla flava.   < Zoologist, 2d ser., v, 1870, p. 2406.

1871. GURNEY, J. H., JR.   Nesting of the Grayheaded Wagtail [Motacilla neglecta] near Newcastle.   < Zoologist, 2d ser., vi, 1871, p. 2483.

1871. GURNEY, J. H., JR.   Grayheaded Wagtail [Motacilla neglecta] at Brighton.   < Zoologist, 2d ser., vi, 1871, p. 2639.

1871. RICKARDS, M. S. C.   White Wagtail [Motacilla alba] at Northam Burrows.   < Zoologist, 2d ser., vi, 1871, p. 2608.

1872. GURNEY, J. H.   [Albinotic] Variety of the Rock Pipit [Anthus rupestris].   < Zoologist, 2d ser., vii, 1872, p. 2943.

1872. HUME, A. O.   The Wagtails of India.   No. 1.   *Stray Feathers*, pp. 26–31.
    Refers to *Motacilla dukhunensis*, *M. personata*, and others of the "pied" group.   I have not seen this article.

1873. ALLEN, J. A.   [Field note on] The Missouri Skylark [Neocorys spraguei].   < *Am. Nat.*, vii, 1873, p. 745.

1873. DOUBLEDAY, H.   [Note on habits of] Ray's Wagtail.   < Zoologist, 2d ser., viii, 1873, p. 3490.

1873. GATCOMBE, J.   A Four-legged Rock Lark [Anthus "petrosus"].   < *Am. Nat.*, vii, 1873, pp. 311, 312.

1873. HUDSON, W. H.   Notes on the Habits of the Pipit [Anthus correndera] of the Argentine Republic.   < *P. Z. S.*, 1873, pp. 771, 772.

1873. WHARTON, C. B.   Ray's Wagtail in Hertfordshire in the Winter.   < Zoologist, 2d ser., viii, 1873, p. 3455.

1873. WHARTON, C. B.   Ray's Wagtail.   < Zoologist, 2d ser., viii, 1873, p. 3526.
    Cf. *Zool.* 2d ser., p. 3490.

1874. INGERSOLL, E.   Discovery of the Water Thrush's [Siurus ludovicianus] Nest in New England.   < *Am. Nat.*, viii, 1874, pp. 238–239.

1874. ROWLEY, G. D.   The Tawny Pipit [Anthus rufescens] at Brighton.   < Zoologist, 2d ser., ix, 1874, p. 3832.

1876. REINHARDT, J.   Motacilla yarrellii skudt i Jylland.   < *Vidensk. Meddel. Naturh. Foren. Kjøbenharn* for Aaret 1876, pp. 203–206.

1877. BROOKS, W. E.   A few Observations on some Species of Anthus and Budytes.   < *Ibis*, 4th ser., i, Apr., 1877, pp. 206–209.
    Anthus neglectus Brooks = *A. blakistoni* Swinhoe, *P. Z. S.*, 1863, p. 90.   *Budytes taivanus* Swinhoe, *Ibis*, 1870, p. 346, a good species.

1877. COUES, E.   Corrections of Nomenclature in the Genus Siurus.   < *Bull. Nutt. Ornith. Club*, ii, No. 2, Apr., 1877, pp. 29–33.
    "Seiurus" to be written *Siurus*. 1. *S. auricapillus*. 2. *S. nævius* (Bodd.) = *S. novebora-censis* (Gm.). 3. *S. motacilla* (Vieill.) = *S. ludovicianus* (Aud.).   Full synonymy of these species.

1877. SEEBOHM, H.   [Anthus seebohmi Dresser = A. gustavi Swinh., P. Z. S., 1863, p. 90.]   < *Ibis*, 4th ser., i, Jan., 1877, pp. 128, 129.

1877. TWEEDDALE, *Marquis of*.   [Note on the occurrence of Anthus gustavi in Celebes.]   < *Ibis*, 4th ser., i, Apr., 1877, p. 258.

1878. BALLOU, W. H.   Large-billed Water Thrush [Siurus motacilla, the nest and eggs of].   < *The Oölogist*, iv, No. 4, June, 1878, p. 27.

1878. BREWER, T. M.   The Titlark (Anthus ludovicianus) in Massachusetts in June.   < *Bull. Nutt. Ornith. Club*, iii, No. 4, Oct., 1878, p. 194.

1878. BREWSTER, W.   Nesting of the Large-billed Water-Thrush (Siurus motacilla [Vieill,] Bp.).   < *Bull. Nutt. Ornith. Club*, iii, No. 3, July, 1878, pp. 133–135.
    Reliable observations on a little-known subject, giving a full account of several nests and eggs.

1878. COUES, E.   Letters on Ornithology.   No. 17—The Aquatic Wood-Wagtail, or New York Water Thrush. (Siurus nævius.) < *The Chicago Field*, Feb. 2, 1878.
From advance sheets of "Birds of the Colorado Valley."

1878. COVERT, A. B.   Nesting of the Large-billed Water Thrush (Siurus ludovicianus).   < *The Oölogist*, iv, No. 2, Apr., 1878, pp. 10, 11.
Full account from observations made in Michigan.

1878. GRAY, A. F.   Abnormal Bird's Eggs [of Siurus auricapillus].   < *Forest and Stream*, xi, Aug. 8, 1878, p. 2.

1878. HOMEYER, E. F. v.   Beiträge zur Gattung Budytes.   < *J. f. O.*, Apr., 1878, pp. 126, 131.

1878. NICHOLSON, F.   On an apparently new Species of American Pipit [Anthus peruvianus].   < *P. Z. S.*, Apr. 2, 1878, pp. 390, 391.
Syn. *A. rufus*, S. & S., *P. Z. S.*, 1868, p. 173; *A. chii*, Tacz., *P. Z. S.*, 1874, p. 506.

1878. SCLATER, P. L.   Preliminary Remarks on the Neotropical Pipits [Anthus].   < *Ibis*, 4th ser., ii, No. 7, July, 1878, pp. 356–367, figg. 1–3, pl. x.
The species here recognized and described with synonymy are: 1. *Anthus bogotensis*, p. 537, fig. 1, wing and foot. 2. *A. chii*, p. 359. 3. *A. rufus*, p. 360. 4. *A. correndera*, p. 362. 5. *A. furcatus*, p. 364, f. 2. 6. *A. nattereri*, sp. n., p. 366, f. 3 (head and foot), pl. x (whole bird). The latter is *A. correndera* of Pelz., *Orn. Bras.*, p. 69, *nec* Vieill.

1879. COUES, E.   Coues on the Nest and Eggs of the Water Thrush (Siurus nævius).   < *The Oölogist*, iv, Mar., 1879, p. 57.
Extracted from "Birds of the Colorado Valley," pt. 1, 1878, pp. 305, 306.

Turdidæ.

1826. NAUMANN, J. F. Unerhörtes Vorkommen eines auslandschen Vogels [Turdus minor Gm. aus Nordamerika] in der Mitte von Deutschland. < *Oken's Isis*, Jahrg. x, 1826, pp. 520, 521.

1828. NAUMANN, [J. F.] Note sur l'Apparition extraordinaire du Turdus minor [Gm., de l'Amérique septentrionale] en Allemagne; par Neumann. . . < *Féruss.* *Bull.*, 2ᵉ sect., xiii, 1828, p. 357.
Extraite de *l'Isis*, 1826, pp. 520, 521.

1833. COX, J. C. [Notice of a living Mocking-bird (Turdus polyglottus, Linn.) in his possession]. < *P. Z. S.*, i, 1833, p. 114.

1837. GOULD, J. [Descriptions of three new Species of Orpheus (O. trifasciatus, O. melanotis, O. parvulus) from the Galapagos.] < *P. Z. S.*, 1837, p. 27.

1838. LAFRESNAYE, [F.] DE. Note sur une espèce nouvelle du genre Moqueur, Orpheus [longirostris]. < *Revue Zoologique*, i, 1838, pp. 54, 55.

1839. LAFRESNAYE, F. DE. G. Moqueur. Orpheus. Swainson. M. a long bec. O. longirostris. Lafresnaye. < *Guér. Mag. de Zool.*, 2ᵉ sér., année 1839, Ois., pp. 1–4, pl. 1.
Décrit pour la première fois dans la *Rev. Zool.*, i, 1838, p. 54.—En suite, une liste de dix espèces du genre Moqueur (*Mimus + Harporhynchus*).

1843. LAFRESNAYE, F. DE. Sur un petit groupe d'oiseaux des Antilles. < *Revue Zoologique*, vi, 1843, pp. 66–68.
Ramphocinclus (g. n.), p. 66; *R. tremulus, R. gutturalis*, pp. 67, spp. nn.
Cf. P. Z. S., 1855, p. 213—*R. tremulus* considered probably = *Stenorhynchus ruficauda* Gould, *P. Z. S.*, 1835 (*Cinclocerthia*).

1843. LESSON, R. P. Note sur le genre d'oiseau appelé Ramphocinclus. < *Revue Zoologique*, vi, 1843, pp. 325–327.

1844. BREWER, T. M. [Facts tending to clear up the confusion and errors in the history of the Hermit Thrush (Turdus solitarius, Wils.)] < *Proc. Bost. Soc. Nat. Hist.*, i, 1844, pp. 190, 191.
Chars. of 3 spp.—*Merula wilsonii* = *T. fuscescens* Steph.; *M. solitaria* = *T. pallasi* Cab.; *M. olivacea* sp. n. = *T. swainsoni* Cab., p. 191. The name "olivacea", moreover, is preoccupied in the genus.

1844. LAFRESNAYE, F. DE. Réponse de M. F. de Lafresnaye aux observations de M. Lesson, sur son genre Ramphocinclus, insérées dans cette Revue, 1843, page 325. < *Revue Zoologique*, viii, 1844, pp. 43–46.
Au sujet du genre *l'Herminierus*, Less., MS.

1844. LAFRESNAYE, [F. DE]. Ueber Orpheus longirostris [u. s. w.]. < *Oken's Isis*, Bd. xxxvii, 1844, p. 409.
Auszug aus *Guér. Mag. de Zool.*, 1839.

1845. LAFRESNAYE, [F.] DE. Sur le Fournier Rosalbin, Furnarius roseus Lesson, Illustrations de zoologie. < *Revue Zoologique*, viii, 1845, pp. 10, 11.
Noting the inaccuracy of the plate, especially as regards the form of the bill, giving the habitat of the bird as Colombia, not Brazil, and discussing the position of the species among the Furnarians. The article is the fifth of the "Mélanges Ornithologiques."

1848. CABOT, S., JR. [Occurrence of Turdus nævius in New Jersey.] < *Proc. Bost. Soc. Nat. Hist.*, iii, 1848, p. 17.

1848. DEBY, J. Note on the occurrence of Turdus minor of Latham, in Belgium. < *Zoologist*, vi, 1848, pp. 1966–1968.

1848. [JARDINE, W.] Turdus xanthoscelus, Jardine [sp. n., from Tobago]. < *Jard. Contrib. Orn.*, 1848, p. 14, pl. i.

1849. HOMEYER, E. F. v. Über die Gattung Turdus. < *Rhea*, Heft ii, 1849, pp. 144-159.

> 21 Arten, monographisch bearbeitet, nebst Synonymik, Kennzeichen, Aufenthalt und Bemerkungen. *TT. varius, lunulatus, auroreus, pallasii, wilsonii, swainsoni, viscivorus, hodgsoni* (sp. n., p. 150), *musicus, pallens, werneri, iliacus, naumanni, fuscatus, ruficollis, atrigularis, sibiricus, pilaris, migratorius, merula*, und *torquatus*.

1850. HARTLAUB, [G.] Description d'une nouvelle espèce de Turdus [aurantiirostris] de Venezuela. < *Rev. et Mag. de Zool.*, ii, 1850, p. 158.

1850. HARTLAUB, G. Note upon Turdus vulpinus, Hartl. < *P. Z. S.*, xviii, 1850, p. 276, pl. (Aves) xxxii.

> Décrit comme espèce nouvelle dans la *Rev. et Mag. de Zool.*, i, 1849, p. 276, provenant de Caraccas; c'est une synonyme de *Furnarius roseus, Less..Ill. Zool.*, pl. 5; c'est-à-dire, de *Rhodinocichla rosea*.

1850. KAUP, J. [J.] Ueber die Bedeckung der Fusswurzel des Turdus migratorius. < *Arch. f. Naturg.*, 1850 (1), pp. 42, 43, pl. ii, fig. i–v.

> Shows the gradual transition with age from the scutellation to the booting of the tarsus.

1850. NAUMANN, J. F. Kritische Bemerkungen über einige in Deutschland seltene Drosselarten. < *Naumannia*, i, Heft iii, 1850, pp. 1–12.

1851. CORDEAUX, W. H. Occurrence of the Mocking Bird of America (Turdus [Mimus] polyglottus) in the County of Kent. < *Zoologist*, ix, 1851, p. 3277.

1851. [JARDINE, W.] Turdus aurantiirostris, Hartlaub. < *Jard. Contrib. Orn.*, 1851, p. 80, pl. lxxii.

1851. NAUMANN, J. F. Vorläufige Anzeige der seit c. 30 und einigen Jahren in Deutschland vorgekommenen, früher hier nicht bemerkten oder übersehenen fremden Drossel-Arten, welche in naturgetrenen Abbildungen und Beschreibungen für die nächsten Supplement-Hefte zu meiner Naturgesch. d. Vögel Deutschlands ausführlicher dargestellt werden sollen. < *Naumannia*, i, Heft iv, 1851, pp. 1–9.

1852. CABANIS, J. [Das Vorkommen von Turdus migratorius in Deutschland, Dec. 1851—ohne Zweifel durch Siberia.] < *Naumannia*, ii, Heft ii, 1852, pp. 122, 123.

1852. HARTLAUB, G. Sur une nouvelle espèce du genre Melanotis [M. hypoleucus], Bonap. (Consp., p. 276). < *Rev. et Mag. de Zool.*, iv, 1852, p. 460.

1852. LAWRENCE, G. N. Mimus melanopterus [n. sp.]. < *Ann. Lyc. Nat. Hist. New York*, v, 1852, pp. 35, 36, pl. ii. (Read Apr. 16, 1849.)

1852. LAWRENCE, G. N. Descriptions of New Species of Birds, of the Genera Toxostoma [Le Contei, p. 121] Wagler, . . . < *Ann. Lyc. Nat. Hist. New York*, v, 1852, pp. 121–123. (Read Sept. 8, 1851.)

> Other spp. here described are a *Tyrannula* and a *Plectrophanes:* title is to be found in full in N. Am. part of this Bibl.

1853. CABANIS, J. Turdus migratorius, Lin. als Gast in Deutschland. < *J. f. O.*, i, 1853, pp. 67–69.

> Gleichfalls über das Vorkommen der genannten Arten und *T. pallasi* in Helgoland.

1854. GOULD, J. Description of a New Bird from Guatemala, forming the type of a new Genus [Malacocichla dryas]. < *P. Z. S.*, xxii, Nov. 28, 1854, pp. 285, 286, pl. (Aves) lxxv.

1855. SCLATER, P. L. Note on the Genus Legriocinclus, Lesson, and its synonyms. < *P. Z. S.*, xxiii, 1855, pp. 212–214.

> *Legriocinclus* Less., 1847 = *Ramphocinclus* Lafr., 1843 = *Cinclocerthia* Gray, 1840 = *Stenorhynchus* Gould, 1835 (preoccupied): these, with *Herminierus* Less. and *Cinclops* Bp., 1854, proposed to be reduced to one group, or at all events to be placed in close juxtaposition. There is also important criticism on the species concerned.

1856. GOULD, J. Description of a New Bird from Guatemala, forming the type of a New Genus [Malacocichla dryas]. < *Ann. Mag. Nat. Hist.*, 2d ser., xvii, 1856, pp. 78, 79.

> From *P. Z. S.*, Nov. 28, 1854, pp. 285, 286.

1856. SCLATER, P. L.   Note on the Genus Legriocinclus, Lesson, and its synonyms.
  < *Ann. Mag. Nat. Hist.*, 2d ser., xviii, 1856, pp. 341–343.
    From *P. Z. S.*, Nov. 27, 1855, pp. 212–214, *q. v.*

1856. [BILLINGS, E.]   On the Robin, or Migratory Thrush (Turdus migratorious [sic]).
  < *Canad. Nat. and Geol.*, i, 1856, pp. 142–146.
    Compiled description and account of distribution and habits, mainly from Wilson.

1858. GOULD, A. A.   [On the Food of the American Robin (Turdus migratorius, Linn.).]
  < *Proc. Boston Soc. Nat. Hist.*, vi, 1858, p. 403.

1858. TREADWELL, D.   [Detailed account of the feeding and growth of the American
  Robin (Turdus migratorius, Linn.).]   < *Proc. Boston Soc. Nat. Hist.*, vi, 1858,
  pp. 396–399.

1859. SCLATER, P. L.   A Synopsis of the Thrushes (Turdidæ) of the New World.   < *P.
  Z. S.*, xxvii, June 28, 1859, pp. 321–347.
    Sketch of the group and tables of geographical distribution of *Turdus*. Systematic synony-
    matic and diagnostic synopsis, with critical annotation of the species: *Catharus*, 7; *Turdus*,
    39; *Cichlerminia*, 1; *Margarops*, 3; *Galeoscoptes*, 3; *Melanoptila*, 1; *Melanotis*, 2; *Rhampho-
    cinclus*, 1; *Cinclocerthia*, 2; *Harporhynchus*, 6; *Oreoscoptes*, 1; *Mimus*, 20.—*Catharus occiden-
    talis*, p. 323; *Turdus pinicola*, p. 334; spp. nn. It is an important revision of the whole subject,
    which should be consulted preparatory to any study of this group.

1859. SCLATER, P. L.   On a new species of Catharus [occidentalis].   < *Ann. Mag. Nat.
  Hist.*, (3), iv, 1859, p. 400.
    From *P. Z. S.*, June 28, 1859, p. 323.

1860. BRYANT, H.   [Note on Turdus minimus Lafr.]   < *Proc. Bost. Soc. Nat. Hist.*,
  vii, 1860, pp. 226, 227.
    This untitled article also describes *Vireo bogotensis*, sp. n., p. 227.

1861. SCLATER, P. L.   Remarks on the Geographical Distribution of the Genus Turdus.
  < *Ibis*, 1861, iii, pp. 277–283, pl. viii.
    Palaearctic 16, Indian 15 (*T. schlegelii*, sp. n., p. —), Aethiopian 9, Australian 5, Nearctic
    12, Neotropical 27. Pl. viii represents *T. fulviventris*.

1861. TREADWELL, [D.]   On the Feeding and Growth of the American Robin [Turdus
  migratorius].   < *Rep. Com'r of Patents for* 1860, *Agric.*, 1861, pp. 88, 89.

1862. JENKS, J. W. P.   [Report upon the habits of the Robin, Turdus migratorius.]
  < *Seventeenth Ann. Rep. Ohio State Board of Agric.*, 1862, pp. 288–291.
    Very full results of investigation upon the food of this species—one of the best contributions
    upon this particular subject extant.

1862. SACC, Dr.   [Einiges über Turdus polyglottus in Gefangenschaft.]   < *Zool.
  Gart.*, iii, 1862, p. 215.

1863. CHIAPELLA, C.   [Histoire détaillée du Merle moqueur, Mimus polyglottus.]
  < *Journal de Bordeaux*, du 22 décembre 1863.
    Pas vue moi-même.

1863. HILL, R.   Notes on the Mimidæ of Jamaica.   < *Proc. Acad. Nat. Sci. Phila.*, xv,
  1863, pp. 304, 305.
    Descriptions; field-notes of habits.

1863. PUTNAM, F. W.   [Nesting of Turdus migratorius on the ground, and on a beam
  connected with the moving machinery of a sawmill.]   < *Proc. Boston Soc.
  Nat. Hist.*, ix, 1863, p. 248.

1863. SCHÜLER, A.   Spottvögel (Turdus polyglottus).   < *Zool. Gart.*, iv, 1863, p. 256.
    Dessen Nahrung, in Gefangenschaft.

1865. BRYANT, H.   Remarks on the Genus Galeoscoptes, Cabanis, with the Characters of two new Genera, and a Description of Turdus plumbeus Lin.   < *Proc.
  Boston Soc. Nat. Hist.*, ix, 1865, pp. 369–372.
    Mimokitta, Mimocichla (Scl., 1859).

1865. CHIAPELLA, C.   La Merle moqueur [Mimus polyglottus], éducations faites a
  Bordeaux.   < *Bull. Soc. Acclim.*, 2 sér., ii, 1865, pp. 466–473.

1865. CHIAPELLA, C. Der amerikanische Spottvogel [Mimus polyglottus] und seine Zucht in Bordeaux. < *Zool. Gart.*, vi, 1865, pp. 424–426.

 Auszug aus d. *Bull. Soc. d'Acclim.*, 8 août 1865, pp. 466–473.

1866. McKAY, A. W. On the Turdus migratorius. < *Rep. Brit. Ass. Adv. Sci.* for 1865, 1866 (*Misc. Comm.*), p. 90.

 A few desultory observations, not entirely correct.

1867. MANGER, —. [Die Katzendrossel (Mimus carolinensis) in Gefangenschaft.] < *Zool. Gart.*, viii, 1867, pp. 191, 192.

1868. ALLEN, J. A. The "Dwarf Thrush" ["Turdus nanus"] again. < *Am. Nat.*, ii, 1868, pp. 488, 489.

 Identifies the supposed Massachusetts example (*tom. cit.*, p. 218) with *T. olivaceus*, and considers the supposed Pennsylvania one (*tom. cit.*, p. 380) to be not distinct from *T. pallasi*.

1868. "A. P. R." The Robin [Turdus migratorius] at Fault. < *Am. Nat.*, ii, 1868, p. 217.

 Failure of the bird's attempts to build a nest under the eaves of a barn.

1868. GARLICK, T. Migrations of Birds [*i. e.*, of Turdus migratorius]. < *Am. Nat.*, ii, 1868, p. 492.

 Reappearance, at Cleveland, Ohio, for five successive years, of an albino of this species.

1868. HUGHES, D. D. Albino Robin [Turdus migratorius]. < *Am. Nat.*, ii, 1868, p. 490.

1868. JACQUES, D. H. The Mocking Bird [Mimus polyglottus]. < *Am. Nat.*, ii, 1868, p. 215.

 Brief note on its singing in winter, and on its breeding.

1868. SAMUELS, E. A. The Dwarf Thrush [Turdus nanus] in Massachusetts. < *Am. Nat.*, ii, 1868, p. 218.

 Cf. Allen, *tom. cit.*, pp. 488, 489.

1868. TRIPPE, T. M. The Dwarf Thrush [Turdus nanus]. < *Am. Nat.*, ii, 1868, p. 380.

 Its supposed occurrence in New Jersey (*cf.* Allen, *tom. cit.*, pp. 488, 489).

1869. ["A. P. R."] The Robin [Turdus migratorius] at Fault. < *Zoologist*, 2d ser., iv, 1869, p. 1604.

 From 'American Naturalist.' June, 1868, p. 217.

1869. BREE, C. R. American Robin [Turdus migratorius]. < *Zoologist*, 2d ser., iv, 1869, p. 1644.

1869. LINDEN, C. Albino Robins [Turdus migratorius]. < *Am. Nat.*, iii, 1869, p. 279.

 Two cases, Buffalo, N. Y.

1869. MAYNARD, C. J. The Dwarf Thrush [Turdus nanus] again. < *Am. Nat.*, ii, 1869, pp. 662, 663.

 The supposed Massachusetts example reaffirmed to be *T. swainsoni*; from which, also, *T. aliciæ* is decided to be not distinct.

1869. RIDGWAY, R. Notices of certain obscurely known species of American Birds. < *Proc. Acad. Nat. Sci. Phila.*, xxi, June, 1869, pp. 125–135, 9 woodcc.

 I.—The North American Wood Thrushes, *Hylocichla*, pp. 127–129. Treating of 7 spp.
 The article also treats of species of II. *Pyranga*, and of III. *Quiscalus*.

1871. ANON. The Mocking-bird [Mimus polyglottus]. < *Appleton's Journ.*, v, Feb., 1871, p. 230.

 Becoming intoxicated by freely partaking of berries of the pride-of-China tree.

1871. ANON. Der peruanische Spottvogel [   ]. < *Aus der Natur*, lv, oder n. F., xliii, 1871, p. 80.

1871. BOARDMAN, G. A. Mocking Bird [Mimus polyglottus] in Maine. < *Am. Nat.*, v, 1871, p. 121.

1872. CABANIS, J. [Turdus auroreus Pall. = T. nævius Gm.] < *J. f. O.*, xx, 1872, p. 157.

1872. COUES, E. Ornithological Query. < *Am. Nat.*, vi, 1872, p. 47.

 Whether certain partial albino *Turdus migratorius* were not offspring of a perfect albino and a normal individual.

1872. COUES, E.   The Nest, Eggs and Breeding Habits of Harporhynchus crissalis.
      < Am. Nat., vi, 1872, pp. 370–371.

1872. DREW, S. A. L.   Reason or Instinct in the Robin [Turdus migratorius]?   < Am.
      Nat., vi, 1872, p. 52.
        Observations on the nesting.

1873. COUES, E.   Some United States Birds, New to Science, and other Things Orni-
      thological.   < Am. Nat., vii, 1873, pp. 321–331, figg. 65–70.
        Peucœa carpalis, p. 322; Harporhynchus bendirei, p. 330, spp. nn.; and, among "other things
      ornithological", a slight monography of Harporhynchus, with figures of the heads of six spp.
      of that genus.

1873. SCLATER, P. L.   [Notice of a New Work on American Birds.]   < P. Z. S., 1873,
      p. 554.
        Notice of the Nomenclator Avium Neotropicalium.—Turdus subcinereus, P. Z. S., 1866, p.
      320 = Colluricincla rufiventris, of Australia. Onipolegus sp. of Cat. A. B., p. 203 = Chasiem-
      pis sandwichensis.

1874. BOYCE, C[AROLINE].   The Robin [Turdus migratorius].   < Am. Nat., viii, 1874,
      pp. 203–208.
        Field notes on Turdus migratorius.

1874. BOYCE, CAROLINE.   Usefulness of the Robin [Turdus migratorius].   < Pop.
      Sci. Monthly, Nov., 1874, p. 124.

1874. BREWER, T. M.   [Remarks on the species of Turdus of the subgenus Hylocichla.]
      < Proc. Bost. Soc. Nat. Hist., xvi, 1874, p. 115.
        Critical; 8 spp. recognized.

1874. CABANIS, J.   [Identität von Turdus apicalis Hartl. und Margarops montanus
      (Lafr.).]   < J. f. O., 1874, pp. 350, 351.

1874. WILSON, ROBERT.   The Mocking-bird [Mimus polyglottus].   < Appleton's
      Journ., xi, June, 1874, p. 776.
        History of the bird woven into a novelette.

1875. ABBOTT, C. C.   Notes on Habits of certain Thrushes [in New Jersey].   < Rod
      and Gun, vi, May 8, 1875, p. 86.
        Read before Nutt. Ornith. Club, April, 25, 1875.

1875. ANON.   [Mimus carolinensis and other garden birds.]   < Rod and Gun, vi, July
      3, 1875, p. 215.

1875. COOPER, J. G.   Notes on Californian Thrushes [of the subgenus Hylocichla].
      < Am. Nat., ix, No. 2, Feb., 1875, pp. 114–116.

1875. GREENWOOD, E. C.   Occurrence of the Mocking-Bird [Mimus polyglottus] in
      Massachusetts.   < Am. Sportsman, v, 1874–5, Mar. 13, p. 370.
        Note added by R. Deane to the effect that this specimen, which was exhibited to the
      Nuttall Ornithological Club, was the fourth taken near Boston, within a few months.

1875–76. INGERSOLL, E.   The Nesting of [certain Turdidæ of North] American Birds.
      I[–IV.].   < Forest and Stream, v, Dec. 16, 1875, p. 291; Dec. 23, 1875, p. 308;
      Dec. 30, 1875, p. 323; Jan. 13, 1876, p. 356.
        I. Turdus migratorius. II. Turdus nœvius. III. Turdus mustelinus. IV. Turdus pallasi.

1876. COUES, E.   Letters on Ornithology.   No. 1.—The Oregon Robin [Turdus næ-
      vius].   < The Chicago Field, June 24, 1876, fig.
        Account of habits, with a figure of the head.
        This series of "Letters", each with its own subhead, runs through several issues of the
      paper, as follows:—No. 1, June 24, 1876; No. 2, Aug. 12, 1876; No. 3, Aug. 26, 1876; No. 4,
      Oct. 7, 1876; No. 5, Nov. 18, 1876; No. 6, Dec. 2, 1876; No. 7, Dec. 9, 1876; No. 8, Dec. 16, 1876;
      No. 9, Dec. 23, 1876; No. 10, Dec. 30, 1876; No. 11, Jan. 6, 1877; No. 12, Jan. 13, 1877; No. 13,
      Feb. 13, 1877; No. 13 [bis = 14], Mar. 17, 1877; No. 15, July 14, 1877; No. 16, July 21, 1877;
      No. 16 bis, Dec. 15, 1877; No. 17, Feb. 2, 1878; No. 18, June 29, 1878; No. 19, Apr. 26, 1879;
      No. 20, May 10, 1879; No. 21, May 17, 1879; No. 22, May 24, 1879; No. 23, June 9, 1879; No.
      24, June 14, 1879; No. 25, June 21, 1879; No. 26, June 28, 1879; No. 27, July 5, 1879; No. 28,
      July 12, 1879; No. 29, July 19, 1879; No. 30, July 26, 1879.—They give popular accounts of
      various North American Birds, in certain cases from advance sheets of the "Birds of the Col-
      orado Valley," and are for the most part illustrated with original woodcut figures. They are
      cited in this Bibliography collectively by the major head under "North America", and also
      individually by minor heads under the several families to which they respectively pertain.

1876. COUES, E.   Letters on Ornithology.   No. 7.—The Catbird [Mimus carolinensis].
< *The Chicago Field*, Dec. 9, 1876, fig.
Biographical, from advance sheets of the *Birds of the Colorado Valley.*

1876. GRAY, A. F.   Strange nesting places [of Turdus migratorius].   < *Forest and Stream*, vi, July 6, 1876, p. 355.

1876. HARTING, J. E.   [Turdus migratorius in England.]   < *The* (London) *Field*, Dec. 23, 1876, p. —.
Not seen.

1876. [INGERSOLL, E.]   The Crissal Thrasher [Harporhynchus crissalis].   < *Forest and Stream*, vii, Oct. 12, 1876, p. 148.
Quotations from letters from Capt. Charles Bendire, concerning breeding habits of the species in Arizona.

1876. MORRIS, R. T.   A Plea for the Robin [Turdus migratorius].   < *Forest and Stream*, vi, June 29, 1876, p, 337.

1876. RAGSDALE, G. H.   Late appearance of the Mocking-bird [Mimus polyglottus, in Cooke Co., Texas].   < *Forest and Stream*, v, Jan. 20, 1876, p. 372.

1876. WOOLDRIDGE, G.   Mocking-bird [Mimus polyglottus] food.   < *Forest and Stream*, vii, Oct. 5,1876, p. 132.

1876. ———.   A Cat Whipped by Robins [Turdus migratorius].   < *Rod and Gun*, vii, Feb. 5, 1876, p. 294.

1877. BAILEY, H. B.   Occurrence for the first time in England of the Robin (Turdus migratorius).   < *Bull. Nutt. Ornith. Club*, ii, No. 4, Oct., 1877, p. 110.
Prepared from Harting's articles, *The Field*, Dec 23, 1876, and the *Zoologist*, Jan., 1877.

1877. BOARDMAN, G. A.   Melanosis [in Turdus migratorius].   < *Forest and Stream*, ix. Sept. 6, 1877, p. 86.

1877. [YOUNG, RAWLINGS.]   Song of the Mocking Bird [described and analyzed].
< *Forest and Stream*, ix, Aug. 16, 1877, p. 24.

1877. HARTING, J. E.   [Turdus migratorius in England.]   < *Zoologist*, —, Jan., 1877, p. —.
Not seen.

1877. INGERSOLL, E.   The Domestic Life of the Brown Thrasher [Harporhynchus rufus].   < *Forest and Stream*, viii, Apr. 12, 1877, p. 145.
An original and complete account.

1877. RIDGWAY, R.   On Geographical Variation in Turdus migratorius.   < *Bull. Nutt. Ornith. Club*, ii, No. 1, Jan., 1877, pp. 8, 9.
Turdus propinquus, subsp. n., p. 9.

1877. TREAT, *Mrs.* M.   Our Mocking-bird [Mimus polyglottus].   < *Forest and Stream*, viii, Mar. 29, 1877, pp. 112, 113.

1878. ALLEN, J. A.   Persistency in Nest-building by a Pair of City Robins [Turdus migratorius].   < *Bull. Nutt. Ornith. Club*, iii, No. 2, Apr., 1878, pp. 103, 104.

1878. ANON.   [Ingenuity of Turdus migratorius.]   < *The Country*, ii, May 18, 1878, p. 57.

1878. BEAL, F. E. L.   Birds' Nests in Unusual Places.   < *Forest and Stream*, x, Mar. 21, 1878, p. 118.
Nest of *Turdus migratorius* on the ground.

1878. BREWER, T. M.   Wilson's Thrush [Turdus fuscescens], with Spotted Eggs and nesting on a Tree.   < *Bull. Nutt. Ornith. Club*, iii, No. 4, Oct., 1878, p. 193.

1878. COUES, E.   Melanism of Turdus migratorius.   < *Bull. Nutt. Ornith. Club*, iii, No. 1, Jan., 1878, pp. 47, 48.

1878. DEANE, R.   Deadly Combat between an Albino Robin [Turdus migratorius] and a Mole.   < *Bull. Nutt. Ornith. Club*, iii, No. 2, Apr., 1878, p. 104.
Covering a narrative of the occurrence from Miss Maria L. Audubon, granddaughter of J. J.

1878. FISHER, A. K. Robins' [Turdus migratorius] Eggs, Spotted. < Bull. Nutt. Ornith. Club, iii, No. 2, Apr., 1878, p. 97.

1878. HUYLER, A. I. A Case of Instinct [of Turdus migratorius]. < Science News, i, No. 2, Nov. 15, 1878, p. 32.

1878. GRAY, A. F. Robin [Turdus migratorius] Nesting Upon the Ground. < Forest and Stream, ix, Jan. 31, 1878, p. 489.

1878. [GRINNALL, G. B.] An Albino Thrush [Turdus pallasi]. < Forest and Stream, x, Feb. 28, 1878, p. 55.

1878. INGERSOLL, E. The nesting habits of rare American thrushes [Harporhynchus]. < The London Field, li, Apr. 20, 1878, p. 453.

> Treating all the United States species of the genus excepting H. rufus.

1878. LAWRENCE, G. N. Characters of a supposed new Species of South-American Thrush [Turdus brunneus]. < Ibis, 4th ser., ii, Jan., 1878, p. 57, pl. i.

> N. B. There is more than one Turdus brunneus of earlier authors. The present belongs to the section of the genus including T. leucomelas, albiventris, &c. If a proper Turdus, stet TURDUS LAWRENCII, nobis, hoc loco, species renovata.

1878. LYLE, D. A. The Robin's [Turdus migratorius] Food. < Am. Nat., xii, No. 7, July, 1878, pp. 448–453.

> Detailed account of the enormous quantity and variety of food consumed by a captive Robin.

1878. READ, M. C. Variations in Robins' [Turdus migratorius] Nests. < Science News, i, No. 2, Nov. 15, 1878, p. 32.

1878. TURNER, H. W. Nesting of the Robin [Turdus migratorius] on the Ground. < Am. Nat., xii, No. 1, 1878, p. 53.

1879. ALLEN, J. A. Odd Behavior of a Robin [Turdus migratorius] and a Yellow Warbler. < Bull. Nutt. Ornith. Club, iv, No. 3, July, 1879, pp. 178–182.

> The curious case given by Miss O. C. Coolidge is here amplified, with account of similar doings of Dendrœca œstiva.

1879. ANON. Nesting of Swainson's Thrush (Turdus swainsoni). < The Oölogist, iv, No. 12, summer, 1879 (an extra number), pp. 93–95, cut.

> In Herkimer County, N. Y. Extended original observations, with cut of nest and eggs.

1879. BOARDMAN, G. A. Interesting Note on Albinism. < Forest and Stream, xiii, Aug. 7, 1879, p. 525.

> Note on albino Hirundo horreorum, and on melanotic Turdus migratorius.

1879. COUES, E. Le Conte's Thrasher (Harporhynchus lecontii). < The Oölogist, iv, No. 12, summer, 1879 (extra number), pp. 99, 100.

> Quoted from the Birds of the Colorado Valley, pt. i, 1878, p. 72.

1879. [COOLIDGE, Miss O. C.] A Robin's [Turdus migratorius] Persistency. < Water-town (N. Y.) Daily Times, May 24, 1879.

> In tapping for several days at a window. See full account of the same case, and another instance of the same behavior in the case of Dendrœca œstiva, Bull. Nutt. Ornith. Club., iv, 1879, p. 178.

1879. HENSHAW, H. W. Remarks upon Turdus pallasi and its Varieties. < Bull. Nutt. Ornith. Club, iv, No. 3, July, 1879, pp. 134–139.

> Carefully distinguishing T. nanus and T. auduboni from T. pallasi proper.

1879. HOLMES, MARY E. Another Lesson from the Robin [Turdus migratorius]. < Science News, i, No. 10, Mar. 15, 1879, pp. 155, 156.

> Referring to M. C. Read's article of similar title (tom. cit., pp. 117, 118), the writer gives her own experiences with a Robin in captivity.

1879. HOLZAPPEL, J. [Occupation by Turdus mustelinus of a nest of Cardinalis vir-ginianus] < The Oölogist, v, No. 1, July, 1879, p. 3.

1879. [INGERSOLL, E.] Nest and Eggs of the Texas Thrasher (Harporhynchus rufus var. longirostris.) < The Oölogist, iv, No. 10, May, 1879, pp. 75, 76, pl. (not num-bered), fig. 3.

> Editorial extracts from the published observations of G. B. Sennett and J. C. Merrill.

1879. "ISSAQUENA." Are Robins [Turdus migratorius] Topers? < *Forest and Stream*, xiii, Sept. 18, 1879, p. 646.

Further discussion from *tom. cit.*, p. 554. The writer considers that the birds gorge themselves with the China berries and become helpless from this cause.

1879. LOCKWOOD, S. Rob: A Bird Biography [Turdus migratorius]. < *Am. Nat.*, xiii, No. 4, Apr., 1879, pp. 359–366.

Very full and entertaining account of the habits of a pet Robin.

1879. LUM, S. K. Notes on the Thrushes [Turdidæ] of Washington Territory. < *Am. Nat.*, xiii, No. 10, Oct., 1879, pp. 629–632.

Field-notes on the habits and local distribution of various species.

1879. RAGSDALE, G. H. Olive-backed Thrush (Turdus swainsoni) in Texas. < *Bull. Nutt. Ornith. Club*, iv, No. 2, Apr., 1879, p. 116.

1879. READ, M. C. A new Lesson from the Robin [Turdus migratorius]. < *Science News*, i, No. 8, Feb. 15, 1879, pp. 117, 118.

With reference to the migrations of the bird.

1879. SENNETT, G. B. The Curve-billed Thrush (Harporhynchus curvirostris), its Nest and Eggs. < *The Oölogist*, iv, No. 10, May, 1879, pp. 74, 75, pl. —, f. 2.

From advance sheets of the paper in *Bull. U. S. Geol. and Geogr. Surv. Terr.*, v, No. 2, Sept. 6, 1879.

1879. ST. CLAIR, [J. W.] St. Clair on the Robin [Turdus migratorius]. < *Forest and Stream*, xiii, Oct. 30, 1879, p. 765.

1879. STAPLES, E. F. Odd. < *Forest and Stream*, xii, June 12, 1879, p. 385.

A Robin (T. migratorius) with the voice of a Whip-poor-will.

1879. T[AYLOR], N. A. Are Robins [Turdus migratorius] Topers? < *Forest and Stream*, xiii, Aug. 14, 1879, p. 544. (See p. 646.)

Denying statement in *Forest and Stream* by J. W. St. Clair (*tom. cit.*, p. 765) that Robins are intoxicated by feeding on the berries of the China tree (*Melia azedarach*).

1879. W. B. A Few Questions Discussed. < *Forest and Stream*, xiii, Sept. 11, 1879, p. 625. (See pp. 544, 646, 765.)

Slightly ornithological. Explains apparent "intoxication" of Robins by stating that they become choked by a China berry of unusual size.

Hydrobatidæ.

1816. V[IEILLOT, L. P.].   Aguassière, Hydrobata.   < *Nouv. Dict. d'Hist. Nat.*, i, 1816, pp. 219, 220.

> *Hydrobata albicollis*, g. sp. n., p. 219.   (*Hydrobata* also in *Analyse*, 1816.   Not *Hydrobates*, Boie, 1822.) Antedated by *Cinclus* Bechst, *Naturg. Vög. Deutschl.*, iii, 1802, p. 808. The latter name is now in almost universal employ. (Not *Cinclus* Gray, *G. of B.*, iii, 549, ex Moehr., 1752, which = *Strepsilas* Illiger, 1811.)

1829. THOMPSON, T.   Birds presented to the Hull Literary and Philosophical Society. < *Loudon's Mag. Nat. Hist.*, ii, 1829, pp. 301, 302.

> A note on *Sternus cinclus* (*Cinclus aquaticus*), which the writer conceives should be written *S. "cinctus"*, because he can make nothing of the word *cinclus!*

1832. "SUBSCRIBER."   The Term Cinclus, as the Epithet in the Name of the Species of Bird called Sturnus Cinclus.   < *Loudon's Mag. Nat. Hist.*, v, 1832, p. 734.

1833. FALK, V.   Bidrag till Strömstarens [Cinclus aquaticus] Natural-Historia. < *Tidsk. f. Jägare o. Naturf.*, ii, 1833, pp. 671–673.

1834. BONAPARTE, C. L.   [Cinclus unicolor = C. pallasii.]   < *Oken's Isis*, Bd. xxvii, 1834, p. 813.

> Auszug aus *Philos. Mag.*, ix, 1831, p. —.

1834. "T. G."   The Water Ouzel [Cinclus aquaticus].   < *Loudon's Mag. Nat. Hist.*, vii, 1834, pp. 540–542.

1834. "TIRO."   The Water Ouzel [Cinclus aquaticus]; its Song and Nest.   < *Loudon's Mag. Nat. Hist.*, vii, 1834, pp. 542, 543.

1835. MORRIS, F. O.   Notices of the Affinities, Habits, and certain Localities of the Dipper (Cinclus aquáticus).   < *Loudon's Mag. Nat. Hist.*, viii, 1835, pp. 374–376.

1835. WATERTON, C.   The Dipper [Cinclus aquaticus].   < *Loudon's Mag. Nat. Hist.*, viii, 1835, pp. 514–516.

> Controversy with F. O. Morris (*op. cit.*, p. 375) respecting the queer notion that Waterton had, that birds do not oil their feathers.

1844. JERDON, A.   Notes on [the habits of Cinclus aquaticus] the Dipper.   < *Zoologist*, ii, 1844, p. 450.

1847. ANON.   Habits of the Water-Ouzel [Cinclus aquaticus].   < *Zoologist*, v, 1847, p. 1875.

> From 'Wild Sports in the Highlands,' p. 198.

1849. OLANS, J.   Note on the Water Ouzel (Cinclus aquaticus).   < *Zoologist*, vii, 1849, p. 2526.

1856. BREHM, [C.] L.   Ueber die Wasserschwätzer, Cinclus, Bechst.   < *Naumannia*, vi, 1856, pp. 178–189.

> Beschreibung, Aufenthalt, Betragen, Nahrung, Fortpflanzung, Feinde, Jagd und Fang. Nutzen.   6 spp.—*C. aquaticus, C. medius, C. meridionalis, C. peregrinus, C. septentrionalis, C. melanogaster.*

1856. COUCH, J.   Particulars of some of the Habits of the Dipper (Cinclus aquaticus). < *Zoologist*, xiv, 1856, pp. 5250, 5251.

1856. GLOGER, C. W. L.   Was den Wasserschwätzer [Cinclus aquaticus] stellenweise ganz vertreibt und die Gebirgs-Bachstelze [Motacilla] ebenda selten macht. < *J. f. O.*, iv, 1856, pp. 502–504.

1856. STEVENSON, H.   Note on the Common Dipper (Cinclus aquaticus) near Norwich.   < *Zoologist*, xiv, 1856, p. 5061.

1857. MATHEWS, M. A.   Velocity of the Flight of the Water Ouzel [Cinclus aquaticus; over 20 miles an hour.]   < *Zoologist*, xv, 1857, p. 5791.

1857. STEVENSON, H. Inquiry respecting the Plumage of the Common Dipper [Cinclus aquaticus]. *< Zoologist*, xv, 1857, p. 5751.

1858. KINAHAN, J. R. On the subaqueous habits of the Water Ouzel (Cinclus aquaticus). *< Nat. Hist. Rev. (Pr. Soc.)*, v, 1858, pp. 91–94.

1859. BREHM, [C.] L. Etwas über das königl. zoologische Museum zu Dresden. *< J. f. O.*, vii, 1859, pp. 470, 471.

   Cinclus leucogaster brachycercus, C. l. macrourus, subspp. nn., p. 471, Siberia.

1859. GOULD, J. On two New Species of Cinclus [C. cashmeriensis, C. sordidus]. *< P. Z. S.*, xxvii, 1859, pp. 493, 494.

1859. SMURTHWAITE, H. Curious Situation for a Dipper's [Cinclus aquaticus] Nest. *< Zoologist*, xvii, 1859, p. 6561.

1860. GOULD, J. On two New Species of Cinclus. *< Ann. Mag. Nat. Hist.*, 3d ser., v, 1860, p. 502.

   From *P. Z. S.*, Dec. 13, 1859, pp. 493, 494, *q. v.*

1860. HOMEYER, A. v. Ein Moment aus dem Leben eines Wasserschwätzerpaares [Cinclus aquaticus]. *< J. f. O.*, viii, 1860, pp. 301, 302.

1863. SAXBY, H. L. Food of the Dipper (Cinclus aquaticus). *< Zoologist*, xxi, 1863, p. 8631.

1865. ALSTON, E. R. Habits of the Water Ouzel [Cinclus aquaticus]. *< Zoologist*, xxiii, 1865, pp. 9432, 9433.

1865. CRISP, E. On the Anatomy and Habits of the Water-Ousel (Cinclus aquaticus). *Proc. Zool. Soc.*, 1865, pp. 49–52.

   This is an important and interesting contribution to the subject.

1865. CRISP, E. On the Anatomy and Habits of the Water-Ousel (Cinclus aquaticus). *< Ann. Mag. Nat. Hist.*, 3d ser., xvi, 1865, pp. 49–52.

   From *P. Z. S.*, Jan. 10, 1865, pp. 49–52, *q. v.*

1867. FEILDEN, H. W. Nesting of the Dipper [Cinclus aquaticus]. *< Zoologist*, 2d ser., ii, 1867, pp. 755, 756.

1867. HARTLAUB, G. [The original description of Cinclus leucogaster Eversm. believed to have been published in that part of the "Addenda ad Zoographiam Rosso-Asiaticam" of which the whole edition was destroyed by fire excepting a very few copies.] *< Ibis*, 2d ser., iii, 1867, p. 383.

1866. RODD, E. H. Nesting of the Dipper [Cinclus aquaticus]. *< Zoologist*, 2d ser., i, 1866, pp. 268, 269.

1867. TRISTRAM, H. B. [The Cinclus which breeds in the Pyrenees is C. melanogaster.] *< Ibis*, 2d ser., iii, 1867, pp. 466, 467.

1867. SALVIN, O. [Note on Cinclus leucogaster Eversm.] *< Ibis*, 2d ser., iii, 1867, pp. 382, 383.

   With reference to the publication of the name in *Tchihatcheff's Voy. Scient. dans l'Altaï Orient.*, 1845, p. 442. Cf. *Ibis*, 1867, pp. 118 and 383.

1867. SALVIN, O. On the Genus Cinclus. *< Ibis*, 2d ser., 1867, iii, pp. 109–122, pl. ii.

   This article is *facile princeps* among those treating of the present family, and remains the leading authority. The species and races are handled upon philosophical principles which were not usually applied to the solution of such questions at that date, and treated with synonymy, description, habitat, and much critical comment. Thirteen forms of the genus are recognized, arranged in five main stems, with *four* more "representative" branches, and four "local" twigs. These are: AQUATICUS, with races (aquaticus), albicollis, and melanogaster, and *cashmiriensis* and *leucogaster* as representative species; SORDIDUS, alone; PALLASI, with (pallasi), marila, and asiaticus as races; MEXICANUS, with *ardesiacus* (p. 121, pl. ii, sp. n.) as its representative species; and LEUCOCEPHALUS with leuconotus as its representative.

   "We thus have five well-marked forms of *Cinclus* :—1. *Cinclus aquaticus*, which consists of three constant but nearly allied local races [1, *aquaticus*, 2, *albicollis*, 3, *melanogaster*] and two more distinct representative species [4, *cashmiriensis*, 5, *leucogaster*], all occupying different geographical areas; 2. [6] *Cinclus sordidus*, which seems to stand alone; 3. *Cinclus pallasi*, represented by three distinguishable races [7, *pallasi*, 8, *marila*, 9, *asiaticus*] occupying distinct districts; 4, *Cinclus mexicanus*, which is represented by two forms [10, *mexi-*

1867. SALVIN, O.—Continued.

canus, 11, ardesiacus] ; and 5. Cinclus leucocephalus, also represented by two members [12, leucocephalus, 13 leuconotus],—the total number of recognizable species being *thirteen*."

Reviewing the whole literature of the family, I make out the following list of nominal species, in alphabetical order, with the references :—

albicollis (HYDROBATA), *Vieill.*, Nouv. Dict., i, 1816, p. 219 . . . . .S. EUR., LEBANON.

albiventris (CINCLUS AQUATICUS var.), *Hempr. & Ehrenb.*, "Symb. Phys., 1820–25, Aves, fol. bb."=*albicollis*.

americanus (CINCLUS), *Sw.*, Fn. Bor.-Am., ii, 1831, p. 173 = *mexicanus* Sw.

aquaticus (CINCLUS), *Bechst.*, Naturg. Vög.Deutschl., iii, 1802, p. 808. . .CENT. EUROPE.

aquaticus (CINCLUS), *Tristr.*, Ibis, 1864, p. 436 = *albicollis* V.

ardesiacus (CINCLUS), *Salv.*, Ibis, 2d ser., iii, 1867, p. 121, pl. ii . . . . .VERAGUA.

asiaticus (CINCLUS), *Sw.*, Fn. Bor.-Am., ii, 1831, p. 174 . . . . .HIMALAYAN ASIA.

bicolor (HYDROBATA), *Vieill.*, ——?

brachycercus (CINCLUS LEUCOGASTER var.), *Brehm*, J. f. O., 1859, p. 471=*leucogaster*.

cashmeriensis (CINCLUS), *Gould*, P. Z. S., 1859, p. 494 . . . . .THIBET.

cinclus (STURNUS), *Linn.*, Syst. Nat., i, 1766, p. 290 = *melanogaster*, Br.

cinclus (STURNUS), *Gm.*, Syst. Nat., i, 1788, p. 803 = *aquaticus* ×.

cinclus var.(STURNUS), *Pall.*, Zoog. R.-A., i, 1831, p. 426 = *leucogaster ?*

cinclus (HYDROBATA), *L. Adams*, P. Z. S., 1858, p. 439 = *cashmiriensis*.

europæus (CINCLUS), *Steph.*, Shaw's G. Z., x, 1817, p. 313 = *aquaticus* ×.

gularis (TURDUS), *Lath.*, Ind. Orn. Suppl., 1802, pl. xl = *aquaticus* ×.

leucocephalus (CINCLUS), *Tschudi*, Arch. f. Naturg., 1844, (1), p. 279 . . . . .PERU.

leucocephalus (CINCLUS), *Lafr.*, Rev. Zool., 1847, p. 68 = *leuconotus*.

leucogaster (CINCLUS), *Eversm.*, "Add. ad Zoog. R.-A."; "Tchihatcheff's Voy., 1845, p. 442"; (*cf.* Ibis, 1867, pp. 117, 118, 382, 383) . . . . .SIBERIA.

leuconotus, *Scl.*, P. Z. S., 1857, p. 274. . . . . .ECUADOR.

macrourus (CINCLUS LEUCOGASTER var.), *Brehm*, J. f. O., 1859, p 471 = *leucogaster*.

maculatus (CINCLUS), *Hodgs.*, "Zool. Misc., 1844, pp. 83, 73" = *asiaticus*.

marila (HYDROBATA), *Swinh.*, "J. N. China Br. Roy. Asiat. Soc. 1859"; Ibis, 1860, p. 187. . . . . .FORMOSA.

medius (CINCLUS), *Brehm*, Naum., vi, 1856, 185 = *aquaticus*.

melanogaster (CINCLUS), *Brehm*, Lehrb. Eur. Vög., i, 1823, p. 289 . . . . . . .N. EUROPE.

meridionalis (CINCLUS), *Brehm*, Naum., vi, 1856, p. 186 = *albicollis*.

mexicanus (CINCLUS), *Sw.*, Philos. Mag., i, 1827, p. 368 . . . . .N. AMERICA.

mortoni (CINCLUS), *Towns.*, Narr., 1839, p. 337 = *mexicanus*.

pallasii (CINCLUS), *Temm.*, Man., i, 1820, p. 177 ; iii, 1835, p. 107 . . . . . .E. ASIA, JAPAN.

pallasii (CINCLUS), *Bp.*, Ann Lyc. N. Y., ii, 1826, p. 439 = *mexicanus*.

pallasi (CINCLUS), *Gould*, "Cent. B., pl. 24" = *asiaticus* Sw.

pallasi (CINCLUS), *Swinh.*, Ibis, iv, 1863, p. 272 = *marila* Swinh.

peregrinus (CINCLUS), *Brehm*, Naum., vi, 1856, p. 187 = *melanogaster*.

rufipectoralis (CINCLUS), *Brehm*, Naum., vi, 1856, p. 186 = *albicollis*.

rufiventris (CINCLUS AQUATICUS var.), *Hempr. & Ehrenb.*, "Symb. Phys., 1820–25," p. —, = *albicollis*.

rupestris (CINCLUS), *Brehm*, Naum., vi, 1856, p. — = *albicollis*.

septentrionalis (CINCLUS), *Brehm*, Lehrb. Eur.Vög., i,1823, p. 287 = *melanogaster* Br.

sordidus (CINCLUS) *Gould*, P. Z. S., 1859, p. 494 . . . . .THIBET.

tenuirostris (CINCLUS), "*Gould*," *Bp.*, Consp. Av., i, 1850, p. 252 = *asiaticus* Sw.

townsendii (CINCLUS), "*Aud.*," *Towns.*, Narr., 1839, p. 340 = *mexicanus*.

unicolor (CINCLUS), *Bp.*, Zool. Journ., iii, 1827, p. 52 = *mexicanus*.

1870. GOULD, J. [Remarks on exhibition of some English specimens of Water-ouzels (Cinclus aquaticus).]   < *P. Z. S.*, xxxviii, 1870, p. 384.

1871. GURNEY, J. H., JR.   Dipper [Cinclus aquaticus] at Rye and Bridlington. < *Zoologist*, 2d ser., vi, 1871, p. 2848.

1874. COUES, [E.]   The Dipper [Cinclus mexicanus].   < *Am. Sportsman*, 1874, p. 97, fig.

Figure and brief notice,

1878. [FITCH, E. H.]   The Water Ouzel or American Dipper.   (Cinclus mexicanus.) < *The Journ. of Sci.*, (Toledo, Ohio), 2d ser., No. 8, Nov., 1878, fig.

Popular biography of the bird, with a cut.

1878. MUIR, J.   The Humming-Bird [*i. e.*, Cinclus mexicanus!] of the California Water-Falls.   < *Scribner's Monthly Mag.*, vol. xv, Feb., 1878, No. 4, pp. 545–554, figs.

Popular, with pretty but marvellous cuts.

Formicariidæ.

1792. SCHRANK, F. V. PAULA. Beschreibung eines seltnen Vogels aus der Gattung der Würger [Lanius surinamensis]. < *Abh. einer Privatgesell. von Naturf. und Oekon. Oberdeutschl.*, 1ster Theil, 1792, pp. 95, 98, pl. vi.

Not seen—nor do I know that it belongs here. But there are no *Laniidæ* in Surinam, and I presume that some Formicarian is meant. *Cf. Meyer's Zool. Annalen*, i, 1794, pp. 56, 137.

1825. LESSON, R. P. Sur deux nouveaux genres d'oiseaux, Formicivora et Drymophila, . . . ; par W. Swainson. . . . < *Féruss. Bull.*, 2ᵉ sect., vi, 1825, pp. 410–411.

Extr. du *Zool. Journ.*, ii, No. 6, Juin, 1825, pp. 145–154.

1825. SUCH, G. Descriptions of some new Brazilian species of the family Laniadæ [*i. e.*, Formicariidæ]. < *Zool. Journ.*, i, 1825, pp. 554–559, pll. suppl. 5–8.

Thamnophilus swainsonii, p. 556, pl. 5; *T. maculatus*, p. 557, pl. 6; *T. vigorsii*, p. 557, pl. 7, 8; *T. leachii*, p. 558; *T. ruficeps*, *Drymophila variegata*, p. 559.

1825. SWAINSON, W. The characters and descriptions of seven Birds belonging to the genus Thamnophilus. < *Zool. Journ.*, ii, 1825, pp. 84–93.

T. bicolor, p. 86; *T. cinnamomeus*, p. 87; *T. fasciatus*, p. 88; *T. torquatus*, p. 89: *T. naevius*, p. 90, vars. *ambiguus* and *pileatus*, p. 91; *T. ferrugineus*, p. 92.

1825. SWAINSON, W. On two new Genera of Birds, Formicivora and Drymophila, with Descriptions of several species. < *Zool. Journ.*, ii, 1825, pp. 145–154.

F. (p. 145) *maculata*, p. 147; *F. nigricollis*, p. 147; *F. brevicauda*, p. 148; *D.* (p. 149) *leucopus*, p. 150; *D. longipes*, *D. trifasciata*, p. 152; *D. atra*, p. 153.

1826. LESS[ON, R. P.]. Caractères et description de divers Oiseaux du genre Thamnophilus; par W. Swainson. . . . < *Féruss. Bull.*, 2ᵉ sec., vii, 1826, p. 108, 109.

Extrait du *Zool. Journ.*, ii, 1825, No. 5, p. 84–93.

1826. LESS[ON, R. P.]. Description de quelques espèces inédites de la famille des Laniadæ [*i. e.*, Formicariidæ], provenant du Brésil; par George Such. . . . < *Féruss. Bull.*, 2ᵉ sect., vii, 1826, p. 245, 246.

Extrait du *Zool. Journ.*, i, No. 4, Janvier 1825, p. 554–559.

1830. SUCH, G. Neue brasilische Laniaden [*i. e.*, Formicariidæ]. < *Oken's Isis*, Bd. xxiii, 1830, pp. 827–829.

Aus der *Zool. Journ.*, i, Nr. iv, 1825, pp. 554–559, *q. v.*

1830. SWAINSON, W. Zwey neue Vögel, Formicivora und Drymophila. < *Oken's Isis*, Bd. xxiii, 1830, pp. 845, 846.

Aus der *Zool. Journ.*, ii, 1825, pp. 145–154, *q. v.*

1830. SWAINSON, W. Charactere mehrerer Thamnophili. < *Oken's Isis*, Bd. xxiii, 1830, pp. 840, 841.

Aus der *Zool. Journ.*, ii, 1825, pp. 84–93, *q. v.*

1835. MÉNÉTRIÉS, E. Monographie de la Famille des Myiotherinae où sont décrites les espèces qui ornent le musée de l'Académie Impériale des Sciences. < *Mém. de l'Acad. Impér. Sci. St.-Pétersb.*, vi sér., vol. iii, pte. ii, (*Sci. Nat.*, i), 1835, pp. 443–543, pll. 1–15.

Myioturdus rex, p. 462. *M. ochroleucus*, p. 464. *M. marginatus*, p. 465, pl. 1. *M. tetema*, p. 466. *M. umbretta*, p. 468. *M. tinniens*, 469. *M. palikour*, sp. renom., p. 470. *M. lineatus*, p. 471. *Myrmothera nematura*, *M. longipes*, p. 474. *M. thamnophiloides*, p. 475. *M. gularis*, p. 476, pl. 2, f. 2. *M. axillaris*, p. 478. *M. unicolor*, sp. n., p. 480, pl. 2, f. 1. *Formicivora nigricollis*, p. 482, pl. 3, f. 1, 2. *F. duluzæ*, sp. n., p. 484, pl. 5, f. 2. *F. pileata*, p. 485. *F. rufimarginata*, p. 487. *F. ferruginea*, p. 488. *F. loricata*, p. 490, pl. 4, f. 1, 2. *F. strigilata*, p. 493. *F. maculata*, p. 494, pl. 5, f. 1. *F. malura*, p. 496. *F. rufa*, pl. 9, f. 1. *F. caerulescens*, p. 499, pl. 6, f. 1, 2. *F. melanaria*, sp. n., p. 500, pl. 7, f. c. *F. alapi*, p. 502. *F. domicella*, p. 503, pl. 7, f. 1, 2, and *b.* *F. atra*, p. 505. *F. maura*, sp. n., p. 506, pl. 7, f. a. *F. ardesiaca*, p. 507. *F. melanura*, sp. n., p. 508, pl. 8, f. 1, 2. *F. capistrata*, p. 509 (Asiatic!). *F. melanothorax*, p. 510 (Asiatic!). *F. pyrrhogenys*, p. 511 (Asiatic!). *F. epilepidota*, *grammiceps*, p. 512 (Asiatic!). *F. leucophrys*,

1835. MÉNÉTRIÉS, E.—Continned.

p. 513 (Asiatic!). *F. gularis*, p. 514 (Asiatic!). *Leptorhynchus* (g. n., p. 515) *guttatus*, sp. n., p. 516, pl. 10, f. 1. *L. striolatus*, p. 517, pl. 10, f. 2. *Oxypyga* (g. n., p. 519) *scansor*, sp. n., p. 520. pl. 11 [= *Sclerurus* Sw., 1827 — *Anabatidæ*]. *Malacorhynchus* (g. n., p. 522) *cristatellus*, sp. n., p. 523, pl. 12 [= *Merulaxis* Less., 1830 — *Pteroptochidæ*]. *M. rhynolophus*, p. 524. *M. albiventris*, sp. n., p. 525, pl. 13, f. 2. *M. speluncæ*, sp. n., p. 527, pl. 13, f. 1. *M. chilensis*, sp. renom., p. 527. *M. indigoticus*, p. 529. *Conopophaga leucotis*, p. 532. *C. dorsalis*, sp. n., p. 533, pl. 14, f. 2. *C. vulgaris*, sp. renom., p. 534, pl. 14, f. 1. *C. nigrogenys*, p. 536, pl. 15, f. 1. *C. melanogaster*, sp. n., p. 537, pl. 15, f. 2. *C. naevia*, p. 538.

1839. LESSON, R. P. Révision de la famille des Fourmilliers (Myiotherideæ). *< Revue Zoologique*, ii, 1839, pp. 135, 136.

1839. LESSON, R. P. Cadre spécifique des oiseaux de la famille des Myiothères. *< Revue Zoologique*, ii, 1839, pp. 225, 226.

31 genres.

1840. BONAPARTE, C. L. Catalogue d'Oiseau du Mexique et du Pérou. *< Rev. Zool.*, iii, 1840, pp. 19, 20.

This is not the catalogue itself, but merely editorial notice of Bonaparte's lately new genus *Scolopacinus*, P. Z. S., 1837, p, 119.

1840. LAFRESNAYE, [F.] DE. Réponse de M. de La Fresnaye aux réflexions ornithologiques de M. Lesson. *< Revue Zoologique*, iii, 1840, pp. 130–132.

1840. LESSON, R. P. Réflexions ornithologiques. *< Revue Zoologique*, iii, 1840, pp. 97, 98.

Au sujet du genre *Ramphocœnus* Vieill.

1842. LAFRESNAYE, F. DE. [Ueber Myothera longirostris s. caudacuta.] *< Oken's Isis*, Bd. xxxv, 1842, p. 56.

Auszug aus d. *Guér. Mag. Zool.*, Bd. iii, 1833, pl. 10.

N. B. This title is misplaced. It should be on p. 531, *anteà*, (*Anabatidæ*).

1845. HARTLAUB, G. Notes ornithologiques. *< Rev. Zool.*, viii, 1845, pp. 342, 343.

Sur le genre *Myrmornis*, établi par J. Hermann (*Tab. Affin. Anim.*, p. 188), en 1783; il serait donc contemporain avec *Formicarius* Bodd., 1783.

1849. STRICKLAND, H. E. Holocnemis nævius, Gmelin. *< Jard. Contrib. Orn.*, 1849, p. 34, pl. xviii.

1853. LAFRESNAYE, F. DE. Mélanges ornithologiques. *< Rev. et Mag. de Zool.*, v, 1853, pp. 337–340.

§ 1. La diagnostique de cinq espèces du genre *Thamnophilus*,—*TT. nævius, coerulescens, maculatus, atripileus* et *tenuipunctatus* (sp. n., p. 239). § 2. Sur l'oiseau de Paradis émeraude, (*Paradisea apoda*).

1854. SCLATER, P. L. Descriptions of Six New Species of Birds of the Subfamily Formicarinæ. *< P. Z. S.*, xxii, 1854, pp. 253–255, pll. (Aves) lxx–lxxiv.

Myrmeciza leucaspis, p. 253, pl. lxx; *M. margaritata*, p. 253, pl. lxxi; *Hypocnemis melanolæna*, p. 254, pl. lxxii, f. 2; *H. melanosticta*, p. 254, pl. lxxiii; *Formicivora caudata*, p. 254, pl. lxxiv; *Pithys erythrophrys*, p. 255, pl. lxxii, f. 1, spp. nn.

1855. SCLATER, P. L. Characters of six new species of the genus Thamnophilus. *< P. Z. S.*, xxiii, 1855, pp. 18, 19, pll. (Aves) lxxix–lxxxii.

T. transandeanus, T. leucauchen, pl. lxxiv, *T. albinuchalis*, p. 18; *T. melanonotus*, pl. lxxx, *T. nigrocinereus*, pl. lxxxi, *T. cæsius*, pl. lxxxii, p. 19.

1855. SCLATER, P. L. Descriptions of some new Species of Ant-Thrushes (Formicariinæ) from Santa Fé di Bogota. *< P. Z. S.*, xxiii, 1855, pp. 88–90, pll. (Aves) xciv–xcviii.

Grallaria hypoleuca, p. 88; *G. modesta*, pl. xciv; *Chamæza mollissima*, pl. xcv; *Formicivora callinota*, pl. xcvi, p. 89; *Dysithamnus semicinereus*, pl. xcvii; *Pyriglena tyrannina*, pl. xcviii, p. 90.

1855. SCLATER, P. L. A Draft Arrangement of the Genus Thamnophilus. *< Edinburgh New Philos. Journ.*, new series, i, 1855, pp. 226–249.

Systematic, synonymatic, descriptive synopsis of 39 spp., with critical comment, introduced by list of 14 doubtful species which have been referred to the genus. *T. ventralis*, p. 244, sp. n. Other lately new spp. were descr. by the writer, P. Z. S., Jan., 1855, pp. 18, 19, *q. v.*

1855. SCLATER, P. L.   A | Draft Arrangement | of the | Genus Thamnophilus, | (Vieillot.) | By | Philip Lutley Sclater, M. A., F. Z. S. | — | (From the Edinburgh New Philosophical Journal, New Series, April 1855.) | — | Edinburgh : | printed by Neill and Company. | — | MDCCCLV.   1 vol.   8vo.   pp. 26.

Treating 39 spp. with synonymy, description, criticism, &c., after a general consideration of the Bush-shrikes, real or nominal.

1856. SCLATER, P. L.   Descriptions of some new Species of Ant-Thrushes (Formicariinæ) from Santa Fé di Bogota.   < *Ann. Mag. Nat. Hist.*, (2), xviii, 1856, pp. 57–59.

From *P. Z. S.*, June 12, 1855, pp. 88–90, *q. v.*

1856. SCLATER, P. L.   Descriptions of Six New Species of Birds of the Subfamily Formicarinæ.   < *Ann. Mag. Nat. Hist.*, 2d ser., xvii, 1856, pp. 63–65.

From *P. Z. S.*, Nov. 28, 1854, pp. 253–255, *q. v.*

1856. SCLATER, P. L.   Characters of six new Species of the genus Thamnophilus.   < *Ann. Mag. Nat. Hist.*, 2d ser., xvii, 1856, pp. 360–362.

From *P. Z. S.*, Jan. 23, 1855, pp. 18, 19, *q. v.*

1857. SCLATER, P. L.   Characters of some apparently New Species of American Ant-Thrushes.   < *P. Z. S.*, xxv, 1857, pp. 46–48.

Formicarius trivittatus, p. 46; *Conopophaga castaneiceps, Hypocnemis elegans*, p. 47; *Myrmeciza hemimelæna, Formicivora hæmatonota*, p. 48.

1857. SCLATER, P. L.   Descriptions of Twelve New or Little-known Species of the South American Family Formicariidæ.   < *P. Z. S.*, xxv, 1857, pp. 129–133, pl. (Aves) cxxvi.

Grallaria ferrugineipectus, G. loricata, p. 129; *Hypocnemis melanopogon, Formicivora melæna, F. urosticta* (pl., f. 1), p. 130; *F. brevicauda, F. hauxwelli* (pl., f. 2), *F. cinerascens*, p. 131; *Herpsilochmus pectoralis, Dysithamnus xanthopterus*, p. 132; *Thamnophilus melanothorax, T. melanoceps*, p. 133, spp. nn.

1857. SCLATER, P. L.   Characters of some apparently New Species of American Ant-Thrushes.   < *Ann. Mag. Nat. Hist.*, 2d ser., xx, 1857, pp. 376–378.

From *P. Z. S.*, Mar. 10, 1857, pp. 46–48, *q. v.*

1857. SCLATER, P. L.   Descriptions of Twelve New or Little-known Species of the South American Family Formicariidæ.   < *Ann. Mag. Nat. Hist.*, 2d ser., xx, 1857, pp. 462–467.

From *P. Z. S.*, June 23, 1857, pp. 129–133, *q. v.*

1858. SCLATER, P. L.   Descriptions of new species of Ant-wrens (Formicivorinae).   < *Ann. Mag. Nat. Hist.*, 3d ser., ii, 1858, pp. 372–374.

From *P. Z. S.*, Apr. 27, 1858.

1858. SCLATER, P. L.   Synopsis of the American Ant-birds (Formicariidæ).   Part I. Containing the Thamnophilinæ.   < *P. Z. S.*, xxvi, 1858, pp. 202–224, pll. (Aves) cxxxix, cxl; Part II. Containing the Formicivorinæ or Ant-Wrens < *tom. cit.*, pp. 232–254, pll. (Aves) cxli, cxlii; Part III. Containing the Third Subfamily Formicariinæ, or Ant-Thrushes < *tom. cit.*, pp. 272–289, pl. (Aves) cxliii.

Very full synonymy, characters, and distribution of all the species, with list of 22 spp. not recognized by the author. *Thamnophilus amazonicus*, p. 214, pl. cxxxix; *Pyrgiptila*, n. g., p. 220; *Myrmotherula* (g. n.) *multostriata*, p. 234, pl. cxli; *Formicivora erythrocerca*, p. 240, pl. cxlii; *Cercomacra* (n. g., p. 244) *nigricans*, p. 245; *Pyriglena maculicauda*, p. 247; *Hypocnemis schistacea*, p. 252; *Gymnocichla*, n. g., p. 274; *Myrmelastes* (g. n., p. 274) *plumbeus*, p. 274, pl. cxliii; *M. nigerrimus*, p. 275; *Grallaricula*, g. n., p. 283, figg., spp. nn.

1858. SCLATER, P. L.   On Two Species of Ant-birds in the Collection of the Derby Museum, at Liverpool.   < *P. Z. S.*, xxvi, 1858, pp. 540, 541.

Myrmeciza exsul, p. 540, sp. n.   The other is *Dysithamnus olivaceus*.

1859. SCLATER, P. L.   On Two Species of Ant-birds in the Collection of the Derby Museum, at Liverpool.   < *Ann. Mag. Nat. Hist.*, 3d ser., iv, 1859, p. 151.

From *P. Z. S.*, Nov. 23, 1858, pp. 540, 541, *q. v.*

1859. SCLATER, P. L.   On two new species of American Ant-Thrushes.   < *Ann. Mag. Nat. Hist.*, 3d ser., iv, 1859, p. 239.

   From *P. Z. S.*, May 11, 1858, pp. 274, 275—extracted from his full paper there, pp. 272–289, *q. v.*

1860. LAWRENCE, G. N.   Descriptions of New Species of Birds of the Genera Myiarchus and Phlogopsis.   < *Ann. Lyc. Nat. Hist. New York*, vii, 1860, pp. 284–286.

   M. panamensis, p. 284; *Ph. McLeannani*, p. 285.

1865. LAWRENCE, G. N.   Descriptions of New Species of Birds of the Families Tanagridæ, Dendrocolaptidæ, Formicaridæ, Tyrannidæ, and Trochilidæ.   < *Ann. Lyc. Nat. Hist. New York*, viii, 1865, pp. 126–135.

   The Formicarians here described are *Dysithamnus striaticeps*, p. 130; *D. rufiventris*, p. 131; *Myrmotherula albigula*, p. 131; *Myrmeciza stictoptera*, p. 132.

1866. LAWRENCE, G. N.   Descriptions of Six New Species of Birds of the Families Hirundinidæ, Formicaridæ, Tyrannidæ, and Trochilidæ.   < *Ann. Lyc. Nat. Hist. New York*, viii, 1866, pp. 400–405.

   The Formicarian is *Thamnophilus leucopygus*, p. 401, Panama.

1868. SCLATER, P. L.   Descriptions of some New or little-known Species of Formicarians.   < *P. Z. S.*, xxxvi, 1868, pp. 571–575, pl. xliii, woodc.

   Thamnophilus nigriceps, Neoctantes (n. g.) *niger*, p. 571, woodc.; *Hypocnemis hypoxantha* (pl. xliii), *Heterocnemis simplex*, p. 573; *Conopophaga gutturalis*, p. 574, spp. nn., with list of 37 spp. of the family.   In the author's collection 178 species of the family were represented by 381 specimens.

1869. SCLATER, P. L., *and* SALVIN, O.   Descriptions of Six New Species of American Birds of the Families Tanagridæ, Dendrocolaptidæ, Formicariidæ, Tyrannidæ, and Scolopacidæ.   < *P. Z. S.*, xxxvii, 1869, pp. 416–420.

   The Formicarians are *Gymnocichla chiroleuca*, p. 417, and *Grallaria princeps*, p. 418; with a list of six spp. of the latter genus.

1872. CABANIS, J.   [Die Thamnophilen-Gattung Diallectes, nebst 2 neuen Arten (D. semifasciatus, D. granadensis).]   < *J. f. O.*, xx, 1872, pp. 233, 234.

1874. PELZELN, A. v.   [Letter relating to "Pithys rufigula Bodd" (cf. Ibis, 1873, 113); = Phæornis obscura (Gm.).]   < *Ibis*, 3d ser., iv, Oct., 1874, pp. 461, 462.

1877. SCLATER, P. L.   Description of two new Ant-birds of the Genus Grallaria, with a List of the known Species of the Genus.   < *Ibis*, 4th ser., i, Oct., 1877, pp. 437–451, pll. viii, ix.

   Many important additions to the group as given by him in *P. Z. S.*, 1858, pp. 202, 232, 272; see also *P. Z. S.*, 1868, p. 571.   In 1842, Lafresnaye had given 9 spp.: in 1873, in the *Nomenclator Av. Neotrop.*, the author and Salvin gave 20.   Here are 27 spp.; among them *G. haplonota*, p. 442, Venezuela, and *G. flavotineta*, p. 445, pl. ix, Antioquia, spp. nn.   *G. ruficeps* figured on pl. viii.   These are all treated with synonymy, diagnosis, habitat, and comment: they are divided into 4 sections—*Grallariæ squamigeræ, reges, uniformes, flammulatæ*.   The genus is made to cover the following names: *Myioturdus* and *Myiotrichus* Boie, *Calobathris* and *Codonistris* Gloger, (*Handb. u. Hilfsb. d. Nat.*, 1842, pp. 304 and 303), and *Hypsibemon* Cab.

Tyrannidæ.

1817. GEOFFROY SAINT-HILAIRE, ÉT.   Description d'un oiseau du Brésil, sous le nom
de Tyran Roi. < *Mém. du Mus. d'Hist. Nat.*, iii, 1817, pp. 275–278.

  Le Tyran huppé de Cayenne, pl. enlum., 289, devenu aujourd'hui la *Muscivora regia* (Gm.)
  ou *coronata* (Müll.).

1821. MAXIMILIAN, —.   Ueber den Fliegenfänger mit verticalen Schwanz-Federn.
Muscicapa Alector. < *Oken's Isis*, Jahrg. v, 1821, pp. 647–649.

  Alectrurus tricolor, Vieill. Gal. Ois., p. 132.

1824. THUNBERG, C. P.   De Genere Megarhyncho. Præs. C. P. Thunberg, Resp. O. A.
Schærström, Gestr. Hels. Upsaleæ, 1824. 4°. pp. 6.

  Opus ipsud nunquam vidi. Confer quod de hac parum cognita dissertatione edidit F.
  Heine, *J. f. O.*, 1859, pp. 337–346.

1826. SWAINSON, W.   On the Tyrant Shrikes [Tyrannidæ] of America. < *Quart.
Journ. Sci. Lit. and Arts, Roy. Inst.*, xx, 1826, pp. 267–285. (*Féruss. Bull.*, 2ᵉ
sect. xiii, 1828, pp. 433–435. *Isis*, 1833, pp. 935, 936.)

  Not seen.

1828. LESSON, [R. P.]   Sur les Pie-Grièches tyrans [Tyrannidæ] de l'Amérique; par
William Swainson. . . . < *Féruss. Bull.*, 2ᵉ sect., xiii, 1828, pp. 433–435.

  Précis de cette monographie: *Edinb. Journ. Sci.*, No. 40, pp. 267–285.

1833. SWAINSON, [W.]   Swainson über die Tyrannen-Würger in America. < *Oken's
Isis*, Jahrg. 1833, pp. 935, 936.

  Auszug aus d. *Quart. Journ. Sci. Roy. Inst.*, xx, 1826, pp. 267–285.

  Diagnostik von 18 Arten *Tyrannus: TT. sulphuratus, pitangua, audax, crinitus, calcaratus* n.,
  crassirostris n., *vociferans* n., *intrepidus, griseus, crudelis* n., *leucotis* n., *cinereus, rufescens* n.?,
  ambulans n., *nengeta* Marc., *savana, longipennis* n.

1837. LAFRESNAYE, F. DE.   Observations sur le Roitelet omnicolor, et sur le méla-
nisme ou la variété noire chez les Oiseaux de proie. (Mém. Soc. Acad. de Falaise, 1835.) < *L'Institut*, v, No. 217, 1837, pp. 230, 231.—Voir *Isis*, 1837, pp. 842,
843. (*Regulus omnicolor* Vieill. = *R. azaræ* Licht. = *Cyanotis azaræ* Gray.)

  Pas vues moi-même; le titre tiré de la *Bibl.* de Carus et Engelm.—Voir *Isis*, 1837, pp. 842,
  843. (*Regulus omnicolor* Vieill. = *R. azaræ* Licht. = *Cyanotis azaræ* Gray.)

1837. LA FRESNAYE, [F.] DE.   Regulus unicolor [sc. omnicolor] aus Brasilien.
< *Oken's Isis*, Bd. xxx, 1837, pp. 842, 843.

  Auszug aus: *L'Institut*, 1837, Nr. 217.

1843. BAIRD, W. M., *and* BAIRD, S. F.   Descriptions of two Species, supposed to be.
new, of the Genus Tyrannula Swainson, found in Cumberland County, Pennsylvania. < *Proc. Acad. Nat. Sci. Phila.*, i, 1843, pp. 283–286.

  T. flaviventris, p. 283; *T. minima*, p. 284.—This is the first scientific paper ever published
  by S. F. Baird.

1844. BAIRD, W. M., *and* BAIRD, S. F.   Descriptions of two species, supposed to be
new, of the genus Tyrannula, (Swainson,) found in Cumberland County, Penn.
< *Sillim. Am. Journ. Sci.*, xlvi, 1844, pp. 273–276.

  T. flaviventris, T. minima; already described, *Proc. Phila. Acad.*, i, 1843, pp. 283–286.

1844. LAFRESNAYE, F. DE.   Mélanges ornithologiques. [iii.] < *Revue Zoologique*,
vii, 1844, pp. 321–325.

  Sur le *Tyrannus monachus* du docteur Hartlaub.

1844. LAFRESNAYE, F. DE.   Sur une nouvelle espèce d'oiseau de la Nouvelle Grenade
décrite par M. Hartlaub sous le nom de Vireo versicolor, dans la Revue de
1843, P. 289. < *Revue Zoologique*, vii, 1844, pp. 46, 47.

  Considérée comme appartenant au genre *Pachyrhynchus* Sw., *Pachyramphus* Gray. Note
  sur l'adoption par M. Hartlaub du genre *Myiobius* Gray.

1844. [LAFRESNAYE, F. DE.]   G. Conophaga. Vieill. C. ruficeps Lafr. < *Guér. Mag.
de Zool.*, 2ᵉ ser., année 1844, Oiseaux, pp. 1, 2, pl. 51.

  Todirostrum ruficeps, Lafr., *R. Z.*, 1843, p. 291 (*Euscarthmus*).

1846. LAFRESNAYE, F. DE. Essai d'une monographie du genre Todirostre de Lesson (Traité d'ornit.). < *Revue Zoologique*, ix, 1846, pp. 360–365.
13 esp.; *Todirostrum flavifrons, T. plumbeiceps*, 361; *T. furcatum, T. palpebrosum*, p. 362; *T. spiciferum, T. squamæcrista*, p. 363, spp. nn.

1847. GAMBEL, W. [Exhibition of an albino specimen of the Wood Pewee (Muscicapa (*i. e.*, Contopus) virens.)] < *Proc. Acad. Nat. Sci. Phila.*, iii, 1847, p. 278.

1848. LAFRESNAYE, F. DE. Sur les genres Attila, Lesson, et Dasycephala Swainson. < *Revue Zoologique*, xi, 1848, pp. 39–48.
Attila, 6 spp. *A. flammulatus*, p. 47, sp. n.

1849. [JARDINE, W.] Tænioptera alpina, Jardine [n. sp.]. < *Jard. Contrib. Orn.*, 1849, p. 47, pl. xxi.

1850. STRICKLAND, H. E. Elænia linteata, Strickland [sp. n.]. < *Jard. Contrib. Orn.*, 1850, p. 121, pl. lxiii.

1851. LAFRESNAYE, F. DE. Sur deux nouvelles espèces de Tyrans d'Amérique. < *Rev. et Mag. de Zool.*, iii, 1851, pp. 470–476.
Saurophagus rufipennis, p. 471; *Scaphorhynchus mexicanus*, p. 473.

1851. SCLATER, P. L. On two new species of Birds of the genus Tænioptera. < *P. Z. S.*, xix, 1851, pp. 193, 194, pll. (Aves) xli, xlii.
T. erythropygia, pl. xli, *T. striaticollis*, pl. xlii; p. 193.

1852. LAWRENCE, G. N. Description of a new species of Tyrannus [cassini]. < *Ann. Lyc. Nat. Hist. N. Y.*, v, 1852, pp. 39, 40, pl. iii, fig. 2. (Read June 3, 1850.)

1852. LAWRENCE, G. N. Descriptions of New Species of Birds, of the Genera . . . Tyrannula [cinerascens, p. 121] Swainson, . . . < *Ann. Lyc. Nat. Hist. N. Y.*, v, 1852, pp. 121–123. (Read Sept. 8, 1851.)
Other spp. here descr. are a *Toxostoma* and a *Plectrophanes*: title is to be found in full in N. Am. part of this Bibl.

1852. STRICKLAND, H. E. V.—On Two Species of·Todirostrum. < *Jard. Contrib. Orn.*, 1852, pp. 41, 42, pl. lxxxv.
T. granadense Hartl., ?—*T. multicolor*, sp. n.

1853. DES MURS, O. Notice sur les Lanius pitangua et sulphuratus dè Linné. < *Rev. et Mag. de Zool.*, v, 1853, pp. 3–8.
L. pitangua L. (*P. E.* 212) = *Scaphirhynchus pitangua* Strickl. *L. sulphuratus* Gm. (*P. E.* 249 et 296) = *Saurophagus sulphuratus* Sw. *Cf. op. cit.*, p. 63.

1853. KAUP, J. [J.] Uebersicht des Genus Cnipolegus, Boie. < *J. f. O.*, i, 1853, pp. 29, 30.
Behandelt 5 Arten, nebst Synonymik und Artkennzeichen. Cf. *J. f. O.*, 1859, pp. 329–337.

1853. LAFRESNAYE, F. DE. [Note sur l'article de M. Des Murs (R. M. Z., Jan., 1853, p. 3,) sur les Lanius pitangua et sulphuratus de Linné.] < *Rev. et Mag. de Zool.*, v, 1853, pp. 63, 64.

1853. SCLATER, P. L. On two new species of Birds of the genus Tænioptera. < *Ann. Mag. Nat. Hist.*, 2d ser., xii, 1853, pp. 213, 214.
From *P. Z. S.*, June 10, 1851, pp. 193, 194.

1855. SCLATER, P. L. On a New Species of the Genus Todirostrum of Lesson [T. nigriceps.] < *P. Z. S.*, xxiii, 1855, pp. 66, 67, pl. (Aves) lxxxiv.
With synopsis of 5 other species. The second figure of the plate is *T. spiciferum*.

1856. SCLATER, P. L. On a New Species of the Genus Todirostrum of Lesson. < *Ann. Mag. Nat. Hist.*, 2d ser., xvii, 1856, p. 428.
From *P. Z. S.*, March 27, 1855, pp. 66, 67.

1857. SCLATER, P. L. On Three New Species of the genus Todirostrum. < *P. Z. S.*, xxv, 1857, pp. 82–84, pl. (Aves) cxxv.
Todirostrum calopterum, p. 82; *T. capitale, T. exile*, p. 83. List of 16 other spp. known to him, and of 6 more which rest on other good authority.

1857. SCLATER, P. L. On Three New Species of the genus Todirostrum. < *Ann. Mag. Nat. Hist.*, 2d ser., xx, 1857, pp. 382, 383.
From *P. Z. S.*, May 12, 1857, pp. 82–84.

1857. SCLATER, P. L.   Description of a new species of Pachyrhamphus [albo-griseus].
    < *Ann. Mag. Nat. Hist.*, 2d ser., xx, 1857, p. 398.
    From *P. Z. S.*, April 28, 1857, p. 78.—N. B. This title should be under *Cotingidæ*, p. 590.

1857. SCLATER, P. L.   On a [lately] new Genus of Birds from Mexico.   < *Ann. Mag.
    Nat. Hist.*, 2d ser., xx, 1857, p. 470.
    From *P. Z. S.*, July 14, 1857, p. 203; the bird is *Camptostoma imberbe*, the description of
    which is extracted to form a special paper, from a paper of wider scope, occupying pp. 201–
    207 of the *P. Z. S.*

1858. BRYANT, H.   [Remarks on the Habits of Muscicapa (*i. e.*, Empidonax) acadica
    and M. flaviventris.]   < *Proc. Boston Soc. Nat. Hist.*, vi, 1858, p. 430.

1858. SCLATER, P. L.   On a new species of Platyrhynchus [Coronatus] from the Rio
    Napo, in the Republic of Ecuador.   < *Ann. Mag. Nat. Hist.*, 3d ser., ii, 1858,
    p. 316.
    From *P. Z. S.*, Jan. 26, 1858, p. 71.

1859. HEINE, F.   Eine wenig bekannte Dissertation Thunberg's ,, De genere Megar-
    hyncho.''   < *J. f. O.*, vii, 1859, pp. 237–346.
    Very complete commentary.   The chars. of Thunberg's 8 spp. are reproduced, followed by
    a bibliography of the genus and of *M. pitanguá*, *M. chrysocephalus* and *M. mexicanus*.

1859. HEINE, F.   Das Genus Cnipolegus Boie.   < *J. f. O.*, vii, 1859, pp. 329–337.
    Full synopsis of 6 spp.   *C. anthracinus*, "Cab." p. 334, sp. n.   Cf. *J. f. O.*, 1853, pp. 29, 30.

1859. SCLATER, P. L.   Descriptions of New Species of the American family Tyran-
    nidæ.   < *P. Z. S.*, xxvii, 1859, pp. 40–46.
    Attila citriniventris, p. 40, with synopsis of 7 spp. of the genus; *Myiodynastes luteiventris*
    Bp., *Myiod. nobilis*, p. 42, with list of 6 spp. of *Myiodynastes*; *Contopus mesoleucus*, *C. sordid-
    ulus*, p. 43, with list of 6 spp. of *Contopus*; *Mitrephorus phæocercus*, p. 44; *Pyrocephalus mexi-
    canus*, p. 45; *Elainia placens*, *Mionectes assimilis*, p. 46.

1859. SCLATER, P. L.   A List of the Tyrant-birds [Tyrannidæ] of Mexico, with de-
    scription of some new species.   < *Ibis*, i, 1859, pp. 436–445, pl. xiv.
    Classification and position of the group; synonymatic and geographical synopsis of 43 spp.
    Empidonax brachytarsus, p. 441; *Cyclorhynchus cinereiceps*, p. 443; *Todirostrum schistacei-
    ceps*, spp. nn.   Pl. represents *Camptostoma imberbe* (fig. 1), and *Mitrephorus phæocercus* (fig. 2).

1860. SCLATER, P. L.   Description of a New Tyrant-bird of the genus Elainea [E.
    riisii] from the Island of Saint Thomas, West Indies.   < *P. Z. S.*, xxviii, 1860,
    pp. 313, 314.

1860. SCLATER, P. L.   Description of a New Tyrant-bird of the genus Elainea [E.
    riisii], from the Island of Saint Thomas, West Indies.   < *Ann. Mag. Nat. Hist.*,
    3d ser., vi, 1860, pp. 439, 440.
    From *P. Z. S.*, June 12, 1860, pp. 313, 314.

1860. SCLATER, P. L.   Descriptions of New Species of the American Family Tyran·
    nidæ.   < *Ann. Mag. Nat. Hist.*, 3d ser., v, 1860, pp. 422–424.
    From *P. Z. S.*, Jan. 25, 1859, pp. 40–46, *q. v.*

1861. HEINE, F.   Ueber Myiozetetes icterophrys n. sp.   < *J. f. O.*, ix, 1861, pp. 197, 198.

1861. PHILIPPI, [R. A.], *and* LANDBE[C]K, [L.]   [Noticias sobre cuatro especies del
    jénero Pepoaza d'Orb. (Agriornis Gould), i sobre el modo de vivir de las dos
    especies chilenas de Dasycephala.]   < *Anal. Univ. Chile*, xix, Nov., 1861, pp.
    —-652.
    The above is a putting together of two subheads of a paper of wider scope, describing vari-
    ous new Peruvian birds, among them *Dasycephala albicauda*, p 618.   The title is introduced
    here on account of its special bearing on *Tyrannidæ*.

1861. SCLATER, P. L.   Index generis Elaineæ ex familia Tyrannidarum additis nova-
    rum specierum diagnosibus.   < *P. Z. S.*, xxix, 1861, pp. 406–408, pl. xli.
    Index Elaineæ generis 17 specierun, adjectis synonymis, locis.   *E. semipagana*, p. 406; *E.
    pallatangæ* (tab. lxi); *E. subplacens*, p. 407; *E. implacens*, p. 408, spp. nn.

1862. SCLATER, P. L.   On Two New Species of Tyrant-birds from Ecuador.   < *P. Z.
    S.*, xxx, 1862, p. 113.
    Ochthoëca citrinifrons, *Mecocerculus gratiosus*.

1862. SCLATER, P. L.   On Two New Species of Tyrant-birds from Ecuador.   < *Ann. Mag. Nat. Hist.*, 3d ser., x, 1862, p. 313.

From *P. Z. S.*, Mar. 25, 1862, p. 113, *q. v.*

1864. PHILIPPI, R. A., *and* LANDBECK, L.   De las Muscisaxicolas Sud-Americanas. < *Anal. Univ. Chile*, xxv, Set. de 1864, pp. 418-439.

This is a subhead of an article of more extended scope. It appears in German in *Arch. f. Naturg.*, 1865, Bd. i, pp. 74-106, *q. v.* The authors treat of 15 spp. of the genus, among which *M. cinerea*, p. 422; *M. rubricapilla*, p. 429; *M. flavivertex*, p. 434; and *M. nigricans*, p. 436, are described as new. *Cf.* Cab., *J. f. O.*, 1860, p. 249, note; Scl., *Ibis*, 1865, p. 59.

1865. BRYANT, H.   [Remarks on the occurrence of Tyrannus verticalis at "Plympton," Me. (*i. e.*, Pembroke, Me.), in October.]   < *Proc. Boston Soc. Nat. Hist.*, x, 1865, p. 96.

1865. LAWRENCE, G. N.   Descriptions of new species of Birds of the Families Paridæ, Vireonidæ, Tyrannidæ, and Trochilidæ, with a note on Myiarchus Panamensis. < *Proc. Acad. Nat. Sci. Phila.*, xvii, 1865, pp. 37-39.

Myiarchus venezuelensis, p. 38.

1865. LAWRENCE, G. N.   Descriptions of New Species of Birds of the Families Tanagridæ, Dendrocolaptidæ, Formicaridæ, Tyrannidæ, and Trochilidæ.   < *Ann. Lyc. Nat. Hist. New York*, viii, 1865, pp. 126-135.

The Tyrannines here described are *Empidonax flavescens*, p. 133, and *Contopus lugubris*, p. 134.

1865. PHILIPPI, R. A., *and* LANDBECK, L.   Monographie der südamerikanischen Muscisaxicolinen.   < *Arch. f. Naturg.*, 1865, Bd. i, pp. 74-106.

This is a subtitle of an article of more extended scope, which originally appeared in Spanish in *Anales Univ. Chile*, xxv, 1864, pp. 418-439, *q. v.* The 15 species treated are *MM. albifrons, cinerea, maculirostris, mentalis, rubricapilla, rufiventris, flavivertex, nigrifrons, striaticeps, frontalis, capistrata, brunnea, flavinucha, albilora, albimentum.*

Among them are four species from the Cordilleras of Chili not described by previous authors, namely: *M. cinerea*, p. 80; *M. rubricapilla*, p. 90; *M. flavivertex*, p. 98; and *M. nigrifrons*, p. 101.—Cf. *Ibis*, 1866, pp. 56-59, and *Zool. Rec.* for 1865, pp. 106, 107.

1866. BURMEISTER, H.   [Extract from a letter relating to certain Tyrannidæ of Buenos Ayres.]   < *P. Z. S.*, xxxiv, 1866, p. 2.

List of ten or twelve species.

1866. LAWRENCE, G. N.   Descriptions of Six New Species of Birds of the Families Hirundinidæ, Formicaridæ, Tyrannidæ and Trochilidæ.   < *Ann. Lyc. Nat. Hist. New York*, viii, 1866, pp. 400-405.

The Tyrant is *Empidonax pectoralis*, p. 402, Panama.

1866. SCLATER, P. L.   Note on the Species of the genus Muscisaxicola.   < *Ibis*, 2d ser., ii, 1866, pp. 56-59.

With special reference to those described by Philippi and Landbeck (*Arch. Naturg.*, 1865, pp. 74-109), making some important criticisms, and giving the diagnoses of 9 species of the genus.

1868. CABANIS, J.   Neue Arten der südamerikanischen Gattung Empidochanes, im Berliner Museum.   < *J. f. O.*, xvi, 1868, pp. 194-196.

E. euleri, p. 195; *E. altirostris, E. argentinus*, p. 196.

1869. HUDSON, W. H.   [Extract from a Letter respecting Lichenops perspicillatus.]   < *P. Z. S.*, xxxvii, 1869, pp. 432, 433.

1869. RIDGWAY, R.   A True Story of a Pet Bird.   < *Am. Nat.*, iii, 1869, pp. 309-312.

Account of the habits of *Tyrannus verticalis* in semi-domestication.

1869. SCLATER, P. L.   Note on the species of the Genus Hirundinea, belonging to the family Tyrannidæ.   < *Ibis*, 2d ser., v, 1869, pp. 195-198, pl. v.

Synonymatic, diagnostic, critical; 3 spp. are discriminated: *H. ferruginea* (Gm.), *H. bellicosa* (V.) and *H. rupestris* (Max.). Pl. v, fig. 1, *H. bellicosa;* fig. 2, *H. ferruginea;* fig. 3, *H. rupestris.*

1869. SCLATER, P. L., *and* SALVIN, O.   Descriptions of Six New Species of American Birds of the Families Tanagridæ, Dendrocolaptidæ, Formicariidæ, Tyrannidæ and Scolopacidæ.   < *P. Z. S.*, xxxvii, 1869, pp. 416-420.

The new Tyrant is *Contopus ochraceus*, p. 419.

1870. SCLATER, P. L. Descriptions of three apparently new Species of Tyrant-birds of the Genus Elainea, with Remarks on other known Species. < *P. Z. S.*, xxxviii, 1870, pp. 831–835, woodcc.

Elainea gigas, p. 831, fig. 1, p. 832; *E. fallax*, p. 832, fig. 2, p. 833; *E. pudica*, p. 833, fig. 3, p. 834. With synopsis of 16 spp. of the genus.

1871. LAWRENCE, G. N. Description of New Species of Birds of the Families Troglo- dytidæ and Tyrannidæ. ' < *Proc. Acad. Nat. Sci. Phila.*, 1871, pp. 233–236.

The Tyrannines here described are: *Myiozetetes grandis*, p. 234, Tumbes, Peru; *Empidonax atrirostris*, p. 234, Venezuela?; and *Myiarchus yucatanensis*, p. 235, Yucatan (= *M. mexicanus* Lawr., *Ann. Lyc. N. Y.*, ix, p. 202, nec Kaup).

1871. SCLATER, P. L. Notes on the Types of Tyrannula mexicana of Kaup and Tyran- nula barbirostris of Swainson. < *P. Z. S.*, xxxix, 1871, pp. 84, 85.

1. *T. mexicana*, Kaup, *P. Z. S.*, 1851, 51 = *Myiarchus cooperi* Bd., *B. N. A.*, 1858; *M. mexi- canus* Bd. = *M. cinerascens* Lawr.—2. *Tyrannula barbirostris* Sw., *Phil. Mag.*, 1827, p. 367, is West Indian, not Mexican, and = *Blacicus tristis* of Gosse.

1871. SCLATER, P. L. Remarks on the Species of the Genera Myiozetetes and Cono- pias, belonging to the family Tyrannidæ. < *P. Z. S.*, xxxix, 1871, pp. 751–756.

8 spp. of *Myiozetetes*, 3 of *Conopias*, the former quite fully treated.

1872. ABBOTT, C. C. Occurrence of the Scissor-tail Flycatcher [Milvulus forficatus] in New Jersey. < *Am. Nat.*, vi, 1872, p. 367.

1872. BREWER, T. M. [Occurrence of Empidonax pusillus in Wisconsin.] < *Proc. Boston Soc. Nat. Hist.*, xiv, 1872, pp. 303, 304.

1872. COUES, E. Occurrence of Couch's Flycatcher [Tyrannus melancholicus couchi] in the United States. < *Am. Nat.*, vi, 1872, p. 493.

1872. COUES, E. Studies of the Tyrannidæ.—Part I. Revision of the Species of Myi- archus. < *Proc. Acad. Nat. Sci. Phila.*, xxiv, 1872, pp. 56–81.

No more published.—Monographic; giving synonymy and characters of 9 spp. and 6 subspp., with much criticism. The author enters at some length into the general characters of the group, laying down several formal propositions applicable to the case, as well as the arbitrary rules which may govern one in the distinguishing between species, varieties, and synonyms.

"With *Myiarchus* are united *Kaupornis, Blacicus,* and *Myionax.* Five supposed species are unknown to the author, who gives the history and synonymy of the remaining nine:— 1. *M. validus*; 2. *M. crinitus*, with three varieties, *a. crinitus*, *β. irritabilis* = *erythrocercus*, Scl. & Salv. (*Zool. Rec.*, iii, p. 83), *mexicanus* and *yucatanensis*, Lawr., *γ. cooperi* (*Zool. Rec.*, viii, p. 58); 3. *M. cinerascens*; 4. *M. tyrannulus* = *panamensis* and *venezuelensis*, Lawr. (*Zool. Rec.*, ii, p. 107); 5. *M. phæocephalus*; 6. *M. lawrencii* = *rufimarginatus*, and *nigricapillus*, Cab.; 7. *M. nigriceps*; 8. *M. stolidus*, with three varieties, *a. stolidus* = *dominicensis*, Bryant, *β. phœbe* = *lucaysiensis* and *bahamensis*, Bryant, *γ. antillarum*; 9. *M. tristis.*" (From *Zool. Rec.*)

1872. HUDSON, W. H. Notes on the Habits of the Churinche (Pyrocephalus rubineus). < *P. Z. S.*, Nov. 5, 1872, pp. 808–810.

An interesting biography.

1872. LOCKWOOD, S. The Kingbird [Tyrannus carolinensis] and Bee Martin. < *Am. Nat.*, vi, 1872, pp. 769, 770.

Occupation by *Tyrannus carolinensis* of a nest of *Progne subis.*

1872. SCLATER, P. L. [Exhibition of a Nest of the Tijereta (Milvulus tyrannus), con- taining eggs of Molothrus bonariensis.] < *P. Z. S.*, 1872, pp. 862, 863.

1873. A[LLEN], J. A. Revision of the American or Tyrant Flycatchers. < *Am. Nat.*, vii, 1873, pp. 35–38.

Extended review of E. Coues's "Studies of the Tyrannidæ, Part I" (*Proc. Acad. Nat. Sci. Phila.*, 1872, pp. 56–81).

1873. BENDIRE, C. Nest, Eggs and Breeding Habits of the Vermilion Flycatcher (Py- rocephalus rubineus var. Mexicanus). < *Am. Nat.*, vii, 1873, pp. 170, 171.

1873. GENTRY, T. G. Observations on Nests of Sayornis fuscus. < *Proc. Acad. Nat Sci. Phila.*, xxv, 1873, pp. 292–294.

An extended account of deviations from the usual style of nest-building.

1873. HERSEY, J. L.   Bees and Kingbirds [Tyrannus carolinensis]. < Am. Nat., vii, 1873, p. 434.

Note from the *American Bee Journal*, to the effect that *Tyrannus carolinensis* eats bees.

1873. HERSEY, J. L.   Bees and King Birds [Tyrannus carolinensis]. < Am. Sportsman, ii, 1873, p. 166; see also *ibid.*, iii, 1873, p. 51.

From *American Bee Journal ; Tyrannus carolinensis* eats the drone hive-bees.

1873. MERRIAM, C. H.   The Olive-sided Flycatcher [Contopus borealis, in New York]. < Am. Nat., vii, 1873, p. 750.

Notes on habits; continued, *op. cit.*, viii, 1874, p. 309.

1873. SCLATER, P. L.   Note on the Genus Ornithion of Hartlaub. < P. Z. S., 1873, pp. 576-578.

Synopsis of 4 spp. of this genus, with which *Camptostoma* Scl. and *Myiopatis* Cab. are considered synonymous. See especially Lawrence, *Ibis*, 1876, p. 497.

1874. BREWER, T. M.   The Olive-sided Fly Catcher [Contopus borealis]. < Am. Sportsman, iv, 1874, p. 198.

Denies the allegation that it is a "rare" species in New England.

1874. CABOT, J. E.   The Olive-sided Flycatcher [Contopus borealis]. < Am. Nat., viii, 1874, p. 240.

Memorandum of the original discovery of the speceis in Massachusetts.

1874. DEANE, R.   Olive-sided Flycatcher [Contopus borealis]. < Am. Nat., viii, 1874, pp. 308-309.

Field-notes.

1874. EDITORIAL.   [Alleged occurrence of Tyrannus dominicensis on Long Island.] < Forest and Stream, ii, July 23, 1874, p. 373.

1874. HALL, F. W.   The Mycharchus [*i. e.*, Myiarchus] crinitus. < Forest and Stream, iii, Dec. 3, 1874, p. 261.

1874. LAWRENCE, G. N.   Descriptions of Two New Species of Birds of the Families Tanagridæ and Tyrannidæ. < Ann. Lyc. Nat. Hist. N. Y., xi, July, 1874, pp. 70-72.

The Tyrannine here described is *Myiarchus flammulatus*, p. 71, from Tehuantepec, Mexico.

1874. MERRIAM, C. H.   The Olive-sided Flycatcher [Contopus borealis]. < Am. Nat., viii, 1874, p. 309.

Further (*op. cit.*, vii, 1873, 750) field-notes.

1874. MORRIS, R. T.   The Crested Fly-catcher [Myiarchus crinitus]. < Forest and Stream, ii, May 14, 1874, p. 213.

1875. BAIRD, S. F.   [Note of the occurrence of Tyrannus verticalis in Maryland, near Washington, D. C.] < Ann. Rep. Smithson. Inst. for 1874, 1875, p. 32.

The original notice of the occurrence. The capture was made by P. L. Jouy; see his Catalogue of the Birds of the District of Columbia, in *Field and Forest*, ii, No. 9, 1877, pp. 154-156, and No. 10, 1877, pp. 178-181.

1876. "BRIDGEPORT."   Cats vs. Birds. < Rod and Gun, vii, Feb. 19, 1876, p. 329.

King-birds whipping a cat. Compare p. 294.

1876. HENSHAW, H. W.   On two Empidonaces, traillii and acadicus. < Bull. Nutt Ornith. Club, i, No. 1, Apr., 1876, pp. 14-17.

With special reference to differences in their geographical distribution, nests, and eggs. The subject is well handled, and the author's remarks have been established by later experiences.

S. F. Baird was the first to fix the species of our smaller Flycatchers with any satisfactory degree of precision. This he did in 1858; since which time, no material modification has been established among the N. Am. species of *Empidonax*. The history, however, of the habits of these birds, especially of their geographical distribution, nesting, and eggs, has been much involved. Little reliance can be placed on the accounts given by Wilson, Nuttall and Audubon; and even since 1858, there have been several mistakes made in the writings of Allen, Brewer and Coues, with reference to the distribution of *acadicus* in New England, and to the nests and eggs of all four of the eastern species. Late papers in the *Nuttall Bulletin*, however, have at length cleared up the confusion; and no one should presume to write on the habits of birds of this genus without consulting the present paper by Henshaw, and the several others in the *Nuttall Bulletin* by Purdie, Osborne, Batchelder and Coues, cited beyond in this bibliography.

1876. LAWRENCE, G. N.   Note on Muscipeta incanescens, Wied.   < *Ibis*, 3d ser., vi, Oct., 1876, pp. 497, 498.
>   Wied's type, now in Amer. Mus. Nat. Hist. New York, examined and found to be very different from *Ornithion imberbe*, which Sclater (*P. Z. S.*, 1873, p. 576) had united with it.

1876. PURDIE, H. A.   The Nest and Eggs of Traill's flycatcher [Empidonax trailli], as observed in Maine.   < *Bull. Nutt. Ornith. Club*, i, No. 3, Sept., 1876, pp. 75, 76

1877. "G. G. H., JR."   The great crested flycatcher.   Myiarchus crinitus—Calamis [*i. e.*, Cabanis].   < *Forest and Stream*, ix, Aug. 23, 1877, p. 44.
>   Observations on nidification.

1877. "GUYON" [   ].   Migration of Kingbirds [Tyrannus carolinensis].   < *Forest and Stream*, viii, May 17, 1877, p. 224.

1877. JUDSON, E. Z. C.   A Plea for the King Bird [Tyrannus carolinensis].   < *Forest and Stream*, ix, Aug. 9, 1877, p. 5.
>   Protection afforded to farm-yard by *Tyrannus carolinensis* through its enmity to hawks.

1877. [SCLATER, P. L., *and* SALVIN, O.]   Lawrence on a new Pitangus [gabbii].   < *Ibis*, 4th ser., i, Oct., 1877, p. 481.
>   Notice of the paper in *Am. Lyc. N. Y.*, xi, Nov., 1876, pp. 288-290.

1877. WHITE, W. H.   King Birds [Tyrannus carolinensis] and Bees.   < *Forest and Stream*, ix, Oct. 4, 1877, p. 186.
>   Kingbirds insatiable devourers of honey-bees.

1878. ALLEN, J. A.   Late Capture of the Yellow-bellied Flycatcher [Empidonax flaviventris] in Massachusetts.   < *Bull. Nutt. Ornith. Club*, iii, No. 2, Apr., 1878, pp. 101, 102.

1878. ANON.   The fork-tailed fly-catcher.   Milvulus Tyrannus (L.) Bp.   < *Familiar Science and Fanciers' Journ.*, i (new series), Feb., 1878, p. 30.   Illustrated.

1878. [FITCH, E. H.]   The Wood Pewee [Contopus virens].   < *The Journ. of Sci.* (Toledo, Ohio), 2d ser., i, No. 2, May, 1878; cut.
>   Popular biography, with a figure.

1878. INGERSOLL, E.   The Linnean Society.   < *The Country*, i, Apr., 20, 1878, p. 371, See vol. ii, p. 9.
>   Secretary's report of meeting; many facts concerning nidification of *Tyrannidæ*.

1878. INGERSOLL, E.   Linnean Society.   < *The Country*, ii, Apr. 27, 1878, p. 9.
>   Report of meeting, and letter from H. A. Purdie concerning breeding of *Empidonax trailli*.

1878. [INGERSOLL, E.]   Linnean Society.   < *Forest and Stream*, x, Apr. 25, 1878, p. 216.   See p. 255.
>   Report of proceedings, and letter from H. A. Purdie in regard to breeding of *Empidonax trailli*.

1878. MERRILL, J. C.   The Occurrence of Myiarchus crinitus var. erythrocercus, Sclat., at Fort Brown, Texas.   < *Bull. Nutt. Ornith. Club*, iii, No. 2, Apr., 1878, p. 99, 100.
>   With an editorial note respecting priority of the discovery; and a note by T. M. Brewer on the eggs of the same bird.

1878. NICHOLAS, G. L.   Perseverance of Pewees [(Sayornis fuscus) in nest-building].   < *Forest and Stream*, xi, Dec. 12, 1878, p. 379.
>   Nest of a pair of *Sayornis fuscus* rebuilt seven times in the same place in one season.

1878. OSBORNE, S. D.   The Nesting of the Yellow-bellied Flycatcher (Empidonax flaviventris).   < *Bull. Nutt. Ornith. Club*, iii, No. 4, Oct., 1878, pp. 187, 188.
>   Confirming H. A. Purdie's description, *op. tom. cit.*, pp. 166-168, both as to situation and structure of the nest, and as to the eggs being spotted.

1878. PECKHAM, B. J.   Nesting of Contopus virens.   < *The Oölogist*, iv, No. 5, July, 1878, p. 34.

1878. PURDIE, H. A.   Traill's Flycatcher [Empidonax trailli].   < *Forest and Stream*, x, May 9, 1878, p. 255.   See p. 216.

1878. PURDIE, H. A. The Nest and Eggs of the Yellow-bellied Flycatcher (Empidonax flaviventris). < *Bull. Nutt. Ornith. Club*, iii, No. 4, Oct., 1878, pp. 166–168.

  Important, being a careful description of an authentic nest and eggs. Much error and uncertainty had prevailed on this subject, even among the leading writers. Both Brewer and Coues had stated the eggs to be white, whereas they are well spotted.

1878. SCLATER, [P. L.] [Remarks on Exhibition of the type of Dicrurus marginatus Blyth, Ibis, 1865, p. 46, = Muscipipra vetula Licht.] < *P. Z. S.*, Mar. 19, 1878, p. 339.

1879. A[LLEN], J. A. Brewer on the Nests and Eggs of Empidonaces. < *Bull. Nutt. Ornith. Club*, iv, No. 4, Oct., 1879, p. 232.

  Notice of the paper in *Proc. Nat. Mus.*, ii, Apr., 1879, pp. 1–10.

1879. ANON. Nest and Eggs of Empidonax trailii. < *The Oölogist*, iv, No. 11, June, 1879, pp, 85, 86.

1879. BATCHELDER, C. F. Nesting of the Yellow-bellied Flycatcher (Empidonax flaviventris. < *Bull. Nutt. Ornith. Club*, iv, No. 4, Oct., 1879, pp. 241, 242.

  Two cases detailed, with full description of the nests and eggs.

1879. BREWER, T. M. Notes on the Nests and Eggs of the eight North American Species of Empidonaces. < *Proc. U. S. Nat. Mus.*, ii, Apr. 29, 1879, pp. 1–10.

  Measurements of all the specimens in the National Museum, in the Coll. T. M. B., and a few others, with descriptions of these, and of various nests. Eggs of *E. minimus, obscurus,* and *hammondi* normally white, unmarked; of *E. flaviventris* normally spotted, sometimes unmarked; of *E. trailli, acadicus, pusillus,* and *difficilis* normally strongly marked.

1879. [COUES, E.] The Nest of Empidonax minimus. < *Temperance Vidette* (newspaper of Terrell, Texas), Nov. 1, 1879.

  Quoted from his *Birds of the Northwest,* 1874, p. 255.

1879. CUNNINGHAM, S. Nest of the Great-crested Flycatcher [Myiarchus crinitus]. < *The Oölogist,* iv, No. 8, Mar., 1879, p. 59.

1879. [GRINNELL, G. B.] Nests and Eggs of the Genus Empidonax. < *Forest and Stream,* xii, July 10, 1879, p. 444.

  Notice of Dr. T. M. Brewer's paper on The Nests and Eggs of the Eight North American Species of *Empidonaces* in *Pr. U. S. Nat. Mus.*, ii, 1879, pp. 1–10.

1879. HAYWARD, R. A Spotted Egg of Empidonax minimus. < *Bull. Nutt. Ornith. Club,* iv, No. 2, Apr., 1879, p. 124.

  Identification of the specimen attested by W. Brewster.

1879. OSBORNE, S. D. Another Nest of the Yellow-bellied Flycatcher (Empidonax flaviventris). < *Bull. Nutt. Ornith. Club,* iv, No. 4, Oct., 1879, pp. 240, 241.

1879. RIDGWAY, R. Descriptions of New Species and Races of American Birds, including a Synopsis of the Genus Tyrannus, Cuvier. < *Proc. U. S. Nat. Mus.*, i, 1878 (pub. May, 1879), pp. 466–486.

  I. The greater part of the paper is occupied with this excellent monography of *Tyrannus,* in which the following species are recognized and fully treated, with synonymy, diagnosis, habitat, and criticism: *TT. magnirostris, rostratus, dominicensis, carolinensis, crassirostris, melancholicus* (β. *couchi,* γ. *satrapa*), *albigularis, apolites, niveigularis, verticalis, vociferans, luggeri* (n. sp., p. 481), and *aurantio-atrocristatus.*—II. *Lichenops perspicillatus,* β. *andinus,* p. 483; *Dacnis pulcherrima,* β. *aureinucha,* p. 484; *Parus rufescens,* β. *neglectus,* p. 485, subspp. nn.

Ampelidæ.

[NOTE.—Nearly all my titles on the genus *Ampelis* were given in *B. Col. Vall.*, i, 1878, pp. 453–459; and are not here reproduced. The family, as constituted by Gray, includes *Myiadestes* and *Phainopepla*.]

1834. HEARNE, J. [Letter on various Zoological Subjects relating to the Island of Hayti.] < *P. Z. S.*, ii, 1834, p. 25.
Note of a bird called the 'Musicien' (*Myiadestes elizabeth*).

1835. TREVELYAN, W. C. The Bohemian Waxwing, or Chatterer [Ampelis garrulus], living in a State of Domestication in England. < *Loudon's Mag. Nat. Hist.*, viii, 1835, pp. 511, 512.

1835. TURNER, H. The Bohemian Waxwing, or Chatterer [Ampelis garrulus], . . . < *Loudon's Mag. Nat. Hist.*, viii, 1835, p. 511.

1835. ANON. The Bohemian Waxwing, or Chatterer [Ampelis garrulus] (p. 511.); the Appendages to its Wings vary in Number in different Individuals: an instance of this. < *Loudon's Mag. Nat. Hist.*, viii, 1835, p. 615.
From *The Carlisle Journal*, January, 1835.

1840. CLARKE, C. [Notes, contained in a letter, relating to a Bird called in Cuba 'The Musician'.] < *P. Z. S.*, viii, 1840, pp. 153, 154.

1845. LAFRESNAYE, F. DE. Sur le Ptilogonys nitens de Swainson, Hypotyme luisant, nob. < *Revue Zoologique*, viii, 1845, pp. 451, 452.
This note forms a part of one of the instalments of the "Mélanges Ornithologiques".

1858. SCLATER, P. L. Note on the Genus Cichlopsis of Cabanis. < *P. Z. S.*, xxvi, 1858, pp. 541–543.
Rectification of synonymy of *C. leucogonys.*—*Phainopepla*, g. n., p. 543.

1861. HEIBERG, P. V. Sidensvandsen [Ampelis garrulus]. < *Tidssk. Pop. Fremst. af Naturv.*, 2en række, iii, 1861, pp. 297–301.

1866. "THE OLD BUSHMAN." The Waxwing [Ampelis garrulus], the Pine Grosbeak. and the Crossbills. < *The Intellectual Observer*, ix, 1866, pp. 345–352.
Interesting field-notes on the first named of these species.

1870. ALLEN, J. A. „Fugle efterstræbte af Frøer." < *Tiddsk. for Pop. Fremst. Naturv.* 4e ser., ii, 1870, p. 80.
Proc. Bost. Soc. Nat. Hist., 1868, p. —.

1876. [INGERSOLL, E.] The Bohemian Waxwing [Ampelis garrulus]. < *Forest and Stream*, vi, Apr. 13, 1876, p. 148.
Observations in Minnesota of P. L. Hatch and Thos. S. Roberts.

1877. LAMB, W. F. Nest and Eggs of Townsend's Flycatcher [Myiadestes townsendi]. < *Bull. Nutt. Ornith. Club*, ii, No. 3, July, 1877, p. 77, 78.

1877. ROWLEY, G. D. Phainoptila melanoxantha, Salvin. *Rowl. Orn. Misc.*, ii, pt. x, Oct., 1877, pp. 439–442, pl. lxxix.
This lately-described species is figured, with copy of the original article, and additional matter from A. Boucard.

1877. SALVIN, O. Description of a New Genus and Species of Oscines from Costa Rica [Phainoptila melanoxantha]. < *P. Z. S.*, Apr. 17, 1877, p. 367.
Provisionally placed near *Ptilogonys*, in *Ampelidæ*.

Cotingidæ.

1769. Vosmaer, A. Description | d'une belle | Grive d'Amerique [Cotinga cayana], | nommée | Quereiva, | Qui vient du | Bresil, | Et se conserve dans le Cabinet de | son altesse Sérénissime | Monseigneur le Prince d'Orange et de Nassau, | Stadhouder He're'ditaire, Gouverneur, Capi- | taine Ge'ne'ral et Amiral des Provinces-Unies | des Pais-Bas, &c. &c. &c. | Par | A. Vosmaer, | Directeur des Cabinets d'Histoire Naturelle & de Curiosités de S. A. S., Membre de | l'Academie Impériale, & Correspondant de l'Académie Royal des Sciences de Paris. | A Amsterdam, | Chez Pierre Meijer, M. DCC. LXIX. 4to. pp. 7. pl.

The bird here described is the *Cotinga cayanensis* of Brisson, ii, p. 344, pl. 34, f. 3, the *Quereiva* Buff. P. E. 624 = *Ampelis cayana* L.

1769. Vosmaer, A. Description | du | Coq-des-Roches | Americain [Rupicola crocea], | Oiseau | d'une merveilleuse beauté, très peu connu encore; apporté de | Surinam, | Pour le Cabinet de | son altesse Sérénissime | Monseigneur le Prince d'Orange et de Nassau, | Stadhouder He're'ditaire, Gouverneur, Capi- | taine Ge'ne'ral et Amiral des Provinces-Unies | des Pais-Bas, &c. &c. &c. | Par | A. Vosmaer, | Directeur des Cabinets d'Histoire Naturelle & de Curiosités de S. A. S., Membre de | l'Académie Impériale, & Correspondent de l'Académie Royal des Sciences de Paris. | A Amsterdam, | Chez Pierre Meijer, | M. DCC. LXIX. 4to. pp. 7, pl.

The bird here described is the *Cocq de Roche* Buff. P. E. 39; *Rupicola* Briss. iv, p. 437, pl. 34, f. 1 = *Pipra rupicola* L.

1823. Thunberg, C. P. Description d'un nouveau genre d'oiseaux [Cotinga]. < *Mém. Soc. Nat. Moscou*, vi, 1823, pp. 175–179.

Pas vue moi-même : le titre tiré de la *Bibl.* de Carus et Engelm.

1823. Thunberg, C. P. Ampelis, cujus novas species præs. C. P. Thunberg p. p., resp. O. Fr. Tullberg, Smol. Upsaliæ. 1823. 4to. pp. 4, 6.

Libellus haud mihi obvius.

1825. Swainson, W. On the genus Psaris of M. Cuvier, with an Account of two new Species. < *Zool. Journ.*, ii, 1825, pp. 354–357.

Ps. cristatus, p. 255; *Ps. niger*, p. 356, spp. nn.

1826. Desm . . . st. [Desmarest, A. G.] Description d'un nouveau genre d'oiseaux découvert dans le Brésil et nommé Cotinga, par C. P. Thunberg. . . . < *Féruss. Bull.*, 2e sec., vii, 1826, p. 248.

Mém. de la Soc. Imp. des Sci. de Moscou, vi, p. 175.

1826. Lesson, [R. P.] Sur le genre Psaris de M. Cuvier, avec la description de deux espèces nouvelles; par William Swainson. . . . < *Féruss. Bull.*, 2e sec., viii, 1826, pp. 442, 443.

Extrait du *Zool. Journ.*, ii, No 7, 1825, pp. 354–357, q. v.

1826. Selby, P. J. An Account of a new or fifth Species of the Genus Psaris [erythrogenys], Cuv. < *Zool. Journ.*, ii, 1826, pp. 483, 484.

1827. Lesson, R. P. Description d'une espèce nouvelle du genre Psaris, de M. Cuvier; par P. J. Selby. . . < *Féruss. Bull.*, 2e sect., xii, 1827, p. 267.

Ps. erythrogenys, Selby; *Zool. Journ.*, ii, 1826, p. 483.

1828. Selby, P. J. Neue Gattung Psaris Cuv., . . . < *Oken's Isis*, Bd. xxi, 1828, pp. 943, 944.

Uebers. aus d. *Zool. Journ.*, ii, 1826, pp. 483, 484; *Ps. erythrogenys*.

1830. Swainson, [W.] Ueber die Sippe Psaris Cuv. < *Oken's Isis*, Bd. xxiii, 1830, p. 1038.

Uebers. aus d. *Zool. Jour.*, Bd. ii, Nr. vii, Oct., 1825, pp. 354–357.

1830. WAGLER, J.   Revisio generis Pipra.   < *Oken's Isis*, Bd. xxiii, 1830, pp. 926-943.

    PP. ignicapilla, lanceolata, p. 931; *aurantia*, p. 935; *auricapilla*, p. 934; *perspicillata*, p. 935; *tyranulus* (sic), p. 940, spp. nn.—Expositio specierum 33, synonymis, descriptionibus et patriis redactarum, pp. 926-941.—Expositio brevior reliquarum specierum 17.

1832. CHILDREN, [J. G.]   [On specimens of the Phytotoma bloxhami, Childr., col
    lected by Mr. Cuming in Chili.]   < *Proc. Comm. Sci. and Corr. Zool. Soc. Lond.*,
    pt. ii, 1832, p. 3.

1832. LAFRESNAYE, F. DE.   Phytotome.   Phytotoma, Molina, Daudin, etc.   < *Guér.*
    Mag. de Zool., 2e année, classe ii, notice v, pl. v.

    Esquisse monographique sur ce genre.   Pl. v, *Phytotoma rutila* V.

1835. CHILDREN, [J. G.]   [Phytotoma bloxhami.]   < *Oken's Isis*, Bd. xxviii, 1835, p.
    365.

    Aus *P. Z. S.*, 1832, p. 3.

1838. EYDOUX, [F.] *et* GERVAIS, [P.]   Sur quelques particularités anatomiques du
    Phytotoma rara de Molina.   < *Guér. Mag. de Zool.*, 8e année, 1838, classe ii,
    notice lxxxvi, pp. 1-4, pl. lxxxvi.

1839. LAFRESNAYE, F. DE.   G. Cotinga.   Ampelis. Lin.   C. a plumes en lamelles.
    Ampelis lamellipennis. De Lafr.   < *Guér. Mag. de Zool.*, 2e sér., année 1839,
    Oiseaux, pp. 1, 2, pl. 9.

    C'est une *Cotinga*, du sous genre *Xipholena* Glog.

1841. PARZUDAKI, C.   Manakin nouveau [Pipra candei], découvert par M. De Maus-
    sion Candé.   < *Revue Zoologique*, iv, 1841, p. 306.

1842. LAFRESNAYE, F. DE.   [Ueber Phytotoma.]   < *Oken's Isis*, Bd. xxxv, 1842, p. 51.

    Aus d. *Mag. de Zool.*, Jahrg. ii, 1832, Klasse ii, Artikel v, Taf. 5.

1843. DES MURS, O.   Notice sur le genre ornithologique rupicola ou coq de roche et
    considérations oologiques.   < *Guér. Mag. de Zool.*, 2e sér., année 1843, Oiseaux,
    pp. 1-10, pl. 37.

    Pl. 37, l'œuf de *Rupicola peruviana*.

1843. GOUDOT, J.   Note sur le nidification du Rupicola peruviana et de l'Eurypyga
    phalenoïdes.   < *Revue Zoologique*, vi, 1843, pp. 1, 2.

1843. GOUDOT, J.   Observations sur l'organisation et les habitudes du coq de roche
    péruvien (Pipra peruviana, Lath.), et du caurale (Ardea helias, Lin.).   < *Guér.*
    Mag. de Zool., 2e sér., année 1843, pp. 1-4, pll. 37, 38.

    Pl. 37, œuf du *Rupicola peruviana*; pl. 38, œuf de l'*Eurypga phalenoïdes*.

1843. LAFRESNAYE, [F.] DE.   G. Cotinga.   Ampelis. L.   C. a croissant.   C. arcuata.
    De Lafresn.   < *Guér. Mag. de Zool.*, 2e sér., année 1843, Oiseaux, pp. 1, 2, pl. 40.

    Rev. Zool., 1843, p. 98.   (*Pyrrhorhynchus*, Lafr., 1849.)

1843. LAFRESNAYE, [F.] DE.   G. Cotinga.   Ampelis. L.   C. a poitrine d'or.   A. aureo-
    pectus. De Lafr.   < *Guér. Mag. de Zool.*, 2e sér., année 1843, Oiseaux, pp. 1, 2,
    pl. 39.

    Rev. Zool., 1843, p. 68.   (*Euchlornis* De Fil., 1846.)

1843. LAFRESNAYE, [F.] DE.   G. Manakin.   Pipra. Linné.   M. chrysoptère.   P. chrys-
    optera. De Lafr.   < *Guér. Mag. de Zool.*, 2e sér., année 1843, Oiseaux, pp. 1, 2,
    pl. 44.

    R. Z. 1843, p. 97.   (*Masius* Bp., 1850.)

1843. PARZUDAKI, [C.]   G. Manakin.   Pipra. Linné.   M. de Candé.   Pipra Candei.
    Parzudaki.   < *Guér. Mag. de Zool.*, 2e sér., année 1843, Oiseaux, pp. pl. 45.

    Revue Zool., iv, 1841, p. 306.   (*Chiromachæris* Cab., 1847.)

1844. EYDOUX, [F.] *and* GERVAIS, [P.]   Anatomisches über Phytotoma.   < *Oken's*
    Isis, Bd. xxxvii, 1844, p. 405.

    Aus *Guér. Mag. de Zool.*, Jahrg. viii, 1838, Klasse ii, Notiz 86, taf. 86.

1847. LAFRESNAYE, [F.] DE.   Sur le Ptilochloris arcuatus (Lanius arcuatus Cuv.), et
    les autres espèces du genre.   < *Revue Zoologique*, x, 1847, pp. 182-185.

1847. PARZUDAKI, C. Description d'une nouvelle espèce du genre Iodopleurus [lege Iodopleura] [d'Isabelle; sic; c'est-à-dire isabellæ] (Lesson). < *Revue Zoologique*, x, 1847, p. 186.

Stet *Iodopleura isabellæ.*

1848. [JARDINE, W.] Tityra surinama, Linnaeus. < *Jard. Contrib. Orn.*, 1848, p. 62, pl. xi.

1849. HARTLAUB, G. Note monographique sur le sous-genre Pyrrhorhynchus. < *Rev. et Mag. de Zool.*, i, 1849, pp. 493–494, pl. 14, f. 1.

Cinq espèces. *Ampelis formosa,* sp. n., pl. 14, f. 1.

1850. SCHOMBURGK, R. Rupicola aurantia (Cuv.) < *Naumannia*, i, Heft ii, 1850, pp. 34–38.

Ein physioiogisch. Beitrag.

1850. WALLACE, A. R. On the Umbrella Bird (Cephalopterus ornatus), "Ueramimbé," L. G. < *P. Z. S.*, xviii, 1850, pp. 206, 207.

Description, habits, and distribution of this species; structure of the crest.

1851. WALLACE, A. R. On the Umbrella Bird (Cephalopterus ornatus), "Ueramimbé," L. G. < *Ann. Mag. Nat. Hist.*, 2d ser., viii, 1851, pp. 428–430.

From *P. Z. S.*, 1850, pp. 206, 207.

1851. SCLATER, P. L. V.—On a new species of Manakin [Pipra flavicollis]. < *Jard. Contrib. Orn.*, 1851, p. 143.

1852. CORNALIA, E. On a New Species of the Family of Ampelidæ [Euchlornis sclateri]. < *Jard. Contrib. Orn.*, 1852, p. 133, pl. ci.

1852. DEVILLE, E., *et* SCLATER, [P. L.]. Description d'une nouvelle espèce de Cotinga [porphyrolæma] provenant de l'expédition de MM. de Castelnau et Deville dans l'Amérique du Sud. < *Rev. et Mag. de Zool.*, iv, 1852, pp. 226, 227.

1853. CORNALIA, E. Note sur une nouvelle espéce du Genre Euchlornis [sclateri]. < *Rev. et Mag. de Zool.*, v, 1853, pp. 104–109, pl. 4.

E. sclateri, p. 107, pl. 4. Notice historique et critique du genre. Tableau synoptique des espèces.

1854. CORNALIA, E. Note sur une nouvelle espèce du genre Euchlornis [sclateri]. < *Bianconi's Repert. Ital. Stor. Nat.*, ii, 1854, p. 55.

Extrait de la *Rev. et Mag. de Zool.*, 1853, p. 107, pl. 4.

1857. GOULD, J. Descriptions of three new and very beautiful species of Birds, from Guatemala [Cotinga amabilis] and from the Island of Lombock. < *P. Z. S.*, xxv, 1857, pp. 64, 65, pl. (Aves) cxxiii.

Cotinga amabilis, p. 64, pl. cxxiii; *Halcyon fulgidus, Pitta concinna,* p. 65.

1857. GOULD, J. Descriptions of three new and very beautiful species of Birds, from Guatemala and from the Island of Lombock. < *Ann. Mag. Nat. Hist.*, 2d ser., xx, 1857, pp. 380, 381.

From *P. Z. S.*, April 28, 1857, pp. 64, 65, *q. v.*

1857. SCLATER, P. L. Review of the species of the South American Sub-family Tityrinæ. < *P. Z. S.*, 1857, pp. 67–80, 2 woodcc.

The subfamily is composed of the two genera *Tityra* and *Pachyrhamphus,* the former with 6, and the latter with 16 spp. With *Tityra* are considered synonymous *Psaris,* Cuv., 1817, and *Erator,* Kaup, 1851. With *Pachyrhamphus* Gray, 1838 (*vice Pachrhynchus,* Spix, 1824) are considered synonymous *Bathmidurus,* Cab., 1847, *Chloropsaris,* Kaup, 1851, and *Platypsaris* and *Callopsaris* Bp., 1854.—The species are treated with synonymy, diagnosis, habitat and critical commentary. Wood-cuts show the wing-structure of each genus. *Pachyrhamphus albogriseus,* p. 78, sp. n.

1857. SCLATER, P. L. Description of a new species of Pachyrhamphus [albo-griseus]. < *Ann. Mag. Nat. Hist.*, 2d ser., xx, 1857, p. 398.

From *P. Z. S.*, Apr. 28, 1857, p. 78.

1859. GOULD J. On the Members of the Genus Rupicola, and whether there be Two or more Species. < *P. Z. S.*, xxvii, 1859, pp. 99, 100.

R. sanguinolenta, p. 100, sp. n.

1860. CRISP, E.   [Exhibition of specimens of the Cock of the Rock (Rupicola crocea)].
    < *P. Z. S.*, xxviii, 1860, p. 98.

1860. GOULD, J.   On the Members of the Genus Rupicola, and whether there be Two
    or more Species.   < *Ann. Mag. Nat. Hist.*, 3d ser., v, 1860, p. 62.
    From *P. Z. S.*, Feb. 8. 1859, pp. 99, 100.

1860, SCLATER, P. L.   Description of a New Species of Manakin [Pipra heterocerca]
    from Northern Brazil.   < *P. Z. S.*, xxviii, 1860, pp. 312, 313.

1860. SCLATER, P. L.   Description of a New Species of Manakin [Pipra heterocerca]
    from Northern Brazil.   < *Ann. Mag. Nat. Hist.*, 3d ser., vi, 1860, pp. 438, 439.
    From *P. Z. S.*, June 12, 1860, pp. 312, 313.

1861. EYTON, T. C.   Note on the Anatomy of Cephalopterus penduliger.   < *Ibis*, iii,
    1861, pp. 57, 58.

1861. SCLATER, P. L.   On a New Species of Bird of the Genus Lipaugus of Boié ⌊L.
    subalaris].   < *P. Z. S.*. xxix, 1861, pp. 209–212.
    With synopsis of 9 spp. of the genus, arranged in the 3 sections of *Lathria, Lipaugus*, and
    Aulia. (N. B. nomen generis Lipaugus nec Lipangus scribendum, scil. λείπειν deficere,αὐγή
    splendor.)

1862. SCLATER, P. L.   Note on Pipra deliciosa.   < *Ibis*, iv, 1862, pp. 175–178, pl. vi.
    Referred to genus *Machœropterus ;* synonymatic synopsis of 4 spp. of this genus; and re-
    print from *P. Z. S.* of his remarks on its wing-structure.

1862. SCLATER, P. L.   On a New Species of Bird of the Genus Lipangus of Boié.
    < *Ann. Mag. Nat. Hist.*, 3d ser., x, 1862, p. 80.
    From *P. Z. S.*, May 28, 1861, pp. 209–212.

1863. SCLATER, P. L.   On a New Species of the Genus Pipra [leucorrhoa] from New
    Grenada.   < *P. Z. S.*, xxxi, 1863, pp. 63, 64, pl. x.

1865. SALVIN, O.   Note on the Costa-Rican Bell-bird (Chasmorhynchus tricaruncu-
    latus, Verreaux) and its allies.   < *Ibis*, 2d ser., i, 1865, pp. 90–95, pl. iii.
    With synonymatic and diagnostic synopsis of the 4 known spp. of the genus. The species
    named is figured.

1866. SCLATER, P. L.   Note on the Distribution of the Species of Chasmorhynchus.
    < *Ibis*, 2d ser., ii, 1866, pp. 406, 407.
    Corrects some previous erroneously assigned localities; compares the distribution of the
    genus with that of *Galbula viridis* and its allies. Four species are treated. *Cf. Intellectual
    Observer,* Jan., 1867, pp. 401–408, on the same subject.

1866. ANON.   Der Glockenvogel [Chasmorhynchus nudicollis].   < *Aus der Natur.*,
    xxxviii, oder n. F., xxvi, 1866, p. 783.
    Grösstentheils nach Watertons ,, Wanderungen " mitgetheilt.

1867. SCLATER, P. L.   The Bell-Birds [Chasmorhynchus] of America.   < *The Intellec-
    tual Observer,* x, 1867, pp. 401–408, 1 col. pl., one woodcut.
    A popular account of these singular birds. The plate illustrates *C. nudicollis.*

1869. SCLATER, P. L.   [Note on Chasmorhynchus variegatus in British Guiana.]
    < *Ibis*, 2d ser., v, 1869, p. 462.

1870. ANON.   Der Glockenvogel [Chasmorhynchus carunculatus].   < *Aus der Natur.*,
    lii, oder n. F., xl, 1870, p. 352.

1872. ZORN, J.   [Eine Siesta am Irura.]   < *Westerm. illustr. deutsche Monatshafte,*
    Juni, 1872, pp. — — —, fig.
    Fig. of *Cephalopterus ornatus.*

1878. SCLATER, P. L.   Revision of the Species of the Cotingine Genus Pipreola.   < *Ibis*,
    4th ser., ii, Apr., 1878, pp. 164–173, pl. vi.
    Monography of 9 spp. regarded as " firmly established ", with notice of two doubtful ones,
    one of these being *P. chlorolepidota*, on which Swainson originally established the genus.
    Euchlorornis Cab. & H., 1859, or *Euchlornis* Filippi, Mus. Med., 1847, = *Pyrorhynchus* Bp.,
    1854, or *Pyrrhorhynchus* Lafr., 1849, = *Pipreola* Sw., 1838. The nine spp. are *riefferi, mela-
    nolœma, viridis, formosa, frontalis* (pl. vi), *sclateri, aureipectus, jucunda, elegans ;* none new.

Vireonidæ.

1843. [LAFRESNAYE, F. DE.] G. Cyclarhis. Cyclarhis. Swainson. (Fam. Laniadae.) Gen. Laniagra, d'Orb. et Lafr. Tangara, Buff. < *Guér. Mag. de Zool.*, 2e sér., année 1843, Ois., pp. 1–4, pl. 33.

Pl. 33, *C. nigrirostris* Lafr. (*R. Z.*, 1842, p. 133). Liste des trois espèces composant le genre.

1851. CASSIN, J. Sketch of the Birds composing the genera Vireo, Vieillot, and Vireosylvia, Bonaparte, with a List of the previously known and descriptions of three new species. < *Proc. Acad. Nat. Sci. Phila.*, v, 1851, pp. 149–154, pll. x, xi.

Vireo, 5 spp.; *V. huttoni*, p. 150, pl. x, f. 1, sp. n.; *Vireosylvia*, 6 spp.; *V. flavoviridis*, p. 152, pl. xi; *V. philadelphica*, p. 153, pl. x, f. 2, spp. nn.

1851. LAFRESNAYE, F. DE. Sur l'oiseau nommé par Brisson Tangara de Saint-Domingue, Tanagra Dominicensis, Tanagra Dominica, par Linné, figuré par Buffon, pl. enl. 156, f. 2, et dont Vieillot a fait son genre Esclave (Dulus), sous le nom de Dulus palmarum. < *Rev. et Mag. de Zool.*, iii, 1851, pp. 583–590.

1851. STRICKLAND, H. E. On the Type of the genus Dulus, Vieill. < *Jard. Contrib. Orn.*, 1851, pp. 103, 104.

Tanagra dominica L., nec *Turdus palmarum* L. *Cf.* Lafr., *Rev. et Mag. de Zool.*, iii, 1851, pp. 583–590. (See Gray's *Handlist*, Nos. 5827 and 7025.)

1852. LYMAN, T. [On the Breeding of the Yellow-breasted Chat (Icteria viridis) in New England.] < *Proc. Boston Soc. Nat. Hist.*, iv, 1852, p. 167.

1852. WOODHOUSE, S. W. Descriptions of new species of Birds of the genera Vireo [atricapilla, p. 60], Vieill., and Zonotrichia, Swains. < *Proc. Acad. Nat. Sci. Phila.*, vi, 1852, pp. 60, 61.

1853. LAWRENCE, G. N. Descriptions of New Species of Birds of the Genera Ortyx Stephens, Sterna Linn., and Icteria [longicauda, p. 4] Vieillot. < *Ann. Lyc. Nat. Hist. N. Y.*, vi, 1853, pp. 1–4.

1857. BREWER, T. M. [On the characters, habits and distribution of Vireosylvia philadelphica of Cassin.] < *Proc. Boston Soc. Nat. Hist.*, ii, 1857, pp. 108–111.

Including a letter from Th. Kumlein, of Wisconsin.

1860. BRYANT, H. [Vireo bogotensis, sp. n.] < *Proc. Bost. Soc. Nat. Hist.*, vii, 1860, p. 227.

The description occurs in an untitled article which also treats of *Turdus minimus* Lafr.

1863. LAWRENCE, G. N. Descriptions of New Species of Birds of the Families Vireonidæ and Rallidæ. < *Proc. Acad. Nat. Sci. Phila.*, xv, 1863, pp. 106, 107.

Vireo atripennis, p. 106, Sombrero. See especially Baird, *Rev. Amer. Birds*, p. 330.

1864. BROWN, E. Occurrence of the Redeyed Flycatcher [Vireo olivaceus] in England. < *Zoologist*, xxii, 1864, pp. 8965–8967.

Extracted from the "Natural History of Tutbury", p. 385.

1864. HADFIELD, H. Notes on the Redeyed Flycatcher [Vireo olivaceus]. < *Zoologist*, xxii, 1864, pp. 9020, 9021.

1865. LAWRENCE, G. N. Descriptions of new species of Birds of the Families Paridæ, Vireonidæ, Tyrannidæ, and Trochilidæ, with a note on Myiarchus Panamensis. < *Proc. Acad. Nat. Sci. Phila.*, xvii, 1865, pp. 37–39.

Hylophilus acuticaudus, p. 37, Venezuela.

1870. BREE, C. R. The Red-eyed Flycatcher [Vireo olivaceus]. < *The London Field*, May 14, 1870.

The writer contends that the *Vireo* captured in England, as described and figured by Mosley in *Nat. Hist. Tutbury* (pl. 6), is *V. altiloquus*, not *V. olivaceus!* A note from "B" appended suggests that the bird may be *Erythrosterna parva!!*

1874. SHARPE, R. B. On a new Genus and Species of Bird from the West Indies. < *P. Z. S.*, xlii, 1874, pp. 427, 428, woodcc. pl. liv.

   Phœnicomanes iora. Considered related to *Phœnicophilus*, and referred with the latter to *Vireonidæ* rather than *Tanagridæ.* But it proved to be an *Iora ;* see *P. Z. S.*, 1875, p. 640.

1875. FINSCH, O. Notes on Phœnicomanes iora, Sharpe, and Abrornis atri-capilla, Blyth. < *P. Z. S.*, Dec. 7, 1875, pp. 640–641.

   Former (*P. Z. S.*, 1874, p. 427) is *Iora lafresnayei* Hartl., *R. Z.*, 1844, p. 401!

1876. DEANE, R. The Philadelphia Vireo [V. philadelphicus] in New England. < *Bull. Nutt. Ornith. Club,* i, No. 3, Sept., 1876, p. 74.

   Summary of its recorded occurrences there.

1876. [INGERSOLL, E.] A Peculiar Bird's Nest [Vireo noveborecensis]. < *Forest and Stream*, vi, May 4, 1876, p. 197.

1877. FOX, W. H. Capture of the Philadelphia Vireo [V. philadelphicus] in New Hampshire. < *Bull. Nutt. Ornith. Club,* ii, No. 3, July, 1877, p. 78.

1878. BATCHELDER, C. F. Spurious Primaries in the Red-eyed Vireo [Vireo oliva-ceus]. < *Bull. Nutt. Ornith. Club,* iii, No. 2, Apr., 1878, pp. 97, 98.

   The writer has apparently measured the quill from the carpal joint, giving dimensions much above those of the exposed portion of the feather.

1878. COOPER, W. A. Notes on the breeding habits of Hutton's Vireo (Vireo huttoni) and the Gray Titmouse (Lophophanes inornatus), with a description of their Nests and Eggs. < *Bull. Nutt. Ornith. Club.*, iii, No. 2, Apr., 1878, pp. 68, 69.

1878. COUES, E. Letters on Ornithology. No. 18.—The Yellow-breasted Chat [Icteria virens]. < *The Chicago Field*, June 29, 1878.

   From advance sheets of "Birds of the Colorado Valley."

1878. SALVIN, O. Note on the Type of Malaconotus leucotis, Swainson. < *Ibis*, 4th ser., ii, No. 8, Oct., 1878, pp. 443–445, pl. xi.

   Swainson's species (*An. Menag.*, 1838, p. 431) is identified with *Vireolanius icterophrys* of Bonaparte, *C. R.*, xxxviii, 1853, p. 380.—Note on *V. dubusi* Verr.

1879. BREWER, T. M. Vireo gilvus and Vireo flavifrons in Northern New England. < *Bull. Nutt. Ornith. Club.*, iv, No. 4, Oct., 1879, p. 237.

1879. BREWSTER, W. Notes upon the Distribution, Habits, and Nesting of the Black-capped Vireo (Vireo atricapillus). < *Bull. Nutt. Ornith. Club,* iv, No. 2, Apr., 1879, pp. 99–103.

   Being the whole history of the species to date, with very full descriptions of nest and eggs.

1879. COUES, E. Note on the Black-capped Greenlet, Vireo atricapillus of Wood-house. < *Bull. Nutt. Ornith. Club.*, iv, No. 4, Oct., 1879, pp. 193, 194, pl. i.

   A perfunctory editorial, written up to the very pretty colored plate, which illustrates a pair of the birds with their nest.

1879. DEANE, R. Vireo atricapillus in Texas. < *Bull. Nutt. Ornith. Club,* iv, No. 1, Jan., 1879, pp. 58, 59.

   The first fresh advices of the species for many years.

Laniidæ.

1781. TENGMALM, P. G. Anmårkningar Vid Lanius Collurio, en liten Rof-fogel. < *Kongl. Vetensk. Acad. Nya Handl.*, ii, 1781, pp. 98–104.

"Veckoskr. f. Läk. o. Naturf. 2:dra B:det. [1781], 280–281" (*v. Friesen*).

1824. SEYFFERTITZ, [A.] v. Beobachtungen über den Würger, Lanius, Linn. aus Briefen des Herrn Freiherrn v. Seyffertitz mit dessen eigenen Worten. < *Ornis*, Heft i, 1824, pp. 54–79.

1824. SWAINSON, W. An Inquiry into the natural Affinities of the Laniadæ, or Shrikes; preceded by some Observations on the present State of Ornithology in this Country. < *Zool. Journ.*, i, 1824, pp. 289–307.

1826. LESSON, R. P. Recherches sur les rapports naturels des Lanianæ on Pies-grièches, . . .; par William Swainson. . . < *Féruss. Bull.*, 2ᵉ sect., vii, 1826, p. 107, 108.

Extrait du *Zool. Journ.*, i, Oct., 1824, pp. 289–307.

1829. "A. N." Peculiar Smell of the Greater Shrike [Lanius excubitor]. < *Loudon's Mag. Nat. Hist.*, ii, 1829, p. 484.

1829. A[UDUBON], J. J. [Note on the manner in which the Shrike (Lanius excubitor) seizes its prey.] < *Loudon's Mag. Nat. Hist.*, i, 1829, p. 93.

1829. FARRAR, W. A Pair of Butcher Birds (Lanius Collurio, m. et-f. ?). < *Loudon's Mag. Nat. Hist.*, ii, 1829, p. 484.

1830. SWAINSON, W. Untersuchung über die natürlichén Verwandtschaften der Laniadæ oder Würger. < *Oken's Isis*, Bd. xxiii, 1830, pp. 419, 420.

Auszug aus d. *Zool. Journ.*, i, Oct., 1824, pp. 289–307.

1831. HOY, J. D. Observations on the British Species of Shrikes [Laniidæ], their Habits, Nidification, &c. < *Loudon's Mag. Nat. Hist.*, iv, 1831, pp. 341–344.

1832. "SOMERSETENSIS." The Butcher Bird (Lanius Collurio). < *Loudon's Mag. Nat. Hist.*, v, 1832, pp. 281, 282.

Note of its habits.

1835. BLYTH, E. Notice of a very remarkable Individual of the Common Shrike (Lànius Collùrio Lin.), with some Observations on this Species of Shrike. < *Loudon's Mag. Nat. Hist.*, viii, 1835, pp. 364–371.

♀ in male plumage.—The following observations are extended and miscellaneous. Editorial note, pp. 371, 372.

1837. GRAY, G. R. Description of a new Subgenus, and some Remarks on Birds belonging to the Family Laniadæ. < *Charlesw. Mag. Nat. Hist.*, i, 1837, pp. 487–490, fig. 61.

Chaunonotus, p. 487; *Hapalophus*, p. 489, genn. nn.

1839. LESSON, R. P. Révision de la Famille des Pies-grièches. < *Revue Zoologique*, ii, 1839, pp. 133, 134.

1839. LESSON, [R. P.] Description d'une nouvelle espèce de Pie-grièche tuée à Oran, (Lanius algeriensis). < *Revue Zoologique*, ii, 1839, pp. 134, 135.

1839. LESSON, R, P. Cadre spécifique des oiseaux de la famille des Laniadées. < *Revue Zoologique*, ii, 1839, pp. 197–199.

46 genres.

1843. DOUBLEDAY, H. Note on the Grey Shrike, (Lanius Excubitor). < *Zoologist*, i, 1843, p. 40.

1843. HARTLAUB, [G.] [Sur une Pie-grièche trouvée en Grèce (Lanius nubicus Licht.).] < *Revue Zoologique*, vi, 1843, p. 159.

1843. HEWETT, W.   Note on the Shrike [Lanius collurio].   < *Zoologist*, i, 1843, p. 352.

1843. JORDAN, W. R. H.   Note on the Red-backed Shrike, (Lanius collurio).   < *Zoologist*, i, 1843, p. 40.

1844. BURLINGHAM, D. C.   Note on the occurrence of the Grey Shrike [Lanius excubitor] at Lynn.   < *Zoologist*, ii, 1844, p. 444.

1844. HEPPENSTALL, J.   Note on the great grey Shrike [Lanius excubitor].   < *Zoologist*, ii, 1844, p. 656.

1844. SPENCER, J. B.   Note on the capture of the Great Grey Shrike [Lanius excubitor, in Britain].   < *Zoologist*, ii, 1844, p. 761.

1845. HOLME, F.   Habits of the Grey and Red-backed Shrikes.   < *Zoologist*, iii, 1845, pp. 1135, 1136.

1845. NORMAN, G.   Occurrence of the great grey-backed Shrike [Lanius excubitor] near Hull.   < *Zoologist*, iii, 1845, p. 1023.

1847. HUNTER, C. B.   Occurrence of the Great Gray Shrike [Lanius excubitor] at Downham.   < *Zoologist*, v, 1847, p. 1637.

1849. BORRER, W., JR.   Occurrence of the Great Gray Shrike [Lanius excubitor] near Shoreham.   < *Zoologist*, vii, 1849, p. 2386.

1849. BREE, C. R.   Occurrence of the Great Gray Shrike [Lanius excubitor] in Suffolk.   < *Zoologist*, vii, 1849, p. 2412.

1849. DUFF, J.   Occurrence of the Great Gray Shrike (Lanius Excubitor) near Bishop's Auckland.   < *Zoologist*, vii, 1849, p. 2386.

1849. LUKIS, J. W.   Occurrence of the Great Gray Shrike (Lanius excubitor) at Heacham, Norfolk.   < *Zoologist*, vii, 1849, pp. 2411, 2412.

1849. MILNER, W. M. E.   Occurrence of the Great Gray Shrike (Lanius Excubitor) near York.   < *Zoologist*, vii, 1849, p. 2452.

1849. RODD, E. H.   Occurrence of the Woodchat (Lanius rufus) at Scilly.   < *Zoologist*, vii, 1849, pp. 2620, 2621.

1849. SMITH, J.   Occurrence of the American Greater Northern Shrike (Lanius borealis) near Aberdeen.   < *Zoologist*, vii, 1849, p. 2495.

1849. SMITH, J.   Error in describing the American Shrike [Lanius borealis].   < *Zoologist*, vii, 1849, p. 2567.

1849. UNWIN, W. C.   Occurrence of the Great Gray Shrike [Lanius excubitor] near Lewes.   < *Zoologist*, vii, 1849, pp. 2452, 2453.

1850. BOND, F.   Occurrence of the Great Gray Shrike (Lanius Excubitor) near London.   *Zoologist*, viii, 1850, p. 2698.

1850. ELLMAN, J. B.   Singular Variety of the Red-backed Shrike (Lanius collurio).   < *Zoologist*, viii, 1850, p. 2698.

1850. GARTH, J. C.   Occurrence of the Great Gray Shrike (Lanius excubitor) near Bedale.   < *Zoologist*, viii, 1850, p. 2649.

1850. GARTH, J. C.   Occurrence of the Greater Northern Shrike (Lanius borealis) near Knaresborough.   < *Zoologist*, viii, 1850, p. 2649.

1850. TOMES, R. F.   Occurrence of the ["]Greater Northern Shrike["] [*i. e.*, Lanius excubitorides] in Warwickshire.   < *Zoologist*, viii, 1850, pp. 2650, 2661 [cf. Zool., 2734].

1850. TOMES, R. F.   Description of Lanius Excubitorides, a new British Shrike; and Correction of an Error [Zool., 2650] respecting Lanius borealis.   < *Zoologist*, viii, 1850, pp. 2734, 2735, fig.

1851. CASSIN, J.   Descriptions of new species of birds of the family Laniadæ, specimens of which are in the collection of the Academy of Natural Sciences of Philadelphia.   < *Proc. Acad. Nat. Sci. Phila.*, v, 1851, pp. 244–246.
    Lanius pallidirostris, p. 244 ; *L. pallens. Laniarius quadricolor*, p. 245 ; *Dryoscopus sublacteus, D. atrialatus*, p. 246.

1851. STRANGEWAYES, R. The Red-backed Shrike, (Lanius Collurio). < *Zoologist,* ix, 1851, p. 3207.

1852. BUXTON, T. F., JR. Occurrence of the Great Ash-coloured Shrike [Lanius excubitor] in Norfolk. < *Zoologist,* x, 1852, p. 3475.

1852. ELLMAN, J. B. Occurrence of the Great Gray Shrike [Lanius excubitor] at Hailsham. < *Zoologist,* x, 1852, p. 3388.

1852. VIERTHALER, R. [Lanius kiek.] < *Naumannia,* Bd. ii, Heft ii, 1852, p. 57.

1853. BONAPARTE, C. L. Monographie des Laniens. < *Rev. et Mag. de Zool.,* v, 1853, pp. 292-295, 432-441.

La synonymie, la patrie et les caractères de 42 espèces des Laniens, traitées d'après la manière de son *Conspectus. Lanius cephalomelus,* p. 436; *L. schwaneri,* p. 437; *Enneoctonus niloticus,* p. 439; *Sigmodus rufiventris,* p. 441.

1853. GURNEY, J. H. Note on the Red-backed Shrike [Lanius rufus] destroying Small Birds. < *Zoologist,* xi, 1853, pp. 3981, 3982.

1853. TOBIAS, R. [Ueber Nester und Eier von Lanius rufus.] < *Naumannia,* iii, 1853, pp. 335, 336.

1854. BREHM, C. L. Der grosse Würger (Lanius excubitor Lin.) und einige seiner Verwandten. < *J. f. O.,* ii, 1854, pp. 143-148.

Characters of *L. rapax* Brhm, *L. excubitor, L. ludovicianus, L. mexicanus* Brhm., n. sp., p. 145; *L. assimilis* A. & E. Brhm., *L. leuconotus* A. & E. Brhm.

1854. PARTRIDGE, H. T. Carnivorous Propensity of the Great Gray Shrike [Lanius excubitor]. < *Zoologist,* xii, 1854, p. 4251.

1856. DIEZEL, C. E. Kampf eines Dorndrehers [Lanius spinitorquus] mit einer Eidechse. < *J. f. O.,* iv, 1856, pp. 84, 85.
Nachschrift von Dr. Gloger.

1857. CASSIN, J. Notes on the North American species of Archibuteo and Lanius, and description of a new species of Toucan, of the genus Selenidera, Gould. < *Proc. Acad. Nat. Sci., Phila.,* ix, 1857, pp. 211-214.

In so far as *Lanius* is concerned, this paper gives a monographic sketch of the (too many) species recognized as North American by the author, these being no fewer than seven in number. Later authors have not succeeded in establishing more than two of these as valid.

1857. CRISP, E. [On a nest found in Suffolk, supposed to be that of Lanius excubitor.] < *P. Z. S.,* xxv, 1857, pp. 219, 220.

1857. HADFIELD, H. W. Note on the Woodchat Shrike (Lanius rufus). < *Zoologist,* xv, 1857, p. 5685.

1857. [WHATELY, R.] The Song of the Butcher-bird [Lanius collurio]. < *Nat. Hist. Rev.,* iv, 1857, pp. 57, 58.

1857. WILSON, J. J. Occurrence of the Great Gray Shrike [Lanius excubitor] near Leeds. < *Zoologist,* xv, 1857, pp. 5362, 5363.

1858. FARREN, W., JR. The Great Gray Shrike (Lanius excubitor) in Cambridgeshire. < *Zoologist,* xvi, 1858, p. 5958.

1858. HOMEYER, A. v. Ueber die verschiedene Färbung der Eier des Lanius collurio. Lin. < *J. f. O.,* vi, 1858, pp. 323, 324.

1858. PÄSSLER, W. Ueber die verschiedene Färbung der Eier des Lanius collurio. < *J. f. O.,* vi, 1858, pp. 43-46.

1859. EDWARD, T. Occurrence of the Great Ash-coloured Shrike (Lanius excubitor) in Banffshire. < *Zoologist,* xvii, 1859, pp. 6491, 6492.

1859. HAWKER, W. H. [Letter on supposed nest and eggs of Lanius excubitor.] < *Ibis,* i, 1859, pp. 330, 331.

1860. EDWARD, T. Occurrence of the Great Ashcoloured Shrike (Lanius excubitor) in Aberdeenshire. < *Zoologist,* xviii, 1860, pp. 6807, 6808.

1860. EDWARD, T. Capture of an Ashcoloured Shrike (Lanius Excubitor) at Sea. < *Zoologist,* xviii, 1860, p. 7235.

1860. GORDON, G.   Occurrence of the Great Gray Shrike (Lanius excubitor) at Forres, N. B.   < *Zoologist*, xviii, 1860, p. 6860.

1860. SAVILLE, S. P.   Occurrence of the Great Ashcoloured Shrike (Lanius excubitor) in Cambridgeshire.   < *Zoologist*, xviii, 1860, p. 6808.

1860. SAVILLE, S. P.   Another Occurrence of the Ashcoloured Shrike [Lanius excubitor] in Cambridgeshire.   < *Zoologist*, xviii, 1860, p. 6808.

1862. DUTTON, J.   Occurrence of the Great Gray Shrike [Lanius excubitor] at Jevington, Sussex.   < *Zoologist*, xx, 1862, p. 7881.

1863. ATKINSON, J. C.   Shrike and Yellowhammer.   < *Zoologist*, xxi, 1863, p. 8484.
   The former impaling the latter.

1863. HARTING, J. E.   Great Gray Shrike (Lanius excubitor) near Newmarket.   < *Zoologist*, xxi, 1863, p. 8444.

1863. MATTHEWS, M. A.   Great Gray Shrike (Lanius excubitor) near Taunton.   < *Zoologist*, xxi, 1863, p. 8444.

1863. MORRIS, W.   The Great Gray Shrike (Lanius Excubitor) at Leyton Marsh.   < *Zoologist*, xxi, 1863, p. 8325.

1864. GORDON, G.   Redbacked Shrike, or Butcher Bird [Lanius rufus], in Forfarshire.   < *Zoologist*, xxii, 1864, p. 9360.

1864. GUNN, T. E.   Great Gray Shrike [Lanius excubitor] near Norwich.   < *Zoologist*, xxii, 1864, p, 9104.

1865. BOULTON, W. W.   Great Gray Shrike [Lanius excubitor] near Beverley.   < *Zoologist*, xxiii, 1865, p. 9418.

1865. GUNN, T. E.   Great Gray Shrike [Lanius excubitor] in Suffolk.   < *Zoologist*, xxiii, 1865, p. 9455.

1865. HODGKINSON, J. B.   Great Gray Shrike [Lanius excubitor] at Preston.   < *Zoologist*, xxiii, 1865, p. 9418.

1866. HARVIE-BROWN, J. A.   Great Gray Shrike [Lanius excubitor] in Stirlingshire.   < *Zoologist*, 2d ser., i, 1866, p. 143.

1866. DUTTON, J.   Great Gray Shrike [Lanius excubitor] at Pevensey.   < *Zoologist*, 2d ser., i, 1866, p. 96.

1866. HARRISON, H.   Great Gray Shrike [Lanius excubitor] near Rochdale.   < *Zoologist*, 2d ser., i, 1866, p. 31.

1866. HOMEYER, A. v.   Lanius collurio als Mäusefänger.   < *J. f. O.*, xiv, 1866, p. 71.

1866. SMITH, A. C.   Great Gray Shrike [Lanius excubitor] in Wiltshire.   < *Zoologist*, 2d ser., i, 1866, p. 308.

1866. TSCHUSI, V. v.   Auch ein Lanius collurio als Mäusefänger.   < *J. f. O.*, xiv, 1866, pp. 212, 213.
   Tom. cit., p. 71.

1867. HOGG, J.   Zoological Notes [on Lanius excubitor].   < *Nat. Hist. Trans. Northumb. and Durh.*, i, 1867, pp. 232, 233.

1867. JENKINSON, J. H.   Great Gray Shrike [Lanius excubitor].   < *Zoologist*, 2d ser., ii, 1867, pp. 555-557.
   Descriptions of and comments on some specimens.

1867. JENKINSON, J. H.   Our Gray Shrikes.   < *Zoologist*, 2d ser., ii, 1867, pp. 605, 606.

1867. RODD, E. H.   The two Great Gray British Shrikes.   < *Zoologist*, 2d ser., ii, 1867, p. 555.

1867. RODD, E. H.   The Lesser Gray Shrike (Lanius minor) a British Bird.   < *Zoologist*, 2d ser., ii, 1867, p. 703.

1868. MÜLLER, KARL.   Beobachtung eines Lanius excubitor.   < *J. f. O.*, xvi, 1868, pp. 178-182
   Lebensweise.

1868. WALDEN, *Viscount.* Note on Lanius melanthes, Swinhoe, and on Lanius cephalomelas, Bp. < *Ibis*, 1868, 2d ser., iv, pp. 68–71.

The former = *L. fuscatus* Less.; the latter = *L. nasutus* Scop.

1869. CLARK-KENNEDY, A. Woodchat in Kent in 1868. < *Zoologist*, 2d ser., iv, 1869, pp. 1863, 1864.

1869. GEDNEY, H. S. The Loggerhead Shrike [Lanius ludovicianus]. < *Am. Nat.*, iii, 1869, pp. 159, 160.

Note on its habits.

1869. GUNN, T. E. Great Gray Shrike [Lanius excubitor] in Norfolk. < *Zoologist*, 2d ser., iv, 1869, p. 1513.

1869. GURNEY, J. H., JR. Great Gray Shrike [Lanius excubitor] at Dover. < *Zoologist*, 2d ser., iv, 1869, p. 1513.

1869. STUBBS, C. E. Great Gray Shrike [Lanius excubitor] at Henley-on-Thames. < *Zoologist*, 2d ser., iv, 1869, p. 1560.

1869. WALDEN, *Viscount.* [On Japanese species of Lanius.] < *Ibis*, 2d ser., v, 1869, p. 242.

1870. COUES, E. Om Tornskadernes Vane at spidde Insekter fortæller den amerikanske Ornithologo Elliot[t] Coues følgende: < *Tidssk. for Populære Fremst. af Naturvidensk.*, 4th ser., ii, 1870, p. 480.

Habits of *Lanius ludovicianus:* from *Proc. Bost. Soc. N. H.*, xii, 1868, pp. 112, 113.

1870. DRESSER, H. E., *and* SHARPE, R. B. Notes on Lanius excubitor and its Allies. < *P. Z. S.*, xxxviii, 1870, pp. 590–600.

A synoptical table of nine closely allied species is given, and their geographical distribution shown. *L. meridionalis*, p. 594; *L. minor*, p. 599, spp. nn. (*L. mollis*, Eversm., is accidentally omitted, *cf. Ann. N. H.*, (4), xvii, p. 78.)

1870. STEVENSON, H. Lesser Gray Shrike [Lanius collurio] in Norfolk. < *Zoologist*, 2d ser., v, 1870, p. 2139.

1871. BOYES, F. Great Gray Shrikes [Lanius excubitor] in East Yorkshire. < *Zoologist*, 2d ser., vi, 1871, pp. 2482, 2483.

1871. HARDING, H. J. Great Gray Shrike [Lanius excubitor]. < *Zoologist*, 2d ser., vi, 1871, p. 2439.

The manner in which it strikes its prey.

1871. HOCKER, J. Ueber die verschiedene Färbung der Eier von Lanius minor. < *J. f. O.*, xix, 1871, p. 464.

The variation in color, as in other species of the genus, depends on the age of the female.

1871. HOLFORD, C. E. Great Gray Shrike [Lanius excubitor] at Ware. < *Zoologist*, 2d ser., vi, 1871, p. 2607.

1871. RICKARDS, M. S. C. Great Gray Shrike [Lanius excubitor] near Clifton. < *Zoologist*, 2d ser., vi, 1871, p. 2726.

1871. ROBSON, S. E. Redbacked Shrike breeding near Wastwater. < *Zoologist*, 2d ser., vi, 1871, p. 2805.

1871. SAXBY, H. L. Great Gray Shrike [Lanius excubitor] in Shetland. < *Zoologist*, 2d ser., vi, 1871, p. 2561.

1872. ANNÉ, A. F. [Der grosse Würger (Lanius excubitor).] < *Zool. Gart.*, xiii, 1872, p. 89.

1872. BOYES, F. Great Gray Shrike [Lanius excubitor] in East Yorkshire. < *Zoologist*, 2d ser., vii, 1872, p. 3064.

1872. GUNN, T. E. Great Gray Shrike [Lanius excubitor] near Yarmouth. < *Zoologist*, 2d ser., vii, 1872, p. 3323.

1872. LOCKWOOD, S. The Great Northern Shrike [Lanius borealis] and the English Sparrows. < *Am. Nat.*, vi, 1872, pp. 236, 237.

Lanius borealis feeding on *Passer domesticus.*

1873. CABANIS, J. [Ueber zwei für die europäische Ornis neue Würger, Lanius major Pall. und L. homeyeri n. sp., und über L. sphenocercus n. sp. aus China.] < *J. f. O.*, 1873, pp. 75, 76 (und folg.).

1873. FREYBURG, *Baron* v. Der rothrückige Würger, Lanius collurio. < *Zool. Gart.*, xiv, 1873, p. 474.

1873. HERBERT, W. H. Great Gray Shrike [Lanius excubitor] near Newbury. < *Zoologist*, 2d ser., viii, 1873, p. 3489.

1873. PURDIE, H. A. Collurio ludovicianus [in Massachusetts]. < *Am. Nat.*, vii, 1873, p. 115.

1873. TRIPPE, T. M. The White-rumped Shrike [Lanius excubitorides]. < *Am. Nat.*, vii, 1873, p. 497.
  Note on the close relationship of this supposed species to *C. ludovicianus.*

1873. WHITAKER, J., JR. Great Gray Shrike [Lanius excubitor, at Lambly]. < *Zoologist*, 2d ser., viii, 1873, p. 3489.

1874. CABANIS, J. [Ueber Lanius excubitor und verwandte Arten und über „Abarten im Allgemeinen"]. *J. f. O.*, 1874, pp. 233–237.

1874. "R. P. C." Notes on the Butcher bird—Collyris [*i. e.*, Lanius] borealis. < *Forest and Stream*, i, Jan. 29, 1874, p. 391.

1875. MAYNARD, C. J. The Loggerhead Shrike (Lanius ludovicianus) in Mass[achusetts]. < *Am. Sportsman*, v, 1874–5, Feb. 13, p. 313.

1875. SCHALOW, H. [Uber die geographische Verbreitung des Pallas'schen Würgers (Lanius major).] < *Ber. über d.* xxi. *Vers. d. deut. Orn.-Ges.*, 1875, pp. 13, 14.

1876. COUES, E. Letters on Ornithology. No. 6.—The Shrike, or Butcher Bird [Lanius borealis]. < *The Chicago Field*, Dec. 2, 1876, fig.
  Brief biography of the species, with cut of the head.

1876. WILSON, T. J. The Butcher-bird in New York. < *Forest and Stream*, vii, Oct. 12, 1876, p. 148.
  Lanius ludovicianus asserted to breed in New York State, and *L. borealis* supposed to.

1877. ANON. Butcher-Birds [(Lanius borealis), as enemies of the English sparrows]. < *Rod and Gun*, ix, Feb. 10, 1877, p. 291.

1877. "F. L. R." The Butcher Bird Once More [Lanius ludovicianus]. < *Forest and Stream*, viii, Mar. 1, 1877, p. 49.

1877. "J. F." The Shrike [in Indiana]. < *Forest and Stream*, vii, Jan. 25, 1877, p. 388.

1877. KEYES, F. H. The Butcher-Bird [(Lanius borealis) eating its prey alive]. < *Forest and Stream*, viii, Feb. 15, 1877, p. 17.

1877. SCHALOW, H. [Letter on a species of Lanius.] < *Ibis*, 4th ser., i, July, 1879, p. 398.
  Maintaining the distinction of *L. phœnicuroides* Severtz. from *L. isabellinus* H. & E. Cf. *tom. cit.*, p. 164.

1878. COUES, E. History of the Shrike's names. < *Science News*, i, No. 1, Nov. 1, 1878, pp. 15, 16.
  Quoted from his *Birds of the Colorado Valley*, pt. i, 1878, pp. 540–542.

1878. EATON, D. H. Nesting of the White-rumped Shrike (Collurio excubitoroides). < *Oölogist*, iv, No. 1, Mar., 1878, p. 2, 3.
  A good account of the subject, from original observations made in New York State.

1878. SCHALOW, H. Das Subgenus Collurio Bp. < *J. f. O.*, Apr., 1878, pp. 133–156.

1879. BAGG, E., JR. The Loggerhead Shrike [Lanius ludovicianus] in Central New York. < *Bull. Nutt. Ornith. Club*, iv, No. 4, Oct., 1879, p. 237.

1879. BREWER, T. M. The Loggerhead Shrike (Collurio ludovicianus) breeding in Northern New England. < *Bull. Nutt. Ornith. Club*, iv, No. 2, Apr., 1879, p. 119.

1879. BREWER, T. M.   The Great Northern Shrike [Lanius borealis] in New England.   < *Bull. Nutt. Ornith. Club*, iv, No. 2, Apr., 1879, pp. 120, 121.

> Controversial, arising from his mistaken reading of a passage in the "Birds of the Colorado Valley," the author of which appends a note pointing out the blunder.

1879. [GRINNELL, G. B.]   Habits of the Butcher Bird [Lanius borealis].   < *Forest and Stream*, xiii, Oct. 2, 1879, p. 684.

> Notice of D. M. Marshall's contribution to the *Journal of Science*.

1879. DEANE, R.   Capture of the Loggerhead Shrike [Lanius ludovicianus] in New Hampshire.   < *Bull. Nutt. Ornith. Club*, iv, No. 2, Apr., 1879, pp. 119, 120.

1879. LANGDON, F. W.   The White-rumped and Loggerhead Shrikes [Lanius ludovicianus, et var. excubitorides] in Ohio.   < *Bull. Nutt. Ornith. Club*, iv, No. 2, Apr., 1879, p. 120.

1879. MARSHALL, D. M.   Notes on the Habits of the Great Northern Shrike [Lanius borealis].   < *The Journal of Science* (newspaper of Toledo, Ohio), n. s., ii, No. 6, Aug., 1879, cut.

> Popular account of habits, with a cut.

1879. MARSHALL, D. M.   [Notes on the Habits of the Great Northern Shrike (Lanius borealis).]   < *The Oölogist*, v, No. 2, Aug., 1879, p. 16.

> Quoted with editorial comment from *The Journal of Science* (Toledo, Ohio), Aug., 1879.

1879. PURDIE, H. A.   The Loggerhead Shrike [Lanius ludovicianus] breeding in Maine.   < *Bull. Nutt. Ornith. Club*, iv, No. 3, July, 1879, pp. 186, 187.

1879. PURDIE, H. A.   Nesting of the Great Northern and Loggerhead Shrikes in Maine.   < *Forest and Stream*, xii, Apr. 3, 1879, p. 166.

> Interesting note on the breeding of *Lanius ludovicianus* in Maine.

1879. PURDIE, H. A.   The Loggerhead Shrike [Lanius ludovicianus] in Maine.   < *Forest and Stream*, xii, May 8, 1879, p. 265.

> Correcting statement in *Forest and Stream*, above cited, that *Lanius borealis* breeds in Maine, and showing that probably *L. ludovicianus*, only, occurs there in summer.

Corvidæ.

1805. BARTRAM, W. Anecdotes of the American Crow. < *Philadelphia Med. and Phys. Journ.*, i., 1805, pp. 89–95; *Nicholson's Journ.*, xii, 1805, pp. 194–198.
Not seen; title from *Roy. Soc. Cat.*

1818. ORD, G. An Account of the Florida Jay, of Bartram [Garrulus cærulescens]. <*Journ. Acad. Nat. Sci. Phila.*, i, 1818, pp. 345–347.

1829. HILL, W. H. The Young of the Raven [Corvus corax]. < *Loudon's Mag. Nat. Hist.*, ii, 1829, p. 403.

1833. D[ENSON?], J. A Magpie the Tips of whose Mandibles crossed each other in the manner the Sides of the Letter x do. < *Loudon's Mag. Nat. Hist.*, vi, 1833, pp. 517, 518.

1835. G[EOFFROY] S[T. HILAIRE, ISID.]. Pie. Pica. Cuv. P. a moustaches blanches. P. mystacalis. G. S. < *Guér. Mag. de Zool.*, 5ᵉ année, 1835, classe ii, notice xxxiv, pl. xxxiv.
Bolivia (*Cyanocorax*).

1836. GODMAN, J. D. American | Natural History. | By | John D. Godman, M. D. | To which is added | his last work, | the Rambles of a Naturalist, | with | a biographical sketch of the author. | In two volumes. | Vol. I [II]. | — | Third edition. | — | Philadelphia : | published by Hogan & Thompson. | — | 1836. 2 vols. 8vo. Vol. I, engr. title-p., pp. i–xxvi (biographical sketch), 1 l. (dedication), pp. v–xiv (preface and introduction), pp. 15–345. Vol. II, engr. title-p., pp. 1–337. Plates in both vols.
Dr. Godman was born at Annapolis, Md., Dec. 20, 1794, and died Apr. 17, 1830. His principal work, "American Natural History," is devoted to Mammals, as is well known. The original edition, in 3 vols. 8vo., was published, vols. i, ii, 1826, Philadelphia, H. C. Carey and I. Lea, and vol. iii, 1828, Philadelphia, Carey, Lea, and Carey. This was reissued in 1831, Philadelphia, Stoddart and Atherton, without alteration, doubtless from the original plates. In 1836 appeared the third edition, as here cited, in *two* vols.; substantially the same as the original, as to main text, but with biographical sketch prefixed to vol. i, and the "Rambles" affixed to vol. ii. This third edition was reissued in 1860, Philadelphia, Uriah Hunt and Son, apparently without alteration, though with new title-page. I have handled all four of these issues.
The "Rambles" are an incomplete series of sketches, composed by the author on his deathbed, and appeared first in a weekly journal published in Philadelphia; but I have never been able to see the original articles. They were first added to this 1836 edition of the "Natural History," and reappear in the 1860 reissue. Nos. x–xii of the "Rambles," pp. 325–337 of both the 1836 and the 1860 editions, are devoted to the natural history of *Corvus americanus;* and these sketches are, upon the whole, the best account we possess of the habits and traits of the bird.

1836. WATERTON, C. Notes on the Habits of the Magpie [Corvus pica]. < *Loudon's Mag. Nat. Hist.*, ix, 1836, pp. 225–229.

1842. LAFRESNAYE, [F.] DE. G. Pie. Pica. Cuvier. P. de San-Blas. P. San-Blasiana. De Lafresn. (Geai de San-Blas, Néboux, Rev. zool., 1840, pp. 290 et 323.) < *Guér. Mag. de Zool.*, 2ᵉ sér., année 1842, oiseaux, pp. 1, 2, pl. 28.

1843. CABOT, S., JR. [Corvus vociferus, sp. n., from Yucatan.] < *Proc. Bost. Soc. Nat. Hist.*, i, 1843, p. 155.

1843. H[EWITT], W. Note on the Habits of the Raven [Corvus corax]. < *Zoologist*, i, 1843, pp. 215–219.

1843. H[EWITT], W. Additional Note on the Raven [Corvus corax]. < *Zoologist*, i, 1843, pp. 305, 306.

1843. HEWITT, W. Note on Magpies, Jays and Crows [Corvidæ]. < *Zoologist*, i, 1843, pp. 350, 351.
Bull. v, 4——6.

1845. ANON. Ferocity of a Magpie [Corvus pica]. < Zoologist, iii, 1845, p. 1072.
From *Lancaster Gazette*, June 21, 1845.

1845. CABOT, S., JR. [Remarks on exhibition of a specimen of Pica melanoleuca from Michigan.] < *Proc. Bost. Soc. Nat. Hist.*, ii, 1845, pp. 73, 74.
Critical comparison with the European bird.

1845. STRICKLAND, H. E. On Cyanocitta, a proposed new genus of Garrulinæ, and on C. superciliosa, a new species of Blue Jay, hitherto confounded with C. ultramarina, Bonap. < *Ann. Mag. Nat. Hist.*, xv, 1845, pp. 260, 261.
The type of the new genus *Cyanocitta* is expressly stated to be *Garrulus cristatus* (Linn.); wrongly given by most American writers as *G. superciliosa=G. californicus.—G. cristatus* is wrongly given by G. R. Gray and others as the type of Swainson's genus *Cyanurus*, 1831, upon the assumption that the first species mentioned by an author under a genus must be considered his type of that genus. But Swainson himself says that *cristatus*, etc., are aberrant members of his genus *Cyanurus*. Therefore, *Cyanurus* Sw., 1831, is a synonym of *Cyanocorax* Boie, 1826, leaving *Cyanocitta* Strickl., 1845, to stand for the *crested* blue jays of America typified by *C. cristatus, stelleri*, etc.—See *P. Z. S.*, 1876, p. 268, note.

1845. STRICKLAND, H. E. Further Notice respecting Cyanocitta superciliosa, a supposed new Species of Blue Jay. < *Ann. Mag. Nat. Hist.*, xv, 1845, pp. 342, 343.
Identified with *Garrulus californicus* Vig.

1846. AGASSIZ, L. [Corvus lugubris, sp. n.] < *Proc. Bost. Soc. Nat. Hist.*, ii, 1846, p. 188.

1846. HUGHES, E. J. R. Habit of the Raven [Corvus corax]. < *Zoologist*, iv, 1846, p. 1366.

1847. AGASSIZ, L. On the Moose and Carabou and on the American Raven [Corvus lugubris]. < *Am. Journ. Sci.*, iii, 1847, p. 436.
From *Proc. Bost. Soc. Nat. Hist.*, 1846, p. 187.

1847. AGASSIZ, L. On the Moose and Carabou, and on the American Raven [Corvus lugubris]. < *Ann. Mag. Nat. Hist.*, xx, 1847, p. 142.
From *Am. Journ. Sci.*, 1847, p. 436.

1848. CASSIN, J. Descriptions of two new Species of the Genus Cyanocorax [C. harrissii, C. concolor], Boie, of which specimens are in the Collection of the Academy of Natural Sciences of Philadelphia. < *Proc. Acad. Nat. Sci. Phila.*, iv, 1848, pp. 26, 27.

1848. PRATER, T. Anecdote of a Magpie (Corvus pica). < *Zoologist*, vi, 1848, p. 2146.

1849. CABOT, S., JR. [On the specific distinctness of Corvus americanus and Corvus corone.] < *Proc. Bost. Soc. Nat. Hist.*, iii, 1849, pp. 104, 105.

1849. ELLMAN, J. B. A Gamekeeper's Stratagem. < *Zoologist*, vii, 1849, p. 2494.
Singular method of attracting magpies,—by cries of a tortured hedgehog.

1849. STRICKLAND, H. E. Cyanocorax nanus, Dubus. ? < *Jard. Contrib. Orn.*, 1849, p. 122, pl. xxxiii.
Provisionally named *C. pumilio*, sp. n.

1850. ANON. A Magpie's delicate attention to its Mistress. < *Zoologist*, viii, 1850, p. 2953.
From *Literary Gazette*, Oct. 12, 1850.

1850. BONAPARTE, C. L. On the Garruline Birds, or Jays; with Descriptions of new species. < *P. Z. S.*, xviii, 1850, pp. 79–86, pl. (Aves) xvii.
This paper requires close attention to catch its drift. The author's "Napoleonic" tendency to transfer, substitute, and otherwise interfere with the genera of other authors, to suit his own notions, is here seen at about its worst: and this abuse of generic nomenclature in *Garrulinæ* has provoked endless confusion.

Gray's *Lophocitta*, 1840, *vice Platylophus* Sw., is applied (p. 79) to *Gurrulus histrionicus* Müll., and *Corvus galericulatus* Cuv.

Garrulus lidthi, p. 80, pl. 17, is a new species; other species of *Garrulus* treated are *G. lanceolatus* Vig., *glandarius* V., *japonicus* Schl., *krynickii* Kalen., *melanocephalus* Bonelli, *brandti* Eversm., and *bispecularis* Vig.

Cyanogarrulus Bp., p. 83, is "dismembered" from *Cyanocorax* Boie, 1826, for *C. cristatus*, etc., becoming thus exactly synonymous with *Cyanocitta* Strickl., 1845.

1850. BONAPARTE, C. L.—Continued.

Cyanocorax Boie is "restricted" to such species as *O. azureus* and *violaceus*.

Xanthura Bp., p. 83, is proposed for *Corvus peruvianus*.

Cissilopha Bp., p. 83, is applied to *C. sanblasiana*.

Cyanurus Sw., 1831, is "transferred" to such species as *Pica bullockii* Wagl., and *P. colliei* Vig.—*Cyanurus dairi, Cyanurus cubo*, p. 84, are new species.

Calocitta is applied to "red-billed, long-tailed, blue magpies."

Cyanocephalus wiedi Bp., "1842", occurs on p. 85; but only the generic name *Cyanocephalus* appeared in 1842.   *Gymnokitta* (g. n., "Max.") occurs in the same paragraph.

Cyanopica Bp., p. 85, with species *C. melanocephala* (Wagl.) *cyaneus* (Pall.) and *cooki* Bp., 1849.

Streptocitta Bp. and *Gazòla* Bp. are respectively proposed to be applied to *Pica albicollis* V., and *Corvus caledonicus*.

1850. C.   Fragments from my note-book.—A bird breathing through its wing. *Family Visitor*, i, 1850, p. 32.

A blue jay with its wing broken, was brought to me to stuff. . . .   Wishing to kill it without injuring its skin or disarranging its feathers, I attempted to strangle it by compressing its neck firmly so that the windpipe was entirely closed, and in this manner I held it several minutes without its presenting any appearance of suffocation or inconvenience, and its thorax contracted and expanded regularly.   Putting it down on the floor it hopped off into a corner, screaming and scolding as usual.   I was sadly puzzled to account for this, till at length I thought of its wing; and on examining it I found the long bone (humerus) broken, and through this it breathed.   After I stopped up this orifice and compressed the windpipe again, it was suffocated in a few moments. . . .   Cleveland, Ohio, Jan. 19, 1850.

1850. CURTLER, M.   Ferocity of the Magpie (Pica caudata).   < *Zoologist*, viii, 1850, pp. 2799, 2800.

1850. MC'INTOSH, J.   Longevity of a Magpie (Pica caudata).   < *Zoologist*, viii, 1850, p. 2824.

1851. BEADLES, H.   Anecdotes of a Raven [Corvus corax].   < *Zoologist*, ix, 1851, pp. 3033, 3034.

1851. BONAPARTE, C. L.   On the Garruline Birds, or Jays; with Descriptions of new species.   < *Ann. Mag. Nat. Hist.*, 2d ser., vii, 1851, pp. 412–419.

From *P. Z. S.*, Apr. 12, 1850, pp. 79–86, *q. v.*

1853. BERNSTEIN, H. A.   De | Anatomia Corvorvm. | Pars prima. | Osteologia. | — | Dissertatio | Inavgvralis zootomica | qvam | consensv et avctoritate | gratiosi Medicorvm ordinis Vratislaviensis | pro | svmmis in Medicina et Chirvrgia honoribvs | rite | capessendis | die XVI. M. Novembris A. MDCCCLIII | Hora IX | palam defendet | avctor | Henricvs Agathon Bernstein. | — | . . . | — | Vratislaviae, | typis Grassii Barthii et Soc. (W. Friedrich).   1 vol. 8vo. pp. i-vi, 1-64 + 1 l.

1854. JAMES, G. P. R.   The Raven [Corvus corax].   < *Harper's Monthly Mag.*, viii, 1854, pp. 463–470.

Anecdotes of its behavior in England.

1855. BERGE, F.   [Ueber die Eier von Corvus corax.]   < *Naumannia*, 1855, p. 110.

1855. FUHLROTT, [C.]   [Varietät der gemeinen Elster, Corvus pica, L.]   < *Naumannia*, 1855, pp. 398–400.

1855. KAUP, J. [J.]   Einige Worte über die systematische Stellung der Familie der Raben, Corvidæ.   (Anh. iii. zu Bericht über d. viii. Jahresvers. d. deut. Orn.-Gesell.)   < *J. f. O.*, 1854, Extrahheft (1855), pp. xlvii-lvi, pl. ii, f. 10.

The family is divided into 5 subfamilies, each of 5 lesser groups (some not yet discovered). The diagrammatic illustration of the author's views is a pentagon (family), pointed with 5 lesser pentagons (subfamilies), rayed into stars by the 25 (actual or theoretical) minor groups. The quinary notion is also indicated in his arrangement of allied families.

1856. MAXIMILIAN.   Ueber die nordamerikanische Elster, (Pica hudsonica Bonap.) < *J. f. O.*, iv, 1856, pp. 197–204.

Elaborate description, with reference to its supposed distinction from *P. melanoleuca*; but some of the alleged differences have been disproved, and none of them have been established.

1857. SMITH, R. B.   Raven Paring [sic] with Crow.   < *Zoologist*, xv, 1857, pp. 5680, 5681.

1858. BREHM, [C.] L.   Die langgeschwänzte Elster, Pica caudata Ray.   < *J. f. O.*, vi, 1858, pp. 173–176.

"Zerfällt nach meiner Ueberzeugung in folgende Arten:" *P. leuconotus* Brm., *P. vulgaris* auct., *P. melanotos* nob., *P. mauritanica* Bp.

1859. SCHLEGEL, H.   Notice sur le Genre Corvus.   < *Bijdragen tot de Dierkunde*, II. Deel, Achtste Aflevering, 1859, pp. 1–16, avec trois planches, dont l'une quadruple, 1, 1 b, 2, 3.

This "notice" is in fact a monograph of the genus; on the whole, the most reliable and satisfactory one we have.   The author's well-known extreme conservatism perhaps never appeared to better advantage than in this case, of a genus of which the rather numerous species are colored so uniformly, and at the same time present so much variation in size and shape. Numberless nominal species are here laid, and the residuum may be considered a safe basis for further study of the genus; for it is extremely unlikely that there are *fewer* good species than this author allows.   Two, *C. advena* and *C. senex*, are figured in colors; while of most of the rest, the heads are shown of life size on the black "quadruple plate" (really two double plates, 1 and 1b).   Here is the list of them all, with the references both to the pages and to the plates, as the publication is not in every library :—

C. crassirostris, cafer, p. 1; *scapulatus, pectoralis*, p. 2; *advena* (sp. n., pl. ii), *cornix*, p. 3; *splendens, corax* (pl i, f. 1, 2), p. 4; *japonensis* (pl. i, f. 3, 4), *culminatus* (pl. i, f. 7), p. 7; *corone* (pl. i, f. 11, 12), *coronoides* (pl. i, f. 13), *umbrinus* (pl. i, f. 14), p. 8; *macrorhynchus* (pl. i, f. 5, 6), *orru* (pl. i, f. 9, 10), *brevipennis* (sp. n., pl. i, f. 8), p. 9; *senex* (pl. iii), *americanus*, p. 10; *solitarius* (pl. i, f. 17), *mexicanus* (pl. i, f. 25), *frugilegus* (pl. i, f. 18), p. 11; *capensis* (pl. i, f. 19), *minor* (pl. i, f. 20) *validissimus* (sp. n., pl. i, f. 21), p. 12; *validus* (pl. i, f. 22), *enca* (pl. i, f. 23), p. 13; *violaceus* (pl. i, f. 24), *ossifragus* (pl. i, f. 27), *leucognaphalus* (pl. 1, f. 28), p. 14; *affinis* (pl. i, f. 26), *monedula*, p. 15; *daiuricus, neglectus* (sp. n.), p. 16.   Cf. *Ibis*, 1860, pp. 189–191.

1860. ANON.   The Magpie Nesting in Confinement.   < *Zoologist*, xviii, 1860, pp. 6920, 6921.

1860. GODMAN, J. D.   American | Natural History | By John D. Godman, M. D. | To which is added | his last work, | The Rambles of a Naturalist, | with a biographical sketch of the author. | In two volumes.   Vol. II. | — | Third edition. | — | Philadelphia : | Uriah Hunt & Son, | 62 North Fourth street. | 1860. 8vo. pp. 337.

This is merely a reissue of the 2 vol. 3d ed. of 1836, *which see*.   The articles on *Corvus americanus* occupy the same pages, 325–337, of vol. ii.

1860. HEINE, F.   Ueber die Gattung Cyanocorax Boie.   < *J. f. O.*, viii, 1860, pp. 113–118.

Systematic synopsis, with diagnoses, synonyms, etc., of 8 spp.—*C. sclateri, C. uroleucus*, p. 115; *C. intermedius*, p. 116, spp. nn. *Argurocatta*, g. n., p. 117, type *Corvus cyanoleucus* Wied.

1862. BARCLAY, W. L.   Three Ravens [Corvus corax] feeding on a dead Hare at Higham.   < *Zoologist*, xx, 1862, p. 7932.

1862. BREE, W. T.   Gathering of Magpies.   < *Zoologist*, xx, 1862, p. 7846.

1862. BREE, C. R.   Notes about Magpies.   < *Zoologist*, xx, 1862, pp. 8162–8164.

1862. GIBSON, B.   Large Flocks of Magpies.   < *Zoologist*, xx, 1862, p. 7881.

1862. HADFIELD, H.   Corvus americanus : Corvus corone of Wilson.   < *Zoologist*, xx, 1862, p. 8282.

Differences from *C. corone* of Europe.

1862. HADFIELD, H.   Gatherings of Magpies.   < *Zoologist*, xx, 1862, pp. 7931, 7932.

1862. THOMPSON, T.   Gathering of Magpies.   < *Zoologist*, xx, 1862, p. 7846.

1863. BREE, C. R.   Magpies Breeding in Confinement.   < *Zoologist*, xxi, 1863, p. 8632.

1864. COX, C. J.   Defence of the Magpie and Rook.   < *Zoologist*, xxii, 1864, pp. 8952–8954.

1864. MORTIMER, T.   Domesticated Magpies.   < *Zoologist*, xxii, 1864, p. 8885.

1864. WALTER, H.   Eine Rabenkrähe mit Kreuzschnabelbildung.   < *Zool. Gart.*, v, 1864, pp. 283–286, figg.

1865. ANON. Grosse Antipathie des Raben [Corvus corax] gegen den Habicnt. < *Aus. der Natur.*, xxxi oder xix, 1865, p. 1860.

1865. DUTTON, J. Destructive Propensities of the Raven [Corvus corax]. < *Zoologist*, xxiii, pp. 9562, 9563.

1865. GOBYNARI, —. Ein alter Rabe [Corvus corax]. < *Zool. Gart.*, vi, 1865, p. 278.

1865. REY, E. [Zucht der Elstervögel (Pica melanoleuca).] < *Zool. Gart.*, vi, 1865, pp. 187–189.

1866. DUTTON, J. Raven [Corvus corax] Nesting in a Cucumber-frame. < *Zoologist*, 2d ser., i, 1866, p. 32.

1866. MATHEW, M. A. An ancient Raven [Corvus corax]. < *Zoologist*, 2d ser., i, 1866, p. 270.

1866. NÖLL, J. F. Ein getäuschter Rabe. < *Zool. Gart.*, vii, 1866, p. 39.

1866. WILLEMOES-SUHM, R. V. Brütende Elsteralbinos [Pica caudata]. < *Zool. Gart.*, vi, 1866, pp. 76, 77.

1867. BECKWITH, R. G. Magpie with Yellow Beak. < *Zoologist*, 2d ser., ii, 1867, pp. 826, 827.
    Supposes the bird's bill colored with yolk of egg.

1867. HARVIE-BROWN, J. A. Magpie with a Yellow Beak. < *Zoologist*, 2d ser., ii, 1867, pp. 877, 878.
    Fears no satisfactory conclusion can be reached.

1867. HARVIE-BROWN, J. A. Magpie with a Yellow Beak. < *Zoologist*, 2d ser., ii, 1867, pp. 706, 707.
    A living bird of this kind observed in Scotland. Very interesting, in its bearing on *Pica nuttalli*.

1867. MATHEW, G. F. Magpie with Yellow Beak. < *Zoologist*, 2d ser., ii, 1867, p. 1016.
    Another case,—a similar bird observed in Devonshire.

1867. NEWTON, A. Magpie with a Yellow Beak. < *Zoologist*, 2d ser., ii, 1867, p. 757.
    Makes the obvious comparison with *Pica nuttalli*. The editor, E. Newman, supposes the bird to be *Pica nuttalli*.

1867. NEWTON, A. Magpie with a Yellow Beak. < *Zoologist*, 2d ser., ii, 1867, p. 913.
    Pertinent observation: "Causes which in America have produced a permanent race of magpies having yellow bills may in Europe have produced a single example having the same peculiarity."

1867. SCHLEGEL, H. Coraces. < *Mus. Hist. Nat. Pays-Bas*, 9e livr., 1867, pp. 1–150.
    "La famille des Coraces comprend les sous-familles des Corvi, Paradiseæ et Coraciæ." (!)
    "The author in this portion of his Catalogue groups together a most heterogeneous assemblage of birds. *Corvidæ*, *Paradiseidæ*, *Oriolidæ*, *Sturnidæ*, but worst of all, *Coraciidæ*, so that it is almost impossible to give here a clear account of them. The *Corvidæ*, in which we include the author's genera *Corvus*, *Nucifraga*, *Pica*, *Cyanocorax*, *Picathartes*, *Pyrrhocorax*, *Garrulus*, *Cissa*, *Glaucopis*, *Chalybæus*, *Cracticus*, and *Lycorax*, appear to be represented in the Leyden Museum by 685 mounted specimens belonging to 116 species . . ." (*Zool. Rec.*, 1867, p. 112.) Cf. *Ibis*, 1867, p. 111.

1868. DUTTON, J. Rook with a crossed Beak. < *Zoologist*, 2d ser., iii, 1868, p. 1459.

1868. ENDICOTT, W. E. Remarkable flight of Crows [Corvus americanus]. < *Am. Nat.*, ii, 1868, p. 381.
    Nearly 100,000, estimated, passing over a point in Maryland, U. S., between 4 and 6 p. m., in April.

1868. HOXIE, W. [Extract from a letter containing observations on the habits of Cyanurus cristatus.] < *Proc. Boston Soc. Nat. Hist.*, xi, 1868, p. 284.

1868. NAUMAN, C. H. Is the Crow [Corvus americanus] a Bird of Prey? < *Am. Nat.*, ii, 1868, p. 491.
    Cf. *tom. cit.*, 664. Note of a crow seizing and carrying off a chicken, *more accipitrino*.

1869. ANON. La Corneille [Corvus americanus] est-elle un oiseau de proie? < *Naturaliste Canadien*, i, 1869, p. 194.
    Affirmé.

1869. BARTHOLF, J. H.   Is the Crow [Corvus americanus] a Bird of Prey?   < *Am. Nat.*, ii, 1869, p. 664.
   Other (cf. *tom. cit.*, 491) instances of the crow seizing and carrying off chickens, like a hawk.

1869. BREWER, T. M.   [Remarks on exhibition of four unspotted eggs of Corvus americanus.]   < *Proc. Boston Soc. Nat. Hist.*, xiii, 1869, pp. 138, 139.

1869. RATHVON, S. S.   The Crow [Corvus americanus] a Bird of Prey.   < *Am. Nat.*, iii, 1869, pp. 102, 103.
   The raptorial propensities of *Corvus americanus* confirmed.

1870. BREWER, T. M.   The Blue Jay Family.   < *Atlantic Monthly*, Apr., 1870, pp. 480–485.

1870. HAMEL, E. D.   Cream-coloured Magpie.   < *Zoologist*, 2d ser., v, 1870, p. 2344.

1871. COUES, E.   The Long-crested Jay [Cyanurus macrolophus].   < *Am. Nat.*, v, 1871, pp. 770–775, fig. 134.
   Extended biography of *Cyanurus macrolophus.*

1871. HORNE, C.   [Destruction of young lambs by] Magpies.   < *Zoologist*, 2d ser., vi, 1871, pp. 2483, 2484.

1871. LÜHDER, W.   Ueber die Raben Neu-Vorpommerns und Rügens.   < *Mitth. a. d. naturw. Ver. v. Neu-Vorp. u. Rüg.*, iii, 1871, pp. 40–52.
   9 spp.

1872. COUES, E.   Observations on Picicorvus columbianus.   < *Ibis*, 3d ser., ii, 1872, pp. 52–59.
   Extended biographical sketch; synonymy, etc.

1872. COUES, E.   Contribution to the History of the Blue Crow [Gymnokitta cyanocephala] of America.   < *Ibis*, ii[3], 1872, pp. 152–158.
   Synonymy, description, and biography.

1872. FRIEDEL, E.   Krähen als Nussdiebe.   < *Zool. Gart.*, xiii, 1872, p. 94.

1873. ALLEN, J. A.   Crows and Ravens.   < *Am. Nat.*, vii, 1873, pp. 743, 744.
   On the local distribution of *Corvus corax* and *C. americanus*, with reference to *tom. cit.*, p. 693.

1873.. BARRETT, M.   On the Migration of Certain Animals as Influenced by Civilization.   < *Am. Nat.*, vii, 1873, pp. 693–695.
   Chiefly on the local dispersion of *Corvus corax* and *C. americanus.*

1873. BARRETT, M.   On the Migration of Certain Animals as influenced by Civilization.   < *Am. Sportsman*, iii, 1873, p. 86.
   Disappearance of *Corvus corax* from Minnesota, and immigration of *C. americanus.*

1873. GIZYCKI, G. V.   Biographie meiner Elster.   < *J. f. O.*, 1873, pp. 35–45.

1873. [SALVIN, O.]   [Reference to the original notice of the Genus Cyanocephalus Bp.]   < *Ibis*, 3d ser., iii, 1873, p. 103.
   Bonaparte proposed the genus *Cyanocephalus* in 1842, in his *Oss. Stat. Zool. Eur. Vert.* 1840–41, p. 17; and named the species by implication, *C. wiedi;* but the word "*wiedi*" does not actually occur there. I have verified Mr. Salvin's reference.

1874. ANON.   [EDITORIAL.]   Possibly a new bird from Oregon.   < *Forest and Stream*, iii, Sept. 10, 1874, p. 68.
   Concluded to be *Picicorvus columbianus;* see *ibid.*, p. 84.

1874. DUBOIS, A.   Remarques Morphologiques sur les Espèces du Sous-genre Xanthoura.   < *Bull. Acad. Roy. de Be'gique*, 2° sér, xxxviii, 1874, pp. ———, fig. (carte).
   L'auteur constate que ce sous-genre ne comprend réellement qu'une seule espèce, très-variable suivant la position géographique qu'occupent les individus qui la composent, de la manière suivante: *Cyanocorax yncas*, Bolivie, Pérou, repub. de l'Équateur; *a, cyanodorsalis* (var. n.), Nouvelle-Grenada centrale et méridionale; *β, cyanocapilla*, nord de la Nouv.-Grenade jusqu'au Guatémala; *γ, cœruleocephala* (var. n.), Vénézuéla; *δ, luxuosa*, Mexique, Texas.

1874. KERR, W. J.   Ravens [Corvus corax] Nesting in North Wales.   < *Zoologist*, 2d ser., ix, 1874, p. 4156.

1874. LEE, A., *Miss.*   Jim Crow.   < *St. Nicholas Mag.*, i, 1874, pp. 647–649, figs. 1-9.
   Amusing account of a pet *Corvus americanus.*

1874. TRIPPE, T. M. The White-necked Raven [Corvus cryptoleucus, field note on]. < *Am. Nat.*, viii, 1874, pp. 429, 430.

1875. ANON. A variegated Crow [Corvus americanus, albinistic]. < *Forest and Stream*, iii, Feb. 4, 1875, p. 405.

1875. COUES, E. [On the nest and eggs of Gymnokitta cyanocephala.] < *Ibis*, 3d ser., v, 1875, pp. 270—.

1875. [PIERCE, G.] A white Crow [Corvus americanus]. < *Forest and Stream*, v, Sept. 23, 1875, p. 100.

1875. [PIERCE, G.]. Rara Avis [albinistic Corvus americanus]. < *Rod and Gun*, vi, Sept. 25, 1875, p. 386.

1876. ANON. Mathematical Faculty of Crows. < *Rod and Gun*, vii, Mar. 4, 1876, p. 363.
Anecdote, from "Portland Advertiser."

1876. ANON. A Thievish Crow [Corvus americanus]. < *Rod and Gun*, viii, July 22, 1876, p. 269.
From the New Bedford, Mass., "Mercury." *Corvus americanus* preying upon fledglings of Robins.

1876. ANON. [Caterpillars' eggs in stomach of Corvus americanus.] < *Rod and Gun*, viii, July 15, 1876, p. 250.

1876. BENDIRE, C. Notes on the Breeding Habits of Clarke's Crow (Picicorvus columbianus), with an Account of its Nest and Eggs. < *Bull. Nutt. Ornith. Club*, i, No. 2, July, 1876, pp. 44, 45.

1876. [COUES, E.] [Anecdote of the intelligence of a Crow (Corvus ossifragus).] < *New York Independent*, Nov. 23, 1876.
A tame bird of this kind, kept in a yard where there was a tub of water containing small fish, snails, etc., for stocking an aquarium, used to alight upon the brim of the tub, and drop bread-crumbs into the water to attract the fish; which it seized as they rose to the surface, and devoured.

1876. FRAZAR, A. M. Intelligence of a Crow [Corvus americanus]. < *Bull. Nutt. Ornith. Club*, i, No. 3, Sept., 1876, p. 76.

1876. "J. F." Crows [Corvus americanus] despoiling heronries. < *Forest and Stream*, vii, Sept. 14, 1876, p. 84.

1876. MORRIS, R. T. Charges against the Crow [Corvus americanus]. < *Forest and Stream*, vi, July 27, 1876, p. 401.

1876. REID, P. Blue Jay [Cyanurus cristatus]. < *Rod and Gun*, vii, Feb. 12, 1876, p. 369.

1876. SCHOCK, O. D. Charges against the Crow [Corvus americanus]. < *Forest and Stream*, vii, Aug. 17, 1876, p. 20.

1876. SCLATER, P. L., *and* SALVIN, O. Notes on some of the Blue Crows of America. < *P. Z. S.*, Feb. 15, 1876, pp. 268–272.
Cyanocitta germana, p. 270, Belize, Piten, Merida, sp. n.; *C. armillata*, γ. *quindiuna*, p. 272, Cordillera of Quindiu, var. n.
Critical notes on *Cyanocitta argentigula*, *C. sanblasiana*, *C. beecheii*, *C. germana* (p. 270, sp. n.), *C. jolyœa* Bp., *C. armillata*, G. R. Gr., of which last are given as subspecies *meridana*, p. 271, *bogotana*, p. 272, and *quindiuna* (subsp. n.), p. 272.—*Cyanocorax ortoni*, Lawr. = *C. mystacalis*, Geoffr.—Special note on the type of the genus *Cyanocitta*, which is *C. cristatus*.

1876. WEBSTER, N. B. Crows [Corvus americanus] seeking Water. < *Field and Forest*, vol. ii, No. 4, Oct., 1876, p. 65.
By pecking into watermelons.

1877. COUES, E. Letters on Ornithology. No. 15.—Curious Crows [Picicorvus columbianus and Gymnokitta cyanocephala]. < *The Chicago Field*, July 14, 1877, 2 figg.
Popular notices of these species, with figures of their heads.

1877. [INGERSOLL, E.] Crows [Corvus americanus]. < *Rod and Gun*, ix, Jan. 27, 1877, p. 266.
> From "New York Tribune."

1877. MILLER, H. The Crow [Corvus americanus]. < *Rod and Gun*, ix, Feb. 24, 1877, p. 329.
> Observations upon habits, capability, and utility.

1877. TENNEY, S. The Raven [Corvus carnivorus] and the Sooty Tern [Sterna fuliginosa] in Williamstown, Massachusetts. < *Am. Nat.*, xi, No. 4, Apr., 1877, p. 243.

1878. EAGLE, C. H. The Fish Crow (Corvus ossifragus, Wils.), on Long Island. < *Bull. Nutt. Ornith. Club*, iii, No. 1, Jan., 1878, p. 47.
> With editorial note by J. A. Allen.

1878. HENSHAW, H. W. Nest and Eggs of the Blue Crow (Gymnokitta cyanocephala). < *Bull. Nutt. Ornith. Club*, iii, No. 3, July, 1878, pp. 112–115.
> Also on the general habits of the bird. Cf. *Ibis*, 1875, p. 270.

1878. [QUAY, T. R.] Crimes of the Crow [Corvus americanus]. < *Forest and Stream*, x, May 2, 1878, p. 236.
> Opinion that the bird is rather injurious than beneficial to the agriculturist.

1878. [WILLARD, S. L.] The Jay of the North; Canada Jay [Perisoreus canadensis]. < *The Oölogist*, iv, No. 2, Apr., 1878, pp. 14, 15.
> Compiled account of the habits of the bird.

1878. [WILLARD, S. L.] Utility of the Crow [Corvus americanus]. < *The Oölogist*, iv, No. 5, July, 1878, p. 38.

1878. WILY, S. B. Nesting of the Canada Jay [Perisoreus canadensis]. < *The Oölogist*, iv, No. 4, June, 1878, p. 27.

1879. BREWER, T. M. The Rocky Mountain Whiskey-Jack (Perisoreus canadensis capitalis). < *Bull. Nutt. Ornith. Club*, iv, No. 4, Oct., 1879, pp. 239, 240.
> On the nest and eggs of this bird, both of which are fully described.

1879. [CORDES, H.] The Crow [Corvus americanus] arraigned. < *Forest amd Stream*, xiii, Oct. 2, 1879, p. 684.

1879. [COUES, E.] The Long Crested Jay-Bird [Cyanurus macrolophus]. < *Hamilton Freeman* (newspaper of Webster City, Iowa), Apr. 9, 1879.
> Editorial reprint, with comment, of the account of that species in "Birds of the Northwest," 1874, pp. 216–218.

1879. FLAGG, W. The Blue Jay [Cyanurus cristatus] in the East. < *Forest and Stream*, xiii, Dec. 18, 1879, p. 907.

1879. [GRINNELL, G. B.] Crows [Corvus americanus] in Caucus. < *Forest and Stream*, July 24, 1879, p. 485.
> Great flight of crows near Harper's Ferry, Va.

1879. [HARRIMAN, M. C.] Corvus corax in New Hampshire. < *Forest and Stream*, xii, Mar. 13, 1879, p. 106.
> Notice of capture of this species near the town of Warner, N. H.

1879. ZEREGA, L. A. Capture of a Fish Crow (Corvus ossifragus) near Seabright, Monmouth County, New Jersey. < *Bull. Nutt. Ornith. Club*, iv, No. 4, Oct., 1879, p. 239.

Addenda to Corvidæ.

1815. CLINTON, DE WITT. An Introductory Discourse delivered on the 4th of May, 1814. < *Trans. Lit. and Philos. Soc. New York*, i, 1815, pp. 21–184. > Note T, p. 129.
> Note T, to this discourse, is on the American Raven, *Corvus corax.*

1825. BONAPARTE, C. [L.] Descriptions of two new species of Mexican Birds. < *Journ. Acad. Nat. Sci. Phila.*, iv, 1825, pp. 387–390.
> At p. 387, *Corvus ultramarinus*; the other is an *Icterus.*

Icteridæ.

1815. CLINTON, DE WITT. An Introductory Discourse delivered on the 4th of May, 1814. < *Trans. Lit. and Philos. Soc. N. Y.*, i, 1815, pp. 21–184. > Note S, pp. 125–128.

Note S, appended to this discourse, treats of the plumages and migrations of the Bobolink, *Dolichonyx oryzivorus*.

1818. ORD, G. Observations on two species of the genus Gracula [G. quiscala, G. barita] of Latham. < *Journ. Acad. Nat. Sci. Phila.*, i, 1818, pp. 253–260.

A critical article, distinguishing the Boat-tailed Grackle (*Quiscalus major* V.) from the Purple Grackle (*Q. purpureus*).

1819. LICHTENSTEIN, K. M. H. Ueber die Gattung Gracula aus der Familie der Krähenvögel (Coraces). < *Abhandl. der Berlin. Akad.*, aus d. Jahren 1816–17, 1819, Phys. Classe, pp. 143–154. (Vorgelesen den 18. Juli 1816.)

This is the original; there is another edition in *Isis*, 1824, pp. 402–406, *q. v.*

The "genus" *Gracula* of this author is very extensive, including birds of several of the families recognized by modern ornithologists, among them the *Icteridæ*.

The species of *Gracula* treated are the following:—*Gracula religiosa*, p. 148; *G. calva*, p. 148; *G. tristis*, p. 148; *G. pagodarum*, p. 148; *G. cristatella*, p. 149 : *G. carunculata*, p. 149, with several others of doubtful character.—The author then proceeds to treat the other Linnean "*Graculæ*", *i. e.*, *Icteridæ*, as follows:—*Quiscala purpurea*, "n. sp"., p. 151 (but Bartram had called it *Gracula purpurea* in 1791!); *Q. fulgida*, n. sp., p. 151; *Q. navicularis*, n. sp., p. 151; *Q. saularis*, p. 151; *Q. jamaicensis*, p. —.

1824. LICHTENSTEIN, K. M. H. Dissertation sur le genre Martin ou Mainate (Gracula); par Lichtenstein. . . < *Féruss. Bull.*, 2e sect., ii, 1824, p. 294.

Extraite des *Abhand. Königl. Acad. Wiss. Berlin* pour les années 1816 et 1817, pp. 143–154.

1824. LICHTENSTEIN, K. M. H. [Abhandlung über Gracula. Auszug aus Abh. Königl. Akad. Wiss. Berlin aus d. Jahren 1816–17, 1819, SS. 143–154.] < *Oken's Isis*, Jahrg. viii, 1824, pp. 402–406.

Die Charaktere der verwandten Sippen, *Corvus, Coracias, Paradisea, Gracula*. Die reinen *Graculæ* sind folgende sechs: *religiosa, calva, tristis, pagodarum, cristatella, carunculata*, p. 403. Zweifelhaft bleiben; *G. grisea* Daud., *GG. gingiiniana, malabarica, icterops* Lath., *G. longirostra* Pall.—*GG. strepera, tibicen* und *varia* Shaw bilden besser eine eigene Sippe den Racken nahe.—*G. cayennensis* Gm. und *G. picoides* Shaw hat Hermann als *Dendrocolaptes* aufgestellt. Die andern *Graculæ* von Linné stellt der Verfasser als *Quiscala* auf: *Q. purpurea* = *G. quiscala* Lath.; *Q. fulgida* Licht. = *Sturnus quiscala* Daud.; *Q. navicularis*; *Q. saularis*; *Q. jamaicensis* = *Sturnus jamaicensis* Daud.

1825. BONAPARTE, C. [L.] Descriptions of two new species of Mexican Birds. < *Journ. Acad. Nat. Sci. Phila.*, iv, 1825, pp. 387–390.

At p. 389, *Icterus melanicterus*; the other is a *Corvus*.

1825. VIGORS, N. A. On the genus Icterus Briss. . < *Zool. Journ.*, ii, 1825, pp. 182–197, pll. suppl. 9, 10.

This, the second instalment of the series of articles entitled "Sketches on Ornithology; or," &c., treats of the family *Icteridæ* as now understood. Here occur the descriptions of *Xanthornus chrysopterus*, sp. n., p. 190, pl. 9, and of *Leïstes* (g.·n., p. 191) *suchii*, sp. n., p. 192, pl. 10. (*Féruss. Bull.*, viii, 1826, pp. 111–113; *Isis*, 1830, 1013–1016.)

1826. BONAPARTE, C. [L.] On the distinction of two species of Icterus, hitherto confounded under the specific name of Icterocephalus. < *Journ. Acad. Nat. Sci. Phila.*, v, 1826, pp. 222–225.

Icterus xanthocephalus, n. sp., p. 223.

1826. LESSON, [R. P.] Esquisses ornithologiques, etc., etc. Du genre Icterus de Brisson; par N. A. Vigors. . . < *Féruss. Bull.*, 2e sect., viii, 1826, pp. 111–113.

Zool. Journ., ii, No. 6, 1825, pp. 182–197.

1827. LESSON, R. P.   Sur les distinctions a établir entre deux espèces d'Icterus, jusqu'a ce jour confondues sous le nom spécifique d'Icterocephalus ; par Ch. Bonaparte. . .   < *Féruss. Bull.*, 2e sect., xii, 1827, pp. 266, 267.
> *Journ. Acad. Phila.*, vi, 1826, pp. 222-225.

1830. VIGORS, N. A.   Ornithologischen Skizzen, Fortsetzung.   < *Oken's Isis*, Bd. xxiii, pp. 1013-1018.
> Uebersetzt aus d. *Zool. Journ.*, vol. ii, Nro. vi, 1825, pp. 182-197.

1836. ORD, G.   Observations on the Cow Bunting [Molothrus ater] of the United States of America.   < *Loudon's Mag. Nat. Hist.*, ix, 1836, pp. 57-71.
> On its oviposition, parasitism, &c.

1837. BREWER, T. M.   Remarks on the positions assumed by George Ord, Esq., in relation to the cow black-bird, (Icterus agripennis [*i. e.*, Molothrus ater]) in Loudon's Magazine for February, 1836.   < *Journ. Bost. Soc. Nat. Hist.*, i, pt. iv, 1837, pp. 418-435.   (Read July 6, 1836.)
> "*Icterus agripennis*" is a name of the Bobolink (*Dolichonyx oryzivorus*), not of the species treated in this paper.

1839. LINSLEY, J. H.   Notice of Vespertilio pruinosus and Icterus [Agelæus] Phoeniceus.   < *Sillim. Am. Journ. Sci.*, xxxvii, 1839, pp. 195, 196.
> On the carnivorous habits of the Blackbird.

1843. CABOT, S., JR.   [Oriolus musicus, sp. n., from Yucatan.]   < *Proc. Bost. Soc. Nat. Hist.*, i, 1843, p. 155.
> This is an *Icterus*, supposed to be the same as that figured by Cassin in *Journ. Phila. Acad.*, ii, 1848, pl. 17 (*giraudii*).

1843. GURNEY, J. H.   Note on the occurrence of the red-winged Icterus [Agelæus phœniceus] near Norwich.   < *Zoologist*, i, 1843, p. 317.

1844. LAFRESNAYE, [F.] DE.   < G. Icterus. Briss. I. guttulatus. Lafresn.   < *Guér. Mag. de Zool.*, 2e sér., année 1844, Oiseaux, pp. 1-4, pl. 52.
> *Icterus mentalis* Lafr., *R. Z.*, 1842, p. 136.

1847. CASSIN, J.   Descriptions of three new species of the genus Icterus (Briss. ;) specimens of which are in the Museum of the Academy of Natural Sciences of Philadelphia.   < *Proc. Acad. Nat. Sci. Phila.*, iii, 1847, pp. 332-334.
> *I. maculi-alatus, I. auricapillus*, p. 332 ; *I. giraudii*, p. 333.

1847. TARRAGON, [L.] DE.   Description d'une nouvelle espèce de Cassique [Cassicus pyrohypogaster], et note sur le Macronix Ameliæ.   < *Revue Zoologique*, x, 1847, pp. 252, 253.

1848. CASSIN, J.   Description of three new species of the genus Icterus, (Briss.); specimens of which are in the Museum of the Academy of Natural Sciences of Philadelphia.   < *Journ. Acad. Nat. Sci. Phila.*, ii, pt. ii, Aug., 1848, art. xi, pp. 137, 138, pll. xvi, xvii.
> *I. maculi-alatus*, p. 137, pl. xvi, f. 1 ; *I. auricapillus*, p. 137, pl. xvi, f. 2 ; *I. giraudii*, p. 138, pl. xvii.   Described the year previous in *Proc. Phila. Acad.*, iii, pp. 332-334.

1850. STRICKLAND, H. E.   Xanthornus prosthemelas, Strickland [sp. n.].   < *Jard. Contrib. Ornith.*, 1850, p. 120, pl. lxii.

1852. LAWRENCE, G. N.   Descriptions of new species of Birds of the genera . . . and Xanthornus [affinis], . . .   < *Ann. Lyc. Nat. Hist. N. Y.*, v, 1852, pp. 112-117, pl. v.   (Read Apr. 28, 1851.)
> Here occurs, in a paper of wider scope, full title of which is in the N. Am. part of this Bibl., the orig. descr. of the above sp., p. 113.

1852. [READ, M. C.]   Cow Blackbird [Molothrus ater].   < *The Family Visitor*, vol. iii, 1852, p. 68.
> A popular article, giving numerous species in the nests of which eggs of the Cowbird have been found.

1853. ANON.   "Could'nt! Cos he Sung so!"   < *Zoologist*, xi, 1853, p. 3982.
> From *Clinton* (U. S.) *Courant*. Note of a young person's inability to throw a stone at *Dolichonyx oryzivorus*, for the reason stated in the title.

1854. GLOGER, C. W. L. Das geschlechtliche Verhältniss bei den nicht selbst brütenden Vögeln. < *J. f. O.*, ii, 1854, pp. 137–143.
> The general relations of parasitic birds illustrated in the case of *Molothrus ater.*

1856. [BILLINGS, E.] On the Bob-link or Rice-Bird, (Dolichonyx orzivora [sic].)
< *Canad. Nat. and Geol.*, i, June, 1856, pp. 233–237.

1861. SCLATER, P. L. [Exhibition of a Specimen of the American Meadow-Starling
(Sturnella magna) shot in Suffolk, England.] < *P. Z. S.*, xxix, 1861, p. 30.

1861. SCLATER, P. L. Notice of the occurrence of the American Meadow-Starling (Sturnella ludoviciana [magna]) in England. < *Ibis*, iii, 1861, pp. 176–180.
> Concludes with observations on the genus and a synopsis of 5 spp., namely: *ludoviciana,
neglecta, hippocrepis* (Cuba), *mexicana* (Mexico), p. 179, and *meridionalis* (South America), p.
179—the two last being new.

1864. JEFFERY, W., JR. The Redwinged Starling [Agelæus phœniceus] in Sussex.
< *Zoologist*, xxii, 1864, p. 8951.

1865. JESSE, W. Redwinged Starling [Agelæus phœniceus] near Liphook. < *Zoologist*, xxiii, 1865, p. 9782.

1865. SHIMER, H. [On a supposed new Species of Icterus from Illinois (=I. spurius).]
< *Trans. Acad. Sci. St. Louis*, ii, pt. ii, 1865, pp. 260, 261.

1866. CASSIN, J. A Study of the Icteridæ. < *Proc. Acad. Nat. Sci. Phila.*, xviii, 1866,
pp. 10–25. (Continued *ibid.*, pp. 403–417, and *op. cit.*, 1867, pp. 45–74.)
> *Agelainæ*: 7 genn., 46 spp.—*Macroagelaius*, p. 13; *Agelaioides*, p. 15; *Erythropsar*, p. 17;
Callothrus, p. 18; *Cyanothrus*, p. 19, subgg. nn. *Dolichonyx fuscipennis*, p. 16; *Molothrus ca-
banisii*, p. 22; *M. rufo-axillaris*, p. 23, spp. nn.

1866. CASSIN, J. A Second Study of the Icteridæ. < *Proc. Acad. Nat. Sci. Phila.*, xviii,
1866, pp. 403–417. (Continued from *ibid.*, pp. 10–25; continued, *op. cit.*, 1867,
pp. 45–74.)
> *Quiscalinæ*: 5 genn., 28 spp.—*Holoquiscalus*, p. 404; *Megaquiscalus*, p. 409; *Euphagus,
Dives*, p. 413; *Idiopsar*, p. 414, gg. nn. *Quiscalus gundlachii, Q. brachypterus*, p. 406; *Q.
mexicanus*, p. 408; *Q. rectirostris*, p. 409; *Idiopsar brachyurus*, p. 414, spp. nn.

1866. EDWARD, T. Redwinged Starling (Sturnus predatorius [Agelæus phœniceus])
in Scotland. < *Zoologist*, 2d ser., i, 1866, p. 310.

1866. MONK, T. J. Redwinged Starling [Agelæus phœniceus] at Brighton. < *Zoologist*, 2d ser., i, 1866, p. 229.

1867. CASSIN, J. A Third Study of the Icteridæ. < *Proc. Acad. Nat. Sci. Phila.*, xix,
1867, pp. 45–74. (Continued from *ibid.*, pp. 403–407, and *op. cit.*, 1866, pp.
10–25.)
> *Icterinæ*, more monographically treated than the other groups were in previous "Studies."
Euopsar, p. 47; *Andriopsar*, p. 49; *Ateleopsar*, p. 53; *Cassiculoides*, p. 54; *Poliopsar*, p. 55;
Melanopsar, p. 56; *Icterioides*, p. 60; *Melanophantes, Aporophantes*, p. 63, genn. nn. *Icterus
graysonii*, p. 48; *Icterus sclateri*, p. 49; *Icterus salvinii*, p. 41; *I. grace-annæ*, p. 52; *Cassicus
melanurus*, p. 66, spp. nn. Cf. *Ibis*, 1868, p. 115.
> Mr. Cassin's "Studies" were protracted and faithful, representing our leading monograph
of this family, notwithstanding that the author pushed his generic subdivision so far, and
described in some cases very slight geographical modifications as distinct species. It was
one of his last works, as this hand paused Jan. 10, 1869.

1867. JESSE, W. Redwinged Starling [Agelæus phœniceus] near Liphook. < *Zoologist*, 2d ser., ii, 1867, p. 913.

1868. BREWSTER, W. A variety of the Blackbird [Agelæus phœniceus]. < *Am. Nat.*,
ii, 1868, pp. 217, 218.
> Marked with orange on the breast.

1868. "F. W." The Crow Blackbird [Quiscalus versicolor] a Robber. < *Am. Nat.*,
ii, Aug., 1868, p. 326.
> Note on breeding, and on stealing the material from other birds' nests.

1868. JACKSON, T. H. The Cow-bunting [Molothrus ater]. < *Am. Nat.*, ii, 1868, p, 490.
> Its eggs found in nests of *Sayornis fuscus, Empidonax acadicus, Icteria viridis*, and *Pyranga
rubra.*

1868. McLAUGHLIN, W. J.   The Yellow-headed Blackbird (Xanthocephalus icterocephalus Baird).   < *Am. Nat.*, ii, 1868, pp. 493, 494.

Biographical note from Centralia, Kansas, with editorial note on geographical distribution.

1869. KEDNEY, H. S.   The Cow Bunting [Molothrus ater].   < *Am. Nat.*, iii, 1869, p. 550.

Plural eggs of *Molothrus ater* in nests of *Zonotrichia leucophrys* and *Contopus virens*.

1869. [" F. W."]   The Crow Blackbird [Quiscalus versicolor] a Robber.   < *Zoologist*,
2d ser., iv, 1869, pp. 1603, 1604.

From 'American Naturalist,' Aug., 1868, p. 326.

1869. RIDGWAY, R.   Notices of certain obscurely known species of American Birds.
< *Proc. Acad. Nat. Sci. Phila.*, xxi, 1869, pp. 125–135, woodcc.

III. The Smaller Quiscali of the United States, pp. 133–135, figg. 1–3; 3 spp.—*Q. æneus*,
sp. n., p. 134, f. 2.

The article also treats of species of I. *Hylocichla* and II. *Pyranga*.   (See under *Turdidæ* and
Tanagridæ.)

1869. STERNBERG, C.   Zur Fortpflanzungsgeschichte des Viehstaares, Molobrus sericeus (Licht.).   < *J. f. O.*, xvii, 1869, pp. 125–136.

Mit Bemerkungen vom Herausgeber.

1869. [STERNBERG, C.]   Fortpflanzung des Viehstaares (Molobrus sericius [lege seri-
ceus]).   < *Aus der Natur*, xlix, oder n. F., xxxvii, 1869, pp. 595–597.

Nach C. Sternberg's Artikel in *J. f. O.*, 1869, pp. 125–136, mitgetheilt.

1869. TRIPPE, T. M.   The Cow Blackbird [Molothrus ater].   < *Am. Nat.*, iii, 1869, pp.
291–294.

An extended notice of the habits of this species, with special reference to the birds in the
nests of which its eggs have been found.

1870. COUES, E.   The Cow Bird [Molothrus ater].   < *Am. Nat.*, iv, 1870, p. 58.

Inquires whether the eggs of *Molothrus ater* vary in any way connected with the character
of the eggs of different birds selected as foster parents, with reference to A. Newton's observations to this effect in case of *Cuculus canorus*.

1870. COUES, E.   The Natural History of Quiscalus major.   < *Ibis*, 2d ser., vi, 1870,
pp. 367–378.

A full account of the habits of the bird as observed by the writer at Fort Macon, North
Carolina.

1870. HOWELL, R.   Blackbirds [Icteridæ] in Winter.   < *Am. Nat.*, iv, 1870, p. 52.

Molothrus ater and *Scolecophagus ferrugineus* in Tioga Co., N. Y.

1870. SAUSSURE, H. DE.   Los Tordos [Icteridæ].   < *La Naturaleza*, i, 1870, pp. 352–
358.

Sobre las costumbres.   "Con esta nombre [tordo] designaron los Españoles un grupo inte-
resante de aves americanas, por tener algunas de sus especies semejanza en cuanto al color,
con los tordos de Europa [Sturnidæ?], de los que sin embargo son de géneros enteramente
distintos."

1871. BREWER, T. M.   [Remarks on exhibition of a nest of Icterus baltimore.]   < *Proc.
Boston Soc. Nat. Hist.*, xiii, 1871, pp. 411, 412.

1871. COUES, E.   The Yellow-headed Blackbird [Xanthocephalus icterocephalus].
< *Am. Nat.*, v, 1871, pp. 195–200, with a fig.

Extended biography of this species, with allusions to various other birds observed in Kansas.

1871. COUES, E.   Bullock's Oriole [Icterus bullocki].   < *Am. Nat.*, v, 1871, pp. 678–682,
fig. 120.

Extended biography.

1871. COUES, E.   Singular albino [of Dolichonyx oryzivorus].   < *Am. Nat.*, v, 1871,
p. 733.

1871. GILLMAN, H.   Albino Swamp Blackbird [Agelæus phœniceus].   < *Am. Nat.*, v,
1871, p. 251.

1871. NEWMAN, E.   On the Occurrence of the American Meadow Lark (Alauda [Stur-
nella] magna of Wilson) in Great Britain.   < *Zoologist*, 2d ser., vi, 1871, pp.
2557–2560.

1872. BARCENA, M. Apuntes para la ornitología Mexicana.—Costumbres del Quiscalus macrourus. < *La Naturaleza*, ii, 1872, pp. 203–207.

1872. BREWER, T. M. [Note on the North American Forms of Quiscalus.] < *Proc. Boston Soc. Nat. Hist.*, xiv, 1872, p. 205.

1872. HALDEMAN, S. S. Note of Icterus baltimore [written in musical notation]. < *Am. Nat.*, vi, 1872, p. 234.

1872. HOLTZ, L. Ueber Molobrus-Eier, zu Cantagallo in Brasilien von Herrn C. Euler gesammelt. < *J. f. O.*, 1872, p. 193–201, pl. 1, fig. i.
   In continuation of the subject from *op. cit.*, 1870, pp. 15–19. The species are not given. Eggs are figured, pl. 1, f. *a–e.*

1872. KEDNEY, H. S. Occurrence of the Orchard Oriole [Icterus spurius] in South Carolina. < *Am. Nat.*, vi, 1872, pp. 49–51.
   With observations on its habits.

1872. LAWRENCE, G. N. Descriptions of New Species of Birds of the Genera Icterus and Synallaxis. < *Ann. Lyc. Nat. Hist. N. Y.*, x, 1872, pp. 184–186.
   Icterus formosus, p. 184 (Tehuantepec).

1872. LOCKWOOD, S. The Baltimore Oriole [Icterus baltimore] and Carpenter-Bee. < *Am. Nat.*, vi, 1872, pp. 721–724.
   Popular account of the manner in which the bird feeds upon *Xylocopa carolina.*

1872. SCLATER, P. L. [Exhibition of a nest of the Tijereta (Milvulus Tyrannus) containing eggs of Molothrus bonariensis.] < *P. Z. S.*, 1872, p. 862.

1873. CABANIS, J. [Ueber Ostinops angustifrons Spix, O. atrovirens d'Orb., und O. atrocastaneus, n. sp.] < *J. f. O.*, 1873, pp. 308, 309.

1873. FOULKS, O. D. The Red-winged Blackbird [Agelæus phœniceus]. < *Am. Sportsman*, iii, 1873, p. 92.

1873. NEWMAN, E. Molothrus sericeus in Devon. < *Zoologist*, 2d ser., viii, 1873, p. 3411.
   Presumed to have escaped from confinement.

1873. ORTON, J. Meadow Lark [Sturnella magna] with Four Legs. < *Am. Nat.*, vii, 1873, p. 175.

1874. "D. S." A Semi-domesticated Blackbird. < *Am. Sportsman*, iv, 1874, p. 28.

1874. "F. S. B." The Western lark—Strunella Neglecta [*i. e.*, Sturnella magna, var. neglecta]. < *Forest and Stream*, ii, Apr. 9, 1874, p. 134.

1874. HUDSON, W. H. Notes on the Procreant Instincts of the three Species of Molothrus found in Buenos Ayres. < *P. Z. S.*, xlii, 1874, pp. 153–174.
   An extended and interesting article, giving much information, with suggestive deductions.

1874. JENKS, J. W. P. Instinct or Reason. < *Am. Sportsman*, v, Dec. 5, 1874, p. 145.
   Sagacity of Orioles (*Icterus baltimore*) in giving extra support to their nest after experience had proved that its fastenings were weak; also, departure from type of architecture to meet an emergency in the case of the Boat-tailed Grakle (*Quiscalus major*).

1874. MAYNARD, C. J. Orchard Oriole (Icterus spurius). < *Am. Sportsman*, iv, 1874, p. 155.
   Occurring at Ipswich, Mass., and breeding at West Meriden, Conn.

1874. MEEHAN, T. [Frugivorous] Habits of the Orchard Oriole [Icterus spurius]. < *Proc. Acad. Nat. Sci. Phila.*, xxvi, 1874, p. 84.

1874. SCLATER, P. L. On Centropsar, an apparently new Form of the Family Icteridæ. < *P. Z. S.*, xlii, Mar. 3, 1874, pp. 175, 176, pl. xxvi, woodcc.
   Centropsar mirus (sane mirabile dictu!), g. sp. n.; cf. *P. Z. S.*, 1875, p. 380.

1875. BATTY, J. H. Natural [history] researches in the Sierras. < *Rod and Gun*, vi, June 5, 1875, p. 146.
   Song and characteristics of *Sturnella magna* var. *neglecta.*

1875. COUES, E. Albino Black-bird [Xanthocephalus icterocephalus]. < *Rod and Gun*, vi, Apr. 10, 1875, p. 24.

1875. "C. S. W." [INGERSOLL, E.] [Information as to the different birds in whose nests Molothrus ater has been observed to lay.] < *Forest and Stream*, v, Dec. 16, 1875, p. 292.

1875. DAVIS, F. J. The Rusty Blackbird. (S[colecophagus]. ferrugineus.) < *Oölogist*, i, pt. 5, 1875, pp. 37, 38, with figure.

1875. DUBOIS, A. Descriptions de quelques Oiseaux Nouveaux. < *Bull. Acad. Roy. Belgique*, 2ᵉ sér., xl, No. 12, Dec., 1875, pp. 13–17.
> Only seen separate.—Of *Icteridæ* there are here described: *Icterus virescens*, p. 15, Mexico; *Icterus xanthornus* var. *dubusii*, p. 16, Panama; and *I. x.* var. *marginalis*, p. 17, Panama. The article also describes *Cyanocitta yucatanica*, sp. n., p. 13.

1875. F[REEMAN], C. M. The Baltimore Oriole [Icterus baltimore]. < *Oölogist*, i, 1875, p. 46.

1875. SCLATER, P. L. [Remarks on exhibition of the typical specimen of Centropsar mirus.] < *P. Z. S.*, June 1, 1875, p. 380.
> Genus fictitum; avis artefacta, capite *Icteri* (*auduboni* ?), caudâ *Agelæi phœnicei*, pedibus *Eremophilæ alpestris*, instructa. Cf. *J. f. O.*, xxii, 1874, p. 458.

1875. ANON. A Word for the Birds [Icteridæ]. < *Rod and Gun*, vi, Sept. 11, 1875, p. 364.
> Reprint from Boston "Advertiser" concerning utility of Blackbirds in destroying army worms.

1876. FOWLER, H. G. Asylums of the Cow-bird [Molothrus ater]. < *Forest and Stream*, vii, Aug. 10, 1876, p. 4.
> List of birds in whose nests eggs of this species have been found; to which is added editorial [INGERSOLL, E.] note.

1876. "FRANK." Black Birds [Icteridæ of New York State]. < *Rod and Gun*, viii, July 15, 1876, p. 244.

1876. INGERSOLL, E. A Summer Bird [Icterus baltimore]. < *Harper's New Monthly Mag.*, liii, p. 574–578; illustration of nest.

1876. RAGSDALE, G. H. Nesting of the Hooded Oriole [Icterus cucullatus] in Cooke County, Texas. < *Oölogist*, ii, No. 8, 1876, p. 57.

1876. ANON. A Golden Robin [Icterus baltimore]. < *Rod and Gun*, viii, Aug. 19, 1876, p. 325.
> Successful amputation of wild oriole's leg. From "Boston Post".

1877. BREWER, T. M. [Remark on the eggs of Molothrus bonariensis.] < *Proc. Boston Soc. Nat. Hist.*, xix, 1877, p. 76.

1877. W[ILLCOX], J. Crow Blackbirds [Quiscalus versicolor] eat fish. < *Forest and Stream*, viii, Apr. 5, 1877, p. 129.

1877. MERRILL, J. C. Notes on [the habits of] Molothrus æneus, Wagl. < *Bull. Nutt. Ornith. Club*, ii, No. 4, Oct., 1877, pp. 85–87.

1877. RAGSDALE, G. H. The Nesting of the Hooded Oriole [Icterus cucullatus] in Cooke Co., Texas. < *Forest and Stream*, vii, Feb. 1, 1877, p. 404.
> From *Oölogist*, ii, 1876, p. 57.

1877. WILLCOX, J. On the [fish-eating] Habits of Quiscalus purpureus. < *Proc. Phila. Acad. Nat. Sci.*, 1877, p. 38.

1878. BAILEY, T. S. That Nondescript Egg. < *The Oölogist*, iv, No. 4. June, 1878, p. 25.
> Decided to be that of *Quiscalus purpureus*. The article also gives an account of a hybrid between *Gallus bankivi* var. and *Numida meleagris*.

1878. BAILEY, T. S. A Stray Egg. < *The Oölogist*, iv, No. 3, May, 1878, p. 19.
> Of *Molothrus ater*, in nest of *Spizella pusilla*.

1878. BARBER, E. A. Ornithological Notes. < *Am. Nat.*, xii, No. 7, July, 1878, pp. 477, 478.
> On peculiarities in oviposition of *Molothrus ater* and *Sturnella magna*.

1878. [WILLARD, S. L.] Flocking of Quiscalus purpureus. < *The Oölogist*, iv, No. 2, Apr., 1878, p. 15.

1878. [WILLARD, S. L.] The Cow-bird [Molothrus ater] a Polygamist. < *The Oölogist*, iv, No. 1, Mar., 1878, p. 7.

1878. [WILLARD, S. L.] A Nondescript Egg. *The Oölogist*, May, 1878, pp. 17–19.
   Supposed to be the produce of *Turdus migratorius* × *Quiscalus purpureus!*

1879. BREWER, T. M. The Cow-Blackbird of Texas and Arizona (Molothrus obscurus). < *Bull. Nutt. Ornith. Club*, iv, No. 2, Apr., 1879, p. 123.
   Dr. J. C. Merrill's correction of "a grave error" of the writer's respecting the eggs of this bird.

1879. [CHAPMAN, W. L.] Albinos [Scolecophagus cyanocephalus?]. < *Forest and Stream*, xiii, Dec. 18, 1879, p. 907.

1879. DUGÈS, E. [Flocking of Molothrus ater (var. obscurus?).] < *The Oölogist*, iv, No. 10, May, 1879, p. 84.
   Quoted from a letter to the Smithsonian Institution, published by S. F. Baird in *Harper's Weekly*: refers to a certain flight supposed to have been 12,000 yards in length, six yards wide, and probably over a yard deep, estimated to contain 9 or 10,000,000 individuals.

1879. EDITORIAL. [Eggs of Molothrus ater in Nests of Turdus migratorius and Quiscalus versicolor.] < *The Oölogist*, iv, No. 10, May, 1879, pp. 78, 79.
   Two untitled paragraphs, from Rev. J. Walton and C. W. Strumberg, with editorial comment.

1879. GRAY, A. F. Albino Bobolink [Dolichonyx oryzivorus]. < *Science News*, i, No. 19, Aug. 1, 1878, p. 304.

1879. INGERSOLL, E. Breeding Habits of the Hooded Oriole [Icterus cucullatus]. < *The Oölogist*, iv, No. 7, Feb., 1879, pp. 49, 50.
   From advance sheets of his "Nests and Eggs of American Birds."

1879. INGERSOLL, E. Breeding Habits of obscure American Birds. The Hooded Oriole [Icterus cucullatus]. < *The Field* (London), liv, No. 1,394, Sept. 13, 1879, p. 374.

1879. RATHBUN, F. R. Golden Bird of Silver Song [*i. e.*, Icterus baltimore]. <*Auburn (N. Y.) Daily Advertiser*, May 21, 1879.
   Popular account of habits.

1879. SENNETT, G. B. The Great-tailed Grackle (Quiscalus macrurus). < *The Oölogist*, iv, No. 7, Feb., 1879, pp. 53, 54.
   Quoted from his paper in *Bull. U. S. Geol. and Geogr. Surv. Terr.*, iv, No. 1, 1878, pp. 1–66; relating to the habits of the bird as observed in Texas.

1879. [WILLARD, S. L.] Two Nests of Icterus baltimore. < *The Oölogist*, iv, No. 6, Jan., 1879, p. 42.

1879. [WILLARD, S. L.] [Eggs of Molothrus ater in nest of Turdus migratorius.] < *The Oölogist*, iv, No. 9, Apr., 1879, p. 65.

Tanagridæ.

1777. ANON. Description d'un nouveau Gros-bec de la Guiane. < *Obs. sur la Phys.* (*Rozier*), x, 1777, pp. 244, 245.

Pas vue moi-même.—N'est-ce pas la *Loxia erythromelas* Gm., c'est-à-dire, *Pitylus erythromelas?*

1792. BOSC, L. Tanagra humeralis. < *Journ. d'Hist. Nat.*, ii, 1792, pp. 179, 180.

Not seen.—I do not know that this comes under *Tanagridæ* as now understood.

1805-18—. DESMAREST, A. G. Histoire Naturelle | des | Tanagras, | des Manakins et des Todiers, | par Anselme-Gaëtan Desmarest; | Avec figures imprimées en couleur, d'après les dessins de Mademoiselle | Pauline de Courcelles, élève de Barraband. | — | Paris, | Garnery, Rue de Seine; | Delachaussée, Rue de Temple, N.º 37. | XIII.=1805. gr. folio, not paged, 72 pll. not numbered.

Published in 12 livraisons, 1805 being the date of the first. The plates, by Mlle. de Courcelles (whom Temminck afterward knew very well as Mme. Knip), are very fine; Desmarest's letterpress is not specially noteworthy. The work, however, is "classic". By some fantasy, or marvellous oversight, in punishment for which the work ought to be banished from good society, not only is the text unpaged, but also are the plates uunumbered. The only clue by which they can be cited is the indirect avis servant de table at the end. According to this, the following is the order of the plates: 1. *Tanagra tatao*. 2. *Motacilla velia*. 3, 4. *Tanagra tricolor*. 5. *T. mexicana*. 6, 7. *T. gyrola*. 8, 9. *T. punctata*. 10. *T. cayana*. 11. *T. peruviana*. 12, 13, 14. *T. gularis*. 15, 16. *T. episcopa*. 17, 18. *T. archepiscopus*, nob. 19, 20. *Pipra musica*. 21, 22, 23. *Tanagra violacea*. 24, 25. *T. chlorotica*. 26. *T. cayenensis*. 27. *Euphonia olivacea*, nob. 28, 29. *Tanagra brasilia*. 30, 31. *Tanagra jacapa*. 32, 33. *T. mississipensis* (sic). 34. *T. rubra*. 35, 36, 37. *T. olivacea* Gm.!!! 38, 39, 40. *T. silens* Lath. 41. *T. pileata*. 42. *T. atra*. 43. *T. magna*. 44. *T. guinanensis*. 45, 46. *T. nigerrima*. 47, 48, 49. *T. cristata*. 59, 51, 52, 53. *Pipra pareola*. 54, 55, 56, 57. *P. aureola*. 58. *P. gutturosa*, nob. 50. *P. leucocapilla*. 60, 61. *P. erythrocephala*. 62–64. *P. serena*. 63–65. *P. gutturalis*. 66. *P. albifrons*. 67. *Todus viridis*. 68. *T. cinereus*. 69. *T. griseus*, nob. 70. *T. maculatus*, nob. 71. *T. sylvia*, nob. 72. *T. platyrynchos* (sic). All these, except those marked nob. and one of Latham, are ascribed to Gmelin; but the identification, in some cases, is very wild.—The genera *Euphonia* and *Ramphocelus* are new.

1826. SWAINSON, W. A Monograph of the genus Tachyphonus, a group of Birds belonging to the Tanagræ L. < *Quart. Journ. Sci. Lit. Arts Roy. Inst.*, xx, 1826, pp. 60–69. (*Féruss. Bull.*, 2e sect., xi, 1827, pp. 111–113.)

Not seen in this form; there is an edition in *Isis*, 1833, pp. 934, 935.

1827. LESSON, [R. P.] Monographie du genre Tachyphonus, . . . ; par William Swainson. . . . < *Féruss. Bull.*, 2e sect., xi, 1827, pp. 111–113.

Précis de cet ouvrage.

1829. LUND, P. W. De genere Euphones præsertim de singulari canalis intestinalis structurâ in hocce avium genere, auctore Dr. P. W. Lund. 8vo. Havniæ, 1829.

Not seen.—Cf. *Froriep's Notizen*, 1830, No. 573; *Férussac's Bull.*, 2e sect., xxii, 1830, p. 121.

1831. ANON. De genere Euphones, praesertim de singulari canalis intestinalis structura in hocce avium genere, auct. Dr. P. W. Lund. Havniæ ap. Brummer. 29. 8. 32. tab. < *Oken's Isis*, Bd. xxiv, 1831, pp. 733, 734.

Uebersicht und Auszug.

1833. BONAPARTE, C. L. Ueber einen neuen Ramphocelus [passerinii] aus Cuba. < *Oken's Isis*, Bd. xxxvi, Jahrg. 1833, p. 755.

1833. SWAINSON, W. Monographie von Tachyphonus. < *Oken's Isis*, Jahrg. 1833, pp. 934, 935.

Auszug aus d. *Quart. Journ. Sci. Roy. Inst.*, xx, 1826, pp. 60–69. Diagnostik von 9 Arten.

1834. SUNDEVALL, C. J. Några arter af Fogelslägtet Euphone. < *Kongl. Svensk. Vetensk.-Acad. Handl. for* 1833, 1834, pp. 308–312, pll. 10, 11.

E. œnea, p. 309, pl. 11, f. 4; *E. xanthogaster*, p. 310, pl. 10, f. 1; *E. chlorotica*, p. 310, pl. 10, f. 2, 3; *E. aurora*, p. 312, pl. 11, f. 5.

1835. JAMESON, R. [Tanagra nigricephala, n. sp.] < *L'Institut*, iii, 1835, p. 316.
Not seen.—This is the Jamaican *Spindalis* (Jard., 1837) *nigricephala*; see Jard. & Selby, *Ill. Orn.*, pl. 9; Des Murs, *Ic. Orn.*, pl. 40; Gosse, *Ill. B. Jam.*, pl. 56.

1837. LAFRESNAYE, F. DE. Notice sur le groupe des Tangaras Rhamphocèles et sur toutes les espèces qui le composent, et description d'une nouvelle espèce de cette division. < *Guér. Mag. de Zool.*, 7e année, 1837, classe ii, notice lxxxi, pp. 1–4, pl. lxxxi.
Six espèces de cette division. Pl. 81, *Rhamphocelus dimidiatus*, sp. n.

1838. BONAPARTE, C. L. Nouvelle espèce d'oiseau du genre Rhamphocèle [Rhamphocelus icteronotus]. < *Revue Zoologique*, i, 1838, p. 8.

1838. LAFRESNAYE, [F.] DE. Nouvelle espèce d'oiseau du genre Rhamphocèle [Rhamphocelus luciani]. < *Revue Zoologique*, i, 1838, p 54.

1839. DUBUS DE GHISIGNIES, V. B. Description d'un Tanagra nouveau [T. lunulata]. < *Bull. Acad. Bruxelles*, via, 1839, p. 439, pl. (*L'Inst.*, vii, No. 310, 1839, p. 428.)
Not seen.

1839. LAFRESNAYE, F. DE. G. Tangara. Tanagra. Linné. (Groupe des Rhamphocèles, Rhamphocelus.) T. (Rh.) de Lucien. T. (Rh.) Luciani. Lafresn. < *Guér. Mag. de Zool.*, 2e sér., année 1839, Ois., pp. 1, 2, pl. 2.

1839. TRUDEAU, J. Description of the White-winged Tanager, (Pyranga leucoptera.) < *Journ. Acad. Nat. Sci. Phila.*, viii, 1839, p. 160.

1840. PASSERINI, [C.] [Note sur la propagation de la Paroaria cucullata en Europe.] < *Revue Zoologique*, iii, 1840, p. 28.

1841. BOISSONNEAU, —. G. Tangara. Tanagra. Linné. (Groupe des Tangaras Euphones.) T. de Vassor. T. vassorii. Boissonneau. < *Guér. Mag. de Zool.*, 2e sér., année 1841, Oiseaux, pp. 1, 2, pl. 23.
Rev. Zool., 1840, p. 4.

1841. HARTLAUB, [G.] Description d'une nouvelle espèce du genre Tangara [T. iridina]. < *Revue de Zoologique*, iv, 1841, p. 305.

1841. LAFRESNAYE, [F.] DE. [Tangara iridina Hartl. = Tanagra velia Vieill.] < *Revue Zoologique*, iv, 1841, pp. 365–367.

1841. PASSERINI, C. Notizie | sulla moltiplicazione in Firenze negli anni 1837. 1838. 1839 | dell'Uccello Americano | Paroaria cucullata | chiamato volgarmente Cardinale | Lette in Pisa | alla sezione di Zoologia della prima riunione degli Scienziati Italiani | il 7 Ottobre 1839 | da Carlo Passerini | [ec., 10 linie] | — | Firenze | tipografia Pezzati | 1841   folio. pp. 8, 1 pl.
La tavola colorata, dei cinque figure, mostra gl' uccelli (il maschio e la femmina), il piccolo, il nido, e l' uova. Cf. *Rev. Zool.*, v, 1842, pp. 280, 281.

1842. LAFRESNAYE, F. DE. Sur quelques Oiseaux. < *Revue Zoologique*, v, 1842, pp. 69, 70.
Certhiparus, g. n., p. 69; *Pyranga bivittata*, sp. n., p. 70.

1843. LAFRESNAYE, [F.] DE. G. Tangara. Tanagra. L. T. (Aglaia) de Parzudaki. T. (Aglaia) Parzudaki. Lafr. < *Guér. Mag. de Zool.*, 2e sér., année 1843, Ois., pp.. 1, 2, pl. 41.
Rev. Zool., 1843, p. 97.

1843. [LAFRESNAYE, F. DE.] G. Tangara. Tanagra. L. T. (Euphone) de prêtre. T. (Euphonia) Pretrei. De Lafr. < *Guér. Mag. de Zool.*, 2e sér., année 1843, Ois., pp. 1, 2, pl. 42.

1843. [LAFRESNAYE, F. DE.] G. Tangara. Tanagra. L. T. (Aglaia) vert noiret. T. (Aglaia) nigroviridis. De Lafr. < *Guér. Mag. de Zool.*, 2e sér., année 1843, Ois., pp. 1, 2, pl. 43.
R. Z., 1843, pp. 97 and 69.

1844. BUCKLER, C. Note on the occurrence of the Red-breasted Tanager [Ramphopis purpureus], near Cheltenham. < *Zoologist*, ii, 1844, p. 444.

1844 LAFRESNAYE, [F.] DE. G. Lamprotes. Swainson. L. albo-cristatus. De Lafresnaye. < *Guér. Mag. de Zool.*, 2e sér., année 1844, Oiseaux, pp. 1, 2, pl. 50.

1846. CABOT, S., JR. [Pyranga roseo-gularis, sp. n.] < *Proc. Boston Soc. Nat. Hist.*, ii, 1846, p. 187.

1846. CABOT, S., JR. Description of Pyranga roseo-gularis, (Rose-throated Tanager.) < *Journ. Boston Soc. Nat. Hist.*, v, pt. iii, 1846, p. 416.

1846. LAFRESNAYE, F. DE. Sur une nouvelle espèce d'Euphone (Euphonia [cinerea]). < *Revue Zoologique*, ix, 1846, pp. 277, 278.

1846. LAFRESNAYE, F. DE. Sur le Ramphocelus Icteronotus du prince Bonaparte. < *Revue Zoologique*, ix, 1846, pp. 365–370.

    Avec synopsis de 10 esp. du genre.

1846. LAFRESNAYE, [F.] DE. Sur le Lanion huppé, Lanio cristatus de Vieillot, et sur une nouvelle espèce du genre Lanion. < *Revue Zoologique*, ix, 1846, pp. 202–206.

    Synopsis de six espèces—*Lanio aurantius*, p. 204, sp. n.

1847. CABOT, S., JR. Pyranga roseo-gularis, a new species from Yucatan. < *Am. Journ. Sci.*, iii, 1847, pp. 436, 437.

    From *Proc. Bost. Soc. Nat. Hist.*, Dec., 1846, p. 187.

1847. CABOT, S., JR. Pyranga roseo-gularis, a new species from Yucatan. < *Ann. Mag. Nat. Hist.*, xx, 1847, p. 143.

    From *Am. Journ. Sci.*, 1847, p. 437.

1847. HARTLAUB, [G.] [Rectification de la synonymie de Tanagra zenoides Lafr.] < *Revue Zoologique*, x, 1847, pp. 417, 418.

1847. LAFRESNAYE, F. DE. Sur les Tanagras gyrola Gmel. (Rouverdin Vieillot) et Zena Gmel. (Bahamensis Brisson) et quelques espèces voisines faciles a confondre avec elles. < *Revue Zoologique*, x, 1847, pp. 275–281.

1848. CASSIN, J. Description of a new Tanagra [nigro-aurita], in the Collection of the Academy of Natural Sciences of Philadelphia. < *Proc. Acad. Nat. Sci. Phila.*, iv, 1848, pp. 85, 86.

1849. [JARDINE, W.] Tanagra cana, Swainson. < *Jard. Contrib. Ornith.*, 1849, p. 19, pl. xvi.

1850. SCLATER, P. L. [Description of Calliste chrysonota, sp. n.] < *Jard. Contrib. Ornith.*, 1850, p. 50, pl. li.

1851. BONAPARTE, C. L. Note sur les Tangaras, leurs affinités, et descriptions d'espèces nouvelles. < *Compt. Rend. de l'Acad. Sci.*, xxxii, 1851, pp. 76–83.

    Calliste bourcieri, C. phoenicotis, C. icterocephala, C. guttulata, p. 76: *Tanagrella rufigula*, p. 77: *Callospiza boliviana*, p. 80, spp. nn.

    The paper is substantially the same (though with some modification) as one in *R. M. Z.* of same date (see next title). It is full of mishaps, many of which were exposed by Sclater, *Jard. Contr. Orn.*, 1851, pp. 93–96.

1851. BONAPARTE, C. L. Note sur les Tangaras, leurs affinités et descriptions d'espèces nouvelles. < *Rev. et Mag. de Zool.*, iii, Mar., 1851, pp. 129–145 ; Apr., 1851, pp. 168–180.

    Calliparœa (g. n.) *bourcieri. C. phoenicotis, Chrysothraupis icterocephala*, p. 129; *Ixothraupis* (g. n.) *guttulata, Tanagrella rufigula*, p. 130, spp. nn.: *Chalcothraupis*, g. n., p. 131. L'auteur donne encore plusieures rectifications relatives aux espèces de la famille et à leur synonymie. *Procnias*, 2 esp. *Pipræida*, 2 esp. *Iodopleura*, 5 esp. *Euphone*, 13 esp.: *E. brevirostris. E. pumila*, p. 136, spp. nn. *Pyrrhuphonia* (g. n., p. 137), 2 esp. *Chlorophonia* (g. n., p. 137), 3 esp. *Cyanophonia* (g. n., p. 138), 2 esp. *Calliste*, 8 esp. *Tatao* (g. n., p. 141), 7 esp. *Chrysothraupis*, 11 esp. *Ixothraupis*, 3 esp. *Chalcothraupis*, 7 esp. *Callospiza*, 4 esp.: *C. boliviana*, sp. n., p. 169; *Tanagra*, 8 esp. *Dubusia gigas*, sp. n., p. 171; *Tachyphonus*, 10 esp.: *T. beauperthuyi*, p. 175, sp. n. *Phœnicothraupis*, 2 esp. *Lanio, Lamprotes, Sericossypha, Pyranga, Ramphocelus ; Dulus ; D. poliocephalus*, p. 178, sp. n. Enfin, description d'une Alouette d'Afrique! *Alauda cinnamomea*, p. 179, sp. n.—Voir *Jard. Contr. Orn.*, 1851, pp. 93–96.

1851. LAFRESNAYE, F. DE. Sur l'oiseau nommé par Brisson Tangara de Saint-Domingue, Tanagra Dominicensis, Tanagra Dominica, par Linné, figuré par Buffon, pl. enl. 156, f. 2, et dont Vieillot a fait son genre Esclave (Dulus), sous le nom de Dulus palmarum. < *Rev. et Mag. de Zool.*, iii, 1851, pp. 583–590.

    There is a curious "snag" here. *Cf.* Strickl., *Jard. Contr. Orn.*, 1851, pp. 103, 104. See Gray's *Handlist*, Nos. 5827 and 7025.

1851. SCLATER, P. L.   On Some New Species of Calliste.   < *Jard. Contrib. Ornith.*, 1851, pp. 21–25, pl. lxix.

  C. virescens, p. 22, pl. lxix, f. 1 ; *C. xanthogastra*, p. 23 ; *C. chrysophrys*, p. 24, pl. lxix, f. 2 ; with chars. of *C. punctata*, Linn.

1851. SCLATER, P. L.   I. Remarks on Prince Canino's Note, "Sur les Tangaras," in the Revue et Magazine de Zoologie, March and April, 1851.   < *Jard. Contrib. Ornith.*, 1851, pp. 93–96.

  Rectifications of synonymy, &c.

1851. SCLATER, P. L.   II. On the Genus Tanagrella.   < *Jard. Contrib. Ornith.*, 1851, pp, 97, 98, pl. lxxiv.

  3 spp.   The pl. represents *T. calophrys*.

1851. SCLATER, P. L.   III. On the genus Chlorochrysa, Bp.   < *Jard. Contrib. Ornith.*, 1851, pp. 99–101, pl. lxxiii.

  2 spp.   Pl. lxxiii, up. fig., *C. calliparœa ;* low. fig., *C. phœnicotis*.

1851. SCLATER, P. L.   Synopsis of the Tanagrine genus Calliste, with Descriptions of New Species.   < *Jard. Contrib. Ornith.*, 1851, pp. 49–73, pl. lxx.

  48 spp., divided in 8 groups.: *C. leucotis*, p. 58, *C. castaneoventris, C. ruficapilla*, p. 61 ; *C. castanonota*, p. 63, *C. lunigera*, p. 65, pl. lxx, f. 2, *C. lamprotis*, p. 65, spp. nn.   The other fig. of pl. lxx is *C. icterocephala* Bp.

1851. SCLATER, P. L.   Synopsis of the genus Euphonia, with descriptions of New species.   < *Jard. Contrib. Ornith.*, 1851, pp. 81–92, pl. lxxv.

  23 spp. + 3 doubtful.   *E. melanura*, p. 86 ; *E. pyrrhophrys*, p. 89, pl. lxxv, f. 2, spp. nn.   The other fig. of same pl. is *E. nigricollis*.

1851. STRICKLAND, H. E.   On two New Species of Euphonia, Desm., allied to E. chlorotica.   < *Jard. Contrib. Ornith.*, 1851, pp. 71–73.

  E. trinitatis, E. strictifrons, p. 72, with synopsis of 5 spp. of the genus.

1851. STRICKLAND, H. E.   On the Type of the genus Dulus, Vieill.   < *Jard. Contrib. Ornith.*, 1851, pp. 103, 104.

  Tanagra dominica L., nec *Turdus palmarum* L.   *Cf* Lafr., *Rev. Mag. Zool.*, iii, 1851, pp. 583–590.

1852. STRICKLAND, H. E.   Description of Iridosornis dubusia (Bon.).   < *Jard. Contrib. Ornith.*, 1852, pp. 127, 128, pl. xciv.

  With important bibliographical criticism.   The pl. is marked "*Pœcilornis rufivertex*."

1853. LAFRESNAYE, F. DE.   [Arremon mystacalis Scl. = A. albifrenatus Boiss. et Lafr.]   < *Rev. et Mag. de Zool.*, v, 1853, pp. 62, 63.

1853. LAFRESNAYE, F. DE.   Sur le genre Ramphocelus, Desm. et trois nouvelles espèces qui lui appartiennent.   < *Rev. et Mag. de Zool.*, v, 1853, pp. 241–246.

  Le genre doit être naturellement subdivisé en deux sections, d'après la forme du bec.: I. *Ramph. macrognathi* (11 spp.).   II. *R. micrognathi* (5 spp.).   *R. magnirostris, R. venezuelensis*, p. 243 ; *R. aterimus*, p. 244.

1854. LAFRESNAYE, F. DE.   Mélanges Ornithologiques.   < *Rev. et Mag. de Zool.*, vi, 1854, pp. 205–209.

  The article relates chiefly to the "subgenus" *Chrysothraupis*, i. e., *Calliste*, pp. 205–208.   *C. sclatteri*, (sic) p. 207, sp. n.

1854. SCLATER, P. L.   Characters of some New or imperfectly-described Species of Tanagers.   < *P. Z. S.*, xxii, 1854, pp. 95–98, pll. (Aves), lxiv, lxv.

  Arremon axillaris. Ramphocelus dorsalis Bp. Mss., *Buthraupis chloronota*, pl. lxiv. p. 97 ; *Euphonia concinna*. pl. lxv, f. 2 : *E. hirundinacea*, pl. lxv, f. 1, p. 98.

1854. SCLATER, P. L.   Descriptions of Two New Tanagers in the British Museum.   < *P. Z. S.*, xxii, 1854, pp. 157, 158, pll. (Aves) lxviii, lxix.

  Chlorospingus melanotis. p. 157, pl. lxviii ; *Tachyphonus xanthopygius*, p. 158, pl. lxix.

1854. SCLATER, P. L.   Description of a new Tanager of the Genus Calliste [C. venusta].   < *P. Z. S.*, xxii, 1854, p. 248.

1854. SCLATER, P. L.   Description of a second species of the Genus Procnias [P. occidentalis].   < *P. Z. S.*, xxii, 1854, p. 249.

1854. SCLATER, P. L.   On a new species of Tanager [Phœnicothraupis gutturalis] in the British Museum.   < *Ann. Mag. Nat. Hist.*, 2d ser., xiii, pp. 24, 25.

  Phœnicothraupis gutturalis, p. 25; with synopsis of 3 spp. of the genus.

1854. SCLATER, P. L.   Tanagrarum | Catalogus Specificus, | auctore | Philippo Lutley Sclater, A. M. | Soc. Zool. Lond. Socio. | Basingstoke, | 1854. 1 vol. 8vo. pp. 16.

  Exhibens nomina generum 41, specierum circ. 240, adjectis cuique auctore et patria, necnon annotationibus 15 ad calcem opusculi.

1855. SCLATER, P. L.   Descriptions of four new or little-known Tanagers.   < *P. Z. S.*, xxiii, 1855, pp. 83–85, pll. (Aves) lxxxix–xcii.

  Arremon erythrorhynchus, p. 83, pl. lxxxix; *Tachyphonus xanthopygius*, p. 83, pl. xc; *Tanagra notabilis*, "Jardine," p. 84, pl. xci; *Saltator arremonops*, "Jardine," p. 84, pl. xcii.

1855. SCLATER, P. L.   Description of a newly discovered Tanager of the Genus Buarremon [leucopterus].   < *P. Z. S.*, xxiii, 1855, p. 214, pl. (Aves) cix.

1855. SCLATER, P. L.   Characters of two New Species of Tanagers.   [Dubusia auricrissa, Iridornis porphyrocephala, pl. cx.]   < *P. Z. S.*, xxiii, 1855, pp. 227, 228, pl. (Aves) cx.

1855. SCLATER, P. L.   Characters of some New or imperfectly-described Species of Tanagers.   < *Ann. Mag. Nat. Hist.*, 2d ser., xvi, 1855, pp. 140–143.

  From *P. Z. S.*, Mar. 28, 1854, pp. 95–98, *q. v.*

1855. SCLATER, P. L.   Description of a new Tanager of the Genus Calliste [venusta].   < *Ann. Mag. Nat. Hist.*, 2d ser., xvi, 1855, p. 150.

  From *P. Z. S.*, Nov. 14, 1854, p. 248.

1855. SCLATER, P. L.   Descriptions of Two New Tanagers in the British Museum.   < *Ann. Mag. Nat. Hist.*, 2d ser., xvi, 1855, pp. 377, 378.

  From *P. Z. S.*, July 25, 1854, pp. 157, 158, *q. v.*

1855. SCLATER, P. L.   Description of a second species of the genus Procnias [occidentalis].   < *Ann. Mag. Nat. Hist.*, 2d ser., xvi, 1855, pl. 380.

  From *P. Z. S.*, Nov. 14, 1854, p. 249.

1856. SCLATER, P. L.   Note on the Zoological Appendix to the 'Report of the U. S. Naval Astronomical Expedition to the Southern Hemisphere,' and on the Geographic Range and Distribution of the Tanagrine Genera Calliste and Euphonia.   < *P. Z. S.*, xxiv, 1856, pp. 18, 19.

  The "Note" refers to a probable mistake in the work named respecting the alleged Chilian habitat of *Calliste cyaneicollis*, *C. gyroloides*, and *Euphonia rufiventris;* states that the *C. "larvata"* figured on pl. 18, f. 2, is not that species, but *C. thalassina*. The article concludes with a tabular exhibit of the geographical distribution of 48 spp. of the genus *Calliste*.

1856. SCLATER, P. L.   Synopsis Avium Tanagrinarum.—A descriptive Catalogue of the known Species of Tanagers.   < *P. Z. S.*, xxiv, 1856, pp. 64–94, 108–132, 230–281.

  40 genn., 272 spp.   Much synonymy and critical commentary.   *Chlorospingus flavirentris*, p. 91; *Nemosia guirina*, *N. insignis*, p. 110; *N. auricollis*, p. 111; *Ramphocelus unicolor*, p. 128; *Calliste vieilloti*, p. 257; *C. cyanescens*, p. 260; *Euphonia fulvicrissa*, p. 276; *E. crassirostris*, p. 277, spp. nn.

1856. SCLATER, P. L.   Synopsis Avium Tanagrinarum. | A Descriptive Catalogue | of the known | Species of Tanagers. | By | Philip Lutley Sclater, M. A., F. Z. S., &c. | — | [From the Proceedings of the Zoological Society, | April 8, 1856.] | — | London : | printed by Taylor and Francis. | Red Lion Court, Fleet Street. | 1856. 1 vol. 8vo. pp. 127.

  Treating 272 spp. under 40 genera, with synonymy, diagnosis, habitat, and criticism

1856. SCLATER, P. L.   On a New Tanager of the Genus Calliste [rufigenis].   < *P. Z. S.*, xxiv, 1856, p. 311.

1856. SCLATER, P. L.   Description of a newly discovered Tanager of the genus Buarremon [leucopterus].   < *Ann. Mag. Nat. Hist.*, 2d ser., xviii, 1856, pp. 350, 351.

  From *P. Z. S.*, Nov. 27, 1855, p. 214.

1856. SCLATER, P. L.   Characters of Two New Species of Tanagers.   < *Ann. Mag. Nat. Hist.*, 2d ser., xviii, 1856, pp. 418, 419.

  From *P. Z. S.*, Dec. 11, 1855, pp. 227, 228, *q. v.*

1856. SCLATER, P. L. Descriptions of four new or little-known Tanagers. < *Ann. Mag. Nat. Hist.*, 2d ser., xvii, 1856, pp. 515–517.

From *P. Z. S.*, May 22, 1855, pp. 83–85.

1857. SCLATER, P. L. Descriptions of some New Species of Tanagers. < *Ann. Mag. Nat. Hist.*, 2d ser., xix, 1857, p. 272.

From *P. Z. S.*, May 13, 1856.

1857. SCLATER, P. L. Description of a New Tanager of the genus Euphonia [E. gouldi]. < *P. Z. S.*, xxv, 1857, p. 66, pl. (Aves) cxxiv.

1857. SCLATER, P. L. Description of a new Tanager [Euphonia gouldi]. < *Ann. Mag. Nat. Hist.*, 2d ser., xx, 1857, pp. 319, 320.

From *P. Z. S.*, Apr. 28, 1857, p. 66.

1857. SCLATER, P. L. A | Monograph | of | the Birds forming | the Tanagrine Genus Calliste; | illustrated by | coloured plates of all the known species. | By Philip Lutley Sclater, M. A., Fellow of Corpus Christi College, Oxford; | Fellow of the Zoological and Linnæan Societies of London; Correspondent | of the Academy of Natural Sciences of Philadelphia; Hon. Member of | the German Ornithological Society; Member of the British and | American Associations for the advancement of Science, etc. | [Publisher's monogram.] | London: | John Van Voorst, Paternoster Row. | MDCCCLVII. | 1 vol. 8vo. Map as frontispiece, pp. xviii, 104, pll. col'd xlv.

Letter-press general, relating to each one of 52 spp., introduced by an essay on the genus, which includes schema generum tanagrinorum, et callistarum schema geographicum. The *pls. are not numbered*; according to the text they are:—Pl. i, f. 1, *tatao*, p. 1; i, f. 2, *cœlicolor*, p. 3; ii, *yeni*, p. 5; iii, *tricolor*, p. 7; iv, *fastuosa*, p. 9; v, *festiva*, p. 11; vi, *cyaneiventris*, p. 13; vii, *thoracica*, p. 15; viii, *schranki*, p. 17; ix, *punctata*, p. 19; x, *guttata*, p. 21; xi, *xanthogastra*, p. 23; xii, *graminea*, p. 25; xiii, *rufigularis*, p. 27; xiv, f. 2, *aurulenta*, p. 29; xiv, f. 1, *sclateri*, p. 31; xv, *pulchra*, p. 33; xvi, *arthusi*, p. 35; xvii, *icterocephala*, p. 37; xviii, *vitriolina*, p. 39; xix, *cayana*, p. 41; xx, *cucullata*, p. 45; xxi, *flava*, ♂, ♀, p. 47; xxii, *pretiosa*, p. 49; xxiii, *melanonota*, ♂, ♀, p. 51; xxiv, *cyanoptera*, p. 53; xxv, *gyrola*, p. 55; xxvi, *gyroloides*, p. 57; xxvii, *desmaresti*, p. 59; xxviii, *brasiliensis*, p. 61; xxix, *flaviventris*, p. 63; xxx, *boliviana*, p. 67; xxxi, *atricœrulea*, p. 69; xxxii, *ruficervix*, p. 71; xxxiii, *atricapilla*, ♂, ♀, p. 73; xxxiv, *argentea*, p. 75; xxxv, *cyanescens*, p. 79; xxxvi, *larvata*, p. 81; xxxvii, *nigricincta*, p. 85; xxxviii, *cyaneicollis*, p. 87; xxxix, *labradorides*, p. 89; xl, *rufigenis*, p. 91; xli, *parzudakii*, p. 93; xlii, *lunigera*, p. 95; xliii, *chrysotis*, p. 97; xliv, f. 1, *xanthocephala*, p. 99; xliv, f. 2, *venusta*, p. 101; xlv, *inornata*, p. 103.—*cyanolœma*, p. 43; *vieilloti*, p. 65; *nigriviridis*, p. 77; *francescae*, p. 83, are not figured. For additions, see *Ibis*, 1863, pp. 450–452.

1858. CASSIN, J. Description of a New Tanager [Calliste lavinia] from the Isthmus of Darien, and note on Selenidera Spectabilis, Cassin. < *Proc. Acad. Nat. Sci. Phila.*, x, 1858, pp. 177, 178.

1858. SCLATER, P. L. Description of a New Tanager of the Genus Euphonia [gouldi]. (P. Z. S., April 28, 1857.) < *J. f. O.*, vi, 1858, p. 73.

Uebersetzt, nebst Anmerk. d. Herausgebers.

1858. SCLATER, P. L. On some New or little-known Species of Tanagers from the Collection of M. Verreaux of Paris. < *P. Z. S.*, xxvi, 1858, pp. 293, 294.

5 spp.—*Chlorospingus castaneicollis*, p. 293; *Calliste cyanotis*, p. 294, spp. nn.

1858. SCLATER, P. L. On two New Species of Tanagers from the Collection of M. Verreaux of Paris. < *Ann. Mag. Nat. Hist.*, 3d ser., ii, 1858, pp. 472, 473.

From *P. Z. S.*, June 8, 1858, pp. 293, 294, *q. v.*

1858. SCLATER, P. L. On Euchætes coccineus, a new genus of Birds. < *Ann. Mag. Nat. Hist.*, 3d ser., ii, 1858, p. 494.

From *P. Z. S.*, Jan. 26, 1858, pp. 73, 74; there forming part of an article of wider scope.

1859. DUBOIS, C. F. Description et figure d'une nouvelle espèce d'Euphonia [cyanodorsalis]. < *Rev. et Mag. de Zool.*, xi, 1859, pp. 49, 50, pl. 2.

1860. JARDINE, W. [Euphonia cyanodorsalis Dubois = E. occipitalis, ♀, P. Z. S., 1856-270.] < *Ibis*, ii, 1860, p. 103.

1863. SALVIN, O. On a New Species of Calliste [dowii] from Costa Rica < *P. Z. S.*, xxxi, 1863, pp. 168, 169.

1863. SCLATER, P. L.   List of recent Additions to the Genus Calliste.   < *Ibis*, v, 1863, pp. 450–452, pl. xii.

> 5 spp. added to the 52 of his well-known monograph (1857); none new; *C. dowii* figured, pl. xii.

1864. LAWRENCE, G. N.   Descriptions of New Species of Birds of the Families Tanagridæ, Cuculidæ, and Trochilidæ, with a Note on Panterpe insignis.   < *Ann. Lyc. Nat. Hist. N. Y.*, viii, 1864, pp. 41–46.

> The Tanagers here described are *Saltator fulviventris*, p. 41, Paraguay; *Tachyphonus tibialis*, p. 41, Costa Rica; and *T. napensis*, p. 42, Rio Napo.

1864. LÉOTAUD, [A.]   Description d'une nouvelle espèce du genre Tachyphonus [albispecularis].   < *Rev. et Mag. de Zool.*, xvi, 1864, pp. 129, 130.

1864. SALVIN, O.   On a New Species of Calliste [dowii] from Costa Rica.   < *Ann. Mag. Nat. Hist.*, 3d ser., xiii, 1864, pp. 104, 105.

> From *P. Z. S.*, May 12, 1863, pp.

1865. BILLOT, E.   Éducation des Cardinaux gris a tête rouge [Paroaria cucullata].   < *Bull. Soc. Acclim.*, 2e sér., ii, 1865, pp. 463–465.

1865. CASSIN, J.   On some Conirostral Birds from Costa Rica in the Collection of the Smithsonian Institution.   < *Proc. Acad. Nat. Sci. Phila.*, xvii, 1865, pp. 169–172.

> The article treats of 22 sp. of *Fringillidæ* and *Tanagridæ*; the new species described are three of the latter family, namely: *Arremon rufidorsalis, Buarremon crassirostris*, p. 170; *Euphonia anneæ*, p. 172.

1865. LAWRENCE, G. N.   Descriptions of New Species' of Birds of the Families Tanagridæ, Dendrocolaptidæ, Formicaridæ, Tyrannidæ, and Trochilidæ.   < *Ann. Lyc. Nat. Hist. New York*, viii, 1865, pp. 126–135.

> *Buarrremon ocai*, p. 126.

1865. SCHMIDT, MAX.   Fortpflanzung des grauen Kardinals [Paroaria cucullata].   < *Zool. Gart.*, vi, 1865, pp. 12–16.

1865. SCLATER, P. L.   Description of a new Species of Tanager of the genus Iridornis [reinhardti].   < *Ibis*, 2d ser., i, 1865, pp. 495, 496, pl. xi.

1868. SCLATER, P. L.   On a recently discovered Tanager of the genus Calliste.   < *Ibis*, 2d ser., iv, 1868, pp. 71, 72, pl. iii.

> *C. sclateri* Cab. *nec* Less.; = *C. cabanisi* Scl., sp. renom.

1869. LINDEN, E.   Zur Ehrenrettung des grauen Kardinals [Paroaria cucullata].   < *Zool. Gart.*, x, 1869, pp. 376–378.

1869. RIDGWAY, R.   Notices of certain obscurely known Species of American Birds.   < *Proc. Acad. Nat. Sci. Phila.*, xxi, June, 1869, pp. 125–135, woodcc.

> II. On the uniformly red species of *Pyranga* (6 spp.), pp. 129–133.   *P. cooperi*, sp. n., p. 130, fig.   The article also treats of species of I., *Hylocichla* and III., *Quiscalus*.

1869. SCLATER, P. L., *and* SALVIN, O.   Descriptions of Six New Species of American Birds of the Families Tanagridæ, Dendrocolaptidæ, Formicariidæ, Tyrannidæ, and Scolopacidæ.   < *P. Z. S.*, xxxvii, 1869, pp. 416–420, pl. xxviii.

> The new Tanager is *Calliste florida*, p. 416, pl. xxviii.

1869. SCLATER, P. L., *and* SALVIN, O.   Descriptions of three new Species of Tanagers from Veragua.   < *P. Z. S.*, xxxvii, 1869, pp. 439, 440, pll. xxxi, xxxii.

> *Buthraupis arcœi*, p. 439, pl. xxxi; *Tachyphonus chrysomelas*, p. 440, pl. xxxii; *Chlorospingus punctulatus*, p. 440.

1870. ALLEN, J. A.   Summer Red Bird [Pyranga æstiva].   < *Am. Nat.*, iv, 1870, p. 56.

> Its occurrence at Amherst, Mass., U. S. A.

1870. CABANIS, J.   Ueber eine neue brasilische Nemosie oder Wald-Tangare, Nemosia Rourei nov. spec.   < *J. f. O.*, xviii, 1870, pp. 459, 460 (pl. i, in Jahrg. 1871).

1870. SCHMIDT, MAX.   Fortpflanzung des grauen Kardinals (Paroaria cucullata).   < *Zool. Gart.*, xi, 1870, pp. 335–341.

1871. ORTON, J.   Correction [of a misstatement respecting Euphonia elegantissima, Am. Nat., iv, 714].   < *Am. Nat.*, v, 1871, p. 378.

1873. BREHM, A. [Singvermögen der Euphonia.] < *J. f. O.*, xxi, 1873, pp. 71, 72.

1873. SALVADORI, T. Descrizione di una nuova specie del genere Euphonia [mesochrysa]. < *Atti della Reale Accad. delle Sci. di Torino*, viii, 1873, p. 193.

1873. SCLATER, P. L. Note on the Pyranga roseogularis of Cabot. < *Ibis*, 3d ser., iii, 1873, pp. 125, 126, pl. iii.

> The colored plate, drawn by R. Ridgway, represents this beautiful species.

1874. DUBOIS, A. Remarque sur la variabilité de certaines espèces du genre Calliste. < *Bull. Acad. Roy. des Sci. de Belgique*, 2ᵉ sér., xxxviii, July, 1874, pp. 124-—.
Pas vu moi-même.

1874. LAWRENCE, G. N. Descriptions of Two New Species of Birds of the Families Tanagridæ and Tyrannidæ. < *Am. Lyc. Nat. Hist. N. Y.*, xi, July, 1874, pp. 70–72.

> The Tanagrine here described is *Phœnicothraupis cristatus*, p. 70, from Bogotá.

1875. SCLATER, P. L. Remarks on the species of the Tanagrine Genus Chlorochrysa. < *Ibis*, 3d ser., v, 1875, pp. 464–467, pl. x.

> 3 spp.—Characters, synonomys, etc. Pl. x, *C. nitidissima.*

1876. SCLATER, P. L. Description of a new Tanager of the Genus Calliste [melanotis], and Remarks on other recently discovered Species. < *Ibis*, 3d ser., vi, Oct., 1876, pp. 407–410, pl. xii.

> *C. melanotis*, p. 408, pl. xi, fig. 1, from Rio Napo, Ecuador = *C. cyanotis* Scl., *Ibis*, 1863, p. 451.—Pl. xi, f. 2, *C. cyanotis.*—Criticisms on various other species. Cf. *Ibis*, 1863, p. 450, and 1868, p. 71.

1877. PELZELN, A. v. Description of a new Species of Calliste, and of a . . . < *Ibis*, 4th ser., i, 1877, pp. 337–339.

> The Tanager here named is *Calliste albertinæ*, p. 337, from Brazil (Natterer).

1878. BREWER, T. M. [Occurrence of Pyranga ludoviciana in Winter in Boston, Mass.] < *Ibis*, 4th ser., ii, Apr., 1878, pp. 204–206.

> Statement occurring in an untitled letter on other subjects.

1878. BREWER, T. M. Rare Visitors. < *Forest and Stream*, x, March 14, 1878, p. 94.
Pyranga ludoviciana at Lynn, Mass., Jan. 20.

1878. INGERSOLL, E. Dr. Coues's Idea of a Tanager. < *The Country*, i, Mar. 23, 1878, p. 310.

> Extract from "The Birds of the Colorado Valley", pt. i, p. 352, with a note as to circumstances of its publication.

1878. SALVADORI, T. [Identity of Euphonia chalcopasta S. & S. with E. mesochrysa Salvad.] < *Ibis*, 4th ser., ii, Apr., 1878, p. 200.

1879. ANON. Comparative Scarcity of the Scarlet Tanager [Pyranga rubra, in New York]. < *The Oölogist*, iv. No. 11, June, 1879, p. 92.

Fringillidæ.

(With *Emberizidæ.*)

1740. LINNÆUS, C.   Doctor Carl Linnæi Beskrifning på Snö-Sparfven.   < *Kongl. Svensk. Vetensk.-Akad. Handl.*, i, 1740, pp. 368–374, tab. i, figg. 9–11.

This, which I have not seen, is the original description of the subsequent *Emberiza nivalis* L. (*Plectrophanes nivalis*).   (Vol. i, for 1839-40, was pub. 1841.)

1743. LINNÆUS, C.   Beskrifning på Snö-sparfwen.   < *Kongl. Swensk. Wetens. Acad. Handl.*, i (1740), 1743, pp. 362–368, pl. i, figg. 9–11.

This is simply the original description of *Emberiza nivalis* in the later edition of the 1st vol. of the *Handlingar.*

1749? LINNÆUS, C.   Beschreibung eines Schneesperlings.   < *Abhandl. d. Schwed. Akad.* auf d. Jahr. 1740, 1749? pp. 134–141, taf. i, figg. 9–11.

This, which I have not seen, is the same description of the subsequent *Emberiza nivalis* in the German version (Kästner) of the *Handlingar.*

1749? SUNDIUS, P.   B. C. D. | Surinamensia Grilliana | [. . .] | curiosis examinanda sistit | Alumnus Oxenstiernianus | Petrus Sundius Nic. fil. | Stockholmiensis. | In audit. Carol. Maj. d. xviii* Junii | Anni MDCCXLIIX [sic] | H. A. M. C. | — | Holmiæ, | Typis Laurentii Salvii. | sm. 4to, 1. p. l., pp. 1–24, 1 pl.

Classis II, Aves, p. 10.   Solum de *Emberizæ* specie tractatur, *Passer caeruleofuscus*, Sloane, *Jam.* ii, p. 311.

1750. LINNÆUS, C.   En Indianisk Sparf. Eller Fringilla capite cæruleo, dorso viridi, abdomine fulvo.   < *Kongl. Svensk. Vetensk.-Acad. Handl.*, xi, 1750, pp. 278–280, pl. vii. fig. 1.

This is the original description of the subsequent *Emberiza ciris* L. (= *Cyanospiza ciris* Baird), erroneously considered as a bird of India.

1750. LINNÆUS, C.   Beschreibung eines indianischen Sperlings, Fringilla, capite caeruleo, dorso viridi, abdomine fulvo.   < *Abhandl. d. Schwed. Akad.* auf d. Jahr 1750, pp. 287, 288.

The same description of the subsequent *Emberiza ciris* L. (*Cyanospiza ciris* Bd.) in the German version of the *Handlingar.*

1757. SCHÖNBERG, A.   Anmärkningar Om Svånska Papegojan, Loxia [enucleator], linea alarum duplici alba. Faun. Sv. N. 176.   < *Kongl. Svensk. Vetensk.-Acad. Handl.*, xviii, 1757, pp. 139–143.

1757. SCHÖNBERG, A.   Anmerkungen über den schwedischen Papagey (Loxia [enucleator]).   < *Abhandl. d. Schwed. Akad.*, auf d. Jahr. 1757, pp. 132–135.

The German version, not seen by me, of the original Swedish.

1773. ANON.   Le Pie-grièche noire de la Caroline [Pipilo erythrophthalmus].   < *Journ. Observ. de Phys.*, ii, 1773, pp. 570, 571.

Not seen: the article is anonymous, nor have I been able to discover the author; whoever he may be, he is not "Le Piegriche" whom Giebel invented in his Bibliography, p. 139.

1774. GÜNTHER, D. F. C.   Vorläufige Nachricht von dem sehr seltenen Nest und den Eyern des Kreuzvogels, oder des Krummschnabels [Loxia curvirostra].   < *Der Naturforscher*, ii, 1774, pp. 66–75.

1778. OTTO, —.   Abhandlung von den Abarten der Kreutzschnabel [Loxia curvirostra], nebst einigen Anmerkungen über die Anordnung der Thière.   < *Der Naturforscher*, xii, 1778, pp. 92–99.

1785–1787. KUHN, —.   Von dem Krünitz oder Krumschnabel (Loxia curvirostra,).   < *Der Naturforscher*, xxi, 1785, p. 197; xxii, 1787, p. 142.

1796. TOLMAN, T.   Account of the Crossbill Bird [Loxia curvirostra americana].   < *The Rural Magazine; or, Vermont Repository*, vol. ii, 1796, p. 475.

Seen only in the reprint, by R. Deane, *Bull. Nutt. Club*, iv, No. 2, Apr., 1876, p. 111.   The breeding of the species in winter is recorded: "they lay their eggs and hatch their young in the middle of winter."

1797. OSBECK, P. Beskrifning på Knorsnäfven (Loxia curvirostra) och dess lefnadssått. < *Kongl. Vetensk.-Akad. Nya Handl.*, xviii, 1797, pp. 298–303.

1822. GREEN, J. Fragments relating to the history of Animals. < *Sillim. Am. Journ. Sci.*, iv, 1822, pp. 309–312.

> Under special subhead "Blue-Yellow Bird.—*Fringilla tristis*", the writer gives a curious supposed case of a specimen of *Chrysomitris tristis* which was dark "indigo" in places where the bird is normally yellow; retaining the black pileum and wing-bars.

1825. BONAPARTE, C. [L.] Description of a new Species of South American Fringilla [F. xanthoroa]. < *Journ. Acad. Nat. Sci. Phila.*, iv, 1825, pp. 350, 351.

1825. COOPER, W. Description of a new species of Grosbeak [Fringilla vespertina, p. 220], inhabiting the Northwestern Territory of the United States. < *Ann. Lyc. Nat. Hist. New York*, i, pt. ii, 1825, pp. 219–222. (Read Jan. 10, 1825.)

> This is the original description of the species, from the Schoolcraft specimen, Saute Ste. Marie, Michigan, Apr., 1823.

1826. COOPER, W. Description of a new Species of Grosbeak [Fringilla vespertina, p. 136], inhabiting the North-western Territory of the United States. < *Thomson's Ann. of Philos.*, new ser., xi, 1826, pp. 134–136.

> Reproduced from *Ann. Lyc. Nat. Hist. New York*, i, 1825, pp. 219–222.

1826. LESS[ON, R. P.] Description d'une espèce nouvelle de Gros-bec [Fringilla vespertina, Coop.], etc., habitant le territoire N.-O. des États-Unis; par William Cooper. . . . < *Féruss. Bull.*, 2e sect., vii, 1826, p. 110.

> Extraite des *Annales du Lycée d'Hist. Nat. de New-York*, i, 1825, pp. 219–222.

1826. LESS[ON, R. P.] Description d'une nouvelle espèce de Fringilla [xanthorea] de l'Amérique méridionale; par Charles Bonaparte. . . . < *Féruss. Bull.*, 2e sect., vii, 1826, p. 249.

> Extraite du *Journ. Acad. Phila.*, iv, 1825, pp. 350, 351.

1826. SELBY, P. J. Description of the Plectrophanes [Centrophanes] Lapponica; a Species lately discovered in the British Islands. < *Trans. Linn. Soc.*, xv, pt. i, 1826, pp. 156–160, pl. i.

> With synonymy, criticism, and notes of habits.

1827. BREHM, [C. L.] Eine neue Art Kreuzschnabel mitlen in Deutschland [Crucirostra bifasciata]. < *Ornis*, Heft iii, 1827, pp. 77–98.

1827. BREHM, C. L. Etwas über die Kreuzschnåbel von Brehm. < *Oken's Isis*, B l. xx, 1827, pp. 704–724.

> *Crucirostra pityopsittacus, C. subpityopsittacus*, p. 703; *C. media*, p 710; *C pinetorum, C. bifasciata*, p. 714; *C. taenioptera*, p. 716; *O. leucoptera*, p 720.

1827. GLOGER, C. [W. L.] Ueber den weisbindigen Kre uzschnabel—Loxia taenioptera—als eigene Art. < *Oken's Isis*, Bd. xx, 1827, pp. 411-418.

1827. GLOGER, C. [W. L.] Noch etwas über Loxia taenioptera. < *Oken's Isis*, Bd. xx, 1827, p. 419, 420.

1827. LESSON, R. P. Description d'une espèce nouvelle de gros-bec [Fringilla vespertina, Coop.], habitant la partie nord-ouest des États-Unis; par William Cooper. . . . < *Féruss. Bull.*, 2e sect., xii, 1827, pp. 267, 268.

> Tiré des *Annal. de Philos.*, xi, 1826, pp. 134–136.

1828. [GLOGER, C. W. L.] Sur le Bec croisé à bandes blanches (Loxia tænioptera), nouvelle espèce: par Constantin Gloger. . . . < *Féruss. Bull.*, 2e sect., xiv, 1828, pp. 116, 117.

> Tiré de *l'Isis*, xx, 1827, pp. 411–418.

1828. L[UROTH, S. G.] Sur les Becs-Croisés (Loxia); par Brehm. . . . < *Féruss. Bull.*, 2e sect., xiv, 1828, pp. 259, 260.

> Tiré de *l'Isis*, xx, 1827, p. 704–724.

1828. [SELBY, P. J.] Description du Plectrophanes [Centrophanes] lapponica, Meyer; espèce nouvelle pour la Faune Brittanique, av. fig.; par P. J. Selby esq. < *Féruss. Bull.*, 2e sect., xiii, 1828, p. 243.

> Tiré des *Trans. Linn. Soc. Lond.*, xv, pp. 156–160.

1828. SELBY, P. J. Beschreibung der Plectrophanes lapponica, kúrzlich in Brittanien entdeckt. < *Oken's Isis*, Bd. xxi, 1828, pp. 1163, 1164.
    Uebersetzt aus d. *Linn. Trans.*, Bd. xv, T. 1, 1826, pp. 156-160.

1828. S . . . s. [STRAUS, —.] Nouvelle espèce de Bec croisé d'Allemagne; par le même [*i. e.*, C. L. Brehm]. . . . < *Féruss. Bull.*, 2e sect., xiv, 1828, p. 260.
    Crucirostra bifasciata—Ornis, 1827, Heft 3, pp. 77-98.

1829. ANON. The Crossbill [Loxia curvirostra]. < *Loudon's Mag. Nat. Hist.*, i, 1829, p. 394.

1829. GLOGER, C. [W. L.] Zur Naturgeschichte des weissbindigen Kreuzschnabels, Loxia tænioptera. < *Nov. Act. Acad. Leop. Carol. Nat. Cur.*, xiv, pt. ii, 1829, pp. 919–942.
    Not seen by me: title from Carus and Engelmann.

1829. "J. W." Flocks of Crossbills [Loxia curvirostra] near Worcester. < *Loudon's Mag. Nat. Hist.*, ii, 1829, p. 268.

1829. YARRELL, W. On the structure of the Beak and its muscles in the Crossbill, (Loxia curvirostra.) < *Zool. Journ.*, iv, 1829, pp. 459–464, pl. xiv, figg. 1-7.

1830. BREHM, C. L. Noch einige Beobachtungen über den zweybindigen Kreuzschnabel, Crucirostra bifasciata. < *Oken's Isis*, Bd. xxiii, 1830, pp. 110–112.

1830. GLOGER, C. [W. L.] Sur l'histoire naturelle du Bec croisé à bandes blanches. (Loxia tænioptera); par Constantin Gloger. . . . < *Féruss. Bull.*, 2e sect., xxii, 1830, pp. 125, 126.
    Extrait des *Nov. Act. Acad. Nat. Cur.*, xiv, 1829, pt. ii, pp. 919-924.

1831. K[UHN, —.] Sur les Becs-croisés de Russie. . . . < *Féruss. Bull.*, 2e sect., xxv, 1831, pp. 353, 354.
    Tiré du nouv. *Magas. d'Hist. Nat.*, etc., de Moscou, février 1829.

1832. COOPER, W. Neue Gattung Kernbeisser [Fringilla vespertina]. < *Oken's Isis*, Bd. xxv, 1832, p. 1073.
    Auszug aus d. *Ann. Lyc. Nat. Hist. New-York*, i, 1825, pp. 219-222.

1832. GREEN, J. Fragmente zur Naturgeschichte. < *Oken's Isis*, Bd. xxv, 1832, p. 1042.
    Aus d. *Amer. Journ. Sci.*, iv, 1822, pp. 309-312, q. v.

1833. CLARKE, W. B. A Bird's [Plectrophanes nivalis] Nest in the Skull of an Esquimaux. < *Loudon's Mag. Nat. Hist.*, vi, 1833, p. 154.
    Cf. tom. cit., p. 524.

1833. CLARKE, W B. A Snow Bunting's [Plectrophanes nivalis] Nest not in the Skull of an Esquimaux. < *Loudon's Mag. Nat. Hist.*, vi, 1833, p. 524.
    Cf. tom. cit., p. 154.

1834. BOIE. J. F. Emberiza [*i. e.*, Centrophanes] lapponica Linn. < *Oken's Isis*, Bd. xxvii, 1832, p. 366.

1834. GERVAIS, [P.] Moineau. Fringilla. Linné. M. de Gay. F. Gayi. Eydoux et Gervais. < *Guér. Mag. de Zool.*, 4e année, 1834, classe ii, notice xxiii, pl. xxiii.

1834. "J. O." The Plectrophanes [Centrophanes] lapponica has been captured, along with Larks, near Preston, Lancashire. < *Loudon's Mag. Nat. Hist.*, vii, 1834, pp. 56, 57.

1835. GARDINER, W. Particulars on a caged Pair of Siskins', or Aberdevines', building Nests and rearing a pair of young Siskins in Confinement; and a Statement of the Fact that the Siskin, wild, has bred about Dundee. < *Loudon's Mag. Nat. Hist.*, viii, 1835, pp. 372–374.

1835. GERVAIS, [P.] Moineau. Fringilla. L. Vieill. M. de Cuba. F. Cubæ. Gervais. < *Guér Mag. de Zool.*, 5e année, 1835, classe ii, notice xliv, pl. xliv.

1836. BROWN, J. S. The Crossbill (Loxia curvirostra). < *Loudon's Mag. Nat. Hist.*, ix, 1836, p. 202.

1836. MORRIS, F. O. Facts on the Habits and personal Characteristics of the Crossbill (Loxia curvirostra Temm.). < *Loudon's Mag. Nat. Hist.*, ix, 1836, pp. 413–416.

1837. CLARKE, J.   Notes on, and Notices of, the Crossbill (Loxia curvirostra Linn.).   < *Charlesw. Mag. Nat. Hist.*, i, 1837, pp. 164–167.
   Habits, nidification, and manners in captivity.

1837. DARWIN, C.   [Remarks upon the Habits of Birds of the Genera Geospiza, Camarhynchus, Cactornis, and Certhidea.]   < *P. Z. S.*, v, 1837, p. 49.

1837. GOULD, J.   [Remarks on a group of Ground Finches from Mr. Darwin's Collection, with characters of the New Species.]   < *P. Z. S.*, v, 1837, pp. 4–7.
   Geospiza magnirostris, G. strenua, G. fortis, G. nebulosa, G. fuliginosa, p. 5; *G. dentirostris, G. parvula, G. dubia, Camarhynchus psittacula, O. crassirostris*, p. 6; *Cactornis scandens, O. assimilis, Certhidea olivacea*, p. 7, genn. et spp. nn.
   A very notable paper, first describing the remarkable *Fringillidæ* of the Galapagos. See Darwin's remarks on them, *ibid.* p. 49.

1837. S[ELBY], P. J.   Loxia curvirostra [in Britain].   < *Mag. of Zool. and Bot.*, i, 1837, pp. 103, 104.

1838. BLYTH, E.   [Remarks on the Plumage and progressive Changes of the Crossbill and Linnet.]   < *P. Z. S.*, vi, 1838, p. 115.

1838. BLYTH, E.   Plumage of the Crossbill [Loxia curvirostra].   < *Charlesw. Mag. Nat. Hist.*, ii, pp. 451, 452.

1839. BROWN, J.   Breeding of the Crossbill [Loxia curvirostra] in Gloucestershire.   < *Charlesw. Mag. Nat. Hist.*, iii, 1839, p. 310.

1839. CHARLESWORTH, E.   [Exhibition of the Nest and Eggs of the Crossbill (Loxia curvirostra).]   < *P. Z. S.*, vii, 1839, p. 60.

1839. CLARKE, J.   Young of Loxia curvirostra, Temm. (Crossbill.)   < *Charlesw. Mag. Nat. Hist.*, iii, 1839, p. 565.
   In Britain.

1839. LONG, H. L.   Notice of the discovery of the Nests and Eggs of the common Crossbill [Loxia curvirostra], near Farnham, Surrey.   With additional Remarks by Mr. Yarrell.   < *Charlesw. Mag. Nat. Hist.*, iii, 1839, pp. 236–239.

1839. LONG, H. L.   Breeding of the Crossbill [Loxia curvirostra] in Surrey.   < *Charlesw. Mag. Nat, Hist.*, iii, 1839, p. 311.

1840. YARRELL, W.   Exhibition of the Snow-Bunting [Plectrophanes nivalis, in perfect summer plumage, shot in England].   < *P. Z. S.*, viii, 1840, p. 59.

1841. [LAFRESNAYE, F. DE.]   G. Passerine. Passerina. Vieillot.   S.–G. Spiza. Bonaparte.   P. (Spiza) de Leclancher.   P. (spiza) Leclancherii. De Lafr.   < *Guér. Mag. de Zool.*, 2e sér., année 1841, Oiseaux, pp. 1, 2, pl. 22.
   Rev. Zool., 1840, p. 260.—En suite de la description specifique, une liste synonymatique de cinq espèces du sousgenre *Spiza*.

1842. BRANDT, J. F.   Note sur les espèces de Loxia (bec croisé) de la Faune de Russie.   < *Bull. Scientif. Acad. Imp. Sci. St.-Pétersb.*, ix, 1842, p. 288.
   1. *L. curvirostra*; 2. *L. pityopsittacus*; 3. *L. leucoptera*.

1842. BRANDT, J. F.   Remarques sur le Passer arctous de Pallas, comme étant vraisemblablement le type de trois différentes espèces d'oiseaux.   < *Bull. Scientif. Acad. Imp. Sci. St.-Pétersb.*, x, for Nov. 26, 1841, pub. 1842, pp. 251–253.
   Fringilla (Linaria) gebleri, p. 251 = *P. arctous*, var. *a*. F. (L.) *brunneonucha*, p. 252 = *P. a.* var. β.   F. (L.) *griseonucha*, p. 252 = *P. a.* var. γ.   Each one of Pallas's three varieties of *Passer arctous* is thus provided with a new name; but as Brandt afterward saw that the word *arctous* itself must stand for one of them, he consequently (*Bulletin* of Feb. 3, 1843, p. 27) transferred his term *gebleri* to an entirely different bird.

1842. LAFRESNAYE, [F.] DE.   G. Catamblyrhynque.   Catamblyrhynchus. De Lafresnaye.   < *Guér. Mag. de Zool.*, 2e sér., année 1843, Oiseaux, pp. 1, 2, pl. 34.
   Pl. 34, *O. diadema* Lafr., *R. Z.*, 1842, p. 301, Bogotá.

1842. SUNDEVALL, C. J.   Om systematiska fördelningen af Passeres (Fringilla, Loxia och Emberiza L.).   < *Förh. Skand. Naturf. o. Läk.*, iii, 1842, pp. 691, 692.
   Not seen.

1843. GREGORY, — DE. [Note relative aux essais pour acclimater Cardinalis virginianus en France.] < *Revue Zoologique*, vi, 1843, p. 127.

1843. HASLAM, S. H.   Note on the occurrence of the Lark Bunting [Centrophanes lapponica] near Milnthorpe. < *Zoologist*, i, 1843, p. 316.

1843. HEPPENSTALL, J.   Note on the Lesser Redpoll [Ægiothus linaria]. < *Zoologist*, i, 1843, p. 353.

1843. JORDAN, W. R. H.   Note on the Crossbill, (Loxia curvirostra) [in Devon]. < *Zoologist*, i, 1843, p. 39.

1843. JERDON, A.   Note on the occurrence of the White-winged Crossbill [Loxia leucoptera] in Scotland. < *Zoologist*, i, 1843, pp. 221, 222.

1843. LAFRESNAYE, [F.] DE.   G. Gros-bec.   Coccothraustes. Cuv. (G. Guiraca. Swainson. S.–G. Piezorina. De Laf.)   G. cendré.   C. cinerea. De Lafr.   < *Guér. Mag. de Zool.*, 2e sér., année 1843, Oiseaux, pp. 1, 2, pl. 30.
    A peculiar form of the *Fringillidæ* from the Galapagos Islands.

1843. LEWCOCK, J.   Notes on the Crossbill's [Loxia curvirostra] breeding in the Holt Forest [Hampshire]. < *Zoologist*, i, 1843, p. 189.

1843. WILLOUGHBY, S.   Note on the Snow Bunting [Plectrophanes nivalis]. < *Zoologist*, i, 1843, p. 352.

1844. BELL, R. J.   Note on the occurrence of the Snow Bunting [Plectrophanes nivalis] at Derby. < *Zoologist*, ii, 1844, p. 569.

1844. BONAPARTE, C. L.   Genus novum Fringillinarum [Bustamantia (capitaurea sp. n.)].   < *Nuov. Ann. Scienze Nat. Bologna*, 2d ser., i, May, 1844, pp. 397–399.
    The genus and species, described as new from Bogotá, are synonymous with *Catamblyrhynchus diadema* Lafr., *R. Z.*, 1842, p. 301.

1844. BRANDT, J. F.   Ueber die Gattungen von Loxia in Russland. < *Oken's Isis*, Bd. xxxvii, 1844, p. 134.
    From *Bull. Sci. Acad. Imp. Sci. St.-Pétersb.*, Bd. ix, 1841, p. 288.

1844. BRANDT, J. F.   Bemerkungen über Passer arctous Pallas, welcher wahrscheinlich der Typus von 3 verschiedenen Gattungen ist.   < *Oken's Isis*, Bd. xxxvii, 1844, pp. 135–137.
    Bull. Sci. Acad. Imp. Sci. St.-Pétersb., Bd. x, auf d. J. 1841, 1842, pp. 251–253, q. v.   *Fringilla (Linaria) gebleri, F. (L.) brunneonucha, F. (L.) griseonucha.*

1844. WARD, J. F.   Ueber das Vorkommen von Pyrrhula enucleator bey Newyork.   < *Oken's Isis*, Bd. xxxvii, 1844, p. 118.
    Ann. Lyc. Nat. Hist. N. Y., iv, p. 51.—Vergl. 1848, WARD, J. F.

1845. BORRER, W., JR.   Occurrence of the Lapland Bunting (Plectrophanes [Centrophanes] Lapponica), near Brighton, Sussex. < *Zoologist*, iii, 1845, p. 825.

1845. CLARK, H.   Occurrence of the Pine Grosbeak [Pinicola enucleator] near Rochdale. < *Zoologist*, iii, 1845, p. 1025.

1845. FITTON, E. [B.]   [Note on the White-winged Crossbill (Loxia leucoptera).]   < *P. Z. S.*, xiii, 1845, p. 91.

1845. FITTON, E. B.   Occurrence of the White-winged Crossbill [Loxia leucoptera] at Exmouth. < *Zoologist*, iii, 1845, p. 1190.

1845. FRERE, H. T.   Occurrence of the Snow Bunting [Plectrophanes nivalis] near Aylsham. < *Zoologist*, iii, 1845, p. 1191.

1845. SUNDEVALL, [C. J.]   Korsnäbbens [Loxia curvirostra] fortplantning.   < *Öfvers. Kongl. Svensk. Vetensk.-Akad. Förhandl. för år* 1845, pp. 131, 132.

1846. BELL, R. J.   Occurrence of the White-winged Crossbill [Loxia leucoptera] at Derby, Nov. 21st, 1845.   < *Zoologist*, iv, 1846, pp. 1247, 1248.

1846. CHARLESWORTH, [E.]   [Nest vom Kreuzschnabel, vom Gipfel einer Fichte.]   < *Oken's Isis*, Bd. xxxix, 1846, p. 618.
    P. Z. S., vii, Mar., 1839, p. 60.

1846. COOPER, J.   Occurrence of the White-winged Crossbill [Loxia leucoptera] near Carlisle.   < *Zoologist*, iv, 1846, p. 1551.

1846. GARTH, J.   Occurrence of the Crossbill [Loxia curvirostra] at Knaresborough. < *Zoologist*, iv, 1846, p. 1367.

1846. HUNTER, C. B.   Nesting of the Lesser Redpoll [Ægiothus linaria] in Norfolk. < *Zoologist*, iv, 1846, p. 1497.

1846. HUNTER, C. B.   Occurrence of the White-winged Crossbill [Loxia curvirostra] near Thetford.   < *Zoologist*, iv, 1846, p. 1498.

1846. NEWTON, A.   On Redpolls [Ægiothus linaria] staying at Thetford throughout the summer.   < *Zoologist*, iv, 1846, pp. 1497, 1498.

1846. SELYS-LONGCHAMPS, E. DE.   Notice sur les Becs-croisés leucoptère et bifascié. < *Bull. Acad. Belgique*, xiii, i, 1846, pp. 324–336 ; *l'Institut*, xiv, No. 660, 1846, pp. 290, 291.
   Pas vue moi-même.

1846. SUNDEVALL, [C. J.]   Loxia bifasciata Br.   < *Öfvers. Kongl. Svensk. Vetensk.- Akad. Förhandl. för år* 1846, pp. 37–40.
   "Efter några underrättelser om Bändel korsnäbbens förekomst, lemnar förf. en öfversigt af de hittills kända 5 arterna af sl. *Loxia*."—v. Friesen, *Öfv. Sver. Orn. Litt.*, 1860, 34.
   Hittills känner man följande arter af slagtet *Loxia* : L. *pityopsittacus*, L. *curvirostra*, L. *fusca* V. [=L. *americana* Wils.], L. *bifasciata*, L. *leucoptera*.

1847. HODGKINSON, J. B.   Occurrence of the White-winged Crossbill [Loxia curvi-rostra] in Cumberland.   < *Zoologist*, v, 1847, p. 1638.

1848. JOHNSON, F. W.   Extreme abundance of the Mealy Redpoll (Fringilla [Ægiothus] canescens) near Ipswich.   < *Zoologist*, vi, 1848, p. 2064.

1848. NEWMAN, E.   Proposed alteration of Name in the Europæan White-winged Crossbill, and Occurrence of the American White-winged Crossbill [Loxia leucoptera] in England.   < *Zoologist*, vi, 1848, p. 2300.

1848. NEWTON, A.   Note on the Mealy Redpoll (Fringilla [Ægiothus] canescens), &c.   < *Zoologist*, vi, 1848, pp. 2144, 2145.

1848 (*prior to*). WARD, J. F.   Notice of the Appearance of the Pine Grosbeak, Pyrr-hula Enucleator, in the Environs of New-York [in winter of 1836–7].   < *Ann. Lyc. Nat. Hist. New York*, iv, 1848, pp. 51, 52.   (Read Dec. 19, 1836. Whole vol. dated 1848.)
   This article must have appeared in 1844 or earlier, as it is noticed in the *Isis* of that year. The date given is that of the completed vol. of the *Annals*.

1849. BREE, C. R.   Occurrence of the Two-barred Crossbill (Loxia bifasciata) in Suf-folk.   < *Zoologist*, vii, 1849, p. 2419.

1849. CATER, W. E.   Arrival of the Snow Bunting (Emberiza [Plectrophanes] nivalis) [in Britain].   < *Zoologist*, vii, 1849, p. 2415.

1849. DUFF, J.   The Crossbill (Loxia curvirostra) nesting in Durham.   < *Zoologist*, vii, 1849, pp. 2526, 2527.

1849. ELLMAN, J. B.   Occurrence of the Hawfinch (Loxia coccothraustes) and Cross-bill (L. curvirostra) at Rye.   < *Zoologist*, vii, 1849, p. 2418.

1849. HULKE, J. W.   Occurrence of the Snow Bunting (Emberiza [Plectrophanes] ni-valis) near Deal.   < *Zoologist*, vii, 1849, p. 2388.

1849. [JARDINE, W.]   Phrygilus unicolor, Tschudi.   < *Jard. Contrib. Orn.*, 1849, p. 46, pl. xx.

1849. MARRIS, R.   Occurrence of the Crossbill [Loxia curvirostra] at Wisbeach.   < *Zo-ologist*, vii, 1849, p. 2527.

1849. [THIENEMANN, F. A. L.]   Der weissbindige Kreuzschnabel.   < *Rhea*, Heft. ii, 1849, pp. 165–171.
   Behandelt *Loxia pityopsittacus*, *curvirostra*, und *leucoptera*, mit kurzer Beschreibung und Aussmessungen einiger Exemplare der drei Formen.

1850. AMHURST, F. K.   Enquiry respecting a [British] Bird's Nest [Ægiothus linaria?
see Zool., 3027].   < *Zoologist*, viii, 1850, p. 2967.

1850. BONAPARTE, C. L., *and* SCHLEGEL, H.   Monographie | des | Loxiens | par | Ch. L.
Bonaparte | et | H. Schlegel. | — | Ouvrage | accompagné de 54 planches colo-
riées. | lithographiées | d'après les dessins | de | M. Bädeker | et autres natu-
ralistes. | — | Leiden et Düsseldorf, | chez | Arnz & Comp. | 1850.   1 vol.   4to.
3 p. ll (title, dedication), pp. i–xviii, 1–55, pll. color. 54.

Descriptive and general account of 41 spp., introduced by a commentary on the inter-rela-
tions of *Fringillidæ*. The "Loxiens" are divided into 3 groups, *Loxiaceæ, Montifringillaceæ*,
and *Linotaceæ.*—*Oriturus, Melanodera,* p. ii; *Lophospiza, Phonipara,* p. iii; *Pyrrholoxia, Cy-
anoloxia,* p. vi; *Chaunoproctus,* p. xiv, appear to be new generic names of Bonaparte's. Pl. 1.
Loxia pityopsittacus ; 2, 3, 4, 5, *L. curvirostra* et vars. ; 6, *L. americana ;* 7, *L. himalayana ;*
8, *L. bifasciata ;* 9, 10, *L. leucoptera ;* 11, 12, *Corythus enucleator ;* 13, *C. subhimachalus ;* 14,
Carpodacus erythrinus ; 15, *C. purpureus ;* 16, 17, *C. frontalis ;* 18, *C. sinaiticus ;* 19, 20, *C.
roseus ;* 21, *C. rhodochrous ;* 22, *C. rhodopeplus ;* 23, *C. thura,* p. 21, n. sp. ; 24, *C. sophia,* p, 22,
n. sp.; 25, *C. rhodochlamys ;* 26. *C. rubicilla ;* 27, 28, *C. puniceus ;* 29, *Pyrrha saturata ;* 30, 31,
Erythrospiza phœnicoptera ; 32, *E. obsoleta ;* 33, *E. githaginea ;* 34, 35, *Uragus sibiricus ;* 36,
U. sanguinolentus ; 37, 38, *Chaunoproctus papa ;* 39, 40, *Hæmatospisa sipahi ;* 41, *Montifrin-
gilla griseinucha ;* 42, *M. brunneinucha ;* 43, *M. tephrocotis ;* 44, 45, *M. arctoa ;* 46, *M. nivalis ;*
47, *Fringalauda nemoricola ;* 48, *Linota cannabina ;* 49, *L. fringillirostris,* n. sp., p. 45; 50, *L.
montium ;* 51, *Acanthis canescens ;* 52, *A. linaria ;* 53, *A. hollbölli ;* 54, *A. rufescens.*

The introductory matter of this work is unmistakably "Napoleonic"; the text is apparently
from the hand of the more conservative and trustworthy author.—There is a reprint of the
"Introduction" in *Jard. Contr. Orn.*, 1851, pp. 27–47—though one issue of this matter might
have been consiuered amply sufficient.

1850. [KIRTLAND, J. P.]   Birds of Winter.   < *The Family Visitor*, i, No. 8, 1850, p. —.
Noting occurrence of certain *Fringillidæ* in Ohio at that season.

1850. [KIRTLAND, J. P.]   Pine Linnet—Linaria pinus.   < *The Family Visitor*, i, No. 18,
1850, p. 140.   See also No. 19, p. 148, and No. 21, p. 164.
Biographical sketch of the species as observed in Ohio.

1850. [KIRTLAND, J. P.]   White-headed Sparrow [Zonotrichia leucophrys].   < *The
Family Visitor*, i, No. 19, 1850, p. 148.   See also No. 21, p. 164.

1850. LANFOSSI, P.   Sovra l' albinismo e melanismo di una Loxia curvirostra e di una
Fringilla cisalpina, e sull' Emberiza rustica Pall.   < *Giorn. dell' Ital. R. Istit.
Lombardo*, ii, 1850, pp. 111–113.
Non veduto per me.

1850. NEWMAN, E.   Occurrence of the Parrot Crossbill (Loxia pityopsittacus) near
London.   < *Zoologist*, viii, 1850, p. 2770.

1851. BREWER, T. M.   [On the occurrence of the Pine Grosbeak (Strobilophaga enucleator) and other Fringillidæ, in the neighbourhood of East Bethel, Vt.]
< *Proc. Boston Soc. Nat. Hist.*, iv, 1851, pp. 42, 43.

1851. HEWITSON, W. C.   Remarkable Bird's [Ægiothus linaria?] Nest.   < *Zoologist*,
ix, 1851, p. 3027.
Cf. *Zool.*, 2967.

1851. [JARDINE, W.]   Monographie des Loxiens.   < *Jard. Contrib. Orn.*, 1851, pp. 27–47.
Note introducing a reprint of the introduction of this work.

1851. LANFOSSI, P.   Sopra varie Fringille appartenenti al sottogenere Linaria de
Brehm.   < *Giorn. dell' Ital. R. Istit. Lombardo*, new ser., iii, 1851, pp. 95–109.
Non veduto per me.

1851. NEWTON, A.   Occurrence of the Parrot Crossbill [Loxia pityopsittacus] in Suffolk and Norfolk.   < *Zoologist*, ix, 1851, p. 3145.

1852. BELL, J.   On the Pipilo Oregonus [n. sp.] as distinguished from the Pipilo
Arcticus of Swainson.   < *Ann. Lyc. Nat. Hist. N. Y.*, v, 1852, pp. 6–8.   (Read
Nov. 27, 1848.)

1852. BREE, C. R.   Note on the Common Red-poll (Linota [Ægiothus] linaria).   < *Zoologist*, x, 1852, pp. 3511, 3512.

1852. ELLMAN, J. B.   Note on the Snow Bunting (Emberiza [Plectrophanes] nivalis). < *Zoologist*, x, 1852, p. 3329.

1852. MCCALL, G. A.   Note on Carpodacus frontalis, (Say,) with description of a new species [C. familiaris] of the same genus, from Santa Fé, New Mexico. < *Proc. Acad. Nat. Sci. Phila.*, vi, 1852, p. 61.

1852. VERREAUX, J.   Description d'une nouvelle espèce d'oiseau du genre Calli- rhynchus [devronis].   < *Rev. et Mag. de Zool.*, iv, 1852, pp. 314–316.
Described from Guayaquil.

1852. LAWRENCE, G. N.   Descriptions of new species of Birds of the genera . . . Em- bernagra [rufivirgata], . . . < *Ann. Lyc. Nat. Hist. N. Y.*, v, 1852, pp. 112– 117, pl. 5. (Read Apr. 28, 1851.)
Here occurs, in a paper of wider scope, full title of which is the N. Amer. part of this *Bibl.*, the orig. descr. of the above sp., p. 112, pl. 5, f. 2.

1852. LAWRENCE, G. N.   Descriptions of New Species of Birds, of the genera . . . Plectrophanes [McCownii, p. 122] Meyer.   < *Ann. Lyc. Nat. Hist. N. Y.*, v, 1852, pp. 121–123.   (Read Sept. 8, 1851.)
Other spp. here described are a *Toxostoma* and a *Tyrannula*: title is to be found in full in the N. Am. part of this *Bibl.*

1852. WOODHOUSE, S. W.   Descriptions of new species of Birds of the genera Vireo, Vieill., and Zonotrichia [cassinii, p. 60], Swains.   < *Proc. Acad. Nat. Sci. Phila.*, vi, 1852, pp. 60, 61.
This is the *Peucœa cassini* of later authors.

1852. WOODHOUSE, S. W.   Description of a new Snow Finch of the genus Struthus [caniceps], Boie.   < *Proc. Acad. Nat. Sci. Phila.*, vi, 1852, pp. 202, 203.

1853. BREHM, [C.] L.   Die Kreuzschnäbel. Crucirostra, Cuv.   < *Naumannia*, iii, 1853, pp. 178–203, 241–256 ; pl. —, figg. 1–20.
I. *Loxia pityopsittacus*: 1, *C. major*, f. 1 ; 2, *C. pityopsittacus*, f. 2 ; 3, *C. subpityopsittacus*, f. 3 ; 4, *C. brachyrhynchos*, f. 4 ; 5, *C. pseudopityopsittacus*, f. 5 ; 6, *C. intercedcns*, f. 6.   II. *Loxia curvirostra*: 1, *C. montana*, f. 9 ; 2, *C. paradoxa*, f. 7 ; 3, *C. media*, f. 8 ; 4, *C. macrorhynchos*, f. "8"; 5, *C. pinetorum*, f. 11.   III. *Crucirostra minuta*: *C. minor*, f. 12.   IV. *Crucirostra rubri- fasciata*; 1, *C. rubrifasciata*, f. 13 ; 2, *C. erythroptera*, f. 14.   V. *Crucirostrœ albifasciatæ*: 1, *C. trifasciata*, f. 15 ; 2, *C. bifasciata*, f. 16 ; *C. tænioptera*, f. 17 ; 4, *C. orientalis*, f. 18 ; 5, *C. assi- milis*, f. 19 ; 6, *C. leucoptera*, f. 20.
In this paper Brehm is very thoroughly himself, carrying out his peculiar views to their logical extreme.   All these "species," real or Brehmian, some of which are here described as new, are very elaborately treated ; and the plate, from nature by J. F. Naumann, is valuable as showing how complete is the graduation in size of bill from the largest to the smallest. Among the twenty "species" here treated, some five or six might be held worthy of recogni- tion by many ornithologists.

1853. BÖCK, —.   Ausfallen der Mauser bei einem Vogel [Centrophanes lapponica] in der Gefangenschaft.   < *J. f. O.*, i, 1853, pp. 207.
Cf. tom. cit., p. 383.

1854. CASSIN, J.   [Remarks on abundance of Loxia leucoptera in the vicinity of Philadelphia, winter of 1853–4.]   < *Proc. Acad. Nat. Sci. Phila.*, vii, 1854, pp. 203, 204.

1854. LANFOSSI, P.   Sopra varie fringille appartenenti al sottogenere Linaria di Brehm. < *Bianconi's Repert. Ital. Stor. Nat.*, ii, 1854, pp. 24–27.
Estratto *Giorn. delle' I. R. Istit. Lombardo di Scienze*, ec., t. iii, pp. 95–109, Milano, 1851.

1854. LANFOSSI, P.   Sovra l'albinismo e melanismi d'una varietà della Loxia curvi- rostra etc.   < *Bianconi's Repert. Ital. Stor. Nat.*, ii, 1854, pp. 9, 10.
Giorn. I. R. Istit. Lombardo di Scienze, ec., t. ii, Milano, 1850, p. 111.

1854. ROBERTS, A.   Occurrence of the Crossbill [Loxia curvirostra] near Scarborough. < *Zoologist*, xii, 1854, pp. 4329, 4330.

1855. BOLD, T. J.   Occurrence of Crossbills [Loxia curvirostra] in Northumberland and Durham.   < *Zoologist*, xiii, 1855, p. 4871.

1855. BOLLE, C. Der Hakengimpel, Pyrrhula Enucleator, Temm. in Amerika. <*Naumannia*, 1855, pp. 424-427.
Aus dem Englischen von Audubon.

1855. BONAPARTE, C. L. [Remarques sur un opuscule de M. le vicomte Dubus de Ghisignies, sur douze espèces inédites de Passereaux chanteurs.] < *Compt. Rend. de l'Acad. Sci.*, xl, 1855, pp. 356, 454, 455.
Note: Kieneria, g. n., p. 356, type "ex-*Pipilo rufipilea*."

1855. COTTLE, T. Coccothraustes vespertina.—Evening Grosbeak. < *Canad. Journ.*, iii, 1855, p. 287.
Historical and descriptive—occurrence of the species in Canada.

1855. DEHNE, A. Loxia leucoptera Gmel. und Loxia bifasciata Brehm. < *Allg. deutsche naturh. Zeitung*, n. F., i, 1855, p. 439.
Nebst Nachschrift von Reichenbach, p. 440.—Nicht mir selbst zugänglich.

1855. GLOGER, C. W. L. Die Liebe zu glänzenden Gegenständen, [u, s. w.]. <*J. f. O.*, iii, 1855, pp. 76-79.
As instanced by Audubon in the case of *Guiraca cœrulea*, etc.

1855. NORMAN, G. Occurrence of large Flocks of Crossbills [Loxia curvirostra] near Hull. < *Zoologist*, xiii, 1855, p. 4808.

1855. STEVENSON, H. The Lapland Bunting (Plectrophanes [Centrophanes] lapponica,) in Norfolk. < *Zoologist*, xiii, 1855, p. 4631.

1856. BOLD, T. J. Crossbill [Loxia curvirostra] breeding in the North of England. < *Zoologist*, xiv, 1856, pp. 5159, 5160.

1856. BREHM, C. L. Etwas über die Leinzeisige, Linaria, Briss. < *Naumannia*, vi, 1856, pp. 173-177.
1) Von rothbrüstigen, *L. longirostris, tenuirostris, holböllii, alnorum, agrorum, betularum et microrhynchus*. 2) Von weissbrüstigen, *L. borealis, robusta, rufescens, dubia, canigularis, assimilis, leuconotus, septentrionalis, flavirostris, pusilla*.

1856. SMITH, J. A. [Note on Ægiothus canescens in the vicinity of Edinburgh.] < *Edinb. New Philos. Journ.*, new ser., iii, 1856, p. 350.

1857. [BILLINGS, E.] On the Natural History of the Rosignol or Song Sparrow, Fringilla [Melospiza] melodia. < *Canad. Nat. and Geol.*, ii, 1857, pp. 47-52.
With chars. and synon., copied from Audubon, of 4 spp. of Canadian *Fringillidæ*.

1857. BONAPARTE, C. L. Observations sur diverses espèces d'Emberiziens et répartition en genres de cette Sous-famille de Passereaux chanteurs conirostres. < *Rev. et Mag. de Zool.*, ix, 1857, pp. 160-166, pl. 7.
La sous-famille se trouve limitée aux genres *Cynchramus, Plectrophanes, Centrophanes, Onychospina, Hypocenter, Fringillaria, Hortulanus, Schœnicla, Emberiza, Buscarla* (type *E. pusilla* Pall.). L'objet principal de ce mémoire est d'illustrer la figure d'un jeune mâle de *Buscarla pityornis* (pl. 7—"*Emberiza scotata*" par une evreur de gravure—voir "errata." p. 209.)

1857. D'URBAN, W. S. M. Notice of the Occurrence of the Pine Grosbeak [Pinicola enucleator] and Bohemian Chatterer, near Montreal. < *Canad. Nat.*, i, Jan., 1857, pp. 465-472, woodc.

1857. LANFOSSI, P. Intorno ai Crocieri a doppia fascia [Loxia bifasciata]. < *Giorn. dell' Ital. R. Istit. Lombardo*, new ser., ix, 1857, pp. 117-127.
Non veduto per me.

1858. BAIRD, S. F. [Ammodromus samuelis, a new Sparrow from California.] <*Proc. Boston Soc. Nat. Hist.*, vi, 1858, pp. 379, 380.

1858. CASSIN, J. [Occurrence of Hesperiphona vespertina in Northern Illinois.] < *Proc. Acad. Nat. Sci. Phila.*, 1858, p. 191.

1858. DOUBLEDAY, H. Plectrophanes nivalis [habits of]. < *Zoologist*, xvi, 1858, pp. 6093, 6094.

1858. HADFIELD, H. W. Emberiza [Plectrophanes] nivalis [habits of]. < *Zoologist*, xvi, 1858, pp. 6239, 6240.

1858. MATTHEWS, M. A.   [Note on habits of] Emberiza [Plectrophanes] nivalis.
   < *Zoologist*, xvi, 1858, pp, 6207, 6208.

1858. SMURTHWAITE, H.   Occurrence of Crossbills [Loxia curvirostra] in Yorkshire.
   < *Zoologist*, xvi, 1858, p. 6309.

1859. ANON.   Occurrence of the Parrot Crossbill (Loxia pityopsittacus) near Brighton.
   < *Zoologist*, xvii, 1859, p. 6329.

1859. BLAKISTON, T.   Scraps from the Far West.   < *Zoologist*, xvii, 1859, pp. 6318-
   6325, 6373-6376.
   Remarks on birds observed in British America between York Factory and Carleton House,
   and as such only properly citable in another connection; noted here for the detailed account
   of *Hesperiphona vespertina* which the paper includes.

1859. BREWER, T. M.   [Note on the occurrence of Coturniculus henslowi in Massachusetts.]   < *Proc. Boston Soc. Nat. Hist.*, vii, 1859, pp. 74, 75.
   Corrects his erroneous statement, tom. cit., p. 21, that *Peucæa æstivalis* had been found
   in Massachusetts.

1859. GOULD, J.   [Exhibition of Crithagra brasiliensis shot in England (probably
   escaped).]   < *P. Z. S.*, xxvii, 1859, p. 100.

1859. GRAYSON, A. J.   The Crimson-necked or House Finch [Carpodacus frontalis].
   < *The Hesperian* (San Francisco, Cal.), ii, Mar., 1859, pp. 7 - —, with pl. of ♂
   and ♀.
   Not seen.

1859. ROGERS, H.   Occurrence of the Snow Bunting (Emberiza [Plectrophanes] nivalis) in the Isle of Wight.   < *Zoologist*, xvii, 1859, p. 6780.

1859. WHEELER, E. S.   [Remarks on exhibition of male and female specimens of
   Ammodromus henslowi, with nest and eggs.]   < *Proc. Boston Soc. Nat. Hist.*,
   vii, 1859, p. 137.

1860. GLOGER, C. W. L.   Die Heimath des weissbindigen Kreuzschnabels in Europa.
   < *J. f. O.*, viii, 1860, pp. 397, 398.
   "*Loxia leucoptera! taenioptera, bifasciata.*

1860. KIRTLAND, J. P.   [Occurrence of Hesperiphona vespertina in Ohio.]   < *Ohio
   Farmer*, March 24, 1860, vol. ix, p. —.
   The original ascription of the species to Ohio; but it had been got in that State in 1847.

1860. SCHNERR, J.   Die Kreuzschnäbel [Loxia curvirostra].   Legende.   < *J. f. O.*,
   viii, 1860, pp. 471, 472.
   Gedicht.

1860. PHILIPPI, R. A.   Ueber zwei vermuthlich neue Chilenischen Enten und über
   Fringilla barbata Mol.   < *Archf. f. Naturg.*, 1860, (1), pp. 24-28.
   Anas iopareia, p. 24.   *Erismatura vittata*, p. 26.   Synonymik von *Chrysomitris barbata.*

1861. BOLLE, C.   Ueber den californischen Hausfinken, Carpodacus familiaris McCall.
   < *J. f. O.*, ix, 1861, pp. 141-147.
   Ins Deutsche übertragen von Dr. C. Bolle aus *Cass. Ill. B. Cal. Texas*, Heft 3, 1853, fig. xiii.

1861. COUES, E.   A Monograph of the Genus Ægiothus, with descriptions of new Species.   < *Proc. Acad. Nat. Sci.*, xiii, 1861, pp. 373-390.
   This is an attempt, not entirely successful, to fix the species of this difficult genus, with
   synonymy, description, and criticism.   The author recognizes seven species: *Æ. rostratus*
   (sp. n., p. 378, Greenland), *canescens, exilipes* (sp. n., p. 385, Arctic America), *linaria, fuscescens*
   (Coues, described as sp. n., in op. tom. cit., p. 222, Labrador), *rufescens*, and *holbölli*.   The last
   two are given as doubtfully distinct from *linaria*.   (*Æ. fuscescens* has since been shown to be
   the dark midsummer plumage of *linaria*, and *rostratus* to bear the same relation to the large
   Greenland form.   *Æ. exilipes* has been usually accepted as a good species, and of late accredited also to boreal continental parts of the old world.)   Cf. *Ibis*, 1862, p. 187.

1861. GLOGER, C. W. L.   Richtige Ansicht eines nordischen Zoologen [Liljeborg] über
   die Färbung der mannlichen Kreuzschnäbel [Loxia curvirostra].   < *J. f. O.*,
   ix, 1861, p. 78.

   Bull. v, 4——8

1861. SCLATER, P. L.   On a New Species of Finch, of the Genus Sycalis [chrysops], from Mexico.   < *P. Z. S.*, xxix, 1861, pp. 376, 377.

1861. W[HEATON], J. M.   Bird Talk.   < *Field Notes*, vol. i, No. 20, May 18, 1861, p. 153.
     Occurrence of various birds, especially *Chondestes grammica*, in Ohio.

1862. BREE, C. R.   Occurrence of the Parrot Crossbill [Loxia pityopsittacus] near Colchester.   < *Zoologist*, xx, 1862, pp. 8032, 8033.

1862. CABANIS, J.   Zur Synonymie einiger Pipilo-Arten.   < *J. f. O.*, x, 1862, pp. 473, 474.
     Pipilo crissalis, fuscus, rutilus, maculatus.

1862. COUPER, W.   Occurrence of the Blue Grosbeak (Guiraca cœrulea, Swainson) at Mille Vaches, Lower St. Lawrence.   < *Canad. Nat. and Geol.*, vii, 1862, p. 319.

1862. GUISE, W. V.   Parrot Crossbill [Loxia pityopsittacus] at Cheltenham.   < *Zoologist*, xx, 1862, p. 7844.

1862. HADFIELD, H.   Of the change of Plumage in the Crossbills [Loxia spp.] and Pine Grosbeak [Pinicola enucleator].   < *Zoologist*, xx, 1862, pp. 8033, 8034.

1862. HADFIELD, H.   Occurrence of the Crossbill [Loxia curvirostra] in England.   < *Zoologist*, xx, 1862, p. 7931.

1862. SCLATER, P. L.   On a new Species of Finch, of the Genus Sycalis [chrysops], from Mexico.   < *Ann. Mag. Nat. Hist.*, 3d ser., ix, 1862, p. 340.
     From *P. Z. S.*, Nov. 26, 1861, pp. 376, 377.

1862. STEVENSON, H.   Occurrence of the Lapland Bunting [Centrophanes lapponica] in Norfolk.   < *Zoologist*, xx, 1862, p. 8032.

1862. TYRER, R., JR.   Occurrence of the Crossbill [Loxia curvirostra] near Eye.   < *Zoologist*, xx, 1862, p. 7881.

1862. VERRILL, A. E.   Description of a Species of Passerella [obscura], supposed to be new, from Anticosti.   < *Proc. Boston Soc. Nat. Hist.*, ix, 1862, pp. 143–146.
     It has not proven to be distinct from *P. iliaca.*

1862. WHEELWRIGHT, [H.]   On the Change of Plumage in the Crossbills [Loxia spp.] and Pine Grosbeak [Pinicola enucleator].   < *Zoologist*, xx, 1862, pp. 8001, 8002.

1863. BLYTH, E.   Note on the Genus Pyrrhula.   < *Ibis*, v, 1863, pp. 440–442, pl. x.
     Sketch of bibliography of the genus, and list of 7 spp. held to compose it.   *P. erythacus* Blyth (*Ibis*, 1862, p. 389) is figured, pl. x.

1863. BLYTH, E.   Parrot Crossbill and Common Crossbill supposed one species.   < *Zoologist*, xxi, 1863, pp. 8327, 8328.

1863. COUES, E.   Additional Remarks on the North American Ægiothi.   < *Proc. Acad. Nat. Sci. Phila.*, xv, 1863, pp. 40, 41.
     Recognizing American representatives of the forms known in Europe as *Æ. holbölli* and *Æ. rufescens.*   For the monograph to which these remarks are additional, see *op. cit.*, 1861, pp. 373–390.

1863. HARTLAUB, G.   Ueber Pipilo virescens n. sp.   < *J. f. O.*, xi, 1863, pp. 228, 229.
     A note of the editor's says that *Tanagra melanops* and *Fringilla scutata* Licht., *Mus. Berol.*, are both this species.

1863. HUCKETT, T.   Parrot Crossbills [Loxia pityopsittacus] at Brandon.   < *Zoologist*, xxi, 1863, p. 8845.

1863. MATHEWS, G. F.   Snow Bunting [Plectrophanes nivalis] near Barnstaple.   < *Zoologist*, xxi, 1863, p. 8845.

1863. SAXBY, H. L.   Snow Bunting [Plectrophanes nivalis] in June.   < *Zoologist*, xxi, 1863, p. 8680.

1863. WHEELWRIGHT, H.   Change of Plumage in the Crossbills [Loxia curvirostra].   < *Zoologist*, xxi, 1863, p. 8492.

1864. BLAKE-KNOX, H.   Nesting of the Lesser Redpole [Ægiothus linaria] at Dalkey.   < *Zoologist*, xxii, 1864, p. 8884.

1864. HAMILTON, J.   Lesser Redpole's [Ægiothus linaria] Nest near Chester.   < *Zoologist*, xxii, 1864, p. 9210.

1864. HOMEYER, A. V.   Notiz zu Crucirostra balearica.   < *J. f. O.*, xii, 1864, p. 224.

1864. RAKE, T. B.   Lesser Redpoles' [Ægiothus linaria] Nests near Birmingham. < *Zoologist*, xxii, 1864. p. 9248.

1864. REEKS, H.   Pine Grosbeak [Pinicola enucleator] at Thruxton.   < *Zoologist*, xxii, 1864, p. 9023.

1864. RODD, E. H.   Snow Bunting [Plectrophanes nivalis] in Summer Plumage near Penzanze.   < *Zoologist*, xxiii, 1864, p. 9109.

1864. SCHWAITZER, F.   Corythus enucleator (Cuv. ex L.) in der Frovinz Posen.   < *J. f. O.*, xii, 1864, pp. 239, 240.

1864. SMITH, C. H.   Crossbills in Bedfordshire.   < *Zoologist*, xxii, 1864, p. 9110.

1865. CASSIN, J.   An Examination of the Birds of the genus Chrysomitris in the Museum of the Academy of Natural Sciences of Philadelphia.   < *Proc. Acad. Nat. Sci. Phila.*, xvii, 1865, pp. 89–94.
      16 spp.   *Pyrrhomitris, Melanomitris*, p. 91; *Pseudomitris*, p. 93, subgenn. nn.   *Ch. bryantii*, p. 91, sp. n.

1865. JESSE, W., JR.   Ornithological Notes [on food of Ægiothus linaria].   < *Zoologist*, xxiii, 1865, p. 9562.

1865. LAMPRECHT, A.   [Ueber epileptische Anfälle von Loxia cardinalis.]   < *Zool. Gart.*, vi, 1865, pp. 228, 229.

1865. WHARTON, C. B.   Snow Bunting [Plectrophanes nivalis] at the Kingsbury Reservoir.   < *Zoologist*, xxiii, 1865, p. 9539.

1866. ALTUM, B.   Kreuzschnäbelzug in Westphalen.   < *J. f. O.*, xiv, 1866, pp. 286, 287.

1866. DUTTON, J.   Snow Bunting [Plectrophanes nivalis] at Beachy Head.   < *Zoologist*, 2d ser., i, 1866, p. 522.

1866. SCHMIDT, MAX.   [Die Fortpflanzung des grünen Kardinals (Gubernatrix cristatella) in Gefangenschaft.]   < *Zool. Gart.*, vii, 1866, pp. 342–345.

1866. STUBBS, C. E.   Crossbills at Henley-on-Thames.   < *Zoologist*, 2d ser., i, 1866, p. 523.

1867. CABANIS, J.   Ueber die systematische Stellung von Sylvia concolor Orb. als Typus einer neuen Gattung Xenospingus.   < *J. f. O.*, xv, 1867, pp. 347–349.

1867. COOKE, N.   Lapland Bunting [Centrophanes lapponica] in Lancashire.   < *Zoologist*, 2d ser., ii, 1867, pp. 558, 559.

1867. DUTTON, J.   Snow Bunting [Plectrophanes nivalis] at Eastbourne.   < *Zoologist*, 2d ser., ii, 1867, p. 792.

1867. GODERICH, —.   Crossbill at Ripon.   < *Zoologist*, 2d ser., 1867, p. 793.

1867. HELLMANN, A.   Zur Frage über die Entstehung der Fichtenabsprunge.   < *Zool. Gart.*, viii, 1867, pp. 350, 351.
      Loxia curvirostra exonerated.   Cf. *tom. cit.*, pp. 12, 79, 476.

1867. JÄCKEL, [A. J.]   Schaarenweises Auftreten des Fichtenkreuzschnabels im Jahre 1866.   < *Zool. Gart.*, viii, 1867, p. 79.
      Cf. *tom. cit.*, pp. 12, 350, 476.

1867. KENNEDY, A. C.   Snow Bunting [Plectrophanes nivalis] at Hunstanton. < *Zoologist*, 2d ser., ii, 1867, p. 559.

1867. MATHEW, G. F.   Snow Bunting [Plectrophanes nivalis] at Sea.   < *Zoologist*, 2d ser., ii, 1867, p. 559.

1867. RÖSE, A.   Sind die Eichhörnchen allein, oder auch Vögel, namentlich die Kreuzschnäbel, bei der Entstehung der sogenannten „Fichtenabsprünge" betheiligt?   < *Zool. Gart.*, viii, 1867, pp. 12–17.
      Loxia curvirostra found not guilty of damaging the shoots of fir-trees.   Cf. *tom. cit.*, pp. 79, 350, 476.

1867. RÖSE, A.   Noch einmal die Frage über Entstehung der sogenannten „Fichtenabsprünge".   < *Zool. Gart.*, viii, 1867, pp. 476–480.
      Loxia curvirostra.   Cf. *tom. cit.*, pp. 12, 79, 350.

1867. Sacc, *Dr.* [Eier des Cardinals (Fringilla cardinalis).] < *Zool. Gart.*, viii, 1867, pp. 440, 441.

1867. Samuels, E. A. Eggs of the Indigo Bird [Cyanospiza cyanea]. < *Am. Nat.*, i, 1867, p. 435.
    Note on the occasional spotting of the eggs of this species.

1867. Sclater, P. L. [Exhibition of Mexican Birds, and Characters of a New Species of Zonotrichia (boucardi).] < *P. Z. S.*, xxxv, 1867, pp. 1, 2, pl. i.

1867. Weir, J. J. Lapland Bunting [Centrophanes lapponica] at Lewisham. < *Zoologist*, 2d ser., ii, 1867, p. 705.

1867. Weir, J. J. Snow Bunting [Plectrophanes nivalis] on Blackheath. < *Zoologist*, 2d ser., ii, 1867, p. 705.

1868. Anon. Common Crossbill in Surrey. < *Zoologist*, 2d ser., iii, 1868, p. 1376.

1868. Anon. Migration of Crossbills. < *Zoologist*, 2d ser., iii, 1868, p. 1377.

1868. Blake-Knox, H. The Crossbill breeding successfully in County Kildare. < *Zoologist*, 2d ser., iii, 1868, pp. 1133, 1134.

1868. Blake-Knox, H. Whitewinged Crossbill [Loxia leucoptera] in the County Dublin. < *Zoologist*, 2d ser., iii, 1868, p. 1376.

1868. Blake-Knox, H. Crossbill in Ireland in 1868. < *Zoologist*, 2d ser., iii, 1868, p. 1377.

1868. Bruhin, T. A. Der Kreuzschnäbel (Loxia curvirostra). < *Zool. Gart.*, ix, 1868, p. 255.
    Um St. Gerold.

1868. Bruhin, T. A. Ungewohnlich zahlreiches Erscheinen des Fichtenkreuzschnabels in Vorarlberg. < *Zool. Gart.*, ix, 1868, p. 118.

1868. Clark-Kennedy, A. Snow Bunting [Plectrophanes nivalis] at Hastings. < *Zoologist*, 2d ser., iii, 1868, p. 1132.

1868. Hammond, W. O. Crossbill at Wingham. < *Zoologist*, 2d ser., iii, 1868, p. 1376.

1868. Möbius, *Dr.* [Kiefernpapageien (Loxia pityopsittacus) bei Kiel am 11. Juli 1868.] < *Zool. Gart.*, ix, 1868, p. 284.

1868. Norman, G. Nesting of the Crossbill. < *Zoologist*, 2d ser., iii, 1868, p. 1255.

1868. Rodd, E. H. Common Crossbill in Cornwall. < *Zoologist*, 2d ser., iii, 1868, pp. 1376, 1377.

1868. Rodd, E. H. Crossbills at Scilly. < *Zoologist*, 2d ser., iii, 1868, p. 1320.

1868. Salvadori, T. Description of a New Species of the Genus Leucosticte [gigliolii]. < *P. Z. S.*, xxxvi, 1868, pp. 579, 580, pl. xliv.
    L. gigliolii, p. 579, pl. xliv, with list of 7 spp. of the genus.

1868. Sclater, P. L., *and* Salvin, O. Descriptions of New or little-known American Birds of the Families Fringillidæ, [etc.] < *P. Z. S.*, xxxvi, 1868, pp. 322-329.
    The full paper comes under the Neotropical (Faunal) department of this Bibliography. It is cited here also, because it relates so largely to the *Fringillidæ*. With *Peucæa notosticta*, sp. n., p. 322, S. Mexico, is given a synopsis of 5 spp. of *Peucæa.—Zonotrichia quinquestriata*, p. 323, sp. n., Mexico.—With *Pyrgisoma cabanisi*, sp. renom., p. 324, and *P. kieneri* Bp., is given a synopsis of 5 spp. of that genus.

1868. Trippe, T. M. Singular variety of the Field Sparrow [Spizella pusilla]. < *Am. Nat.*, i, 1868, pp. 614, 615.
    Partial albino.

1868. Walker, T. C. Crossbills at Leicester. < *Zoologist*, 2d ser., iii, 1868, pp. 1421, 1422.

1869. Angus, W. C. On the Occurrence of the Whitethroated Sparrow (Zonotrichia albicollis) in Aberdeenshire. < *Zoologist*, 2d ser., iv, 1869, pp. 1547-1549.
    Cf. *P. Z. S.*, 1870, p. 52.

1869. CLIFTON, *Lord.* Goldfinch, Mealy Redpole and Lesser Redpole in Kent. < *Zoologist*, 2d ser., iv, 1869, p. 1600.

1869. COUES, E. On Variation in the Genus Ægiothus. < *Proc. Acad. Nat. Sci. Phila.*, xxi, 1869, pp. 180–189.

> Discusses the climatic and other causes operative in this case, endeavoring to fix the limits of individual and geographical variation in its bearing upon the determination of the species of the genus. The article is supplementary to the author's monograph of the genus, in the same *Proceedings*, 1861, pp. 373–390, *q. v.*

1869. GUNN, T. E. Crossbills in Surrey. < *Zoologist*, 2d ser., iv, 1869, p. 1721.

1869. GUNN, T. E. Cirl Buntings and Crossbills in Devonshire. < *Zoologist*, 2d ser., iv, 1869, p. 1721.

1869. LAWRENCE, G. N. Description of Seven New Species of American Birds from various localities, with a note on Zonotrichia melanotis. < *Proc. Acad. Nat. Sci. Phila.*, Dec., 1868, pp. 359–362. (Pub. 1869.)

1869. LE MOINE, J. M. Le Cardinal. < *Naturaliste Canadien*, i, 1869, pp. 225–231.
Biographique.

1869. MAYNARD, C. J. Capture of the Centronyx Bairdii [*i. e.*, of Passerculus princeps] at Ipswich [Mass.]. < *Am. Nat.*, iii, 1869, pp. 554, 555.

1869. MÜLLER, K. Beobachtung über Ernährung von Loxia taenioptera. < *J. f. O.*, xvii, 1869, pp. 105, 106.

1869. SCHACHT, H. Ungewöhnliches, zahlreiches Auftreten der Kreuzschnäbel im Sommer 1866 [in mehreren Gegenden Deutschlands]. < *Zool. Gart.*, x, 1869, pp. 31, 32.

1869. SKINNER, A. Crossbills near Faversham. < *Zoologist*, 2d ser., iv, 1869, p. 1561.

1869. SMITH, C. Common Crossbill near Taunton. < *Zoologist*, 2d ser., iv, 1869, p. 1514.

1869. THURN, E. F. IM. Painted Bunting in Oxfordshire. < *Zoologist*, 2d ser., iv, 1869, p. 1865.

1869. WONFOR, T. W. The Redpole building in Brighton. < *Zoologist*, 2d ser., iv, 1869, p. 1801.

1869. WONFOR, T. W. Crossbills in Sussex. < *Zoologist*, 2d ser., iv, 1869, p. 1561.

1870. ABBOTT, C. C. Song of the Song-sparrow [Melospiza melodia]. < *Am. Nat.*, iv, 1870, p. 378.

1870. ALCOTT, W. P. Albino Snow Bird [Junco hyemalis]. < *Am. Nat.*, iv, 1870, p. 376.

1870. ANON. Be-mired Crossbills. < *Zoologist*, 2d ser., v, 1870, p. 2383.
From the 'Lynn Advertiser,' Oct. 15, 1870.

1870. BOND, F. Lapland Bunting [Centrophanes lapponica] near London. < *Zoologist*, 2d ser., v, 1870, p. 2061.

1870. BOND, F. Correction of an Error [respecting Centrophanes lapponica]. < *Zoologist*, 2d ser., v, 1870, p. 2022.

1870. "C. F. W., JUN." Snow Bunting [Plectrophanes nivalis] in Middlesex. < *Zoologist*, 2d ser., v, 1870, p. 2407.
From *The* (London) *Field*, Nov. 12.

1870. NAUMANN, C. H. Oological. < *Am. Nat.*, iv, 1870, p. 442.

> Fruitless incubation for 3 weeks of an egg of *Numida meleagris* by *Cardinalis virginianus*, and variation in number of eggs of the latter bird.

1870. NEWTON, A. [Exhibition of a skin of the North-American Zonotrichia albicollis shot in Scotland.] < *P. Z. S.*, xxxviii, 1870, p. 52.

> This is the case previously reported by W. C. Angus, *Zoologist*, 2d ser., iv, 1869, pp. 1547–1549. Another case of the same occurrence is subsequently noticed, with a colored figure, by G. D. Rowley, in *Rowl. Orn. Misc.*, ii, pt. v, 1876, pp. 75, 76, pl. xlvi, f. 3.

1870. NEWTON, A.   On the Northern Range of the Lesser Redpoll.   < *Zoologist*, 2d ser., v, 1870, p. 2223.

1870. RICKARDS, M. S. C.   Snow Bunting [Plectrophanes nivalis] on the Severn Bank.   < *Zoologist*, 2d ser., v, 1870, p. 2140.

1870. WALLIS, H. M.   Snow Bunting [Plectrophanes nivalis] at Aldeburgh.   < *Zoologist*, 2d ser., v, 1870, p. 1981.

1871. CABANIS, J.   [Notiz über die Gattung Pyrrhula und die in Sibirien vorkommenden Arten.]   < *J. f. O.*, xix, 1871, pp. 316–319.
> Diagnostic synopsis of 9 spp. Cf. *Ibis*, 1871, p. 232; *J.f. O.*, p. 315.

1871. GURNEY, J. H.   Early Occurrence of the Snow Bunting [Plectrophanes nivalis] in Suffolk.   < *Zoologist*, 2d ser., vi, 1871, p. 2849.

1871. JONES, J. M.   Cardinal Grosbeak [Cardinalis virginianus].   < *Am. Nat.*, v, 1871, p. 176.
> At Halifax, Nova Scotia, Jan. 31, 1871.

1871. SCLATER, P. L.   A Revision of the Species of the Fringilline Genus Spermophila.   < *Ibis*, 3d ser., i, 1871, pp. 1–23, pll. i, ii.
> Very complete; analysis, synonymy, diagnosis, habitat of 24 spp. known to the author, with critical commentary; 11 other spp. similarly treated; remarks on geographical distribution of the genus. Pl. i, f. 1, 2, *S. nigrorufa*, ♂, ♀; fig. 3, *S. pileata*. Pl. ii, f. 1, 2, *S. aurita*; f. 3, *S. ocellata*.

1872. BOYES, F.   [On the usual resorts of the] Lesser Redpoll.   < *Zoologist*, 2d ser., vii, 1872, p. 3313.

1872. CABANIS, J.   [Ueber Pyrrhula cassini und P. cineracea n. sp. aus Sibirien.]   < *J. f. O.*, xx, 1872, pp. 315, 316.

1872. HÜGEL, A. v.   Redpole Breeding in Lancashire.   < *Zoologist*, 2d ser., vii, 1872, pp. 3147, 3148.

1872. LEACH, H. R.   Snow Bunting [Plectrophanes nivalis, Sept. 20, 1872, between Hunstanton and Thornham].   < *Zoologist*, 2d ser., vii, 1872, p. 3313.

1872. MAYNARD, C. J.   A New Species of Passèrculus [princeps] from Eastern Massachusetts.   < *Am. Nat.*, vi, 1872, pp. 637, 638.
> *P. princeps*, n. sp., the same formerly supposed to be *Centronyx bairdii* (*cf. op. cit.*, iii, 513, 554, 631; vi, 307). With a note on *Thalasseus havelli = Sterna forsteri*.

1872. NICHOLSON, F.   Lesser Redpoll and Twite.   < *Zoologist*, 2d ser., vii, 1872, p. 3235.

1872. PORRITT, G. T.   Redpoll breeding at Huddersfield.   < *Zoologist*, 2d ser., vii, 1872, p. 3235.

1872. RIDGWAY, R.   On the Occurrence of a Near Relative of Ægiothus flavirostris [var. brewsteri, n. v.] at Waltham, Mass.   < *Am. Nat.*, vi, 1872, pp. 433, 434.

1872. ROWLEY, G. D.   [Remarks on exhibition of a specimen of Zonotrichia albicollis, taken near Brighton.]   < *P. Z. S.*, June 4, 1872, p. 681.
> For a previous occurrence of this species in Great Britain, cf. *P. Z. S.*, 1870, p. 52. For further notice of the present case, cf. *Rowl. Orn. Misc.*, ii, pt. v, 1876, p. 75, pl. xlvi, f. 3.

1872. SCLATER, P. L.   A Revision of the Species of the Fringilline Genus Sycalis.   < *Ibis*, 3d ser., ii, 1872, pp. 39–48, pll. ii, iii.
> Of the 20 species assigned to the genus in Gray's 'Hand-list,' the author has not seen 2: the remaining 18 are merged in 10, the diagnostic characters, synonymy, and distribution of which are given. One receives a new name (*Sycalis pelzelni*, p. 42). Pl. ii, f. 1, *S. chrysops*; f. 2, *S. lutea*. Pl. iii, *S. aureiventris*, ♂, ♀.

1873. "AIKEN, C. E." [*i. e.*, RIDGWAY, R.—cf. Bull. Essex Inst., v, 1873, p. 190.] A New Species of Sparrow [Centronyx ochrocephalus, Aiken].   < *Am. Nat.*, vii, 1873, pp. 236, 237.
> Afterward determined to be *C. bairdi*.

1873. B[AIRD], S. F.   Note on Cassin's Pyrrhula [P. cassini, Bd.].   < *Am. Nat.*, vii, 1873, p. 239.
> With reference to Cabanis's recent remarks: cf. *J. f. O.*, 1871, p. 318; 1872, p. 315; 1873, p. 314.

1873. BREWER, T. M. [Exhibition of a pair of Plectrophanes maccowni from "California," *i. e.*, Colorado.] < *Proc. Boston. Soc. Nat. Hist.*, xv, 1873, p. 311.

1873. CABANIS, J. [Berichtigungen über Pyrrhula cineracea und P. cassini.] < *J. f. O.*, 1873, pp. 314, 315.
Cf. *J. f. O.*, 1871, p. 318; 1872, p. 315.

1873. COUES, E. Notice of a Rare Bird [Coturniculus lecontii]. < *Am. Nat.*, vii, 1873, pp. 748, 749.
Rediscovery of the species, in Dakota; amended description of adult and young; notice of habits.

1873. EDWARDS, W. H. Snowbird [Junco hyemalis, breeding on Graylock Mountain]. < *Am. Nat.*, vii, 1873, p. 745.

1873. FISCHER, J. v. Fortschreitender Albinismus. < *Zool. Gart.*, xiv, 1873, pp. 115, 116.
Cannabina linota, Plectrophanes nivalis.

1873. MAPES, H. H. The Rose-breasted Grosbeak (Guiraca ludoviciana). < *Am. Nat.*, vii, 1873, p. 493.
A field-note on the destruction of *Doryphora* 10-*lineata* by this species.

1873. SCHACHT, H. Cardinal (Cardinalis virginianus) und Kirschkernbeisser (**Lox.** coccothraustes). < *Zool. Gart.*, xiv, 1873, p. 355.

1873. SCOTT, D. [W.] Centronyx "ochrocephalus," Aiken. < *Am. Nat.*, vii, 1873, pp. 564, 565.
Validity of this species denied.—*Harporhynchus bendirii* considered probably the same as *H. curvirostris* var. *palmeri.*

1873. TENNEY, S. The Black Snowbird [Junco hyemalis] breeds in the Graylock Range. < *Am. Nat.*, vii, 1873, p. 634.

1873. TRIPPE, T. M. The Painted Bunting [Plectrophanes pictus]. < *Am. Nat.*, vii, 1873, p. 500.
A field-note.

1874. BATTY, J. H. Eggs and nest of the Yellow bird [Chrysomitris tristis]. < *Forest and Stream*, ii, April 16, 1874, p. 149.

1874. BREWSTER, W. Spizella breweri(?) in Massachusetts. < *Am. Nat.*, viii, 1874, pp. 366, 367.

1874. CORBIN, G. B. Lesser Redpoll and Siskin. < *Zoologist*, 2d ser., ix, 1874, p. 4034.

1874. CLARK-KENNEDY, A. W. M. On the Occurrence of Emberiza [Plectrophanes] nivalis in full Summer Plumage [in Great Britain]. < *Zoologist*, 2d ser., ix, 1874, p. 3914.

1874. COUES, E. New Variety of the Blue Grosbeak [Goniaphea coerulea var. eurhyncha, Mexico]. < *Am. Nat.*, viii, 1874, p. 563.

1874. COUES, E. The Snow-Bird [Junco hyemalis] as a Sparrow. < *Field and Stream* (newspaper of Chicago, Ill.), Apr. 4, 1874.
With reference to its coming under the provisions of a game-law.

1874. DYBOWSKI, B. Notiz über die Ostsibirischen Pyrrhula-Arten. < *J. f. O.*, 1874, pp. 39–45, pl. i.
Pl. i, *P. cineracea.—P. coccinea.*

1874. GUNN, T. E. Lesser Redpoll breeding near Norwich. < *Zoologist*, 2d ser., ix, 1874, pp. 4117, 4118.

1874. HANF, P. B. Beobachtungen der Fortpflanzung des Fichten-Kreuzschnabels im Winter 1871/72 und 1872/73. < *Verh. (Abh.) k.-k. zool.-bot. Ges. Wien*, xxiv. 1874, pp. 211–216.

1874. HENSHAW, H. W.   Synopsis of the Genus Junco.   < *Rep. Ornith. Specs. Coll. in* 1871, 1872 *and* 1873 (Expl. W. 100 Merid.   8vo.   Washington, 1874), pp. 113, 114.

> Scarcely citable as a separate article, as it occurs in a report having a much wider scope. It is well, however, to thus call attention to this one among several essays on this perplexing genus.

1874. KERR, W. J.   Crossbills in Denbighshire.   < *Zoologist*, 2d ser., ix, 1874, p. 4156.

1874. NATION, W.   On the Habits of Spermophila simplex.   < *P. Z. S.*, xlii, 1874, pp. 329, 330.

1874. NEWTON, A.   The Lesser Redpoll not in Spitsbergen.   < *Zoologist*, 2d ser., ix, 1874, pp. 3880, 3881.

1874. RIDGWAY, R.   Description of a new bird [Leucosticte atrata] from Colorado. < *Am. Sportsman*, iv, 1874, p. 241.

1874. SWINHOE, R.   [Note on the species of Pyrrhula from the Kurile Islands and Japan.]   < *Ibis*, 3d ser., iv, 1874, pp. 463, 464.

1875. ALLEN, J. A.   [Note on Ammodromus candacutus var. nelsoni, n. var., from Illinois.]   < *Proc. Bost. Soc. Nat. Hist.*, xvii, 1875, pp. 292–294.

1875. "BEVERLY, FRED." [*i. e.*, F. A. OBER.]   The pine grosbeak—(Pinicola Canadensis) [*i. e.*, enucleator].   < *Forest and Stream*, iv, Mar. 4, 1875, p. 54.

1875. [COUPER, W.]   Ornithological Curiosity.   < *Montreal Herald* (newspaper) of Mar. 30, 1875.

> Notices nest of *Loxia leucoptera*, containing nearly fledged young, in the snow.

1875. CRITTENDEN, G. W.   [Pinicola enucleator in Massachusetts.]   < *Forest and Stream*, iv, Feb. 18, 1875, p. 23.   See also vol. iii, p. 389.

1875. HÖPFNER, P.   Briefliche Mittheilungen [über den Hakengimpel (Pinicola enucleator)].   < *Ber. uber d. xxi. Vers. d. deut. Orn.-Ges.*, 1875, pp. 101–103.

1875. "L. W. L."   The pine bullfinch [Pinicola enucleator].   < *Forest and Stream*, iii, Feb. 4, 1875, p. 405.   See vol. iv, p. 22.

1875. MAYNARD, C. J.   A New Species of Finch [Ammodromus melanoleucus] from Florida.   < *Am. Sportsman*, v, Jan. 16, 1875, p. 248.

> This is the bird before described by R. Ridgway (*Bull. Essex Inst.*, v, Dec., 1873, p. 198) as *A. maritimus* var. *nigrescens*.

1875. RIDGWAY, R.   A Monograph of the Genus Leucosticte, Swainson; or, Gray-crowned Purple Finches.   < *Bull. U. S. Geol. Surv.*, 2d ser., No. 2, May 14, 1875, pp. 53–82.

> History—Bibliography—Material examined—Discussion of races and varieties—Geographical Distribution—Habits.   Then the species monographed are: *L. atrata*, *L. tephrocotis*, *L. t.* vars. *littoralis* and *griseinucha*, *L. australis*, *L. brunneinucha*.
> The article is very complete, entering fully into the characters of all these forms of the genus.   It became the occasion of a protracted discussion between the author and J. A. Allen: cf. *Bull. U. S. Geol. and Geogr. Surv. Terr.*, ii, 1876, pp. 345–350; *Field and Forest*, ii, 1876, pp 37–43, and 76–79.

1875. S[ENNETT], G. B.   Albino Linnet [Ægiothus linaria].   < *Forest and Stream*, iv May 13, 1875, p. 215.

1875. SILL, J. M. B.   The Western Nonpareil [Cyanospiza versicolor] in Michigan < *Am. Nat.*, ix, No. 12, 1875, p. 665.

1875. ANON.   Pine Grosbeaks [Pinicola enucleator].   < *Forest and Stream*, iv, Apr. 15 1875, p. 149.   [Reprinted from Meadville (Pa.) "Republican."]

1875. ANON.   The Confined Purple Finch [Carpodacus purpureus].   < *Oölogist*, 1875, p. 5.

1876. ALLEN, J. A.   Sexual, Individual, and Geographical Variation in Leucosticte tephrocotis.   < *Bull. U. S. Geol. Surv. Terr.*, ii, No. 4, July, 1876, pp. 345–350.

Treating the puzzling genus from the reverse of Ridgway's perspective, and reaching different results. Cf. *op. cit.*, 2d ser., No. 2, May 14, 1875, pp. 53–82; *Field and Forest*, ii, 1876, pp. 37–43, 76–79.

1876. ALLEN, J. A.   Sexual Variation in the Genus Leucosticte.   < *Field and Forest*, ii, No. 5, Nov., 1876, pp. 76–79.

Rejoinder to Ridgway's reply (*Field and Forest*, ii, 1876, pp. 37–43) to Allen's critique (*Bull. U. S. Geol. Surv. Terr.*, ii, 1876, pp. 345–350) of Ridgway's monograph (*Bull. U. S. Geol. Surv. Terr.*, 2d ser., No. 2, May 14, 1876, pp. 53–82), claiming that the main point at issue has been substantially conceded by Mr. Ridgway.

1876. BICKNELL, E. A.   The Crossbill [Loxia curvirostra var. americana] breeding at Riverdale, N. Y.   < *Am. Nat.*, x, No. 4, 1876, p. 237.

1876. BREWSTER, W.   The Ipswich Sparrow [Passerculus princeps] in New Brunswick.   < *Bull. Nutt. Ornith. Club*, i, No. 2, July, 1876, p. 52.

1876. BURROUGHS, J.   Notes from Our Correspondents.   < *Forest and Stream*, v, Jan. 13, 1876, p. 356.

Pinicola enucleator on the Hudson in winter.

1876. C[OUES], E.   Breeding Range of the Snow-Bird [Junco hyemalis].   < *Am. Nat.*, x, No. 2, Feb., 1876, pp. 114, 115.

On mountains in Southwestern Virginia.

1876. GILLMAN, H.   Protective Resemblance in the Yellow-Bird [Chrysomitris tristis].   < *Am. Nat.*, x, No. 2, 1876, pp. 115, 116.

Color of the birds assimilating with that of flowers of *Verbascum thapsus*.

1876. HENSHAW, H. W.   Genus Junco, Wagler.   Synopsis of the genus.   < *Rep. Geogr. and Geol. Expl. and Surv. West 100th Meridian* (4to, Washington, "1875" = 1876), vol. v, chap. iii, pp. 264–273.

Scarcely citable as a separate article, as it is part of the general report on the Ornithology of the Survey. It is well, however, thus to call attention to one of several essays on this genus, especially as some of the colored plates illustrate the species. The author recognizes the following forms of the genus:—A. *J. hyemalis*, with var. *aikeni*. B. *J. oregonus*, with var. *annectens*. C. *J. cinereus*, with vars. *alticola, dorsalis*, and *caniceps*.—Pl. viii, *J. annectens*. Pl. ix, *J. dorsalis*. Pl. x, *J. cinereus*.

1876. [INGERSOLL, E.]   Pine finch.   < *Forest and Stream*, vii, Oct. 12, 1876, p. 147.

Inquiry whether *Chrysomitris spinus* of Europe does not regularly visit New Brunswick during midwinter.

1876. RIDGWAY, R.   "Sexual, Individual and Geographical Variation" in the Genus Leucosticte.   < *Field and Forest*, ii, No. 3, Sept., 1876, pp. 37–43.

Continuation of the discussion with Mr. J. A. Allen of the much-vexed question respecting the species of this genus:—See *Bull. U. S. Geol. Surv. Terr.*, No. 2, May 14, 1875, and *op. cit.*, vol. ii, No. 4, July, 1876, pp. 345–350. In the present paper the author goes further into the subject, and concludes that he has "no hesitation" in asserting the distinct North American species of the genus to be *L. griseinucha* Brandt, *L. tephrocotis* Sw., *L. atrata* Ridgw., and *L. australis* Allen. The article is somewhat controversial. Cf. *Ibis*, 1878, p. 104.

1876. ROWLEY, G. D.   Zonotrichia albicollis, Bonap.   (The American White-throated Sparrow.)   < *Rowl. Orn. Misc.*, ii, pt. v, Oct., 1876, pp. 75, 76, pl. xlvi, f. 3.

Captured near Brighton, England, 22d Mar., 1872.—A previous occurrence of the same species in Great Britain, in Scotland, is recorded by Newton, *P. Z. S.*, 1870, p. 52, and by Rob. Gray, *B. of West Scotland*, p. 138, plate. This was taken 17th Aug., 1867, and in Mar., 1868, a notice of the occurrence was communicated by Mr. Angus to the Nat. Hist. Soc. of Glasgow, and a description with a plate was afterwards published in the *Proceedings* of that Society.

1876. SCOTT, D. [W.]   The proper specific name of the Song Sparrow.   < *Am. Nat.*, x, No. 1, Jan., 1876, pp. 17, 18.

Melospiza fasciata ex *Fringilla fasciata* Gm.; synonymy given. (See Bd., *B. N. A.*, 1858, p. 477.)

1877. BAILEY, H. B.   Occurrence of Le Conte's Bunting (Coturniculus lecontei Bon.) in Iowa.   < *Bull. Nutt. Ornith. Club*, ii, No. 1, Jan., 1877, pp. 26, 27.

1877. BAILEY, H. B.   Occurrence of Passerculus princeps in New York.   < *Bull. Nutt. Ornith. Club*, ii, No. 3, July, 1877, pp. 78, 79.

1877. BREWER, T. M.   A New Bird [Centrophanes ornata] to Massachusetts.   < *Bull. Nutt. Ornith. Club*, ii, No. 3, July, 1877, p. 78.

1877. BREWSTER, W.   Northern Range of the Sharp-tailed Finch (Ammodromus caudacutus).   < *Bull. Nutt. Ornith. Club*, ii, No. 1, Jan., 1877, p. 28.

1877. BREWSTER, W   Two undescribed nests of California Birds.   < *Bull. Nutt. Ornith. Club*, ii, No. 2, Apr., 1877, pp. 37, 38.
    Carpodacus purpureus var. *californicus*, Peucœa ruficeps.

1877. COALE, H. K.   MacCown's Longspur [Rhynchophanes maccowni] in Illinois.   < *Bull. Nutt. Ornith. Club*, ii, No. 2, Apr., 1877, p. 52.

1877. COALE, H. K.   Junco oregonus in Illinois.   < *Bull. Nutt. Ornith. Club*, ii, No. 3, July, 1877, p. 82.

1877. COVERT, A. B.   Nesting of the rose-breasted grosbeak, (Goniaphea ludoviciana).   < *Forest and Stream*, viii, April 12, 1877, p. 145.
    A variety of eggs with ground color white instead of green.

1877. HARVIE-BROWN, J. A.   Ægiothus exilipes in Europe.   < *Bull. Nutt. Ornith. Club*, ii, No. 2, Apr., 1877, pp. 51, 52.

1877. [INGERSOLL, E.]   [Calamospiza bicolor reported from Ipswich, Mass.]   < *The Country*, i, Dec. 27, 1877, p. 115.

1877. INGERSOLL, E.   The Song Sparrows of North America.   < *The* (London) *Field*, l, Nov. 10, 1877, p. 544.
    Elaborate and original biography of *Melospiza meloda*.

1877. LENGERKE, J. v.   [Early arrival of Plectrophanes nivalis in New Jersey.]   < *The Country*, i, Dec. 29, 1877, p. 115.   See p. 79.

1877. RAGSDALE, G. H.   Plectrophanes Lapponicus [Centrophanes lapponica] in Texas.   < *Oölogist*, ii, No. 11, pp. 79, 80.

1877. RIDGWAY, R.   Mrs. Maxwell's Colorado Museum.   Additional Notes.   < *Field and Forest*, iii, No. 1, July, 1877, p. 11.
    Supplementary to a more general article, ending at *op. cit.*, vol. ii, p. 214; these "additional notes" relating entirely to unusually colored specimens of *Junco caniceps* and *J. annectens*.

1877. SCLATER, P. L.   Note on the South-American Song-Sparrows.   < *Ibis*, 4th ser., i, Jan., 1877, pp. 46–48, pl. i.
    Remarks on *Zonotrichia pileata*, Z. canicapilla (p. 1, f. 1), and Z. strigiceps (pl. 1, f. 2).

1878. ALLEN, J. A.   The Lark-Bunting (Calamospiza bicolor) in Massachusetts.   < *Bull. Nutt. Ornith. Club*, iii, No. 1, Jan., 1878, p. 48.

1878. ALLEN, J. A.   Rufous-headed Sparrow (Peucæa ruficeps) in Texas.   < *Bull. Nutt. Ornith. Club*, iii, No. 4, Oct., 1878, pp. 188, 189.

1878. ALLEN, J. A.   The Snow-Bird [Junco hyemalis] in Summer on Mount Wachusett [Mass.].   < *Bull. Nutt. Ornith. Club*, iii, No. 4, Oct., 1878, p. 192.

1878. ANON.   Birds [Crossbills?] Hatched in February.   < *Forest and Stream*, x, Mar. 7, 1878, p. 75.

1878. ANON.   [Nesting of Crossbills.]   < *Forest and Stream*, x, Apr. 4, 1878, p. 156.

1878. BAGG, E., JR.   Lincoln's Finch (Melospiza lincolni) breeding in Hamilton County, N. Y.   < *Bull. Nutt. Ornith. Club*, iii, No. 4, Oct., 1878, pp. 197, 198.

1878. BREWER, T. M.   [Occurrence of Centrophanes ornata in Massachusetts.]   < *Proc. Boston Soc. Nat. Hist.*, xix, for May, 1877, pub. Jan., 1878, pp. 239, 240.
    Specimen in the Museum of the Society, shot by C. W. Townsend, July 28, 1878, near Magnolia. Cf. *Bull. Nutt. Ornith. Club*, ii, No. 3, July, 1877, p. 78.

1878. BREWER, T. M.   [Occurrence of Centrophanes lapponica in Massachusetts.]   < *Proc. Boston Soc. Nat. Hist. for* Oct. 3, 1877, xix, pub. Feb., 1878, p. 257.
    Specimen shot in Swampscott, May 1, 1877.

1878. BREWER, T. M. [Occurrence of Ammodromus maritimus in Massachusetts.] < *Proc. Boston Soc. Nat. Hist.*, xix, for Dec. 6, 1877, pub. Feb., 1878, p. 260.

1878. BREWER, T. M. [Letter relating to the Nest and Eggs of Zonotrichia coronata.] < *Ibis*, 4th ser., ii, Jan., 1878, pp. 117, 118.
Fully described, as being the first authentic specimen known.

1878. BREWER, T. M. The Black-throated Bunting (Euspiza americana) [nesting in Massachusetts]. < *Bull. Nutt. Ornith. Club*, iii, No. 4, Oct., 1878, pp. 190, 191.

1878. BREWER, T. M. The White-crowned Sparrow [Zonotrichia leucophrys] breeding in Vermont. < *Bull. Nutt. Ornith. Club*, iii, No. 4, Oct., 1878, p. 195.

1878. BREWER, T. M. Notes on Junco caniceps and the closely allied Forms. < *Bull. Nutt. Ornith. Club*, iii, No. 2, Apr., 1878, pp. 72–75.

1878. BREWER, T. M. The Seaside Finch (Ammodramus maritimus) in Eastern Massachusetts. < *Bull. Nutt. Ornith. Club*, iii, No. 1, Jan., 1878, p. 48.

1878. BREWER, T. M. Nest and Eggs of Zonotrichia coronata. < *Bull. Nutt. Ornith. Club*, iii, No. 1, Jan., 1878, pp. 42, 43.

1878. BREWER, T. M. Song of Hepburn's Finch (Leucosticte littoralis, Baird). < *Bull. Nutt. Ornith. Club*, iii, No. 4, Oct., 1878, pp. 189, 190.
Observations of C. Bendire in Oregon.

1878. BROWN, N. C. The Sharp-tailed Finch (Ammodramus caudacutus) in Maine. < *Bull. Nutt. Ornith. Club*, iii, No. 2, Apr., 1878, pp. 98, 99.

1878. "CARNIFEX, JOHN" (*pseudon.*). Some Western Sparrows. < *The Country* (newspaper of N. Y.), July 20, 1878.
Treating of species of *Plectrophanes, Passerculus bairdi, Calamospiza bicolor*, etc.

1878. COOPER, W. A. Notes on the breeding habits of Carpodacus purpureus var. californicus, with a Description of its Nest and Eggs. < *Bull. Nutt. Ornith. Club*, iii, No. 1, Jan., 1878, pp. 8–10.

1878. COUES, E. Note on Passerculus bairdi and P. princeps. < *Bull. Nutt. Ornith. Club*, iii, No. 1, Jan., 1878, pp. 1–3, pl. i.
Perfunctory letter-press for the plate; but gives complete synonymy of the two species, the former of which is figured on the colored plate.

1878. COUES, E. Pipilo erythrophthalmus with Spotted Scapulars. < *Bull. Nutt. Ornith. Club*, iii, No. 1, Jan., 1878, pp. 41, 42.
With editorial note by J. A. Allen.

1878. COVERT, A. B. Rare Birds [in Michigan]. < *Science News*, i, No. 4, Dec. 15, 1878, p. 64.
Junco oregonus, J. caniceps, and others.

1878. DEANE, R. Coturniculus henslowi in New Hampshire. < *Bull. Nutt. Ornith. Club*, iii, No. 1, Jan., 1878, p. 39.

1878. "E. C. M." A Cardinal Grosbeak [Cardinalis virginianus] in Central Park. < *Forest and Stream*, x, Apr. 4, 1878, p. 156.

1878. [FITCH, E. H.] The Field Sparrow. (Spizella Pusilla.) < *The Journ. of Sci.* (Toledo, Ohio), 2d ser. i, No. 7, Oct., 1878, cut.
Popular biography, with a figure.

1878. GENTRY, [T. G.] The Rose-breasted Grosbeak [Goniaphea ludoviciana]. < *The Oölogist*, iv, No. 4, June, 1878, p. 30.
Notes on the habits of the bird.

1878. HENSHAW, H. W. On the Species of the genus Passerella. < *Bull. Nutt. Ornith. Club*, iii, No. 1, Jan., 1878, pp. 3–7.
Reduces them all to subspecies of *P. iliaca.*

1878. INGERSOLL, E. Breeding habits of the Goldfinch [Chrysomitris tristis]. < *Forest and Stream*, x, July 11, 1878, p. 442.

1878. JONES, J. M. Cardinal Grosbeak [Cardinalis virginianus] in Nova Scotia in Winter. < *Forest and Stream*, x, May 16, 1878, p. 275.

1878. KOCH, E. G.   Breeding of the Snow bird [Junco hyemalis] in Pennsylvania.
    < *Forest and Stream*, x, July 4, 1878, p. 422.

1878. LAWRENCE, N. T.   The Ipswich Sparrow (Passerculus princeps) on Long Island,
    N. Y.   < *Bull. Nutt. Ornith. Club*, iii, No. 2, Apr., 1878, p. 102.

1878. MERRIAM, C. H.   Breeding of the Pine Linnet [Chrysomitris pinus] in Northern
    New York.   < *Forest and Stream*, x, July 18, 1878, p. 463.
        Giving a full account, from original observations.

1878. MORAN, G. H.   Breeding Snow-Birds [Junco hyemalis].   < *Forest and Stream*,
    xi, Oct. 17, 1878, p. 222.
        In mountains of North Carolina and Georgia.

1878. "M[ERRIAM?], C. H."   Winter Range of the American Goldfinch [Chrysomitris
    tristis].   < *Forest and Stream*, x, May 30, 1878, p. 319.
        Northward to Warner, N. H.

1878. NICHOLAS, G. W.   [Northern Range of Cardinalis virginianus.]   < *The Country*,
    i, Feb. 23, 1878, p. 244.

1878. PURDIE, H. A.   The Lark-Finch (Chondestes grammaca) again in Massachusetts.
    < *Bull. Nutt. Ornith. Club*, iii, No. 1, Jan., 1878, p. 44.
        Cf. *Proc. Essex Inst.*, i, 1856, p. 224.

1878. PURDIE, H. A.   The Black-throated Bunting (Euspiza americana) nesting in
    Massachusetts.   < *Bull. Nutt. Ornith. Club*, iii, No. 1, Jan., 1878, p. 55.

1878. RAGSDALE, G. H.   The Painted Lark Bunting (Plectrophanes pictus) in Texas.
    < *Bull. Nutt. Ornith. Club*, iii, No. 2, Apr., 1878, p. 92.

1878. RIDGWAY, R.   Eastward range [to Washington, D. C.] of Chondestes grammaca.
    < *Bull. Nutt. Ornith. Club*, iii, No. 1, 1878, pp. 43, 44.

1878. [SCLATER, P. L., *and* SALVIN, O.]   Ridgway on the genus Leucosticte.   < *Ibis*,
    4th ser., ii, Jan., 1878, p. 104.
        Notice of the paper in *Field and Forest*, ii, 1876, pp. 37-43.

1878. S[TERLING], E.   An Explanation wanted [of gravel in a Song Sparrow's nest].
    < *Forest and Stream*, xi, Dec. 19, 1878, p. 400.

1878. STOCKWELL, G. A.   An early Bird indeed.   < *Am. Nat.*, xii, No. 6, June, 1878,
    p. 399.
        Spizella socialis nesting Mar. 21 in Michigan.

1878. [WILLARD, S. L.]   Reflections upon the Habits of the Purple Finch [Carpoda-
    cus purpureus].   < *The Oölogist*, iv, No. 2, Apr., 1878, pp. 13, 14.

1878. [WILLARD, S. L.]   Studies on Certain Fringillidæ.—The Grass Finch [Poœcetes
    gramineus].   < *The Oölogist*, iv, No. 4, June, 1878, p. 31.
        Notes on the habits of the bird.

1878. [WILLARD, S. L.]   Studies on Certain Fringillidæ.—The Tree Sparrow [Spizella
    monticola].   < *The Oölogist*, iv, No. 5, July, 1878, pp. 37, 38.

1878. WILLISTON, S. W.   A Foster-Father.   < *Forest and Stream*, xi, Aug. 8, 1878, p. 2.
        Tame *Cardinalis virginianus* rearing orioles in his cage.

1879. ALLEN, J. A.   The Evening Grosbeak [Hesperiphona vespertina] in New Mex-
    ico.   < *Bull. Nutt. Ornith. Club*, iv, No. 4, Oct., 1879, p. 237.

1879. ATKINS, H. A.   The Snowbird (Junco hyemalis) in Southern Michigan in Sum-
    mer.   < *Bull. Nutt. Ornith. Club*, iv, No. 4, Oct., 1879, p. 238.

1879. BREWER, T. M.   The Sharp-tailed Finch—Ammodromus caudacutus,—its Nest,
    and Eggs.   < *The Oölogist*, iv, No. 6, Jan., 1879, pp. 41, 42.
        Very full account.

1879. BREWER, T. M.   A Word in Defence.   < *Bull. Nutt. Ornith. Club*, iv, No. 3, July,
    1879, pp. 191, 192.
        Merely controversial, with E. Coues, with respect to the position of *Hesperiphona vesper-
        tina* in the *List of the Birds of New England*, published by the latter in 1868, occasioned by
        a remark made in "The History of the Evening Grosbeak," *tom. cit.*, p. 75. An editorial
        note appended states that the person in mention declines to reply.

1879. BREWSTER, W. Notes on the Habits and Distribution of the Rufous-crowned Sparrow (Peucæa ruficeps). < *Bull. Nutt. Ornith. Club*, iv, No. 1, Jan.. 1879, pp. 47, 48.
From the observations of C. A. Allen of Nicasio, Cal.

1879. CADY, W. B. Curious Death of a Bird [Spizella socialis]. < *Science News*, i, No. 15, June 1, 1879, p. 240.
Strangled by a thread from the nest.

1879. COUES, E. Southward Range of Centrophanes lapponica. < *Bull. Nutt. Ornith. Club*, iv, No. 4, Oct., 1879, p. 238.
Fort Smith, Arkansas.

1879. COUES, E. Nest and Eggs of the Clay-colored Bunting [Spizella pallida]. < *The Oölogist*, iv, No. 7, Feb., 1879, p. 50.
Quoted from the "Birds of the Northwest."

1879. COUES, E. Nest and Eggs of the Chestnut-collared Bunting [Plectrophanes ornatus]. < *The Oölogist*, iv, No. 10, May, 1879, p. 79.
Quoted from "Birds of the Northwest."

1879. COUES, E. History of the Evening Grosbeak [Hesperiphona vespertina]. < *Bull. Nutt. Ornith. Club*, iv, No. 2, Apr., 1879, pp. 65–75.
By permission, from advance MS. of *Birds of the Colorado Valley*, Part II. Very full on the geographical distribution and habits of the species, as well as its appearance in previous literature of the subject, the record of which is given, together with a copious synonymy.

1879. [COUES, E.] nest and Eggs of the Chestnut-collared Bunting [Plectrophanes ornatus]. < *The Temperance Vidette* (newspaper of Terrell, Texas) of Sept. 20, 1879.
Quoted from *The Oölogist*, iv, No. 10, May, 1879, p. 79.

1879. DAVIS, F. J. Yellow-winged Sparrow [Coturniculus passerinus]. < *The Oölogist*, iv, No. 6, Jan., 1879, p. 47.
Notes on the nest and eggs of this species.

1879. DEANE, R. Record of the Breeding of Crossbills [Loxia curvirostra americana] in Northern Vermont in 1796. < *Bull. Nutt. Ornith. Club*, iv, No. 2, Apr., 1879, pp. 121, 122.
Interesting record respecting *Loxia curvirostra americana*, from "The Rural Magazine; or, Vermont Repository," vol. ii, 1796, p. 475, by Thomas Tolman.

1879. DEANE, R. Nesting of the Black-throated Bunting (Euspiza americana) in Massachusetts. < *Bull. Nutt. Ornith. Club*, iv, No. 2, Apr., 1879, pp. 122, 123.

1879. HENSHAW, H. W. Melospiza meloda and its Allies. < *Bull. Nutt. Ornith. Club*, iv, No. 3, July, 1879, pp. 155–160.
A very full discussion of the intricate forms of this stock, distinguishing 8 varieties: *MM. meloda, fallax, heermanni, samuelis, mexicana, gattata, rufina*, and *insignis*.

1879. JEFFRIES, W. A. Ægiothus exilipes in Massachusetts. < *Bull. Nutt. Ornith. Club*, iv, No. 2, Apr., 1879, p. 121.

1879. JEFFRIES, W. A. The Ipswich Sparrow (Passerculus princeps, Maynard). < *Bull. Nutt. Ornith. Club*, iv, No. 2, Apr., 1879, pp. 103–106.
Treated as not specifically distinct from *P. savanna*.

1879. PEARSALL, R. F. Notes on the Purple Finch [Carpodacus purpureus]. < *Bull. Nutt. Ornith. Club*, iv, No. 2, Apr., 1879, p. 122.

1879. PECKHAM, B. J. [Nesting of Pipilo erythrophthalmus off the Ground.] < *The Oölogist*, iv, No. 6, Jan., 1879, p. 43.

1879. RAGSDALE, G. H. Song of Cassin's Finch [Peucæa cassini]. < *Science News*, i, No. 9, Mar. 1, 1879, pp. 134, 135.

1879. RAGSDALE, G. H. Pensile Nests of the Painted Bunting [Cyanospiza ciris]. < *Science News*, i, No. 17, July 1, 1879, p. 272.

1879. RAGSDALE, G. H. Nesting of the Snowbird [Junco hyemalis] in Eastern Tennessee. < *Bull. Nutt. Ornith. Club*, iv, No. 4, Oct., 1879, pp. 238, 239.

1879. RIDGWAY, R. On a new species of Peucæa [illinoensis] from Southern Illinois and Central Texas. < *Bull. Nutt. Ornith. Club*, iv, No. 4, Oct., 1879, pp. 218–222.

Extended critical comparison with its allies, and G. H. Ragsdale's notes on its habits.

1879. RIDGWAY, R. [Letter on Peucæa illinoensis.] < *Temperance Vidette* (Texas newspaper), Oct. 11, 1879.

1879. RIDGWAY, R. Henslow's Bunting (Coturniculus henslowi) near Washington. < *Bull. Nutt. Ornith. Club*, iv, No. 4, Oct., 1879, p. 238.

1879. ROBERTS, T. S. Note on Hesperiphona vespertina. < *Bull. Nutt. Ornith. Club*, iv, No. 4, Oct., 1879, pp. 237, 238.

The lateness (May 19) of its departure in the spring from Minnesota, where it winters.

1879. SABIN, W. W. [Nesting of Pipilo erythrophthalmus off the Ground.] < *The Oölogist*, iv, No. 6, Jan., 1879, p. 43.

1879. SMITH, G. S[TUART]. Nesting of the Black-throated Bunting (Euspiza americana) < *The Oölogist*, iv, No. 8, Mar., 1879, pp. 58, 59.

1879. SMITH, G. S[TUART]. Nesting of the Sharp-tailed Finch (Ammodromus caudacutus). < *The Oölogist*, iv, No. 9, Apr., 1879, pp. 66, 67.

From original observations in Massachusetts.

1879. [WILLARD, S. L.] Studies on Certain Fringillidæ.—The Savannah Sparrow [Passerculus savanna]. < *The Oölogist*, v, No. 2, Aug., 1879, p. 14.

1879. [WILLARD, S. L.] Studies on Certain Fringillidæ.—The White-throated Sparrow [Zonotrichia albicollis]. < *The Oölogist*, iv, No. 9, Apr., 1879, p. 71.

1879. [WILLARD, S. L.] Studies on Certain Fringillidæ.—The Black Snow Bird [Junco hyemalis]. < *The Oölogist*, iv, No. 11, June, 1879, p. 90.

1879. [WILLARD, S. L.?] Nest and Eggs of Carpodacus purpureus. < *Temperance Vidette* (newspaper of Terrill, Texas), Nov. 22, 1879.

Copied from *The Oölogist*.

1879. W[ILLIAMS, *Mrs.* J.] The Potato Bug Bird [*i. e.*, Goniaphea ludoviciana]. < *Forest and Stream*, xiii, Nov. 20, 1879, p. 827.

In the issue of the same paper of Dec. 18, 1879, appeared letters from " M." [A. C. McElwrath], T. S. Roberts, and S. A. Forbes identifying the bird referred to by Mrs. Williams as above, and testifying to its usefulness in destroying *Doryphora* 10-*lineata*, The same important fact had been noticed by W. H. Mapes, *Am. Nat.*, vii, 1873, p. 493.

Alaudidæ.

1778. PALLAS, P. S.   Den Mongoliska Lärkan (Alauda mongolica), en rar Fogel från Östra Sibirien, funnen och beskrifven af P. S. Pallas. $<$ *Kongl. Svensk. Vetensk.-Akad. Händl.*, 1778, pp. 201–203, pl. vii, f. 2.

1778. PALLAS, P. S.   Die Mongolische Lerche, Alauda mongolica. $<$ *Abhandl. d. Schwed. Akad.*, xl, f. 1778, pp. 193–195, pl. —.
Not seen.

1814. LEISLER, J. P.   Die kurzzehige Lerche (Alauda brachydactyla). $<$ *Ann. d. Wetter. Ges. f. d. ges. Naturk.*, iii, 1814, pp. 357–359, pl. —.
Not seen.

1835. GARDINER, W.   Some Skylarks [Alauda arvensis] were Singing on the Wing on Sept. 27. 1834. in Scotland. $<$ *Loudon's Mag. Nat. Hist.*, viii, 1835, p. 614.

1836. LAFRESNAYE, F. DE.   Alouette. Alauda. Lin. Certhilauda. Swainson.—Sirli. Lesson. $<$ *Guér. Mag. de Zool.*, 6e année, 1836, classe ii, notices lviii, lix, pp. 1–8, pll. lviii, lix.
Alauda albo-fasciata, p. 3 $=$ Certhilauda a., pl. 58.—A. rufo-palliata, p. 4 $=$ Certhilauda r., pl. 59.—Sur les Alouettes à long bec de l'Amérique méridionale, pp. 6, 7 ; monographie de six espèces.

1838. SYKES, [W. H.]   [On the Calandra Lark.] $<$ *P. Z. S.*, vi, 1838, pp. 113, 114.
Made type of Londra, g. n., with remarks on its affinities.

1839. WATERHOUSE, G. R.   [Description of a New Species of Lark from China (Alauda sinensis).] $<$ *P. Z. S.*, vii, 1839, pp. 60, 61.

1843. BROWN, E.   Enquiry.—Does the Female Sky-lark [Alauda arvensis] ever sing ? $<$ *Zoologist*, i, 1843, p. 219.

1844. BRIGGS, J. J.   Remarks upon [the habits of] the Skylark [Alauda arvensis]. $<$ *Zoologist*, ii, 1844, pp. 657, 658.

1844. FISHER, W. R.   Note on the migration of Larks [Alauda arvensis] at Yarmouth. $<$ *Zoologist*, ii, 1844, p. 452.

1845. STREATFIELD, J. F.   Anecdote of a Lark's Nest. $<$ *Zoologist*, iii, 1845, p. "1065," *i. e.*, 1075.

1846. RODD, E. H.   Occurrence of the Crested Lark (Alauda cristata), near Penzance. $<$ *Zoologist*, iv, 1846, p. 1497.

1846. WATERHOUSE, [G. R.]   [Eine Lerche aus China, Alauda sinensis.] $<$ *Oken's Isis*, Bd. xxxix, 1846, p. 618.
P. Z. S., vii, 1839, p. 60.

1847. SLADEN, E. H. M.   Supposed New British Lark [Alauda isabellina, sp. n.] $<$ *Zoologist*, v, 1847, p. 1697.

1850. SMITH, J.   Occurrence of the Wood Lark (Alauda arborea) in Scotland. $<$ *Zoologist*, viii, 1850, pp. 2849–2851.

1851. GURNEY, J. H.   Occurrence of the Shore Lark (Alauda [Eremophila] alpestris) near Yarmouth. $<$ *Zoologist*, ix, 1851, p. 2985.

1851. RODD, E. H.   Occurrence of the Continental Crested Lark near Penzance. $<$ *Zoologist*, ix, 1851, p. 3033.

1852. POWYS, T. L.   The Shore Lark (Alauda [Eremophila] alpestris) breeding in Devonshire. $<$ *Zoologist*, x, 1852, p. 3707.

1854. ALLIS, T. H.   Occurrence of the Shore Lark (Alauda [Eremophila] alpestris) in Yorkshire. $<$ *Zoologist*, xii, 1854, pp. 4251, 4252.

1854. GORGAS, J.   Importation of Sky-larks [Alauda arvensis, in the United States]. $<$ *Rep. Comm. Patents for* 1853, *Agric.*, 1854, pp. 70, 71.

1854. RODD, E. H.   Occurrence of the Short-toed Lark (Alauda brachydactyla) at Scilly.   < *Zoologist*, xii, 1854, p. 4477.

1855. HELLMANN, A.   Otocorys [Eremophila] alpestris bei Gotha erlegt.   < *J. f. O.*, iii, 1855, p. 181.

1855. OLPH-GALLIARD, L.   [Die Feldlerche, Alauda arvensis, setzt sich auf Bäume.] < *Naumannia*, 1855, p. 215.

1856. BREHM, [C. L.]   [Ueber die Ammerlerchen (Melanocorypha).]   < *Naumannia*, vi, 1856, pp. 374–376.
   1. *M. calandra*, a) *albigularis*, b) *megarhynchos*, c) *subcalandra*; 2. *semitorquata*; 3. *rufescens*. Auch zeigt d. Verf. 2 kurzzehige Lerchenarten vor, *Calandrella ferrunginea* [sic] A. Brhm., und *C. brachyptera*.

1858. BREHM, [C.] L.   Etwas über die Haubenlerchen, Galerita, Boje.   (Alauda cristata, L., et undata, L.)   < *Naumannia*, viii, 1858, pp. 204–213.
   1. *Galerita cristata nigricans, G. c. major, G. c. vulgaris, G. c. pagorum, G. c. viarum, G. c. karinthiaca, G. c. pallida, G. c. planorum, G. c. gallica, G. c. tenuirostris, G. c. augustistriata, G. c. maculata, G. c. altirostris, G. c. undata, G. c. rufescens.* 2. *G. abyssinica.* 3. *G. flava, G. f. tenuirostris, G. f. crassirostris.* 4. *G. lutea.* 5. *G. theklae.*

1858. SCHILLING, H.   Ueber das Vorkommen von Alauda [Eremophila] alpestris in Pommern.   < *Naumannia*, viii, 1858, pp. 60–63.

1859. SWINHOE, R.   Description of the small Chinese Lark [Alauda cœlivox, Swinh.]. < *Zoologist*, xvii, 1859, pp. 6723–6727.

1860. LOCHE, —.   Description de deux nouvelles espèces d'Alouettes découvertes dans le Sahara algérien par le commandant Loche, directeur du muséum d'histoire naturelle d'Alger.   < *Rev. et Mag. de Zool.*, xii, 1860, pp. 148–151, pl. 11.
   Calandrella reboudia, p. 149, pl. xi, f. 1; *Galerida randoni*, p. 150, pl. xi, f. 2—les deux décrites en 1858 par Loche, *Cat. Mamm. et Ois. de l'Algérie*, pp. 83–85.

1861 [HARRIS, S. D.]   Note.   < *Field Notes*, i, No. 12, Mar. 23, 1861, p. 92.
   Introduction of *Alauda arvensis* in Ohio in 1851.

1861. VIAN, J.   Notice sur l'Alouette pispolette, Alauda pispoletta, Pall. et Bp.. et sur l'Alouette, Alauda brachydactyla, Temm., Calandrella brachydactyla, Bp. < *Rev. et Mag. de Zool.*, xiii, 1861, pp. 346–353.

1862. BARTLETT, J. P.   Occurrence of the Short-toed Lark (Alauda brachydactyla) and other rare Birds in Hampshire.   < *Zoologist*, xx, 1862, pp. 7930, 7931.

1862. SAXBY, H. L.   Notes upon the Migration and Song of the Skylark [Alauda arvensis].   < *Zoologist*, xx, 1862, p. 8281.

1862. STEVENSON, H.   [Letter on occurrence of Eremophila alpestris in Norfolk, England.]   < *Ibis*, iv, 1862, pp. 189, 190.

1862. STEVENSON, H.   [Letter on another (Ibis, iv, 189) occurrence of Eremophila alpestris in Norfolk, England].   < *Ibis*, iv, 1862, p. 303.

1862. STEVENSON, H.   Another [Zool., 1845, 7931] Shore Lark [Eremophila alpestris] in Norfolk.   < *Zoologist*, xx, 1862, pp. 8090, 8091.

1863. DES MURS, O.   Note sur les espèces du genre Pyrrhulauda et leur œuf.   < *Rev. et Mag. de Zool.*, xv, 1863, pp. 209–212.

1863. GATCOMBE, J.   Occurrence of the Calandra Lark [Alauda calandra] in Devon. < *Zoologist*, xxi, 1863, p. 8768.

1863. NEWMAN, H. W.   Skylarks [Alauda arvensis] congregating in October [in England.]   < *Zoologist*, xxi, 1863, p. 8326.

1863. REICHENBACH, L.   Frühes [8 Feb., 1861] Nisten der Feldlerche, Alauda arvensis.   < *J. f. O.*, 1863, xi, p. 155.

1863. ROBERTS, A. W.   The Shore Lark (Alauda [Eremophila] alpestris) near Lowestoft.   < *Zoologist*, xxi, 1863, p. 8446.

1864. TYRER, R., JR.   A Yellow Skylark [Alauda arvensis].   < *Zoologist*, xxii, 1864, p. 8950.

1865. EEDLE, T.   Shore Lark [Eremophila alpestris] near London.   < *Zoologist*, xxiii, 1865, p. 9782.

1865. GURNEY, J. H.   Note on a Deformity in the Bill of a Sky Lark [Alauda arvensis].   < *Zoologist*, xxiii, 1865, p. 9467.

1865. RAMSAY, E. P.   Note on the Nidification of Mirafra horsfieldi.   < *P. Z. S.*, Nov. 28, 1865, pp. 689, 690.

1866. ANON.   Food of Larks.   < *The Intellectual Observer*, viii, 1866, p. 480.   (From *Proc. Roy. Soc.*, No. 78.)
Regards grass the chief food in winter.

1866. WATKINS, M. G.   The Sky Lark [Alauda arvensis].   < *Zoologist*, 2d ser., i, 1866, p. 498.
Quotation from *Milton's L'Allegro*.

1867. BOND, F.   Wood Lark at Brighton.   < *Zoologist*, 2d ser., ii, 1867, p. 792.

1867. CLARK-KENNEDY, A.   Young Lark feeding other young ones.   < *Zoologist*, 2d ser., ii, 1867, p. 949.

1867. CLIFTON, *Lord*.   Wood Lark in Kent.   < *Zoologist*, 2d ser., ii, 1867, p. 705.

1867. JEFFREY, W., JR.   Wood Lark in West Sussex.   < *Zoologist*, 2d ser., ii, 1867, p. 756.

1867. ROWLEY, G. D.   Shore Larks [Eremophila alpestris] in Suffolk.   < *Zoologist*, 2d ser., ii, 1867, p. 560.

1867. WEST, E.   Black Sky Lark [Alauda arvensis].   < *Zoologist*, 2d ser., ii, 1867, p. 705.

1868. CLIFTON, *Lord*.   Wood Lark [at Eton].   < *Zoologist*, 2d ser., iii, 1868, p. 1132.

1868. DUTTON, J.   White Lark [Alauda arvensis] near Eastbourne.   < *Zoologist*, 2d ser., iii, 1868, p. 1132.

1868. HENSMAN, H. P.   Longevity [21 years] of a Caged Lark.   < *Zoologist*, 2d ser., iii, 1868, p. 1254.

1869. GORDON, C.   Shore Lark [Eremophila alpestris] in Captivity.   < *Zoologist*, 2d ser., iv, 1869, pp. 1513, 1514.

1869. GUNN, T. E.   White Sky Lark [Alauda arvensis] in Confinement.   < *Zoologist*, 2d ser., iv, 1869, p. 1599.

1869. GURNEY, J. H., JR.   Calandra Lark near Exeter.   < *Zoologist*, 2d ser., iv, 1869, p. 1599.

1870. BOND, F.   Siberian Lark at Brighton.   < *Zoologist*, 2d ser., v, 1870, p. 2022.

1870. BORRER, W.   Shore Lark [Eremophila alpestris] near Weymouth.   < *Zoologist*, 2d ser., v, 1870, p. 2101.

1870. BOYES, F.   Shore Larks [Eremophila alpestris] in East Yorkshire.   < *Zoologist*, 2d ser., v, 1870, p. 2101.

1870. GUNN, T. E.   Buff Variety of Skylark [Alauda arvensis].   < *Zoologist*, 2d ser., v, 1870, p. 2101.

1870. MONK, T. J.   Shore Lark [Eremophila alpestris] near Newhaven.   < *Zoologist*, 2d ser., v, 1870, p. 2140.

1870. NEWMAN, E.   Shore Larks [Eremophila alpestris] near London.   < *Zoologist*, 2d ser., v, 1870, pp. 2406, 2407.

1870. RAMSEY, R. G. W.   Shore Lark [Eremophila alpestris] at St. Andrews.   < *Zoologist*, 2d ser., v, 1870, p. 2022.

1870. RAMSEY, R. G. W.   Shore Larks [Eremophila alpestris] near Dunbar.   < *Zoologist*, 2d ser., v, 1870, p. 2101.

1870. ROWLEY, G. D.   Correction of an Error [Zool. s. s. 1984; Alauda sibirica].   < *Zoologist*, 2d ser., v, 1870, p. 2066.

Bull. v, 4——9

1871. BOYES, F.   Migration of Larks in East Yorkshire.   < *Zoologist*, 2d, ser., 1871, pp. 2639, 2640.

1871. MOOR, E. C.   White Larks.   < *Zoologist*, 2d ser., vi, 1871, pp. 2640, 2641.

1871. SHARPE, R. B.   On the Alauda bimaculata of Ménétriés.   < *Am. Mag. Nat. Hist.*, 4th ser., viii, 1871, pp. 179–181.

1872. ANON.   Sky Larks [Alauda arvensis] breeding in an Aviary.   < *Zoologist*, 2d ser., vii, 1872, p. 3186.

1872. HUME, A. O.   The Skylarks of India.   < *Stray Feathers*, i, pp. 38–41.
    All the Indian species of *Alauda* are referred to *A. arvensis* and *A. malabarica*. The latter includes *A. gulgula*, *A. malabarica* (vera), *A. triborhyncha*, as subspecies, each with a separate habitat, as well as a fourth from the central provinces, to which no name is given. (Cf. *Ibis*, 1873, pp. 221, 222.)—Not seen: title and comment from *Zool. Rec.*

1873. CORBIN, G. B.   Migration of the Sky Lark [Alauda arvensis].   < *Zoologist*, 2d ser., viii, 1873, p. 3647.

1873. GREGSON, C. S.   [Albinotic and Melanotic] Varieties of the Skylark [Alauda arvensis].   < *Zoologist*, 2d ser., viii, 1873, p. 3412.

1873. HOMEYER, E. F. V.   Monographische Beiträge über einige Gruppen der Lerchen (Alaudidæ).   < *J. f. O.*, 1873, pp. 186–209.
    Genn. *Hierapterhina, Melanocorypha, Pallasia*, n. g., p. 190, *Alauda, Calandrella* (*C. immaculata* Brhm. MSS., sp. n., 194), *Calandritis* (*C. heinei*, sp. n., p. 197), *Ammomanes, Chorys, Galerita* (*G. microcristata*, sp. n., p. 64); 23 Aiten. Cf. *Zool. Rec.*, x, p. 64.

1873. HOMEYER, E. F. V.   Notiz über Calandritis heinei Nob.   < *J. f. O.*, 1873, pp. 425, 426.

1873. LILFORD, *Lord*.   [Occurrence of Calandrella reboudia near Seville, Spain.   < *Ibis*, 3d ser., iii, 1873, p. 98.

1874. BURROUGHS, J.   Mellow England.   < *Scribner's Monthly*, vol. viii, 1874, pp. 559–571.
    Contains short account of English skylark, notes upon its possible introduction into the United States, and a comparison of the singing of English and American birds.

1874. ROPE, G. T.   Early Nesting of Sky Lark [Alauda arvensis, in Suffolk].   < *Zoologist*, 2d ser., ix, 1874, p. 4034.

1875. COUES, E.   Letters on Ornithology.   No. 4.—The Horned or Shore Lark [Eremophila alpestris].   < *The Chicago Field*, Oct. 7, 1876, fig.
    On the habits of this species.

1877. INGERSOLL, E.   [Inquiry as to introduction of English] Sky Larks [into the U. S.].   < *Forest and Stream*, viii, Mar. 8, 1877, p. 65.   See p. 129.

1877. WILLICOTT, W.   What becomes of our foreign song-birds.   < *Forest and Stream*, viii, Apr. 5, 1877, p. 129.
    Reply to question asked by E. Ingersoll (p. 65) concerning skylarks introduced from England to U. S., stating that acclimatization was attempted, several years previous, but none were now known to survive.

1878. ALLEN, J. A.   Early Nesting of the Shore Lark [Eremophila alpestris] near Indianapolis, Ind.   < *Bull. Nutt. Ornith. Club*, iii, No. 4, Oct., 1878, p. 189.
    Young were well grown April 24. (The bird has been known to nest in the N. W. States before the snow was off the ground.)

1878. DAVIS, F. J.   Nesting of the Horned Lark (Eremopila [sic] cornuta) in Central New York.   < *The Oölogist*, iv, No. 2, Apr., 1878, p. 9, cut.

1878. HOWEY, J. M.   Breeding of the Shore Lark [Eremophila alpestris] in Western New York.   < *Bull. Nutt. Ornith. Club*, iii, No. 1, Jan., 1878, p. 40.

1878. JONES, H. T.   Breeding of the Shore Lark [Eremophila alpestris] in Western New York.   < *Bull. Nutt. Ornith. Club*, iii, No. 4, Oct., 1878, p. 189.
    Quite common near Rochester, N. Y.; nest with incubated eggs June 6. (Cf. *op. tom. cit.*, p. 40, and *loc. cit.*)

Picidæ.

1701. [MÉRY, J.]   De rebus ad Historiam Animalium pertinentibus.   < *Reg. Scient. Acad. Hist. Paris (Duhamel ed.)*, i, 1701, pp. 380–385, fig.
　　De structurâ Pici linguæ. *Ann.* 1695.

1716. WALLER, R.   A Description of that curious Natural Machine, the Wood-Peckers Tongue, &c.   < *Philos. Trans.*, xxix, 1716, pp. 509–522, tab. i, figg. 1–9.
　　Remarkably complete and pertinent, for the time. The writer also takes occasion to criticize and review various authors who had written upon the same subject.

1730. HIRE, [P.] DE LA.   Explication mécanique du mouvement de la langue du Pivert.   < *Mém. de l'Acad. Roy. des Sciences Paris*, ix, 1730, pp. 238–240, fig.

1733. MÉRY, J.   Observations sur les mouvemens de la langue du Piver [Picus].   < *Mém. de l'Acad. Roy. des Sci. pour l'année* 1709, 1733, pp. 85–91, pl. 3.

1740. LINNÆUS, C.   Carl Linnæi Beskrifning på en ny Fogel: Picus pedibus tridactylis.   < *Kongl. Svensk. Vetensk.-Akad. Handl.*, i, 1740, pp. 222–224.

1742. MÉRY, [J.]   Observations on the motions of the tongue of the wood-pecker.   < *Hist. and Mem. of the Roy. Acad., for* 1709, *English Abridgment*, iii, 1742, pp. 183–190, pl. iii, figs. 1–3.

1743. LINNÆUS, C.   Beskrifning på en ny Fogel: Picus pedibus tridactylis.   < *Kongl. Swensk. Wetens. Acad. Handl.*, i (1740), 1743, pp. 214–216.

1803. DAUDIN, F. M.   Description d'une nouvelle espèce de Pic trouvée à Porto-Rico.   < *Ann. du Mus. d'Hist. Nat.*, ii, 1803, pp. 285, 286, pl. 51.
　　Picus portoricensis, p. 286, pl. 51.

1821. SWAINSON, W.   Observations on the Genus Picus of Linnæus, with Descriptions of two New Species from the Interior of Brazil.   < *Mem. Wernerian Nat. Hist. Soc.*, iii, 1821, pp. 288–293.
　　Read Mar., 1820. *P. chrysosternus*, p. 289; *P. braziliensis*, p. 291.

1824. BERTHOLD, A. A.   Einigen Notizen aus der Anatomie und Physiologie des Spechtes im Allgemeinen, des Grasspechtes (Picus viridis) aber insbesondere.   < *Oken's Isis*, Jahrg. viii, 1824, pp. 555–558.

1826. LESS[ON, R. P.]   Observations sur le genre Picus de Linnæus, et description de deux espèces nouvelles de l'intérieur du Brésil, . . . par William Swainson. . .   < *Féruss. Bull.*, 2ᵉ sec., vii, 1826, pp. 250, 251.
　　Mem. of the Wernerian Soc., iii, 1821, p. 288.

1832. GOULD, J.   [On a New Species of Woodpecker, Picus imperialis.]   < *P. Comm. Sci. Z. S.*, ii, 1832, pp. 139, 140.
　　"California", the alleged locality, is incorrect.

1833. GOULD, J.   [Characters of a New Species of Woodpecker (Picus flavinucha).]   < *P. Z. S.*, i, 1833, p. 120.

1835. GOULD, J.   Neuer Specht [Picus imperialis], aus Californien in der Nähe von Mexico; grosser als alle andern.   < *Oken's Isis*, 1835, p. 433.
　　Aus d. *P. Comm. Sci. Z. S.*, 1832, p. 139.

1837. TRUDEAU, J.   Description of a New Species of Woodpecker [Picus auduboni].   < *Journ. Acad. Nat. Sci. Phila.*, vii, 1837, pp. 404–406.

1840. BOISSONNEAU, —.   Nouvelle espèce du genre Pic [Picus rivolii].   < *Rev. Zool.*, iii, 1840, pp. 36, 37.

1843. LAFRESNAYE, [F.] DE.   G. Pic. Picus. Linn. P. de Magellan. P. magellanicus ♀ (King. in the Zool. journ., 1827, p. 430). P. jubatus de Lafr., Rev. zool., 1841, p. 242.   < *Guér. Mag. de Zool.*, 2ᵉ sér., année 1843, Oiseaux, pp. 1, 2, pl. 31.

1844. CABOT, S., JR.   [Picus dubius, P. parvus, P. yucatanensis (p. 164), spp. nn. from Yucatan.]   < *Proc. Bost. Soc. Nat.*, i, 1844, pp. 164, 165.

1844. KESSLER, K.   Beitraege zur Naturgeschichte der Spechte.   < *Bull. Soc. Imp. Nat. Moscou*, xvii, pt. i, 1844, pp. 285–362, pll. x–xiii, nebst Karte.   (Auch separatabdruckt, 8°, Riga, 1844, pp. 80, 4 Taf.)

> 1te Abtheil. Osteologie, pll. x, xi.   2te Abth. Ueber die Befiederung der Spechte, nebst einigen Bemerkungen über die Bürzeldrüse, die Schleimdrüsen, und der Zungenapparat, pll. xii, xiii.

1845. LAFRESNAYE, F. DE.   Sur la genre Picumne, de Temminck, pl. coloriées.   < *Rev. Zool.*, viii, 1845, pp. 1–10.

> A subhead of the Mélanges Ornithologiques.   This is an important piece of monography, making many criticisms and rectifications.   Nine species are recognized: *P. cayennensis* (ex Briss.), sp. n., *P. temminckii* (= *P. exilis* Temm.), sp. n., *P. exilis* Licht. (= *P. lichtensteinii*, sp. n.), *P. buffonii* (ex Pl. Enl. 786, f. 1), sp. n., p. 6; *P. pygmæus* (Licht.), *P. albo-squamatus* d'Orb. & Lafr.), *P. olivaceus*, Lafr., *P. cinnamomius* Lafr., *P. d'Orbignyanus* Lafr., p. 7. These species are ranged in four sections according to their coloration.

1845. LAFRESNAYE, [F.] DE.   Recticatations [sic] et additions à la monographie du Genre Picumnus.   < *Rev. Zool.*, viii, 1845, p. 111.

> Voir *tom. cit.*, pp. 1–11.

1845. MALHERBE, A.   Notice sur quelques espèces de Pics de Brésil.   < *Mém. de la Soc. Roy. de Liège*, ii, 1846, pp. 65–70.

> Pas vue moi-même; j'ai tiré le titre de la *Bibl.* de Carus et Engelmann.

1845. MALHERBE, A.   Description de trois espèces nouvelles du genre Picus, Linné.   < *Rev. Zool.*, viii, 1845, pp. 373–377.

> *P. (Leuconotopicus) stricklandi*, p. 373; *P. (L.) jardinii*, p. 374; *P. (L.) numidicus*, p. 375.

1845. MALHERBE, A.   Description de sept espèces nouvelles du genre Picus, Linné.   < *Rev. Zool.*, viii, 1845, pp. 399–406.

> *P. (Chloropicus) pyrrhogaster*, 399; *P. (Brachypternopicus) rubropygialis*, *P. (Chloropicus) kirkii*, p. 400; *P. (C.) rufoviridis*, p. 401; *P. (C.) xanthoderus*, p. 402; *P. (Chrysoptilopicus) smithii*, p. 403; *P. (Brachypternopicus) chrysonotus*, p. 404.

1847. GAMBEL, W.   [Note on a tridactyle woodpecker from Georgia, like P. pubescens.]   < *Proc. Acad. Nat. Sci. Phila.*, iii, 1847, p. 278.

> Same as subsequently described by W. L. Jones under name of *P. lecontei*.

1848. JONES, W. L.   Description of a new Species of Woodpecker [Picus Le Contei].   < *Ann. Lyc. Nat. Hist. New York*, iv, 1848, pp. 489, 490, pl. xvii.   (Read Mar. 13, 1847.)

> It proved to be *P. pubescens* accidentally lacking one toe.   Meanwhile, however, Bonaparte distinguished himself by making a new genus *Tridactylia* for it (*Cons. Zygod.*, 1854, 8).

1849. BIRD, W. F. W.   The New British Woodpecker [Picus villosus; cf. Zool. 2496] killed in Yorkshire.   < *Zoologist*, vii, 1849, pp. 2527, 2528.

1849. HIGGINS, E. T.   Occurrence of a supposed new British Woodpecker [Picus villosus; cf. Zool. 2527] near Whitby.   < *Zoologist*, vii, 1849, pp. 2496, 2497.

1849. MALHERBE, A.   Description de quelques nouvelles espèces de Picinées (Picus, Linn.).   < *Rev. et Mag. de Zool.*, i, 1849, pp. 529–544.

> *Picus wilsonii*, *P. temminckii*, p. 529; *P. mitchellii*, p. 530; *P. cinereigula*, p. 531; *Dendropicos hartlaubii*, p. 532; *D. lafresnayi*, p. 533; *Celeopicos smaragdinicollis*, *Phaiopicos blythii*, p. 534; *P. jerdonii*, p. 535; *Mesopicos desmuri*, p. 537; *M. cecilii*, p. 538; *Chloropicas guerini*, p. 539; *Chrysopicos cailliautii*, p. 540; *Geopicos campestroides*, p. 541; *Zebrapicus pucherani*, *Melampicos flavigula*, p. 542.

1850. MALHERBE, A.   Description de quelques espèces de Picinées; (Genus Picus, Linn).   < *Rev. et Mag. de Zool.*, ii, 1850, pp. 154–158.

> *Chloropicos isidori*, p. 154; *Chrysopicos atricollis*, p. 156, spp. nn.

1850. MALHERBE, A.   Nouvelle Classification des Picinées ou Pics, devant servir de base à une Monographie de ces Oiseaux Grimpeurs, accompagnée de planches peintes. Metz. Impr. de Lamont. July 1850. 8vo. pp. 56.

> Pas vue moi-même.   Extraite des *Mém. de l'Acad. Nat. dé Metz.*—Voir la revue de l'ouvrage par M. H. E. Strickland, inserée dans les *Contrib. Ornith. de Jardine*, 1851, pp. 17–20.

1851. BIRD, W. F. W.   Note on the Figure [Zool., 2986] of the Hairy Woodpecker (Picus villosus).   < *Zoologist*, ix, 1851, pp. 3034, 3035.

1851. NEWMAN, E. Description of the Hairy Woodpecker [Picus villosus], chiefly copied from Wilson's 'American Ornithology.' < *Zoologist*, ix, 1851, pp. 2985–2988, fig.

1851. S[TRICKLAND], H. E. Nouvelle Classification des Picinées ou Pics, . . . par M. Alfred Malherbe. 8vo. Metz, July, 1850. < *Jard. Contrib. Orn.*, 1851, pp. 17–20.
Short critical review, with a concordance of Malherbe's generic names.

1852. MALHERBE, A. Description de nouvelles espèces de Picidæ. < *Rev. et Mag. de Zool.*, iv, 1852, pp. 550–555.
Chloropicos caroli, p. 550; *Geopicos chrysoïdes*, p. 553.

1853. CASSIN, J. Descriptions of new species of Birds of the genera Melanerpes Swainson, and Lanius Linnæus. < *Journ. Acad. Nat. Sci. Phila.*, 2d ser., ii, pt. iii, Jan., 1853, art. xxiv, pp. 257, 258, pll. xxii, xxiii.
Descr. orig. *Pr. Phila. Acad.*, v, 1850–51, pp. 106, 244, 245.—Pl. xxii, *Melanerpes albolarvatus*, before described as *Leuconerpes albolarvatus*, *Pr. Phila. Acad*, v, 1850, p. 106. Pl. xxiii, f. 1, *Lanius pallidirostris ;* f. 2, *L. pallens.*

1854. LAFRESNAYE, F. DE. Sur une nouvelle espèce du genre Picumnus, Temminck. < *Rev. et Mag. de Zool.*, 1854, pp. 208, 209.
A sub-head of an article entitled "Mélanges Ornithologiques," *ibid.*, pp. 205–209; the remainder of the article relating chiefly to *Chrysothraupis* (i. e., *Calliste*). The new *Picumnus* is *P. squamulatus*, p. 208.

1854. MALHERBE, A. Nouvelles espèces de Picidae. < *J. f. O.*, ii, 1854, pp. 171, 172.
P. nataliae, p. 171; *P. cabanisi*, p. 172.

1854. MALHERBE, A. Description d'une nouvelle espèce [Indopicus carlotta] de la famille des Picidæ (Picus Linn.). < *Rev. et Mag. de Zool.*, vi, 1854, pp. 379, 380.

1854–5. MURRAY, A. On a curious habit of a Californian Woodpecker (Melanerpes formicivorus). < *Proc. Roy. Phys. Soc.*, i, 1854, pp. 1——; 1855, pp. 18——.
Not seen: the above title is probably not literally correct.

1855. ANON. Melanerpes formicivorus (Swainson). < *Edinb. New Philos. Journ.*, new ser., i, 1855, pp. 376, 377.
Containing an extract on its nut-storing habits, from Cassin's "Birds of California and Texas."

1855. MURRAY, A. On a curious habit [storing acorns in holes in bark] stated to have been observed in one of the Woodpeckers [Melanerpes formicivorus] in California. < *Edinb. New Philos. Journ.*, new ser., i, 1855, pp. 363–364.

1855. PUCHERAN, —. Note sur le Picus atrothorax Less. < *Rev. et Mag. de Zool.*, 2e sér., vii, 1855, pp. 21, 22.
Ce n'est qu'une synonyme de *Picus varius* L. (*Sphyrapicus varius* de Baird).

1856. ANTINORI, O. Picus cruentatus, Antinori, n. sp. < *Naumannia*, vi, 1856, pp. 411–414, Taf.

1856. [BILLINGS, E.] On the Species of Woodpeckers observed in the vicinity of the City of Ottawa [Canada]. < *Canad. Nat. and Geol.*, i, 1856, pp. 176–189.
Eleven spp.—Various compiled accounts.

1856. BURMEISTER, H. Ueber die brasilianischen Spechte [Picidæ]. < *Abhandl. Naturf. Gesellsch. zu Halle*, Bd. iii, Jahrg. 1555, 1856, Sitzungsber., pp. 31, 32.
Nicht mir selbst zugänglich.—Titel aus Carus and Engelmann.

1856. WEINLAND, D. F. Observations on a new genus of Tænioides [(Liga punctata), from the small intestine of Picus auratus]. < *Proc. Boston Soc. Nat. Hist.*, vi, 1856, pp. 59–63.

1857. GADAMER, [H.] Picus tridactylus [in Westgothland brütend]. < *Naumannia*, vii, 1857, Heft i, p. 86.

1858. BOLLE, C. Merkwürdige Wintermagazine zweier Spechte Nordwest-amerikas. Nach Cassin und de Saussure mitgetheilt. < *J. f. O.*, vi, 1858, pp. 316–323.
Colaptes rubricatus, Melanerpes formicivorus.

1858. BRIDGES, T. Notes on Californian Birds. With Remarks by P. L. Sclater.
P. Z. S., xxvi, 1858, pp. 1–3, pl. (Aves) cxxxi.
    Picus rubrigularis Scl., p. 2, pl. 131, sp. n. [= *P. williamsonii*, Newb., *P. R. R. Rep.*, vi, part
    iv, 1857, p. 89, pl. 34, up. fig., no descr. = *P. thyroideus* Cass., ♂].

1858. [CABANIS, J.] Dendromus meriani keine Species, sondern ein Artefact. < *J. f.*
O., vi, 1858, p. 416.

1858. MALHERBE, A. Monographie des Picidés [u. s. w.] < *Naumannia*, viii, 1858, pp.
360–363.
    Prospectus.

1858. SCLATER, P. L. Description of a new species of Woodpecker [Melanerpes rubri-
gularis] discovered by Mr. Thomas Bridges in Northern California. < *Ann.
Mag. Nat. Hist.*, 3d ser., i, 1858, p. 127.
    Cf. *P. Z. S.*, 1858, p. 2.

1859. MARSH, G. S. Occurrence of the Goldenwinged Woodpecker [Colaptes auratus]
in England. < *Zoologist*, xvii, 1859, p. 6327.

1859. PICKARD-CAMBRIDGE, O. Note on a new British Woodpecker [Picus pubescens].
< *Zoologist*, xvii, 1859, p. 6444.

1860. CLIFFORD, E. A. [On Sphyrapicus varius.] < *Prairie Farmer*, April, 1860, and
fig. in a subsequent No. of this newspaper.

1860. G[UÉRIN]-M[ÉNÉVILLE]. Monographie des Picidés. . . . par Alfred Malherbe
. . . < *Rev. et Mag. de Zool.*, xii, 1860, pp. 85–87.

1860. REINHARDT, J. En Bemærkning om den Berettigelse, hvorned Picus tridactylus er anfört i Fortegnelsen paa de i Danmark trufne Fugle. < *Vidensk. Meddel. Naturhist. Foren. Kjøbenhavn for Aaret*, 1859, 1860, pp. 97–102.

1860. SCLATER, P. L. On a new Species of Bird (Chloronerpes sanguinolentus). < *Ann.
Mag. Nat. Hist.*, 3d ser., vi, 1860, p. 80.
    From *P. Z. S.*, Jan. 25, 1859.

1861–62. MALHERBE, A. Monographie | des | Picidées | ou Histoire Naturelle | des |
Picidés, Picumnines, Yungines ou Torcols | comprenant | dans la première
partie, | L'origin mythologique, les mœurs, les migrations, l'anatomie, la phy-
siologie, la répartition géographique, | les divers systèmes de classification de
ces oiseaux grimpeurs zygodactyles, ainsi qu'un | dictionnaire alphabétique
des auteurs et des ouvrages cités par abréviation ; | dans la deuxième partie,
| La synonymie, la description en latin et en français, l'histoire de chaque
espèce, ainsi qu'un | dictionnaire alphabétique et synonymique latin de toutes
les espèces; | par | Alf. Malherbe | [etc., 6 lignes.] | — | Texte [Planches]—
Vol. I [-IV] | Metz—1861 [1862] | — | Typographie de Jules Verronnais, Im-
primeur de la Société | d'Histoire Naturelle de la Moselle | 4 vols. folio. (2
vols. texte, 2 vols. pll. color.) Texte, Vol. I, 1861, 1 p. l., pp. i–lxx (+ 6 ll. in-
terpol.), 1–214. Texte, Vol. II, 1862, 1 p. l., pp. 1–325. Planches, Vol. III,
1861, 1 p. l., pp. 1–8, pll. i–lx. Planches, Vol. IV, 1862, 1 p. l., pp. 1–6, pll.
lxi–cxxi.

1861. TREMBLY, J. B. The old time birds. < *Field Notes* (newspaper, Columbus,
Ohio), i, No. 9, Mar. 2, 1861, p. 65.
    Note of the continuance of *Hylatomus pileatus* in N. W. Ohio.

1861. WIEPKEN, C. F. Zur Naturgeschichte der Melanerpes melanopogon Licht. aus
Californien. < *Bericht über d. xiii. Versamml. der deutsch. Ornith. Gesellsch.*,
Apr., 1861, pp. 94–—.
    This article, which I have seen, though the above title is taken at second hand, refers to
    the habit the bird has of storing up acorns.

1862. LAPHAM, I. A. [Letter on the habits of Sphyrapicus varius.] < *Proc. Boston
Soc. Nat. Hist.*, ix, 1862, pp. 55, 56.

1863. BOUVÉ, T. T. [Remarks on the injury done to a house by Sphyrapicus varius.]
< *Proc. Boston Soc. Nat. Hist.*, ix, 1863, pp. 248, 249.

1863. CABANIS, J.; *and* HEINE, F. Museum Heineanum. | — | Verzeichniss | der | ornithologischen Sammlung | des | Oberamtmann | Ferdinand Heine | auf | Gut St. Burchard | vor Halberstadt. | Mit kritischen Anmerkungen und Beschreibung fast | sämmtlicher bekannten Arten systematisch bearbeitet | von | Dr. Jean Cabanis, | erstem Custos der königlichen zoologischen Sammlung in Berlin | und | Ferdinand Heine, | Stud. philos. | — | IV. Theil, | die | Klettervögel | enthaltend. | Heft 2: Spechte [Picidæ]. | — | Halberstadt, 1863. | In Commission der Frantz'schen Buchandlung (G. Loose). 8vo. Titel, pp. 1–180.

    Auch unter dem Halbtitel: Museum | Ornithologicum | Heineanum. | — | Pars IV. | Scansores. | — | Sectio II. | Picidæ.

    Die neuen genera und species dieser Arbeit sind folgende: *Pipiscus, Nannopipo*, p. 9; *Craugiscus*, p. 10; *Picumnus lepidotus*, p. 14; *P. azarae*, p. 20; *Dendrocoptes*, p. 41; *Liopipo*, p. 44; *Dendrotypes*, p. 46; *D. nesiotes*, p. 49; *Xylurgus*, p. 50; *X. subrufinus*, p. 50; *Xylocopus*, p. 51; *Baeopipo*, p. 54; *Dryobates homorus*, p. 65; *Threnopipo*, p. 70; *Cactocraugus*, p. 72; *Dictyopipo, Xenocraugus*, p. 74; *Cladoscopus*, p. 80; *Scapaneus*, p. 90; *Oniparchus*, p. 98; *Ipocrantor*, p. 99; *Phloeotomus*, p. 102; *Thriponax*, p. 105; *T. jerdoni*, p. 105; *Xylolepes*, p. 108; *Lepocestes*, p. 110; *Ipophilus*, p. 113; *Ipoctonus* (Heine, 1860) *lepidus*, p. 118; *Thripias*, p. 121; *Ipagrus*, p. 123; *Ipopatis*, p. 129 (*Stictocraugus* Heine, 1860); *Onipotheres*, p. 131; *Camponomus*, p. 137; *Phaeonerpes reichenbachi*, p. 141; *Campias*, p. 145; *C. agilis*, p. 147; *C. sedulus*, p. 153; *C. hilaris*, p. 154; *Craugasus*, p. 157; *Chrysoptilus punctipennis*, p. 163; *Geciniscus*, p. 174.

    Most of these genera are useless and burdensome synonyms, resulting from the authors' purism in rejecting prior names not "classical" in form—a practice totally indefensible, unless in exceptional cases.

    The original scope of the *Mus. Hein.*, as begun by Cabanis alone in 1850, was much enlarged in later parts by Cabanis & Heine. Thus, Theil IV. (Scansores), of which this Heft 2 consists of the *Picidæ*, amounts to a monography of the several families treated. Elaborate Latin descriptions of all the species in the collection are given, with a copious synonymy of each; and many other species are also as fully treated in German, in the foot-notes, which latter form a running commentary, especially full in synonymy and in criticism of the literary infelicities of previous writers who misspelled or misformed their generic names. The authors are careful to express their surprise at these "barbarisms" with the note of exclamation, and, what is more to the point, to give the etymology of the many new names they are pleased to invent for themselves. Cf. *Ibis*, 1865, p. 101.

1863. CASSIN, J. Notes on the Picidæ, with descriptions of new and little known species. < *Proc. Acad. Nat. Sci. Phila.*, xv, 1863, pp. 194–204, 322–328.

    61 spp. critically treated. *Picus orizabæ, P. vagatus*, p. 196; *Polipicus* (g. n., p. 196) *elliotii; Campethera vestita*, p. 197; *Chrysopicus malherbei*, p. 198; *Campephilus bairdii*, p. 322, spp. nn.; *Campethera chrysura*, var. *lineata*, p. 327, n. var.

1863. CASSIN, J. Descriptions of new and little known species of Birds of the family Picidæ in the Museum of the Academy of Natural Sciences of Philadelphia. < *Journ. Acad. Nat. Sci. Phila.*, v, pl. iv, Nov., 1863, art. x, pp. 457–461, pll. li–lii.

    Pl. li, f. 1, *Polipicus elliotii* (descr. orig. *Proc. Acad.*, 1863, 197): f. 2, *Campethera vestita* descr. orig. *l. c.*): f. 3, *Chrysopicus malherbei* (descr. orig. *l. c.*, 198). Pl. lii, f. 1, *Picus vagatus* (descr. orig. *l. c.*, 196); fig. 2, *Celeus mentalis* (descr. orig. *op. cit.*, 1860, 13).

1863. [LAPHAM, I. A.] The Sapsucker [Sphyrapicus varius]. < *Zoologist*, xxi, 1863, pp. 8767, 8768.

    From *Proc. Bost. Soc. Nat. Hist.*, ix, 1862, p. 55.

1865. BRYANT, H. Remarks on Sphyropicus varius Linn. < *Proc. Boston Soc. Nat. Hist.*, x, 1865, pp. 93–95.

    Description of hyoid apparatus, in comparison with that of *Picus villosus* and *Colaptes auratus*, and conclusions drawn as to peculiar habits of the bird.

1865. HOY, P. R. The Sapsuck [Sphyrapicus varius]. < *Trans. Illinois State Agric. Soc. for 1861–4*, v, 1865, pp. 730–734, pl.

    Habits, food, and peculiarities of hyoid apparatus. Treats also of other *Picidæ*, etc.

1866. JACKSON, C. T. [Notes on the Habit of Melanerpes formicivorus of hoarding acorns.] < *Proc. Boston Soc. Nat. Hist.*, x, 1866, p. 227.

1866. LORD, J. K. North Western Woodpeckers. < *The Intellectual Observer*, ix, 1866, pp. 321–333, 1 col. pl.

    Pl. of *Picus albolarvatus*, ♂, ♀.

1866. SUNDEVALL, C. J. Conspectum Avium Picinarum | edidit | Carolus J. Sundevall | Custos Musei Zool. Stockholmiensis. | — | Stockholmiæ 1866. | Samson & Wallin. 1 vol. 8vo. pp. i–xiv, 1–116.

    Præmonenda, pp. iii–vi; Index Operis Malherbei, pp. vii–xii; Distributio Picorum geographica, pp. xii–xiv; Conspectus Picorum. pp. 1–3: Pici species, pp. 4–94.—Picumnus, pp. 95–106.—Iynx, pp. 107–109.—Nomina et synonyma specialia Picorum, exclusis Picumnis et Iyngibus, pp. 110–115. Synopsis subgenerum Pici, pp. 115, 116.

    Pici species adprobatae 254: incertæ et spuriæ 24. Picumni species 28. Iyngis species 4.

    Synopsis subdivisionum generis Pici: Series I, *Angusticolles*, 1) *Principales*, 2) *Squamicipites*, 3) *Parvicaudati*, 4) *Auricipites*. Series II, *Securirostres*, 5) *Nigrovarii*, 6) *Intermedii*, 7) *Passerini*, 8) *Fulviscapi*, 9) *Menstrui*, 10) *Fuscorubidi*, 11) *Debilipedes*, 12) *Subvirides*. Series III, *Ligonirostres*, 13) *Dominicani*, 14) *Nigropicti*, 15) *Albofasciati*, 16) *Guttiventres*, 17) *Mesospili*, 18) *Flavinuchales*, 19) *Virides*, 20) *Chrysuri*, 21) *Aratores*, 22) *Canipilei*, 23) *Rivolii*, 24) *Aurati*, 25) *Flavifasciati*, 26) *Campestres*. Series IV, *Nudinares*, 27) *Sultanei*, 28) *Auropalliati*, 29) *Fulvicristati*, 30) *Acutirostres*.

    Picumni genus in tribus 5 divisum: 1) Picumni enormes, 2) normales, 3) subnormales, 4) abnormes, 5) innormales.

    Iyngis generis divisiones desunt.

    Species omnes Picinarum auctori obviæ optime describuntur, characteribus specierum et subspecierum datis, adjectisque synonymis, auctorum citationibus, locis, et notis variis; et suum cuique proprium locum in serie analytica adhibet auctor.

    Picorum species novæ sequentes in hoc opere descriptæ: *P. canifrons*. p. 26; *P. hedenborgii* (= *P. murinus* Sund., 1850. *nec* Malh., 1845), p. 31; *P. rubidus* (= *reichenbachi* Mus. Hein. *nec* Malh.), p. 35; *P. albipes*, p. 37; *P. scotochlorus*, p. 48; *P. imberbis* (= *Malherbei* Cass. 1863, *nec* Gray), p. 194; *P. submexicanus* (= *mexicanoides* Lafr.), p. 72; *P. flavilumbis*, p. 74; *P. pholidotus* (= *mentalis* Cass. *nec* Temm.). p. 87; *P. squamigularis*, p. 89.

    Picorum subspecies novæ ut sequuntur: *P. (rubricollis) occidentalis*, p. 6; *P. (lineatus) occidentalis*, p. 8; *P. (canente) orientalis* et *occidentalis*, p. 11: *P. (villosus) major, medius, minor*, p. 16; *P. (minor) borealis*. p. 26: *P. (varius) occidentalis*. p. 34: *P. (goertan) occidentalis*, p. 46; *P. (chrysurus) occidentalis* et *meridionalis*, p. 64: *P. aurato-mexicanus*, p. 72: *P. (sultaneus) major, indica*, p. 79; *minor*, p. 80: *P. (javanensis) major, minor*, p. 83.

    Picumnorum species novæ: *P. micromegas*. p. 95: *P. asterias*, p. 97; *P. spilogaster*, p. 100; *P. guttifer*. p. 101; *P. squamifer*. p. 102: *P. sagittatus*, p. 103; *P. nebulosus*, p. 103.

    Iynges novæ nullæ, sed Iyngis torquillæ formæ novæ septemtrionalis et meridionalis describuntur p. 108.

    Specierum Picorum cognitarum 254 sunt Americanæ 132, Europæo-Asiaticæ 90, Africæ propriæ 32.

    Inter species Pici incertæ et spuriæ sunt 15 dubiæ, 2 defectu partium non agnitæ, 3 aliorum generum Pico confusæ, 4 arte compositæ.

    "This useful publication consists of a masterly digest of M. Malherbe's great 'Monographie des Picidées,' published at Metz between 1859 and 1862. Each species is fully described, references being made to the works in which it is figured (when such is the case), and its habitat stated. Excellent indices are also added. The *Picidæ* are divided into three genera only . . . —a very different treatment of the family from that of most modern authors. We think it needless to indicate the precise limits of the smaller groups of species, or their relation to the too numerous so-called genera which have been lately instituted: for the work is one which must be consulted by any one working up the family, and its last pages contain a concise synopsis of their contents . . . The whole of this careful work is in Latin." (*Zool. Rec.*. iii. p. 77). *Cf.* also *Ibis*, 1866, pp. 415, 416.

1868. BERENDT, C. H. Report of Explorations in Central America. < (*Twenty-second*) *Ann. Rep. Smith. Inst.* (for 1867), 1868, pp. 420–426.

    Allusion to habits of a Woodpecker.

1868. KEDZIE, W. K. The Golden-winged Woodpecker [Colaptes auratus]. < *Am. Nat.*, ii, 1868, p. 382.

    Laying of 33 eggs by one pair, upon repeated spoliation of their nest.

1868. ————. Saftsugende Træpikkere. < *Tidssk. Pop. Frems. af Naturv.*, 3°. Række, v, 1868, pp. 345–347.

    "Sap-sucking Woodpeckers."

1869. BARRY, W. E.   The Woodpecker [Picus pubescens] and Sheldrake [Mergus sp.].
    < *Am. Nat.*, ii, 1869, pp. 660–662.
    Biographical notes.

1869. FOWLER, A.   The Golden-winged Woodpecker [Colaptes auratus].   < *Am. Nat.*,
    iii, 1869, pp. 422–427.
    Account of the habits of this species and of *Picus pubescens.*

1869. SAUSSURE, H. DE.   Los Picos [Picidæ].   < *La Naturaleza*, i, 1869, pp. 129–133.
    Traducido por D. Jesus Sanchez.   Sobre las costumbres del "*Colaptes rubricatus*" [i. e.,
    Melanerpes formicivorus?].

1871. STROOP, L. J.   Habits of the Red-headed Woodpecker [Melanerpes erythro-
    cephalus].   < *Am. Nat.*, iv, 1871, p. 692.
    Twenty-two individuals consecutively destroyed while trying to nest in a church-steeple.

1872. CABANIS, J.   [Ueber Centurus polygrammus.]   < *J: f. O.*, xx, 1872, pp. 157, 158.

1872. GARROD, A. H.   Note on some of the Cranial Peculiarities of the Woodpeckers.
    < *Ibis*, 3d ser., ii, 1872, pp. 357–360, woodc.
    With special reference to the presence of a bone believed to be the vomer, absence of which
    had been asserted.   The bone he mentions is situated between the palatals.

1872. THOMPSON, J. M.   The Sapsucker [Centurus carolinus].   < *Appleton's Journ.*,
    viii, Dec., 1872, p. 631.

1873. TRIPPE, T. M.   The Golden-winged Woodpecker [Colaptes auratus].   < *Am.
    Nat.*, vii, 1873, p. 498.
    Red feathers in the black cheek-patches of a male of this species from New Jersey.

1873. WHITE, C. A.   Woodpeckers [Melanerpes erythrocephalus] Tapping Sugar Trees.
    < *Am. Nat.*, vii, 1873, p. 496.
    Observed to tap sound *Acer saccharinum*, for the purpose, apparently, of feeding on the sap.

1874. FERNALD, C. H.   The Red-headed Woodpecker in Maine (Melanerpes erythro-
    cephalus Sw.).   < *Am. Nat.*, viii, 1874, pp. 437, 438.

1876. BREWSTER, W.   [Habits of] the Yellow-bellied woodpecker (Sphyrapicus va-
    rius).   < *Bull. Nutt. Ornith. Club*, i, No. 3, Sept., 1876, pp. 63–70.

1876. HERRICK, H.   Notes from Our Correspondents.   < *Forest and Stream*, v, Jan. 13,
    1876, p. 356.
    Melanerpes erythrocephalus revisiting Northern New Jersey.

1876. [INGERSOLL, E.]   A provident woodpecker (Melanerpes formicivorus).   < *Forest
    and Stream*, vii, Sept. 7, 1876, p. 68.

1876. [NEWCOMB, R. L.]   Notes from Our Correspondents.   < *Forest and Stream*, v,
    Jan. 13, 1876, p. 356.
    Deformity in tongue of *Colaptes auratus.*

1876. SALVIN, O.   [Exhibition of piece of trunk of a pine tree from Guatemala per-
    forated by Melanerpes formicivorus.]   < *P. Z. S.*, May 2, 1876, p. 414.

1877. ALDRICH, C.   The Red-Headed Woodpecker [Melanerpes erythrocephalus] Car-
    nivorus.   < *Am. Nat.*, xi, No. 5, May, 1877, p. 308.

1877. "ARROW."   The Red-Headed Woodpecker as an Egg-Sucker.   < *Forest and
    Stream*, Nov. 8, 1877, p. 256.

1877. BOUDWIN, G.   Red-Headed Woodpeckers [Melanerpes erythrocephalus].   < *For-
    est and Stream*, viii, July 26, 1877, p. 420.

1877. CALVIN, S.   On Changes of Habit among Woodpeckers.   < *Am. Nat.*, xi, No. 8,
    Aug., 1877, pp. 471, 472.

1877. COUES, E.   Letters on Ornithology.   No. 12.—Woodpeckers [Picidæ].   < *The
    Chicago Field*, Jan. 13, 1877, p. 348, figg. 6.
    General account of various North American species, with original figures of the heads of
    Picus villosus, Sphyrapicus thyroideus, ♂, ♀, *Melanerpes torquatus, M. formicivorus*, and *Co-
    laptes auratus.*

1877. LYLE, D. A.   Notes on the Breeding habits of the Golden-winged Woodpecker [Colaptes auratus].   < *Am. Nat.*, xi, No. 12, Dec., 1877, pp. 747–750.

Very close observation.   Note by E. Coues, on the molestation of this large bird by English Sparrows (*Passer domesticus*).

1877. [SCOTT, W. E. D.]   Migration of Woodpeckers [Picidæ].   < *The Country*, i, Nov. 10, 1877, p. 31

1878. ALDRICH, C.   Red-headed Woodpecker [Melanerpes erythrocephalus] eating Grasshoppers.   < *Bull. Nutt. Ornith. Club*, iii, No. 4, Oct., 1878, p. 189.

Communicated by E. C[oues].   The birds caught *Caloptenus spretus* on open prairie, half a mile from timber.

1878. ANON.   [Death of a woodpecker by fixing its bill in a piece of wood.]   < *The Country*, i, March 9, 1878, p. 261.

1878. BAILEY, H. B.   Some New Traits for the Red-headed Woodpecker [Melanerpes erythrocephalus).   < *Bull. Nutt Ornith. Club*, iii, No. 2, Apr., 1878, p. 97.

Their storing grasshoppers in cracks of wood.

1878. B[REWER], T. M.   Picoides Arcticus.   < *Forest and Stream*, xi, Oct. 31, 1878, p. 259.   See p. 300.

Correcting misstatement on p. 239.

1878. "I. N."   Fly-catching woodpeckers.   < *The Country*, i, Feb. 9, 1878, p. 213.

1878. MERRIAM, C. H.   Nesting of the Banded Three-toed Woodpecker (Picoides americanus) in Northern New York.   < *Bull. Nutt. Ornith. Club*, iii, No. 4, Oct., 1878, p. 200.

1878. "WILL."   The Woodpecker [Melanerpes erythrocephalus] as a Flycatcher.   < *Forest and Stream*, ix, Jan. 17, 1878, p. 451.

1879. ALDRICH, C.   Habits of the Red-headed Woodpecker [Melanerpes erythrocephalus].   < *Am. Nat.*, xiii, No. 8, Aug., 1879, p. 522.

With special reference to the grasshopper-eating proclivities of the bird.

1879. CALVIN, S.   On Changes of Habit among Woodpeckers [Picidæ].   < *The Oölogist*, iv, No. 11, June, 1879, pp. 91, 92.

From *Am. Nat.*, xi, No. 8, p. 471.

1879. HOYT, B. F.   Nesting under Difficulties [in the case of Colaptes auratus].   < *Science News*, i, No. 17, July 1, 1879, p. 272.

Interesting note of the finding of "six young fl.ckers (*Colaptes auratus*) in a hole which their parents had dug in the hard dry earth of a perpendicular river bank.   This hole was about six inches deep and contained no grass or lining of any kind."

1879. LINDAHL, J.   Some New Points in the Construction of the Tongues of Woodpeckers [Picidæ].   < *Am. Nat.*, xiii, No. 1, Jan., 1879, pp. 43, 44, fig.

In *Gecinus viridis* the cornua of the hyoid bone extend far into the nasal cavity of the upper mandible.   Asymmetry of the hyoid cornua in other species (but this is well known).

1879. MAYNARD, C. J.   The Food of Woodpeckers [Picidæ].   < *Scientific Farmer* (Boston), iv, No. 4, Apr., 1879, pp. 50, 51, 2 cuts.

The figures illustrate bark bored by *Melanerpes formicivorus* to insert acorns, and the stomach of *Colaptes auratus*.

1879. RAGSDALE, G. H.   Lewis Woodpecker [Asyndesmus torquatus] in Middle Texas.   < *Temperance Vedette* (Terrell, Tex.), Aug. 2, 1879.

1879. RAGSDALE, G. H.   Centurus aurifrons.   < *Science News*, i, No. 20, Aug. 15, 1879, p. 320.

On its local distribution in Texas.

1879. RAGSDALE, G. H.   Centurus aurifrons.   < *Temperance Vedette* (newspaper of Terrell, Texas), Sept. 13, 1879.

From *Science News*.   On the local distribution of the species in Texas.

1879. RAGSDALE, G. H.   Lewis' Woodpecker [Asyndesmus torquatus] in Middle Texas.   < *Science News*, i, No. 13, May 1, 1879, p. 208.

1879. SMITH, Q. C.   Woodpeckers and Road-runners [Geococcyx californianus].   < *Temperance Vedette* (newspaper of Terrell, Texas), Nov. 1, 1879.

1879. WINTLE, E. D.   Pileated Woodpecker [Hylotomus pileatus] in Canada.   < *Forest and Stream*, xiii, Jan. 1, 1879, p. 946.

Trochilidæ.

1671. [WINTHROP, J.]   A further Accompt of the Stellar Fish; formerly described in Numb. 57, p. 1153; with the Addition of some other Curiosities.   < *Philos. Trans.*, vi, 1671, pp. 2221–2224.

P. 2223, description of nest and eggs of the bird subsequently known as *Trochilus colubris;* nest weighed 24 grains; one egg about 5 grains, the other 3½ grains.

1693. GREW, N.   The Description of the American Tomineius, or Humming Bird, communicated by Nehemiah Grew, M. D. and Fellow of the Royal Society.   < *Philos. Trans.*, xvii, 1693, pp. 760, 761.

Description by Mr. Hamersly, of Coventry; vague and general, but pointing to the bird afterward known as *Trochilus colubris.*

1693. GREW, N.   A Query put by Dr. N. Grew, concerning the food of the Humming Bird; occasioned by the Description of it in the Transactions. Numb. 200. < *Philos. Trans.*, xvii, 1693, p. 815.

Whether it be juice of flowers, or small insects. The question was thus opened very early.

1698. BULLIVANT, B.   Part of a Letter from Mr. Benjamin Bullivant, at Boston, in New England; to Mr. James Petiver, Apothecary, and Fellow of the Royal Society, in London.   Concerning some Natural Observations he had made in those Parts.   < *Philos. Trans.*, xx, 1698, pp. 167, 168.

Feeding a "Hum-bird" (*i. e., Trochilus colubris*) in captivity with honey.

1777. ————.   Description d'un Oiseau-Mouche.   < *Obs. et Mém. sur la Phys.* (*Rozier,*) ix, 1777, pp. 466, 467, fig.

Pas vue moi-même—le titre tiré de Carus and Engelmann.

1778. BADIER, —.   Sur la nourriture des Colibris [Trochilidæ].   < *Obs. et Mém. sur la Phys.*, xi, 1778, pp. 32, 33.

Not seen.

1802. AUDEBERT, J. B., *and* VIEILLOT, L. P.   Histoire | Naturelle | et Générale | des Colibris, | Oiseaux-Mouches, | Jacamars et Promerops ; | [mut. mut.] | Par J. B. Audebert et L. P. Vieillot. | — | A Paris, | chez Desray, Libraire, Rue Hautefeuille, N° 36. | An XI = 1802. | [De l'imprimerie de Crapelet.] **gr.** folio. 2 vols. Vol. I, 2 p. ll., pp. i–x, 1–128, pll. 1–70; pp. 1–8, pll. 1–6; pp. 1–28, pll. 1–9. Vol. II, 2 p. ll., pp. 1–128, pll. 1–88 ; pp. 1–40, pll. 1–16.

Contents of Vol. I.

Oiseaux dorés | ou | a reflets métalliques. | — | Tome Premier. | 1 leaf, backed with Crapelet's imprint.

Title-page of Vol. I, as above, 1 leaf, backed blank.

Advertisement, pp. i–viii.   List of subscribers, pp. ix, x.   Preface, pp. 1–4.

Histoire Naturelle des Colibris et des Oiseaux-Mouches, pp. 5–128, pll. 1–70.

Histoire Naturelle | des Jacamars. | Par L. P. Vieillot. | pp. 1–8, pll. 1–6.

Histoire Naturelle | des Promerops. | Par L. P. Vieillot, Naturaliste-Voyageur. | pp. 1–22, pll. 1–9.

Table générale des matières [pour les Colibris, les Jacamars et les Promerops], pp. 23–28.

Contents of Vol. II.

Oiseaux dorés | ou | a reflets métalliques. | — | Tome second. | 1 leaf, backed with Crapelet's imprint.

Title page of Vol. II, as follows : | Histoire Naturelle | et Générale | des Grimpereaux | et | des Oiseaux de Paradis. | Par J. B. Audebert et L. P. Vieillot. | — | A Paris, | chez Desray, Libraire, Rue Hautefeuille, N° 36. | An XI = 1802. | 1 leaf, backed blank.

Histoire Naturelle des Grimpereaux Souï-Mangas. pp. 1–68, pll. 1–41.

Histoire Naturelle des Grimpereaux Guit-guits. pp. 69–84, pll. 42–51.

Histoire Naturelle des Grimpereaux Héoro-taires. pp. 85–106, pll. 52–71.

1802. AUDEBERT, J. B., *and* **VIEILLOT, L. P.—Continued.**

Histoire Naturelle des Grimpereaux.   pp. 107–128, pll. 72–88.

Histoire Naturelle | des | Oiseaux de Paradis. | pp. 1–34, pll. 1–16.

Table générale des matières.   pp. 35–40.

The composition of the whole work is not evident at first sight.   As consisting of two vols. folio, the general title is simply OISEAUX DORÉS OU À REFLETS MÉTALLIQUES, by Audebert and Vieillot, and such is the preliminary half-title printed on the first leaf of each vol.

But the full title-page of Vol. I is as above given.   It includes the Colibris and Oiseaux-Mouches (= *Trochilidæ*), by both authors; then the Jacamars (*Galbulidæ*) by Vieillot, separately paged and half-titled, plates separately numbered; then the Promerops (*Upupidæ, Promeropidæ*, etc.) by Vieillot, also half-titled, separately paged, and the plates separately numbered. The vol. closes with a table of contents of the whole, continuously paged with Promerops.

Vol. II is still more composite as to the birds treated, but has only two paginations and two numerations of plates.   The preliminary title is Oiseaux dorés, etc., as before, Vol. II. The full-page title is as given above under "Contents"; but the "Grimperaux" of the full title are subdivided by a sort of chapter-headings into "Grimpereaux Souï-Mangas", "Grimpereaux Guit-guits", "Grimpereaux Héoro-taires", and "Grimpereaux"; continuously paged, their plates continuously numbered.   Then the "Oiseaux de Paradis" are half-titled, separately paged, and their plates separately numbered.   The vol. closes with a table of contents of the whole, continuously paged with Oiseaux de Paradis.

The "Grimpereaux" are a most miscellaneous lot of birds, about equal to the Linnæan *Certhia*; including *Meliphagidæ, Cœrebidæ, Sylvicolidæ, Dendrocolaptidæ*, etc.   The Paradise birds are less composite, but still include others than the *Paradiseidæ* of modern authors.

The work is said to have been published in 32 livraisons, the dates of which are unknown to me.   The date above given is that of the title-page of each vol., being the completion of the work.   There are said to be actually 192 places, though the ostensible series is 70 + 6 + 9 + 88 + 16 = 189.   The edition is said to have been of 200 copies.   There are said to have been also 100 copies printed on vellum, and 10 copies printed with gold instead of black ink.   In the copy examined, in the Libr. Phila. Acad., the names on the plates are all in gold.

Fortunately or otherwise, no scientific nomenclature is used in this luxurious work.   It should be used in connection with Vieillot's article "Colibri" in *Nouv. Dict. d'Hist. Nat.*, vii, 1817, which see.

1804. BARTON, B. S.   Facts relative to the Food of the Humming-Bird [Trochilus colubris].   < *Barton's Med. and Phys. Journ.*, part i, vol. i, 1804, pp. 88, 89.

"— that the *Trochilus* does actually subsist, in part, upon the different species of insects."

1817. V[IEILLOT, L. P.]   Colibri, Trochilus, Lath.   < *Nouv. Dict. d'Hist. Nat.*, vii, 1817, pp. 340–376, pll. B 38, B 19.

In Audebert and Vieillot's ouvrage de luxe, *Oiseaux dorés ou à reflets métalliques*, which was completed in 1802, no scientific names are given to the Hummers and other glittering birds so beautifully depicted; but in the present article, Vieillot names many species in due form, with references to the plates of the *Ois. dor..* as follows:—*T. caudacutus*, V., p. 247; *T. multicolor*. Lath., p. 347; *T. azar*, V.. p. 347; *T. superciliosus*, Lath., p. 347 (pll. 17, 18 of *Ois. Dor.*); *T. fuscus*, V.. p. 348; *T. galeritus*, Lath., p. 348; *T. cinereus*, Lath., p. 348 (pl. 5 of *O. D.*), *T. leucurus*, Lath., p. 348; *T. nigricollis*, V., p. 349; *T. fulvifrons*, Lath., p. 349; *T. flavifrons*, Lath., p. 349; *T. granatinus*, Lath., p. 350 (pl. 4 of *O. D.*); *T. aurulentus*, Audeb., p. 350 (pll. 12, 13 of *O. D.*); *T. elegans*, Audeb., p. 351 (pl. 14 of *O. D.*); *T. pectoralis*, Lath., p. 351; *T. para diseus*, Lath., p. 352; *T. cristatellus*, Lath., p. 352; *T. hirsutus*. p. 352 (pl. 20 of *O. D.*); *T. thau mantias*, Lath., p. 353; *T. mango*, Lath., p. 353 (pl. 7 of *O. D.*); *T. mango;* var., p. 353; *T. quad ricolor*, V., p. 353; *T. viridis*, V., p. 354 (pl. 41 of *O. D.*); *T. torquatus*, Lath., p. 354; *T. atrica pillus*, V., p. 354; *T. polytmus*, Lath., p. 355 (pl. 47 of *O. D.*); *T. pella*. Lath., p. 355 (pll. 2, 3 of *O. D.*); *T. exilis*, Lath., p. 356; *T. atrigaster*, V., p. 356 (pl. 65 of *O. D.*); *T. punctatus*, Lath., p. 357 (pl. 8 of *O. D.*); *T. viridis*, V. [not *viridis* of p. 354], p. 357 (pl. 15 of *O. D.*); *T. brasiliensis*, Lath., p. 357 (pl. 19 of *O. D.*); *T. holosericeus*, Lath., p. 357 (pl. 6 of *O. D.*); *T. violaceus*, Lath., p. 358; *T. punctulatus*, Lath., p. 358; *T. amethystinus*, Lath., p. 358; *T. albirostris*, V., p. 359 (pl. 45 of *O. D.*); *T. serrirostris*, V., p. 359; *T. cinereus*, V., p. 359; *T. mellivorus*, Lath., p. 360 (pll. 22. 23, 24 of *O. D.*); *T. obscurus*, Lath., p. 361; *T. splendidus*, V., p. 361; *T. ourissia*, Lath., p. 361; *T. carbunculus*, Lath., p. 361 (pl. 5 of *O. D.*); *T. cœruleus*, V., p. 361 (pl. 40 of *O. D.*); *T. maculatus*, V., p. 361 (pl. 44 of *O. D.*); *T. ruficollis*, V., p. 362; *T. leucogaster*, Lath., p. 363 (pl. 43 of *O. D.*); *T. mellisugus*, Lath., p. 363 (pl. 39 of *O. D.*); *T. maximus*, Lath., p. 364; *T. ornatus*, Lath., p. 364 (pl. 49 of *O. D.*); *T. cristatus*, Lath., p. 365; *T. pileatus*, Lath., p. 365 (pl. 63 of *O. D.*); *T. latipennis*, Lath., p. 365 (pl. 21 of *O. D.*); *T. longirostris*, V., p. 366 (pl. 59 of *O. D.*); *T. macrorus*, Lath., p. 366; *T. forficatus*, Lath., p. 366 (pl. 60 of *O. D.*); *T. magnificus*, V., p. 367; *T. marmoratus*, V., p. 367; *T. maugœus*, V., p. 368 (pl. 37 of *O. D.*); *T. auritus*, Lath., p. 368 (pl 25, 26 of *O. D.*); *T. minimus*, Lath., p. 369; *T. ruber*. Lath.. p. 369; *T. cyanurus* V.. p. 369; *T. glaucopis*,

1817. V[IEILLOT], L. P.—Continued.

Lath., p. 370 ; *T. ruficaudatus*, V., p. 370 (pll. 27, 28 of *O. D.*) ; *T. platurus*, Lath., p. 370 (pl. "98" of *O. D.*); *T. colubris*, Lath., p. 371 (pll. 31, 32, 33 of *O. D.*) ; *T. rubineus*, Lath., p. 371 ; *T. moschitus*, Lath., p. 372 (pl. 55 of *O. D.*) ; *T. saphirinus*, Lath., p. 373 (pll. 35, 57, 58 of *O. D.*) ; *T. bicolor*, Lath., p. 373 (pl. 36 of *O. D.*) ; *T. collaris*, Lath., p. 374 (pll. 61, 62 of *O. D.*) ; *T. leucocrotaphus*, V., p. 374 ; *T. cyanocephalus*, Lath., p. 375 ; *T. viridissimus*, var., p. 375 (pl. 40 of *O. D.*); *T. guianensis*, Lath., p. 375 ; *T. furcatus*, Lath., p. 376 (pl. 34 of *O. D.*). The article acquires consequence from thus furnishing a technical nomenclature to the *Oiseaux Dorés*. Most, if not all, of the species marked " V." are technically new. Many of the rest, attributed to Latham, are really Gmelinian, Linnæan, or other names.—See 1802, AUDEBERT and VIEILLOT.

1822. MAXIMILIAN, —. Ueber die Nahrung der Fliegenvögel (Trochilus) [Trochilidæ]. < *Oken's Isis*, Jahrg. vi, 1822, pp. 470–472.

1824. BULLOCK, [W.] Ueber Colibris. < *Fror. Notiz.*, ix, No. 183, 1824, pp. 100–104.

Nicht mir selbst zugänglich—Titel aus C. u. E. *Bibl.* Aus dessen ,, Six Months' Residence in Mexico " (London, 1824).

1824. WILSON, —. Note sur l'anatomie de l'Oiseau-mouche. < *Bull. Sc. Médic.*, —, 1824, pp. 9– —.

Not seen—title from Giebel.

1827. VOIGT, —. W. Bullock über die Colibri's. (Aus dessen : Six Month's Residence in Mexico etc. London 1824.) < *Ornis*, Heft iii, 1827, pp. 98–111.

1828. [LESSON, R. P.] Histoire Naturelle des Oiseaux-Mouches ; par R. P. Lesson. . . . < *Féruss. Bull.*, 2ᵉ sect., xv, 1828, pp. 303, 304.

Extrait du Prospectus de cet ouvrage.

1828. RENNIE, J. Nahrung des Colibri. < *Fror. Notiz.*, xxiii, No. 488, 1828, p. 54.

Nicht mir selbst zugänglich—Titel aus Carus u. Engelmann.

1829. ANON. Histoire naturelle des oiseaux mouches, par Lesson. Paris chez A. Bertrand. 29, gr. 8 ; libr. 1, 2 ; pl. illum. < *Oken's Isis*, Bd. xxii, 1829, p. 785.

1829. ANON. Histoire naturelle des Oiseaux-Mouches ; par M. R. P. Lesson. . . . < *Féruss. Bull.*, 2ᵉ sect., xvii, 1829, pp. 123, 124.

1829. ANON. Histoire naturelle des Oiseaux-Mouches ; par R. P. Lesson, . . . < *Féruss. Bull.*, 2ᵉ sect., xvi, 1829, pp. 281, 282.

1829. ANON. Histoire naturelle des Oiseaux-Mouches : par R. P. Lesson. . . . < *Féruss. Bull.*, 2ᵉ sect., xix, 1829, pp. 352, 353.

1829. ANON. Histoire naturelle des Oiseaux-Mouches, etc. ; par M. R. P. Lesson, . . . *Féruss. Bull.*, 2ᵉ sect., xvi, 1829, pp. 462, 463.

This and the four preceding anonymous titles of similar character are simply notices of the livraisons of the work as they successively appeared ; some of them are signed "D."

1829. LESSON. R. P. Histoire Naturelle | des | Oiseaux-Mouches, | ouvrage orné de planches | dessinées et gravées par les meilleurs artistes, | et dédié | A S. A. R. Mademoiselle ; | Par R. P. Lesson, | [etc., 8 lignes. | [Quotation.] | — | Paris. | Arthus Bertrand, Libraire, | éditeur du voyage autour du monde du capitaine Duperrey, | Rue Hautefeuille, Nº 23. | No date. (1829.) 8vo. pp. i–xlvj, 1–223; pll. color. 1–85, + 48 bis (86 plates in all).

Published in 17 livraisons, beginning Jan. 1829 ; and ending Sept., 1829. This is the original series of Lesson's illustrations of Humming-birds, from which the two succeeding ones and Index Général are to be carefully distinguished. pp. i–xlvj, title, dedication, advertisement (latter dated 10 janvier 1829). and tableau des espèces décrites et figurées dans cette histoire naturelle (mai 1829) ; 1–223, the regular text ; to this belongs the original series of 1–85 (86) plates. This set of plates and accompanying text is citable as one work under the above title, commonly called "Oiseaux-Mouches." The work is found bound in 1 vol., text and plates ; or in 2 vols., one of letter-press, the other of plates ; or text bound with that of Lesson's two other series of Hummers, the "Colibris" and the "Trochilidées." The plates are either plain or colored ; or both, in duplicate sets. Compare the other titles given beyond, at 1830–31, and 1832. same author.

The *Trochilidæ* figured and described in this work are:—Plate 1. *Ornismya petasophora.* p. 37. 2, *O. superba*, p. 40. 3, *O. tristis*, p. 43. 4, *O. rivolii*, p. 48. 5, *O. cyanopogon*, p. 50. 6, *O. cora*, p. 52. 7, 8, *O. chrysolopha*, p. 55. 9, *O. arsennii*, p. 60. 10, 11, *O. aurita*, p. 63. 12, 13,

1829. LESSON, R. P.—Continued.

O. amazili, p. 67. 14, *O. sephaniodes*, p. 69. 15, *O. heteropygia*, p. 72. 16, *O. nattererii*, p. 75. 17, *O. cephalatra*, p. 78. 18, *O. furcata*, p. 82. 19, *O. vesper*, p. 85. 20, *O. temminckii*, p. 88. 21, 22, *O. mellivora*, p. 90. 23, 24, *O. delalandi*, p. 95. 25, *O. hirundinacea*, p. 98. 26, *O. langs-dorffii*, p. 102. 27, 28, *O. sapho*, p. 205. 29, 30, *O. mesoleuca*, p. 110. 31, 32, *O. cristata*, p. 113. 33, *O. simplex*, p. 119. 34, *O. simplex*, p. 121. 35. *Campylopterus ensipennis*, p. 124. 36, *Tro-chilus falcatus*, p. 126. 37, *T. recurvirostris*, p. 129. 38, 39, *T. lugubris*, p. 132. 40, *Ornismya platura*, p. 136. 41, *O. ornata*, p. 139. 42, 43, *O. strumaria*, p. 143. 44, 45, 46, *O. rubinea*, p. 146. 47, *O. amethystina*. 48, 48 bis, *O. colubris*, p. 151. 49, 50, *O. bicolor*, p. 161. 51, *O. audeberti*, p. 164. 52, 53, 54, *O. moschita*, p. 166. 55, 56, 57, *O. sapphirina*, p. 172. 58, 59, *O. glaucopis*, p. 175. 60, *O. viridis*, p. 178. 61, *O. erythronotos*, p. 181. 62, *O. tephrocephalus*, p. 182. 63, *O. albicollis*, p. 184. 64, *O. vieillotii*, p. 186. 65, *O. prasina*, p. 188. 66, 67, *O. sasin*, p. 190. 68, 69, *O. maugei*, p. 194. 70, *O. swainsonii*, p. 197. 71, *O. cyanea*, p. 199. 72, *Trochilus multicolor*, p. 201. 73, *Ornismya waglerii*, p. 203. 74, *O. anna*, p. 205. 75, *O. viridissima*, p. 207. 76, *O. albiventris*, p. 209. 77, *O. brevirostris*, p. 211. 78, *O. albirostris*, p. 212. 79, *O. minima*, p. 213. 80, *O. clementiœ*, p. 216. 81, generic characters. 82, 83, 84, 85, nests. The Tableau des espèces records 58 spp., all under "*Ornismya*," nob., p. x, but rearranged under the "tribes" *Cynanthus* Sw., p. xj; *Phœthornis* Sw., p. xviij; *Platurus*, nob., p. xxij; *Lam-pornis* Sw., p. xxiij; *Lophornis*, nob., p. xxvij; *Camphylopterus* Sw.; to which 58 spp. there are added (Sept., 1829) *O. clemenciœ*, which was figured pl. 80, but omitted from the Tableau, and *O. cyanocephalus*, nob., p. xlv. Nearly all these species are described as if new—Lesson even giving them new specific names when he quotes older ones, a common practice with this author.

1829. LYON, *Capt.* Extract of a Letter from Capt. Lyon, R. N., Corr. Memb. Z. S., &c., to a Friend in England, dated Gongo Soco, Brazil, 17th March, 1829. < *Zool. Journ.*, v, 1829, pp. 1, 2, figs. 1, 2.

Relating to the nidification of a species of Humming-bird, which increased the capacity of the nest with the growth of the young.

1829. RENNIE, J. Food of the Humming bird. < *Loudon's Mag. Nat. Hist.*, i, 1829, pp. 371, 372.

1830. ANON. Histoire naturelle des Oiseaux Mouches; par R. P. Lesson . . . < *Féruss. Bull.*, 2ᵉ sect., xxi, 1830, pp. 142 and 320.

1830. [LESSON, R. P.] Histoire naturelle des Colibris, suivie d'un supplément à l'His-toire naturelle des Oiseaux-Mouches; par R. P. Lesson. . . . < *Féruss. Bull.*, 2ᵉ sect., xxii, 1830, pp. 323–325.

Prospectus.

1830–31. LESSON, R. P. Histoire Naturelle | des Colibris, | suivie | d'un supplément | a l'histoire naturelle | des | Oiseaux-Mouches; | ouvrage orné de planches | des-sinées et gravées par les meilleurs artistes, | et dédié | A M. le Baron Cuvier. | Par R. P. Lesson. | [Quotation, 9 lignes.] | — | Paris. | Arthus Bertrand, Li-braire, | éditeur du voyage autour du monde du capitaine Duperrey, | Rue Hautefeuille, Nº 23. | No date. (1830–31.) 8vo. pp. i–x, 1–196; pll. 1–25, 12 bis, 13 bis (Colibris), 1–39 (Suppl. Ois.-Mouches) = 66 plates in all.

Published in 13? livraisons, monthly or thereabouts, each of 5 or 6 plates and accompanying letter-press, beginning Oct., 1830, and ending Dec., 1831. This is the second series of Les-son's Hummers, consisting of "Colibris" and "Supplément Oiseaux-Mouches," the two por-tions of this work being continuously paged, but the two sets of plates being separately enumerated: pp. i–x, title, dedication, and preface; pp. 1–90, text of Colibris; pp. 91–192, text of Suppl. Ois.-Mouch.; pp. 193–196, Indexes to each; pll. 1–25, 12 *bis*, 13 *bis*, for Colibris, pll. 1–39 for Suppl. Ois.-Mouches. The text of this work is citable as "Col. et Suppl. Ois.-Mouch.," but in citing the plates, it must be specified which series is meant. Compare same author at 1829 and 1832.

The following are figured and described in "Colibris:"—Pl. 1, *Ramphodon* (g. n.) *macu-latum*, p. 18. 2, 3, 4, 5, *Trochilus pella*, pp. 21, 27, 31, 33. 6, 7, *T. superciliosus*, pp. 35, 38. 8, *T. squalidus*, p. 40. 9, *T. rufigaster*, p. 43. 10, *T. auratus*, p. 46. 11, *T. viridis*, p. 50. 12, 12 bis, *T. gramineus*, pp. 52, 56. 13, 13 bis, 14, *T. mango*, pp. 58, 62, 64. 15, *T. nitidus*, p. 66. 16, 17, 18, 19, *T. aurulentus*, pp. 68, 71, 73, 74. 20, *T. holosericeus*, p. 76. 21, *T. hirsutus*. 22, *T. leu-curus*. 23, *T. simplex*, p. 86. 24, *T. prevostii*, p. 87. 25, Détails anatomiques et caractères des Colibris.

In the "Suppl. Ois.-Mouches" are described and figured the following:—Pl. 1, *Ornismya du-pontii*, p. 100. 2, *O. audenetii*, p. 102. 3, *O. anais*, p. 104. 4, *O. chrysura*, p. 107. 5, *O. sepha-nioides*, p. 109. 6, *O. simplex*, p. 111. 7, *O. anna*. 8, *O. clemenciœ*, p. 115. 9, 10, *O. cyano-pogon*, pp. 117, 119. 11, 12, 13, *O. sasin*, pp. 121, 123, 124. 14, *O. tricolor*, p. 125. 15, *O. pampa*,

1830–31. LESSON, R. P.—Continued.

p. 127. 16, *O. langsdorffii*, p. 129. 17, 18, *O. cyanocephala*, pp. 132, 134. 19, *O. delalandii*, p. 136. 20, 21, 22, *O. amethystina*, pp. 138, 141, 142. 23, *O. cyanea*, p. 143. 24, *O. avocetta*, p. 145. 25, *O. eriphile*, p. 148. 26, *O. wiedii*, p. 150. 27, *O. arsennii*, p. 152. 28, 29, *O. arsenoe*, pp. 154, 156. 30, *O. oenone*, p. 157. 31, *O. platura*, p. 159. 32, *O. chrysolopha*, p. 162. 33, *O. superba*, p. 164. 34, *O. recurvirostris*, p. 166. 35, *O. nuna*, p. 169. 36, *O. dumerilii*, p. 172. 37, 38, *O. canivetii*, pp. 174, 177. 39, *O. hirundinasea*, p. 179.

1830. LODDIGES, [G.] [Cephallepis, g. n.] $< P. Z. S.$, i, 1830, p. 12.

1830. SCHIEDE, —, *and* DEPPE, —. Humming Bird and Insects at a great height on the Volcano of Orizaba. $< Edinb. New Philos. Journ.$, viii, 1830, pp. 203, 204.

1830. VIGORS, N. A. [Characters of a New Species of Humming-bird, Trochilus loddigesii Gould.] $< P. Z. S.$, i, 1830, p. 12.

1831. ANON. Histoire naturelle des Oiseaux-Mouches, par R. P. Lesson. . . . $< Féruss. Bull.$, 2ᵉ sect., xxiv, 1831, pp. 200–202.
This is simply one of the many notices of Lesson's works on Hummers which appeared in this Bulletin during the progress of the publication.

1831. ANON. Histoire naturelle des Colibris, . . . ; par R. P. Lesson. . . . $< Féruss. Bull.$, 2ᵉ sect., xxiv, 1831, p. 202.

1831. ANON. Histoire naturelle des Colibris, . . . ; par R. P. Lesson. . . . $< Fé. russ. Bull.$, 2ᵉ sect., xxv, 1831, pp. 118, 119.

1831. ANON. Les Trochilidées ou les Colibris, et les Oiseaux-Mouches; par R.-P. Lesson. . . . $< Féruss. Bull.$, 2ᵉ sect., xxvi, 1831, pp. 77–79.
Prospectus.

1831. LYON, *Capt.* [Ueber das Nest der Colibri.] $< Oken's Isis$, Bd. xxiv, 1831, p. 714.
Auszug aus den *Zool. Journ.*, Bd. v, No. xvii, 1829, pp. 1, 2.

1831. VIGORS, N. A. [Remarks on exhibition of several species of Humming-birds.] $< Philos. Mag.$, ix, 1831, p. 62.
From *P. Z. S.*, i, Dec. 14, 1830, p. 12, *q. v.* for an n. sp.

1832. LESSON, R. P. Les | Trochilidées | ou | les Colibris | et | les Oiseaux-Mouches, | suivis d'un Index Général, | dans lequel sont décrites et classées méthodiquement toutes les races | et espèces du genre Trochilus. | Ouvrage orné de planches | dessinées et gravées par les meilleurs artistes, | par R. P. Lesson. | Splendet ut sol. | Marcgrave. | — | Paris. | Arthus Bertrand, Libraire, | éditeur du voyage autour du monde par le Capitaine Duperrey, | rue Hautefeuille, nº 23. | No date. (1832.) 8vo. pp. i–iv, 1–171, i–xliij (Index Général), pll. 1–66.

The Index separately titled as well as paged, thus : Index | Général et Synoptique des oiseaux | du | Genre Trochilus, | Par R. P. Lesson. | — | Paris. | Arthus Bertrand, Libraire, | éditeur du voyage autour du monde par le capitaine Duperrey, | rue Hautefeuille, nº 23. | — | M DCCC XXXII. 8vo. pp. i–xliij.

Published in 13? livraisons, monthly or thereabouts, each of 5 plates and accompanying letter-press. The "Colibris" was finished in Dec., 1831, and the preface to the "Trochilidées" is dated 1831: but probably nothing appeared until 1832, which latter is the date of completion of the work, on the title of the Index Général. Compare same author, at 1829 and 1830–31.
In this, the third and last series of Lesson's Hummers, are described and figured :—Plate 1, *O. colubris*. p. 1. 2, *Troch. longuemareus*, p. 15. 3, *T. mazeppa*, p. 18. 4, *O. cristata*, p. 20. 5, *T. buffonii*, p. 31. 6, *O. vesper*, p. 33. 7, *O. viridissima*, p. 35. 8, 9, 10, 11, *O. vieillotii*, pp. 37, 41, 44, 46. 12, *O. petasophora*, p. 48. 13, *T. davidianus*, p. 50. 14, *O. sapphirina*, p. 53. 15, *O. moschita*, p. 55. 16, 17, *O. bicolor*, pp. 58, 60. 18, *T. bourcieri*, p. 62. 19, *T. intermedius*, p. 65. 20, 21, *T. pella*, pp. 68, 70. 22, *O. cyanea*, p. 72. 23, *O. avocetta*, p. 74. 24. *O. ornata*, p. 77. 25, 26, 27, *O. amethystoides*, pp. 79, 81, 83. 28, 29, *O. orthura*, pp. 85, 88. 30, nid de l'ois.-mouche Améthyste, avec son œuf., p. 90. 31, *T. eurynome*, p. 91. 32, *O. albiventer*, p. 94. 33, *O. viridis*, p. 96. 34, *O. superba*, p. 99. 35, *O. langsdorffii*, p. 101. 36, *O. gouldii*, p. 103. 37, *O. underwoodii*, p. 105. 38, *O. kingii*, p. 107. 39, 40, *O. cora*, pp. 109, 111. 41, *O. delalandii*, p. 113. 42, *O. atala*, p. 115. 43, *O. sasin*, p. 117. 44, *O. guy*, p. 119. 45, *O. mesoleuca*, p. 122, 46, 47, *T. eusipennis*, pp. 124, 127. 48, *O. vesper*, p. 129. 49, *O. sapho*, p. 131. 50, *T. stokesii*, p. 135. 51, *T. loddigesii*, p. 138. 52, *O. amethystina*, p. 140. 53, *O. coeligena*, p. 141. **54**, *O.*

1832. LESSON, R. P.—Continued.

viridis, p. 144. 55, 56, *Ramphodon anais*, pp. 146, 148. 57, *Ornismya! anais*, p. 151. 58, *O. cristata* (nid), p. 153. 59, *O. petasophora*, p. 154. 60, *O. tricolor*, p. 156. 61, *O. nattererii*, p. 158. 62, *T. longuemareus*, p. 160. 63, 64, *O. montana*, pp. 161, 163. 65, *O. kieneri*, p. 165. 66, *O. swainsonii*, p. 167.

In the Index Général, 1832, the 110 spp. treated in all three of Lesson's series of Hummers are rearranged systematically, according to the author's classification, in 27 "races" and sundry "tribes," with short characters and synonymy. *Lesbia* Less., p. xvij; *Cœligena* Less., p. xviij.

These three books may be found bound in different ways: generally, with text of all three together, and plates in three separate vols. Index Général belongs to "Trochilidées," as per title of the latter, but is separately titled and paged. There are in the whole series 86 + 66 + 66 = 218 plates, but only about 110 species are treated. There are both plain and colored issues of the plates—both together, in the copy examined.

These three books are hard to get the hang of; the titles are so curiously mixed up that there is endless confusion in citing them, especially at second-hand. The three separate series are perfectly distinct works, bibliographically speaking, yet represent a single monograph of the Hummers, with titles enough alike to be confusing, yet not different enough to be distinctive until they are studied out. The following summary may therefore be useful:

LESS., "Ois.-Mouch.", pp. i-xlvj, 1-233, pll. 1-48, 48 *bis*., 49-85 (86 plates). Date, 1829.

LESS., "Colibris et Suppl. Ois.-Mouch.", pp. i-x, 1-196 (*Colibris*, pp. 1-90; *Suppl. O.-M.*, pp. 91-192). *Colibris*, pll. 1-12, 12 *bis*, 13 *bis*, 14-25. *Suppl. O.-M.*, pll. 1-39 (66 plates in the two series). Date, 1830-'31.

LESS., "Trochilidées," pp. i-iv, 1-171, pll. 1-66. Date, 1832.

Index Général, pp. i-xliij, no plates. Date, 1832.

Lesson's work on the Hummers is notable as one of the earliest extensive monographies of this extraordinary family of birds, being only preceded by that of Audebert and Vieillot. It treats, however, of only about one-third of the species now known, and its claims as a contribution to science are not of the highest. The plates are finely finished, being good work of this French kind, and when colored become very pretty pictures; but the technic of the work, as already hinted, is of moderate merit. Many new species and several new genera are named, and various species are renamed even when the author knew and cited their prior designations—a reprehensible habit which Lesson not seldom indulged.

It appears from *Rev. Zool.*, iii. 1840, p. 71, that Lesson intended to publish a fourth vol.; but it remained ined.

1832. LODDIGES, G. [Characters of Four New Species of Humming-birds from Popayan, in the Collection of John Gould.] < *P. Z. S.*, ii, 1832, pp. 6, 7.

Trochilus tyrianthinus, p. 6; *T. eurypterus*, *T. flavescens*, *T. gouldii*, p. 7.

1832. LODDIGES, G. [Exhibition and characters of several Humming Birds from Popayan.] < *Philos. Mag.*, xi, 1832, p. 461.

From *P. Z. S.*, Jan. 10, 1832, pp. 6, 7, *q. v.*

1832. WATERTON, C. Humming-birds. < *London's Mag. Nat. Hist.*, v, 1832, pp. 473-476.

Miscellaneous notes of habits.

1832. WATERTON, C. The Green Humming-bird. < *London's Mag. Nat. Hist.*, v, 1832, pp. 675, 676.

1832. WHITE, A. Ueber Colibris. < *Fror. Notiz.*, xxxv, No. 750, 1832, pp. 20-25.

Nicht mir selbst zugänglich—Titel aus Car. und Eng.

1833. JARDINE, W. The | Naturalists' Library. | Ornithology. | Vol. I [II]. | Humming-Birds. | By | Sir William Jardine, Bart. | F. R. S. E. F. L. S. &c. &c. | Edinburgh: | W. H. Lizars, and Sterling and Kenney; | Longman, Rees, Orme, Brown, Green, and | Longman, London; | and W. Curry, Jun. and Co. Dublin. | — | 1833. 2 vols. 16 mo. Vol. I: a green half-cover-title, 1 leaf; a notice, 1 leaf; advts., pp. 1-6; half-title, 1 leaf; portrait of Linnæus: engr. col'd title, backed blank; full title as above, backed with W. Ballantyne & Co.'s imprint; contents, pp. i-iii; blank, p. iv; advt., pp. 1-10; half-title to memoir of Linnæus, pp. 11, 12; memoir of Linnæus, pp. 13-48; regular text of Humming-birds, pp. 49-147, with pll. col'd 1-34: advts., pp. 1-32 and pp. 1-8. Vol. II, not handled by me.

1833. JARDINE, W.—Continued.

"The Naturalists' Library," which reached about 40 vols. through several years, was started in 1833 with Jardine's "Humming-Birds," in 2 vols. The above is the full title and collation of the original issue, in cheap binding and loaded with advts., differing materially from the later reissue, when the many vols. were systematically rearranged, Mammals first, then Birds, &c. In the final rearrangement, these two Humming-Bird vols. become "Humming-Birds.—Part I [II]", and form Vols. VI, VII. The main text, and the plates, are identical in any issues; but the titles and the furnishings differ. (Compare next title.)

"The Naturalists' Library" was a publisher's enterprise; but the weight of the editor's name, the excellence of the text, and the beauty of the plates, rendered it a very notable work, of no less scientific merit than popular interest and usefulness.

1833. JARDINE, W.   The | Naturalist's Library. | Edited by | Sir William Jardine, Bart., | F. R. S. E., F. L. S., etc., etc., | Vol. VI [VII]. | — | Ornithology. | Humming Birds.—Part I [II]. | By the Editor. | — | Edinburgh : | W. H. Lizars, [etc.] n. d. [1833.] 2 vols. 16mo. Vol. VI: portrait of Linnæus; eng. col'd title; other title; contents, 2 leaves; pp. i–xxxii, 25–191, cuts, pll. col'd 1–34. Vol. VII : portrait of Pennant; eng. col'd title; other title; contents, 2 leaves; pp. 1–192, cuts, pll. col'd, 1–30.

Being Vols. I, II, of the original issue. The date here given is that of the original issue; I do not know exactly when the reissue was made. On the systematic rearrangement of the many vols. of the series, the Hummers, originally Vols. I and II, became "Humming-Birds, Part I [II]," and then formed Vols. VI, VII, of the rearranged series. (Compare last title.)

These two vols. contain memoirs of Linnæus (Vol. VI) and of Pennant (Vol. VII), and otherwise consist of a monograph of *Trochilidæ*; the text by Jardine, the illustrations by Lizars.

Vol. VI: *Ramphodon nœvius*, pl. 1; *Troch. avocetta*, pl. 2; *T. recurvirostris*, pl. 3; *T. rufigaster*, pl. 4; *T. colubris*, pl. 5; *T. anna*, pl. 6; *T. cyaneus*, pl. 7; *T. prasina*, pl. 8; *T. quadricolor*, pl. 9; *T. delalandii*, pl. 10; *T. moschitus*, pl. 11; *T. sephanoides*, pl. 12; *T. petasophorus*, pl. 13; *T. scutatus*, pl. 14; *T. ornatus*, pls. 15, 16; *T. audenetii*, pl. 17; *T. chalybeus*, pl. 18; *T. magnificus*, pls. 19, 20; *T. cornutus*, pls. 21, 22; *T. furcatus*, pl. 23; *T. vesper*, pl. 24; *T. cora*, pl. 25; *T. dupontii*, pl. 26; *T. enicurus*, pl. 27; *T. saphirinus*, pl. 28; *T. leucotis*, pl. 29; *T. mellivorus*, pl. 30; *T. multicolor*, pl. 31; *T. gramineus*, pls. 32, 33; *T. latipennis*, pl. 34 (name *Campylopterus latipennis* on pl.).

Vol. VIII: *T. thalassinus*, pls. 1, 2 (*T. auris* on pl.); *T. gigas*, pl. 3; *T. coelegena*, pl. 4; *T. stokesii*, pl. 5; *T. loddigesii*, pl. 6; *T. delalandii*, ♀, pl. 7; *T. orthura*, pl. 8; *T. amethystoides*, pl. 9 (*T. amethystina* on pl.); *TT. rubineus, montana*, no pl.; *T. langsdorffii*, pl. 10; *T. rufus*, pl. 11; *T. gouldii*, pl. 12; *T. tricolor*, pl. 13; *T. lucifer*, pl. 14 (*T. cyanopogon* on pl.); *T. petasophorus*, pl. 15; *T. wagleri*, pl. 16; *TT. bicolor, mangerii, glaucopis, cœruleus, swainsonii, erythronotus, cyanogenys, atala*, no pl.; *T. mesoleucus*, pl. 17; *TT. squamosus, albicollis, superbus*, no pl.; *T. rivolii*, pl. 18; *T. buffonii*, pl. 19; *T. mango*, pl. 20; *TT. viridis, holosericeus, leucurus, aurulentus, hypophœus*, no pl.; *T. polytmus*, pl. 21; *T. underwoodii*, pl. 22; *T. sparganurus*, pl. 23; *T. nuna*, no pl.; *T. pella*, pls. 24, 25; *T. superciliosus*, pls. 26, 27; *T. eurynome*, pl. 28; *T. guy, T. intermedius, bourcieri, squalidus, longuemareus, rufigaster, davidianus*, no pl.; *T. hirsutus*, pl. 29; *T. mazeppa*, no pl.; *T. swainsoni*, pl. 30. The synopsis, which follows, is briefly synonymatic and descriptive, adopting Swainson's five subfamilies. This series of illustrations, coming after Lesson's works on the same subject, furnish a valuable check on the species so indiscriminately described as new by the latter, to the great prejudice of others, especially Vieillot.

1833. LA LLAVE, P. DE.   [Memoria sobre algunas especies nuevas del género Trochilus.] < *Registro Trimestre*, vol. ii = núm. 5, Enero de 1833, pp. 39–50.

T. cohuatl, p. 47; *T. xicotencal*, p. 48; *T. tzacatl*, p. 48; *T. papantzin*, p. 48; *T. topiltzin*, p. 49.

This article has no title, and appears to be little known. I commend it to notice, as containing descriptions of five new Hummers, the names of which, given in due Linnæan form, doubtless antedate others now in general employ.

1833. SCHREIBERS, C. V.   [Neue Arten von Trochilus.] < *Oken's Isis*, Bd. xxxvi, 1833, pp. 534, 535.

„ Regierungs-Rath von Schreibers aus Wien legte eine Probe des von ihm beabsichtigten, gemeinschaftlich mit den österreichischen Naturforschern herausgegebenen Werkes vor, worinn die von den Oesterreichern in Brasilien neu entdeckten Thiere beschrieben und abgebildet werden sollen. Dieselbe besteht in dem ersten Hefte des ornithologischen Theiles, welcher die Beschreibung und Abbildung zweyer neuer Trochilus-Arten enthält, die er dem Könige und der Königinn von Ungarn zu Ehren *Trochilus regis* und *Trochilus reginae* nennt, und führet den Titel: *Collectanea qd faunam Brasiliae.*"

1833. SCHREIBERS, C.'v.   Caroli a Schreibers | Muscorum Regio-Caesareo-Aulicorum
ex Hist. Nat. Praefecti etc., | Collectanea | ad | Faunam Brasiliae. | — | Nova
Genera et Species animalium, | a naturae scrutátoribus Caes. Austriacis in Bra-
silia collectorum, | descripta et iconibus illustrata. | — | Fasciculus I. | — |
Viennae. | Impensis Editoris. | 1833.   Folio.   Cover-title, other title, pp. 1–4,
pl. 1.

No more published.—The above is the cover-title of the publication as a whole, of which
the present piece is Fasciculus I. To this theré is special title as follows: Collectanea | ad
Ornithologiam Brasiliae. | — | Beyträge zur Vögelkunde Brasiliens. | — | Neue Arten von
Blumenspechten, Colibri; | beschrieben | von | Karl von Schreibers. | — | Wien. | Auf Kos-
ten des Herausgebers. | MDCCCXXXIII. [Gedruckt bey Anton Strauss's sel. Witwe.]
The 4 pages of text are devoted to the description of two new species of *Trochilidæ*, viz:
T. regis, p. 1, pl. 1, f. 1 and 1 a; and *T. reginæ*, p. 3, pl. i, f. 2. Besides these, the Plate gives—
fig. a, *T. ornatus*; f. b., *T. magnificus*; f. c., *T. strumarius*.
There is no other ornithological matter. Cf. *Isis*, 1833, pp. 534, 535.

1834. BARNES, *Mrs.* —. [Note on the rearing of a species of Humming-bird (Mellisuga humilis?)]   < *P. Z. S.*, ii, 1834, p. 33.

1834. GUILDING, L.   Facts on Humming-Birds, their Food, the Manner in which they
take it, and on their Habits; with Directions for preserving the Eggs of
Humming-Birds, and the Forms of the Bodies of Spiders, and Pupæ and
Larvæ of Insects.   < *Loudon's Mag. Nat. Hist.*, vii, 1834, pp. 569–573.

1834. VIGORS, N. A.   [Trochilus loddigesii.]   < *Oken's Isis*, Bd. xxvii, 1834, p. 814.
Auszug aus *Philos. Mag.*, ix, 1831, p. 62.

1835. BARNES, [*Mrs* —.] [Colibri aus Jamaica.]   < *Oken's Isis*, Bd. xxviii, 1835, p.
1026.
Auszug aus den *P. Z. S.*, ii, 1834, p. 33.

1835. GERVAIS, [P.] Oiseaux-mouches. Ornismya. Less.   < *Guér. Mag. de Zool.*,
5e année, 1835, class ii, notices xli, xlii, pll. xli, xlii.
O. ricordii, Gerv., pll. xli, xlii, n. sp.

1835. GERVAIS, [P.] Oiseau-mouche. Ornismya. O. cinnamomon. O. cinnamomeus. Gervais.   < *Guér. Mag. de Zool.*, 5e année, 1835, classe ii, notice xliii, pl.
xliii.

1835. GUILDING, L.   Ueber die Nahrung des Colibris.   < *Fror. Notiz.*, xliii, No. 930,
1835, pp. 71, 72.
Nicht mir selbst zugänglich. Titel aus Carus und Euglm. Aus dessen ,. Facts on Humming-Birds," u. s. w., in *Loudon's Mag. Nat. Hist.*, vii, 1834, pp. 569–573.

1835. LODDIGES, G.   [Vier Arten der Trochilidæ.]   < *Oken's Isis*, Bd. xxviii, 1835,
pp. 367, 368.
Auszug aus den *P. Z. S.*, ii, 1832, pp. 6, 7, *q. v.*

1837. ANON.   Lesson's Werke über die Colibri.   < *Oken's Isis*, Bd. xxx, 1837, p. 94.

1837. CHAMBERS, R.   [On the Habits and Geographical Distribution of Humming-
Birds.]   < *P. Z. S.*, v, 1837, p. 37.
Merely a note of a paper read.

1837. CHAMBERS, R.   Observations on the Humming-Bird.   < *Charlesw. Mag. Nat.
Hist.*, i, 1837, pp. 592–596, fig. 70. (Auch in: *Froriep's Notizen*, iv, No. 84, 1837,
pp. 289–292.)
"These remarks are only those of an ardent admirer of nature, not of an ornithologist."

1838. GEOFFROY SAINT-HILAIRE, [ISID.] Note sur l'ostéologie des Oiseaux-Mouches,
envoyée de Liége.   < *Compt. Rend. de l'Acad. Sci.*, vi, 1838, pp. 880–883.
1°. Unité de plan et modifications dans les détails de l'appareil hyoïdien.—2°. Unité de
plan et modifications dans les detaìls de l'appareil sternal chez les Oiseaux-mouches, et les
grands voiliers, les Frégates.

1838. GEOFFROY SAINT-HILAIRE, [ISID.] [Note sur l'Ostéologie des Oiseaux-mouches.]
< *Revue Zoologique*, i, 1838, p. 99.
Extraite des *Comptes Rend. à l'Acad. Sci. Paris*, vi, 1838, pp. 880–883, *q. v.*

1838. LESSON, [R.] P.   Espèces nouvelles d'oiseaux mouches.   < *Revue Zoologique*, i, 1838, pp. 314, 315.

> 12 espèces, dont quelqu'unes récemment décrites: *Ornismya arsinœ, O. fanny, O. vesper, O. nuna, O. vestita, O. helianthea*, p. 314; *O. parzudhaki* (sic), *O. zemès, O. lumachella, O. rhami, O. senex, Trochilus inaïs*, p. 315.

1839. BOISSONNEAU, —.   Nouvelles espèces d'Oiseaux-Mouches de Santa-Fé de Bogota   < *Revue Zoologique*, ii, 1839, pp. 354–356.

> *Ornismya temminckii, O. ensifera, O. microrhyncha*, p. 354; *O. paulinœ, O. heteropogon*, p. 355. Toutes les espèces ici décrites sont figurées, *Guér. Mag. de Zool.*, 1840, pll. 12–16, q. v.

1839. BOURCIER, J.   Description de quelques espèces nouvelles d'Oiseaux-Mouches.   < *Revue Zoologique*, ii, 1839, pp. 294, 295.

> *Ornismya costae, O. allardi*, p. 294; *O. jourdanii*, p. 295.

1839. CHAMBERS, [R.]   Ueber die Lebensart und die geographische Verbreitung der Colibri.   < *Oken's Isis*, Bd. xxxii, 1839, p. 144.

> *P. Z. S.*, London, Marz 28, 1837, p. 37.

1839. LATTRE, — DE, *and* LESSON, [R. P.]   Oiseaux-Mouches nouveaux ou très-rares, découverts par M. De Lattre dans son voyage en Amérique et décrits par MM. De Lattre et Lesson.   < *Revue Zoologique*, ii, 1839, pp. 13–20.

> *Ornysmia* (sic) *campylopterus*, De L., p. 14; *O. lessonii*, De L., p. 15; *O. heloisa*, Less. et De L., p. 15; *O. abeillei*, Less. et De L., p. 16; *O. henrica*, Less. et De L., *O. phœbé*, Less. et De L., p. 17; *O. De Lattrei*, Less., p. 19; *Trochilus pretrei*, Less. et De L., *T. eliza*, Less. et De L., p. 20, spp. nn.

1840. BOISSONNEAU, —.   G. Oiseau-mouche.   Ornismya. Lesson. [mut. mut.]   < *Guér. Mag. de Zool.*, 2e sér., année 1840, Oiseaux, pp. 1, 2, 1, 2, 1, 2, 1, 2, 1, 2, pll. 12, 13, 14, 15, 16.

> *O. heteropogon*, pl. 12; *O. paulinœ*, pl. 13; *O. temminckii*, pl. 14; *O. ensifera*, pl. 15; *O. microrhyncha*, pl. 16.   Toutes les espèces déjà décrites, *Rev. Zool.*, 1839, pp. 354, 355, q. v.

1840. BOURCIER, J.   Descriptions et figures de trois espèces nouvelles d'Oiseau-Mouches.   < *Ann. Sc. Phys. Soc. d'Agric. de Lyon*, iii, 1840, pp. 225–228, 5 pll.

> Not seen—title from C. & E. *Bibl.*

1840. BOURCIER, [J.]   Oiseau-Mouche nouveau [Ornismya heliordor].   < *Revue Zoologique*, iii, 1840, p. 275.

1840. FRASER, L.   [Characters of new Species of Humming-birds.]   < *P. Z. S.*, viii, 1840, pp. 14–19.

> *Trochilus exortis*, p. 14; *T. cupreoventris, T. uropygialis, T. coruscus*, p. 15; *T. brachyrhynchus, T. derbianus, T. aurcogaster*, Lodd. MSS., p. 16; *T. fuscicaudatus, T. cyanopterus*, Lodd. MSS., *T. gibsoni* Lodd. MSS., p. 17; *T. angustipennis, T. parvirostris, T. flavicaudatus, T. melanogenys, T. tyrianthinus*, Lodd. MSS., p. 18.

1840. FRASER, L.   [Characters of new Species of Trochilidæ.]   < *Annals of Nat. Hist.*, vi, 1840, pp. 151–155.

> From *P. Z. S.*, Feb. 11, 1840, pp. 14–19, q. v.

1840. LESSON, [R. P.]   Oiseaux-mouches rares ou nouveaux, communiqués par MM. Longuemare et Parzudaki, faisant partie du t. IV inédit de l'histoire naturelle des Oiseaux-mouches de M. Lesson.   < *Revue Zoologique*, iii, 1840, pp. 71–74.

> 13 spp.—*Ornismya pouchetti, O. sylphia, Campylopterus rufus*, spp. nn. ?

1841. BOURCIER, J.   Description de l'adulte de l'Ornysmia Bonapartei.   < *Revue Zoologique*, iv, 1841, p. 177.

1841. LONGUEMARE, G. DE.   Oiseau-mouche nouveau [Ornismya Clarisse].   < *Revue Zoologique*, iv, 1841, p. 306.

> Fig. *Guér. Mag. de Zool.*, 1842, pl. 26.

1842. BOURCIER, J.   Descriptions de quelques espèces nouvelles d'Oiseaux-Mouches.   < *Ann. Sc. Phys. Soc. d'Agric. de Lyon*, v, 1842, pp. 307–310, 4 pll.

> Pas vues moi-même—le titre tiré de la *Bibl.* de Carus et Engelmann.

1842. BOURCIER, J.   Descriptions de quelques espèces nouvelles d'Oiseaux-Mouches.   < *Ann. Sc. Phys. Soc. d'Agric. de Lyon*, v, 1842, pp. 344, 345, 3 pll.

> Pas vues moi-même—le titre tiré de la *Bibl.* de Carus et Engelmann.

1842. BOURCIER, J.   Description de trois espèces nouvelles d'Oiseaux-mouches.   < *Revue Zoologique*, v, 1842, pp. 373, 374.

> *Ornismya aline, O. julie, O. mulsant*, p. 373.

1842. DUBUS DE GHISIGNIES, V. B.   Diagnoses spécifiques de trois espèces nouvelles d'Oiseaux-Mouches de la Colombie.   < *Bull. Acad. Bruxelles*, ix, i, 1842, pp. 524–526.

> Pas vues moi-même—le titre est tiré Carus et Engelmann.

1842. LONGUEMARE, G. DE.   G. Oiseau-mouche.   Ornismia.   Cuvier.   O. M. Clarisse. O. Clarisse. De Longuemare.   < *Guér. Mag. de Zool.*, 2ᵉ sér., année 1839, Oiseaux, pp. 1, 2, pl. 26.

> Descr. orig. *Rev. Zool.*, 1841, p. 306.

1843. BOURCIER, [J.]   Description de deux nouvelles espèces d'Oiseaux-Mouches de Colombie.   < *Revue Zoologique*, vi, 1843, p. 2.

> *Ornismya colombica, O. poortmani.*

1843. BOURCIER, [J.]   Oiseaux Mouches nouveaux ou mal connus.   < *Revue Zoologique*, vi, 1843, pp. 70–73.

> *Trochilus prunellei*, p. 70; *T. cupripennis, T. anthophilus*, p. 71; *T. guimeti, T. guerini, T. barroti*, p. 72.

1843. BOURCIER, J.   Oiseaux-mouches nouveaux.   < *Revue Zoologique*, vi, 1843, pp. 99–104.

> *Trochilus prevostii*, p. 99; *T. cyanifrons, T. goudoti*, p. 100; *T. chrysogaster, T. cyanotus. T. geoffroyi*, p. 101; *T. leadbeateri*, p. 102; *T. fallax, T. riefferi, T. viridigaster*, p. 103.

1843. BOURCIER, J.   Descriptions de quelques espèces nouvelles d'Oiseaux-Mouches.   < *Ann. Sc. Phys. Soc. d'Agric. de Lyon*, vi, 1843, pp. 36–49, 6 pll.

> Pas vues moi-même—le titre tiré de Carus et Engelmann.

1843. BOURCIER, J., *and* MULSANT, E.   Descriptions et figures de plusieurs espèces nouvelles d'Oiseaux-mouches.   < *Ann. Sc. Phys. Soc. d'Agric. de Lyon*, vi, 1843, pp. 36–49.

> Pas vues moi-même—le titre ci-dessus tiré du *Roy. Soc. Cat.*

1843. LATTRE, [A.] DE.   Description d'un Oiseau-Mouche nouveau, Ornismya Helenae.   < *Revue Zoologique*, vi, 1843, p. 133.

> L'Écho du monde savant.

1843. LODDIGES, G.   [On some Species of Humming Birds.]   < *P. Z. S.*, xi, 1843, p. 122.

> Brief but pointed rectification of synonymy of 9 spp. of *Ornismya*.

1845. CABOT, S., JR.   [Remarks on exhibition of Ornismia (sic) canivetii.]   < *Proc. Bost. Soc. Nat. Hist.*, ii, 1845, p. 55.

1845. CABOT, S., JR.   [Trochilus yucatanensis, sp. n.]   < *Proc. Bost. Soc. Nat. Hist.*, ii, 1845, pp. 74, 75.

1845. G[UÉRIN-]M[ÉNÉVILLE, F. E.]   [Note sur les] Descriptions et figures de plusieurs espèces nouvelles d'Oiseaux-mouches, par MM. J. Bourcier et E. Mulsant [Ann. des Sci., vi, 1843].   < *Revue Zoologique*, viii, 1845, pp. 343, 344.

1845. PARZUDAKI, [E.]   Nouvelle espèce d'oiseau mouche [Ornysmia (sic) isaacsonii].   < *Revue Zoologique*, viii, 1845, p. 95.

1845. PARZUDAKI, [E.]   Nouvelle espèce d'Oiseau-Mouche [Ornysmia (sic) lindenii].   < *Revue Zoologique*, viii, 1845, p. 253.

1846. BOURCIER, J.   Description de nouvelles espèces de Trochilidées.   < *Revue Zoologique*, ix, 1846, pp. 312–314.

> *Trochilus addæ*, p. 312; *T. turnerii, T. lumachellus*, p. 313.

1846. BOURCIER, J.   Description de vingt espèces d'Oiseaux-Mouches.   < *Revue Zoologique*, ix, 1846, pp. 314–316, pll. 3, 4.

> Tel est le titre d'un mémoire que cet ornithologiste et M. Mulsant ont inséré dans les *Ann. Soc. Roy. d'Agr. de Lyon*. Ici se trouvent seulement les descriptions de deux espèces—*T. conversii*, p. 314, pl. 3; *T. victoriæ*, p. 315, pl. 4—suivies d'un liste des autres.

1846. BOURCIER, J., *and* MULSANT, E.   Descriptions de vingt espèces nouvelles d'Oiseaux-Mouches.   < *Ann. Sc. Phys. Soc. d'Agric. de Lyon*, ix, 1846, pp. 313–332,
3 pll.
Not seen—title from E. & C.

1846. GOULD, J.   [Descriptions of three New Species of the Family of Trochilidæ.]
< *P. Z. S.*, xiv, 1846, pp. 44, 45.
Trochilus coruscans, p. 44; *T. flabelliferus, T. strophianus*, p. 45.

1846. GOULD, J.   On twenty [*i. e.*, seventeen] New Species of Trochilidæ or Humming
Birds.   < *P. Z. S.*, xiv, 1846, pp. 85–90.
T. pyra, T. smaragdinus, p. 85; *T. gracilis, T.* (*ocreatus*, g. n.) *rufocaligatus, T. ligonicaudus*,
p. 86; *T. cupricauda, T. æneocauda, T. violifer*, p. 87; *T. cyanopectus, T. aurescens, T. fulviventris*, p. 88; *T. nigrofasciata, T. ruficeps, T. inornata, T. regulus*, p. 89; *T. hypoleucus, T. hispïdus*,
p. 90: cf. *tom. cit.*, pp. 44, 45, for the three others.

1846. GOULD, J.   [On three new species of Trochilidæ.]   < *Ann. Mag. Nat. Hist.*, xviii,
1846, pp. 129, 130.
From *P. Z. S.*, May 12, 1846, pp. 44, 45, *q. v.*

1846. GOULD, J.   On twenty [*i. e.*, seventeen] new species of Trochilidæ or Humming
Birds.   < *Ann. Mag. Nat. Hist.*, xviii, 1846, pp. 419–425.
From *P. Z. S.*, Sept. 22, 1846, pp. 85–90, *q. v.*

1846. GULLIVER, G.   [Note on the Size of the Blood-Córpuscles of Birds, with Measurements by Dr. Davy of the Blood-Corpuscles of some Fishes and of a Humming-
Bird.]   < *P. Z. S.*, 1846, pp. 26–28.
Corpuscles of Hummer 1-2666th × 1-4000th of an inch; long diameter of nucleus very nearly
1-4000th.   Temperature about 105°.

1846. LATTRE, A. DE, *and* BOURCIER, J.   Description de quinze espèces nouvelles de
Trochilidées, faisant partie des collections rapportées par M. Ad. De Lattre,
dont les précédentes excursions ont déjà enrichi plusieurs branches de l'histoire naturelle, et provenant de l'intérieur du Pérou, des républiques de
l'Équateur, de la Nouvelle-Grenade et de l'isthme de Panama.   < *Revue Zoologique*, ix, 1846, pp. 305–312.
Trochilus chimborazo, T. wilsoni, p. 305; *T. mosquera, T. derbyi*, p. 306; *T. grayi, T. lutetiæ*,
p. 307; *T. edward, T. williami*, p. 308; *T. herrani, T. saul*, p. 309; *T. cuvierii, T. fannyi*, p. 310;
T. saucerottei. T. labrador, T. mocoa, p. 311.

1847. BOURCIER, J.   Description de quinze espèces de Trochilidées du cabinet de M.
Loddiges.   < *P. Z. S.*, xv, 1847, pp. 42–47.
T. mirabilis, T. aquila, p. 42; *T. millerii, T. schreibersii, T. matthewsii*, p. 43; *T. watertonii*
(all from Lodd. MSS.), *T. evelynæ*, p. 44; *T. johannæ, T. conradii, T. yarrelli*, p. 45; *T. spencei,
T. ruckeri, T. doubledayi*, p. 46; *T. mitchellii, T. norrisii*, p. 47, spp. nn.

1847. BOURCIER, J.   Description de quinze espèces de Trochilidées du cabinet de M.
Loddiges.   < *Revue Zoologique*, x, 1847, pp. 253–261.
Extraite des *Proc. Soc. Zool. de Londres*, 1847, pp. 42–47, *q. v.*

1847. BOURCIER, J.   Description de deux espèces nouvelles de Trochilidées.   < *P. Z.
S.*, xv, 1847, p. 48.
Trochilus caroli, T. georginæ.

1847. BOURCIER, J.   Description de deux espèces nouvelles de Trochilidées.   < *Revue
Zoologique*, x, 1847, pp. 260, 261.
Extraite des *Proc. Soc. Zool. Londres*, 1847, p. 48, *q. v.*

1847. BOURCIER, J.   Description des nouvelles espèces de Trochilidées.   < *Revue Zoologique*, x, 1847, pp. 401, 402.
Extraite des *Ann. Soc. Roy. de Lyon*, t. x.

1847. BOURCIER, J., *and* MULSANT, E.   Description d'une espèce nouvelle d'Oiseau-
Mouche.   < *Ann. Sc. Phys. Soc. d'Agric. de Lyon*, x, 1847, p. 136.
Pas vue moi-même—le titre tiré de la *Bibl.* de Car. et Englm.

1847. BOURCIER, J., *and* MULSANT, E.   Description de trois espèces nouvelles d'Oiseaux-Mouches.   < *Ann. Sc. Phys. Soc. d'Agric. de Lyon*, x, 1847, pp. 623, 624, 1 pl.
Pas vue moi-même—le titre tiré de la *Bibl.* de Car. et Englm.

1847–48. GOULD, J. Drafts for an arrangement of the Trochilidæ, [&c.—the rest of the title is modified in succeeding Parts.] < *P. Z. S.*, xv, 1847, pp. 7–11, 16, 17, 30, 31, 94–96 ; xvi, 1848, pp. 11–14.

> Synopsis of *Petasphora ; P. iolata*, sp. n., p. 9; *Oreotrochilus*, g. n.; *O. leucopleurus, O. me-lanogaster*, spp. nn , p. 10, with synopsis of the genus; *T. calliope*, sp. n., p. 11. Synopsis of *Eriopus*, n. g., p. 16; *Cometes*, n. g.; *C. phaon*, sp. n., p. 31; *Metallura, Doryfera*, genn. nn., pp. 94, 95; *D. violifrons, Lophornis reginæ*, spp. nn., p. 95; *Trochilus cæruleogaster*, sp. n.. p. 96. In 1848: *Helianthea eos*, g. sp. n., p. 11; *Aglaeactis caumatonotus, Heliangelus mavors*, genn. spp. nn., p. 12; *Thalurania viridipectus*, gen. sp. n.; *Campylopterus obscurus*, sp. n., p. 13; *Trochilus caligatus*, sp. n.; *Oxypogon*, g. n., p. 14.

1847–48. GOULD, J. Drafts for a new arrangement of the Trochilidæ [etc., mut. mut.]. < *Ann. Mag. Nat. Hist.*, xix, 1847, pp. 401–405, 408, 409, 421, 422; xx, 1847, pp. 283–285 ; 2d ser., ii, 1848, pp. 62–66.

> From *P. Z. S.*, 1847–48, *q. v.*

1848. BOURCIER, J., *and* MULSANT, [E.] Descriptions de quelques nouvelles espèces d'Oiseaux-Mouches. < *Revue Zoologique*, xi, 1848, pp. 269–275.

> *Trochilus cephalus*, p. 269; *T. castelnaudii*, p. 270; *T. pucherani*, p. 271; *T. josephinæ, T. de-villei.* p. 272; *T. phaeton, T. amaryllis*, p. 273; *T. eucharis, T. alice*, p. 274.

1848. GOSSE, P. H. Ueber das langgeschwänzte Colibri auf Jamaica. < *Fror. Notiz.*, 3 Reihe, vi, No. 121, 1848, pp. 167–169.

> Nicht mir selbst zugänglich—Titel aus Carus u. Engelmann.

1849. BOURCIER, J., *and* MULSANT, E. [*Trochilus pichincha*, n. sp.] < *Mém. Acad. Lyon*, ii, 1849, pp. 427, 428.

> Pas vu moi-même. Titre tiré de C. & E.

1849. BOURCIER, J., *and* MULSANT, E. Description d'une nouvelle espèce d'Oiseau-Mouche [*Trochilus pichincha*]. < *Rev. et Mag. de Zool.*, 2e sér., i, Dec., 1849, pp. 625, 626.

> Lué à *l'Acad. des Sc.*, etc., *de Lyon*, le 17 juillet 1849.

1849. GOSSE, P. H. Descriptions of two new Birds from Jamaica. < *Ann. Nat. Hist.* 2d ser., iii, 1849, pp. 257–259.

> *Trochilus maria*, p. 258; *Elania* (sic) *cotta*, p. 257.

1849. GOULD, J. Description of Two New Species with the characters of a New Ge-nus of Trochilidæ. < *P. Z. S.*, xvii, 1849, pp. 95, 96.

> *Heliodoxa* (g. n., p. 95) *jacula*, p. 96; *Eriopus simplex*, p. 96.

1849–61. GOULD, J. A Monograph | of | The Trochilidæ, | or | Family of Humming-Birds. | By | John Gould, F. R. S., | [etc., 8 lines.] | In Five Volumes. | Vol. I[–V]. | London : | printed by Taylor and Francis, Red Lion Court, Fleet Street. | Published by the Author, 26 Charlotte Street, Bedford Square. | [1849–]1861. | [The author reserves to himself the right of translation.] | Five vols. folio. Vol. I, title 1 l., dedication 1 l., list of plates 1 l., pp. i–cxxviii (list of subscribers, preface, introduction, etc.), with unnumbered pll. 1–41, and unpaged folios accompanying them. Vol. II, title 1 l., list of plates 1 l., with unnumbered pll. 42–116, and unpaged folios accompanying them. Vol. III, title 1 l., list of plates 1 l., with pll. 117–203, and unpaged folios accom-panying them. Vol. IV, title 1 l., list of plates 1 l., with pll. 204–283, and unpaged folios accompanying them. Vol. V, title 1 l., list of plates 1 l., with pll. 284–360, and unpaged folios accompanying.

> The above is the permanent title, furnished on the completion of the work, with the colla-tion of the five vols. in which it is designed that the 25 parts in which the work was pub-lished be bound. The cover-title is a little different, as follows :—
>
> A | Monograph | of the | Trochilidæ | or | Humming Birds. | Dedicated with permission to | Her Royal Highness, The Princess Royal of England. | By | John Gould, F. R. S., &c. | — | Part I[–XXV]. | — | Contents. | [mut. mut.] | London : | published by the author, . . . [mut. mut.] | [Price Three Guineas.] | June 1st, 1849 [–September 1st. 1861]. Part I. June 1st. 1849, 15 pll. and text. Part II, Nov. 1st, 1851, 15 pll. and text. Part III, May 1st, 1852. 15 pll. and text. Part IV, Oct. 1st, 1852, 15 pll. and text. Part V. May 1st. 1853, 15 pll. and text. Part VI. Oct. 1st, 1853, 15 pll. and text. Part VII, May 1st. 1854, 15 pll. and text. Part VIII, Oct. 1st, 1854, 15 pll. and text. Part IX. May 1st. 1855, 15 pll. and text. Part X. Sept. 1st. 1855, 15

1849-61. GOULD, J.—Continued.

pll. and text. Part XI, May 1st, 1856, 15 pll. and text. Part XII, Sept. 1st, 1856, 15 pll. and text. Part XIII, May 1st, 1857, 15 pll. and text. Part XIV, Sept. 1st, 1857, 15 pll. and text. Part XV, May 1st, 1858, 15 pll. and text. Part XVI, Sept. 1st, 1858, 15 pll. and text. Part XVII, May 1st, 1859, 15 pll. and text. Part XVIII, Sept. 1st, 1859, 15 pll. (of 16 spp.) and text. Part XIX, May 1st, 1860, 15 pll. and text. Part XX, Sept. 1st, 1860, 15 pll. and text. Part XXI, May 1st, 1861, 15 pll. and text. Part XXII, July 1st, 1861, 15 pll. and text. Part XXIII, Sept 1st, 1861, 15 pll. and text. Part XXIV, Sept. 1st, 1861, 15 pll. and text. Part XXV, no pll., 5 titles for 5 vols, 1 dedication, pp. i-cxxviii, being List of Subscribers, Preface, Introduction, Explanation of Abbreviations and Lists of Generic and Specific names, with 5 ll. of Lists of Plates, one for each vol.—In all, 360 unnumbered plates, and about or exactly as many unpaged folios of text, *plus* the titles, etc., furnished with Part XXV.

The unnumbered plates and unpaged folios of text are designed to be rearranged in making up the five volumes in a systematic sequence given in the "Introduction"; this and the lists of plates being the only clue to the citation of the plates by number. Each of the vols. is dated "1861" on the permanent title-page; but each vol. consists of plates and text published in other years, the appearance of the plates having been according to no systematic arrangement of the genera and species. To preserve dates of publication of the plates, I first give a list of the species according to their appearance in the successive Parts, and then quote the Plates by their numbers in the made-up volumes, according to the sequence indicated in the Introduction.

PART I, June 1st, 1849.—Trochilus polytmus, Oreotrochilus estellæ, O. leucopleurus, O. adelæ, Phaëthornis eurynome, P. eremita, Pterophanes temminckii, Docimastes ensiferus, Spathura underwoodi, S. peruana, S. rufocaligata, Oxypogon guerini, O. lindeni, Tryphæna duponti, Augastes scutatus.   (15 spp.)

PART II, Nov. 1st, 1851.—Topaza pella, T. pyra, Oreotrochilus chimborazo, O. pichincha, Eutoxeres aquila, E. condamini, Glaucis ruckeri, Calothorax helisdori, C. mulsanti, Florisuga mellivora, F. flabellifera, F. atra, Augastes lumachellus, Phaethornis griseogularis, Mellisuga minima.   (15 spp.)

PART III, May 1st, 1852.—Eustephanus galeritus, Cynanthus cyanurus, C. smaragdicaudus, Grypus nævius, Selasphorus rufus, S. scintilla, S. platycercus, Eriocnemis simplex, Campylopterus rufus, C. hyperythrus, Hylocharis cyaneus, H. sapphirinus, Lophornis **chalybeus**, Calothorax yarrelli, Thaumatias chionurus.   (15 spp.)

PART IV, Oct. 1st, 1852.—Thaumastura enicura, Cometes sparganurus, C. phaon, Ramphomicron microrhyncha, R. stanleyi, R. heteropogon, R. ruficeps, R. herrani, Phaethornis guy, P. yaruqui, P. syrmatophorus, P. hispidus, P. pygmæus, Threnetes leucurus, T. antoniæ.   (15 spp.)

PART V, May 1st, 1853.—Heliotrypha viola, Petasphora anais, P. iolata, P. cyanotis, P. thalassina, P. serrirostris, P. coruscans, P. delphinæ, Heliomaster longirostris, H. constanti, H. pinicola, H. angelæ, H. mesoleucus, Chlorostilbon prasinus, Phaëthornis bourcieri.   (15 spp.

PART VI, Oct. 1st, 1853.—Eupetomena hirundinacea, Clytolæma rubinea, Urosticte benjamini, Dorifera ludoviciæ, D. johannæ, Heliothrix auritus, H. auriculatus, H. barroti, Eriocnemis cupreiventris, E. mosquera, E. luciani, Schistes geoffroyi, S. albogularis, Aphantochroa cirrhochloris, Phaëthornis intermedius.   (15 spp.)

PART VII, May 1st, 1854.—Lesbia amaryllis, Calothorax micrurus, Eustephanus feruandensis, E. stokesi, Gouldia langsdorffi, G. popelairi, G. conversi, Bourcieria torquata, B. fulgidigula, B. inca, Phaëthornis pretrei, P. augusti, P. anthophilus, Hypuroptila buffoni, H. cæruleogaster.   (15 spp.)

PART VIII, Oct. 1st, 1854.—Diphogena (sic) iris, Selasphorus? heloisæ, Cephalepis delalandi, C. loddigesi, Helianthea typica, H. bonapartei, Myiabeillia typica, Panoplites jardini, P. matthewsi, P. flavescens, Cæligena typica, C. purpurea, Eriocnemis lugens, Delattria henrici, Phaëthornis striigularis.   (15 spp.)

PART IX, May 1st, 1855.—Heliangelus clarissæ, H. strophianus, H. amethysticollis, H. spencei, H. mavors, Patagona gigas, Thaumatias brevirostris, T. affinis, Cyanomyia quadricolor, Delattria clemenciæ, D. vividipallens, Leucippus chionogaster, Adelomyia melanogenys, A. floriceps, Glaucis dohrni.   (15 spp.)

PART X, Sept. 1st, 1855.—Lophornis ornatus, L. gouldi, L. magnificus, L. regulus, L. reginæ, L. helenæ, Helianthea eos, H. violifera, Eriocnemis aureliæ, Campylopterus delattrei, C. pampa, Gouldia lætitiæ, Phaethornis philippi, Leucochloris albicollis, Adelomyia? castaneiventris.   (15 spp.)

PART XI, May 1st, 1856.—Eugenia imperatrix, Heliactin cornuta, Avocettula recurvirostris, Avocettinus eurypterus, Calypte annæ, C. helenæ, C. costæ, Rhodopis vespera, Lamprolaima rhami, Cyanomyia cyanocephala, Cæligena wilsoni, Glaucis hirsuta, Thalurania watertoni, T. glaucopis, Adelomyia inornata.   (15 spp.)

PART XII, Sept. 1st, 1856.—Aglæactis cupripennis, A. pamela, Thaumatias albiventris, T. linnæi, Chrysolampis moschitus, Calothorax fanny, Eugenes fulgens, Lesbia gouldi, Campy-

1849-61. GOULD, J.—Continued.

lopterus lazulus, C. cuvieri, Urochroa bougueri, Lampornis mango, Leucippus fallax, Calliphlox amethystina, Saucerottia cyanifrons. (15 spp.)

PART XIII, May 1st, 1857—Thaumastura elizæ, T. coræ, Lafresnaya flavicauda, L. gayi, Helianthea lutetiæ, Ionolaima schreibersi, Circe latirostris, Aglæactis castelnaui, Orthorhynchus cristatus, O. exilis, Amazilia pristina, A. cerviniventris, A. corallirostris, Chlorostibon auriceps, Thalurania wagleri. (15 spp.)

PART XIV, Sept. 1st, 1857.—Calothorax cyanopogon, C. calliope, C. rosæ, Trochilus alexandri, Eulampis jugularis, E. holosericeus, E. chlorolæmus, Campylopterus ensipennis, Cœligena prunelli, Eucephala cærulea, E. grayi, Eupherusa eximia, Klais guimeti, Phaethornis longuemarus, P. adolphi. (15 spp.)

PART XV, May 1st, 1858.—Eriocnemis derbianus, E. nigrivestis, E. isaacsoni, Trochilus colubris, Phaethornis obscura, P. viridicaudata, Lampornis gramineus, L. porphyrurus, L. veraguensis, L. aurulentus, L. prevosti, Cometes? glyceria, Heliopædica melanotis, Erythronota edwardi, E. niveiventris. (15 spp.)

PART XVI, Sept. 1st, 1858.—Phaiolaima rubinoides, Heliodoxa jacula, Discura longicauda, Phaëthornis superciliosus, P. cephalus, Sternoclyta cyaneipectus, Thalurania furcata, T. columbica, T. venusta, T. eriphile, T. verticeps, Microchera albocoronata, Chrysobronchus virescens, C. virdicaudus, Chrysuronia eliciæ. (15 spp.)

PART XVII, May 1st, 1859.—Metallura cupreicauda, M. æneicauda, M. tyrianthina, M. smaragdinicollis, M. williami, Eriocnemis vestitus, E. alinæ, Heliothrix phaïnolærna, H. purpureiceps, Campylopterus villavicencis, Chrysuronia œnone, C. humboldti, C. josephinæ, Sporadinus elegans, Phaëthornis amaura. (15 spp.)

PART XVIII, Sept. 1st, 1859.—Ionolaïma frontalis, Bourcieria conradi, Juliamyia typica, Damophila amabilis, Spathura melananthera, Oreotrochilus melanogaster, Thaumatias leucogaster, T. chionopectus, T. milleri, Amazilia Dumerili, A. leucophæa, A. cyanura, Hylocharis lactea, Phaëthornis oseryi, P. nigricinctus, P. episcopus. (16 spp. on 15 pll.)

PART XIX, May 1st, 1860.—Spathura cissiura, Calothorax pulchra, Heliotrypha parzudaki, Chlorostilbon caniveti, Phaiolaima aequatorialis, Sapphironia goudoti, S. cæruleogularis, Campylopterus latipennis, C. obscurus, Chrysuronia chrysura, Thaumatias caudidus, Erythronota antiqua, Calliphlox mitchelli, Amazilia riefferi, A. devillei. (15 spp.)

PART XX, Sept. 1st, 1860.—Lophornis verreauxi, Lesbia eucharis, L. nuna, L. gracilis, Heliodoxa leadbeateri, H. otero, Cyanomyia franciæ, C. violiceps, C. cyanocollis, Chlorostilbon aliciæ, C. poortmani, C. atala, Amazilia viridigaster, Circe doubledayi, Sporadinus riccordi. (15 spp.)

PART XXI, May 1st, 1861.—Clytolæma? aurescens, Heliopædica xantusi, Thalurania refulgens, T. nigrofasciata, T. tschudii, Oreopyra leucaspis, Calothorax evelynæ, C. jourdani, Aphantochroa gularis, Eriocnemis squamata, E. godini, Panterpe insignis, Lampornis viridis, Heliodoxa jamesoni, Chlorostilbon angustipennis. (15 spp.)

PART XXII, July 1st, 1861.—Chlorostilbon phaëthon, C. osberti, Phæoptila sordida, Thaumatias viridiceps, Amazilia beryllina, A. ocai, Hypuroptila urochrysia, Cometis? caroli, Erythronota sophæ, Eucephala cæruleo-lavata, E. smaragdo-cærulea, E. chlorocephala, E. hypocyanea, Grypus spixi, Glaucis melanura. (15 spp.)

PART XXIII, Sept. 1st, 1861.—Loddigesia mirabilis, Schistes personatus, Eriocnemis d'orbignyi, Thaumatias nitidifrons, Amazilia alticola, A. yucatanensis, A. castaneiventris, Ramphomicron vulcani, Diphlogæna aurora, Selasphorus floresii, Campylopterus roberti, Metallura primolinus, Phaethornis fraterculus, P. zonura, Erythronota saucerottei. (15 spp.)

PART XXIV, Sept. 1st, 1861.—Lophornis dellattrei, Threnetes cervinicauda, Glaucis fraseri, G. affinis, G. mazeppa, G. lanceolota, Erythronota feliciæ, E. ? elegans, Calothorax decoratus, Lamphornis virginalis, Adelomyia maculata, Orthorhynchus ornatus, Smaragdochrysis iridescens, Sporadinus maugæi, Phlogophilus hemileucurus. (15 spp.)

PART XXV, Sept. 1st, 1861.—No plates.

(Above names, copied as printed on covers, may not be literally the same as engraved on each plate.—To the 361 spp. figured in these parts, others are added in Part XXV, without plates; these are given in the systematic enumeration beyond.)

The sytematic enumeration of the species by plates, according to the make-up of the five volumes, is as follows (the asterisk indicates Gould's genera and species, whether here new or not; a page given instead of a plate signifies that the species is an unfigured one published in Part XXV, 1861):—

VOL. I., with the paged letter-press, &c., and pll. 1-41.—Grypus nævius, pl. 1; spixi, 2; Eutoxeres aquila, 3; condaminei. 4: Glaucis hirsuta, 5; mazeppa, 6; affinis, 7; *lanceolata, 8; *melanura, 9; dohrni, 10; ruckeri, 11; *fraseri, 12; *Threnetes leucurus, 13; *cervinicauda, 14; antoniæ, 15: Phaëthornis eurynome, 16; malaris, 17; consobrina (p. xl) ; *fratercula, 18; longirostris, 19; *syrrnatophora, 20; *boliviana (p. xl); philippi, 21; *hispida, 22; oseryi, 23; anthophila, 24; bourcieri, 25; guyi, 26; emiliæ (p. xli) ; yaruqui, 27; superciliosa, 28; augusti, 29; squalida [=intermedius on pl.], 30: Pygmornis longuemari [=Phaethornis longuemarus of pl.],

1849-61. GOULD, J.—Continued.

31; amaura [=Phaethornis on pl.], 32; aspasiæ [=Phaëth. *viridicaudata on pl.], 33; *zonura [=Phaëthornis on pl.], 34; adolphi [=Phaëth. on pl.], 35; *griseogularis [=Phaethornis on pl.], 36; *striigularis [=Phaethornis on pl.], 37; idaliæ [=Phaethornis *obscura on pl.], 38; nigricincta [=Phaeth. on pl.], 39, f. 1; *episcopus [=Phaethornis on pl.], 39, f. 2; rufiventris (p. xliv); *eremita [=Phaeth. on pl.], 40; pygmæus [=Phaethornis on pl.], 41.

VOL. II, pll. 42-116.—*Eupetomena macrura [E. hirundinacea on pl.], 42; Sphenoproctus [= Campylopterus cr pl.] pampa, 43; curvipennis (p. xlv); Campylopterus lazulus, 44; hemileucurus [=delattrei on pl.], 45; ensipennis, 46; splendens, 47, up. fig.; villavicencis, 47, low. fig.; latipennis, 48; *æquatorialis (p. xlvii); *obscurus, 49; rufus, 50; hyperythrus, 51; *Phaeochroa [Campylopterus on pl.] cuvieri, 52; roberti, 53; *Aphantochroa cirrhochloris, 54; *gularis, 55; Dolerisca [= Leucippus on pl.] fallax, 56; *cervina (p. xlviii); *Urochroa bougueri, 57; *Sternoclyta cyaneipectus, 58; *Eugenes fulgens, 59; Coeligena [=Delattria on pl.] clemenciæ, 60; Lamprolaema rhami, 61; Delattria henrici, 62; viridipallens, 63; *Heliopædica melanotis, 64; xantusi, 65; Topaza pella, 66; pyra, 67; *Oreotrochilus chimborazo, 68; pichincha, 69; estellæ, 70; *leucopleurus, 71; *melanogaster, 72; adelae, 73; Lampornis mango, 74; *iridescens (p. liii); prevosti, 75; *veraguensis, 76; gramineus, 77; viridis, 78; purulentus, 79; virginalis, 80; porphyrurus, 81; Eulampis jugularis, 82; holosericeus, 83; chlorolæmus, 84; *longirostris (p. lv); Lafresnaya flavicaudata, 85; gayi, 86; saulæ (p. lv); *Doryfera johannæ, 87; ludoviciæ, 88; *rectirostris (p. lvi); Chalybura [=Hypuroptila on pl.], 89; *urochrysia [=Hypuroptila on pl.], 90; *cæruleogastra [=Hypuroptila on pl.], 91; *isauræ (p. lvii); *Iolæma frontalis, 92; schreibersi, 93; *Heliodoxa *jacula, 94; jamesoni, 95; Leadbeatera otero, 96; *splendens (p. lviii); grata, 97; Aithurus [=Trochilus on pl.] polytmus, 98; *Thalurania glaucopis, 99; watertoni, 100; furcata, 101; *furcatoides (p. lx); forficata (p. lx); *refulgens, 102; *tschudii, 103; *nigrofasciata, 104; *venusta, 105; columbica, 106; *verticeps, 107; fanniæ (p. lx); eriphyle, 108; wagleri, 109; *Panoplites jardini, 110; flavescens, 111; matthewsi, 112; Florisuga mellivora, 113; *flabelliferą, 114; *atra, 115; *Microchera *albocoronata, 116.

VOL. III, pll, 117-203.—Lophornis ornatus, 117; gouldi, 118; magnificus, 119; *regulus, 120; *lophotes (p. lxiii); delattrei, 121; *reginæ, 122; helenæ, 123; Polemistria [= Lophornis on pl.] chalybea, 124; verreauxi [=Lophornis on pl.], 126; Discura longicauda, 126; Prymnacantha [=Gouldia on pl.] popelairi, 127; Gouldia langsdorffi, 128; conversi, 129; letitiæ, 130; Trochilus colubris, 131; alexandri, 132; Mellisuga minima, 133; *Calypte costæ, 134; annæ, 135; helenae, 136; Selasphorus rufus, 137; *scintilla, 138; floresii, 139; platycercus, 140; Atthis heloisæ, 141; *Stellula [Calothorax on pl.] *calliope, 142; Calothorax cyanopogon, 143; *pulcher, 144; *Acestrura [=Calothorax on pl.] mulsanti, 145; *decorata [=Calothorax on pl.], 146; heliodori [=Calothorax on pl.], 147; *micrura [= Calothorax on pl.], 148; Chætocercus [=Calothorax on pl.] rosæ, 149; jourdani [=Calothorax on pl.], 150; Myrtis [=Calothorax on pl.] fanniæ, 151; yarrelli [=Calothorax on pl.], 152; Thaumastura coræ, 153; Rhodopis vespera, 154; Doricha elizæ, 155; evelynæ, 156; enicura, 157; *Tryphaena duponti, 158; Calliphlox amethystina, 159; amethystoides (p. lxx); mitchelli, 160; *Loddigesia *mirabilis, 161; *Spathura underwoodi, 162; melananthera, 163; *peruana, 164; *rufocaligata, 165; *cissiura, 166; Lesbia gouldi, 167; *gracilis, 168; nuna, 169; amaryllis, 170; eucharis, 171; Cynanthus cyanurus, 172; *caelestis (p. lxxii); mocoa [=*smaragdicaudus on pl.], 173; *Cometes sparganurus, 174; *phaon, 175; glyceria, 176; caroli, 177; *Pterophanes temminckii, 178; *Aglæactis cupripennis, 179; aequatorialis (p. lxxiv); *parvula (p. lxxiv); *caumatonotus (p. lxxiv); castelnaudi, 180; pamelæ, 181; *Oxypogon guerini, 182; lindeni, 183; Ramphomicron heteropogon, 184; stanleyi, 185; *vulcani, 186; herrani, 187; *ruficeps, 188; microrhynchum, 189; *Urosticte benjamini, 190; *Metallura *cupreicauda, 191; *aeneicauda, 192; williami, 193; primolii, 194; tyrianthina, 195; *quitensis (p. lxxvii); smaragdinicollis, 196; Adelomyia inornata, 197; melanogenys, 198; *maculata, 199; Avocettula eurypterus, 200; Avocettula recurvirostris, 201; Anthocephala [=Adelomyia on pl.] floriceps, 202; castaneiventris [=Adelomyia on pl.], 203.

VOL. IV, pll. 204-283.—Chrysolampis moschitus, 204; Orthorhynchus cristatus, 205; *ornatus, 206; exilis, 207; Cephalepis delalandi, 208; *loddigesi, 209; Klais guimeti, 210; Myiabeillia typica, 211; Heliactin cornuta, 212; Heliothrix aurita, 213; auriculata, 214; *phainolæma, 215; barroti [=purpureiceps on pl.], 216; *violifrons [=barroti on pl.], 217; Schistes geoffroyi, 218; *personata, 219; *albigularis, 220; *Augastes scutatus, 221; lumachellus, 222; Petasophora serrirostris, 223; anais, 224; *iolata, 225; *coruscans, 226; thalassina, 227; cyanotis, 228; adelphinac, 229; Polytmus [=Chrysobronchus on pl.] virescens, 230; viridissimus [=Chrysobronchus viridicaudus on pl.], 231; Patagona gigas, 232; *Docimastes ensiferus, 233; *Eugenia imperatrix, 234; *Helanthea typica, 235; bonapartei, 236; *eos, 237; lutetiæ, 238; *violifera, 239; *Heliotrypha parzudaki, 240; *viola, 241; *Heliangelus clarissæ, 242; *strophianus, 243; spencei, 244; amethysticollis, 245; *mavors, 246; *Diphlogenia *iris, 247; *aurora, 248; *Clytolæma rubinea, 249; *aurescens, 250; Bourciera torquata, 251; *fulgidigula, 252; insectivora (p. xc); conradi, 253; *inca, 254; Lampropygia coeligena [Coeligena typica on pl.], 255; *boliviana (p. xc); purpurea [Coeligena on pl.], 256; prunellei [Coeligena on pl.], 257; wilsoni, 258; Heliomaster longirostris, 259; stuartæ (p. xci); sclateri (p. xcii); *pallidiceps (p. xcii);

1849–61. GOULD, J.—Continued.

constanti, 260; leocadiæ [*pinicola on pl.], 261; Lepidolarynx [Heliomaster on pl.] mesoleucus, 262; Calliperidia [Heliomaster on pl.] angelæ, 263; *Oreopyra *leucaspis, 264; Eustephanus galeritus, 265; stokesi, 266; fernandensis, 267; Phæolæma rubinoïdes, 268; *æquatorialis, 269; Eriocnemis cupreiventris, 270 and 271 [latter being E. *simplex]; isaacsoni, 272; luciani, 273; mosquera, 274; vestita, 275; nigrivestis, 276; godini, 277; d'orbignyi, 278; derbiana, 279; alinæ, 280; *squamata, 281; *lugens, 282; aureliae, 283.

VOL. V, pll. 284–360.—Cyanomyia quadricolor, 284; *violiceps, 285; cyanocephala, 286; *guatemalensis (p. xcvi); franciæ, 287; *cyanicollis, 288; *Hemistilbon *ocai, 289; norrisi (p. xcvii): Leucippus chionogaster, 290; Leucochloris albicollis, 291; Thaumatias candidus, 292; *chionopectus, 293; leucogaster, 294; *viridiceps, 295; milleri, 296; nitidifrons, 297; *cæruleiceps (p. xcviii); brevirostris, 298; *affinis, 299; *chionurus, 300; albiventris, 301; linnæi, 302; *fluviatilis (p. xcix); *apicalis (p. xcix); *maculicaudus (p. xcix); Amazilia pristina, 303; *alticola 304; dumerili, 305; leucophæa, 306; Pyrrhophæna cinnamomea [=Amazilia corallirostris on pl.], 307; yucatanensis [= Amazilia on pl.], 308; *cerviniventris [=Amazilia on pl.], 309; *castaneiventris [=Amazilia on pl.], 310; riefferi [=Amazilia on pl.], 311; beryllina [= Amazilia on pl.], 312; devillei [=Amazilia on pl.], 313; viridigaster [=Amazilia on pl.], 314; iodura (p. ci); *cyanura [=Amazilia on pl.], 315; Erythronota antiqua, 316; feliciæ, 317; edwardi, 318; *nigriventris, 319; *elegans, 320; Saucerottia typica [Erythronota saucerottei on pl.], 321; sophiæ [=Erythronota on pl.], 322; warszewiczi (p. ciii): Hemithylaca [=Saucerottia on pl.] cyanifrons, 323; *Eupherusa eximia, 324; Chrysuronia œnone, 325; josephinae, 326; neera (p. civ); *cæruleicapilla (p. civ); humboldti, 327; eliciae, 328; chrysura, 329; Eucephala grayi, 330; *smaragdo-cærulea, 331; chlorocephala, 332; *cærulo-lavata, 333; *scapulata (p. cv); *hypocyanea, 334; cærulea, 335; cyanogenys (p. cv); Panterpe insignis, 336; Juliamyia typica, 337; feliciana (p. cvi); *Circe latirostris, 338; doubledayi, 339; *Phæoptila *sordida, 340; *zonura (p. cvii); Damophila *amabilis, 341; Hylocharis sapphirina, 342; lactea, 343; cyanea, 344; Sapphironia goudoti, 345; *cæruleigularis, 346; Sporadinus elegans, 347; ricordi, 348; maugæi, 349; Chlorolampis [Chlorostilbon on pl.] *auriceps, 350; caniveti [Chlorostilbon on pl.], 351; osberti [Chlorostilbon on pl.], 352; salvini (p. cix); *Chlorostilbon augustipennis, 353; haeberlini (p. cx); phaëthon, 354; aureiventris (p. cx); prasinus, 355; *igneus (p. cxi); atala, 356; daphne (p. cxi); *peruanus (p. cxi); *napensis (p. cxi); *brevicaudatus (p. cxi); chrysogaster (p. cxi); assimilis (p. cxii); nitens (p. cxii); Panychlora [Chlorostilbon on pl.] alicæ, 357; euchloris (p. cxii); stenura (p. cxiii); poortmani [Chlorostilbon on pl.], 358; *Smaragdochrysis *iridescens, 359; *Phlogophilus *hemileucurus, 360.

(*Note.*—The above list being drawn up by turning the pages of the Introduction, the asterisk may be misplaced in some instances, if the author has omitted to place his name after his own genera and species, or has placed it after any names for which he is the authority only in as far as the combination of the generic with the specific term is concerned. I have preferred to take this list rather than that of the plates alone, as this represents the final views of the author, and gives many species not figured; the species here catalogued being 416 in number, while the plates number 360. In many cases the generic, and sometimes the specific, names are here different from those printed in the body of the work and engraved on the plates; but all these discrepancies I have taken due note of in the brackets.)

1849. [JARDINE, W.] Oreotrochilus jamesonii [n. sp.], Jardine. October, 1849. < *Jard. Contrib. Orn.*, 1849, p. 67, pl. xliii.

See also note, *Contrib.* for 1850, p. 27.

1849. PARZUDAKI, [E.] Description et figure d'une [récemment] nouvelle espèce d'Oiseau-Mouche de la République de Venezuela. < *Rev. et Mag. de Zool.*, i, 1849, pp. 273, 274, pl. 8.

Ornysmia (sic) *lindenii*, Parz., *R. Z.*, 1845, p. 253.

1849. SALLÉ, A. [Description d'une nouvelle espèce d'Oiseau-Mouche (Ornismia (sic) catharinæ).] < *Rev. et Mag. de Zool.*, i, 1849, p. 498.

1850. BONAPARTE, C. L. Note sur les Trochilidés. < *Compt. Rend. de l'Acad. Sci. Paris*, xxx, 1850, pp. 379–383.

Lafresnaya, Delattria, Bourciera, Saucerottia, Loddigiornis, Gouldic, sont des genres nouveaux ou récemment décrits (1849).

1850. BONAPARTE, C. L. Note sur les Trochilidés. < *Rev. et Mag. de Zool.*, ii, 1850, pp. 243–245.

Extraite des *Comptes Rendus de l'Acad. des Sc. de Paris*, séance du 1er avril 1850, *q. v.*

1850. GOULD. J. On six new species of Humming Birds. < *P. Z. S.*, xviii, 1850, pp. 162–164.

Trochilus scintilla, T. chionura, p. 162; *T. venusta, T. coeruleogularis, T. castaneoventris,* p. 163; *T. niveoventer,* p. 164.

1850. [JARDINE, W.] Trochilus allardi, Bourc. < *Jard. Contrib. Orn.*, 1850, p. 81, and p. 151, pl. lv.

1850. [JARDINE, W.] Ornithology of Quito. < *Jard. Contrib. Orn.*, 1850, pp. 1–3.
The piece consists of notices of 8 spp. of *Trochilidæ*.

1851. ANON. Ueber die Verbreitung der Colibris. < *Fror. Tagsb.*, no. 339 (Zool. Bd., ii), 1851, p. 120.
Not seen—title from Carus and Engelmann.

1851. BOURCIER, J. Note sur onze espèces nouvelles de Trochilidées. < *Compt. Rend. de l'Acad. Sci.*, xxxii, 1851, pp. 186–188.
Trochilus bougueri, T. godini, p. 186; *TT. condamini, yaruqui, pichincha, stanleyi, benjamini, jardini, villaviscensis, jamesoni, duchassaini*, p. 187, recueillies par lui en 1849 et '50 dans la République de l'Équateur.—Note sur ce sujet par M. Isid. Geoffroy St.-Hilaire, p. 188.

1851. BOURCIER, J. Note sur onze espèces nouvelles de Trochilidées. < *Rev. et Mag. de Zool.*, iii, Feb., 1851, pp. 96–98.
Extraite des *Comptes Rendus de l'Acad. des Sc. de Paris*—séance du 10 février, 1851, *q. v.*

1851. BOURCIER, J., *and* MULSANT, E. Description d'une nouvelle espèce d'Oiseau-Mouche [Trochilus stanleyi]. < *Ann. Sc. Phy. Soc. d'Agric. de Lyon*, nouv. sér., iii, 1851, pp. 199–203. (Aussi séparément, 8vo, pp. 5.)
Not seen—title from Carus and Engelmann.

1851. GEOFFROY SAINT-HILAIRE, ISID. [Note sur les onze espèces nouvelles de Trochilidées de M. Bourcier.] < *Compt. Rend. de l'Acad. Sci.*, xxxii, 1851, p. 188.

1851. GOULD, J. On some new species of Trochilidæ. < *P. Z. S.*, xix, 1851, pp. 115, 116.
Trochilus (—?) amabilis, Phaëthornis griseogularis, p. 115.

1851. GOULD, J. On six new species of Humming Birds. < *Ann. Mag. Nat. Hist.*, 2d ser., viii, 1851, pp. 341–343.
From *P. Z. S.*, June 25, 1850, pp. 162–164, *q. v.*

1851. GOULD, J. Description of Three New Species of Humming-Birds. < *Jard. Contrib. Orn.*, 1851, pp. 139, 140.
Phaethornis syrmatophora, p. 139; *Schistes albogularis, Eriopus lugens*, p. 140.

1851. [JARDINE, W.] Trochilus (Thalurania) verticeps, Gould. [n. sp.] < *Jard. Contrib. Orn.*, 1851, p. 79, pl. lxxi.

1851. [JARDINE, W.] Trochilus (Spathura) melananthera, Jardine. < *Jard. Contrib. Orn.*, 1851, pp. 111, 112, pl. lxxx.

1851. JERRARD, P., *and* BAILEY, F. W. N. The Humming Bird Keepsake. A Book of Bird Beauty. The Birds painted among Nests and Flowers by Paul Jerrard. The Poetry by F. W. N. Bailey, written expressly for this work. London: P. Jerrard. 1851. 4to.
Not seen—title from Carus and Engelmann.

1852. BOURCIER, J., *and* MULSANT, E. Description d'une nouvelle espèce d'Oiseau-Mouche. < *Ann. Sc. Phys. Soc. d'Agric. de Lyon*, nouv. ser., iv, 1852, pp. 139–144.
Not seen—title from Carus and Engelmann.

1852. DEVILLE, E. Observations faites en Amérique sur les mœurs de différentes espèces d'Oiseaux-Mouches, suivies de quelque notes anatomiques et de mœurs sur l'Hoazin, le Caurale et la Savacou. < *Rev. et Mag. de Zool.*, iv, 1852, pp. 208–226, pl. 9.
Sur les mœurs de dix espèces du genre *Ornismyia ;* sur l'*Opisthocomus cristatus* (pl. 9), l'*Eurypyga helias* et la *Cancroma cochlearia.*

1852. GOULD, J. Descriptions of Three New Species of Humming Birds. < *Jard. Contrib. Orn.*, 1852, pp. 135–137.
Ramphomicron vulcani, p. 135, Bolivia; *Bourcieria inca*, p. 136, Bolivia; *Trochilus (——?) auriceps*, p. 137, Mexico.

1852. GOULD, J. On the genus Thalurania. < *P. Z. S.*, xx, 1852, pp. 8, 9.
List of 11 spp., with their habitats; *T. refulgens*, p. 9, sp. n.

1852. MARTIN, W. C. L.   A | General History | of | Humming-Birds, | or the | Trochilidæ : | with especial reference to the | collection of J. Gould, F. R. S., &c. | now exhibiting in the | Gardens of the Zoological Society of London. | By | W. C. L. Martin, | late one of the Scientific Officers of the Zoological | Society of London. | — | London : | H. G. Bohn, York Street, Covent Garden. | 1852. 1 vol. sm. 16mo. pp. i–vii, 1 l., pp. 1–232, frontisp. and pll. col'd, 1–3, 3 *, 4–14.

I also find this work cited as "12mo., 1853"; but this may not indicate a different edition. The work seems to have been designed as a sort of continuation of, or supplement to, the Humming-birds of Jardine's *Naturalist's Library;* and it was in fact afterward made one of the vols. of that notable collection.   I have handled the vol. both as a separate work and as one of the *Nat. Libr. ;* the title and collation are identical, excepting that the date is carefully erased in the *Nat. Libr.* binding.   When found in this connection there is absolutely nothing to show what vol. of the series it is intended for.—Omitting the unnumbered vol. called "General History of Man," it would make Vol. XLI of the *Nat. Libr.;* counting the *Gen. Hist. of Man* as one, it would be Vol. XLII; there being 40 vols. of the series without either of these two.—But the copy examined is stamped on the back "Hummingbirds, Vol. III"; going by this token, the work makes Vol. VII *bis* of the Bird Series, the two regular Humming-bird volumes being respectively Vols. VI and VII.

It is a modest treatise of much merit, as the author's name would lead us to anticipate. The arrangement of the genera is according to Bonaparte.   Some 175 spp. altogether are treated, and, on the 15 (not 14) colored plates and the frontispiece are figured the following: Frontisp., *Docimastes ensiferus.*   Pl. 1, *Petasophora iolata ;* 2, *Heliothrix auritus;* 3, *Campylopterus obscurus;* 3*, Topaza pyra ;* 4, *Bourciera torquata ;* 5, *Aglæactis cuprcipennis ;* 6, *Helianthea eos ;* 7, *Chrysuronia œnone ;* 8, *Heliangelus mavors ;* 9, *Oreotrochilus chimborazo ;* 10, *Ramphomicron heteropogon ;* 11, *Oxypogon lindeni ;* 12, *Spathura underwoodii ;* 13, *Eriopus cupreiventris ;* 14, *Gouldia conversi.*

1853. BOURCIER, J.   Nouvelle espèce du genre Metallura [primolinus], Gould.   < *Rev. et Mag. de Zool.,* v, 1853, pp. 295. 296.

1853. GOULD, J.   Descriptions of Five New Species of Humming Birds.   < *P. Z. S.,* xxi, 1853, pp. 61, 62.

Helianthea iris, H. aurora, Heliangelus viola, Trochilus (——?) cyanocollis, p. 61 ; *T. (— ?) floriceps,* p. 62.

1853. GOULD, J.   Observations on the Nests of Humming Birds [Trochilidæ].   < *P. Z. S.,* xxi, 1853, p. 100.

1853. GOULD, J.   Descriptions of Two New Species of Humming Birds from Peru.   <'*P. Z. S.,* xxi, 1853, p. 109.

Spathura cissiura, Calothorax micrurus.

1853. GOULD, J.   On some new species of Trochilidæ.   < *Ann. Mag. Nat. Hist.,* 2d ser., xi, 1853, pp. 466, 467.

From *P. Z. S.,* Mar. 25, 1851, pp. 115, 116, q. v.

1853. MÜNTER, W.   Abwesenheit der Furcula am Skelet eines Trochilus.   < *Zeitschr. gesammt. Naturwiss.,* i, 1853, p. 18.

Not seen—title from Giebel.

1853. VERREAUX, J., *and* VERREAUX, E.   Note du genre Lophornis Ch. Bp.—Lophornis Verreauxii Bourc.   < *Rev. et Mag. de Zool.,* v, 1853, p. 193, pl. 6.

1854. BONAPARTE, C. L.   Tableau [sic] des Oiseaux-Mouches.   < *Rev. et Mag. de Zool.,* vi, Mai, 1854, pp. 248–257.   (Aussi séparément, Paris, Raçon, 1854 ; 8vo, pp. 12.)

Conspectus Trochilorum: 80 genres, 322 espèces: "le squelette de mes études sur les Oiseaux-Mouches."   Les noms seulement, sans descriptions.

The year 1854 was a sad one for the Hummers.   Two deadly assaults were made upon the literature of the family, by Bonaparte in France, and by Reichenbach in Germany; with the result of making confusion worse confounded in the generic nomenclature.   Both these authors opened the flood-gates, and fairly inundated the subject with numberless new names. few of which were needed, none of which were characterized with regard for proprieties, and some of which duplicated each other.   What with these authors' extravagancies, and the still further loosening of the reins of judicious moderation in the hands of Mulsant in 1866 and subsequently, the Hummers were probably as badly abused as any family of birds whatever.   They have been fairly overwhelmed with a mass of synonymy.   There are to-day scarcely fewer genera of Hummers than species; and, if we count the different application

1854. BONAPARTE, C. L.—Continued.

of the same name by different authors and the varying orthography of names, there are actually more generic names than there are species in this family!

I regard Bonaparte's services to the science of Ornithology to have ceased in 1850. The sum total of his after contributions to the subject, to the time when death cut short his schemes, is not only a worthless but a pernicious aggregate. In his latter years, Bonaparte simply played chess with birds, with himself for king: *le roi s'amuse!* Scheme followed scheme, tableau tableau, conspectus conspectus, with perpetual changes, incessant coining of new names, often in mere sport—it was nothing but turning a kaleidoscope. It may have been fun for him, but it was death to the subject. Besides his pedantries and his pleasantries, he had two very bad habits, neither of them any better than a trick, by which he juggled other authors out of the way to make room for himself. Under a thin pretence of making due grace to his peers, he would take their names, invest them with a new significance, and place "Bp." after such names in their new association; and then bestow a new name upon the genus thus deprived of its rightful designation—killing two birds with one stone. Again, he usually took a specific name for a generic one, and to the species thus left nameless he would give a new name—scoring two for himself again. When, as sometimes happened, these two tricks fell together, he was enabled to write "Bp." four times where it should not once have appeared. Add to all this that he was utterly regardless of orthography—often wrote the same name in different ways—quoted others' names so carelessly as to make them look like new names—renamed the same thing often in mere forgetfulness—made genera in joke, for a chance for a pun, or to compliment a friend—and let the most slovenly printing pass—with all this, I say, we have a state of things that is a disgrace to himself, a scandal to science, and only to be adequately characterized by the word abominable.

The present article may stand in illustration of the justness of my censure. It is one of four in which within as few years Bonaparte disarranged the Hummers. There is his article in the *Consp. Av.* 1849; one in the *Compt. Rend.* 1850; one in the *Ann. Sc. Nat.* 1854; and the present. He calls it only "the skeleton" of his studies; we may wonder what it would be if filled out. It is a mere list of the names of 80 genera and 322 species. It is impossible for any one who has not made a special study of the Hummers to tell which are here new names and which are not. Many are here used for the first time, and many others, both of his own and of others', are used in such novel application, or are so differently spelled, that they become *de jure* new names. I give the following list, being those that have "Bp." after them:—

Myiaetina, Doleromyia, Leucippus, Orthornis, Guyornis, p. 249. *Pygmornis,* p. 250. *Leadbeatera, Heliomastes, Ornithomyia, Bourcieria,* p. 251. *Coeligena, Lafresnaya, Chrysobronchus, Heliotryppha* (sic; Gould), *Eriocnemys* (sic; Reich.), p. 252. *Ramphomicron, Myiabeillia, Adelomyia, Florisuga, Delattria,* p. 253. *Cyanomyia, Amazilius, Chrysuronia.* p. 254. *Saucerottia, Sporadinus, Thaumantias, Juliamyia,* p. 255. *Sapphironia, Avocettinus, Cephalepis* (sic; Lodd.), *Loddiggiornis, Discura,* p. 256. *Thaumastura, Lophorinus, Gouldia, Gouldomyia,* p. 257.

It is directly pertinent to the subject of Bonaparte's abuse of names in this family to refer to his other schemes, which are not formally citable in this part of my Bibliography.

In the *Ann. Sc. Nat.,* 4th ser., i, 1854, Bonaparte has inserted one of his perpetual conspectus, embracing *Trochilidæ.* Here he is not only at the tricks I have exposed, but commits an ultra-Napoleonic piece of fatuity: namely, citing a number of names as if Reichenbach's, which the latter never published (see Elliot, *Class. and Syn. Troch.,* 1879, p. 188). Consequently the reproach of them falls upon Bonaparte. Such are *Aline, Mosqueria, Luciania, Derbomyia,* etc.

Bonaparte was seldom thoughtful enough of the convenience of others to indicate whether a "Bp." name was newly proposed or not; and it is consequently not easy for any one to decide upon the original reference to be given in such cases. Thus, in his "Note sur les Trochilidés," in *Comp. Rend. (vide suprà,* 1850), he has a number of names; and I notice that Mr. Elliot quotes this place and date as the original reference to them. Most if not all of them, however, occur in his *Consp. Av.* of date 1849.

As the latter is a general work which does not come in this portion of my Bibliography, I will here give a list of the Bp. genera in it—being those which Gray correctly attributes to "Bp. 1849" in his *Handlist:*—

Phaëtornis (= *Phaethornis,* Sw.), p. 67; *Lafresnaya, Doryfera* (= *Dorifera,* Gld.), p. 68; *Colibri, Heliotrix* (= *Heliothryx,* Boie), p. 69; *Delattria, Leadbeatera, Heliomaster,* p. 70; *Caeligena* (ex. Less), *Leucippus, Bourcieria, Florisuga,* p. 73; *Avocettinus, Chrysuronia,* p. 75; *Saucerottia, Amazilius,* p. 77; *Thaumatias,* p. 78; *Ramphomicron,* p. 79; *Sephanoides* (ex. Less.), p. 82; *Cephalepis* (ex. Lodd.), p. 83; *Discosura,* p. 84; *Thaumastura,* p. 85; *Gouldia,* p. 86.

1854. BOURCIER, J. Nouvelle espèce du genre Hylocharis [chlorocephalus]. Boie.
    < *Rev. et Mag. de Zool.,* vi, 1854, pp. 457, 458.

1854. GOULD, J. Description of a New Species of Humming Bird, from Quijos [Threnetes cervinicauda]. $<$ *P. Z. S.*, 1854, xxii, p. 109.

1854. GOULD, J. On the Genus Thularania. $<$ *Ann. Mag. Nat. Hist.*, 2d ser., xiii, 1854, pp. 228, 229.

From *P. Z. S.*, Jan. 13, 1852, pp. 8, 9, *q. v.*

1854. GOULD, J. On a New Species of Cometes [mossia]; a Genus of Humming-Birds. $<$ *Rep. Brit. Assoc. Adv. Sci. for* 1853, xxiii, 1854 (*Misc. Comm.*), p. 68.

Not described here. (See *Athen.*, 24th Sept., 1853.)

1854. REICHENBACH, L. Aufzählung der Colibris oder Trochilideen in ihrer wahren natürlichen Verwandtschaft, nebst Schlüssel ihrer Synonymik. $<$ *J. f. O.*, 1853, *Extrah.*, Marz, 1854, besondere Beilage, pp. 1–24.

General remarks; Tabular view of Genera under 16 subfamilies of 4 groups; Criticism of generic names; List of Species; Synonymatic key to the same; New Species, as follows:— *Coeligena warszewizii, C. sagitta, Chlorestes maculicollis, C. euchloris,* p. 23; *Lesbia gorgo, Steganura spatuligera, S. remigera, Amazilia leucophoea,* p. 24.

I regret to perceive that either Mr. Elliot or myself is mistaken respecting the date of this paper, the former having uniformly cited the many new genera of Reichenbach's as of 1853. Gray gives them correctly, as of 1854. The paper is a special supplement to the extra number of the *J. f. O.* for 1853; but the *Extraheft* dates 1854. Moreover, Cabanis, the editor, who surely should know, gives the exact date as March, 1854. The article was presented to the seventh annual meeting of the German Ornithological Society, held at Halberstadt, July 11–14, 1853.

It is curious that Reichenbach and Bonaparte twice crossed each other's paths in their coining of many new names for the Hummers. The portions of the *Av. Syst. Nat.* of the former, and of the *Consp. Av.* of the latter, which contain the *Trochilidæ*, both date 1849. Again, in 1854, both brought forward numberless new names. In the former case I do not know with which author lies actual priority; in the latter, Reichenbach takes precedence, Bonaparte's article having appeared in May, 1854.

If the reader will refer to my remarks upon Bonaparte's article of 1854, he will be prepared for no very favorable judgment of mine respecting the present paper of Reichenbach's. Of the immense number of new generic names which the German author here inflicts upon the *Trochilidæ* it cannot be that many are either necessary or desirable; many are mere synonyms, and none whatever are characterized. Not a few, however, take precedence over those of Bonaparte. I give the following list of the names which are Reichenbach's—most of which are here new, though some were proposed by him in 1849—there being no distinction made between them.

Avocettula, p. 6; *Damophila, Chlorestes, Smaragditis,* p. 7; *Riccordia, Discura, Steganura, Tilmatura,* p. 8; *Chrysolampis, Sappho, Eriocnemis, Engyete. Threptria, Phemonoë, Hemistephania, Phaiolaima, Ionolaima, Lamprolaima,* p. 9; *Agyrtria, Uranomitra, Leucochloris, Chalybura, Cyanophaia, Eucephala, Cyanochloris,* p. 10; *Margarochrysis, Boissonneaua, Platystylopterus, Floresia, Sericotes, Pampa, Saepiopterus, Prognornis,* p. 11; *Mulsantia, Bellatrix, Heliactinia, Popelairia. Rhamphomicron* (ex. Bp.), *Parzudakia, Lamprurus, Anactoria, Diotima, Atthis, Doricha, Rhodopis, Calliperidia,* p. 12; *Myrtis, Archilochus, Lipidolarynx, Klais, Baucis. Telesiella, Praxilla, Petasophora,* p. 12; *Eustephanus, Eremita, Ptyonornis, Ametrornis, Thaumaste,* p. 14; *Eutoxeres,* p. 15.

1855. ANON. [Review of parts vii, viii of Gould's Trochilidæ.] $<$ *Nat. Hist. Rev.*, ii. 1855, pp. 3–8.

1855. GOULD, J. On two New Species of Humming Birds. $<$ *P. Z. S.*, xxiii, 1855, pp. 86, 87.

Heliothrix purpureiceps, p. 87, Popayan; *H. phaïnolœma,* p. 87, Rio Napo.

1855. GOULD, J. On a new Genus and Species of Trochilidæ [Eugenia imperatrix] from Ecuador. $<$ *P. Z. S.*, xxiii, 1855, p. 192.

1855. GOULD, J. Descriptions of Five New Species of Humming Birds. $<$ *Ann. Mag. Nat. Hist.*, 2d ser., xv, 1855, pp. 146, 147.

From *P. Z. S.*, Apr. 12, 1853, pp. 61, 62, *q. v.*

1855. GOULD, J. Observations on the Nests of Humming Birds. $<$ *Ann. Mag. Nat. Hist.*, 2d ser., xv, 1855, pp. 157, 158.

From *P. Z. S.*, July 26, 1853, p. 100.

1855. GOULD, J. Description of a New Species of Humming Bird, from Quijos. $<$ *Ann. Mag. Nat. Hist.*, 2d ser., xvi, 1855, pp. 278, 279.

From *P. Z. S.*, May 9, 1854, p. 109.

1855. GOULD, J.   Descriptions of two new Species of Humming Birds, from Peru.
    < Ann. Mag. Nat. Hist., 2d ser., vx, 1855, pp. 318, 319.
        From P. Z. S., Nov. 22, 1853, p. 109.

1855. LAWRENCE, G. N.   Description of a New Species of the Humming Bird of the
    Genus Mellisuga Brisson [M. albo-coronata], with a note on Trochilus aquila
    Bourcier.   < Ann. Lyc. Nat. Hist. New York, vi, 1855, pp. 137–142, pl. iv.

1855. REICHENBACH, L.   Trochilinarum Enumeratio ex affinitate naturali reciproca
    prima ducta provisoria. Leipzig. J. Hofmeister. 1855. 8vo.
        Not seen.

1856. ADAMS, H. G.   Humming Birds described and illustrated; with an introductory
    sketch of their structure, plumage, habits, haunts, etc. By H. G. Adams.
    With 8 coloured plates. London: Groombridge. 1856. 1 vol. 8vo. pp.
    104, pll. 8.
        Not seen: title from Carus and Engelmann. Bibl. (Young Naturalist's Library.)

1856. BOURCIER, J.   Description d'une espèce nouvellement connue d'Oiseau-mouche
    du genre Pygmornis [amaura] (Conspectus Trochilorum, prince Ch. Bona-
    parte), famille des Trochilidés, sousfam. 175 Phætorninés.   < Rev. et Mag. de
    Zool., viii, 1856, pp. 552, 553.

1856. BOURCIER, J., and MULSANT, E.   [Trochilus idaliæ, T. aspasiæ, spp. nn.]
    < Ann. Soc. Linn. de Lyon, n. s.,iii, 1856, pp. 187–189.
        Pas vu moi-même—le titre est tiré de la Bibl. de Carus et Engelmann.

1856. GOULD, J.   On two New Species of Humming Birds belonging to the genus
    Amazilius.   < P. Z. S., xxiv, 1856, pp. 150, 151.
        A. cerviniventris, p. 150, Cordova ; A. castaneiventris, p. 150, Bogotá.

1856. GOULD, J.   On a new genus and species of Trochilidæ [Eugenia imperatrix]
    from Ecuador.   < Ann. Mag. Nat. Hist., 2d ser., 1856, pp. 270, 271.
        From P. Z. S., Nov. 13, 1855, p. 192.

1856. GOULD, J.   On two new Species of Humming-Birds.   < Ann. Mag. Nat. Hist., 2d
    ser., xvii, 1856, pp. 518, 519.
        From P. Z. S., June 12, 1855, pp. 86, 87, q. r.

1857. ANON.   The Canadian Humming Bird [Trochilus colubris].   < Canad. Journ.,
    ii, 1857, pp. 382, 383.
        Note of Gould's carrying them toward England.

1857. GOULD, J.   Descriptions of Three New Species of the Genus Phaëthornis, Fam-
    ily Trochilidæ.   < P. Z. S., xxv, 1857, pp. 14, 15.
        Phaëthornis viridicaudata, P. episcopus, P. obscura, p. 14.

1857. GOULD, J.   On two New Species of Humming Birds belonging to the genus
    Amazilius.   < Ann. Mag. Nat. Hist., 2d ser., xix, 1857, p. 352.
        From P. Z. S., June 10, 1856, pp. 150, 151, q. v.

1857. GOULD, J.   Descriptions of Three New Species of the Genus Phaëthornis, Fam-
    ily Trochilidæ.   < Ann. Mag. Nat. Hist., 2d ser., xix, 1857, pp. 493, 494.
        From P. Z. S., Jan. 27, 1857, pp. 14, 15, q. v.

1858. LAWRENCE, G. N.   Descriptions of Seven New Species of Humming Birds.
    < Ann. Lyc. Nat. Hist. New York, vi, 1858, pp. 258–264.
        Phæthornis moorei, p. 258; Ph. villosus, p. 259; Ph. atrimentalis, Ph. nigricinctus, p. 260;
        Glaucis affinis. p. 261; Campylopterus splendens, p. 262; Ionolaima frontalis, p. 263.

1858. S[TIMPSON], W.   Humming Bird of the U. States.   < Am. Journ. Sci., xxv, 1858,
    pp. 294, 295.
        T. colubris.—From Ann. Mag. N. H., 2d ser., xx, p. 520.

1859. BOURCIER, J., and MULSANT, E.   [Lophornis verreauxi.]   < Ann. Sc. Phys. Soc.
    d'Agric. de Lyon, iii, 1859, p. 364.
        Not seen—title from Giebel. (Some mistake here?)

1859. GOULD, J.   Descriptions of four new Species of Humming-birds from Mexico.
    < Ann. Mag. Nat. Hist., 3d ser., iv, 1859, pp. 96–98.
        Amazilia ocai, p. 96, Xalapa; Calothorax pulchra, Cyanomyia violiceps, C. ? sordida, p. 97
    Oaxaca.

1859. H[INCKS], W.   A monograph of the Trochilidæ, or Humming Birds.   < *Canad.*
Journ., iv, 1858, pp. 47–50.
Review of portions of Gould's work.

1859. JAMESON, W., *and* FRASER, L.   Notes on some of the Humming-birds of Ecuador figured in Mr. Gould's Monograph.   < *Ibis*, i, 1859, pp. 399, 400.
Brief field-notes on 9 spp.

1860. BRYANT, H.   [Note on Trochilus bahamensis.]   < *Proc. Boston Soc. Nat. Hist.*,
vii, 1860, p. 317.

1860. CABANIS, J., *and* HEINE, F.   Museum Heineanum. . . .   III. Theil, die Schrill-
vogel . . .   Halberstadt, 1860.   > Fam. Trochilidæ, pp. 1–81.

Though scarcely citable as a separate article, I notice this portion of the *Mus. Hein.* here
for the many new names of Hummers it gives, as follows:—*Dolerisca*, p. 6; *Pygmornis rufiven-*
tris (for *rufigaster* V.), p. 7; *Toxoteuches*, p. 11; *Sphenoproctus*, p. 11; *Loxopterus*, p. 13; *Oro-*
trochilus (for *Oreotrochilus* Gould), p. 15; *Chrysolampis reichenbachi*, p. 31; *Thalurania for-*
ficata (for *furcatoides* Gould), p. 24; *Sporadicus*, p. 25; *Agyrtria niveipectus* (for *chionopectus*
Gld.), p. 33; *Pyrrhophœna*, p. 35; *P. suavis*, p. 36; *Hemithylaca*, p. 37; *H. hoffmanni*, p. 38;
H. warscewiczi, p. 38; *Uranomitra lessoni*, p. 41; *Chrysurisca*, p. 42; *Panterpe*, p. 43; *P.*
insignis, p. 43; *Chlorolampis*, p. 47; *C. salvini*, p. 48; *C. smaragdina*, p. 48; *Prasitis*, p. 49;
Pauychlora, p. 46; *P. aurata*, p. 50; *P. stenura*, p. 50; *Aïthurus*, p. 50; *Entima*, p. 51; *Spar-*
ganura, p. 52; *Psalidoprymna*, p. 52; *Heliomaster sclateri*, p. 54; *Cephalolepis* (for *Cephallepis*
Lodd.), p. 61; *Polemistria*, p. 63; *Prymnacantha*, p. 64; *Urolampra*, p. 68; *U. chloropogon*, p.
68; *Agaclyta*, p. 70; *A. aequitorialis*, p. 72; *Adelisca*, p. 72; *Anthocephala*, p. 72; *Heliotryphon*
(for *Heliotrypha*), p. 74; *Streblorhamphus*, p. 76; *Opisthoprora*, p. 76; *Hypermetra*, p. 80.

The high character of this publication is too well known to require comment here.   These
authors offer a notable contrast to some who could be named, and who would suffer by comparison, in the great care they take for the correct and precise orthography of words according to their classical etymology.   Many of the above new names, in fact, have their origin in
the practice of these authors to discard altogether, or at least to emend, any name not classical in form.   Commendable as is this care in the coining of new words, it is perhaps going
to an extreme to reject all words, otherwise unobjectionable, which are not formed in the
same manner.

1860. GOULD, J.   Descriptions of twenty-two New Species of Humming-Birds.   < *P.*
Z. S., xxviii, 1860, pp. 304–312.

Grypus spixi, Glaucis melanura, p. 304; *Phaëthornis zonura, Augasma smaragdineum*, p.
305; *Eucephala cœruleo-lavata, E. hypocyanea*, p. 306; *Erythronota? elegans, Thaumatias virid-*
iceps, T. cœruleiceps, p. 307; *T. nitidifrons, Chlorostilbon melanorhynchus, C. acuticaudus*, p. 308;
C. osberti, Calothorax decoratus, Amazilia alticola, p. 309; *Phlogophilus* (g. n.) *hemileucurus,*
Calliphlox? iridescens, Aphantochroa? gularis, p. 310; *Eriocnemis squamata, Schistes person-*
atus, p. 311; *Thalurania tschudii, Oreopyra leucaspis*, p. 312.

1860. GOULD, J.   Descriptions of twenty-two New Species of Humming-Birds.   < *Ann.*
Mag. Nat. Hist., 3d ser., vi, 1860, pp. 301–309.
From *P. Z. S.*, June 12, 1860, pp. 304–312, *q. v.*

1860. LAWRENCE, G. N.   Descriptions of three new species of Humming-birds of the
Genera Heliomaster, Amazilia, and Mellisuga.   < *Ann. Lyc. Nat. Hist. New*
York, vii, Apr., 1860, pp. 107–111.
H. stuartæ, p. 107, Bogotá; *A. xantusii*, p. 109, Cape St. Lucas; *M. merrittii*, p. 110, Veragua.
[The "*Mellisuga merrittii*" = *Klais guimeti.*]

1860. LAWRENCE, G. N.   Description of a New Species of Bird of the genus Phaeton,
also of a New Species of Humming Bird of the Genus Heliopaedica.   < *Ann.*
Lyc. N. Y., vii, Apr., 1860, pp. 142–145.
The Hummer is named *H. castaneocauda*, p. 145; it is from Cape St. Lucas, and is the same
as *Amazilia xantusii. Id. ibid.*, p. 109.

1860. OCA, R. M. DE.   The Mexican Humming-Birds.   < *Proc. Acad. Nat. Sci. Phila.*,
xii, 1860, pp. 47, 48, 80, 81, 551–553.
Descriptions of, and field notes on, 4 spp. in three separate papers: No. 1, *Campylopterus*
delattrei; No. 2, *Cyanomyia cyanocephala;* No. 3, *Campylopterus pampa* and *Thaumasturo*
elizæ.   (Title of Nos. 2 and 3 modified to "The Hummingbirds of Mexico".)

1860. SALVIN, O.   Notes on the Humming-birds of Guatemala.   < *Ibis*, ii, 1860, pp
259–272.
More or less extended biographical notes on 23 spp., with remarks upon several others.

1861. BREWER, T. M. [Remarks on exhibition of two nests of Trochilus colubris.] < *Proc. Boston Soc. Nat. Hist.*, vii, 1861, p. 426.

1861. GEOFROY, L. DE. Note sur les Trochilidées, (Oiseaux-Mouches—Tominejas) de la Nouvelle Grenade.—Par Mr. L. de Geofroy, Secrétaire de la Légation de France á Bogotá. < *Contribuciones de Colombia a las Ciencias i a las Artes publicadas con la cooperacion de la Sociedad de Naturalistas Neo-Granadinos, por E. Uricoechea, Año Segundo*, 1861, pp. 1–16 (8vo, Bogotá, imprenta de El Mosaico; Londres, Trübner & Co).

> The piece of the "Contribuciones" handled consists only of the above cover-title and of Geofroy's article, which treats briefly of 64 spp., mostly with reference to their habits, &c. The list is dressed after Bonaparte's, with Gould's names also, when different, and with the native appellations; the whole preceded by some general considerations.
> Cf. *Ibis*, 1862, p. 188.

1861. GOULD, J. Descriptions of Two New Species of Humming-Bird, belonging to the Genus Hypuroptila. < *P. Z. S.*, xxix, 1861, pp. 198, 199.

> *H. urochrysa*, p. 198; *H. isauræ*, p. 199.

1861. GOULD, J. Descriptions of Two New Species of Humming-Birds belonging to the Genus Hypuroptila. < *Ann. Mag. Nat. Hist.*, 3d ser., viii, 1861, pp. 268, 269.

> From *P. Z. S.*, May 14, 1861, pp. 198, 199, *q. v.*

1861. GOULD, J. An | Introduction | to | The Trochilidæ, | or | Family of Humming-birds. | By John Gould, F. R. S., &c. &c. | London : | printed for the author, | by Taylor & Francis, Red Lion Court, Fleet street. | 1861. 8vo. 4 p. ll., pp. i–iv, 1–216.

> Synonymatic list, with primary reference to the pll. of the folio work, habitat, and miscellaneous critical and biographical comment on the 416 spp. and 123 genn. presented. Species given without a reference are: *Phaethornis boliviana*, p. 42; *Eulampis longirostris*, p. 69; *Dorifera rectirostris*, p. 71; (*Stellula*, p. 90:) *Cynanthus cœlestis*, p. 102; *Metallura quitensis*, p. 112 (*descr. nulla*); *Cyanomyia guatemalensis*, p. 148; (*Hemistilbon*, p. 149;) *Chrysuronia cœruleicapilla*, p. 165 (*descr. nulla*); *Circe*, p. 168; *Phœoptila*, p. 169; *Eucephala scapulata*, p. 166; *Phœoptila zonura*, p. 170; *Chlorostilbon igneus*, p. 176; *C. peruanus, C. napensis*, p. 177; *C. brevicaudatus.*

1862. ANON. Die Kolibris. < *Aus der Natur.*, xix, oder n. F. vii, Jan.-März 1862, pp. ——.

> Not seen.

1862. CRISP, E. On some points relating to the Anatomy of the Humming-bird (Trochilus colubris). < *P. Z. S.*, xxx, 1862, pp. 208–210.

1862. GOULD, J. [Exhibition and Description of two New Species of Humming-birds from Ecuador, of a New Fregilus from the Himalayas, and of a new Prion.] < *P. Z. S.*, Apr. 8, 1862, pp. 124, 125.

> The Hummers named are *Heliothrix longirostris* and *Aphantochroa hyposticta*, p. 124.

1862. GOULD, J. [On new Trochilidæ, a new Fregilus, and a new Prion.] < *Ann. Mag. Nat. Hist.*, 3d ser., x, 1862, pp. 315–317.

> From *P. Z. S.*, April 8, 1862, pp. 124, 125, *q. v.*

1862. LAWRENCE, G. N. Descriptions of Six New Species of Birds of the Families Charadridæ, Trochilidæ, and Caprimulgidæ. < *Ann. Lyc. Nat. Hist. New York*, vii, Feb., 1862, pp. 455–460.

> The *Trochilidæ* here described are *Thalurania luciæ*, p. 456, and *Chlorostilbon insularis*, p. 457, both from the Tres Marias Isls.; *Trochilus aurigularis*, p. 458, loc. ignot.; *Sapphironia luminosa*, p. 458, N. Granada.

1863. BENVENUTI, H. Description de quatre nouvelles espèces de la famille des Trochilidæ, provenant de la Nouvelle-Grenade et d'une nouvelle Sylvia du Brésil. < *Rev. et Mag. de Zool.*, xv, 1863, pp. 206–208.

> *Polytmus ceciliæ, Mellisuga judith, M. salvadorii, M. ridolfii, Sylvia picciolii*, p. 207.—Traduction franç. d'un opuscule, petit in-4° de 16 pages, Florence, impr. royale, 1863. Voir le titre ci-dessous, 1866, BENVENUTI, E.

1863. CRISP, E. On some Points relating to the Anatomy of the Humming-bird (Trochilus colubris). < *Ann. Mag. Nat. Hist.*, 3d ser., xii, 1863, pp. 70–72.

> From *P. Z. S.*, June 24, 1862, pp. 208–210.

1863. GOSSE, P. H. The Humming Bird's Tongue. < *Zoologist*, xxi, 1863, pp. 8485, 8486, figg. 1, 2.

1863. GOULD, J. On a New Genus of Humming Birds [Androdon aequatorialis, sp. n.]. < *Ann. Mag. Nat. Hist.*, 3d ser., xii, 1863, pp. 246, 247.

1863. HEINE, F. Trochilidica. < *J. f. O.*, xi, 1863, pp. 173–217.

> An extended and elaborate critical review.—*Dnophera*, p. 175; *Aspasta*, p. 179; *Polyplancta*, p. 182; *Eranna*, p. 187; *Eratina*, p. 190; *Polyerata*, p. 194; *Eratopis*, p. 191; *Erasmia*, p. 191; *Cloanges*, p. 200; *Polyonymus*, p. 206; *Thaumatoëssa*, p. 209; *Tricholopha*, p. 209; *Polyaena*, p. 215, genn. nn. *Thalurania subfurcata*, p. 181; *Agyrtria terpna*, p. 184; *A. compsa*, p. 185; *Hemithylaca braccáta*, p. 193; *Chlorostilbon egregius*, p. 197; *Lesbia margarethæ*, p. 213; *Docimastes schliephackei*, p. 215, spp. nn.

1863. WALLACE, A. R. Who are the Humming Bird's Relations? < *Zoologist*, xxi, 1863, pp. 8486–8491.

> *Cypselidae*, not *Nectariniidæ*.

1864. BURMEISTER, H. Sobre los Picaflores descriptos por D. Felix de Azara. < *Anales del Mus. Publ. de Buenos Aires*, 1, Entrega primera, 1864, pp. 67–70.

> This is the original form of the paper; see the German paper of same date. Cf. *Ibis*, 1865, p. 535; *P. Z. S.*, 1865, p. 467. See 1867, BURMEISTER, H.

1864. LAWRENCE, G. N. Descriptions of New Species of Birds of the Families Tanagridæ, Cuculidæ, and Trochilidæ, with a Note on Panterpe insignis. < *Ann. Lyc. Nat. Hist. New York*, viii, 1864, pp. 41–46.

> The *Trochilidæ* here described are *Urochroa leucura*, p. 43, Ecuador; *Urosticte ruficrissa*, p. 44, Ecuador; and *Ramphomicron olivaceus*, p. 44, Bolivia.

1865. BURMEISTER, H. [Extract from a letter concerning Heliomaster angelæ.] < *P. Z. S.*, 1865, pp. 466, 467.

1865. BURMEISTER, H. Ueber die von Azara beschriebenen Kolibri-Arten. < *J. f. O.*, xiii, 1865, pp. 225–229. Nachtrag dazu, *J. f. O.*, 1866, pp. 88–90.

> Azara's No. 289 = *Agyrtria albiventris*; Nos. 290, 291 = *Hylocharis ruficollis*; Nos. 292, 293, 294 = *H. bicolor* (lege *flavifrons*); Nos. 295, 296 = *Lampornis mango*; No. 298, unbestimmtbar; Nos. 297, 299 = *Heliomaster angelae*. (Vergl. *Zool. Rec.* a. d. J. 1865, p. 100; *Ibis*, 1865, p. 535; *P. Z. S.*, 1865, p. 467.)

1865. LAWRENCE, G. N. Descriptions of new species of Birds of the Families Paridæ, Vireonidæ, Tyrannidæ, and Trochilidæ, with a Note on Myiarchus panamensis. < *Proc. Acad. Nat. Sci. Phila.*, xvii, Jan., 1865, pp. 37–39.

> The Hummers here described are *Chalybura æneicauda*, p. 38, Venezuela; *C. carnioli* and *Panychlora parvirostris*, p. 39, Costa Rica.

1865. LAWRENCE, G. N. Descriptions of New Species of Birds of the Families Tanagridæ, Dendrocolaptidæ, Formicaridæ, Tyrannidæ, and Trochilidæ. < *Ann. Lyc. Nat. Hist. New York*, viii, 1865, pp. 126–135.

> The Hummer here described is *Eupherusa niveicauda*, p. 134.

1865. SCLATER, P. L. [Exhibition of specimens of Heliomaster angelæ, with notes thereupon by Prof. Burmeister.] < *P. Z. S.*, xxxiii, 1865, pp. 466, 467.

1866. BENVENUTI, E. Descrizione di quattro nuove specie della famiglia dei Trochilidi provenienti dalla Nuova Granata e di una nuova specie di Dendroica del Brasile con l'aggiunta di una nota riguardante la Fauna Toscana. < *Annali R. Museo di Fisica e Storia Nat. di Firenze* per il 1865, nuova serie, i, 1866, pp. 197–209.

> *Polytmus (Campylopterus) ceciliae*, p. 202; *Mellisuga (Panaplites) judith*, p. 203; *M. (Cynanthus) salvadorii*, p. 204; *M. (Eriocnemis) ridolfi*, p. 205; *Dendroica picciolii*, p. 207.
>
> This is the title as taken direct from the *Annali* for 1865, dated 1866; but the article must have appeared, in substance at least, with the names of all these new species, as early as 1863; being noticed in French in the *Rev. et Mag. de Zool.* of that year, xv, pp. 206–208; where it is described as a sm. 4to of 16 pp., Florence, 1863. I have not seen it in that form, nor of such date.— Compare same author, 1863. (See especially *Ibis*, 1876, pp. 5–11.)

1866. BURMEISTER, H. Ueber die von Azara beschriebenen Kolibri-Arten. Nachtrag [*J. f. O.*, 1865, pp. 225–229]. < *J. f. O.*, 1866, pp. 88–90.

1866. LAWRENCE, G. N. Characters of Seven New Species of Birds from Central and South America, with a Note on Thaumatias chionurus. < *Ann. Lyc. Nat. Hist. New York*, viii, 1866, pp. 344–350.

Besides the Hummer mentioned in the text there are described as new *Phœthornis cassinii*, p. 347, and *Eupherusa cupreiceps*, p. 348.

1866. LAWRENCE, G. N. Descriptions of Six New Species of Birds of the Families Hirundinidæ, Formicaridæ, Tyrannidæ, and Trochilidæ. < *Ann. Lyc. Nat. Hist. New York*, viii, 1866, pp. 400–405.

The Hummers here described are *Heliodoxa henryi*, p. 402, Costa Rica; *Thaumatias viridicaudus*, p. 404, Buenaventura; *Amazilia (Pyrrhophœna) graysoni*, p. 404, Tres Marias Islands. Cf. *Ibis*, 1867, p. 247.

1866. MULSANT, E., VERREAUX, J., *and* VERREAUX, E. Essai d'une Classification Méthodique des Trochilidées ou Oiseaux-Mouches. < *Mém. Soc. Imp. des Sci. Nat. de Cherbourg*, xii, 1866, pp. 152–240. (Separate, 8vo, Paris, 1866, pp. 98.)

Not seen.—Cf. *Ibis*, 1867, pp. 126–129; and especially *Zool. Rec.* for 1866, pp. 83–85, from which I took title and comment, before I handled the separate, which see (next title).

This work is designed to furnish an analytical arrangement of the family, and to characterize the several groups composing it. The *Trochilidæ* are primarily divided into two tribes, the Trochiliens and the Ornismiens, distinguished by characters drawn from the upper mandible. The Trochiliens form two sections, each of them with several branches, and the branch "Leucoliares" being further subdivided; and the Ornismiens similarly contain two divisions, each subdivided. The whole are arranged in 70 genera, including 29 subgenera, so great a reduction of the 123 genera recognized by Gould, in 1861, that "we should be inclined to look upon Prof. Mulsant's arrangement as an improvement, but for the belief that his reduction in their number *seems* to be obtained in some cases by totally ignoring certain of his predecessor's divisions, while, on the other hand, the use of so many groups larger than genera deprives the present work of a very desirable simplicity; but the fact, which is highly creditable to him, remains to be mentioned that characters which are more or less definite are assigned to each group of species, whether larger than a genus or less, named or unnamed." 11 new genera and 13 new subgenera are proposed; others are used in a sense very different from that attributed to them by Gould. There is great liberty taken with the spelling. 370 spp. are enumerated, among them 4 new ones without description—a most reprehensible practice. The work is announced as merely the precursor of a larger one on the same subject.

Leucolia, p. 31; *Ariana*, p. 36; *Euclosia*, p. 63; *Callidice*, p. 65; *Erebenna*, p. 66; *Bellona*, p. 75; *Paphosia*. p. 75; *Telamon*, p. 75; *Uralia*, p. 81; *Amathusia*, p. 85; *Zephyritis*, p. 87, are new genera; and *Dyrinia*, *Egolia*, *Elvira*, *Emilia*, *Eupogonus*, *Galenia*, *Halia*, *Manilia*, *Mesophila*, *Momus*, *Osalia*, *Philodice*, and *Polymnia* are new subgenera. *Amazilia lessoni*, p. 35 = *A. pristina* of Gould; *Diphlogœna (Helianthea) lessoni*, p. 61 = *Lampropygia cœligena* + *L. boliviana* of Gould; *Bellona hectoris*, p. 75 = *Orthorhynchus ornatus* of Gould; *Zephyritis (Calypte) elvirœ*, p. 88 = *Calypte helenœ* of Gould.

1866. MULSANT, E., VERREAUX, J., *and* VERREAUX, E. Essai | d'une | Classification Méthodique | des | Trochilidées | ou | Oiseaux-Mouches, | par E. Mulsant, | Sous-Bibliothécaire de la ville de Lyon, Professeur d'histoire naturelle au Lycée, | Président de la Société linnéene, etc., | et | Jules Verreaux, | Attaché au Muséum d'histoire naturelle de Paris, | Edouard Verreaux, | Marchand-naturaliste. | — | Paris, | F. Savy, Libraire, Rue Hautefeuille, 24, || Deyrolle, Rue de la Monnaie, 19, | Verreaux, Place Royale, 9. | [1866.] 1 vol. 8vo. pp. 98.

Extrait des Mémoires de la Société Impériale des Sciences Naturelles de Cherbourg, t. xii, 1866. Cherbourg, Imp. Bedelfontaine et Syffert.

1866. SCLATER, P. L. [Exhibition of some specimens of Eustephanus fernandensis and E. stokesi.] < *P. Z. S.*, xxxiv, 1866, pp. 556, 557.

Including extracts from a letter by E. L. Landbeck on the *Trochilidæ* of Juan Fernandez.

1867. BURMEISTER, H. Suplemento á las noticias sobre los Picaflores de d. Félix de Azara. < *Anal. Mus. Publ. Buenos Aires*, i, Entrega segunda, 1867, p. 86 (última página).

"La última página de la primera Entrega debe suprimirse por estar reimpressa en la segunda Entrega." This "suplemento" is therefore on the last page (86) of Entrega i, 1864; but only appeared with Entrega ii, 1867. See 1864, BURMEISTER, H.

1867. LAWRENCE, G. N. Descriptions of New Species of Trochilidæ. < *Ann. Lyc. Nat. Hist. New York*, viii, May, 1867, pp. 483–485.

Doricha bryantœ, p. 483; *Oreopyra venusta*, p. 484; *O. cinereicauda*, p. 485; all three from Costa Rica.

1868. GOULD, J. Descriptions of two new species of Humming-Birds. < *Ann. Mag. Nat. Hist.*, 4th ser., i, 1868, pp. 322, 323.

   Eriocnemis smaragdinipectus, p. 322, Ecuador; *Gouldia melanosternon*, p. 323, Peru.

1868. GOULD, J. On some additional species of Eutoxeres. < *Ann. Mag. Nat. Hist.*, 4th ser., i, 1868, pp. 455–457.

   Eutoxeres heterura, p. 457, sp. n., from Central Ecuador, and *E. salvini*, p. 457, sp. n., from Veragua and Costa Rica.

1868. MILLINGTON, L. A. An albino Humming-Bird [Trochilus colubris ?]. < *Am. Nat.*, ii, 1868, p. 110.

1868. MILLINGTON, L. A. An Albino Humming Bird [Trochilus colubris ?]. < *Zoologist*, 2d ser., iii, 1868; p. 1343.

   From the "American Naturalist," April, 1868.

1868. SALVIN, O. [On the probable identity of Heliomaster spectabilis Lawr. (cf. Ibis, 1868, 115) with Eugenes fulgens.] < *Ibis*, 2d ser., iv, 1868, p. 251.

1869. BEULLOCH, —. El Pájaro-mosca [Trochilus]. < *La Naturaleza*, i, 1869, pp. 61–69.

   Traducido y anotado por D. Jesus Sanchez. "La primera noticia acerca de estas aves data del año 1558, y se encuentra en 'Las singularidades de la Francia antártica' (Brasil)".

1869. GOULD, J. Description of a New Genus and Species of the Family Trochilidæ. < *P. Z. S.*, xxxvii, 1869, pp. 295, 296.

   Oreonympha nobilis, p. 295, Tinta, Peru.

1869. GOULD, J. Descriptions of five new species of birds from Queensland, Australia; and a new Humming-bird from the Bahamas. < *Ann. Mag. Nat. Hist.*, 4th ser., iv, Aug., 1869, pp. 108–112.

   Not seen.—The Hummer is *Doricha lyrura*, p. 112; from Inagua, Dr. H. Bryant.

1870. A[LLEN], J. A. [Identification of a specimen of Trochilus colubris.] < *Am. Nat.*, iv, 1870, p. 576.

1870. BAIRD, S. F. Agency of Humming-birds in fertilizing Plants. < *Harper's New Monthly Mag.*, xl, 1870, p. 940.

1870. ELLIOT, D. G. Description of a new Species of Humming-bird of the Genus Chrysolampis [chlorolæma]. < *Ann. Mag. Nat. Hist.*, 4th ser., vi, 1870, p. 346.

1870. GOULD, J. [Remarks on a Collection of Humming-birds made by Mr. Buckley in Ecuador, and Descriptions of two new Species.] < *P. Z. S.*, xxxviii. 1870, pp. 803, 804.

   Chætocercus bombus, Thalurania hypochlora, p. 804, both from Citado, Ecuador; with list of 30 spp.

1870. GOULD, J. On a supposed new Species of Humming-bird [Eustephanus leyboldi] from the Juan-Fernandez Group of Islands. < *Ann. Mag. Nat. Hist.*, 4th ser., vi, 1870, p. 406.

1871. ELLIOT, D. G. Descriptions of two new Species of Humming-birds belonging to the Genera Eupherusa and Cyanomyia. < *Ann. Mag. Nat. Hist.*, 4th ser., viii, 1871, pp. 266, 267.

   E. poliocerca, p. 266, Putla, Mexico; *C. viridifrons*, p. 266, Mexico.

1871. GOULD, J. Descriptions of six new Humming-Birds. < *P. Z. S.*, xxxix, 1871, pp. 503–505.

   Helianthea osculans, Heliangelus squamigularis, p. 503; *Heliomaster albicrissa, Lesbia chlorura*, p. 504; *Eriocnemis russata, Polytmus leucorrhous*, p. 505.

1871. GOULD, J. On a new Species of Humming-bird belonging to the Genus Spathura [solstitialis]. < *Ann. Mag. Nat. Hist.*, 4th ser., viii, 1871, pp. 61, 62.

1871. JOHNSON, L. The Humming Bird [Trochilus colubris]. < *Am. Nat.*, v, 1871, pp. 309, 310.

   Notes of nidification at Bradford, Massachusetts.

1871. LAWRENCE, G. N. Descriptions of three New Species of American Birds, with a Note on Eugenes spectabilis. < *Ann. Lyc. Nat. Hist. N. Y.*, x, 1871, pp. 137–140.

   The specific validity of *Eugenes spectabilis* reaffirmed.

1872. ELLIOT, D. G. Description of a supposed new Species of Humming Bird of the Genus Eriocnemis. < *Ibis*, 3d ser., ii, 1872, pp. 293–295.

E. *dyselius*, p. 294; list of 14 spp. of the genus.

1872. ELLIOT, D. G. The Humming-birds of the West Indies. < *Ibis*, 3d ser., ii, 1872, pp. 345–357.

General characteristics of the trochilidine *Ornis*; synonymatic and critically annotated synopsis of 18 spp., with tabular view of their distribution in each of the islands.

1872. GOULD, J. Descriptions of two new Species of Humming-Birds. < *Ann. Mag. Nat. Hist.*, 4th ser., ix, 1872, pp. 195, 196.

Heliangelus micraster, Chlorostilbon pumilus, p. 195.

1872. GOULD, J. Description of three new Species of Humming-birds. < *Ann. Mag. Nat. Hist.*, 4th ser., x, 1872, pp. 452, 453.

Iolæma whitelyana, Adelomyia chlorospila, p. 452; *A. cervina*, p. 453.

1873. ANON. The Ruby-throated Humming Bird [Trochilus colubris]. < *Am. Sportsman*, iii, 1873, p. 54. See also p. 251.

1873. ANON. A Humming-bird Fight. < *Kingston* [N. Y.] *Freeman*, Sept. 5th, 1873.

Between two individuals of *Trochilus colubris*. Quoted in *Am. Sportsm.*, ii, 1873, p. 187.

1873? BOUCARD, A. Notes sur quelques Trochilidés. 8vo. pp. 16.

Presentées à la Société linnéene de Lyon, les 10 février 1873 et séances suivantes.

1873. GOULD, J. On a new Genus and Species [Hylonympha macrocerca] of the Family Trochilidæ. < *Ann. Mag. Nat. Hist.*, 4th ser., xii, 1873, p. 429.

1873–77. MULSANT, E., *and* VERREAUX, E. Histoire Naturelle des Oiseaux-Mouches ou Colibris constituant la famille des Trochilidés. Par E. Mulsant et feu Edouard Verreaux. Ouvrage publiée par la Société Linnéene de Lyon. Paris. 1873–77. 4 vols. 4to. Pub. par livr.

I have only seen the first two livraisons, and therefore cannot give the full title and collation of this great work.—Vol. I, Livr. 1, 2, 1873; 3, 4, 1874: pp. i–vi, 1–343, pll. xv. Vol. II, Livr. 1, 2, 1875; 3, 4, 1876. Vol. III, Livr. 1, 2, 1876; 3, 4, —? Vol. IV, Livr. 1–4, —? It is said to have been completed in 1877. Cf. *Ibis*, 1874, pp. 453, 454.

1873. SALVIN, O., *and* ELLIOT, D. G. Notes on the Trochilidæ. The genus Phaethornis. < *Ibis*, 3d ser., iii, 1873, pp. 1–14.

In this and subsequent papers of the same character, forming in effect a series, but with modified caption, the synonymy, distribution, and diagnoses are very elaborately treated, with much critical commentary, and lists of specimens examined. The present article treats in such manner of 14 spp. of the genus named.

1873. SALVIN, O., *and* ELLIOT, D. G. Notes on the Trochilidæ. The Genera Pygmornis, Glaucis, and Threnetes. < *Ibis*, 3d ser., iii, 1872, pp. 269, 279.

Pygmornis, 8 spp.; *Glaucis*, 1 sp.; *Threnetes*, 4 spp.

1873. SALVIN, O., *and* ELLIOT, D. G. On two Species of Trochilidæ of the Genus Lophornis. < *Ibis*, 3d ser., iii, 1873, pp. 279, 280.

L. gouldi; L. stictolophus (= *reginae* Gould, *nec* Schreibers), p. 280, sp. renom.

1873. SALVIN, O., *and* ELLIOT, D. G. Notes on the Trochilidæ. The Genus Thalurania. < *Ibis*, 3d ser., iii, 1873, pp. 353–361.

11 spp., with 2 others not known to the authors.

1873. WHITELY, H. Notes on Humming-birds collected in High Peru. < *P. Z. S.*, 1873, pp. 187–191.

Field-notes on 17 spp. For later notes see *tom. cit.*, p. 784, and *op. cit.*, 1874, p. 675.

1873. WHITELY, H. Additional Notes on Humming-birds collected in High Peru. < *P. Z. S.*, 1873, p. 784.

Field-notes on 5 spp. For other notes see *tom. cit.*, p. 187, and *op. cit.*, 1874, p. 675.

1874. ELLIOT, D. G. Description of an apparently new Species of Bird belonging to the Family Trochilidæ, of the Genus Eucephala. < *Ibis*, 3d ser., iv, 1874, pp. 87–89.

E. subcaerulea, sp. n. List of 9 spp. of the genus.

1874. ANON. The Pugnacity of the Humming Bird. < *Am. Sportsman*, iii, 1874, p. 251. See also Vol. II, 1873, p. 187.

1874. ELLIOT, D. G.   Remarks on some Typical Specimens of the Trochilidæ, with a Description of one new Genus.   < *Ibis*, 3d ser., iv, 1874, pp. 261-264.

A. von Pelzeln's types from the Vienna Museum. *Ptoshoptera*, p. 261, gen. n., based on *Thalurania iolæma* Pelz. The other species remarked upon are *Cephalepis beekii*, p. 262; *Argyrtria meliphila*, p. 263; *A. media*, p. 263; and *Thalurania lerchi*.

1874. ELLIOT, D. G.   Notes on the Trochilidæ.   The Genus Helianthus.   <*Ibis*, 3d ser., iv, 1874, pp. 330-335.

8 spp. critically treated.

1874. " H. A."   The Humming Bird [Trochilus colubris] and her Nest.   < *Am. Sportsman*, iii, 1874, p. 381.

Bird protected its nest during a storm by leaves temporarily fastened above it.

1874-75. OCA, R. M. DE.   Ensayo ornitologico de la familia Trochilidæ o sea de los Colibries o Chupamirtos de Mexico.   < *La Naturaleza*, iii, 1874, pp. 15-31, 59-66, 99-106; iii, 1875, pp. 159-167, 203-211, 299-304; 12 láminas.

Also separate, 1 vol., 4to, Mexico, 1875, *q. v.*

1874. PARTRIDGE, I. H.   Humming-Birds.   < *Pop. Sci. Monthly*, July, 1874, pp. 277-287, figg. 1-5.

General popular account.

1874. "READER."   A Tame Humming Bird [Trochilus colubris].   <*Am. Sportsman*, iv, 1874, p. 75.

1874. S[CLATER], P. L.   [List of seven species of Trochilidæ procured by Mr. H. Whitely in High Peru.]   < *P. Z. S.*, Dec. 1, 1874, p. 676.

Merely a foot-note to one of Mr. Whitely's articles on Peruvian *Trochilidæ*.

1874. VILLADA, M. M.   Troquilideos [Trochilidae] del valle de México—su descripcion y sinonimia adoptada por el profesor Jhon [sic] Gould, con algunas notas sobre sus costumbres.   < *La Naturaleza*, ii, 1874, pp. 339-369, pl. 1.

1874. WHITELY, H.   Further Notes on Humming-birds collected in High Peru.   < *P. Z. S.*, Dec. 1, 1874, pp. 675, 676.

On the habits of *Lesbia nuna*, *Acestrura mulsanti*, *Oreonympha nobilis*, and *Bourcieria inca*. Note by P. L. S[clater] giving list of seven spp. collected by Mr. Whitely in High Peru. For Mr. Whitely's earlier notes see *P. Z. S.*, 1873, pp. 187 and 784.

1875. ELLIOT, D. G.   Notes on the Trochilidæ.   The Genera Chlorostilbon and Panychlora.   <*Ibis*, 3d ser., v, Apr., 1875, pp. 149-172.

Monographic; much criticism, synonymy, &c. *Chlorostilbon*, 8 spp. *Panychlora*, 3 spp.

1875? BOUCARD, A.   Notes sur les Trochilidés du Mexique.   8vo.   pp. 16.

Présentées à la Société linnéene de Lyon, le 11 janvier, 1875.—P. 14, Liste générale des Trochilidés du Mexique; p. 15, Errata de ses premières notes (1873).

1875. MULSANT, E.   Catalogue des Oiseaux-Mouches ou Colibris.   Lyons, Paris and London.   1875.   8vo.   pp. 32.

Not seen. According to the *Zool. Rec.*, a number of new generic names occur in this list, some but not all of which were afterward characterized in the same author's *Hist. Nat. des Ois.-Mouches*, then in course of publication. They are as follows: *Alsosia*, p. 17; *Amalsia*, p. 29; *Aurinia*, p. 27; *Calligenia*, p. 20; *Dialia*, p. 27; *Eudosia*, p. 20; *Eudosia* (bis), p. 32; *Engyete*, p. 21; *Eupogonus*, p. 26; *Helymus*, p. 23; *Himalia*, p. 28; *Himelia*, p. 7; *Hypolia*, p. 17; *Idas*, p. 27; *Lavinia*, p. 24; *Leucaria*, p. 29; *Lisoria*, p. 11; *Methon*, p. 7; *Myrmia*, p. 32; *Mytinia*, p. 28; *Nania*, p. 21; *Niche*, p. 21; *Nodalia*, p. 23; *Peratus*, p. 23; *Pholoe*, p. 22; *Polyplaneta*, p. 17; *Saturia*, p. 21; *Sericotes*, p. 15; *Timolia*, p. 23; *Tricholopha*, p. 27.

1875. OCA, R. M. DE.   Ensayo ornitológico | de los | Troquilideos ó Colibries de México | por Rafael Montes De Oca | Miembro de la Sociedad Mexicana de Historia Natural, Profesor de Dibujo, | Pintura en Cristal, é idiomas | publicado | con la proteccion del Ministerio de Fomento | Inter folia frvctvs | Mexico | imprenta de Ignacio Escalente, | Bajos de San Agustin num. 1. | — | 1875.   1 vol. 4to.   2 p. ll. (title and dedication), pp. 1-58 (text), 1 l. (index); portrait of author (frontisp.), and 46 figg. col'd on 12 pll.   (Separate from *La Naturaleza*, iii, 1874-5.)

Introduccion, pp. 1-4; idea general de dichas aves y uso que hacan de sus plumas los antiguos Méxicanos, pp. 5, 6; descripcion de los Colibries que se encuentran en México (48 especies), pp. 6-58; Indice, pp. 59, 60.

1876. COOPER, J. G. Early Nesting of the Anna Humming-Bird [Calypte anna]. < *Am. Nat.*, x, No. 1, Jan., 1876, pp. 48-50.

1876. ELLIOT, D. G. Remarks on some Type Specimens of Trochilidæ from the Museums of Neuchâtel and Florence. < *Ibis*, 3d ser., vi, No. xxi, Jan., 1876, pp. 5-11.
    Bourcieria insectivora (Tschudi). *Heliodoxa leadbeateri* (Bourc.). *Leucippus leucogaster* (Tschudi).—*Mollisuga judith*, Benv. = *Paroplites flavescens. M. salvadorii*, Benv. = *Cynarthus cyanurus* ♀. *M. ridolfii*, Benv. = *Eriocnemis vestita* ♀.

1876. ELLIOT, D. G. Notes on the Trochilidæ. The Genus Lampropygia. < *Ibis*, 3d ser., vi, Jan., 1876, pp. 54-60.
    Critical notes on 7 spp. *L. columbiana*, p. 57, sp. n.

1876. ELLIOT, D. G. Notes on the Trochilidæ. The Genera Cyanomyia and Heliotrypha. < *Ibis*, 3d ser., vi, July, 1876, pp. 311-319.
    Of the former 7 and of the latter 3 spp. are distinguished, with synonymy and criticism.

1876. ELLIOT, D. G. Notes on the Trochilidæ. The Genera Heliothrix, Calliphlox, Catharma [g. n.], and Petasophora. < *Ibis*, 3d ser., vi, Oct., 1876, pp. 394-407.
    Heliothrix, 3 spp.; *Calliphlox*, 2 spp.; *Catharma*, 1 sp.; *Petasophora*, 6 spp.; with synonymy, diagnosis, and criticism.

1877. BEAL, W. J. Fertilization of Flowers by Birds [*i. e.*, by Trochilus colubris]. < *Am. Nat.*, xi, No. 12, Dec., 1877, p. 754.

1877. BOUDWIN, G. The ruby-throated humming bird [Trochilus colubris]. < *Forest and Stream*, viii, June 7, 1877, p. 280.
    Account of the nidification.

1877. ELLIOT, D. G. Review of the Specimens of Trochilidæ in the Paris Museum, brought by D'Orbigny from South America. < *Ibis*, 4th ser., i, 1877, pp. 133-142.
    D'Orbigny's were among the most important of the earlier collections of these difficult birds, and the present paper, drawn up from their examination, is specially valuable. Comparatively few of the species, described as new by D'Orb. and Lafr., stand, most being provided with earlier names by Vieillot, Lesson, etc. *Thaumatias neglectus*, sp. n., p. 140 = *Ornismya bicolor* D'Orb. & Lafr. Upwards of 30 spp. are accounted for.

1877. ELLIOT, D. G. [Amazilia lucida, sp. n.] < *Ann. Mag. Nat. Hist.*, 4th ser., xx, 1877, pp. 404 - —.
    Not seen. Cf. *Ibis*, 1878, p. 113.

1877. ELLIOT, D. G. Remarks on Selasphorus alleni, Henshaw. < *Bull. Nutt. Ornith. Club.*, ii, No. 4, Oct., 1877, pp. 97-102. 2 figs.
    Contends that *S. alleni* is the true *S. rufus* Gm., and names *S. henshawi* (p. 102) what Henshaw had considered to be *S. rufus*. Cf. *op. cit.*, iii, 1878, p. 11.

1877. HENSHAW, H. W. Description of a new species of Humming-Bird from California. < *Bull. Nutt. Ornith. Club.*, ii, No. 3, July, 1877, pp. 53-58, 2 figs.
    Selasphorus alleni, p. 53, compared at much length with *S. platycercus*.

1877. HENSHAW, H. W. Notes on the Habits of the Green-backed California Humming Bird. Selasphorus Alleni, (Henshaw). < *Field and Forest*, iii, No. 6, Dec., 1877, pp. 95-98.

1877. LAWRENCE, G. N. Note on Doricha enicura (Vieill). < *Bull. Nutt. Ornith. Club*, ii, No. 4, Oct., 1877, p. 108, 109.
    The so-called "*Doricha enicura* (Vieill.)," which had been ascribed to the U. S., proves to have been *Calothorax lucifer* (Sw.) ♀. See Henshaw, *Amer. Sportsm.*, v. Feb. 20, 1875, p. 328, and *Rep. Expl. W. 100th Merid.*, Vol. V, p. 381.

1877. LAWRENCE, G. N. Descriptions o' New Species of Birds of the Families Trochilidæ and Tetraonidæ. < *Ann. N. Y. Acad. Sci.*, i, Dec., 1877, pp. 50-52.
    Sporadinus bracei, p. 50, Bahamas; *Orthorhynchus emigrans*, p. 51, Venezuela; *Cyrtonyx sumichrasti*, p. 51, Tehuantepec. (Cf. *Ibis*, 1878, p. 468.)

1877. MERRILL, J. C. A Humming Bird [Amazilia cerviniventris] new to the Fauna of the United States. < *Bull. Nutt. Ornith. Club*, ii, No. 1, Jan., 1877, p. 26.

1877. MULSANT, E. Description d'une espèce nouvelle de Trochilidé. < *Ann. Soc. Linn. Lyon*, Oct. 12, 1877, pp. — - —.

Not seen. *Arinia* (g. n.) *boucardi*, p. —, Costa Rica. Cf. *Ibis*, 1878, p. 469.

1877. SALVADORI, T. Description of a . . . and of a new Humming-bird of the Genus Heliangelus. < *Ibis*, 4th ser., i, July, 1877, pp. 337–339.

The Hummer here described is *Heliangelus taczanowskii*, p. 338, from Bogotá (Münsberg).

1877. [SCLATER, P. L., *and* SALVIN, O.] Mulsant's 'Histoire Naturelle des Oiseaux-Mouches.' < *Ibis*, 4th ser., i, Apr., 1877, p. 244.

Review of parts of that work. Cf. *Ibis*, 1875, p. 510.

1878. ALLEN, C. A. An Albino Anna Humming-Bird [Calypte anna]. < *Bull. Nutt. Ornith. Club*, iii, No. 4, Oct., 1878, pp. 192, 193.

1878. COUES, E. Nest and Eggs of Selasphorus platycercus. < *Bull. Nutt. Ornith. Club*, iii, No. 2, Apr., 1878, p. 95.

Communicated by E. A. Barber.

1878. ELLIOT, D. G. Notes on the Trochilidæ. The Genus Thaumatias. < *Ibis*, 4th ser., ii, Jan., 1878, pp. 35–53.

One of the most extensive and important of this writer's numerous critical reviews of Hummers, analyzing and describing no fewer than 21 spp. which he considers to belong here, among them *T. nigricauda*, p. 47, and *T. nitidicauda*, p. 48, spp. nn. The author considers that these birds should be called by Reichenbach's name of *Argyrtria*; a view from which the editors dissent.

1878. ELLIOT, D. G. Description of a new Species of Humming-bird, from Mr. Gould's Collection, belonging to the Genus Iolæma [luminosa Gould MS.]. < *Ibis*, 4th ser., ii, No. 6, Apr., 1878, p. 188.

1878. HENSHAW, H. W. Additional Remarks on Selasphorus alleni. < *Bull. Nutt. Ornith. Club*, iii, No. 1, Jan., 1878, pp. 11–15.

Defends and re-establishes his original position respecting *S. rufus* and *S. alleni*. Cf. *op. cit.*, 1877, pp. 53 and 97.

1878. RIDGWAY, R. On a new Humming Bird (Atthis ellioti) from Guatemala. < *Proc. U. S. Nat. Mus.*, i, 1878, pp. 8–10, 2 figg.

The new species is carefully compared with its nearest relative, *A. heloisæ*, the characters and synonymy of which are also given; and both are figured in outline in the cuts.

1879. A[LLEN], J. A. Elliot's Synopsis of the Trochilidæ. < *Bull. Nutt. Ornith. Club*, iv, No. 4, Oct., 1879, pp. 230–232.

Review of that work.

1879. BALLOU, W. H. A Hummer's [Trochilus colubris] Meal. < *Am. Nat.*, xiii, No. 2, Feb., 1879, p. 127.

Lapping sirup "as a dog would lap water."

1879. BURROUGHS, J. Does the Humming-Bird [Trochilus colubris] sing? < *Science News*, i, No. 5, Jan. 1, 1879, p. 89.

Answered affirmatively by "an intelligent Vermont lady."

1879. DALL, W. H. On the Use of the generic Name Gouldia in Zoology. < *P. Z. S.*, Feb. 4, 1879, pp. 131, 132.

Not available in Ornithology, being preoccupied in Conchology. Another genus of *Trochilidæ*, *Halia* M. & V., is in like case. *Doryfera* is antedated by *Doryphora*. (*Glaucus* Bruch, *Laridæ*, and *Gnathodon* Jardine, *Columbidæ*, both also preoccupied in mollusks.)

1879. ELLIOT, D. G. Smithsonian Contributions to Knowledge. | —317— | A | Classification | and | Synopsis of the Trochilidæ. | By | Daniel Giraud Elliot, F. R. S. E., Etc. | — | Washington City : | published by the Smithsonian Institution. | [March, 1879.] 4to. cover-title, pp. i-xii, 1–277, figg. 1–127. (Forming a part of Vol. xxiii of the *Smiths. Contr. Knowl.*)

The above is the cover-title; the regular title is the same, excepting the words "[March, 1879.]", in place of which is "[Accepted for publication, January, 1878.]". Printed at Philadelphia, by Collins. Title and preface, pp. i-vi; contents, pp. vii-xii; main text, pp. 1–248, with 127 figures. Appendix: key to the 120 genera, pp. 249–256. Index of 120 genera adopted, pp. 257, 258; index of 339 generic names mentioned, pp. 259–262; index of 426 species adopted, pp. 263, 268; index of 880 specific names mentioned, pp. 269–277. Apr., 187 to p. 8; July,

1879. ELLIOT, D. G.—Continued.

1878, to p. 40; Aug., 1878, to p. 80; Sept., 1878, to p. 136; Oct., 1878, to p. 144; Nov., 1878, to p. 160; Dec., 1878, to p. 208; Jan., 1879, to p. 248; appendix and furnishings, March, 1879.

This great work treats formally of the genera and species of the family, giving extensive synonymy, description, habitat, and general comment in nearly every case. It is evidently prepared with care, by one exceptionally familiar with a subject so fascinating and so peculiarly difficult as is that of the present family. It is a monograph in a high sense of that term, and one which places the matter in a state more satisfactory than that in which it had been left by Gould and other leading specialists.

The author recognizes 120 genera in this family, making a very judicious reduction in number from the 339! generic names mentioned in the work; no fewer than 219 being reduced to synonyms. In like conservative manner, the species regarded as valid are 426 in number, out of 880 nominal ones which the author accounts for, leaving 454, or more than half, as synonyms. Such treatment as this is *prima facie* evidence of the merit of the author's work and trustworthiness of his results; for a similar reduction of nominal species is the usual result of a critical study of the current lists of species and genera in nearly every group in ornithology. There is a running commentary through the work on the systematic position and relations of the generic forms; and analyses of the species of each genus, greatly facilitating their determination.

Nearly all the genera, at least, and some of the leading specific forms, are illustrated by outline figures of head, wing, and tail, showing details of external form. There are 127 such figures, or, on an average, a little more than one to each genus treated.

The author's previous study of this group may be inferred from the list of 15 papers, either by himself alone or in joint authorship with Salvin, published in the *Ibis*, 1872-1878 (see above for these). These papers discuss, more at length than the present Synopsis does, the occasion for many of the author's conclusions, particularly in the matter of nomenclature and synonymy.

New names proposed are: *Floricola,* p. 82, *Callipharus,* p. 211, and *Iache,* p. 234, genn. nn.; *Petasophora rubrigularis,* p. 51, and *Bourcieria assimilis,* p. 78, spp. nn.

Extracts from the Preface will further elucidate the plan and scope of the work:—"In the following Synopsis I have given every species of Humming-bird known to me, that in my opinion is entitled to a separate rank, and even of these, it is possible that future information will compel us to place some of them among the synonymes of others. Although the Family contains a certain number of groups, composed of species having more or less relationship with each other, I have not seen my way very clear to the recognition of any subfamilies as has been done by other writers. . . . In the present Synopsis, the recognition of genera has been carried to the farthest limit that seemed practicable, and in every case it has been attempted to give structural characters for the genera which have been acknowledged. . . . The arrangement here given of the species composing this Family is, I am aware, very different from all those heretofore proposed. It is not, however, the result of guess or imagination, but has been arrived at by a careful comparison of the different species themselves, for of the 426 acknowledged as distinct in this Synopsis, about 380 are continued in the great collection, by the assistance of which this book has been written, and of the remaining ones, with but few exceptions, I have carefully examined the types. . . . In the present work, both Genera and Species have been critically examined, and it has been found necessary to make some important and very unexpected changes, especially in the first of these divisions; but it is believed that in every instance a satisfactory explanation is given for thus deviating from the course, which, when judged by the law of priority, had been ascertained to be incorrect, although perhaps sanctioned in some degree by custom. . . . The synonymy is that which, in the majority of cases, refers to a passage in the work cited, that gives some desirable information regarding the species. . . . The chief exceptions to this are the lists of Bonaparte and Reichenbach, which, on account of the many genera first proposed in them, could not be passed over. The value of synonymy has not been deemed to consist in its great length.—The same may be said of the descriptions of the species. Usually one of a genus has been pretty thoroughly described, but I have thought it best, in the majority of cases, to give simply the differences that may exist in allied species, . . . The asterisk, placed before the names of certain species indicates that it [*i. e.,* the species in mention] is not contained in my collection. . . . The drawings which illustrate the generic characters, are with few exceptions, all made from specimens contained in my collection." And I may add, as the author omits to do so, that that they were all drawn by Mr. R. Ridgway.

This "Classification and Synopsis of the Trochilidæ" is likely to supplant previous monographs as the leading authority on the subject.

1879. SCLATER, P. L. [Thaumasius taczanowskii, g. sp. n., Peru.] < *P. Z. S.,* Feb. 18, 1879, pp. 145, 146.

The genus *Thaumasius,* though intended as an emendation of *Thaumatias,* is in effect a new genus: see *Ibis,* 1879, p. 451.

1879. [SCLATER, P. L., *and* SALVIN, O.] Elliot's Classification of the Trochilidæ.
< *Ibis*, 4th ser., iii, Oct., 1879, pp. 479, 480.
> Notice of the work.

ADDENDUM TO TROCHILIDÆ.

Trochilidine literature is extensive, and most of it is "special"—that is, represented by books and papers exclusively devoted to this group of birds. Hummers are very peculiar birds, and their study may almost be said to form a particular department of ornithology—in fact, the word "Trochilidist" has been coined to designate those who pay special attention to this branch of the science; and there are few ornithologists who, however great their general acquirements, can be considered experts in this study. As the plan of this Bibliography, consequently, permits an exceptionally complete exposition of Trochilidine literature, certain points which appear upon consideration of the whole subject may not improperly be here noted, as preliminary to the list of the genera of Hummingbirds with which this Addendum concludes.

Hummers were of course unknown to the ancients, whose τρόχιλος or *trochilus* is believed to have been one of the Plovers (*Charadriidæ*). Misled by the false analogy of small size, slender bill, and glittering plumage, some comparatively modern authors have confounded these exclusively American birds with certain Old World forms, as the *Cinnyridæ* for instance. But as a rule the *Trochilidæ* have been recognized as one of the most perfectly circumscribed groups in ornithology. The literature of the subject dates back to the "heroic age"; the first mention of any bird of this family is said to have been made in 1558, and can scarcely have been earlier. Scattered notices of such birds appeared in various works relating to America during the remainder of the xvi. and the whole of the xvii. century; but it was not until toward the close of the latter that special papers upon the subject appeared; the oldest one which I have seen dating 1693, when Hamersly* described the "American Tomineins" in the *Philos. Trans.* The xviii. century gave us almost nothing of this kind; but notices multiplied in various historical, geographical, and narrative works relating to America; while during the latter half of this century—that is to say, in the Linnæan period—several formal accounts of *Trochilidæ* formed a part of the systematic treatises on ornithology; notably, those of Linnæus, Brisson, Buffon, Gmelin, and Latham; but the sum is small, and the substance meagre, of all that was learned of the birds prior to 1800.

In 1758, when Linnæus applied his system consistently to birds, in the x. ed. of the *Syst. Nat.*, he used the classic word *Trochilus* for a genus coextensive with the modern family *Trochilidæ*, and catalogued 18 species, mostly based upon descriptions or figures furnished by Seba, Brown, Sloane, Catesby, Edwards, Clusius, and Albin; with references also to the *Mus. Ad. Fr.* In the xii. ed., 1766, this number was increased to 22, with many additional references, as to Marcgrave, Willughby, Ray, and especially Brisson.

In 1760, the last-named famous ornithologist gave us what may be deemed the first extended, or in any sense "monographic" account of *Trochilidæ*. Studiously collating the already numerous notices scattered through works of the character I have mentioned, as well as through the illustrated and other natural history treatises of his predecessors in ornithology, he was enabled to describe with his customary elaboration no fewer than 36 species, and to present a copious bibliography. He also made the first tenable genera of Hummers after *Trochilus*, dividing the whole family into two groups, *Polytmus* and *Mellisuga*—one containing large species with curved bills, the other small species with straight bills. In this action of Brisson's we see the origin of the curious fashion which so long endured among French writers—that of distinguishing "Colibris" from "Oiseaux-mouches" among *Trochilidæ*. It is also notable as the starting-point of a generic subdivision of the group which was destined at length to reach the farcical and scandalous extreme of some 350 genera for few more than 400 known species.

In 1779, Buffon adopted the same two divisions of "Colibris" and "Oiseaux-mouches," presenting 19 species of the former, and 24 of the latter group: a total of 43 *Trochilidæ*. If we except the mere naming and describing of some additional species by Gmelin and Latham, nearly all that had been learned of the birds up to the close of the last century was reflected in the works of these two famous French authors.

In 1788, the industrious but indiscriminate and incompetent compiler of the xiii. ed. of the *Syst. Nat.* produced a total of 65 species of *Trochilus*. None were described except at second-hand, but to many of them binomial names were first affixed. Two years afterward 65 species of *Trochilus* were recorded in the *Ind. Orn.* of Latham.†

We are thus brought, by the stepping-stones, of but few works requiring special mention here, to the opening of the xix. century, which saw Audebert and Vieillot's luxurious work. *Ois. Dorés;* perhaps the first ornithological work which undertook to reproduce metallic reflections of plumage. The feathery Iris of these exquisite creatures is always fascinating, and there are no more favorable subjects for glittering plates. The work, indeed, was not exclusively a monograph of the Hummers,

---

* By a clerical error, and my own oversight, this paper stands accredited to Dr. Grew. Winthrop's earlier (1671) paper in the same *Trans.* does not relate exclusively to the Hummingbird.

† The viii. vol., 1812, of Shaw's *Gen. Zool.*, gave 70 species of *Trochilus.*

but the *Histoire Naturelle des Colibris et des Oiseaux-mouches* formed a large part of the undertaking. Scientific names were not used in the *Ois. Dor.;* but a technical nomenclature of the subjects of the work was furnished by Vieillot in 1817.

The first great illustrated work on Hummers exclusively was Lesson's, published in parts, from 1829 to 1832, the parts being afterward grouped in three separately titled volumes. This author described and figured in colors upward of 100 (about 110) species, many of which were actually new, and to many more of which new names were given. A very few genera, additional to or in place of Brisson's, had meanwhile been proposed; but Lesson was the first to introduce any considerable number of new generic names. Many of those, however, which Gray and others have since cited as generic, were certainly not used or intended as such by Lesson, being simply vernacular designations of certain "tribes" and "races" among which he distributed the *Trochilidæ*: such words as "Bleuets" and "Queues étroites", for example. French authors were (and I think many of them still are) such sinners in spelling, that it is not always easy to say what words of theirs they would have us take as technical. Possessing a copious and voluble vocabulary, largely supplemented by gesture-speech, or shrug-language, and violating in their articulation the usual powers of written characters, they not only acquired a trick of Gallicizing technical words, but they also cultivated a characteristic habit of rising superior to orthography. If Vieillot could write *Cripsirina* for *Cryptorhina* without flinching, we need not wonder that Lesson invented *Ornismya*, which he defended as against *Ornithomyia*, or that some of his successors reached the height of *Ornysmia!*

The Hummers have always been objects of study peculiarly agreeable to French ornithologists. Their daintiness, so to speak, seems to suit the national genius. French literature, therefore, figures in the written history of these birds to an extent greater than that observable in any other family of birds. About the time we have reached, however, several English names became prominent in the present connection: as those of Swainson, Vigors, Loddiges, and especially Jardine—for Gould had not then begun the work which was afterward to identify his name with Trochilidine literature. Swainson had already classified the Hummers as a part of his general scheme, describing some new species and establishing certain genera. In 1833, and thus upon the heels of Lesson's memoirs, Sir William Jardine prepared his monography, to the valuable and agreeable text of which Lizars contributed beautiful illustrations. The home of the Hummers was heard from the same year in La Llave's *Memoria;* and Schreibers's *Collectanea* of same date consisted only of these birds. From this time until the beginning of Gould's great work in 1849 appeared no monographic treatise on *Trochilidæ*. But the period was one of great activity, among both English and French writers: the accumulation of material was rapid and incessant, and many papers of these years described new genera and species, though too often hastily and inadequately. In England, Gould and Fraser were busy with their materials. In France, the writings of Lesson continued; Bourcier became prominent in the number of his papers; while Boissoneau, De Lattre, Gervais, Longuemare and others made their respective contributions. This was the period of accumulation rather than of elaboration; numberless new names were introduced, but among them were many synonyms, both generic and specific; little or no systematic revision of the subject being effected, unless Gould's *Draft Arrangement*, the precursor of his *Monograph*, be considered of such character.

The thirteen years, 1849–61, during which Gould's work was pending, marked the next period in the history of the subject. The preparation of this great work held its author, already recognized as the leading Trochilidist, to his subject: and the appearance of successive parts served as a continual stimulus to others to move in the same direction. The author published many papers describing cursorily new objects about to be depicted in his magnificent folios; and several French ornithologists, notably Bourcier and Mulsant, were little behind him in this respect. The period was also marked by the appearance in England of Martin's *General History*, in some sense a continuation of Jardine's work. It was furthermore characterized by the malignant epidemic which we may call the genus-itch; which broke out simultaneously in 1849, from two foci of contagion, in France and in Germany, and proved disastrous in the extreme. The infection reappeared in an aggravated form in 1854, and Trochilidine literature has never entirely recovered from its effect.

Many genera of Hummers, notably Swainson's, Lesson's, and Gould's, had been found acceptable, and, indeed, necessary; but the most embarrassing results attended the steps of some authors who coined names on the glancing of a feather in this beautiful group of birds. As just stated, serious difficulty began in 1849, in those parts of Bonaparte's *Conspectus* and of Reichenbach's *Systema* which treat of *Trochilidæ*; and in 1854 each of these authors increased it immeasurably, the one in his *Tableau*, the other in his *Aufzählung*. But I have on previous pages sufficiently commented upon this matter.

The completion of Gould's splendid monument closed this period of accumulation. The subject had grown rapidly, and had become unmanageable. Some authors had simply amused themselves in "playing chess" with the names of Hummers, and many had pressed forward with new species upon insufficient examination of known material, or inadequate regard for what others had published. The fog of synonymy had completely enveloped the subject. It was hazardous to enter it, and it seemed almost hopeless to attempt to lift it. The *Monograph* represented, therefore, rather a broad and secure basis for future investigation than any final accomplishment. It gave a series of 360 colored plates of about as many species, real or nominal, with accompanying descriptive letter-press: other species added in the *Introduction* raising the total to 416, referred to 123 genera. But many new names, generic and specific, were still to see the light; many others were to sink into synonymy: the nomenclature was

till shifting; in short, studious and judicious systematic revision of the whole subject was impera-
tively demanded. If Gould's work made this necessity apparent, it also immeasurably contributed to
the desired result.

Previous to this Gouldian period American writers did next to nothing for the special literature of
the family; but during this time, and subsequently, many new species were described by Lawrence.
In 1860, and therefore just before the period closed, Germany brought a fascicle of the *Museum Heineanum* to bear upon the subject, many new genera, and some new species being described by Cabanis
and Heine. In 1863, the *Trochilidica* of the last-named author appeared in the *J. f. O.*, with a similar
result. In 1866, MM. Mulsant and Verreaux's *Essai d'une Classification Méthodique* appeared as the
precursor of a more elaborate work then contemplated, containing fresh accessions to the number of
genera with which the family was destined to be burdened, and a rearrangement of the whole group.
This decade, 1861–70, saw also a fair number of minor papers, calling, however, for no special remark
here. It represented flood-tide in the mere describing of species, and their rearrangement in futile
genera; the ebb necessarily followed.

The state of the case at that moment was faithfully reflected in Gray's *Handlist*. This catalogued
469 species, real or nominal, distributed in 163 genera or subgenera, and carrying a load of synonymy
amounting in the aggregate to perhaps 800 specific and 300 generic names. This, it will be remem-
bered, is irrespective of the endless combinations of generic and specific names, which, were they
counted, might represent a total of several thousand binomial names which have been imposed upon a
family of birds consisting of few more than 400 known species, conveniently referable to about one-
fourth as many modern genera!

Such a state of things as this inevitably tended toward a healthy reaction; and during the last decade, the accessions of new names have been fairly offset by the reduction of others to synonyms. It
is true that the *Histoire Naturelle des Oiseaux-Mouches* of MM. Mulsant and Verreaux, and M. Mulsant's *Catalogue*—these being among the most notable publications of this period—can scarcely be
regarded as tending in this direction, viewing the many additional new names which they present.
Having seen neither of these treatises, I cannot judge of their claims to be considered as advancing or
improving the science. But it cannot be doubted that the patient and faithful study which Messrs. D.
G. Elliot and O. Salvin have of late applied to the amelioration of Trochilidine affairs has done much
toward the needed reform. These skilful ornithologists have published numerous papers reviewing
different groups of Hummers, under the most advantageous circumstances as regards handling material and examining literature; and their criticisms have been of the greatest service, not only in
defining genera and species, but in sifting synonymy and settling nomenclature. Mr. Elliot's labors
have borne their final fruit in his *Classification and Synopsis of the Trochilidæ*. However qualified a
success the experts may conclude this performance to be, it is certainly a great boon to the working
ornithologist, and a faithful reflection of the present state of our knowledge respecting the exquisite
creatures to the elucidation of whose history it is devoted.

With this rapid glance at the origin, progress, and present state of Trochilidine literature, I pass to
an alphabetical Index of the Genera of Trochilidæ, the preparation of which has given me no little trou-
ble. I shall not regret the drudgery, however, if the list of names shall seem to bear out and justify
the remarks in which I have indulged on this point, and be of any practical use to the working ornithologist. I have taken great pains to make the list complete and accurate, having personally made
or verified very nearly every reference, excepting those of Mulsant and Verreaux's *Histoire Naturelle*,
and Mulsant's *Catalogue*.

Index Generum Trochilidarum.

Abeillia BP., 1849: *Consp. Av.*, p. 79 (in text).

Acestrura GOULD, 1861: *Introd.*, 8vo, p. 91. [p, 72.

Adelisca CAB. and HEINE, 1860: *Mus. Hein.*, iii,

Adelomyia BP., 1854: *Rev. Mag. Zool.*, p. 253.

Agaclyta CAB. and HEIN., 1860: *Mus. Hein.*, iii,

Agapeta HEINE, 1863: *J. f. O.*, p. 178.   [p. 70.

Aglaeactis GOULD, 1848: *P. Z. S.*, p. 12.   [p. 69.

Aglaiactis CAB. and HEIN., 1860: *Mus. Hein.*, iii,

Agyrtria REICH., 1855: *Troch. Enum.*, p. 7.

Agyrtria REICH., "1854."   [p. 50.

Aithurus CAB. and HEIN., 1860: *Mus. Hein.*, iii,

Aline "REICH.", BP., 1854: *Ann. Sc. Nat.*, p. 137.

Alosia MULS., 1875: *Cat. Ois.-Mouches*, p. 17.

Amalasia MULS., 1875: *Cat. Ois.-Mouches*, p. 29.

Amalusia MULS , 1877: *Hist. O.-M.*, iv, p. 15.

Amathusia MULS. and VERR., 1866: *Class. Troch.*,

Amazilia REICH., 1849: *Syst. Av.*, pl. xxxix. [p. 85.

Amazilicus BP., 1850: *Compt. Rend.*, p. 382.

Amazilis LESS., 1832: *Ind. Gén. Troch.*, p. xxvii.

Amazillis SCL. and SALV., 1859.

Amazilius BP., 1849: *Consp. Av.*, p. 77.

Ametrornis REICH., 1854: *Aufz. Col.*, p. 14.

Amizilis GRAY.

Anactoria REICH., 1854: *Aufz. Col.*, p. 12.

Anais "BP., 1854." (*Ubi?*)

Androdon GOULD, 1863: *Ann. Mag. N. H.*, 2d ser., xii, p. 246.

Anisoterus MULS. and VERR., 1873: *Hist. Nat. O.- M.*, i, p. 72.

Anthocephala CAB. and HEIN., 1860: *Mus. Hein.*, iii, p. 72.

Anthracothorax BOIE, 1831: *Isis*, p. 545.

Aphantochroa GOULD, 1853: *Monog.*, pt. vi.

Archilochus REICH., 1855: *Troch. Enum.*, p. 10.

Ariana MULS. and VERR., 1866: *Class. Troch.*, p. 36.

Arinia MULS., 1877: *Ann. Soc. Linn. Lyon*, Oct.,

Aspasta HEIN., 163: *J. f. O.*, p. 179.   [1877, p. —.

Atthis REICH., 1854: *Aufz. Col.*, p. 12.

Augasma GOULD, "MS."

Augaste MULS. and VERR., 1866.

Augastes GOULD, 1851: *Monog.*, pt. ii.
Aurinia MULS., 1875: *Cat. Ois.-Mouches*, p. 27.
Avocetta AGASS. (nec BRISS.).
Avocettes LESS., 1832: *Ind. Gén.*, p. —.
Avocettina MULS. and VERR., 1866.
Avocettinus BP., 1854: *R. M. Z.*, p. 256, nec 1849.
Avocettinus BP., 1849: *Consp. Av.*, p. 75.
Avocettula REICH., 1849: *Syst. Av. Nat.*, vl. xxxix.

Basilenna CAB. and HEIN., 1860: *Mus. Hein.*, iii,
Basilina REICH., "1849." [p. 44, nec BOIE.
Basilinna BOIE, 1831: *Isis*, p. 546.
Baucis REICH., 1854: *Aufz. Col.*, p. 13.
Bellatrix BOIE, 1831: *Isis*, p. 544.
Bellona MULS. and VERR., 1866: *Class. Troch.*, p. 75.
Bleuets LESS., 1832: *Ind. Gén.*, p. —.
Boissoneaua REICH., CAB. and HEIN., 1860: *Mus. Hein.*, iii, p. 74.
Boissonneaua REICH., 1854: *Aufz. Col.*, p. 11.
Bourcieria BP., 1849: *Consp. Av.*, p. 73.

Caeligena BP., 1849: *Consp. Av.*, p. 73.
Callidice MULS. and VERR., 1866: *Class Troch.*, p. 65.
Calligenia MULS., 1875: *Cat. O.-M.*, p. 20.
Calliperidia REICH., 1854: *Aufz. Col.*, p. 12.
Callipharus ELLIOT, 1879: *Class. Troch.*, p. 211.
Calliphlox BOIE, 1831: *Isis*, p. 544.
Callopistria "REICH.", BP., 1854: *Ann. Sc. Nat.*,
Callothorax BP., 1854: *R. M. Z.*, p. 257. [p. 137.
Calothorax GRAY, 1840: *Cat. G. of B.*, p. 13.
Calothorax GRAY, 1848: *G. of B.*, i, p. 110.
Calothorax REICH., 1854: *Aufz. Col.*, p. 13.
Calypte GOULD, 1856: *Monogr.*, pt. xi.
Campylopterus SW., 1827: *Zool. Journ.*, p. 358.
Catharma ELLIOT, 1876: *Ibis*, p. 400.
Cephalepis BP., 1849: *Consp. Av.*, p. 83.
Cephallepis LODD., 1830: *P. Z. S.*, p. 12. [p. 61.
Cephalolepis CAB. and HEIN., 1860: *Mus. Hein.*, iii,
Chætocercus GRAY, 1853: *Cat. G. of B.*, p. 22.
Chalcostigma REICH., 1854: *Aufz. Col.*, p. 12.
Chalybura REICH., 1854: *Aufz. Col.*, p. 10.
Chloanges HEIN., 1863: *J. f. O.*, p. 200.
Chlorestes REICH., 1854: *Aufz. Col.*, p. 7.
Chlorolampis CAB. and HEIN., 1860: *Mus. Hein.*, iii,
Chlorostilbon GOULD, 1853: *Monog.*, pt. v. [p. 47.
Chlorostilbon BP., 1854: *R. M. Z.*, p. 255.
Chrysobronchus BP., 1854: *R. M. Z.*, p. 252.
Chrysolampis BOIE, 1831: *Isis*, p. 546.
Chrysomirus MULS., 1875: *Cat.*, p. 13.
Chrysures LESS., 1832: *Ind. Gén.*, p. —. [p. 42.
Chrysurisca CAB. and HEIN., 1860: *Mus. Hein.*, iii,
Chrysuronia BP., 1849: *Consp. Av.*, p. 75.
Chrysurus BP., 1850: *Compt. Rend.*, p. 382.
Circe GOULD, 1861: *Introd.*, 8vo, p. 168.
Clotho MULS., 1875: *Cat. O.-M.*, p. 9.
Clytolæma GOULD, 1853: *Monog.*, pt. vi.
Cœligena LESS., 1832: *Ind. Gén.*, p. xviij.
Cœligena BP., 1854: *R. M. Z.*, p. 252.
Coeligena TSCHUDI, 1844: *Fn. Peru.*, p. 39, nec LESS.
Colibri SPIX, 1824: *Av. Bras.*, p. 80.
Colibri BP., 1849: *Consp. Av.*, i, p. 69.
Colibris PELZ.. 1856.
Colubris REICH., 1849: *Syst. Av.*, pl. xl.
Cometes GOULD, 1847: *P. Z. S.*, p. 31.
Conradinia REICH., 1854: *Aufz. Col.*, p. 10.
Cora "REICH.", BP., 1854: *Ann. Sci. Nat.*, p. 138.
Corinnes LESS., 1832: *Ind. Gén.*, p. —.

Crinis MULS., 1873: *Hist. Nat.*, i, p. 178.
Culampis LESS., 1832: *Ind. Gén.*, p. vii.
Cyanochloris REICH., 1854: *Aufz. Col.*, p. 10.
Cyanomyia BP., 1854: *R. M. Z.*, p. 254.
Cyanophaia REICH., 1854: *Aufz. Col.*, p. 10. [p.138.
Cyanopogon "REICH.", BP., 1854: *Ann. Sci. Nat.*,
Cynanthus SW., 1827: *Zool. Journ.*, p. 357.
Cynanthus LESS., 1829: *Tabl. O.-M.*, p. xi.
Cynanthus BOIE, 1831: *Isis*, p. 547.
Cynanthus SW., 1837: *Class. B.*, ii, p. 330.
Cynanthus TSCHUDI, 1844: *Consp.*, p. 36.
Cynanthus BP., 1849: *Consp. Av.*, p. 81.

Damophila REICH., 1854: *Aufz. Col.*, p. 7.
Delattria BP., 1849: *Consp. Av.*, p. 70. [p. 137.
Delphinella "REICH.", BP., 1854: *Ann. Sci. Nat.*,
Derbomyia "REICH.", BP., 1854: *Ann. Sci. Nat.*,
Derbyomyia GRAY, 1855. [p. 137.
Dialia MULS., 1875: *Cat. Ois.-Mouch.*, p. 27.
Diotima REICH., 1854: *Aufz. Col.*, p. 12.
Diphlogæna GOULD, 1861: *Introd.*, 8vo, p. 133.
Diphogena GOULD, 1854: *Monog.*, pt. viii.
Discosura BP., 1849: *Consp. Av.*, p. 84.
Discura REICH., 1854: *Aufz. Col.*, p. 8.
Dnophera HEIN., 1863: *J. f. O.*, p. 175.
Docimaster BP., 1849: *Consp. Av.*, p. 74.
Docimastes, GOULD, 1849: *Monog.*, pt. i.
Dolerisca CAB. and HEIN., 1860: *Mus. Hein.*, iii, p. 6.
Doleromyia BP., 1854: *R. M. Z.*, p. 249.
Dolicha HEIN., 1863: "*J.f. O.*, p. 208."
Doricha REICH., 1854: *Aufz. Col.*, p. 12.
Dorifera BP., 1849: *Consp. Av.*, p. 68.
Doryfera GOULD, 1847: *P. Z. S.*, p. 95. [p. 77.
Doryphora CAB. and HEIN., 1860: *Mus. Hein.*, iii,
Dyrinia MULS. and VERR., 1866: *Class. Troch.*, p. 88.

Egolia MULS. and VERR., 1866: *Class. Troch.*, p. 86.
Elisa "REICH.", BP., 1854: *Ann. Sci. Nat.*, p. 138.
Elvíra MULS. and VERR., 1866: *Class. Troch.*, p. 32.
Elvira MULS., 1875: *Cat. O.-M.*, p. 9.
Emeraudes LESS., 1832.
Emilia MULS. and VERR., 1866: *Class Troch.*, p. 41.
Endoxa HEIN., 1868: *J. f. O.*, p. 179.
Engyete REICH., 1854: *Aufz. Col.*, p. 9.
Entima CAB. and HEIN., 1860: *Mus. Hein.*, iii, p. 51.
Epherusa MULS. and VERR., 1866.
Eranna HEIN., 1863: *J. f. O.*, p. 187.
Erasmia HEIN., 1863: *J. f. O.*, p. 191.
Eratina HEIN., 1863: *J. f. O.*, p. 190.
Eratopis HEIN., 1863: *J. f. O.*, p. 191.
Erebenna MULS. and VERR., 1866, *Class Troch.*,
Eremita REICH., 1854: *Aufz. Col.*, p. 14. [p. 66.
Eriocnemis REICH., 1849: *Syst. Av.*, pl. xl.
Eriocnemys BP., 1854: *R. M. Z.*, p. 252.
Eriona MULS., 1875: *Cat. O.-M.*, p. 28.
Eriopus GOULD, 1847: *P. Z. S.*, p. 16.
Erythronota GOULD, 1861: *Introd.*, 8vo, p. 160.
Eucephala REICH., 1854: *Aufz. Col.*, p. 6.
Euclosia MULS. and VERR., 1866: *Class. Troch.*,
Eudosia MULS., 1875: *Cat. O.-M.*, p. 20. [p. 63.
Eudosia (bis), MULS., 1875: *Cat. O.-M.*, p. 32.
Eugenes GOULD, 1854: *Monog.*, pt. xii.
Eugenia GOULD, 1855: *P. Z. S.*, p. 192.
Eulampís BOIE, 1831: *Isis*, p. 547.
Eulidia, MULS., 1877: *Hist. Nat.*, iv, p. 114.
Eupetomena GOULD, 1853: *Monog.*, pt. vi.
Eupherusa GOULD, 1857: *Monog.*, pt. xiv.

Eupogonus MULS. and VERR., 1866: *Class. Troch.*, p. 72.

Eustephanus REICH., 1849: *Syst. Av.*, pl. xl.

Eutoxeres REICH., 1849: *Syst. Av.*, pl. xl.

Floresia REICH., 1854: *Aufz. Col.*, p. 11.

Floricola ELLIOT, 1879: *Class. and Syn. Troch.*,

Florisuga BP., 1849: *Consp. Av.*, p. 73.   [p. 82.

Galenia MULS. and VERR., 1866: *Class. Troch.*, p. 47.

Glaucis BOIE, 1831: *Isis*, p. 545.

Glaucopes LESS., 1832: *Ind. Gén.*, p. —.

Glaucopis BURM., 1856: *Th. Bras.*, ii, p. 333.

Gouldia BP., 1849: *Consp. Av.*, p. 86.

Gouldomyia BP., 1854: *R. M. Z.*, p. 257.

Grypus SPIX, 1824: *Av. Nov.*, p. 79.

Guimetia "REICH.", BP., 1854: *Ann. Sc. Nat.*,

Guyornis BP., 1854: *R. M. Z.*, p. 249.   [p. 137.

Halia MULS. and VERR., 1866: *Class. Troch.*, p. 61.

Heliactin BOIE, 1831: *Isis*, p. 546.

Heliactinia REICH., 1849: *Syst. Nat.*, pl. —.

Heliactinus BURM., 1856: *Th. Bras.*, ii, p. 356.

Heliangelus GOULD, 1848: *P. Z. S.*, p. 12.

Helianthea GOULD, 1848: *P. Z. S.*, p. 11.

Heliodoxa GOULD, 1849: *P. Z. S.*, p. 95.

Heliodoxa REICH., 1854: *Aufz. Col.*, p. 9.

Heliomaster BP., 1849: *Consp. Av.*, p. 70.

Heliomastes BP., 1854: *R. M. Z.*, p. 251.

Heliopædica GOULD, 1858: *Monog.*, pt. xv.

Heliopedica SCL. and SALV., "1859."

Heliothrix STRICKL., "1841."

Heliothrys GRAY, "1840": *List G., of B.*, p. 14.

Heliothryx BOIE, 1831: *Isis*, p. 547.

Heliotrypha GOULD, 1853: *Monog.*, pt. v.

Heliotryphon CAB. and HEIN, 1860: *Mus. Hein.*,

Heliotryppha BP., 1854: *R. M. Z.*, p. 252.   [iii, p. 60.

Helymus MULS., 1875: *Cat. O.-M.*, p. 23.

Hemistephania REICH., 1854: *Aufz. Col.*, p. 9.

Hemistilbon GOULD, 1861: *Introd.*, 8vo, p. 149.

Hemithylaca CAB. and HEIN., 1860: *Mus. Hein.*, iii,

Himelia MULS., 1875: *Cat. O.-M.*, p. 7.   [p. 37.

Homophania REICH., 1854: *Aufz. Col.*, p. 10.

Homophania CAB. and HEIN., 1860: *Mus. Hein.*,

Huppés LESS., 1832: *Ind. Gén.*   [iii, p. 79.

Hylocharis BOIE, 1831: *Isis*, p. 546.

Hylocharis GRAY, 1848: "*Gen. of B.*, i, p. 114."

Hylonympha GOULD, 1873, *Ann. Mag. N. H.*, xii,

Hylocharis BP., 1854: *R. M. Z.*, p. 255.   [p. 429.

Hypermetra CAB. and HEIN., 1860: *Mus. Hein.*,

Hypochrysia REICH., 1854: *Aufz. Col.*, p. 9.   [p. 80.

Hypolia MULS., 1875, *Cat. O.-M.*, p. 17.

Hypophania REICH., 1854: *Aufz. Col.*, p. 11.

Hypuroptila GOULD, 1854: *Monog.*, pt. vii.

Iache ELLIOT, 1879: *Class and Syn. Troch.*, p. 234.

Idas MULS., 1875: *Cat. Ois.-Mouch.*, p. 27.

Iolæma GOULD, 1861: *Introd.*, 8vo, p. 73.

Ionolæma GOULD, 1857: *Monog.*, pt. xiii.

Ionolaima REICH., 1854: *Aufz. Col.*, p. 9.

Jacobines LESS., 1832: *Ind. Gén.*, p. —.

Juliamyia BP., 1854: *R. M. Z.*, p. 255.

Kampylopterus SPIX.

Klais REICH., 1854; *Aufz. Col.*, p. 13.

Lafresnaya BP., 1849: *Consp. Av.*, p. 68.

Lampornis SW., 1827: *Philos. Mag.*, i, p. 422.

Lampornis LESS., 1829: *Tabl. O.-M.*, p. xxiii.

Lampornis REICH., 1849: *Syst. Av.*, pl. xxxix.

Lampraster TACZ., 1874: *P. Z. S.*, p. 140.

Lamprolæma GOULD, 1861.

Lamprolaima REICH., 1854: *Aufz. Col.*, p. 9.

Lampropogon BP., 1854: *R. M. Z.*, p. 252.

Lampropygia REICH., 1854: *Aufz. Col.*, p. 10.

Lamprurus REICH., 1854: *Aufz. Col.*, p. 12.

Lavania MULS., 1875: *Cat. Ois.-Mouch.*, p. 24.

Lavinia MULS., 1877: *Hist. O.-M.*, iii, 106.

Leadbeatera BP., 1849: *Consp. Av.*, p. 70.

Leobia MULS., 1876: *Hist. O.-M.*, iii, p. 297.

Lepidopyga REICH., 1855: "*Troch. Enum.*, p. 7."

Lepidolarynx REICH., 1854: *Aufz. Col.*, p. 13.

Lepidopyga REICH., 1855: *Troch. Enum.*, p. 7.

Lepidoria MULS. and VERR., 1866: *Class Troch.*,

Lepidololopha REICH., "1854".   [p. 61.

Lesbia LESS., 1832: *Ind. Gén.*, p. xvij.

Lesbia BP., 1854: *R. M. Z.*, p. 252, nec LESS.

Lesbia CAB. and HEIN., 1860: *Mus. Hein.*, nec LESS.

Leucaria MULS., 1875: *Cat. Ois.-Mouch.*, p. 31.

Leucippus BP., 1849: *Consp. Av.*, p. 73.

Leucochloris REICH., 1854: *Aufz. Col.*, p. 10.

Leucodora MULS., 1873: *Hist. O.-M.*, i, p. 309.

Leucolia MULS. and VERR., 1866: *Class. Troch.*,

Lisoria MULS., 1875: *Cat. O.-M.*, p. 11.   [p. 31.

Loddigesia GOULD, "1850".   [p. 381."

Loddigiornis BP., "1850": *Compt. Rend.*, 1850,

Loddiggiornis BP., 1854: *R. M. Z.*, p. 256.

Lophorinus BP., 1854: *R. M. Z.*, p. 257.

Lophornis LESS., 1829: *Tabl. Ois.-Mouch.*, p. xxvii.

Lophornis TSCHUDI, 1844: *Fn. Peru.*, p. 39, nec LESS.

Loxopterus CAB. and HEIN., 1860: *Mus. Hein.*, iii,

Luciania "REICH.", BP., 1854: "*Ann. Sci. Nat.*,   [p. 13.

Lucifer REICH., 1849: *Syst. Nat.*, p. xxxix. [p. 137.

Lucifers LESS., 1832: *Ind. Gén.*, p. —.

Lumachellus BP., "1854."

Manilla MULS. and VERR., 1866: *Class. Troch.*, p. 86.

Margarochrysis REICH., 1854: *Aufz. Col.*, p. 11.

Marsyas MULS., 1875: *Cat. O.-M.*, p. 13.

Mellisuga BRISS., 1760: *Orn.*, iii, p. 694.

Mellisuga BOIE, 1831: *Isis*, p. 545.

Mellisuga GRAY, "1841."

Mellisuga GRAY, 1848: *G. of B.*, i, p. 112.

Mellisuga, MULS. and VERR., 1866.

Merion MULS., 1875: *Hist. Nat.*, ii, p. 92.

Mesophila MULS. and VERR., 1866: *Class. Troch.*,

Metallura GOULD, 1847: *P. Z. S.*, p. 94.   [p. 17.

Metallura BP., 1854, nec GOULD.

Methon MULS., 1875: *Cat. O.-M.*, p. 7.

Microchera GOULD, 1861: *Introd.*, 8vo, p. 82.

Milornis MULS., 1873: *Hist. Nat.*, i, p. 77.

Momus MULS. and VERR., 1866: *Class. Troch.*, p. 19.

Mosqueria "REICH.", BP., 1854: *Ann. Sci. Nat.*,

Mulsantia REICH., 1854: *Aufz. Col.*, p. 12. [p. 137.

Myiabeillia BP., 1854: *R. M. Z.*, p. 253.

Myiabellia "SCL."

Myiaetina BP., 1854: *R. M. Z.*, p. 249.

Myiornis AGASS. (emend. from **Ornismya**).

Myletes MULS., 1873: *Hist. Nat.*, i, p. 284.

Myrmia MULS., 1875: *Cat. O.-M.*, p. 32.

Myrtes CAB. and HEIN., 1860: *Mus. Hein.*, iii, p. 59.

Myrtis REICH., 1854: *Aufz. Col.*, p. 13.

Mythinia MULS., 1876: *Hist. Nat. O.-M.*, iii, p. 235.

Mytinia Muls., 1875: *Cat. Ois.-Mouch.*, p. 28.

Nania Muls., 1875: *Cat. O.-M.*, p. 21.
Niche Muls., 1875: *Cat. O.-M.*, p. 21.
Nodalia Muls., 1875: *Cat. O.-M.*, p. 23.

Ocreatus Gould, 1846: *P. Z. S.*, p. 86.　　[p. 76.
Opisthoprora Cab. and Hein., 1860: *Mus. Hein.*, iii,
Oreonympha Gould, 1869: *P. Z. S.*, p. 295.
Oreopyra Gould, 1860: *P. Z. S.*, p. 312.
Oreotrochilus Gould, 1847: *P. Z. S.*, p. 10.
Oriotrochilus Reich., 1849.　　[p. 91.
Ornismya Muls. and Verr., 1866: *Class. Troch.*,
Ornismya Less., 1829: *Tabl. O.-M.*, p. x.
Ornismyia of some.
Ornithomyia Bp., 1854: *R. M. Z.*, p. 251.
Ornithomya Less., 1832.
Ornysmia of some Frenchmen.　　[p. 15.
Orotrochilus Cab. and Hein, 1860: *Mus. Hein.*, iii,
Orthorhynchus Cuv., "1799–1800."
Orthorhynchus Ill., 1811: *Prod.*, p. 209.
Orthorhynchus Burm., 1856: *Thier. Bras.*
Orthornis Bp., 1854: *R. M. Z.*, p. 249.
Osalia Muls. and Verr, 1866: *Class. Troch.*, p. 92.
Oxypogon Gould, 1848: *P. Z. S.*, p. 14.

Pampa Reich., 1854: *Aufz. Col.*, p. 11.
Panoplites Gould, 1854: *Monog.*, pt. yiii, October.
Panichlora Muls. and Verr.　　[p. 43.
Panterpe Cab. and Hein., 1860: *Mus. Hein.*, iii,
Panychlora Cab. and Hein., 1860: *Mus. Hein.*, iii, p. 49.
Paphosia Muls. and Verr., 1866: *Class. Troch.*,
Parzudakia Reich., 1854: *Aufz. Col.*, p. 12. [p. 75.
Patagona Gray, 1840: *List G. of B.*, p. 18.
Patagons Less., 1832: *Ind. Gén.*, p. —.
Peratus Muls., 1875: *Cat. O.-M.*, p. 23.
Petasophora Gray, 1840: *List G. of B.*, p. 13.
Petasophorus Muls. and Verr., 1866.
Phæochroa Gould, 1861: *Introd.*, 8vo, p. 55.
Phæolæma Bp., 1854.
Phæoptila Gould, 1861: *Introd.*, p. 169.
Phaëthornis Sw., 1831: *Fn. Bor.-Am.*, ii, p. 322.
Phaëtornis Bp., 1849: *Consp. Av.*, p. 67.
Phætornis Gray, 1848.
Phaiolaima Reich., 1854: *Aufz. Col.*, p. 9.
Phemonoë Reich., 1854: *Aufz. Col.*, p. 9.
Phœthornis Sw., 1827: *Zool. Journ.*, p. 357.
Phœtornis Less., 1832: *Ind. Gén. Troch.*, p. xiv.
Phœtornis Tschudi, 1844: *Consp.*, p. 37.　　[p. 86.
Philodice Muls. and Verr., 1866: *Class. Troch.*,
Phlogophilus Gould, 1860: *P. Z. S.*, p. 310.
Pholoe Muls., 1875: *Cat. O.-M.*, p. 22.
Phrethornis Boie, 1831: *Isis*, p. 548.
Pilonia Muls., 1876: *Hist. Nat.*, iii, p. 4.
Placophorus Muls., 1873: *Hist. Nat.*, i, p. 137.
Platurus Less., 1829: *Tabl. O.-M.*, p. xxij.
Platystylopterus Reich., 1854: *Aufz. Col.*, p. 11.
Polemistria Cab. and Hein., 1860: *Mus. Hein.*, iii,
Polyæna Hein., 1863: *J. f. O.*, p. 215.　　[p. 63.
Polyerata Hein., 1863: *J. f. O.*, p. 194.
Polymnia Muls. and Verr., 1866: *Class Troch.*,
Polyonymus Hein., 1863: *J. f. O.*, p. 206.　　[p. 91.
Polyplaneta Hlin., 1863: *J. f. O.*, p. 182.
Polythmus Less., 1832: *Ind. Gén. Troch.*, p. xvi.
Polythmus Less., 1832: *Ind. Gén.*, p. xvi.
Polytmus Vieill., 1807.

Polytmus Gray, 1849: *List G. of B.*, p. —.
Polytmus Reich., 1849: *Syst. Av.*, pl. xxxix.
Polytmus Briss., 1760: *Orn.*, iii, p. 666.　　[p. 123.
Polyxemus Muls., 1877: *Hist. Nat. O.-M.*, iv,
Popelairia Reich., 1854: *Aufz. Col.*, p. 12.
Prasites Gray: *Ubi?*
Prasitis Cab. and Hein., 1860: *Mus. Hein.*, iii, p. 49.
Praxilla Reich., 1854: *Aufz. Col.*, p. 13.
Prognornis Reich., 1854: *Aufz. Col.*, p. 11.
Prymnacantha Cab. and Hein., 1860: *Mus. Hein.*, iii, p. 64.
Psalidoprymna Cab. and Hein., 1860: *Mus. Hein.*,
Pterophanes Gould, 1849: *Monog.*, pt. i. [iii, p. 72.
Ptochoptera Elliot, 1874: *Ibis*, p. 261.
Ptyonornis Reich., 1854: *Aufz. Col.*, p. 14.
Pygmornis Bp., 1854: *R. M. Z.*, p. 250.
Pygornis Muls.and Verr.,1866: *Class.Troch.*,p.18.
Pyrrhophæna Cab. and Hein., 1860: *Mus. Hein.*, iii, p. 35.

Queues-étroites Less., 1832: *Ind. Gén.*, p. xxxi.

Ramphodon Less., 1830: *Hist. Nat. Col.*, p. 18.
Ramphomicron Bp., 1849: *Consp. Av.*, p, 79.
Rhamphodon Less.
Rhamphomicron auct.　　[iii, p. 70.
Rhamphomicrus Cab. and Hein.,1860: *Mus. Hein.*
Rhodopis Reich., 1854: *Aufz. Col.*, p. 12.
Riccordia Reich., 1854: *Aufz. Col.*, p. 10.
Rubis Less., 1832: *Ind. Gén.*, p. —.

Sæplopterus Reich., 1854: *Aufz. Col.*, p. 11.
Saphos Less., 1832: *Ind. Gén.*, p. —.
Sapphironia Bp., 1854: *R. M. Z.*, p. 256.
Sapphironia "Gould, 1861".
Sapphironia Bp., 1854: *R. M. Z.*, p. 256.
Saphirs Less., 1832: *Ind. Gén.*, p. —.
Sappho Reich., 1849: *Syst. Av.*, pl. xl.
Saturia Muls., 1875: *Cat. O.-M.*, p. 21.
Saucerottia Bp., 1849: *Consp. Av.*, p. 77.
Schistes Gould, 1851: *Jard. Cont. Orn.*, p. 140.
Selasopheruss Reich., 1855: *Troch. Enum.*, p. 11.
Selasphorus Sw., 1831: *Fn. Bor.-Am.*, ii, p. 496.
Selosphorus Bp., 1849: *Consp. Av.*, p. 82.
Séphaniodes Less., 1832: *Ind. Gén.*, p. xxix.
Sephanoides Bp., 1849: *Consp. Av.*, p. 82.
Sericotes Reich., 1854: *Aufz. Col.*, p. 11.
Smaragdites Less., 1832: *Ind. Gén.*, p. xxix.
Smaragdites Muls. and Verr., 1866.
Smaragdites Boie, 1831: *Isis*, p. 547.
Smaragdites Reich., 1849: *Syst. Av.*, pl. xl.
Smaragdites Boie, 1831: *Isis*, p. 547.
Smaragditis Reich., 1854: *Aufz. Col.*, p. 7.
Smaragdochrysis Gould.,1861: *Introd.*,8vo, p. 161.
Sparganura Cab. and Hein., 1860: *Mus. Hein.*, iii,
Spathura Gould, 1849: *Monog.*, pt. i.　　[p. 52.
Sphenoproctus Cab. and Hein., 1860: *Mus. Hein.*, iii, p. 11.
Sporadicus Cab. and Hein., 1860: *Mus. Hein.*, iii.
Sporadinus Bp., 1854: *R. M. Z.*, p. 255.
Steganura Reich., 1854: *Aufz. Col.*, p. 8.
Steganurus Reich., 1849: *Syst. Av.*, pl. xl.
Steilula Gould, 1861: *Introd.*, 8vo, p. 90.
Stellura Muls. and Verr.,1866: *Class. Troch.*, p. 88.
Sternoclyta Gould, 1858: *Monog.*, pt. xvi.
Stokæsiella Bp., "1854."
Stokosiella Bp., 1854: "*Ann. Sci. Nat.*, p. 138."

Streblorhamphus, CAB. and HEIN., 1860: *Mus.*
Strophiolæmus GOULD, "1853". [*Hein.*, iii, p. 76.

Telamon MULS. and VERR., 1866: *Class. Troch.*,
Telaphorus MULS., 1874: *Hist. Nat.*, i, p. 257. [p. 75.
Telesiella REICH., 1854: *Aufz. Col.*, p. 13.
Telesilla CAB. and HEIN., 1860: *Mus. Hein.*, p. 27.
Thalucania BOURC., 1856.
Thalurania GOULD, 1848: *P. Z. S.*, p. 13.
Thaluronia GRAY, 1849.
Thaumantias BP., 1854: *R. M. Z.*, p. 255.
Thaumasius SCLAT., 1879: *P. Z. S.*, p. 145.
Thaumaste REICH., 1854: *Aufz. Col.*, p. 14.
Thaumastura BP., 1849: *Consp. Av.*, p. 85.   [1849.
Thaumastura BP., 1850: *Compt. Rend.*, p. 383, nec
Thaumatias BP., 1850: *Compt. Rend.*, xxx, p. 382.
Thaumatias BP., 1849: *Consp. Av.*, p. 78.
Thaumatias GOULD, 1861: *Introd.*, 8vo, p. 151.
Thaumatessa HEIN., 1863: *J. f. O.*, p. 209.
Tholucania HARTL., 1857: *Arch. f. Nat.*, p. 49.
Threnetes, GOULD, 1853: *Monog.*, pt. iv.

Threptria REICH., 1854: *Aufz. Col.*, p. 9.
Tilmatura REICH., 1854: *Aufz. Col.*, p. 8.
Timolia MULS., 1875: *Cat. O.-M.*, p. 23.
Topaza GRAY, 1840: *List G. of B.*, p. 13.
Topazes LESS., 1832: *Ind. Gén.*, p. —.
Toxoteuches CAB. and HEIN., 1860: *Mus. Hein.*, iii,
Tricholopha HEIN., 1863: *J. f. O.*, p. 209.   [p. 11.
Trochilus LESS., 1766: *S. N.*, i, p. 189.
Tryphæna GOULD, 1849: *Monog.*, pt. i.

Ulysses MULS., 1875: *Cat. O.-M.*, p. 12.
Uralia MULS. and VERR., 1866: *Class. Troch.*, p. 81.
Urania "FITZ." (*fide* GRAY).
Uranomitra REICH., 1854: *Aufz. Col.*, p. 10.
Urochroa GOULD, 1856: *Monog.*, pt. xii.
Urolampra CAB. and HEIN., 1860: *Mus. Hein.*, iii,
Urosticte GOULD, 1853: *Monog.*, pt. vi.   [p. 68.

Vestipes LESS., 1832: *Ind. Gén.*, p. —.

Zephyritis MULS. and VERR., 1866: *Class. Troch.*,
Zodalia MULS., 1876: *Hist. Nat.*, iii, p. 231. [p. 87.

Cypselidæ.

1793. BRUYN, S. J.   A Letter on the Retreat of Swallows [Chætura pelagica], and the Torpid State of certain Animals, in Winter. $<$ *Mem. Amer. Acad. Arts and Sci.*, ii, 1793, pp. 96–99.

This is the earliest notice I have seen of the now well-known fact that immense collections of the bones, feathers, and excrement of Swifts are occasionally found in hollow trees to which the birds have been wont to resort by thousands for a series of years. A late anonymous writer (very well known to me, however,) in the *N. Y. Independent* of Oct. 7, 1875, has a paragraph on the subject, in which he seems inclined to believe that our Chimney Swift may not impossibly hybernate in such retreats. See also 1853, THOMPSON, Z.

1817. S. B. D.   To the editors of the American Monthly Magazine. $<$ *Am. Month. Mag.*, ii, 1817, p. 32.

On the débris of *Chætura pelagica* in hollow trees.

1817. WOOD, J.   [On the débris of Chætura pelagica in hollow trees.] $<$ *Am. Month. Mag.*, i, 1817, p. 292.

1826. JENNER, —.   Annual return of migrating Birds to the same spot. $<$ *Sillim. Am. Journ. Sci.*, x, 1826, p. 192.

From *Brewster's Journal.*

1839. TOWNSEND, J. K   Description of a New Species of Cypcelus [Cypcelus vauxii] from the Columbia River. $<$ *Journ. Acad. Nat. Sci. Phila.*, viii, 1839, p. 148.

Citators of this bird's name may observe that Townsend did not call it *Cypselus vauxi.*

1841. JOHNSON, H.   Chætura ruficollis [n. sp.]; Cayenne. $<$ *Ann. Mag. Nat. Hist.*, vii, 1841, p. 351.

1845. BRYDGES, H. J. J.   Description of a supposed new Swift. $<$ *Zoologist*, iii, 1845, p. 939.

From Jamaica   Not named.

1848. STREUBEL, A. B.   Die Cypseliden des Berliner Museums. $<$ *Oken's Isis*, Bd. xli, 1848, pp. 348–373.

Monographisch bearbeitet.—*C. parvus* (Licht.), p. 351; *C. caffer* (Licht.), p. 352; *C. abessynicus*, p. 354, sp. n. *Pseudoprocne*, g. n., p. 357. *Hemiprocne torquata*, p. 342, sp. n.; *H. temminckii*, p. 368, sp. n.; *H. fumigatus*, Natt. MS., sp. n., p. 366. *Cypseloides*, g. n., p. 366; *Salangana*, g. n., p. 368; *Chelidonia*, g. n., p. 370; *Hemiprocne fucivora*, p. 369.

1853. THOMPSON, Z.   [Remarks on exhibition of a mass of débris of Chætura pelagica from interior of a "Swallow tree" in Vermont.] $<$ *Proc. Boston Soc. Nat. Hist.*, iv, 1853, p. 299.

1857. KENNERLY, C. B. R.   Description of a new Species of Cypselus [C. borealis] collected on the North Western Boundary Survey, Archibald Campbell, Esq., Commissioner. $<$ *Proc. Acad. Nat. Sci. Phila.*, ix, 1857, pp. 202, 203.

1863. SALVIN, O.   [Panyptila sancti jeromæ, sp. n.] $<$ *Ibis*, v, 1863, p. 239.

Cf. *Panyptila sancti hieronymi, P. Z. S.*, 1863, p. 190, pl. 23.

1863. SCLATER, P. L.   On the American Spine-tailed Swifts of the Genus Chætura. $<$ *P. Z. S.*, xxvi, 1863, pp. 98–102, pl. xiv, fig. 1.

Synonymatic and diagnostic synopsis, with criticism, of 8 spp. *C. cinireiventris* is figured.

1865. SCLATER, P. L.   Notes on the genera and species of Cypselidæ. $<$ *P. Z. S.*, 1865, pp. 593–617, figg. 1–10, pll. xxxiii, xxxiv.

This notable article opens with an account of the structure of the sternum and digits in various species of the family, illustrated with ten figures. The family is divided into two subfamilies, *Cypselinæ* and *Chæturinæ*, the former having the tarsi feathered, and the ratio of the phalanges abnormal; the latter with the opposite of these characters. The species of *Cypselinæ* are all referred to the two genera *Cypselus* and *Panyptila*, the latter exclusively American. The *Chæturinæ* are divided into four genera, *Chætura, Cypseloides, Collocalia,*

1865. SCLATER, P. L.—Continued.

and *Dendrochelidon.* Forty-eight species, two of them new, are reviewed, with synonymy, diagnosis, habitat, and criticism, as follows:—

CYPSELINÆ. I. *Cypselus.* A. Old World. a. Fork-tailed. 1. *C. melba.* 2. *C. æquatori-alis.* 3. *C. apus.* 4. *C. pacificus.* 5. *C. leuconyx.* 6. *C. unicolor.* 7. *C. caffer.* 8. *C. parvus.* 9. *C. batassiensis.* 10. *C. infumatus,* sp. n., p. 602, Borneo. b. Even-tailed. 11. *C. subfur-catus.* 12. *C. affinis.* B. New World (*Tachornis*). 13. *C. phœnicobius.* 14. *C. squamatus* (pl. 33). 15. *C. andicola.* 16. *C. montivagus.* II. *Panyptila.* 1. *P. cayanensis.* 2. *P. sancti-hieronymi.* 3. *P. melanoleuca.* CHÆTURINÆ. III. *Chætura.* A. Majores. a. Asiatic (*Hi-rundinapus*). 1. *C. caudacuta.* 2. *C. gigantea.* b. American (*Hemiprocne*). 3. *C. semicol-laris.* 4. *C. biscutata,* sp. n., p. 609, pl. 34 (e Natt. MS., Brazil). 5. *C. zonaris.* B. Minores. a. American. 6. *C. pelasgia.* 7. *C. vauxii.* 8. *C. poliura.* 9. *C. cinereiventris.* 10. *C. spini-cauda.* 11. *C. rutila.* b. African. 12 *C. sabini.* 13. *C. cassini.* c. Asiatic. 14. *C. sylvatica.* 15. *C. coracina.* IV. *Cypseloides.* 1. *C. senex.* 2. *C. fumigatus.* 3. *C. niger.* 4. *C. borealis.* V. *Collocalia:* merely a list of 6 spp., after Wallace. VI. *Dendrochelidon.* 1. *D. mystacea.* 2. *D. wallacii.* 3. *D. klecho.* 4. *D. coronata.* 5. *D. comata.*

1865. SCLATER, P. L. [Letter relating to various Cypselidæ.] < *Ibis*, 2d ser., i, 1865, pp. 234, 235.

1867. SCLATER, P. L. Bemerkungen über die Genera und Species der Cypseliden. Aus den ,, Proceedings of the Zoological Society of London, June 27, 1865 " übersetzt. < *J. f. O.*, xv, 1867, pp. 112–141.

1869. FOWLER, A. The Chimney Swallow [Chætura pelagica]. < *Am. Nat.*, iii, 1869, pp. 8–13.

Account of its habits.

1873. SEARS, J. H. Chimney Swallow [Chætura pelagica]; Change in Place of Nest-ing. < *Am. Nat.*, vii, 1873, pp. 751, 752.

1874. MERRIAM, C. H. The Chimney Swift [Chætura pelagica]; Change in Place of Nesting. < *Am. Nat.*, viii, 1874, pp. 367, 368.

1874. SALVIN, O. [On the breeding of Panyptila sancti-hieronymi at San Geronimo, Guatemala; etc.] < *Ibis*, 3d ser., iv, Apr., 1874, p. 188.

Not seen.

1875. ANON. [On the possible hybernation of Chætura pelagica in hollow trees.] < *N. Y. Independent*, Oct. 7, 1875.

1877. GRAY, A. F. Chimney Swallow. Chimney Swift. Chætura pelagica.—Baird. < *Forest and Stream*, ix, Nov. 8, 1877, p. 215.

1878. [FITCH, E. H.] The Swifts [Cypselidæ]. *Journ. of Sci.* (Toledo, Ohio), n. s., i, No. 1, Apr., 1878, cut.

Characters of two subfamilies, *Cypselinæ* and *Chæturinæ;* figure of *Panyptila saxatilis.*

1878. LAWRENCE, G. N. Description of a New Species of Cypselidæ, of the Genus Chaetura [dominicana]. < *Ann. New York Acad. Sci.*, i, No. 8, 1878, pp. 255, 256. (Read Nov. 11, 1877.)

1879. ANON. Nest of the Chimney Swift (Chætura pelasgia). < *The Oölogist*, v, No. 2, Aug., 1879, pp. 9, 10, cut.

Very good original observations, illustrated with a figure of the nest and eggs.

1879. MERRIAM, [C. H.] How the Chimney Swallows [Chætura pelagica] did Congre-gate. < *The Oölogist*, v, No. 1, July, 1879, pp. 6, 7.

Quoted from his " Review of the Birds of Connecticut " in *Trans. Conn. Acad.*, iv, 1877, p. 50.

Caprimulgidæ.

1817. HUMBOLDT, A. v. Sur le Steatornis [caripensis], nouveau genre d'Oiseau nocturne. < *Bull. Sci. Soc. Philom*, 1817, pp. 51, 52.

Pas vu moi-même—le titre tiré de Carus et Engelmann.

1818. HUMBOLDT, A. v. [Ueber einen Nachtvogel Guacharo genannt (d. h., Steatornis caripensis).] < *Oken's Isis*, Jahrg. ii, 1818, p. 411.

Aus d. *Verh. Acad. Wiss. Paris*, 1817.

1831. SW[AINSON, W.] The pectinated Claw of the Goatsucker. < *Loudon's Mag. Nat. Hist.*, iv, 1831, pp. 275, 176.

Smiles at the simplicity of J. Rennie in supposing the comb useful in removing insect parasites.

1831. ANON. The Night Hawk [Chordeiles virginianus]. < *D. J. Browne's The Naturalist*, i, No. x, Oct., 1831, pp. 301–309.

Chiefly compiled from Wilson. The article continues with a similar notice of the Whippoorwill, *Antrostomus vociferus*.

1831. ANON. The Whip-poor-will [Antrostomus vociferus] and Night Hawk [Chordeiles virginianus]. < *D. J. Browne's The Naturalist*, i, No. xi, Nov., 1831, pp. 334, 335.

Determining that these are really two distinct species.

1832. WATERTON, C. Answer to the Question at p. 603 [tom. cit.] on the Nightjar's [Caprimulgus europæus] transporting its Eggs, as suggested by Audubon's declaration of the Carolina Goatsucker's [Antrostomus carolinensis] so doing. < *Loudon's Mag. Nat. Hist.*, v, 1832, pp. 726, 727.

1834. L'HERMINIER, [F.] Mémoire sur le Guacharo (Steatornis caripensis (Humboldt)). < *Nour. Ann. du Mus. d'Hist. Nat.*, iii, 1834, pp. 321–331, pl. 15.

Planche coloriée, in-fol., grosseur nat.—Rapport: *L'Inst.*, ii, 1834, No. 74, p. 330.

1834. MATHEWS, A. Information on the Habits of a Species of Caprimulgus (or of some closely allied Genus) which inhabits the Neighbourhood of Lima. < *Loudon's Mag. Nat. Hist.*, vii, 1834, pp. 633, 634. With Note by the Editor, pp. 634–637.

1835. DON, D. The Species of Caprimulgus which inhabits the Neighbourhood of Lima, noticed by Mr. Matthews in [op. cit.] VII. 633., and technically described in 635., is, doubtless, the C. americànus of Wilson's "American Ornithology," vol. V. t. 40. fig. 1. < *Loudon's Mag. Nat. Hist.*, viii, 1835, p. 470.

Which it doubtless is not.

1836. L'HERMINIER, [F.] Note additionelle au mémoire sur le Guacharo de la caverne de Caripe (Steatornis Caripensis. Humb.) < *Compt. Rend. de l'Acad. Sci.*, ii, 1836, pp. 67–71.

1836. L'HERMINIER, F. Note sur le Guacharo de la caverne de Caripe (Steatornis caripensis Humb.). < *Ann. Sci. Nat.*, 2e sér., Zool., vi, pp. 60–64.

Not seen—this vol. missing from the set of the *Ann.* handled. Paper said to be also in *Fror. Nat.*, Bd. 1, No. 1082, 1836, pp. 49–51.

1836. ROULIN, —. Existence du guacharo [Steatornis caripensis] dans la province de Bogota. < *Compt. Rend. de l'Acad. Sci.*, ii, 1836, pp. 94–96.

Extraite d'une lettre. (*L'Inst.*, iv, No. 168, 1836, pp. 241, 242; *Ann. Sci. Nat.*, 2e sér., vi, 1836, pp. 115–117.)

1838. GOULD, J. Icones Avium, | or | Figures and Descriptions | of | new and interesting Species of Birds | from various parts of the World. | By | John Gould, F. L. S., &c. | Forming | a supplement | to his previous works. | — | Part. II. | — | Monograph of the Caprimulgidæ, | Part I. | [Contents.] | London : | printed by Richard and John E. Taylor, Red Lion Court, Fleet Street. | Pub-

1838. GOULD, J.—Continued.

lished by the author, 20, Broad Street, Golden Square. | August, 1838. folio, 8 plates, unnumbered, each with a sheet of letterpress, unpaged.

Part I contained 10 plates of miscellaneous birds. The present Part begins a monograph which was abandoned. Only these two parts of "Icones Avium" appeared.

This beginning of a monograph of the *Caprimulgidæ* contains: 1. *Amblypterus anomalus.* 2. *Nyctidromus derbianus.* 3. *Semeiophorus (Macrodipteryx?) vexillarius.* 4. *Lyncornis cerviniceps.* 5. *Lyncornis macrotis.* 6. *Lyncornis temminckii.* 7. *Batrachostomus* (Gould, g. n. ?) *auritus.* 8. *Nyctibius pectoralis.*

1838. SAINT-VINCENT, BORY DE. Sur l'existence du Guacharo (Steatornis [caripensis]), à l'île de la Trinité. < *Compt. Rend. de l'Acad. Sci.*, vii, 1838, pp. 474–478.

D'après une lettre de M. Hautessier. Avec des renseignements sur les mœurs de l'oiseau.

1839. HAUTESSIER, ST. CYR. Notice historique sur l'existence du Guacharo [Steatornis caripensis] qui a été découvert dans les cavernes des Bouches à la Trinidad. < *Actes Soc. Linn. Bordeaux*, xi, 1839, pp. 98– —.

Pas vue moi-même—le titre tiré de Giebel.

1839. HAUTESSIER, [ST. CYR.] [Ueber Steatornis caripensis, mit Nest und Eyern, aus Trinidad.] < *Oken's Isis*, Bd. xxxii, 1839, pp. 382, 383.

L'Institut, Nr. 249, 1838, p. 326.

1842. LAFRESNAYE, [F. DE.] Ueber die Caprimulgiden. < *Oken's Isis*, Bd. xxxv, 1842, p. 219.

Mag. de Zoöl., Bd. iii, 1837.

1842. MUELLER, J. Anatomische Bemerkungen über den Quacharo, Steatornis caripensis v. Humb. < *Müller's Arch. Anat. Phys.*, ix, 1842, pp. 1–11, pl. 1.

Gelesen in d. k. Akad. Wiss. zu Berlin am 13. Mai 1841. *Berlin. Monatsb.*, 1841, pp. 172–179; *L'Inst.*, ix, No. 408, 1841, p. 357.

1843. DES MURS, O. Considérations oologiques sur le genre d'oiseaux nommé Guacharo. (Steatornis de Humbold [sic]?). < *Revue Zoologique*, vi, 1843, pp. 33–37.

1844. FUNCK, N. Notice sur le Steatornis caripensis. < *Bull. Acad. Bruxelles*, xi, 1844, pp. 371–377.

L'Institut, xiii, 1845, No. 598, pp. 216, 217.

Pas vue moi-même—le titre tiré de la *Bibl.* de Carus et Engelmann. La notice se trouve aussi inserée dans l'*Isis* d'Oken, 1848, q. v.

1846. GOULD, J. [On a new species of Nyctibius (bracteatus).] < *P. Z. S.*, xiv, 1846, p. 1.

1846. GOULD, J. [Nyctibius bracteatus.] < *Ann. Mag. Nat. Hist.*, xvii, 1846, p. 476.

From *P. Z. S.*, Jan. 13, 1846, p. 1.

1846. L'HERMINIER, [F.] Ueber Steatornis caripensis in der Provinz Cumana. < *Oken's Isis*, Bd. xxxix, 1846, p. 552.

Nouv. Ann. Mus. d'Hist. Nat., Tom. iii, 1834, pp. 321–331, pl. 15.

1846. REICHENBACH, [L.]. Neuer Caprimulgus in Ungarn. < *Allgemein. Naturh. Zeitung*, 1846, pp. 269– —.

Not seen. Said to contain a list of the known species of *Caprimulgidæ. Chordeiles wiederspergii*, sp. n., p. —.

1848. CABOT, S., JR. [On a species of Chordeiles from Surinam (C. labeculatus?)] < *Proc. Bost. Soc. Nat. Hist.*, iii, 1848, pp. 55, 56.

1848. FUNCK, N. Ueber den Guacharo (Steatornis caripensis). < *Oken's Isis*. Bd. xli, 1848, pp. 1018, 1019.

Auszug aus d. *Bull. Acad. Roy. Bruxelles*, xi, 1844, pp. 371–377.

1849. CASSIN, J. Descriptions of new species of birds of the Family Caprimulgidæ, specimens of which are in the Collection of the Academy of Natural Sciences of Philadelphia. < *Proc. Acad. Nat. Sci. Phila.*, iv, 1849, pp. 236–239.

Hydropsalis limbatus, p. 236; *H. segmentatus, Antrostomus serico-caudatis* (sic), p. 238.

1849. L'HERMINIER, [F.] Notes sur la classification méthodique du Guacharo (Steatornis [caripensis]), . . . < *Rev. et Mag. de Zool.*, xii, (2e sér., i), 1849, pp. 321–328.

1850. CASSIN, J.   Descriptions of new species of Birds of the Family Caprimulgidæ.
    < *Ann. Mag. Nat. Hist.*, 2d ser, v, 1850, pp. 310–313.
    From *Proc. Phila. Acad.*, iv, 1849, pp. 236–239.

1851. CASSIN, J.   Catalogue | of the | Caprimulgidæ | in the collection of | the Academy of Natural Sciences | of Philadelphia. *Published with Proc. Acad. Nat. Sci. Phila.*, v, Nov. 1, 1851, not paged. Also separate, 8vo, one signature (foll. 8).
    Synonymatic.

1851. CASSIN, J.   Notes of an examination of the Birds composing the family Caprimulgidæ, in the Collection of the Academy of Natural Sciences of Philadelphia. < *Proc. Acad. Nat. Sci. Phila.*, v, 1851, pp. 175–190.
    Stenopsis, p. 179; *Lurocalis*, p. 189, gg. nn. The 'notes' are a critical running commentary on all the New World forms, with mention of all the species which had come under the writer's observation. An early, if not the first notice of the special subject at all to be called critical.

1852. CASSIN, J.   Monograph of the Birds composing the genera Hydropsalis, Wagler, and Antrostomus, Nuttall. < *Journ. Acad. Nat. Sci. Phila.*, ii, pt. ii, Jan. 1852, art. xiv, pp. 113–124, pll. xiii, xiv.
    Hydropsalis, 6+1 spp. Pl. xiv gives sections of tail-feathers of *H. limbatus, H. lyra, H. segmentatus, H. psalurus. Antrostomus*, 6+2 spp. Pl. xiii, *A. serico-caudatus.*

1854. BREWER, T. M.   [Remark on exhibition of an egg of the Chuck-will's-widow (Antrostomus carolinensis).] < *Proc. Bost. Soc. Nat. Hist.*, v, 1854, p. 56.

1858. BOLLE, K.   Drei Ziegenmelker [Caprimulgidæ] Nordamerikas. < *Naumannia*, viii, 1858, pp. 150–163.
    Aus dem Englischen des Audubon—*Caprimulgus [Antrostomus] carolinensis, C. [A.] vociferus, C. [Chordeiles] virginianus.*

1860. HADFIELD, H.   Note on the Piramidigs of Jamaica (Chordeiles). < *Zoologist*, xviii, 1860, p. 6976.

1860. PHILIPPI, R. A., *and* LANDBECK, L.   Beschreibung zweier neuen Chilenischen Vögel aus den Geschlechtern Procellaria und Caprimulgus. < *Arch. f. Naturg.*, 1860, (1), pp. 279–284.
    Caprimulgus andinus, p. 270; *Thalassidroma segethi*, p. 282.

1861. GOULD, J.   Description of a New Species of the Family Caprimulgidæ [Chordeiles? pusillus]. < *P. Z. S.*, xxix, 1861, p. 182.

1861. GOULD, J.   Description of a New Species of the Family Caprimulgidæ. < *Ann. Mag. Nat. Hist.*, 3d ser., viii, 1861, p. 262.
    From *P. Z. S.*, April 23, 1861, p. 182.

1861. PHILIPPI, R. A., *and* LANDBECK, L.   Descripcion de una nueva especie de pájaros del jénero Chotacabra o Caprimulgus [andinus, p. 31]. < *Anales Univ. Chile*, xviii, Enero 1861, pp. 29–33.

1865. PELZELN, A. v.   Ueber zwei neue Caprimulgiden aus Brasilien. < *Verhandl. d. k.-k. zool.-bot. Ges. zu Wien*, xv, 1865, *Abhandl.*, pp. 985–988.
    Hydropsalis ypanemæ (Natt.) und *H. pallescens* (Natt.).

1866. PELZELN, A. v.   Zwei neue Caprimulgiden aus Brasilien. < *J. f. O.*, xiv, 1866, pp. 46–49.
    Aus *Verh. k.-k. Zool.-bot. Ges. Wien*, xv, 1865, *Abhandl.*, pp. 985–988. *Hydropsalis ypanemæ, H. pallescens.*

1866. SCLATER, P. L.   Notes on the American Caprimulgidæ. < *P. Z. S.*, xxxiv, 1866, pp. 123–145, pll. xiii, xiv, woodcc.
    This is the most important paper on the special subject, being a monographic sketch of the group, with reference to classification as based upon anatomical structure, to geographical distribution, and to the determination of the genera and species. After referring to the leading authorities upon the subject, the writer remarks upon the whole family and its geographical distribution, and proposes to divide it into two sections, readily distinguished by the structure of the feet. In one of the these, *Caprimulginæ* proper, the outer digit has only four phalanges, and the claw of the third or middle digit is pectinated; while in the other the same claw is not peculiar, and the fourth digit has the usual number of phalanges, five. The sternum also offers important characters, as was shown by Blanchard. (*Ann. du Mus.*

1866. SCLATER, P. L.—Continued.

    xi, 1859, pp. 104–108.) The anatomical characters in mention are figured in the woodcuts, pp. 124–126. *Podargus* and allied forms, such as *Nyctibius*, may require to be separated as a distinct family. The *Caprimulgidæ* are divided upon the foregoing considerations into 3 subfamilies : 1, *Podarginæ* (*Podargus, Batrachostomus, Ægotheles, Nyctibius*); 2, *Steatornithinæ* (single genus); 3, *Caprimulginæ*, (a) *Glabrirostres* (*Podager, Lurocalis, Chordiles, Lyncornis, Eurystopodus*), and (b) *Setirostres* (*Caprimulgus, Scotornis, Macrodipteryx, Antrostomus, Stenopsis, Hydropsalis, Heleothreptus, Nyctidromus, Siphonorhis*). The American forms are treated in a synonymatic and diagnostic list of 42 spp., with critical and biographical remarks, and a table of geographical distribution.—*Stenopsis ruficervix*, sp. n., p. 140, pl. xiv : *Antrostomus parvulus* Gould, pl. xiii.

    The paper is translated in *J. f. O.*, 1867, pp. 252–278.

1866. SCLATER, P. L.   Additional Notes on the Caprimulgidæ.   < *P. Z. S.*, xxxiv, 1866, pp. 581–590, pll. xlv, xlvi.

    In continuation of *P. Z. S.*, 1866, pp. 123–145, *q. v.* Anatomy of *Podargus.—Antrostomus ornatus*, p. 586, pl. 45 ; *S. langsdorfi* Pelz., *S. platura* Pelz., p. 589, spp. nn. Pl. 46 represents *Antrostomus maculicaudus. Stenopsis leucura* (V.) renamed *S. candicans* Pelz., p. 588.

1867. SCLATER, P. L.   Bemerkungen über die amerikanischen Caprimulgiden. (Uebersetzt aus den P. Z. S., 27 Feb. 1866.)   < *J. f. O.*, xv, 1867, pp. 252–278.

    Vergleich d. Originalausgabe, *l. c.*, 1866.

1868. MOORE, N. B.   Note on Chordeiles virginianus.   < *Proc. Bost. Soc. Nat. Hist.*, xii, 1868, p. 127.

    Occurrence of a pebble "of considerable size" in its stomach.

1868. SALVADORI, T.   Due nuove specie di uccelli della famiglia dei Caprimulgidi.   < *Atti della Soc. Ital. di Sci. Naturali*, xl, fasc. iii, Sept. 16, 1868, pp. 447 – —.

    Stenopsis macrorhyncha, Scotornis nigricans, both from South America. I cannot give the pages, as I have only seen repaged oversheets. 8vo. pp. 4.

1868. SCLATER, P. L.   [Exhibition of the egg of the Guacharo (Steatornis caripensis).]   < *P. Z. S.*, xxxvi, 1868, pp. 73, 74.

1869. GOERING, A.   Escursion a algunas cuevas hasta ahora no esploradas, (al sureste de Caripe.)   < *Vargasia*, núm. 5, 1869, pp. 124–128, con una lámina.

    Una visita á la célebre Cueva del Guáchero (*Steatornis caripensis*). Cf. *Ibis*, 1870.

1869. HEPBURN, J.   [Identifies the "booming swallow" (cf. Ibis, 1867, 126) with Chordeiles virginianus.]   < *Ibis*, v, 2d ser., 1869, pp. 126, 127.

1869. KÖNIG-WARTHAUSEN, R.   Bemerkungen über die Fortpflanzung einiger Caprimulgiden.   < *J. f. O.*, xvi, 1868, pp. 361–388, pl. ii, f. 3.   (Publicirt 1869.)

    The concluding Heft of the Journ. for 1868 was not published till May, 1869. Cf. *Zool. Rec.* for 1868, p. 29; for 1869, 56.

    The plate represents eggs of *Stenopsis bifasciatus.*

    The paper is an interesting one, with much on the literature of the subject, and very full treatment of 28 spp., "According to the colour of the Eggs the birds may be arranged in *four* groups—those laying (1) glossy eggs with a white ground, blotched with brownish- or bluish-gray, (2) very glossy eggs with a greenish-white ground, spotted and streaked with greenish-brown and gray, (3) dull and delicate eggs with a pale reddish cream-coloured or lively-flesh-coloured ground marked with yellowish-red and violet-grey, and (4) unspotted eggs more or less white. The first of these is the prevailing type, especially in the northern hemisphere and the temperate districts of the Old World; the second is the northern type of the New World; the third the southern type, especially in the New World, and the fourth the Polynesian type, which is special for the *Podarginæ* and *Steatornithinæ*. The accounts of the different species are given in much detail and with great apparent accuracy." (*Zool. Rec.*, 1869, p. 57.)

1870. PELZELN, A. v.   [Rectification of Zool. Record, v, p. 74, in respect of certain Neotropical Caprimulgidæ.]   < *Ibis*, 2d ser., vi, 1870, p. 296.

1871. "FAIRFAX."   The Notes of the Whipporwill [Antrostomus vociferus].   < *Am. Nat.*, v, 1871, pp. 438, 439.

1873. BREWER, T. M.   Color of the Eggs of Caprimulginæ.   < *Am. Nat.*, vii, July, 1873, pp. 434, 435.

    With reference to a statement made by E. Coues, *tom. cit.*, p. 325.

1873. GARROD, A. H. On some Points in the Anatomy of Steatornis. < *P. Z. S.*, June 3, 1878, pp. 526–535, figg. 1–4.

> Relating almost entirely to the pterylosis (figured) and the anatomy of the soft parts, especially the digestive organs, trachea, carotid arteries and certain muscles, the skull being also described and figured so far as to make it comparable with those in Huxley's paper on the classification of birds (*P. Z. S.*, 1867). The article is an important one. The pterylosis more closely resembles that of the *Strigidæ* than that of the *Caprimulgidæ*, and the genus should be made the type of a distinct family.

1873. MURIE, J. Fragmentary Notes on the Guacharo or Oil-Bird (Steatornis caripensis). < *Ibis*, 3d ser., iii, 1873, pp. 81–84.

> A 'scrupulously exact' description of the outside of the bird.

1873. SCOTT, D. [W.] The North American Goatsuckers [Caprimulgidæ]. < *Am. Nat.*, vii, 1873, pp. 669–675.

> Biographical notes, with analytical synopsis of the species.

1878. [FITCH, E. H.] The Whippoorwill. (Antrostomers Vocifereus [sic].) < *The Journ. of Sci.* (Toledo, Ohio), 2d ser., i, No. 4, July, 1878, suppl. sheet, cut.

> Popular biography of the bird, with a figure.

1878. ROCKWELL, C. A Tough Young Night Hawk [Chordeiles virginianus]. < *Forest and Stream*, xi, Aug. 22, 1878, p. 46.

> *Chordeiles virginianus* hatching from an egg which had been broken and "stirred up" by the writer.

1879. [FITCH, E. H.] The Night Hawk [Chordeiles popetue]. < *The Journ. of Sci.* (Toledo, Ohio), 2d ser., i, No. 11, Feb., 1879, cut.

> Popular biography, with a figure.

1879. MAYNARD, C. J. Nest of the Chuck-will's-widow [Antrostomus carolinensis]. < *The Oölogist*, v, No. 1, July, 1879, p. 2.

Todidæ.

1833. LAFRESNAYE, F. DE. Sur le genre Todier, Todus. L. < *Guêr. Mag. de Zool.*, 3ᵉ année, 1833, classe ii, notice xi, pl. xi.

Todus viridis Gm., pl. xi.

1842. LAFRESNAYE, F. DE. [Ueber Todus.] < *Oken's Isis*, Bd. xxxv, 1842, p. 56.

Mag. de Zool., iii, 1833.

1847. LAFRESNAYE, F. DE. Mélanges ornithologiques sur le Todier vert, Todus viridis des auteurs. < *Revue Zoologique*, x, 1847, pp. 326–333.

4 spp.—*TT. viridis, dominicensis, portoricensis, mexicanus.*

1851. LAFRESNAYE, F. DE. Mélanges ornithologiques.—Sur une nouvelle espèce de Todier (Todus [augustirostris]). < *Rev. et Mag. de Zool.*, iii, 1851, pp. 477–479.

1872. MURIE, J. On the skeleton of Todus, with Remarks as to its Allies. < *P. Z. S.*, May 21, 1872, pp. 664–680, pl. lv, 20 figg.

Describes in great detail the skeleton of *Todus viridis*, and shows that the bird is a Coccygomorph, its nearest living allies being the *Momotidæ* and *Alcedinidæ*, but having also Muscicapine, Meropine, Galbuline, and Bucconine tendencies, as shown by its habits, food, and other peculiarities.

"It may be presumed that *Todus* comes of Halcyonine lineage, though its organization places it in juxtaposition with the Motmots. It moreover offers structure so truly Passerine as to mask its more direct allies; and such exterior points deceived the older naturalists or were too strongly insisted upon." A very elaborate and philosophical memoir.

1872. SCLATER, P. L. Observations on the Systematic Position of the Genera Peltops, Eurylæmus, and Todus. < *Ibis*, 3d ser., ii, Apr., 1872, pp. 177–180, figg. 1–4.

I. That *Peltops* should be referred to the family *Muscicapidæ*. II. That the *Eurylæmidæ* should be assigned to the order *Passeres*. III. That the *Todidæ* should be constituted a family of *Coccygomorphæ*, in the immediate neighbourhood of the *Momotidæ*.

1874. SHARPE, R. B. On the Genus Todus. < *Ibis*, 3d ser., iv, 1874, pp. 344–355, pl. xiii.

Chronological summary of literature of the subject: synonymatic, descriptive, etc., synopsis of 5 spp. *Todus pulcherrimus*, p. 353, pl. xiii, f. 3, sp. n. Pl. xiii, figg. 1, 2, *T. subulatus.*

Momotidæ.

1841. JARDINE, W. Horæ Zoologicæ. No. III. On the History and Habits of the Birds composing the Genus Prionites of Illiger. < *Ann. Mag. Nat. Hist.*, vi, 1841, pp. 321–328, figg.

1841. LESSON, R. P. Description des Oiseaux du genre Momot Briss. < *Actes Soc. Linn. de Bordeaux*, xii, 1841, pp. 187–—.

Pas vue moi-même. Titre tiré de Carus et Engelmann.

1843. CABOT, S., JR. [Momotus yucatacensis, sp. n., from Yucatan.] < *Proc. Bost. Soc. Nat. Hist.*, i, 1843, p. 156.

This was subsequently identified with *M.* (*Eumomota* Scl. 1857) *superciliaris* Sandb.

1849. STRICKLAND, H. E. Momotus gularis, Lafresnaye. < *Jard. Contrib. Orn.*, 1849, p. 33, pl. xvii.

1851. SCHOMBURGK, R. Prionites Momota, Ill. < *Naumannia*, i, Heft iv, 1851, pp. 21–24.

Aus der Leben.

1853. SCLATER, P. L. Notes sur deux novelles espèces du genre Momot (momotus). < *Rev. et Mag. de Zool.*, v, 1853, pp. 489, 490.
Momotus semirufus, *M. subrufescens*, p. 489.

1854. GOULD, J. Description of a New Species of Momotus [castaneiceps]. < *P. Z. S.*, xxii, 1854, p. 154.

1855. GOULD, J. Description of a New Species of Momotus. < *Ann. Mag. Nat. Hist.*, 2d ser., xvi, 1855, pp. 273, 274.

From *P. Z. S.*, July 25, 1854, p. 154.

1857. SCLATER, P. L. Review of the species of the Fissirostral Family Momotidæ. < *P. Z. S.*, xxv, 1857, pp. 248–260, pl. (Aves) cxxviii.

4 genera, 17 spp., and 4 others doubtful. *Eumomota*, p. 257, g. n. *Momotus microstephanus*, *M. nattereri*, p. 251, spp. nn. A very complete account of the group. The pl. represents *Prionirhynchus carinatus*.

1863. SCHLEGEL, H. Momotus. < *Mus. Hist. Nat. Pays-Bas.*, 4e livr., Juil., 1863, pp. 1–8.

The group here treated is made to consist of the *Momotidæ* and *Todidæ* of authors; there are given 13 spp. of the single genus *Momotus*, and 2 of *Todus*.

1872. MURIE, J. On the Motmots [Momotidæ] and their Affinities. < *Ibis*, 3d ser., ii, 1872, pp. 383–412, pll. xiii–xv.

I. Skull and sternum of *Momotus lessoni*. II. Cranium, etc., of *M. brasiliensis*. III. Osteology of *M. ruficapillus*. IV. *Eumomota superciliaris*—skeleton generally. V. The alliances of the *Momotidæ* osteologically considered. (These are with the *Todidæ*, the two families constituting a section of Syndactyle birds proposed to be called *Serratirostres*.) VI. Compendium of facts and opinions on the Motmots. VII. Conclusions derivative from data given. Pls. xiii–xv represent anatomical details and bills.

"Describes the skull and sternum of *Momotus lessoni*, and in detail the skeleton of *Baryphthengus ruficapillus* and *Eumomota superciliaris*. A comparison is then made of the osteology of the *Momotidæ* with that of the *Todidæ*, *Coraciidæ*, *Meropidæ*, *Alcedinidæ*, and other families; and after a consideration of various facts as to habits, structure, and geographical distribution, and of opinions as to their supposed affinities, arrives at the conclusion that the four families just named best accord with the *Momotidæ*, and of them the *Todidæ* are most akin. If it is necessary to group them more nearly, Mr. Blyth's term "Serratirostres" (*Mag. Nat. Hist.*, new ser., ii, p. 422) may be used. Only four genera of *Momotidæ* (*Momotus, Baryphthengus, Hylomanes* and *Eumomotus*) seem well established." (*Zool. Rec.*)

1873. SALVIN, O. On the Tail-Feathers of Momotus. < *P. Z. S.*, 1873, pp. 429–433, figg. 4.

Mode of formation of the "racket"; cf. *Ibis*, 1872, p. 383. The birds are stated to nibble the feathers.

1878. GARROD, A. H.   On the Systematic Position of the Momotidæ.   < *P. Z. S.* Jan., 15, 1878, pp. 100–102, figg. A, B.

Cf. *P. Z. S.*, 1874, p. 123: errors there made here corrected.   Colic cœca absent; minute tuft on oil-gland, or none.   Such being the case, *Momotidæ* must be placed with the *Piciformes* as defined by Garrod, instead of with *Passeriformes*.   *Momotidæ* scarcely separable as a family from *Todidæ*.   A pterylographic peculiarity favors the reference of the family to *Piciformes*.   Syrinx of *Momatus lessoni* figured, 2 views.

Trogonidæ.

1832. LA LLAVE, PABLO DE. Memoria sobre el Quetzaltototl, género nuevo de Aves [Pharomachrus mocinno, g. sp. n.]. < *Registro Trimestre* (Mexico), i, núm. 1, Enero de 1832, pp. 43–49.

1833. GOULD, J. [Description of the Female of Trogon pavoninus, Spix.] < *P. Z. S.*, i, 1833, p. 107.

1834. GOULD, J. [Characters of three New Species of Trogon (T. erythrocephalus, T. malabaricus, and T. elegans) in the Collection of the Society.] <*P. Z. S.*, ii, 1834, pp. 25, 26.

1834. GOULD, J. [Description of Trogon pavoninus, ♀.] < *Lond. and Edinb. Philos. Mag.*, iv, 1834, pp. 59, 60.
From *P. Z. S.*, Sept. 10, 1833, p. 107.

1835. GOULD, J. [Characters of several New Species of Trogon (Trogon resplendens, T. ambiguus, T. citreolus).] < *P. Z. S.*, iii, 1835, pp. 29, 30.

1835. GOULD, J. [On Trogonidæ.] < *Lond. and Edinb. Philos. Mag.*, vii. 1835, p. 226.
From *P. Z. S.*, Mar. 10, 1835, pp. 29–30.

1835. GOULD, [J.] Viele Vögel. < *Oken's Isis*, Bd. xxviii, 1835, pp. 1024, 1025.
Proc. Zool. Soc. Lond., 1834, p. 25. *Trogon erythrocephalus, T. malabaricus, T. elegans.*

1836. GOULD, J. [Exhibition of Trogon resplendens and T. pavoninus.] < *P. Z. S.*, iv, 1836, p. 12.

1837. BONAPARTE, C. L. [On the Habits of the Long-tailed Trogon (Trogon resplendens, Gould).] < *P. Z. S.*, v, 1837, p. 101.

1837. GOULD, [J.] Ueber Trogon. < *Oken's Isis*, Bd. xxx, 1837, pp. 121, 122.
Proc. Zool. Soc. Lond., 1835, p. 29. *Trogon resplendens, T. ambiguus, T. citreolus.*

1837. ORBIGNY, A. D'. Couroucou. Trogon. Linnee. Antisien. Antisianus. D'Orb. < *Guér. Mag. de Zool.*, 7ᵉ année, 1837, classe ii, notice lxxxv, pl. lxxxv.

1838. BLYTH, E. [Observations on the Structure of the Feet of the Trogonidæ.] < *P. Z. S.*, vi, 1838, p. 20.

1838. BONAPARTE, C. L. Dell' Uccello messicano quezalt e dei Trogonidi cui apparti-ente. < *Nuovi Ann. Sci. Nat. Bologna*, ii, 1838, pp. 5–12.
Trogon paradiseus, "nob.", p. 6.—Caratteri della famiglia e della sottofamiglia, p. 8.—Caratteri di ciascuno dei cinque generi *Trogon, Harpactes, Apaloderma, Temnurus, Calurus*, p. 10.

1838? BONAPARTE, C. L. Dell' Uccello Messicano | Quezalt | e dei Trogonidi | cui Ap-partiene | di Carlo Luc. Bonaparte | principe di Musignano | Memoria estratta | dal 7.º fasc. dei nuovi annali delle Scienze Naturali | n. d. n. p. 8vo. pp. 10.

1838. BONAPARTE, C. L. Observations on the Long-tailed Trogon [T. paradiseus]. < *Charlesw. Mag. Nat. Hist.*, ii, 1838, pp. 229–231.

1838. GOULD, J. [Trogon resplendens et pavonicus.] < *Oken's Isis*, Bd. xxxi, 1838, p. 172.
Auszüge aus *Proc. Zool. Soc. Lond.*, iv, 1836, p. 12.

1838. GOULD, J. A monograph of the Trogonidæ or family of Trogons. London. 1838. 1 vol. imp. folio. pll. 38.
This is the date of completion of the orig. ed. of the monograph, a copy of which I have yet to see. Nor can I now give dates of the 3 parts in which it appeared. There is a 2d ed., a very different publication, 1868–75, *q. v.*

1839. BONAPARTE, C. L. Ueber den mexicanischen Vogel Quezalt aus der Gruppe der Trogoniden. < *Oken's Isis*, Bd. xxxii, 1839, pp. 611–614.
Uebersetz. aus *Nuovi Annali delle Scienze naturali, Bologna* ii, 1838, pp. 5–12.

1841. CLARKE, C. [Exhibition of Trogon temnura.] < *P. Z. S.*, ix, 1841, p. 53.

1842. GOULD, J. On two new Species of Trogon and a new species of Toucan from the Cordillerian Andes. < *Ann. Mag. Nat. Hist.*, ix, 1842, pp. 236–239.

  Trogon personata, p. 237; *T. auriceps*, p. 238; *Pteroglossus castaneorhynchus*, p. 238.

1843. LATTRE, A. DE. Note sur les mœurs du Couroucou Pavonin, et détails sur les contrées qu'il habite. < *Revue Zoologique*, vi, 1843, pp. 163–165.

  L'Écho du Monde Savant.

1845. GOULD, J. [Description of a new Trogon (T. puella).] < *P. Z. S.*, xiii, 1845, p. 18.

1847. LAFRESNAYE, [F.] DE. Mélanges ornithologiques sur le Trogon Xalapensis (Couroucou de Xalapa), Brd. Dubus; Esquisses ornithologiques, 1re livrais., Pl. II, et sur les Couroucous en général. < *Revue Zoologique*, x, 1847, pp. 180–182.

1849. DEVILLE, E., *et* DES MURS, O. Note sur une nouvelle espèce de Couroucou (Trogon ramoniana), et sur le Trogon meridionalis. < *Rev. et Mag. de Zool.*, i, 1849, pp. 331–333.

1856. FRASER, L. [Exhibition of a number of Birds, from the collection of T. C. Eyton, Esq.] < *P. Z. S.*, xxiv, 1856, pp. 368, 369.

  Trogon eytoni, Juida eytoni, spp. nn.

1856. GOULD, J. Description of a New Trogon and a New Odontophorus. < *P. Z. S.*, xxiv, 1856, pp. 107, 108.

  Trogon aurantiiventris, p. 107; *Odontophorus veraguensis*, p. 107.

1857. BOGDANOW, A. Note sur le pigment rouge des plumes du Calurus auriceps, Gould. < *Rev. et Mag. de Zool.*, ix, 1857, pp. 511–514.

1857. GOULD, J. Description of a new Trogon [aurantiiventris] and a new Odontophorus [veragnensis]. < *Ann. Mag. Nat. Hist.*, 2d ser., xix, 1857, pp. 110, 111.

  From *P. Z. S.*, May 13, 1856, pp. 107, 108.

1860. SALVIN, O. [Exhibition of the eggs of the Quesal (Pharomachrus paradiseus).] < *P. Z. S.*, xxviii, 1860, p. 374.

1861. LA LLAVE, PABLO DE. Mémoires d'histoire naturelle du docteur D. Pablo de la Llave, extraits du Registro trimestre publié à Mexico en 1832. < *Rev. et Mag. de Zool.*, xiii, 1861, pp. 23–33.

  Contient une traduction Française, par A. Sallé, d'un mémoire sur le Quetzaltototl (*Pharomachrus mocinno*) par Señor de la Llave, accompagnée des notes du traducteur. Voir 1832.

1861. SALVIN, O. Quesal-shooting in Vera Paz. < *Ibis*, iii, 1861, pp. 138–149.

  Narrative of an expedition to procure *Pharomachrus paradiseus*.

1868-75. GOULD, J. A | Monograph | of | the Trogonidæ, | or | Family of Trogons. | By | John Gould, F. R. S. &c. | — | London : | printed by Taylor and Francis, Red Lion Court, Fleet Street. | Published by the Author, 26 Charlotte Street, Bedford Square. | [1868–] 1875. 1 vol. folio. pp. i–xx (title, dedication, preface, introduction, synopsis); list of plates 1 leaf; pll. colored, 1–4, 4a, 5–46, each with a sheet or more of letterpress. Pub. in — Parts.

  Orig. ed. pub. —— to 1838. This second edition is really a different publication, all the plates being redrawn, and many more species being figured. Some of the plates are reproduced from the author's *Birds of Asia*. They are as follows:

  1. *Pharomacrus mocinno*. 2. *P. antisianus*. 3. *P. fulgidus*. 4, 4a. *P. auriceps*. 5. *P. pavoninus*. 6. *Euptilotis neoxenus*. 7. *Trogon mexicanus*. 8. *T. ambiguus*. 9. *T. elegans*. 10. *T. personatus*. 11. *T. puella*. 12. *T. aurantiiventris*. 13. *T. collaris*. 14. *T. atricollis*. 15. *T. tenellus*. 16. *T. caligatus*. 17. *T. meridionalis*. 18. *T. ramonianus*. 19. *T. variegatus*. 20. *T. behni*. 21. *T. viridis*. 22. *T. chionurus*. 23. *T. bairdii*. 24. *T. aurantius*. 25. *T. surucura*. 26. *T. citreolus*. 27. *T. melanocephalus*. 28. *T. clathratus*. 29. *T. melanurus*. 30. *T. macrurus*. 31. *T. massena*. 32. *Tmetotrogon roseigaster*. 33. *Prionotelus temnurus*. 34. *Hapaloderma narina*. 35. *H. constantia*. 36. *H. diardi*. 37. *H. hasumba*. 38. *H. fasciatus*. 39. *H. ardens*. 40. *H. davauceli*. 41. *H. rutilus*. 42. *H. hodgsoni*. 43. *H. erythrocephalus*. 44. *H. reinwardti*. 45. *H. mackloti*. 46. *H. oreskios*. Cf. *Ibis*, 1870, p. 118.

1871. LA LLAVE, PABLO DE. El Pharomachrus mocinno su descripcion y fundamentos de este género de aves. < *La Naturaleza*, ii, 1871, pp. 17, 18.

  Apéndice al artículo anterior, *ibid.*, pp. 14–16.

1871. SAUSSURE, H. DE.   Los Curucús [Trogonidæ].   < *La Naturaleza*, ii, 1871, pp. 14–16.

Sobre las costumbres.

1872. BREWER, T. M.   [Remarks on exhibition of Pharomachrus mocinno.]   < *Proc. Boston Soc. Nat. Hist.*, xv, 1872, p. 152.

1874. TURATI, *Count, and* SALVADORI, T.   Description of a New Trogon of the Genus Pharomacrus [xanthogaster].   < *P. Z. S.*, Nov. 17, 1874, p. 652.

1877. BOUCARD, A.   Notes on Pharomacrus costaricensis.   < *Rowl. Orn. Misc.*, iii, pt. xi, Nov., 1877, pp. 21–28.

Very full on the habits of the bird.

Alcedinidæ.

1845. THOMPSON, W. Occurrence of the Belted Kingfisher, Alcedo Alcyon, Linn., in Ireland. < *Ann. Mag. Nat. Hist.*, xvi, 1845, p. 430.

1846. NEWMAN, E. Occurrence of the Great Belted Kingfisher [Ceryle alcyon] in Ireland. < *Zoologist*, iv, 1846, p. 1212.

1846. THOMPSON, W. Additional note on the Belted Kingfisher, Alcedo Alcyon, Linn., obtained in Ireland. < *Ann. Mag. Nat. Hist.*, xvii, 1846, pp. 69, 70.

1852. CASSIN, J. Catalogue | of the | Halcyonidæ | in the collection of | the Academy of Natural Sciences | of Philadelphia. | < *Published with the Proc. Acad. Nat. Sci. Phila.*, vol. vi; dated Nov. 1, 1852; not paged. Also separately, 8vo, foll. 10.
Synonymatic.

1863. SCHLEGEL, H. Alcedines. < *Mus. Hist. Nat. Pays-Bas*, 3ᵉ livr., Mai, 1863, pp. 1–52.
The Kingfishers are all ranged in two genera, *Alcedo* and *Dacelo*, corresponding nearly with the subfamilies of other authors; there being treated of the former 32 spp., and 46 of the latter, represented by a total of 544 specimens in the Leyden Museum. *A. picturata*, p. 16; *Dacelo grayi*, p. 37, spp. nn.
See same author at 1874.

1868. ENDICOTT, W. E. The Belted Kingfisher [Ceryle alcyon]. < *Am. Nat.*, ii, 1868, p. 218.
Note on the mode of nesting.

1868. FOWLER, A. The Belted Kingfisher [Ceryle alcyon]. < *Am. Nat.*, ii, 1868, pp. 403–405.
On the breeding-habits, nest and eggs.

1868. MARCH, P. G. Kingfisher's [Ceryle alcyon] Nest again [with reference to preceding accounts in the same Journal]. < *Am. Nat.*, ii, 1868, p. 490.
Description of two nests.

1868–71. SHARPE, R. B. A Monograph | of | the Alcedinidæ: | or, | Family of Kingfishers. | By | R. B. Sharpe, F. L. S. &c., | Librarian to the Zoological Society of London, Member of the German Ornithologists' Society, &c., &c. | — | Perque dies placidos hiberno tempore septem | Incubat alcyone pendentibus æquore nidis. | Ovid, Met. xi. 745. | — | London : | published by the author. | — | 1868–71. 1 vol. 4to. not paged, plates not numbered. Title, 1 l.; dedication, 1 l.; contents, list of plates and introduction, pp. i–lxxii, with 1 plate of generic details and 1 map. Text, unpaged, 304 pp. Plates, unnumbered, 120. Index, pp. i–xii. List of subscribers, 1 page. Published in 15 parts, 1868–1871, as follows:—
Part I, July 1, 1868; II, Oct. 1, 1868; III, Jan. 1, 1869; IV, Apr. 1, 1869; V, July 1, 1869; VI, Oct. 6, 1869; VII, Jan. 1, 1870; VIII, Apr. 1, 1870; IX, July 1, 1870; X, XI, Oct. 1, 1870; XII, Nov. 1, 1870; XIII, Dec. 1, 1870; XIV, XV, Jan. 1, 1871; the last containing the permanent title, introduction, and other furnishings.
According to the table of contents the pages and plates are citable as follows:
Alcedo ispida, p. 1, pl. 1; *bengalensis*, p. 11, pl. 2; *grandis*, p. 19, pl. 3; *malaccensis*, p. 21, pl. 4; *asiatica*, p. 23, pl. 5; *quadribrachys*, p. 25, pl. 6; *semitorquata*, p. 27, pl. 7; *euryzona*, p. 29, pl. 8; *beryllina*, p. 31, pl. 9. *Corythornis vintzioides*, p. 33, pl. 10; *cristata*, p. 35, pl. 11; *cæruleocephala*, p. 39, pl. 12. *Alcyone azurea*, p. 41, pl. 13; *pulchra*, p. 45, pl. 14; *diemensis*, p. 47 (no pl.); *leasoni*, p. 49, pl. 15; *affinis*, p. 51, pl. 15; *pusilla*, p. 53, pl. 16; *cyanopectus*. p. 55, pl. 17. *Ceryl guttata*, p. 57, pl. 18; *lugubris*, p. 59 (no pl.); *rudis*, p. 61, pl. 19; *maxima*, p. 67, pl. 20; *sharpi* p. 71, pl. 21; *torquata*, p. 73, pl. 22; *stellata*, p. 77 (no pl.); *alcyon*, p. 79, pl. 23; *amazonia*, p. 8 pl. 24; *cabanisi*, p. 87, pl. 25; *americana*, p. 89, pl. 26; *inda*, p. 91, pl. 27; *superciliosa*, p. 93, p 28. *Pelargopsis melanorhyncha*, p. 95, pl. 29; *amauroptera*, p. 97, pl. 30; *leucocupilla*, p. 99, p 31; *gouldi*, p. 101, pl. 32; *fraseri*, p. 103, pl. 33; *gurial*, p. 105, pl. 34; *malaccensis*, p. 107 (no pl.); *burmanica*, p. 109, pl. 35; *floresiana*, p. 111, pl. 36. *Ceyx philippensis*, p. 113, pl. 37; *solitari*

1868–71. SHARPE, R. B.—Continued.

p. 115, pl. 38: *melanura*, p. 117, pl. 39; *tridactyla*, p. 119, pl. 40; *rufidorsa*, p. 121, pl. 41; *sharpii*, p. 123, pl. 42; *dillwynni*, p. 125, pl. 43; *cajeli*, p. 127, pl. 44; *wallacei*, p. 129, pl. 45; *lepida*, p. 131, pl. 46; *uropygialis*, p. 133, pl. 47. *Ceycopsis fallax*, p. 135, pl. 48. *Ispidina madagascariensis*, p. 137, pl. 49; *leucogastra*, p. 139, pl. 50; *picta*, p. 141, pl. 51; *natalensis*, p. 145, pl. 52; *ruficeps*, p. 147, pl. 53; *lecontei*, p. 149, pl. 54. *Syma torotoro*, p. 151, pl. 55; *flavirostris*, p. 153, pl. 56. *Halcyon coromanda*, p. 155, pl. 57; *badia*, p. 159, pl. 58; *smyrnensis*, p. 161, pl. 59; *gularis*, p. 165, pl. 60; *cyanoventris*, p. 167, pl. 61; *pileata*, p. 169, pl. 62; *erythrogastra*, p. 171, pl. 63; *semicaerulea*, p. 173, pl. 64; *albiventris*, p. 177, pl. 65; *orientalis*, p. 181, pl. 66; *chelicutensis*, p. 183, pl. 67; *senegaloides*, p. 157, pl. 68; *cyanoleuca*, p. 189, pl. 69; *senegalensis*, p. 191, pl. 70; *dryas*, p. 193, pl. 71; *malimbica*, p. 195, pl. 72; *albicilla*, p. 197, pl. 73; *leucopygia*, p. 199, pl. 74; *nigrocyanea*, p. 201, pl. 75; *lazuli*, p. 203, pl. 76; *diops*, p. 205, pl. 77; *macleayi*, p. 207, pl. 78; *pyrrhopygia*, p. 211, pl. 79; *cinnamomina*, p. 213, pl. 80; *australasiæ*, p. 215, pl. 81; *lindsayi*, p. 217, pl. 82; *concreta*, p. 219, pl. 83; *hombroni*, p. 221, pl. 84; *sacra*, p. 223, pl. 85; *juliae*, p. 227, pl. 86; *chloris*, p. 229, pl. 87; *sordida*, p. 233, pl. 88; *forsterii*, p. 235, pl. 89; *vagans*, p. 237, pl. 90; *sancta*, p. 239, pl. 91; *funebris*, p. 243, pl. 92. *Todirhamphus veneratus*, p. 245, pl. 93; *recurvirostris*, p. 247, pl. 94; *tutus*, p. 249, pl. 95. *Carcineutes pulchellus*, p. 251, pl. 96; *melanops*, p. 253, pl. 97. *Monachalcyon monachus*, p. 255, pl. 98. *Caridonax fulgidus*, p. 257, pl. 99. *Tanysiptera sylvia*, p. 259, pl. 100; *doris*, p. 263, pl. 101; *emiliæ*, p. 265, pl. 102; *sabrina*, p. 267, pl. 103; *nympha*, p. 269, pl. 104; *ellioti*, p. 271, pl. 105; *hydrocharis*, p. 273, pl. 106; *acis*, p. 275, pl. 107; *margarethæ*, p. 277, pl. 108; *nais*, p. 279, pl. 109; *galeata*, p. 281, pl. 110; *riedeli*, p. 283, pl. 111. *Ducelo gigas*, p. 285, pl. 112; *leachi*, p. 289, pl. 113; *cervina*, p. 291, pl. 114; *occidentalis*, p. 293, pl. 115; *gaudichaudi*, p. 295, pl. 116; *tyro*, p. 297, pl. 117. *Cittura sanghirensis*, p. 299, pl. 118; *cyanotis*, p. 301, pl. 119. *Melidora macrorhina*, p. 303, pl. 120.

In addition to these plates of species, there is one of generic details, 27 figures, and a map of family relationships.

The introduction includes elaborate essays on the classification of the family, with diagnoses of all the genera and species recognized, and on the geographical distribution, as well as an important résumé of the literature of the subject. The family is divided into two subfamilies, *Alcedininæ*, with 5 genera and 41 spp., and *Daceloninæ*, with 14 genera and 84 spp.

The monograph is a model one; it at once became and remains the leading authority on the subject, and forms the corner-stone of the author's high reputation.

Cf. *Ibis*, 1868, pp. 472, 473; 1869, pp. 215, 216; 1870, pp. 121, 122, 506, 507; *J. f. O.*, 1870, pp. 377–380; *Am. Nat.*, iii, 1869, pp. 149, 150.

1869. DAVIS, H. The Kingfisher in Winter [*Ceryle alcyon*, in Minnesota]. < *Am. Nat.*, iii, 1869, p. 389.

1869. RIDGWAY, R. The Belted Kingfisher [*Ceryle alcyon*] again. < *Am. Nat.*, iii, 1869, pp. 53, 54.

Observations on the nidification of *Ceryle alcyon*, with reference to conflicting statements in this journal.

1869. WILLIAMS, C. E. Nest of the Belted Kingfisher [*Ceryle alcyon*]. < *Am. Nat.*, ii, 1869, pp. 614, 615.

Note on two nests, with reference to discussion between W. Wood and W. E. Endicott.

1870. HUGHES, D. D. The Kingfisher's [*Ceryle alcyon*] Nest. < *Am. Nat.*, iii, 1870, p. 616.

Notes on several nests of *Ceryle alcyon*.

1870. FINSCH, O. R. B. Sharpe's Monographie der Alcedinidæ. < *J. f. O.*, xviii, 1870, pp. 377–380.

1873. ABBOTT, C. C. Feeding Habits of the Belted Kingfisher [*Ceryle alcyon*]. < *Zoologist*, 2d ser., viii, 1873, pp. 3527, 3528.

From 'Nature,' Mar. 13.

1873. ANON. Kingfishers and Fish. < *Am. Sportsman*, ii, 1873, p. 187.

Method in which *Ceryle alcyon* handles and swallows its prey discussed.

1873. BREED, E. E. The Kingfisher [*Ceryle alcyon*]. < *Am. Nat.*, vii, 1873, p. 634.

On the way in which its food is prepared for deglutition.

1874. SCHLEGEL, H. Revue de la Collection des Alcedines faisant partie du Musée des Pays-Bas. < *Mus. Nat. Hist. Pays-Bas*, 11e livr., Juin, 1874, pp. 1–48.

See the original article, to which this is supplementary, 1863.

1878. BICKNELL, E. P. [Migrations of Kingfisher (*Ceryle alcyon*).] < *The Country*, i, Feb. 16, 1878, p. 229.

1878. BROWN, N. C. [Late stay of Kingfisher (Ceryle alcyon) in New England.]
< *The Country*, i, Jan. 26, 1878, p. 181.

1878. COUES, E. Habits of the Kingfisher (Ceryle alcyon). < *Bull. Nutt. Ornith. Club*,
iii, No. 2, Apr., 1878, p. 92.
Fruit-eating: communicated by Mrs. Mary Treat.

1879. SHAW, C. J. The Belted King Fisher. (Ceryle Alcyon.) < *Journ. of Sci.* (Toledo, Ohio), n. s., ii, No. 8, Dec., 1879.
Nesting habits.

Capitonidæ.

[In this family I give all the titles I possess.]

1798. SPARRMAN, A. Bucco atro-flavus: Et nytt fogel species ifrån Sierra Liona, beskrifvit. < *Kongl. Vetensk.-Acad. Nya Handl.*, xix, 1798, pp. 305–307, pl. ix.

1836. LAFRESNAYE, F. DE. Barbion. Micropogon. Temm. B. soufré. B. sulphuratus. Lafresn. < *Guér. Mag. de Zool.*, 6e année, 1836, classe ii, pp. 1–5, notice lx, pl. lx.

    Pl. 60, *Micropogon sulphuratus.*—En suite, une liste de sept espèces américaines, asiatiques et africaines du genre.

1837. RÜPPELL, [E.] A Notice of the Phytotoma tridactyla of Abyssinia. < *P. Z. S.*, v, 1837, p. 50.

    Proposes to call *Pogonias brucei* what had been named by Stanley *Bucco saltii.*

1842. HARTLAUB, [G.] Description d'une nouvelle espèce du genre Barbu [Bucco malaccensis], suivie de la liste de toutes les espèces connues de ce genre. < *Revue Zoologique*, v, 1842, pp. 336, 337.

    27 espèces.

1849. DEVILLE, E., *and* DES MURS, O. Notice sur le Barbu orangé de Pérou (Capito Peruvianus); sur le Barbu de la Gnyane [sic] (C. erythrocephalus ou Cayanensis) et sur une variété intermédiare ou espèce nouvelle (C. amazonicus?). < *Rev. et Mag. Zool.*, i, 1849, pp. 161–176.

    Petite monographie.

1849. LAFRESNAYE, F. DE. Description et figure d'une [récemment] nouvelle espèce d'Oiseau du genre Micropogon de Temminck. < *Rev. et Mag. Zool.*, i, 1849, pp. 116, 117, pl. 4.

    M. bourcieri, Lafr., *R. Z.*, 1845, p. 179.

1849. LAFRESNAYE, F. DE. Description et figure d'une [récemment] nouvelle espèce d'Oiseau du genre Micropogon de Temminck. < *Rev. et Mag. Zool.*, i, 1849, pp. 176, 177, pl. 6.

    M. hartlaubii, Lafr., *R. Z.*, 1845, p. 180.

1850. [JARDINE, W.] Megalaima capistratus, Eyton [n. sp. ?]. < *Jard. Contrib. Orn.*, 1850, p. 29, pl. xlv.

1855. [JARDINE, W.] Tetragonops ramphastinus (Jardine). < *Edinb. New Philos. Journ.*, new ser., ii, 1855, p. 404.

1858. SCLATER, P. L. On a new species of Barbet from the Upper Amazon. < *Ann. Mag. Nat. Hist.*, 3d ser., i, 1858, p. 235.

    From *P. Z. S.*, Nov. 24, 1857, p. 267. The new species is *Eubucco aurantiicollis*, described among other birds in a paper on Bates's Upper Amazon collections.

1859. VERRAUX, J. Description d'une nouvelle espèce de Barbu [Laimodon albiventris] de l'Afrique occidentale. < *P. Z. S.*, xxvii, 1859, pp. 393–400, pl. (Aves) clvii.

    Suivie de l'indication synonymatique de 24 espèces africaines.

1861. SCLATER, P. L. On the American Barbets (Capitonidæ). *Ibis*, iii, 1861, pp. 182–190, pl. vi.

    Synonymatic, diagnostic, and geographical synopsis of 12 spp. of *Capito* and 1 sp. of *Tetragonops* (pl. vi), with critical remarks.

1862. SCLATER, P. L. Additional [Ibis, 1861, 182] Notes on the American Barbets. < *Ibis*, iv, 1862, pp. 1, 2, pl. i.

    Capito maculicoronatus.

1864. SCLATER, P. L. On a new Species of Tetragonops [frantzii]. *Ibis*, vi, 1864, pp. 371, 372, pl. x.

1865. FRANTZIUS, A. v. [Extract from a letter relating to Tetragonops frantzii.] < *Ibis*, 2d ser., i, 1865, p. 551.

Bull. v, 4——13

1865. MILNE-EDWARDS, A.   Rapport sur quelques acquisitions nouvelles faites par la galerie ornithologique du Muséum.   *< Nouv. Arch. du Mus. d'Hist. Nat. de Paris*, liv, 1865, *Bull.*, pp. 75–78, pll. iii–v.

> *Capito quinticolor* Elliot, p, —, pl. iv, f. 1, N. Grenada; *Buthraupis edwardsii* Elliot, p, —, pl. iv, f. 2, N. Grenada; *Sitta villosa* Verr., pl. v, f. 1, China.

1867. SCLATER, P. L.   Barbets [Capitonidæ] and their Distribution.   *< Intellectual Observer*, Nov.. 1867, pp. 241–246, pl.

> A popular account of the leading peculiarities of the family *Capitonidæ*, illustrated with a plate representing *Megalæma asiatica*.

1870. MARSHALL, C. H. T., *and* MARSHALL, G. F. L.   [Megalæma humii, n. sp.]   *< Ibis,* 2d ser., vi, 1870, pp. 536–538.

1870. MARSHALL, C. H. T., *and* MARSHALL, G. F. L.   Notes on the Classification of the Capitonidæ.   *< P. Z. S.*, xxxviii, 1870, pp. 117–120, figg. 1–6.

> The family is primarily divided into the three subfamilies *Pogonorhynchinæ*, *Megalæminæ*, and *Capitoninæ*; the first represented in Africa and America, the second in Africa and Asia, the third in Africa, Asia, and America. Several of the current genera are rearranged or reorganized; *Stactolæma*, g. n., p. 118, type *Buccanodon anchietæ*, Bocage, Africa. The heads of this species, of *Barbatula leucolæma*, *Xylobucco duchaillui*, *X. scolopacea*, *Trachyphonus margaritatus*, and *T' purpureus*, are figured.

1870–71. MARSHALL, C. H. T., *and* MARSHALL, G. F. L.   A Monograph of the Capitonidæ or Scansorial Barbets. . . .   London. 1870, 1871.   roy. 8vo.   Pub. in 9 parts. Parts i–v, 1870; Parts vi–ix, 1871.

> Not seen.
>
> According to the *Zool. Rec.*, whence I take the title and comment herewith presented, Part V contains the Preface and Introduction, the latter beginning with a dissertation on the theory of evolution, which is followed by an account of the literature relating to the special subject, to which succeeds a chapter on the classification and geographical distribution.
>
> The species figured are as follows:
>
> Part I. *Megalæma virens*, *M. versicolor*, *M. henrici*, *Calorhamphus lathami*, *Tricholæma hirsuta*, *Trachyphonus margaritatus*, *Capito maculicoronatus*, *C. aurovirens.* Part II. *Pogonorhynchus dubius*, *Tetragonops frantzii*, *Xylobucco duchaillui*, *Trachyphonus cafer*, *Capito bourcieri*, *Megalæma lineata*, *M. hodgsoni*, *M. flavifrons.* Part III. *Megalæma zeylanica*, *M. caniceps*, *M. nuchalis*, *M. faber*, *M. australis*, *Xantholæma rubricapilla*, *Stactolæma anchietæ*, *Pogonorhynchus leucocephalus.* Part IV. *Megalæma viridis*, *M. asiatica*, *M. oorti*, *M. phæostriata*, *Trachyphonus goffini*, *T. purpuratus*, *T. squamiceps*, *Barbatula leucotis.* Part V. *Megalæma chrysopogon*, *Xantholæma hæmacephala*, *Capito aurantiicollis*, *Psilopogon pyrolophus*, *Calorhamphus fuliginosus*, *Pogonorhynchus abyssinicus*, *P. torquatus*, *P. bidentatus.* Part VI. *Pogonorhynchus rolleti*, *P. diadematus*, *P. melanocephalus*, *Megalæma inornata* (Zool. Rec., vii, p. 43), *Gymnobucco bonapartii*, *Xantholæma malabarica*, *Barbatula bilineata*, *B. atroflava*, and *Capito versicolor.* Part VII. *Xantholæma rosea*, *Megalæma javensis*, *M. mystacophonus*, *M. humii* (Zool. Rec., vii, p. 43), and *M. franklini*, *Tetragonops rhamphastinus*, *Gymnobucco calvus*, and *Xylobucco scolopaceus.* Part VIII. *Megalæma armillaris*, *M. chrysopsis*, *M. corvina*, *Pogonorhynchus vieilloti*, *P. leucomelas*, *Capito richardsoni*, *C. niger*, and *C. auratus.* Part IX. *Pogonorhynchus melanopterus*, *P. undatus*, *Barbatula leucolæma*, *B. pusilla*, *B. subsulphurea*, *B. chrysocoma*, *B. uropygialis*, *Capito glaucogularis*, *C. quinticolor*, *Megalæma legrandierii*, *M. duvauceli*, and *M. cyanotis.*
>
> Cf. *Ibis*, 1870, pp. 505, 506; 1871, pp. 451, 452; and *Zool. Rec.* for 1870 and 1871.

1870. [NEWTON, A.]   [Announcement of the Messrs. Marshall's Monograph of the Capitonidæ.]   *< Ibis*, 2d ser., vi, 1870, p. 156.

1870. SWINHOE, R.   The Large Barbet [Megalæma marshallorum n. sp.] of the Himalayas in want of a Name!   *< Ann. Mag. Nat. Hist.*, 4th ser., vi, 1870, p. 348.

1872. MARSHALL, C. H. T., *and* MARSHALL, G. F. L.   [Note on the validity of Megalæma marshallorum.]   *< Ibis*, 3d ser., ii, 1872, p. 327.

1873. LLOYD, J. H.   On a new Species of Barbet [Megalæma sykesi] from Western India.   *< Ibis*, 3d ser., iii, 1873, pp. 124, 125.

Bucconidæ.

1836. GOULD, J. [Characters of a new species of Tamatia (T. bicincta).] < *P. Z. S.*, iv, 1836, pp. 80, 81.

1845. LAFRESNAYE, F. DE. Description de deux nouvelles espèces d'Oiseaux. < *Revue Zoologique*, viii, 1845, pp. 179, 180.

Micropogon bourcierii, p. 179; *M. hartlaubi*, p. 180.

1850. LAFRESNAYE, F. DE. Description et figure d'une nouvelle espèce de **Barbacou** [*Monasa mystacalis*]. < *Rev. et Mag. Zool.*, ii, 1850, pp. 215, 216, pl. 3.

Avec la description d'une autre nouvelle espèce, *M. axillaris*, p. 216.

1851. CASSIN, J. Descriptions of new species of Birds of the genera Galbula and Bucco, Briss., specimens of which are in the collection of the Academy of Natural Sciences of Philadelphia. < *Journ. Acad. Nat. Sci. Phila.*, v, Feb. 1851, pp. 154, 155, pll. vii, viii.

The new *Bucco* here described and figured is *B. ordii*, p. 154, pl. viii, from Venezuela.

1853. SCLATER, P. L. Descriptions of New Species of Bucconidæ. < *P. Z. S.*, xxi, 1853, pp. 122–124, pll. l, li.

Bucco radiatus, p. 122, pl. l; *B. striatipectus*, *Malacoptila fulvogularis*, *M. substriata* (pl. li), *M. aspersa*, p. 423.

1854. SCLATER, P. L. A Synopsis of the Fissirostral family Bucconidæ. < *Ann. Mag. Nat. Hist.*, 2d ser., xiii, 1854, pp. 353–365, 474–484.

Very complete, giving synonymy, diagnosis, geographical distribution, and much critical matter. *Bucco*, 15 spp.; *Malacoptila*, 12 spp.; *Monasa*, 4 spp.; *Chelidoptera*, 2 spp.

1854. SCLATER, P. L. Synopsis | of | the | Fissirostral Family | Bucconidæ, | accompanied by four coloured plates | of hitherto unfigured Species. | By | Philip Lutley Sclater, M. A., F. Z. S., | Fellow of Corpus Christi College, Oxford. | — | Reprinted, with Additions, from the | Annals and Magazines of Natural History, | 2nd Series, 1854.. | — | London: | Samuel Highley, 32 Fleet Street. | 1854. 1 vol. 8vo. pp. 24, pll. 4.

In this excellent monograph the author, after reviewing the previous arrangements of the group, especially insisting upon the separation of the family from the Scansorial Barbets or *Capitonidæ*, and noting their restriction to tropical America, divides the species into four genera: 1) *Bucco* with *Tamatia*, *Chaunornis* and *Cyphos* as subgenera, 2) *Malacoptila* with *Nonnula* as a subgenus, 3) *Monasa*, 4) *Chelidoptera*. *Bucco* has 15 spp., *Malacoptila* 12, *Monasa* 4, *Chelidoptera* 2. These 33 species are carefully worked out, with all the synonomy the author was able to discover (excepting that relating to *Capito senilis* Tschudi = *Bucco senilis* Poeppig MS.), diagnosis, habitats, and critical comment. The species figured are *Bucco ruficollis*, pl. 1; *B. bicinctus*, pl. 2; *B. lanceolatus*, pl. 3; *Chelidoptera albipennis*, pl. 4. The name *Nonnula* Scl. is new or recently so. Several lately new species of Sclater's were described in the *P. Z. S.* for Dec. 13, 1853.

1855. SCLATER, P. L. Characters of some apparently New Species of Bucconidæ, accompanied by a geographical Table of the family. < *P. Z. S.*, xxiii, 1855, pp. 193–196, pll. cv, cvi.

Bucco hyperrhynchus, pl. cv; *B. dysoni* "Gray", p. 193; *B. pulmentum* Bp. et Verr. MSS., pl. cvi; *Monasa peruana* Bp. et Verr. MSS., *Bucco picatus*, p. 194; *Malacoptila nigrifusca*, p. 195, spp. nn. 5 genera, 40 spp.

1855. SCLATER, P. L. Descriptions of New Species of Bucconidæ. < *Ann. Mag. Nat. Hist.*, 2d ser., xv, 1855, pp. 292–294.

From *P. Z. S.*, Dec. 13, 1853.

1856. SCLATER, P. L. Characters of some apparently New Species of Bucconidæ. < *Ann. Mag. Nat. Hist.*, 2d ser., xviii, 1856, pp. 260–263.

From *P. Z. S.*, Nov. 13, 1855.

1861. GIEBEL, C. G. Zur Osteologie der Gattung Monasa. < *Zeitschr. f. d. gesammt. Naturwiss.*, xviii, 1861, pp. 121— —.

Nicht mir selbst zugänglich.

1862. SCLATER, P. L.   On a New Species of Malacoptila [M. poliopsis] from Western Ecuador.   < *P. Z. S.*, xxx, 1862, pp. 86, 87, pl. viii.

1863. GOFFIN, A.   Buccones.   < *Mus. Hist. Nat. Pays-Bas*, 2ᵉ livr., Janv., 1863, pp. 1–66; 3ᵉ livr., 1863, pp. 67–98.

The group "Buccones" of this author, who may have caught a spirit of retrograde classification from the Director of the Leyden Museum, consists of the two very distinct families of *Capitonidæ* and *Bucconidæ,*—the distinction between which, however, is recognized by the primary division of the group into two, according as the rectrices are 10 (*Capitonidæ*) or 12 (*Bucconidæ*) in number; equivalent respectively to the "scansorial" and "fissirostral" Barbets.   Of the former are treated 11 spp. of *Pogonorhynchus*, 34 of *Megalaima*, 1 *Tetragonops*, 11 of *Capito*, and 1 *Calorhamphus*.   Of the latter are given 11 spp. of *Bucco*, 4 of *Malacoptila*, 3 of *Monasa*, and 1 of *Chelidoptera*.   The groups are, together, represented by 300 specimens in the Leyden Museum.   Various species, not represented in the Collection, are also treated in the foot-notes.

1868. SCLATER, P. L., *and* SALVIN, O.   Descriptions of New or Little-known American Birds of the Families Fringillidæ, Oxyrhamphidæ, Bucconidæ, and Strigidæ. < *P. Z. S.*, xxxvi, 1868, pp. 322–329, pl. xxix.

Monasa grandior, sp. n., p. 327.

Galbulidæ.

1768. VOSMAER, A. Description | d'un petit | Alcyon d'Amerique, | d'une beauté admirable, | N'ayant presque point de queuë, pourvû de deux doigts | de devant, & de deux de derrière [   ]; | Apporté de la Colonie Hollandoise, nommée | Les Berbices ; | Et qui se conserve dans le Cabinet de | Son Altesse Sérénissime | Monseigneur le Prince d'Orange et de Nassau, | Stadhouder He′-re′ditaire, Governeur, Capi- | taine Ge′ne′ral et Amiral des Provinces-Unies | des Pais-Bas, &c. &c. &c. | Par | A. Vosmaer, | Directeur des Cabinets d'Histoire Naturelle & de Curiosités de S. A. S., Membre de | l'Académie Impériale, & Correspondant de l'Académie Royale des Sciences de Paris. | A amsterdam, | Chez Pierre Meijer, | MDCCLXVIII.   4to.   pp. 6, pl. 1.

1768. VOSMAER, A. Description | d'un | Alcyon d'Amerique, | à longue quenë [   ], | Ayant deux doigts de devant, & deux de derrière, | d'une espèce belle et rare, si ce n'est même inⅽonnuë, | Apporté de la Colonie Hollandoise, nommée | Les Berbices ; | Et qui se conserve dans le Cabinet de | son Altesse Sérénissime | Monseigneur le Prince d'Orange et de Nassau, | Stadhouder He′re′ditaire, Gouverneur, Capi- | taine Ge′ne′ral et Amiral des Provinces-Unies | des Pais-Bas, &c. &c. &c. | Par | A. Vosmaer, | Directeur des Cabinets d'Histoire Naturelle & de Curiosités de S. A. S., Membre de | l'Académie Impériale, et Correspondant de l'Académie Royale des Sciences de Paris. | a Amsterdam, | Chez Pierre Meijer, | MDCCLXVIII. | 4to.   pp. 9, pl. 1.

1851. CABANIS, [J.] Galbula. <*Ersch und Grub. Encyclop.*, erste Sect., lii, 1851, pp. 307–311.

> A concise monograph of the family, treating the following genera and species :
> I. GALBULA. 1, *viridis*; 2, *viridicauda*; 3, *ruficauda*; 4, *rufoviridis*, p. 308, sp. n. ; 5, *tombacea*; 6, *albirostris*; 7, *cyanopogon*, p. 309, sp. n. ; 8, *paradisea*; 9, *leucogastra*; 10, *albiventris*; 11, *albogularis*; 12, *lugubris*. II. CAUAX. 1, *tridactylus*. III. CAUECIAS, p. 310, g. n. 1, *leucotis*. IV. LAMPROPTILA (*vice Lamprotila* Sw., 1837). 1, *grandis*; 2, *boërsii*.

1851. CASSIN, J. Descriptions of new species of birds of the genera Galbula and Bucco, Briss., specimens of which are in the collection of the Academy of Natural Sciences of Philadelphia. < *Proc. Acad. Nat. Sci. Phila.*, v, 1851, pp. 154, 155, pll. vii, viii.

> G. *cyanicollis*, p. 154, pl. vii, from Pará; B. *ordii*, p. 154, pl. viii.

1852. SCLATER, P. L. VI.—Synopsis of the Genus Galbula. < *Jard. Contrib. Orn.*, 1852, pp. 29–33.

> 11 spp. G. *maculicauda*, p. 29; G. *inornata*, p. 32, spp. nn.

1852. SCLATER, P. L. VII.—On a new species of Galbula [G. melanogenia]. < *Jard. Contrib. Orn.*, 1852, p. 61, pl. xc.

1852. SCLATER, P. L. VIII.—Further Remarks on the Galbulidæ. < *Jard. Contrib. Orn.*, 1852, pp. 93–95, pl. xc.

> 4 spp. of *Galbula* (G. *melanogenia*, pl. xc); notes on spp. of *Jacamaralcyon*, *Galbalcyrhynchus*, *Jacamerops*, *Galbuloides*.

1853. SCLATER, P. L. A Synopsis of the Galbulidæ by Philip Lutley Sclater, M. A., F. Z. S.   8vo.   pp. 10, and cover.

> Reprinted, with additions, from *Jard. Contrib. Orn.*, for 1852. The author recognizes of *Galbula* 11 spp., of *Jacamaralcyon* 2, of *Jacamerops* 2, of *Galbuloides* and *Galbalcyrhynchus* each one. In using this synopsis the author's later paper, *P. Z. S.*, 1855, pp. 13–16, should be consulted for some important rectifications.—The cover of this publication gives some valu able bibliographical data respecting that erratic publication, *Jardine's Contrib. Orn.* for 1848–52. It appears that the Contributions were begun in the middle of 1848, during which year three parts appeared; in 1849, seven parts were published, forming a volume, with 27 plates; in 1850, seven parts, forming a volume, with 21 plates; in 1851, six parts, forming a volume, with 14 plates; in 1852, seven parts, with 20 plates, forming a volume.

1853. TRISTRAM, H. B.   Occurrence of the Jacamar (Galbula ruficauda) in Lincolnshire.   < *Zoologist*, xi, 1853, pp. 3906, 3907.

1855. SCLATER, P. L.   Remarks on the Arrangement of the Jacamars (Galbulidæ),
with Descriptions of some New Species.   < *P. Z. S.*, xxiii, 1855, pp. 13–16, pl.
(Aves) lxxvii.

> 6 genn., 20 spp. *Galbula fuscicapilla*, p. 13, pl. lxxvii; *Urogalba amazonum*, p. 14; *Brachy-
galba melanosternum*, p. 15, spp. nn.   Besides these new species the paper includes some important rectifications resulting from investigations made since the writer's 'Synopsis' of
1853 appeared, and a table of Geographical Distribution.   The genus *Galbuloides* is eliminated
as probably fictitious.

1856. SCLATER, P. L.   Remarks on the Arrangement of the Jacamars (Galbulidæ),
with Descriptions of some New Species.   < *Ann. Mag. Nat. Hist.*, 2d ser., xvii,
1856, pp. 70–73.

> From *P. Z. S.*, Jan. 9, 1855, pp. 13–16

Rhamphastidæ.

1773. ————————. Naturgeschichte des grossschnablichten Pfeffervogels.　< *Berlin. Samml.*, Bd. v, 1773, pp. 294-302.

Not seen—title from Carus and Engelmann.

1795. SPALOWSKI, J. J. A.　Beschreibung und Abbildung der Ramphastos viridis und momota L.　< *Neuere Abhandlungen der K. Böhmer. Gesellsch.*, ii, 1795, pp. 172-178, 2 pll.

Not seen.

"1803–1818." LEVAILLANT, F.　Histoire Naturelle | des Oiseaux de Paradis | et des Rolliers, | suivie de celle des Toucans et des Barbus, | par | François Lavaillant. | Tome premier [second; et un troisième (Promerops, Guépiers)]. | [Monogram.] | Paris, | Chez $\left\{\begin{array}{l}\text{Denné le jeune, Libraire, rue Vivienne, n}^\circ\text{. 10.} \\ \text{Perlet, Libraire, rue de Tournon [mut. mut.].}\end{array}\right.$ | 1806. ["1803–1818."] 3 vols.　gr. in-fol.　196 planches coloriées et les doubles en noir, savoir :—

[*Vol. I.*]

Histoire Naturelle des Oiseaux de Paradis et des Rolliers, suivie de celle des Toucans et des Barbus, [etc.]　Vol. I.　Faux titre, titre, pp. 1–153, i, ii, pll. 1–56.

Histoire Naturelle des Oiseaux de Paradis.　pp. 1–68, pll. 1–24.　[PARADISEIDÆ, etc.]

Histoire Naturelle des Rolliers et des Geais.　pp. 69–116, pll. 25–39.　[CORACIIDÆ, MOMOTIDÆ, etc.]

Histoire Naturelle des Geais.　pp. 117–153, pll. 40–56.　[CORVIDÆ, COTINGIDÆ, etc.]

[*Vol. II.*]

Histoire Naturelle des Oiseaux de Paradis et des Rolliers, suivie de celle des Toucans et des Barbus, [etc.]　Vol. II.　Faux titre, titre, pp. 1–133, i, ii, 1 feuillet, pll. 1–57.

Histoire Naturelle des Toucans.　pp. 1–46, pll. 1–18.　[RHAMPHASTIDÆ.]

Histoire Naturelle des Barbus.　pp. 47–106, pll. 19–46.　[CAPITONIDÆ, BUCCONIDÆ.]

Histoire Naturelle des Jacamars.　pp. 107–126, pll. 47–54.　[GALBULIDÆ.]

Additions aux articles des Barbus proprements dits.　pp. 127–133, pll. 55–57.

[*Vol. III.*]

Histoire Naturelle | des Promerops | et des Guépiers, | par | F. Levaillant, | faisante suite | a celle des Oiseaux de Paradis, | par le même.　Faux titre, 1 feuillet; pp. 1–81, 1–67, 1–38, 39–52, i, ij., pll.

1ère PARTIE.　Histoire Naturelle des Promerops.　pp. 1–81, pll. 1–32.

2ème PARTIE.　Histoire Naturelle des Guépiers.　pp. 1–67, pll. 1–20.　[MEROPIDÆ.]

3ème PARTIE.　Histoire Naturelle des Couroucous, et des Touracous.　pp. 1–38, pll. 1–20.　[TROGONIDÆ, MUSOPHAGIDÆ.]

SUPPLEMENT aux différents genres d'oiseaux décrits dans les deux premiers volumes.　pp. 39–52, pll. A, AA, B, C, D, E, F, G, h, K, L.

The whole of this series of splendid monographs forms three large folio volumes, with nearly 200 colored plates, duplicated in black.　The titles of Vols. I and II are identical; the title of the third is entirely changed, and does not show on its face that it is not of a different work.　The three, however, are uniform, and form parts of one work.　It is, in fact, the continuation of Levaillant's *Hist. Nat. Ois. de l'Amérique et des Indes* (itself a supplement to the

"1803–1818" LEVAILLANT, F.—Continued.

Ois. de l'Afrique), which was announced in 1801 to appear in parts, with 240 plates; only one volume of that, however, came out, with 49 plates. That was, in effect, two monographs, of the *Bucerotidæ* and *Cotingidæ;* and the present Iconography continues the same system of monographing successive groups of birds; though, unfortunately, the author's groups do not correspond with any recognized modern families.

Volume I is consecutively paged and the plates are continuously numbered throughout. It has two Parts. The first is a monograph of *Paradiseidæ*, the second of *Coraciidæ, Momotidæ*, certain *Corvidæ*, etc.

Volume II, titled identically with Vol. I, and likewise with a continuous pagination and consecutive numbering of plates throughout, has several monographs, of *Rhamphastidæ, Capitonidæ, Bucconidæ, Galbulidæ*, etc.

Vol. III is less homogeneous. In the first place, the several memoirs are separately paged, and their respective series of plates are separately enumerated. In the next place, it has supplementary matter relating to the subjects treated in the two preceding volumes—this supplement being paged continuously with the last part of the main text, and its plates being lettered instead of numbered. There are three "Parts" in this Volume:—1. *Promerops* (a miscellaneous assortment, *Certhia*, etc.). 2. *Meropidæ*. 3. *Trogonidæ* and *Musophagidæ*.

I indicate thus the general bearing of the several treatises which compose this Iconography; though, as already said, few if any of Levaillant's groups correspond exactly with modern families.

Owing to its extensive and varied composition the work is not an easy one to cite tersely; and it is to be found quoted in such various and loose fashion as to convey the impression that there are as many distinct works as there are monographs in the single one. Figures and descriptions had best be all cited by the leading words "OIS. DE PARAD.", giving Vol. I. II, III, as the case may be, and in the instance of the last volume citing also name of the monograph or supplement.

The date of the work is in endless question. I have never yet been able to fix it. The date on the titles of all three of the volumes is the same, 1806; but the work appeared in parts, during several years. According to Engelmann, there were 33 livraisons, running from 1803 to 1818; but he gives no sufficient particulars. The date is of less consequence, however, as the author uses no scientific names, and therefore raises no question of priority of nomenclature.

The number of plates is ostensibly $56 + 57 + 32 + 20 + 20 + 11 = 196$, but there may be some interpolations. Engelmann gives 198. I have not made the actual count.

1815. TRAILL, T. S. Some Observations on the Bill of the Toucan; in a Letter to the Right Hon. Sir Joseph Banks, Bart., K. B. P. R. S. H. M. L. S. < *Trans. Linn. Soc.*, xi, pt. ii, 1815, pp. 288, 289.

Controverting the notion of its hollowness; noting its great vascularity, and probable use as a delicate organ of smell.

1818. TRAILL, T. S. Tukanschnabel, von Sf. [lege T. S.] Traill. < *Oken's Isis*, Jahrg., ii, 1818, pp. 1921, 1922.

From *Tr. Linn. Soc.*, xi, 1815, p. 288, *q. v.*

1820. SWAINSON, W. Description of two new Birds of the genus Pteroglossus. < *Quart. Journ. Sci. Lit. and Art*, Roy. Inst., ix, 1820, pp. 266–268.

Not seen. The species are *Pt. torquatus*, p. —, and *Pt. sulcatus*, p. —.

1825. BRODERIP, W. J. Observations on the Manners of a live Toucan [Rhamphastos erythrorhynchus], now exhibited in this country. < *Zool. Journ.*, i, 1825, pp. 484–488; also p. 591.

1825. LESSON, R. P. Observations sur les habitudes et la manière de vivre d'un Toucan qu'on montre actuellement en Angleterre; par W. J. Broderip. . . . < *Féruss. Bull.*, 2e sect., vi, 1825, p. 413.

Zool. Journ., Janvier 1825, pp. 484–488.

1826. VIGORS, N. A. On some species of the Ramphastidæ. < *Zool. Journ.*, ii, 1826, pp. 466–483, pl. suppl. 17.

This is a subhead of a much more extensive paper, entitled "Sketches in Ornithology;" &c., which runs through several vols. and years of the periodical cited.

Here occur the descriptions of *Ramphastos ariel*, p. 466, and *Pteroglossus bitorquatus*, p. 481, pl. 17, spp. nn., with much other matter relating to the family at large. (*Féruss. Bull.*, x, 1827, pp. 155–157; *Isis*, 1830, pp. 1060–1065.)

1827. AG. DESM—ST. Suite des Esquisses ornithologiques, ou Observations sur les véritables affinités de quelques groupes d'oiseaux, par M[*i. e.*, N]. A. Vigors.— Sur quelques espèces de Ramphastidées. < *Féruss. Bull.*, 2ᵉ sect., x, 1827, pp. 155–157.

> *Zool. Journ.*, ii, 1826, pp. 466–483.

1827. ANON. Systema Avium. Auctor Dr. I. Wagler. Stuttgartiae apud Cotta. 1827. 8. < *Oken's Isis*, Bd. xx, 1827, pp. 864–873.

> The peculiar plan of the work is illustrated by a transcript of Wagler's treatment of the genus *Rhamphastos*—14 spp.—nearly the whole of the present article being devoted to the exhibit of that genus.

1828. BRODERIP, W. J. Bemerkungen über das Betragen eines lebendigen Tukans [Rhamphastos] in London. < *Oken's Isis*, Bd. xxi, 1828, pp. 939, 940.

> Uebers aus d. *Zoological Journal*, i, 1825, Bd. i, Nr. 47, pp. 484–488, 591.

1830. VIGORS, N. A. Ornithologischen Skizzen. Ueber die Verwandtschaft einiger grösserer Vôgelgruppen. < *Oken's Isis*, Bd. xxiii, 1830, pp. 1060–1064.

> *Zoological Journal*, Nro. viii, Januar 1826 (vol. ii), pp. 466–483. Ueber einige Arten der Ramphastiden.

1832. OWEN, R. [On the Anatomy of Ramphastos ariel, Vig.] < *P. Z. S.*, ii, 1832, pp. 42–46.

1833–35. GOULD, J. A Monograph of the Ramphastidæ or Family of the Toucans. London. Published by the Author. 1833–1835. folio. Pub. in 3 parts. 52 colored plates.

> Not seen! There is a 2d ed. 1854, and Suppl. 1855, *q. v.* There is also a German version by Sturm and Sturm, 1841——.

1833. GOULD, J. [Characters of a New Species of Toucan (Pteroglossus ulocomus).] < *P. Z. S.*, i, 1833, p. 38.

1833. GOULD, J. [Characters of three New Species of Toucan (Rhamphastos and Pteroglossus).] < *P. Z. S.*, i, 1833, pp. 69, 70.

> *R. swainsonii*, p. 69; *R. culminatus, P. hypoglaucus*, p. 70.

1833. GOULD, J. [Characters of a New Species of Toucan (Pteroglossus castanotis).] < *P. Z. S.*, i, 1833, pp. 119, 120.

1834. ANON. A Monograph, etc.—Monographie des Toucans; par M. J. Gould, in-fol., Londres, 1833. < *Ann. des Sci. Nat.*, 2ᵉ sér., i, 1834, p. 256.

> L'annonce de l'ouvrage.

1834. GOULD, J. [Characters of the Genera and Species of the Family Rhamphastidæ, Vig.] < *P. Z. S.*, ii, 1834, pp. 72–79.

> This is the most extensive and complete of the earlier notices of the family, treating in all of 22 species.

1834. GOULD, J. [Characters of a New Species of Toucan (Pteroglossus hæmatopygus).] < *P. Z. S.*, ii, 1834, p. 147.

1835. GOULD, J. [Exhibition of a living Red-billed Toucan (Rhamphastos erythrorhynchus, Gmel.).] < *P. Z. S.*, iii, 1835, p. 21.

1835. GOULD, J. [On a New Species of Toucan (Rhamphastidæ, Vig.—Aulacorhynchus derbianus).] < *P. Z. S.*, iii, 1835, p. 49.

1835. GOULD, J. [Characters of New Toucans and Araçaris (Rhamphastidæ), with a Synoptic Table of the Species of the Family.] < *P. Z. S.*, iii, 1835, pp. 156–160.

> *Rhamphastos citreopygus, R. osculans*, p. 156; *Pteroglossus pluricinctus, P. humboldtii, P. nattereri, P. reinwardtii, P. langsdorffii*, p. 157; *P. pavoninus*, p. 158. With analytical diagnosis of the species of the family.

1835. GOULD, J. [On Rhamphastidæ.] < *Lond. and Edinb. Philos. Mag.*, vii, 1835, pp. 64 and 228.

> From *P. Z. S.*, Dec. 9, 1834, and Apr. 14, 1835.

1835. GOULD, J. [Zeigt einen Toucan, mit merkwürdigen Federn auf dem Kopf, u. s. w.] < *Oken's Isis*, Bd. xxvⁿi, 1835, pp. 523, 524.

> *P. Z. S.*, 1833, p. 38.

1835. GOULD, J.   Drey neue Vögel [Rhamphastidæ].   <*Oken's Isis*, Bd. xxviii. 1835, pp. 535, 536.
  From *Z. P. S.*, 1833, pp. 69, 70.

1835. GOULD, J.   Ein neuer Toucan [Pteroglossus castanotis], nahe verwandt mit Pteroglossus aracari et regalis.   <*Oken's Isis*, Bd. xxviii, 1835, p. 550.
  P. Z. S. London, 1833, p. 119.   Beschreibung von *Picus flavinucha* folgt.

1835. GOULD, J.   Rhamphastidæ Vig.   <*Oken's Isis*, Bd. xxviii, 1835, pp. 1032-1038.
  Uebersetzung: *Proc. Zool. Soc. Lond.*, ii, 1834, pp. 72-79.

1835. GOULD, J.   Ein neuer Toucan [Pteroglossus haematopygus], von Strickland mitgetheilt aus Südamerica.   <*Oken's Isis*, Bd. xxviii, 1835, p. 1060.
  Proc. Zool. Soc. Lond., ii, 1834, p. 147.

1835. OWEN, R.   Anatomie von Ramphastos ariel Vig.   <*Oken's Isis*, Bd. xxviii, 1835, pp. 373, 374.
  Aus d. *P. Z. S.*, 1832, pp. 42-46.

1836. GOULD, J.   Uebersicht der Rhamphastiden.   <*Arch. f. Naturg.*, ii, (1), 1836, pp. 307-311.
  Nach *P. Z. S.*, 1835, p. 156, *seq.*, mitgetheilt.

1837. GOULD, J.   Ueber Ramphastiden.   <*Oken's Isis*, Bd. xxx, 1837, pp. 188-191.
  Uebersetzung: *Proc. Zool. Soc. Lond.*, 1835, pp. 156-160.

1837. GOULD, J.   Ein neuer Toucan.   <*Oken's Isis*, Bd. xxx, 1837, p. 123.
  Proc. Zool. Soc. of Lond., 1835, p. 49.

1837. NATTERER, J.   [On a New Species of Araçari (Pteroglossus Gouldii).]   < *P. Z. S.*, v, 1837, p. 44.

1837. EDITORIAL.   A Monograph of the Family Ramphastidæ.   By J. Gould, F. L. S. Three parts, folio, 1833-36, London.   <*Mag. of Zool. and Bot.*, i, 1837, pp. 187-192.
  Extended review.

1839. WATERHOUSE, G. R. . [Description of a New Species of Toucan (Pteroglossus nigrirostris).]   < *P. Z. S.*, vii, 1839, pp. 111, 112.

1840. FRASER, L.   [Exhibition of some specimens of the true Pteroglossus Azarae of Wagler and Viejllot.]   < *P. Z. S.*, viii, 1840, pp. 60, 61.

1841-4-. GOULD, J.   (*Ed. Sturm.*)   Monographie der Ramphastiden oder Tukanartigen Vögel. Aus dem Englischen übersetzt, mit Zusätzen und einigen neuen Arten vermehrt von J. H. C. F. Sturm und J. W. Sturm. . . . Nürnberg, 1841-4-.
  This I have not seen, and can say little about. According to my information, it is in sm. folio, and was published in Parts. Parts i-iii are cited as of 1841, '42; Part iv as of 1847; there are said to be 5 Parts, each of ten colored lithographic plates and as many sheets of letter-press. I should judge by the title that the work is much modified from the original. See *Isis*, 1842, p. 235; 1843, p. 558; 1848, p. 695.

1842. ANON.   Gould's Monographie der Ramphastiden, aus dem Englischen übersetzt, mit Zusätzen und einigen neuen Arten vermehrt von H. und G. Sturm. Nürnberg, Pamerstrasse S. Nr. 709. Hft. II. 1841. Kl. Fol. T. 10.   < *Oken's Isis*, Bd. xxxv, 1842, pp. 235, 236.

1842. GOULD, J.   On two new Species of Trogon and a new species of Toucan from the Cordillierian Andes.   < *Ann. Mag. Nat. Hist.*, ix, 1842, pp. 236-239.
  Pteroglossus castaneorhynchus, p. 238.

1843. ANON.   J. Gould's Monographie der Ramphastiden oder tukanartigen Vögel, aus dem Englischen übersetzt, mit Zusätzen und einigen neuen Arten vermehrt von Fr. u. W. Sturm. Nürnberg. Hft. III. 1842. Kl. Fol. S. 20. Taf. 10. ill.   < *Oken's Isis*, Bd. xxxvi, 1843, p. 558, 559.

1843. GOULD, J.   [On two New Species of Birds from the collection formed by Sir Edward Belcher.]   < *P. Z. S.*, xi, 1843, pp. 15, 16.
  Pteroglossus erythropygius, Pterocles personatus, p. 15, spp. nn.

1843. GOULD, J.   [On an extensive Series of Toucans, with characters of two New Species.]   < *P. Z. S.*, xi, 1843, pp. 147, 148.
  Rhamphastos citreolæmus, Pteroglossus pœcilosternus, p. 147. spp. nn.

1844. GOULD, J. [On two new species of Ramphastidæ.] < *Ann. Mag. Nat. Hist.,* xiv, 1844, pp. 61, 62.
From *P. Z. S.*, Dec. 12, 1843.

1848. ANON. J. Gould's Monographie der Ramphastiden oder tukanartigen Vögel, übersetzt und mit Zusätzen und neuen Arten vermehrt von Fr. und W. Sturm. Nürnberg bey den Verfassern 1847. Heft IV. Kl. Fol. < *Oken's Isis*, Bd. xli, 1848, p. 695.

1849. [MITCHELL, D. W.] [Report of the purchase of a specimen of Rhamphastos carinatus.] < *P. Z. S.*, xvii, 1849, p. 94.

1853. GOULD, J. Description of a new species of Aulacorhamphus [cæruleogularis]. < *P. Z. S.*, xxi, 1853, p. 45.

1854. GOULD, J. A Monograph | of | the Ramphastidæ, | or | Family of the Toucans. | By | John Gould, F. R. S., | [etc., 7 lines.] | London: | printed by Taylor and Francis, Red Lion Court, Fleet street. | Published by the author, 20, Broad street, Golden Square. | 1854. 1 vol. folio. pp. 1–28 (title, &c., and introduction); 51 colored plates with as many sheets of letter-press; 1 uncolored plate (details) with 4 pp. of text.

> This a second edition, "with new drawings of the old species, and figures and descriptions of no less than eighteen others", making 51 in all. The original edition was published in 1833–35, containing 33 species. There is a supplement, 1855. There is a German version of the orig. ed., 1841 *seq.*
>
> The introduction gives a general account of the family, the species of which are so brilliantly illustrated in the colored plates. An additional plate, uncolored, with 4 pages of text, represents anatomical observations. The plates are as follows:
>
> 1. *R. toco;* 2. *R. carinatus;* 3. *R. brevicarinatus;* 4. *R. tocard;* 5. *R. ambiguus;* 6. *R. erythrorhynchus;* 7. *R. inca;* 8. *R. cuvieri;* 9. *R. citreolœmus;* 10. *R. osculans;* 11. *R. culminatus;* 12. *R. ariel;* 13. *R. vitellinus;* 14. *R. discolorus.* 15. *Pteroglossus araçari;* 16. *P. wiedi;* 17. *P. pluricinctus;* 18. *P. pœcilosternus;* 19. *P. castanotis;* 20. *P. torquatus;* 21. *P. erythropygius;* 22. *P. humboldti;* 23. *P. inscriptus;* 24. *P. viridis.* 25. *Beauharnasius ulocomus;* 26. *B. bitorquatus;* 27. *B. sturmi;* 28. *B. azaræ;* 29. *B. flavirostris;* 30. *B. mariæ.* 31. *Selenidera maculirostris;* 32. *S. gouldi;* 33. *S. langsdorffi;* 34. *S. nattereri;* 35. *S. reinwardti;* 36. *S. piperivora.* 37. *Andigena laminirostris;* 38. *A. hypoglaucus;* 39. *A. nigrirostris;* 40. *A. cucullatus;* 41. *A. bailloni;* 42. *Aulacoramphus sulcatus;* 43. *A. derbianus;* 44. *A. castaneorhynchus;* 45. *A. hœmatopygius;* 46. *A. cœruleocinctus;* 47. *A. prasinus;* 48. *A. wagleri;* 49. *A. albivittata;* 50, *A. atrogularis;* 51. *A. cœruleogularis.*—Plate uncolored of details.
>
> *Grammarhynchus*, g. n., p. 26.

1855. GOULD, J. Description of a New Species of Aulacorhamphus. < *Ann. Mag. Nat. Hist.*, 2d ser., xv, 1855, pp. 390, 391.
From *P. Z. S.*, Feb. 22, 1853, p. 45.

1857. CASSIN, J. Notes on the North American species of Archibuteo and Lanius, and description of a new species of Toucan, of the genus Selenidera, Gould. < *Proc. Acad. Nat. Sci. Phila.*, ix, 1857, pp. 211–214.
The new Toucan is named *S. spectabilis*, p. 214.

1858. CASSIN, J. Description of a New Tanager from the Isthmus of Darien, and note on Selenidera Spectabilis, Cassin. < *Proc. Acad. Nat. Sci. Phila.*, x, 1858, pp. 177, 178.

1858. CASSIN, J. Descriptions of New Species of Birds of the genera Selenidera, Gould, and . . . < *Journ. Acad. Nat. Sci. Phila.*, iv, pt. i, Dec. 1858, pp. 5–8, pll. i–iii.
> *Selenidera spectabilis*, pl. i, originally described in *Proc. Phila. Acad.*, 1857, p. 214.—(The remainder of the paper relates to *Numida* and *Phasidus*, and the title will be found in full under *Numididæ*.)

1858. GOULD, J. [On a New Species of Toucan (Andigena spilorhynchus).] < *P. Z. S.*, xxvi, 1858, pp. 149, 150.

1858. GOULD, J. On a new species of Toucan. < *Ann. Mag. Nat. Hist.*, 3d ser., ii, 1858, p. 388.
From *P. Z. S.*, March 23, 1858.

1865. SCHMIDT, MAX.   [Einiges über Ramphastos discolorus Gm.]   < *Zool. Gart.*, v, 1865, pp. 267, 268.

1866. GOULD, J.   Description of a New Species of Toucan belonging to the Genus Aulacoramphus [A. cyanolæmus].   < *P. Z. S.*, xxxiv, 1866, p. 24.

1867. CASSIN, J.   A Study of the Rhamphastidæ.   < *Proc. Acad. Nat. Sci. Phila.*, xix, 1867, pp. 100–124.

Monographic.   5 genn., 64 spp.   *Burhynchus*, p. 102; *Tucanus*, p. 104; *Ramphodryas*, p. 106; *Boillonius*, p. 114; *Ramphastoides*, p. 117, subgg. nn.   No new species are described.   Cf. *Zool. Rec.*, iv, 1867, p. 88.

1867. SCHMIDT, MAX.   [Einiges über Ramphastos im Gefangenschaft.]   < *Zool. Gart.*, viii, 1867.

1870. STEVENS, R. P.   The Toucan's Beak.   < *Am. Nat.*, iv, 1870, pp. 622, 623.

On the adaptation and uses of the organ in *Rhamphastidæ*.

1871. STEVENS, R. P.   Tukanens Næb.   < *Tidssk. for populære Fremst. af Naturvidensk.*, 4e ser., iii, 1871, p. 80.

„Spørgsmaalet: i hvilket Øjemed har Tukanen sit ejendommelige Næb.‟

1876. GURNEY, J. H., JR.   Toucans in England in the Seventeenth Century.   < *Zoologist*, 2d ser., xi, Mar., 1876, pp. 4838, 4839.

Extracts from Plot's *Nat. Hist. Oxfordshire*, 1677, and Leigh's *Nat. Hist. Lancashire*, 1700.

Cuculidæ.

[NOTE.—The literature of this family is extensive, but much of it relates to *Cuculus canorus* alone, or is otherwise excluded from presentation here.]

1832. KAUP, J. [J.] Saurothera marginata. Eine neue Art aus Mexico. *< Oken's Isis,* Bd. xxv, 1832, pp. 991, 992, pl. xxvi.

1833. CAWDOR, *Lord.* [Exhibition of a Coccygus carolinensis killed in Wales.] *< P. Z. S.*, i, 1833, p. 26.

1835. BOTTA, P. E. Description du Saurothera californiana. *< Nouv. Ann. du Mus. d'Hist. Nat.*, iv, 1835, pp. 121–124, pl. (color.) 9.

1835. THOMPSON, W. [Coccygus americanus in Great Britain.] *< P. Z. S.*, iii, 1835, pp. 83, 84.

1837. SWAINSON, W. On the Natural History and Relations of the Family of Cuculidæ or Cuckoos, with a view to determine the series of their variation. *< Mag. of Zool. and Bot.*, i, 1837, pp. 213–225, 430–437.
It suffices to remark of this article that it is quinarian.

1839. JARDINE, W. Horæ Zoologicæ. No. I. On the History and Habits of Crotophaga. *< Ann. Nat. Hist.*, iv, 1839, pp. 160–171, figg. 1, 2.

1840. JARDINE, W. Horæ Zoologicæ. No. II. The History and Habits of Crotophaga continued from page 171, by the Notes of Mr. Schomburgk on the Manners of the Birds of Guiana. *< Ann. Nat. Hist.*, iv, 1840, pp. 318–322.

1844. JARDINE, W. Uber das Betragen der Kielschnabel (Keel-Bils, Crotophaga). *< Oken's Isis*, Bd. xxxvii, 1844, pp. 913–918.
Ann. Nat. Hist., iv, 1839, pp. 160–171, and 318–322.

1844. SWAINSON, W. Ueber die Naturgeschichte und die Verwandschaften der Cuculidae. *< Oken's Isis*, Bd. xxxvii, 1844, pp. 512, 513.
Mag. Zool. and Bot. Lond., Bd. i, Hft. iii, 1837, pp. 213–225, 430–437.

1847. LAFRESNAYE, [F.] DE. Sur le Saurothera vetula (Tacco Vieillard) de Vieillot. *< Revue Zoologique,* x, 1847, pp. 353–360.
4 esp. *S. jamaicensis*, p. 354; *S. dominicensis*, p. 355, spp. nn.

1849. VERREAUX, J., *and* DES MURS, O. Nouvelle espèce de Coucou [Cuculus macrourus] se rapprochant du genre Piaya. *< Rev. et Mag. Zool.*, ¼, 1849, p. 276.
The species is identified by Gray with *Dromococcyx phasianellus* (Spix) of Brazil.

1849. GRAY, G. R. Description of a new species of the genus Cultrides [C. rufipennis]. *< P. Z. S.*, xvii, 1849, p. 63, (Aves) pl. x.
From Mexico. (The genus is a synonym of *Neomorphus* Gloger, 1827.)

1850. GRAY, G. R. Description of a new species of the genus Cultrides [C. rufipennis.] *< Ann. Mag. Nat. Hist.*, 2d ser., v, 1850, p. 224.
From *P. Z. S.*, Apr. 24, 1849, p. 63.

1852. STRICKLAND, H. E. On a new species of Coccyzus [C. pumilus] from Trinidad. *< Jard. Contrib. Orn.*, 1852, p. 28, pl. lxxxii.

1854. GLOGER, C. W. L. Ein seltsamer Zug in der Fortpflanzung der amerikanischen Kuckuke [Coccygus americanus]. *< J. f. O.*, ii, 1854, pp. 219–232.
Mainly from Audubon and Nuttall.

1854. HARTLAUB, G. Beiträge zur exotischen Ornithologie. *< J. f. O.*, ii, 1854, pp. 409–421.
Descriptions of various birds, with critical comment; and, in particular, a review of numerous species of *Cuculidæ*.

1855. JONES, J. C. [Communication presenting a specimen of Geococcyx (mexicanus?).] *< Proc. Boston Soc. Nat. Hist.*, v, 1855, p. 258.

1860. REINHARDT, J.   Bemærkninger om Redebygningen og Forplantningsforholdene hos Crotophaga-Slægten.   8vo.   pp. 31.

Aftryk af *Oversigt over det Kgl. danske Vidensk. Selsk. Forhandlinger* o. s. v., Januar 1860.

1862–63. CABANIS, J., *and* HEINE, F.   Museum Heineanum. | — | Verzeichniss | der | ornithologischen Sammlung | des | Oberamtmann | Ferdinand Heine | auf | Gut St. Burchard | vor | Halberstadt. | Mit kritischen Anmerkungen und Beschreibungen fast | sämmtlicher Arten | systematisch bearbeitet | von Dr. Jean Cabanis, | erstem Custos der königlichen zoologischen Sammlung in Berlin | und | Ferdinand Heine, | Stud. philos. | — | IV. Theil, | die Klettervögel | enthaltend. | Heft I: Kuckuke und Faulvögel. | — | Halberstadt, 1862–63. | In Commission der Frantz'schen Buchhandlung (G. Loose).   8vo.   2 p. ll., pp. 1–229.

Auch unter d. Titel: Museum | Ornithologicum | Heineanum. | — | Pars IV. Scansores. | Sectio I. | Cuculidæ.   Argornithidæ.

The greater part of this Heft is occupied with the *Cuculidæ* (to p. 122), and these sheets all date 1862.   The rest consists of the *Bucconidæ* (pp. 123–128 in 1862, rest in 1863) to p. 153, *Trogonidæ* to p. 212 (1863), and *Galbulidæ* to p. 229 (1863).   The new names proposed are as follows:

CUCULIDÆ (1862).   *Lamprococcyx*, p. 11; *L. chrysochlorus*, p. 11; *Chalcococcyx*, p. 15; *Penthoceryx*, *Misocalius*, p. 16; *Cacangelus*, p. 17; *Cacomantis threnodes*, p. 19; *C. infaustus*, p. 23; *Heteroscenes*, p. 26; *Hiracococcyx*, p. 27; *H. sparverinus*, p. 28; *Caliechthrus*, p. 31; *Cuculus leptodetus*, p. 34; *C. canorinus*, p. 35; *Eudynamis chinensis* [sic—*lege sinensis*], p. 52; *Ceuthmochares*, p. 60; *Rhopodytes*, p. 61; *Rhamphococcyx*, p. 65; *Glaucococcyx*, p. 71; *Cochlothraustes*, p. 74; *Coccygus nesiotes*, p. 78; *Nesococcyx*, p. 79; *Pyrrhococcyx mesurus*, p. 83; *P. guianensis*, p. 85; *P. pallescens*, p. 86; *Acentetus*, p. 102; *Centrococcyx*, p. 109; *C. moluccensis*, p. 113; *Pyrrhocentor*, p. 117; *P. unirufus*, p. 118; *Nesocentor*, p. 118.

BUCCONIDÆ (1863—none new in 1862).   *Malacoptila aequatorialis*, p. 134; *M. blacica*, p. 137; *Nystalus*, p. 139; *Hypnelus*, p. 143; *Nothriscus*, p. 146; *Argicus*, p. 148; *Notharchus*, p. 149.

TROGONIDÆ (1863).   *Pyrotrogon orrhophaeus*, p. 156; *Orescius* (= *Oreskios*, Bp.), p. 161; *Trogon virginalis*, p. 173; *T. propinquus*, p. 175; *Pothinus*, p. 180; *Aganus*, p. 184; *A. crissalis*, p. 190; *? A. devillei*, p. 191; *Harpalophorus*, p. 199; *Troctes*, p. 201; *T. mesurus*, p. 202; *Tanypeplus*, p. 205; *Leptuas*, p. 206.

GALBULIDÆ (1863).   *Brachycex*, p. 214; *Urocex*, p. 216; *Caucalias*, p. 218.

1863. HEINE, F.   Cuculidina.   < *J. f. O.*, xi, 1863, pp. 349–358.

Lamprococcyx chrysites, *L. resplendens*, p. 350; *Cacomantis dysonymus*, *C. querulus*, *Cuculus telephonus*, p. 352; *Coccyzusa gracilis*, p. 356, spp. nn.—*Thamnias*, p. 357; *Eutroctes*, p. 358, new generic names in other groups.

1864. SCHLEGEL, H.   Cuculi.   *Mus. Hist. Nat. Pays-Bas*, 5e livr., 1864, pp. 1–86.

The *Cuculi* of this author are a superfamily group, consisting of the *Indicatoridæ, Leptosomatidæ, Musophagidæ, Coliidæ* and *Opisthocomidæ!* of authors, besides the *Cuculidæ* proper. Each of these families is treated as if of a single genus, excepting the last-named, in which the author allows several.   The 122 species treated are represented in the collection by 842 specimens.

1864. SCLATER, P. L.   On the Species of the American genus Coccyzus.   < *P. Z. S.*, xxxii, 1864, pp. 119–122.

Synonymatic, diagnostic, and critical synopsis of 8 spp.   *C. bairdi*, p. 120, sp. n.

1864. SCLATER, P. L.   Notes on the Species of Cuckoos of the Genus Neomorphus.   < *P. Z. S.*, 1864, pp. 249, 250.

Diagnosis of two species.

1866. SCLATER, P. L.   On a New American Cuckoo of the Genus Neomorphus [N. salvini].   < *P. Z. S.*, xxxiv, 1866, pp. 59, 60, pl. v.

With synopsis of 3 spp.

1869. WALDEN, *Lord*.   On the Cuculidæ described by Linnæus and Gmelin, with a sketch of the Genus Eudynamis.   < *Ibis*, 2d ser., v, 1869, pp. 324–346, pl. x.

The author rightly holds that the old names must be either identified or disposed of.   He handles the subject critically and patiently, accounting for most of the names.

"Of the 22 Linnæan species of *Cuculus*, 3 belong to other families, and 11 of the remaining 19 have been more or less satisfactorily identified, leaving 8 undetermined.   Of these, 2 seem to be beyond hope at present; but the names of the last 6 can, it is shown, be referred without much fear of error to the species for which they were intended.   The 2 Linnean species

1869. WALDEN, *Lord*—Continued.

    of *Crotophaga* are identical. Gmelin named 24 species and 10 varieties of *Cuculus* in addition to those given by Linnæus, besides 2 species which belong to other families, 2 which really are Cuckoos though placed in other genera, and 1 *Crotophaga*. Of these 29 only 9 can, from one cause or another, retain Gmelin's names. The genus *Eudynamis* is specially treated, 9 species being recognized, one of which *E. ransomi*, Bp. (*Consp. Av.*, i, p. 101) is figured." (*Zool. Rec. for* 1869, p. —.)

1870. SCLATER, P. L. Further [cf, P. Z. S., 1864, pp. 119 seq.] Notes on the Cuckoos of the Genus Coccyzus. < *P. Z. S.*, xxxviii, 1870, pp. 165–169.

    Synonymatic and diagnostic synopsis of 8 spp., with critical commentary.

1871. DRESSER, H. E. [Exhibition of a specimen of Coccyzus americanus found in Great Britain.] < *P. Z. S.*, xxxix, 1871, p. 299.

1872. SCLATER, P. L. [Remarks on Exhibition of a Skin of the Yellow-billed Cuckoo (Coccyzus americanus) from Buenos Ayres.] < *Proc. Zool. Soc. London*, 1872, p. 496.

1872. SCLATER, P. L. [Remarks on Exhibition of a specimen of Coccyzus erythrophthalmus killed in Ireland.] < *Proc. Zool. Soc. London*, 1872, p. 681.

    The same specimen formerly recorded (*Zoologist*, p. 2943) as *C. americanus*. The only other instance of the occurrence of this bird in Europe is stated to be in Italy (Bolle, *J. f. O.*, 1858, p. 457; Selys-L., *Ibis*, 1870, p. 452; Salvadori, *Fn. Ital.*, 1871, p. 42).

1872. BLAKE-KNOX, H. American Cuckoo [Coccygus erythrophthalmus] in Ireland. < *Zoologist*, 2d ser., vii, 1872, p. 2943.

    Erroneously given as *C. americanus:* cf. P. Z. S., 1872, p. 681.

1872. CLERMONT, *Lord*. Blackbilled American Cuckoo [Coccygus erythrophthalmus] in Ireland. < *Zoologist*, 2d ser., vii, 1872, p. 3022.

1873. CABANIS, J. [Coccygus euleri, n. sp. aus Brasilien.] < *J. f. O.*, 1873, pp. 72, 73.

1873. COUES, E. Range of the Geococcyx californianus. < *Am. Nat.*, vii, 1874, p. 751.

1873. LAWRENCE, G. N. Remarks on Neomorphus pucherani and its Allies. < *Ibis*, 3d ser., iii, 1873, pp. 287–295.

    Historical. Descriptive synopsis of 4 spp. of the genus.

1874. ANON. [The Road-runner—Geococcyx californianus.] < *Am. Sportsman*, iv, 1874, p. 395.

    From San Luis Obispo, Cal., *Tribune*.

1874. HUDNUT, J. O. The Paisano [Geococcyx californianus] not the Chiacalaca [Ortalida sp.] < *Field and Stream* (newspaper of Chicago, Ill.), Apr. 4, 1874.

1875. ANON. The Bird Road-Runner [Geococcyx californianus.] < *Rod and Gun*, vi, Sept. 25, 1875, p. 396.

    Reprint from St. Helena, Cal., *Star*.

1875. BENNER, F. Is the yellow-billed cuckoo parasitic? < *Forest and Stream*, v Sept. 16, 1875, p. 83.

1875. DUBOIS, A. Note sur un Coccyzus tué en Belgique. < *Bull. Acad. Roy. Belgique*, xxxix, Jan., 1875, pp. 9–11.

    Pas vue moi-même. Un individu du *C. americanus* tué dans le Bois-de-Lessines, le 22 Oct 1874.

1875. "PARVUS." American Cuckoo. < *Rod and Gun*, vii, May 1, 1875, p. 75.

    Mere statement of fact that the American species make nests of their own.

1876. CHAMBERS, V. T. The Chapparal Cock. < *Am. Nat.*, x, No. 6, 1876, p. 373.

    Request for information respecting food of *Geococcyx californianus*.

1878. BENDIRE, C. Breeding habits of Geococcyx californianus. < *Bull. Nutt. Ornith. Club*, iii, No. 1, Jan., 1878, p. 39.

1878. JONES, J. M. Nesting of Cuckoo [(Coccygus erythrophthalmus) near Halifax, N. S.]. < *Forest and Stream*, xi, Oct. 10, 1878, p. 204.

1879. BREWER, T. M.   Parasitic Birds [Cuculidæ].   < *The Oölogist*, iv, No. 11, June, 1879, p. 85.

1879. BRYANT, W. E.   Love-making in the Road-Runner [Geococcyx californianus]. < *Science News*, i, No. 7, Feb. 1, 1879, p. 112.

1879. MILLER, *Miss* F.   Strange Story of a California Bird [Geococcyx californianus]. < *Bull. Nutt. Ornith. Club*, iv, No. 2, Apr., 1879, pp. 109, 110.
    Habits as observed in semi-domestication.

Psittacidæ.

1733. DUVERNEY, J. G. Anatomie. < *Hist. de l'Acad. Roy. des Sci. de Paris* pour l'année 1682, i, 1733, pp. 344, 345.

Sur le bec d'un Perroquet, p. 344.

1752. CERATI, *l'Abbe.* [Observation sur l'âge auquel peuvent parvenir les Perroquets.] < *Hist. de l'Acad. Roy. des Sci.* pour l'année 1747, 1752, pp. 57, 58.

Une espèce de Cacatua—près de cent-vingt années.

1753. ISNARD, A. D. DE. [Observation sur un Perroquet qui pondit un œuf en France.] < *Hist. de l'Acad. Roy. des Sci.* pour l'année 1727, 1753, pp. 25, 26.

1801–05. LEVAILLANT, F. Histoire Naturelle | des Perroquets, | par François Levaillant. | — | Tome premier [second]. | [Monogram.] | A Paris, | Chez Levrault, Schoell et Ce, rue de Seine S. G. | — | Strasbourg, de l'imprimerie de Levrault. | An xii (1804). [1801–1805.] Pub. livr. I–XXIV, titled and paged for 2 vols. folio. Vol. I, half-title, title, dedication, preface, each 1 leaf. Text pp. 1–135, 1 leaf (table) ; pll. col'd 1–71. Vol. II, half-title, title, each 1 leaf. Text pp. 1–111 ; pll. 72–139.

This is the earliest of the great Parrot Monographs ; a splendid work, worthy associate of the others from the same celebrated source. The two volumes of 139 plates, describing 90 species of the family, were followed in 1837–38 by a third (supplementary) volume by Bourjot St. Hilaire, with 111 plates of 88 species ; to which a fourth vol. of 48 plates and about as many species was added by De Souancé in 1857–58, these together making by far the most extensive Iconography of the Parrots extant.

It is to be always regretted, for Levaillant's sake, that, while he described so carefully and so brilliantly figured numberless species of birds, many of them before unknown, he did not in any of his four great works use the system of nomenclature which would have entitled him to full recognition. He is the real author of very many new species to which systematic names were later applied by Vieillot and others, who consequently get all the perfunctory credit that should have gone to Levaillant. Buffon, Brisson and Levaillant are the three great French names in ornithology which are not citable for species.

The beautiful plates of this work were drawn from nature, engraved and printed in colors under the direction of Bouquet. The text (as is not very often the case with Iconographies like this) is much more than a brief description of the objects represented, occupying usually more than one leaf to a plate, and going into many particulars concerning the species of this family. The whole work forms the corner-stone of the special literature of *Psittacidæ*.

1801. MOROZZO, [C. L.] Letter from Count Morozzo to C. Lacepede, respecting a Parrot hatched at Rome ; together with some Observations on the duration of the Life of these Birds. < *Tilloch's Philos. Mag.*, xii, 1801, pp. 235–246.

From *Journ. de Physique*, Ventose, An 10.

I. History of the laying and incubation of a pair of Brazilian Parrots. II. Their habits, attachment, mode of rearing their young. III. Description of ♂, ♀, and young (== Amazon Parrot of Barrere, *Fr. Equinox.*, p. 144). IV. Instances of some Parrots which have laid in Europe. V. Conjectures on the duration of the life of Parrots, including a table of the iuration of incubation and life of several birds, and periods of gestation in several mammals, in comparison with the duration of their life.

1802. MOROZZO, [C. L.] Histoire d'un Perroquet né à Rome, suivie de quelques observations sur la durée de la vie des oiseaux. < *Journ. de Phys., Chim., et Hist. Nat.*, liv, 1802, pp. 180–193.

L'histoire de ces Perroquets, et celle de leur ponte et de leur incubation.—Leurs habitudes, amours, et la manière d'élever leurs petits.—Description de ces oiseaux.—Conjectures sur la vie des perroquets, etc. ; "j'en ai vu un moi-même qui étoit depuis 75 ans dans la même maison." Table de la durée de l'incubation, et de la vie de plusieurs oiseaux.

1803. MOROZZO, C. L. Relation De deux fétus produits par les mêmes perroquets qui dans l'année 1801 ont donné un petit, à Rome. < *Journ. de Phys., Chim., et Hist. Nat.* lvi, 1803, pp. 347–350.

1820. KUHL, H. H. Kuhl, Ph. Dr. Ac. C. L. C. N. C. S. | Conspectus Psittacorum. |
Cum specierum definitionibus, novarum descriptionibus, | synonymis et circa
patriam singularum naturalem | adversariis, | adjecto indice museorum, ubi
earum | artificiosae exuviae servantur. | Cum Tabulis III. aeneis pictis. | [n. d.,
n. p.; Bonnae, 1820.] 1 vol. 4to. pp. 104, pll. iii.

Novis Actis Acad. Cæs. Leop.-Carol. Nat. Cur., vol. x, pars i, 1820, pp. 4–104.

De speciebus 209 Psittacorum tractat auctor celeberrimus, quarum novas "circa 40, nusquam descriptas" continet monographia sua. Species signo †notatas vidit ipse et sec. naturam descripsit.

Species omnes ad genus *Psittaci* unicum relatæ sunt, hoc genere in sect. vi. diviso, sc., 1, *Ara;* 2, *Convrvs* (p. 4); 3, *Psittacvla;* 4, *Psittacus* ipse; 5, *Kakadoe!* (p. 11); 6, *Probosciger* (p. 13).—I. *Ara*, A, colore coccineo, spp., 1–3; B, colore caeruleo, 4, 5; C, colore viridi, 6–10. II. *Convrvs*, A, Americani, 11–28; B, Africani, 29–33; C, Asiatici, 34–61; D, Australes, 62–92. III. *Psittacvla*, A, Americani, 93–102; B, Africani, 103–105; C, Asiatici, 106–115; D, Australes, 116–119. IV. *Psittacus*, A, Americani, 120–144; B, Africani, 145–147; C, Asiatici, 148–150; D. Australes, 151, 152. V. *Kakadoe*, A, Indici, 153–156; B, Australes, 157–164. VI. *Probosciger*, 165, 166.—Psittaci patriæ incertae, 167–171.—Psittaci dubii, aut auctori incogniti, ab aliis descripti, 172–209.

Species sequentes sanè novas asterisco notavi; reliquæ forsan prius descriptæ.

10. *Psittacus illigeri*, Temm. et Kuhl, p. 19 (=*P. fuscatus*, Mus. Berol. nomine inepto). 24. *P. viridissimus*, Temm. et Kuhl, p. 25. 63. *P. platurus*, Temm. et Kuhl, p. 43. 67. *P. *erythronotus,* p. 45. 72. *P. *auriceps,* p. 46. 75. *P. *chlorolepidotus,* p. 48. 77. *P. *ultramarinus,* p. 49. 78. *P. *chrysostomus,* p. 50, pl. i. 82. *P. *spurius,* p. 52. 84. *P. *cyanomelas,* p. 53. 86. *P. icterotis,* Temm. et Kuhl, p. 54. 90. *P. *brownii,* p. 56. 94. *P. *st. thomae,* p. 58. 104. *P. *swinderniamos,* p. 62, pl. ii ("*swinderianus,*" lapsu). 111. *P. simplex,* p. 66. 113. *P. *micropterus,* p. 67. 125. *P. brachyurus,* Temm. et Kuhl, p. 72. 127. *P. *maximiliani,* p. 72. 133. *P. cyanotis,* Temm. et Kuhl, p. 77. 134. *P. *erythrurus,* p. 77. 148. *P. *spadiceocephalus* (!), p. 84. 158. *P. *tenuirostris,* p. 88. 15.9 *P. *eos,* p. 88. 162. *P. *temminkii* (sic), p. 89. 164. *P. *leachii,* p. 91, pl. iii. 166. *P. *goliath,* p. 92. 168. *P. *bitorquatus.* p. 92. 171. *P. *fuscicollis,* p. 95

12. *P. auricapillus,* "Licht.," p. 20. 15. *P. leucotis,* "Licht.," p. 21. 96. *P. surdus,* "Ill.," p. 59. 97. *P. melanonotus,* "Licht.," p. 59. 102. *P. vulturinus,* "Ill.," p. 62. 121. *P. leucogaster,* "Ill.," p. 70.

De Vaillanti opere "Histoire Naturelle des Perroquets," pp. 102–104.

Exemplum hujusce opusculi quod examinavi in *Biblioth. Reip. Amer.* olim cl. Okeno d. d. auctor, ut patet notâ msc. ante titulum: ,,Herrn Hofrath Dr Oken vom V'fs.''

1821. KUHL, H. [Auszüge aus seinem Conspectus Psittacorum.] <*Oken's Isis,* Jahrg. v, 1821, pp. 951–962.

Die Originalausgabe ist enthalten in den *Neue Verh. der Kaiserl.-Leop.-Carol. Acad.*, Bd. x., Abth. i, 1820, pp. 4–104; auch besonders gedruckt, 4to, Bonnæ, 1820. Der obige Aufsatz besteht nur aus einer Synopsis der Gattungen und einem Verzeichniss der Arten, nebst einem Anhange des Herausgebers über die Levaillant'sche ,,Naturgeschichte der Papageien.''

1821. TEMMINCK, C. J. Account of some new Species of Birds of the Genera Psittacus and Columba, in the Museum of the Linnean Society. < *Trans. Linn. Soc.*, xiii, pt. i, 1821, pp. 107–130.

Psittacus cookii, p. 111; *P. solandri.* p. 113; *P. nasicus,* p. 115; *P. flavigaster,* p. 116; *P. baueri,* p. 118; *P. brownii,* p. 119; *P. multicolor,* p. 119; *P. icterotis,* p. 120; *P. venustus,* p. 121; *P. pulchellus,* p. 122; *Columba dilopha,* p. 124; *C. magnifica,* p. 125; *C. leucomela,* p. 126; *C. scripta,* p. 127; *C. humeralis,* p. 128; *C. phasianella,* p. 129. Memoir in French.

1822. EDITORIAL. Notice regarding the History and Distribution of the genus Psittacus or Parrot. <*Edinb. Philos. Journ.*, vii, 1822, pp. 398–401.

1823. DESM[AREST], A. [G.] Notice sur les Aras Bleus nés en France, et acclimatés dans le dép. du Calvados; par M. J.-V. Lamouroux. . . . <*Féruss. Bull.*, 2e sect., ii, 1823, pp. 451, 452.

Extraite des *Mém. Soc. Linn. de Paris*, ii, 1823?, pp. 155–162.

1823. GABRIAC, MARQUIS DE. Notice Sur la Ponte faite à Paris par des Perruches de l'Amérique méridionale, de l'espèce dite Pavouane, dans les mois de juillet et d'août de l'année 1822. < *Mém du Mus. d'Hist. Nat.*, x, 1823, pp. 309–313.

Addition à la notice précédente, par Geoffroy-St.-Hilaire, pp. 314–316.

1823? LAMOUROUX, J. V. F.   Notice Sur des aras bleus nés en France et acclimatés dans le departement du Calvados.   < *Mém. Soc. Linn. de Paris*, ii, 1823?, pp. 155–162.

1823. V.–Y.   Conspectus Psittacorum. . . . Auct. H. Kuhl.   < *Féruss. Bull.*, 2e sect., iv, 1823, p. 208, 209.
> Revue de cet ouvrage.

1824. DESM[AREST, A. G.]   Description de quelques espèces d'oiseaux des genres Perroquet et Pigeon du Muséum de la Société linnéenne de Londres ; par M. C. J. Temminck.   < *Féruss. Bull.*, 2e sec., i, 1824, p. 278, 279.
> Extr. des *Trans. Linn. Soc.*, xiii, pt. i, p. 107.

1824. PAYRAUDEAU, B. C.   Notice sur la ponte faite a Paris par·des Perruches de l'Amérique méridionale, de l'espèce dite Pavouane, dans les mois de juillet et d'août de l'année 1822 ; par M. le Mis. de Gabriac, . . . < *Féruss. Bull.*, 2e sect., ii, 1824, p. 203.
> Extraite des *Mém. du Mus. d'Hist. Nat.*, x, 1823, pp. 309–313.•

1824-25. VIGORS, N. A.   Descriptions of some rare, interesting, or hitherto uncharacterized subjects of Zoology.   < *Zool. Journ.*, i, 1824, pp. 409–418, 526–542, pll. 13, 14, 16; pll. suppl. 1–4; ii, 1825, pp. 234–241, pl. 8.
> *Muscicapa lathami*, p. 410, pl. 13, n. sp.; *Anthus richardi*, Vieill., p. 411, pl. 14; *Psittacula kuhli*, p. 412, pl. 16, n. sp.; *Platycercus* (g. n.?, p. 527) *pacificus*, Lath., pl. suppl. 1; *P. auriceps*, Kuhl, pl. 2; *P. ulietanus*, Lath., pl. 3; *Psittacus pyrhopterus*, Lath., pl. 4; Vol. ii, *Anthropoides stanleyanus*, p. 234, pl. 8.

1825. [ANON.]   Notice regarding the Breeding of the Peacock Parrot of South America [in confinement].   < *Edinb. Philos. Journ.*, xii, 1825, pp. 184, 185.
> From *Bulletin Universel.* Cf. *Mém. du Mus. d'Hist. Nat.*, x, 1823, pp. 309–313, and *Féruss. Bull.*, 2e sect., ii, 1824, p. 203.

1825. VIGORS, N. A.   On a new genus of Psittacidæ.   < *Zool. Journ.*, ii, 1825, pp. 387–390.
> This is a subhead, being part of the third instalment (pp. 368–405) of the series of papers entitled "Sketches on Ornithology; or," etc.
> The new genus is *Psittacara*, p. 387; of which are described *Ps. frontatus*, p. 389, and *Ps. lichtensteinii*, p. 390, spp. nn.
> *Féruss. Bull.*, ix, 1826, pp. 91, 92; *Isis*, 1830, pp. 1043–1045.

1826. LESSON, R. P.   Sur un genre nouveau de la famille des Perroquets; par Vigors. . . . < *Féruss. Bull.*, 2e sect., ix, 1826, p. 91, 92.
> *Psittacara.* Extrait du *Zool. Journ.*, ii, 1825, pp. 357–390, q. v.

1826. LESSON, [R. P.]   Description de quelques objets de zoologie rares, intéressans ou mal décrits; par N. A. Vigors . . . < *Féruss. Bull.*, 2e sect., vii, 1826, p. 105.
> *Zool. Journ.*, iv, Janv. 1825, p. 526.

1826. LESSON, R. P.   Esquisses ornithologiques, etc.; observations sur le groupe des Psittacidæ, et sur les Perroquets connus des anciens; par N. A. Vigors. . . . < *Féruss. Bull.*, 2e sect., vii, 1826, pp. 111, 112.
> "*Zool. Journ.*, avril 1825, p. 37."

1827. VIGORS, N. A.   A Reply to some Observations in the "Dictionnaire des Sciences Naturelles," upon the newly characterized groups of the Psittacidæ.   < *Zool. Journ.*, iii, 1827, pp. 91–123.

1829. MICHEL, —.   Les Perroquets, | leur éducation physique et morale ; | ouvrage | dans lequel on établit des moyens pour les | guérir de leurs maladies. | Par Michel, | Bachelier ès-lettres, | ancien oiseleur du roi de Westphalie. | Paris. | Audot, Libraire-Éditeur, | rue des Maçons-Sorbonne, N°. 11. | 1829. 1 vol. 18mo. 2 p. ll., pp. 1–146, 1 l.

1829. TEMMINCK, C. J.   Notice sur quelques espèces nouvelles d'oiseaux des genres Psittacus et Columba dans le Muséum de la Société linnéenne par C. J. Temminck. (Lin. transact. xiii. P. 1. p. 107.).   < *Oken's Isis*, Bd. xxii, 1829, pp. 1194–1209.
> Le mémoire ici se trouve réproduit en entier, des *Linn. Soc. Trans.*, 1821, q. v.

1830. VIGORS, N. A. Seltene Gegenstände aus der Zoologie [Papageyen aus Australien]. < *Oken's Isis*, Bd. xxiii, 1830, pp. 824, 825.

Aus der *Zool. Journ.*, Vol. i, Nr. iv, 1825, p. 526.

1830. VIGORS, N. A. Ornithologische Skizzen. Fortsetzung. Ueber die den Alten bekannten Papageyen. < *Oken's Isis*, Bd. xxiii, 1830, pp. 831–839.

Aus der *Zool. Journ.*, Vol. ii, Nr. 5, April 1825, p. 37.

1830. VIGORS, N. A. Psittacara, neue Sippe der Psittaciden. < *Oken's Isis*, Bd. xxiii, 1830, pp. 1043–1045.

Uebers. aus. d. *Zool. Journ.*, ii, 1825, pp. 387–390.

1831. BENNETT, E. T. Observations on the Hyacinthine Maccaw. < *London's Mag. Nat. Hist.*, iv, 1831, pp. 211–213.

Technical and historical.

1832. LEAR, E. Illustrations | of | the family of | Psittacidæ, | or | Parrots: | the greatest part of them | species hitherto unfigured, | containing forty-two lithographic plates, | drawn from life, and on stone, | By Edward Lear, A. L. S. | — | London: | published by E. Lear, 61 Albany street, Regent's Park. | — | 1832. 1 vol. folio. Title, list of subscribers, dedication, list of plates, each 1 leaf; and 42 colored plates.

These plates are the most beautiful illustrations of Parrots, drawn with art as well as with fidelity to nature. There is no text. The following is a list of the plates:

1. *Psittacus badiceps.* 2. *Plyctolophus rosaceus.* 3. *P. galeritus.* 4. *P. sulphureus.* 5. *P. leadbeateri.* 6. *Calyptorhynchus baudini.* 7. *Macrocercus aracanga.* 8. *M. ararauna.* 9. *M. hyacinthinus.* 10. *Psittacara patachonica.* 11. *P. leptorhyncha.* 12. *P. nana.* 13. *Nanodes undulatus.* 14, 15. *Platycercus erythropterus.* 16. *P. tabuensis.* 17. *P. baueri.* 18. *P. barnardi.* 19. *P. palliceps.* 20. *P. brownii.* 21, 22. *P. pileatus.* 23, 24. *P. stanleyii.* 25. *P. unicolor.* 26. *P. pacificus.* 27. *Palæornis novæ-hollandiæ.* 28. *P. melanura.* 29. *P. anthopeplus.* 30. *P. rosaceus.* 31. *P. columboides.* 32. *P. cucullatus.* 33. *P. torquatus.* 34. *Trichoglossus rubritorquis.* 35. *T. matoni.* 36. *T. versicolor.* 37. *Lorius domicella.* 38. *Psittacula kuhlii.* 39. *P. tarantæ.* 40. *P. torquata.* 41. *P. rubrifrons.* 42. *P. swinderiana.*

1832. WAGLER, [J.] Monographia | Psittacorum. | Auctor | [Joannes] Wagler. | [n. d. n. p. München. 1832.] 4to. Halb-titel, 1 Blatt, Vorwort 2 Blätter, pp. 469–750, Taf. illum. xxii–xxvii.

The pagination and also the numeration of the plates show this book to be a part of something else. It is extracted from the *Denksch. Acad. München*, i, 1832, without indication of the fact. Wagler's pieces mostly have some mechanical defect of date, title, pagination, or other, showing either ignorance or negligence of the requirements of workmanlike printing.

Gedrängter Ueberblick der Geschichte der Papageien, p. 469; Die Papageien der Alten, p. 470; Die Pap. Asiens, p. 474; Die Pap. Africa's, p. 476; Die Pap. America's, p. 478; Die Pap. Australiens, p. 481. Gedrängter Vergleich der Pap. mit dem Nagern und Einiges über ihre Stellung im natürlichen Systeme, p. 483.—Conspectus systematicus generum et specierum ex ordine Psittacorum, adjectis generum characteribus, pp. 489–505. *Polytelis*, p. 489; *Nymphicus, Prioniturus*, p. 490; *Deroptyus, Euphema*, p. 492; *Charmosyna*, p. 493; *Eos, Coriphilus*, p. 494; *Domicella, Eclectus, Psittacodis*, p. 495; *Pionus*, p. 497; *Nasiterna*, p. 498; *Triclaria, Sittace*, p. 499; *Tanygnathus, Coracopsis*, p. 501; *Dasyptilus*, p. 502; *Corydon, Cacatua*, p. 504; *Licmetis, Nestor*, p. 505, are genera, apparently new, of Wagler's.

Exposito specierum, pp. 506–697, gives the full description of the species, among which are doubtless many new ones; but none are marked as such.

Characteres specierum ex ordine Psittacorum, pp. 698–738; Psittaci auctori dubii, pp. 739–747; Index, pp. 748–750.

Pl. xxii, *Eclectus linnaei*; xxiii, *Psittacodis paragua*; xxiv, f. 1, *Pionus vulturinus*, f. 2, *Sittace euops*; xxv, *Sittace pachyrhyncha*; xxvi, *Sittace glauca*; xxvii, *Calyptorhynchus stellatus.*

1834. VIGORS, N. A. [Kein Gabelbein bei Psittacus, u. s. w.] < *Oken's Isis*, Bd. xxvii, 1834, p. 820.

Auszug aus *Philos. Mag.*, Bd. ix, 1831.

1835. PÖPPIG, [E.] Psittacus cyanolyseos Mol. < *Arch. f. Naturg.*, i, (1,) 1835, pp. 87, 88.

Cf. Poeppig, *Reise in Chili*, u. s. w., i, 1835, p. 451.

1836. SELBY, P. J.   The | Naturalist's Library. | Edited by | Sir William Jardine, Bart., | F. R. S. E., F. L. S., etc., etc. | Vol. X. | — | Ornithology. | Parrots. | By Prideaux John Selby, Esq., | F. R. S. E., F. L. S., M. W. S., etc., etc. | — | Edinburgh: | W. H. Lizars, [etc.]. [No date. 1836.] 1 vol. sm. 12mo. Portrait of Bewick, eng. col'd title, other title, contents, each 1 leaf, pp. 7–219, cuts, pll. col'd 1–30 (+ portrait and vignette = 32 pll.).

Being Vol. VI of general arrangement.   Contains memoir of Bewick, likewise of D'Aubenton, and an account of *Psittaci*.

Pl. 1, *Palæornis barrabandi*; 2, *alexandri*; 3, *malaccensis*. 4, *Arara patagonica*. 5, *Microcercus militaris*; 6, *M. ararauna*; 7, *M. aracanga*. 8, *Psittacara nobilis*. 9, *Psittacus festivus*; 10. *Ps. erythacus*. 11, *Agapornis swinderianus*. 12, *Nestor hypopolius*. 13, *Plyctolophus leadbeateri*; 14, *P. sulphureus*. 15, *Calyptorynchus stellatus*. 16, *Microglossus aterrimus*. 17, *Dasyptilus pequetii*. 18, *Lorius domicillus*. 19, *Charmosyna papuensis*. 20, *Trichoglossus swainsonii*; 21, *T. versicolor*; 22, *T. pyrrhopterus*. 23, *Coriphilus kuhlii*. 24, *Psittaculus galgulus*. 25, *Platycercus pennantii*; 26, *P. palliceps*. 27, *Nanodes venustus*; 28, *N. undulatus*. 29, *Pezoporus formosus*. 30, *Nymphicus novæ hollandiæ*.

This is rather sketchy, an outline of the family, with figures of the leading types.

1836. VIGORS, N. A.   [Characters of two new Parrots (Psittacus augustus and P. guildingii).] < *P. Z. S.*, iv, 1836, p. 80.

1836. WHITE, W. H.   Facts on the Measure of the Length of Life of a Species of Parrot; with Suggestions for ascertaining the Average Period of Existence of the whole Animal Creation; and an Anecdote of a Parrot. < *Loudon's Mag. Nat. Hist.*, ix, 1836, pp. 347–349.

1837–38. BOURJOT ST.-HILAIRE, A.   Hoistoire Naturelle | des Perroquets, | troisième volume | (supplémentaire), | pour faire suite aux deux volumes de Levaillant, | contenant les espèces laissées inédites par cet auteur ou récemment découvertes. | Ouvrage destiné | a compléter une monographie figurée de la famille des Psittacidés, le texte renfermant la | classification, la synonymie, et la description de chaque espèce ; | suivi d'un index général des espèces décrites dans tout l'ouvrage ; | par le docteur | Al. Bourjot Saint-Hilaire, | Professeur du Zoologie au Collège Royale de Bourbon. | Les figures lithographiées et coloriées avec soin | par | M. Werner, | Peintre attaché au Muséum d'Histoire Naturelle. | — | Paris, | Chez F. G. Levrault, Libraire Éditeur, rue de la Harpe, n.º 81. | Strasbourg, | même maison, rue des Juifs, n.º 33. | 1837–1838. 1 vol. in-fol. grand jésus. pp. i–xlii (faux titre, titre, dédicace, préface, introduction, index generalis Psittacorum, table, liste des auteurs); Planches coloriées 111, avec le texte non paginé. Pub. par. livr. (29.)

Engelmann cites the work by a somewhat different title, beginning "Collection des Perroquets", etc., and gives 1835–39 as dates of the appearance of 29 livraisons. Above title is from a bound copy in Libr. Phila. Acad. ; the wrappers of the parts not being preserved, I cannot give their respective dates.

As expressly stated in the title, this Iconography is designed as a third (supplementary) volume to Levaillant's *Histoire Nat. de Perroçuets*, 2 vols, 1801–5. A fourth companion volume was added to the series of illustrations in 1857–58, by De Souancé.

The plates of the present series are as follows :—Pl. 1, *Psittacus bengalensis* ; 2, *P. torquatus* ; 3, 3 bis, *P. colomboides* ; 4, *P. barrabandi* ; 5, *P. melanurus* ; 6, *P. rosaceus* ; 7, *P. anthopeplus* ; 8, *P. undulatus* ; 9, *P. rufifrons* ; 10, *P. chrysostomus* ; 11, *P. auriconus* ; 11 bis, *P. novæ hollandiæ* ; 12, *P. cornutus* ; 13, *P. illigerii* ; 14, *P. glauca* ; 15, *P. glauca minor* ; 16, *P. cobaltina* (nob.) ; 17, *P. cæruleo-frontata* ; 18, *P. gouarouba* ; 19, *P. patagonica* ; 20, *P. nanday* ; 21, *P. lepthorhinca* (sic) ; 22, *P. nobilis* ; 23, *P. xanthoptera* ; 24, *P. nana* ; 25, *P. tiriba* ; 26, *P. variegata melanura* ; 27, *P. perlata* ; 28, *P. ninus* ; 29, *P. flaviventris* ; 30, *P. icterotis* ; 31, *P. palliceps* ; 32, *P. barnardi* ; 33, *P. brownii* ; 34, *P. viridis unicolor* ; 35, 35 bis, *P. erythropterus* ; 36, *P. pacificus* ; 37, *P. novæ zealandiæ* ; 38, *P. tabuensis* ; 39, *P. purpureocephalus* ; 40, *P. coeruleo-barbatus* (nob.) ; 41, *P. dorso-cærulens* (nob.) ; 42, 42 bis, *P. aurcapillus* ; 43, *P. euteles* ; 44, 44 bis, *P. iris* ; 45, *P. aurifrons* ; 46, *P. placens* (nob.) ; 47, *P. xanthopterigius* (sic) ; 48. *P. toui gutture luteo* ; 49, *P. gregarius* ; 50, *P. passerinus* ; 51, *P. scintillatus* ; 52, *P. versicolor* ; 53. 53 bis. *P. spatuliger* ; 54, *P. flavirostris* ; 55, 55 bis, 56, *P. mitratus* ; 57, *P. cyanogaster* ; 58, *P. leucogaster* ; 59, *P. vulturinus* ; 60, *P. senilis* ; 61, *P. meyeri* ; 62, *P. accipitrinus* ; 63, *P. augustus* ; 64, *P. guildingii* ; 65, *P. columbinus* ; 66, *P. pretrei* ; 67, *P. pecqueti* ; 68, *P. novae zealandiæ* ; 69, *P. productus* ; 70, *P. funereus* ; 71, 71 bis,

1837–38. Bourjot St.-Hilaire, A.—Continued.

P. banksianus ; 72, 72 bis, *P. temminckii ;* 73, *P. baudinii ;* 74, *P. rosea ;* 75, 75 bis, 75 ter, *P. rubrogaleata ;* 76, *P. tenuirostris ;* 77, *P. leadbeateri ;* 78, *P. rubrocristata* (nob.) ; *79, P. sulfureus major ;* 80, *P. sulfureus minor ;* 81, *P minor philippinarum ;* 82, *P. albo-cristata ;* 83, *P. interfringillacea ;* 84, *P. Florentis* (nob.) *Desmarestii ;* 86, *P. griseifrons* (nob.) ; 87, *P. rubrifrons ;* 88, *P. cyano-pileata ;* 89, *P. Philippensis vel coula cissi ;* 90, *P. rubricollis vel pullaria guienensis ;* 91, *P. roseicollis ;* 92, *P. malaccensis ;* 93, *P. huetii ;* 94, *P. loxia ;* 95, *P. melanonota ;* 96, *P. cana ;* 97, *P. torquato-squamata ;* 98, *P. swinderiana ;* 99, *P. tarantae ;* 100, *P. pygmœus.*

There are some interpolations in this series; but not all those presented as such in the table are actually present. I make out 111 plates by actual count. They were executed by Werner.

The nomenclature is very lax, scarcely satisfying the requirements of a system. The names in the text do not always correspond with those in the table, from which I have taken the above list; and the author's way of using names is difficult to make out, or see the point of. Only French names are engraven on the plates. This laxity or carelessness is a serious blemish upon an otherwise very praiseworthy and valuable monograph. There is about a leaf of text, descriptive, etc., to each plate.

"Many of the plates are original, others are copied from Spix, Temminck, or Lear; they are executed on stone, and though inferior to the works of Gould and Lear, they are perhaps the best ornithological lithographs which have issued from the French press. The text of this work is prepared with considerable care, but the nomenclature wants precision, the latin names being often wrongly spelled, and the principles of binomial nomenclature often departed from. Thus the genus *Palæornis* is in one instance designated *Psittacus,* in another *Psittacus sagittifer,* and in a third *Conurus sagittifer,* with the addition in each case of a specific name." (*Strickl. Rep. Brit. Assoc. for* 1844, 1845, p. 198.)

1838. Anon. Disquisitiones anatomicæ Psittacorum, diss. inaug. auct. M. J. Thuet. Turici, apud Orell. 1838. 4. 36. T. 2. < *Oken's Isis,* Bd. xxxi, 1838, p. 231.

1838. Thuet, M. J. Disquisitiones anatomicæ Psittacorum. Dissertatio inauguralis. Turici. Orellii, Fuesslini et Soc. 1838. 4to. pp. 36. pll. 2.

Not seen.

1838. Vigors, N. A. [Psittacus augustus, Ps. guildingii.] < *Oken's Isis,* Bd. xxxi, 1838, p. 195.

Aus *P. Z. S.,* iv, 1836.

1839. Rousseau, L. F. E. Note sur un nouvel os découvert dans la tête des Perroquets. < *Revue Zoologique,* ii, 1839, pp. 352, 353, pl. 2, figg. 3, 4, 5.

Désigné sous le nom de l'os Inter-carré-tympano-auditif.

1840. Jacquemin, [E.] [Sur un os observé par M. E. Rousseau dans la mâchoire des Perroquets et décrit comme nouveau par cet anatomiste.] < *Compt. Rend. de l'Acad. Sci.,* x, 1840, pp. 139, 140.

L'auteur sonpçonne que cet os n'est autre chose qu'une pièce qu'il a lui-même indiqué dans son Mémoire sur la Corneille.

1840. Rousseau, [L. F. E.] Sur un os nouvellement découvert dans la mâchoire des perroquets. < *Compt. Rend. de l'Acad. Sci.,* x, 1840, pp. 251, 252.

Voir *C. R., tom. cit.,* p. 139.

N'est point, comme l'a supposé M. Jacquemin, une piece dépendante du système des canaux aériens du squelette, mais une piece propre aux oiseaux du genre *Psittacus.*

1840. Rousseau, [L. F.] E. [Observations au sujet de l'os que l'on trouve à la tête des Perroquets.] < *Revue Zoologique,* iii, 1840, pp. 57–59.

Voir *op. cit.,* ii, 1839, p. 352.

1842–55. Brehm, C. L. Monographie | der | Papageien | oder | vollständige Naturgeschichte aller bis jetzt | bekannten Papageien mit getreuen und | ausgemalten Abbildungen, | im Vereine mit andern Naturforschern | herausgegeben | von | C. L. Brehm | Pfarrer zu Renthendorf, der Kaiserl. Leopoldinischen Akademie Naturforscher und mehrerer gelehrten und | naturwissenschaftlichen Gessellschaften mit- oder Ehrenmitgliede. | — | Jena | August Schmid, | Paris | Treuttel et Würtz, Rue de Lille No. 17. | 1842 [–1855]. folio. pub. in Parts. 1 Heft, 1842 ; 2 Heft, 1843 ; 3 Heft, 1845 ; 4 Heft, 1853 ; 5 Heft, 1852 ; 6 Heft,

1842-55. BREHM, C. L.—Continued.

1853; 7 Heft, 1853; 8 Heft, 1853; 9 Heft, 1853; 10 Heft, 1854; 11 Heft, 1854; 12 Heft, 1854 ; 13 Heft, 1855; 14 Heft, 1855.

The copy examined of this work consists of 2 prel. pages (title and dedication), pp. 1-60 of text, and 70 colored plates. It appears to be incomplete, the text breaking off abruptly in the middle of a sentence on page 60, at species 34, already calling for plate 72; it has covers of the 14 Hefte above indicated bound in at the end. The dates on these covers are mostly in manuscript, presumably of some one who knows, but I cannot vouch for their accuracy; in fact, there seems to be some oversight, as the dates do not all follow consecutively the successive issues of the Parts. The text consists of a general account of each species, chiefly synonymatic, descriptive, and critical. The plates are as follows:—

Pl. 1, *Psittacus macao ;* 2, *P. aracanga ;* 3, *P. tricolor ;* 4, *P. hyacynthinus ;* 5, *P. militaris.* 6, *Arara hyacinthiacus ;* 7, *A. ararauna ;* 8, *A. buffonii* (Brehm, page 6) ; 9, *A. purpureo-dorsalis ;* 10, *A. macawuanna ;* 11, *A. severus ;* 12, *A. macrognathos ;* 13 missing (=*Anadorhynchos maximiliani,* see *Arara hyacinthinus*) ; 14, *Aratinga carolinae-augustae ;* 15, *Arat. haemorrhous ;* 15 bis, *Arathinga chrysocephalus ;* 16, *Aratinga aurifrons ;* 17, *A. luteus* sive *garauba ;* 18, f. 1, *A. caixana,* f. 2, *A. ninus ;* 19, *A. cyanogularis ;* 20, *A. aureus ;* 21, *A. xanthopterus ;* 22, *A. acutirostris ;* 23, *A. flaviventer ;* 24, *A. latus ;* 25, *A. fasciatus ;* 26, *A. melanunus* (sic) ; 27, *A.* "*guianensis*" (so lettered, being *A. nobilis* of the text, p. 21) ; 28, *A. guianensis ;* 29, 30, *A. pertinax ;* 31, *A. virescens ;* 32, *Psittaculus passerinus ;* 33 (numbered 34 by mistake, see text, p. 26), *Ps. xanthopterygius ;* 34, *P. gregarius ;* 35, *P. tui ;* 36, *P. swinderianus ;* 37, *Psittacus xantops* (sic) ; 38, *P. columbinus ;* 39, *P. malachitaceus ;* 40, *P. pumilio ;* 41, 42, *P. pileatus, ♂, ♀* (42 being *P. diadema* of text, p. 33) ; 43, *P. diadema* (43 being *senilis* of text, p. 34) ; 44, *P. senilis* (44 being *pulverulentus* of text, p. 34) ; 45, *P. pulverulentus ;* 46, *P. senilis ;* 47, *P. accipitrinus ;* 48, *P. menstruus ;* 49, *P. cestivus* (for *œstivus*) ; 50, *P. amazonicus ;* 51, *P. amazoninus ;* 52, *P. melanocephalus ;* 53, *P. barabandi ;* 54, *P. bouqueti ;* 55, *P. cyanotis ;* 56, *P. aureus,* Bechst., nec L. ; 57, *P. autumnalis ;* 58, *P. paradisi ;* 59, *P. cervicalis ;* 60, *P. mascarinus ;* *61, *P. menstruus, ♀ ;* *62, *P. senegalus ;* *63, *P. gramineus ;* *64, *P. melanocephalus ;* *65, *P. geoffrayi* (sic) ; 66, *P. crythacus* (for *erythacus*) ; 67, *P. domicella ;* 68, *P. cyanurus ;* 69, *P. guebiensis ;* 70, *P. ochruptenus* (sic). Those asterisked uncolored in copy examined. Text of p. 60 calls for—Pl. 71, *P. garrulus ;* Pl. 72, *P. unicolor ;* these not found.

Since the above was written I have fortunately found a copy in the original cover-titles, giving further particulars, as follows:—

Heft I, 1842, title, pp. 1-4, pll. 1-5; II, 1843, pp. 5-8, pll. 6-10 ; III, 1845, pp. 9-12, pll. 11-15; IV, 1853, pp. 13-16, pll. 16-20 ; V, 1852, pp. 17-20, pll. 21-25 ; VI, 1853, pp. 21-24, pll. 26-30 ; VII, 1853, pp. 25-28, pll. 31-35 ; VIII, 1852, pp. 29-32, pll. 36-40 ; IX, 1853, pp. 33-36, pll. 41-45 ; X, 1854, pp. 37-40, pll. 46-50; XI, 1854, pp. 41-44, pll. 51-55 ; XII, 1854, pp. 45-48, pll. 56-60 ; XIII, 1855, pp. 49-52, pll. 61-65 ; XIV, 1855, pp. 53-56, pll. 66-70.

Comparison of these two copies shows that there are in this work 14 perfect Parts, of pp. 56 and pll. 70 ; and also a 15th incompleted Part, raising the text to pp. 60, but apparently lacking pll. 71 and 72, called for by the text.—I handled the bound copy in the Congressional Libr., the other in the Libr. of the Phila. Acad.

1842. KUHLMANN, H.   De absentia furculae in Psittaco pullario et de regione animalium vertebratorum humerali praecipue avium.   Dissertatio inauguralis medica.   Auctore Henrico Kuhlmann.   Kiliæ.   1842.

Haud mihi obvia.

1845. DES MURS, O.   Notes sur une espèce de Perruche nouvelle.   < *Revue Zoologique,* viii, 1845, p. 449.

1846. ANON.   The | Parrot-Keeper's | Guide. | — | Comprising, | the Natural History of | Macaws, Cockatoos, Parrots, Lories, | Parokeets, and Love-Birds; | with | general observations on the best modes of treatment, | the diseases to which they are subject, and | methods of cure, &c. | — | By an experienced dealer. | [Figure.] | London : | Thomas Dean & Co. Threadneedle-Street.   1 vol.   16mo. [n. d.   1846.]   pp. 48, 6 col'd pll., and other illustrations.

1847. LAFRESNAYE, F. DE.   Quelques oiseaux nouveaux de Bolivie et de Nouvelle-Grenade.   < *Revue Zoologique,* x, 1847, pp. 65-76.

Les trois oiseaux ici décrits sont de la famille des *Psittacidés—Ara rubro-genys,* p. 65; *A. castaneifrons,* p. 66 ; *Pionus melanotis,* p. 67.

1849. [JARDINE, W.]   Pionus gulielmi, Jardine [n. sp.].   < *Jard. Contrib. Orn.,* 1849, pp. 64, 65, pl. xxviii.

1849. VERREAUX, J., *and* DES MURS, O.   Description d'une nouvelle espèce de Perroquet [Pionus fuscicapillus].   < *Rev. et Mag. de Zool.*, i, 1849, p. 58.

1850. BONAPARTE, C. L.   Nouvelles espèces ornithologiques.   < *Compt. Rend. de l'Acad. Sci.*, xxx, 1850, pp. 131–139, 291–295.

Première Partie, Perroquets (y comprise *Lophornis* (i. e., *Diphyllodes*) *respublica*, sp. n., p. 131, note; voir note, p. 291.—*Paradiseidæ*). *Conurus xanthogenius*, p. 132; *Barrabandius*, p. 133; *Trichoglossus forsteni*, p. 134; *Chalcopsitta* (g. n., 1849) *rubiginosa*, p. 134; *Eos cyanogenia, E. semilarvata, Eclectus cornelia*, p. 135; *Psittacodis intermedius, Tanygnathus mulleri*, p. 136; *Poiocephalus magnirostris, Geoffroyus cyanicollis, G. personatus*, p. 137; *Plyctolophus parvulus*, p. 139, sont des espèces nouv. ou récemment décrites.—Seconde Partie, *Accipitres* (*Cathartidæ, Vulturidae, Gypaetidæ, Gypohieracidæ, Gypogeranidæ*), point d'espèces nouvelles.

1850. BONAPARTE, C. L.   Nouvelles espèces ornithologiques.   < *Rev. et Mag. de Zool.*, ii, 1850, pp. 124–127.

Extraites des *Compt. Rend. de Acad. des Sci. de Paris*, séance du 11 février, 1850.—Aperçu général de l'ordre des Psittacidés; sept sous-familles.

1854. BONAPARTE, C. L.   Tableau des Perroquets.   < *Rev. et Mag. de Zool.*, vi, 1854, pp. 145–158.

§1. Critique sur les espèces décrites par MM. Masséna et De Souancé, *R. M. Z.*, 1854, pp. 71–74; *Graydidascalus*, gen. n., p. 147.   §2. Monographie du genre *Pionus*, pp. 148, 149; *P. corallinus*, p. 149.   §3. Conspectus Psittacorum, pp. 149–158; *Cyanopsitta, Ararauna, Aracanga, Rhyncopsitta*, p. 149; *Cyanoliseus, Nandayus, Heliopsitta, Eupsittula, Microsittace, Miropsitta*, p. 150; *Tirica, Psittovius, Evopsitta, Œnochrus*, p. 151; *Pionopsitta, Belurus*, p. 152; *Prosopeia, Purpureicephalus, Barnardius, Barrabandius, Cyanoramphus*, p. 153; *Poliopsitta*, p. 154; *Urodiscus, Stavorinus, Eolophus*, p. 155; *Chalcopsitta*, p. 156; *Psitteuteles, Glossopsitta*, p. 157, "Bp."

—4 familles, 15 sous-familles, 78 genres, 316 espèces; les genres et les espèces introduits pour la première fois (mais sans descriptions) se trouvent précédés d'un astérisque. *Trichoglossus massena, T. verreauxius*, p. 157, spp. nn., avec descr.

This paper is conceived in the same fatuous spirit, and executed with the same disreputable result, as that on the *Trochilidæ*, which I have criticised adversely in this Bibliography.

1854. MASSÉNA, —, *and* SOUANCÉ, [C.] DE.   Description de quelques nouvelles espèces d'oiseaux de la famille des Psittacidés.   < *Rev. et Mag. de Zool.*, vi, 1854, pp. 71–74.

Ara auritorques, Conurus icterotis, C. rubrolarvatus, p. 71; *C. chrysogenys, C. callipterus*, p. 72; *C. devillei, C. molinæ, Psittacus selinoides*, p. 73; *Ps. cobaltinus*, p. 74. Cf. *op. cit.*, 1854, pp. 146–148.

1855. CASSIN, J.   Description of new species of Psittacidæ, in the collection of the Academy of Natural Sciences of Philadelphia.   < *Journ. Acad. Nat. Sci. Philada.*, iii, pt. ii, Dec., 1855 (extra copies printed Nov., 1855), art. xii, pp. 153–156, pll. xii, xiii, xiv.

Ara auricollis, pl. xii (descr. orig. *Proc. Acad.*, 1853, p. 372). *Chrysotis viridigenalis*, pl. xiii (descr. orig. *Proc. Acad.*, 1853, p. 371). *Psittacula lineola*, pl. xiv, f. 1 (descr. orig. *Proc. Acad.*, 1853, p. 372). *Brotogeris aurifrons*, n. sp., p. 155, pl. xiv, f. 2. *Prioniturus flavicans* (descr. orig. *Proc. Acad.*, 1853, p. 373) fig. nulla. *Palaeornis gironieri* Verr. (= *P. viridicollis*, descr. orig. *Proc. Acad.*, 1853, p. 373), fig. nulla.

1856. BLANCHARD, É.   Des caractères ostéologiques chez les Oiseaux de la famille des Psittacides.   < *Compt. Rend. de l'Acad. Sci.*, xliii, 1856, pp. 1097–1100.

Extrait par l'auteur.

1856. SOUANCÉ, C. DE.   Catalogue des perroquets de la collection du prince Masséna d'Essling, duc de Rivoli, et observations sur quelques espèces nouvelles ou peu connues de Psittacidés.   < *Rev. et Mag. de Zool.*, viii, 1856, pp. 56–64, 152–158, 208–226.

"Ne voulant, dans cet opuscule, considérer cet ordre d'Oiseaux que sous le point de vue spécifique, nous laisserons de côté toute idée de la classification générale, nous bornant à suivre celle adoptée par S. A. le prince Ch. Bonaparte dans son Conspectus Psittacorum." (*Rev. et Mag. de Zool.*, 1854, pp. 145–158.)—*Psittacara hahni*, p. 58; *P. chloroptera, P. maugei*, p. 59; *Chrysotis chloronota*, p. 153; *C. coccineifrons*, p. 154; *Poeocephalus aubryanus*, p. 216; *Loriculus regulus*, p. 222; *L. bonapartei*, p. 222; *Nestor esslingii*, p. 223.—218 spp.

1856. SOUANCÉ, C. DE.   [Description d'une nouvelle espèce de Perroquet, Myiopsitta tigrina.]   < *Rev. et Mag. de Zool.*, viii, 1856, p. 144.

1857. BLANCHARD, É. Nouvelles observations sur les caractères ostéologiques chez les oiseaux de la famille des Psittacides. < *Compt. Rend. de l'Acad. Sci.*, xliv, 1857, pp. 518-521.

1857. BLANCHARD, É. Nouvelles observations sur les caractéres ostéologiques chez les Oiseaux de la famille des Psittacides. < *Rev. et Mag. de Zool.*, ix, 1857, pp. 112, 113.

> Résumé d'un travail lu à l'Acad. de Paris, séance du 9 mars 1857.

1857. BONAPARTE, C. L. Remarques du Prince Bonaparte à propos des observations de M. Emile Blanchard sur les caractères ostéologiques chez les Oiseaux de la famille des Psittacides. < *Compt. Rend. de l'Acad. Sci.*, xliv, 1857, pp. 534-539.

> *Myiopsitta catherina*, p. 538.

1857. BONAPARTE, C. L. Remarques à propos des observations de M. E. Blanchard Sur les caractères ostéologiques chez les Oiseaux de la famille des Psittacides. < *Rev. et Mag. de Zool.*, ix, 1857, pp. 113-117.

1857. BONAPARTE, C. L. Tableau des genres de Perroquets disposés en series parallèles. < *Comp. Rend. de l'Acad. Sci.*, xliv, 1857, pp. 595-597.

1857. MAXIMILIAN, PRINZ VON WIED. Ueber den Papagei von Nord-America. Psittacus (Conurus) carolinensis, Lin. < *J. f. O.*, v, 1857, pp. 97-105.

> Elaborate description and account of geographical distribution and habits.

1857. SCLATER, P. L. Notes on an unnamed Parrot [Chrysotis sallæi] from the Island of St. Domingo, now living in the Society's Gardens; and on some other Species of the same Family. < *P. Z. S.*, xxv, 1857, pp. 224-226, pl. (Aves) cxxvii.

1857. SOUANCÉ, C. DE. Descriptions de trois nouvelles espèces de Perroquets. < *Rev. et Mag. de Zool.*, ix, 1857, pp. 97, 98.

> *Conurus astec* [sic], *Pyrrhura hoematotis* [sic], p. 97; *Cyanoramphus malherbi*, p. 98.

1857-58. SOUANCÉ, C. DE. Iconographie | des | Perroquets | non figurés dans les publications de Levaillant et de M. Bourjot Saint-Hilaire | par | M. Charles de Souancé | avec la coopération de | S. A. le prince Bonaparte, et de M. Émile Blanchard | — | Histoire Naturelle des Perroquets. | — | Paris | P. Bertrand | Libraire-Éditeur | Rue de l'Arbre-sec, 22 | — | 1857 [1858]. 1 vol. in fol. grand jésus. Faux titre, 1 feuillet; titre, 1 feuillet; introduction, 1 feuillet (2 pages); le Texte non paginé, 48 feuillets; et 48 Planches coloriées. (Publiée par livr. i-xii, 1857, 1858.)

> Levaillant a publié les figures et descriptions de 90 espèces de Perroquets, dans son *Hist. Nat. des Perroq.*, en deux vols. in-fol. 1801-1805. En 1837-38, M. Bourjot St.-Hilaire a représenté 88 autres espèces, dans son ouvrage, rédigé sur le même plan, *Hist. Nat. des Perroq.*, qui forme la suite ou le troisième vol. (supplémentaire) de l'Iconographie de Levaillant. Cette Iconographie dé M. de Souancé forme le quatrième volume de *l'Hist. Nat. des Perroq.* de Levaillant et M. Bourjot St.-Hilaire. Elle contient les figures des espèces qui ne se trouvent pas dans les trois volumes publiés par les deux auteurs, accompagnées d'une courte description, et des détails anatomiques. L'auteur a trouvé les matériaux de son ouvrage d'abord dans la riche collection de son oncle, le prince d'Essling, dans celle du Jardin des Plantes à Paris, et dans les divers musées de France et de l'étranger.
>
> Voici la liste des planches: Pl. I, f. 1, *Anodorhynchus leari*; f. 2, *A. glaucus*. II. *Sittace primoli*. III, *S. rubrigenis*. IV, *Evopsitta acuticauda*. V, *Rhynchopsitta pachyrhyncha*. VI. *Psittacara hahni*. VII, *Evopsitta euops*. VIII, *E. maugei*. IX, *Conurus petzii*. X, *C. cactorum*. XI, *C. chrysophrys*. XII, *C. aztec, C. nanus*. XIII, *C. weddellii*. XIV, *Pyrrhura luciani*. XV, *P. molinæ*. XVI, *P. devillei*. XVII, *P. calliptera*. XVIII, *P. haematotis*. XIX, *Psittacara icterotis*. XX, *Evopsitta wagleri*. XXI, *Evopsitta mitrata*. XXII, *E. erythrogenys*. XXIII, *Bolborhynchus aymara*. XXIV, f. 1, *B. orbignesia*; f. 2, *B. aurifrons*. XXV, *Pyrilia amazonina*. XXVI, *P. typica*. XXVII, *Chrysotis auripalliata*. XXVIII, *C. poecilorhyncha*. XXIX, *C. chloronota*. XXX. *C. albifrons*. XXXI, *C. viridigenalis*. XXXII, *C. diadema*. XXXIII, *C. hypochondrica*. XXXIV, f. 1, *Pionus siy*; f. 2, *P. maximiliani*. XXXV, *P. chalcopterus*. XXXVI, *P. seniloides*. XXXVII, *Urochroma purpurata*. XXXVIII, *U. surda*. XXXIX, *Psittacula guianensis*. XL, *P. cœlestis*. XLI, *P. conspicillata*. XLII. *P. cyanopygia*. XLIII, *Palæornis schisticeps*. XLIV, *P. calthropæ*

1857-58. Souancé, C. de.—Continued.

XLV, *Tanygnatus mulleri.* XLVI, *T. sumatranus.* XLVII, *Barnardius zonarius.* XLVIII, (énumérée à tort LXXIX) *Oyanoramphus malherbi.*

(NOTE.—Carus announces the work as of two parts: 1) *His'. Nat.*, 1 vol., 8vo, to be pub. in 1859, and, 2) *Iconogr.*, 1 vol., fol. or 4to, with about 120 pll., in 30 monthly parts; but all I know of the work is as above.)

1858. Sclater, P. L.   Notes on an unnamed Parrot [Chrysotis sallæi] from the Island of St. Domingo; and on some other Species of the same Family. < *Ann. Mag. Nat. Hist.*, 3d ser., i, 1858, pp. 223-226.

From *P. Z. S.*, Nov. 10, 1857, pp. 224-226.

1858. Sclater, P.·L.   Verzeichniss der in den Gärten der zoologischen Gesellschaft zu London lebenden Papageien. < *Naumannia*, viii, 1858, pp. 201-204.

77 spp.

1859. Sclater, P. L.   Descriptions of two new Species of American Parrots. < *Ann. Mag. Nat. Hist.*, 3d ser., iv, 1859, pp. 224-226.

Conurus holochlorus, p. 224; *C. xantholœmus*, p. 225. List of 9 Mexican spp. of the family.

1859. Gray, G. R.   List | of the | Specimens of Birds | in | the collection | of the | British Museum. | By G. R. Gray, F. L. S., F. Z. S., etc. | Part III.   Section II. Psittacidæ. | Printed by order of the Trustees. | London: 1859.   1 vol.   sm. 12mo.   2 p. ll., pp. 1-110, 1-8 (advts.).

This List catalogues the specimens of Parrots in the British Museum, exemplifying by letters *a, b, c,* &c., the locality and source whence each has been derived. The scientific value of the treatise rests in the extensive synonymy of the genera and species which is given. Cf. *Ibis*, 1859, pp. 320, 321.

1859. Wallace, A. R.   Correction of an Important Error affecting the Classification of the Psittacidæ. < *Ann. Mag. Nat. Hist.*, 3d ser., iii, 1859, pp. 147, 148.

Domicella is brush-tongued, like *Trichoglossus* and *Eos.*

1860. Blanchard, É.   Observations sur le système dentaire chez les Oiseaux. < *Compt. Rend. de l'Acad. Sci.*, 1, 1860, pp. 540-542.

Recherches sur divers *Psittacides.*

1862. Förster, A.   [Scrophulöse Drüse eines Papageies (Psittacus amazonicus).] < *Zool. Gart.*, iii, 1862, p. 66.

1862. Neubert, W.   Ueber Züchtung von Papageien in Deutschland. < *Zool. Gart.*, iii, 1862, pp. 57-61, 76-78.

1863. Finsch, O.   Naamlijst der in de Diergaarde levende Papagaaijen. < *Nederl. Tijdschr. voor de Dierk.*, 1863, pp. vi-xxiv.

Not seen.

1863. Weinland, D. F.   Unsere Arara's. < *Zool. Gart.*, iv, 1863, pp. 244, 247, figg. 1-5.

1864. Aucapitaine, H.   Longévité des Perroquets. < *Rev. et Mag. de Zool.*, xvi, 1864, pp. 409-411.

1864. Cabanis, J.   Eine neue Papageien-Art von Bogota, Conurus (Gnathosittaca) Heinei. < *J. f. O.*, xii, 1864, pp. 414-416.

1864. Sacc, Dr.   [Begattung von Platycercus eximius.   Neuer Amazon-Papagei. Perroquet tapiré.] < *Zool. Gart.*, v, 1864, p. 21.

1864. Schlegel, H.   Psittaci. < *Mus. Hist. Nat. Pays-Bas*, 5e livr., 1864, pp. 1-166.

The Parrots, represented in the Leyden Museum by 1,204 specimens, referred by the author to 259 spp., none of which are described as new, are here treated under 19 genera, among them *Amazona*, Less.

There is a second article of similar character, 1874, *q. v.*

1864. Schmidt, Max.   Das Federnagen der Papageien. < *Zool. Gart.*, v, 1864, pp. 177-181.

1864. Sclater, P. L.   Characters of Three New American Parrots. < *P. Z. S.*, xxiv, 1864, pp. 297, 298, pl. xxiv.

Conurus rhodogaster, Natt. mss., p. 298, pl. xxiv; *Brotogerys chrys· sema*, Natt. mss. p. 298. *Chrysotis finschi*, p. 298.

1865. [ANON.] Langes Leben der Papageien. < *Aus der Natur,* xxxi, oder n. F., **xix,** 1865, pp. 175, 176.

1865. SCHMIDT, MAX. Die Nachtheile eiserner Sitzstangen für Papageien. < *J. f. O.,* xiii, 1865, p. 354.

1865. SCLATER, P. L. [Remarks on a rare Parrot (Chrysotis augusta) from Dominica.] < *P. Z. S.,* xxxiii, 1865, pp. 437, 438.

1866. FINSCH, O. Die geographische Verbreitung der Papageien. < *Peterm. Geogr. Mittheil.,* 1867 (pub. 1866), pp. 3–7 (mit einer Karte von A. Petermann).
Nicht mir selbst zugänglich.

1866. GUYON, —. Des animaux disparus de la Martinique et de la Guadeloupe depuis notre établissement dans ces îles. < *Compt. Rend. de l'Acad. Sci.,* lxiii, 1866, pp. 589–597.
Des Aras, des Perroquets et des Perruches.

1866. [GUYON, —.] Ueber die Thiere, die auf den Inseln Martinique und Guadeloupe seit der Besitznahme durch die Franzosen verschwunden sind. < *Aus der Natur,* xxxviii, oder n. F., xxvi, 1866, pp. 730, 733.
Auszug aus den *Compt. Rend.,* lxiii, 1866, pp. 589–597, *q. v.*

1867. [FINSCH, O.] Geographische Verbreitung der Papageien. < *Aus der Natur,* xxxix, oder n. F., xxvii, 1867, pp. 107–111.

1867–68. FINSCH, O. Die Papageien, | monographisch bearbeitet | von | Otto Finsch, | Conservator der zoologischen Sammlung der Gesellschaft ,, Museum " zu Bremen, früher | Assistent am Reichs-Museum zu Leiden, correspondirendes Mitglied der | Zoological Society zu London und anderer gelehrter Gesell- schaften. | — | Erster Band. | Mit einer Karte und einer lithographirten Tafel. | — | Leiden, E. J. Brill. | 1867. | . . . . | Zweiter Band. | Erste [zweite] Haelfte. | Mit 5 nach der Natur lithographirten und colorirten Tafeln und | Uebersichts-Tabellen zur Geographischen Verbreitung. | Leiden, E. J. Brill. | 1868. 2 vols. 8vo. Vol. I, 1867, pp. xii, 361 + 1, 1 map, 1 pl. Vol. II, 1868, pp. vii + 22, 996 + 3, 5 pll. col'd, 1 table; this vol. published in 2 parts, con- tinuously paged, same date.
Vol. I. Vorwort; Erklärungen; Allgem. Naturg. d. Papag. (Geschichtliches u. liter- arischer Ueberblick—Aeusseres Leben—Verbreitung—Geistesanlagen—Gestalt und äussere Werkzeuge—Federn—Anatomie—Systematik); Specielle Naturg. d. Papag; Karte; Pl. I, Scelet von *Ps. erythacus* und Schadel von *Plect. sulfureus* u. *Euphema pulchella.* Vol. II. Vorwort; Uebers.-Tabellen zur geogr. Verbreit.; Specielle Naturg. fortzetzt.; Anhang (Dubiöse Arten, etc.); Pl. II, *Brotogerys subcœrulea;* Pl. III, *B. chrysosema;* Pl. IV, *Chrysotis guatemalœ;* Pl. V, *Coryllis exilis;* Pl. VI, *Domicella fuscata.*—*Bolborhynchus luchsii,* ii, p. 121, sp. n.
Very complete. The first part general; historical and literary view of the subject; bibli. ographical abstract; biographical account; geographical distribution, illustrated by maps (pl. I); on the wit, external structure, pterylography and anatomy, and systematic arrange- ment; list of genera and species. In the second part each species is treated in great detail— 1 "family"; 5 subfamilies; 26 genera, 350 + 4 spp., besides 41 doubtful ones.
Cf. *Zool. Rec.,* iv, 1867, pp. 83–85; v, 1868, pp. 69–70; *Zool. Gart.,* 1867, pp. 318–320; *Ibis,* 2d ser., v, 1869, pp. 223–225.

1867. NIEMEIER, W. Zur Verfärbung von Conurus carolinensis. < *Zool. Gart.,* viii, 1867, p. 268.

1867. NOLL, F. C. Die Papageien, monographisch bearbeitet von Otto Finsch. Lei- den, E. J. Brill 1867, ———?
Review.—My copy of this title, I suspect, is defective: it looks to me like a title from *Zool. Gart.,* with the reference omitted through oversight; but I cannot verify.

1867. SCHLEGEL, F. Uebersicht der Papageien unserer zoologischen Gärten. < *Zool. Gart.,* viii, 1867, pp. 32–34, 72–75.

1867. SCHLEGEL, F. Nachtrag zur Uebersicht der Papageien unserer zool. Gärten. < *Zool. Gart.,* viii, 1867, pp. 229–231.
Vergl. *tom. cit.,* pp. 32–34, 72–75. Diese zwei Artikel geben ein Namen-Verzeichniss von 130 in verschiedenen zool. Gärten in Europa lebenden Arten.

1867. SCLATER, P. L. Notes upon some Parrots living in the [London Zoological] Society's Menagerie. < P. Z. S., Feb. 14, 1867, pp. 183-185, pl. xvi.

Comparative diagnoses of *Ara ambigua* and *A. militaris*. Plate of *Lorius chlorocercus*. Critical remarks on various species of *Cacatua*.

1868. [FINSCH, O.] Papegoiernes geografiske Udbredning. < *Tidssk. Pop. Frems. af Naturv.*, 3e række, v, 1868, pp. 340-345.

1868. [FINSCH, O.] Uebersichts-Tabellen zur geographischen Verbreitung der Papageien. Abgeschlossen am 15. Juni 1868. [Von Dr. Otto Finsch. n. d. n. p. 1868.] 8vo. 11 unpaged leaves.

This brochure, without author's name, date, or place of publication, is apparently extracted from Finsch's celebrated monograph. It gives in tabular form the distribution of *Psittacidæ* under the six principal heads of America, Africa, Asia, East Indian regions, Australia, and Polynesia.

1869. BARBOZA DU BOCAGE, J. V. Museu Nacional de Lisboa | — | Secção Zoologica | — | Catalogo das Collecções Ornithologicas | — | Psittaci—Papagaios. | Accipitres—Aves de Rapina. | — | Junho de 1869 | [Arms.] | Lisboa | Imprensa Nacional | 1869 8vo. pp. 62.

" . . . enceto agora a publicação dos catalogos das collecções zoologicas do museu du Lisboa. Os primeiros que se póde levar á conclusão comprehendem duas ordens de aves, os *Psittacideos* ou *papagaios* e as *Aves de rapina*. Estes catalogos foram redigidos pelo sr. José Augusto de Sousa, . . . Os *Psittacideos* [pp. 7-28] constam de 204 especies e as *Aves de rapina* de 223."

1871. LAWRENCE, G. N. [Notes on Central American Psittacidæ, with reference to O. Salvin's paper, tom. cit., p. 86 seq.] < *Ibis*, 3d ser., i, 1871, pp. 249-251.

1871. REINHARDT, J. [Note on the habitat of Ara macao, with reference to O. Salvin's paper, tom. cit., pp. 86-100.] < *Ibis*, 3d ser., i, 1871, p. 362.

1871. REY, E. [Der Carolinenpapagei (Conurus carolinensis) in Gefangenschaft.] < *Zool. Gart.*, xii, 1871, pp. 280-283.

1871. SALVIN, O. On the Psittacidæ of Central America. < *Ibis*, 3d ser., i, 1871, pp. 86-100, pl. iv.

Critical commentary, with special reference to geographical distribution, upon 27 spp. of 9 genn. *Conurus finschi*, p. 91, pl. iv, sp. n. (Cf. Lawrence, *tom. cit.*, pp. 249-251, and Reinhardt, *ibid.*, p. 362.)

1872. DODGE, N. S. A chapter on Parrots. < *Appleton's Journ.*, viii, Oct., 1872, p. 431.

1872. DORNER, H. Die Papageien-Ausstellung der zoologischen Gärten zu Hamburg. Hamburg. 1872. 1 vol. 8vo. pp. 48.

Short descriptions of 78 spp., living on exhibition—which, with the other matter of the book, are apparently from O. Finsch's monograph.

1872. REY, E. [Ein- und Ausfliegen von Papageien, Conurus carolinensis.] < *Zool. Gart.*, xiii, 1872, pp. 123, 124.

1872. SCHMIDT, MAX. Fortpflanzung des Mönchsittichs (Bolborhynchus monachus) in Gefangenschaft. < *Zool. Gart.*, xiii, 1872, pp. 257-264.

In the Zoological Garden at Frankfort.

1873. FINSCH, O. On a new American Parrot, of the Genus Chrysotis [C. bodini]. < *P. Z. S.*, 1873, pp. 569, 570, pl. xlix.

1873. STRICKER, W. Geschichtliche Mittheilungen über den Handel mit Papageien und die Zähmung derselben in Europa bis zum Ende des Mittelalters. < *Zool. Gart.*, xiv, 1873, pp. 266, 267.

1874. CABANIS, J. [Chrysotis canipalliata, sp. n.] < *J. f. O.*, xxii, 1874, pp. 105, 106.

1874. CABANIS, J. [Chrysotis panamensis, sp. n.] < *J. f. O.*, xxii, 1874, p. 349.

1874. FINSCH, O. On an apparently new Species of Parrot [Psittacula andicola] from Eastern Peru. < *P. Z. S.*, xlii, 1874, pp. 90, 91.

1874. SCHLEGEL, H.   Revue de la Collection des Perroquets (Psittaci) faisant partie du Musée des Pays-Bas. *< Mus. Hist. Nat. Pays-Bas*, 11ᵉ livr., Mai, 1874, pp. 1–84.

> In this review of the subject since 1864 (*q. v.*) are treated the specimens, now 2,237 in number, of the Leyden Collection. *Psittacula diophthalma aruensis*, p. 33.

1874. SCLATER, P. L.   [Report on recent additions to the Society's Menagerie.] *< P. Z. S.*, xlii, 1874, p. 206, pl. xxxiv.

> *Chrysotis finschi*, pl. xxxiv.

1874. WALDEN, *Lord.*   A Reply to Mr. Allan Hume's Review of 'Die Papageien' of Dr. Otto Finsch. *< I bis*, 3d ser., iv, 1874, pp. 270–299.

> A terribly incisive castigation, delivered with an unfaltering hand—with how much justice, readers of both articles may judge.

1875. FINSCH, O.   Ueber drei neue Vögelarten. *< J. f. O.*, 1875, pp. 411– —.

> The article includes the description of *Chrysotis nattereri*, p. —, from Brazil.

1875. SCLATER, P. L.   On some rare Parrots living in the Society's Gardens. *< P. Z. S.*, Feb. 2, 1875, pp. 59, 62, figg. 1, 2, pll. x, xi.

> Treating of *Cacatua goffini*, pl. x, and fig. 1 in text, *C. sanguinea* (fig. 2) and *C. gymnopis*; also, *Chrysotis bouqueti*, pl. xi, from Santa Lucia, and various South American species. Whole series in the menagerie, 186 specimens of 115 spp.

1875. [SCLATER, P. L.]   [Addition of Chrysotis xantholora to the Society's Menagerie.] *< P. Z. S.*, Mar. 16, 1875, p. 157, pl. xxvi.

1875. [SCLATER, P. L.]   [On additions to the Society's Menagerie in March, 1875.] *< P. Z. S.*, Apr. 20, 1875, pp. 316, 317.

> Various birds, among them *Chrysotis bouqueti* (see *P. Z. S.*, 1874, p. 323; 1875, p. 59, pl. xi), from Santa Lucia, W. I.

1875. SCLATER, P. L.   [Report on additions to the Society's Menagerie, with Remarks on Chrysotis xantholora.] *< P. Z. S.*, Mar. 16, 1875, pp. 156, 157, pl. xxvi.

> The Parrot named is figured on the plate cited. There is no other bird matter.

1875. SELLER, W. J.   A Talking Parrot. *< Rod and Gun*, vii, Dec. 18, 1875, p. 179.

1875. WICKHAM, H. A.   [Letter on the occurrence of Ara hyacinthina near Santarem, Brazil.] *< P. Z. S.*, Dec. 7, 1875, pp. 633, 634.

1876. GARROD, A. H.   Notes on the Anatomy of certain Parrots. *< P. Z. S.*, June 20, 1876, pp. 691, 692.

> Brief observations on numerous species, some of them neotropical.

1876. GREGORY, J. A.   A wonderful Parrot. *< Forest and Stream*, vii, Dec. 14, 1876, p. 292.

1876. SCLATER, [P. L.]   [Ara couloni, sp. n.] *< P. Z. S.*, Feb. 15, 1876, pp. 255, 256, fig.

> Being *Conurus illigeri*, Tsch., *Fn. Peru, Aves*, p. 271, and in part *Sittace maracana*, Finsch, *Pap.*, i, p. 420.

1876. [NEWCOMB, R. L.]   A musical Parrot. *< Forest and Stream*, vii, Dec. 7, 1876, p. 276.

1877. COUES, E.   Western Range [to Kansas and Colorado] of Conurus carolinensis. *< Bull. Nutt. Ornith. Club*, ii, No. 2, Apr., 1877, p. 50.

1877. GARROD, A. H.   Note on the Absence or Presence of a Gall-bladder in the family of the Parrots [Psittacidæ]. *< P. Z. S.*, Nov. 20, 1877, p. 793.

> Present in *Cacatua* and its allies. Also, present in some *Columbidæ.* It had been denied to both these families.

1877. SCLATER, P. L.   On the American Parrots of the Genus Pionus. *< Rowl. Orn. Misc.*, iii, pt. xi, Nov., 1877, pp. 5–10, pll. lxxx, lxxxi.

> *P. corallinus*, pl. 80; *P. tumultuosus*, pl. 81.

1878. BURMEISTER, H.   Notes on Conurus hilaris and other Parrots of the Argentine Republic. *< P. Z. S.*, Jan. 15, 1878, pp. 75–77.

> Extended account of a long-tailed Parrot (not named); correction of mistakes in Finsch's work respecting various Argentine and Brazilian species.

1878. [SCLATER, P. L.] [On Addition of Ara spixi? to the Society's **Menagerie, in** November, 1878.] < *P. Z. S.*, Dec. 3, 1878, p. 976, pl. lxi.

1879. ANON. New Facts about Parrots [Psittacidæ]. < *Forest and Stream*, Oct. **16,** 1879, p. 737.

> Reprinted from *Pittsburgh Leader*.

1879. SCLATER, P. L. Remarks on some Parrots living in the Society's Gardens. < *P. Z. S.*, Mar. 18, 1879, pp. 299–301, pl. xxviii.

> The series consisted of 170 individuals of 98 spp., 6 of which are here remarked upon—2 spp. of *Brotogerys*, 3 of *Palæornis*, and *Caica xanthomera*, which latter is figured.

1879. SCLATER, [P. L.] [Remarks on exhibition of Ara glauca from **Corrientes.**] < *P. Z. S.*, June 17, 1879, p. 551.

Strigidæ.

1822. EDMONSTON, L. Observations on the Snowy Owl, (Strix Nyctea, Linn.)
 $<$ *Mem. Wernerian Nat. Hist. Soc.*, iv, pt. i, 1822, pp. 157–160.
  Read Mar., 1822. Relating to its distribution and habits.

1826. GARNOT, P. Observations sur le Chat-huant couleur de neige (Strix Nyctea)
 par Laurence Edmonston. . . . $<$ *Féruss. Bull.*, 2e sec., vii, 1826, pp. 106, 107.
  Mem. Wernerian Soc., iv, 1822, pp. 157–160.

1829. HEAD, T. The Biscacho, or Coquimbo Owl (Strix cunicularia). $<$ *Loudon's*
 Mag. Nat. Hist., i, 1829, p. 285, fig. 150.
  From *Head's Rough Notes*, p. 82.

1830. GEOFFROY ST.-HILAIRE, ISID. Remarques sur les caractères et la classification
 des Oiseaux de proie nocturnes, et Description d'un genre nouveau sous le
 nom de Phodilus. $<$ *Ann. des Sci. Nat.*, xxi, 1830, pp. 194–203.
  Division de la famille en 2 sections—§ I. Les genres chez lesquels il n'existe point de disque autour de la face, 1º *Noctua*, 2º *Bubo*, 3º *Phodilus*, g. n., p. 199. § II. Ceux chez lesquels
  le disque est complet ou presque complet, 1º *Syrnium*, 2º *Ulula*, 3º *Strix*.—Chouette Calong,
  Pl. Col. 318, = *Strix badius*, Horsf. = *Phodilus badius*, p. 203.

1833. HOY, J. D. The Short-eared Owl (Strix brachyotus Lath.) breeds in the County
 of Norfolk. $<$ *Loudon's Mag. Nat. Hist.*, vi, 1833, pp. 150, 151.

1834. BREE, W. T. [On Shakespeare's Notice of the Owl's Manner of Flight.]
 $<$ *Loudon's Mag. Nat. Hist.*, vii, 1834, p. 593.

1835. NEILL, P. The Snowy Owl (Stríx nýctea), an Individual of, has been taken
 alive at Orkney, and was alive on May 9. 1835, at Canonmills, near Edinburgh. $<$ *Loudon's Mag. Nat. Hist.*, viii, 1835, p. 508.

1837. DENNY, H. [Letter on the occurrence of the Snowy Owl (Nyctea nivea) at
 Selby, Yorkshire.] $<$ *P. Z. S.*, v, 1837, p. 45.

1838. CABOT, S. [JR.] Observations on the plumage of the Red and Mottled Owls
 (Strix asio). $<$ *Journ. Bost. Soc. Nat. Hist.*, ii, pt. i, 1838, pp. 126–128.
  Supposing the difference to be due to age—*S. naevia* juv., *S. asio* ad. The true interpretation of the phenomenon (dichromatism, independent of age, sex, or season) was not made
  until many years afterward.

1838. DENNY, H. Surnia Nyctea, Dumeril. $<$ *Mag. of Zool. and Bot.*, ii, 1838, p. 93.
  Its occurrence Feb. 13, 1838, in Britain.

1838. THOMPSON, W. On the Snowy Owl, Surnia nyctea, Dumeril. $<$ *Annals of Nat.*
 Hist., i, 1838, pp. 241–245.
  Description, and habits in confinement.

1839. LESSON, R. P. Description d'une nouvelle espèce de Syrnium [S. ocellatum].
 $<$ *Revue Zoologique*, ii, 1839, pp. 289–290.

1839. MICHENER, E. A few Facts in relation to the Identity of the Red and Mottled
 Owls, &c. $<$ *Journ. Acad. Nat. Sci. Phila.*, viii, 1839, pp. 53–56.

1839. THOMPSON, W. Note on the Migration of the Snowy Owl, Surnia nyctea,
 Dum. $<$ *Annals of Nat. Hist.*, iii, 1839, pp. 107–110.

1842. ABBOTT, S. L. [On a specimen of Syrnium cinereum from Massachusetts.]
 $<$ *Proc. Bost. Soc. Nat. Hist.*, i, 1842, pp. 57, 58.

1843. GERARD, —. Chouette. $<$ *Dict. Nouv. d'Hist. Nat.*, iii, p. 631.
  Not seen. The article Chouette in this dictionary is specially mentioned by Wagner, as
  "one of the best of the ornithological articles contained in the present part." The author
  regards the commonly received genera as subgenera, and does not enter upon species.

1843. VAN BENEDEN, P. J. Note sur l'oreille externe de quelques oiseaux de proie
 nocturnes. $<$ *Mem. Soc. Roy. Sci. Liège*, i, 1843, pp. 121–124, pl. 3.
  Pas vue moi-même.

1844. CASSIN, J. [On the frequent occurrence of Strix nyctea in the vicinity of Philadelphia during the winter of 1843–4.] < *Proc. Acad. Nat. Sci. Phila.*, ii, 1844, pp. 19, 20.

1844. FAYRER, —. [Letter from, accompanied by two specimens of Strix nyctea.] < *P. Z. S.*, xii, 1844, p. 19.

1844. PUCHERAN, *Dr.* Considérations générales sur les oiseaux de proie nocturnes et description de quelques espèces peu connues de cet ordre, de la collection du musée de Paris. < *Arch. du Mus. d'Hist. Nat.*, iv, 1844, pp. 311–343, pll. xxii–xxiv.

> *Scops rutilus*, p. 326, pl. 22 (*Rev. Mag. Zool.*, 1849, p. 29); *Bubo madascariensis*, p. 328, pl. xxiii (*Otus madag.*, Smith, *S. Afr. Quart. Jour.*, ii, 1835, 316); *Bubo magellanicus*, auct., p. 331; *Otus stygius*, p. 336, pl. xxiv (*Nyctalops stygius*, Wagl., *Isis*, 1832, p. 1221); *Syrnium ocellatum*, p. 339 (Less., *R. Z.*, ii, 1839, p. 289).

1844. THOMPSON, W. Ueber Surnia nyctea, geschossen in September 1837. in einem Steinbruch in der Grafschaft Down. < *Oken's Isis*, Bd. xxxvii, 1844, pp. 582, 583.

> From *Ann. Nat. Hist.*, 1838, p. 241.

1844. THOMPSON, W. Ueber die Wanderung der Schnee-Eule (Surnia nyctea). < *Oken's Isis*, Bd. xxxvii, 1844, pp. 748, 749.

> *Ann. Nat. Hist.*, iii, 1839, p. 107.

1845. LILLJEBORG, W. [Om Stryx nyctea.] < *Öfvers. Kongl. Vetensk.-Akad. Förhandl. för år 1844*, 1845, p. 212, 213.

1846. VAN BENEDEN, [P. J.] Ueber das äussere Ohr der Eulen. < *Oken's Isis*, Bd. xxxix, 1846, p. 157.

> *Mém. Soc. Roy. Sci. Liège*, Tom. i, pt. i, 1843, pp. 121–124, pl. 3.

1847. CABOT, S., JR. [Occurrence of Syrnium cinereum in Vermont and Massachusetts.] < *Proc. Bost. Soc. Nat. Hist.*, ii, 1847, p. 206.

1848. CASSIN, J. Descriptions of Owls, presumed to be undescribed, specimens of which are in the collection of the Academy of Natural Sciences of Philadelphia. < *Proc. Acad. Nat. Sci. Phila.*, iv, 1848, pp. 121–125.

> *Ephialtes sagittatus*, p. 121; *E. watsonii*, p. 123; *Syrnium albogularis, S. virgatum*, p. 124.

1848. CURTLER, M. Occurrence of the Short-eared Owl (Strix brachyotus) near Worcester. < *Zoologist*, vi, 1848, p. 2063.

1848. KAUP, J. J. Uebersicht der Eulen (Strigidae). < *Oken's Isis*, Bd. xli, 1848, pp. 753–774.

> *Sceloglaux, Hieracoglaux, Spiloglaux, Microptynx*, p. 768; *Microglaux, Pholeoptynx, Taenioglaux, Pisorhina, Megascops, Acnemis, Ptilopsis, Pseudoscops*, p. 769; *Rhinostrix, Phasmaptynx, Pseudoptynx, Megastrix*, p. 770; *Pulsatrix*, p. 771.—Zusätze zu den *Falconidæ, Isis*, 1847, 616. (Vergl. 1851-52, u. 1859, KAUP, J. J.)

1849. CASSIN, J. Descriptions of Owls presumed to be undescribed. < *Ann. Mag. Nat. Hist.*, 2d ser., iv, 1849, pp. 225–229.

> From *Proc. Acad. Phila.*, iv, 1848, pp. 121–125.

1849. PUCHERAN, *Dr.* Observations sur les types peu connues du Musée de Paris.—Rapaces nocturnes. < *Rev. et Mag. de Zool.*, i, 1849, pp. 17–28.

> Types de MM. Vieillot et Lesson.

1850. CASSIN, J. Descriptions of Owls, presumed to be new species, in the collection of the Academy of Natural Sciences of Philadelphia. < *Journ. Acad. Nat. Sci. Phila.*, ii, pt. i, Nov., 1850, art. iv, pp. 51–54, pll. iii, iv, v.

> Already described, *Proc. Acad.*, iv, Dec., 1848, p. 124; iv, Feb., 1849, p. 157. Pl. iii, *Syrnium virgatum;* pl. iv, *S. albogularis;* pl. v, *Nyctale harrisii.* See same author at 1852.

1850. ELLMAN, J. B. Note on the Long and Short-eared Owls (Strix otus and brachyotus). < *Zoologist*, viii, 1850, p. 2698.

1850. FOOTIT, W. F. Occurrence of the Snowy Owl (Strix nyctea) in the north of Scotland. < *Zoologist*, viii, 1850, p. 2923.

1850. GURNEY, J. H.   Occurrence of the Snowy Owl (Strix nyctea) in Norfolk. < *Zoologist*, viii, 1850, p. 2765.

1850. GURNEY, J. H.   Occurrence of the Snowy Owl [Nyctea nivea] in Norfolk. < *Zoologist*, viii, 1850, p. 2765.

1851. CASSIN, J.   [Note on the Plumages of Ephialtes asio (Gm.).]   < *Proc. Acad. Nat. Sci. Phila.*, v, 1851, p. 236.
   Specimens establishing the identity of *E. nœvia* and *E. asio.*

1851–52. KAUP, J. J.   Monograph of the Owls—Strigidæ, by T. T. [sic] Kaup.   < *Jard. Contrib. Orn.*, 1851, pp. 119–130; 1852, pp. 103–122.
   Of the same character as the author's Monog. *Falconidæ.* Many of the generic names are now or lately new, but are not so indicated. See the original, *Isis*, 1848, pp. 753-774. There is a later memoir by the same on the same, 1859, *q. v.*

1852. CASSIN, J.   Description of Owls presumed to be new species, specimens of which are in the collection of the Academy of Natural Sciences of Philadelphia. < *Journ. Acad. Nat. Sci. Phila.*, ii, pt. ii, Jan., 1852, art. xii, pp. 95–97, pl. xii.
   Orig. descr. *Proc. Acad.*, iv, 1848, pp. 121, 123.—Pl. xii, f. 1, *Ephialtes watsonii;* f. 2, *E. sagittatus.* See same author at 1850.

1852. GERBE, Z.   Observations sur la Chouette Tengmalm (Strix Tengmalmi, Gmel.). < *Rev. et Mag. de Zool.*, iv, Avril, 1852, pp. 172–174.
   Sous-titre de ses *Mélanges Zoologiques*, pp. 161-174 et suiv.

1852. HOY, P. R.   Descriptions of two species of Owls, presumed to be new, which inhabit the State of Wisconsin.   < *Proc. Acad. Nat. Sci. Phila.*, vi, 1852, pp. 210, 211.
   Nyctale kirtlandii, p. 210 ; *Bubo subarcticus*, p. 211. (Neither of these is new.)

1852. KAUP, [J. J.]   [Notice of paper read by: "On the Classification of the Strigidæ." To be published in the Society's Transactions.]   < *P. Z. S.*, xx, 1852, p. 88.
   It appeared in 1859, *q. v.*

1853. COUPER, W.   Naturalist's Calendar, for November and December, Toronto, 1853. < *Canad. Journ.*, ii, 1853, pp. 124, 125.
   Notice of *Strix nyctea.*

1854. GLOGER, C. W. L.   Das Fische-Fangen der Schnee-Eule, Strix nyctea(!) L., beschrieben von Audubon. < *J. f. O.*, ii, 1854, pp. 378, 379.
   Translation of passages in *Orn. Biog.*, iv, pp. 436-438.

1854. GLOGER, C. W. L.   Eine Schnee-Eule [Nyctea nivea] weit auf dem Meere; [u. s. w.]   < *J. f. O.*, ii, 1854, pp. 477, 478.
   An extract from Audubon's *Orn. Biog.*, Vol. V, Appendix, pp. 382, 383, with remarks by the translator.

1854. GLOGER, C. W. L.   Eine Warnigung von Seiten Andubon's vor Täuschungen [u. s. w.].   < *J. f. O.*, ii, 1854, pp. 479, 480.
   An extract from Audubon's *Orn. Biog.*, Vol. V, p. 386, with comments by the translator, respecting *Strix nebulosa*, etc.

1855. NEWMAN, E.   Occurrence of the Snowy Owl [Nyctea nivea] in Averdeenshire. < *Zoologist*, xiii, 1855, p. 4761.

1856. BREWER, T. M.   [On the Short-eared Owl of North America (Brachyotus cassinii, sp. n.).]   < *Proc. Bost. Soc. Nat. Hist.*, v, 1856, p. 321.
   This is, I think, Dr. Brewer's first and last appearance in the rôle of species-making, and an entirely unsuccessful one.

1857. [BILLINGS, E.]   On the Great Horned Owl, Bubo virginianus.   < *Canad. Nat. and Geol.*, i, 1857, pp. 443–447, fig.

1857. [BILLINGS, E.]   The Snowy Day Owl.   Surnia Nyctea.   < *Canad. Nat. and Geol.*, i, 1857, pp. 447–450.

1857. BISHOP, N. H.   The Burrowing Owl of South America.   (Athene cunicularia. Molina.)   *Proc. Bost. Soc. Nat. Hist.*, vi, 1857, pp. 204-206.
   Habits.

1857. GADAMER, —.   Strix nyctea.   < *Naumannia*, vii, 1857, Heft i, pp. 84, 85.

1857. GRAHAM, D.   Snowy Owls [Strix nyctea] in the Western Islands.   < *Zoologist*, xv, 1857, p. 5831.

1857. H[INCKS], W.   Canadian Strigidæ.   < *Canad. Journ.*, ii, 1857, pp. 219, 220.
Recapitulation of the species.

1858. BREHM, [C.] L.   Die Schleierkäuze.   Strix, Lin.   < *Naumannia*, viii, 1858, pp. 214–220.
> 1. *Strix flammea*; a. *obscura*; b. *vulgaris*; c. *adspersa*; d. *guttata*.   2. *S. margaritata*.   3. *S. paradoxa* Brm., p. 217.   4. *S. splendens*.   5. *S. kirchhoffii*, nob., p. 219.   6. *S. maculata*, nob., p. 220.

1858. BREHM, [C.] L.   Die Steinkäuze.   Athene, Boje, Noctua, Cuv. (Strix psilodactyla, L.   Strix passerina, Gm., L.   Strix noctua, Retz.)   < *Naumannia*, viii, 1858, pp. 221–230.
> 1. *A. longicauda* Brm., p. 221.   2. *A. major* Brm., p. 222.   3. *A. passerina*; a. *psilodactyla*; b. *vulgaris*; c. *leucophrys*.   4. *A. vidali*, nob., p. 224.   5. *A. indigena* Brm., p. 226.   6. *A. intercedens* Brm., p. 227.   7. *A. meridionalis*.   8. *A. ferruginea*, nob., p. 229.

1859. KAUP, J. J.   Monograph of the Strigidæ.   < *Trans. Zool. Soc. Lond.*, iv, pt. vi, 1859, art. xviii, pp. 201–260, pll. lvi, lvii (generic details of structure).
> Dr. Kaup was specially occupied for some years with the birds of prey, publishing meanwhile numerous papers.   Three of these are upon *Strigidæ—Isis*, 1848; *Contr. Orn.*, 1851–52, and the present one.   He coined many new generic names for these birds, several of which have proven available; but his work cannot be considered of great merit or utility, and would be scarcely remembered were it not for the new genera proposed.   His classification is hopelessly vitiated by his 'quinarian' freaks, and his way of working out species has the reverse of felicitous result.   I should not be disposed to take issue with any one who might go so far as to consider the author in mention a magnificent failure.

1859. XANTUS, J.   Catalogue of Birds collected in the vicinity of Fort Tejon, California, with a description of a new species of Syrnium [occidentale, p. 193].   < *Proc. Acad. Nat. Sci. Phila.*, xi, 1859, pp. 189–193.

1862. H[INCKS], W.·   The Snowy Owl [in Canada].   < *Canad. Journ.*, vii, 1862, p. 522.

1862. PASSMORE, S.   To the Editor of the Leader.   < *Canad. Journ.*, vii, 1862, p. 523.
On *Strix nyctea* in Canada.

1862. "STRIX."   To the Editor of the Leader.   < *Canad. Journ.*, vii, 1862, pp. 522–523.
On *Strix nyctea* in Canada.

1863. BOULTON, W. W.   Occurrence of the Snowy Owl in Sutherlandshire, and of the Honey Buzzard in Inverness-shire.   < *Zoologist*, xxi, 1863, p. 8765.

1863. HADFIELD, H.   Snowy Owl (Strix nyctea).   < *Zoologist*, xxi, 1863, pp. 8718, 8719.

1863. PELZELN, A. v.   Ueber vier von Natterer in Brasilien gesammelte noch unbeschriebene Vögelarten.   < *Verh. k.-k. zool.-bot. Gesellsch. Wien*, xiii, Oct. 10, 1863, pp. 1125–1130.
> *Syrnium superciliare*, p. 1125 (*Strix superciliaris* on p. 1126); and three species of *Tinamidæ*.

1863. SAVILLE, S. P.   Note on the Shorteared Owl.   < *Zoologist*, xxi, 1863, p. 8818.

1863. SAXBY, H. L.   Notes on the Snowy Owl.   < *Zoologist*, xxi, 1863, pp. 8633–8639.

1863. SCHLEGEL, H.   Oti   < *Mus. Hist. Nat. Pays-Bas*, 2ᵉ livr., Déc., 1862, pp. 1–30. (Pub. 1863.)
> Article dated Dec., 1862, and possibly out that year in loose sheets, but the whole livr. not published till 1863.
> This author's "Oti," or Eared Owls, include the genera *Otus*, *Bubo*. and *Scops*, there being treated of the first 5, of the second 18, and of the third 10 spp., with certain subspp. of these genera respectively.   These species are represented in the Leyden Museum by 185 specimens, of a synonymatic and descriptive list of which the article consists.   *Bubo orientalis minor*, p. 13; *Scops zorca asiaticus* et *africanus*, p. 20, subspp. nn.

1863. SCHLEGEL, H.   Striges   < *Mus. Hist. Nat. Pays-Bas*, 2ᵉ livr., Déc., 1862, pp. 1–46. (Pub. 1863.)
> Article dated Dec., 1862; possibly out in loose sheets that year; but the livr. not published till 1863.

1863. SCHLEGEL, H.—Continued.

The 264 specimens of "Striges" contained in the Leyden Museum are here treated, with synonymy and description, as representing 6 spp. of *Strix*, 21 of *Ulula*, and 26 of *Noctua*. *Strix flammea americana*, p. 4; *Noctua hirsuta philippensis*, p. 26; *N. perlata capensis*, p. 37, subspp. nn.—The group is that of Owls without ear-tufts, as distinguished from the tufted species, the latter being the "Oti" of this author.

1863. WHEELWRIGHT, H.   Notes on the Hawk Owl (Strix funerea), and Tengmalm's Owl (Strix Tengmalmi) as observed in Lapland.   <*Zoologist*, xxi, 1863, pp. 8442–8444.

1864. ARMISTEAD, J. J.   The Shorteared Owl [Strix brachyotus] perching.   <*Zoologist*, xxii, 1864, p. 8876.

1865. LORD, J. K.   The Pigmy Owl.   Glaucidium gnoma, Wagler.   . . .   <*The Intellectual Observer*, vii, 1865, pp. 409–413.

1867. ELLIOT, D. G   Description of an apparently new species of Owl, of the Genus Scops [S. kennicottii].   <*Proc. Acad. Nat. Sci. Phila.*, xix, 1867, pp. 99, 100.

1867. WARD, H.   Snowy Owl [in Caithness] and Honey Buzzard [in Coventry].   <*Zoologist*, 2d ser., ii, 1867, p. 912.

1868. ALLEN, J. A.   Notes on the Red and Mottled Owls [Scops asio].   <*Am. Nat.*, ii, 1868, pp. 327–329.

The question discussed and their identity snown.

1868. ANON.   Snowy Owl in Inverness-shire.   <*Zoologist*, 2d ser., iii, 1868, p. 1457.

From the 'Inverness Advertiser.'

1868. FOWLER, A.   The Mottled Owl [Scops asio].   <*Am. Nat.*, ii, 1868, p. 109.

Continues the controversy between himself and E. A. Samuels (*op. cit.*, i, 1867, p. 496, and ii, 1868, p. 47).

1868. GURNEY, J. H., JR.   Snowy Owls in Shetland.   <*Zoologist*, 2d ser., iii, 1868, p. 1374

1868. HARVIE-BROWN, J. A.   Snowy Owl off the Scotch Coast.   <*Zoologist*, 2d ser., iii, p. 1058.

1868. MAYNARD, C. J.   The Mottled Owl [Scops asio] in confinement.   <*Am. Nat.*, ii, 1868, pp. 73–77.

Extended notice, with introductory note by E. A. Samuels.

1868. RATHVON, S. S.   The Barn Owl [Strix pratincola] in Pennsylvania.   <*Am. Nat.*, ii, 1868, p. 489.

Account of a nesting place at Lancaster, Pa.

1868. SCLATER, P. L., *and* SALVIN, O.   Descriptions of New Species of Birds of the Families Dendrocolaptidæ, Strigidæ, and Columbidæ.   <*P. Z. S.*, xxxvi, 1868, pp. 53–60, pl. v, woodcc.

The new Owls described are *Syrnium fulvescens*, p. 58, and *Scops barbarus*, p. 56, woodcut; and a synopsis of 7 spp. of the latter genus is also given.

1868. SCLATER, P. L., *and* SALVIN, O.   Descriptions of New or Little-known American Birds of the Families Fringillidæ, Oxyrhamphidæ, Bucconidæ, and Strigidæ.   <*P. Z. S.*, xxxvi, 1868, pp. 322–329, pl. xxix.

The Owl described and figured is *Gymnoglaux lawrencii*, p. 328, pl. xxix; a synonymatic synopsis of 3 spp. of this genus is also given.

1868. WOOD, W.   The Mottled Owl [Scops asio].   <*Am. Nat.*, ii, 1868, pp. 370–374.

On the changes of plumage, and habits.

1868. WRIGHT, C.   A Comical Owl [Glaucidium siju].   <*Am. Nat.*, ii, 1868, pp. 420–422.

Habits of an individual in confinement.

1869. BREWSTER, W.   The Mottled Owl again.   <*Am. Nat.*, iii, 1869, pp. 334, 335.

Notes on the habits of *Scops asio* in captivity.

1869. CANFIELD, C. S.   Habits of the Burrowing Owl of California [Athene cunicularia].   <*Am. Nat.*, ii, 1869, pp. 583–586.

Chiefly on the kind of association with *Spermophilus beecheyi*, and on the nesting.

1869. EULER, C.   Notes on the Brazilian species of Strigidæ. $<$ J. f. O., xvii, 1869, pp. 242–249.

1869. GUNN, T. E.   Early Nesting of the Barn Owl in Norfolk. $<$ Zoologist, 2d ser., iv, 1869, p. 1721.

1869. HÜGEL, A. DE.   Snowy Owl in Ross-shire. $<$ Zoologist, 2d ser., iv, 1869, p. 1863.

1869. LINDEN, C. S.   Nyctale albifrons [i. e., N. acadica juv.]. $<$ Am. Nat., iii, 1869, p. 556.
    Capture of an individual at Buffalo, New York.

1870. ANON.   Nos Hiboux. $<$ Naturaliste Canadien, ii, 1870, pp. 197–206, pl. i.
    Sur les Strigidæ du Canada. Pl. I, Syrnium nebulosum (d'après Audub.).

1870. CLIFTON, Lord.   Supposed [entirely uncertain] Occurrence of the American Mottled Owl [Scops] at Cobham, Kent. $<$ Zoologist, 2d ser., v, 1870, p. 2138.

1870. CLIFTON, Lord.   Supposed Occurrence of Strix asio in Kent. $<$ Zoologist, 2d ser., v, 1870, p. 2343.
    Reaffirmed.

1870. GURNEY, J. H.   Supposed Occurrence of the American Mottled Owl [Scops asio] in Kent. $<$ Zoologist, 2d ser., v, 1870, p. 2221.
    Leaves it open.

1870. HADFIELD, H.   Supposed Occurrence of the American Mottled Owl [Scops asio] in Kent. $<$ Zoologist, 2d ser., v, 1870, p. 2181.
    Doubtful.

1870. HADFIELD, H.   Supposed Occurrence of Strix asio in Kent. $<$ Zoologist, 2d ser., v, 1870, p. 2382.
    Criticises his lordship severely. Editor interferes to stay further proceedings.

1870. HAWKINS, H. S.   [On the nesting of Nyctea nivea in Labrador.] $<$ Ibis, 2d ser., vi, 1870, p. 298.

1870. STREETS, T. H.   [On asymmetry in the skull of an owl.] $<$ Proc. Acad. Nat. Sci. Phila., 1870, p. 73.

1871. ANON.   Hiboux [se montrent très communs à Quebec]. $<$ Naturaliste Canadien, iii, 1871, p. 28.

1871. ASHBY, R.   Snowy Owl in County Mayo. $<$ Zoologist, 2d ser., vi, 1871, p. 2765.

1871. CLIFTON, Lord.   Note on the alleged Identity of the American Red Owl [Scops asio] with the Mottled Owl [Scops asio]. $<$ Zoologist, 2d ser., vi, 1871, p. 2606.
    Returns to the charge with a flank movement.

1871. COLLETT, R.   On the Asymmetry of the Skull in Strix tengmalmi. $<$ P. Z. S., xxxvi, 1871, pp. 739–743, woodcc.

1871. HADFIELD, H.   Mottled and Red Owl [Scops asio]. $<$ Zoologist, 2d ser., vi, 1871, pp. 2680, 2681.
    Flank movement ineffectual; charge resumed. Editor dismisses both belligerents forever.

1871. KESSLER, G.   Die Schnee-Eule [Nyctea nivea] auf Hiddens-Oee erlegt. $<$ J. f. O., xix, 1871, p. 224.

1871. VERRILL, A. E.   Occurrence of Kirtland's Owl [Nyctale "albifrons," i. e., N. acadica juv.] in Maine. $<$ Am. Nat., v, 1871, p. 119.

1872. COLLETT, R.   Om Kraniets Assymetri hos Nyctala tengmalmi. $<$ Vidensk. Selsk. Forh. Christ., 1872, pp. 68–73, woodcc.
    Mainly a translation of his paper in P. Z. S., 1871, p. 739.

1872. COUES, E.   A New Bird [Glaucidium ferrugineum] to the United States. $<$ Am. Nat., vi, 1872, p. 370.

1872. ELLIOT, D. G.   On Nyctale kirtlandi. $<$ Ibis, 3d ser., ii, 1872, pp. 48–52.
    Identifies it with N. tengmalmi; full synonymy and description. But cf. Ridgway, Am. Nat., 1872, pp. 283–285.

1872. GURNEY, J. H., JR.   Snowy Owl at Southrepps, Norfolk.   < *Zoologist*, 2d ser., vii, 1872, p. 2912.

1872. RIDGWAY, R.   Relationship of the American White-fronted Owl.   < *Am. Nat.*, vi, 1872, pp. 283–285.

> Critical examination (with ref. to Elliot, *Ibis*, Jan., 1872) of *N. albifrons*, which is determined to be *N. acadica* juv.   Characters and synonyms of this species and *N. tengmalmi.*

1872. WHITAKER, J., JR.   Abundance of Shorteared Owls in Nottinghamshire.   < *Zoologist*, 2d ser., vii, 1872, p. 2992.

1873. A[LLEN], J. A.   The White-fronted Owl in Canada.   < *Am. Nat.*, vii, 1873, pp. 427–429.

> Maintains that this is *Nyctale acadica* juv.

1873. RIDGWAY, R.   Revision of the . . . and the Strigine Genus, Glaucidium.   < *Proc. Boston Soc. Nat. Hist.*, xvi, 1873, pp. 73–106.

> For full title and comment, see under FALCONIDÆ, same date and author.

1873. WHITAKER, J., JR.   Shorteared Owl in Nottinghamshire.   < *Zoologist*, 2d ser., viii, 1873, p. 3489.

1874. COUES, E.   Pet Owls [Bubo virginianus].   < *Am. Sportsman*, iii, 1874, p. 354.

1874. GRATOR, A.   Captive Owl fed by its Mate.   < *Am. Sportsman*, iii, 1874, p. 213.

1874. GURNEY, J. H.   Nidification of the Snowy Owl in Confinement.   < *Zoologist*, 2d ser., ix, 1874, p. 4154.

1874. HUDSON, W. H.   On the Habits of the Burrowing Owl (Pholeoptynx cunicularia).   < *P. Z. S.*, xlii, 1874, pp. 308–311.

1874. RIDGWAY, R.   Discovery of a Burrowing Owl in Florida.   < *Am. Sportsman*, iv, No. 14, July 4, 1874, p. 216, fig. 1.

> Description of *Speotyto cunicularia* var. *floridana*, var. n., with account of habits.   Remarks upon geographical distribution of American birds, and peculiarities of Florida in this respect.

1874. RIDGWAY, R.   Two Rare Owls [Syrnium occidentale, Micrathene whitneyi] from Arizona.   < *Am. Nat.*, vii, No. 4, Apr., 1874, pp. 239, 240.

> The article includes a notice of *Asturina plagiata.*

1875. ANON [EDITORIAL].   [Capture of Speotyto hypogæa in New York City.]   < *Forest and Stream*, v, Aug. 12, 1875, p. 4.

1875. DEANE, R.   Occurrence of the burrowing Owl in [Newburyport,] Massachusetts.   < *Rod and Gun*, vi, May 15, 1875, p. 97.

> Read before *Nutt. Ornith. Club*, May 6; notes also other rarities.

1875. GURNEY, J. H.   On the Snowy Owl [Nyctea nivea] nesting in Confinement.   < *Zoologist*, 2d ser., x, Aug., 1875, p. 4573.

1875. GURNEY, J. H.   Further Note [Zool., s. s., 4573] on the Young of the Snowy Owl [Nyctea scandiaca] hatched in Confinement.   < *Zoologist*, 2d ser., x, Oct., 1875, pp. 4663, 4664.

1875. GURNEY, J. H.   [On the breeding of Nyctea nivea in confinement.]   < *Ibis*, 3d ser., v, 1875, pp. 517, 518.

1875. "PETE."   The Great Horned Owl (Bubo virginianus) [attacks a dog].   < *Rod and Gun*, vii, Dec. 11, 1875, p. 163.

1875. RIDGWAY, R.   More About the Florida Burrowing Owl [Speotyto cunicularia var. floridanus].   < *Rod and Gun*, vi, Apr. 3, 1875, p. 7.   (See also *Am. Sportsman* for July 4, 1874.)

1875. SHARPE, R. B.   Contributions to a History of the Accipitres.   The Genus Glaucidium.   < *Ibis*, 3d ser., v, 1875, pp. 35–59, pll. i, ii.

> Elaborate, critical, with special reference to R. Ridgway's paper on same subject (*Pr. Bost. Soc.*, xvi, 1873, pp. 91–106).   9 spp. *G. griseiceps*, p. 41, pl. ii, f. 2; *G. ridgwayi*, p. 58, spp. nn.; pl. i, *G. gnoma;* pl. ii, f. 1, *G. pumilum.*

1875. SHARPE, R. B.   Contributions to a History of the Accipitres.   The Genus Strix of Linnaeus, and its Type.   < *Ibis*, 3d ser., v, 1875, pp. 324–328.

> *Strix* is left for *S. flammea.*   But see especially NEWTON, *Ibis*, 1876, pp. 94–104.

1875. SHARPE, R. B.   Catalogue | of the | Striges, | or | Nocturnal Birds of Prey, | in the | collection | of the | British Museum. | By R. Bowdler Sharpe. | London: | printed by order of the Trustees. | 1875. 1 vol. 8vo. pp. i–xii, 1–326, pll. i–xv, and numberless cuts in text.

This is the second vol. of the new Catalogue of the Birds of the British Museum, entitled as follows: Catalogue | of the | Birds | of the | British Museum. | Volume II. | London: | printed by order of the Trustees. | 1875. It catalogues 1,090 specimens of Owls, of which there are in the Museum 153 species, leaving 37 desiderata of the 190 spp. supposed to be known. The plan of the work, as was, that on the *Falconidæ*, which forms Vol. I, is much more highly developed than was that of the old Brit. Mus. Catalogues, being in fact a considerable monograph of the birds of which the work treats. The author regards the *Striges* as an order, which he divides into two families, *Bubonidæ* and *Strigidæ*, according to the structure of the feet and sternum; the latter family containing only the genera *Strix* ("Barn Owls") and *Phodilus*. The *Bubonidæ* are divided into the two subfamilies, *Buboninæ* and *Syrniinæ*, according to the structure of the ear-conch and facial disc. Analyses of all the genera are given, and the species are very elaborately described, with extensive synonymy, geographical distribution, and critical comment. Fourteen genera of *Buboninæ* and three of *Syrniinæ* are recognized. Analytical keys to the species, as well as to the genera, are presented. Whatever may be said of the author's general attitude in classification, and in discrimination of species, his work is obviously very carefully and faithfully done.

The following appear to be new names: *Scops stictonotus*, p. 54; *S. rufipennis*, p. 60; *S. bouruensis*, p. 73; *S. albiventris*, p. 78; *S. guatemalæ*, p. 112; *Syrnium spilonotum* ("Gray, descr. nulla"), p. 277.

The plates are as follows: I, *Scotopelia bouvieri*. II, *Bubo shelleyi*. III, f. 1, *Scops capensis*; f. 2, *S. stictonotus*. IV, f. 1, *S. malayanus*; f. 2, *S. gymnopodus*. V, *S. magicus*. VI, *S. leucospilus*. VII, f. 1, *S. morotensis*; f. 2, *S. bouruensis*. VIII, f. 1, *S. albiventris*; f. 2, *S. mendanensis*. IX, *S. guatemalæ*. X, *S. hypogramma*. XI, f. 1, *Ninox hantu*; f. 2, *N. ochracea*. XII, f. 1, *N. fusca*; f. 2, *N. squamipila*. XIII, f. 1, *Glaucidium cobanense*; f. 2, *G. tephronotum*. XIV, *Strix flammea*.

1875. "SPEOTYTO FLORIDANUS." Adventures of a Scientific Owl. < *Am. Sportsman*, v, Mar. 27, 1875, p. 401.

Humorous history of *Speotyto floridanus*. The bird, confined in the Smithsonian Tower, destroyed the type specimen *Helminthophaga leucobronchialis;* cf. COUES, *B. C. V.*, pt. i, 1878, p. 213.

1875. "WOLVERENE." My Owl [Scops asio], etc. < *Am. Sportsman*, v, 1875, Feb. 20, p. 347.

1876. ANON. [Nyctea nivea unusually abundant at Boston.] < *Forest and Stream*, vii, Nov. 23, 1876, p. 245. (See p. 261.)

1876. ANON. [Nyctea nivea at Norfolk, Va., and in South Carolina.] < *Forest and Stream*, vii, Dec. 7, 1876, p. 276. (See pp. 245, 261.)

1876. BOIES, A. H.   A Wary Owl [Nyctea nivea?]. < *Rod and Gun*, ix, Nov. 25, 1876, p. 116.

1876. "CAU." The Snowy Owls [at Boston]. < *Forest and Stream*, vii, Nov. 30, 1876, p. 261. (See p. 245.)

1876. CLARK-KENNEDY, A. J.   Barn Owl and Shrew. < *Zoologist*, 2d ser., xi, May, 1876, pp. 4922, 4923.

1876. DUNBAR, S. M.   Bad Place for Owls. < *Rod and Gun*, ix, Nov. 25, 1876, p. 116.

Various species at Baldwinsville, N. Y.

1876. GATCOMBE, J.   Occurrence of the Snowy Owl on Dartmoor. < *Zoologist*, 2d ser., xi, May, 1876, pp. 4921, 4922.

1876. GURNEY, J. H., JR.   Claws of the Hawk Owl. < *Zoologist*, 2d ser., xi, Feb., 1876, p. 4795.

1876. GURNEY, J. H., JR.   Barn Owl and Shrew. < *Zoologist*, 2d ser., xi, Apr., 1875, p. 4871.

1876. GURNEY, J. H., JR.   Barn Owl and Rat. < *Zoologist*, 2d ser., xi, Apr., 1876, p. 4871.

1876. GURNEY, J. H., JR.   On the Snowy Owl Nesting in Confinement. < *Zoologist*, 2d ser., xi, Aug., 1876, pp. 5041, 5042.

1876. HOWELL, T. H.   The Short-eared Owl [in Illinois].   *< Forest and Stream*, vii, Nov. 30, 1876, p. 261.   (See p. 342.)

1876. "J. B. S."   The Arctic Owl [Nyctea nivea?].   *< Forest and Stream*, vii, Nov. 16, 1876, p. 230.

1876. MITFORD, R.   Barn Owl and its Castings.   *< Zoologist*, 2d ser., xi, Mar., 1876, p. 4832.
>Cf. *op. cit.*, p. 4870.

1876. MITFORD, R.   Owl-pellets: Correction of an Error.   *< Zoologist*, 2d ser., xi, Apr., 1876, p. 4870.
>Cf. *op. cit.*, p. 4832.

1876. MURRAY, H. B.   Snowy Owl in County Fermanagh.   *< Zoologist*, 2d ser., xi, Apr., 1876, p. 4871.

1876. NEWTON, A.   On the Assignation of a Type to Linnæan Genera, with especial reference to the Genus Strix.   *< Ibis*, 3d ser., vi, Jan., 1876, pp. 94–104.

>The opinion expressed by the writer (*Yarr. Br. B.*, 4th ed., i, p. 150) having been demurred to by Salvin (*Ibis*, 1875, pp. 66, 67) and Sharpe (*ibid.*, pp. 324–328), this occasion is taken to reconsider the matter, and reiterate the views on nomenclature already expressed.   It is an important paper in its bearing on the general question, discussing certain principles touching nomenclature at large, aside from the special case of *Strix*.   The author has decided views on the subject, and adheres to certain rules with such thorough consistency that he scarcely provides for some emergencies which may arise, and appear to many persons to require some elasticity of application of a principle he would make inflexible.   He fortifies his position with his usual cogency of argument and his conspicuous scholarly attainments.
>
>Prof. Newton finds that, among the 78 genera of Linn. *S. N.*, 1766, there are only 12 which Linnæus can be considered to have invented: *Rhamphastos*, *Buceros*, *Procellaria*, *Diomedea*, *Phaeton*, *Palamedea*, *Mycteria*, *Cancroma*, *Parra*, *Didus*, *Menura*, *Pipra*.   He doubts not that had Linnæus known our modern practice, he would have designated as the type of each of his genera that species to which the name he adopted as generic had formerly been specifically applied; this seeming so obvious that he wonders at G. R. Gray and others who invented the arbitrary rule of selecting the first-named Linnæan species as the type of the genus under which it stands.   He finds it curious that so few Linnæan genera, such as *Vultur*, *Falco* and *Psittacus* (and 9 others) had been used by pre-Linnæan writers in a generic sense.   The authors whence Linnæus derived his genera are Gesner, Belon, Aldrovandus, Clusius, Johnston, Brown, Barrére, Klein, Moehring, Brisson, and perhaps one or two others.
>
>Following out his principle, the author determines the types of 56 Linnæan genera to be as follows (to save space I simply couple the generic and specific terms): *Strix stridula, Lanius* excubitor, *Buphaga* africana, *Crotophaga* ani, *Corvus* corax, *Oriolus* galbula, *Paradisea* apoda, *Bucco* capensis, *Cuculus* canorus, *Jynx* torquilla, *Picus* martins, *Sitta* europæa, *Alcedo* ispida, *Merops* apiaster, *Upupa* epops, *Certhia* familiaris, *Trochilus* colubris, *Alca* torda, *Procellaria* pelagica, *Diomedea* exulans, *Pelecanus* onocrotalus, *Plotus* anhinga, *Phaeton* æthereus, *Rhynchops* nigra, *Sterna* hirundo, *Phoenicopterus* ruber, *Platalea* leucorodia, *Mycteria* americana, *Cancroma* cochlearia, *Ardea* cinerea, *Tantalus* loculator, *Recurvirostra* avocetta, *Hæmatopus* ostralegus, *Fulica* atra, *Parra* jacana, *Rallus* aquaticus, *Psophia* crepitans, *Otis* tarda, *Struthio* camelus, *Didus* ineptus, *Pavo* cristatus, *Meleagris* gallopavo, *Crax* alector, *Phasianus* colchicus, *Numida* meleagris, *Alauda* arvensis, *Sturnus* vulgaris, *Turdus* viscivorus, *Ampelis* garrulus, *Loxia* curvirostra, *Tanagra* tatao, *Fringilla* cœlebs, *Muscicapa* grisola, *Pipra* leucocilla, *Hirundo* rustica, *Caprimulgus* europæus.
>
>Out of those 56 genera, only *Strix* and three or four others have, from the author's way of regarding them, a type other than that commonly assigned to them.
>
>The case of *Strix* is then elaborately discussed, and the author maintains, in summing his answer to his critics,
>
>"(1) That the type, according to the modern notion, of the Linnæan genus *Strix*, is clearly and indisputably *S. stridula.*
>
>"(2) That in subdividing a genus Brisson's right to affix its original name to the portion of it he chose is not affected by his exceptional position as regards specific names, and that the type of his restricted genus *Strix* is also *S. stridula.*
>
>"(3) That should ornithologists, in the teeth of the law, persist in disregarding this right, there is a strong probability, which may at any moment become a certainty, of its being indefeasably established without reference to any exception whatever."

1876. NICHOLLS, H.   Abundance of the Shorteared Owl near Kingsbridge.   *< Zoologist*, 2d ser., xi, Mar., 1876, pp. 4831, 4832.

1876. RIDGWAY, R.   The Genus Glaucidium.   *< Ibis*, 3d ser., vi, Jan., 1876, pp. 11–17, pl. i.

> *Cf.* Ridway, *Proc. Bost. Soc.*, xvi, 1873, pp. 91–106, and Sharpe, *Ibis*, 3d ser., v, Jan., 1875, pp. 35–39; the latter being a review of the former. "The present paper represents the conclusions arrived at after a careful reconsideration of the subject, with much additional material, and the benefit of Sharpe's monograph, . . ." The author here allows *GG. gnoma, jardini, nanum, ferrugineum, pumilum,* and *siju,* all of which are analyzed, and several of which are described at length, with synonymy. The plate gives *G. jardini,* in its two phases of coloration.

1876. [SALVIN, O.]   [Notice of Sharpe's Catalogue of the Striges in the British Museum.]   *< Ibis*, 3d ser., vi, Apr., 1876, pp. 273, 274.

1876. SHARPE, R. B.   On the Geographical Distribution of Barn Owls.   *< Rowl. Orn. Misc.*, pt. iv, May, 1876, pp. 269–298, 3 maps; pt. v, Oct., 1876, pp. 1–21.

> In this article Mr. Sharpe goes much further into the subject of the distribution, local names, etc., of *Strix flammea* and its allies, than he did in the *Brit. Mus. Cat.*, ii, pp. 294–296, where his general conclusions are stated. He divides the birds into the true Barn Owls and the Grass Owls, of which latter two African and Asiatic species are known. Map I shows the distribution of the different races of *Strix flammea;* Map II the ranges of *S. novæ hollandicæ, S. tenebricosa,* and *S. castanops;* Map III, of *S. candida, S. capensis,* and *S. thomensis*—these three being the Grass Owls.

1876. SHARPE, R. B.   [Remarks on Exhibition of a British-killed specimen of Surnia ulula.]   *< P. Z. S.*, Apr. 4, 1876, pp. 334, 335.

1877. ANON.   [Nyctea nivea on its southward migration invariably accompanied by Ptarmigans.]   *< Forest and Stream*, viii, Feb. 22, 1877, p. 33.

1877. BREWER, T. M.   A new Form of Surnia [ulula] to New England.   *< Bull. Nutt. Ornith. Club*, ii, No. 3, July, 1877, p. 78.

1877. COALE, H. K.   Notes on [occurrences, etc., of] Nyctale acadica.   *< Bull. Nutt. Ornith. Club*, ii, No. 3, July, 1877, pp. 83, 84.

1877. DEANE, R.   Probable Breeding of the Acadian Owl (Nyctale acadica) in Massachusetts.   *< Bull. Nutt. Ornith. Club*, ii, No. 3, July, 1877, p. 84.

1877. DEANE, R.   Unusual abundance of the Snowy Owl (Nyctea scandiaca) in New England.   *< Bull. Nutt. Ornith. Club*, ii, No. 1, Jan., 1877, p. 9–11.

1877. FRAZAR, A. M.   The Mottled Owl [Scops asio] as a Fisherman.   *< Bull. Nutt. Ornith. Club*, ii, No. 3, July, 1877, p. 80.

1877. RAGSDALE, G. H.   An Inquiry [concerning identity of supposed Speotyto cunicularia var. hypogæa, Cs.].   *< Forest and Stream*, viii, Feb. 22, 1877, p. 33.

1877. "R. T. G." [*and* EDITOR].   A tough owl [colliding with railway train].   *< Forest and Stream*, vii, Feb. 1, 1877, p. 405.

1877. [SCLATER, P. L.]   [Note on the abundance of Nyctea nivea in Europe and America in the winter of 1876–77.]   *< P. Z. S.*, Jan. 2, 1877, p. 1.

1877. [SCLATER, P. L.]   [On addition of a Mexican Eared Owl (Asio mexicanus) to the Society's Menagerie.]   *< P. Z. S.*, Mar. 6, 1877, pp. 159, 160.

> Important synonymatic note on the name here used.

1877. [SCLATER, P. L., *and* SALVIN, O.]   Irruption of Snowy Owls [Nyctea nivea] from the North.   *< Ibis*, 4th ser., i, Jan., 1877, pp. 131, 132.

> Occurring in the United States.

1878. ANON.   The Acadian Owl [Nyctale acadica].   *< The Oölogist*, iv, No. 5, July, 1878, p. 38.

> Note of its habits as observed in Central New York.

1878. ABBOTT, C. C.   The barn owl.   *< The Country*, i, Mar. 2, 1878, p. 260.

1878. ALLEN, C. A.   The Pygmy Owl (Glaucidium californicum).   *< Bull. Nutt. Ornith. Club*, iii, No. 4, Oct., 1878, p. 193.

> Note of habits. Mobbed by small birds.

1878. [FITCH, E. H.]   The Great Grey Owl. (Syrnium cinereum.)   *< The Journ. of Sci.* (Toledo, Ohio), 2d ser., i, No. 5, Aug., 1878, cut.

> Popular biography, with an excellent figure.

1878. JASPER, T. The Barred Owl (Syrnium nebulosum). < *The Oölogist*, iv, No. 3, May, 1878, pp. 21, 22.

A notice of the habits of this species, from his ' Birds of North America,' Part 6.

1878. LAWRENCE, G. N. On the Members of the Genus Gymnoglaux. < *Ibis*, 4th ser., ii, Apr., 1878, pp. 184–187.

The author maintains "three well-marked species,"—*nudipes* Daud., from Porto Rico; *newtoni* Lawr., from St. Croix and St. Thomas; and *lawrencei*, S. and S., from Cuba,—which are described and compared. Editors incline to differ.

1878. RIDGWAY, R. A Review of the American Species of the Genus Scops. < *Proc. U. S. Nat. Mus.*, i, 1878, pp. 85–117.

This is an elaborate article, in which the several American species are described at full length and critically discussed, upon more material than appears to have been commanded by previous writers. The six species recognized are thrown into three groups, according to the feathering of the feet.—A, *S. nudipes* alone, with toes and lower half or more of tarsus bare; B, with *SS. brasilianus, barbarus,* and *flammeolus,* with toes alone, or merely lower end of tarsus, completely naked; C, *SS. asio* and *cooperi* (n. sp., p. 116), with toes strongly bristled, sometimes densely feathered, at base. *S. nudipes* stands alone, without subspecies. Of *S. brasilianus* are recognized subspp. *brasilianus, atricapillus, ustus, guate-malæ,* and *cassini* (subsp. n., p. 102). *SS. barbarus* and *flammeolus* have no subspecies. Of *S. asio* are recognized subspp. *asio, maccalli, kennicotti, floridanus,* and *maxwelliæ. S. cooperi* has no subspp. Besides these six distinct forms, with their several races, the author treats *S. trichopsis,* Wagl., as a doubtful form. The descriptions given are very elaborate, and the synonymy is copious. Cf. *Ibis,* 1879, p. 209.

1878. [SCOTT, W. E. D.] [Attacks by Scops asio upon human beings.] < *The Country,* i, Feb. 23, 1878, p. 245.

1878. [SCOTT, W. E. D.] Winter Notes. Owls. < *The Country,* i, 1878, pp. 229, 244.

1878. "SUBSCRIBER." [Attack upon a man by] Another Vicious Owl. < *Forest and Stream,* x, Mar. 14, 1878, p. 95.

1878. WILLISTON, S. W. The Prairie Dog, Owl [Speotyto cunicularia hypogæa] and Rattlesnake. < *Am. Nat.,* xii, No. 4, Apr., 1878, pp. 203–208:

1879. ANON. [COOPER, J. G.?] The Great Gray Owl [Syrnium cinereum]. < *.Pacific Rural Press,* xvii, No. 1, Jan. 4, 1879, p. 9, fig.

Compiled account of the species, and a very good figure, from Baird, Brewer and Ridgway's *Hist. N. A. Birds.*

1879. BALLOU, W. H. Does the Snowy Owl [Nyctea nivea] Breed in the United States ? < *Am. Nat.,* xiii, No. 8, Aug., 1879, pp. 524, 525.

Asserting as a fact that the bird is seen along Lake Ontario throughout the year, and that in the "North Woods" of New York the writer once saw a young Snowy Owl not nearly full-fledged.

1879. COOPER, W. A. Notes on the Breeding Habits of the California Pygmy Owl (Glaucidium californicum), with a Description of its Eggs. < *Bull. Nutt. Ornith. Club,* iv, No. 2, Apr., 1879, pp. 86, 87.

Note by J. A. A[llen] refers to *Pr. Bost. Soc. Nat. Hist.,* xix, 1877, p. 232, as the only previous account of the eggs of this species, based on the same specimens as here described.

1879. DEANE, R. Capture of a Third Specimen of the Flammulated Owl (Scops flam-meola) in the United States, and first Description of its Nest. < *Bull. Nutt. Ornith. Club,* iv, No. 3, July, 1879, p. 188.

1879. HAWES, C. A. Nesting of the Barred Owl (Syrnium nebulosum). < *The Oölo-gist,* iv, No. 10, May, 1879, pp. 77, 78.

From original observations made near Boston, Mass.

1879. KING, M. B. A. A Family Arrangement [Bubo virginianus]. < *Science News,* i, No. 16, June 15, 1879, p. 256.

Occurrence of five young, apparently of different ages, in one nest.

1879. [WOOD, C. S.] Scops flammeola. < *Colorado Springs Gazette* [daily newspaper], Sept. 3, 1879.

First publication of the exhibition by C. E. Aiken of the fourth specimen of this species known from the United States.

Falconidæ.

[NOTE.—Among papers on Birds of Prey there are not a few relating to more than one of the recognized families of this order. As I have no head under which to range articles on *Raptores* in general, I bring under *Falconidæ* the titles relating to American Raptores, excepting those treating exclusively of *Strigidæ* or of *Cathartidæ.*]

1781. MERREM, B.   Anatomische Beschreibung des weissköpfigen Adlers.   < *Vermischte Abhandl. zur Thiergesch. Göttingen*, —, 1781, pp. 145-—.

Not seen—the title from Giebel.

1784. HUBER, [J.]   Observations | sur le vol des | Oiseaux de Proie, | Par M. Huber, de Genève. | Accompagnées de figures, dessinées par l'Auteur. | [Dessin.] | A Genève, | Chez Paul Barde, Imprimeur-Libraire. | — ¡ M. DCC. LXXXIV.
1 vol.   4to in size and by signatures, 8vo type-bed, pp. 51, with 6 folded pll.

1784. ÖDMAN, S.   Fiskljusens (Falconis Haliæti) Hushållning och Historia.   < *Kongl. Vetensk. Acad. Nya Handl.*, v, 1784, pp. 301-309.

1784. ÖDMAN, S.   Falco albicilla, Svet. Hafs-örn.   < *Nova Acta Reg. Soc. Sc. Upsal.*, iv, 1784, pp. 225-238.

Not seen.

1798. CARLSON, G. v.   Tal med Utkast till Falk-Slägtets [Falconidæ] i synnerhet de Svenska Arternas, Indelning och Beskrifning; hållet för K. Vet. Akad. vid Praesidii nedläggande d. 31 Jan. 1798 af Gust. v. Carlson.   Stockholm.   1798.   8vo.   pp. 30.

Not seen.

1798. LJUNGH, S. I.   Beskrifning på Svarta Örnen, Falco Fulvus canadensis [Aquila chrysaëtus], en ny Recrüt för Fauna Svecica.   < *Kongl. Vetensk. Acad. Nya Handl.*, xix, 1798, pp. 235-240.

In Swedish and Latin.

1801-02. WACHTMEISTER, H.   Försök til Svenske Falk-Arters beskrifning och bestämmande.   < *Kongl. Vetensk. Acad. Nya Handl.*, xxii, 1801, pp. 171-207 ; xxiii, 1802, pp. 249-274.

FF. albicilla, fulvus, nœvius?, haliaëtus, lagopus, islandicus, gyrfalco, milvus, buteo, apivorus, æruginosus, rufus, pp. 171-207, 1801.—*FF. palumbarius, gallinarius, peregrinus,* ——*?,* ——*?, subbuteo, tinnunculus, lithofalco, nisus,* pp. 249-274, 1802.

1809. CUVIER, FRÉD.   Du Pygargue et de l'orfraie, Falco pygargus et falco ossifragus, Linnæus.   < *Ann. du Mus. Hist. Nat.*, xiv, 1809, pp. 301-313.

Sur les noms que les anciens ont donné aux aigles dont ils ont parlé, et sur l'application de ces noms aux espèces que nous connoissons—Comparaisons des descriptions que les anciens ont donné—Le pygargue et l'orfraie paroissent être de la même espèce, et ce dernier nom doit être conservé.

1810. SAVIGNY, J. C.   Système | des | Oiseaux | de l'Egypte et de la Syrie, | présenté a l'Assemblée Générale de la Commission, | le 29 Août 1808, | Par Jules-César Savigny, Membre de l'Institut de l'Egypte. | [Dessin.] | A Paris, | de l'imprimerie Imperriale [sic]. | — | M. DCCC. X.   1 vol.   folio.   pp. 1-54, 1-16.

Petite édition, revue par l'auteur, tirée à 30 exemplaires.   Extraite de la *Descr. de l'Égypte, Partie Systématique, Oiseaux de l'Égypte et de la Syrie.*   Exemplaire dans la *Bibliothèque de l'Acad. des Sc. Nat. de la Philadelphie,* inscrite "à M. Latreille, comme un témoignage des sentimens de l'auteur" (autographe de l'auteur), plus tard présentée à l'Académie par M. le Dr. T. B. Wilson.

The copy of this extremely rare piece consists of 54 + 16 pages folio, including the two titles.   The full title is transcribed above.   The prel. title is: Oiseaux | de l'Égypte et de la Syrie. | — | Partie Systématique. | With it is bound 16 pages of "Observations," half-titled as follows: Observations | sur | le Système des Oiseaux | de l'Égypte et de la Syrie. | The 54 pages are extracted from the general work on Egypt, apparently for the purpose of following them up with the "Observations." These are in defense of the "Système," which had been critized in high places.

1810. SAVIGNY, J. C.—Continued.

The first order, *Raptores*, of Savigny's System, appeared in 1809 in the first livraison of the general work, and was intended to form part of a considerable treatise. It is here that we find the several new generic names of Savigny's for Birds of Prey. In this extract of 1810 the 17 genera which the author adopts are characterized on pp. 8, 9. They are as follows :—

VULTURES.—1. *Gyps.*   2. *Ægypius.*   3. *Neophron.*   4. *Phene.*

ACCIPITRES.—5. *Aquila.*   6. *Haliœetus* (observe the original orthography of this name). 7. *Milvus.*   8. *Circus.*   9. *Dœdalion.*   10. *Pandion.*   11. *Elanus.*   12. *Falco.*

ULULÆ.—13. *Noctua.*   14. *Scops.*   15. *Bubo.*   16. *Syrnium.*   17. *Strix.*

The species of these genera are given as follows ; they include many new names :— 1. *Gyps vulgaris*, p. 11.   2. *Ægypius niger*, p. 14.   3. *Neophron percnopterus*, p. 16.   **Phene** *ossifraga*, p. 18 ; 5. *P. gigantea*, p. 20.   6. *Aquila heliaca*, p. 22 ; 7. *A. fulva*, p. 22 ; 8. *A. melanœetos*, p. 24.   9. *Haliœetus nisus*, p. 26.   10. *Milvus ictinus*, p. 28 ; *M. œtolius*, p. 29.   12. *Circus œruginosus*, p. 30 ; 13. *C. rufus*, p. 31 ; 14. *C. gallinarius.*   15. *Dœdalion palumbarius*, p. 33 ; 16. *D. fringillarius*, p. 34.   17. *Pandion fluviatilis*, p. 36.   18. *Elanus cœsius*, p. 38. 19. *Falco tinnunculus*, p. 39 ; 20. *F. smirillus* ; 21. *F. communis.*   22. *Noctua glaux.*   23. *Scops ephialtes.*   24. *Bubo otus* ; 25. *B. ascalaphus.*   26. *Syrnium ululans.*   27. *Strix flammea.*

The text consists chiefly (besides brief characters of the species and genera) of a most elaborate and erudite synonymy of the names applied to these birds by ancient and modern authors.

The interesting copy handled is annotated in Savigny's handwriting, and was formerly presented by him to Latreille.

1818. WILSON, J.   Observations on some Species of the Genus Falco of Linnæus. < *Mem. Wernerian Nat. Hist. Soc.*, ii, pt. ii, 1818, pp. 569–617.

Read Feb., 1817.—An elaborate and carefully prepared criticism, not to be overlooked in any study of the subject, in spite of errors now fully apparent.—Specific distinction of *Falco fulvus* and *F. chrysaëtus* maintained.   Identity of *Falco albidus* Gm. and *F. variegatus* with *F. apivorus.*—Significance of the terms "Haggard" and "Gentle" or "Gentil."—Discussion of *Falco gentilis*, considered as "one of the numerous varieties of the "Common Falcon."—On *Falco palumbarius.*—History of *F. communis*, to which *FF. peregrinus, hornotinus, fuscus, leucocephalus, albus, gibbosus, rubens, maculatus*, and *niger*, all of Brisson, and perhaps some other names, are considered referable.

1820. KUHL, H.   [Gehirn einer] Aquila ossifraga (IV.).   < *Van Hasselt und Kuhl's Beit. zur Vergl. Anat.*, ii^te Abtheil., 1820, pp. 60, 61, pl. iv, f. 1–3, pl. v.

Pl. iv, f. 4–6, dasselbe des *Psittacus aestivus.*

1822. GREEN, J.   Falco leucocephalus—Bald Eagle.   < *Sillim. Am. Journ. Sci.*, iv, 1822, pp. 89, 90.

Note of capture of a specimen.

1823. SELBY, P. J.   Some Observations on the Falco chrysaëtos and F. fulvus of Authors, proving the Identity of the two supposed species.   < *Mem. Wernerian Nat. Hist. Soc.*, iv, pt. ii, 1823, pp. 428–433, fig. on p. 431.

With reference to J. Wilson's article in the same Memoirs, 1823, *q. v.*   The author makes the point plain.

1823. WILSON, J.   Remarks on the different Opinions entertained regarding the specific Distinction, or Identity, of the Ring-tailed and Golden Eagles.   < *Mem. Wernerian Nat. Hist. Soc.*, iv, pt. ii, 1823, pp. 434–448.

"Notwithstanding the arguments which have been brought forward by Mr SELBY and other competent judges," the writer adheres to his opinion of their specific distinctness, and supports his views at great length.

1824. [BREHM, C. L.]   Der nordische Seeadler. (Weisschwänzige Seeadler. Beinbrecher.)   Aquila borealis, Brehm. (Aquila albicilla et ossifraga. Falco albicilla et ossifragus, Linn.)   < *Ornis*, Heft i, 1824, pp. 1–19.

1824. VIGORS, N. A.   Sketches in Ornithology : or, [etc.]   < *Zool. Journ.*, i, 1824, pp. 308–446 ; [etc.]

This is the first instalment of a series of articles under the above head, running through several vols. and years of the periodical.   It is subtitled : On the Groups of the *Falconidæ.* (pp. 312–346.)

This portion treats of the *Falconidæ*, which are analyzed and classified upon the quinary plan, being divided into 5 stirpes—*Accipitrina, Falconina, Buteonina, Milvina, Aquilina.* Further comment upon the article is therefore superfluous.   *Harpagus*, g. n., p. 327.

1825. LESSON, [R.] P.   Quelques Observations sur les Falco chrysaetos et fulvus, qui prouvent l'identité de ces deux espèces; par P.-J. Selby. . . .   < *Féruss. Bull.*, 2ᵉ sect., vi, 1825, pp. 96, 97.
Extrait des *Mém. Wern. Soc.*, iv, pt. ii, 1823, pp. 428-433, *q. v.*

1825. LESSON, [R.] P.   Remarques sur diverses opinions émises sur la distinction spécifique, ou sur l'identité des Aigles commun et doré; par James Wilson. . . .   < *Féruss. Bull.*, 2ᵉ sect., vi, 1825, p. 97.
Extrait des *Mém. Wern. Soc.*, iv, pt. ii, 1823, pp. 434-448, *q. v.*

1825. LESSON, R. P.   Esquisses ornithologiques, ou observations sur les rapports qui existent dans un des groupes les plus nombreux en espèces d'oiseaux; par N.-A. Vigors, jun. . . .   < *Féruss. Bull.*, 2ᵉ sect., vi, 1825, pp. 406-408.
Extrait du *Zoological Journal*, i, Oct., 1824, pp. 308-446; cette partie des "Esquisses" renfermant la classification "quinaire" des Falconidés.

1825. VIGORS, N. A.   On a new genus of Falconidæ [Gampsonyx swainsonii, sp. n., p. 69].   < *Zool. Journ.*, ii, No. 5, Apr., 1825, pp. 65-70.
A subhead, being part of the 2d instalment of "Sketches in Ornithology; or," etc. Cf. *Féruss. Bull.*, 2ᵉ sect., vii, 1826, p. 106; *Isis*, 1830, pp. 839, 840.

1825. VIGORS, N. A.   On a new genus of Falconidæ [Nauclerus riocourii, p. 386, sp. n.].   < *Zool. Journ.*, ii, No. 7, Oct., 1825, pp. 385-387.
A subhead, being part of the fourth instalment (pp. 368-405) of the series of papers entitled "Sketches on Ornithology; or," etc. Cf. *Féruss. Bull.*, ix, 1826, p. 91; *Isis*, 1830, pp. 1042, 1043.

1826. LESSON, R. P.   Esquisses ornithologiques, etc., sur un genre nouveau des Falconidæ; par M. N. A. Vigors. . . .   < *Féruss. Bull.*, 2ᵉ sect., vii, 1826, p. 106.
Gampsonix (sic) *swainsonii.—Zool. Journ.*, ii, No. 5, Avril, 1825, p. 65.

1826. LESSON, [R. P.]   Sur un nouveau genre de la famille des Faucons; par Vigors. . . .   < *Féruss. Bull.*, 2ᵉ sect., ix, 1826, p. 91.
Nauclerus riocourii.—Extrait du *Zool. Journ.*, ii, 1825, pp. 385-387.

1829. AUDUBON, J. J.   Notes on the Bird of Washington (Falco washingtoniana), or Great American Sea Eagle (fig. 53).   < *Loudon's Mag. Nat. Hist.*, i, 1829, pp. 115-120.

1829. JOHNSON, J.   Vision of Birds of Prey.   < *Loudon's Mag. Nat. Hist.*, ii, 1829, p. 473.
From *Medico-Chirurgical Review*.

1829. "T. F."   An Arrangement of the different Species of Falcons found in Great Britain.   < *Loudon's Mag. Nat. Hist.*, i, 1829, pp. 217-221, figg. 85-90.
14 spp., under 6 sections.

1830. BENNETT, [E. T.]   [Polyborus ? hypoleucus, sp. n.]   < *P. Z. S.*, Dec. 14, 1830, p. 13.

1830. BREHM, C. L.   Die grossen Adler mit befiederten Füssen von Brehm.   < *Oken's Isis*, Bd. xxiii, 1830, pp. 96-106.
Aquila fulva, A. melanaetos, A. chrysaetos "Brehm".

1830. VIGORS, N. A.   Gampsonyx [swainsonii], eine neue Sippe der Falconiden.   < *Oken's Isis*, Bd. xxiii, 1830, pp. 839, 840.
Aus d. *Zool. Journ.*, ii, 1825, p. 65.

1830. VIGORS, N. A.   Nauclerus [riocourii], neue Sippe der Falconiden.   < *Oken's Isis*, Bd. xxiii, 1830, pp. 1042, 1043.
Uebers. d. *Zool. Journ.*, ii, 1825, p. 385.

1831. ANON.   The Bald Eagle [Haliaëtus leucocephalus].   < *D. J. Browne's The Naturalist*, i, No. xii, Dec., 1831, pp. 359-367.
Popular account, chiefly compiled from Wilson.

1831. AUDUBON, J. J.   An account of the habits of the American Goshawk (Falco palumbarius, Wils.).   < *Edinb. Journ. Nat. Geogr. Sci.*, iii, 1831, pp. 145-147.
Not seen.

1831. BENNETT, [E. T.]   [Remarks on two specimens of Polyborus hypoleucus which had been living in the Society's Garden.]   < *Philos. Mag.*, ix, 1831, pp. 63, 64.
From *P. Z. S.*, Dec. 14, 1830, p. 13.

1831. BLACKWALL, J.   On an undescribed Bird of the Family Falconidæ [Gampsonyx holmii].   < *Philos. Mag.*, x, 1831, pp. 264, 265.

1831. HOY, J. D.   Peregrine Falcon.   < *Loudon's Mag. Nat. Hist.*, iv, 1831, pp. 146, 147.
   Falco peregrinus at Thetford, England.

1832. [FRIES, B. F.]   Om Jagt-Falken [F. gyrfalco]. Med planche.   < *Tidsk. f. Jägare o. Naturf.*, i, 1832, pp. 352–363, med. kol. fig.
   Not seen ?

1832. HOY, J. D.   The White-tailed Eagle [Haliaëtus albicilla] breeds in Captivity.   < *Loudon's Mag. Nat. Hist.*, v, 1832, pp. 278, 279.

1832. "J. M."   Great Harpy Eagle.   < *Loudon's Mag. Nat. Hist.*, v. 1832, p. 452.
   One said to have been sent from Mobile, Florida (*i. e.*, Alabama), in Sept., 1828.

1832. R[AFINESQUE], C. S.   Description of a new Eagle from South America, Aquila dicronyx or Macarran Eagle.   < *Atlantic Journ. and Friend of Knowl.*, i, No. 2, 1832, p. 63.
   From Buenos Ayres; 3 feet long, expanse 9 feet, bill 4 inches, etc. Seen living in a collection. *Thrasaëti?*—or what ?

1832. SÖDERBERG, C.   Ornithologiska Bidrag.   < *Tidsk. f. Jägare o. Naturf.*, i, 1832, pp. 114–117, fig.
   Descr. *Haliaëti albicillæ*, ♂ juv., cum fig.

1833. HOLMSTEDT, J.   Underrättelse om en tam Hafsörn [Haliaëtus albicilla].   < *Tidsk. f. Jägare o. Naturf.*, ii, 1833, p. 476.

1833. HOY, J. D.   Observations on the Iceland and Ger Falcons (Falco islandicus), tending to show that these Birds are of two distinct Species.   < *Loudon's Mag. Nat. Hist.*, vi, 1833, pp. 107–110.

1834. BENNETT, [E. T.]   [Ueber Polyborus ? hypoleucus.]   < *Oken's Isis*, Bd. xxvii, 1834, p. 815.
   Auszug aus *Philos. Mag.*, ix, 1831, p. 63.

1834. BLACKWALL, J.   Neue Falke aus Brasilien [Gampsonyx holmii].   < *Oken's Isis*, Bd. xxvii, 1834, p. 830.
   Aus *Philos. Mag.*, Bd. ix, 1831, p. 264.

1834. "J. C."   Of the Forked-tail Kite.   < *Loudon's Mag. Nat. Hist.*, vii, 1834, p. 511.
   In Essex County, England.

1834. LAFRESNAYE, F. DE.   Cymindis.   Cymindis. Cuvier.   C. bec en hameçon.   C. hamatus. Illig., Temminck.   (En livrée particulière avant celle de l'adulte.)   < *Guér. Mag. de Zool.*, 4e année, 1834, classe ii, notice xx, pl. xx.

1834. LAFRESNAYE, F. DE.   Cymindis.   Cymindis. Cuv.   C. bec en croc.   C. uncinatus. Tem.   col. 103, 104 et 115 (En livrée jusqu'alors non décrite.)   < *Guér. Mag. de Zool.*, 4e année, classe ii, notice xxi, pl. xxi.

1834. LAFRESNAYE, F. DE.   Cymindis.   Cymindis. Cuvier.   C. a manteau noir. Cuv.— Petit autour de Cayenne. Buff.—Falco Cayennensis. L. Gmel.   (Dans la livrée qui précède celle de l'adulte, qui est la Buse mantelée, Falco pallatus, Pr. Max. Tem., col. 204; et le Cymindis busoïde, C. buteonides. Lesson, Traité, p. 55.)   < *Guér. Mag. de Zool.*, 4e année, 1834, classe ii, notice xxii, pl. xxii.

1836. ANON.   A Falco [Pandion] Haliætus L. shot near Oxford.   < *Loudon's Mag. Nat. Hist.*, ix, 1836, p. 597.

1836. DENNIS, G. E.   The Osprey [Pandion haliaëtus].   < *Loudon's Mag. Nat. Hist.*, ix, 1836, pp. 202, 203.
   Anecdote, from *Morning Chronicle*, Dec. 1, 1835.

1836. DUGMORE, H.   [Note on Haliaëtus albicilla in confinement.]   < *P. Z. S.*, iv, 1836, p. 49.

1836. TURNER, H.   Sea Eagle (Aquila [Haliaëtus] albicilla).   < *Loudon's Mag. Nat. Hist.*, ix, 1836, p. 203.
   From *Bury and Suffolk Herald*, Dec. 16, 1835.

1837. BREHM, C. L.   Ueber das Betragen der männlichen Raubvögel gegen ihr brütendes Weibschen und die Jungen.   < *Oken's Isis*, Bd. xxx, 1837, pp. 367–374.
Versammlung der Naturforscher und Aerzte zu Jena am 18. September 1836.

1837. HAMILTON, H.   [Letter announcing a donation of a Chilian Eagle.]   < *P. Z. S.*, v, 1837, p. 67.

1837. YARRELL, W.   [Exhibition of a Quill, filled with a species of Pediculus, from the wing of a Harpy Eagle (Thrasaëtus harpya).]   < *P. Z. S.*, v, 1837, p. 127.

1838. HANCOCK, J.   Occurrence of Falco Islandicus in England.   < *Annals of Nat. Hist.*, ii, 1838, p. 159.

1838. HANCOCK, J.   Remarks on the Greenland and Iceland Falcons, showing that they are distinct Species.   < *Annals of Nat. Hist.*, ii, 1838, pp. 241–250, pl. x.
Carefully distinguishing the two.   This article is usually referred to with much respect for its accuracy.

1838. ROBERTSON, C.   [Letter on the capture of a Peregrine Falcon at sea.]   < *P. Z. S.*, vi, 1838, p. 77.

1838. THOMPSON, W.   Golden and Sea Eagle, Aquila chrysaëtos and A. [Haliaëtus] albicilla [in Ireland].   < *Charlesw. Mag. Nat. Hist.*, ii, 1838, p. 164.

1838. THOMPSON, W.   Bald Eagle, Haliaëtus leucocephalus, Savig.   < *Charlesw. Mag. Nat. Hist.*, ii, 1838, pp. 164, 165.
Note of habits.

1838. TOWNSEND, T.   Capture of the White-tailed Eagle, (Falco albicilla: Penn. Mont. Haliætus albicilla, Selby), on the Suffolk Coast, February 22nd, 1838.   < *Charlesw. Mag. Nat. Hist.*, ii, 1838, pp. 292, 293.

1839. DUGMORE, H.   Capture of an Eagle [Haliaëtus albicilla] at Swaffham.   < *Charlesw. Mag. Nat. Hist.*, iii, 1839, p. 198.

1839. HANCOCK, J.   Remarks on the Greenland and Iceland Falcons.   < *Rep. Brit. Assoc. Adv. Sci. for* 1838, vii, 1839 (*Misc. Comm.*), p. 106.

1839. LAFRESNAYE, [F.] DE.   Nouvelle classification des oiseaux de proie ou rapaces.   < *Revue Zoologique*, ii, 1839, pp. 193–196.
Ire fam. *Vulturidæ;* 1re sousfam. *Didinæ,* 2e *Cathartinæ,* 3e *Vulturinæ,* 4e *Gypaetinæ;* IIe fam. *Falconidæ,* avec 7 sousfamilles; IIIe fam. *Gypoaeranidæ.*

1839. LESSON, R. P.   Tableau de la famille des oiseaux Accipitres (Raptores).   < *Revue Zoologique*, ii, 1839, pp. 132, 133.
Ire sect., *Diurnes,* 4 fam.; IIe sect., *Nocturnes,* 1 fam.

1839. WEISSENBORN, W.   Curious capture of a White-headed Eagle [Haliaëtus albicilla].   < *Charlesw. Mag. Nat. Hist.*, iii, 1839, pp. 197, 198.

1839. WIEGMANN, A. F. A.   Ueber den Seeadler (Falco [Haliaëtus] albicilla).   < *Preuss. Provinzlabl.*, xxii, 1839, pp. 525–536.
Mir nicht zugänglich.

1841. BELANY, J. C.   A | Treatise | upon | Falconry. | In two parts. | By | James Cockburn Belany. | [Quotations, 7 lines.] | Berwick-upon-Tweed:—printed for the author. | 1841.   1 vol.   8vo.   pp. i–xii, 1–278, 1–6; frontisp.
Part First. Containing Observations upon the Nature, Antiquity, and History of Falconry, pp. 1–116.
Part Second. Containing Notices of the different Hawks used in British Hawking, the Proper Method of Keeping, Training, and Flying the Birds, the Apparatus belonging to the Art, &c., pp. 117–277.
Terms in Falconry, pp. 1–6.

1841. JAMESON, R.   On the Affinities of the Falconidæ.   < *Calcutta Journ. Nat. Hist.*, i, 1841, pp. 307–324.   (Auch in d. *Isis*, 1843, pp. 810–812.)
Not seen.

1841. SCHLEGEL, H.   Abhandlungen | aus dem | Gebiete | der Zoologie und Vergleich-
enden Anatomie, | von | H. Schlegel. | — | 1 Heft. | — | Leiden, | A. Arnz &
Comp. | 1841. | Zu beziehen durch alle solide Buchhandlungen des In- und
Auslandes.   1 vol.   4to.   2 p. ll., pp. 1–44, 1–12, 1–20, 1 l., pll. i–xv.

> This consists of 3 separately paged articles, the first two upon *Cetacea*, the third (perhaps
> better citable separately) as follows: III. Beschreibung einiger neuen grossen Edelfalken,
> aus Europa und dem Nordlichen Afrika, pp. 1–20, pll. x–xv.—*Falco feldeggii*, p. 3, pll. x, xi, *F.
> tanypterus*, Licht., p. 8, pll. xii, xiii.—Fortzetzung: *F. jugger*, p. 13, pl. xv. Folgt schliesslich
> eine Uebersicht aller bekannten grossen Edelfalken: A, Langswänzige Arten, 9 spp.—1. *F.
> candicans*, Gm.; 1a, *F. c. islandicus*; 2, *F. gyrfalco*; 3, *F. subniger*, Gr.; 4, *F. mexicanus*, Licht.
> M. B., p. 15, sp. n.; 5, *F. hypoleucos*, Gould; 6, *F. tanypterus*, Licht.; 7, *F. lanarius*; 7a, *F. l.
> alphanet*, pl. xiv ; 7b, *F. l. cervicalis*, Licht. M. B., p. 17; 8, *F. saeer*; 9, *F. jugger.* B, Kurz-
> schwänzige Arten.—1, *F. communis;* 1a, *F. c. americanus*, p. 19; 1b, *F. c. australis*, p. 19; 1c,
> *F. c. indicus;* 1d, *F. c. minor ;* 2, *F. peregrinoides.*

1841. YARRELL, [W.]   [Eine Schwungfeder vom Harpy-Eagle (Harpyia destructor).]
< *Oken's Isis*, Bd. xxxiv, 1841, p. 942, 943.

> *Proc. Zool. Soc. Lond.*, Nov. 14, 1837, p. 127.

1842. HALDEMAN, S. S.   [Proposed Changes of Nomenclature of certain Genera.]
< *Proc. Acad. Nat. Sci. Phila.*, i, 1842, pp. 187, 188.

> In ornithology, one only—*Anopaia*, p. 188, g. n. = *Harpyia*, Cuv., preoccupied.

1842. LAFRESNAYE, [F.] DE.   Description d'un nouveau genre d'Oiseau de proie [Har-
pyhaliætus].   < *Revue Zoologique*, v, 1842, p. 173.

1842. LESSON, [R. P.]   Nouveau Genre d'Oiseau de proie [Carnifex].   < *Revue Zoologique*, v, 1842, pp. 378–380.

> *L'Écho du Monde Savant*, 9e année, p. 1081.
> Ce n'est qu' une synonyme de *Micrastur.*

1843. EDMONSTON, T., JR.   Note on the capture of the Sea Eagle (Haliaëtos albicilla)
in Shetland.   < *Zoologist*, i, 1843, pp. 36–39.

1843. HEPPENSTALL, J.   The Osprey, (Pandion Haliaëtos) [near Sheffield].   < *Zoologist*, i, 1843, pp. 14, 15.

1843. JAMESON, R.   Ueber die Verwandtschaften der Falconiden.   < *Oken's Isis*, Bd.
xxxvi, 1843, pp. 810–812.

> *Calcutta Journ. Nat. Hist.*, 1841, p. 307.

1844. FRASER, L.   [Description of three New Species of Birds.]   < *P. Z. S.*, Feb. 27,
1844, pp. 37, 38.

> Among them "*Lagopus*" *ferrugineus*, p. 37 = *Archibuteo ferrugineus* (Licht.) from Mexico.
> Very curiously, the two authors here concerned independently selected the same name for
> the species.   Lichtenstein has priority, having described his bird as *Falco (Buteo) ferrugi-
> neus* from California in 1839 (*Abhandl. Berlin. Akad. aus d. Jahre* 1838, p. 428.)

1844. FRASER, L.   [On three lately new Species of Birds.]   < *Ann. Mag. Nat. Hist.*,
xiv, 1844, pp. 452, 453.

> *Lagopus ferrugineus, Psittacus Timneh, Plyctolophus citrino-cristatus.* From *P. Z. S.*, Feb.
> 27, 1844, pp. 37, 38, *q. v.*

1844. GERBE, Z.   Note sur un OEuf d'Aigle, recueilli dans le département de l'Aube et
attribué avec doute à l'Aigle royal (Aquila chrysaetos).   < *Revue Zoologique*,
vii, 1844, pp. 440, 441.

1844. GRAY, G. R.   [List of Birds in the British Museum.   Part I.—Raptores.   London: 1844.]

> This is the date of the orig. ed., the title of which I cannot give, having yet to see a copy.
> There is a 2d ed., 1848, *q. v.*

1844. HANCOCK, J.   Bemerkungen über den Unterschied des grön- und isländischen
Falken.   < *Oken's Isis*, Bd. xxxvii, 1844, pp. 668–671.

> *Ann. Nat. Hist.*, Bd. ii, No. x, 1838, pp. 241–250, *q. v.*

1844. HARDY, J.   Quelques observations sur le Faucon pélerin, Falco peregrinus,
Linn., faites dans l'arrondissement de Dieppe.   < *Revue Zoologique*, vii, 1844,
pp. 289–291.

1844. HARRIS, £. [Exhibition of a specimen of Cymindis hamatus from Florida.] < *Proc. Acad. Nat. Sci. Phila.*, ii, 1844, p. 65.

1844. MANSELL, T. Occurrence of the Osprey [Pandion haliaëtus] near Farnham. < *Zoologist*, ii, 1844, p. 443.

1844. NEWTON, A. Note on the occurrence of the Sea Eagle [Haliaëtus albicilla] at Elden, near Thetford. < *Zoologist*, ii, 1844, p. 443.

1844. NORMAN, G. Note on the occurrence of the Rough-legged Buzzard [Archibuteo lagopus] at Hull. < *Zoologist*, ii, 1844, p. 491.

1845. BARLOW, J. W. Occurrence of the Golden Eagle [Aquila chrysaëtus] in Cheshire. < *Zoologist*, iii, 1845, p. 1022.

1845. BOLD, T. J. Occurrence of the Iceland Falcon [Falco islandicus] and Rough-legged Buzzard [Archibuteo lagopus] in Northumberland. < *Zoologist*, iii, 1845, p. 935.

    With quotation of more detailed statements from *Morning Chronicle*, Feb. 6, 1845.

1845. DES MURS, O. Notice sur le genre Aigle Aquila. < *Revue Zoologique*, viii, 1845, pp. 271–274.

1845. EDITORIAL. Falco islandicus [shot near the North Tyne]. < *Ann. Mag. Nat. Hist.*, xv, 1845, pp. 213, 214.

1845. GURNEY, J. H. The supposed Chaunting Falcon [= Circus cyaneus]. < *Zoologist*, iii, 1845, p. 1022.

1845. KAUP, J. J. Ueber Falken. Mit besonderer Berücksichtigung der im Museum der Senckenbergischen naturforschenden Gesellschaft aufgestellten Arten. < *Mus. Senckenb.*, Bd. iii, Heft iii, 1845, pp. 229–262.

    This article, which I have not seen, appears to be the first of several by this author on the same subject; it is noticed in *Isis*, 1846, pp. 315, 316, and may be regarded as the forerunner of the ,, Monographien der Genera der Falconidæ '' in *Isis*, 1847, pp. 39–80, 83–121, 161–212, 241–283, 325–386, 954, 955; 1848, pp. 772–774; ''Monograph of the *Falconidæ*'' in *Jard. Contr. Orn.*, 1849, pp. 68–121; 1850, pp. 51–80; and ,, Corrigirte Uebersicht der *Falconidæ*,'' in *Arch. f. Naturg.*, 1850, (i), pp. 27–41; *qq. vv.*—In the course of these several publications many new names are proposed, conferring some vitality upon a set of papers which would otherwise be only consulted now from motives of curiosity by one desiring to know to what lengths the quinarian craze may carry its victims. I give these new names, or many of them, under head of the *Isis* article, 1847–48, *q. v.* See also same author at 1849–50, and 1850.

1845. LAFRESNAYE, [F.] DE. Sur le Falco isidori, Desmurs; Revue Zool. 1845, p. 175. < *Revue Zoologique*, viii, 1845, pp. 209–211.

1845. ROBERTSON, C. [Ueber Falco peregrinus.] < *Oken's Isis*, xxxviii, 1845, p. 374.

    Proc. Zool. Soc. Lond., vi, 1838, p. 77.

1845. ROSS, F. W. L. Occurrence of the Osprey [Pandion haliaëtus] in Devonshire. < *Zoologist*, iii, 1845, p. 1190.

1845. SLADEN, E. Supposed occurrence of the Chanting Falcon ["Falco musicus"— *i. e.*, Circus cyaneus] in Suffolk. < *Zoologist*, iii, 1845, pp. 935, 936.

    From *Kentish Gazette*, Mar. 18, 1845.

1846. ANON. Ueber Falken mit besondere Berichtigung der im Museum der senkenbergischen naturforschenden Gesellschaft aufgestellten Arten von Dr. Kaup Inpector des zoologischen Museums zu Darmstadt. (Museum senkenbergianum. III.) 1845. 4. 231–262. < *Oken's Isis*, Bd. xxxix, 1846, pp. 315, 316.

1846. HALLOWELL, E. On the Anatomy [Osteology] of Harpyia destructor, Cuv., o: Harpy Eagle of South America. < *Proc. Acad. Nat. Sci. Phila.*, iii, 1846, pp 84–88.

1846. LAFRESNAYE, F. DE. Mélanges ornithologiques. < *Revue Zoologique*, ix, 1846 pp. 124–133.

    Sur les genres *Aviceda* (Swainson), *Lophotes* (Lesson), *Lépidogenys* (Gould), et sur deu nouvelles espèces du genre *Aviceda; A. verreauxii*, p. 130; *A. butéoïdes*, p. 133.

1846. THIENEMANN, F. A. L.   Kritische Revision der europäischen Jagdfalken.   < *Rhea,* Heft i, 1846, pp. 44–98, pll. i, ii.

,, Vortreffliche, die reiche Literatur des Gegenstandes kritisch bewältegende Arbeit."— 1, *Falco gyrfalco,* Alb. Mag., p. 50.   2, *F. cyanopus,* Gesn., p. 62, pll.   3, *F. rubeus* [sic], Alb. Mag., p. 72.   4. *F. gentilis,* p. 77.—*F. subbuteo,* p. 87; *F. æsalon,* p. 89; *F. sacer,* p. 91.—A. *F. sacer.*   B. *F. montanarius.*   C. *Falcones lanarii.*

1846. TYZENHAUZ, C.   Remarques sur les Aigles d'Europe.   < *Revue Zoologique,* ix, 1846, pp. 322–326.

7 espèces, des genres *Aquila* et *Haliaëtus.*

1846. WOLLEY, J.   Occurrence of the Rough-legged Buzzard [Archibuteo lagopus] in Nottinghamshire and Derbyshire.   < *Zoologist,* iv, 1846, p. 1247.

1847. ANON.   Occurrence of the Golden Eagle [Aquila chrsyaëtus] near Hungerford.   < *Zoologist,* v, 1847, p. 1695.

1847. CASSIN, J.   Description of a new rapacious Bird [Cymindis wilsonii] in the Museum of the Academy of Natural Sciences of Philadelphia.   < *Proc. Acad. Nat. Sci. Phila.,* iii, 1847, pp. 199, 200.

1847. CASSIN, J.   Description of a new rapacious Bird in the Museum of the Academy of Natural Sciences of Philadelphia.   < *Am. Journ. Sci.,* iv, 1847, pp. 285, 286.

Cymindis wilsonii; from *Proc. Acad. Nat. Sci. Phila.,* iii, 1847, p. 199.

1847. CASSIN, J.   Description of a new rapacious Bird in the Museum of the Academy of Natural Sciences of Philadelphia.   < *Ann. Mag. Nat. Hist.,* xx, 1847, p. 356.

Cymindis wilsonii; from *Am. Journ. Sci.,* Sept., 1847, p. 285.

1847. CASSIN, J.   Description of a new rapacious Bird in the Museum of the Academy of Natural Sciences of Philadelphia.   < *Journ. Acad. Nat. Sci. Phila.,* i, pt. i, Dec., 1847, pp. 21–23, pl. vii.

Cymnidis wilsonii, figured.   Cf. *Proc. Acad. Nat. Sci. Phila.,* Apr., 1847, p. 199.

1847. DES MURS, O.   Notice sur le Falco (Spizaetus) ornatus Daudin,. et l'Harpya (Spiz) braccata de Spix.   < *Revue Zoologique,* x. 1847, pp. 315–326.

S. spixii, sp. n. propos., p. 325.

1847–48. KAUP, J. J.   Monographien der Genera der Falconidae.   < *Oken's Isis,* Bd. xl, 1847, pp. 39–80, pll. i, ii; pp. 83–121, 161–212, 241–283, 325–386, 954, 955; xli, 1848, pp. 772–774.

Subfam. I. *Falconinæ—Hierax, Tinnunculus, Harpagus, Falco, Jeracidea.* II. *Milvinae— Ictinia, Nauclerus, Circus, Elanus, Milvus.* III. *Accipitrinæ—Spizaetus, Nisus, Geranospiza, Aster, Asturina.* IV. *Aquilinæ—Aquila, Helotarsus, Circaëtus, Pandion, Haliaetus.* V. *Buteoninæ—Buteo, Pernis, Polyborus, Rostrhamus, Ibicter* [sic].

Polihierax, p. 47; *Poecilornis* (Kaup, 1843), p. 49; *Tichornis* (Kaup, 1843), p. 51; *Aesalon,* p. 59; *Gennaia* (Kaup, 1845), p. 69; *Poecilopteryx,* p. 86; *Glaucopteryx,* p. 99; *Spilocircus,* p. 101; *Spizacircus,* p. 103; *Lophoictinia* (1845), p. 113; *Hydroictinia,* p. 114; *Gypoictinia,* p. 114; *Lophaetus,* p. 165; *Spizaetus,* p. 165; *Pternura,* p. 168; *Hieraspiza,* p. 169; *Tachyspiza,* p. 172; *Scelospiza,* p. 173; *Urospiza,* p. 180; *Geranospiza* (1846), p. 183; *Lophospiza* (1843), p. 187; *Leucospiza* (1843), p. 197; *Leucopternis,* p. 210; *Hieraetus,* p. 243; *Pteroaetus,* p. 245; *Onychaetus* (1843), p. 245; *Uroaetus,* p. 252; *Circaetus,* 256; *Ictinoaetus* (1843), p. 275; *Heteroaetus,* p. 278; *Pontaetus,* p. 279; *Thalassaetus,* p. 283; *Tachytriorchis,* p. 328; *Poecilopternis,* p. 329; *Ichthyoborus,* p. 333; *Regerhinus,* p. 344; *Odontriorchis,* p. 346; *Aetotriorchis,* p. 358, are some of Kaup's new or lately new genera.   See same author at 1845, 1849–50, and 1850.

Nachträge und kritische Uebersichten der vorhandenen Synopsen, pp. 360–363, über *Falco concolor* und *F. eleonorae.*—Systemat. Uebersicht, pp. 363–374.   Uebersicht der Arten Azara's, pp. 374–376.   Revision der von Vieillot in der *Ency. Méth.* aufgezahlten *Falconidæ,* pp. 376–383.   Erklärung der·Abbild., pp. 384–386.   Nachträge und Correctionen, pp. 954, 955.   Zusätze (1848), pp. 772–774.

1847. TSCHUDI, J. J. v.   The Gyr-Falcon [sic; i. e., Milvago chimango].   < *Zoologist,* v, 1847, p. 1806.

From "Travels in Peru".   Cf. *Zool.,* 2018.

1848. BOWLES, *Admiral.*   [Letter from, announcing the presentation of three living specimens of Haliaëtus aguia (Temm.), and a male Condor, by Rear-Admiral Sir George Seymour.]   < *P. Z. S.,* xvi, 1848, p. 112.

Bull. v, 4——16

1848. CARLETON, J. W.   Natural History of the Hawk Tribe.   Illustrated by A. Henning.   London: D. Bogue.   1848.   18mo.   pp. 112.

Not seen—title from Carus and Engelmann.

1848. DES MURS, O.   Complément de la notice sur la spécification distincte du Spizaetus braccatus (Harpya braccata, Spix) d'avec le Spizaetus ornatus (Falco ornatus, Daudin) et le Spizaetus tyrannus (Falco tyrannus, Temm.).   <Revue Zoologique, xi, 1848, pp. 35–39.

1848. [GRAY, G. R.]   List | of the | Specimens of Birds | in | the collection | of the | British Museum. | [By George Robert Gray.] | — | Second edition. | — | Part I.—Accipitres. | Printed by order of the Trustees. | London: 1848.   1 vol. sm. 12mo.   pp. i–viii, 1–120.

Orig. ed. 1844.   This is the list of the *Accipitres*, 2d ed., giving an extensive synonymy of each species and genus, and the localities whence were derived the specimens in the British Museum; being one of the several partial lists, or lists of particular groups, which preceded and led up to the same author's famous *Hand List*.

1848. JOHNSON, F. W.   Occurrence of the Rough-legged Buzzard (Falco [Archibuteo] lagopus) in Suffolk.   <Zoologist, vi, 1848, p. 2063.

1848. LAFRESNAYE, [F.] DE.   Sur le Spizaëtus tyrannus, Tem.   <Revue Zoologique, xi, 1848, pp. 134–138.

1849. BURROUGHES, T. H.   Occurrence of the Rough-legged Buzzard (Buteo [Archibuteo] lagopus) in Norfolk.   <Zoologist, vii, 1849, p. 2452.

1849. DUFF, J.   Occurrence of the Osprey (Falco [Pandion] Haliæetus) near Bishop's Auckland.   <Zoologist, vii, 1849, p. 2452.

1849. ELLMAN, J. B.   Occurrence of the Osprey [Pandion haliaëtus] at Udimore, Sussex.   <Zoologist, vii, 1849, p. 2346.

1849. ELLMAN, J. B.   Golden Eagle (Aquila chrysaëtos) near Rye.   <Zoologist, vii, 1849, p. 2409.

1849. GARTH, J. C.   Occurrence of the White-tailed Eagle (Haliæetus albicilla) in Somersetshire.   <Zoologist, vii, 1849, p. 2409.

1849. HULKE, J. W.   White-tailed Eagle [Haliaëtus albicilla] at Deal.   <Zoologist, vii, 1849, p. 2409.

1849-50. KAUP, [J. J.]   Monograph of the Falconidæ, Systematically arranged by Dr. T. T. [sic] Kaup.   <Jard. Contrib. Ornith., 1849, pp. 68–121; 1850, pp. 51–80.

"Dr. Kaup has sent us his Monograph of the Falconidæ, translated by himself from that Journal [*Oken's Isis*] of 1847, as improved in 1848."—*Editor*.   The first article is occupied with classificatory speculations of the most general character, relating not only to the present subject but to birds in general; in the second portion of the paper the family is systematically treated on the quinarian plan, and elaborated down to species.   There is nothing to show whether various of the author's generic terms are really new in this paper, or whether they had already been in print in the *Isis* or elsewhere.   The latter is doubtless the case.—See this author at 1845, 1849–50, and 1850.

1849. KNOX, A. E.   Capture of the Sea Eagle (Haliæëtos albicilla) in Sussex.   <Zoologist, vii, 1849, p. 2386.

1849. LAFRESNAYE, F. DE.   Mélanges ornithologiques.   <Rev. et Mag. de Zool., i, 1849, pp. 385–391.

Sur quelques synonymies nouvelles à appliquer à des espèces d'oiseaux de proie anciennement connues.   *Hypomorphnus leucurus*, sp. n., p. 388.

1849. THORNCROFT, T.   Peregrine Falcons (Falco peregrinus) at Beachy Head.   <Zoologist, vii, 1849, pp. 2494, 2495.

1850. BELL, T.   Occurrence of the Peregrine Falcon (Falco peregrinus) at Selborne.   <Zoologist, viii, 1850, p. 2764.

1850. BOLD, T. J.   Occurrence of the Osprey (Pandion Haliætus) in Northumberland.   <Zoologist, viii, 1850, p. 2824.

1850. BONAPARTE, C. L. [Suite à nouvelles espèces ornithologiques.] < *Rev. et Mag. de Zool.*, ii, 1850, pp. 241–243.

 Acad. des Sc. de Paris, séance du 11 Mars. *Raptores*—quatre familles.

1850. BREHM, [C.] L. Einige Bemerkengen über europäische und nordostafrikanische Vögel und Beschreibung einiger neuen Vögelarten. < *Naumannia*, i, Heft iii, 1850, pp. 22–31.

 Vultur fuscus (nec Gm.!), p. 23; *Aquila fuscicapilla, A. fusca*, p. 24; *A. unicolor*, p. 26; *A. fuscoatra*, p. 27; *A. suonaevia*, p. 30, "Brm."

1850. CASSIN, J. Descriptions of new species of the Genera Micrastur, . . . < *Journ. Acad. Nat. Sci. Phila.*, i, pt. iv, Jan., 1850, art. xxiv, pp. 295–297, pll. xl, xli.

 Micrastur guerilla, heretofore described, here figured, pl. xl.

1850. CURTLER, M. Occurrence of the Peregrine Falcon (Falco peregrinus) near Worcester. < *Zoologist*, viii, 1850, p. 2698.

1850. DUFF, J. Occurrence of the Osprey [Pandion haliaëtus] at Hartlepool. < *Zoologist*, viii, 1850, p. 2764.

1850. [KIRTLAND, J. P.] The Eagle. < *The Family Visitor*, i, No. 2, 1850, p. 15.

 On *Aquila chrysaëtus* and *Haliaëtus leucocephalus* in Ohio.

1850. KAUP, [J. J.] Corrigirte Uebersicht der Falconidæ. < *Arch. f. Naturg.*, xvi, 1850, (1), pp. 27–41.

 Verzeichniss nebst Synonymik von 191 Arten—39 *Falconinæ*, 28 *Milvinæ*, 51 *Accipitrinæ*, 40 *Aquilinæ*, 33 *Buteoninæ. Cypselopteryx*, p. 31; *Pterocircus*, p. 32; *Geranopus*, p. 35, und vielleicht andere genn. nn. Vergl. 1845, 1847-48, 1849-50, KAUP, J. J.

1850. MORRIS, B. R. Peregrine Falcon [Falco peregrinus] shot near Market Weighton. < *Zoologist*, viii, 1850, p. 2648.

1850. NEWMAN, E. Occurrence of the Osprey (Falco [Pandion] haliæëtos) near Colchester. < *Zoologist*, viii, 1850, p. 2764.

1850. NEWMAN, E. Golden Eagle [Aquila chrysaëtus, in Scotland]. < *Zoologist*, viii, 1850, p. 2764.

1850. PUCHERAN, *Dr.* Études sur les types peu connus du Musée de Paris. < *Rev. et Mag. de Zool.*, ii, 1850, pp. 1–14, 81–94, 208–215.

 Troisième article. *Rapaces diurnes.* A. Types de Cuvier. B. Types de Vieillot. C. Types de Lesson.

1850. SMITH, C. J. Occurrence of the Osprey (Falco [Pandion] haliæetos) at Toddington, Bedfordshire. < *Zoologist*, viii, 1850, p. 2967.

1850. WEBB, G. J. Capture of the Peregrine Falcon (Falco peregrinus) near Marlborough. < *Zoologist*, viii, 1850, p. 2648.

1850. WENDENBURG, H. [Aquila (Haliaëtus) albicilla am Eisleber See.] < *Naumannia*, i, Heft ii, 1850, p. 100.

1851. BOND, F. Occurrence of the Iceland Falcon [Falco islandicus] in Rossshire. < *Zoologist*, ix, 1851, pp. 3275, 3276.

1851. BUXTON, T. F. Occurrence of the Gyrfalcon (Falco Gyrfalco) in Norfolk. < *Zoologist*, ix, 1851, p. 3028.

1851. CORDEAUX, W. H. Occurrence of the Golden Eagle (Aquila chrysaëtos) in Herefordshire. < *Zoologist*, ix, 1851, p. 3027.

1851. ELLMAN, J. B. Occurrence of the Jer Falcon at Mayfield, Sussex. < *Zoologist*, ix, 1851, p. 3233.

1851. GURNEY, J. H. Occurrence of the Osprey [Pandion haliaëtus] in Norfolk. < *Zoologist*, ix, 1851, p. 3145.

1851. HARPER, J. O. Occurrence of the Osprey [Pandion haliaëtus] in Norfolk. < *Zoologist*, ix, 1851, p. 3207.

1851. KAUP, J. [J.] Vertheidigung meines Systems der Falken und Eulen gegen den Conspectus des Prinzen Ch. Bonaparte. *Arch. f. Naturg.*, 1851, (1), pp. 75–114.

 Kaup laborirt nach wie vor an der Monomanie der Fünfzahl.

1851. KENNER, T. ·Occurrence of the Roughlegged Buzzard (Buteo [Archibuteo] lagopus) on Marlboro' Downs. < *Zoologist,* ix, 1851, p. 3054.

1851. RODD, E. H.   Occurrence of the Osprey [Pandion haliaëtus] at the Land's End. < *Zoologist,* ix, 1851, p. 3300.

1851. WEBB, G. J.   Occurrence of Peregrine Falcons [Falco peregrinus] near Oxford. < *Zoologist,* ix, 1851, p. 3112.

1852. BURTON, R. F.   Falconry | in the | Valley of the Indus. | By Richard F. Burton, | Lieut. Bombay Army. | Author of "Goa and the Blue Mountains," etc. | [Monogram.] | London : | John Van Voorst, Paternoster Row. | — | M. DCCC. LII.   1 vol.   12mo.   pp. i–xii, 2 ll., pp. 1–107, frontisp. (by Wolf), and 3 pll.

Very entertaining narrative of his sport in India, well written, and of excellent authority. The writer is "convinced that the race of round or short-winged hawks has been unduly depreciated, and that by selecting good birds and by careful training, excellent sport is to be got out of them"—as one would readily believe, from seeing Wolf's spirited "Goshawk and Gazelle", or reading the author's "A Day with the Shahbaz." Cf. *Zool.,* 1852, pp. 3569-3576.

1852. EVANS, J.   Occurrence of the Osprey [Pandion haliaëtus] near Derby.   < *Zoologist,* x, 1852, pp. 3474, 3475.

1853. CASSIN, J.   Synopsis of the Species of Falconidæ whioh inhabit America north of Mexico; with descriptions of [a] new species.   < *Proc. Acad. Nat. Sci. Phila.,* vi, 1853, pp. 450–453.

Synonymatic.   *Buteo bairdii,* "Hoy", p. 451.—Cont. with modified title, 1855, *q. v.*

1853. GARDNER, J.   Occurrence of the Osprey (Falco [Pandion] Haliætus) at Weybridge.   < *Zoologist,* xi, 1853, p. 4072.

1853. DES MURS, O.   Description d'une nouvelle espèce de Phalcobéne, Phalcobænus carunculatus.   < *Rev. et Mag. de Zool.,* v, 1853, pp. 154, 155.

1853. WEBB, G. J.   The Osprey (Falco [Pandion] Haliætus) in Surrey.   < *Zoologist,* xi, 1853, p. 3753.

1854. BOLD, T. J.   Rough-legged Buzzard [Archibuteo lagopus] killed on the North Tyne.   < *Zoologist,* xii, 1854, p. 4251.

1854. BONAPARTE, C. L.   [Tableau méthodique des Oiseaux rapaces.]   < *Compt. Rend. de l'Acad. Sci.,* xxxix, 1854, p. 230.

Présentation du mémoire.   Voir *R. M. Z.,* vi, 1854, pp. 530-544.

1854. BONAPARTE, C. L.   Tableau des Oiseaux de proie.   < *Rev. et Mag. de Zool.,* vi, 1854, pp. 530–544.

Seulement une liste méthodique des noms, 146 genres, 451 espèces.   Les genres *Lophogyps,* p. 530; *Chiquera,* p. 535; *Smithiglaux,* p. 544, sont indiqués comme nouvellement introduits.

1854. HANCOCK, J.   Note on the Greenland and Iceland Falcons.   < *Ann. Mag. Nat. Hist.,* 2d ser., xiii, 1854, pp. 110–112.

Corroborative of his views of 1838, and rectificative of the description of *F. grœnlandicus.*

1854. SEALY, A. F.   Occurrence of the Rough-legged Buzzard (Buteo [Archibuteo] lagopus) and Peregrine Falcon (Falco peregrinus) in Cambridgeshire.   < *Zoologist,* xii, 1854, p. 4165.

1855. CASSIN, J.   Notes on North American Falconidæ, with descriptions of new Species.   < *Proc. Acad. Nat. Sci. Phila.,* vii, 1855, pp. 277–284.

25 spp.   *Buteo calurus, B. elegans,* p. 281; *B. oxypterus,* p. 282, spp. nn.   See 1853, CASSIN, J.

1855. FRITSCH, A.   Bemerkungen über einige Falkenarten.   < *J. f. O.,* iii, 1855, pp. 266–270.

F. laniarius, F. communis, F. peregrinoides, F. eleonoræ, F. concolor, F. ardesiacus.

1855. KJÄRBÖLLING, [N.]   Ueber die hochnordischen Edelfalken.   < *Naumannia,* v, 1855, pp. 489–493.

. *Falco groenlandicus, F. islandicus, F. gyrfalco.*

1855. KNEELAND, S., JR.   [Remarks on exhibition of a Golden or Ring-tailed Eagle (Aquila chrysaëtus).]   < *Proc. Bost. Soc. Nat. Hist.,* v, 1855, pp. 272, 273.

1855. PÄSSLER, W. Bemerkenswerthes in Bezug auf die Färbung der Raubvögel-Eier. < *J. f. O.*, iii, 1855, pp. 209–214.

„1) Ein und dasselbe Weibchen legt stets ahnliche, ja, ich möchte sagen, gleich gefärbte Eier; und 2) Abänderungen, welche man bei einer Art findet, trifft man auch bei anderen Arten."

1855. SCHLEGEL, H. [An der Frage über die Falken, besonders die Edelfalken.] < *Naumannia*, v, 1855, pp. 251–254.

„Das Verzeichniss aller mir bekannten Arten "—40 spp.

1855. STRICKLAND, H. E. Ornithological Synonyms. | By the late Hugh Edwin Strickland, M. A., | F. R. S., F. R. G. S., F. G. S., | Deputy Reader in Geology in the University of Oxford, etc. | — | Edited by Mrs. Hugh E. Strickland | and | Sir W. Jardine, Bart., F. R. S. E., L. S., &c. | — | Vol. I. | Accipitres. | London : | John Van Voorst, Paternoster Row. | MDCCCLV. 1 vol. 8vo. pp. xlvi, 222.

An extensive but far from complete synonymy of 370 + 3 spp., not entirely free from inaccuracies, but prepared with great care, and of great practical utility. The list of works quoted in the introduction is a convenient index to research. No second volume has appeared.

1855. WALLENGREN, G. D. J. [Ueber Falco gyrfalco, islandicus, und candicans.] < *Naumannia*, v, 1855, pp. 247–249.

1856. BREHM, [C. L.] [Einige Wörte über die eigentlich europäischen Wanderfalken.] < *Naumannia*, vi, 1856, pp. 326–332.

I. Aechte Wanderfalken: 1. *F. peregrinus cornicum, F. per. abietii. s, F. per. grisewentris, F. per. leucogenys*, p. 227; *F. per. orientalis*, subsp. un. 2. *F. barbarus.* II. Unächte Wanderfalken: 1. *F. cervicalis*, Mus. Berol., *F. biarmicus* Nob., p. 330; *F. tanypterus* Brm., p. 331.

1856. BREWER, T. M. [Observations on the California Red-tailed Hawk (Buteo montanus).] < *Proc. Bost. Soc. Nat. Hist.*, v, 1856, pp. 385, 386.

1856. COOKE, M. C. Occurrence of the Peregrine Falcon [Falco communis] near Norwich. < *Zoologist*, xiv, 1856, p. 5058.

1856–57. MÜLLER, J. W. V. Der Jagdfalke und die Falkenbaize. < *J. f. O.*, iv, 1856, pp. 497–502; v, 1857, pp. 169–174.

I. *F. candicans.* II. Die Falkenbaize.

1856. STEVENSON, H. Occurrence of the Sea Eagle (Haliaëtus albicilla) in Norfolk. < *Zoologist*, xiv, 1856, p. 4946.

1856. URBAN, W. S. M. D'. Occurrence of the Whitetailed Eagle (Falco [Haliaëtus] albicilla) in Devonshire. < *Zoologist*, xiv, 1856, p. 5096.

1856. VERREAUX, J. Note sur un Nouveau Genre [Urubitornis, de la Nouvelle Grenade] des Oiseaux de Proie. < *P. Z. S.*, xxiv, 1856, pp. 145, 146.

1857. BARRON, C. Occurrence of the Whitetailed Eagle [Haliaëtus albicilla] near Haslar. < *Zoologist*, xv, 1857, p. 5426.

1857. BLASIUS, J. H. Aphorismen über Falken. < *Naumannia*, vii, 1857, pp. 223–264. Sehr vollständig.

1857. BLASIUS, J. H. Ueber die Wiehen Europa's. < *Naumannia*, vii, 1857, pp. 307–324.

Behandelt *Cirus aëruginosus, C. cyaneus, C. pallidus, C. cineraceus*—4 Arten.

1857. CASSIN, J. Notes on the North American species of Archibuteo and Lanius, and description of a new species of Toucan, of the genus Selenidera, Gould. < *Proc. Acad. Nat. Sci. Phila.*, ix, 1855, pp. 211–214.

The author recognizes 3 species of the genus *Archibuteo*, one of them being the previously little-known *A. ferrugineus* (Licht.).

1857. ERHARD, Dr. [Aquila fulva beim Horste, u. s. w.] < *Naumannia*, vii, 1857, Hft. i, pp. 87, 89.

1857. G[RAYSON], A. J. The white breasted Squirrel Hawk.—(Buteo californica [sp. n.].) < *Hutchings's California Magazine*, Mar., 1857, pp. 393–396, fig.

Described as a new species under the above name. It is the *Archibuteo ferrugineus* (Licht.) or the *Lagopus ferrugineus*, Fraser. The article is mainly devoted to the habits of the bird, but also gives a recognizable description and figure.

1857. MIDDENDORFF, [A. T.] v. [Falco peregrinus auf ebener Erde horstend.] $<$ *Naumannia*, vii, Heft ii, 1857, p. 181.

1858. BREHM, A. E.   Die Geieradler und ihr Leben. $<$ *Mittheil. aus der Werkstälte der Natur*, 1es u. 2tes Heft, 1858.

> Nicht mir selbst zugänglich.—„ In instructives und anzienender Weise schildert A. Brehm , die Geieradler und ihr Leben '; . . . Die Subspecies werden gut beschrieben." (*Hartl.*)

1858. CASSIN, J.   [Occurrence of Falco polyagrus at Rock Island, Illinois, east of the Mississippi River.]· $<$ *Proc. Acad. Nat. Sci. Phila.*, x, 1858, p. 1.

1858. HOCKER, J.   Ueber den Standort des Horstes der Kornweihe (Circus cyaneus). $<$ *Naumannia*, viii, 1858, pp. 505, 506.

1858. JÄGER, C.   Aquila [Haliaëtus] albicilla in der Wetterau. $<$ *Naumannia*, viii, 1858, pp. 507, 508.

1858. PELZELN, A. v.   Ueber Gold- und Steinadler. $<$ *Verh. d. zool.-bot. Ver. Wien*, viii, 1858, pp. — – —, Taf. i.

> Pl. i, *Aquila chrysaëtos*, Pall.

1858. RICHARDSON, J.   Occurrence of the Peregrine Falcon [Falco peregrinus] in Yorkshire. $<$ *Zoologist*, xvi, 1858, p. 6058.

1858. SCHNELL, F. H.   Der Taubenhabicht.   Eine monographische Schilderung seines Lebens in der Vogelwelt. $<$ *Jahrb. d. Vereins für Naturk. im Herzogth. Nassau*, Nr. 12, pp. 342–356.

> Nicht mir selbst zugänglich.

1858. SCLATER, P. L.   On some New or little-known Species of Accipitres, in the collection of the Norwich Museum. $<$ *P. Z. S.*, xxvi, 1858, pp. 128–133.

> *Buteo zonocercus*, p. 130; *Syrnium albitarse*, Gray, p. 131; *Scops usta*, p. 132, spp. nn. Figured. *Tr. Z. S.*, 1859, q. v. Lists of spp. of *Urubitinga*, *Syrnium*, and *Scops*.

1858. SCLATER, P. L.   Note on the Variation of the Form of the Upper Mandible in a Rapacious Bird [Urubitinga unicincta]. $<$ *P. Z. S.*, xxvi, 1858, p. 150, woodcc.

1858. SCLATER, P. L.   Description of a new Species of the Genus Buteo [fuliginosus] from Mexico. $<$ *P. Z. S.*, xxvi, 1858, p. 356.

1858. SCLATER, P. L.   On some New or little-known species of Accipitres, in the Collection of the Norwich Museum. $<$ *Ann. Mag. Nat. Hist.*, 3d ser., ii, 1858, pp. 225–229.

> From *P. Z. S.*, Mar. 9, 1858, pp. 128–133, q. v.

1858. SCLATER, P. L.   On the Variation of the Form of the Upper Mandible in a Rapacious Bird. $<$ *Ann. Mag. Nat. Hist.*, 3d ser., ji, 1858, pp. 163, figg. 2.

> From *P. Z. S.*, Mar. 23, 1858, p. 150.

1859. CREWE, H. R.   Occurrence of the Peregrine Falcon (Falco peregrinus) in Derbyshire. $<$ *Zoologist*, xvii, 1859, p. 6779.

1859. GOULD, J.   [Exhibition of all the known Species of the genus Elanus, with description of a New Species (E. hypoleucus).] $<$ *P. Z. S.*, xxvii, 1859, pp. 126, 127.

1859. HINCKS, W.   The Family of Falconidæ. $<$ *Canad. Journ.*, iv, Nov., 1859, pp. 443–449.

> 15 Canadian spp.

1859. SCLATER, P. L.   Description of a new Species of the Genus Buteo [fuliginosus] from Mexico. $<$ *Ann. Mag. Nat. Hist.*, 3d ser., iii, 1859, p. 78.

> From *P. Z. S.*, July 13, 1858, p. 356.

1859. SCLATER, P. L.   On some New or little-known Species of Accipitres in the Collection of the Norwich Museum. $<$ *Trans. Zool. Soc.*, iv, pt. vi, 1859, pp. 261–266 pll. 59–61.

> Descr. orig. *P. Z. S.*, 1858, pp. 128–133, the species being here figured in colors.—Pl. 59, *Bute zonocercus;* pl. 60, *Syrnium albitarse;* pl. 61, *Scops usta.*

1859. SCLATER, P. L.   Description of a New Species of the genus Buteo (B. fuligi nosus) from Mexico. $<$ *Trans. Zool. Soc. Lond.*, iv, pt. vi, 1859, p. 267, pl. 62.

> Descr. orig. *P. Z. S.*, 1858, p. 356.

1859. STEVENSON, H. A Peregrine Falcon (Falco peregrinus) killed by the Telegraph-wires. < *Zoologist*, xvii, 1859, p. 6779.

1860. CREWE, H. H. Occurrence of the Osprey (Falco [Pandion] haliæëtus) in Derbyshire. < *Zoologist*, xviii, 1860, p. 6889.

1860. DUTTON, J. Whitetailed Eagle (Falco [Haliaëtus] albicilla) near Eastbourne. < *Zoologist*, xviii, 1860, pp. 6888, 6889.

1860. DUTTON, J. Peregrine Falcon (Falco peregrinus) near Eastbourne. < *Zoologist*, xviii, 1860, p. 6889.

1860. EDITORIAL. [J. Cassin's Remarks on Ictinia, with editorial comment.] < *Ibis*, ii, 1860, pp. 103, 104.

1860. GLOGER, C. W. L. Die grössere Länge der Schwung- und Schwanzfedern bei den jungen Adlern [u. s. w.]. < *J. f. O.*, viii, 1860, pp. 209–211.
     Aquila, Haliaëtus.

1860. GLOGER, C. W. L. Der Seeadler [Haliaëtus albicilla] auf dem Wasser. < *J. f. O.*, viii, 1860, pp. 470, 471.
     Nilss. Sk. Fn. Fog., i, p. 61.

1860. OWEN, ROBERT. On the Habits of the Swallow-tailed Kite (Elanoides furcatus) in Guatemala. < *Ibis*, ii, 1860, pp. 240–243.

1860. PELZELN, A. v. Zur naheren Kenntniss des Morphnus guianensis (Daud.) < *J. f. O.*, viii, 1860, pp. 337–340.

1860. ROBERTS, A. Occurrence of the Osprey (Falco [Pandion] haliæetus) at Sherburne. < *Zoologist*, xviii, 1860, p. 7104.

1860. SCLATER, P. L. On an undescribed Species of Hawk [Accipiter collaris, Kaup, Mus. Brit.] from New Granada. < *Ibis*, ii, 1860, pp. 147–149, pl. vi.

1860. SCLATER, P. L. On the Eggs of Two Raptorial Birds from the Falkland Islands. < *Ibis*, ii, 1860, pp. 24–28, pl. i.
     Pl. i, fig. 1, *Milvago australis;* fig. 2, *Cathartes* sp., wrongly identified as *Milvago australis;* fig. 3, *Buteo erythronotus.*

1860. TAYLOR, J. Note on Falco Islandicus and F. Grœnlandicus. < *Rep. Brit. Assoc. Adv. Sci. for* 1859, 1860 (*Misc. Comm.*), p. 158.
     Confirming J. Hancock's determination.

1860. WILSON, W. Occurrence of the Roughlegged Buzzard (Falco [Archibuteo] lagopus) at King's Lynn. < *Zoologist*, xviii, 1860, p. 6889.

1861. BRYANT, H. Remarks on the variations of plumage in Buteo borealis, Auct., and Buteo harlani, Aud.? < *Proc. Bost. Soc. Nat. Hist.*, viii, 1861, pp. 107–119.
     Extended description and criticism of the various current nominal species, which are to be reduced to one or the other of these two. But the "*Buteo harlani* Aud.?" of this paper is not of Aud., being *B. swainsoni* Bp. Cf. *Ibis*, 1862, pp. 184, 185.

1861. SCLATER, P. L. Note on Milvago carunculatus and its allied species. < *Ibis*, iii, 1861, pp. 19–23, pl. i.
     Full description from Des Murs' MSS. ined., with critical observations on the genus.

1861. SCLATER, P. L. On a rare Species of Hawk, of the Genus Accipiter [pectoralis] from South America. < *Ibis*, iii, 1861, pp. 313, 314, pl. x.

1861. NORDMANN, A. v. Aquila Fulva L. (Goldadler) im Gefecht. < *Zool. Gart.*, ii, 1861, p. 68.
     Bull. Soc. Imp. Natur. Moscou, 1860, p. 7.

1861. ORDE, J. W. P. [Letter on the breeding of Aquila chrysaëtus in a fir-tree in Perthshire.] < *Ibis*, iii, 1861, pp. 112, 113.

1861. ORDE, J. W. P. [Note on an Hierofalco shot Oct., 1860, on North Uist.] < *Ibis*, iii, 1861, p. 415.

1862. BLASIUS, J. H. Über die nordischen Jagdfalken [Hierofalco]. < *J. f. O.*, x, 1862, pp. 43–59.
     An elaborate examination of the question, with extended descriptions of various forms.

1862. CHENU, J. C., *and* DES MURS, O. La | Fauconnerie | Ancienne et Moderne | par |
J. C. Chenu et O. Des Murs | — | Supplément au tome deuxième | des | Leçons
Élémentaires sur l'Histoire Naturelle des Oiseaux | [Dessin.] | Paris | Librairie
L. Hachette et Cie | 77, Rue Saint-Germain, 77 | — | 1862. 1 vol. in-12°. faux-
titre, titre, et pp. 1–176, figg. 1–45, + 7; exemplaires en couleur ou en noir.

> Aperçu historique, p. 1—Description des Faucons, p. 47, figg. 7–21—Éducation des Oiseaux
> de vol, p. 79—Observations sur le vol des Oiseaux, p. 131—Liste alphabétique des termes de
> Fauconnerie, p. 151.

1862. PELZELN, A. V. [On the habitat of Accipiter pectoralis (Brazil).] < *Ibis*, iv,
1862, p. 194.

1862–63. PELZELN, A. V. Uebersicht der Geier und Falken der kaislerlichen ornithologischen Sammlung. < *Verh. (Abh.) k.-k. zool.-bot. Ges. Wien*, xii, 1862, Abth.
ii, pp. 123–192; xiii, 1863, pp. 585–636.

> Enthaltend das systematische Verzeichniss der in der Kaiserl. Ornith. Samml. aufbe-
> wahrten *Vulturidæ*, *Cathartidæ* und *Falconidæ*. Der Uebersicht ist im Allgemeinen das von
> G. R. Gray (in: *G. of B.* und *List of G. of B.*, 1855) System zu Grunde gelegt, ohne jedoch
> einzelne Abänderungen auszuschliessen. Am Schlusse hat der Verf. die reichen und werth-
> vollen von Natterer während seiner Reise gemachten und in dem Cataloge (msc.) seiner
> brasilischen Sammlung enthaltenen Notizen über die von ihm gesammelten Arten der hier
> besprochenen Gruppen zusammengestellt.—*Handschriftliche Notizen* von J. Natterer, pp. 171–
> 191 (1862), 631–636 (1863).—Cf. *Ibis*, 1864, p. 123.

1862. RORERTS, A. Occurrence of the Golden Eagle [Aquila chrysaëtus] near Driffield. < *Zoologist*, xx, 1862, p. 7880.

1862. SAVILLE, S. P. Occurrence of the Peregrine Falcon [Falco peregrinus] in Cambridgeshire. < *Zoologist*, xx, 1862, p. 7843.

1862. SCHLEGEL, H. Falcones < *Mus. Hist. Nat. Pays-Bas*, 1re livr. Août 1862, pp. 1–36.

> Treats of 35 spp. and several subspp., all referred to the genus *Falco*; constituting a synon-
> ymatic and descriptive catalogue of the 337 specimens of *Falconinæ* in the Leyden Museum.

1862. SCHLEGEL, H. Aquilae < *Mus. Hist. Nat. Pays-Bas*, 1^e livr., Sept., 1862, pp. 1–24.

> Treats of 20 species of "Eagles", namely: 8 referred to the genus *Aquila*, 11 to *Haliaëtus*,
> and 1 to *Pandion*; representing a synonymatic descriptive list of the 182 specimens con-
> tained in the Leyden Museum.

1862. SCHLEGEL, H. Astures < *Mus. Hist. Nat. Pays-Bas*, 1^e livr., Sept., 1862, pp. 1–5*.

> The "*Astures*" of this author include *Gypogeranus*, which remarkable form is ranged in the
> genus *Astur* itself!—a piece of "conservatism" so extreme as to be justly reprehensible, and
> to tend to bring the author's faculty of discernment into discredit—unless, indeed, he in-
> tended by such course to satirize some of his contemporaries. Fifty-five species are treated,
> of the three genera *Spizaëtus* (9), *Astur* (18), and *Nisus* (27).—*Nisus verreauxii*, p. 37, sp. n.

1862. SCHLEGEL, H. Asturinae < *Mus. Hist. Nat. Pays-Bas*, 1^e livr., Sept., 1862, pp. 1–14.

> Treating of 15 spp. of one genus, *Asturina*, represented by 52 specimens in the Leyden
> Museum.

1862–63. SCHLEGEL, H. Buteones < *Mus. Hist. Nat. Pays-Bas*, 1^e livr., Août 1862, pp.
1–4; 2^e livr., 1863, pp. 5–30.

> Whole article dated Aug., 1862, and pp. 1–4 pub. that year; pp. 5–30, in livr. 2, not pub. as a
> whole till 1863, though the loose signatures may have been out in 1862. The "*Buteones*", 31
> in number, are referred to the 2 genera *Buteo* (23) and *Circaetus* (8). A descriptive and synony-
> matic list of 193 specimens in the Leyden Museum.—*Buteo cabanisii*, p. 11, sp. n.? *Circaetus
> bacha celebensis*, p. 27, sp. n.? The series of articles on the Raptores continues in the 2^e livr.,
> 1863; and there is a general review of the whole subject, of date 1873.

1862. SCLATER, P. L. Note on Falco circumcinctus [P. Z. S. 1851, 42], a rare Bird of
Prey from South America. < *Ibis*, iv, 1862, pp. 23–25, pl. ii.

> Cf. *Falco punctipennis*, Burm., *J. f. O.*, 1860, p. 242.

1863. ALLIS, T. H. The Osprey [Pandion haliaëtus] near Bury St. Edmunds. < *Zoologist*, xxi, 1863, pp. 8677, 8678.

1863. BAKER, J. Osprey [Pandion haliaëtus] in Cambridgeshire. < *Zoologist*, xxi,
1863, p. 8813.

1863. BAKER, J. Marsh [Circus æruginosus] and Montagu's [Circus cineraceus] Harriers in Norfolk. < *Zoologist*, xxi, 1863, p. 8765.

1863. BLAKE-KNOX, H.   Marsh Harrier [Circus æruginosus], Peregrine Falcon [F. peregrinus], Iceland Falcon [F. grœnlandicus, see Zool. 8678], &c., in Ireland. < *Zoologist*, xxi, 1863, p. 8523.
Notice, also, of *Falco æsalon* and *Alca alle*.

1863. BODINUS, *Dr.*   [Tuberculose bei Raubvögeln, u. s. w.]   < *Zool. Gart.*, iv, 1863, pp. 68–71.

1863. BOULTON, W. W.   The Roughlegged Buzzard (Falco [Archibuteo] lagopus) in Yorkshire.   < *Zoologist*, xxi, 1863, p. 8441.

1863. DUTTON, J.   Hen Harrier (Falco [Circus] cyaneus) at Eastbourne.   < *Zoologist*, xxi, 1863, p. 8484.

1863. KENT, R.   The Roughlegged Buzzard (Falco [Archibuteo] lagopus) and Hen Harrier (Falco [Circus] cyaneus) at Ashburnham Park.   < *Zoologist*, xxi, 1863, p. 8442.

1863. HARTING, J. E.   Peregrine Falcon (Falco peregrinus) at Haverfordwest. < *Zoologist*, xxi, 1863, p. 8523.

1863. HARTING, J. E.   The Osprey [Pandion haliaëtus] near Uxbridge.   < *Zoologist*, xxi, 1863, p. 8813.

1863. HOMEYER, A. V.   Kampf eines Seeadlers [Haliaëtus albicilla] mit einem Fuchse. Mit Zusatz von Dr. Gloger.   < *J. f. O.*, xi, 1863, pp. 155–159.

1863. MAXIMILIAN, PRINZ VON WIED.   Ueber das vollkommene Gefieder des Morphnus guianensis.   < *J. f. O.*, xi, 1863, pp. 1–3.

1863. PELZELN, A. V.   Ueber die Färbung des Morphnus guianensis (Daud.) und M. Harpyia (L.).   < *J. f. O.*, xi, 1863, pp. 121–132.

1863. RODD, E. H.   Occurrence of the Osprey [Pandion haliaëtus] near Hayle. < *Zoologist*, xxi, 1863, p. 8841.

1863. RODD, E. H.   Marsh Harrier [Circus æruginosus] in the Scilly Isles.   < *Zoologist*, xxi, 1863, p. 8841.

1863. SAVILLE, S. P.   Roughlegged Buzzard (Falco [Archibuteo] lagopus) in Cambridgeshire.   < *Zoologist*, xxi, 1863, p. 8441.

1863. SAXBY, H. L.   Iceland Falcon (Falco islandicus) in Shetland.   < *Zoologist*, xxi, 1863, p. 8484.

1863. SAXBY, H. L.   The Osprey [Pandion haliaëtus] in Shetland.   < *Zoologist*, xxi, 1863, p. 8677.

1863. SCHLEGEL, H.   Milvi   < *Mus. Hist. Nat. Pays-Bas*, 2e livr., Oct., 1862, pp. 1–12, (Pub. 1863.)
This monograph is dated Oct., 1862, and the sheet may have been out that year, but the livr. was not pub. as a whole until 1863.
Milvus (6), *Elanoïdes* (2), *Elanus* (6), *Ictinia* (2) = 16 spp., represented by 79 specimens, a list of which is given, with synonymy and description. *Elanus intermedius*, p. 7, sp. n.

1863. SCHLEGEL, H.   Pernes   < *Mus. Hist. Nat. Pays-Bas*, 2e livr., Nov., 1862, pp. 1–10. (Pub. 1863.)
Memoir dated Nov., 1862, and the sheet may have been out that year; but this livraison not pub. as a whole until 1863.   Treats of *Pernis* (2), *Baza* (4), *Macheirhamphus* (1), *Cymindis* (2) = 9 spp., represented in the Leyden Museum by 43 specimens.

1863 SCHLEGEL, H.   Polybori   < *Mus. Hist. Nat. Pays-Bas*, 2e livr., Nov., 1862, pp. 1–10.   (Pub. 1863.)
This memoir is dated Nov., 1862, and may have been out that year; but the livraison containing it was not pub. till 1863.   Treats of 5 spp of *Polyborus* and 4 of *Ibicter* (sic), represented by 28 specimens in the Leyden Museum.

1863. SCHLEGEL, H. Vultures < *Mus. Hist. Nat. Pays-Bas,* 2ᵉ livr., Nov., 1862, pp. 1–12.

> Article dated Nov., 1862, and may have been out that year, but the livr. not pub. till 1863.
> The "Vultures" of the author, whose classificatory instincts are anachronistic, tending always to retrogression, include the very distinct group of *Cathartidæ* with the Old World Vulturines.—There are here treated 6 spp. of *Cathartidæ* in the single genus *Cathartes,* with 2 of *Neophron,* 6 (including several subspp.) of *Vultur,* and 1 (with a subsp.) of *Gypaëtus;* represented by 94 specimens in the Leyden Museum.

1863. SCHLEGEL, H. Circi < *Mus. Hist. Nat. Pays-Bas,* 2ᵉ livr., Dec., 1862, pp. 1–12. (Pub. 1863.)

> The article is dated Dec., 1862, and the signature (13) may have been distributed that year; but the livr. was not pub. till 1863.
> It treats of eleven spp. and one subsp. of the genus *Circus,* represented by 118 specimens in the Leyden Museum, being a synonymatic and descriptive list thereof.

1863. [SCHLEGEL, H.] Aves Rapaces. Résumé Général. 31 Décembre 1862. < *Mus. Hist. Nat. Pays-Bas,* 2ᵉ livr., 1863, 1 feuille.

> A large loose folded sheet, not paged, issued with livr. 2ᵉ, giving a tabular view of the author's system of classification of the *Rapaces,* according to which the several articles are recommended to be bound, viz: *Oti* (No. 11), *Striges* (No. 12), *Falcones* (No. 2), *Circi* (No. 13), *Aquilæ* (No. 3), *Astures* (No. 4), *Asturinæ* (No. 5), *Buteones* (No. 6), *Milvi* (No. 7), *Pernes* (No. 8), *Polybori* (No. 9), *Vultures* (No. 10).—Also noting additions to the collection, bringing the total of species to 333, of specimens to 2,002.

1863. SCLATER, P. L. Note on the Occurrence of the European Sea-Eagle [Haliaëtus albicilla] in North America. < *P. Z. S.,* xxxi, 1863, pp. 251–253.

> But cf. *P. Z. S.,* 1865, p. 731.

1863. STEVENSON, H. The Roughlegged Buzzard (Buteo [Archibuteo] lagopus) on the Norfolk Coast. < *Zoologist,* xxi, 1863, p. 8325.

1863. WHEELWRIGHT, H. The Norwegian Jer-Falcon (Falco Jer-falco norvegicus of Wooley, "rip-spenning," Lap., "jagt falk," Sw.). < *Zoologist,* xxi, 1863, pp. 8439–8441.

1863. WHEELWRIGHT, H. The Roughlegged Buzzard [Archibuteo lagopus]. < *Zoologist,* xxi, 1863, pp. 8441, 8442.

1864. ADOLPHI, R. [Haltung der Raubvögel.] < *Zool. Gart.,* v, 1864, p. 21.

1864. ALLEN, J. A. Notes on the Habits and Distribution of the Duck Hawk, or American Peregrine Falcon [Falco peregrinus], in the Breeding Season, and Description of the Eggs [from Mt. Tom, Mass.]. < *Proc. Essex Inst.,* iv, 1864, art. x, pp. 153–161.

1864. ANON. A Jerfalcon shot in the South of Scotland. < *Zoologist,* xxii, 1864, p. 8875.

1864. BLASIUS, R. Die Adler. (Beilage xi. zum Berichte über die xiv. Versamml. der Deutsch. Ornith. Gesellsch.) < *J. f. O.,* xi, 1863, besond. Beigabe, pp. 76–106. (Pub. 1864.)

> Full descriptions, with extensive tables of measurement, of 7 spp.

1864. BLASIUS, J. H. Zur Unterscheidung des Dunenkleides der Raubvögel. < *J. f. O.,* xii, 1864, pp. 276–289.

> a. Der untere Theil des Laufs ist mit Netztafeln besetzt, der obere befiedert (*Falco, Elanus, Pandion, Circaetos, Pernis*). b. Der Lauf ist bis zur Zehenwurzel befiedert (*Aquila, Archibuteo*). c. Die unteren Thiele des Laufs sind vorn mit umfassenden Quertafeln besetzt, die oberen vorn befiedert (*Buteo vulgaris, Haliaëtus, Milvus, Astur, Circus*). Many specific distinctions of European diurnal and nocturnal *Raptores* are also systematically drawn.

1864. BOULTON, W. W. Osprey [Pandion haliaëtus] near Beverley. < *Zoologist,* xxii, 1864, pp. 9207–9209.

1864. BOULTON, W. W. Peregrine Falcon [Falco peregrinus] at Flamborough. < *Zoologist,* xxii, 1864, p. 9209.

1864. DUTTON, J. Peregrine Falcons [Falco peregrinus] taken at Beachy Head and Seaford Cliffs. < *Zoologist,* xxii, 1864, p. 9209.

1864. GUNN, T. E.   Whitetailed Eagle [Haliaëtus albicilla] near Wymondham. *<Zoologist*, xxii, 1864, p. 9019.

1864. GURNEY, J. H.   A | Descriptive Catalogue | of | the Raptorial Birds | in the | Norfolk and Norwich Museum, | compiled and arranged | by | John Henry Gurney. | — | Part One: | containing | Serpentariídæ, Polyboridæ, Vulturidæ. | — | London : | John Van Voorst, Paternoster Row. | Norwich : Matchett and Stevenson, Market-place. | 1864.   1 vol.   roy.   8vo (4to by sigs.).   pp. i-vi, 7–90.

> Mr. Gurney's high name as an authority on Birds of Prey, and his accomplishments as a writer, render anything he has to say upon this subject important and interesting.
> Lists of 157 specimens, as well as 30 species, are given, with very full particulars on geographical distribution, food, nidification, general habits, colors of soft parts, etc.—constituting a treatise, rather than a catalogue, of the highest authority. Cf. *Ibis*, 2d ser., i, 1865, p. 99.

1864. HODGKINSON, J. B.   Osprey [Pandion haliaëtus] near Preston. *< Zoologist*, xxii, 1864, p. 8875.

1864. HOMEYER, E. v.   Raubvögelhorste [werden zu häufig von den verschiedensten Raubvögeln bewohnt]. *< J. f. O.*, xii, 1864, pp. 218, 219.

1864. HUSSEY, H.   Eagles in the Highlands. *< Zoologist*, xxii, 1864, pp. 9206–9207.

1864. LUNGERSHAUSEN, L.   [Haltung der kleineren Raubvögel.] *< Zool. Gart.*, v, 1864, pp. 265, 267.

1864. NEWTON, A.   Ootheca Wolleyana : | An illustrated Catalogue | of | the collections of Birds' Eggs | formed by the late | John Wolley, Jun., M. A., F. Z. S. | Edited from the original notes | by | Alfred Newton, M. A., F. L. S., etc. | — | Part I. Accipitres. | — | London : | John Van Voorst, Paternoster Row. | M. DCCC. LXIV.   1 vol.   8vo.   pp. i-viii, 1–180, with 1 l. of list of plates, col'd pll. ix (eggs), and A–I (landscape, nests, &c.).

> This work has been recognized as extremely accurate and reliable, the greatest possible pains having been taken to secure these results by the distinguished editor, who moreover based his work upon the collections and field-notes of one of the most conscientious and laborious of naturalists, and an oölogist of large experience. The Catalogue enters upon great detail in describing and illustrating the large series of the eggs of *Accipitres* collected by Mr. Wolley, and in presenting the record of his experiences in the field. There are treated no fewer than 55 species of the Western Palæarctic region, with many colored figures of eggs, and views of the nests, &c. Pl. I, *Neophron percnopterus;* II–IV, *Aquila chrysaëtus;* V, VI, *Pandion haliaëtus;* VIII, *Falco gyrfalco;* IX, figs. 1-4, *Nyctale tengmalmi;* 5-8, *Surnia ulula;* 9-12, *Syrnium lapponicum.*

1864. PAMPLIN, W.   The Osprey [Pandion haliaëtus] in North Wales. *< Zoologist*, xxii, 1864, p. 9039.

1864. PRATT, H.   The Whitetailed Eagle [Haliaëtus albicilla] at Shoreham. *< Zoologist*, xxii, 1864, p. 8875.

1864. ROWLAND, W. H.   Whitetailed Eagle [Haliaëtus albicilla] in Savernake Forrest. *< Zoologist*, xxii, 1864, p. 9020.

1864. SWINHOE, R.   Natural-History Notes, principally from Formosa. *< Zoologist*, xxii, 1864, pp. 9224–9229.

> Only ornithological in a paragraph on *Pandion.*

1865. ANON.   Für Jagdfreunde. *< Zool. Gart.*, vi, 1865, p. 75.

> Note on *Falco islandicus* and *Haliaëtus albicilla.*

1865. BOWER, W.   Whitetailed Eagle [Haliaëtus albicilla] in Sussex. *< Zoologist*, xxiii, 1865, p. 9465.

1865. BRUNTON, T.   Peregrine Falcon [Falco peregrinus] breeding on the Antrim Coast. *< Zoologist*, xxiii, 1865, p. 9625.

1865. BRYANT, H.   Remarks on the Type of Buteo insignatus Cassin. *< Proc. Boston Soc. Nat. Hist.*, x, 1865, pp. 90, 91.

> Identified with *B. swainsoni.*

1865. Cassin, J. Notes on Some New and little known Rapacious Birds. < *Proc. Acad. Nat. Sci. Phila.*, xvii, 1865, pp. 2-5.

> *Polyborus audubonii*, p. 2, sp. n.; *Spilornis bacha; Haliaetus blagrus; Limnastus africanus*, sp. n., p. 4; *Otus stygius*.

1865. Crewe, H. H. [On Pandion haliaëtus, &c.] < *Ibis*, 2d ser., i, 1865, pp. 113, 114.

1865. Gravil, H. Peregrine Falcon and Merlin at Epworth. < *Zoologist*, xxiii, 1865, p. 9538.

1865. Mathew, M. A. Osprey [Pandion haliaëtus] near Exeter. < *Zoologist*, xxiii, 1865, p. 9847.

> From *Exeter and Plymouth Gazette*, Oct. 6, 1865.

1865. Newcome, E. C. [Buteo lineatus, shot Feb. 26, 1863, at Kingussie, Inverness-shire, Scotland.] < *Ibis*, 2d ser., i, 1865, p. 549.

1865. Rocke, J. [On Pandion haliaëtus breeding in Scotland; cf. Ibis, 1865, p. 9.] < *Ibis*, 2d ser., i, 1865, p. 360.

1865. Sclater, P. L. Description of a New Accipitrine Bird [Leucopternis princeps] from Costa Rica. < *P. Z. S.*, May 9, 1865, pp. 429, 430, pl. xxiv.

1865. Sclater, P. L. [Correction of some previous remarks (P. Z. S., 1863, p. 251) on the supposed occurrence of Haliaëtus albicilla in America.] < *P. Z. S.*, xxxiii, 1865, p. 731.

1866. Angus, W. C. Osprey [Pandion haliaëtus] and Golden Eagle [Aquila chrysaëtus] in Aberdeenshire. < *Zoologist*, 2d ser., i, 1866, p. 497.

1866. Dilke, C. W. [Letter on the occurrence of Falco gyrfalco near Farnham.] < *P. Z. S.*, xxxiv, 1866, p. 2.

1866. Gunn, T. E. Peregrine Falcon [Falco peregrinus] in Suffolk. < *Zoologist*, 2d ser., i, 1866, p. 96.

1866. Gunn, T. E. Roughlegged Buzzard [Archibuteo lagopus] in Suffolk. < *Zoologist*, 2d ser., i, 1866, p. 142.

1866. Harrison, H. Osprey [Pandion haliaëtus] at Rostherne Mere. < *Zoologist*, 2d ser., i, 1866, p. 30.

1866. Harrison, H. Jerfalcon at Crosby Ravensworth. < *Zoologist*, 2d ser., i, 1866, p. 30.

1866. Harrison, H. Jerfalcons near Biddulph. < *Zoologist*, 2d ser., i, 1866, pp. 30, 31.

1866. Homeyer, A. v. Zwei Notizen über Falco peregrinus. < *J. f. O.*, xiv, 1866, p. 426.

> Lebensweise.

1866. Homeyer, A. v. Notiz über Aquila albicilla und Grus cinerea. < *J. f. O.*, xiv, 1866, p. 426.

> Kampf zwischen Seeadler und Kranich.

1866. Kratzsch, H. Vortrag über die Raubvögel. < *Mittheil. aus dem Osterlande*, xvii, pp. 204-210.

> Mir nicht zugänglich.

1866. Lang, C. Osprey [Pandion haliaëtus] in Sussex. < *Zoologist*, 2d ser., i, 1866, p. 495.

> From the "Field."

1866. Mathew, M. A. Hen Harrier [Circus cyaneus] near Barnstaple. < *Zoologist*, 2d ser., i, 1866, p. 267.

1866. Sclater, P. L. On a New Species of the Genus Accipiter [ventralis] from New Granada. < *P. Z. S.*, May 8, 1866, pp. 302-304.

> With a synonymatic and critically annotated list of nine American species of the genus.

1866. Smith, H. E. Roughlegged Buzzard [Archibuteo lagopus] in South Yorkshire. < *Zoologist*, 2d ser., i, 1866, p. 31.

1867. ANON. Osprey [Pandion haliaëtus] near Cork. < *Zoologist*, 2d ser., ii, 1867, p. 912.
From the "Field."

1867. BEAL, W. J. Novel way of shooting Eagles [Haliaëtus leucocephalus]. < *Am. Nat.*, i, 1867, p. 439.
On horse-back.

1867. BRUHIN, P. T. A. Originelles Mittel gegen Raubvögel. < *Zool. Gart.*, viii, 1867, pp. 238, 239.

1867. CLIFTON, *Lord.* Peregrine Falcon [Falco peregrinus] in Kent. < *Zoologist*, 2d ser., ii, 1867, pp. 631, 632.

1867. DUTTON, J. Peregrine Falcon [Falco peregrinus] breeding at Beachy Head. < *Zoologist*, 2d ser., ii, 1867, p. 791.

1867. ELWES, H. J. [On probable attack of Aquila chrysaëtus upon Falco peregrinus.] < *Ibis*, 2d ser., iii, 1867, pp. 143, 144.

1867. FEILDEN, H. W. Nesting of the Peregrine Falcon [Falco peregrinus]. < *Zoologist*, 2d ser., ii, 1867, p. 702.

1867. FEILDEN, H. W. Nesting of the Peregrine [Falcon, Falco peregrinus] in Stirlingshire. < *Zoologist*, 2d ser., ii, 1867, pp. 790, 791.

1867. GUNN, T. E. Osprey [Pandion haliaëtus] in Norfolk. < *Zoologist*, 2d ser., ii, 1867, p. 823.

1867. GURNEY, J. H. [Commentary on various Raptores, mentioned in papers by S. F. Baird, R. C. Beavan, and E. Newton, in Ibis, July, 1867.] < *Ibis*, 2d ser., iii, 1867, pp. 464–466.

1867. HARVIE-BROWN, J. A. Baldheaded Eagle [Haliaëtus leucocephalus] in Achill. < *Zoologist*, 2d ser., ii, 1867, pp. 562, 563.
The facts "can scarcely be considered conclusive."

1867. HARVIE-BROWN, J. A. Roughlegged Buzzard [Archibuteo lagopus] in Dumfriesshire. < *Zoologist*, 2d ser., ii, 1867, pp. 604, 605.

1867. HOMEYER, A. V. Notizen über Falco peregrinus. < *J. f. O.*, xv, 1867, p. 143.
Lebensweise.

1867. ROBERTS, G. Nesting of the Peregrine [Falcon, Falco peregrinus] in Yorkshire. < *Zoologist*, 2d ser., ii, 1867, pp. 947, 948.

1868. FOWLER, A. The Osprey, or Fish Hawk [Pandion carolinensis]. < *Am. Nat.*, ii, 1868, pp. 192–195.
Biographical.

1868. GUNN, T. E. Osprey [Pandion haliaëtus] in Norfolk. < *Zoologist*, 2d ser., iii, 1868, pp. 1176, 1177

1868. GUNN, T. E. Peregrine Falcon [Falco peregrinus] at Hareland: Parasitical Worms. < *Zoologist*, 2d ser., iii, 1868, pp. 1217, 1218.

1868. GURNEY, J. H. [Note on the breeding of Haliaëtus albicilla in Mantchouria.] < *Ibis*, 2d ser., iv, 1868, pp. 129, 130.

1868. HADFIELD, H. Diagnostics of the Roughlegged Buzzard [Archibuteo lagopus]. < *Zoologist*, 2d ser., iii, 1868, pp. 1057, 1058.

1868. HALDEMANN, S. S. The Eagle [Haliaëtus spp.] a Fisher. < *Am. Nat.*, i, 1868, pp. 615, 616.
Haliaëtus spp. fish for themselves, not being always despoilers of *Pandion*; etymology and orthography of the generic name: *Haliaëtus*, and less properly in science the poetic form *Haliæëtus*, but never *Haliætus*.

1868. [HOMEYER, A. V.?] Kampf zwischen Adler und Fuchs. < *Aus. der Natur*, xlv, oder n. F., xxxiii, 1868, p. 544.

1868. RODD, E. H. Roughlegged Buzzard [Archibuteo lagopus] near Truro. < *Zoologist*, 2d ser., iii, 1867, p. 1058.

1869. BARBOZA DU BOCAGE, J. V.   Museu Nacional de Lisboa | — | Secção Zoologica | — | Catalogo das Collecções Ornithologicas | — | Psittaci—Papagaios. | Accipitre—sAves de Rapina. | — | Junho de 1869. | [Arms.] | Lisboa | Imprensa Nacional | 1869 8vo. pp. 62.

> ". . . enceto agora a publicação dos catalogos das collecções zoologicas do museu de Lisboa. Os primeiros que se pôde levar à conclusão comprehendem duas ordens de aves, os *Psittacideos* ou *papagaios* e as *Aves de rapina*. Estes catalogos foram redigidos pelo sr. José Augusto de Sousa, . . . Os *Psittacideos* constam de 204 especies e as *Aves de rapina* [pp. 29–62] de 223." Cf. *Ibis*, 1870, pp. 134, 135.

1869. BREE, C. R.   Whitetailed Eagle [Haliaëtus albicilla] in Suffolk.   < *Zoologist*, 2d ser., iv, 1869, pp. 1558, 1559.

1869. CLIFTON, *Lord*.   Peregrine Falcon [Falco peregrinus] in Kent.   < *Zoologist*, 2d ser., iv, 1869, p. 1598.

1869. GRAVIL, J. F., JR.   Osprey [Pandion haliaëtus] at Epworth.   < *Zoologist*, 2d ser., iv, 1869, p. 1559.

1869. GRAVIL, J. F., JR.   Peregrine Falcon [Falco peregrinus] at Epworth.   < *Zoologist*, 2d ser., iv, 1869, p. 1559.

1869. GRAVIL, J. F., JR.   Hen Harrier [Circus cyaneus] at Epworth.   < *Zoologist*, 2d ser., iv, 1869, p. 1560.

1869. GREGSON, C. S.   The Peregrine Falcon [Falco peregrinus] breeding in Lancashire.   < *Zoologist*, 2d ser., iv, 1869, p. 1846.

1869. GUNN, T. E.   Capture of an Osprey [Pandion haliaëtus] in the North Sea.   < *Zoologist*, 2d ser., iv, 1869, p. 1512.

1869. GUNN, T. E.   Roughlegged Buzzard [Archibuteo lagopus] in Suffolk.   < *Zoologist*, 2d ser., iv, 1869, p. 1513.

1869. GUNN, T. E.   Peregrine Falcon [Falco peregrinus] and Merlin [F. æsalon] in Norfolk.   < *Zoologist*, 2d ser., iv, 1869, p. 1513.

1869. GUNN, T. E.   Roughlegged Buzzard [Archibuteo lagopus] in Norfolk.   < *Zoologist*, 2d ser., iv, 1869, pp. 1598, 1599.

1869. GUNN, T. E.   Osprey [Pandion haliaëtus] in Norfolk.   < *Zoologist*, 2d ser., iv, 1869, p. 1721.

1869. "G. W. L."   [On a hawk catching an owl.]   < *Am. Nat.*, ii, 1869, p. 670.

> Two sentences, stating the fact, and asking if it is a common thing.

1869. HOY, P. R.   [On the nidification of Cooper's Hawk (Accipiter cooperi).]   < *Proc. Boston Soc. Nat. Hist.*, xii, 1869, pp. 396, 397.

1869. [NEWTON, A.]   [Extracts from a letter from T. M. Brewer, relating to his mistake of an Egg for that of Falco columbarius, &c. Cf. Ibis, 1868, p. 347.]   < *Ibis*, 2d ser., v, 1869, pp. 422, 423.

1869. SCLATER, P. L., *and* SALVIN, O.   Notes on the Species of the Genus Asturina.   < *P. Z. S.*, xxxvii, 1869, pp. 129–134.

> Systematic synopsis of 7 spp., with synonymy, diagnosis, and criticism. *A. ruficauda*, p. 133, sp. n.

1869. SCLATER, P. L., *and* SALVIN, O.   Notes on the Species of the Genus Micrastur.   < *P. Z. S.*, xxxvii, 1869, pp. 364–369.

> Synonymatic and diagnostic synopsis of 7 spp., with critical commentary.

1869. SKINNER, A.   Roughlegged Buzzard [Archibuteo lagopus] near Faversham.   < *Zoologist*, 2d ser., iv, 1869, p. 1559.

1869. STEVENSON, H.   Golden Eagle [Aquila chrysaëtus] in Norfolk.   < *Zoologist*, 2d ser., iv, 1869, p. 1863.

1869. WONFOR, T. W.   Whitetailed Eagle [Haliaëtus albicilla] in Sussex.   < *Zoologist*, 2d ser., iv, 1869, p. 1512.

1869. WONFOR, T. W.   Peregrine Falcon [Falco peregrinus] in Sussex.   < *Zoologist*, 2d ser., iv, 1869, p. 1559.

1869. WONFOR, T. W. Peregrine Falcon [Falco peregrinus] near Brighton. *< Zoologist*, 2d ser., iv, 1869, p. 1598.

1869. WOOD, W. [Habits of] The Red-tailed Hawk [Buteo borealis]. *< Am. Nat.,* iii, 1869, pp. 393–397.

1870. ABBOTT, C. C. The Marsh Harrier [Circus hudsonius]. *< Am. Nat.,* iv, 1870, 377.

1870. ABBOTT, C. C. Curious Conduct of a Sharp-shinned Hawk [Accipiter fuscus]. *< Am. Nat.,* iv, 1870, pp. 439, 440.
  Gathering and preparing grass for its nest.

1870. ALLEN, J. A. What is the "Washington Eagle"? *< Am. Nat.,* iv, 1870, pp. 524–527.
  It is stated to be *Haliaëtus leucocephalus.*

1870. ALLISON, T. Anecdote of the Sparrow-hawk [Falco sparverius]. *< Am. Nat.,* iv, 1870, p. 53.

1870. BLAKE-KNOX, H. Osprey [Pandion haliaëtus] in County Kerry. *< Zoologist,* 2d ser., v, 1870, p. 2406.

1870. BROOKE, V. [On the occurrence in Ireland of Astur atricapillus.] *< Ibis*, 2d ser., vi, 1870, pp. 538, 539.

1870. COLLETE, J. R. The Osprey (Pandion haliaëtus [carolinensis]). *< Am. Nat.,* iv, 1870, p. 57.
  A biographical note.

1870. GUNN, T. E. Hen Harrier [Circus cyaneus] in Suffolk. *< Zoologist,* 2d ser., v, 1870, p. 1980.

1870. GUNN, T. E. Harriers [Circus cyaneus] in Norfolk. *< Zoologist,* 2d ser., v, 1870, p. 2382.

1870. GURNEY, J. H. [Circus "hudsonius" of Ibis, 1868, p. 356 = C. melanoleucus.] *< Ibis*, 2d ser., vi, 1870, pp. 444, 445.

1870. HART, W., *and* SON. Osprey [Pandion haliaëtus] at Poole. *< Zoologist,* 2d ser., v, 1870, p. 2382.

1870. HARVIE-BROWN, J. A. [On sites of the nests of Falco peregrinus in Scotland.] *< Ibis*, 2d ser., vi, 1870, p. 297.

1870. NEWTON, A. [Exhibition of Skins of Falcons from Alaska, referred to F. islandicus.] *< P. Z. S.,* xxxviii, 1870, p. 384.

1870. RIDGWAY, R. A New Classification of the North American Falconidæ, with Descriptions of Three New Species. *< Proc. Acad. Nat. Sci. Phila.,* xxii, 1870, pp. 138–150.
  6 subfamilies. *Pandion* referred to *Milvinæ.*—Analytical tables of chars. of the groups, genera, and most of the species. *Onychotes,* pp. 142, 149, g. n. ; *O. gruberi,* pp. 142, 149 ; *Falco richardsonii,* pp. 145, 147 ; *F. leucophrys,* pp. 140, 147, spp. nn. Cf. *Ibis,* 1871, pp. 460, 461.
  The classification is based chiefly on the characters afforded by the structure of the "superciliary process of the lachrymal bone," whether rudimentary and not visible from the outside, or whether developing a superciliary shield. The author later very materially modified his views, upon further consideration of the general osteological structure of the family (cf. *Bull. U. S. Geol. and Geogr. Surv.,* 2d ser., No. 4, June 10, 1875, pp. 225–231, pll. xi–xviii).

1870. RODD, E. H. Iceland Falcon [Falco islandicus] in Cornwall. *< Zoologist,* 2d ser., v, 1870, pp. 2017, 2018.

1870. RODD, E. H. The Iceland Jer Falcon [Falco islandicus] in Cornwall. *< Zoologist,* 2d ser., v, 1870, p. 2060.

1870. ROWLEY, G. D. [Anecdote of a] Hen Harrier [Circus cyaneus]. *< Zoologist,* 2d ser., v, 1870, p. 2343.

1870. STEARNS, W. A. The Pigeon Hawk [i. e., Falco sparverius, not Falco columbarius as supposed.] *< Am. Nat.,* iv, 1870, p. 439.
  Note of breeding at Amherst, Mass., U. S. A. (cf. *op. cit.,* v, p. 56.)

1870. WOOD, W.   Falconry.   < *Am. Nat.*, iv, 1870, pp. 74–82.
A short popular sketch of the subject, chiefly historical.

1870. WOODMAN, W.   The Nesting of the Fish Hawk [Pandion carolinensis.]   < *Am. Nat.*, iv, 1870, pp. 559, 560.
Criticism of E. A. Samuels's statement.

1871. ABBOTT, C. C.   The Nest of the Pigeon Hawk [Falco columbarius.]   < *Am. Nat.*, v, 1871, pp. 248–250.
Ref. to T. M. Brewer, *tom. cit.*, p. 56, and W. A. Stearns, *op. cit.*, iv, p. 439.

1871. ALLEN, J. A.   The Migration of Hawks.   < *Am. Nat.*, v, 1871, p. 173.
Confirms W. Wood's observations (*op. cit.*, iv, pp. 759, 760).

1871. BOYES, F.   Marsh Harrier [Circus æruginosus] in East Yorkshire.   < *Zoologist*, 2d ser., vi, 1871, p. 2847.

1871. BOYES, F.   Ospreys [Pandion haliaëtus] in East Yorkshire.   < *Zoologist*, 2d ser., vi, 1871, p. 2847.

1871. BREWER, T. M.   The ["]Pigeon Hawk["].   < *Am. Nat.*, v, 1871, pp. 56, 57.
Corrects misstatement of W. Stearns, *op. cit.*, iv, p. 439.

1871. BROOKE, A. B.   Graylag Goose and American Goshawk [Astur atricapillus, in Ireland].   < *Zoologist*, 2d ser., vi, 1871, pp. 2524, 2525.

1871. CAREY, C. B.   Whitetailed Eagle [Haliaëtus albicilla] in Alderney.   < *Zoologist*, 2d ser., vi, 1871, p. 2866.

1871. GUNN, T. E.   Roughlegged Buzzard [Archibuteo lagopus] near Yarmouth.   < *Zoologist*, 2d ser., vi, 1871, p. 2847.

1871. HADFIELD H.   [On the characters of the European and American] Roughlegged Buzzard.   < *Zoologist*, 2d ser., vi, 1871, pp. 2764, 2765.

1871. HOMEYER, E. F. VON.   Monographische Beiträge.   I. Gennaja und Falco Kaup.   < *J. f. O.*, xix, 1871, pp. 39–56.
Commentary on what the writer considers the established species: *FF. tanypterus, cervicalis, jugger; peregrinus, minor, calidus, peregrinator, melanogenys, peregrinoides.*

1871. JARVIS, W.   The Duck Hawk [Falco communis, breeding in White Mountains of New Hampshire].   < *Am. Nat.*, v, 1871, p. 662.

1871. NEWTON, A.   On certain species of Falconidæ, Tetraonidæ, and Anatidæ.   < *Proc. Acad. Nat. Sci. Phila.*, 1871, pp. 94–100.
Discussing the Great Northern Falcon question, and recognizing three species—*Falco candicans, islandicus, gyrfalco,* the comparative diagnoses of which are given.

1871. REEKS, H.   [Distinction of American and European] Roughlegged Buzzard.   < *Zoologist*, 2d ser., vi, 1871, p. 2726.

1871. RODD, E. H.   Marsh Harrier [Circus æruginosus] at St. Mary's, Scilly.   < *Zoologist*, 2d ser., vi, 1871, p. 2847.

1871. SAUNDERS, H.   [Exhibition of, and Remarks upon, a series of Birds of the genus Aquila.]   < *P. Z. S.*, xxxvix, 1871, pp. 37–39.

1871. SMITH, C.   Marsh Harrier [Circus æruginosus] in Somersetshire.   < *Zoologist*, 2d ser., vi, 1871, pp. 2866, 2867.

1871. STEARNS, W. A.   The Pigeon Hawk.   Correction [of misstatement made by writer, op. cit., iv, p. 439, the species being F. sparverius, not F. columbarius].   < *Am. Nat.*, v, 1871, p. 253.

1871. WOOD, W.   The Game Falcons of New England.   < *Am. Nat.*, v, 1871, pp. 80–87.
Relates chiefly to *Falco communis*—biographical, descriptive, etc.

1871. WOOD, W.   Migration of Hawks.   < *Am. Nat.*, iv, 1871, pp. 759, 760.
Note on the large flights occasionally observed.

1872. BUCKLEY, H.   On some new or rare Birds' Eggs.   < *P. Z. S.*, May 7, 1872, pp. 625, 626.
Falco polyagrus, Elanoides furcatus, Ictinia mississippiensis.

1872. CABANIS, J.   [Gruppe der Würgfalken, Pnigohierax (n. g.) laniarius, jugger, und mexicanus.]   < *J. f. O.*, xx, 1872, pp. 156, 157.

1872. CAREY, C. B.   Another Whitetailed Eagle [Haliaëtus albicilla] in Guernsey. < *Zoologist* 2d ser., vii, 1872, p. 2911.

1872. COUCH, J.   Foot of the Whitetailed Eagle [Haliaëtus albicilla].   < *Zoologist*, 2d ser., vii, 1872, p. 2911.

1872. DRESSER, H. E.   [Remarks on exhibition of Skins of various Eagles (Aquila).] < *P. Z. S.*, 1872, pp. 863–865.

1872. FEILDEN, H. W.   Ospreys [Pandion haliaëtus] in Hampshire.   < *Zoologist*, 2d ser., vii, 1872, pp. 2991, 2992.

1872. HADFIELD, H.   Golden Eagle [Aquila chrysaëtus] in the Isle of Wight.   < *Zoologist*, 2d ser., vii, 1872, pp. 3309–3311.

1872. RICKARDS, M. S. C.   Whitetailed Eagle [Haliaëtus albicilla] in Gloucestershire.   < *Zoologist*, 2d ser., vii, 1872, p. 2991.

1872. SALVIN, O.   A further Revision of the Genus Leucopternis, with a Description of a new Species.   < *Ibis*, 1872, pp. 239–243, pl. viii.
　　10 spp.   *Leucopternis plumbea*, p. 240, pl. viii, sp. n.

1873. ANON.   A battle in the air [between "large brown eagles"].   < *Forest and Stream*, i, Sept. 11, 1873, p. 71.

1873. ANON.   Whitetailed Eagle [Haliaëtus albicilla] near Rye.   < *Zoologist*, 2d ser., viii, 1873, p. 3411.
　　From "Field," Nov. 30.

1873. BECK, T.   Peregrine [Falcon, Falco peregrinus] near Scarborough.   < *Zoologist*, 2d ser., viii, 1873, p. 3802.

1873. BOLLE, C.   [Haliaëtus albicilla in der Mark.]   < *J. f. O.*, 1873, p. 74.

1873. "FRED BEVERLY" [FRED. A. OBER].   The Peregrine Falcon (Falco anatum). < *Forest and Stream*, i, Oct. 30, 1873, p. 181.

1873. GILPIN, J. B.   On the Eagles of Nova Scotia.   < *Trans. Nova Scotia Inst. Nat. Sci.*, iii, pt. iii, 1872 (pub. 1873), pp. 202–208.
　　2 spp.—*Aquila chrysœtos* [sic], *Halieatus* [sic] *leucocephalus*.

1873. GILPIN, [J.] B.   Variation in the Tarsal Envelope of the Bald Eagle [Haliaëtus leucocephalus].   < *Ann. Nat.*, vii, 1873, pp. 429, 430.
　　With editorial note by E. Coues.

1873. GREEN, C. A.   Sea Eagle [Haliaëtus albicilla] in Jersey.   < *Zoologist*, 2d ser., viii, 1873, p. 3411.

1873. GURNEY, J. H., JR.   Osprey [Pandion haliaëtus] at Hempstead.   < *Zoologist*, 2d ser., viii, 1873, pp. 3367, 3368.

1873. HERSCHEL, J.   The Flight of the Eagle.   < *Forest and Stream*, i, Sept. 18, 1873, p. 85.

1873. HOOPES, B. A.   Description of a new variety of Buteo [borealis var kriderii]. < *Proc. Acad. Nat. Sci. Phila.*, xxv, 1873, pp. 238, 239, pl. 5.

1873. HOOPES, B. A.   [Description of a new species of hawk, Buteo borealis var. kriderii.]   < *Forest and Stream*, i, Oct. 16, 1873, p. 150.

1873. MAYNARD, C. J.   Blue Kite—Everglade Kite.   So-for-fun-i-kar [Rostrhamus sociabilis].   < *Am. Sportsm.*, iii, 1873, p. 181.
　　Biography, from his "Birds of Florida", 4to, Salem.

1873. NEWTON, A.   On the Great Northern Falcons.   < *Ann. Mag. Nat. Hist.*, 4th ser., xii, 1873, pp. 485–487.
　　Protests against the "retrograde" opinion of R. B. Sharpe, *P. Z. S.*, 1873, pp. 414–419; confirming that of J. Hancock, *Ann. Mag.*, 2d ser., xiii, pp. 110–112, and *Ann. N. H.*, ii, 1838, pp. 241–250.

1873. RIDGWAY, R.   Catalogue of the Ornithological Collection of the Boston Society of Natural History.   Part II.   Falconidæ.   < *Proc. Bost. Soc. Nat. Hist.*, xvi, 1873, pp. 43–72.

1873. RIDGWAY, R.—Continued.

Part I was A. Hyatt on *Spheniscidæ, op. cit.*, xiv, p. 237.—A simple catalogue, with reference to the locality, when known, of each specimen, which is mentioned by the Society's number, the original number of the Lafresnaye Collection, when any, being also given; numbers of species according to Gray's *Hand List* also affixed. *Rhynchofalco*, p. 46; *Antenor*, p. 63, nn. subgg. Cf. Coues, *Am. Nat.*, 1874, pp. 541-546.

1873. RIDGWAY, R. Revision of the Falconine Genera, Micrastur, Geranospiza and Rupornis, and the Strigine Genus, Glaucidium. < *Proc. Bost. Soc. Nat. Hist.*, xvi, 1873, pp. 73–106.

Published as an "Appendix" to the author's catalogue of the *Falconidæ* of the Boston Society, *tom. cit.*, pp. 43–72. An elaborate article, with characters and synonymy of the genera and species, analytical tables, etc., based upon examination of an unusually large series of specimens. *Micrastur*, 5 spp.; *Geranospiza*, 2 spp.; *Rupornis*, 2 spp.; *Glaucidium*, 8 spp.; besides several "varieties" of each of these genera excepting the first. There is much rectification of synonymy according to the views of the writer, which are not in entire accord with those of other authors. Cf. Coues, *Am. Nat.*, 1874.

Glaucidium is treated on pp. 91–106. This is the first elaborate monograph of the genus, and led to the subsequent revisions of the group by Mr. Sharpe (1875) and Mr. Ridgway (1876). (See *anteà* under *Strigidæ*.) The species allowed in this monograph are *G. passerinum* var. *californicum* (= *G. gnoma*). *G. pumilum*, *G. lansbergii* (= rufous phase of *G. jardinii*), *G. jardinii*, *G. ferrugineum*, *G. infuscatum* (= *G. ferrugineum*), *G. infuscatum* var. *gnoma* (= *G. ferrugineum*), *G. nanum*, and *G. siju*. *G. lansbergii* is described as new, (but has been determined to be the rufous phase of *G. jardinii*).—The rectifications here given in parenthesis are derived from the author's later study.

1873. SCHLEGEL, H. Revue de la Collection des Oiseaux de Proie faisant partie du Musée des Pays-Bas. < *Mus. Nat. Hist. Pays-Bas*, 10e livr., Juillet 1873, pp. 1–156.

The author here reviews the whole subject, which he had previously gone over in 1862-3, but has not apparently much to add to science, though noting the increase of the Museum.

Otus capensis major, p. 3; *Noctua hirsuta minor*, p. 24; *Falco neglectus*, p. 43; *Astur henstii*, p. 62; *Baza celebensis*, p. 135, spp. nn.

1873. SHARPE, R. B. On the Falco arcticus of Holböll, with Remarks on the changes of Plumage in some other Accipitrine Birds. < *P. Z. S.*, 1873, pp. 414–419, pl. xxxix.

F. holboelli, p. 415, sp. n. The pl. shows changes of plumage in *Falco, Cymindis*, and *Accipiter*. Cf. especially Newton, *Ann. Mag. Nat. Hist.*, xii, 1873, pp. 485-487.

1873. STEENSTRUP, J. Om de Mærker, som Knoklerne i Fuglenes ophulkede Foderboller bære af Opholdet i Fuglenes Maver, samt om disse Mærkers Betydning for Geologien og Archæologien. < *Vidensk. Meddel. Naturhist. Foren. Kjöbenhavn* for Aaret 1872 (1873), pp. 211–236, pl. iv.

This is the full text of the article, a résumé of which, in French, is given in the same volume, pp. 28–36, and also in *Gerv. Journ. de Zool.*, iii, 1873, pp. 488-498.

1873. STEENSTRUP, J. Sur les marques que portent les os contenus dans les pelotes rejetées par les oiseaux de proie et sur l'importance de ces marques pour la géologie et l'archéologie. < *Vidensk. Meddel. Naturhist. Foren. Kjöbenhavn* for Aaret 1872 (1873), pp. 28–36, pl. iv.

1873. STEENSTRUP, J. Sur les marques que portent les os contenus dans les pelotes rejetées par les oiseaux de proie et sur l'importance de ces marques pour la géologie et l'archéologie. < *Gerv. Journ. de Zool.*, ii, 1873, pp. 488-498, pl. xx.

Analyse, faite par l'auteur, de son Mémoire inséré dans le *Vidensk. Meddel. fra den Naturh. Foren. i Kjöbenh.* for Aaret 1872, 1873, p. 211-236, pl. iv.

1873. WOOD, W. The Game Falcons of New England. The Pigeon Hawk [Falco columbarius]. < *Am. Nat.*, vii, 1873, pp. 340–345.

A biography of this species.

1874. ANON. An Eagle's struggle with a Girl. < *Am. Sportsman*, iii, 1873-4, p. 375.

Quoted from Jacksonville, Florida, *Republican* (newspaper). An eagle attacks a child 14 years old.

1874. ANON. Singular Capture of an Eagle. < *Zoologist*, 2d ser., ix, 1874, p. 3953.

From *Inverness Advertiser*.

1874. BARRINGTON, R. M. Golden Eagle [Aquila chrysaëtus] at Powerscourt. < *Zoologist,* 2d ser., ix, 1874, p. 3952.

1874. CLARK-KENNEDY, A. J. An Osprey [Pandion haliaëtus] carrying off Young Chickens. < *Zoologist,* 2d ser., ix, 1874, pp. 3996, 3997.

1874. COUES, E. Habits and Characteristics of Swainson's Buzzard [Buteo swainsoni]. < *Am. Nat.,* viii, 1874, pp. 282–287.
Extended description and biography.

1874. GUNN, T. E. Marsh Harrier [Circus æruginosus] in Suffolk. < *Zoologist,* 2d ser., ix, 1874, p. 4117.

1874. HADFIELD, H. Peregrines [Falco peregrinus] in the Isle of Wight. < *Zoologist,* 2d ser., ix, 1874, pp. 4032, 4033.

1874. HARVIE-BROWN, J. A. Osprey [Pandion haliaëtus] carrying off Chickens. < *Zoologist,* 2d ser., ix, 1874, p. 4117.

1874. "NIMROD." [JARVIS, W.] The Peregrine Falcon (Falco Peregrinus). < *Am. Sportsman,* iii, 1874, p. 323.

1874. RUFF, M. D. Fish-Hawks [Pandion carolinensis) and their Nests. < *St. Nicholas Mag.,* i, 1874, pp. 79–82, one illust.

1874. SHARPE, R. B. Catalogue | of the | Accipitres, | or | Diurnal Birds of Prey, | in the | collection | of the | British Museum. | By | R. Bowdler Sharpe. | London: | printed by order of the Trustees. | 1874. ¹ vol. pp. i–xiv, 1–480, pll. i–xiv, numberless cuts in text.

This is the first volume of the New British Museum Catalogue of Birds, the title of the work as one of the series being: Catalogue | of the | Birds | of the | British Museum. | Volume I. | London: | printed by order of the Trustees. | 1874. The scope of these new Catalogues is greatly enlarged over that of previous ones, and much beyond the requirements of a mere list: being, in fact, a series of monographs of the different groups treated. The present volume, like that on the Owls, is by Mr. Sharpe. It contains a very full account of all the known species of Diurnal Birds of Prey, 377 in number, of which only about 25 are wanting in the collection. These are elaborately described, with extensive synonymy, analytical keys to the species and genera, &c. Many details of structure are illustrated by the woodcuts, and a number of species are figured in colors. The total number of specimens handled is 2,466.

The author's classification has been much criticised. He divides the *Raptores* into three suborders, *Falcones, Pandiones,* and *Striges.* The *Pandiones* include only the two genera *Pandion* and *Polioaëtus.* The *Falcones* are made to consist of two families, *Falconidæ* and *Vulturidæ.* The latter include the *Cathartidæ,* certainly more different from *Vulturidæ* than these are from *Falconidæ.* The *Falconidæ* are divided into *Polyborinæ, Accipitrinæ, Buteoninæ, Aquilinæ, Falconinæ.* Under the first of these subfamilies are ranged *Cariama!* and *Serpentarius.* These birds are treated under 80 genera, of which the following 9 are new: *Lophogyps,* p. 15; *Œnops,* p. 25; *Urotriorchis,* p. 83; *Erythrocnema,* p. 84; *Heterospizias,* p. 160; *Buteola,* p. 201; *Lophotriorchis,* p. 255; *Henicopernis,* p. 241; *Microhierax,* p. 366. The following species are figured:

Pl. I. *Gyps kolbi.* II. f. 1, *Œnops falklandica;* f. 2, *Œ. urubitinga.* III. *Astur macroscelides.* IV. f. 1, *A. soloensis;* f. 2, *A. cuculoides.* V. *A. wallacii.* VI. f. 1, *A. toussenelii;* f. 2, *Accipiter hartlaubii.* VII. f. 1, *Buteo plumipes;* f. 2, *Archibuteo strophiatus.* VIII. *Buteo ferox.* IX. *Spilornis pallidus.* X. f. 1, *Baza magnirostris;* f. 2, *B. erythrothorax.* XI, f. 1, *B. sumatrensis;* f. 2, *B. cuculoides.* XII. *Falco minor.* XIII, *Hierofalco holbœlli.* XIV. f. 1, *Cerchneis alopex;* f. 2, *C. zoniventris.*

1874. SUNDEVALL, C. J. Fornyad Anordnung av Dagroofoglarna (Dispositio nova Accipitrum Hemeroharpagorum). < *Öfvers. af Kongl. Vetensk.-Akad. Förh.,* 1874, pp. 21–29.
Not seen:—*Plangus neogæus,* p. 28.

1874. UNWIN, W. H. On the Breeding of the Golden Eagle (Aquila chrysaëtos) in North-western India. < *P. Z. S.,* xlii, 1874, pp. 208–212.

1874. WOOD, W. The Game Falcons of New England. The Sparrow Hawk [Falco sparverius]. < *Am. Nat.,* viii, 1874, pp. 266–270.
Biographical notice.

1875. ANON. Hawking. < *Rod and Gun,* vi, Aug. 14, 1875, p. 294.
Reprint from the *London Quarterly.*

1875. ANON. [Eagles in Pennsylvania.] < *Rod and Gun,* vi, Nov. 20, 1875, p. 124.

1875. ANON. Whitetailed Eagle [Haliaëtus albicilla] in Northamptonshire. < *Zoologist,* 2d ser., x, Feb., 1875, p. 4337.
From *The Field,* Jan. 16, 1875.

1875. "AUDUBON" [*pseudon.*]. Eagles [Haliaëtus leucocephalus] on the Susquehanna. < *Forest and Stream,* v, Nov. 25, 1875, p. 243.

1875. AUDUBON, J. J. The Golden Eagle, Aquila chrysaetus, Linn. < *The Oölogist,* i, 1875, pp. 68, 69.
Quoted from his work.

1875. BLASIUS, W. [Ueber die nordischen Jagdfalken.] < *Ber. über d. xxi. Vers. d. deut. Orn.-Ges.,* 1875, pp. 17, 18.

1875. BOARDMAN, G. A. [Haliaëtus leucocephalus catching its own fish.] < *Forest and Stream,* iv, Feb. 18, 1875, p. 22.

1875. "BOB." Great Flight of Hawks. < *Rod and Gun,* vii, Oct. 2, 1875, p. 3.

1875. CLARK-KENNEDY, A. J. Whitetailed Eagle [Haliaëtus albicilla] in Norfolk. < *Zoologist,* 2d ser., x, Nov., 1875, p. 4690.

1875. CLARK-KENNEDY, A. J. Osprey [Pandion haliaëtus] in Suffolk. < *Zoologist,* 2d ser., x, Nov., 1875, p. 4690.

1875. CORBIN, G. E. Osprey [Pandion haliaëtus] in Hampshire. < *Zoologist,* 2d ser., x, Nov., 1875, p. 4690.

1875. D[AVIS], F. J. Nest and Eggs of the Broad-winged Hawk. (Buteo pennsylvanicus.) < *The Oölogist,* i, 1875, p. 2.

1875. DRESSER, H. E. Notes on Falco labradorus, Aud., Falco sacer, Forster, and Falco spadiceus, Forster. < *P. Z. S.,* Mar. 2, 1875, pp. 114–117.
1. *F. labradorus* is distinguished as a good species. *F. sacer* is queried as a synonym of *F. gyrfalco. F. spadiceus,* which Sharpe and Ridgway had each referred to *Archibuteo sanctijohannis,* and of which Vieillot had made a *Buteo spadiceus,* is identified with *Circus hudsonius.*

1875. [FITCH, E. H.] The Swallow-tailed Kite. (Nauclerus forficatus.) < *The Scientific Monthly* (Toledo, Ohio), i, No. ii, 1875, pp. 41–44, fig.
Popular account.

1875. G[RAY], A. F. [Haliaëtus leucocephalus in Massachusetts.] < *Forest and Stream,* iv, Feb. 18, 1875, p. 22.

1875-79. GURNEY, J. H. Notes on a 'Catalogue of the Accipitres in the British Museum,' by R. Bowdler Sharpe (1874). < *Ibis,* 3d ser., v, Jan., 1875, pp. 87–96; Apr., 1875, pp. 221–236; July, 1875, pp. 353–370, pl. vi; Oct., 1875, pp. 468–484.— vi, Jan., 1876, pp. 65–77, pl. iii; Apr., 1876, pp. 230–243; July, 1876, pp. 364–376; Oct., 1876, pp. 467–493.—4th ser., i, Apr., 1877, pp. 209–236; July, 1877, pp. 325–333; Oct., 1877, pp. 418–437.—ii, Jan., 1878, pp. 84–102, pl. ii; Apr., 1878, pp. 145–164: July, 1878, pp. 352–356; Oct., 1878, pp. 451–466.—iii, Apr., 1879, pp. 71–84; July, 1879, pp. 330–341; Oct., 1879, pp. 464–470. (Continued in 1880.)
Accipiter ovampensis, 1875, pl. vi. *Buteo hypospodius,* 1876, pl. iii. *Dryotriorchis spectabilis,* 1878, pl. ii.
This is a very notable series of papers, forming a critical review of Mr. Sharpe's work, from a hand long specially practised in this department of ornithology. Containing as it does many elaborate discussions of doubtful points and extended descriptions of specimens, as well as other add itions to and corrections of Mr. Sharpe's Catalogue, it is almost necessarily to be consulted by any one using the work of the last-named author.

1875. HENSHAW, H. W. Avi-Fauna—A Correction. < *Rod and Gun,* vi, Apr. 24, 1875, p. 57.
Capt. Bendire's discovery of *Urubitinga anthracina* in Arizona.

1875. INGERSOLL, E. Eagles. < *Forest and Stream,* v, Nov. 4, 1875, p. 195.
Bald eagle reported as carrying away children and lambs in Pennsylvania.

1875. "J. H. D." "Cave Aquilam." < *Rod and Gun,* vi, May 8, 1875, p. 91.
"Large brown eagle" seizing ducks shot by gunners.

1875. MATHEW, M. A.   Flight of a Male Peregrine at an old Male Hen Harrier.   < *Zoologist*, 2d ser., x, Jan., 1875, pp. 4296, 4297.

1875. "NIMROD." [JARVIS, W.]   The Swallow-tailed hawk [Elanoides forficatus]. < *Forest and Stream*, v, Oct. 21, 1875, p. 163.
Merely descriptive of plumage and habit.

1875. "NIMROD." [JARVIS, W.] [Haliaëtus leucocephalus capturing its own fish.] < *Forest and Stream*, iii, Jan. 28, 1875, p. 389.

1875. RIDGWAY, R.   The Sparrow hawk or American Kestrel [Tinnunculus sparverius].   < *Rod and Gun*, vi, July 3, 1875, pp. 209 and 220.

1875. RIDGWAY, R.   Notice of a very rare Hawk [Onychotes gruberi].   < *Rod and Gun*, vi, May 1, 1875, p. 65.

1875. RIDGWAY, R.   On Nisus cooperi (Bonaparte), and N. gundlachi (Lawrence). < *Proc. Acad. Nat. Sci. Phila.*, 1875, pp. 78–88.
A very elaborate article, descriptive, synonymatic and critical, in which the distinction of these two species is maintained. The synonymy is very copious.

1875. RIDGWAY, R.   On the Buteonine Subgenus Craxirex, Gould.   < *Proc. Acad. Nat. Sci. Phila.*, 1875, pp. 89–119.
Very complete treatment, with copious synonymy, exhaustive description, and much critical comment, of 6 spp.: *Buteo* (*Craxirex*) *galapagoensis, poliosomus, erythronotus, albicaudatus, swainsoni*, and *pennsylvanicus*, which are all the species the author allows to stand in this particular group, distinguished from typical *Buteo* (type *vulgaris*) by having only three instead of four outer primaries emarginate on their inner webs. *Tachytriorchis* and *Poecilopternis* of Kaup are regarded as strictly synonymous. The group is considered peculiar to America, four of the species being neotropical.

1875. RIDGWAY, R.   Outlines of a Natural Arrangement of the Falconidæ.   < *Bull. U. S. Geol. Surv. Terr.*, 2d ser., No. 4, June 10, 1875, pp. 225–231, pll. xi–xviii.
Divided into *Falconinæ* and *Buteoninæ*: *Falconinæ* subdivided into *Falcones, Polybori, Micrastures, Herpetotheres*. Cf. *Ibis*, 1875, pp. 498–500.
Compare same author, *Pr. Phila. Acad.*, 1870, pp. 138–150. That former classification is here very decidedly modified, upon broader consideration of the osteology of the family, with special reference to characters afforded by the sternum and shoulder-girdle, many of the features of which are illustrated on the plates.

1875. "ROAMER."   Eagles [Haliaëtus leucocephalus].   < *Forest and Stream*, iv, Mar. 4, 1875, p. 55.

1875. SHARPE, R. B.   Contributions to a History of the Accipitres.   Notes on Birds of Prey in the Museum at the Jardin des Plantes and in the Collection of Mons. A. Bouvier.   < *Ibis*, 3d ser., v, Apr., 1875, pp. 253–261.
Notes on 12 spp. *Microhierax sinensis* (David, MSS.), p. 254; *Syrnium davidi*, p. 256; *Glaucidium tephronotum, Scotopelia bouvieri*, p. 260, spp. nn. List of 6 spp. of *Carine*, 28 spp. of *Ninox*, 24 spp. of *Glaucidium*.

1875. WHITAKER, J.   Peregrine Falcon in Nottinghamshire.   < *Zoologist*, 2d ser., x, July, 1875, p. 4537.

1875. WILLMOTT, C.   Golden Eagle [Aquila chrysaëtus] near Chatteris.   < *Zoologist*, 2d ser., x, Nov., 1875, p. 4703.

1876. BARRINGTON, R. M.   Golden Eagles trained to capture Wolves and Foxes. < *Zoologist*, 2d ser., xi, Nov., 1876, p. 5162.

1876. BREWSTER, W.   Winter habits of buzzard hawks.   < *Forest and Stream*, vi, Feb. 10, 1876, p. 3.

1876. BROWNE, MONTAGU.   Osprey [Pandion haliaëtus] near Birmingham.   < *Zoologist*, 2d ser., xi, Jan., 1876, p. 4759.

1876. CARTWRIGHT, D. W.   A plucky eagle.   < *Rod and Gun*, viii, Apr. 22, 1876, p. 55.
Anecdote from "Western Wild Animals."

1876. CHARBONNIER, H. J.   Greenland Falcon in Scotland.   < *Zoologist*, 2d ser., xi, June, 1876, p. 4954.

1876. C[LARKE], S. C. Fish hawks and eagles [in Florida]. < *Forest and Stream*, vii, Dec. 7, 1876, p. 276. See vol. viii, p. 4.

1876. CLARK-KENNEDY, A. J. Whitetailed Eagle in Suffolk. < *Zoologist*, 2d ser., xi, Dec., 1876, p. 5178.

1876. CONCH, J. Greenland or Iceland Falcon in Guernsey. < *Zoologist*, 2d ser., xi, June, 1876, pp. 4953, 4954.

1876. COPE, W. J. Peregrine Falcons breeding on the Yorkshire Coast. < *Zoologist*, 2d ser., xi, July, 1876, p. 5000.

1876. CORDEAUX, J. Food of Peregrine, &c. < *Zoologist*, 2d ser., xi, Mar., 1876, pp. 4828, 4829.

1876. COUES, E. Letters on Ornithology. No. 9.—The Red-tailed Buzzard [Buteo borealis] and other Hawks. < *Chicago Field*, vi, No. 19, Dec. 23, 1879, p. 301, fig.
    Popular notice of North American *Falconidæ*, with fig. of head of species named.

1876. DRESSER, H. E. Falco labradorus. (Labrador Falcon.) < *Rowl. Ornith. Misc.*, pt. iii, Jan., 1876, pp. 185–191, pll. xxiv, xv.
    Maintaining the validity of this species in an extended article, illustrated with colored figures of adult and young.

1876. GURNEY, J. H., JR. Peregrine in the City of Norwich. < *Zoologist*, 2d ser., xi, Feb., 1876, p. 4795.

1876. GURNEY, J. H., JR. Notes on the Roughlegged Buzzard. < *Zoologist*, 2d ser., xi, Mar., 1876, p. 4829.

1876. GURNEY, J. H., JR. Plumage of the Roughlegged Buzzard. < *Zoologist*, 2d ser., xi, May, 1876, p. 4921.

1876. GURNEY, J. H., JR. Roughlegged Buzzard. < *Zoologist*, 2d ser., xi, May, 1876, p. 4921.

1876. GURNEY, J. H., JR. Variety of the Sea Eagle. < *Zoologist*, 2d ser., xi, July, 1876, p. 5000.

1876. GURNEY, J. H., JR. Falco peregrinus in Egypt. < *Zoologist*, 2d ser., Aug., 1876, p. 5041.

1876. GURNEY, J. H., JR. Sternum of the Peregrine Falcon. < *Zoologist*, 2d ser., xi, Sept., 1876, p. 5079.

1876. HADFIELD, H. Roughlegged Buzzard. < *Zoologist*, 2d ser., xi, May, 1876, pp. 4920, 4921.

1876. "H. W." The Red-tailed Hawk. < *Forest and Stream*, v, Jan. 6, 1876, p. 340.

1876. [INGERSOLL, E.] American Falconidæ, etc. < *Forest and Stream*, vi, Apr. 13, 1876, p. 148.
    Review of R. Ridgway's papers in *Bull. U. S. Geol. and Geog. Surv. Terr.*, ii, No. 2, 1876.

1876. JACOB, E. Osprey [Pandion haliaëtus] in County Waterford. < *Zoologist*, 2d ser., xi, Jan., 1876, p. 4759.

1876. MATHEW, M. A. Archibuteo Sancti-Johannis. < *Zoologist*, 2d ser., xi, Apr., 1876, p. 4870.
    Its possible occurrence in England.

1876. MAYNARD, C. J. The Common Buzzard Hawk (Buteo vulgaris) of Europe in North America. < *Bull. Nutt. Ornith. Club*, i, No. 1, Apr., 1876, pp. 2–6.
    But see *tom. cit.*, No. 2, July, 1876, p. 32.

1876. McNICHOL, N. Iceland Falcon in Caithness. < *Zoologist*, 2d ser., xi, 1876, p. 4920.

1876. NEWMAN, E. The Eagles of Poetry and Prose. < *Zoologist*, 2d ser., xi, Nov., 1876, pp. 5133, 5136.
    This posthumous fragment appears to have been written with some idea that it should form the commencement of a popular work to be entitled 'British Bird Biography'—an idea probably abandoned, as no continuation has been found.

1876. RAMSAY, E. P.   Catalogue | of the | Australian Accipitres | or | Diurnal Birds of Prey | inhabiting Australia, | in the | Collection of the Australian Museum | at | Sidney, N. S. W. | By | E. Pierson Ramsay, F. L. S., C. M. Z. S., &c., &c. | Curator of the Museum, Sidney. | — | Sidney : | printed by order of the Minister of Justice and Public Instruction. | — | 1876.   pp. i–viii, 1 leaf, pp. 1–64, • 1–3.

> There is another title of this little brochure, according to which it is Part I of a Catalogue of Australian Birds in the Museum.   It is highly wrought for a catalogue—quite in the style of the *Brit. Mus. Catalogues*, treating 27 spp. with description, synonymy, &c.—these being, in fact, all the Diurnal Birds of Prey known to the author to inhabit Australia.

1876. RICHARDSON, W.   Roughlegged Buzzard in Yorkshire.   < *Zoologist*, 2d ser., xi, Jan., 1876, p. 4760.

1876. RIDGWAY, R.   Regarding Buteo vulgaris in North America.   < *Bull. Nutt. Ornith. Club*, i, No. 2, July, 1876, pp. 32–39.

> Critical discussion of the question, with special reference to *tom. cit.*, No. 1, p. 2.

1876. RIDGWAY, R.   Studies of the American Falconidæ.   By Robert Ridgway.   Monograph of the Polybori.   < *Bull. U. S. Geol. Surv. Terr.*, 2d ser., No. 6, Feb. 8, 1876, pp. 451–473, pll. 22–26.

> The genera of *Polybori* are recognized as *Polyborus, Phalcobœnus, Milvago*, and *Ibycter*, monography of the species of each of which is given, illustrated with details of form on the 5 plates.   *Polyborus lutosus*, p. 459, sp. n.

1876. RIDGWAY, R.   Studies of the American Falconidæ.   < *Bull. U. S. Geol. and Geogr. Surv. Terr.*, ii, No. 2, Apr. 1, 1876, pp. 91–182, pll. 30, 31.

> In this, the third paper of the series (all published in this *Bull.*), numerous genera are studied with care, the results of investigation constituting a monography of each one of them. *Nisus*, pp. 91–131; *Geranoaëtus*, pp. 131–133; *Onychotes*, pp. 134, 135; *Herpetotheres*, pp. 136–138, pll. 30–31, giving details of *H. cachinnans*; *Heterospizias*, pp. 139, 140; *Buteogallus*, p. 141; *Busarellus*, pp. 142–144; *Thrasaëtus*, pp. 145, 146; *Morphnus*, pp. 147–149; *Gampsonyx*, pp. 150, 151; *Leptodon*, pp. 152–155; *Regerhinus*, pp. 156–160; *Antenor*, pp. 161–165; *Spiziastur*, p. 166; *Urubitinga*, p. 167–173; *Leucopternis*, pp. 174–179; *Elanoides*, pp. 180–182.   The descriptions are elaborate, in most cases, and the synonymy is very copious.

1876. RIDGWAY, R.   Studies of the American Falconidae.—Monograph of the Genus Micrastur.   < *Proc. Acad. Nat. Sci. Phila.*, Dec. 28, 1875, pp. 470–502, figg. 1–9. (Pub. 1876.)

> Elaborate treatment of 6 spp. of the genus, with copious synonymy, extended descriptions, and critical comment; much also on the literature of the subject.   The species recognized as valid are 7 in number, viz : *M. melanoleucus, mirandollii, guerilla, zonothorax, ruficollis, pelzelni*, sp. n., p. 494, *concentricus*.   Details of heads, feet, and wings are figured.   The appendix, pp. 500–502, gives biographical notes on *M. melanoleucus*, by A. J. Grayson.—The author afterward reviewed his work in *Ibis*, 1876, pp. 1–5, *q. v.*   See also his original paper on the genus, *Proc. Bost. Soc.*, xvi, 1873, pp. 73–106.

1876. RIDGWAY, R.   Second Thoughts on the Genus Micrastur.   < *Ibis*, 3d ser., Jan. 1876, pp. 1–5.

> Results of examination of the entire series of the smaller members of this genus in the Mus. Salvin-Godman, modifying views before given in *Proc. Bost. Soc.*, xvi, 1873, pp. 73–106, and *Proc. Phila. Acad.*, 1875 (pub. 1876), pp. 470–502, *qq. vv.*   The spp. now admitted are *MM. melanoleucus, mirandollii, guerilla, zonothorax, ruficollis, pelzelni*, and *concentricus*, all of which are analyzed, with critical determinations of the names of old authors, and a special description of *M. pelzelni* Ridgw.

1876. ROCKE, J.   Greenland Falcon in North Wales.   < *Zoologist*, 2d ser., xi, May, 1876, pp. 4919, 4920.

1876. ROWLEY, G. D.   Falconry.   < *Rowl. Orn. Misc.*, pt. iv, May, 1876, pp. 213–222, pll. xxvii–xxix.

1876. [SCLATER, P. L.]   [On Young Caracaras (Polyborus sp.) in remarkable plumage.]   < *P. Z. S.*, Apr. 4, 1876, p. 333, pl. xxv.

> The species here left in doubt was afterward determined to be *P. tharus*, juv., in an abnormal phase of coloring.   Cf. *P. Z. S.*, 1878, pp. 230–232.

1876. SCLATER, J.   Plumage of the Roughlegged Buzzard.   < *Zoologist*, 2d ser., xi, June, 1876, p. 4955.

1876. VENNOR, H. G.   Our Birds of Prey, | or the | Eagles, Hawks, and Owls | of | Canada. | By | Henry G. Vennor, F. G. S. | Of the Geological Survey of Canada. | With 30 Photographic Illustrations by Wm. Notman. | — | R. Worthington, 750 Broadway, New York. | Montreal : | published by Dawson Brothers. | — | 1876. 1 vol. sm. 4to. pp. i–viii, 1–154, with 30 photog. pll.

> An interesting and valuable treatise in so far as it is largely based upon original observations and personal experiences, though the technic of the work is decidedly behind the times. The photographic illustrations must be regarded as an experiment not entirely successful, being for the most part taken from very badly stuffed specimens.—Pl. 1, Duck Hawk. 2, Pigeon Hawk. 3, Gyr Falcon. 4, same, dark variety. 5, Sparrow Hawk. 6, 7, American Goshawk, ad. and young. 8, Cooper's Hawk. 9, Sharp-shinned Hawk. 10, Red-tailed Buzzard. 11, Red-shouldered Buzzard. 12, same, young. 13, Broad-winged Buzzard. 14, Rough-legged Buzzard. 15, same, black variety. 16, Marsh Hawk. 17, Golden Eagle. 18, Bald Eagle. 19, Osprey. 20, Great Horned Owl. 21, Screech Owl. 22, Long-eared Owl. 23, Short-eared-Owl. 24. Great Gray Owl. 25, Barred Owl. 26, Sparrow Owl. 27, Acadian Owl. 28, 29, Snowy Owl. 30, Hawk Owl.

1876. WHITAKER, J. Kite, Hen Harrier and Hobby in Nottinghamshire. < Zoologist, 2d ser., xi, Jan., 1876, p. 4760.

1876. WHITAKER, J. Roughlegged Buzzard at Rufford. < Zoologist, 2d ser., xi, Apr., 1876, p. 4870.

1876. WOOD, W. The game Falcons of New England: the Goshawk [Astur atricapillus]. < Am. Nat., x, No. 3, 1876, pp. 132–135.

> A good popular account of the habits of this species.

1876. YUILLE, S. Hen Harrier in Northumberland. < Zoologist, 2d ser., xi, Sept., 1876, p. 5079.

1877. A[LLEN], J. A. Ridgway's "Studies of the American Falconidæ." < Bull. Nutt. Ornith. Club, ii, No. 3, July, 1877, pp. 70–73.

> Extended review of several of Ridgway's late papers on this subject, in Bull. U. S. Geol. Surv. Terr., Proc. Phila. Acad., and Proc. Bost. Soc.

1877. BOUDWIN, G. Peregrine falcon (Falco Peregrinus). < Forest and Stream, viii, Apr. 19, 1877, p. 161.

> Falco anatum feeding upon the pigeons around St. Peter's Church, Philadelphia.

1877. C[LARKE], S. C., and "DOM PEDRO" [QUAY, T. R.]. "Does the Osprey ever take dead fish?" < Forest and Stream, viii, Feb. 8, 1877, p. 4.

> Letters detailing affirmative instances. See vol. vii, p. 276.

1877. CORY, C. B. The Black Gyr-Falcon (Falco sacer var. labradora) in Massachusetts. < Bull. Nutt. Ornith. Club, ii, No. 1, Jan., 1877, p. 27.

1877. COUES, E. Eastward Range [to Illinois] of the Ferruginous Buzzard (Archibuteo ferrugineus). < Bull. Nutt. Ornith. Club, ii, No. 1, 1877, p. 26.

1877. COUES, E. Letters on Ornithology. No. 13.—The Harrier [Circus hudsonius]. < The Chicago Field, Feb. 3, 1877, fig.

> Notice of habits, etc.

1877. "DOM PEDRO" [QUAY, T. R.]. Does the Osprey [Pandion haliaëtus] ever take dead fish? < Forest and Stream, viii, May 17, 1877, p. 224.

1877. "FLORIDA." Audacity in Hawks. < Forest and Stream, viii, June 14, 1877, p. 300.

1877. GIBBS, R. M. W. A Rare Bird [Buteo harlani]. < The Naturalist and Fancier (of Grand Rapids, Michigan), Aug., 1877, p. 31.

> Description, by R. Ridgway, of a specimen from Gainesville, Texas, Nov. 16, 1876.

1877. HARRINGTON, B. J. A very rare bird [dark variety of gyrfalcon, in Montreal]. < Canadian Naturalist, viii, Apr., 1877, p. 249.

1877. MURDOCH, J. The Pigeon-Hawk (Falco columbarius) at Sea. < Bull. Nutt. Ornith. Club, ii, No. 3, July, 1877, p. 79.

1877. RAGSDALE, G. H. Capture of Buteo harlani (Aud.) in Texas. < Forest and Stream, ix, Aug. 16, 1877, p. 24.

1877. "ROAMER" [   ]. Does the Osprey Ever Take Dead Fish ? < *Forest and Stream*, vii, Jan. 11, 1877, p. 357.

1877. "ROAMER" [   ]. Ospreys Taking Dead Fish. < *Forest and Stream*, viii, June 14, 1877, p. 300. See pp. 4, 113.

1877. "ROAMER" [   ]. Ospreys taking dead fish. < *Forest and Stream*, viii, Mar. 29, 1877, p. 113. See p. 4, 224, 300.

1877. [SCOTT, W. E. D.] A Strange Flight of Hawks. < *The Country*, i, Dec. 8, 1877, p. 79.
    Brief remarks on the migratory habits of hawks, *à propos* of a contextual paragraph quoted.

1878. A[LLEN], J. A. Sharpe's "Catalogue of the Birds in the British Museum." < *Bull. Nutt. Ornith. Club*, iii, No. 2, Apr., 1878, pp. 77–79.
    Review of the parts of the work (vols. i and ii) relating to *Falconidæ* and *Strigidæ*.

1878. ANON. The Bird of America [Haliaëtus leucocephalus]. < *Mining and Scientific Press* (newspaper of San Francisco), xxxvii, No. 25, Dec. 21, 1878, p. 393.
    A popular biographical sketch.

1878. ANON. The Harpy Eagle (Harpya destructor). < *The Oölogist*, iv, No. 4, June, 1878, pp. 28–30.
    Account of habits, quoted from *Knight's Museum of Animated Nature*, i, p. 259.

1878. [BENDIRE, C.] Golden Eagle [Aquila chrysaëtus]. < *Familiar Science and Fancier's Journ.*, new ser., v, Apr., 1878, p. 88.
    Cowardly behavior in presence of danger to nest.

1878. BREWSTER, W. Occurrence of a Second Specimen of Swainson's Buzzard (Buteo swainsoni) in Massachusetts. < *Bull. Nutt. Ornith. Club*, iii, No. 1, Jan., 1878, pp. 39, 40.

1878. COUES, E. Swallow-tailed Kite [Elanoides forficatus] in Dakota in Winter. < *Bull. Nutt. Ornith. Club*, iii, No. 3, July, 1878, p. 147.
    Occurrence at Fort Sisseton, Dakota, during nearly the whole winter, according to observations of Dr. C. E. McChesney, U. S. A.

1878. INGERSOLL, E. [Report of discussion upon habits of eagles at] The Linnean Society. < *The Country*, i, Apr. 13, 1878, p. 354.

1878. GOSS, N. S. Breeding of the Duck Hawk [Falco communis var. anatum] in trees. < *Bull. Nutt. Ornith. Club*, iii, No. 1, Jan., 1878, pp. 32–34.

1878. GURNEY, J. H. Notes on a Specimen of Polyborus lately living in the Society's Gardens. < *P. Z. S.*, Feb. 19, 1878, pp. 230–232.
    The same individual as described and figured in *P. Z. S.*, 1876, p. 333, pl. 25, here decided to be *P. tharus* juv., in an abnormal phase of coloring.

1878. GURNEY, J. H. [Falco of Ibis, 1877, p. 149 and p. 397, from Socotra, proved to be F. peregrinus.] < *Ibis*, 4th ser., ii, July, 1878, p. 380.

1878. "JOHN." [J. FOWLER.] An Epicurean Eagle. < *Forest and Stream*, x, May 30, 1878, p. 319.
    Bald eagles feeding on lambs; four albino robins mating and building nests.

1878. MEARNS, E. A. The Golden Eagle [Aquila chrysaëtus] in the Hudson Highlands. < *Bull. Nutt. Ornith. Club*, iii, No. 2, Apr., 1878, pp. 100, 101.

1878. MEARNS, E. A. The White-headed Eagles [Haliaëtus leucocephalus] of the Hudson Highlands. < *Forest and Stream*, x, July 4, 1878, p. 421; July 18, 1878, pp. 462, 463.

1878. MERRILL, J. C. Buteo Albi-Caudalus [sic]. < *Forest and Stream*, x, July 11, 1878, p. 443.
    Notice of the capture of *Buteo albocaudatus*, new to the U. S. Fauna, at Fort Brown, Texas.

1878. OSWALD, F. L. The Home of the Harpy Eagle [Thrasaëtus destructor]. < *Am. Nat.*, xii, No. 3, 1878, pp. 146–157.
    Full account of the habits of *Thrasaëtus destructor*, as observed in Mexico. An interesting article.

1878. PENNOCK, C. J. Relaying of Hawks in the same Nest when robbed. < *Bull. Nutt. Ornith. Club*, iii, No. 1, Jan., 1878, p. 41.

1878. STEARNS, R. E. C. A Strange Flight of Hawks [in California]. < *Am. Nat.*, xii, No. 3, 1878, pp. 185, 186.

1878. WOOD, W. The Birds of Connecticut. No. 4. White-headed Eagle: Bald Eagle. Haliaëtus leucocephalus (Linn.) Sav. < *Familiar Sci. and Fancier's Journ.*, v, No. 4, Apr., 1878, pp. 73–75.

1878. WOOD, W. The Birds of Connecticut. No. 5. Fish Hawk: Osprey. Pandion haliaëtus, (Linn.) Sav. < *Familiar Sci. and Fancier's Journ.*, v, No. 5, May, 1878, pp. 93, 94.

1879. ANON. Notes on the Nesting Habits of the Sparrow Hawk (Falco Sparverius). < *The Oölogist*, iv, No. 8, Mar., 1879, p. 58.

1879. ANON. Nesting of Accipiter fuscus. < *The Oölogist*, iv, No. 10, May, 1879, p. 76, pl. —, f. 4.

1879. ANON. The Caracara Eagle [Polyborus tharus auduboni]. < *The Oölogist*, iv, No. 10, May, 1879, p. 83.
  Compiled notice of its habits.

1879. ANON. The Marsh Harrier (Circus hudsonius). < *Temperance Vedette* (newspaper of Terrill, Texas), Nov. 22, 1879.
  A few paragraphs on the habits of this species.

1879. BOARDMAN, G. A. Capture of Two Escaped Prisoners. < *Forest and Stream*, xiii, Nov. 27, 1879, p. 848.
  Notes shooting of specimen of *Haliaëtus leucocephalus* with a steel trap attached to its leg, and of "gray duck" (? *Chaulelasmus streperus*) with a string tied to its leg.

1879. BREWER, T. M. A Mistake Corrected. < *Forest and Stream*, Oct. 9, 1879.
  Respecting date of first publication of *Buteo albocaudatus* as a bird of the United States, in *op. cit.* of July 11, 1878, not in *The Country* of July 13, 1878.

1879. COUES, E. A Correction. < *Bull. Nutt. Ornith. Club*, iv, No. 4, Oct., 1879, p. 242.
  Of his mistake in proposing to substitute the name *Buteo aquilinus* for *Falco borealis* Gm.

1879. DAVIS, F. J. Nesting of Buteo pennsylvanicus in a Hemlock Tree. < *The Oölogist*, iv, No. 7, Feb., 1879, p. 51.

1879. [FITCH, E. H.] The Swallow-tailed Kite [Elanoides forficatus]. < *The Journ. of Sci.* (Toledo, Ohio), 2d ser., i, No. 12, Mar., 1879, cut.
  Popular biography, with a figure.

1879. [GILBERT, E. S.] The Hawk's Spiral Flight. < *Science News*, i, No. 11, Apr. 1, 1879, pp. 171, 172.
  Digest of observations of C. Darwin and J. B. Holder.

1879. GURNEY, J. H. Note upon Three American Raptorial Birds apparently new to Science. < *Ibis*, 4th ser., iii, Apr., 1879, pp. 171–178, pl. iii.
  Micrastur amaurus, p. 173; *Morphnus tæniatus*, p. 176, pl. 3; *Buteo pœcilochrous*, p. 176.

1879. [INGERSOLL, E.] [On the Breeding Habits of Buteo lineatus.] < *Science News*, i, No. 9, Mar. 1, 1879, p. 138.
  Editorial report of a meeting of the Linnæan Society of New York, Jan. 25, 1879, giving the observations of S. D. Osborne on the subject.

1879. JOHNSON, F. E. Capture of the Golden Eagle [Aquila chrysaëtus] at Gravesend, L. I. < *Bull. Nutt. Ornith. Club*, iv, No. 3, July, 1879, p. 189.

1879. PURDIE, H. A. MacFarlane's Gerfalcon (Falco gyrfalco sacer) in Maine. < *Bull. Nutt. Ornith. Club*, iv, No. 3, July, 1879, pp. 188, 189.

1879. SALE, C. J. Early Nesting of Eagles. < *Forest and Stream*, xii, May 8, 1879, p. 265.
  Nest of *Haliaëtus leucocephalus* completed Jan. 20 in Virginia.

1879. STEVENS, F. Nesting of Buteo zonocercus in New Mexico. < *Bull. Nutt. Ornith. Club*, iv, No. 3, July, 1879, p. 189.

1879. WARREN, B. H.   Diurnal Rapacious Birds of Chester County [Pennsylvania].
< *Daily Local News*, vii, No. 154, May 16, 1879, 3 columns.
Treating of 15 spp. of *Falconidæ*.

1879. [VENNOR, H. G.]   The Dark Gyr Falcon [Falco sacer labradorus].   < *Forest and Stream*, xii, June 26, 1879, p. 406.
Notice of specimens in the writer's collection.

1880. MARSHALL, D. M.   Notes on the Habits of the Bald Eagle.   (Haliattus Leucocephalus.)   < *Journ. of Sci.* (Toledo, Ohio), n. s., iii, No. 2, Feb. 15, 1880, cut.

1880. RIDGWAY, R.   Description of the adult plumage of Hierofalco gyrfalco obsoletus.   < *Bull. Nutt. Ornith. Club*, v, No. 2, Apr., 1880, pp. 92–95.
This is the dark American continental form of Gyr Falcon, named *F. labradora* by Audubon, here identified with *F. obsoletus* Gm., and varietally distinguished from the other races.

Cathartidæ.

1694. SLOANE, H.   An Account of a prodigiously large Feather of the Bird Cuntur, brought from Chili and supposed to be a kind of Vultur; and of the Coffee-Shrub.   < *Philos. Trans.*, xviii, 1694, pp. 61–64.

   Quill of the bird afterward known as *Sarcorhamphus gryphus*.

1772. ———.   Naturgeschichte des Geierkönigs [Sarcorhamphus papa].   < *Berlin. Samml.*, iv, 1772, pp. 173–179.

   Nicht mir selbst zugänglich.

1789. WALBAUM, J. J.   Vom dem Geyerkönig [Sarcorhamphus papa].—§. 1., Der Kopf des Geyerkönigs nach der Natur dargestellet und beschrieben.   < *Schriften Berlin. Gesell. Naturf. Freunde*, ix, 1789, pp. 246–256, pl. 8.

180-. GEOFFROY ST. HILAIRE, É.   Observations sur le Vautour royal (Vultur [Sarcorhamphus] papa) dans premier age.   < *Bull. Sci. Soc. Philom.*, iii, An xii (180-), p. 189.

   Pas vues moi-même.

1808. HUMBOLDT, A. v.   Versuch einer Naturgeschichte des Condor (Vultur [Sarcorhamphus] gryphus L.).   < *Beob. aus d. Zool. u. Vergl. Anat.*, 2 Lief., 1808.

   Nicht mir selbst zugänglich.

1811. HUMBOLDT, A. DE.   Essai sùr l'Histoire Naturelle du Condor, ou du Vultur [Sarcorhamphus] gryphus de Linné.   < *Recueil d'Obs. Zool. Anat.*, i, 1811, pp. 26–45, pll. viii, ix.

   Lu à la première class de l'Institut de France, le 13 oct. 1806.

   The miscellaneous work by Humboldt and Bonpland, entitled "Collections of Observations in Zoology and Comparative Anatomy," etc., appeared in several languages and at different dates.   I have only seen a French version, "Recueil d'Observations," etc., the first vol. of which, dated 1811, contains, among several distinct papers, one by Humboldt on the os hyoides and larynx of birds, and one by the same on the Condor, as above given.   The full title of the works comes in a different department of this Bibliography.

.1826. AUDUBON, J. J.   Account of the Habits of the Turkey Buzzard (Vultur [Cathartes] aura), particularly with the view of exploding the opinion generally entertained of its extraordinary power of Smelling.   < *Edinb. New Philos. Journ.*, ii, 1826, pp. 172–184.   (*Fror. Not.*, xvii, No. 359, 1827, pp. 97–106.)

   This very notable article opened a protracted discussion, in which the writer's views met with no little opposition and ridicule.   The paper includes circumstantial recital of experiments made, and general account of the habits of the bird.

1826. HEAD, F. A.   Ueber die Stärke und das zähe Leben der Condor's [Sarcorhamphus gryphus] Südamerika's.   < *Froriep's Notizen*, xv, No. 324, 1826, pp. 246–248.

   Nicht mir selbst zugänglich.

1827. AUDUBON, J. J.   Account of the Carrion Crow, or Vultur [Cathartes] atratus.   < *Edinb. Journ. Sci.*, vi, 1827, pp. 156–161.   (*Fror. Not.*, xvij, No. 357, 1827, pp. 65, 70.)

   Extended notice of the habits of this species.

1827. ANON.   Living Condor [Sarcorhamphus gryphus] at Paris.   < *Philos. Mag.*, i, 1827, p. 473.

1827. PAYRAUDEAU, B. C.   Notice sur les Couroumous ou Vautours de la Guiane; par M. J.-A.-A. Noyer. . . .   < *Féruss. Bull.*, 2e sect., xii, 1827, pp. 129–131.

   Précis: *Annales Marit. et Colon*, janv. et févr. 1826, p. 96.

1828. DOUGLAS, D.   Observations on the Vultur [Cathartes] Californianus of Shaw.   < *Zool. Journ.*, iv, 1828, pp. 328–330.

   Description and account of habits.

1828. L[UROTH], S. G.   Observations sur le Vultur [Cathartes] atratus; (par J. J. Audubon.) . . .   < *Féruss. Bull.*, 2e sect., xiii, 1828, p. 239, 240.

Précis de ces observations, inserées dans *Edinb. Journ. Sci.*, janv., 1827, pp. 156–161.

1830. HARLAN, R.   Notice of an Anatomical Peculiarity observed in the Structure of the Condor of the Andes; (Vultur [Sarcorhamphus] gryphus, Linn.)   < *Trans. Amer. Philos. Soc.*, 2d ser., iii, 1830, p. 466.

Merely a note on the digestive organs, the "peculiarity" of which is not obvious.

1830. HUMBOLDT, A. V.   On the Lofty Flight of the Condor [Sarcorhamphus gryphus].   < *Edinb. New Philos. Journ.*, viii, 1830, pp. 142, 143.

From *Tableaux de la Nature*, ii, pp. 72–78.

1830. HUNTER, P.   Powers of Smell ascribed to the Vulture [Cathartes aura].   < *Loudon's Mag. Nat. Hist.*, iii, 1830, p. 449.

1831. DOUGLAS, D.   Ueber Vultur [Cathartes] californianus Shaw.   < *Oken's Isis*, Bd. xxiv, 1831, pp. 110–112.

Aus d. *Zool. Journ.*, iv, 1828, pp. 328–330.

1831. LESS[ON, R. P.]   Note sur une particularité anatomique de la structure du Condor (Vultur [Sarcorhamphus] gryphus, L.); par R. Harlan. . . .   < *Féruss. Bull.*, 2e sect., xxvii, 1831, pp. 188, 189.

Extraite des *Trans. Amer. Philos. Soc.*, 2e sér., iii, 1830, p. 466.

1832. AUDUBON, J. J.   Lebensart von Vultur [Cathartes] aura (Turkey Buzzard).   < *Oken's Isis*, Bd. xxv, 1832, p. 687.

Auszug aus *Edinb. New Philos. Journ.*, Bd. ii, 1826, Heft 3, p. 172–184.

Only a 4-line paragraph here.

1832. LUND, [P. W.]   Sur la conformation particulière du Jabob cher l'Urubu (Percnopterus [Cathartes] Jota Bonap.).   < *Ann. des Sci. Nat.*, xxv, 1832, pp. 333–336, pl. xi.   (*Fror. Notizen*, xxv, No. 750, 1832, pp. 17–20.)

1832. WATERTON, C.   On the Faculty of Scent in the Vulture [Cathartes aura].   < *Loudon's Mag. Nat. Hist.*, v, 1832, pp. 233–241.

1833. GRANT, R. E.   [On the Cloaca of the female Condor (Sarcorhamphus gryphus).]   < *P. Z. S.*, i, 1833, p. 78.

1833. HUNTER, P.   The Means by which the Vulture (Vultur [Cathartes] Aura L.) traces its Food.   < *Loudon's Mag. Nat. Hist.*, vi, 1833, pp. 83–88.

With extracts from Audubon's article in the *Edinb. New Philos. Journ.*, ii, 1826, pp. 172–184.

1833. WATERTON, C.   The Means by which the Turkey Buzzard (Vultur [Cathartes] Aura L.) traces its Food.   < *Loudon's Mag. Nat. Hist.*, vi, 1833, pp. 162, 163.

1833. WATERTON, C.   Remarks on Mr. Audubon's "Account of the Habits of the Turkey Buzzard (Vultur [Cathartes] Aura), particularly with the View of exploding the Opinion generally entertained of its extraordinary Powers of Smelling."   < *Loudon's Mag. Nat. Hist.*, vi, 1833, pp. 163–171.

Cf. *Edinb. New Philos. Journ.*, ii, 1826, pp. 172–184.

1834. GOURCY-DROITAUMONT, F.   Einiges über den Condor, oder Kuntur, Vultur gryphus Linn., Sarcoramphus gryphus Dumeril.   < *Oken's Isis*, Bd. xxvii, 1834, pp. 407–411.

Nachschrift von Brehm, pp. 411, 412.

1835. GRANT, [R. E.]   Cloake eines weiblichen Condors [Sarcorhamphus gryphus].   < *Oken's Isis*, Bd. xxviii, 1835, p. 537.

P. Z. S., i, 1833, p. 78.

1836. MACKAY, R.   [Letter on the habits of Sarcorhamphus papa.]   < *P. Z. S.*, iv, 1836, p. 107.

1836. RENGGER, J. R.   Notiz Über die Aasvögel.   < *Arch. f. Naturg.*, ii, 1836, (1), p. 104.

Aus dessen *Reise nach Paraguay*, 1835, p. 229.

1837. MACKAY, R.   [On the habits of Sarcorhamphus papa.]   < *Lond. and Edinb. Philos. Mag.*, x, 1837, pp. 479, 480.

From *P. Z. S.*, Nov. 8, 1836, p. 107.

1837. MACKAY, [R.] Sur les mœurs du Vultur [Sarcorhamphus] papa L. < *L'Insti-tut*, v, No. 218, 1837, p. 263.

 Pas vu moi-même: le titré de Carus et Engelmann. Article extr. des *P. Z. S.*, 1836, p. 107.

1837. OWEN, RICHARD. [Dissection of the Head of the Turkey Buzzard (Cathartes aura) and that of the Common Turkey.] < *P. Z. S.*, v, 1837, pp. 34, 35.

1837. SELLS, W. [On the Habits of Cathartes aura.] < *P. Z. S.*, v, 1837, pp. 33, 34.

1837. SELLS, W., *and* OWEN, R. Extract from the "Proceedings of the Zoological Society" relating to the Habits of the Vultur [Cathartes] Aura. < *Charlesw. Mag. Nat. Hist.*, i, 1837, pp. 638–641.

 Mr. W. Sells' paper, with R. Owen's anatomical notes.

1838. MACKAY, "L." [*i. e.*, R.] Ueber die Lebensart des Vultur [Sarcorhamphus] papa. < *Oken's Isis*, Bd. xxxi, 1838, p. 207.

 Auszüge aus *Proceedings of the zoological society of London*, iv, November 1836, p. 107.

1838. OWEN, RICHARD. Dissection de la tête du Vultur [Cathartes] aura. < *L'Insti-tut*, vi, No. 243, 1838, pp. 277, 278.

 Pas vue moi-même. Extr. des *P. Z. S.*, 1837, pp. 34, 35.

1838. SCHOMBURGK, R. H. On the Habits of the King of the Vultures (Sarcorrham-phus papa). < *Annals of Nat. Hist.*, ii, 1838, pp. 255–260. (*Fror. Notizen*, ix, No. 195, 1838, pp. 289–293.)

1838. SELLS, W. [Sur les mœurs du Vultur (Cathartes) aura.] < *L'Institut*, vi, No. 243, 1838, p. 277..

 Pas vu moi-même. Voir *P. Z. S.*, 1837, pp. 33, 34.

1839. SELLS, W. Ueber das Betragen von Vultur [Cathartes] aura. < *Oken's Isis*, Bd. xxxii, 1839, p. 143.

 P. Z. S. London, März 14, 1837, pp. 33, 34.

1844. SCHOMBURGK, R. [H.] Ueber die Lebensart des Geyerkönigs (Sarcoramphus papa). < *Oken's Isis*, Bd. xxxvii, 1844, pp. 673, 674.

 Ann. Nat. Hist., ii, 1838, pp. 255–260.

1845. CASSIN, J. Description of a new Vulture [Cathartes burrovianus] in the Mu-seum of the Academy of Natural Sciences of Philadelphia. < *Proc. Acad. Nat. Sci. Phila.*, ii, 1845, p. 212.

1846. ANON. [Exhibition of a fœtal Condor.] < *P. Z. S.*, xiv, 1846, p. 44.

1846. ANON. [Exhibition of a fœtal Condor.] < *Ann. Mag. Nat. Hist.*, xviii, 1846, p. 129.

 From *P. Z. S.*, May 12, 1846.

1847. GOSSE, P. H. John-Crow Vulture, (Turkey-buzzard, Wilson; Cathartes aura, Vulture aura, Linn; Cathartes aura Illiger.) Ann. pl. 151. < *Edinb. New Philos. Journ.*, xliii, 1847, pp. 90–94.

 Extract from "The Birds of Jamaica," p. 1. On its habits, especially with reference to the senses of sight and smell.

1847. TSCHUDI, J. J. [v.] The Condor [Sarcorhamphus gryphus] of the Cordillera. < *Edinb. New Philos. Journ*, xlii, 1847, pp. 387–389.

 Extract from his "Travels in Peru," p. 300.

1847. TSCHUDI, J. J. v. The Condor [Sarcorhamphus gryphus]. < *Zoologist*, v, 1847, pp. 1772, 1773.

 Extract from "Travels in Peru."

1847. TSCHUDI, J. J. [v.] Sur le condor [Sarcorhamphus gryphus] des cordillères. < *Arch. des Sc. Phys. et Nat.*, vi, 1847, pp. 177, 178.

 Voyages au Pérou, p. 300; *Edinb. New Phil. Journ.*, avril 1847, pp. 387–389.

1848. TOWNSEND, J. K. Popular Monograph of the Accipitrine Birds of N[orth] A[merica].—No. I [II]. < *Lit. Rec. and Journ. Linn. Assoc. of Penna. College*, iv, 1848, pp. 249–255, 265–272.

 Only these two Numbers of the "Monograph" appeared, consisting of extended general accounts of *Cathartes* [*Sarcorhamphus*] *gryphus*, *C. californianus*, *C. aura*, and certain *Fal-conidæ*.

1850. WYMAN, J.   [Note on substances probably dropped by Cathartes aura during flight.]   < *Proc. Boston Soc. Nat. Hist.*, iii, 1850, p. 289.

1851. CABOT, S., JR.   [On the sense of smell in Vultures [Cathartidæ].   < *Proc. Bost. Soc. Nat. Hist.*, iv, 1851, p. 118.

1853. DES MURS, O.   Observations sur un nom spécifique: Catharte citadin, Lesson, Vultur urbis incola, Riccord, Cathartes urbis incola, Lesson, omis jusqu'à ce jour dans toutes les synonymies des espèces du genre Catharte.   < *Rev. et Mag. de Zool.*, v, 1853, pp. 146–154.

1855. TAYLOR, A. S.   Note on the Great Vulture of California (Cathartes vel Sarcoramphus Californianus).   Communicated by J. H. Gurney, Esq.   < *Zoologist*, xiii, 1855, pp. 4632–4635.

1856. MAXIMILIAN, PRINZ VON WIED.   Ueber den nordamerikanischen rothköpfigen Urubu, (Cathartes aura Audub.   Bonap.)   < *J. f. O.*, iv, 1856, pp. 119–124.
   Elaborate description, etc.

1857. BOLLE, C.   Der californische Condor, Sarcorhamphus californianus.   < *J. f. O.*, v, 1857, pp. 50–54.
   Nach A. S. Taylor, aus dem *Zoologist*, 1855, pp. 4632–4635.

1859. EDITORIAL.   [Extract from an article in the San Francisco Herald, by A. S. Taylor, on Cathartes californianus.]   < *Ibis*, i, 1859, pp. 469, 470.

1859. TAYLOR, A. S.   The egg and young of the California Condor [Cathartes californianus].   < *Hutchings's Cal. Mag.*, iii, 1859, pp. 537–——, fig.
   Not seen.—Woodcut of young and egg.   Also, the "Great Condor of California," p. 540.

1859–61. TAYLOR, A. S.   The Great Condor of California (Cathartes californianus).   < *Hutchings's Cal. Mag.*, iv, July, 1859, pp. 17–——; Aug., 1861, pp. ——, with cut of the bird.
   Not seen.

1860. ABBOTT, C. C.   [The egg figured in Ibis, ii, 1860, pl. 1, f. 2, as that of Milvago australis is "undoubtedly that of Cathartes aura."]   < *Ibis*, ii, 1860, p. 432.

1860. SCLATER, P. L.   [Exhibition of the egg of the King Vulture (Gyparchus papa).]   < *P. Z. S.*, xxviii, 1860, pp. 193, 194.

1860. SCLATER, P. L.   Note on the Egg and Nestling of the Californian Vulture [Cathartes californianus].   < *Ibis*, ii, 1860, p. 278, pll. viii (egg), ix (nestling).
   Cf. *op. cit.*, 1859, p. 469.

1860. TAYLOR, A. S.   Notes on the Queleli, a rare Bird of Sonora; the King of the Zopolites; and Bartram's Vulture.   < *Zoologist*, xviii, 1860, pp. 6798–6805.
   Curious and in part mythical account of some Mexican species of *Cathartidæ*.

1866. SCLATER, P. L.   [Notice of a specimen of the Californian Vulture (Cathartes californianus) recently added to the Society's Menagerie.]   < *P. Z. S.*, xxxiv, 1866, p. 366.

1867. GURNEY, J. H.   [On the colored sclerotic ring of Cathartes californianus.]   < *Ibis*, 2d ser., iii, 1867, p. 254.

1868. BAIRD, S. F.   [Letter relating to a drawing of a young Cathartes californianus.]   < *P. Z. S.*, xxxvi, 1868, pp. 183, 184, woodc.

1869. SAUSSURE, H. DE.   El Zopilote [Cathartes].   < *La Naturaleza*, i, 1869, pp. 17–26.
   "Observaciones sobre las costumbres de las aves de México"; artículo traducido del frances por Don J. M. A., y anotado por D. Alfonso Herrera.

1869. HERRERA, A.   Adiciones al artículo el Zopilote [Cathartes].   < *La Naturaleza*, i, 1869, pp. 51, 52.
   Sobre las costumbres.

1870. "J. L. B."   Turkey Buzzard.   < *Am. Nat.*, iv, 1870, p. 375.
   Note on *Cathartes aura* feeding upon *Mephitis mephitica*.

1870. NAUMAN, C. H.   An Albino Turkey Buzzard (Cathartes aura Illig.) . . .   < *Am. Nat.*, iv, 1870, p. 376.
   Also, an albino *Anas obscura*.

1871. CATON, J. D.   Turkey Buzzard [Cathartes aura]. < *Am. Nat.*, iv, 1871. p. 762.
Note on sense of smell in *Cathartes aura.*

1871. ORTON, J.   On the Condors [Cathartidæ] and Humming-birds of the Equatorial Andes. < *Ann. Mag. Nat. Hist.*, 4th ser., viii, 1871, pp. 185–192.

1871. ORTON, J.   The Vultures [Cathartidæ] and Humming Birds of Tropical America. < *Canad. Nat. & Quart. Journ.*, n. s., v, 1871, pp. 357–360.
See *Amer. Nat.*, v, Oct., 1871, pp. 619–626.

1873. CATON, J. D.   Sense of Smell in the Turkey Buzzard [Cathartes aura]. < *Am. Sportsman*, iii, 1873, p. 87.

1873. LYNCH, W. F.   A Condor Hunt. < *Am. Sportsman*, ii, 1873, p. 58.

1873. SHARPE, R. B.   On a New Species of Turkey Vulture from the Falkland Islands, and a New Genus of Old World Vultures. < *Ann. Mag. Nat. Hist.*, 4th ser., xi, Feb., 1873, pp. — — —.
Not seen.
Catharista falklandicas, p. 133; *Pseudogyps*, g. n., p. 133.

1874. COPE, E. D.   Annual Report | upon the | Geographical Explorations and Surveys West of the | one hundredth meridian, | in California, Nevada, | Utah, Arizona, Colorado, New Mexico, | Wyoming, and Montana, | by George M. Wheeler, | first lieutenant of Engineers, U. S. A.; | being | Appendix FF | of the Annual Report of the Chief of Engineers for 1874. | — | Washington: | Government Printing Office. | 1874. 8vo. pp. 130, map.
Report of E. D. Cope, pp. 115–130.—Only ornithological in describing *Cathartes umbrosus*, n. sp. foss., p. 130. (The species may prove to belong to some other group of *Raptores*.)

1874. COUES, E.   The Californian Vulture [Cathartes californianus]. < *Am. Sportsman*, iv, 1874, p. 160.
Mainly quoted from account of Alex. S. Taylor, *San Francisco Herald*, May 5, 1859.

1875. ANON.   Several mooted questions. < *Forest and Stream*, iv, Feb. 11, 1875, p. 5.
Cathartes aura in Vermont.

1875. ANON.   Eggs and Nest of the Condor [Sarcorhamphus gryphus]. < *Oölogist*, i, 1875, p. 66.

1875. EAGLE, C. H.   Buzzards [Cathartidæ] in Maine. < *Forest and Stream*, iii, Jan. 14, 1875, p. 357.

1875. GURNEY, J. H.   [With reference to remarks on the races of the Condor, Ibis, 1875, p. 91.] < *Ibis*, 3d ser., v, 1875, pp. 269, 270.

1875. HADFIELD, H.   Instinct of Birds: Olfactory Power of the Vultures. < *Zoologist*, 2d ser., x, Mar., 1875, pp. 4373–4376.
On the question of the comparative power of the senses of sight and smell, the former being considered the one most employed in the search for food.

1875. MOSES, J. T. C.   Turkey Buzzards [Cathartes aura at Grand Menan Isl., Maine]. < *Forest and Stream*, v, Aug. 26, 1875, p. 36.

1876. SLERLING, E.   Queer fish, skunk and buzzards. < *Rod and Gun*, vii, Mar. 4, 1876, p. 359.
Account of tame *Cathartes aura.*

1877. [COUES, E.]   Birds. < *The Mirror* (Baltimore, Md.), June 1, 1877.
Editorial extracts from the "Birds of the Northwest", relating to certain North American *Falconidæ* and *Cathartidæ.*

1877. [COUES, E.]   Birds. < *The Mirror* (Baltimore, Md.), July 1, 1877, p. 4.
Editorial extracts from the "Birds of the Northwest", relating to certain *Cathartidæ.*

1877. [COUES, E.]   Birds. < *The Mirror* (Baltimore, Md.), Aug. 1, 1877, pp. 4, 5.
Biography of *Cathartes aura*, from "Birds of the Northwest".

1877. LANGDON, F. W.   Occurrence of the Black Vulture or Carrion Crow [Cathartes atratus] in Ohio. < *Bull. Nutt. Ornith. Club*, ii, No. 4, Oct., 1877, p. 109.
Only record of such occurrence since Audubon's.

1878. ANON. Vultures and Turkey Buzzards. < *Forest and Stream*, xi, Oct. 31, 1878, p. 259.

Reprinted from "Florida Star."

1878. KITE, W. A Skunk eaten by Turkey-buzzards [Cathartes aura]. < *Am. Nat.*, xii, No. 12, Dec., 1878, p. 821.

1878. SMITH, G. STUART. The Condor [Sarcorhamphus gryphus]. < *Oölogist*, iv, No. 5, July, 1878, pp. 39, 40.

Compiled account of habits.

1880. ANON. The Condor [Sarcorhamphus gryphus]. < *Temperance Vedette* (newspaper of Terrill, Texas), Mar. 20, 1880.

Popular notice, copied from ——.

1880. RIDGWAY, R. Notes on the American Vultures (Sarcorhamphidæ), with Special Reference to their Generic Nomenclature. < *Bull. Nutt. Ornith. Club*, v, No. 2, Apr., 1880, pp. 77–84.

This is an attempt to fix the generic names, which, though comparatively few in number, have been almost inextricably involved, through the conflicting usages of authors who hold to different rules for the adoption of genera. By a kind of "process of elimination", the author determines the following names, with their types: 1, *Sarcorhamphus* Dum., 1806, for the Condor; 2, *Gyparchus* Gloger, 1842, for the King Vulture; 3, *Pseudogryphus* Ridgw., 1874, for the Californian Vulture; 4, *Cathartes* Ill., 1811, for the Turkey Buzzard; 5, *Catharista* Vieill., 1816, for the Black Vulture. The synonyms of each of these are given, with the references. Remarks are made upon *Sarcorhamphus æquatorialis* and *S. gryphus*, *Pseudogryphus californianus*, *Cathartes burrovianus* and *C. pernigra*.

Columbidæ.

1735. MOORE, J. Columbarium, etc.

> Not seen.—This is the date of the orig. ed. of the famous work, which passed to many eds.; see the American, 1874. There is a verbatim reprint by W. B. Tegetmeier, London, 1879. Cf. *Ibis*, 1879, p. 219.
>
> "The chief interest of Moore's 'Columbarium' consists in the careful descriptions of the different races of the domestic Pigeon as they existed in 1735, enabling a comparison to be made with those of the present day. The alterations produced by careful breeding, carried on for 150 generations, can thus be traced."

1759. KALM, P. Beskrifning på de vilda Dufvor, Som somliga år i så otrolig stor myckenhet Komma til de Södra Engelska nybyggen i Norra America. < *Kongl. Svensk. Vetensk.-Acad. Handl.*, xx, 1759, pp. 275–295.

> The *Ectopistes migratorius* of authors.

1774. PORTAL, —. [Sur un Pigeon qui avoit deux anus; et sur un autre qui avoit une double trachée-artère.] < *Hist. de l'Acad Roy. des Sci.* pour l'année 1771, 1774, p. 38.

1765. ANON. A | Treatise | on | Domestic Pigeons; | comprehending | [etc., 31 lines.] | London : | Printed for and Sold by C. Barry, in Ingram Court, Fenchurch- | street. Sold likewise by P. Stevens, near Stationers Hall, Ludgate- | street; A. Webley, Holborn; and J. Walters, Charing-Cross. | M. DCC LXV. 1 vol. pp. i–xvi, 1–144, frontisp., and 13 pll.

1806. CAVANILLES, A. J. Natural History of the domestic Pigeons of Spain, particularly in the Province of Valentia. < *Tilloch's Philos. Mag.*, xxv, 1806, pp. 112–122.

> From *Bibliothèque Physico-Économique*, No. 3, 1805. Classification, with summary characters of the various breeds, followed by an amplification of the same and general remarks on habits, &c.

1808–11. TEMMINCK, C. J. Histoire Naturelle | Générale | des Pigeons; | par C. J. Temminck, | Directeur de l'Académie Royale des Sciences et des Arts de Harlem, et Membre | de plusieurs Sociétés d'Histoire Naturelle. | Avec figures en couleurs, | peintes par Mademoiselle Pauline de Courcelles, | gravées, imprimées et retouchées sous sa direction. | — | Paris, | Garnery, Rue de Seine, Ancien Hôtel Mirabeau. | — | 1808[-1811]. 1 vol. folio. Prel. Title (Histoire Naturelle | des Pigeons | et des Gallinacés), 1 leaf; Temminck's Dedication to the King of Holland, 1 leaf; Title, 1 leaf; Introduction, pp. i–x; Temminck's Discourse on Pigeons, pp. 7–22; Text, pp. 23–41, 1–128, 1–30; Index, pp. i–xvj; Table, pp. i–iii; with 87 plates, in three series, 1–11; 1–25, 25 bis, 26–59; 1–16. [OR,]

1808–11. KNIP, *Madame*. Les Pigeons, | par Madame Knip, | née Pauline de Courcelles, | premier peintre d'Histoire Naturelle | de S. M. l'Impératrice Reine Marie-Louise. | Le texte par C. J. Temminck, | Directeur de l'Académie des Sciences et des Arts de Harlem, etc. | [Monogram.] | A Paris, |

Chez { Mme Knip, Auteur et Éditeur, Rue de Sorbonne, Musée des Artistes. | Garnery, Libraire, Rue de Seine, Hôtel Mirabeau, n° 6. |

— | De l'imprimerie de Mame. | M. DCCC XI. 1 vol. folio. Prel. Title (Les Pigeons), 1 leaf, Knip's new Title, 1 leaf; Knip's Discourse on Pigeons, pp. 1–14; Text, pp. 23–41, 1–128, 1–30; Table, pp. i–iii; with 87 plates, in three series, 1–11; 1–25, 25 bis, 26–59; 1–16.

> This work is one of the curiosities of literature. Owing to the cause célèbre between the two ostensible authors, we have in effect the same work by two different authors, with two different title-pages, above transcribed. By comparing the two preceding paragraphs, the difference between the two forms of the work may be perceived.
>
> The work was originally published in 15 livraisons, 1808–1811. At the 9th livraison, 1811,

1808-11. TEMMINCK, C. J., *or* KNIP, *Madame*—Continued.

Madame Knip accomplished a piece of truly feminine finesse, by which she stole it from Temminck. To do this, she changed the cover-title of the 9th and following livraisons, and made sundry other alterations to suit her purpose. With the 15th livraison she furnished new title-pages of the whole work, substituted a new *Discours sur les Pigeons*, and directed the binder to suppress Temminck's title-pages, his entire Introduction, his Index, and his *Discours*. To account for the break in the pagination of the text between p. 23 and p.41, she even went so far as to declare it was a typographical error. This was certainly a bold trick, regardless of consequences. But no such piracy as seems to have suited the lady's taste could hope to pass without detection; and Temminck immediately published an indignant réclamation, exposing and protesting against the fraud. What may have gone on under the surface would doubtless be even more curious than what has transpired, but the historical facts are sufficiently novel.

There is a unique copy of this work in the Library of the Philadelphia Academy, from the *Bibliothèque de J. B. Hazard*, preserving all the original cover-titles, and giving some manuscript notes explaining the whole affair. These I shall transcribe beyond.

The first eight livraisons appeared under the following cover-title, 1808-1810:—

Histoire | Naturelle | des Pigeons. | — | [. . .] Livraison. | — | A Paris, | chez Garnery, Rue de Seine, Ancien Hôtel Mirabeau. | — | De l'imprimerie de Mame Frères, | Rue de Pot-de-Fer, no 14. | 1809 [1810].

Though the date on the title is 1808, that on livr. 1, 2, 3, 4, 5 is 1809, and perhaps none of the work appeared before 1809. The date on livraisons 6, 7, 8 is 1810. With the 9th livraison Madame Knip stole the work, altering the cover-title to—

Les Pigeons, | par Madame Knip, | née Pauline de Courcelles, | Premier Peintre d'Histoire Naturelle | de S. M. l'Impératrice Reine Marie-Louise. | Le texte par C. J. Temminck, | Directeur de l'Académie des Sciences et des Arts de Harlem, etc. | — | [. . .] Livraison. Prix 40 francs. | — | Chaque livraison, accompagnée de son texte, est composée de six figures en couleurs | d'après les dessins de l'Auteur, gravées, imprimées, et retouchées sous sa direction. | L'Histoire Générale des Pigeons aura quinze livraisons formant un volume. | A Paris, | Chez { Mme Knip, Auteur et Éditeur, Rue de Sorbonne, Musée des Artistes. | — | De l'imprimerie de Mame. | Garnery, Rue de Seine, Hôtel Mirabeau, no 6. | M. DCCC XI.

The unique copy examined is invaluable in containing Hazard's msc. "Notes Bibliographiques." I think it advisable to publish these notes, as further explaining the transaction. It is to be understood that this copy forms two volumes—one, Temminck's, without the main text, and with the plates uncolored, but with all the suppressed pieces of the work; the other, Knip's, with the substituted titles and discourse, the main text, and the plates colored. (The plates were issued in two series, colored and plain.) The following is Hazard's MS.:—

"NOTES

Bibliographiques sur l'exemplaire de l'Histoire Naturelle des Pigeons, que j'ai dans ma Bibliothèque.

"Cet exemplaire est unique, non seulement par les différentes pièces qu'il contient, qui l'ont fait diviser en deux volumes; mais encore par la beauté des épreuves des doubles figures, et par les portraits qui y ont été ajoutés.

"On sait que cet ouvrage a été rédigé, pour le texte, par *M. Temminck*, et pour les figures, par *Mademoiselle Pauline de Courcelles*, depuis *Madame Knip ;* que ce ne devait être que la première partie d'un ouvrage plus considérable (*l'Histoire Générale des Pigeons et des Gallinacés*), qui devait avoir trois volumes; que d'après les arrangemens particuliers des auteurs, *Madame Knip* est demeurée propriétaire de l'ouvrage des Pigeons; qu'elle y a fait des suppressions et des additions pour ne conserver que ce qui était relatif aux Pigeons, et qu'il n'y a eu qu'un petit nombre d'exemplaires (douze) délivrés au Public, tels qu'ils étaient sortir des mains de *M. Temminck*, d'après le plan général de l'ouvrage; on trouvera ces détails dans la réclamation de M. Temminck, . . .

"Voici la note des pièces qui composent les deux volumes.

"1er Volume. [Temminck's.]

"1o. Faux titre général de l'ouvrage *Histoire Naturelle des Pigeons et des Gallinacés*, au verso est jointe une lettre autographe de *Madame Knip*, née *Pauline de Courcelles*, qui m'envoie les pièces qui ont été supprimées: un feuillet. [La lettre a été retirée plus tard.—E. C.]

"2o. Réclamation de *M. Temminck*, contre *Madame Knip*, pièce manuscrite, extraite du tome troisième de *l'Histoire Naturelle générale des Pigeons et des Gallinacés*, en trois volumes in-8o, 1813-1815: une feuille.

"3o. Avis au Relieur sur les pièces à supprimer et à remplacer par d'autres: un feuillet.

"4o. Faux titre général et titre de l'ouvrage. . . . Ces titres ont été supprimés plus tard: une feuille, 4 pages.

"5o. Un très beau portrait de Louis Napoleon, roi de Hollande, dessiné par Grégorius

1808–11. Temminck, C. J., *or* Knip, *Madame—Continued.*

d'après la buste de *Casteillier*, gravé par *L. C. Ruotte*, et auquel *M. Temminck* avait dédié son ouvrage: un feuillet, 2 pages.

"6º. Épître dédicatoire de *M. Temminck*, au roi de Hollande, supprimée à tous les exemplaires, par l'auteur lui-même : un feuillet, 2 pages.

"7º. Introduction de *M. Temminck*, sur l'ordre générale des Gallinacés ; sur la dernière page, est *l'extrait du Rapport fait à l'Institut national, classe des sciences physiques et mathématiques*, par MM. *Lacépède et Cuvier*, sur les figures coloriées de *Mademoiselle Pauline de Courcelles.* L'introduction étant générale a été supprimée dans l'histoire des Pigeons : 10 pages.

"8º. Discours sur l'ordre des Pigeons : 16 pages. Ce discours, paginé 7–22, devait faire suite aux 6 pages du titre et de l'épître dédicatoire ; l'introduction qui le précède y avait été ajoutée après l'impression. Il a aussi été supprimé et remplacé par un autre, extrait de celui-ci, que l'on trouvera indiqué dans le volume suivant.

"9º. 87 planches des Pigeons, figures noires, avant la lettre, exemplaire d'amateur ; épreuves que *Madame Knip* a bien voulu me choisir et sur lesquelles elle a mis, elle-même, les noms des Pigeons, au crayon. J'ai divisé les trois sections par des titres séparés : Les Colombars, Les Colombes, Les Colombi-Gallines.

"10º. Index (ornithologique) : 16 pages. Cet Index a aussi été supprimé.

"11º. Table : une feuille. Cet Table indiquant les pièces supprimées, a été suprimé aussi et réimprimé pour le volume suivant.

"12º. Enfin, j'ai conservé à ce volume, soit en tête, soit à la fin, les titres-enveloppes des huit premières livraisons, qui portent le premier titre d'Histoire naturelle des Pigeons, sous les dates 1809–1811. Ce n'est qu'à la neuvième livraison que Madame Knip les a changés ainsi qu'ils sont dans le second volume.

"2ᵉ Volume. [Knip's.]"

"1º. Nouveau Faux-Titre, Les Pigeons, et Titre du volume . . . ; un feuille, 4 pages.

"2º. Un très beau portrait, en couleurs, de Marie-Louise, archiduchesse d'Autriche, Impératrice de France, Reine d'Italie, dessiné d'après le buste de *Bosio*, par *Durand Duclos*, gravé par *L. C. Ruotte*: L'Ouvrage lui avait été présenté par *Madame Knip*, et avait valu à cette dernière le titre du premier peintre d'Histoire Naturelle de Sa Majesté. Ce portrait a été ajouté par moi.

"3º. Le nouveau *Discours sur l'ordre des Pigeons*, 14 pages ; on trouve sur la quatorzième l'extrait du Rapport de l'Institut qui, dans le volume précédent, est à la suite de l'Introduction supprimée.

"4º. Les 87 figures coloriées des Pigeons formant les trois séries, épreuves que *Madame Knip* a bien voulu me choisir, elle-même ; elles sont placées en face de leurs descriptions, dans le texte.

"5º. Le texte, commençant page 23, avec les Columbars, première division, et faisant suite au Discours sur l'ordre des Pigeons, du volume précédent, finit page 41 ; quelques erreurs typographiques dans la pagination ont été corrigées avec soin, à la plume. Le texte recommence page 1, avec les Colombes, deuxième division, et se termine page 128. Il recommence encore page 1, avec les Colombi-Gallines, troisième division, et finit page 30.

"La différence de pagination du texte avec les pièces liminaires de ce volume, résultant du pièce supprimée, du volume précédent, a été indiqué par *Madame Knip* comme une faute d'impression, au verso du faux titre.

"6º. La table, qui a été réimprimée, et qui n'indique plus, en tête la Dédicace et l'Introduction, et à la fin l'Index ornithologique, qui ont été supprimés.

"7º. J'ai conservé aussi, à ce volume, comme au précédent, soit en tête, soit à la fin, les titres-enveloppes du livraison 9 à 15 et dernière, sous la date de 1811, qui diffèrent de ceux du précédent, par le titre nouveau, par plus d'étendue et plus d'ornemens typographiques."

The errors of pagination in the first set of pages, from 37 to 41, have been corrected so neatly with the pen in this copy that I cannot make out what they were. The series of plates is consecutive, 1 to 86, with 25 bis = 87 ; but pl. xxxiii is wrongly numbered xxxi, and pl. xlvii is numbered lxvii. The following is a list of the plates—those with the asterisk being Temminck's species:—

I. Colombars.—Pl. 1, 2, *Columba militaris**; 3, *C. australis*; 4, *C. psittacea**; 5, 6, *C. aromatica*; 7, *C. calva**; 8 9, *C. abyssinica*; 10, 11, *C. vernans.*

II. Colombes.—Pl. 1, *Columba spadicea*; 2, *C. palumbus*; 3, 4, *C. oenea*; 5, *C. arquatrix**; 6, *C. armillaris**; 7, *C. littoralis**; 8, *C. chalcoptera*; 9, *C. cristata**; 10, *C. cariba*; 11, *C. oenas*; 12, *C. livia*; 13, *C. leucocephala*; 14, *C. speciosa*; 15, *C. portoricensis**; 16. *C. guinea*; 17, *C. madagascariensis*; 18, *C. gymnoptalmos*; 19, *C. franciæ*; 20, *C. rubricapilla*; 21, *C. auricularis**; 22, *C. elegans**; 23, *C. cincta**; 24, *C. rufina**; 25, 25 bis, *C. aurita**; 26, *C. javanica*; 27, *C. jambos*; 28, 29, *C. violacea**; 30, *C. melanocephala*; 31, *C. larvata**; 32, *C. holosericea*; 33, *C. superba**; 34, 35, *C. purpurata*; 36, *C. tympanistra**; 37, *C. cœrulea**; 38 39,

1808–11. TEMMINCK, C. J., *or* KNIP, *Madame*—Continued.

   C. afra; 40, *C. bitorquata**; 41, *C. vinacea**; 42, *C. turtur*; 43, *C. tigrina**; 44, *C. risoria*; 45, *C. cambayensis*; 46, *C. alba**; 47, *C. malaccensis*; 48, 49, *C. migratoria*; 50, *C. carolinensis*; 51, *C. dominicensis*; 52, *C. maugeus**; 53, 54, *C. capensis*; 55, *C. erythroptera*; 56, *C. mystacea**; 57, *C. godefrida**; 58, *C. cinerea**; 59, *C. squamosa**.
   III. Colombi-Gallines.—Pl. 1, *Columba coronata*; 2, *C. nicobarica*; 3, *C. cyanocephala*; 4, *C. montana*; 5, 6, *C. martinica*; 7, *C. erythrotorax**; 8, 9, *C. cruenta*; 10, *C. frontalis**; 11, *C. carunculata**; 12, *C. talpacoti**; 13, 14, *C. passerina*; 15, *C. hottentota**; 16, *C. minuta*.
   There is a continuation of this work, by Knip, text by Prévost, 1838–4-, forming ostensibly a second volume.

1813–15. TEMMINCK, C. J. .Histoire Naturelle Générale | des | Pigeons | et des | Gallinacés, | par | C. J. Temminck, | Chevalier de l'ordre Impérial de | la Réunion, Directeur de la | Société des Sciences à Harlem, | et Membre de plusieurs | sociétés d'histoire naturelle. | Ouvrage en trois volumes. | Accompagné de | Planches Anatomiques. | — | Tome Premier [Second, Troisième]. | — | — | à Amsterdam, | chez J. C. Sepp & Fils, | et à Paris, | chez C. Dufour, | 1813 [1815]. | à l'Imprimerie de H. O. Brouwer, heerenmarkt | No. 5. à Amsterdam. 3 vols. 8vo. Vol. I, 1813, frontisp., pp. 1–499 + 1 p. Vol. II, 1813, pp. 1–477 + 1 p. Vol. III, 1815, 1 p. l., pp. 1–757 + 1 p., pll. i–xi.

   The 1st vol. treats of the Pigeons, the other two of the *Gallinaceæ* (incl. *Tinamidæ*, etc.); at end of 1st and 3d vol. is an "index", or synopsis of the .species treated, with characters, synonymy, and habitat of each. The plates bound at end of 3d vol. pertain to vols. ii and iii; the frontisp. of vol. i to the *Columbæ*. This is a very well known and "standard" treatise.

   Vol. I is really the text of Temminck's plates, *Hist. Nat. Génér. des Pigeons*, folio, Paris, 1808–1811 (for circumstances of the case see above). *Columba militaris*, p. 39; *psittacea*, p. 47; *aromatica* var., p. 53: *calva*, p. 63; *arquatrix*, p. 93; *armillaris*, p. 97; *littoralis*, p. 99; *cristata*, p. 108; *picazuro*, p. 111; *maculosa*, p. 113; *gymnophtalmos* (sic), p. 225; *auricularis*, p. 236; *elegans*, p. 240; *cincta*, p. 243; *rufina*, p. 245; *aurita*, p. 247; *violacea*, p. 260; *larvata*, p. 267; *holosericea*, p. 269; *mystacea*, p. 275; *superba*, p. 277; *tympanistria*, p. 287; *cœrulae* (sic), p. 290; *geoffroii* (sic), p. 297; *cinerea*, p. 299; *bitorquata*, p. 301; *vinacea*, p. 303; *picturata*, p. 315; *tigrina*, p. 317; *alba*, p. 333; *squamosa*, p. 336; *maugei*, p. 363; *erythrotorax* (siĆ), 405; *carunculata*, p. 415; *talpacoti*, p. 421; *picui*, p. 435; *miniata*, p. 460; *brunnea*, p. 475—"*mihi*".

   Vol. II. *Pavo cristatus primus*, p. 27; *Gallus sonneratii*, p. 246; *morio*, p. 253; *lanatus*, p. 256; *furcatus*, p. 261; *ecundatus* (sic), *primus*, p. 267; *macartneyi*, p. 273; *Phasianus colchicus hybridus*, p. 319; *torquatus primus*, p. 326; *satyrus*, p. 349; *Lophophorus refulgens*, p. 355; *Polyplectron chinquis*, p. 363; *Argus giganteus*, p. 410—"*mihi*".

   Vol. III. *Pauxi galeata*, p. 1; *Pauxi mitu*, p. 8; *Crax rubra*, p. 21; *C. carunculata*, p. 44; *Penelope parrakoua*, p. 85; *Tetrao saliceti*, p. 208; *Pterocles arenarius*, p. 240; *Pt. bicinctus*, p. 247; *Pt. quadricinctus*, p. 252; *Pt. setarius*, p. 256; *Pt. tachypetes*, p. 274; *Syrrhaptes pallasii*, p. 282; *Perdix clamator*, p. 298; *adansonii*, p. 305; *longirostris*, p. 323; *thoracica*, p. 335; *gularis*, p. 401; *oculea*, p. 408; *dentata*, p. 419; *borealis*, p. 436; *sonnini*, p. 451; *Coturnix perlata*, p. 470; *australis*, p. 474; *textilis*, p. 512; *excalfactoria*, p. 516; *grisea*, p. 523; *novæ guineæ*, p. 524; *Cryptonix* (sic) *coronatus*, p. 526; *rufus*, p. 534; *Tinamus rufescens*, p. 552; *maculosus*, p. 557; *tao*, p. 569; *undulatus*, p. 582; *adspersus*, p. 585; *obsoletus*, p. 588; *lataupa*, p. 590; *st*ı*igulosus*, p. 594; *nanus*, p. 600; *Hemipodius nigrifrons*, p. 610; *pugnax*, p. 612; *nigricollis*, p. 619; *thoracicus*, p. 622; *tachydromus*, p. 626; *maculosus*, p. 631; *fasciatus*, p. 634; *Turnix hottentottus*, p. 636—"*mihi*"

   The majority of all the birds in these three volumes are thus described as new; a large part of the rest are credited to Latham. Temminck's names are barbarous in many cases, most of those given in the French vernacular being horrid; but that has always been the style with the French ornithologists.

   Vol. III concludes with a statement from Temminck of the circumstances under which his folio work on the Pigeons appeared—which is not only important as a bibliographical matter, but delightful as a bit of gossip. In explanation both of the present publication and of the folio work on the Pigeons, I here give the substance of his grievance as set forth by him:

   The present work, says Temminck, was intended to appear in folio, with colored plates, The first volume of the folio edition appeared at Paris in 1808 and was completed in 1811, under the direction of Mlle. Pauline de Courcelles, afterward Madame Knip, a very accomplished natural history artist, all of whose works attest her distinguished talents. This lady was charged with the supervision of the engraving, 47 drawings having been made by her from specimens of Pigeons in the Paris Museum, and 40 others copied by her from M. Prêtre's designs, the latter made under Temminck's supervision. The first livraison appeared in 1808, with the same general title as the present edition; Mlle. de Courcelles being properly credited with her part of the work in the following terms: "Aves figures en couleurs peintes par Mademoiselle Pauline de Courcelles, gravées, imprimées et retouchées sous sa direction."

1813-15. TEMMINCK, C. J.—Continued.

No sooner was the work completed than Madame Knip, "the ingrate", saw fit to replace the title with another in which she appeared as the author, her concoction being in the following terms: ". . . les Pigeons par Madame Knip, née Pauline de Courcelles, première peintre d'histoire naturelle de S. M. l'Impératrice et Reine. Le texte par C. J. Themminck [sic].—Se vend à Paris, chez l'auteur, Rue Serbonne. Musée des Artistes." She suppressed 40 pages of text, which would have told against her, and did the same for the 16 double-column pages of the Latin index. The work thus mutilated was presented to Queen Marie Louise, and secured for Mad. Knip some favors her ambition had long coveted. Nevertheless, to keep Temminck in the dark, the lady had the wit to send him some perfect copies, properly titled. It had been agreed that he was to have eight copies; these eight, he says, and four others which bear the date 1808 and have the Latin index, "sont les seuls approuvés par moi"—whence it appears that there are only twelve perfect and authorized copies of the folio work extant! The aggrieved author found out the artful woman's trick when he went to Paris to publish the part of the work relating to the *Gallinæ;* but it was too late. He could obtain no redress; the plot was backed up by royalty; journalists refused his "réclamations", even his reply to an article which the lady published—and which, I suppose, if I could lay my hands on it, would tell quite another story. Such, in brief, is Temminck's own version of the affair which determined him to publish the present 8vo ed. For further particulars relating to the folio work, see under that head, 1808-11.

1824. BOITARD, [P.] *and* CORBIÉ, —. Les Pigeons | de | Volière et de Colombier, | ou | Histoire Naturelle et Monographie | des Pigeons domestiques, | renfermant | la nomenclature et la description de toutes les races | et variétés constantes connues jusqu'à ce jour; la | manière d'établir des colombiers et volières; d'élever, | soigner les pigeons, etc., etc. | Dédiée a son Altesse Royale | Madame la Duchesse de Berry, | par MM. Boitard et Corbié. | Avec vingt-cinq figures de pigeons peints d'après nature. | A Paris, | Chez { Audot, Libraire-Éditeur, rue de Maçons-Sor- | bonne, n°. 11. | { Corbié, Oiselier de S. A. R. madame la duchesse | de Berry, quai de la Mégisserie, n°. 66. | — | 1824. 1 vol. 1 p. l., pp. i-viij, 1-240, pll. 1-25, + 1.

Histoire générale des pigeons—Origine des pigeons domestiques—Du croisement des races—Nourriture—Accouplement—De la ponte et de l'incubation—Des pigeonneaux—Du jeune pigeon et de la connaissance des sexes—Maladies des pigeons—Du colombier—Manière de peupler le colombier—Soins à donner au colombier—De la colombier—Ustensiles—De la volière—Soins à donner à la volière—Dégâts et utilité des pigeons.

Partie 2ᵉ, Monographie des Pigeons de volière—Pigeons de la première-vingt-quatrième race.—Colombes tourterelles.—Tourterelle des bois, à collier, et blanche.

1825. DESM[ARE]ST, [A. G.] Les Pigeons de volière et de Columbier, . . .; par MM. Boitard et Corbie. . . . < *Féruss. Bull.,* 2ᵉ sect., iv, 1825, pp. 258-260.

1827. AUDUBON, J. J. Notes on the Habits of the Wild Pigeon of America, Columb. [Ectopistes] migratoria. < *Edinb. Journ. Sci.,* vi, 1827, pp. 257-265. (*Froriep Notizen,* xvii, 1827, col. 257-262.)

Read before the Roy. Soc. Edinb., Feb. 19, 1827.

1827. L[UROTH], S. G. Observations sur les habitudes du Pigeon sauvage d'Amériqu (Columba [Ectopistes] migratoria); par J.-J. Audubon. . . . < *Féruss. Bull* 2ᵉ sect., xii, 1827, pp. 125, 126.

Précis, tiré de l'*Edinb. Journ. of Science,* vi, avril 1827, pp. 257-265.

1828. ANON. Sur les Columba domestica, livia et Amaliae; par M. Brehm. . . < *Féruss. Bull.,* 2ᵉ sect., xiv, 1828, pp. 260, 261.

Précis, tiré de *l'Isis,* xxi, 1828, pp. 136-141.

1828. BREHM, C. L. Ueber Columba domestica, livia et Amaliae. < *Oken's Isis,* xxi, 1828, pp. 136-141.

1829. [EDITORIAL.] Notice respecting a Pigeon which continued to live two da without Brain and upper part of Spinal Marrow. < *Edinb. New Phil Journ.,* vii, 1829, p. 372.

Note on M. Desportes's communication to Acad. Sci. Paris.

1829. FLEMING, [J.] Description of the Passenger Pigeon [Ectopistes migratoriu < *Loudon's Mag. Nat. Hist.,* i, 1829, p. 488.

1829. "J. M." Columba [Ectopistes] migratoria (the Wild Pigeon). < *Loudon's Mag. Nat. Hist.*, ii, 1829, pp. 369, 370.

Quotations from the Rochester, N. Y., *Genesee County Register*, Dec., 1828; *Susquehanna County Register*, May, 1829, and *New York Med. and Phys. Journ.*, ii, p. 210.

1832. ANON. Mode of decoying Wild Pigeons [Ectopistes migratorius] in New England. < *Loudon's Mag. Nat. Hist.*, v, 1832, pp. 452, 453.

From *Silliman's Journal.*

1833. HUNT, J. [Note on the Breeding of the Passenger Pigeon (Ectopistes migratorius, Swains.), in the Society's Menagerie.] < *P. Z. S.*, i, 1833, p. 10.

1835. ANON. Passenger Pigeon [Ectopistes migratorius, at Baffin's Bay, lat. 73¼° N.]. < *Edinb. New Philos. Journ.*, xx, 1835, p. 209.

From *Ross's Voyage.*

1835. ANON. The Carrier-Pigeon. A Society of Pigeon Fanciers, at Ghent, give an Annual Prize for the Best Carrier Pigeon. < *Loudon's Mag. Nat. Hist.*, viii, 1835, p. 619.

1835. SELBY, P. J. The | Naturalist's Library. | Edited by | Sir William Jardine, Bart., | F. R. S. E., F. L. S., etc., etc. | Vol. IX. | — | Ornithology. | Pigeons. | By Prideaux John Selby, Esq., | F. R. S. E., F. L. S., M. W. S., etc., etc. | — | Edinburgh : | W. H. Lizars, [etc.] [1835.] 1 vol. sm. 12mo. Portrait of Pliny, eng. col'd title, contents, 1 leaf, pp. 17–252, cuts, pll. 1–30 (+ portrait and vignette = 32 pll.).

Being Vol. V of the general arrangement. "The Pigeons, . . . are now, in accordance with their true affinities, admitted into the order of the Rasores, or Gallinaceous Birds, of which they form one of the five great groups or divisions, the other four being represented by the Pavonidæ, Tetraonidæ, Struthionidæ, and Cracidæ"—in spite of which opening, the book continues well.—Pl. 1, *Vinago aromatica;* 2, *V. oxyura;* 3, *Ptilinopus purpuratus;* 4, *P. monachus;* 5, *P. cyanovirens;* 6, *Carpophaga* (Selby, p. 112) *magnifica;* 7, *C. oceanica;* 8, *Columba phasianella;* 9, *C. spadicea;* 10, *C. dilopha;* vignette, *C. palumbus;* 11, *C. œnas;* 12, *C. livia;* 13, var. *tremula latecauda;* 14, *C. cucullata jacobina;* 15, var. *gutturosa subrubicunda;* 16, *C. turcica;* 17, *Turtur risorius;* 18, *T. ? lophotes;* 19, *Ectopistes migratoria;* 20, *E. ? capensis;* 21, *Phaps* (Selby, p. 194) *chalcoptera;* 22, *Chœmepelia* (sic) *talpicoti* (sic); 23, *Peristera tympanistria;* 24, *P. jamaicensis* (named *rufaxilla* on pl.); 25, *P. martinica* (named *cuprea* on pl.); 26, *P. larvata;* 27, *Geophilus* (Selby, p. 214) *cyanocephalus;* 28, *G. carunculatus;* 29, *G. nicobaricus;* 30, *Lophyrus coronatus.* "Miscellaneous observations on the rearing, feeding, and management of domestic pigeons" concludes the volume.

1838-4-. KNIP, *Madame, and* PRÉVOST, F. Les Pigeons, | par Madame Knip, | née Pauline de Courcelles, | le texte par Florent Prévost, | Aide Naturaliste et Chef des Travaux Zoologiques au Muséum | d'Histoire Naturelle. | — | Tome Second. | — | A Paris, | Chez { Mᵐᵉ Knip, auteur des dessins, et éditeur, Bellizard, Dufour et Cⁱᵉ, Libraires, Rue Rue de Bac, Nᵒ 17. | de Verneuil, 1 bis. | — | Typographie de Firmin Didot Frères, Rue Jacob, 56. [n. d. 1838–184-.] 1 vol. folio. Prel. title, 1 leaf; title, 1 leaf; table, 1 leaf (2 pages); text, pp. 1–113. Plates, 1–60, colored.

This is ostensibly Vol. II of the Temminck-Knip work; but, appearing many years afterward, with text by another person, it is in effect a different work altogether, though in continuation of the same subject, and prepared in the same style. The volume examined in the Libr. Phila. Acad. is bound uniform with Hazard's unique copy of Temminck-Knip; but unfortunately the cover-titles of the livraisons are not preserved, so that I cannot give the dates. It stands announced for 15 livraisons of 4 plates each, and, according to Engelmann, livrs. 1–12 appeared 1838–43.

The following is a list of the plates :

Pl. 1. *Columba puella.* 2. *leucotis.* 3. *zoeœ.* 4. *porphyria.* 5. *humeralis.* 6. *reinwaratsii.* 7. *humilis.* 8. *cyanovirens.* 9. *rufigaster.* 10. *sieboldii.* 11. *gularis.* 12. *olax.* 13. *lophotes.* 14. *pulchella.* 15. *pinon.* 16. *janthina.* 17. *viridis.* 18. *denisea.* 19. *dilophus.* 20. *dussumieri.* 21. *perlata.* 22. *boliviana.* 23. *xanthura.* 24. *oceanica.* 25. *magnifica.* 26. *venusta.* 27. *gelastes.* 28. *leucomela.* 29. *radiata.* 30. *oxyura.* 31. *modesta.* 32. *aymera.* 33. *scripta.* 34. *rosacea.* 35. *picturata.* 36. *ruficeps.* 37. *capistrata.* 38. *capellei.* 39. *picui.* 40. *luctuosa.* 41. *macquarii.* 42. *superba.* 43. *laurivora.* 44. *locutrix.* 45. *histrionica.* 46. *manadensis.* 47. *forsterii.* 48. *cruziana.* 49. *sphenura.* 50. *leuconota.* 51. *histrionica.* 52. *pha-*

1838-4-. KNIP, *Madame, and* PRÉVOST, F.—Continued.

sianella. 53. *monacha.* 54. *hyogaster.* 55. *Colombigallina linearis.* 56. *Columba mullerii.* 57. *rivolii* (nobis). 58. *plumifera.* 59. *nuna.* 60. *mayeri.*

In the text the species are only given under their French vernacular names. But the technical names are graven on the plates, and also given in the table.

1839. WEISSENBORN, [W.] [Letter relating to a Pigeon destitute of Organs of Vision. < *P. Z. S.*, vii, 1839, p. 175.

1840. HUNTER, J. On a Secretion in the crop of breeding Pigeons, for the nourishment of their young. < *Obs. Anim. Œcon.*, Amer. ed., 1840, pp. 149–151.

Orig. ed., 1786.

1844. CABOT, S., JR. [Note on Columba trudeaui.] < *Proc. Bost. Soc. Nat. Hist.*, i, 1844, p. 183.

1847. McCALL. G. A. Description of a supposed new species of Columba [solitaria], inhabiting Mexico, with some account of the habits of the Geococcyx viaticus, Wagler. < *Proc. Acad. Nat. Sci. Phila.*, iii, July, 1847, pp. 233–235.

1847. McCALL, G. A. Description of a supposed new species of Columba [solitaria] inhabiting Mexico. < *Am. Journ. Sci.*, iv, 1847, p. 421.

From *Proc. Acad. Nat. Sci. Phila.*, iii, 1847, p. 233.

1850. [KIRTLAND, J. P.] Wild Pigeon—Ectopistes migratoria. < *The Family Visitor*, i, No. 17, 1850, p. 133.

1,285 netted one day near Circleville, Ohio.

1851. EATON, J. M. Dedicated to the young and inexperienced fancier | of the Almond Tumbler. | — | A | Treatise | on the art of | Breeding and Managing | the | Almond Tumbler. | — | By John Matthews Eaton | — | [Quotation.] | — | Published for the author, | 7, Islington Green, London. | — | 1851. 1 vol. 8vo. pp. i–vi, 7–49 + 1 p. Followed by Notes on a treatise on the art of breeding and managing the Almond Tumbler. By an old Fancier. pp. i–viii.

1851. HARTLAUB, "P." [*i. e.*, G.] Sur une nouvelle espèce de Colombe [Zenaida innotata] de Chili. < *Rev. et Mag. de Zool.*, iii, 1851, p. 74.

1852. EATON, J. M. Dedicated to the young and inexperienced Fancier | of tame, domesticated, and fancy Pigeons. | — | A | treatise | on the art of | breeding and managing | Tame, Domesticated, and Fancy Pigeons, | carefully compiled from, the best authors, with observations, containing | all that is necessary to be known of tame, domesticated, and fancy pigeons. | — | By John Matthews Eaton, | Author of the Almond Tumbler. | — | [Quotation.] | — | Published for, and to be obtained of, the author, | 7 Islington Green, London. | — | 1852. 1 vol. 8vo. pp. i–xxii, 23–88.

This is an annotated reprint of John Moore's Columbarium (London, 1735), the full title-page of which makes p. ix of the present tract, the preceding pp. being Eaton's preliminary matter. His annotations are in the form of foot-notes throughout the tract, sometimes occupying the whole page, as pp. 59, 60, 61. Moore's tract ends at p. 80, and Eaton's concludes the vol.

1852. EATON, J. M. [Plates accompanying a treatise on Fancy Pigeons, by J. M. Eaton.] 4to and fol. size. London: published Dec. 8, 1852. 6 plates, colored.

No title-page; plates not numbered. 1, Almond Tumbler, 4to; 2, Black Mottle, 4to; 3, Bald Head, 4to; 4, Beard, 4to; 5, Carrier, folio, folded. 6, Powter, folio, folded. I suppose these plates belong to Eaton's treatise of same date, *q. v.*, but there is nothing to show this.

1852. WOODHOUSE, S. W. Description of a new species of Ectopistes [marginella]. < *Proc. Acad. Nat. Sci. Phila.*, vi, 1852, pp. 104, 105.

1854-55. BONAPARTE, C. L. Coup d'œil sur l'ordre des Pigeons. < *Compt. Rend. de l'Acad. Sci.*, xxxix, 1854, pp. 869–880, 1072–1078, 1102–1112; xl, 1855, pp. 15–24, 96–102, 205–215.

1854.—*Phalacrotreron*, p. 872; *Butreron, Crocopus*, p. 873; *Osmotreron*, p. 874; *Leucotreron, Thouarsitreron, Lamprotreron*, p. 876; *L. apicalis*, p. 876; *Cyanotreron, Ramphiculus, Jotreron, Kurutreron, Omeotreron*, p. 878; *O. batilda*, p. 878; *Globicera*, p. 1072; *G. tarrali, G. sundevalli,*

1854-55. BONAPARTE, C. L —Continued.

G. rubricera, "Gray", p. 1073; *Carpophaga chalybura, C. ochropygia, Ptilocolpa,* p. 1074; *Pt. carola, Pt. grieseipectus,* "Gray", p. 1075; *Ducula paulina,* "Temm.", *D. basilica,* "Temm.", *Hemiphaga,* p. 1076; *Myristicivora grisea,* "Gray", p. 1078: *Leucomeloena, Trocaza, Turturoena,* p. 1104; *Stictoenas dilloni,* p. 1105; *Palumbœnas,* p. 1107; *Columba (Chlorœna) albilinea,* "Gray", p. 1108; *Chlorœnas spilodera,* "Gray", p. 1109; *Crossophthalmus reichenbachi,* p. 1110; *Macropygia doreya,* p. 1111; *M. carteretia, Turacœna, Reinwardtœna typica,* p. 1112.

    1855.—*Streptopelia,* p. 17; *Aplopelia,* p. 18; *Chalcopelia,* p. 19; *Chamaepelia granatina, C. albivitta, C. trochila, C. amazilia,* p. 21; *Talpacotia,* p. 22; *Chamaepelia rufipennis,* Gray, *Ch. godinœ,* p. 22; *Columbula* p. 22; *Metriopelia, M. gymnops,* Gray, p. 23; *M. inornata,* Gray, p. 24; *Scardafella, S. inca, Uropelia,* p. 24; *Zenaidura, Z. marginella,* p. 96; *Zenaida bimaculata,* "Gray", *Z. hypoleuca,* Gray, *Z. ruficauda,* Gray, p. 97; *Z. pentheria, Z. stenura,* p. 98; *Leptoptila verreauxi, L. dubusi,* p. 99; *Geotrygon chrysia,* p. 100; *G. bourcieri, G. saphirina,* p. 101; *Osculatia, Starnoenas,* p. 102; *Pampusana,* p. 207; *Chalcophaps augusta,* p. 209; *Chrysauchœna,* p. 210; *Phapitreron amethystina,* p. 214; *Globicera microcera, Ducula pistrinaria,* p. 215.— Tableau! p. 212. (Coup de théâtre!! "À moi la cargaison"!!!)

1854. BONAPARTE, C. L.   Coup d'œil sur les Pigeons.   < *Rev. et Mag. de Zool.,* vi, 1854, pp. 680, 681.

    Résumé de la commencement de la troisième partie de son ouvrage présenté à l'Acad. de Paris, séance du 11 déc. 1854.

1854. DESPORTES, E. H.   Observation de longévité d'un pigeon.   < *Ann. des Sci. Nat.,* 4e sér., ii, 1854, pp. 249-254.

1855. GREENLEAF, P. H.   Observations on the Flight of the American Passenger Pigeon [Ectopistes migratorius], at Madison, Ind., March, 1855.   < *Proc. Bost. Soc. Nat. Hist.,* v, 1855, pp. 181, 182.

1856. [BILLINGS, E.]   On the Pigeon, (Ectopistes Migratoria.)   < *Canad. Nat. and Geol.,* i, June, 1856, pp. 168-176.

    Compilation from Wilson.

1856. BONAPARTE, C. L.   Additions et Corrections au Coup d'œil sur l'Ordre des Pigeons, et à la partie correspondante du Conspectus Avium.   < *Compt. Rend. de l'Acad. Sci.,* xliii, 1856, pp. 833-841, 942-949.

    Thouarsitreron minor, Drepanoptila, p. 834; *Ducula concolor, Palumbus excelsus,* p. 836; *Trocaza bouvryi,* p. 837; *Columba eversmanni,* p. 838.   Voir 1854-55, même auteur.

1856. BONAPARTE, C. L.   Additions et corrections au Coup d'œil sur l'ordre des Pigeons et à la partie correspondante du Conspectus Avium.   < *Rev. et Mag. de Zool.,* viii, 1856, p. 535, et pp. 538, 539.

    Voici seulement la Note qui précède ces additions, et la conclusion générale.

1857-58. BONAPARTE, C. L.   Iconographie | des Pigeons | non figurés par Mme Knip (Mlle Pauline de Courcelles) | dans les deux volumes de MM. Temminck et Florent Prevost | par Charles-Lucien Bonaparte | — | Ouvrage servant d'illustration a son | Histoire Naturelle des Pigeons | — | Paris | P. Bertrand, Libraire-Éditeur | Rue de l'Arbre-sec, 22 | 1857 [1858]. 1 vol. in-fol. grand jésus. Faux titre, 1 feuillet; titre, 1 feuillet; table des matières, 1 feuillet; avis de l'éditeur, 1 feuillet; lettre à Moquin-Tandon, 4 pages; Clavis systematis et Conspectus generum, 6 pages; 55 planches coloriées renfermant 66 figures, avec le texte non paginé, 59 feuillets. (Livraisons i-xii, 1857, 1858.)

    "La quatrième livraison de notre Iconographie venait de paraître, lorsque la mort a frappé son savant auteur. Il n'y avait donc que 20 planches de publiées; mais nous avions entre les mains 35 lithographies prêtes, dont plusieurs déjà coloriées, et tous les dessins originaux, approuvés par le Prince, qui avaient servi ou devaient servir de modèles au coloriage. Nous avions aussi les descriptions correspondantes, les unes imprimées, les autres en cours d'épreuves. . . . Nous nous sommes trouvé possesseur des éléments de plus de sept nouvelles livraisons. Nous les avons publiées successivement, dans l'espace de dix mois. . . . M. Moquin-Tandon a bien voulu revoir toutes les épreuves, texte et planches. Réunies aux quatre premières, ces livraisons composent un total de 55 planches, renfermant 66 figures. . . . Comme trois de nos planches renferment deux espèces, et que nous avons donné dans la seconde livraison la *Lettre à M. Moquin-Tandon,* et dans la sixième le *Clavis Systematis,* le *Conspectus generum* et le *Conspectus geographicus,* les figures se sont trouvées en avance sur les descriptions. Force a été d'ajouter, pour compléter l'ouvrage, une douzième livraison

1857–58. BONAPARTE, C. L.—Continued.

sans Planches. Le nombre des Pigeons figurés dans cette *Icongraphie* s'élève donc à 58. . . . Nous ferons observer que les espèces publiées par le Prince Charles Bonaparte appartiennent principalement aux premiers groupes de l'ordre des Pigeons, et forment aussi des séries complètes, par example, celles des Tréronés et des Ptilopés." (*Avis de l'éditeur*, le 1er juillet 1858.)

Owing to these circumstances the work is in fact an unfinished one. It was announced to appear in 30 livraisons, of 150 plates (5 to a livraison). Only 12, however, were published—4 in 1857, and the remaining 8 from Sept., 1857, to July, 1858. The numbering of the plates is with reference to the whole series of 150, only 55 of which appeared; and is consequently not continuous. The 55 plates are accompanied by about as many sheets of letter-press. The following is a list of them (I cannot separate them in sets according to livraisons, nor give exact dates; but the first 20 appeared in 1857, livrs. 1–4, and the remainder in 1857 and 1858):

Pl. 1. *Phalacrotreron delalandi; a, P. abyssinnica.* 2. *P. crassirostris.* 3. *P. nudirostris; a, P. calva.* 4. *Sphenocercus apicaudus.* 5. *S. cantillans.* 6. *Treron curvirostra.* 7. *T. aromatica.* 8. *T. nepalensis.* 8. *Crocopus viridifrons.* 11. fig. 1, *Osmotreron pompadora;* fig. 2, *O. malabarica.* 12. *O. malabarica.* 13. *O. vernans.* 14. *Ramphiculus occipitalis.* 15. *Lamprotreron porphyrea.* 16. *Trerolœma leclancheri.* 17. *Thouarsitreron leucocephala.* 18. *T. diadema.* 19. *Ptilopus purpuratus.* 20. *P. flavicollis.* 21. *P. swainsoni.* 22. fig. 1, *P. clementinœ;* fig. 2. *P. mercieri.* 23. *P. roseicapillus.* 24. fig. 1, *P. ewingi;* fig. 2, *P. clementinœ.* 25. *P. greyi.* 26. *P. mariœ.* 28. *Iotreron viridis.* 29. fig. 1, *Kurutreron oopa;* fig. 2, *K. chrysogaster.* 31. *Chrysœna luteovirens.* 32. *Erythrœna madagascariensis.* 33. *Serresius galeatus.* 34. *Globicera myristicivora.* 35. *G. pacifica.* 36. *G. microcera.* 38. *G. tarrali.* 39. *G. rubricera.* 40. *G. sundevalli.* 42. *Carpophaga chalybura.* 45. *C. perspicillata.* 51. *Ptilocolpa griseipectus.* 57. *Palumbus torquatus.* 58. *P. casiotis.* 61. *Dendrotreron hodgsoni.* 62. *Leucomelœna norfolciensis.* 69. *Trocaza laurivora.* 70. *T. bouvryi.* 75. *Columba rupestris.* 102. *Turtur isabellinus.* 116. *Osculatia sapphirina.* 119. *Leptoptila jamaicensis.* 121. *Talpacotia rufipennis.* 125. fig. 1, *Peristera cinerea;* fig. 2, *P. geoffroyi.* 126. *P. mondetoura.* 133. *Zenaida auriculata.* 134. *Z. hypoleuca.* 140. *Didunculus strigirostris.*

The livraisons in which these plates and their accompanying text appeared may be seen by the table of contents in the work. They were published not in the above order nor in any other; nor did the sheets of text always appear with the plates to which they respectively pertain. The text is very briefly descriptive of the subjects of the beautiful plates.

1857. BREHM, C. L. Die | Naturgeschichte und Zucht | der Tauben | oder vollständige Beschreibung aller europäischen wilden und zah- | men Taubenarten und ihrer Abänderungen, ihrer Wohnorte | und Sitten, ihrer Nahrung and Fortpflanzung, ihrer Be- | handlung und Pflege, ihres Nutzens und Schadens, ihrer | Feinde und Krankheiten. | — | Für Taubenzüchter und Ornithologen | von | Christian Ludwig Brehm, | [etc.] | — | Weimar, 1857. | Verlag und Druck von Bernh. Friedr. Voight. 1 vol. 8vo. 1 p. l., pp. i–xii, 1–177, + 1½ ll. advts.

Columbarum conspectus systematicus, pp. 7–13. The main part of the work is a complete treatment of each species and variety of European and domesticated Pigeon. Many varietal names of Brehm's occur, some doubtless new here; but it is seldom desirable and never necessary to cite his useless synonyms.

1858. [EDITORIAL.] Unusual migration of Wild Pigeons [Ectopistes migratorius]. < *Canad. Nat. and Geol.*, iii, 1858, pp. 150, 151.

1866. WYMAN, J. [Account of the dissection of a young domestic pigeon.] < *Proc. Boston Soc. Nat. Hist.*, xi, 1866, pp. 24, 25.

1867. HILL, R. Note on Geotrygon sylvatica, Gosse. < *Proc. Acad. Nat. Sci. Phila.*, xix, 1867, pp. 130, 131.

Habits; with suggested relation to *Didus*.

1867. NEWMAN, E. Notices of New Books. < *Zoologist*, 2d ser., ii, 1867, pp. 929–943.

Review of Tegetmeier's 'Pigeons, their Structure, Habits and Varieties.'

1867. TEGETMEIER, W. B. Pigeons, their Structure, Habits and Varieties. By W. B. Tegetmeier, F. L. S. With Coloured Illustrations of the Varieties by Harrison Weir. London. Routledge. 1867. 8vo.

Not seen. Cf. *Zoologist*, 2d ser., ii, 1867, pp. 929–943. The many domesticated breeds of *Columba livia* are very fully treated.

1868. HARRIS, E. D. The Structure, Flight and Habits of the different varieties of the Domesticated Pigeon. < *Proc. Boston Soc. Nat. Hist.*, xi, 1868, pp. 355–360.

1868. SCLATER, P. L., *and* SALVIN, O. Descriptions of New Species of Birds of the Families Dendrocolaptidæ, Strigidæ, and Columbidæ. < *P. Z. S.*, xxxvi, 1868, pp. 53–60, pl. v, woodcc.

The new Pigeons are described as *Leptoptila plumbeiceps* and *L. cerviniventris*, p. 59, and a synopsis of 8 spp. of the genus is given.

1868. VOIT, —. Beobachtungen nach Abtragung der Hemisphären des Grosshirns bei Tauben. < *Sitzungsb. Akad. Wissensch. München*, ii, 1868, pp. 105–108.

Not seen.

1869. VOIT, —. Observations sur l'ablation des hémisphères cérébraux des pigeons. < *Institut*, No. 1828, 12 Jan., 1869; *Ann. Sc. Nat.*, 5ᵉ sér., xi, pp. 90–92.

Not seen.

1871. SALVADORI, T. Nuove specie di Uccelli dei generi Criniger, Picus ed Homoptila Nov. Gen. < *Atti della R. Acad. delle Scienze di Torino*, vi, 1871, pp. 128–132.

Homoptila decipiens, g. sp. n., p. 131, ex Brasiliâ.—Genus novum genere *Leptoptilæ* differt tantum remige prima apicem versus minime attenuata.

1872. ANON. Wild Pigeon [Ectopistes migratorius] roost in Maryland. < *Am. Sportsman*, ii, 1872, p. 42.

From *Baltimore Gazette*, Oct. 11, 1872.

1872. BAIRD, S. F. Restoration of excised brain in pigeons. < *Harper's New Monthly Mag.*, xlv, 1872, p. 632.

1873. ANON. Carrier Pigeons < *Forest and Stream*, i, Aug. 14, 1873, p. 5.

Use of these birds by newspapers.

1873. SANCHEZ, J., *and* VILLADA, M. M. Palomas viajeras [Ectopistes migratorius]. < *La Naturaleza*, ii, 1873, pp. 250–255.

Nota sobre las que ultimamente han emigrado a México; emigracion, descripcion, costumbres. Con noticia por el Sr. Don Ant. del Castillo.

1873. SCHLEGEL, H. Aves Columbæ. < *Mus. Nat. Hist. Pays-Bas*, 10ᵉ livr., mars, 1863, pp. 1–!80.

This is one of the most extensive and elaborate monographs of the series. It treats of the *Columbidæ* (including *Didunculus*) under the following genera: *Ptilopus*, 48 spp. ; *Treron*, 24 spp. ; *Columba*, 11 spp. ; *Lepidoenas*, 6 spp. ; *Stictoenas*, 7 spp. ; *Janthoenas*, 7 spp. ; *Chloroenas*, 8 spp. ; *Carpophaga*, 32 spp. ; *Macropygia*, 9 spp. ; *Turtur*, 25 spp. ; *Geopelia*, 7 spp. ; *Peristera*, 22 spp. ; *Chalcophaps*, 2 spp. ; *Melopelia*, 2 spp. ; *Phaps*, 7 spp. ; *Henicophaps*, 1 sp. ; *Phlegoenas*, 3 spp. ; *Leptoptila*, 13 spp. ; *Starnoenas*, 9 spp. ; *Didunculus*, 1 sp. ; *Goura*, 2 spp. ; *Otidiphaps*, 1 sp. ; *Caloenas*, 1 sp.

Ptilopus neglectus, p. 7; *P. cinctus lettiensis*, p. 35. *Columba palumbus himalayana*, p. 66. *Chloroenas fallax*, p. 80. *Carpophaga geelvinkiana*, p. 86; *C. luctuosa*, p. 102. *Macropygia reinwardtii minor*, p. 106; *M. turtur*, p. 110; *Turtur neglectus*, p. 122; *T. fallax*, 124; *Peristera lansbergii*, p. 139, spp. nn.

1874. ANON. Carrier Pigeons [employed as news-transporters]. < *Am. Sportsman*, v, Nov. 14, 1874, p. 99.

1874. ANON. Pigeon-catching. < *Am. Sportsman*, v, Oct. 10, 1874, p. 23.

Methods of netting *Ectopistes migratorius*; quoted from *Lewiston* (Maine) *Journal*.

1874. ANON. The Great Pigeon [Ectopistes migratorius] Roost of 1874. < *Am. Sportsman*, iv, 1874, p. 275.

Quoted from New York *World*.

1874. "A. G. D." Passenger Pigeons [Ectopistes migratorius]. < *Am. Sportsman*, iv, 1874, p. 298.

General discussion of breeding habits; and of decrease in numbers, supported by quotations and statistics.

1874. "F. P." Nesting of Wild Pigeons [Ectopistes migratorius, in Wisconsin]. < *Am. Sportsman*, iv, 1874, p. 171. See also p. 194.

1874. GARROD, A. H. On some Points in the Anatomy of the Columbæ. < *P. Z. S.*, xlii, 1874, pp. 249–259.

On the number of rectrices, and presence or absence of the oil-gland, the cœca, and the ambiens muscle. Classification of the group on these points. *Pterocles* and *Syrrhaptes* are included among *Columbæ*.

1874. HEDDON, J. Will pigeons [Ectopistes migratorius] play out? < *Am. Sportsman,* iv, 1874, p. 362.

Great diminution in numbers of *Ectopistes migratorius.*

1874. "H. K." The Wild Pigeon [Ectopistes migratorius]. < *Am. Sportsman,* iv, 1874, p. 387. See also pp. 171, 194, 243, 298, and 339.

1874. MOORE, J. Columbarium; | or, | The Pigeon-House : | being | an introduction | to a | Natural History | of | Tame Pigeons, | giving an | account of the several species known in England, | with the method of breeding them, their | distempers and cures. | — | [Quotation.] | | — | By John Moore. | — | London: | Printed for J. Wilford, behind the Chapter-House in St. Paul's Church-Yard. | 1735. | — | Reprinted by Jos. M. Wade, | Fanciers' Journal Office, Philadelphia, 1874. 1 vol. 16mo. pp. i-x, 1–64 + 7 ll. advts., many cuts.

"Moore's work on Pigeons was, no doubt, the first, and is really the most important, work ever written on this subject, . . . 'The work is out of print [very naturally—1735], and very scarce, only two or three copies are known to be in existence at the present time.'

" . . . in May, 1874, we began its publication in the columns of the *Fanciers' Journal,* which circumstance has created a demand for this reprint in book form.

"The original work was not illustrated; and, in order to make it more valuable to young fanciers, *we have embellished it with a series of illustrations* by that well-known artist, Mr. J. W. Ludlow." (*Extracts from American Publisher's Preface.*)

There are many editions of the famous original, among them a literal reprint by Tegetmeier, 1879.

1874. LINCECUM, G. The Nesting of Wild Pigeons [Ectopistes migratorius]. < *Am. Sportsman,* iv, 1874, p. 194. See also pp. 171, 243, 298, 339, and 387.

Description of food and breeding habits.

1874. "M. T." Passenger Pigeons [Ectopistes migratorius]. < *St. Nicholas Mag.,* i, 1874, p. 15.

Migrations in Minnesota.

1874. SEARS, J. H. Breeding of Wild Pigeon [Ectopistes migratorius, in Essex County, Mass.]. < *Am. Sportsman,* iv, 1874, p. 155.

1875. ALIX, E. Garrod (A. H.): Sur quelques points de l'anatomie des Colombés. (Proceed. Zool. Soc. London, 1874, p. 249.) < *Gerv. Journ. de Zool.,* —, 1875, pp. ———.

Résumé des observations de M. Garrod, insérées dans les *P. Z. S.,* 1874, pp. 249–259, *q. v.*

1875. ANON. A Pigeon [Ectopistes migratorius] Roost. < *Rod and Gun,* vi, Oct. 9, 1875, p. 27.

1875. CARLETON, J. F. The breeding habits of pigeons [Ectopistes migratorius]. < *Forest and Stream,* iv, Aug. 5, 1875, p. 406.

1875. "G. D. B." The pigeon [Ectopistes migratorius] roost near Corning [N. Y.]. < *Forest and Stream,* iv, May 27, 1875, p. 252.

1876. ADAMS, J. W. Wild pigeons [Ectopistes migratorius, yet numerous] in Massachusetts. < *Forest and Stream,* vii, Sept. 28, 1876, p. 116. See pp. 104, 184.

1876. ANON. [W. M. TILESTON.] Protecting wild pigeons [Ectopistes migratorius]. < *Forest and Stream,* vii, Oct. 26, 1876, p. 184. See p. 104.

1876. ANON. Homing Pigeons [exported from France to New York]. < *Rod and Gun,* viii, Aug. 19, 1876, p. 326.

Reprinted from "L'Epervier."

1876. GUNN, C. W. The Ectopistes migratoria, Sw. Wild Pigeon. < *Oölogist,* ii, No. 4, 1876, p. 29, 30.

1876. [INGERSOLL, E.] The Protection of Wild Pigeons [Ectopistes migratorius]. < *Forest and Stream,* vii, Sept. 21, 1876, p. 104. See p. 184.

Comments and statistics on the progressive destruction of this species.

1876. OWEN, T. M. Wild Pigeons [Ectopistes migratorius]. < *Rod and Gun,* viii, June 3, 1876, p. 148.

Statistics as to capture of living and dead specimens of this species in Ohio and Michigan for shooting matches and market.

1876. REID, P.   Pigeons [Ectopistes migratorius]—Food in Crop.   < *Rod and Gun,* vii, Jan. 8, 1876, p. 227.   See also p. 277.
   Explaining "rice" found in pigeon's stomachs, supposed by Audubon and others to prove enormous velocity of the bird's flight.

1876. STERLING, E.   Passenger Pigeons [Ectopistes migratorius] and Rice.   < *Rod and Gun,* vii, Jan. 29, 1876, p. 277.
   Reply to Reid, concerning "rice in crops", and velocity of flight. See p. 227.

1876. "TOM TRAMP."   A pigeon [Ectopistes migratorius] roost.   < *Rod and Gun,* viii, June 3, 1876, p. 149.
   Breeding of, and statistics of capture and decrease of this species in Illinois.

1877. COUES, E.   Melopelia leucoptera in Colorado.   < *Bull. Nutt. Ornith. Club,* ii, No. 3, July, 1877, p. 83.

1877. COUES, E.   Leptoptila albifrons, a Pigeon new to the United States Fauna.   < *Bull. Nutt. Ornith. Club,* ii, No. 3, July, 1877, pp. 82, 83.
   Taken in Texas by G. B. Sennett. Soon afterward made type of a new genus, *Æchmoptila,* Coues, *Bull. U. S. Geol. Surv. Terr.,* iv, No. 1, 1878, p. 48 (= *Engyptila,* Sundev., *Tentamen,* 1872, p. 156.)

1877. ROWLEY, G. D.   Geotrygon costaricensis (Lawrence).   < *Rowl. Orn. Misc.,* iii, pt. xi, Nov., 1877, pp. 43–46, pl. lxxxvii.
   Copy of orig. descr. in *Ann. N. Y. Lyc.,* ix, 1868, p. 136, with a colored fig. of the bird, and notes by A. Boucard.

1878. FIROR, V. M.   Chamœpelia passerina.   < *Familiar Science and Fancier's Journ.,* n. s., v, Apr., 1878, p. 86.

1878. GRINNELL, G. B.   The Ground Dove (Chamæpeleia passerina) in New York.   < *Bull. Nutt. Ornith. Club,* iii, No. 3, July, 1878, p. 147.
   In New York City, Oct., 1862; specimen identified by J. W. Audubon; now first recorded.

1878. McL[ELLAN, I.]   The Wild or Passenger Pigeon (Columba [Ectopistes] migratoria).   < *Forest and Stream,* ix, Jan. 31, 1878, p. 488.

1878. OWEN, T. M.   Among the Pigeons [Ectopistes migratorius, in Ohio].   < *Forest and Stream,* x, May 23, 1878, p. 297.

1878. ROWLEY, G. D.   Chlorœnas subvinacea.   Lawrence.   < *Rowl. Orn. Misc.,* iii, pt. xii, Jan., 1878, pp. 75, 76, pl. xci.
   Copy of orig. descr. in *Ann. N. Y. Lyc. Nat. Hist.,* ix, Apr., 1868, p. 135, with colored plate, and a note from A. Boucard.

1878. ROWLEY, G. D.   Geotrygon rufiventris, Lawrence.   < *Rowl. Orn. Misc.,* iii, pt. xii, Jan., 1878, pp. 77, 78, pl. xcii.
   Copy of orig. descr. in *Ann. Lyc. Nat. Hist. N. Y.,* xi, 1875, with a colored plate, and note by A. Boucard.

1878. ROWLEY, G. D.   Leptoptila cassini, Lawrence.   < *Rowl. Orn. Misc.,* iii, pt. xii, Jan., 1878, pp. 79, 80, pl. xciii.

1878. STERLING, E.   [Acorns of the black-jack oak as] Food of the Wild Pigeon [Ectopistes migratorius].   < *Forest and Stream,* x, Mar. 14, 1878, p. 95.

1879. KNAPP, H.   Statement about the Wild Pigeon [Ectopistes migratorius].   < *Forest and Stream,* xii, Mar. 27, 1879, p. 146.
   Taken from some Central New York newspaper, either Buffalo or Rochester, I think.

1879. McQUILLEN, J. H.   Recovery of all the Faculties in a Pigeon from which four-fifths of the upper portion of the Cerebrum had been removed.   < *Proc. Acad. Nat. Sci. Phila.,* Oct., 1878, (pub. 1879), pp. 342–346.

1879. THOMPSON, F. J.   Incubation [of Ectopistes migratorius] under Difficulties.   < *Forest and Stream,* xii, May 8, 1879, p. 265.
   Account of its breeding, in March, in an open air aviary in the Cincinnati Zoological Garden.

Cracidæ.

1733. PERRAULT, C.   Description anatomique de trois Cocqs Indiens [Cracidæ].
   < Mém. de l'Acad. Roy. des Sci. depuis 1666 jusq. 1699, iii, pt. i, 1733, pp. 221–
   231, pl. 33, 34.
   Mitu-poranga of Marcgrave.

1757. PERRAULT, C.   Anatomische Beschreibung dreier indianischer Hühner [Cra-
   cidæ].   < Abhandl. Königl. Französich Akad., i, 1757, pp. 259–——.
   Nicht mir selbst zugänglich: Titel aus Giebel. Uebers. d. *Mém. de l'Acad. Roy. Paris*,
   1666–1699, iii, pt. i, 1733, pp. 221–231.

1830. WAGLER, J.   Revisio generis Penelope.   < Oken's Isis, Bd. xxiii, 1830, pp. 1109–
   1112.
   Important: "may be regarded as the earliest scientific article (in a modern sense) upon
   this subject." Describes 18 spp., in three sections, A, B, C, corresponding exactly to the
   genera *Pipile, Penelope,* and *Ortalida.* "His excellent diagnoses materially assist us in
   identifying Spix's species." Seven new species are described, namely: *P. pileata* (Licht.,
   M. B.), p. 1109; *P. purpurascens,* p. 1110; *P. albiventris, P. ruficeps,* p. 1111; *P. vetula, P. poliocephala, P. canicollis* (after Azara), p. 1112. All these are considered valid by Sclater and
   Salvin.

1831. ANON.   Revue du genre Penélope; par M. Wagler.   < Féruss. Bull., 2e sect.,
   xxiv, 1831, pp. 367, 368.
   Ici se trouve seulement la description genérique, avec une énumération des espèces: tirée
   de l'*Isis*, 1830, pp. 1109–1112, q. v.

1831. YARRELL, W.   [On the Tracheæ of Cracidæ.]   < P. Z. S., i, 1831, pp. 33, 34.
   Crax yarrelli, sp. n., p. 33, descr. nullâ. See Bennett, *Gard. and Menag. Zool. Soc.,* 1835,
   p. 227, where first described, and figured.

1831. YARRELL, W.   [On the Sterno-trachæal Muscles of Ourax mitu.]   < P. Z. S.,
   i, 1831, p. 59.

1833. PORTER, R. T.   [Letter relating to Cracidæ from Caracas.]   < P. Z. S., 1833,
   p. 114.

1833. YARRELL, W.   [On the Trachea of the Penelope Guan, Temm.]   < P. Z. S., i,
   1833, p. 3.

1835. YARRELL, W.   [Ueber die Luftrohre von Penelope Guan, Temm.]   < Oken's Isis,
   1835, p. 517.
   Nicht mir selbst zugänglich.—Aus d. *P. Z. S.,* 1833, p. 3.

1836. HERON, R.   [On the breeding of Curassows (Cracidæ) in confinement at Stub-
   ton.]   < P. Z. S., iv, 1836, p. 1.

1836. HERON, R.   [On the breeding of Curassows (Cracidæ) in confinement at Stub-
   ton.]   < Lond. and Edinb. Philos. Mag., ix, 1836, p. 141.
   From *P. Z. S.,* Jan. 12, 1836, p. 1.

1838. HERON, R.   Brüten von Crax rubra im letzten Sommer.   < Oken's Isis, Bd
   xxxi, 1838, p. 168.
   Aus d. *P. Z. S.,* iv, 1836, p. 1.

1840. FREMBLY, J.   [Notice of forwarding of Penelope pileata to the Society.]   < P
   Z. S., viii, 1840, p. 131.

1842. CABOT, S., JR.   [On the Paraqua Guan or Phasianus motmot.]   < Proc. Bosto
   Soc. Nat. Hist., i, 1842, pp. 76, 77.

1846. HERON, R.   [Note on the Genus Crax.]   < P. Z. S., xiv, 1846, p. 67.

1848. [JARDINE, W.]   Ortalida ruficauda, Jardine.   < Jard. Contrib. Orn., 1848, p
   16, 17, woodc. pl. iii.
   Anatomical.

1848. [JARDINE, W.]　Penelope cristata.　< *Jard. Contrib. Orn.*, 1848, pp. 16, 17, woodc. pl. viii.
　　　Anatomical.

1850. FRASER, L.　On new Birds in the Collection at Knowsley.　< *P. Z. S.*, xviii, 1850, pp. 245, 246, pll. (Aves) xxv–xxix.
　　　Palæornis derbianus, p. 245, pl. xxv; *P. erythrogenys*, p. 245, pl. xxvi; *Crax alberti*, p. 246, pll. xxvii, xxviii; *Penelope niger*, p. 246, pl. xxix. On these *Cracidæ*, see *P. Z. S.*, 1870, p. 509.

1854. POMME, —.　Sur les Hoccos et les Marails, extrait d'une lettre addressée a M. Is. Geoffroy Saint-Hilaire.　< *Bull. Soc. Acclim.*, i, 1854, pp. 139–143.

1854. BARTHÉLEMY-LAPOMMERAYE, —.　Note sur l'acclimatation et domestication du Hocco [Crax alector].　< *Bull. Soc. Acclim.*, i, 1854, pp. 123–126.

1854. BARTHÉLEMY-LAPOMMERAYE, —.　Sur la reproduction du Hocco en France, extrait d'une lettre addressée a M. Is. Geoffroy Saint-Hilaire : Addition à la note présentée à la Société zoologique d'Acclimatation dans la séance du 10 mars 1854.　< *Bull. Soc. Acclim.*, i, 1854, pp. 406–408.

1857. MARTIN, L.　Das klimatische Abandern der grossen süd- und mittelamerikanischen Hühner-Arten [Crax, Urax, Penelope].　< *J. f. O.*, v, 1857, pp. 70–72.

1858. BARTHÉLEMY-LAPOMMERAYE, —.　Sur la reproduction du Hocco lettre addressée a M. le Président de la Société impériale zoologique d'acclimatation.　< *Bull. Soc. Acclim.*, v, 1858, pp. 483, 484.

1859. LE LONG, J.　Extrait de la lettre de M. Le Long, membre de la Société, annonçant le don de plusieurs oiseaux [Cracidæ].　< *Bull. Soc. Acclim.*, vi, 1859, p. 487.

1860. GRAY, G. R.　Synopsis of the Species of the Gènus Penelope.　< *P. Z. S.*, xxviii, 1860, pp. 269–272.
　　　14 spp.　Diagnosis, synonymy, and habitat.　*P. nigricapilla*, *P. lichtensteinii*, p. 269; *P. sclateri*, *P. bridgesi*, p. 270, spp. nn.

1860. SALVIN, O.　History of the Derbyan Mountain-Pheasant (Oreophasis derbianus).　< *Ibis*, ii, 1860, pp. 248–253.

1860. SCLATER, P. L.　[Exhibition of specimens of Oreophasis derbianus, from the Volcan de Fuego, Guatemala.]　< *P. Z. S.*, xxviii, 1860, p. 184.

1861. BARTHÉLEMY-LAPOMMERAYE, —.　Ueber die Einführung und Zähmung der Hoccos [Cracidæ].　< *Zool. Gart.*, ii, 1861, pp. 110–112.

1861. KRÜGER, A.　[Ueber Penelope sp.]　< *Zool. Gart.*, ii, 1861, p. 133.

1861. POMME, —.　Ueber die Hoccos und Jakhühner [Cracidæ].　< *Zool. Gart.*, ii, 1861, pp. 163–165.
　　　Bull. Soc. d'Acclim., i, 1854, pp. 139–143.

1862. BARTHÉLEMY-LAPOMMERAYE, —.　Notice sur l'éducation du Hocco de la Guyane (Crax globicera).　< *Bull. Soc. Acclim.*, ix, 1862, pp. 861–871.

1865. AQUARONE, P.　Note sur l'éducation des Hoccos [Cracidæ].　< *Bull. Soc. Acclim.*, 2e sér., ii, 1865, pp. 449–462, fig.

1865. AQUARONE, P.　Die Zucht der Hokkos [Cracidæ].　< *Zool. Gart.*, vi, 1865, pp. 428–430.
　　　Auszüge aus d. *Bull. Soc. d'Acclim.*, ii, 1865, pp. 449–462.

1866. AQUARONE, P.　Notice complémentaire sur l'éducation des Hoccos [Cracidæ]. Lettre addressée a M. le Directeur du Jardin d'Acclimatation du Bois de Boulogne.　< *Bull. Soc. Acclim.*, 2e sér., iii, 1866, pp. 25–28.

1866. GRAY, G. R.　On a New Species of Penelope [greeyii], lately living in the Society's Gardens.　< *P. Z. S.*, xxxiv, 1866, p. 206, pl. xxii.

1870. SCLATER, P. L., *and* SALVIN, O.　Synopsis of the Cracidæ.　< *P. Z. S.*, xxxviii, 1870, pp. 504–544.
　　　This is a very complete memoir, remaining to date the leading autnority on the subject, as may be judged from the following synopsis :
　　　§ 1. Introductory Remarks, p. 504: on the systematic position and relations of the family.

1870. SCLATER, P. L, *and* SALVIN, O.—Continued.

§ 2. Brief Chronological Account of the Writings of the Principal Authorities on the *Cracidæ*, pp. 505-512: an analysis of the literature of the subject, noting principal articles in works of wider scope, as well as special papers. Of this I give the following condensation:

1766. LINN., *Syst. Nat.*, i.   Five species: *Crax* (g. n.) *rubra, globicera*, ——, ——, and *Phasianus motmot.*

1780 (about). *Pl. Enl.* 86 = *Crax daubentoni;* 125 = *C. globicera* ♀ ; 78 = *Pauxi galeata;* 338 = *Penelope marail.*

1783. BODDAERT, *Tabl. P. E.   Phasianus katraka* sp. n. = P. E. 146 = *Ortalida motmot.*

1784. JACQUIN, *Beyt. Gesch. Vög.   Crax cumanensis*, pl. 19 ; *C. pipile*, pl. 11.

1786. MERREM, *Ic. Av.*, fasc. 2dus, p. 40.   *Crax*, L. ; *Penelope*, g. n., type *P. jacupema ; Ortalida*, g. n., type *Phas. motmot*, L. [On this name, see especially WHARTON, *Ibis*, 1879, p. 450.] *P. jacupema* and *P. leucolophos* figured.

1788. GMELIN, *Syst. Nat.   Penelope cristata, P. cumanensis, P. marail, P. satyra* (a *Ceriornis*), *P. vociferans, Phasianus parraka.*

1790. LATHAM, *Ind. Orn.   Crax galeata*, n. sp. = *C. pauxi*, L.

1811. HUMBOLDT, *Rec. Obs. Zool.*, i, p. 4.   *Phasianus garrulus* sp. n. (= *Ortalida garrula.*)

1815. TEMM., *Pig. et Gall.*, vol. ii.   *Pauxi*, g. n. ; *Crax carunculata, Penelope obscura, P. superciliaris*, spp. nn.

1823. TEMM., *Pl. Col.*, livr. 26.   *Ourax* = *Pauxi ; O. mitu* figured.

1825. SPIX, *Av. Bras.*, vol. ii.   *Crax fasciolata, urumutum, tomentosa, blumenbachii, globulosa, rubrirostris, tuberosa, Penelope jacuacu, jacucaca, jacutinga, jacupeba, jacupemba, guttata, araucuan*, described and figured.

1828. LESSON, *Man. Orn.*, vol. ii.   *Penelope aburri, Ortalida goudoti, Crax albini*, spp. nn.

1830. WAGLER, Revisio generis *Penelope*. [See the paper in this Bibliography, anteà, 1830.]

1831. LESSON, *Tr. Orn.   Mitu*, g. n., p. 485.

1832. WAGLER, *Isis.   Salpiza, Chamaepetes*, genn. nn.

1833. MAXIMILIAN, *Beit. Naturg. Bras.   Crax rubrirostris, Penelope superciliaris, P. leucoptera, P. araucuan.*

1835. BENNETT, *Gard. and Menag. Zool. Soc.*   Descr. and figs. of 6 spp.; *Crax yarrelli*, orig. descr., but see *P. Z. S.*, 1831, p. 33.

1841. STRICKL., *Ann. Nat. Hist.*, vii.   *Mitu*, Less., changed to *Mitua*, p. 36.

1844. GRAY, *Gen. of B.*, iii. 34 + 3 spp. of *Cracidæ.   Oreophasis derbyanus*, g. sp. n., p. 485, pl. 121.

1844-46. TSCHUDI, *Fn. Peru.   Crax temminckii, Penelope aspersa, P. rufiventris*, spp. nn.

1846. GRAY, J. E., *Knowsley Menag.*   Four col'd pll. of *Penelope superciliaris, P. pileata, P. pipile, P. purpurascens.*

1847. JARDINE, *Ann. Nat. Hist.   Ortalida ruficauda*, sp. n.

1850. FRASER, *P. Z. S.   Crax alberti, Penelope nigra*, spp. nn.

1852. REICHENBACH. *Av. Syst. Nat.   Penelops, Aburria*, genn. nn.

1856. BONAPARTE, *Compt. Rend.*, Tableaux Gallinacés.   *Pipile* (g. n.) *argyrotes, Ortalida montaguii*, spp. nn.

1856. BURMEISTER, *Syst. Uebers. Th. Bras.*, vol. iii.   On *P. nothicrax*, g. n., p. 347.

1858. PELZELN. *Penelope cujubi*, Natt. MS.

1858. BAIRD, *Birds N. Amer.   Ortalida maccallii*, sp. n.

186-. REICHENBACH, *Vollst. Naturg. Tauben.*   Four new spp. of *Crax*, one n. sp. of *Penelope Crax* divided into *Crax, Mituporanga* (g. n.), *Crossolaryngus* (g. n.), and *Sphæro laryngus ; Penelopsis* = *Penelops*, Reich., *Av. Syst. Nat.; Penelopina*, g. n.

1866. GRAY, *P. Z. S.   Penelope greeyii*, sp. n.

1867. GRAY, *Gallinæ Br. Mus.   Penelope jacquini, Ortalida superciliaris, O. bronzina, O plumbeiceps, O. wagleri, O. cinereiceps, Crax sclateri, C. daubentoni*, spp. nn.

1867. SALVIN, *P. Z. S.   Chamaepetes unicolor*, sp. n.

1869. CABANIS, *J. f. O.   Ortalida frantzii*, sp. n.

§ 3. Synopsis of the species of *Cracidæ*, pp. 512-541.   The 52 spp. known to the authors are divided into 3 subfamilies: 1) *Cracinæ*, with 4 genera (*Crax, Nothocrax, Pauxi, Mitua*); 2) *Penelopinæ*, with 7 genera (*Stegnolæma* (g. n., p. 521), *Penelope, Penelopina. Pipile, Aburria Chamæpetes, Ortalida* (*O. ruficrissa*, sp. n., p. 538)); 3) *Oreophasinæ*, 1 g. sp.—The species are elaborately worked up, with copious synonymy, diagnosis, distribution, and criticism.

§ 4. Geographical Distribution of the *Cracidæ*, pp. 541-544.

1871. BURMEISTER, [H.] [Extracts from a letter on Messrs. Sclater and Salvin's Synopsis of the Cracidæ (P. Z. S., 1870, p. 504).]   < *P. Z. S.*, xxxix, 1871, pp. 701, 702

Relating chiefly to the geographical distribution of certain species.

1871. SCLATER, P. L. [On additions to the Society's Menagerie.]   < *P. Z. S.*, xxxix, 1871, pp. 36, 37.

Pipile cumanensis.

1872. ANON. Les Marails. < *Bull. Soc. Acclim.*, 2ᵉ sér., ix, 1872, p. 692.

1873. SCLATER, P. L. [Notice of a paper on the Curassows (Cracidæ).] < *P. Z. S.*, xli, 1873, p. 557.

1874. SUMMERHAYES, W. [Letter on Curassows (Cracidæ) met with in Venezuela.] < *P. Z. S.*, xlii, 1874, pp. 419, 420.

1875. FUNCK, N. [Letter stating Pauxis galeata var. rubra, of Tr. Zool. Soc., ix, pl. 53, to be true P. galeata ♀.] < *P. Z. S.*, Nov. 16, 1875, p. 566.

1877. GADOW, H. Anatomische Beschreibung der Hoccohühner (Cracidæ Vig.). < *J. f. O.*, Apr., 1877, pp. 181–190.

1877. ROWLEY, G. D. [Note on the egg of Pauxis galeata.] < *P. Z. S.*, Nov. 6, 1877, p. 684.

1878. SCLATER, [P. L.] [Notice of supplementary Memoir on the Cracidæ.] <*P. Z. S.*, June 18, 1878, p. 656.
     To be pub. in *Trans. Zool. Soc.*

1879. REINHARDT, J. [Letter relating to Mitua salvini, Reinhardt, Vid. Medd. Nat. For. i Kjöbenh., Jan. 8, 1879.] < *P. Z. S.*, Feb. 4, 1879, pp. 108, 109.
     Remarks by Mr. Sclater agreeing to the validity of the curious species, and placing it next to *M. tomentosa*, with the differential characters.

Meleagrididæ.

1699. FLOYER, J. A Relation of two Monstrous Pigs, with the resemblance of Humane Faces, and two young Turkeys [Meleagris gallopavo] joined by the Breast. < *Philos. Trans.*, xxi, 1699, pp. 431–435.

1781. PENNANT, T. An Account of the Turkey [Meleagris gallopavo]. < *Philos. Trans.*, lxxi, pt. i, 1781, pp. 67–81, pl. iii.

Very complete. The pl. represents a malformation of the leg.

1789. ÖDMANN, S. Om en Kalkontupp [Meleagris gallopavo], som utlegat Hönsägg. < *Kongl. Vetensk.-Acad. Nya Handl.*, x, 1789, pp. 236–238.

Anmärkning därvid af G. v. Carlson, *ibid.*, p. 239.

1789. CARLSON, G. V. Anmärkning [om en Kalkontupp (Meleagris gallopavo), som utlegat Hönsägg]. < *Kongl. Vetensk.-Acad. Nya Handl.*, x, 1879, p: 239.

1791. BARTRAM, W. [The Wild Turkey of the United States binomially named Meleagris occidentalis at p. 83, M. americanus at p. 290 bis.] < *Trav. in Fla.*, etc., orig. ed., 1791, pp. 83 and 290 *bis.*

Though not properly citable as a separate article, I introduce this title to give the reference to the original names and descriptions of the bird—the name *M. gallopavo* L. being based upon the domestic race, subsequently renamed *M. mexicana* by Gould.

1799. ÖDMANN, [S.] Remarkable Instance of a Turkey Cock [Meleagris gallopavo] hatching Eggs. < *Tilloch's Philos. Mag.*, iii, 1799, pp: 309, 310.

Af *Kongl. Vetensk.-Acad. Nya Handl.*, x, 1789, pp. 236–238.

1805. [BARTON, B. S.] [On the occurrence of two distinct species of Meleagris in North America.] < *Barton's Med. and Phys. Journ.*, part i, vol. ii, 1805, pp. 162, 163.

Referring to a memoir read before the Amer. Philos. Soc., in which the author shows that there are two distinct species of *Meleagris*—one, the common domesticated Turkey, *M. gallopavo* of Linnæus, "which was altogether unknown in the countries of the old world before the discovery of America"; the other, "the common wild Turkey of the United States," to which the author of the memoir gives the name of *Meleagris palawa*, sp. n. After Bartram's notice of 1791, Barton's is the earliest to decide upon the existence of two species.

1805. [BARTON, B. S.] [On the food of the common wild Turkey of the United States, Meleagris palawa.] < *Barton's Med. and Phys. Journ.*, part i, vol. ii, 1805, pp. 163, 164.

1815. CLINTON, DE WITT. An Introductory Discourse delivered on the 4th of May, 1814. < *Trans. Lit. and Philos. Soc. New York*, i, 1815, pp. 21–184. > Note S, pp. 125–128.

Note S, appended to the discourse, treats of the origin of the domestic Turkey, *Meleagris gallopavo.*

1820. CUVIER, G. Description d'une nouvelle espèce de dindon de la baie de Honduras. (Meleagris ocellata. Cuv.) < *Mém. du Mus. d'Hist. Nat.*, vi, 1820, pp. 1–4, pl. i.

La notice de cette espèce se trouve reprodulte dans les *Ann. Génér. Sc. Phys.*, vii, 1820, pp. 145, 146; Brugnatelli, *Giorn. di Fis.*, iv, Dec. 2, 1821, p. 164.

1826. BONAPARTE, C. L. Ueber den wilden Truthahn [Meleagris americana]. < *Froriep's Notizen*, xiii, No. 275, 1826, pp. 165–170.

Nicht mir selbst zugänglich: Titel aus Carus and Engelmann.—Wahrscheinlich einer Auszug aus dessen *Amer. Ornith.*

1832. ANON. Turkeys [Meleagris gallopavo] eat Caterpillars which feed on Tobacco; and Hogs eat the poisonous Root of Cassava (Janipha manihot). < *Loudon's Mag. Nat. Hist.*, v, 1832, pp. 472, 473.

1836. HILDRETH, S. P. [Wild Turkeys (Meleagris americana) in the Kanawha Valley, Virginia.] < *Sillim. Am. Journ. Sci.*, xxix, 1836, p. 85.

1837. OWEN, RICHARD. [Dissection of the head of the Common Turkey (Meleagris gallopavo).] $<$ *P. Z. S.*, v, 1837, pp. 34, 35.
With that of *Cathartes aura.*

1839. OWEN, RICHARD. [Geruchsnerven des Truthuhns (Meleagris gallopavo).] $<$ *Oken's Isis*, Bd. xxxii, 1839, p. 144.
Auszug aus d. *P. Z. S.*, v, 1837, pp. 34, 35.

1842. CABOT, S., JR. [On Meleagris ocellata.] $<$ *Proc. Bost. Soc. Nat. Hist.*, i, 1842, pp. 73, 74.

1842. CABOT, S., JR. [Remarks on Meleagris gallopavo, etc.] $<$ *Proc. Bost. Soc. Nat. Hist.*, i, 1842, pp. 80, 81.

1842. CABOT, S., JR. Observations on the characters and habits of the Ocellated Turkey, (Meleagris ocellata, Cuv.) $<$ *Journ. Bost. Soc. Nat. Hist.*, iv, pt. ii, 1842, pp. 246–251.

1844. GÉRARD, —. Notice sur les Dindons [Meleagris gallopavo]. Paris. 1844. 8vo. pp. 12.
Pas vue moi-même: le titre tiré de Carus et Engelmann.

1848. FISHER, W. R. On the supposed Occurrence of Turkeys' [Meleagris gallopavo] Bones at Lough Gûr. $<$ *Zoologist*, vi, 1848, pp. 2064, 2065.

1849. CHEVASSU, F. Nouvel art d'élever, de multiplier et d'engraisser les Dindons [Meleagris gallopavo], contenant . . . Paris. Tissot. 1849. 18mo. pp. 36.
Pas vu moi-même: le titre tiré de Carus & Engelmann.

1856. GOULD, J. On a new Turkey, Meleagris mexicana. $<$ *P. Z. S.*, xxiv, 1856, pp. 61–63.
Subsequently determined to be the stock whence the domestic bird descended, and hence a synonym of *M. gallopavo* Linn.

1856. GOULD, J. A new species of Turkey [Meleagris mexicana] from Mexico. $<$*Am. Journ. Sci.*, xxii, 1856, p. 139.
From *P. Z. S.*, 1856, pp. 61–63.

1856. [GOULD, J.] A new Species of Turkey [Meleagris mexicana] from Mexico. $<$ *Edinb. New. Philos. Journ.*, n. s., iv, 1856, pp. 371, 372.
From *Am. Journ. Sci.*, xxii, July, 1856, p. 139; this from *P. Z. S.*, 1856, pp. 61–63.

1857. BRYANT, H. [On the supposed new species of Turkey (Meleagris mexicana) recently described by Mr. Gould.] $<$ *Proc. Bost. Soc. Nat. Hist.*, vi, 1857, pp. 158, 159.

1857. [FROST, J.] Der Indianer und der wilde Truthahn [Meleagris americana]. $<$ *Interessante Abenteuer unter den Indianern*, u. s. w., Phila., 1857, pp. 251–254.
Zur Lebensweise.

1857. GOULD, J. On a new Turkey, Meleagris mexicana. $<$ *Ann. Mag. Nat. Hist.*, 2d ser., xix, 1857, pp. 107–110.
From *P. Z. S.*, Apr. 8, 1856, pp. 61–63.

1857. LE CONTE, J. Observations on the Wild Turkey, or Gallapavo sylvestris, of Ray. $<$ *Proc. Acad. Nat. Sci. Phila.*, ix, 1857, pp. 179–181.
Distinction between wild and tame Turkeys in habits and physical characters.

1860. SCHMIDT, MAX. Nachrichten aus dem Zoologischen Garten [über Meleagris gallopavo]. $<$ *Zool. Gart.*, i, 1860, pp. 87, 88.

1861. SCLATER, P. L. Note on the Ocellated Turkey [Meleagris ocellata] of Honduras. $<$ *P. Z. S.*, xxix, 1861, pp. 402, 403, pl. xl.

1863. OEFELE, —, V. Zweckmässige Fütterung und Haltung von Truthühnern [Meleagris gallopavo]. $<$*Zool. Gart.*, iv, 1863, pp. 169–172.

1863. SACC, *Dr.* Sur le Dindon (Meleagris gallopavo). $<$ *Bull. Soc. Acclim.*, x, 1863, pp. 663– —.

1867. BAIRD, S. F.   The Origin of the Domestic Turkey [Meleagris gallopavo].   < *Report U. S. Agric. Dept. for* 1866, 1867, pp. 288–290.

> Held to be descended from the stock named *M. mexicana*, by Gould, in 1856; the proposition being that there are two species in the United States.

1868. HOYNINGEN-HUENE, A.   Notiz über Meleagris gallopavo.   < *J. f. O.*, xvi, 1868, p. 358.

> Lebensweise.

1869. D[ELONDRE], A. A.   Le Dindon huppé (Crested Turkey).   < *Bull. Soc. Acclim.*, 2e sér., vi, 1869, pp. 727, 728.

> Extrait de *The Field*, le 17 juillet 1869, p. 46.

1869. GUNN, T. E.   Vitality of a Turkey [Meleagris gallopavo].   < *Zoologist*, 2d ser., iv, 1869, p. 1722.

1870. ROGER, E.   Reproduction des Dindons Sauvages d'Amérique en liberté.   Lettre adressée a M. Geoffroy Saint-Hilaire.   < *Bull. Soc. Acclim.*, 2e sér., vii, 1870, pp. 264–266.

18—-72. ELLIOT, D. G.   A | Monograph | of the | Phasianidæ | or | Family of the Pheasants. | By | Daniel Giraud Elliot, | [etc., 7 lines.] | — | Volume I [II]. | — | [18—-] 1872: | published by the author, 27 West Thirty-third Street, New York. | [Taylor and Francis, Red Lion Court, London, imp. text. H. and N. Hanhart, imp. plates. J. Wolf, del. J. Smit, lith. J. D. White, pinx.] Vol. I, 18—, Title, 1 leaf. Dedication, 1 leaf. List subscribers, preface, introduction, explanation, list of plates, pp. i-xl. Plates i-xxix, xxix bis, xxx-xxxii, with one or more unpaged sheets of letter-press to each. Vol. II, 18—, Title, 1 leaf. List of plates, 1 leaf. Plates i-xiii, xiii bis, xiv-xlvii, with one or more unpaged sheets of letter-press to each. (A few additional sheets of subfamily characters in both vols.) Plates i, ii, plain: the rest colored. 81 plates in all.

> The work is not paged nor are the plates numbered: the only clue to the plates is the printed list. This may be conceded to be the most superb, as it is also the most extensive, of Mr. Elliot's great Iconographies. Among the birds represented are some of the most gorgeous objects in ornithology. The plates of *Pavo muticus* and *Meleagris ocellata* are incomparable except with some of the other splendid effects of Wolf's art.

> The Introduction goes quite fully into the history of the family, their geographical distribution, etc.

> Vol. I.—Plates 1, 2. Generic details. 3. *Pavo cristatus.* 4. *P. nigripennis.* 5. *P. muticus.* 6. *Polyplectron thibetanum.* 7. *P. bicalcaratum.* 8. *P. germaini.* 9. *P. emphanum.* 10. *P. chalcurum.* 11. *Argus giganteus.* 12. *A. grayi.* 13. Feathers of *A. ocellatus* and *A. bipunctatus.* 14. *Crossoptilon thibetanum.* 15. *C. drouyni.* 16. *C. mantchuricum.* 17. *C. auritum.* 18. *Lophophorus impeyanus.* 19. *L. lhuysi.* 20. *L. sclateri.* 21. *Tetraophasis obscurus.* 22. *Ceriornis satyra.* 23. *C. melanocephala.* 24. *C. temmincki.* 25. *C. caboti.* 26. *C. blythi.* 27. *Pucrasia macrolopha.* 28. *P. duvaucelii.* 29. *P. xanthospila.* 29 bis. *C. darwini.* 30. *Meleagris gallopavo.* 31. *M. mexicana.* 32. *M. ocellata.*

> Vol. II.—Pl. 1. *Phasianus shawi.* 2. *P. colchicus.* 3. *P. insignis.* 4. *P. mongolicus.* 5. *P. torquatus.* 6. *P. formosanus.* 7. *P. decollatus.* 8. *P. elegans.* 9. *P. versicolor.* 10. *P. wallichii.* 11. *P. reevesi.* 12. *P. soemmeringi.* 13. *P. soemmeringi* var. *scintillans.* 13 bis. *Calophasis ellioti.* 14. *Thaumalea amherstiæ.* 15. *T. picta.* 16. *T. obscura.* 17. Hybrid. 18. *Euplocamus albocristatus.* 19. *E. melanotus.* 20. *E. horsfieldi.* 21. *E. nycthemerus.* 22. *E. andersoni.* 23. *E. lineatus.* 24. *E. prælatus.* 25. *E. swinhoei.* 26. *E. ignitus.* 27. *E. nobilis.* 28. *E. erythrophthalmus.* 29. *E. pyronotus.* 30. *Ithaginis cruentus.* 31. *I. geoffroyi.* 32. *Gallus ferrugineus.* 33. *G. lafayetti.* 34. *G. sonnerati.* 35. *G. varius.* 36. *Phasidus niger.* 37. *Agelastes meleagrides.* 38. *Acryllium vulturinum.* 39. *Numida meleagris.* 40. *N. coronata.* 41. *N. mitrata.* 42. *N. ptilorhyncha.* 43. *N. granti.* 44. *N. verreauxi.* 45. *N. cristata.* 46. *N. pucherani.* 47. *N. plumifera.*

> It thus appears that the *Phasianidæ* of this author include the African family *Numididæ*, and the American *Meleagrididæ*.

1872. ANON.   The Wild Turkey [Meleagris americana].   < *Am. Sportsman*, ii, 1872, p. 10.

1873. ANON.   [EDITORIAL.]   The Wild Turkey [Meleagris americana].   < *Forest and Stream*, i, Oct. 9, 1873, p. 137.

1873. CATON, J. D.   The Senses of Sight and Hearing in the wild Turkey [Meleagris americana] and the common Deer.   < *Am. Nat.*, vii, 1873, p. 431.

1873. "OBSERVER."   Wild Turkeys [Meleagris americana, in Northern Maryland]. < *Forest and Stream*, i, Dec. 18, 1873, p. 290.

1875. ANON.   [Der Truthahn (Meleagris gallopavo) als jagdbares Wild.]   < *Aus der Natur*, lxvi, oder n. F., liv, 1875, p. 267.

1875. "BOB WHITE."   Wild Turkey (Meleagris gallopavo [americana]).   < *Am. Sportsman*, v, Jan. 30, 1874-75, p. 279.

1875. HUBBARD, J. H.   Wild Turkeys [Meleagris americana] Playing Out.   < *Rod and Gun*, vi, Apr. 24, 1874, p. 58.
   Statistics of destruction of these birds in Michigan.

1875. JACKSON, J. B. S.   [Exhibition of a curiously malformed Sternum of Meleagris gallopavo, presenting a cavity through which the intestine passed.]   < *Proc. Bost. Soc. Nat. Hist.*, xviii, 1875, p. 454.

1875. "KEYSTONE, F. F. V."   Wild turkey [Meleagris americana] trapping and hunting.   < *Forest and Stream*, iv, Mar. 11, 1875, p. 67.

1876. [STOCKWELL, G. A.]   Game of Michigan.   Wild Turkey.—Meleagris gallipavo [i. e., americana], Meleagris mexicana.   < *Rod and Gun*, ix, Nov. 4, 1876, p. 65.
   Writing under the pseudonym "ARCHER," this person ran a long course of literary imposture, chiefly on the game birds of America, in the columns of the *Chicago Field*, the *London Field*, and doubtless elsewhere, until his gross plagiaries were at length exposed.   None of his writings that have come under my observation have the slightest claim to be regarded. (See COUES, *Chicago Field*, Nov. 29, 1879, and "ARCHER," *ibid.*, Dec. 20, 1879.

1877. ANON.   Hon. J. D. Caton's Domesticated Wild Turkeys (Meleagris gallopavo americana).   < *Forest and Stream*, ix, Oct. 18, 1877, p. 207.

1877. ANON. [EDITORIAL.]   Domesticated Wild Turkeys [Meleagris americana]. < *Forest and Stream*, ix, Dec. 13, 1877, p. 366.

1877. "BOB WHITE."   Wild Turkeys [habits of Meleagris americana].   < *Forest and Stream*, ix, Aug. 30, 1877, p. 64.

1877. CATON, J. D.   The Wild Turkey [Meleagris americana] and its Domestication. < *Am. Nat.*, xi, No. 6, 1877, pp. 321-330.

1878. "W. H. R."   Birds towering [e. g., Wild Turkeys, Meleagris americana]. < *Forest and Stream*, x, May 2, 1878, p. 235.

1879. COUES, E.   The Origin of the Turkey [Meleagris gallopavo].   < *Forest and Stream*, xiii, Jan. 1, 1879, p. 947.
   Chiefly on the early history of the Domestic Turkey in Europe, the origin of which species is held to be the Mexican bird.   The article includes copious extracts from Bennett's *Gard. and Menag. Zool. Soc. London.*

Tetraonidæ.

1729. ROBERG, L. Diss. phys. de Lagopode gallinacea et congeneribus. Præs. L. Roberg, Resp. M. Lithenius, W. Gothus. Upsaliæ. 1729. 4to. pp. 26.
Not seen.

1755. EDWARDS, G. A Letter to Mr. Peter Colluson, F. R. S. concerning the Pheasant of Pensylvania, and the Otis Minor. < *Philos. Trans. for* 1754, xlviii, pt. ii, 1755, pp. 499–503, pll. xv, xvi.
A fair account and figure of the Ruffed Grouse, subsequently the *Tetrao umbellus* or *Bonasa umbellus* of authors.

1774. BARRINGTON, D. Observations on the Lagopus or Ptarmigan. < *Philos. Trans. for* 1773, lxiii, 1774, pp. 224–230.
General structure and relationships, and habits.

1776. MONTIN, L. Tvänne arter af Snöripan [Lagopus]. < *Physiogn. Sällsk. Handl.*, i, 1776, pp. 150–155.
Not seen.

1782. LAPEYROUSE, P. DE. Histoire naturelle du Lagopède (Tetrao Lagopus). < *Hist. et Mém. de l'Acad. de Toulouse*, i, 1782, pp. 111–127.
Pas vue moi-même—le titre tiré de Carus et Engelmann.

1784? LAPEYROUSE, P. DE. Histoire Naturelle du Lagopède. Toulouse. 1784? 4to. pp. 17.
Pas vue moi-même.—Voir 1782, même auteur.

1825. EDITORIAL. Winter Change of Colour of the Ptarmigan [Lagopus]. < *Edinb. Philos. Journ.*, xiii, 1825, p. 390.
Note on Faber's and Boie's opinions.

1827. BONAPARTE, C. L. Notice of a nondescript Species of Grouse [Tetrao urophasianus], from North America. < *Zoological Journ.*, iii, 1827, pp. 212, 213.

1828. ANON. Notice sur une espèce non décrite de Coq de bruyère, habitant l'Amérique du Nord; par M. Charl. Luc. Bonaparte. . . . < *Féruss. Bull.*, 2e sect., xiv, 1828, p. 117.
Extraite du *Zool. Journ.*, iii, 1827, pp. 212, 213.

1828. NILSSON, S. Ripors ömsning af Klor. < *Vetensk.-Akad. Årsb. i Zool.*, 1828, pp. 104–106.
On *Lagopus*: not seen by me.

1828. NILSSON, S. Ripors fjäderömsning. < *Vetensk.-Akad. Årsb. i Zool.*, 1828, pp. 106, 107.
On *Lagopus*: not seen by me.

1828. SCOULER, J. Account of the Tænia found in the Intestines of the Common Grouse (Tetrao [Lagopus] scoticus). < *Edinb. New Philos. Journ.*, vi, 1828, pp. 81–83.

1829. DOUGLAS, D. Observations on some Species of the Genera Tetrao and Ortyx, natives of North America; with Descriptions of Four new Species of the former, and Two of the latter Genus. < *Trans. Linn. Soc.*, xvi, pt. iii, 1829, pp. 133–149. ("Read" Dec. 16, 1828; pub. in 1829, though whole vol. dates 1833.)
This paper is wrongly given in most bibliographies as dating 1833—obviously so, for it is reprinted in 1829, and reviewed in *Oken's Isis* and in *Férussac's Bull.* in 1830.
Tetrao urophasianus Bp., *Zool. Journ.*, iii, 1827, p. 212, fully described, p. 133. *T. urophasianellus*, p. 136; *T. sabini*, p. 137; *T. franklinii*, p. 139; *T. richardsonii*, Sab. MS., p. 141. *Ortyx picta*, p. 143; *O. douglassii*, Vig. MS., p. 145. There are given full accounts of the habits of some of these species; with field-notes on various other N. A. *Tetraonidæ*.
Abstracts in *Philos. Mag.*, v, 1829, pp. 73, 74; *Edinb. New Philos. Journ.*, 1830, pp. 372–376; *Féruss. Bull.*, xx, 1830, pp. 326–331; *Oken's Isis*, xxxiii, 1830, pp. 917–920.

1829. DOUGLAS, D.   Observations on some species of the Genera Tetrao and Ortyx, natives of North America, with descriptions of four [lately] new species of the former, and two of the latter genus.   *< Philos. Mag.*, v, 1829, pp. 73, 74.

From *Trans. Linn. Soc.*, xvi, pt. iii, 1829, pp. 133-149, *q. v.*

1830. BONAPARTE, C. L.   Ueber einen neuen Tetrao [urophasianus] aus Nordamerica.   *< Oken's Isis*, Bd. xxiii, 1830, p. 1160.

Aus d. *Zool. Journ.*, iii, 1827, pp. 212, 213.

1830. BONAPARTE, C. L.   General Observations on the Birds of the Genus Tetrao; with a Synopsis of the species hitherto known.   *< Trans. Amer. Philos. Soc.*, 2d ser., iii, 1830, pp. 383-394.

3 genn. *Bonasia*, 2 spp.; *Tetrao*, 8 spp.; *Lagopus*, 3 spp.

1830. DOUGLAS, D.   Ueber einige nordamericanische Gattungen von Tetrao u. Ortyx.   *< Oken's Isis*, Bd. xxiii, 1830, pp. 917-920.

Uebersetzt aus d. *Linn. Trans.*, xvi, pt. iii, 1829, pp. 133-149, *q. v.*

1830. [DOUGLAS, D.]   Observations sur quelques espèces des genres Tetrao et Ortyx, de l'Amérique septentrionale.   *< Féruss. Bull.*, 2e sect., xx, 1830, pp. 326-331.

Précis, par Lesson, de l'article inseré dans les *Trans. Linn. Soc.*, xvi, pte. iii, 1829, pp. 133-149, *q. v.* Les descriptions des espèces nouvelles se trouvent reproduites ici.

1830. [DOUGLAS, D.]   Account of several New Species of Grouse (Tetrao) from North America.   *< Edinb. New Philos. Journ.*, viii, 1830, pp. 372-376.

Anonymous article. See DOUGLAS, D., 1829 and 1830.

1833. ANON.   Rip-Jagt. [Lagopus.]   *< Tidsk. f. Jägare och Naturf.*, Årg. ii, 1833, pp. 641-657, fig.

Not seen.

1834. GRÖNLAND, C.   Några ord om Fjell-Ripan [Lagopus].   *< Tidsk. f. Jäg. och Naturf.*, Årg. iii, 1834, pp. 850, 851.

Not seen—title from Carus and Engelmann.

1836. ARAGO, —.   Observations sur la température des animaux par de très grands froids.   *< Ann. des Sci. Nat.*, 2e sér., v, 1836, pp. 375, 376.

Gelinotte noir d'Amérique, Lagopède des Saules.

1836. AUDUBON, J. J.   Naturgeschichte des Cupido-Huhns (The Pinnated Grous, Tetrao Cupido.   L.)   *< Arch. f. Naturg.*, ii, 1836, (1), pp. 164-175.

Aus dessen *Ornith. Biog.*, ii, p. 490, *seq.*

1836. KOCH, T.   Beobachtungen über das Cupido-Huhn Tetrao Cupido L. (Prairie-Henn, Ruster.)   *< Arch. f. Naturg.*, ii, 1836, (1), pp. 159-163.

Ich weiss nicht was es heissen soll, dass der Verf. „Henn, Ruster" sagt. Soll es veilleicht „ Hen, Rooster."

1837. SKAIFE, J.   Domestication of Grouse [Lagopus britannicus].   *< Charlesw. Mag. Nat. Hist.*, i, 1837, p. 608.

1839. CHARLTON, E.   On Tetrao Rakelhahn.   *< Rep. Brit. Assoc. Adv. Sci. for 1838*, vii, 1839 (*Misc. Comm.*), p. 107.

Considered as a hybrid between *T. urogallus* and *T. tetrix.*

1839. CHARLTON, [E.]   [Tetrao Rakkelhan Temm. n'est qu'un hybride entre le Lagopède Ptarmigan ♀ et le Coq de bruyère.]   *< Revue Zoologique*, ii, 1839, p. 154.

1846. CABOT, S., JR.   [Measurements of some of the internal organs of Tetrao cupido.]   *< Proc. Boston Soc. Nat. Hist.*, ii, 1846, p. 120.

1848. BLADON, J.   Extremely large Red Grouse (Lagopus Scoticus).   *< Zoologist*, vi, 1848, p. 2023.

1848. WEBSTER, T.   Another extremely large Red Grouse (Lagopus Scoticus).   *< Zoologist*, vi, 1848, p. 2066.

1850. JONES, J. M.   Food of the Red Grouse (Tetrao [Lagopus] Scoticus).   *< Zoologist*, viii, 1850, p. 2652.

1854. CAIRE, *L'Abbe.*   [Note relative aux changements du plumage du Tetrao lagopus.]   *< Rev. et Mag. de Zool.*, vi, 1854, pp. 694-697.

1854. GLOGER, C. W. L.   Wie rasch hühnerartige [e. g., Bonasa umbellus] Vögel
sich im Schnee verbergen konnen.   < *J. f. O.*, ii, 1854, pp. 382, 383.
Nach *Audubon's Ornith. Biogr.*

1855. CABOT, S., JR.   [On the distribution of Tetrao (Cupidonia) cupido and other species of Grouse in New England.]   < *Proc. Bost. Soc. Nat. Hist.*, v, 1855, p. 154.

1856. GLOGER, C. W. L.   Wie oft mag das Alpen-Schneehuhn (Lagopus alpinus Nils.)
mausern.   < *J. f. O.*, iv, 1856, pp. 461–464.

1857. B[ILLINGS], E.   Notes on the Natural History of the Mountain of Montreal.
< *Canad. Nat. and Geol.*, ii, 1857, pp. 92–101.
Only ornithological in giving an account of habits of *Bonasa umbellus.*

1858. ATKINSON, J. C.   Contributions towards a Biography of the Red Grouse [Lago-
pus scoticus].   < *Zoologist*, xvi, 1858, pp. 6257–6264.

1858. BOND, F.   The Red and Willow Grouse [Lagopus spp.].   <*Zoologist*, xvi, 1858,
pp. 6264, 6265.

1858. GOULD, J.   On a New Species of Ptarmigan [Lagopus hemileucurus].   <*P. Z. S.*,
xxvi, 1858, pp. 354, 355.

1858. NEWMAN, E.   The Red and Willow Grouse [Lagopus spp.].   < *Zoologist*, xvi,
1858, p. 6264.

1858. NORMAN, G.   Is the Red Grouse [Lagopus scoticus] of Britain really distinct
from the Norwegian Willow Grouse?   < *Zoologist*, xvi, 1858, pp. 6209, 6210.

1858. NORMAN, G.   The Red Grouse and the Willow Grouse [considered identical].
< *Zoologist*, xvi, 1858, pp. 6242, 6243.
With note by E. Newman.

1858. NORMAN, G.   Red and Willow Grouse [Lagopus spp.].   < *Zoologist*, xvi, 1858,
p. 6266.

1858. SMITH, A. C.   The Red and Willow Grouse [Lagopus spp.].   < *Zoologist*, xvi,
1858, p. 6265.

1859. GOULD, J.   On a [lately] New Species of Ptarmigan [Lagopus hemileucurus].
< *Ann. Mag. Nat. Hist.*, 3d ser., iii, 1859, pp. 75–77.
From *P. Z. S.*, July 13, 1858, pp. 354, 355.

1861. SUCKLEY, G.   Description of a new species of North American Grouse [Pedio-
cætes kennicottii].   < *Proc. Acad. Nat. Sci. Phila.*, xiii, 1861, pp. 361–363.
This is the boreal form of the genus, later identified by Elliot with the original *Tetrao
phasianellus,* L.

1862. ELLIOT, D. G.   Remarks on the Species composing the Genus Pediocaetes,
Baird.   < *Proc. Acad. Nat. Sci. Phila.*, xiv, 1862, pp. 402–404.
Distinguishing the northern form, under name of *P. phasianellus* ex Linn., from the south-
ern, to which the name *P. columbianus* ex Ord is applied.

1862. WOOD, T. W.   [Remarks on the peculiarities of the Habits of the Pinnated
Grouse (Tetrao [Cupidonia] cupido).]   < *P. Z. S.*, xxx, 1862, p. 153.

1864. COOPER, J.   The Red Grouse and Willow Grouse [Lagopus spp.].   < *Zoologist*,
xxii, 1864, pp. 9045, 9046.

1864. ELLIOT, D. G.   Prospectus of a Monograph of the Tetraoninæ, or Family of the
Grouse.   < *Am. Journ. Sci.*, xxxvii, 1864, pp. 437, 438.

1864. ELLIOT, D. G.   Remarks upon a proposed Arrangement of the Family of Grouse
and New Genera added.   < *Proc. Acad. Nat. Sci. Phila.*, xvi, 1864, p. 23.
Recognizing 9 genera of *Tetraoninæ,* of which *Dendragapus* and *Falcipennis* are named
as new; *Falcipennis hartlaubii,* sp. renom.

1864. NORMAN, G.   The Willow Grouse and Red Grouse [Lagopus spp.].   <*Zoologist*,
xxii, 1864, pp. 9044, 9045.

1864. REEKS, H.   The Willow Grouse and the Red Grouse [Lagopus spp.].   <*Zoologist*, xxii, 1864, pp. 8955–8957.

1864. SMITH, A. C. The Red Grouse and Willow Grouse [Lagopus spp.]. < *Zoologist*, xxii, 1864, pp. 9113, 9114.

1864–65. ELLIOT, D. G. A | Monograph of the Tetraoninae, | or | Family of the Grouse. | By | Daniel Giraud Elliot, | [etc., 4 lines.] | New York: | published by the Author, No. 27 West Thirty-third Street. [1864] 1865. | 1 vol. imp. folio. Title, dedication, list of subscribers, preface, each 1 leaf; introduction, 4 leaves; explanations, list of plates, each 1 leaf; 27 unnumbered colored plates, each with 1 sheet of letter-press, unpaged. Pub. in 5 parts.

> The second of the author's well-known series of magnificent monographs, succeeding that of the *Pittidæ.* The work is modelled after the plan of Mr. Gould's various folio publications. It originally appeared in 5 parts—parts i, ii, 1864; iii–v, 1865. Twenty-three species are treated, under 10 genera. The apparently new names proposed were previously established by the author in the *Proc. Phila. Acad.*, 1864, p. 23. Pl. 1, *Bonasa umbellus;* 2, *B. umbelloides;* 3, *B. sabinei;* 4, *B. sylvestris;* 5, *Tetrao urogallus;* 6, *T. urogalloides;* 7, *Dendragapus obscurus;* 8, *D. richardsonii;* 9, *Canace canadensis;* 10, *C. franklinii;* 11, *Falcipennis hartlaubi;* 12, *Lyrurus tetrix;* 13, *Centrocercus urophasianus;* 14, *Pediœcætes* (sic—lege *Pediœcetes*) *columbianus;* 15, *P. phasianellus;* 16, *Cupidonia cupido;* 17, 18, *Lagopus albus;* 19, *L. scoticus;* 20, *L. persicus;* 21, 22, *L. mutus;* 23, *L. rupestris;* 24, *L. hyperboreus;* 25, *L. leucurus;* 26, 27 (marked i, ii), eggs of 17 species. The plates of Part I were Nos. 13, 7, 14, 10, 2, 25; of Pt. II, 3, 9, 12, 15, 4, 19; Pt. III, 16, 5, 8, 20, 17, 18; Parts IV and V, published together, contained the rest. The above numeration of the plates is according to a sheet of letter-press introduced with the completion of the work, in 1865; the sequence indicated being different from that in which they first appeared. The title is quoted from the made-up vol. Cf. *Ibis*, 1865, pp. 228, 345; 1866, pp. 213, 214; *Zool. Rec.* for 1864 and for 1865.

1867. DOUBLEDAY, H. The Willow Grouse and Red Grouse [Lagopus spp.]. < *Zoologist*, 2d ser., ii, 1867, pp. 707, 708.

1867. NORMAN, G. The Willow Grouse and Red Grouse [Lagopus spp.] perching. < *Zoologist*, 2d ser., ii, 1867, p. 607.

1867. NORMAN, G. Red Grouse and Willow Grouse [Lagopus spp.]. < *Zoologist*, 2d ser., ii, 1867, p. 758.

1868. FOWLER, A. The Ruffed Grouse [habits of Bonasa umbellus]. < *Am. Nat.*, ii, 1868, pp. 365–367.

1869. GRAINGER, J. B. White Partridges (? Ptarmigan) near Ganton, Yorkshire. < *Zoologist*, 2d ser., iv, 1869, p. 1951.

1869. RAYMOND, R. On the drumming of the Ruffed Grouse [Bonasa umbellus]. < *Am. Nat.*, iii, 1869, p. 105.

> Criticises and dissents from statements of a writer in *Harper's Magazine* for October, 1868, on the mode of producing the peculiar sound made by this bird.

1869. WILSON, J. G. Among the Prairie Chickens [Cupidonia cupido]. < *Appleton's Journ.*, ii, Dec., 1869, p. 522.

1870. BELL, A. S. Reported probable occurrence of the Ptarmigan [Lagopus sp.] in Yorkshire. < *Zoologist*, 2d ser., v, 1870, p. 2062.

1870. HARTING, J. E. Reported Occurrence of the Ptarmigan [Lagopus sp.] in Yorkshire. < *Zoologist*, 2d ser., v, 1870, p. 2023.

1870. LUPEL, *Comte de.* Acclimatation d'un nouveau Gibier pris dans la classe des Oiseaux; la petite Grousse d'Écosse. < *Bull. Soc. Acclim.*, 2e sér., vii, 1870, pp. 122–126.

1871. JAYCOX, T. W. [Bonasa jobsii, n. sp.] < *Cornell Era* (newspaper of Ithaca, N. Y.), iv, Dec. 8, 1871, p. 182.

> Cf. *op. cit.*, Jan. 19, 1872; *Am. Nat.*, vi, 1872, pp. 172, 300, 303; *Ibis*, 1872, p. 191.

1871. NEWTON, A. [On the specific validity of Lagopus hemileucurus.] < *Ibis*, 3d ser., i, 1871, p. 249.

1871. NEWTON, A. On certain species of Falconidæ, Tetraonidæ, and Anatidæ. [Communicated by Mr. Coues.] < *Proc. Acad. Nat. Sci. Phila.*, July 4, 1871, pp. 94–100.

> The *Tetraonidæ* here noticed are species of *Lagopus*, which are critically discussed, pp. 96–98, four European species being held to be distinct.

1872. [ALLEN, J. A.] Ornithological Blunders [Bonasa jobsii]. <*Am. Nat.*, vi, 1872, pp. 303, 304.
Ref. to *op. cit.*, vi, 1872, p. 172, on *Bonasa jobsii;* supplemented by editorial comments.

1872. ANON. Grouse[Cupidonia cupido]-shooting in Iowa. <*Am. Sportsman*, ii, 1872, p. 34.

1872. [COUES, E.] An Ornithological Blunder [Bonasa jobsii]. <*Am. Nat.*, vi, 1872, pp. 172, 173.
Editorial publication of extracts from a letter relating to *Bonasa jobsii*, Jaycox, *Cornell Era*, iv, Dec. 8, 1871, p. 182.

1872. "DOGWHIP." [SMITH, L. H.] Destruction of the Pinnated Grouse [Cupidonia cupido]. <*Am. Sportsman*, ii, 1872, p. 37. See also pp. 60, 84, 98, 116, 131, 151.
Discussion of laws applying to the shooting of *Cupidonia cupido;* and comparison of that species with *Bonasa umbellus.*

1872. WILDER, B. G. The Last of "Bonasa jobsii." <*Am. Nat.*, vi, 1872, pp. 300–303.
Letters from S. F. Baird, E. Coues, and other contributions to the subject, with reference to *Am. Nat.*, vi, 1872, p. 172.

1873. ANON. Grouse [Lagopus sp.] Driving. <*Am. Sportsman*, ii, 1873, p. 134.
Extracted from *Blackwood's Magazine.* Increase of Grouse on Yorkshire moors caused by the custom of "driving".

1873. ANON. The Partridge (Tetrao [Bonasa] umbellus). <*Am. Sportsman*, iii, 1873, p. 193.

1873. "C. J. W." Breeding Prairie Chickens [Cupidonia cupido]. <*Am. Sportsman*, ii, 1873, p. 182. See also p. 346.
Quoted from "Poultry Bulletin"; domestication of this species deemed impracticable.

1873. COLLET, R. [Bastard von Lagopus lapponicus × Tetrao tetrix.] <*Bericht. über d. xx. Versamml. d. deutschen Orn.-Ges.*, 1873, p. 27.

1873. GOEBEL, H. Einige Worte über den Farbenwechsel des Lagopus albus. <*J. f. O.*, 1873, pp. 422–425.

1873. [GRINNELL, G. B.] A Day with the Sage Grouse [Centrocercus urophasianus]. <*Forest and Stream*, i, Nov. 6, 1873, p. 196.

1873. "OLD HAND." [Pinnated Grouse (Cupidonia cupido) shooting in Iowa.] <*Forest and Stream*, i, Dec. 4, 1873, p. 268.

1873. RIDGWAY, R. The Grouse and Quails of North America. Discussed in relation to their variation with habitat. <*Forest and Stream*, i, Dec. 18, 1873, pp. 289, 290.

1873. "V." A Rare case of Albinoism [in Cupidonia cupido]. <*Am. Sportsman*, iii, 1873, p. 75.
Six out of a brood of fourteen having albinistic marks.

1873. WHITE, J. Canadian Partridge [Canace canadensis]. <*Am. Sportsman*, ii, 1873, p. 171. See also ensuing paragraph.
Instances of poisoning following the eating of the flesh of this species.

1874. ANON. Importation of pinnated and ruffed grouse [Cupidonia cupido and Bonasa umbellus] into England. <*Forest and Stream*, ii, April 16, 1874, p. 152. See also p. 233.

1874. ANON. [EDITORIAL.] Prairie Fowl [Cupidonia cupido] in England. <*Forest and Stream*, iii, Aug. 20, 1874, p. 24. See Vol. ii, p. 408.
Failure to introduce them into England, and comments thereon.

1874. ANON. The pinnated grouse [Cupidonia cupido] in England. <*Forest and Stream*, ii, Aug. 6, 1874, p. 408. See Vol. iii, p. 24.
Failure of attempt to introduce them into England.

1874. BARBER, L. A Grouse [Bonasa umbellus] Hiding in Water. <*Am. Sportsman*, iv, 1874, p. 203.

1874. BATTY, J. H. The Dusky Grouse (Tetrao Obscurus). <*Am. Sportsman*, iii, 1874, p. 342.

1874. BATTY, J. H. How the Ruffed Grouse [Bonasa umbellus] drums. $<$ *Am. Sportsman*, iii, 1874, p. 379. See also p. 322, and iv, pp. 7, 38.
    Reply to Mr. Ridgway's article on the same subject, p. 322. Maintains that the drumming noise is made by striking together the exterior surfaces of the wings above the back.

1874. BATTY, J. H. Has the Ruffed Grouse [Bonasa umbellus] Ceased to Fear the Presence of Man? $<$ *Am. Sportsman*, iv, 1874, p. 38.
    Reply to Wm. Brewster concerning timidity of *Bonasa umbellus;* and maintaining the theory advocated *ibid.*, iii, p. 322.

1874. BATTY, J. H. The White-tailed ptarmigan—Lagopus leucurus. $<$ *Forest and Stream*, i, Jan. 29, 1874, p. 390.

1874. BREWER, T. M. [Description of the Egg of Lagopus leucurus.] $<$ *Forest and Stream*, ii, Mar. 26, 1874, p. 103.

1874. BREWER, T. M. Note on the Nesting and Eggs of Lagopus leucurus. $<$ *Proc. Bost. Soc. Nat. Hist.*, xvi, 1874, pp. 348, 349.
    MS. from T. M. Trippe; locality near Idaho Springs, Colorado; date June 28, 1873; altitude 1,000 feet above timber-line.

1874. BREWSTER, W. The Ruffed Grouse [Bonasa umbellus] again. $<$ *Am. Sportsman*, iv, 1874, p. 74. See also p. 7.
    Reply to Mr. Batty (*ibid.*, p. 38) in further explanation of drumming of *Bonasa umbellus.*

1874. BREWSTER, W. The Drumming of the Ruffed Grouse [Bonasa umbellus]. $<$ *Am. Sportsman*, iv, 1874, p. 7.
    Confirming observations recorded *ibid.*, iii, p. 322, and controverting theory expressed *ibid.*, iii, p. 379. The present writer maintains that the drumming is produced by forcible downward stroke of the wings.

1874. "E. M. M." Drumming of the Ruffed Grouse [Bonasa umbellus]. $<$ *Am. Sportsman*, iv, 1874, p. 28.

1874. "CORPORAL." The Ruffed Grouse [Bonasa umbellus]. $<$ *Am. Sportsman*, iv, 1874, p. 108.

1874. FERGUSON, N. Introduction of Pinnated Grouse [Cupidonia cupido]. A Theory. $<$ *Am. Sportsman*, iii, 1874, p. 245. See also p. 182.
    Suggestions as to introducing it into the Eastern States.

1874. H[ARVEY], M. The Ptarmigan [Lagopus spp.] of Newfoundland. $<$ *Forest and Stream*, ii, Aug. 6, 1874, p. 404.
    General account of *Lagopus albus* and *L. rupestris.*

1874. "HI! ON!" The Sharp-tailed Grouse [Pediœcetes phasianellus]. $<$ *Am. Sportsman*, iii, 1874, p. 231. See also pp. 267 and 315.

1874. H[OLBERTON], W. C. Pinnated grouse [Cupidonia cupido] for New Jersey. $<$ *Forest and Stream*, ii, Apr. 9, 1874, p. 131.
    Account of former abundance of this Grouse in New Jersey.

1874. "K." Mountain Grouse [Canace obscurus]. $<$ *Am. Sportsman*, v, Oct. 24, 1874, p. 49.

1874. M[CELWRAITH, A?]. Pinnated Grouse—[Cupidonia] Cupido. $<$ *Am. Sportsman*, iv, 1874, p. 83.

1874. "R. H. B." Habits of the Pinnated Grouse [Cupidonia cupido]. $<$ *Am. Sportsman*, iii, 1874, p. 346. See also p. 182.

1874. RIDGWAY, R. Why and How does the Ruffed Grouse [Bonasa umbellus] drum. $<$ *Am. Sportsman*, iii, 1874, p. 322.
    This article gave rise to an animated discussion, each part of which will be found catalogued under its own title, printed on p. 379 of Vol. iii, and pp. 3, 7, 28, 38, 74, and 108 of Vol. iv.

1874. RIDGWAY, R. A remarkable peculiarity [slight muscularity of the gizzard] of Centrocercus Urophasianus. $<$ *Am. Nat.*, viii, 1874, p. 240.

1874. [SMITH, GREENE.] Pinnated Grouse (Prairie Hens [Cupidonia cupido]). $<$ *Forest and Stream*, ii, July 2, 1874, p. 324.
    Experience with this species in confinement.

1874. "VETERAN." The sage cock [Centrocercus urophasianus]. < Forest and Stream, ii, Mar. 12, 1874, p. 66.

1874. "VETERAN." The blue grouse [Canace obscurus]. < Forest and Stream, ii, May 21, 1874, p. 230.
    Circumstantial observations upon habits.

1874. [WESTCOTT, C. S.] Do pinnated grouse [Cupidonia cupido] remain in "packs" all the season? < Forest and Stream, iii, Oct. 1, 1874, p. 116.
    Affirmed

1875. ANON. Pinnated grouse [Cupidonia cupido] in England. < Forest and Stream, v, Aug. 12, 1875, p. 4.
    Reprinted from "Land and Water."

1875. ANON. The sharp-tailed grouse—(Pediœcetes Phasianettus—Elliot). < Forest and Stream, v, Oct. 7, 1875, p. 131.

1875. ANON. Sagacity of the Partridge [?]. < Rod and Gun, vi, Aug. 21, 1875, p. 315.

1875. ANON. Disease in grouse. < Rod and Gun, vi, Apr. 17, 1875, p. 41.
    Quoted remarks of Andrew Wilson at Edinburgh University.

1875. ANON. [EDITORIAL.] Quail and pinnated grouse [introduced] in England. < Forest and Stream, iv, Apr. 15, 1875, p. 153.

1875. B[ANES], J. DE. The Ruffed Grouse [Bonasa umbellus]. < Forest and Stream, iv, May 13, 1875, p. 213.
    Circumstantial biography.

1875. CARDE, B. F. S. Singular boldness of a partridge [Bonasa umbellus]. < Forest and Stream, v, Nov. 25, 1875, p. 243.

1875. "FRED." Calling of pinnated grouse [Cupidonia cupido]. < Rod and Gun, vi, June 19, 1875, p. 183.

1875. "MORTIMER." Grouse [Bonasa umbellus, acclimated] on Staten Island. < Forest and Stream, iv, Feb. 11, 1875, p. 11.

1875. "ROAMER." Cock grouse [Bonasa umbellus] protecting nests. < Forest and Stream, iv, July 1, 1875, p. 326.

1876. ANON. Early Nidification of Ruffed Grouse [Bonasa umbellus, April 29]. < Forest and Stream, vi, May 18, 1876, p. 233.

1876. COUES, E. On the Breeding-habits, Nest, and Eggs, of the White-tailed Ptarmigan (Lagopus leucurus). < Bull. U. S. Geol. Surv. Terr., 2d ser., No. 5, Jan. 8, 1876, pp. 263-266.
    From fresh material from Southern Colorado, here fully described.

1876. "GIPSEY." A Lucky partridge [Bonasa umbellus]. < Forest and Stream, vi, Feb. 10, 1876, p. 4.

1876. "J." Self-protection in the grouse [Bonasa umbellus]. < Forest and Stream, vi, Aug. 3, 1876, p. 418.

1876. "PENOBSCOT." [LIBBEY, D. S.] Winter Habits of the Ruffed Grouse [Bonasa umbellus]. < Forest and Stream, v, Jan. 13, 1876, p. 356.

1876. SCOTT, DAVID. The Drumming of the Ruffed Grouse. (Bonasa umbellus.) < Field and Forest, ii, No. 4, Oct., 1876, pp. 57-60.
    The writer concludes in the hope of discovering, "ere long," how and why it is done.

1876. STANTON, W. Singular Incident. < Forest and Stream, vii, Nov. 9, 1876, p. 212.
    Bonasa umbellus crashing through two windows and an intervening room.

1877. ALDRICH, C. Destruction of Birds [Cupidonia cupido] by Telegraph Wires. < Am. Nat., xi, No. 11, Nov., 1877, pp. 636, 637.
    Referring to E. Coues's observations on the subject at large, the writer instances Prairie Chickens in further illustration of the fact.

1877. ALDRICH, C. Destruction of Birds [Cupidonia cupido] by Telegraph Wires. < The Country, i, Dec. 8, 1877, p. 79.
    Reprinted from Am. Nat., Nov., 1877, pp. 636, 637.

1877. ANON. [EDITORIAL.] Are the Prairie Chickens [Cupidonia cupido] Going to California? < *Forest and Stream*, ix, Dec. 27, 1877, p. 397.
> Reported westward migration [later shown to be erroneous].

1877. ANON. Taming Prairie Chickens [Cupidonia cupido]. < *Rod and Gun*, ix, Mar. 17, 1877, p. 374.
> Reprinted from "Canadian Gentleman."

1877. ANON. Save the Prairie Chickens [Cupidonia cupido]. < *Rod and Gun*, ix, Mar. 31, 1877, p. 409.
> Reprinted from St. Paul (Minn.) "Pioneer-Press."

1877. "AWAHSOOSE." [ROBINSON, R. E.] A few words concerning ruffed grouse [Bonasa umbellus]. < *Forest and Stream*, ix, Dec. 6, 1877, p. 346.

1877. BREWSTER, W. An undescribed Hybrid between two North American Grouse. < *Bull. Nutt. Ornith. Club*, ii, No. 3, July, 1877, pp. 66–68.
> *Cupidonia cupido* × *Pediœcetes columbianus;* named *C. cupidini-columbiana*, p. 68.

1877. COUES, E. Letters on Ornithology. No. 13 [bis = 14].⹃[Cupidonia cupido as a destroyer of] Grasshoppers. < *The Chicago Field*, Mar. 17, 1877, fig.
> Urging the important services of this bird as one of the natural agencies by which *Caloptenus spretus* is held in check.

1877. [EDITORIAL.] Frank Schley's American Partridge and Pheasant Shooting. < *Rod and Gun*, ix, Feb. 3, 1877, p. 279.
> Review of above-mentioned work, published by Baughman Bros., Frederick, Md., 1877.

1877. INGERSOLL, E. Notes of the U. S. Geological Survey—No. 1. < *Forest and Stream*, viii, July 19, 1877, p. 407.
> Observations upon *Centrocercus urophasianus*.

1877. LAWRENCE, G. N. A Note on Cupidonia cupido var. pallidicinctus, Ridgway. < *Bull. Nutt. Ornith. Club*, ii, No. 2, Apr., 1877, p. 52.
> Recognizing this variety among the Prairie Chickens brought to Eastern market.

1877. MURDOCK, A. American Grouse. < *Forest and Stream*, ix, Aug. 23, 1877, p. 44.
> Criticisms upon certain alleged habits.

1877. "MONON." [LAURIE, J.] Cupidonia Cupido.—How the Prairie Chickens Woo. < *Forest and Stream*, ix, Nov. 22, 1877, p. 307.

1877. "PENOBSCOT." [LIBBEY, D. S.] Habits of the Ruffed Grouse [Bonasa umbellus]. < *Forest and Stream*, ix, Sept. 27, 1877, p. 143.

1877. S[MITH], J. T. B. The Ruffed Grouse [Bonasa umbellus]—A Query. < *Forest and Stream*, ix, Sept. 6, 1877; p. 85.
> Female parent transporting her young.

1877. "STONY ISLAND." Ruffed Grouse [Bonasa umbellus] Shooting. < *Rod and Gun*, ix, Feb. 10, 1877, p. 290.

1877. WILLIAMS, W. H. An interesting question [respecting Bonasa umbellus]. < *Forest and Stream*, ix, Dec. 13, 1877, p. 366.
> Is there a disparity in numbers between the sexes of Ruffed Grouse?

1878. ANON. Ruffed Grouse's [Bonasa umbellus] Drumming. < *Forest and Stream*, ix, Jan. 10, 1878, p. 430.
> The operation not entirely confined to the pairing season.

1878. ANON. [EDITORIAL.] Ruffed Grouse [Bonasa umbellus] in Texas. < *Forest and Stream*, x, May 9, 1878, p. 256.

1878. ———. Habits of the Ruffed Grouse [Bonasa umbellus]. < *Forest and Stream*, ix, Jan. 17, 1878, p. 450; Jan. 24, 1878, p. 469; x, Mar. 7, 1878, p. 76; Mar. 21, 1878, p. 177.
> This head covers a series of letters from a dozen or more correspondents on the subject of the habits of the Ruffed Grouse, with special reference to the "drumming" of that bird.

1878. ———. [Discussion and correspondence relative to alleged] Prairie chickens in California and Colorado. < *Forest and Stream*, x, May 23, 1878, p. 296. See p. 175.

1878. "AWAHSOOSE." [ROBINSON, R. E.] Eccentricities of the Ruffed Grouse [Bonasa umbellus]. < Forest and Stream, xi, Nov. 21, 1878, p. 321.

1878. COOPER, J. G. Californian Prairie Chickens. < Bull. Nutt. Ornith. Club, iii, No. 2, Apr., 1878, p. 96.

Being *Pediœcetes columbianus* instead of the alleged *Cupidonia cupido*. There was a good deal of newspaper matter on the subject about this time, all founded in error, the supposed P.ai.ie Chickens west of the Rocky Mountains being Sharp-tailed Grouse.

1878. COUES, E. The Willow Grouse [Lagopus albus] in New York. < Bull. Nutt. Ornith. Club, iii, No. 1, Jan., 1878, p. 41.

1878. [GRINNELL, G. B.] About our Grouse. < Forest and Stream, xi, Oct. 31, Nov. 7, 14, 21, and Dec. 5, 1878, pp. 259, 280, 299, 300, 319, 320, 360.

Notes on the habits of the less known *Tetraonidæ* of North America.

1878. HENSHAW, H. W. Prairie chickens in Nevada. < Forest and Stream, x, Apr. 11, 1878, p. 175. See p. 296.

Cupidonia cupido not extending its range westward.

1878. "J. N." A singular combat [between a male Tetrao canadensis and a dung-hill Cock]. < Forest and Stream, x, Feb. 14, 1878, p. 18.

1878. NELSON, E. W. The Rock Ptarmigan (Lagopus rupestris) in the Aleutian Islands. < Bull. Nutt. Ornith. Club, iii, No. 1, Jan., 1878, p. 38.

1878. NEWTON, A. [Remarks on Exhibition of a supposed hybrid between Lagopus scoticus and L. mutus.] < P. Z. S., Nov. 5, 1878, p. 793.

1878. "PENOBSCOT." [LIBBEY, D. S.] Drumming of the Ruffed and Canada Grouse [Bonasa umbellus, Canace canadensis]. < Forest and Stream, xi, Sept. 19, 1878, p. 131.

1878. "RUFFED GROUSE." Habits of the Ruffed Grouse [Bonasa umbellus]. < Forest and Stream, x, 1878, pp. 215, 274. See pp. 76, 117.

Letters also from "Awahsoose" (R. E. Robinson), and "D. C. M."

1878. "SANGER." Two Sides to the Question [of preponderance of males over females in Bonasa umbellus]. < Forest and Stream, ix, Jan. 31, 1878, p. 489.

1878. "SNAPSHOT." The Grouse Family [Tetraonidæ] of Oregon. < San Francisco Chronicle, Jan. 20, 1878.

Biographical.

1878. STEARNS, R. E. C. The Prairie Chicken in California. < Am. Nat., xii, No. 2, 1878, p. 124, 125.

Supposed to be *Cupidonia*—proved afterward to be *Pediœcetes*.

1879. ANON. The Partridge fly. < Forest and Stream, xi, Jan. 9, 1879, p. 462.

Discussion by the editor, "Straight-bore" (Morton Robinson), and C. H. Hope, of a parasite of *Bonasa umbellus*, supposed to belong to genus *Hippobosca*.

1879. ANON. The Ruffed Grouse [Bonasa umbellus]: a semi-soliloquy. < The Oölogist, v, No. 1, July, 1879, p. 1.

Poem.

1879. BENDIRE, C. Notes on the Dusky Grouse (Canace obscurus). < The Oölogist, iv, No. 12, summer 1879 (extra number), pp. 98, 99.

From his paper on *Birds of Southeastern Oregon*, in *Proc. Bost. Nat. Hist. Soc.*

1879. B[REWER], T. M. Not Pinnated Grouse. < Forest and Stream, xi, Jan. 2, 1879, p. 441.

Denying that *Cupidonia cupido* has strayed to the Pacific Slope.

1879. B[YERS], W. N. The Sage Grouse [Centrocercus urophasianus]. < Forest and Stream, xi, Jan. 2, 1879, p. 440.

1879. B[YERS], W. N. The Flesh of the Sage Grouse [Centrocercus urophasianus]. < Forest and Stream, xii, May 22, 1879, p. 307.

Reply to editorial comments on previous article on this topic, the writer protesting against the manner in which the discussion of the question was closed.

1879. CLARK, M. W. Domesticated Ruffed Grouse [Bonasa umbellus]. < *Forest and Stream,* xii, May 29, 1879, p. 326.

1879. C[LARKE], S. C. Habitat of Sharp-tailed Grouse [Pediœcetes phasianellus columbianus]. < *Forest and Stream,* xiii, Oct. 9, 1879, p. 705.

1879. CREIGHTON, R. J. Exportation of Quail [i. e., Cupidonia cupido]. < *Forest and Stream,* xii, Mar. 13, 1879, p. 120.
　　History of the lot of Pinnated Grouse shipped from Kansas to New Zealand.

1879. "DINGO." Pinnated Grouse [Cupidonia cupido] for New Zealand. < *Forest and Stream,* xii, Feb. 13, 1879, p. 31.
　　Notice of a shipment of 28 birds of this species for New Zealand.

1879. DUTTON, J. W. Drumming of the Canada Grouse [Canace canadensis]. < *Forest and Stream,* xii, Nov. 20, 1879, p. 827.

1879. [GRINNELL, G. B.] Not Pinnated Grouse [Cupidonia cupido]. < *Forest and Stream,* xi, Jan. 2, 1879, p. 440.
　　Editorial remarks replying to statement of a correspondent that "prairie chickens" are found in Nevada, pointing out the fact that evidence of the occurrence of *Cupidonia cupido* so far west is still wanting.

1879. [GRINNELL, G. B.] Grouse [Cupidonia cupido] For New Zealand. < *Forest and Stream,* xii, Mar. 13, 1879, p. 119.

1879. [GRINNELL, G. B.] Drumming of the Spruce Partridge [Canace canadensis]. < *Forest and Stream,* xiii, Sept. 11, 1879, p. 625.

1879. HARDY, M. Notes on the Habits of the Ruffed Grouse [Bonasa umbellus]. < *The Temperance Vedette* (newspaper of Terrell, Texas), Dec. 6, 1879.
　　Quoted from *The Oölogist.*

1879. R[ICH], J. G. Drumming of the Canada Grouse [Canace canadensis]. < *Forest and Stream,* xiii, Oct. 2, 1879, p. 684.

1879. [SAMUELS, E. A.] Canada Grouse, Tetrao canadensis. Linnæus. < *Town and Country* (monthly newsp., Boston, Mass.), i, No. 10, Oct., 1879, p. 1, fig.
　　A short notice, with a figure from the author's 'Birds of New England', after Audubon.

1879. "TRANSIT" [RICHARDS, —,] and "INCOG." [GRINNELL, M.] The Flesh of the Sage Grouse [Centrocercus urophasianus]. < *Forest and Stream,* xii, Mar. 6, 1879, p. 85.
　　Different opinions as to the gastronomic quality of this bird's flesh.

1879. W[EBSTER], J. W. Destruction of Ruffed Grouse [Bonasa umbellus] in Connecticut. < *Forest and Stream,* xiii, Oct. 2, 1879, p. 684.
　　Destruction of the young of this species by the larvæ of *Olfersia americana,* Leach.

1879. WRIGHT, M. M. How the Ruffed Grouse [Bonasa umbellus] Drums. < *Town and Country, the People's Monthly Journal* (Boston), i, No. 3, Mar., 1879.
　　The wings beat the air, but neither the body of the bird, nor the log, nor each other.
　　As may be seen from many of the foregoing titles, there was for a time considerable discussion in the sporting papers and elsewhere, respecting the mechanics and acoustics of this remarkable operation; and the same subject has often been taken up in general works which have occasion to treat of the Ruffed Grouse. Opinions have been advanced: 1) That the outsides of the wings strike each other over the bird's back; 2) that the insides of the wings strike the bird's body; 3) that the wings strike the log or other hard object on which the bird stands; 4) that the wings beat the air with such rapidity as to produce the vibrations in which the "drumming" sound consists. It would appear to be impossible that the peculiar sound should be produced in any other than one of these four ways; and the balance of evidence is in favor of the last named, as held by the present writer and others.

Perdicidæ.

1830. VIGORS, N. A. [Observations on the Genus Ortyx, with characters of two New Species—O. neoxenus, O. affinis, p. 3.] < *P. Z. S.*, i, 1830, pp. 2–4.

1831. "J. C." Notice of an Attempt to naturalise the Virginia Partridge [Ortyx virginiana] in England. < *Loudon's Mag. Nat. Hist.*, iv, 1831, pp. 16–18, fig. 8.

1831. [EDITORIAL]. [Abstract of Mr. Vigor's remarks on a Gallinaceous group (Ortyginæ) of America which supplies in that continent the place of the Quails of the Old World.] < *Philos. Mag.*, ix, 1831, pp. 54, 55.

From *P. Z. S.*, Nov. 4, 1830, pp. 2–4.

1832. LLAVE, P. DE LA. Sobre tres especies nuevas del género Tetrao [Ortyginæ]. < *Registro Trimestre* (Mexico), i, núm. 2, Abril de 1832, pp. 141–145.

The genus *Tetrao* is here equivalent to three modern genera of *Ortyginæ* or *Odontophorinæ*. None of the species here described as new is really so. *Tetrao marmorata*, p. 144, is *Dendrortyx macroura* (Jard. and Selby); *T. cristata*, p. 144, is *Callipepela squamata* (Vig.); and *T. guttata*, p. 145, is *Cyrtonyx massena* (Less.) There is a French translation in *R. M. Z.*, xiii, 1861, pp. 425–429.

1833. D[ENSON], J. The Virginian Partridge [Ortyx virginiana]. < *Loudon's Mag. Nat. Hist.*, vi, 1833, p. 153.

On its introduction in England.

1834. VIGORS, [N. A.] Ueber die Wachteln [Ortyginæ] der neuen Welt. < *Oken's Isis*, Bd. xxvii, 1834, p. 806.

Auszug aus *Philos. Mag.*, Bd. ix, 1831, pp. 54, 55.

1836. GOULD, J. [Characters of a New Species of Ortyx (ocellatus) from Mexico.] < *P. Z. S.*, iv, 1836, pp. 75, 76.

1837. GOULD, J. [On a New Species of Ortyx (plumifera) from the collection of the late Mr. David Douglas.] < *P. Z. S.*, v, 1837, p. 42.

1839. GOULD, J. [Ortyx plumifera n. sp. aus Californien.] < *Oken's Isis*, Bd. xxxii, 1839, p. 145.

Aus *P. Z. S.*, v, Apr. 11, 1837, p. 42.

1841. CONTRAINE, F. Observations sur le Conin sonnini . . . < *Bull. Acad. Bruxelles*, 2e sér., viii, 1841, pp. 113–116.

Pas vues moi-même.

1842. GOULD, J. [On various New Species of Ortyx.] < *P. Z. S.*, x, 1842, pp. 181–184.

O. nigrogularis, p. 181; *O. pectoralis, O. castanea*, p. 182; *O. stellata*, p. 183.

1843. CABOT, S., JR. [On a species of Ortyx (nigrogularis) discovered by him in Yucatan.] < *Proc. Bost. Soc. Nat. Hist.*, i, 1843, p. 151.

Cf. *Stephens' Incidents of Travel in Yucatan*, i, App., p. 474.

1843. GOULD, J. [Descriptions of Ortyx parvicristatus and O. marmoratus, spp. nn.] < *P. Z. S.*, xi, 1843, pp. 106, 107.

1843. GOULD, J. Descriptions of four New Species of Ortyx. < *P. Z. S.*, xi, 1843, pp. 132–134.

Ortyx leucophrys, p. 132; *O. fasciatus, O. leucotis*, p. 133; *O. strophium*, p. 134.

1843. GOULD, J. [New Species of Ortyx.] < *Ann. Mag. Nat. Hist.*, xii, 1843, pp. 284–286.

From *P. Z. S.*, Dec. 13, 1842.

1843. [RÉDACTEUR.] [Extrait d'un article sur la Caille des États-Unis, Perdix borealis Temm. (Ortyx virginiana), publié dans les Mémoires de la Soc. d'Agric. de l'Aube, 1842.] < *Revue Zoologique*, vi, 1843, pp. 223, 224.

1844. DENNY, H. Ortyx virginiana in Norfolk. < *Ann. Mag. Nat. Hist.*, xiii, 1844, pp. 405, 406.

1845. GOULD, J.   A Monograph of the Sub-family Odontophorinæ, or Partridges of America.   < *Rep. Brit. Assoc. Adv. Sci. for* 1844, 1845 (*Misc. Comm.*), pp. 61, 62.

Here only a notice of the monograph, including an abstract of some points given respecting the birds themselves.

1847. ABERT, J. W.   [On the Habits of Ortyx (Callipepla) squamata, Vigors, as observed in New Mexico.]   < *Proc. Acad. Nat. Sci. Phila.*, iii, 1847, pp. 221, 222.

1848. GAMBEL, W.   Description of a new Mexican Quail [Ortyx thoracicus].   < *Proc. Acad. Nat. Sci. Phila.*, iv, 1848, p. 77.

1849. GAMBEL, W.   Description of a [lately] new Mexican Quail [Ortyx thoracicus].   < *Ann. Mag. Nat. Hist.*, 2d ser., iii, 1849, pp. 317, 318.

From *Proc. Acad. Nat. Sci. Phila.*, iv, 1848, p. 77.

1850. GOULD, J.   A Monograph | of | The Odontophorinæ, | or | Partridges of America. | By John Gould, F. R. S., | [etc., etc.] | London: | printed by Richard and John E. Taylor, Red Lion Court, Fleet street. | Published by the author, 20, Broad street, Golden Square. | 1850.   1 vol.   folio.   pp. 23 of introd., rest not paged; pll. col'd 32.

7 genn., 35 spp., 32 of which are figured.   Pl. I, *Ortyx virginianus* ; II, *O. cubanensis* ; III, *O. castaneus* ; IV, *O. nigrogularis* ; V, *O. pectoralis* ; VI, *O. coyolcos* ; VII, *Cyrtonyx* (n. g., p. 14) *massena* ; VIII, *C. ocellatus* ; IX, *Eupsychortyx* (n. g., p. 15) *cristatus* ; X, *E. leucotis* ; XI, *E. sonninii* ; (*E. affinis* not fig.); XII, *E. parvicristatus* ; XIII, *E. leucopogon* ; XIV, *Philortyx* (n. g., p. 17) *fasciatus* ; XV, *Callipepla picta* ; XVI, *C. californica* ; XVII, *C. gambeli* ; XVIII. *O. elegans*; (*O. douglassi* not fig.) ; XIX, *C. squamata* ; XX, *Dendrortyx* (n. g., p. 20) *micrurus*; XXI, *D. leucophrys* ; XXII, *D. barbatus* ("Licht. Mus. B."); XXIII, *Odontophorus guianensis* ; (*O. marmoratus* not fig.); XXIV, *O. pachyrhynchus* ; XXV, *O. speciosus* ; XXVI, *O. dentatus* ; XXVII, *O. stellatus* ; XXVIII, *O. guttatus* ; XXIX, *O. balliviani* ; XXX, *O. columbianus* ; XXXI, *O. strophium* ; XXXII, *O. lineolatus.*

1850. JONES, J. M.   Note on the Californian Quail [Lophortyx californica].   < *Zoologist*, viii, 1850, p. 2852.

1850. REEVES, W. W.   Occurrence of the Virginian Colin (Coturnix Marylandica [Ortyx virginiana]) near Tunbridge Wells.   < *Zoologist*, viii, 1850, p. 2700.

1850. REEVES, W. W.   Occurrence of the Virginian Colin (Perdix Marylandica [Ortyx virginiana]) near Tunbridge Wells.   < *Zoologist*, viii, 1850, p. 2771.

1853. LAWRENCE, G. N.   Descriptions of New Species of Birds of the Genera Ortyx [texanus, p. 1] Stephens, Sterna Linn., and Icteria Vieillot.   < *Ann. Lyc. Nat. Hist. N. Y.*, vi, 1853, pp. 1–4.

1854. PRÉVOST, F.   Note sur l'acclimatation du Colin houï [Ortyx virginiana] de l'Amérique du Nord.   < *Bull. Soc. Acclim.*, i, 1854, pp. 247–251.

Avec une liste des Colins, Perdrix et Tétras susceptibles d'être acclimatés comme gibiers.

1854. SAULNIER, —.   Sur le Colin de Californie [Lophortyx californica] et sa reproduction, extrait d'une lettre addressée a M. le Président de la Société zoologique d'acclimatation.   < *Bull. Soc. Acclim.*, i, 1854, pp. 303–305, fig.

1855. COEFFIER, —.   Le Colin houi [Ortyx virginiana] vulgairement nommé Perdrix d'Amérique, Extrait d'une lettre addressée à M. le comte d'Fprémesnil.   < *Bull. Soc. Acclim.*, ii, 1855, pp. 143–146.

1856. GOULD, J.   Description of a New Trogon and a New Odontophorus [veraguensis, p. 107].   < *P. Z. S.*, xxiv, 1856, pp. 107, 108.

1857. WIEPKEN, C. F.   Ein brütendes Männchen von Callipepla [Lophortyx] californica.   < *Naumannia*, vii, 1857, pp. 264–266.

1859. GOULD, J.   On a new species of Odontophorus [erythrops].   < *P. Z. S.*, xxvii, 1859, pp. 98, 99.

1860. ELLIOT, D. G.   Description of a new species of Eupsychortyx [leucofrenatus].   < *Ann. Lyc. Nat. Hist. New York*, vii, 1860, pp. 106, 107, pl. iii.

1860. GOULD, J.   On a [lately] new species of Odontophorus [erythrops].   < *Ann. Mag. Nat. Hist.*, 3d ser., v, 1860, p. 72.

From *P. Z. S.*, Feb. 8, 1859, pp. 98, 99.

1860. GOULD, J.   Description of a New Species of American Partridge [Eupsychortyx hypoleucus].   < *P. Z. S.*, xxviii, 1860, pp. 62, 63.

1860. GOULD, J.   Description of a [lately] New Species of American Partridge [Eupsychortyx hypoleucus].   < *Ann. Mag. Nat. Hist.*, 3d ser., vi, 1860, p. 77.
From *P. Z. S.*, Jan. 24, 1860, pp. 62, 63.

1860. GOULD, J.   Description of a new Odontophorus [melanonotus].   < *P. Z. S.*, xxviii, 1860, p. 382.

1860? VERREAUX, J.   Description d'une nouvelle espèce d'oiseau [Cyrtonyx sallaei].   < *Arcana Naturae (Paris)*, i, 1860?, p. —, pl. iv.
Not seen.—The bird is named *Cyrtonyx sallaei*, and is from Mexico.

1861. LAURENCE, A.   Note sur l'acclimatation des Colins [Ortyx virginiana] en liberté.   < *Bull. Soc. Acclim.*, viii, 1861, pp. 20–24.

1861. LLAVE, PABLE DE LA.   Sur trois espèces nouvelles du genre Tetrao [Ortyginæ].   < *Rev. et Mag. de Zool.*, xiii, 1861, pp. 425–429.
Extrait, traduit du *Registro Trimestre*, i, No. 2, Mexico, 1832, pp. 141–145.—*Tetrao marmorata* (= *Dendrortyx macroura*), *T. cristata* (= *Callipepla squamata*), et *T. guttata* (= *Cyrtonyx massena*).   Voir 1832, même auteur.

1861. GOULD, J.   Description of a [lately] new Odontophorus [melanonotus].   < *Ann. Mag. Nat. Hist.*, 3d ser., vii, 1861, p. 149.
From *P. Z. S.*, Nov. 13, 1860, p. 382.

1861. NEWTON, A.   [Gives J. Reinhardt's views on the Ortyges of St. Thomas.]   < *Ibis*, iii, 1861, pp. 114, 115.

1862. NEWTON, A.   [Remarks on exhibition of a Nest containing seventeen hatched-out eggs of Ortyx virginiana.]   < *P. Z. S.*, xxx, 1862, p. 2.

1863. FREYBURG, *Baron* v.   [Fortpflanzung der californischen Wachtel (Lophortyx californica) in Gefangenschaft, u. s. w.]   < *Zool. Gart.*, iv, 1863, pp. 231, 232; 234–237.

1864. FREYBERG, *Baron* v.   [Noch ein Wort über californische Wachteln (Lophortyx californica).]   < *Zool. Gart.*, v, 1864, pp. 298, 299.

1864. LAURENCE, A.   Reproduction des Colins de Californie [Lophortyx californica] en liberté.   Lettre adressée a M. le président de la Société impériale d'acclimatation.   < *Bull. Soc. Acclim.*, 2e sér., i, 1864, pp. 402–407.

1865. BUSSIÈRE DE NERCY, —.   Note sur le Colin de Californie [Lophortyx californica] et son acclimatation en France.   < *Bull. Soc. Acclim.*, 2e sér., ii, 1865, pp. 637, 638.

1866. BUSSIÈRE DE NERCY, —.   Note sur une épidémie qui a sévi sur le Colin de Californie [Lophortyx californica].   < *Bull. Soc. Acclim.*, 2e sér., iii, 1866, pp. 599–602.

1866. BUSSIÈRE DE NERCY, —.   Bemerkung über das Feldhuhn [Lophortyx californica] von Californien und seine Acclimatisation in Frankreich.   < *Zool. Gart.*, vii, 1866, pp. 110, 111.

1866. COUES, E.   Field Notes on Lophortyx gambeli.   < *Ibis*, 2d ser., ii, 1866, pp. 46–55.
A considerable biography of the species, from original observations in Arizona.

1866. [FREYBERG, — v.]   [Ueber die Acclimatisation des kalifornischen Rebhuhns (Lophortyx californica).]   < *Zool. Gart.*, vii, 1866, pp. 269, 270.
Vergl. *tom. cit.*, pp. 110, 111.

1868. STEPHENSON, J. W.   Virginian Colin [Ortyx virginiana] at St. Mary's Cray, Kent.   < *Zoologist*, 2d ser., iii, 1868, p. 1059.

1869. FOWLER, A.   The Virginia Partridge [Habits of Ortyx virginiana].   < *Am. Nat.*, iii, 1869, pp. 535–539.

1869. GEOFFROY SAINT-HILAIRE, A. Note sur les succès obtenus par MM. Louis Coignet et Léon Hennecart dans la multiplication des Colins de Californie [Lophortyx californica] en liberté. < *Bull. Soc. Acclim.*, 2e sér., vi, 1869, pp. 509–514.

1869. GEOFFROY SAINT-HILAIRE, A. [Sur l'éclosion des Colins; réponse à M. Deschamps.] < *Bull. Soc. Acclim.*, 2e sér., vi, 1869, pp. 707, 708.

1869. [THORPE, T. B.] Bob White [Ortyx virginiana]. < *Harper's New Monthly Mag.*, xxxix, Sept., 1869, pp. 505–512, figs. 1–6.
An account of this species and its congeners.

1870. WILSON, S. M. [Escaped] Californian Quail [Lophortyx californica] in Sussex. < *Zoologist*, 2d ser., v, 1870, pp. 2383, 2384.

1871. FREYBERG, *Baron* v. Züchtung der nordamerikanischer Baumwachteln [Ortyx virginiana]. < *Zool. Gart.*, xii, 1871, pp. 90, 91.

1872. WHITAKER, J., JR. [Escaped] Virginian Colin [Ortyx virginiana] in Nottinghamshire. < *Zoologist*, 2d ser., vii, 1872, p. 2994.

1873. "AMATEUR." Partridge vs. Quail. A Reply to Snap Shot. < *Am. Sportsman*, iii, 1873, p. 106. See also ibid., p. 11.
Concerning vernacular name of *Ortyx virginiana*.

1873. ANON. Quail catching in Syria. < *Am. Sportsman*, iii, 1873, p. 108.

1873. ANON. [EDITORIAL.] Eastern quail [Ortyx virginiana] in California. < *Am. Sportsman*, ii, 1873, p. 87.
Success of attempt to acclimate *Ortyx virginiana* on the Pacific coast.

1873. ANON. [EDITORIAL.] Take care of "Bob White" [Ortyx virginiana, in winter]. < *Am. Sportsman*, ii, 1873, p. 73.

1873. ANON. [EDITORIAL.] Suppression of Scent in Birds. < *Scribner's Monthly*, vi, 1873, p. 760.
Quoted from Tegetmeier.

1873. "CYPRESS, J., JR." [W. P. HAWES], "H", *and* "FRANK FORESTER" [W. H. HERBERT]. A Controversy concerning the genera and distinctions of Quail and Partridge. < *Am. Sportsman*, iii, 1873, pp. 98, 114, 130, 148, 162, 180.
This series of letters, in which much of the natural history of the *Perdicidæ* and *Tetraonidæ* is brought out, was reprinted from the *New York Mirror* and the *American Turf Register and Sporting Magazine*, to which they were addressed during 1840.
It forms a part of the interminable floating literature which evidences the absolute impossibility of teaching sportsmen at large whether a quail is a partridge, or whether a partridge is a quail, or whether one or the other or neither of these is a pheasant, or whether—but I forbear. The many titles bearing upon this subject will show how hopeless is the case. Scientists have not seldom attempted to set sportsmen right, but have generally had to give it up.

1873. "DAVID, JR." The Partridge. < *Am. Sportsman*, ii, 1873, p. 135. See also p. 166.
Comparison of the European *Perdix* with American *Ortyx*.

1873. "E. E. E." The California Partridge [Lophortyx californica]. < *Am. Sportsman*, ii, 1873, p. 83.
Proposed acclimation of this species in the Eastern U. S.

1874. ALLEN, J. M. Quail [Ortyx virginiana] eating pine-cone seeds. < *Am. Sportsman*, iv, 1874, p. 171.

1874. ANON. [EDITORIAL.] A name for the Quail [Ortyx virginiana]. < *Am. Sportsman*, iii, 1874, p. 248.
Urges adoption of "bob-white" as a distinctive name of this species.

1874. ANON. [EDITORIAL.] Quail [Ortyx virginiana] Bred and Breeding in the city. < *Forest and Stream*, ii, June 18, 1874, p. 292.

1874. ANON. The California quail [Lophortyx californica]. < *Forest and Stream*, iii, Aug. 27, 1874, p. 37.

1874. ANON. Quail [Ortyx virginiana] food [and manner of feeding]. < *Forest and Stream*, iii, Oct. 22, 1874, p. 164.

1874. COUES, [E.] Compliments of Mr. & Mrs. Robert White. < *Am. Sportsman*, iv, 1874, p. 65.
    Accompanying portraits of male and female *Ortyx virginiana*.

1874. "E." Do quail [Ortyx virginiana] eat chinch bugs? < *Forest and Stream*, ii, Apr. 30, 1874, p. 180.

1874. "HOMO." [C. S. WESTCOTT.] "Do quail [Ortyx virginiana] voluntarily retain their scent." < *Forest and Stream*, i, Jan. 29, 1874, p. 390.
    The negative maintained.

1874. "PIONEER." The scent question. < *Forest and Stream*, ii, Aug. 6, 1874, p. 405.
    With respect to *Lophortyx californica*.

1874. "SCOTIA." Migration of Bob White [Ortyx virginiana]. < *Am. Sportsman*, iii, 1874, p. 290.

1874. TREETON, J. [Escaped] Virginian Quail [Ortyx virginiana] in Northampton-shire. < *Zoologist*, 2d ser., ix, 1874, p. 3835.

1874. "T. S. D." Albino Bob White [Ortyx virginiana]. < *Am. Sportsman*, iii, 1874, p. 283.

1874. WANMAKER, E. S. Do quail [Ortyx virginiana] withhold their scent? < *For-est and Stream*, ii, Apr. 30, 1874, p. 180. See p. 276.
    Believes that a quiet, sitting bird would be readily overlooked by the dog; but that it could not voluntarily retain its scent. Much correspondence between gunners precedes and fol-lows for several months, little of which has any permanent value, or brings out any new facts upon the subject.

1875. ANON. [Feeding habits of Ortyx virginiana]. < *Rod and Gun*, vi, July 3, 1875, p. 215; Aug. 7, p. 281.
    Reprint. See also pp. 330, 370.

1875. ANON. Fertile Albinos. [Ortyx virginiana]. < *Forest and Stream*, iv, Mar. 11, 1875, p. 69.
    Reprinted from St. Louis "Republican", Mar. 3, 1875.

1875. BARNES, J. B. The Perdicidæ [of America]. < *Forest and Stream*, iii, Jan. 21, 1875, p. 372.

1875. ESTEY, T. H. White California quail [Lophortyx californica]. < *Forest and Stream*, iv, Feb. 11, 1875, p. 5.

1875. EVERTS, M. G. An Open Letter [concerning the Migratory Quail (Coturnix communis) of Europe, and the feasibility of its introduction into the United States]. < *Am. Sportsman*, v, Jan. 23, 1875, p. 264.

1875. GOLDSMITH, M. The migrating quail [Coturnix communis]. < *Rod and Gun*, vi, May 1, 1875, p. 65.
    Habits, etc., in Europe; with reference to its introduction into America.

1875. H[OLBERTON], W. C. Quail [Ortyx virginiana, in winter]. < *Forest and Stream*, iv, Feb. 18, 1875, p. 24.

1875. "HOMO." [C. S. WESTCOTT.] A new variety of quail [Ortyx hoopesii sp. n.]. < *Forest and Stream*, v, Nov. 25, 1875, p. 243.
    Editorial note appended, stating it to be abnormal plumage of *Ortyx virginiana*.

1875. "J. K. O." California Quail [Lophortyx californica, can probably be intro duced into Eastern States]. < *Rod and Gun*, vi, June 19, 1875, p. 187.

1875. "PROTECTOR." How to raise quail [Ortyx virginiana]. < *Forest and Stream*, iii, Jan. 7, 1878, p. 345, 4 cuts.

1875. "RECAPPER." [T. O. ABBOTT.] Protect the American Quail [Ortyx virgini-ana]. < *Am. Sportsman*, v, Mar. 13, 1875, p. 378. See also p. 346.

1875. "T. C. A." Protect the American Quail [Ortyx virginiana]. < *Am. Sports-man*, v, Feb. 20, 1875, p. 346. See also p. 378.

1875. "WAHKONZA." Dearth of Quail [Ortyx virginiana]. *< Am. Sportsman,* v, Mar. 20, 1875, p. 394.

1876. "ALPHA." The Quail [Ortyx virginiana] Question. *< Rod and Gun,* viii, Apr. 29, 1876, p. 67.
Scent concealed by crouching bird.

1876. ANON. Migratory Quail [importation of Coturnix communis into the United States]. *< Forest and Stream,* vi, Mar. 30, 1876, p. 115.

1876. ANON. The Migration of the quail [Coturnix communis, at Malta]. *< Rod and Gun,* viii, July 8, 1876, p. 231.
Quoted from London "Times."

1876. ANON. [HALLOCK, C.] [Success in] Taming quail [Ortyx virginiana]. *< Forest and Stream,* vii, Oct. 5, 1876, p. 137.

1876. ——. Quail [Ortyx virginiana], etc. *< Rod and Gun,* viii, Apr. 15, 1876, p. 34.
Several letters upon the question of their withholding scent.

1876. "ARKANSAS." Quail [Ortyx virginiana, migratory or not?] *< Rod and Gun,* vii, Feb. 12, 1876, p. 307.

1876. BREWSTER, W. Can quail [Ortyx virginiana] withhold their scent? *< Rod and Gun,* vii, Feb. 26, 1876, p. 344.
Considers this power possessed by certain individual birds—not necessarily by all of certain bevies.

1876. "C. F. W. B." Do Quail [Ortyx virginiana, withhold scent?], etc. *< Rod and Gun,* viii, May 13, 1876, p. 99.
Views of German sportsmen.

1876. "CORDUROY", *and* OTHERS. Can Quail [Ortyx virginiana] Withhold Their Scent? *< Rod and Gun,* vii, Mar. 25, 1876, p. 402.
"CORDUROY" denies the power, and thinks concealment and the state of the weather furnish an explanation. BLUNT, GEORGE W., says No; scent naturally does not leave the bird while it remains quiet. "PERDIX CHICAGOENSIS" affirms it, as a conscious act by the bird, which can control the escape of scent from its skin at certain times.

1876. COUES, [E.] Dr. Coues upon Quail, etc. *< Rod and Gun,* viii, Apr. 1, 1876, p. 9.
Cannot voluntarily withhold scent; that is to say, by any act of conscious volition. But certain actions of the birds, without design, result in the retention of the effluvium—which may also be favored or hindered by certain surroundings, as state of the atmosphere.

1876. "HARRY." In the Woods. *< Rod and Gun,* vii, Jan. 8, 1876, p. 226.
Comments upon article "Bob-white" in *Harper's New Monthly Magazine* (xxxix, 1869, pp. 505-512, figs. 1-6), and additional notes on *Ortyx virginiana.*

1876. [INGERSOLL, E.] Red-legged Partridges [imported into the United States]. *< Forest and Stream,* v, Feb. 3, 1876, p. 404.

1876. LINDEN, C. The Scent of Birds [Ortyx virginiana]. *< Rod and Gun,* viii, Apr. 1, 1876, p. 6.
Discussion of the subject of withholding scent by quail.

1876. LOUDON, F. Can Quail [Ortyx virginiana] withhold their Scent? *< Rod and Gun,* vii, Feb. 26, 1876, p. 339.
Believes they can.

1876. "OLD GUNNER." Quail [Ortyx virginiana], Guns, etc. *< Rod and Gun,* vii, Feb. 26, 1876, p. 338.
Quail do at times withhold their scent; and certain bevies are marked by peculiar habits.

1876. "READER." Quails [Ortyx virginiana] Withholding Their Scent. *< Rod and Gun,* vii, Mar. 11, 1876, p. 371.
Bird retains odor upon its feet by covering them the instant it alights so closely that air cannot escape from beneath the feathers; certain bevies inherit this particularly; and the practice is specially observable in those bevies most assailed by hawks.

1876. "BOB WHITE." Quail [Ortyx virginiana] Withholding Scent. < *Rod and Gun*, vii, Mar. 11, 1876, p. 371.

Facts showing its improbability.

1876. "RECAPPER." [T. C. ABBOTT.] Can quail [Ortyx virginiana] withhold their scent? < *Rod and Gun*, vii, Feb. 12, 1876, p. 312.

Believes it is possible, and voluntary, but a peculiarity of some bevies more than of others. This gave rise to much discussion, for which see pages 338, 339, 344, 370, 371, 386, 402, 406; *ibid.*, vii, pp. 2, 6, 9, 34, 67, 99, 134, and the general conclusion reached was, that no voluntary retention of scent was possible; but that the quiet or activity, state of mind and age of the bird—varying with different bevies—as well as atmospheric influences, affected the condition of the scent to such an extent as sometimes to almost wholly obliterate it.

1876. "RED-WING." [A. I. HUYLER.] Quails [Ortyx virginiana] eat Skunk-cabbage [Symplocarpus fœtidus] seeds. < *Forest and Stream*, vi, Apr. 6, 1876, p. 133.

1876. SALVIN, O. On two additional Species of Central-American Odontophorinæ. < *Ibis*, 3d ser., vi, July, 1876, pp. 379, 380.

Eupsychortyx leucotis, Gould, *P. Z. S.*, 1843, p. 133, and *Odontophorus cinctus*, sp. n., p. 379.

1876. "SPY." Can Quail [Ortyx virginiana] Withhold Their Scent. < *Rod and Gun*, vii, Feb. 26, 1876, p. 338.

Can withhold scent voluntarily, and do so when frightened. See p. 312.

1876. TAGGART, D. Quail [Ortyx virginiana] Raising. < *Forest and Stream*, vii, Oct, 26, 1876, p. 179.

Reprinted from "Fanciers' Journal".

1876. [TILESTON, W. M.] Quail [Ortyx virginiana] Shooting. < *Forest and Stream*. vii, Nov. 16, 1876, p. 232.

Habits of *Ortyx virginiana* from a sportsman's point of view.

1876. "TONIC." [?M. M. BENSCHOTER.] Can Quail [Ortyx virginiana] Withhold their Scent? < *Rod and Gun*, vii, Mar. 11, 1876, p. 370.

Answers in the negative, and supposes atmospheric conditions and other circumstances to explain alleged retention.

1876. "T. UMBELLUS." Do quail [Ortyx virginiana, withhold their scent?] etc. < *Rod and Gun*, viii, May 27, 1876, p. 134.

1876. "VIRGINIA," *and* OTHERS. Can Quail [Ortyx virginiana] Withhold Their Scent? < *Rod and Gun*, vii, Mar. 18, 1876, p. 386.

"VIRGINIA" denies that a dog's nose can be "so saturated with scent as that new birds are not perceived"; thinks odor of pine needles disguises birds' scent, but doubts whether it can be retained. "REX" considers that adult birds can withhold scent, by compressing their feathers into an air-tight envelope of the body, through which no effluvium can pass from the body. "RIPPLE" denies the power, and argues the case circumstantially at length. "NORTHWEST" considers that the birds that escape the dog would all be found after a few moments. "DRY LAND" denies that they can withhold scent voluntarily, but that hiding and other circumstances account for the retention.

1876. "WOLVERINE." Powder, Quail and McLellan. < *Rod and Gun*, vii, Mar. 25, 1876, p. 406.

Remarks upon withholding of scent, and "reasoning powers" of *Ortyx virginiana*.

1876. ANON. [EDITORIAL.] [Successful acclimatation of Ortyx virginiana in Nevada.] < *Rod and Gun*, vii, Mar. 25, 1876, p. 407.

1876. YOUNGS, J. E. A pet quail [Ortyx virginiana] in New York [for nine years]. < *Forest and Stream*, vii, Oct. 19, 1876, p. 164.

1876. "YUBA DAM". Quail [Ortyx virginiana] Withholding Scent. < *Rod and Gun*, Apr. 1, 1876, p. 2.

If they do appear to withhold scent, it is owing to atmospheric conditions and density of cover.

1877. ALLIN, E. Treatment of Quail [Ortyx virginiana] in Confinement. < *Forest and Stream*, viii, Feb. 15, 1877, p. 21.

1877. ANON.   An Albino Quail [Ortyx virginiana].   < *Forest and Stream*, ix, Dec. 20, 1877, p. 381.

> From "Bucks County Gazette".

1877. ANON.   Migrations of Quails [Ortyx virginiana].   <*The Country*, i, Dec. 15, 1877, p. 91.

> Letter condensed from "Scientific American " concerning inability of this species to fly across the Mississippi river near Natchez.

1877. ANON.   Migratory Quails [Coturnix communis] for Vermont.   < *Forest and Stream*, viii, June 28, 1877, p. 341.

> Account from Rutland (Vt.) "Herald" of arrival of Quail from Sicily, to be acclimatized by the Hon. M. G. Everts; and remarks on breeding native Quail in this country from the Nashville (Tenn.) "Rural Sun."

1877. ————.   Quail [Coturnix communis] at Sea.   < *Forest and Stream*, ix, Nov. 22, 1877, p. 306.   See pp. 327, 345.

> Letters concerning their occurrence on Atlantic Coast.

1877. ————.   Those Migratory quail [Coturnix communis].   < *Forest and Stream*, ix, Dec. 6, 1877, p. 345.   See pp. 306, 327, 380, 397.

> Letters from M. G. Everts, W. Hapgood, and "Staunch", with editorial remarks, concerning their colonization in Vermont.

1877. COUES, E.   Quail [Coturnix communis] at Sea.   < *Forest and Stream*, ix, Nov. 29, 1877, p. 327.

> Information wanted concerning Quail mentioned on p. 306; distinctions between European and American "Quail."

1877. [COUES, E.]   Birds.   < *The Mirror* (Baltimore, Md.), Oct. 1, 1877, p. 10; Nov. 1, 1877, p. 5.

> Notices of certain North American *Perdicidæ*, from his "Birds of the Northwest."

1877. HAPGOOD, W.   Game birds of New England.   European quail [Coturnix communis].   < *Forest and Stream*, ix, Aug. 9, 1877, p. 10.

1877. HARRINGTON, H.   Can the Partridge [Ortyx virginiana] withhold his scent?   < *Forest and Stream*, ix, Nov. 22, 1877, p. 306.

> Affirmed, through power of bird to compress its plumage, which is non-conducting of scent.

1877. HOUGHTON, G. H.   Breeding season for quail [Ortyx virginiana].   < *Forest and Stream*, viii, July 26, 1877, p. 421.

1877. LAWRENCE, G. N.   Descriptions of New Species of Birds of the Families Trochilidæ and Tetraonidæ.   < *Ann. N. Y. Acad. Sci.*, i, Dec., 1877, pp. 50–52.

> The gallinaceous bird here described is *Cyrtonyx sumichrasti*, p. 51, Sta Efigenia, Tehuantepec.

1877. READY, J. A.   Those Quail [Coturnix communis] Not All Gone to Sea.   < *Forest and Stream*, ix, Dec. 27, 1877, p. 397.

1877. ROWLEY, G. D.   Odontophorus cinctus (Salvin).   < *Rowl. Orn. Misc.*, iii, pt. xi, Nov., 1877, pp. 39–41, pl. lxxxi.

> Copy of the orig. descr., with colored fig. of the bird, and notes on habits by A. Boucard.

1877. [GRINNELL, M.]   Save the Quail [Ortyx virginiana].   < *Forest and Stream*, vii, Jan. 18, 1877, p. 376.

> While suffering from rigors of winter.

1877. VANDYKE, T. S.   California Quail [Lophortyx californica] for the East.   < *Rod and Gun*, ix, Mar. 17, 1877, p. 71.   See also p. 401.

> Habits of Quail of Pacific Coast, and qualities fitting them for successful introduction into the Eastern States.

1877. "VERDE MONTE."   Migratory Quail [Coturnix communis].   < *Forest and Stream*, viii, Aug. 2, 1877, p. 447.

> Details of M. G. Everts' successful introduction of them in Vermont.

1878. ANON.   Inability of American Quail [Ortyx virginiana] to Fly Across Wide Rivers [doubted].   < *Forest and Stream*, x, Apr. 18, 1878, p. 196.   See pp. 255, 319.

1878. BROWN, F. C.   Nesting of the Messina Quail [Coturnix communis, in Connecticut and Massachusetts.]   < *Forest and Stream*, xi, Aug. 8, 1878, p. 2.   See p. 56.

1878. "C. R."   Flight of Quail over Water [and sagacity in escape].   < *Forest and Stream*, x, May 9, 1878, p. 255.   See pp. 196, 319.

1878. "E."   [Ortyx virginiana in Maine in December.]   < *The Country*, i, Mar. 2, 1878, p. 261.

1878. [EDITORIAL.]   European quail [Coturnix communis] for [introduction into] America.   < *The Country*, ii, June 22, 1878, p. 132.

1878. [EDITORIAL.]   More European quails [Coturnix communis, imported for naturalization].   < *The Country*, ii, July 6, 1878, p. 163.

1878. E[LLZEY], M. G.   Inability of our Quail [Ortyx virginiana] to Make Long Flights.   < *Forest and Stream*, x, May 30, 1878, p. 319.   See pp. 196, 255.

1878. EVERTS, M. G.   Successful breeding of the Messina quail (Coturnix communis) in New England.   < *Forest and Stream*, xi, Aug. 22, 1878, p. 56.   See p. 2.

1878. "GREENWOOD".   Wintering quail.   < *Forest and Stream*, x, Feb. 28, 1878, p. 55.

1878. INGERSOLL, E.   American Quails [Ortyx virginiana] for English Preserves.   < *The* [London] *Field*, li, Feb. 9, 1878, p. 152.
   Circumstantial history of the species, with remarks upon its adaptation to residence in England.

1878. "KENTUCKIAN."   [Successful] Domestication of Quail [Ortyx virginiana].   < *Forest and Stream*, xi, Oct. 3, 1878, p. 179.

1878. MITCHELL, H. M.   California mountain quail [Oreortyx picta, able to acclimatize in the Eastern States].   < *Forest and Stream*, ix, Jan. 3, 1878, p. 413.

1878. [NEWBY, J. B.]   Early nesting of Quail [Ortyx virginiana, Jan. 20].   < *Forest and Stream*, x, Feb. 7, 1878, p. 3.

1878. "ORTYX."   The migratory quail [Coturnix communis] at home.   < *Forest and Stream*, x, June 20, 1878, p. 379.

1878. S[WAINSON], J.   The Gray partridge (Perdix Cinerea) [suitable to introduce into U. S.]   < *Forest and Stream*, x, May 2, 1878, p. 235.   See p. 296.

1879. ANON.   Migratory Quail [Coturnix communis].   < *Forest and Stream*, xiii, Jan. 1, 1879, p. 951.

1879. ANON.   Migratory Quail [Coturnix communis].   < *Forest and Stream*, xii, Mar. 20, 1879, p. 126.
   Encouraging report as to the success of the experiment of acclimatizing this species.

1879. ANON.   The California Quail [Lophortyx californica].   < *Forest and Stream*, xiii, Dec. 11, 1879, p. 894.
   Reprinted from San Francisco (Cal.) *Bulletin*.

1879. ———.   The Migratory Quail [Coturnix communis].   < *Forest and Stream*, xiii, Aug. 14, 1879, p. 544.
   Reports from Maine (J. Wight [Wright]) and Canada (J. D. Nevin) of the nesting of the recently imported "migratory quail"; with brief editorial introduction.

1879. ———.   The Migratory Quail [Coturnix communis].   < *Forest and Stream*, xiii, Dec. 25, 1879, p. 927.
   A composite article, consisting of five letters from correspondents, H. P. Tovey, Carl F. Brown, U. S. Consul at Messina, W. H. Williams, and "J. W. S." The information given is encouraging to those interested in the successful acclimatization of this species.

1879. BACON, F.   Migratory Quail [Coturnix communis].   < *Forest and Stream*, xiii, Oct. 16, 1879, p. 725.
   Report of successful rearing of these birds in America from stock imported the previous spring.

1879. "BOBOLINK."   [E. G. ROCK.]   Habits of the Migratory Quail [Coturnix communis.]   < *Forest and Stream*, xi, Jan. 30, 1879, p. 522.
   Compiled from different sources.

1879. BOHON, J. T.   Domestication of Quail [Ortyx virginiana].   <*Forest and Stream,* xii, May 8, 1879, p. 266.

> Short account of raising of them with common fowls until they had attained their full size.

1879. EDITOR, *and* OTHERS.   Importation of Game Birds [Coturnix communis]. <*Forest and Stream,* xii, June 19, 1879, p. 390.

> A made-up article, consisting of reports from various quarters of the success attending the importation of the migratory Quail, with editorial introduction. The reports come from Maine (James Wright), New Hampshire ("Mont Clare"), Massachusetts (Horace P. Tobey), New York (Arnold Stub, M. D., and C. H. Bitting), and Pennsylvania (H. Holdane, "Jot", and Byron Cracroft). In all cases the birds arrived in good order and promised to do well.

1879. EDITOR.   To Breed Quail [Ortyx virginiana].   <*Forest and Stream,* xiii, Aug. 7, 1879, p. 525.

1879. EDITOR.   Migratory Quail [Coturnix communis].   <*Forest and Stream,* xiii, Aug. 28, 1879, p. 585.

> Proposed prohibition of netting these birds in Messina.

1879. ENGLERT, M., *and* ROUSSEL, A. C.   [Breeding of Ortyx virginiana in confinement.]   <*Forest and Stream,* xii, Feb. 6, 1879, p. 6.

1879. HENRY, S. H.   Migratory Quail [Coturnix communis] in New Jersey.   <*Forest and Stream,* xii, June 26, 1879, p. 412.

1879. LINDEN, C., [*and* EDITOR.]   New Protection for Quail [Ortyx virginiana]. <*Forest and Stream,* xii, Feb. 13, 1879, p. 31.

> Proposed plan for protecting this species, with editorial comments.

1879. "MILES".   Domestication of Quail [Ortyx virginiana].   <*Forest and Stream,* xiii, Aug. 7, 1879, p. 525.

1879. [REYNOLDS, C. B.]   The Migratory Quail [Coturnix communis].   <*Forest and Stream,* xii, June 26, 1879, p. 412.

> Brief remarks on the habits of the bird, to introduce woodcut taken from *Morris' British Birds.*

1879. R[HODES], W., *and* TOBEY, H. P.   Migratory Quail [Coturnix communis]. <*Forest and Stream,* xiii, Dec. 11, 1879, p. 891.

> A query by W. R., and an answer by Mr. Tobey, giving some information as to the game qualities of these birds.

1879. SAMUELS, E. A.   The Virginia Partridge, or Common Quail.   Ortyx virginianus —Bonaparte.   <*Town and Country, People's Monthly Journal* (Boston, Mass.), i, No. 3, Mar., 1879.

> Extended popular account of habits.

1879. TOBEY, H. P., *and* BROWN, C. F.   Importation of Migratory Quail [Coturnix communis].   <*Forest and Stream,* xii, Feb. 20, 1879, p. 52.

> Letter from Mr. Tobey inclosing one from C. F. Brown, U. S. consul at Messina, giving directions for obtaining these birds for importation to America.

1879. TOBEY, H. P.   Importation of Migratory Quail [Coturnix communis].   <*Forest and Stream,* xii, Mar. 13, 1879, p. 120.

> Letter giving information in regard to importing these birds.

1879. TOBEY, H. P.   Cost of Importing Migratory Quail [Coturnix communis]. <*Forest and Stream,* xii, Mar. 20, 1879, p. 126.

1879. VIBERT, P.   Importation of European Partridge..   <*Forest and Stream,* xii, June 26, 1879, p. 412.

> Advocating it.

1879. WEST, MARK (? *pseudonym*).   Migratory Quail [Coturnix communis].   <*Forest and Stream,* xiii, Aug. 28, 1879, p. 585.

> Observed near New Haven, Conn.

1879. WOODMAN, M. S.   Migratory Quail [Coturnix communis] in New Hampshire. <*Forest and Stream,* xii, June 26, 1879, p. 412.

> Report of the progress of their acclimatation in that State.

Charadriidæ.

1774. ASCANIUS, P.   Beskrivelse over en Norsk Sneppe [Charadrius sp.] et söedyr
< *Trondhjemske Vid. Selsk. Skr.*, v, 1774, p. 153.

Not seen : title from Carus and Engelmann.

1807. GEOFFROY ST.-HILAIRE, [É.]   Observations sur les habitudes attribuées par
Hérodote aux Crocodiles du Nil.   < *Ann. du Mus. d'Hist. Nat.*, ix, 1807, pp.
373-387.

Sur le *Trochilus* des anciens, *Charadrius ægyptius*, Hasselq., pp. 382-384.

1814. NILSSON, S.   Analecta Ornithologica.   Pars II.   Charadrios Sveciæ sistens.
Præs. Sv. Nilsson, Resp. J. M. Roselius, Gothob. Lundæ. 1814. 4ot. pp.
31-42.

Haud mihi obvia.—Pars I, vide sub Motacillidis, hujusce bibliographiæ.

1825. KAUP, J. J.   Beyträge zur Ornithologie.   < *Oken's Isis*, Jahrg. ix, 1825, pp. 1395,
1396 [i. e., 1375, 1376], pl. xiv.

Ueber die Gattungen *Charadrius* und *Vanellus*.   *C. semipalmatus*, p. "1396" (*i. e.*, 1376),
Taf. xiv (Kopf und Fuss).

1826. S[TRAU]S, —.   Matériaux pour l'Ornithologie ; par M. Kaup. . . .   < *Féruss.
Bull.*, 2e sect., viii, 1826, pp. 276, 277.

Extrait de l'*Isis*, 1825, p. "1395"=1375, pl. 14 ; sur les genres *Charadrius* et *Vanellus*.

1827. GEOFFROY ST.-HILAIRE, [É.]   Mémoire sur deux espèces d'aminaux nommés
Trochilus et Bdella par Hérodote, leur guerre, et la part qu'y prend le Crocodile.   < *Mém. du Mus. d'Hist. Nat.*, xv, 1827, pp. 459-474.

Examen du texte d'Hérodote à leur sujet—Confirmation des faits observés par cet histo-
rien—Sur le *Trochilus* (Pluvier des modernes)—Examen des services rendus par le *Trochilus*
au Crocodile, analogue à ceux du Todier au même reptile à St.-Domingue—Considérations
sur les services réciproques que se rendent les animaux et inductions relatives aux pheno-
mènes de l'instinct.

1828. GEOFFROY ST.-HILAIRE, [É.]   Ueber den Zustand der Naturgeschichte bey den
(alten und neuern) Aegyptiern, vorzüglich hinsichtlich des Crocodills.   < *Oken's
Isis*, Bd. xxi, 1828, pp. 1076-1086.

Uebers. *Rev. Encyc.*, mai 1828.—P. 1083, ,, Was solte man vom *Trochilus* denken ? "—*Charadrius ægyptius* Hasselq.

1828. GEOFFROY ST.-HILAIRE, [É.]   An account of the services which the little bird
called Trochilos [Ægialitis ægyptius (Hasselq.)] renders to the Crocodile.
< *Edinb. Journ. Sci.*, ix, 1828, pp. 68-72.

1829. HAWKINS, T.   A Species of Plover   < *Loudon's Mag. Nat. Hist.*, ii, 1829, p. 207.

1829. "J. B."   Food of the Lapwing [Vanellus cristatus].   < *Loudon's Mag. Nat.
Hist.*, ii, 1829, pp. 113, 114.

1829. "M."   Food of the Lapwing [Vanellus cristatus].   < *Loudon's Mag. Nat. Hist.*,
i, 1829, p. 496.

1832. CLAYTON, G.   The Kentish Plover not a variety of the Ring Plover, or Dul-
willy, as it is asserted to be in Rennie's Montagu's Ornithological Dictionary.
< *Loudon's Mag. Nat. Hist.*, v, 1832, pp. 80, 81.

1833. "T. K."   A remarkable Variety of the Peewit [Vanellus cristatus].   < *Loudon's
Mag. Nat. Hist.*, vi, 1833, p. 519.

1834. GOULD, J.   [Characters of a New Species of Plover (Vanellus albiceps) collected by Lieut. Allen in Western Africa.]   < *P. Z. S.*, ii, 1834, p. 45.

1835. [GOULD, J.]   [Ueber Vanellus albiceps.]   < *Oken's Isis*, Bd. xxviii, 1835, p. 1029.

From *P. Z. S.*, 1834, p. 45.

1835. DOUBLEDAY, H. [Charàdrius minor has been taken in Britain; Grounds of Proof of the Correctness of Identifying the Birds so deemed as it.] < *Loudon's Mag. Nat. Hist.*, viii, 1835, pp. 615–617.

1835. STRICKLAND, A. [Charàdrius minor; the Accuracy of deeming it a Bird of Britain questioned, with Reasons.] < *Loudon's Mag. Nat. Hist.*, viii, 1835, p. 510.

1836. YARRELL, W. [Breeding of Charadrius morinellus at Skiddaw, England.] < *P. Z. S.*, iv, 1836, pp. 1, 2.

1837. L'HERMINIER, F. Edicnème. Ædicnemus, Temminck. E. Vocifer. Æ. vocifer. L'Herminier. < *Guér. Mag. de Zool.*, 7⁰ année, 1837, classe ii, notice lxxxiv, pp. 1–6, pl. lxxxiv.

1838. HEYSHAM, T. C. Some Observations on the Habits of the Dottrel, (Charadrius [Eudromias] Morinellus, Linn.) made in Cumberland, during the Summer of 1835. < *Charlesw. Mag. Nat. Hist.*, ii, 1838, pp. 295–304.

1839. [GOULD, J.] Erythrogonys [cinctus, sp. n.] Gould. Neue Gattung der Wadvögel. < *Arch. f. Naturg.*, 1839, (1), p. 397.
> From *P. Z. S.*, 1837, p. 155, where it occurs as part of a paper describing many new Australian birds.

1843. HEWETT, W. Note on the Golden Plover [Charadrius pulvialis]. < *Zoologist*, i, 1843, pp. 362, 363.
> On its breeding and other habits.

1843. HEWETT, W. Note on the Eggs of the Stone Curlew [Œdicnemus crepitans]. < *Zoologist*, i, 1843, p. 363.

1843. HEWETT, W. Note on the habits of the Dottrell [Eudromias morinellus]. < *Zoologist*, i, 1843, p. 363.

1843. RODD, E. H. Note on the early breeding of the Ring Plover [Ægialitis hiaticula, in the Scilly Islands]. < *Zoologist*, i, 1843, p. 190.

1844. FRASER, L. [On Birds from Chile, and description of Leptopus mitchellii, g. sp. n.] < *P. Z. S.*, xii, 1844, p. 157.
> The genus *Leptodactylus* is proposed in event that *Leptopus* is preoccupied.

1844. HURRY, W. C. Ueber Herodots Trochilus und Crocodil. < *Oken's Isis*, Bd. xxxvii, 1844, p. 889.
> *Edinb. New Philos. Journ.*, xxix, 1840, p. 197.

1845. POOLE, J. Occurrence of the Norfolk Plover [Œdicnemus crepitans] in Co. Wexford. < *Zoologist*, iii, 1845, p. 876.

1845. RODD, E. H. Norfolk Plover [Œdicnemus crepitans] wintering in Cornwall. < *Zoologist*, iii, 1845, p. 876.

1846. CHENNELL, F. A. Incubation of the Ringed Plover (Ægialitis hiaticula). < *Zoologist*, iv, 1846, p. 1212.

1847. HUGHES, E. J. R. Enquiry respecting the rearing of a Lapwing [Vanellus cristatus]. < *Zoologist*, v, 1847, p. 1872.

1848. CLIBBORN, J. Enquiry respecting the Migration of Plovers (Charadrius pluvialis and cinereus). < *Zoologist*, vi, 1848, p. 2023.

1848. FISHER, W. R. Migration of Plovers [in England]. < *Zoologist*, vi, 1848, p. 2066.

1848. GOATLEY, T. Note on the Great Plover (Œdicnemus crepitans). < *Zoologist*, vi, 1848, p. 2147.

1848. GOATLEY, T. Migration of the Golden Plover (Charadrius pluvialis). < *Zoologist*, vi, 1848, p. 2147.

1848. MORRIS, B. R. Note on the Great Plover (Œdicnemus crepitans). < *Zoologist*, vi, 1848, pp. 2146, 2147.

1848. RODD, E. H. Great Plover (Œdicnemus crepitans) wintering in Cornwall. < *Zoologist*, vi, 1848, p. 2023.

1848. POOLE, J. Peewit (Vanellus cristatus) destructive to the Wireworm. <Zoologist, vi, 1848, p. 2023.

1850. FOSTER, T. W. Occurrence of the Dotterel Plover (Charadrius [Eudromias] morinellus) at and near Wisbech. < Zoologist, viii, 1850, p. 2853.

1850. GARTH, J. C. Occurrence of the Little Ringed Plover (Charadrius minor [Ægialitis curonica]) near Whixley. < Zoologist, viii, 1850, p. 2953.

1850. STRICKLAND, H. E. On the occurrence of Charadrius virginiacus, Borkh., at Malta. < Ann. Mag. Nat. Hist., 2d ser., v, 1850, pp. 40–42.

1851. ELLMAN, J. B. Occurrence of the Little Ringed Plover [Ægialitis curonica] at Shoreham, Sussex. < Zoologist, ix, 1851, p. 3279.

1851. JÄGER, —. Beobachtung über den Gold-Regenpfeiffer. (Charadrius auratus Suk.) < Württemb. Naturw. Jahreshefte, vii, Jahrg. 1851, p. 264.
       Nicht mir selbst zugänglich: Titel aus Carus und Engelmann.

1852. PÄSSLER, W. [Aus der Leben von Charadrius minor (Ægialitis curonica).] < Naumannia, ii, Heft i, 1852, pp. 95, 96.

1852. POWYS, T. L. Occurrence of the Ring Dotterel (Charadrius [Ægialitis] Hiaticula) near Oxford. < Zoologist, x, 1852, p. 3476.

1852. RODD, E. H. Occurrence of the Kentish Plover [Ægialitis cantiana] near Penzance. < Zoologist, x, 1852, p. 3453.

1853. GARLAND, J. Occurrence of the Dotterel (Charadrius [Eudromias] Morinellus) near Dorchester. < Zoologist, xi, 1853, p. 4053.

1853. GURNEY, J. H. Note on the occurrence in Sweden of Pluvianus Ægyptius. < Zoologist, xi, 1853, p. 4096.

1853. IRBY, L. H. Occurrence of the Stone Curlew (Œdicnemus crepitans) near Thetford. < Zoologist, xi, 1853, p. 3909.

1854. WARREN, —. [Exhibition of Charadrius minor (Ægialitis curonica) from Clontarf Island.] < Nat. Hist. Rev. (Proc. Soc.), i, 1856, p. 34.

1855. HARTLAUB, G. Ueber Chettusia crassirostris de Filippi. < J. f. O., iii, 1855, p. 427.

1855. LÜBBERT, —. [Ein ungefähr acht Tage alter Œdicnemus crepitans.] < Naumannia, 1855, p. 109.

1858. GURNEY, J. H. Note on a Lapwing's [Vanellus cristatus] Egg with Two Yolks. < Zoologist, xvi, 1858, p. 6144.

1858. RODD, E. H. Occurrence of the Great Plover [Œdicnemus crepitans] at Penzance. < Zoologist, xvi, 1858, p. 6009.

1858. RODD, E. H. Occurrence of the Kentish Plover [Ægialitis cantiana] near Penzance. < Zoologist, xvi, 1858, p. 6097.

1860. GLOGER, C. W. L. Der Alpen-Regenpfeifer (Charadrius [Eudromias] morinellus) auf dem Riesengebirge wieder vorhanden. < J. f. O., viii, 1860, p. 159.

1862. CREWE, H. H. [Letters on the occurrence of Charadrius (Eudromias) morinellus at Tringhoe, England.] < Ibis, iv, 1862, pp. 390, 391.

1862. SAVILLE, S. P. Occurrence of the Norfolk Plover [Œdicnemus crepitans] in Cambridgeshire, with a few Remarks upon its Habits. < Zoologist, xx, 1862, pp. 8168, 8169.

1862. SCLATER, P. L. Notice of the supposed occurrence of the American Kill-deer Plover (Ægialites vociferus) in Great Britain. < Ibis, iv, 1862, pp. 275–277.
       River Avon, in Apr., 1857. Table of 11 out of 38 North American Grallæ which have been found in Europe.

1863. SAXBY, H. L. Colour of the Eggs of the Golden Plover [Charadrius pluvialis]. < Zoologist, xxi, 1863, p. 8725

1864. BOULTON, W. W.   Great Plover or Stone Curlew [Œdicnemus crepitans] near Beverley. $<$ *Zoologist*, xxii, 1864, pp. 9282, 9283.

1864. COINDE, J. L.   Note pour servir à l'histoire des Oiseaux insectivores. $<$ *Rev. Zool.*, 1864, pp. 5, 6.

> On the diet of a bird belonging "à la famille des échassiers riverains du genre chevalier." Not seen; title from *Zool. Rec.*

1864. CORDEAUX, J.   Gray Plover [Squatarola helvetica] on the Lincolnshire Coast. $<$ *Zoologist*, xxii, 1864, p. 9115.

1864. HARTING, J. E.   The little Ringed Plover [Ægialitis curonica] at Kingsbury, Middlesex. $<$ *Zoologist*, xxii, 1864, pp. 9283–9285.

1864. NORMAN, G.   Eggs of the Thickknee Plover [Œdicnemus crepitans]. $<$ *Zoologist*, xxii, 1864, p. 9114.

1864. SCHWAITZER, F.   Charadrius [Eudromias] morinellus in der Provinz Posen. $<$ *J. f. O.*, xii, 1864, p. 314.

1865. SCHLEGEL, H.   Cursores. $<$ *Mus. Nat. Hist. Pays-Bas*, 17e livr., Mars 1865, pp. 1–80.

> The "Cursores" of this author consist of four very distinct families, the *Otididæ*, *Glareolidæ*, *Charadriidæ*, and *Hæmatopodidæ*.
> Of *Otididæ* are described 18 spp., all referred to the single genus *Otis*.
> Of *Glareola* are treated 5 spp., and of *Cursorius* 7 spp.
> *Strepsilas* with 3 spp. and *Hæmatopus* with 6 spp.
> The greater part of the memoir is of course devoted to the charadrian group, of which are described 7 spp. of *Œdicnemus*, 21 of *Charadrius*, 4 of *Morinellus*, 3 of *Pluvialis*, 13 or *Vanellus*, and 9 of *Lobivanellus*.
> The whole group is represented by a total of 750 specimens in the Leyden Museum.

1866. BREHM, A. E.   Zur Naturgeschichte des weisschwänzigen Kiebitzes, (Chaetusia [sic] leucura).   *J. f. O.*, xiv, 1866, pp. 386–388.

1866. MONK, T. J.   Little Ringed Plover [Ægialitis curonica] near Lewes. $<$ *Zoologist*, 2d ser., i, 1866, p. 229.

1866. RODD, E. H.   Occurrence of the Stone Curlew or Great Plover [Œdicnemus crepitans] at the Land's End. $<$ *Zoologist*, 2d ser., i, 1866, pp. 34, 35.

1866. SHORTO, J., JR.   Stone Curlew [Œdicnemus crepitans] near Dorchester. $<$ *Zoologist*, 2d ser., i, 1866, p. 389.

1867. HERKLOTZ, O.   Oedicnemus crepitans. $<$ *Verh. (Abh.) k.-k. zool.-bot. Ges. Wien*, xvii, 1867, pp. 619–622.

> Lebensweise.

1867. SHORTO, J., JR.   Golden and Green Plovers (see Zool. S. S. 690). $<$ *Zoologist*, 2d ser., ii, 1867, p. 759.

1867. STUBBS, C. E.   Lapwings [Vanellus cristatus] at Henley-on-Thames. $<$ *Zoologist*, 2d ser., ii, 1867, p. 829.

1868. BLAKE-KNOX, H.   Thickkneed Plover [Œdicnemus crepitans] in the County of Dublin. $<$ *Zoologist*, 2d ser., iii, 1868, p. 1134.

1868. RODD, E. H.   Occurrence of the Common Dotterel [Eudromias morinellus] at the Lizard. $<$ *Zoologist*, 2d ser., iii, 1868, p. 1423.

1869. CORDEAUX, J.   On the Variation in Colour of the Axillary Plume of the Golden Plover [Charadrius pluvialis]. $<$ *Zoologist*, 2d ser., iv, 1869, pp. 1601, 1602.

1869. HARTING, J. E.   [Exhibition of a skin of Anarhynchus frontalis.] $<$ *P. Z. S.*, xxxvii, 1869, p. 360.

1869. HARTING, J. E.   On rare or little-known Limicolæ.   [Part I.] $<$ *Ibis*, 2d ser., v, 1869, pp. 304–310, fig., and pl. viii.

> This, the first instalment of a series of articles with above caption, without subhead, treats monographically of *Anarhynchus frontalis*.

1869-73. HARTING, J. E.   On rare or little-known Limicolæ. [Parts I–V.]   < *Ibis*,
2d ser., v, 1869, pp. 304–310, fig. and pl. viii, 426–434, figg. and pl. xii; 2d ser.,
vi, 1870, pp. 201–213, pll. v, vi, 378–392; 3d ser., iii, 1873, pp. 260–269, pll. viii, ix.

An important series of papers, very full, and making many rectifications of synonymy and
other criticisms. They are divisible into parts, each one of which will be found entered in
this Bibliography under head of the family to which the birds treated in the successive
instalments respectively belong.—1869, pp. 304–310, treats of *Anarhynchus frontalis* (pl. 8);
1869, pp. 426–434, of *Eurynorhynchus pygmæus* (pl. 12); 1870, pp. 201–213, of *Eudromias asiaticus* (pl. 5), *E. veredus* (pl. 6); 1870, pp. 378–392, of *Ægialitis geoffroyi*, *Æ. mongolicus;* 1873,
pp. 260–269, *Ægialitis varius* (pl. 8), *Æ. sanctæ helenæ*, n. sp., p. 266 (pl. 9) =*pecuarius* ex St.
Helenâ auct. Thus all five papers, excepting the second, treat of *Charadriidae.*

1869. HARTLAUB, G.   On Anarhynchus [frontalis].   < *P. Z. S.*, xxxvii, 1869, pp. 433–
436.

History and characters of the genus; synonymy and description of the species.

1869. HORNE, C. [On the habits of Lobivanellus goensis.]   < *Ibis*, 2d ser., v, 1869,
pp. 454–456.

1869. JARDINE, W. [Note on the bill of Anarhynchus frontalis.]   < *Ibis*, 2d ser., v,
1869, pp. 461, 462.

1869. MATHEW, M. A.   Dotterel [Eudromias morinellus] near Weston.   < *Zoologist*,
2d ser., iv, 1869, p. 1802.

1870. GURNEY, J. H., JR.   Gray Plover [Squatarola helvetica] at Blakeney.   < *Zoologist*, 2d ser., v, 1870, p. 2384.

1870. MOSLEY, O.   Golden Plover [Charadrius pluvialis] on the Dove.   < *Zoologist*,
2d ser., v, 1870, p. 1981.

1870. NEWTON, A. [Exhibition of a Chick of Anarhynchus frontalis.]   < *P. Z. S.*,
xxxviii, 1870, pp. 673, 674, woodc.

1870. HARTING, J. E.   On rare or little-known Limicolæ. [Part III.]   < *Ibis*, 2d
ser., vi, 1870, pp. 201–213, pll. v, vi.

The third instalment of the series, continued from *op. cit.*, v, 1869, p. 434. It treats of *Eudromias asiaticus* (pl. v), and *E. veredus* (pl. vi).

1870. HARTING, J. E.   On rare or little-known Limicolæ. [Part IV.]   < *Ibis*, 2d
ser., vi, 1870, pp. 378–392.

The fourth instalment of the series, continued from *tom. cit.*, p. 213. It treats of *Ægialitis
geoffroyi* and *Æ. mongolica.*

1870. SWINHOE, R.   On the Plovers of the Genus Ægialites found in China.   < *P. Z.
S.*, xxxviii, 1870, pp. 136–142, pl. xii.

8 spp. *Æ. hartingi*, p. 136, pl. xii; *Æ. dealbatus*, p. 138, spp. nn.

1871. HARVIE-BROWN, J. A.   Ringed Plover [Ægialitis hiaticula] breeding Inland.
< *Zoologist*, 2d ser., vi, 1871, p. 2851.

1871. CHALK, W. J.   Large Flock of Golden Plover [Charadrius pluvialis] at Bedford.
< *Zoologist*, 2d ser., vi, 1871, p. 2806.

1871. EDWARDES, L.   Ringed Plover [Ægialitis hiaticula] breeding at a distance
from the Coast.   < *Zoologist*, 2d ser., vi, 1871, p. 2770.

1871. GURNEY, J. H., JR.   Dotterel [Charadrius morinellus] at Dungeness.   < *Zoologist*, 2d ser., vi, 1871, p. 2851.

1871. HARTING, J. E.   Ringed Plover [Ægialitis hiaticula] breeding at a distance from
the Coast.   < *Zoologist*, 2d ser., vi, 1871, p. 2807.

1871. MITFORD, R.   Ring Dotterel breeding Inland.   < *Zoologist*, 2d ser., vi, 1871, p.
2851.

1871. POWER, F. D.   Dotterels [Eudromias morinellus] in Somersetshire.   < *Zoologist*,
2d ser., vi, 1871, p. 2441.

1871. OGDEN, J. A.   Synopsis of the Genus Chettusia (Lobivanellus), with a Description of a New Species.   < *Proc. Acad. Nat. Sci. Phila.*, 1871, pp. 194–196, pl. i.

A short, imperfect sketch, including 16 species, one being *C. nivifrons*, sp. n., from Fazo-
glou, p. 196. See especially Finsch, *op. cit.*, 1872, p. 32.

1871. RODD, E. H.   Kentish Plover [Ægialitis cantiana] near Penzance.   < *Zoologist*, 2d ser., vi, 1871, p. 2806.

1872. ANGUS, W. C.   Ringed Plover [Ægialitis hiaticula] breeding at a distance from the Coast.   < *Zoologist*, 2d ser., vii, 1872, pp. 2905, 2906.

1872. FINSCH, O.   On Charadrius asiaticus and Ch. damarensis.   < *Ibis*, 3d ser., ii, 1872, pp. 144–147.

> Synonymatic and critical. The determinations differ from those of J. E. Harting, *op. cit.*, 1870, p. 206, *q. v.*

1872. FINSCH, O.   Remarks on the "Synopsis of the genus Chettusia (Lobivanellus), with a description of a new Species by J. A. Ogden."   < *Proc. Acad. Nat. Sci. Phila.*, xxiv, 1872, p. 32.

> *Chettusia nivifrons* Ogd. = *C.* [*Limnetes*] *crassirostris;* and other rectifications, with addition of 8 species of the genus to those given by Ogden, *op. cit.*, 1871, pp. 194–196, *q. v.*

1873. CABANIS, J.   [Chettusia leucura bei Sarepta erlegt.]   < *J. f. O.*, 1873, p. 80.

1873. DURNFORD, H.   Remarkable Posture of the Norfolk Plover [Œdicnemus crepitans].   < *Zoologist*, 2d ser., viii, 1873, p. 3693.

1873. HARTING, J. E.   [Eudromias tenuirostris Hume = Ægialitis hartingi Swinh. = Charadrius placidus Gray.]   < *Ibis*, 3d ser., iii, 1873, pp. 324–327.

1873. HARTING, J. E.   On rare or little-known Limicolæ.   [Part V.]   < *Ibis*, 3d ser., iii, 1873, pp. 260–269, pll. viii, ix.

> The fifth and concluding instalment of the series, continued from *op. cit.*, 2d ser., vi, p 392. It treats of *Ægialitis varias* (pl. viii), and of *Æ. sanctæ-helenæ*, n. sp., p. 266, pl. ix   The latter is *pecuarius* auct. ex St. Helenâ.

1874. HARTING, J. E.   On the Lapwing of Chili [Vanellus occidentalis, p. 451, sp. n.].   < *P. Z. S.*, lxii, 1874, pp. 449–452.

1874. HARTING, J. E.   On the Eggs of some little-known Limicolæ.   < *P. Z. S.*, xlii, 1874, pp. 454–460, pl. lx.

> 23 spp., of which the following are figured: fig. 1, *Glareola lactea;* 2, *Pluvianus ægyptius;* 3, *Hoplopterus ventralis;* 4, *Ægialitis pecuarius;* 5, *Æ. tricollaris;* 6, *Æ. falklandicus;* 7, *Æ. collaris;* 8, *Æ. ruficapillus;* 9, *Æ. nigrifrons;* 10, *Himantopus novæ-zelandiæ;* 11, *Anarhynchus frontalis.*

1875. DRESSER, H. E.   [Occurrence of Charadrius fulvus (verus) in Great Britain.]   < *Ibis*, 3d ser., v, 1875, pp. 513, 514.

1875. DRESSER, H. E.   Notes on the Nest and Egg of Hypolais caligata and on the Egg of Charadrius asiaticus, Pall., together with Remarks on the latter Species and Charadrius veredus, Gould.   < *P. Z. S.*, Feb. 16, 1875, pp. 97, 98.

> The distinction of these two species of *Charadrius* maintained.

1875. HARVIE-BROWN, J. A.   [On the Eggs of Anarhynchus frontalis described in P. Z. S., 1874, 454.]   < *Ibis*, 3d ser., v, 1875, p. 519.

1876. BOYES, F.   Stone Curlew [Œdicnemus crepitans].   < *Zoologist*, 2d ser., xi, Apr., 1876, p. 4882.

1876. GURNEY, J. H., JR.   Stone Curlew [Œdicnemus crepitans].   < *Zoologist*, 2d ser., xi, Feb., 1876, p. 4801.

1876. GURNEY, J. H., JR.   The Eye of the Little Ringed Plover [Ægialitis curonica].   < *Zoologist*, 2d ser., xi, Feb., 1876, p. 4801.

1876. RODD, E. H.   Common Dotterel [Eudromias morinellus] near Penzance.   < *Zoologist*, 2d ser., xi, Oct., 1876, p. 5125.

1876. WHEEEER, F.   White Peewit [Vanellus cristatus].   < *Zoologist*, 2d ser., xi, May, 1876, p. 4928.

1877. GARROD, A. H.   Notes on the Anatomy and Systematic Position of the Genera Thinocorus and Attagis.   < *P. Z. S.*, May 1, 1877, pp. 413–418, figg.

> Nearest related to *Oursorius* and *Glareola.*
> This does not come strictly under head of *Charadriidæ;* but I wish it to appear here.

1877. HOWELL, M. A. The American golden plover [Charadrius fulvus virginicus.]
< *Forest and Stream*, viii, Mar. 1, 1877, p. 49.
Habits of the species.

1878. EAGLE, C. H. Capture of Ægialitis meloda var. circumcincta, Ridg., on Long
Island. < *Bull. Nutt. Ornith. Club*, iii, No. 2, Apr., 1878, p. 94.

1878. GARROD, A. H. On the trachea of Tantalus loculator and of Vanellus cayennensis. < *P. Z. S.*, May 21, 1878, pp. 625–629, figg. 1, 2.
The parts named of each of these species are figured on the woodcuts in text.

1879. DUTCHER, W. Wilson's Plover [Ægialitis wilsonia] on Long Island, N. Y.
< *Bull. Nutt. Ornith. Club*, iv, No. 4, Oct., 1879, p. 242.

Chionididæ.

1836. BLAINVILLE, M. H. D. DE. Sur la place que doit occuper dans le système orni-thologique le genre Chionis ou Bec-en-fourreau. < *Comptes Rend. de l'Acad. Sci.*, iii, 1836, pp. 155–164.

Pas vu moi-même.

1836. BLAINVILLE, M. H. D. DE. Mémoire sur la place que doit occuper dans le sys-tème ornithologique le genre Chionis ou Bec-en-fourreau. < *Ann. des Sci. Nat.*, 2e sér., vi, 1836, pp. 97–106.

This I have seen, and in fact have closely studied; but the title is taken at second-hand, and may not be literally correct.

Various previous writers upon the subject had either passed over the systematic position of *Chionis* as not determined, or, in attempting its determination, had in turn considered the bird as grallatorial, natatorial, and gallinaceous, and had placed it in one or another of the recognized families, or had made of it a distinct family. The present author, writing at a time when only three specimens of *Chionis alba* were known to him to have existed, describes briefly the external parts of this species, and in more detail the osteology, the material for the study of the latter being an incomplete skeleton obtained through M. Baillon from M. P. E. Botta, who also contributed some details of the visceral anatomy. Relying chiefly upon the characters of the sternum in classification, M. De Blainville made the bird out to be an échassier, closely related to *Hæmatopus*. The reasons for his conclusions are stated cate-gorically in thirteen propositions on p. 106. The position here taken is defended with learn-ing and ingenuity, and has been until recently very generally accepted without question.—Cf. *Bull. U. S. Nat. Mus.*, No. 3, 1876, pp. 86–88.

1841. HARTLAUB, G. Nouvelle espèce de Bec en fourreau (Chionis [minor]). < *Revue Zoologique*, iv, 1841, pp. 5, 6; v, 1842, pl. 2, figg. 2, 2a, 2b.

Cette espèce est devenue plus tard le type du genre nouveau *Chionarchus* de MM. Kidder et Coues, *Bull. U. S. Nat. Mus.*, n°. 3, 1876, p. 116, *q. v.* Elle a été figurée par M. G. R. Gray, *Gen. Birds.*

1858. EYTON, T. C. Note on the Skeleton of the Sheath-bill (Chionis alba). < *P. Z. S.*, xxvi, 1858, pp. 99, 100.

Inclines to place it with *Glareola*.

1858. EYTON, T. C. Note on the Skeleton of the Sheath-bill (Chionis alba). < *Ann. Mag. Nat. Hist.*, 3d ser., ii, 1858, p. 67.

From *P. Z. S.*, Feb. 23, 1858, pp. 99, 100.

1869. CUNNINGHAM, R. O. On Chionis alba. < *Journ. Anat. and Physiol.*, Nov., 1869, pp. 87–89, pl. vii.

A brief description, illustrated by figures, of the principal digestive organs, and larynx.

1870. CUNNINGHAM, R. O. On Chiaris [sic] alba. < *Rep. Brit. Assoc. Adv. Sci. for* 1869, 1870, (*Misc. Comm.*), p. 111.

Anatomical notes on *Chionis alba*.

1867. SCLATER, P. L. [Exhibition of a skin of Chionis minor.] < *P. Z. S.*, xxxv, 1867, p. 891.

From the Crozet Islands, being that mentioned by E. L. Layard in *Ibis*, 1867, p. 458.

1871. NEWTON, A. [Egg of Chionis minor figured.] < *P. Z. S.*, Jan. 17, 1871, p. 57, pl. iv, f. 7.

Not properly citable as a separate article: the notice occurs in a paper entitled, "On some New or Rare Birds' Eggs", running pp. 55–58, pl. iv, figg. 1–8 of the periodical in mention.

1876. KIDDER, J. H. An interesting Bird [Chionis minor]. < *Popular Science Monthly*, viii, No. 48, Apr., 1876, pp. 657–665, figs. 1–3.

Popular account of the history, characters, and habits of this species.

1876. [KIDDER, J. H.] The Natural History of Kerguelen Island. < *Am. Nat.*, x, No. 8, 1876, pp. 481–484.

Editorial, prepared from Dr. Kidder's paper. *Chionis minor* the only bird treated.

1876. KIDDER, J. H., *and* COUES, E.   A study of Chionis minor with reference to its Structure and Systematic Position.   < *Bull. U. S. Nat. Mus.*, No. 3, 1876, pp. 85–116.

   After De Blainville's original memoir of 1836 on the anatomy and taxonomy of *C. alba*, this article is the principal authority on the structure and systematic position of the family *Chionididæ*. The species studied is *C. minor*, not only fully endorsed as to its specific validity, but raised to the rank of a separate genus (*Chionarchus*, g. n., p. 116). The taxonomic value of the family is also raised to equivalency with the major groups indicated by Huxley by the termination -*morphæ*, under the style of *Chionomorphæ* (p. 115).

   The article opens with a review of the literature of the whole subject, from Forster's founding of the genus *Chionis* in 1788, to date, De Blainville's paper being specially noted (pp. 85–90). The description of *C. minor* follows (pp. 91, 92); the anatomy of the same species continues (pp. 92–107) with an account of the principal muscles and viscera, and a description of the whole skeleton. A "Statement of Conclusions deduced from the foregoing" concludes the paper. De Blainville's views of the near relationship of *Chionis* to *Hæmatopus* are criticized and dissented from. "In summing external characters, therefore, we see how exactly *Chionis* stands between grallatorial and natatorial birds, retaining slight but perfectly distinct traces of several other types of structure" (p. 109). "We thus find in *Chionis* a connecting link, closing the narrow gap between the plovers and gulls of the present day. In our opinion, this group represents the survivors of an ancestral type from which both gulls and plovers have descended. And this opinion is strongly supported by the geographical isolation of its habitat, affording but few conditions favorable to variation" (p. 114). *Chionis* being consequently not referable to either of the two superfamily groups between which it stands, the group *Chionomorphæ* is established for its reception, and defined—the Chionomorphs "constituting exactly the heretofore unrecognized link between the Charadriomorphs and Cecomorphs, nearer the latter than the former, and still nearer the common ancestral stock of both." Of the two recognized species, *C. minor* is decided to be "undoubtedly nearest to the ancestral type," and is therefore named *Chionarchus minor*.

   Other observations on *Chionis minor*, by Dr. Kidder, are found *ibid.*, p. 7; and in *op. cit.*, No. 2, 1875, pp. 1-—; but these are not separate articles. I am under the impression that one or more special papers on *Chionis* appeared after 1876; but if so, I have not indexed the periodicals in which they are contained.

Hæmatopodidæ.

1773. ————. Beschreibung des Austernsammlers [Hæmatopus ostralegus]. <*Berlin. Sammlgn.*, v, 1773, pp. 517–519.
  Nicht mir selbst zugänglich : Titel aus Carus und Engelmann.

1783. OTTO, B. C. Der Steindreher [Tringa (Strepsilas) interpres]. <*Abhandl. Naturf. Gesell. Halle*, i, 1783, pp. 111–120.
  Nicht mir selbst zugänglich : Titel aus Carus und Engelmann.

1826. [BOIE, F.] On the Plumage of the Oyster Catcher [Hæmatopus ostralegus].
  < *Thomson's Ann. Philos.*, new ser., xi, 1826, pp. 71, 72.
  Editorial note of Boie's observations.

1833. EVANS, J. A puzzling Specimen of the Oyster-catcher (Hæmatopus ostralegus L.). < *Loudon's Mag. Nat. Hist.*, vi, 1833, pp. 152, 153.
  From *Hereford Journal*, Dec. 5, 1832.

1834. G[OATLEY], T. The Account of the Oyster Catcher [Hæmatopus ostralegus].
  <*Loudon's Mag. Nat. Hist.*, vii, 1834, pp. 151, 152.
  Cf. *op. cit.*, vi, p. 151.

1846. CHENNELL, F. A. Occurrence of the Oyster-Catcher [Hæmatopus ostralegus] inland. < *Zoologist*, iv, 1846, p. 1212.

1846. HALL, T. Longevity of the Oyster Catcher [Hæmatopus ostralegus, æt. 30].
  < *Zoologist*, iv, 1846, p. 1501.

1848. CABOT, S., JR. [Comparison of the American and European Oyster-catcher (Hæmatopus).] < *Proc. Bost. Soc. Nat. Hist.*, iii. 1848, pp. 43, 44.
  The former was named *H. palliatus* by Temminck, *Man. Orn.*, ii, p. 532.

1848. CABOT, S., JR. American and European Oyster-catcher. < *Am. Journ. Sci.*, vi, 1848, p. 433.
  From *Proc. Bost. Soc.*, iii, 1848, pp. 43, 44.

1849. CURTLER, M. Occurrence of the Oyster-catcher (Hæmatopus ostralegus) in Worcestershire. < *Zoologist*, vii, 1849, p. 2455.

1850. GARTH, J. C. Turnstone [Strepsilas interpres] associating with Pigeons. < *Zoologist*, viii, 1850, p. 2652.

1858. JÄGER, C. [Hæmatopus ostralegus am Main.] < *Naumannia*, viii, 1858, p. 169.

1863. SAXBY, H. L. Green Variety of the Oystercatcher's [Hæmatopus ostralegus] Egg. < *Zoologist*, xxi, 1863, p. 8725.

1864. NEWMAN, H. W. Is the Turnstone [Strepsilas interpres] near Flamborough and Filey in July? < *Zoologist*, xxii, 1864, pp. 9362, 9363.

1867. CLARK-KENNEDY, A. Plumage of the Oystercatcher [Hæmatopus ostralegus].
  < *Zoologist*, 2d ser., ii, 1867, pp. 607, 608.

1868. HARVIE-BROWN, J. A. Plumage of the Oystercatcher [Hæmatopus ostralegus].
  < *Zoologist*, 2d ser., iii, 1868, p. 1178.

1879. "MOWITCH." Black Oyster Catcher [Hæmatopus niger]. < *Forest and Stream*, xiii, No. 14, Nov. 6, 1879, p. 785.
  Its occurrence in British Columbia.

Scolopacidæ.

1765. STRÖM, H.   Beskrivelse voor en Norsk Strand sneppe, kaldet Fiöre-pist [Tringa sp.].   < *Kong. Norske Vidensk.-Selsk. Skrift.*, iii, 1765, pp. 440–445.
Not seen.

1767. STRÖM, H.   [Beschreibung einer nordischen Strandschnepfe, Fiöre-pist genannt (Tringa sp.).]   < *Drontheim. Ges. Schrift.*, iii, 1767, pp. 395–400.
Not seen.   Transl. from *Kong. Norske Vidensk.-Selsk. Skrift.*,iii, 1765, pp. 440–445.

1794. MARKWICK, W.   Additional Remarks on the Wood Sandpiper, Tringa [Totanus] glareola.   < *Trans. Linn. Soc.*, ii, 1794, p. 325.
The original remarks are in a paper "On the migrations of certain Birds," etc., in *Trans. Linn. Soc.*, 1791, pp. 118–130, pl. xi.   The species is here considered as a variety of *T. ochropus* (written *ocropus*).   See same view in *Loudon's Mag. Nat. Hist.*, v, 1832, pp. 81, 82.

1794. [MARKWICK, W.]   Ueber Linnés braungefleckten Strandlaufern, (Tringa [Totanus] Glareola.)   < *Meyer's Zool. Annalen*, i, 1794, pp. 331–383, pl. vi.
Auszug aus *Trans. Linn. Soc.*, 1791, p. 128, pl. xi.

1805. VAUGHAN, J., *and* MILLIGAN, R.   Facts and Observations relative to the North-American Woodcock [Philohela minor].   < *Barton's Med. and Phys. Journ.*, part i, vol. ii, 1805, pp. 68–70.
The behavior of the bird during the mating season.

1816. THUNBERG, C. P.   Platalaea pygmæa, vidaré beskrifven, med figur.   < *Kongl. Vetensk.-Acad. Handl.*, 1816, pp. 194–198, pl. vi.

1818. RAFINESQUE, C. S.   General Account of the Discoveries made in the Zoology of the Western States.   < *Amer. Monthly Mag.*, iv, 1818, pp. 106, 107.
Page 106, *Symphemia*, g. n., named, no descr.   It is described, and its type named *S. atlantica*, sp. n., in *Journ. de Phys.*, lxxxviii, 1819, p. 418.

1823. KAUP, [J. J.]   Brehm's Schnepfe, Scolopax Brehmii Kaup [sp. n.].   < *Oken's Isis*, Jahrg. vii, 1823, p. 1147.

1823. MORRISON, —.   The Woodcock [Scolopax rusticola].   < *Edinb. Philos. Journ.*, x, 1823, pp. 198, 199.
On the migration of this species.

1824. STRAUS, —.   Mémoire sur le Scolopax Brehmii; par M. Kaup. . . .   < *Féruss. Bull.*, 2ᵉ sect., i, 1824, p. 183.
Extrait de l'*Isis*, Bd. vii, 1823, p. 1147.

1825. [MORRISON, —.]   Sur la Bécasse [Scolopax rusticola].   < *Féruss. Bull.*, 2ᵉ sect., vi, 1825, pp. 98, 99.
Extrait de l'*Edinb. Philos. Journ.*, x, 1823, pp. 198, 199; sur les migrations de cet oiseau.

1825. VIGORS, N. A.   A description of a new Species of Scolopax [sabini] lately discovered in the British Islands; . . .   < *Trans. Linn. Soc. London*, xiv, pt. iii, 1825, pp. 556–562, pl. xxi.
The paper is of more extended scope, and the full title will be found in the Fourth (British) Instalment of this Bibliography.   The new Snipe is figured on the plate.

1825. VIGORS, N. A.   [Scolopax sabini.]   < *Philos. Mag.*, lxv, 1825, pp. 433–437.
This is only a catch-title. which I cannot verify at present printing.   I had the full title, but it is lost or mislaid.   See preceding title.

1826. LESS[ON, R. P.].   Description d'une nouvelle espèce de Scolopax [sabini], découverte récemment dans les îles brittaniques, . . .   < *Féruss. Bull.*, 2ᵉ sect., vii, 1826, pp. 250, 251.
Vigors, *Trans. Linn. Soc. London*, xiv, pt. iii, 1825, pp. 556–562.

1828. [EDITORIAL.]   [Note on Yarrell's Description of a Species of Tringa (Tryngites rufescens) new to Europe.]   < *Philos. Mag.*, iv, 1828, p. 61.
See *Trans. Linn. Soc.*, xvi, pt. iii, pub. 1829, pp. 109–113, pl. xi.

1828. GRABA, C. T.   Tringa longirostra [n. sp.].   < *Oken's Isis*, Bd. xxi, 1828, pp. 107, 108.

1828. [GRABA, C. T.]   Nouvelle espèce du genre Tringa [longirostra]; . . .   < *Féruss. Bull.*, 2ᵉ sect., xv, 1828, p. 393.
  Extraite de l'*Isis*, Bd. xxi, 1828, pp. 107, 108.

1829. "A. C. R."   Scolopax Sabini.   < *Loudon's Mag. Nat. Hist.*, ii, 1829, p. 207.
  Cf. *op. cit.*, viii, 1835, p. 614.

1829. BREE, W. T.   Breeding of Woodcocks [Scolopax rusticola] in England.   < *Loudon's Mag. Nat. Hist.*, ii, 1829, pp. 86, 87.
  Including notices from the *Coventry Mercury*, June 1, 1828, the *Aberdeen Chronicle*, and the *Belfast Chronicle*.

1829. HILL, W. H.   The sound or call of some kind of Bird [Gallinago ?].   < *Loudon's Mag. Nat. Hist.*, ii, 1829, p. 100.

1829. HUNTER, P.   Scolopax Sabini.   < *Loudon's Mag. Nat. Hist.*, ii, 1829, pp. 288, 289.
  Refers "A. C. R." (*tom. cit.*, p. 207) to a figure in Bewick, p. 416, last edition.

1829. "H. V. D."   Descriptive and Historical Notices of British Snipes.   < *Loudon's Mag. Nat. Hist.*, ii, 1829, pp. 143-148, figg. 32-39.
  4 spp. carefully discriminated. The modest author concludes his article thus: "It is by such communications as the above, that in my opinion your Magazine may be rendered most valuable."—Cf. *op. cit.*, iii, 1830, pp. 27-30, figg. 2-4.

1829. "J. F."   The Bird [Gallinago] with a Sound like the Bleating of a Goat.   < *Loudon's Mag. Nat. Hist.*, ii, 1829, p. 207.

1829. "J. G. C."   The Bird [Gallinago] with the Sound like the Bleating of a Goat.   < *Loudon's Mag. Nat. Hist.*, ii, 1829, p. 207.

1829. "J. M."   [Call and Answer of certain species of Scolopacidæ.]   < *Loudon's Mag. Nat. Hist.*, i, 1829, p. 297, figg. 157, 158.

1829. "J. V. S."   The Sound of a Bird [Gallinago] resembling the Bleating of a Goat.   < *Loudon's Mag. Nat. Hist.*, ii, 1829, p. 208.

1829. VIGORS, N. A.   Beschreibung einer neuen Gattung Scolopax [sabini] der brittischen Inseln, . . .   < *Oken's Isis*, Bd. xxii, 1829, pp. 1107-1109.
  Aus d. *Trans. Linn. Soc.*, xiv, pt. iii, 1825, pp. 556-562, pl. xxi.

1829. YARRELL, W.   Description of a Species of Tringa [Tryngites rufescens], killed in Cambridgeshire, new to England and France.   < *Trans. Linn. Soc.*, xvi, pt. iii, 1829, pp. 109-113, pl. xi.   (Pt. iii pub. 1829; whole vol. dated 1833.)
  With a list of 13 late additions to British ornithology. See 1828, EDITORIAL.

1829. "YOUR CONSTANT READER."   The Solitary Snipe [Gallinago major].   < *Loudon's Mag. Nat. Hist.*, ii, 1829, p. 302.
  Mutilated note of the length of its bill.

1830. BREE, W. T.   Distinction of Sex in the Woodcock [Scolopax rusticola].   < *Loudon's Mag. Nat. Hist.*, iii, 1830, p. 147.

1830. HARVEY, J. A.   A Snipe of a novel Colour . . .   < *Loudon's Mag. Nat. Hist.*, iii, 1830, pp. 436, 437.

1830. HAYWARD, J.   The Snipe's Beak.   < *Loudon's Mag. Nat. Hist.*, iii, 1830, pp. 449, 450.

1830. "S. T. P."   Supplement to the "Descriptive and Historical Notice of British Snipes," in the Seventh Number of the Magazine of Natural History.   (Vol. II. p. 143.) In a Letter to the Conductor.   < *Loudon's Mag. Nat. Hist.*, iii, 1830, pp. 27-30, figg. 2-4.
  Macrorhamphus griseus and *Gallinago sabinii*. Cf. *op. cit.*, ii, 1829, pp. 143-148, figg. 32-39.

1830. [YARRELL, W.]   Beschreibung von Tringa [Tryngites] rufescens, in England vorgekommen, von W. Yarrell (Linn. transact. XVI. 1. 109. tb. II).   < *Oken's Isis*, Bd. xxiii, 1830, pp. 910-912.

1831. [BREE, W. T.]   Caractère servant à distinguer les deux sexes de la bécasse ordinaire.   (Scolopax rusticola); par W. F. Bree.   < *Féruss. Bull.*, 2e sect., xxiv, 1831, p. 368.
> Extrait du *Magaz. of Nat. Hist.*, iii, mars 1830, p. 147.

1831. "A SUBSCRIBER."   The Snipe's Beak.   < *Loudon's Mag. Nat. Hist*, iv, 1831, p. 383.
> Its use.

1831. GRAY, J. E.   [On Rhynchæa capensis and R. picta, sp. n.]   < *P. Z. S.*, i, 1831, p. 62.

1831. GRAY, [J. E.]   [Remarks on exhibition of specimens of Rhynchæa picta, lately n. sp.]   < *Philos. Mag.*, x, 1831, pp. 56, 57.
> From *P. Z. S.*, Apr. 26, 1831, p. 62.

1832. MACKENZIE, F.   [On the Breeding of Scolopax rusticola in Scotland.]   < *P. Z. S.*, ii, 1832, pp. 133, 134.

1832. [MACKENZIE, F.]   The Woodcock (Scolopax rusticola L.) resides through the Year, and breeds in Scotland.   < *Loudon's Mag. Nat. Hist.*, v, 1832, p. 570.

1832. SÖDERBERG, C.   Några ord om dubbla Becassinen (Scolopax [Gallinago] major).   < *Tidsk. f. Jägare o. Naturf.*, i, 1832, pp. 177–181.
> Not seen.

1832. G[OATLEY], T.   Identity of the Green Sandpiper [Totanus ochropus] and the Wood Sandpiper [Totanus glareola].   < *Loudon's Mag. Nat. Hist.*, v, 1832, pp. 81, 82.

1832. WATERTON, C.   The Woodcock [Scolopax rusticola].   < *Loudon's Mag. Nat. Hist.*, v, 1832, pp. 725–727.
> On the mode of transporting its young.

1833. D[ENSON], J.   A tame Godwit [Limosa sp.] destroyed by a wild Raven.   < *Loudon's Mag. Nat. Hist.*, vi, 1833, p. 145.

1833. DESJARDINS, J. [F.]   [Abstract of the Third Report of the Proceedings of the "Société d'Histoire Naturelle de l'Isle Maurice."]   < *P. Z. S.*, i, 1833, p. 117.
> Notice of the reading of a paper relating to *Totanus glottis* Cuv.

1833. DOUBLEDAY, E.   Green Sandpiper (Totanus ochropus.)   < *Loudon's Mag. Nat. Hist.*, vi, 1833, pp. 149, 150.

1833. EKSTRÖM, C. U.   Morkull [Scolopax rusticola]-Jagt.   < *Tidsk. f. Jägare o. Naturf.*, ii, 1833, pp. 449–460, fig.
> Not seen.

1833. MACKENZIE, F.   [On the breeding of Scolopax rusticola at Conan, Ross-shire.]   < *Lond. and Edinb. Philos. Mag.*, ii, 1833, pp. 68, 69.
> From *P. Z. S.*, July 24, 1832, pp. 133, 134.

1833. "T. G."   Sandpipers breed about Clitheroe, Lancashire.   < *Loudon's Mag. Nat. Hist.*, vi, 1833, pp. 148, 149.

1834. BERRY, H.   The Purre [Tringa cinclus] Breeds at Martin Mere, an extensive Water and Swamp in Lancashire.   < *Loudon's Mag. Nat. Hist.*, vii, 1834, p. 599.
> Cf. *op. cit.*, ix, 1836, pp. 326, 327.

1834. GRAY, [J. E.]   [Ueber Rhynchæa picta.]   < *Oken's Isis*, Bd. xxvii, 1834, p. 825.
> Auszug aus *Philos. Mag.*, x, 1831, pp. 56, 57.

1835. "A CONSTANT READER."   A Notice of an Unusual Individual of the Common Woodcock (Scólopax rusticola L.), or of an Individual of a Distinct Species   < *Loudon's Mag. Nat. Hist.*, viii, 1835, pp. 612, 613.

1835. BREE, W. T.   [Date of the Appearance of the Woodcock (Scolopax rusticola in Inland Localities.]   < *Loudon's Mag. Nat. Hist.*, viii, 1835, pp. 611, 612.

1835. BREHM, C. L.   Die Sumpfschnepfen.   Telmatias Boje.   < *Oken's Isis*, Bd. xxviii, 1835, pp. 116–126.
> 11 Arten.—*T. brehmii, salicaria, stagnatilis, gallinago, septentrionalis, rivalis, faeroensis, brachypus, lacustris, peregrina,* ——.—*T. salicaria*, Artkennzeichen, Beschreibung, Zergliederung, Aufenthalt, Betragen, Nahrung, Fortpflanzung.—*T. alticeps*, p. 123.

1835. BREHM, C. L.   Etwas über die Waldschnepfen.   Scolopax Linné, Cuvier, Boje, Brehm.   < *Oken's Isis*, Bd. xxviii, 1835, pp. 126, 127.

1835. GUILDING, L.   The Woodcock [Scolopax rusticola] occasionally breeds in Britain.   < *Loudon's Mag. Nat. Hist.*, viii, 1835, p. 612.

1835. GUILDING, L.   The Scólopax Sabìni (II. 207 [in reply to the query there].)   < *Loudon's Mag. Nat. Hist.*, viii, 1835, p. 614.

1835. MACKENZIE, F.   Ueber das Brüten von Scolopax rusticola.   < *Oken's Isis*, Bd. xxviii, 1835, p. 432.
  P. Z. S., 1832, pp. 133, 134; *Philos. Mag.*, 1833, pp. 68, 69.

1835. PALLISER, F.   [Early? Time of the Year for the Occurrence of a Nest of Young Woodcocks (Scolopax rusticola) in Britain.]   < *Loudon's Mag. Nat. Hist.*, viii, 1835, p. 612.

1835. "T. G."   A Pair of a Species of Bird, presumed to be Sabine's Snipe, (Scólopax Sabìni Vigors), shot in Lancashire.   < *Loudon's Mag. Nat. Hist.*, viii, 1835, pp. 613, 614.

1836. ANON.   The Woodcock [Scolopax rusticola].   < *Loudon's Mag. Nat. Hist.*, ix, 1836, pp. 543, 544.

1836. HODGSON, B. H.   [On the Scolopacidæ of Nipâl.]   < *P. Z. S.*, iv, 1836, pp. 7, 8.
  Gallinago heterura, G. solitaria, G. nemoricola, p. 8, spp. nn.

1836. HODGSON, B. H.   [On the Scolopacidæ of Nipâl.]   < *Lond. and Edinb. Philos. Journ.*, ix, 1836, pp. 143, 144.
  From *P. Z. S.*, Jan. 12, 1836, pp. 7, 8, *q. v.*

1836. SALMON, J. D.   The Purre's (Tringa Cinclus) Breeding at Martin Mere, Lancashire.   < *Loudon's Mag. Nat. Hist.*, ix, 1836, pp. 326, 327.
  Cf. *op. cit.*, vii, 1834, p. 599.

1836. WILLIAMSON, W. C.   Nests of the Woodcock [Scolopax rusticola] in England.   < *Loudon's Mag. Nat. Hist.*, ix, 1836, p. 543.

1836. YARRELL, W.   [Occurrence of Macrorhamphus griseus near Carlisle, England.]   < *P. Z. S.*, iv, 1836, pp. 1, 2.

1837. BLYTH, E.   The Green Sandpiper [Totanus ochropus, as a British Bird].   < *Charlesw. Mag. Nat. Hist.*, i, 1837, pp. 605, 606.

1837. EDITORIAL.   [Third occurrence in Britain of] Macrorampus [sic] griseus.   < *Mag. of Zool. and Bot.*, i, 1837, p. 104.

1837. EDITORIAL.   Tringa pectoralis, Buonap. [in Britain, near Yarmouth.]   < *Mag. of Zool. and Bot.*, i, 1837, p. 200.

1837. READ, W. H. R.   Woodcock [Scolopax rusticola] shot in July [in Britain].   < *Charlesw. Mag. Nat. Hist.*, i, 1837, p. 52.

1837. SALMON, J. D.   New Tringa [platyrhyncha], shot near Yarmouth.   < *Charlesw. Mag. Nat. Hist.*, i, 1837, p. 54.

1837. SKAIFE, J.   Two Specimens of the Green Sandpiper [Totanus ochropus] shot in August [in Lancashire].   < *Charlesw. Mag. Nat. Hist.*, i, 1837, p. 555.

1838. BLYTH, E.   Native Woodcocks.   < *Charlesw. Mag. Nat. Hist.*, ii, 1838, p. 396.

1838. HODGSON, [B. H.]   Ueber einige Scolopaciden aus Nipal.   < *Oken's Isis*, Bd. xxxi, 1838, p. 170.
  Auszüge aus *Proc. Zool. Soc. Lond.*, iv, 1836, p. 7, *q. v.*

1838. HORNSCHUCH, [C. F.], *und* SCHILLING, —.   Ornithologische Beiträge aus dem Zoologischen Museum der Universität zu Greifswald.   < *Arch. f. Naturg.*, 1838, (1), pp. 167–190.
  1. Ueber *Limosa meyeri* Leisl. und *Limosa rufa* Briss.   Sehr vollständig.

1838. "W. L."   Woodcocks [Scolopax rusticola] breeding in Ross-shire.   < *Charlesw. Mag. Nat. Hist.*, ii, 1838, pp. 347, 348.

1839. FULLER, A. E.   [Letter relating to the Breeding of Woodcocks (Scolopax rusticola) in Sussex.]   < *P. Z. S.*, vii, 1839, p. 111.

1839. KUTORGA, S.   Zwei Beobachtungen von Knochenbrüchen bei den Heerschnepfen (Scolopax gallinago [Gallinago media]).   < Bull. Soc. Imp. Nat. Moscou, xii, 1839, pp. 197–202, pl. xix.

1839. REINHARDT, J.   Om Ynglepladsen for Tringa platyrhyncha.   < Krøyer's Natur-hist. Tidsk., ii, 1839, pp. 431, 432.
  See Tidsk. for Naturvidensk, 5te Bind, p. 86.

1839. THOMPSON, W.   On the Breeding of the Woodcock (Scolopax rusticola, Linn.), in Ireland.   < Ann. Nat. Hist., ii, 1839, pp. 337–348.

1839. WILMOT, E. E.   Breeding of the Woodcock [Scolopax rusticola] in England.   < Charlesw. Mag. Nat. Hist., iii, 1839, p. 255.

1840. GURNEY, J. H.   Red-breasted Snipe [Macrorhamphus griseus, near Yarmouth, England].   < Ann. Mag. Nat. Hist., vi, 1840, p. 236.

1841. PARKINSON, J.   [Observations on the Habits of the Woodcock (Scolopax rusticola) with relation to the exactness of its migrations.]   < P. Z. S., ix, 1841, p. 79.

1841. REINHARDT, [J.]   Von der Brütestelle der Tringa platyrrhyncha.   < Oken's Isis, Bd. xxxiv, 1841, p. 416, 417.
  Krøyer's Naturh. Zeitsch., Bd. ii, Heft 4, 1839, pp. 431, 432.   Vergl. auch J. F. Naumann, Arch. f. Naturg., 1838, Bd. i, pp. 361 folg.

1842. HARTLAUB, G.   Notice sur l'Eurinorhynchus pygmæus Bonaparte.   < Revue Zoologique, v, 1842, pp. 36–38, pl. 2, fig. 1.
  Une petite monographie.

1842. PARKINSON, J.   [Letter on the tendency of the Woodcock [Scolopax rusticola] to return to the same spot.]   < Ann. Mag. Nat. Hist., ix, 1842, p. 344.
  From P. Z. S., Oct. 12, 1841, p. 79.

1843. ATKINSON, J. C.   Notes on the Redshank [Totanus calidris].   < Zoologist, i, 1843, pp. 233–237, fig.

1843. BROWN, E.   Note on the more frequent occurrence of the Woodcock [Scolopax rusticola, in Britain].   < Zoologist, i, 1843, p. 249.

1843. FISHER, W. R.   Note on the occurrence of the Buff-breasted Sandpiper [Tryn-gites rufescens] at Yarmouth.   < Zoologist, i, 1843, p. 363.

1843. FISHER, W. R.   Note on the Pigmy Curlew [Tringa subarquata] and Dunlin [T. alpina]   < Zoologist, i, 1843, p. 316.

1843. HEPPENSTALL, J.   Note on [the habits of] Woodcocks, and Snipes [Scolopacidæ].   < Zoologist, i, 1843, p. 15.

1843. HEWETT, W.   Anecdote of a Woodcock [Scolopax rusticola, in defense of her young].   < Zoologist, i, 1843, p. 362.

1843. JORDAN, R. C. R.   Note on [the breeding of] the Common Snipe [Gallinago media].   < Zoologist, i, 1843, p. 362.

1843. LEWCOCK, J.   Note on the Woodcock's [Scolopax rusticola] breeding in the Holt Forest, Hampshire.   < Zoologist, i, 1843, p. 189.

1843. [PARKINSON, J.]   Note on the occurrence of a [partially albinotic Scolopax rusticola] Woodcock near Torrington, for five successive years.   < Zoologist i, 1843, pp. 80, 81.
  From P. Z. S., 1841, p. 79.

1843. RODD, E. H.   Note on the occurrence of the Wood Sandpiper [Totanus glareola at Penzance.   < Zoologist, i, 1843, p. 189.

1843. RODD, E. H.   Note on the occurrence of the Dusky Sandpiper [Totanus fuscus in Cornwall.   < Zoologist, i, 1843, pp. 363, 364.

1843. SELBY, [P. J.]   Note on the occurrence of Woodcocks [Scolopax rusticola] a Twizell House, in July, 1842.   < Zoologist, i, 1843, p. 80.
  From Annnal Address of the President of the Berwickshire Nat. Club, Sept. 28, 1842.

1844. AUSTIN, T.   On the habits of the Godwit [Limosa sp.].   < *Ann. Mag. Nat. Hist.*, xiv, 1844, pp. 382, 383.

1844. BOND, F.   Note on rare Waders [Tringa subarquata and Totanus glottis] occurring at Kingsbury Reservoir.   < *Zoologist*, ii, 1844, p. 767.

1844. HEPPENSTALL, J.   Note on a Woodcock [Scolopax rusticola].   < *Zoologist*, ii, 1844, p. 667.

1844. HUSSEY, A.   Note on the Food of the Snipe tribe [Scolopacidæ].   < *Zoologist*, ii, 1844, p. 576.

1844. THOMPSON, W.   [Note on the breeding of the Woodcock (Scolopax rusticola) in Ireland.]   < *Rep. Brit. Assoc. Adv. Sci. for* 1843, xiii, 1844, (*Misc. Comm.*), p. 71.

1844. THOMPSON, W.   Ueber das Brüten von Scolopax rusticola in Irland.   < *Oken's Isis*, Bd. xxxvii, 1844, p. 730.
    Ann. Nat. Hist., Bd. ii, No. xi, 1839, pp. 337-348.

1845. CABOT, S., JR.   [Occurrence of Scolopax noveboracensis (Macrorhamphus griseus) in Massachusetts.]   < *Proc. Bost. Soc. Nat. Hist.*, ii, 1845, p. 46.

1845. COOPER, J.   On the Noise made by the Snipe [Gallinago].   < *Zoologist*, iii, 1845, pp. 1192, 1193.

1845. EVERSMANN, E.   Nachricht ueber eine noch unbeschriebene Sumpfschnepfe (Scolopax [hyemalis]) aus dem Altai Gebirges.   < *Bull. Soc. Imp. Nat. Moscou*, xviii, pt. i, 1845, pp. 257–262, pl. vi.

1845. FRERE, H. F.   Flight of the Woodcock [Scolopax rusticola].   < *Zoologist*, 1845, pp. 876, 877.

1845. HORNE, C.   A young Woodcock [Scolopax rusticola] shot on Cairn Monarin.   < *Zoologist*, iii, 1845, p. 1137.

1845. KNOX, A. E.   Occurrence of Sabine's Snipe [Gallinago sabinii] in Sussex.   < *Zoologist*, iii, 1845, p. 1025.

1845. NEWTON, A.   Occurrence of the Spotted Redshank [Totanus fuscus] at Elden.   < *Zoologist*, iii, 1845, p. 877.

1846. COOPER, J.   On the Noise made by the Snipe [Gallinago media].   < *Zoologist*, iv, 1846, pp. 1552–1554.

1846. DAVIS, R., JR.   Occurrence of Sabine's Snipe [Gallinago sabinii] near Clonmel.   < *Zoologist*, iv, 1846, pp. 1500, 1501.

1846. FISHER, W. R.   Note on the Sound produced by the Common Snipe [Gallinago media].   < *Zoologist*, iv, 1846, p. 1501.

1846. RODD, E. H.   Occurrence of the Buff-breasted Sandpiper (Tringa [Tryngites] rufecens), at Penzance.   < *Zoologist*, iv, 1846, p. 1500.

1846. RODD, E. H.   Occurrence of Tringa Schinzii [i. e., T. bonapartii] near Penzance.   < *Zoologist*, iv, 1846, p. 1554.

1846. ROSS, W. F. L.   Snipe [Gallinago gallinula] in captivity.   < *Zoologist*, iv, 1846, p. 1331.

1846. SCLATER, P. L.   Occurrence of Sabine's Snipe [Gallinago sabinii] in Hampshire.   < *Zoologist*, iv, 1846, p. 1300.

1847. COGSWELL, C.   A tame Snipe [Gallinago media].   < *Zoologist*, v, 1847, pp. 1640, 1641.

1847. FRERE, H. T.   Note on the Common Sandpiper [Tringoides hypoleucus] and Woodcock [Scolopax rusticola].   < *Zoologist*, v, 1847, p. 1876.

1847. SMITH, JAMES, Rev.   Occurrence of the Bar-tailed Godwit [Limosa rufa] near Banff.   < *Zoologist*, v, 1847, p. 1910.

1847. [ST. JOHN, C.]   Migration of the Woodcock [Scolopax rusticola].   < *Zoologist*, v, 1847, p. 1877.
    From his " Wild Sports in the Highlands."

1848. BOLD, T. J.   Occurrence of the Green Sandpiper (Totanus ochropus) at Cambo, Northumberland. < *Zoologist*, vi, 1848, p. 2066.

1848. COOKE, N.   Description of a Sandpiper [Totanus glareola?] which was shot near Bootle, in September, 1847. < *Zoologist*, vi, 1848, pp. 2303, 2304.

1848. FALCONER, A. P.   Woodcocks (Scolopax rusticola) drowned in crossing the Channel. < *Zoologist*, vi, 1848, pp. 2023, 2024.

1848. FISHER, W. R.   Enquiry respecting the Egg of the Greenshank [Totanus glottis]. < *Zoologist*, vi, 1848, p. 2024.

1848. FISHER, W. R.   Egg of the Greenshank (Totanus Glottis). < *Zoologist*, vi, 1848, pp. 2147, 2148.

1848. GOATLEY, T.   Nest of the Woodcock (Scolopax rusticola). < *Zoologist*, vi, 1848, p. 2148.

1848. HIGGINS, E. T.   Occurrence of the Spotted Sandpiper (Totanus [Tringoides] macularius) in Yorkshire. < *Zoologist*, vi, 1848, p. 2147.

1848. MILNER, W. M. E.   Egg of the Greenshank (Totanus glottis). < *Zoologist*, vi, 1848, p. 2066.

1848. MILNER, W. M. E.   Egg of the Greenshank (Totanus glottis). < *Zoologist*, vi, 1848, p. 2230.

1848. NEWTON, A.   Woodcock's (Scolopax rusticola) breeding in Norfolk. < *Zoologist*, vi, 1848, p. 2148.

1848. RODD, E. H.   Occurrence of Temminck's Stint (Tringa Temminckii) near Penzance. < *Zoologist*, vi, 1848, p. 2259.

1848. ROUNDELL, H.   Occurrence of Temminck's Stint [Tringa temmincki] near Oxford. < *Zoologist*, vi, 1848, p. 1969.

1849. DUFF, J.   Occurrence of the Spotted Sandpiper (Totanus [Tringoides] macularius) near Bishop's Aukland. < *Zoologist*, vii, 1849, p. 2499.

1849. FOSTER, T. W.   Occurrence of the Black-tailed Godwit (Limosa melanura) on Guyhirn Wash. < *Zoologist*, vii, 1849, p. 2499.

1849. ELLMAN, J. B.   Occurrence of the Bar-tailed Godwit (Limosa rufa) in December, and the Landrail (Crex pratensis) in December and February [in England]. < *Zoologist*, vii, 1849, p. 2419.

1849. ELLMAN, J. B.   Occurrence of the Little Stint (Tringa minuta) at Rye. < *Zoologist*, vii, 1849, p. 2529.

1849. ELLMAN, J. B.   Occurrence of the Little Stint (Tringa minuta) at Rye. < *Zoologist*, vii, 1849, p. 2569.

1849. GURNEY, J. H.   [Supposed] Occurrence of the Pectoral Sandpiper (Tringa pectoralis) near Yarmouth. < *Zoologist*, vii, 1849, p. 2392.
    Cf. *Zoologist*, p. 2568.

1849. GURNEY, J. H.   Correction of an Error respecting the Pectoral Sandpiper [Zool. p. 2392]. < *Zoologist*, vii, 1849, p. 2568.

1849. HANSELL, P. E.   The Jack Snipe (Scolopax [Gallinago] gallinula) breeding in Norfolk. < *Zoologist*, vii, 1849, p. 2456.

1849. HIGGINS, E. T.   Occurrence of the Spotted Sandpiper [Tringoides macularius] near York. < *Zoologist*, vii, 1849, p. 2456.

1849. HULKE, J. W.   Departure [from Deal] of the Snipe (Scolopax gallinago [Gallinago media]) in 1849. < *Zoologist*, vii, 1849, p. 2421.

1849. J[ARDINE], W.   Gallinago brehmi [shot at Jardine Hall]. < *Ann. Mag. Nat. Hist.*, 2d ser., iv, 1849, p. 382.

1849. MILNER, W. M. E.   Occurrence of the Spotted Sandpiper (Totanus [Tringoides macularius) at Whitby. < *Zoologist*, vii, 1849, pp. 2455, 2456.

1849. MORRIS, B. R.   Note on the Tail-feathers of the Green Sandpiper (Totanus ochropus).   *< Zoologist*, vii, 1849, p. 2352.

1849. RODD, E. H.   Occurrence of Temminck's Stint (Tringa Temminckii) near Penzance.   *< Zoologist*, vii, 1849, p. 2591.

1849. TOMES, R. F.   Occurrence of Scolopax [Gallinago] Brehmi in Scotland.   *< Zoologist*, vii, 1849, p. 2621.

1850. BOND, F.   Occurrence of Scolopax [Gallinago] Brehmi (?) near London.   *< Zoologist*, viii, 1850, pp. 2703, 2704.

1850. BREHM, [C.] L.   Ueber die europäischen Arten des Genus Calidris Illiger.   *< Naumannia*, i, Heft ii, 1850, pp. 66–69.
    C. mülleri, p. 66, n. sp.; *C. americana, C. arenaria, C. grisea.*

1850. ELLMAN, J. B.   Occurrence of the Great Snipe (Scolopax [Gallinago] major) at Lewes.   *< Zoologist*, viii, 1850, p. 2703.

1850. FOSTER, T. W.   Occurrence of the Black-tailed Godwit (Limosa melanura) near Wisbech.   *< Zoologist*, viii, 1850, p. 2853.

1850. FOSTER, T. W.   Occurrence of the Whimbrel (Numenius Phæopus) at Sutton.   *< Zoologist*, viii, 1850, p. 2853.

1850. GREEN, I.   Occurrence of the Wood Sandpiper [Totanus glareola] at Woolwich.   *< Zoologist*, viii, 1850, p. 2853.

1850. HIGGINS, E. T.   The Supposed New Snipe [Gallinago brehmi].   *< Zoologist*, viii, 1850, pp. 2800, 2801.

1850. HULKE, J. W.   Occurrence of the Curlew Sandpiper (Tringa subarquata) and Temminck's Stint (Tringa Temminckii), &c., at Shingle End, near Deal.   *< Zoologist*, viii, 1850, pp. 2923, 2924.

1850. [JARDINE, W.]   Scolopax brehmi.   *< Jard. Contrib. Orn.*, 1850, pp. 17, 18, pl. xl.

1850. JONES, J. M.   The Snipe (Scolopax gallinago [Gallinago media]) in South Lancashire.   *< Zoologist*, viii, 1850, pp. 2771, 2772.

1850. SMITH, JAMES, *Rev.*   Note on the [habits of the] Sanderling (Calidris arenaria).   *< Zoologist*, viii, 1850, p. 2915.

1851. ELLMAN, J. B.   Occurrence of the Little Stint [Tringa minuta] at Pevensey, Sussex.   *< Zoologist*, ix, 1851, p. 3279.

1851. ELLMAN, J. B.   Occurrence of the Wood Sandpiper [Totanus glareola] at Newhaven, Sussex.   *< Zoologist*, ix, 1851, p. 3279.

1851. ELLMAN, J. B.   Occurrence of the Spotted Redshank [Totanus fuscus] at Eastbourne, Sussex.   *< Zoologist*, ix, 1851, p. 3279.

1851. ELLMAN, J. B.   Occurrence of Temminck's Stint [Tringa temmincki] at Newhaven, Sussex.   *< Zoologist*, ix, 1851, p. 3279.

1851. HANSELL, P. E.   The Great Snipe (Scolopax [Gallinago] major) breeding in Norfolk.   *< Zoologist*, ix, 1851, p. 3175.

1851. HUSSEY, A.   Woodcock [Scolopax rusticola] Breeding in Sussex.   *< Zoologist*, ix, 1851, pp. 2989, 2990.

1851. IRBY, L. H.   Occurrence of the Wood Sandpiper (Totanus glareola) at Yarmouth.   *< Zoologist*, ix, 1851, p. 3035.

1851. NEWMAN, E.   White Specimen of the Knot [Tringa canutus].   *< Zoologist*, ix, 1851, p. 3116.

1851. NEWTON, E.   Occurrence of the Spotted Redshank [Totanus fuscus] in Suffolk.   *< Zoologist*, ix, 1851, p. 3279.

1851. REEVES, W. W.   Woodcock [Scolopax rusticola] breeding in Sussex.   *< Zoologist*, ix, 1851, pp. 3115, 3116.

1851. RODD, E. H.   Flight of Woodcocks [Scolopax rusticola] at the Land's End.   *< Zoologist*, ix, 1851, p. 3300.

1851. RODD, E. H. Occurrence of the Little Stint (Tringa minuta) at Scilly. < *Zo-ologist*, ix, 1851, p. 3279.

1852. ANON. Woodcock's [Scolopax rusticola] Nest. < *Zoologist*, x, 1852, p. 3579.
From the "Sussex Express," July 31, 1852.

1852. BELL, J. [G.] Observations on the Limosa Scolopacea of Say. < *Ann. Lyc. Nat. Hist. New York*, v, 1852, pp. 1–3. (Read Oct. 9, 1848. Whole vol. pub. 1852.)
Renames it *Scolopax longirostris*, sp. n. See 1852, LAWRENCE, G. N.

1852. BELL, T. Occurrence of the Spotted Redshank (Totanus fuscus) at Selborne.
< *Zoologist*, x, 1852, p. 3330.

1852. BIRD, W. F. W. Instances of the Woodcock (Scolopax rusticola) breeding in
England. < *Zoologist*, x, 1852, pp. 3578, 3579.

1852. BLYTH, E. Illustrations of Indian Ornithology. II. Rhynchea bengalensis.
< *Jard. Contrib. Orn.*, 1852, pp. 52, 53, pl. lxxxix, f. 1, 2, 3.

1852. GURNEY, J. H. Note on the Sandpiper [Actiturus bartramius?] described by
Mr. Reid [Zool., p. 3330]. < *Zoologist*, x, 1852, p. 3388.

1852. HAWKINS, R. W. Nesting of the Woodcock [Scolopax rusticola] in Stafford-shire. < *Zoologist*, x, 1852, p. 3579.

1852. IRBY, L. H. Occurrence of the Wood Sandpiper (Totanus glareola) at Yar-mouth. < *Zoologist*, x, 1852, p. 3504.

1852. KAPLICK, [L. v.] Zur Naturgeschichte der Waldschnepfe, Scolopax rusticola.
L. < *Naumannia*, ii, Heft ii, 1852, pp. 79–81.

1852. LAWRENCE, G. N. Observations on the preceding Paper [i. e., Observations on
the Limosa Scolopacea of Say, by John Bell]. < *Ann. Lyc. Nat. Hist. New
York*, v, 1852, pp. 4, 5, pl. i. (Read Jan. 9, 1849. Whole vol. pub. 1852.)
Restores Say's name, *scolopacea*, to the species named *Scolopax longirostris* by Bell, and re-fers it to the genus *Macror[h]amphus*. The species is here figured. See 1852, BELL, J. G.

1852. LEEMING, J. G. Occurrence of the Curlew Sandpiper [Tringa subarquata] at
Fleetwood. < *Zoologist*, x, 1852, p. 3331.

1852. LEEMING, J. G. Occurrence of the Little Stint [Tringa minuta] at Fleetwood.
< *Zoologist*, x, 1852, p. 3331.

1852. NORMAN, A. M. Occurrence of the Great Snipe (Scolopax [Gallinago] major)
at Botley. < *Zoologist*, x, 1852, p. 3330.

1852. PÄSSLER, W. Berichtigung [Naumannia, i, Heft ii, 1850, p. 50]. < *Nauman-nia*, ii, Heft i, 1852, p. 95.
Dass nicht *Totanus glareola*, sondern *T. ochropus*, auf Bäumen niste.

1852. PRÄLLE, W. A. E. Ueber das Meckern der Becassine, Scolopax gallinago [Gal-linago media]. < *Naumannia*, ii, Heft i, 1852, pp. 24–26.

1852. REID, H. Inquiry respecting a Species of Sandpiper [Actiturus bartramius? in
Great Britain; see Zool., p. 3388]. < *Zoologist*, x, 1852, pp. 3330, 3331.

1852. RODD, E. H. Occurrence of the Wood Sandpiper [Totanus glareola] at Land's
End. < *Zoologist*, x, 1852, p. 3454.

1852. WOODHOUSE, S. W. Description of a new species of Numineus [sic—N. occi
dentalis] (Moehr.) < *Proc. Acad. Nat. Sci. Phila.*, vi, 1852, pp. 194, 195.

1853. BALDAMUS, E. [Die Waldschnepfe (Scolopax rusticola) . . .] < *Naumannia*
iii, 1853, pp. 453, 454.

1853. BREE, C. R. Note on the abundance of Woodcocks [Scolopax rusticola] in par-ticular Localities. < *Zoologist*, xi, 1853, p. 3807.

1853. BUXTON, E. C. Note on Woodcocks [Scolopax rusticola] nesting in Sutherland
shire, and carrying their Young in their Claws. < *Zoologist*, xi, 1853, p. 401?

1853. GARLAND, J. Note on the Woodcock, (Scolopax rusticola). < *Zoologist*, x
1853, p. 4124.

1853. GURNEY, J. H.   Note on the occurrence of the Knot Sandpiper (Tringa cinerea) on the Norfolk Coast, in the Summer Plumage. < *Zoologist*, xi, 1853, p. 3946.

1853. HAWKER, W. H.   Note on Woodcocks' [Scolopax rusticola] Nests in the Forest of Bere, and in Highden Wood, Hants. < *Zoologist*, xi, 1853, pp. 3909, 3910.

1853. IRBY, L. H.   Notes on the Habits of the Green Sandpiper, (Totanus ochropus). < *Zoologist*, xi, 1853, pp. 3988, 3989.

1853. JOHNSON, J.   Note on the abundance of Woodcocks [Scolopax rusticola, near Huddersfield]. < *Zoologist*, xi, 1853, p. 3909.

1853. KING, E. L.   Occurrence of the Green Sandpiper (Totanus ochropus) near Lynn. < *Zoologist*, xi, 1853, p. 3807.

1853. KNAPP, W.   Woodcock [Scolopax rusticola] breeding in England. < *Zoologist*, xi, 1853, p. 3754.

1853. MATTHEWS, A.   [Critical] Remarks on Scolopax Delamotti. < *Zoologist*, xi, 1853, pp. 3729–3733.

1853. NEWTON, A.   Note on the supposed Abundance of Woodcocks (Scolopax rusticola) in Norfolk. < *Zoologist*, xi, 1853, pp. 3754, 3755.

1853. PICKARD-CAMBRIDGE, O.   Woodcocks [Scolopax rusticola] breeding in this [England] country. < *Zoologist*, xi, 1853, pp. 3910, 3911.

1853. RODD, E. H.   Unusually large Woodcock [Scolopax rusticola]. < *Zoologist*, xi, 1853, p. 3754.

1853. RODD, E. H.   Occurrence of Temminck's Stint (Tringa Temminckii) near Penzance. < *Zoologist*, xi, 1853, p. 4053.

1853. TRISTRAM, H. B.   Occurrence of the Great Snipe (Scolopax major) near Durham. < *Zoologist*, xi, 1853, p. 3911.

1854. [BALDAMUS, E.]   [In Betreff der Waldschnepfe, Scolopax rusticula . . .] < *Naumannia*, iv, 1854, pp. 395, 396.

1854. MORE, A. G.   Bartram's Sandpiper [Actiturus bartramius] as a British Bird. < *Zoologist*, xii, 1854, pp. 4254, 4255.

1854. RODD, E. H.   Occurrence of the American Stint (Tringa pusilla [minutilla]) near Penzance. < *Zoologist*, xii, 1854, pp. 4296–4298.

1854. WESTERMAN, G. F.   Beschrijving van Tringa [Prosobonia] leucoptera. < *Bijdrag. tot de Dierk.*, Deel i, Zesde Aflevering, pp. 51, 52, met eene Afbeelding.

1855. ALTUM, B.   Ueber das Meckern der Bekassine [Gallinago media]. < *Naumannia*, 1855, pp. 362–371.

1855. ATKINSON, J. C.   Memorandum on the Habits of the Jack Snipe [Gallinago gallinula]. < *Zoologist*, xiii, 1855, pp. 4656–4660.

1855. BOLD, T. J.   Occurrence of the Pectoral Sandpiper (Tringa pectoralis) on the Coast of Northumberland. < *Zoologist*, xiii, 1855, p. 4808.

1855. BOLD, T. J.   Occurrence of the Ruff (Tringa [Machetes] pugnax ♂) at Prestwick Carr, Northumberland. < *Zoologist*, xiii, 1855, p. 4560.

1855. COOKE, N.   Occurrence of the Pigmy Curlew (Tringa subarquata) and Little Stint (T. minuta) near Warrington. < *Zoologist*, xiii, 1855, p. 4560.

1855. GADAMER, [H.]   2. Zur Naturgeschichte des Numenius arquata. < *Naumannia*, v, 1855, pp. 92–94.

1855. JÄCKEL, [A. J.]   Berichtigung. < *Naumannia*, 1855, pp. 112, 113.
    Cf. L. Ziegler, *Federwild-Jagd* (Hannover, 1846), p. 174, über das Meckern der Bekassine, *Scolopax gallinago* [Gallinago media].

1855. MÜLLER, — v.   [Ueber Scolopax rusticula, major, gallinago, gallinula. und Limicola pygmæa.] < *Naumannia*, v, 1855, pp. 105–107.

1855. NEWMAN, E.   Remarkable Variety of the Woodcock [albinotic Scolopax rusticola]. < *Zoologist*, xiii, 1855, p. 4631.

1855. RODD, E. H.   Occurrence of the Solitary Snipe [Gallinago major] near Penzance.
   < Zoologist, xiii, 1855, p. 4895.

1855. RODD, E. H.   Supposed New Snipe.   < Zoologist, xiii, 1855, p. 4704.
   Cf. Zoologist, xx, 1862, p. 7938.

1856. GLOGER, C. W. L.   Auch der ·Uferläufer (Actitis hypoleuca) sitzt zuweilen auf
   Bäumen, . . .   < J. f. O., iv, 1856, pp. 382, 384.

1856. HADFIELD, H. W.   Gray Longbeak (Macrorhamphus griseus) [in the Isle of
   Wight].   < Zoologist, xiv, 1856, p. 5251.

1856. JÄCKEL, [A.] J.   Noch ein Wort über das Schnurren der Becassine [Gallinago
   media].   < J. f. O., iv, 1856, pp. 85–94.

1856. JÄCKEL, [A. J.]   [Ueber Limicola pygmæa.]   < Naumannia, vi, 1856, p. 528.

1856. RODD, E. H.   Remarkable Flight of Woodcocks [Scolopax rusticola].   < Zoologist, xiv, 1856, pp. 4946, 4947.

1856. STEVENSON, H.   Note on the Broadbilled Sandpiper [Tringa platyrhyncha] in
   Norfolk.   < Zoologist, xiv, 1856, p. 5160.

1856. WALLENGREN, H. D. J.   Berichtigung.   < Naumannia, vi, 1856, p. 428.
   Catoptrophorus semipalmatus betreffend.

1857. GADAMER, [H.]   Noch einmal das Meckern der Bekassine [Gallinago media].
   < Naumannia, vii, 1857, Heft i, pp. 83, 84.

1857. GRAHAM, D.   The Great Snipe (Scolopax [Gallinago] major) shot near York.
   < Zoologist, xv, 1857, p. 5833.

1857. HOFFMANN, J.   Die Waldschnepfe [Scolopax rusticola] falzt und nistet zwei-
   mal im Jahr.   < Naumannia, vii, 1857, Heft ii, pp. 79–82.

1857. JÄCKEL, [A.] J.   Das Schnurren oder Mäckern der Bekassine [Gallinago media].
   < Naumannia, vii, 1857, Heft i, pp. 21–33.

1857. MÜNCHHAUSEN, B. v.   [Scolopax rusticula in trockner Haide, . . .]   < Naumannia, vii, 1857, Heft ii, pp. 83, 84.

1857. NICHOLLS, H.   The Buffbreasted Sandpiper (Tringa [Tryngites] rufescens) and
   Brown Snipe (Scolopax [Macrorhamphus] grisea) in Devonshire.   < Zoologist, xv, 1857, p. 5791.

1857. RODD, E. H.   Occurrence of Temminck's Stint (Tringa Temminckii) at Scilly.
   < Zoologist, xv, 1857, p. 5832.

1857. RODD, E. H.   Occurrence of the Brown Snipe (Scolopax [Macrorhamphus] grisea) at Scilly.   < Zoologist, xv, 1857, pp. 5832, 5833.

1857. RODD, E. H.   Occurrence of the Great Snipe [Gallinago major] at Land's End.
   < Zoologist, xv, 1857, p. 5856.

1857. SALVIN, O.   Note on the Sabine's Snipe [Gallinago sabinii] killed in Norfolk.
   < Zoologist, xv, 1857, pp. 5593, 5594.

1857. SCHACH, C. F.   Ueber das Meckern der Becassine [Gallinago media].   < Mittheil. aus d. Osterl., xiii, 1857, pp. 193–198.
   Not seen—title from Carus and Engelmann.

1857. STEVENSON, H.   Occurrence of Sabine's Snipe (Scolopax [Gallinago] Sabini) in
   Norfolk.   < Zoologist, xv, 1857, pp. 5427, 5428.

1857. STEVENSON, H.   Beautiful [albinotic] Variety of the Common Woodcock [Sco-
   lopax rusticola].   < Zoologist, xv, 1857, p. 5365.

1857. TACZANOWSKY, —.   [Gallinago major kämpft wie Machetes pugnax.]   < Naumannia, vii, 1857, p. 182.

1858. BALDAMUS, E.   Einige neue oder weniger bekannte Eier.   < Naumannia, viii,
   1858, pp. 252, 253, Taf. ii.
   Totanus fuscus, fig. 1; T. glottis, f. 2; Limicola pygmæa, f. 3.

1858. BUCKLEY, H.   Occurrence of the Wood Sandpiper [Totanus glareola] near Birmingham.   < Zoologist, xvi, 1858, p. 6266.

1858. GADAMER, H.   Das Balzen der Scolopax [Gallinago] major.   < *J. f. O.*, vi, 1858, pp. 235–237.

1858. JÄCKEL, [A. J.]   Ueber das Schnurren der Bekassine [Gallinago media].   < *Naumannia*, viii, 1858, pp. 490–495.

1858. KÖNIG-WARTHAUSEN, R.   [Eier von Numenius arquatus.]   < *Naumannia*, viii, 1858, pp. 508, 509.

1858. MEVES, W.   On the Snipes' "neighing" or humming noise, and on its Tail-feathers' systematic value.   < *P. Z. S.*, xxvi, 1858, pp. 199–202, woodcc.
    Contains remarks by the translator, J. Wolley, Jr.

1858. MEVES, W.   On the Snipe's "neighing" or humming noise and on its Tail-feathers' systematic value.   < *Ann. Mag. Nat. Hist.*, 3d ser., 1858, pp. 303–306.
    From *P. Z. S.*, Apr. 13, 1858, pp. 199–202.

1858. STEVENSON, H.   Occurrence of the Broad-billed Sandpiper (Tringa platyrhynca [sic]) for the third time in Norfolk.   < *Zoologist*, xvi, 1858, p. 6096.

1858. THOMPSON, W.   Occurrence of the Pigmy Curlew [Tringa subarquata] at Weymouth.   < *Zoologist*, xvi, 1858, p. 6244.

1859. BUXTON, T. F.   Woodcock's [Scolopax rusticola] Nest in Norfolk.   < *Zoologist*, xvii, 1859, p. 6562.

1859. GRAY, G. R.   [Exhibition of a drawing of Tringa pectoralis.]   < *P. Z. S.*, xxvii, 1859, p. 130.

1859. HARTLAUB, G.   Ueber Eurinorhynchus pygmaeus (Lin.)   < *J. f. O.*, vii, 1859, pp. 325–329.
    History, synonymy, description.

1859. MATHEWS, M. A.   Notes on the Wood Sandpiper [Totanus glareola] and Dunlin [Tringa alpina].   < *Zoologist*, xvii, 1859, pp. 6728, 6729.

1860. BORGGREVE, B.   Auch ein Wort über das Meckern der Bekassine [Gallinago media].   < *J. f. O.*, viii, 1860, pp. 63–73.
    Vergl. einige Bemerkungen zu diesem Aufsatze von Jäckel, in diesem Journale, Jahrg. 1862, S. 212 und folgg.

1860. LILLJEBORG, W.   Notiz über Linné's Original-Exemplar der Platalea pygmaea. (Anmerkung des Herausgebers.)   < *J. f. O.*, viii, 1860, pp. 299, 230.
    Eurynorhynchus pygmæus.   Cf. *J. f. O.*, 1860, p. 460.

1860. [MEVES, W.?]   En Notits om Bekkasinerne [Gallinago].   < *Tidssk. Pop. Fremst. af Naturv.*, 2en Række, ii, 1860, p. 444.
    Cf. *op. cit.*, iii, 1861, p. 302.   See 1858, MEVES, W.

1860. PARFITT, E.   Snipes in Summer [in Bridgwater, England].   < *Zoologist*, xviii, 1860, p. 7172.

1860. PELZELN, A. v.   Notiz über Linné's Original-Exemplar der Platalea pygmaea.   < *J. f. O.*, viii, 1860, pp. 460, 461.
    Eurynorhynchus pygmæus.   Cf. *J. f. O.*, 1860, p. 299.

1860. RODD, E. H.   Occurrence of the Buffbreasted Sandpiper (Tringa [Tryngites] rufescens) near the Land's End.   < *Zoologist*, xviii, 1860, p. 7236.

1860. SAVILLE, S. P.   Great Mortality amongst Woodcocks (Scolopax rusticola).   < *Zoologist*, xviii, 1860, p. 6982.

1860. SAVILLE, S. P.   Occurrence of the Whimbrel (Numenius phæopus) in Cambridgeshire.   < *Zoologist*, xviii, 1860, p. 7146.

1860. VERREAUX, J. P.   Description d'un Oiseau nouveau [Micropalama tacksanowskia].   < *Rev. et Mag. de Zool.*, xii, 1860, pp. 206, 207, pl. xiv.
    Later identified with *Pseudoscolopax semipalmatus.*

1861. BRUN, A.   Nogle Bemærkninger i Anledning af en Notits om Beccassinerne, i dette Tidsskrifts 2det Bind for 1860.   < *Tidssk. Pop. Fremst. af Naturv.*, 2en Række, iii, 1861, pp. 302–310, fig. p. 306.
    Musical notation.   Cf. *op. cit.*, ii, 1860, p. 444.

1861. Coues, E.   A Monograph of the Tringeæ of North America.   < *Proc. Acad. Nat. Sci. Phila.*, xiii, 1861, pp. 170–205.

This paper becomes somewhat conspicuous in the literature of *Scolopacidæ*, owing to the fact that we have no great monographs or iconographies in this family of birds. It is the "maiden" effort of a very youthful author, who appears to have been too timid and too inexperienced to do any very brilliant blundering. On this account we may perhaps justify Dr. Sclater's very generous mention of Mr. Coues's as a "name new to ornithologists, but not the less heartily welcome as that of a recruit to our ranks, who begins by fighting his first fight well, and against a very hard subject" (*Ibis*, 1862, p. 84). We may add on our own account that no material modification of the specific determinations of North American Sandpipers has since been made. Two or three additional species have since been ascertained to inhabit this country; but otherwise, the species stand very nearly as Mr. Coues left them twenty years ago. The following genera and species are treated, with synonymy, diagnosis, description, habitat, and general criticism:

1. *Micropalama himantopus* (Bp.) Bd.   2. *Ereunetes pusillus* (L.) Cass.   3. *Tringa canutus* L.   4. *Calidris arenaria* (L.) Ill.   5. *Arquatella maritima* (Brünn.) Bd.   6. *Ancylocheilus subarquata* (Güld.) Kaup.   7. *Pelidna americana* (Cass.) Coues.   (*P. pacifica*, Coues, n. sp. prob., p. 189.)   8. *Actodromas minutilla* (V.) Coues.   9. *Actodromas bairdii* Coues, n. sp., p. 194.   10. *Actodromas maculata* (V.) Cass.   11. *Actodromas (Heteropygia* sive *Delopygia*, subg. n., p. 190) *bonapartei* (Schl.) Cass.   12. *Actodromas (Heteropygia) cooperi* (Bd.) Coues.   Three species attributed to North America by other authors are noticed and discarded: *Actodromas minuta*; *A. temminckii*; *Limicola pygmæa*. The new species, *A. bairdi*, has been considered invalid by Schlegel, who evidently knew nothing about it. The specific distinction of *Pelidna americana* from *P. alpina* is very questionable, and not now generally conceded.

The Sandpipers ascribed to North America since the appearance of this monograph are the following: 1. *Ereunetes occidentalis* Lawr., *Pr. Phila. Acad.*, 1864, p. 107: doubtfully distinct from *E. pusillus*. 2. *Tringa ptilocnemis* Coues, *Elliott's Rep. Pribylov Islands*, 4to, 1873, not paged; this is *T. crasirostris* Dall, *Am. Nat.*, viii, 1873, p. 635, and *T. gracilis* Harting, *P. Z. S.*, 1874, p. 242, pl. 40. It has proved to be an *Arquatella*, and very near *A. maritima*. 3. *Arquatella couesi*, Ridgw., *Bull. Nutt. Ornith. Club*, v, 1880, p. 160.

No second second specimen of *Tringa cooperi* has ever come to light. The new species of this paper, *A. bairdii*, has proved to be a very common bird of North and South America, before confounded with *bonapartii*, from which it is utterly different. It may have had a prior name, but none such has been established. The suggested "*Pelidna pacifica*" has never been confirmed. The races of *Ereunetes* remarked upon have not since been recognized and are doubtless invalid. Dr. Coues and some others have since adopted Vieillot's name, *fuscicollis*, for what is here called *bonapartii*; but the applicability of the name to this species seems doubtful.—W. S.

1861. "C. W."   Die Kampfhähne [Machetes pugnax, in Gefangenschaft]. . . .   < *Zool. Gart.*, ii, 1861, p. 116.

1861. Gadamer, H.   Das Balzen von Scolopax rusticula.   < *J. f. O.*, ix, 1861, p. 217.

1861. Gloger, C. W. L.   Das Balzen von Scolopax rusticula betreffend.   < *J. f. O.*, ix, 1861, pp. 289, 290.

1862. Barclay, W. L.   Occurrence of the Green Sandpiper [Totanus ochropus] at Leyton.   < *Zoologist*, xx, 1862, p. 7939.

1862. Blake-Knox, H.   The Common Sandpiper [Tringoides hypoleucus] a Diver.   < *Zoologist*, xx, 1862, pp. 8195, 8196.

1862. Blakiston, T.   Occurrence of the Knot [Tringa canutus] in Lancashire in August, and its Eastern Range.   < *Zoologist*, xx, 1862, p. 8287.

1862. Bond, F.   Note on Sabine's Snipe [Gallinago sabini].   < *Zoologist*, xx, 1862, p. 8000.

1862. Bond, F.   Jack Snipe [plumage of Gallinago gallinula].   < *Zoologist*, xx, 1862, p. 8000.

1862. Gatcombe, J.   Variety of Snipe [Zool., p. 4704].   < *Zoologist*, xx, 1862, pp. 7938, 7939.

1862. Gatcombe, J.   Note on Sabine's Snipe [Gallinago sabinii].   < *Zoologist*, xx, 1862, p. 8035.

1862. Green, G. C.   The Sandpiper [Tringoides hypoleucus] a Diver.   < *Zoologist*, xx, 1862, p. 8283.

1862. HARVIE-BROWN, J. A.   The Sandpiper [Tringoides hypoleucus] a Diver.   < *Zoologist*, xx, 1862, p. 8237.

1862. HOLLIS, W.   Snipes' Nests in Oxfordshire.   < *Zoologist*, xx, 1862, p. 8169.

1862. HORSFALL, W. C.   Occurrence of the Great Snipe [Gallinago major] near Malham, in Yorkshire.   < *Zoologist*, xx, 1862, p. 8196.

1862. JÄCKEL, A. J.   Einige Bemerkungen zu dem Aufsatze: ,,Auch ein Wort über das Meckern der Bekassine von B. Borggreve" in diesem Journale, Jahrg. 1860, S. 63 ff.   < *J. f. O.*, x, 1862, pp. 212–223.

1862. LEVEN, R. W.   The Sandpiper [Tringoides hypoleucus] a Diver.   < *Zoologist*, xx, 1862, p. 8237.

1862. MAWSON, G.   Woodcock [Scolopax rusticola] breeding near Keswick, Cumberland   < *Zoologist*, xx, 1862, p. 8196.

1862. RODD, E. H.   [Occurrence of Gallinago sabinii in full plumage in Cornwall.]   < *P. Z. S.*, xxx, 1862, p. 13.

1862. RODD, E. H.   Examination of a Specimen of Sabine's Snipe [Gallinago sabinii].   < *Zoologist*, xx, 1862, pp. 7882, 7883.

1862. RODD, E. H.   Re-examination of Sabine's Snipe [Gallinago sabinii].   < *Zoologist*, xx, 1862, p. 7938.

1862. RODD, E. H.   Correction of an Error [Zool., p. 7882, respecting Scolopax sabinii].   < *Zoologist*, xx, 1862, p. 7938.

1862. SAXBY, H. L.   Unusual Situation of a Sandpiper's [Tringoides hypoleucus] Nest.   < *Zoologist*, xx, 1862, p. 8169.

1862. SAXBY, H. L.   Occurrence of the Curlew Sandpiper [Tringa subarquata] at Rochester.   < *Zoologist*, xx, 1862, p. 8237.

1862. VIAN, J.   Notice sur quelques jeunes Oiseaux d'Europe.   < *Rev. et Mag. de Zool.*, xiv, 1862, pp. 369–371, pl. 15, f. 1.
   Limosa cinerea.

1862. WAGNER, C.   [Fang der Kampfhähne (Machetes pugnax).]   < *Zool. Gart.*, iii, 1862, pp. 173, 174.

1863. BLAKE-KNOX, H.   On the Diving of the Sandpiper [Tringoides hypoleucus].   < *Zoologist*, xxi, 1863, pp. 8632, 8633.

1863. BLAKE-KNOX, H.   The Sandpiper [Tringoides hypoleucus] Diving.   < *Zoologist*, xxi, 1863, pp. 8493, 8494.

1863. BOULTON, W. W.   Jack Snipe [Gallinago gallinula] shot on the River Hull.   < *Zoologist*, xxi, 1863, p. 8770.

1863. BOULTON, W. W.   Ruff (Machetes pugnax ♂) shot near Beverley.   < *Zoologist*, xxi, 1863, p. 8827.

1863. BOULTON, W. W.   Occurrence of the Green Sandpiper [Totanus ochropus] near Beverley.   < *Zoologist*, xxi, 1863, p. 8771.

1863. GRILL, J. W.   Macht der Strandpfeiffer, Totanus hypoleucus Lin., immer eine ,,Runde"?   < *J. f. O.*, xi, 1863, pp. 159, 160.

1863. HADFIELD, H.   American Snipe [called Scolopax americanus; qu. Gallinago wilsoni?].   < *Zoologist*, xxi, 1863, pp. 8446, 8447.

1863. HADFIELD, H.   The Sandpiper [Tringoides hypoleucus] a Diver.   < *Zoologist*, xxi, 1863, p. 8447.

1863. HADFIELD, H.   Common Snipe (Scolopax gallinago [Gallinago media]).   < *Zoologist*, xxi, 1863, p. 8494.

1863. HADFIELD, H.   The Sandpiper [Tringoides hypoleucus] a Diver.   < *Zoologist*, xxi, 1863, pp. 8524–8526.

1863. HARTING, J. E.   The Curlew Sandpiper [Tringa subarquata] near Yarmouth.   < *Zoologist*, xxi, 1863, pp. 8827, 8828.

1863. HARVIE-BROWN, J. A.   Sandpiper [Tringoides hypoleucus] Diving.   < *Zoologist*, xxi, 1863, p. 8770.

1863. HORSFALL, W. C.   Occurrence of the Solitary Snipe [Gallinago major] near Leeds.   < *Zoologist*, xx, 1863, p. 8330.

1863. LEVEN, R. H.   The Sandpiper [Tringoides hypoleucus] a Diver.   < *Zoologist*, xxi, 1863, p. 8691.

1863. NEWTON, A.   On the Breeding of the Green Sandpiper (Helodromas ochropus).   < *P. Z. S.*, xxxi, 1863, pp. 529-532.
On trees, in Thrushes' nests, etc.

1863. RODD, E. H.   Occurrence of Temminck's Stint [Tringa temmincki] at Scilly.   < *Zoologist*, xxi, 1863. p. 8827.

1863. RODD, E. H.   The Spotted Redshank (Totanus fuscus) in Cornwall.   < *Zoologist*, xxi, 1863, p. 8827.

1863. ROGERS, H.   Reeves [Machetes pugnax ♀] in the Isle of Wight.   < *Zoologist*, xxi, 1863, p. 8827.

1863. SAXBY, H. L.   Woodcock (Scolopax rusticola) in Shetland.   < *Zoologist*, xxi, 1863, p. 8494.

1863. SAXBY, H. L.   Five Eggs in the Nest of a Common Snipe [Gallinago media].   < *Zoologist*, xxi, 1863, p. 8691.

1863. SAXBY, H. L.   Redshank [Totanus calidris] breeding in Shetland.   < *Zoologist*, xxi, 1863, p. 8725.

1863. STEVENSON, H.   Blacktailed Godwit (Limosa melanura) at Yarmouth.   < *Zoologist*, xxi, 1863, p. 8330.

1863. SWINHOE, R.   [Exhibition of a rare Wader, Pseudoscolopax semipalmatus.]   < *P. Z. S.*, xxxi, 1863, p. 181.

1864. ARMISTEAD, J. J.   Occurrence of the Little Stint [Tringa minuta] near Leeds.   < *Zoologist*, xxii, 1864, p. 9289.

1864. BOULTON, W. W.   Solitary Snipe [Gallinago major] near Beverley.   < *Zoologist*, xxii, 1864, pp. 8890, 8891.

1864. BOULTON, W. W.   Ruff and Reeve [Machetes pugnax ♂ ♀] near Beverley.   < *Zoologist*, xxii, 1864, p. 9362.

1864. BOULTON, W. W.   Knot [Tringa canutus] and Bartailed Godwit [Limosa lapponica], in Summer Plumage, at Filey.   < *Zoologist*, xxii, 1864, p. 9362.

1864. BRUNTON, T.   Early Breeding of the Woodcock [Scolopax rusticola, in Perth].   < *Zoologist*, xxii, 1864, p. 9119.

1864. CLARKE, J. A.   Sanderling [Calidris arenaria] at Gravesend.   < *Zoologist*, xxii, 1864, pp. 9329, 9330.

1864. CORDEAUX, J.   Note on the Whimbrel [Numenius phæopus] on the Lincolnshire Coast.   < *Zoologist*, xxii, 1864, p. 9115.

1864. CORDEAUX, J.   Curlew Sandpiper [Tringa subarquata] and Dunlin [T. alpina] on the Lincolnshire Coast.   < *Zoologist*, xxii, 1864, p. 9118.

1864. CORDEAUX, J.   Note on the Appearance of the Little Stint [Tringa minuta] i the Humber.   < *Zoologist*, xxii, 1864, p. 9330.

1864. DUTTON, J.   Bartram's [Actiturus bartramius] and the Purple Sandpipe [Tringa maritima] in Sussex.   < *Zoologist*, xxii, 1864, p. 9118.

1864. GUNN, T. E.   Ruff and Reeves [Machetes pugnax ♂ ♀] in Norfolk.   < *Zoologist*, xxii, 1864, p. 9290.

1864. GUNN, T. E.   Occurrence of the Greenshank [Totanus glottis] near Norwich   < *Zoologist*, xxii, 1864, p. 9290.

1864. HARVIE-BROWN, J. A.   Reeve [Machetes pugnax ♀] killed near Grangemout   < *Zoologist*, xxii, 1864, p. 9118.

1864. JEFFREY, W. Blacktailed Godwit [Limosa melanura] and Spotted Redshank [Totanus fuscus] near Chichester. < *Zoologist*, xxii, 1864, p. 9289.

1864. MATHEWS, M. A. Ruff [Machetes pugnax ♂] at Weston-Super-Mare. < *Zoologist*, xxii, 1864, p. 8961.

1864.. MEYER, R. [Schneeweisse Waldschnepfe (Scolopax rusticola).] < *Zool. Gart.*, v, 1864, p. 203.

1864. NEWTON, A. On the Breeding of the Green Sandpiper (Helodromas ochropus). < *Zoologist*, xxii, 1864, pp. 9115–9118.
From *P. Z. S.*, Dec. 8, 1863.

1864. NEWTON, A. On the Breeding of the Green Sandpiper (Helodromas ochropus). < *Ann. Mag. Nat. Hist.*, 3d ser., xiv, 1864, pp. 221–224.
From *P. Z. S.*, Dec. 8, 1863, pp. 529–532, *q. v.*

1864. POWER, W. H. Occurrence of the Ruff [Machetes pugnax] and Curlew Sandpiper [Tringa subarquata] at Kingsbury Reservoir, Middlesex. < *Zoologist*, xxii, 1864, p. 9289.

1864. ROGERS, H. Little Stint [Tringa minuta] in the Isle of Wight. < *Zoologist*, xxii, 1864, p. 8891.

1865. ATKINSON, J. C. Young Snipes. < *Zoologist*, xxiii, 1865, p. 9793.

1865. BECKMANN, L. Der Oberschnabel der Waldschnepfe [Scolopax rusticola]. < *Zool. Gart.*, vi, 1865, pp. 130–133, figg. 4.
Power and mode of inflection of the upper mandible. Cf. *Zool. Rec.*, i, p. 93.

1865. BLAKE-KNOX, H. Malformation of a Snipe's Beak. < *Zoologist*, xxiii, 1865, p. 9564.

1865. GUNN, T. E. Abundance of Woodcocks [Scolopax rusticola] in Norfolk. < *Zoologist*, xxiii, 1865, pp. 9468, 9469.

1865. GURNEY, J. H. Note on the Purple Sandpiper [Tringa maritima]. < *Zoologist*, xxiii, 1865, p. 9468.
Cf. *tom. cit.*, p. 9541.

1865. HADFIELD, H. Plumage of the Ruff [Machetes pugnax ♂]. < *Zoologist*, xxiii, 1865, pp. 9628, 9629.

1865. HODGSON, C. B. Snipe Nesting in Warwickshire. < *Zoologist*, xxiii, 1865, p. 9628.

1865. JESSE, W. Snipe Nesting in Liphook. < *Zoologist*, xxiii, 1865, p. 9793.

1865. LUNEL, G. Note sur le Bécasseau platyrhynque, Tringa platyrhyncha, et description d'un caractère nouveau observé chez cet Oiseau. < *Bull. Soc. Ornith. Suisse*, i, 1865, pp. 31–37, pl. i.
Not seen.—The new character is nudity of the chin.

1865. MATHEW, M. A. Abundance of Jack Snipe [Gallinago gallinula] during the past Winter. < *Zoologist*, xxiii, 1865, p. 9564.

1865. MATHEW, M. A. Snipe [Gallinago media, in England] in the middle of July. < *Zoologist*, xxiii, 1865, p. 9733.

1865. MATHEW, M. A. Woodcock [Scolopax rusticola, in England] in July. < *Zoologist*, xxiii, 1865, p. 9733.

1865. MATHEW, M. A. The Ruff [Machetes pugnax ♂] on the Northam Burrows, North Devon. < *Zoologist*, xxiii, 1865, p. 9848.

1865. POWER, W. H. Curlew Sandpiper [Tringa subarquata] at Kingsbury Reservoir. < *Zoologist*, xxiii, 1865, p. 9848.

1865. POWER, W. H. Temminck's Stint [Tringa temmincki] near Rainham, Kent. < *Zoologist*, xxiii, 1865, p. 9848.

1865. PRYOR, M. R. Solitary Snipe [Gallinago major] near Thetford. < *Zoologist*, xxiii, 1865, p. 9564.

1865. RODD, E. H.   Curlew Tringa [subarquata]; Change of Plumage.   < *Zoologist*, xxiii, 1865, pp. 9793, 9794.

1865. RODD, E. H.   Ruffs and Reeves [Machetes pugnax ♂ ♀] in Cornwall.   < *Zoologist*, xxiii, 1865, pp. 9564, 9565.

1864-65. SCHLEGEL, H.   Scolopaces.   < *Mus. Nat. Hist. Pays-Bas*, 5ᵉ livr., 1864, pp. 1-86; 6ᵉ livr., 1864, pp. 87-102; 7ᵉ livr., 1865, pp. 103-112.

> The birds of this group are treated under the genera *Scolopax* (3 spp.), *Gallinago* (16), *Rhynchaea* (2), *Prosobonia* (1), *Limosa* (8), *Tringa* (17), *Phalaropus* (3), *Totanus* (12), *Actitis* (4), *Numenius* (10), *Recurvirostra* (3), and *Himantopus* (5)—rather an improvement upon the author's custom of classifying, though we still miss some important genera. There are enumerated a total of 1,280 specimens in the Leyden Museum. Cf. *Ibis*, 1865, p. 533.

1866. ANGUS, W. C.   Wood Sandpiper [Totanus glareola] in Aberdeenshire.   < *Zoologist*, 2d ser., i, 1866. pp. 524, 525.

1866. BISCHOFSHAUSEN, R. V.   Beitrag zur Naturgeschichte der Waldschnepfe.   (Scolopax rusticola.)   < *Zool. Gart.*, vii, 1866, pp. 187-191.

1866. BLAKE-KNOX, H.   The Buffbreasted Sandpiper [Tryngites rufescens] in Belfast.   < *Zoologist*, 2d ser., i, 1866, p. 457.

1866. BROOKING-ROWE, J.   Large Snipe.   < *Zoologist*, 2d ser., i, 1866, p. 97.

1866. BULLMORE, W. K.   On the Occurrence of Bartram's Sandpiper [Actiturus bartramius] near Falmouth.   < *Zoologist*, 2d ser., i, 1866, pp. 37-40.

> A notice of the same appeared in the London 'Times' of Nov. 14, 1865.

1866. DUTTON, J.   Purple Sandpiper [Tringa maritima] at Eastbourne.   < *Zoologist*, 2d ser., i, 1866, p. 145.

1866. GATCOMBE, J.   The Purple Sandpiper [Tringa maritima, in Cornwall and Devon].   < *Zoologist*, 2d ser., i, 1866, pp. 96, 97.

> From the London "Field" of Jan. 13, 1866.

1866. GUNN, T. E.   Solitary Snipe [Gallinago major] in Suffolk.   < *Zoologist*, 2d ser., i, 1866, p. 40.

1866. HARVIE-BROWN, J. A.   Ruff [Machetes pugnax ♂] near Grangemouth.   < *Zoologist*, 2d ser., i, 1866, p. 524.

1866. LEGGE, W. V.   [On the nesting of Totanus calidris in Kent and Essex, England.]   < *Ibis*, 2d ser., ii, 1866, pp. 420, 421.

1866. LOWE, J.   Temminck's Stint [Tringa temmincki] at King's Lynn.   < *Zoologist*, 2d ser., i, 1866, p. 457.

1866. POWER, W. H.   Temminck's Stint [Tringa temmincki] at Rainham.   < *Zoologist*, 2d ser., i, 1866, p. 311.

1866. POWER, W. H.   Late Stay of the Snipe [Gallinago media, at Rainham].   < *Zoologist*, 2d ser., i, 1866, p. 311.

1866. POWER, F. D.   Wood Sandpiper [Totanus glareola] at Kingsbury Reservoir.   < *Zoologist*, 2d ser., i, 1866, p. 457.

1866. SMEE, A. H.   Occurrence of the Purple Sandpiper [Tringa maritima] at Shoreham.   < *Zoologist*, 2d ser., i, 1866, p. 190.

1866. SMITH, A. P.   Hard Fate of a Woodcock [Scolopax rusticola, impaled on an arrow-shaped weather-cock].   < *Zoologist*, 2d ser., i, 1866, p. 271.

1866. WHARTON, C. B.   Whimbrel [Numenius phæopus] at the Kingsbury Reservoir.   < *Zoologist*, 2d ser., i, 1866, p. 271.

1867. ALTUM, B.   Die Waldschnepfe [Scolopax rusticola].   Ein monographischer Beitrag zur Jagdzoologie von Dr. Julius Hoffmann, Stuttgart, K. Thienemann's Verlag.   < *J. f. O.*, xv, 1867, pp. 110-112.

> Uebersicht.

1867. ANON.   Sneppereder i Træer.   < *Tidssk. Pop. Fremst. af Naturv.*, 3e Række, iv, 1867, p. 354.

> Nidification of *Totanus ochropus* in trees. See 1863 and 1864, NEWTON, A.

1867. ANON. Singular Habit of the Woodcock [Scolopax rusticola].   < *Zoologist*, 2d
ser., ii, 1867, p. 635.
From the London 'Field.' Elevating and spreading the tail like a turkey.

1867. AUSTIN, H. Dunlins [Tringa alpina] at Kingsbury Reservoir.   < *Zoologist*, 2d
ser., ii, 1867, p. 829.

1867. CLARK-KENNEDY, A. Greenshank [Totanus glottis] and Wood Sandpiper [To-
tanus glareola] near Aldeburgh.   < *Zoologist*, 2d ser., ii, 1867, p. 950.

1867. CLARK-KENNEDY, A. Curlew Sandpiper [Tringa subarquata] near Aldeburgh,
Suffolk.   < *Zoologist*, 2d ser., ii, 1867, p. 950.

1867. CLARK-KENNEDY, A. Pigmy Curlew [Tringa subarquata] at Aldeburgh.   < *Zoologist*, 2d ser., ii, 1867, p. 991.

1867. HOFFMANN, J. Die Waldschnepfe [Scolopax rusticola]. Ein monographischer
Beitrag zur Jagdzoologie von Dr. Julius Hoffmann. Stuttgart. K. Thienemann's Verlag. 1867. 8vo. pp. 151.
Nicht mir selbst zugänglich.—Vergl. *J. f. O.*, 1867, pp. 110–112; *Zool. Gart.*, 1867, pp. 445–
448; *Ibis*, 1868, pp. 109, 110. Soll sehr vollständig und überaus gewissenhaft geschrieben
sein.—Enthalt gleichfalls Bemerkungen über *Philohela minor*.

1867. JÄCKEL, [A. J.] Die Waldschnepfe [Scolopax rusticola]. Ein monograph-
ischer Beitrag zur Jagdzoologie von Dr. Julius Hoffmann. . . .   < *Zool.
Gart.*, viii, 1867, pp. 445–448.
Uebersicht.

1867. JESSE, W. Green Sandpiper [Totanus ochropus] near Ingatestone, Essex.
< *Zoologist*, 2d ser., ii, 1867, p. 915.

1867. POWER, F. D. Extraordinary Flock of Wood Sandpipers [Totanus glareola] at
Rainham, Kent.   < *Zoologist*, 2d ser., ii, 1867, p. 991.

1867. POWER, W. H. Redshank [Totanus calidris] in Breeding Plumage in January.   < *Zoologist*, 2d ser., ii, 1867, p. 708.

1867. POWER, W. H. Early appearance of Jack Snipe [Gallinago gallinula, in Kent].
< *Zoologist*, 2d ser., ii, 1867, pp. 1016, 1017.

1867. SCHLOTTHAUBER, —. Numenius arcuatus mit monströsem Schnabel lebend beobachtet.   < *J. f. O.*, xv, 1867, pp. 358–360.

1867. SHORTO, J., JR. Great Snipe [Gallinago major] near Dorchester.   < *Zoologist*,
2d ser., ii, 1867, p. 608.

1868. ADAMSON, C. M. Solitary Snipe [Gallinago major] in Devonshire.   < *Zoologist*, 2d ser., iii, 1868, p. 1461.

1868. ADAMSON, C. M. Solitary Snipe [Gallinago major, in England].   < *Zoologist*,
2d ser., iii, 1868, p. 1461.
From the London ' Field.'

1868. ADAMSON, C. M. Solitary Snipe [Gallinago major] in Hampshire.   < *Zoologist*, 2d ser., iii, 1868, p. 1461.

1868. ANON. Solitary Snipe [Gallinago major] in Wiltshire.   < *Zoologist*, 2d ser., iii,
1868, p. 1461.
From the London 'Field.'

1868. BOND, F. Early Breeding of the Common Snipe [Gallinago media] in Sussex
in 1868.   < *Zoologist*, 2d ser., iii, 1868, p. 1256.

1868. CORDEAUX, J. Further Remarks on the Green Sandpiper [Totanus ochropus]
breeding in North Lincolnshire.   < *Zoologist*, 2d ser., iii, 1868, p. 1459.

1868. DUTTON, J. Purple Sandpiper [Tringa maritima] near Beachy Head.   < *Zoologist*, 2d ser., iii, 1868, p. 1098.

1868. GUNN, T. E. White Woodcock [Scolopax rusticola] in the North of Yorkshire.
< *Zoologist*, 2d ser., iii, 1868, p. 1220.

1868. GUNN, T. E. White Woodcock [Scolopax rusticola]: Correction of an Error
[Zool., s. s., p. 1220].   < *Zoologist*, 2d ser., iii, 1868, p. 1422.

1868. GURNEY, J. H.   Fawn-coloured Snipe.   < *Zoologist*, 2d ser., iii, 1868, p. 1459.

1868. GURNEY, J. H., JR.   Great Snipe [Gallinago major] near Christchurch.   < *Zoologist*, 2d ser., iii, 1868, p. 1422.

1868. HOFFMANN, W. J.   The Jack-snipe [i. e., Tringoides macularius?].   < *Am. Nat.*, ii, 1868, pp. 216, 217.
    On removal of the young by the ♀ parent, in her beak, when disturbed.

1868. "J. M. H."   Wilson's Snipe [Gallinago wilsoni].   < *Am. Nat.*, ii, 1868, p. 489.
    On the frequent perching of this species in trees.

1868. MATHEW, G. F.   Blacktailed Godwit [Limosa melanura] in Devonshire.   < *Zoologist*, 2d ser., iii, 1868, p. 1459.

1868. MATHEW, G. F.   Whimbrel [Numenius phæopus] in January.   < *Zoologist*, 2d ser., iii, 1868, p. 1135.

1868. MATHEW, G. F.   Solitary Snipes [Gallinago major] near Parracombe.   < *Zoologist*, 2d ser., iii, 1868, p. 1461.

1868. MATHEW, M. A.   Solitary Snipe [Gallinago major] on Dartmoor.   < *Zoologist*, 2d ser., iii, 1868, pp. 1460, 1461.

1868. MOOR, E. C.   Woodcock [Scolopax rusticola] killed by Telegraph-wires.   < *Zoologist*, 2d ser., iii, 1868, p. 1220.

1868. [POPE, W. A.]   A Perching Snipe [Gallinago wilsoni].   < *Am. Nat.*, ii, 1868, p. 329.
    An observation of W. A. Pope's to this effect, from *Land and Water*, and American ornithologists' attention called to the circumstance.

1868. POWELL, A. P. E.   Solitary Snipe [Gallinago major] on Salisbury Plain.   < *Zoologist*, 2d ser., iii, 1868, p. 1461.

1868. RODD, E. H.   Occurrence of the Greenshank [Totanus glottis] and Reeve [Machetes pugnax ♀] at the Land's End.   < *Zoologist*, 2d ser., iii, 1868, p. 1256.

1868. RODD, E. H.   Spring Moulting of the Jack Snipe [Gallinago gallinula].   < *Zoologist*, 2d ser., iii, 1868, p. 1220.

1868. RODD, E. H.   The Great Snipe [Gallinago major]: Number of Tail-feathers.   < *Zoologist*, 2d ser., iii, 1868, p. 1482.

1868. SHORTO, J., JR.   Jack Snipe [Gallinago gallinula, near Dorchester] in August.   < *Zoologist*, 2d ser., iii, 1868, p. 1059.

1868. SMITH, CECIL.   Blacktailed Godwit [Limosa melanura] in Somersetshire.   < *Zoologist*, 2d ser., iii, 1868, p. 1178.

1868. STEPHENSON, J. W.   Solitary Snipe [Gallinago major] in Sussex.   < *Zoologist*, 2d ser., iii, 1868, p. 1482.

1868. WATSON, W.   Sabine's Snipe [Gallinago sabinii].   < *Zoologist*, 2d ser., iii, 1868, pp. 1422, 1423.
    A query respecting the characters of the supposed species.

1869. B[OARDMAN], G. A.   Perching of Wilson's Snipe [Gallinago wilsoni].   < *Am. Nat.*, iii, 1869, p. 222.
    Confirms W. A. Pope's observations on this habit of the bird, *Am. Nat.*, ii, 1868, p. 329.

1869. CASTLE, W. W.   [Perching] Habits of Snipes [Gallinago wilsoni and Philohela minor].   < *Am. Nat.*, ii, 1869, p. 663.

1869. GUNN, T. E.   Purple Sandpiper [Tringa maritima] in Suffolk.   < *Zoologist*, 2d ser., iv, 1869, p. 1722.

1869. GUNN, T. E.   Solitary Snipe [Gallinago major] near Norwich.   < *Zoologist*, 2d ser., iv, 1869, p. 1722.

1869. GUNN, T. E.   Green Sandpiper [Totanus ochropus] on the Norfolk Coast.   < *Zoologist*, 2d ser., iv, 1869, p. 1866.

1869. GUNN, T. E.   Greenshank [Totanus glottis] near Yarmouth.   < *Zoologist*, 2d ser., iv, 1869, p. 1921.

1869. GURNEY, J. H., JR. Correction of an error: Parasite of Sabine's Snipe [Gallinago sabinii]. < *Zoologist*, 2d ser., iv, 1869, pp. 1562, 1563.

1869. GURNEY, J. H., JR. Blacktailed Godwit [Limosa melanura] at Hickling. < *Zoologist*, 2d ser., iv, 1869, p. 1802.

1869. HART, W., *and* SON. Sabine's Snipe [Gallinago sabinii] (?) at Christchurch. < *Zoologist*, 2d ser., iv, 1869, p. 1722.

1869. HARTING, J. E. On rare or little-known Limicolæ. [Part II.] < *Ibis*, 2d ser., v, 1869, pp. 426–434, figg. and pl. xii.

> Continued from *tom. cit.*, p. 310. This second instalment of the series of articles treats monographically of *Eurynorhynchus pygmœus.*
>
> Parts I, III, IV, V, treat of various species of *Charadriidæ*, as stated in previous pages of this Bibliography, where they are all duly entered. But in citing the whole series collectively, as consisting of five papers, dating 1869–73 (see *anteà*, p. 838), I have overlooked a sixth paper, on *Recurvirostra*, 1874 (see *posteà*, p. 875). Please make the necessary correction, in ink, in your copy of this Bibliography.

1869. RICKARDS, M. S. C. Purple Sandpiper [Tringa maritima] at Weston-super-Mare. < *Zoologist*, 2d ser., iv, 1869, p. 1645.

1869. RODD, E. H. American Stint [Tringa minutilla] at Northam Burrows. < *Zoologist*, 2d ser., iv, 1869, p. 1920.

1869. ROWLEY, G. D. White Woodcock [Scolopax rusticola]. < *Zoologist*, 2d ser., iv, 1869, p. 1645.

1869. SCLATER, P. L., *and* SALVIN, O. Descriptions of Six New Species of American Birds of the Families Tanagridæ, Dendrocolaptidæ, Formicariidæ, Tyrannidæ, and Scolopacidæ. < *P. Z. S.*, xxxvii, 1869, pp. 416–420.

> The new Snipe is *Gallinago imperialis*, p. 419.

1869. TEMPLER, R. B. A Buffcoloured Woodcock [Scolopax rusticola]. < *Zoologist*, 2d ser., iv, 1869, p. 1602.

1869. [THORPE, T. B.] The Woodcock [Philohela minor]. < *Harper's New Monthly Mag.*, xxxix, 1869, pp. 640–647, figs. 1–4.

> Natural history and methods of capture.

1869. WARD, E. [Exhibition of a specimen of a melanotic variety of the Common Woodcock (Scolopax rusticola).] < *P. Z. S.*, xxxvii, 1869, p. 473.

1870. ANON. Weight of Snipe. < *Zoologist*, 2d ser., v, 1870, p. 2069.

> From the London 'Field,' Jan. 22, 1870.

1870. BLAKE-KNOX, H. Esquimaux Curlew [Numenius borealis] in Dublin Market. < *Zoologist*, 2d ser., v, 1870, pp. 2408, 2409.

1870. BLAKE-KNOX, H. Ruff [Machetes pugnax ♂] in Dublin. < *Zoologist*, 2d ser., v, 1870, p. 2410.

1870. BRANDRETH, H. P. Woodcock [Scolopax rusticola] on the 19th of March [at Standish Rectory] < *Zoologist*, 2d ser., v, 1870, p. 2141.

1870. BROWNE, A. M. Curlew Sandpiper [Tringa subarquata] near Aberyst-with. < *Zoologist*, 2d ser., v, 1870, p. 2409.

1870. CABANIS, J. [Ueber Bildung und Anzahl der seitlichen Steuerfedern bei Gallinago, und über G. heterocerca n. sp.] < *J. f. O.*, xviii, 1870, pp. 235, 236.

1870. COUES, E. Foot-notes from a Page of Sand. < *Am. Nat.*, iv, 1870, pp. 297–303.

> A popular account of tracks made on the sea-shore by *Ereunetes pusillus*, and how to identify them.

1870. GUNN, T. E. Ruff [Machetes pugnax ♂] in Norfolk. < *Zoologist*, 2d ser., v, 1870, p. 2103.

1870. GUNN, T. E. Wood Sandpipers [Totanus glareola] and Greenshanks [Totanus glottis] in Norfolk. < *Zoologist*, 2d ser., v, 1870, p. 2384.

1870. GUNN, T. E. Solitary Snipe [Gallinago major] in Norfolk. < *Zoologist*, 2d ser., v, 1870, p. 2384.

1870. GURNEY, J. H., JR.   Woodcock [Scolopax rusticola] and Godwit [Limosa ——].
        < Zoologist, 2d ser., v, 1870, p. 2345.

1870. HARTING, J. E.   [Exhibition of a specimen of Totanus fuscus.]   < P. Z. S.,
        xxxviii, 1870, p. 221.

1870. HARTING, J. E.   [Occurrence of Tringa bairdii, Coues, at Walvisch Bay, S.
        Africa, Oct. 24, 1863.]   < Ibis, 2d ser., vi, 1870, pp. 151, 152.

1870. HORNE, C.   Jack Snipe [Gallinago gallinula] in a Norwood Garden.   < Zoolo-
        gist, 2d ser., v, 1870, p. 2141.

1870. "J. W. D."   Sabine's Snipe [Gallinago sabinii].   < Zoologist, 2d ser., v, 1870, p.
        2103.
        From the 'Field.'

1870. MOOR, E. C.   Green Sandpiper [Totanus ochropus] at Hasketon.   < Zoologist,
        2d ser., v, 1870, p. 2105.

1870. RICKARDS, M. S. C.   The American Stint [Tringa minutilla] at Northam Bur-
        rows.   < Zoologist, 2d ser., v, 1870, p. 2025.

1870. RICKARDS, M. S. C.   American Stint [Tringa minutilla, at Northam Burrows].
        < Zoologist, 2d ser., v, 1870, p. 2385.

1870. RODD, E. H.   Blacktailed Godwit [Limosa ægocephala] in Summer Plumage
        at Scilly.   < Zoologist, 2d ser., v, 1870, p. 2182.

1870. RODD, E. H.   British Sandpipers at Scilly.   < Zoologist, 2d ser., v, 1870, pp. 2345,
        2346.

1870. RODD, E. H.   Pectoral Stint or Sandpiper [Tringa maculata] at Scilly.   < Zo-
        ologist, 2d ser., v, 1870, p. 2346.

1870. RODD, E. H.   [Another case of Tringa maculata] Pectoral Sandpiper at Scilly.
        < Zoologist, 2d ser., v, 1870, p. 2346.

1870. RODD, E. H.   Buffbreasted Sandpiper [Tryngites rufescens] at Scilly.   < Zo-
        ologist, 2d ser., v, 1870, p. 2346.

1870. RODD, E. H.   Schinz's Stint [Tringa bonapartii] at Scilly.   < Zoologist, 2d ser.,
        v, 1870, pp. 2384, 2385.

1870. RODD, E. H.   Schinz's Stint [Tringa bonapartii] at the Lizard.   < Zoologist, 2d
        ser., v, 1870, p. 2409.

1870. SMEE, A. H.   Woodcock [Scolopax rusticola] in August.   < Zoologist, 2d ser.,
        v, 1870, p. 2384.

1870. SMEE, A. H.   Little Stint [Tringa minuta], &c., near Leigh.   < Zoologist, 2d
        ser., v, 1870, p. 2385.

1870. SMITH, CECIL.   Ruff [Machetes pugnax ♂] in Somersetshire.   < Zoologist, 2d
        ser., v, 1870, p. 2103.

1870. SMITH, CECIL.   Schinz's Sandpiper [Tringa bonapartii] in North Devon.   < Zo-
        ologist, 2d ser., v, 1870, p. 2409.

1870. SMITH, CECIL.   Sternum of Schinz's Sandpiper [Tringa bonapartii].   < Zoolo-
        gist, 2d ser., v, 1870, p. 2409.

1871. BATES, B.   Schinz's Sandpiper [Tringa bonapartii] at Eastbourne.   < Zoologist,
        2d ser., vi, 1871, p. 2442.

1871. BLAKE-KNOX, H.   Little Stint [Tringa minuta] on the Dublin Coast.   < Zoolo-
        gist, 2d ser., vi, 1871, p. 2609.

1871. BROOKE, V.   [Remarks upon exhibition of a specimen of Numenius borealis
        from Sligo, Ireland.]   < P. Z. S., xxxix, 1871, p. 299.

1871. DESFONTAINES, G.   La Ganga [Actiturus bartramius] de México.   < La Natu-
        raleza, ii, 1871, pp. 154-158.
        Charactéres genéricos y especificos—costumbres y habitos.

1871. FOWLER, A.   Woodcocks and Moles.   < *Am. Nat.*, iv, 1871, pp. 761, 762.
    Philohela minor supposed to prevent the increase of *Soricidæ*.

1871. FULLER, O.   The Stilt Sandpiper [Micropalama himantopus] in Massachusetts.
    < *Am. Nat.*, v, 1871, p. 727.

1871. GUNN, T. E.   Solitary Snipes [Gallinago major] in Norfolk.   < *Zoologist*, 2d ser.,
    vi, 1871, p. 2852.

1871. GUNN, T. E.   Ruffs and Reeves [Machetes pugnax ♂ ♀] at Yarmouth.   < *Zoologist*, 2d ser., vi, 1871, p. 2852.

1871. GURNEY, J. H., JR.   The Wader at Whitby [*i. e.*, Machetes pugnax, Zool., s. s.,
    p. 2772.]   < *Zoologist*, 2d ser., vi, 1871, p. 2806.
    Vanellus gregarius or *Machetes pugnax?* As will be seen by several titles below, the
    "Whitby Wader" occasioned considerable correspondence before it was finally determined
    to be *Machetes pugnax*. ♂, juv.

1871. GURNEY, J. E., JR.   Ruffs [Machetes pugnax ♂, at Romney Bay, near Lydd].
    < *Zoologist*, 2d ser., vi, 1871, p. 2852.

1871. HARTING, J. E.   [Remarks upon exhibition of a specimen of the so-called Sabine's Snipe.]   < *P. Z. S.*, xxxix, 1871, p. 39.
    "*Gallinago sabinii*" = *G. gallinula*, melanotic.

1871. HARTING, J. E.   The Whitby Wader [Machetes pugnax].   < *Zoologist*, 2d ser.,
    vi, 1871, pp. 2851, 2852.

1871. LEACH, H. R.   Temminck's Stint [Tringa temmincki] at Aldeburgh.   < *Zoologist*, 2d ser., vi, 1870, p. 2871.

1871. MATHEW, M. A.   Schinz's Sandpiper [Tringa bonapartii] at Barnstaple.
    < *Zoologist*, 2d ser., vi, 1871, pp. 2441, 2442.

1871. MITFORD, R. H.   Ruff and Reeve [Machetes pugnax ♂] in Middlesex.   < *Zoologist*, 2d ser., vi, 1871, p. 2806.

1871. NEWTON, A.   [Exhibition of some rare European Birds' Eggs.]   < *P. Z. S.*,
    xxxix, 1871, pp. 546, 547.
    Calidris arenaria remarked upon.

1871. POWER, F. D.   Ruff [Machetes pugnax ♂] in Middlesex.   < *Zoologist*, 2d ser., vi,
    1871, p. 2852.

1871. RICKARDS, M. S. C.   Green Sandpiper [Totanus ochropus] at Scilly.   < *Zoologist*, 2d ser., vi, 1871, p. 2485.

1871. RICKARDS, M. S. C.   Pectoral Sandpiper [Tringa maculata] at Braunton Burrows.   < *Zoologist*, 2d ser., vi, 1871, pp. 2808, 2809.

1871. RICKARDS, M. S. C.   Greenshank [Totanus glottis] and Green Sandpiper [Totanus ochropus] near Barnstable.   < *Zoologist*, 2d ser., vi, 1871, pp. 2809, 2810.

1871. RICKARDS, M. S. C.   Wood Sandpiper [Totanus glareola] at Braunton Burrows.
    < *Zoologist*, 2d ser., vi, 1871, p. 2851.

1871. RODD, E. H.   Yellowshanked Sandpiper [Totanus flavipes] near Marazion.
    < *Zoologist*, 2d ser., vi, 1871, pp. 2807, 2808.

1871. RODD, E. H.   Snipe-shooting at St. Mary's, Scilly.   < *Zoologist*, 2d ser., vi, 1871,
    p. 2852.

1871. SIMPSON, M.   Name of a Wader [*i. e.*, Machetes pugnax].   < *Zoologist*, 2d ser.,
    vi, 1871, p. 2772.

1871. SIMPSON, M.   The Whitby Wader [Totanus bartramius? *i. e.*, Machetes pugnax].
    < *Zoologist*, 2d ser., vi, 1871, p. 2870.

1871. SMITH, CECIL.   Wood Sandpiper [Totanus glareola] in Somersetshire.   < *Zoologist*, 2d ser., vi, 1871, p. 2441.

1871. TACZANOWSKI, L.   Notiz über die ostsibirischen Numenius-Arten.   < *J. f. O.*,
    xix, 1871, pp. 56–61.
    NN. arquata, australis, nasicus.

1871. TACZANOWSKI, L.   Nachtrag zur Notiz [tom. cit. 56] über die ostsibirischen Numenius-Arten. < *J. f. O.*, xix, 1871, pp. 395, 396.

1871. TUCK, T. G. Blackwinged Stilt [i. e., Totanus calidris] near Bury St. Edmunds. < *Zoologist*, 2d ser., vi, 1871, p. 2684.
    See *op. cit.*, vii, 1872, p. 3064, where identified as above.

1871. TUCK, T. G. Spotted Sandpiper [Tringoides macularius] near Bury St. Edmunds. < *Zoologist*, 2d ser., vi, 1871, p. 2684.

1872. BOND, F. The Whitby Wader [Machetes pugnax]. < *Zoologist*, 2d ser., vii, 1872, p. 2905.
    At length determined to be *Machetes pugnax*, ♂, juv.

1872. BOYES, F. Snipes [Gallinago sp.] "Drumming" in Winter. < *Zoologist*, 2d ser., vii, 1872, p. 2994.

1872. CORBIN, G. B. Woodcock [Scolopax rusticola] Breeding in the New Forest. < *Zoologist*, 2d ser., vii, 1872, p. 3260.

1872. DURNFORD, H. Sanderlings [Calidris arenaria] at the Mouth of the Mersey. < *Zoologist*, 2d ser., vii, 1872, p. 3149.

1872. FEILDEN, H. W. Woodcocks [Scolopax rusticola] breeding in Wolmar Forest. < *Zoologist*, 2d ser., vii, 1872, p. 3188.

1872. FEILDEN, H. W. Sabine's Snipe [Gallinago sabinii] in Scotland. < *Zoologist*, 2d ser., vii, 1872, p. 3188.

1872. GURNEY, J. H., JR. Whimbrel [Numenius phæopus] near Stratford and Dunlin [Tringa alpina] near Leamington. < *Zoologist*, 2d ser., vii, 1872, p. 3273.

1872. HARTING, J. E. Supposed Occurrence of Wilson's Snipe in Cornwall [Zool. s. s., 3149]. < *Zoologist*, 2d ser., vii, 1872, pp. 3273, 3274.
    It was only a var. of *G. media*. But an authentic instance of occurrence of *G. wilsoni* in England is here noted.

1872. HÜGEL, A. V. Woodcock [Scolopax rusticola] breeding in the New Forest. < *Zoologist*, 2d ser., vii, 1872, p. 3236.

1872. LEACH, H. R. Sanderlings [Calidris arenaria] and Cockle [attached to its foot]. < *Zoologist*, 2d ser., vii, 1872, p. 3314.

1872. MATHEW, G. F. Greenshanks [Totanus glottis], &c., near Newton. < *Zoologist*, 2d ser., vii, 1872, p. 2945.

1872. PICKARD-CAMBRIDGE, O. Snipe [Gallinago sp.] "Drumming" on the 2nd of February. < *Zoologist*, 2d ser., vii, 1872, pp. 2993, 2994.

1872. RICKARDS, M. S. C. [Musky] Scent of Wood Sandpiper [Totanus glareola]. < *Zoologist*, 2d ser., vii, 1872, p. 2945.

1872. RODD, E. H. Wilson's Snipe [i. e., Gallinago media] in Cornwall. < *Zoologist*, 2d ser., vii, 1872, p. 3149.
    See *ibid.*, p. 3273.

1872. STEVENS, S. Spotted Redshank [Totanus fuscus] near Arundel. < *Zoologist*, 2d ser., vii, 1872, p. 3316.

1872. TUCK, T. G. Redshank [Totanus calidris] recorded [Zool. s. s., 2684] as Blackwinged Stilt. < *Zoologist*, 2d ser., vii, 1872, p. 3064.

1873. ANON. Woodcock [Scolopax rusticola] at Clapton. < *Zoologist*, 2d ser., viii, 1873, p. 2529.

1873. ANON. [Manner of "boring" of Philohela minor.] < *Forest and Stream*, i, Nov. 27, 1873, p. 251.

1873. BLASIUS, W. [Ueber Gallinago heterocerca Cab.] < *Ber. über d. xx. Versamml. d. Deutsch. Orn.-Ges.*, 1873, p. 11.

1873. CORBIN, G. B. Whimbrel [Numenius phæopus] in the New Forest. < *Zoologist*, 2d ser., viii, 1873, pp. 3651, 3652.

1873. CORDEAUX, J. On the Migration and Habits of the Curlew Sandpiper (Tringa subarquata, Güldenstaedt). < *Zoologist*, 2d ser., viii, 1873, pp. 3720-3722.

1873. DALL, W. H. Addition to the Avi-fauna of North America. < *Am. Nat.*, vii, 1873, pp. 634, 635.
> Tringa "*crassirostris*", [i. e., *T. ptilocnemis* Coues,] in the Aleutian Islands.

1873. DURNFORD, H. Dark Variety of the Common Snipe [Gallinago media]. < *Zoologist*, 2d ser., viii, 1873, p. 3529.

1873. FOULKS, O. D. The Woodcock [Philohela minor]. < *Am. Sportsman*, ii, 1873, p. 178.
> Biography.

1873. HARVIE-BROWN, J. A. Curlew Sandpiper [Tringa subarquata], Ruffs and Reeves [Machetes pugnax, ♂ ♀, near Falkirk], &c. < *Zoologist*, 2d ser., viii, 1873, p. 3803.

1873. LILFORD, *Lord*. [Occurrence of Numenius hudsonicus in the Coto de Doñana, Spain.] < *Ibis*, 3d ser., iii, 1873, p. 98.

1873. "MASSACHUSETTS" *and* "BORER". Where Woodcock [Philohela minor] moult. < *Am. Sportsman*, ii, 1873, p. 172. See also p. 178.

1873. PRÄLLE, [W. A. E.] [Ueber Telmatias gallinula L.-Eier aus Hannover.] < *Ber. über d. xx. Versamml. d. Deutsch. Orn.-Ges.*, 1873, pp. 5-7.

1873. ROPE, G. T. Nesting of the Woodcock [Scolopax rusticola] in Suffolk. < *Zoologist*, 2d ser., viii, 1873, p. 3616.

1873. STÖLKER, C. Die gemeine Sumpf- oder Heerschnepfe, Bekassine (Scolopax gallinago L.) in Gefangenschaft. < *Zool. Gart.*, xiv, 1873, pp. 477, 478.
> In „ Ornithologische Beobachtungen, " St. Gallen, 1873.

1873. "W. E. H." [Late breeding of Philohela minor.] < *Am. Sportsman*, iii, 1873, p. 70.

1873. WHITAKER, J., JR. Spotted Redshank [Totanus fuscus, in Beetwood Park]. < *Zoologist*, 2d ser., viii, 1873, p. 3492.

1874. "A. M." Arrival of Woodcock [Philohela minor, at Fort Lee, New Jersey]. < *Am. Sportsman*, ii, 1874, p. 412.

1874. ANON.. [EDITORIAL.] The Scarcity of Woodcock [Philohela minor]. < *Forest and Stream*, iii, Dec. 10, 1874, p. 277.

1874. "A. W." Woodcock [Philohela minor] Carrying their Young. < *Am. Sportsman*, iv, 1874, p. 139.
> Nestlings supposed to attach themselves to parent. Compare iii, p. 379, and iv, pp. 10, 75, 92. It was about this time that the curious fact that the bird transports her young when in danger began to be noticed in this country; though long known in case of *Scolopax rusticola* (see *Zoologist*, xi, 1853, p. 4017). Various writers describe the manner in which they suppose it to be done—not easy to determine, in the nature of the case. According to the most reliable observations, the bird holds the young one so closely to her abdomen, between her legs, that the two appear as one body; thus apparently giving rise to the supposition of "A. W." that the young "attach themselves to the parent." A plate has lately been published (*Zoologist*, 3d ser., iii, 1879, p. 433) figuring the European Woodcock (*Scolopax rusticola*) flying with a young one in her claws, remote from her body, much as a hawk would carry a chicken. But there is doubtless a difference in this respect; for the text of the same article speaks of another case in which the little one was held tightly to the body of the mother, between her thighs, exactly as the American bird has been seen to do. The two species probably do not differ from each other in the way they do it, though this may not be always exactly the same in either.

1874. BATTY, J. H. Woodcock [Philohela minor] killing themselves. < *Am. Sportsman*, iv, 1874, p. 76.

1874. BREWSTER, W. Love-Notes of the Woodcock [Philohela minor]. < *Am. Sportsman*, iv, 1874, p. 19. See also pp. 41, 92.
> Singing on the wing after sunset.

1874. COUES, E.   New Species of North American Bird [Tringa ptilocnemis].   <*Am. Nat.*, viii, 1874, pp. 500, 501.

> Reproduction of the description of *Tringa ptilocnemis*, Coues, from H. W. Elliott's *Rep. Prybilov Islands*, 4to, 1873, App., not paged—the original being nearly inaccessible.

1874. DURNFORD, H.   Malformation in Upper Mandible of a Redshank [Totanus calidris].   <*Zoologist*, 2d ser., ix, 1874, pp. 3999, 4000.

1874. "DRY LAND."   Late woodcock [Philohela minor]   <*Forest and Stream*, iii, Dec. 3, 1874, p. 267.

> *Philohela minor* and *Gallinago wilsoni* at Salem, Mass., in December.

1874. "E. H. L."   Curious trick of a woodcock [Philohela minor].   <*Am. Sportsman*, iii, 1874, p. 379.   See also iv, p. 10.

> Parent woodcock carrying young in her beak.

1874. HARTING, J. E.   On a new Species of Tringa [Tringa gracilis] from Alaska.   <*P. Z. S.*, xlii, 1874, pp. 242–244, pl. xl.

> The pl. shows also bill, feet, and tail of *T. alpina* and *T. crassirostris*.—The species was later identified with *T. ptilocnemis*, Coues.

1874. "HOMO."   [C. S. WESTCOTT.]   Upland Plover [Actiturus bartramius] Shooting.   <*Am. Sportsman*, iv, 1874, p. 231.

1874. "HOMO."   [C. S. WESTCOTT.]   The Summer moult of Woodcock [Philohela minor].   <*Forest and Stream*, ii, March 19, 1874, p. 86.

1874. "HOMO."   [C. S. WESTCOTT.]   Woodcock [Philohela minor] and Woodcock Shooting.   <*Forest and Stream*, iii, Oct. 8, 1874, p. 131.

1874. "HOMO."   [C. S. WESTCOTT.]   Snipe [Gallinago wilsoni] and Snipe Shooting.   <*Forest and Stream*, iii, Oct. 22, 1874, p. 163.

1874. "H. P. S."   Early Woodcock [Philohela minor].   <*Am. Sportsman*, iii, 1874, p. 395.

> At Troy, N. Y., March 7.

1874. "PHILOHELA."   Woodcock [Philohela minor] in Boston [Boylston street].   <*Am. Sportsman*, iv, 1874, p. 91.

1874. "HERBERT".   The Song of the Woodcock [Philohela minor].   <*Am. Sportsman*, iv, 1874, p. 92.

> Sings at evening (see p. 19) and carries young by clasping it between the thighs (see p. 75).

1874. LAMBERTON, A. B.   The American Snipe [Gallinago wilsoni].   <*Am. Sportsman*, iv, 1874, p. 99 and p. 115.   See p. 155.

1874. MATHEW, G. F.   Green Sandpiper [Totanus ochropus, in Great Britain].   <*Zoologist*, 2d ser., ix, 1874, p. 4159.

1874. PERSSE, A.   Sabine's Snipe [Gallinago sabinii] in County Galway.   <*Zoologist*, 2d ser., ix, 1874, p. 3836.

1874. ROBINSON, E.   White Woodcock [Scolopax rusticola] in Ireland.   <*Zoologist*, 2d ser., ix, 1874, p. 3915.

1874. ROBERTS, G., EDSON, —, *and* NEWMAN, E.   Communications and Extracts concerning the Marsh Sandpiper (Totanus stagnatilis of Bechstein).   <*Zoologist*, 2d ser., ix, 1874, pp. 4054–4056.

1874. RODD, E. H.   Woodcocks [Scolopax rusticola] in the Scilly Isles.   <*Zoologist*, 2d ser., ix, 1874, p. 4260.

1874. "SETTER."   Woodcock [Philohela minor] carrying their young.   <*Am. Sportsman*, iv, 1874, p. 10.

> *Philohela minor* carrying its young on its back in flight; also in its claws; confirming observation of "E. H. L.", *ibid.*, iii, p. 379.   See also p. 139.

1874. SHAW, J.   Solitary Snipe [Gallinago major] in Lancashire.   <*Zoologist*, 2d ser., ix, 1874, p. 3836.

> From 'Field,' Oct. 4, 1873.

1874. "TIMBERDOODLE." A Woodcock [Philohela minor] Out of Place. < *Am. Sportsman*, iv, 1874, p. 28.

1874. "W. B." German Sporting Notes. < *Am. Sportsman*, iv, 1874, p. 75.
    Philohela minor carries its young, holding them with its claws, between its legs. Compare iv, p. 10, and iii, p. 379.

1874. WHITAKER, J. Bartailed Godwit [Limosa lapponica] in Nottinghamshire. < *Zoologist*, 2d ser., ix, 1874, p. 4199.

1874. "WING NOTE". Ideas of a Georgia Sportsman [as to sounds made by Gallinago wilsoni, while descending]. < *Am. Sportsman*, iv, 1874, p. 155.

1874. WYMAN, L. [Habits of Actiturus bartramius in Massachusetts.] < *Forest and Stream*, i, Jan. 8, 1874, p. 342.

1875. "ALIQUIS." The Woodcock [Philohela minor] as a song bird. < *Forest and Stream*, iv, June 3, 1875, p. 262.

1875. ANON. Artifices of the Woodcock [Philohela minor]. < *Forest and Stream*, iv, April 22, 1875, p. 167. See also p. 215.

1875. ANON. [EDITORIAL.] Instinct in the Woodcock [Philohela minor]. < *Forest and Stream*, iv, June 10, 1875, p. 279.
    Carrying young in its claws.

1875. ANON. [TILESTON, W. M.] Tame Snipe. < *Forest and Stream*, v, Sept. 9, 1875, p. 68.
    Successful experiments in keeping Snipe in various parts of the world.

1875. ANON. [EDITORIAL.] The Woodcock [Philohela minor]. < *Rod and Gun*, vi, April 17, 1875, p. 40. See also p. 67.
    Need of legislative protection. The volume contains frequent allusion to, and arguments for, this measure, from various correspondents.

1875. ANON. [EDITORIAL.] [Characteristics and pseudonyms of Tringa maculata.] < *Rod and Gun*, vi, April 17, 1875, p. 42.

1875. DE BANES, J. Habits of the Woodcock [Philohela minor]. < *Forest and Stream*, iv, March 25, 1875, p. 101.
    Full biography, from observations in Western New York.

1875. "E. E. E." First Snipe [Gallinago wilsoni, at Elkton, Md.]. < *Rod and Gun*, vi, Apr. 3, 1875, p. 10.

1875. "E. R." Artifices of Woodcock [Philohela minor]. < *Forest and Stream*, iv, July 1, 1875, p. 326. See also p. 127, 215.

1875. COFFIN, C. E. Confidences of Woodcock [Philohela minor, on the nest]. < *Forest and Stream*, v, Sept. 9, 1875, p. 68. See also p. 4.

1875. "GEO. H. M." Traits of Woodcock [Philohela minor]. < *Forest and Stream*, iv, May 13, 1875, p. 215. See pp. 167, 215.

1875. GUNN, T. E. Solitary Snipe [Gallinago major] in Norfolk. < *Zoologist*, 2d ser., x, Oct., 1875, pp. 4665, 4666.

1875. GUNN, T. E. Spotted Redshank [Totanus fuscus] in Norfolk. < *Zoologist*, 2d ser., x, Oct., 1875, p. 4666.

1875. GURNEY, J. H., JR. Green Sandpiper [Totanus ochropus] at Northrepps. < *Zoologist*, 2d ser., x, Nov., 1875, p. 4697.

1875. HODGKINSON, J. B. Brown Snipe near Southport. < *Zoologist*, 2d ser., x, Feb., 1875, p. 4341.

1875. INGERSOLL, E. Remarkable success in taming Woodcocks [Philohela minor]. < *Forest and Stream*, v, Dec. 2, 1875, p. 260.

1875. LINDEN, C. Preservation of Woodcock [Philohela minor]. < *Rod and Gun*, vi, May 1, 1875, p. 67. See also p. 40.
    General natural history.

1875. "RECAPPER." [T. C. ABBOTT.] The American Woodcock [Philohela minor]. < *Forest and Stream*, iv, Apr. 1, 1875, p. 117.

1875. WEBSTER, F. S. Gallinago Wilsoni [at Troy, N. Y.]. < *Forest and Stream*, iv, Mar. 18, 1875, p. 85.

1875. WHITAKER, J. Curlew [Numenius arquatus] in Nottinghamshire. < *Zoologist*, 2d ser., x, Mar., 1875, p. 4382.

1875. [WILLARD, S. L.] The American Woodcock, Philohela minor. < *Oölogist*, i, 1875, p. 71.

1875. [WILLARD, S. L.] The Solitary Sandpiper. (Rhyacophilus solitarius.) < *Oölogist*, i, 1875, p. 45.

1876. ANON. Woodcock [Philohela minor] on her nest. < *Forest and Stream*, vi, May 25, 1876, p. 250, fig.

1876. BALFOUR, T. G. Whimbrel [Numenius phæopus] in Wiltshire. < *Zoologist*, 2d ser., xi, Nov., 1876, p. 5166.

1876. "B. L." Woodcock [Philohela minor] in the South. < *Rod and Gun*, viii, Sept. 16, 1876, p. 389.

1876. BOYES, F. Green Sandpipers [Totanus ochropus] near Beverley. < *Zoologist*, 2d ser., xi, Nov., 1876, p. 5168.

1876. BOYES, F. Woodcock [Scolopax rusticola] migrating in July. < *Zoologist*, 2d ser., xi, Nov., 1876, pp. 5166, 5167.

1876. BREWSTER, W. Occurrence of the Curlew Sandpiper [Tringa subarquata] in Massachusetts. < *Bull. Nutt. Ornith. Club*, i, No. 2, July, 1876, pp. 51, 52.

1876. COOPER, J. Curious Habit of the Common Sandpiper [Tringoides hypoleucus]. < *Zoologist*, 2d ser., xi, Oct., 1876, pp. 5125, 5126.

1876. CORDEAUX, J. Great Snipe [Gallinago major] in Perthshire. < *Zoologist*, 2d ser., xi, Nov., 1876, p. 5167.

1876. COUES, E. European Woodcock [Scolopax rusticola] Shot in Virginia. < *Forest and Stream*, vi, Apr. 27, 1876, p. 180.
This and the next title refer to the same instance.

1876. COUES, E. The European Woodcock [Scolopax rusticola] shot in Virginia. < *Am. Nat.*, x, No. 6, June, 1876, p. 372.

1876. COUES, E. The Woodcock (Philohela minor). < *Rod and Gun*, viii, July 8, 1876, p. 227, fig.
From his "Birds of the Northwest." See also p. 260.

1876. "CANONICUS." Nature and Habits of the Woodcock [Philohela minor]. < *Rod and Gun*, viii, May 20, 1876, p. 114, and May 27, 1876, p. 134.

1876. DRESSER, H. E. On a new Species of Broadbilled Sandpiper [Limicola sibirica]. < *P. Z. S.*, June 20, 1876, pp. 674, 675.

1876. GATCOMBE, J. Great Snipe [Gallinago major] in Devon. < *Zoologist*, 2d ser., xi, Oct., 1876, p. 5126.

1876. GURNEY, J. H., JR. Dunlins [Tringa alpina] Inland. < *Zoologist*, 2d ser., x, Feb., 1876, p. 4802.

1876. GURNEY, J. H., JR. Woodcock's [Scolopax rusticola] Mode of Carrying Young. < *Zoologist*, 2d ser., xi, Mar., 1876, p. 4844.

1876. GURNEY, J. H., JR. Bartailed Godwit [Limosa lapponica]. < *Zoologist*, 2d ser., xi, Aug., 1876, p. 5046.

1876. GURNEY, J. H., JR. Woodcock [Scolopax rusticola] migrating in July. < *Zoologist*, 2d ser., xi, Sept., 1876, p. 5083.

1876. GURNEY, J. H., JR. The Redshank [Totanus calidris] at Northrepps. < *Zoologist*, 2d ser., xi, Sept., 1876, p. 5083.

1876. GURNEY, J. H., JR. Green Sandpiper [Totanus ochropus] at Northrepps. < *Zoologist*, 2d ser., xi, Sept., 1876, p. 5083.

1876. GURNEY, J. H., JR.   Green Sandpiper [Totanus ochropus] at Northrepps.   < *Zoologist*, 2d ser., xi, Oct., 1876, p. 5125.

1876. HARTING, J. E.   Bartram's Sandpiper [Actiturus bartramius].   < *Rod and Gun*, viii, Apr. 29, 1876, p. 71.
   From London *Field* of Mar. 25, 1876.

1876. KERRY, F.   Knot [Tringa canutus] and Green Sandpiper [Totanus ochropus] at Aldeburgh.   < *Zoologist*, 2d ser., xi, Sept., 1876, p. 5083.

1876. MATHEW, G. F.   Bartailed Godwit [Limosa lapponica].   < *Zoologist*, 2d ser., xi, Jan., 1876, p. 4764.

1876. "REX." [S. J. MILLS.]   Woodcock [Philohela minor].   < *Rod and Gun*, viii, July 22, 1876, p. 260.
   Notes on spring voice of this species. See p. 22.

1876. RODD, E. H.   Sabine's Snipe [Gallinago sabinii] near Penzance.   < *Zoologist*, 2d ser., xi, Feb., 1876, pp. 4801, 4802.

1876. RODD, E. H.   Note on Sabine's Snipe (Scolopax [Gallinago] Sabini).   < *Zoologist*, 2d ser., xi, Nov., 1876, pp. 5142-5145.
   On its specific validity.

1876. [SCOTT, W. E. D.]   A Key to our Shore Birds.—II.   < *Forest and Stream*, Aug. 10, 1876.
   This second instalment of an analysis, for the use of sportsmen, of the North American *Limicolæ*, gives brief characters of all the *Scolopacidæ*.

1876. "SNIPE."   Early Snipe.   < *Rod and Gun*, vii, Feb. 5, 1876, p. 290.
   Gallinago wilsoni (?) at Baltimore Jan. 16.

1877. ANON.   Woodcock [Philohela minor].   < *Rod and Gun*, ix, Mar. 10, 1877, p. 360.
   Its ability to endure much rigorous weather.

1877. B[RACKETT, A. E.]   Jack Snipe in Colorado.   < *Forest and Stream*, ix, Dec. 27, 1877, p. 397.

1877. "BOURGEOISE."   Woodcock [Philohela minor] a la Bourgeoise.   < *Forest and Stream*, viii, July 26, 1877, p. 421.

1877. [BREWER, T. M.]   The Nesting of the Snipe [Gallinago wilsoni, in southern localities].   < *Forest and Stream*, ix, Dec. 27, 1877, p. 397.   See pp. 285, 326.

1877. BREWER, T. M.   The Willet [Symphemia semipalmata, breeding along the Atlantic coast of the United States].   < *Forest and Stream*, ix, Sept. 27, 1877, p. 144.

1877. HARTING, J. E.   [Remarks on Exhibition of a variety of the common Snipe, Gallinago media.]   < *P. Z. S.*, June 19, 1877, p. 533.
   Showing the so-called *G. sabinii* to be a melanism of this species.

1877. HUIDEKOPER, E.   Breeding of Wilson Snipe [Gallinago wilsoni, at Meadville, Pa.].   < *Forest and Stream*, ix, Nov. 29, 1877, p. 326.   See p. 285.

1877. HOYT, R. D.   The Woodcock [Philohela minor, breeding] in Florida.   < *Forest and Stream*, viii, Apr. 5, 1877, p. 129.   See p. 82.

1877. [MERRIAM, C. H.]   Breeding of Wilson Snipe [Gallinago wilsoni].   < *Forest and Stream*, ix, Nov. 5, 1877, p. 285.   See p. 326.
   Report of its breeding in Connecticut; from his "Review of the Birds of Connecticut," 1877, p. 105.

1877. SEVERANCE, J. A.   Nomenclature [of Gallinago wilsoni corrected].   < *Forest and Stream*, viii, Apr. 5, 1877, p. 128.

1878. ABBOTT, C. C.   The English Snipe [Gallinago wilsoni] in New Jersey.   < *The Country*, i, Jan. 26, 1878, p. 180.
   Breeding at Trenton, N. J.; specimens supposed to have been unable, through injury, to go northward; note appended by W. E. D. Scott, doubting this explanation.

1878. "ANO."   Early Birds.   < *Forest and Stream*, x, Apr. 25, 1878, p. 216.
   Woodcock breeding at Painesville, Ohio, Apr. 7.

1873. [APPLETON, G. L.]   A Large Woodcock [weight nine ounces].   < *Forest and Stream*, x, Mar. 14, 1878, p. 95.

It is not impossible that this and some similar records of unusually large Woodcock shot in the United States have actual reference to the European *Scolopax rusticola*.

1878. BREWER, T. M.   The Stilt Sandpiper (Micropalama himantopus).   < *Bull. Nutt. Ornith. Club*, iii, No. 3, July, 1878, p. 148.

Its frequent occurrence on Long Island, according to observations of G. N. Lawrence.

1878. BREWER, T. M.   Eggs of the Solitary Sandpiper (Rhyacophilus solitarius Bp.).   < *Bull. Nutt. Ornith. Club*, iii, No. 4, Oct., 1878, p. 197.

Important as being doubtless the first description of an authentic egg of this species. The supposed egg had occasionally been reported before, but never with positive identification, that of *Tringoides macularius* or *Ægialitis vocifera* having been usually mistaken for it.

1878. BREWER, T. M.   Notes on the Occurrence of Micropalama himantopus in New England.   < *Proc. Bost. Soc. Nat. Hist.*, xix, for Oct. 3, 1877, pub. Jan. Feb., 1878, pp. 252–256.

This is quite an extensive paper, giving the particulars of various occurrences.

1878. BROWN, N. C.   The Stilt Sandpiper (Micropalama himantopus) at Portland, Maine.   < *Bull. Nutt. Ornith. Club*, iii, No. 2, Apr., 1878, p. 102.

1878. [CHUBB, J.]   Early Snipe [Gallinago wilsoni, at Cleveland, Ohio].   < *Forest and Stream*, x, Mar. 28, 1878, p. 135.

1878. HEAD, J. F.   Breeding of the Woodcock [Philohela minor] in Georgia.   < *Bull. Nutt. Ornith. Club*, iii, No. 3, July, 1878, p. 151.

Communicated by E. C[oues]; comment by W. Brewster on its breeding in Florida.

1878. "J. M. W."   Woodcock [Philohela minor] killed by Telegraph Wires.   < *Familiar Sci. and Fanciers' Journ.*, v, No. 5, May, 1878, p. 94.

1878. [WILLARD, S. L.]   "Tip-up" [Tringoides macularius].   < *The Oölogist*, iv, No. 3, May, 1878, pp. 22, 23.

Notice of its habits, mostly quoted from Coues's "Birds of the Northwest."

1878. WOOD-MASON, J.   On the Structure and Development of the Trachea in the Indian Painted Snipe (Rhynchæa capensis).   < *P. Z. S.*, June 18, 1878, pp. 745–751, figg. 1, 2, pl. xlvii.

Peculiarly convoluted trachea in the ♀. This sex offers reversal of secondary sexual characters and instincts—being larger and more richly colored than the ♂, having the trachea tortuous instead of simple, deputing the duty of incubation to the ♂, and doing the courting business herself. The parts in mention are figured.

1879. BREWER, T. M.   The Eggs of the Curlew Sandpiper (Tringa subarquata).   < *Bull. Nutt. Ornith. Club*, iv, No. 3, July, 1879, p. 190.

Doubtless a mistake. In *Ibis*, 1879, p. 375, Dr. Brewer makes the same statements. H. W. Feilden criticizes the statements in *Ibis*, 1879, p. 468; and the case is reviewed at length by J. E. Harting, *Zool.*, Mar., 1880, p. 104. The bird may have been *Tringa canutus* or *Phalaropus fulicarius*. Authentic eggs of *Tringa subarquata* continue to be unknown.

1879. COUES, E.   Letters on Ornithology.   No. 19.—The Curlews [Numenius spp.] of North America.   < *The Chicago Field*, Apr. 26, 1879.

Matter rearranged from accounts of three species in "Birds of the Northwest."

1879. COUES, E.   Letters on Ornithology.   No. 25.—The Solitary Tattler; Wood Tattler.   Totanus Solitarius.   < *The Chicago Field*, June 21, 1879.

From "Birds of the Northwest."

1879. COUES, E.   Letters on Ornithology.   No. 26.—Semipalmated Tattler, Willet, Stone Snipe.   (Totanus Semipalmatus.)   < *The Chicago Field*, June 28, 1879.

From "Birds of the Northwest."

1879. COUES, E.   Letters on Ornithology.   No. 27.—Bartramian Sandpiper or Tattler; Upland Plover.   Actiturus Bartramius.   < *The Chicago Field*, July 5, 1879.

From "Birds of the Northwest."

1879. COUES, E.   Letters on Ornithology.   No. 28.—The Buff-Breasted Sandpiper Tryngites Rufescens.   < *The Chicago Field*, July 12, 1879, p. 348.

.From "Birds of the Northwest."

1879. COUES, E.   Letters on Ornithology.   No. 29.—The Great Marbled Godwit. Limosa Fedoa.   < *The Chicago Field*, July 19, 1879.
> From "Birds of the Northwest."

1879. DEANE, R.   Additional Captures of the Curlew Sandpiper [Tringa subarquata] in New England.   < *Bull. Nutt. Ornith. Club*, iv, No. 2, Apr., 1879, p. 124.
> Adding two to the three previously recorded.

1879. DWIGHT, J., JR.   The Stilt Sandpiper (Micropalama himantopus) on the New Jersey Coast.   < *Bull. Nutt. Ornith. Club*, iv, No. 1, Jan., 1879, p. 63.

1879. EDITORIAL.   [F. SATTERTHWAITE.]   A Plea for Woodcock [Philohela minor]. < *Forest and Stream*, xiii, Aug. 14, 1879, p. 550.
> Against the shooting of this species during the summer months.

1879. ELLZEY, M. G., *and* SQUIRE, G. R.   Do Woodcock [Philohela minor] Breed Twice a Year?   < *Forest and Stream*, xii, July 10, 1879, p. 444.
> Letters confirming the position taken by Geo. Bird Grinnell, that Woodcock do usually, in the Middle States, rear two broods each season.

1879. [GRINNELL, G. B.]   Woodcock [Philohela minor] Breed Twice.   < *Forest and Stream*, xii, May 1, 1879, p. 250.
> Defence of statement that Woodcock usually rear two broods in a season, with some of the observations on which this assertion is based.

1879. [HARTING, J. E.]   On some little-known Habits of the Woodcock [Scolopax rusticola].   < *Zoologist*, 3d ser., iii, Nov., 1879, pp. 433–440, pl. iii.
> With special reference to the transportation of the young by the parent. The plate figures the parent flying with the young in her feet, away from the body, as a hawk would carry its prey. The text bears this out, but other passages of the same article speak of the young being pressed to the parent's body, clasped between her legs. See 1874, "A. W."

1879. J. C. H.   Breeding of Woodcock [Philohela minor].   < *Forest and Stream*, xii, May 22, 1879, p. 307.
> Notice of the killing, on the wing, of four young woodcock, Mar. 31, 1878, at Fayetteville, N. C. (By typographical error, as noticed in the next issue of *Forest and Stream*, the note above given was dated Fayetteville, N. Y.)

1879. "PORTSA."   Are Woodcock [Philohela minor] Nocturnal?   < *Forest and Stream*, xi, Jan. 23, 1879, p. 502.

1879. SAMUELS, E. A.   Wilson's Snipe.   Gallinago Wilsonii—(Bonaparte.)   < *Town and Country* (monthly newspaper of Boston, Mass.), i, No. 4, Apr., 1879, cut.
> An extended notice of the habits of this species, with sporting anecdote. Being No. 3 of a series of papers entitled "Our Game Birds."

1879. SAMUELS, E. A.   The Woodcock.   Philohela minor.   < *Town and Country* (monthly newspaper of Boston, Mass.), i, No. 5, May, 1879, cut.
> Popular biographical sketch.

1879. S[TERLING], J. W.   The Second Brood of Woodcock [Philohela minor].   < *Forest and Stream*, xiii, Oct. 2, 1879, p. 684.

1879. YOUNG, C. H.   More White Woodcock [Philohela minor].   < *Forest and Stream*, Apr. 10, 1879, p. 185.

Note.

In *Ibis*, Oct., 1879, p. 453, in an article not citable under *Scolopacidœ*, as it refers to various other birds, H. T. Wharton has shown that the proper specific name of the European Woodcock is *rusticula*, not *rusticola*, though the latter is almost invariably used. Though aware of this before these pages were printed, I preferred to use the latter in my brackets, as being that which the authors themselves of the various papers did or would employ.

Recurvirostridæ.

1835. Du Bus de Ghisignies, V. B.   Description d'un nouveau genre d'Oiseaux de l'ordre des Échassiers [Leptorhynchus pectoralis, sp. n.].   < Bull. Acad. Brux., ii, 1835, pp. 419, 420, pl.
Pas vue moi-même: le titre tiré de Carus et Englemann.

1835. Du Bus de Ghisignies, V. B.   Description d'un nouveau genre d'Oiseaux de l'ordre des Échassiers [Leptorhynchus pectoralis].   < L'Institut, iii, No. 103, 1835, p. 138.
Pas vue moi-même: le titre tiré de Carus et Englemann.

1835. Dubus [de Ghisignies, V. B.]   Leptorhynque.   Leptorhynchus.   Dubus. Nouveau genre d'Oiseaux de l'ordre des Échassiers.   < Guér. Mag. de Zool., 5e année, 1835, classe ii, notice xlv, pl. xlv.
Leptorhynchus pectoralis, nuper g. sp. n., pl. 45.—Mémoire presenté à l'Acad. Roy. de Bruxelles, séance du 17 janv. 1835.

1835. Dumortier, —.   [Rapport sur le mémoire intitulé: Description d'un nouveau genre d'Oiseaux de l'ordre des Échassiers (Leptorhynchus pectoralis).]   < L'Institut, ii, 1835, pp. 72–74.
Pas vue moi-même.

1841. Gould, J.   [Description of a New Species of Himantopus (Novæ Zelandiæ) from New Zealand.]   < P. Z. S., ix, 1841, p. 8.

1843. Fisher, W. R.   Note on the occurrence of the Avocet [Recurvirostra avocetta] near Yarmouth.   < Zoologist, i, 1843, p. 148.

1844. Du Bus [de Ghisignies, V. B.]   Neuer Sumpfvogel, Leptorhynchus pectoralis aus Neuholland.   < Oken's Isis, Bd. xxxvii, 1844, pp. 330, 331.
Aus d. Bull. Acad. Roy. Bruxel., Bd. ii, 1835, q. v.

1844. Mansell, T.   Note on the occurrence of the Stilt Plover [Himantopus leucocephalus?] in New South Wales.   < Zoologist, ii, 1844, p. 454.

1845. Ross, F. W. L.   Beak and Legs of the Avocet [Recurvirostra avocetta].   < Zoologist, iii, 1845, p. 1191.

1847. Rodd, E. H.   Occurrence of the Avocet [Recurvirostra avocetta] at the Land's End.   < Zoologist, v, 1847, p. 1910.

1849. Benson, H.   Occurrence of the Avocet [Recurvirostra avocetta] near Ramsgate.   < Zoologist, vii, 1849, p. 2455.

1849. Duff, J.   Occurrence of the Avocet (Recurvirostra avocetta) at the Tees Mouth.   < Zoologist, vii, 1849, p. 2591.

1849. Ellman, J. B.   Occurrence of the Avocet [Recurvirostra avocetta] in Romney Marsh.   < Zoologist, vii, 1849, p. 2455.

1849. Ellman, J. B.   Occurrence of the Avocet (Avocetta recurvirostra) in Romney Marsh.   < Zoologist, vii, 1849, pp. 2528, 2529.

1849. Gurney, J. H.   Occurrence of the Avocet (Avocetta recurvirostra) near Lynn.   < Zoologist, vii, 1849, p. 2455.

1851. Harper, J. O.   Occurrence of the Avocet (Recurvirostra Avocetta) at Sandwich, in Kent.   < Zoologist, ix, 1851, p. 2980.

1851. Harper, J. O.   Occurrence of the Avocet (Recurvirostra Avocetta) at Yarmouth.   < Zoologist, ix, 1851, p. 3208.

1851. Selys-Longchamps, E. de.   Note sur la famille des Recurvirostridées.   < Bull. de l'Acad. Roy. de Bruxelles, xviii, i, 1851, pp. 5–15.
Pas vue moi-même: le titre tiré de la Bibl. de Carus et Engelmann.

1851. SELYS-LONGCHAMPS, E. DE.   Note sur la famille des Recurvirostridées.   <*L'In-stitut*, xix, No. 913, 1851, p. 211.
    Pas vue moi-même.

1852. IRBY, L. H.   Occurrence of the Avocet [Recurvirostra avocetta] at Yarmouth.   < *Zoologist*, x, 1852, p. 3504.

1856. FOOTIT, W. F.   Occurrence of the Avocet [Recurvirostra avocetta] near New-ark.   < *Zoologist*, xiv, 1856, pp. 5251, 5252.

1856. NEWMAN, E.   Occurrence of the Stilt Plover (Himantopus melanopterus) at Bosham, in Sussex.   < *Zoologist*, xiv, 1856, p. 4946.

1856. WOLLEY, G.   Occurrence of the Avocet [Recurvirostra avocetta] in Notting-hamshire.   < *Zoologist*, xiv, 1856, p. 5280.

1857. MATTHEWS, H.   Occurrence of the Avocet (Recurvirostra avocetta) near New-ark.   < *Zoologist*, xv, 1857, pp. 5364, 5365.

1858. GARDNER, J.   Occurrence of the Avocet (Recurvirostra avocetta) in Kent.   < *Zoologist*, xvi, 1858, p. 5921.

1859. JÄGER, G.   Herr Professor Dr. G. Jäger bespricht die Lebensweise eines Exem-plares von Recurvirostra avocetta.   < *Verh. d. k.-k. zool.-bot. Ges. Wien*, ix, 1859, pp. 98-101.

1859. KNOX, A. E.   On the Habits of the Black-winged Stilt [Himantopus melanop-terus], as observed on its occurrence in Sussex.   < *Ibis*, i, 1859, pp. 395-397.

1860. KNOX, A. E.   On the Habits of the Black-winged Stilt [Himantopus melanop-terus], as observed on its occurrence in Sussex.   < *Zoologist*, xviii, 1860, pp. 6979, 6980.
    From *Ibis*, i, 1859, pp, 395-397.

1864. JEFFREY, W., JR.   Avocet [Recurvirostra avocetta] near Chichester.   < *Zoolo-gist*, xxii, 1864, p. 9211.

1867. HACKETTS, W. A.   Avocet [Recurvirostra avocetta] in the County Cork.   < *Zoologist*, 2d ser., ii, 1867, p. 635.
    From the 'Field,' Jan. 12.

1867. RAMSEY, E. P.   Note on the Eggs of the Australian Stilt-Plover (Himantopus leucocephalus).   < *P. Z. S.*, xxxv, 1867, p. 600.

1867. THOMPSON, W.   Occurrence of the Avocet [Recurvirostra avocetta] near Wey-mouth.   < *Zoologist*, 2d ser., ii, 1867, p. 759.

1868. TRISTRAM, H. B.   [Questions distinctness of Recurvirostra sinensis from R. avocetta.]   < *Ibis*, 2d ser., iv, 1868, p. 133.

1869. HART, W., *and* SON.   Avocet [Recurvirostra avocetta] at Portsmouth [England].   < *Zoologist*, 2d ser., iv, 1869, p. 1562.

1870. FEILDEN, H. W.   [Additional (Ibis, 1870, 145) information on the breeding of Himantopus candidus.]   < *Ibis*, 2d ser., vi, 1870, p. 295.

1870. HUME, A. [O.]   [On the breeding, nest, and eggs of the Indian Black-winged Stilt, Himantopus candidus.]   < *Ibis*, 2d ser., vi, 1870, pp. 145-147.

1871. GATCOMBE, J.   Avocet [Recurvirostra avocetta] in Cornwall.   < *Zoologist*, 2d ser., vi, 1871, p. 2810.

1874. HARTING, J. E.   On rare or little-known Limicolæ.   [Part VI.]   < *Ibis*, 3d ser., iv, 1874, pp. 241-261, pl. ix.
    Treats very fully of the species of *Recurvirostra*. The pl. represents *R. andina*.

1875. BULLER, W. L.   On the Genus Himantopus in New Zealand.   < *Trans. and Proc. New Zealand Inst. for* 1874, vii, 1875, pp. 220-224.
    Treats of *HH. leucocephalus, novæ-zealandiæ,* and *albicollis,* the latter sp. n., p. 224.

1875. GURNEY, J. H., JR.   Plumage of the Stilt [Himantopus candidus].   < *Zoologist*, 2d ser., x, Nov., 1875, p. 4697.

1876. WARREN, R.   Avocet [Recurvirostra avocetta] in Ireland.   < *Zoologist*, 2d ser., xi, Jan., 1876, pp. 4764, 4765.

Phalaropodidæ.

1758. EDWARDS, G. An Account of a new-discovered Species of the Snipe or Tringa [*i. e.*, Phalaropus fulicarius]. < *Philos. Trans. for* 1757, 1, pt. i, 1758, pp. 255–257, pl. vi.

"Grey Coot-footed Tringa"=*Phalaropus fulicarius* of later authors. The plate also illustrates the bill of the Red-necked Phalarope, *Lobipes hyperboreus* of systematists.

1807. SIMMONDS, T. W. Observations respecting a Species of Phalarope, and some other rare British Birds. < *Trans. Linn. Soc.*, viii, 1807, pp. 264–269.

Phalaropus williamsii, p. 264, sp. n. [It is *Lobipes hyperboreus*.]

1832. ALLIS, T. Grey Phalarope [Phalaropus fulicarius, near York, England]. < *Loudon's Mag. Nat. Hist.*, v, 1832, p. 589.

1832. COUCH, J. The Grey Phalarope [Phalaropus fulicarius, in Great Britain]. *Loudon's Mng. Nat. Hist.*, v, 1832, pp. 729, 730.

1832. JORDAN, W. R. Notes on the Gray Phalarope (Tringa lobata, Lin. [Phalaropus fulicarius]). < *Loudon's Mag. Nat. Hist.*, v, 1832, p. 282.

1833. SCOULER, J. Grey Phalarope [Phalaropus fulicarius, in Scotland]. < *Loudon's Mag. Nat. Hist.*, vi, 1833, p. 515.

1846. COOPER, J. Occurrence of the Gray Phalarope [Phalaropus fulicarius] near Preston. < *Zoologist*, iv, 1846, p. 1552.

1846. GURNEY, J. H. Occurrence of the Red-necked Phalarope [Lobipes hyperboreus] in Norfolk. < *Zoologist*, iv, 1846, p. 1552.

1846. MURCH, E. Occurrence of the Gray Phalarope [Phalaropus fulicarius] near Honiton. < *Zoologist*, iv, 1846, p. 1552.

1846. RODD, E. H. Occurrence of the Gray Phalarope [Phalaropus fulicarius] near Penzance. < *Zoologist*, iv, 1846, p. 1552.

1847. BEADLES, J. N. Occurrence of the Gray Phalarope [Phalaropus fulicarius] at Mitcheldean. < *Zoologist*, v, 1847, p. 1697.

1847. GOATLEY, T. Occurrence of the Gray Phalarope (P. lobatus [Phalaropus fulicarius]), near Chipping Norton. < *Zoologist*, v, 1847, p. 1640.

1847. HUNTER, C. B. Occurrence of the Gray Phalarope [Phalaropus fulicarius] at Wretham. < *Zoologist*, v, 1847, p. 1640.

1850. LEWINS, R. Occurrence of the Grey Phalarope (Phalaropus lobatus [fulicarius]) in Northumberland. < *Zoologist*, viii, 1850, p. 2853.

1851. ELLMAN, J. B. Occurrence of the Red-necked Phalarope (Phalaropus [Lobipes] hyperboreus) at Lewes. < *Zoologist*, ix, 1851, p. 3035.

1852. GURNEY, S., JR. Occurrence of the Gray Phalarope (Phalaropus platyrrhynchus [fulicarius]) at Carshalton. < *Zoologist*, x, 1852, p. 3331.

1853. HUSSEY, A. Occurrence of the Red-necked Phalarope [Lobipes hyperboreus] at Rottingdean. < *Zoologist*, xi, 1853, pp. 4096, 4097.

1854. GLOGER, C. W. L. Das eigenthümliche Brüt-Verhaltniss der Wassertreter (Phalaropus) und seine Analogie. < *J. f. O.*, ii, 1854, pp. 89–91.

1854. RODD, E. H. Occurrence of the Red-necked Phalarope [Lobipes hyperboreus] near Penzance. < *Zoologist*, xii, 1854, p. 4526.

1854. MILNER, W. M. E. Red-necked Phalarope [Lobipes hyperboreus] killed near York. < *Zoologist*, xii, 1854, p. 4441.

1860. DUNN, J.   Occurrence of the Gray Phalarope [Phalaropus fulicarius] in Orkney.   < *Zoologist*, xviii, 1860, p. 6812.

1860. RODD, E. H.   Occurrence of the Red Phalarope [Phalaropus fulicarius] at Scilly.   < *Zoologist*, xviii, 1860, p. 7236.

1860. WILLIAMS, D.   Occurrence of the Gray Phalarope (Phalaropus platyrhynchus [fulicarius]) at Swansea.   < *Zoologist*, xviii, 1860, p. 6891.

1862. ROGERS, H.   Occurrence of the Gray Phalarope [Phalaropus fulicarius] in the Isle of Wight.   < *Zoologist*, xx, 1862, p. 8283.

1863. DUTTON, J.   The Gray Phalarope [Phalaropus fulicarius] at Brighton.   < *Zoologist*, xxi, 1863, p. 8331.

1863. JEFFERY, W., JR.   The Rednecked Phalarope [Lobipes hyperboreus] near Chichester.   < *Zoologist*, xxi, 1863, p. 8828.

1863. KERR, J.   Gray Phalarope [Phalaropus fulicarius] near Greenock.   < *Zoologist* xxi, 1863, p. 8828.

1863. STEVENSON, H.   The Gray Phalarope (Phalaropus platyrhynchus [fulicarius]) in Norfolk.   < *Zoologist*, xxi, 1863, p. 8331.

1864. OSBORNE, H., JR.   Gray Phalarope [Phalaropus fulicarius] in Caithness.   < *Zoologist*, xxii, 1864, p. 8890.

1866. BLAKE-KNOX, H.   Gray Phalarope [Phalaropus fulicarius] in Dublin Bay.   < *Zoologist*, 2d ser., i, 1866, pp. 500, 501.

1866. DUTTON, J.   Gray Phalarope [Phalaropus fulicarius] at Eastbourne.·   < *Zoologist*, 2d ser., i, 1866, p. 499.

1866. DUTTON, J.   Gray Phalarope [Phalaropus fulicarius] at Eastbourne, &c.   < *Zoologist*, 2d ser., i, 1866, p. 525.

1866. HESSE, B.   Gray Phalarope [Phalaropus fulicarius] in Hackney Marshes.   < *Zoologist*, 2d ser., i, 1866, p. 499.

1866. KIRBY, H. T. M.   Gray Phalarope [Phalaropus fulicarius] at Mayfield.   < *Zoologist*, 2d ser., i, 1866, p. 499.

1866. MATHEW, M. A.   Gray Phalarope [Phalaropus fulicarius] at Weston-super-Mare and at Budleigh Salterton.   < *Zoologist*, 2d ser., i, 1866, pp. 499, 500.

1866. RODD, E. H.   Red Lobefoot [Rednecked Phalarope] [Lobipes hyperboreus] at Scilly.   < *Zoologist*, 2d ser., i, 1866, p. 501.
   Brackets in original title around the words "Rednecked Phalarope".

1867. GUNN, T. E.   The Gray Phalarope [Phalaropus fulicarius] in Norfolk.   < *Zoologist*, 2d ser., ii, 1867, p. 1016.

1867. GURNEY, J. H., JR.   A Summary of the Occurrences [about 250 specimens] of the Grey Phalarope [Phalaropus fulicarius] in Great Britain during the Autumn [Aug. 20–Oct. 8] of 1866.   By J. H. Gurney, jun.   London : 1867. 8vo.   pamph.   pp. 24, map.
   Not seen.—Cf. *Zoology*, s. s., pp. 917–919; *Ibis*, 1868, p. 101.

1867. HAWKER, T. A.   Gray Phalarope [Phalaropus fulicarius] at Shoreham.   < *Zoologist*, 2d ser., ii, 1867, pp. 561, 562.

1867. MATHEW, M. A.   Gray Phalarope [Phalaropus fulicarius] at Barnstaple.   < *Zoologist*, 2d ser., ii, 1867, p. 562.

1868. GUNN, T. E.   Rednecked Phalarope [Lobipes hyperboreus] in Norfolk.   < *Zoologist*, 2d ser., iii, 1868, p. 1482.

1869. GATCOMBE, J.   Rednecked Phalarope [Lobipes hyperboreus] in the Neighbourhood of Plymouth.   < *Zoologist*, 2d ser., iv, 1869, p. 1920.

1869. PRESTON, T. A.   Rednecked Phalarope [Lobipes hyperboreus] at Marlborough.   < *Zoologist*, 2d ser., iv, 1869, p. 1951.

1869. WONFOR, T. W. Gray Phalarope [Phalaropus fulicarius] in Sussex. < *Zoologist*, 2d ser., iv, 1869, p. 1920.

1870. BLAKE-KNOX, H. Gray Phalaropes [Phalaropus fulicarius] in County Dublin. < *Zoologist*, 2d ser., v, 1870, p. 2410.

1870. BROWNE, A. M. Gray Phalarope [Phalaropus fulicarius] in Wales. < *Zoologist*, 2d ser., v, 1870, p. 2410.

1870. GOATLEY, T. H. Gray Phalarope [Phalaropus fulicarius] near Southampton. < *Zoologist*, 2d ser., v, 1870, p. 2385.

1870. HARTING, J. E. On the Immigration of the Gray Phalarope (Phalaropus fulicarius) and the Recent Occurrence of this Species in Sussex. < *Zoologist*, 2d ser., v, 1870, pp. 1972–1975.
 Extracted from 'The Field' of Nov. 13, 1869.

1870. MATHEW, M. A. Gray Phalaropes [Phalaropus fulicarius] in North Devon: Moulting of Birds. < *Zoologist*, 2d ser., v, 1870, pp. 2385, 2386.

1870. MATHEW, M. A. Abundance of the Gray Phalarope [Phalaropus fulicarius]. < *Zoologist*, 2d ser., v, 1870, p. 2410.

1870. SMITH, CECIL. Gray Phalaropes [Phalaropus fulicarius] in Somerset. < *Zoologist*, 2d ser., v, 1870, p. 2410.

1870. SMITH, CECIL. Gray Phalarope [Phalaropus fulicarius] at Bishops Lydeard. < *Zoologist*, 2d ser., v, 1870, p. 2385.

1871. BALKWILL, F. H. Phalaropes [Phalaropus ——] in Plymouth Sound. < *Zoologist*, 2d ser., vi, 1871, pp. 2442, 2443.

1871. BRYDGES, H. J. J. Gray Phalarope [Phalaropus fulicarius] at Boultibrook. < *Zoologist*, 2d ser., vi, 1871, p. 2852.

1871. SMITH, CECIL. Bird-batting. < *Zoologist*, 2d ser., vi, 1871, p. 2438.
 Capture of *Phalaropus fulicarius*.

1871. SMITH, CECIL. Gray Phalarope [Phalaropus fulicarius] near Taunton. < *Zoologist*, 2d ser., vi, 1871, p. 2442.

1871. STUBBS, C. E. Gray Phalarope [Phalaropus fulicarius] near Henley-on-Thames. < *Zoologist*, 2d ser., vi, 1871, p. 2442.

1873. BOYES, F. Rednecked Phalarope [Lobipes hyperboreus] in East Yorkshire. < *Zoologist*, 2d ser., viii, 1873, p. 3371.

1873. CORBIN, G. B. Gray Phalarope [Phalaropus fulicarius, on the Hampshire coast] and Pike. < *Zoologist*, 2d ser., viii, 1873, p. 3492.

1873. MATHEW, M. A. Gray Phalarope [Phalaropus fulicarius] in Winter Plumage. < *Zoologist*, 2d ser., viii, 1873, p. 3454.

1874. NORGATE, F. Rednecked Phalarope [Lobipes hyperboreus] at Salthouse, Norfolk. < *Zoologist*, 2d ser., ix, 1874, p. 4159.

1874. CLARK-KENNEDY, A. J. Gray Phalarope [Phalaropus fulicarius] in Cheshire. < *Zoologist*, 2d ser., ix, 1874, p. 4239.

1874. CLOGG, S. Gray Phalarope [Phalaropus fulicarius] in Cornwall. < *Zoologist*, 2d ser., ix, 1874, p. 4239.

1875. WHITAKER, J. Gray Phalarope [Phalaropus fulicarius] in Nottinghamshire. < *Zoologist*, 2d ser., x, Feb., 1875, p. 4342.

1876. A[LLEN], J. A. Field and Forest. < *Bull. Nutt. Ornith. Club*, i, No. 3, Sept., 1876, p. 71.
 Notice of this periodical, Vol. II, No. 1, the only ornithological article it contains being on *Steganopus wilsoni*. See 1876, KUMLEIN, A. L.

1876. GATCOMBE, J. Early Occurrence of the Gray Phalarope [Phalaropus fulicarius] in Devon. < *Zoologist*, 2d ser., xi, Sept., 1876, pp. 5083, 5084.

1876. KUMLEIN, A. L.   On the Habits of Steganopus wilsoni.   < *Field and Forest,* ii, No. 1, July, 1876, pp. 11, 12.

1876. NICHOLLS, R. P.   Gray Pharalope [Phalaropus fulicarius] near Kingsbridge. < *Zoologist,* 2d ser., xi, Feb., 1876, p. 4802.

1877. NELSON, E. W.   A Contribution to the Biography of Wilson's Phalarope [Steganopus wilsoni].   < *Bull. Nutt. Ornith. Club,* ii, No. 2, Apr., 1877, pp. 38–43.
>   Very full on its habits, especially on its breeding.

1878. COUES, E.   The Northern Phalarope [Lobipes hyperboreus] in North Carolina. < *Bull. Nutt. Ornith. Club,* iii, No. 1, Jan., 1878, pp. 40, 41.

1878. MURDOCH, J.   Phalarope,—An Etymological Blunder.   < *Bull. Nutt. Ornith. Club,* iii, No. 3, July, 1878, pp. 150, 151.
>   Contends that the word should be written *Phalaridopus,* being from φαλαρίς, gen. -ίδος, "a coot", and πούς, "foot", not the adj. φαλαρὸς, "white", as "Phalaropus" would seem to indicate. "Nevertheless," as the writer, who has well taken his point, continues, "the name has served so long as a distinguishing mark of the genus, that it would be by no means advisable to attempt to make an exchange for the etymologically correct form"; especially as the form "Phalaropus" represents no very great degree of contraction. Moreover, as the writer does not state, φαλαρίς, a coot, and φαλαρὸς, bright, white, shining, or otherwise conspicuous, are etymologically the same, the former substantive being derived from the latter adjective and having been applied to the bird because of its conspicuously colored bill; there being this additional reason for not insisting upon the change. Brisson certainly invented "Phalaropus" to mean "coot-footed," but the φάλαρα of the Greeks were any ornaments with which a thing might be furnished, as the gems of a tiara, the studs of a helmet, the caparisons of a horse, etc.; and "Phalaropus" is therefore not so far out of the way after all, for a bird whose feet are remarkably "ornamented" or appendaged.

1878. WILLISTON, S. W.   On the adult male plumage of Wilson's Phalarope. (Steganopus Wilsoni Sab.)   < *Trans. Kansas Acad. Science for* 1877–8, vi, 1878, p. 39.
>   "What has hitherto been considered the young plumage of this bird, has been confounded with [that of] the adult male." Description follows, with other remarks.

Heliornithidæ.

1840. BRANDT, J. F.   Einige Bemerkungen über Podoa und ihr Verhältniss zu Fulica, Podiceps und den Steganopoden.   < *Mém. de l'Acad. St.-Pétersb.*. vi sér., v tome, ii pte., *Sc. Nat.*, iii, 1840, pp. 197–202, pll. xi, xii.

A subtitle, being the third part of his series entitled: Beiträge zur Kenntniss der Naturg. Vögel u. s. w.—*Podoa* is associated with *Fulica*, in the order *Natatores*.

1848. GRAY, G. R.   Description of a new species of Podica [P. personata].   < *P. Z. S.*, xvi, 1848, p. 90.

1849. GRAY, G. R.   Description of a new species of Podica [P. personata].   < *Ann. Mag. Nat. Hist.*, 2d ser., iii, 1849, pp. 311, 312.

From *P. Z. S.*, June 13, 1848, p, 90.

1861. GIEBEL, C. G.   Ueber Podoa surinamensis.   < *Zeitsch. f. d. gesammt. Naturwiss.*, xviii, 1861, pp. 424– —.

Nicht mir selbst zugänglich.—Enthaltend anatomisches.

1867. SCHLEGEL, H.   Urinatores   < *Mus. Hist. Nat. Pays-Bas*, 9e livr., avril 1867, pp. 1–52.

This group, as made up by the author, consists of the five families *Spheniscidæ, Alcidæ, Colymbidæ, Podicipidæ,* and *Heliornithidæ,* of three of which only a single genus is admitted. *Spheniscus,* 12 species.

In the *Alcidæ,* with 3 genera, are treated of *Alca,* 9 spp.; *Simorhynchus,* 6 spp.; *Lunda,* 3 spp.   *Colymbus,* with 3 spp.   *Podiceps,* with 12 spp.   *Heliornis,* with 3 spp.

Parridæ.

1832. GEOFFROY ST.-HILAIRE, ISID. Jacana, Parra. Lin. < *Guér. Mag. de Zool.*, 2ᵉ année, 1832, classe ii, notice vi, pl. vi.

Parra albinuca [sic], pl. vi, sp. n. ; Madagascar. [*Metopodius.*]

1856. SCLATER, P. L. On the species of the American genus Parra. < *P. Z. S.*, xxiv, 1856, pp. 282, 283.

The American birds of the genus *Parra*, with their Old World representatives of the genera *Metopodius*, *Hydralector*, and *Hydrophasianus*, are considered to constitute a natural group related to the *Rallidæ*, but remarkable for the extreme elongation of the toes. The article is a synopsis of five spp., with synonymy, diagnosis, and habitat : 1, *P. jacana*, L. 2, *P. intermedia*, Bp., sp. n., p. 282, Venezuela. 3, *P. melanopygia*, sp. n., p. 283, New Grenada. 4, *P. hypomelæna*, Gr. & Mitch. 5, *P. gymnostoma*, Wagl.

1857. SCLATER, P. L. On the Species of the American genus Parra. < *Ann. Mag. Nat. Hist.*, 2d ser., xix, 1857, pp. 410, 411.

From *P. Z. S.*, July 8, 1856, pp. 282, 283, *q. v.*

1864. GOULD, J. Description of the Egg of Parra gallinacea [Hydralector cristata]. < *P. Z. S.*, Dec. 13, 1864, p. 661.

1865. GOULD, J. Description of the Egg of Parra gallinacea [Hydralector cristata]. < *Ann. Mag. Nat. Hist.*, 3d ser., xvi, 1865, p. 70.

From *P. Z. S.*, Dec. 13, 1864, p. 661.

Rallidæ.

[Including *Gallinula, Fulica, Aramus, Notornis, Aphanapteryx*, etc.]

1717. LIMPRECHT, J. A.   De Fulica recentiorum minore Gesneri.   < *Ephem. Acad. Nat. Cur.*, Cent. 5 et 6, 1717, pp. 212–217.

> Haud mihi cognitus: titulus e Caro et Engelm.

1721. HOFFMANN, M.   De Fulica dissecta.   < *Ephem. Acad. Nat. Cur.*, Cent. 9 et 10, 1721, App., pp. 469, 470.

> Non mihi obvius: titulus e Caro et Engelm.

1734. PERRAULT, C.   Description anatomique d'une Poule Sultane [Porphyrio]. < *Mém. de l'Acad. Roy. des Sci.* depuis 1666 jusq. 1699, iii, pt. iii, 1734, pp. 50–57, pll. 11, 12.

1744–50. HASSELQUIST, F.   Fulica.   Linnaei Syst. Nat. p. 28.   < *Acta Reg. Soc. Sci. Upsal.*, v, 1744–50, pp. 22, 23.

> Haud mihi obvia.

1757. PERRAULT, C.   Anatomische Beschreibung einer Sultanshenne [Porphyrio]. < *Abhandl. Königl. Französisch. Akad.*, ii, 1757, pp. 277– —.

> Mir nicht zugänglich.—Teutsch. Übers. d. *Mém. de l'Acad. Paris*, iii, pt. iii, 1734, p. 50.

1813. LJUNGH, S. I.   En ny Fogel, Rallus Paykullii, beskrifven.   < *Kongl. Vetensk. Acad. Handl.*, 1813, pp. 258–260, pl. v.

1817. BARTON, B. S.   Some Account of the Tantalus Ephouskyca [sp. n.], a rare American Bird.   < *Trans. Linn. Soc.*, xii, pt. i, 1817, pp. 24–27, pl. i.

> This is the "Crying-bird" of Bartram, *Trav. in Fla.*, ed. of 1791, p. 147, "*Tantalus pictus*," *ibid.*, p. 293=*Aramus giganteus* Bp.=*A. pictus*, Coues, *Pr. Phila. Acad.*, 1875, p. 354.

1821. FLEMING, J.   On the Water-Rail [Rallus aquaticus].   < *Mem. Wernerian Nat. Hist. Soc.*, iii, 1821, pp. 174–182.   (Read Nov., 1819.)

> Notes a spine on the wing of *Rallus aquaticus*, and consequently associates the genus with *Parra* and *Palamedea*. Monographic account of the species, followed by a synoptical view of the British species of *Rallus, Ortygometra, Gallinula*, and *Fulica*.

1823. MORRISON, —.   Hybernation of the Corncrake (Rallus Crex [Crex pratensis]). < *Edinb. Philos. Journ.*, viii, 1823, pp. 414, 415.

> Three individuals stated to have been found torpid in a heap of manure.

1829. "B."   Rallus aquaticus.   < *Loudon's Mag. Nat. Hist.*, ii, 1829, p. 302.

> Complaint of the figure given, *op. cit.*, i, p. 289.

1830. ANON.   Spur on the wing of the Rallus Crex [Crex pratensis].   < *Edinb. New Philos. Journ.*, viii, 1830, p. 204.

> See above, 1821, FLEMING, J.

1831. BREHM, C. L.   Die kleinen europäischen Rohrhühner [Porzana spp.].   < *Oken' Isis*, Bd. xxiv, 1831, pp. 705–710.

> *Gallinula minuta* Br.; *G. minutissima*, Pethényi und Brehm. Vergleichung der *G. pusill* und *G. minutissima*.

1832. "A. B."   A white Water-Rail [Rallus aquaticus].   < *Loudon's Mag. Nat. Hist.*, v, 1832, p. 384.

1832. ALLIS, T.   Food of the Water Rail (Rallus aquaticus Linn.).   < *Loudon's Mag. Nat. Hist.*, v, 1832, p. 732.

1832. ANON.   The Gallinule (Gallinula chloropus Latham), a Percher, and exceller for Food.   < *Loudon's Mag. Nat. Hist.*, v, 1832, pp. 381, 382.

1832. "A. R. Y."   The Gizzard of the Corncrake (Rallus crex L., Ortygometra cre Fleming [Crex pratensis]).   < *Loudon's Mag. Nat. Hist.*, v, 1832, pp. 731, 73

1832. BLACKWALL, J.   Descriptions of two Birds, hitherto uncharacterized, belonging to the Genera Crex and Rallus.   < *Edinb. Journ. Sci.*, n. s., vi, 1832, pp. 77, 78.
   C. pygmæa, p. 77, North America; *Rallus bicolor*, p. 78, Brazil? [The former is *Porzana jamaïcensis.*]

1832. BREE, W. T.   The Gallinule (Gallinula chloropus Latham) a Percher and good for Food.   < *Loudon's Mag. Nat. Hist.*, v, 1832, p. 730.   With note by "J. D[enson]."

1832. DOVASTON, J. F. M.   The Rallus Crex [Crex pratensis], or Corncrake.   < *Loudon's Mag. Nat. Hist.*, v, 1832, pp. 298, 299.
   Characters of its gizzard.

1832. "E. P. T."   Is the Water Rail (Rallus aquaticus) migratory or not?   < *Loudon's Mag. Nat. Hist.*, v, 1832, p. 397.

1832. G[OATLEY], T.   Is the Water Rail (Rallus aquaticus Linn.) migratory or not?   < *Loudon's Mag. Nat. Hist.*, v, 1832, pp. 732, 733.
   Yes.

1832. "H. B."   The Waterhen (Gallinula chloropus Latham), when disturbed on its Eggs, covers them before it leaves them.   < *Loudon's Mag. Nat. Hist.*, v, 1832, p. 731.

1832. K[NOX], T.   The Water Rail (Rallus aquaticus, p. 68.).   < *Loudon's Mag. Nat. Hist.*, v, 1832, p. 299.
   Nature of its food.

1832. K[NOX], T.   The Spotted Gallinule (Gallinula Porzana Latham [Porzana maruetta]).   < *Loudon's Mag. Nat. Hist.*, v, 1832, p. 731.

1832. K[NOX], T.   Does the Landrail or Corncrake (Ortygometra Crex Flem. [Crex pratensis]) breed in the South of England?   < *Loudon's Mag. Nat. Hist.*, v, 1832, p. 732.
   Yes.

1833. "RUSTICUS."   [NEWMAN, E.]   "The Daker" is a Name for the Corncrake [Crex pratensis].   < *Loudon's Mag. Nat. Hist.*, vi, 1833, p. 279.

1834. "J. M. B."   A Second Brood of Waterhens adopted and catered for by the Individuals of the First Brood.   < *Loudon's Mag. Nat. Hist.*, vii, 1834, pp. 244, 245.

1835. BLACKWALL, J.   Zwei neue Vögel [Crex pygmæa und Rallus bicolor].   < *Oken's Isis*, Bd. xxviii, 1835, p. 316.
   Auszug aus *Edinb. Journ. Sci.*, neue Folge, Bd. vi, 1832, pp. 77, 78.

1838. SMITH, J.   Nest and Eggs of the Water Rail (Rallus aquaticus).   < *Annals of Nat. Hist.*, ii, 1838, p. 78.

1841. BARTHÉLEMY [DE LA POMMERAYE], —.   Note sur la Foulque caronculée [Fulica carunculata].   < *Revue Zoologique*, iv, 1841, p. 307.

1841. LEIB, G. C.   [On the Nest and Eggs of Fulica americana and Anas discors.]   < *Proc. Acad. Nat. Sci. Phila.*, i, 1841, pp. 124, 125.

1842. LAFRESNAYE, [F.] DE.   Description d'un [récemment] nouveau genre d'Oiseaux [Gallirallus brachypterus].   < *Guér. Mag. de Zool.*, 2e sér., année 1842, Oiseaux, pp. 1–4, pl. 24.
   Rev. Zool., 1841, p. 243.—[Ce n'est qu'une synonyme du genre *Ocydromus* Wagl.]

1842. SEZEKORN, E. W.   Ueber das ungewöhnlich zahlreiche Vorkommen des Crex pratensis im Herbste 1841.   < *Jahresb. d. Ver. f. Naturk. in Cassel*, vi, 1842, pp. 9–11.
   Nicht mir selbst zugänglich.

1843. KIDD, W.   Enquiry respecting the Water-rail [Rallus aquaticus].   < *Zoologist*, i, 1843, pp. 148, 149.

1844. ATKINSON, J. C.   Notes on [the habits of] the Moorhen [Gallinula chloropus].   < *Zoologist*, ii, 1844, pp. 497–499.

1844. ATKINSON, J. C.   Further Remarks on the Power of the Moorhens [Gallinula chloropus], &c. to keep the body submerged.   <*Zoologist*, ii, 1844, pp. 756-761.

1844. ATKINSON, J.   Note on the Water-rail [Rallus aquaticus].   < *Zoologist*, ii, 1844, p. 766.

1844. BARTLETT, J. P.   Notes on the Water-rail [Rallus aquaticus].   <*Zoologist*, ii, 1844, p. 669.

1844. DES MURS, O.   Notice et considérations oologiques sur la classification du genre ornithologique Courlan ou Courliri (Buff.), pl. enlum., 848; Ardea, Gm. ; Scolopax, Lin. ; Numenius, Briss.   < *Guér. Mag. de Zool.*, 2ᵉ sér., année 1844, Oiseaux, pp. 1-8, pll. 46, 47, 48.

  Pl. 46, Oeuf du Courlan, *Aramus scolopaceus*. Pl. 47, Oeuf de la Gruë commune *Grus cinerea*. Pl. 48, Oeuf du *Numenius arcuatus*. Voir 1846, même auteur.

1844. FISHER, W. R.   Note on the Migration of the Water-rail [Rallus aquaticus].   < *Zoologist*, ii, 1844, p. 766.

1844. FRERE, H. T.   Note on the Water-rail [Rallus aquaticus].   < *Zoologist*, ii, 1844, pp. 794, 795.

1844. HUSSEY, A.   Note on [the habits of] the Water Rail [Rallus aquaticus].   < *Zoologist*, ii, 1844, pp. 575, 576.

1844. SCLATER, P. L.   Note on the Water-rail [Rallus aquaticus].   < *Zoologist*, ii, 1844, p. 669.

1844. "W. H. S."   Notes on the Moorhen [Gallinula chloropus].   < *Zoologist*, ii, 1844, pp. 667-669.

1845. ATKINSON, J. C.   Corrections of the Rev. J. C. Atkinson's Paper on the Moorhen [Gallinula chloropus] (Zool. 756).   < *Zoologist*, iii, 1845, p. 877.

  Merely literal, and of no consequence.

1845. BARLOW, T. W.   Migration of the Water Rail [Rallus aquaticus].   < *Zoologist*, iii, 1845, p. 1025.

1845. GEE, T.   Moorhen's [Gallinula chloropus] power of keeping its body under water.   < *Zoologist*, iii, 1845, p. 877.

1845. GOATLEY, T.   Migration of the Water-rail [Rallus aquaticus].   < *Zoologist*, iii, 1845, p. 876.

1845. GOULD, J.   [Fulica australis, a new grallatorial Bird from Australia.]   < *P. Z. S.*, xiii, 1845, pp. 2, 3.

1845. GOULD, J.   [Fulica australis.]   < *Ann. Mag. Nat. Hist.*, xvi, 1845, p. 49.

  From *P. Z. S.*, Jan. 14, 1845, pp. 2, 3.

1845. HUSSEY, A.   Migration of the Land-rail [Crex pratensis].   <*Zoologist*, iii, 1845, p. 876.

1845. "W. H. S."   Further [Zool. 667] Notes on Moorhens [Gallinula chloropus].   < *Zoologist*, iii, 1845, pp. 877, 878.

1846. ATKINSON, J. C.   Submergence of the Moorhen [Gallinula chloropus].   < *Zoologist*, iv, 1846, pp. 1325-1327.

1846. ATKINSON, J. C.   Further [Zool. 1325] remarks on the submergence of Water-birds.   < *Zoologist*, iv, 1846, pp. 1395-1398.

1846. DES MURS, O.   Note rectificative d'un article inséré dans le Magasin de zoologie de 1844, 36ᵉ livraison, sur la classification du genre Courlan ou Courlili, Numenius guaranna [sic] (Briss.).   < *Revue Zoologique*, ix, 1846, pp. 164-167.

  Voir *op. cit.*, 1844, pp. 1-8.

1846. EYTON, T. C.   Description anatomique du courlan (Aramus scolopaceus Bon.).   < *Arch. des Sci. Phys. et Nat.*, i, 1846, pp. 229, 230.

  Résumé de la description, extrait des *Ann. Mag. Nat. Hist.*, janvier 1846.

1846. "W. H. S."   Note on the Water-rail [Rallus aquaticus].   < *Zoologist*, iv, 1846, pp. 1299, 1300.

1846. "W. H. S." Further Notes on the Moorhen [Gallinula chloropus], in reply to Mr. Atkinson. < *Zoologist*, iv, 1846, pp. 1369-1371.

1847. BIRD, W. F. W. Capture of the Little Crake [Porzana minuta] in Norfolk. < *Zoologist*, v, 1847, p. 1777.

1847. THOMPSON, W. Occurrence of Baillon's Crake (Crex [Porzana] Bailloni) in Ireland. < *Zoologist*, v, 1847, p. 1877.
      From *Ann. Mag. Nat. Hist.*, xx, p. 169.

1848. ELLMAN, J. B. Occurrence of the Little Crake (Crex pusilla [Porzana minuta]) at Seaford. < *Zoologist*, vi, 1848, p. 2148.

1848. JOHNSON, F. W. Variety of Moor-hen (Gallinula chloropus). < *Zoologist*, vi, 1848, p. 2067.

1848. MANTELL, [G. A.] [On the localities whence were obtained the specimens of Notornis, etc., described by Owen, tom. cit., pp. 1–10.] < *P. Z. S.*, Jan. 11, 1848, pp. 11, 12.
      Scilicet, Dinornis, Palapteryx, Notornis, Nestor.

1848. MANTELL, [G. A.] Débris d'oiseaux fossiles de la Nouvelle-Zélande. < *Arch. des Sci. Phys. et Nat.*, vii, 1848, p. 337.
      Geol. Soc. Lond., 2 et 23 février; *Athanæum*, 26 février et 11 mars, 1848.

1848. [MANTELL, G. A.] Notices of the Fossil Bones of the Ancient Birds of New Zealand, (in letters dated Jan. 19 and 26, 1848, from Dr. G. A. Mantell to the Senior Editor.) < *Am. Journ. Sci.*, 2d ser., v, No. 15, May, 1848, p. 431.

1848. [MANTELL, G. A.] On the Fossil Bones of the Ancient Birds of New Zealand, (in letters, dated January 19 and 26, 1848, from Dr. G. A. Mantell to Professor Silliman Senior.) < *Edinb. New Philos. Journ.*, xlv, 1848, pp. 196, 197.
      From *Am. Journ. Sci.*, 2d ser., v, No. 15, May, 1848, p. 431.

1848. OWEN, R. On the remains of the gigantic and presumed extinct wingless or terrestrial Birds of New Zealand (Dinornis and Palapteryx), with indications of two other genera (Notornis [g. n.] and Nestor). < *P. Z. S.*, Jan. 11, 1848, pp. 1–10.
      After discussing the *Dinornithidæ* at some length, the author describes g. n. *Notornis*, without, however, naming the form specifically. It afterward became *N. mantelli.*

1848. OWEN, R. On the remains of the gigantic and presumed extinct wingless or terrestrial Birds of New Zealand (Dinornis and Palapteryx), with indications of two other genera (Notornis and Nestor). < *Ann. Mag. Nat. Hist.*, 2d ser., ii, 1848, pp. 53–62.
      From *P. Z. S.*, Jan. 11, 1848, pp. 1–10, *q. v..*

1849. BAIKIE, W. B. The Landrail (Crex pratensis) remaining in England during Winter. < *Zoologist*, vii, 1849, p. 2499.

1849. DES MURS, O. Notice et Considérations oologiques sur le genre ornithologique Poule-Sultane, Fulica Porphyrio (L.). < *Rev. et Mag. Zool.*, i, 1849, pp. 439–444.

1849. HULKE, J. W. Moorhens [Gallinula chloropus] roosting in Trees. < *Zoologist*, vii, 1849, p. 2621.

1849. LAFRESNAYE, F. DE. Mélanges ornithologiques. [Sur le genre Ocydromus.] < *Rev. et Mag. de Zool.*, i, 1849, pp. 433–439.
      Y a-t-il réellement plusieurs espèces de ce genre (*Gallirallus*), ou n'a-t-on point regardé comme telles de livrées d'âge ou de sexe d'une seule espèce?

1849. MANTELL, G. A. Sur des débris d'oiseaux fossiles recueillis à la Nouvelle-Zélande. < *Arch. des Sc. Phys. et Nat.* Genève, x, 1849, pp. 77–79.
      Extrait du *Quart. Journ. Geolog. Soc.*, numéro d'août 1848, p. 225, sur les genres *Dinornis, Palapteryx, Aptornis, Notornis,* et *Nestor.*

1849. MANTELL, G. A. On the Fossil Remains of Birds collected in various parts of New Zealand by Mr. Walter Mantell, of Wellington. < *Am. Journ. Sci.*, 2d ser., vii, 1849, pp. 28–44.
      From *Quart. Journ. Geol. Soc.*, London, No. 15, Aug., 1848. On the genera *Dinornis, Palapteryx, Aptornis, Notornis,* and *Nestor.*

1849. MORRIS, F. O.   The Moorhen (Gallinula chloropus) roosting in Willow-trees.
      < *Zoologist*, vii, 1849, pp. 2591, 2592.

1849. OWEN, R.   On Dinornis (Part III.): containing a description of the Skull and
      Beak of that Genus, and of the same characteristic parts of Palapteryx, and
      of two other Genera of Birds, Notornis and Nestor, forming part of an exten-
      sive series of Ornithic remains discovered by Mr. Walter Mantell, at Wain-
      gongoro, North Island of New Zealand.   < *Trans. Zool. Soc. Lond.*, iii, pt. vi,
      1849, pp. 345-378, pll.
            Notornis mantelli, sp. n. ?

1849. WEDDERBURN, J. N.   Occurrence of the Landrail (Crex pratensis) in Bermuda.
      < *Zoologist*, vii, 1849, p. 2591.

1850. BREE, W. T.   Habits of the Moorhen (Gallinula chloropus).   < *Zoologist*, viii,
      1850, p. 2801.

1850. BONAPARTE, C. L.   [Présentation d'une figure d'un Oiseau (le Notornis mantelli
      d'Owen) trouvé vivant dans la Nouvelle-Zélande.]   < *Compt. Rend. de l'Acad.
      Sci.*, xxxi, 1850, p. 770.

1850. EDITORIAL.   New Bird [Notornis mantelli] from New Zealand.   < *Ann. Mag.
      Nat. Hist.*, 2d ser., vi, 1850, p. 398.

1850. EVANS, A.   On some of the Habits of the Waterhen (Gallinula chloropus).
      < *Zoologist*, viii, 1850, pp. 2704, 2705.

1850. GOULD, J.   Remarks on Notornis Mantelli.   < *P. Z. S.*, xviii, 1850, pp. 212-214,
      pl. (Aves) xxi.
            The living bird is here described, with a colored figure of the head, of natural size.

1850. HODGKINSON, J. B.   Variety of the Corn Crake (Crex pratensis).   < *Zoologist*,
      viii, 1850, p. 2772.

1850. MANTELL, G. A.   Notice of the Discovery by Mr. Walter Mantell in the Middle
      Island of New Zealand, of a living specimen of the Notornis [mantelli], a
      Bird of the Rail family, allied to Brachypteryx, and hitherto unknown to
      naturalists except in a fossil state.   < *P. Z. S.*, xviii, 1850, pp. 209-212.

1851. HARPER, J. O.   Carnivorous propensity of the Water Rail (Rallus aquaticus).
      < *Zoologist*, ix, 1851, p. 2990.

1851. HULKE, J. W.   Occurrence of Baillon's Crake (Crex [Porzana] Baillonii) near
      Deal.   < *Zoologist*, ix, 1851, p. 3035.

1851. MANTELL, [G. A.]   Sur un oiseau [Notornis mantelli] vivant de la Nouvelle-
      Zélande qu'on avait cru n'exister qu'a l'état fossile.   < *Arch. des Sci. Phys. et
      Nat. Genève*, xvi, 1851, pp. 73, 74.
            Ann. and Mag. Nat. Hist., Nov., 1850.

1851. MANTELL, G. A.   Notice of the discovery by Walter Mantell, Esq., of Welling-
      ton, in the Middle Island of New Zealand, of a living specimen of Notornis
      [mantelli], a bird of the Rail Family, allied to Brachypteryx, and hitherto
      known to naturalists only by its fossil remains.   < *Am. Journ. Sci.*, xi, 1851,
      pp. 102-105.

1851-52. MANTELL, G. A.   [Notizen über den lebenden Notornis mantelli.]   < *Froriep's
      Tagsber.*, No. 296, 1851 (*Zool.*, Bd. ii), pp. 57-59; No. 587 (*Zool.*, Bd. iii), 1852,
      pp. 97-101.
            Nicht mir selbst zugänglich.

1851. VARNHAM, W.   Landrail [Crex pratensis] in February.   < *Zoologist*, ix, 1851,
      p. 3115.

1852. GOULD, J.   Remarks on Notornis Mantelli.   < *Ann. Mag. Nat. Hist.*, 2d ser., ix,
      1852, pp. 234-236.
            From *Proc. Zool. Soc.*, Nov. 12, 1850, pp. 212-214, *q. v.*

1852. GOULD, J.   Remarks on Notornis Mantellii.   < *Trans. Zool. Soc. Lond.*, iv, pt.
      ii, 1852, pp. 73, 74, pl.

1852. IRBY, L. H. Occurrence of the Little Crake (Crex pusilla [Porzana minuta]) in Norfolk. < *Zoologist*, x, 1852, p. 3477.

1852. MANTELL, G. A. Notice of the discovery of a living specimen of the Notornis [mantelli]. <*Ann. Mag. Nat. Hist.*, 2d ser., ix, 1852, pp. 231-234.
From *Proc. Zool. Soc.*, Nov. 12, 1850.

1852. MANTELL, G. A. Notice of the Discovery by Mr. Walter Mantell in the Middle Island of New Zealand, of a living specimen of the Notornis [mantelli], a Bird of the Rail family, allied to Brachypteryx, and hitherto unknown to Naturalists, except in a Fossil state. <*Trans. Zool. Soc. Lond.*, iv, pt. ii, 1852, pp. 69-72.

1853. BONAPARTE, C. L. [Note sur une nouvelle espèce de Foulque, Fulica cornuta.] < *Compt. Rend. de l'Acad. Sci.*, xxxvii, Dec. 19, 1853, p. 925.
L'oiseau plus tard nommé *Lycornis* (g. n.) *cornuta*, Bp., *Ann. Sci. Nat.*, 4ᵉ ser., i, 1854, p. 46; *Compt. Rend.*, xliii, p. 600.

1853. GURNEY, J. H. Note on a Wingless Bird said to inhabit the Island of Tristan d'Acunha. < *Zoologist*, xi, 1853, p. 4017.

1853. WODZICKI, C. Einige Worte gewissenhafter Beobachtungen über die Fortpflanzung des Rallus aquaticus, Lin. < *Naumannia*, iii, 1853, pp. 267-276.

1854. BRYANT, H. [Remarks on Exhibition of the peculiarly formed Trachea of the Courlan (Aramus scolopaceus [giganteus]).] < *Proc. Boston Soc. Nat. Hist.*, v, 1854, pp. 20, 21.

1854. GLOGER, C. W. L. Das zweimalige Brüten der Gallinula chloropus. < *J. f. O.*, ii, 1854, pp. 189-191.
Cf. *op. cit.*, 1853, pp. 450, 451.

1854. GURNEY, S., JR. Waterhen [Gallinula chloropus] carrying her Young in her Feet. < *Zoologist*, xii, 1854, p. 4367.

1854. HARTLAUB, G. Kritische Revision der Gattung Fulica Lin. < *J. f. O.*, i, 1853, *Extrah.*, (1854), pp. 73-89.
12 spp., very fully treated, with description, extended synonymy, distribution, and criticism. *F. stricklandi*, p. 75, sp. n.

1854. PARTRIDGE, H. T. Extraordinary Propensity of a Moorhen [Gallinula chloropus]. < *Zoologist*, xii, 1854, p. 4255.

1854. POWYS, T. L. Note on the late abundance of the Spotted Crake (Crex porzana [Porzana maruetta]). < *Zoologist*, xii, 1854, p. 4165.

1854. TRISTRAM, H. B. Occurrence of the Little Olivaceous Gallinule (Ortygometra pusilla [Porzana minuta]) at Balbriggan. <*Zoologist*, xii, 1854, pp. 4298, 4299.

1855. BALDAMUS, [E.] [Notiz über Gallinula chloropus.] < *Naumannia*, v, 1855, p. 413.

1855. CASSIN, J. [Remarks on Exhibition of a specimen of Crex pratensis shot in New Jersey.] < *Proc. Acad. Nat. Sci. Phila.*, vii, 1855, p. 265.

1856. BALDAMUS, E. [Fulica cristata.] < *Naumannia*, vi, 1856, p. 424, Taf. —.

1856. HADFIELD, H. W. Note on the Spotted Crake (Crex Porzana [Porzana maruetta]). < *Zoologist*, xiv, 1856, p. 5064.

1856. HADFIELD, H. W. Little Crake (Crex pusilla [Porzana minuta]) in the Isle of Man. < *Zoologist*, xiv, 1856, p. 5280.

1856. ROEDERN, *Graf.* Ueber die Eier von Ortygometra pygmaea [Porzana minuta]. < *Naumannia*, vi, 1856, pp. 402-404.

1857. HOMEYER, A. v. Seltsames Nesterbauen der Gallinula chloropus. < *J. f. O.*, v, 1857, pp. 373, 374.

1857. RODD, E. H. The Land Rail (Gallinula crex [Crex pratensis]) in Scilly. < *Zoologist*, xv, 1857, p. 5832.

1858. PHILIPPI, R. A. Kurze Beschreibung einer neuen Chilenischen Ralle [Rallus ulignosus]. < *Arch. f. Naturg.*, 1858, (1), pp. 83, 84.

1858. RODD, E. H.   Occurrence of Baillon's Crake (Gallinula [Porzana] Baillonii) near the Land's End.   < *Zoologist*, xvi, 1858, p. 6210.

1858. SALMON, [J. D.]   [Exhibition of Crex (Porzana) bailloni, and its Eggs, from Cambridgeshire.]   < *P. Z. S.*, xxvi, 1858, p. 560.

1858. SCHLEGEL, H.   H. Schlegel, über einige ausgestorbene riesige Vögel von den maskarenischen Inseln, als Anhang zu seiner Geschichte der Dodo's.   (Mittheilungen der Königl. holländischen Akademie der Wissenschaften, Abtheilung Naturkunde, Theil vii, Seite 116.)   Aus dem Holländischen übersetzt von Dr. Ed. v. Martens.   < *J. f. O.*, vi, 1858, pp. 367–381.
Nebst Bemerk. des Uebersetzers, pp. 379-381.

1858. SMURTHWAITE, H.   Occurrence of the Spotted Crake (Gallinula porzana [Porzana maruetta]) near Richmond, Yorkshire.   < *Zoologist*, xvi, 1858, p. 6224.

1859. BOLLE, C.   Zur Oophagie der Rallen [Rallidæ].   < *J. f. O.*, vii, 1859, pp. 237, 238.

1859. SEALY, A. F.   Occurrence of Baillon's Crake [Porzana bailloni] and its Nesting in England.   < *Zoologist*, xvii, 1859, pp. 6329, 6330.

1861. NEWTON, A.   Description of a New Species of Water-Hen (Gallinula [pyrrhorrhoa, p. 19]) from the Island of Mauritius.   < *P. Z. S.*, xxix, 1861, pp. 18, 19.

1861. NEWTON, A.   Description of a [lately] New Species of Water-Hen (Gallinula [pyrrhorrhoa]) from the Island of Mauritius.   < *Ann. Mag. Nat. Hist.*, 3d ser., vii, 1861, pp. 417, 418.
From *P. Z. S.*, Jan. 8, 1861, pp. 18, 19.

1861. PHILIPPI, R. A., *and* LANDBECK, L.   Sobre las especies chilenas del jénero Tulica [sic—lege Fulica].   < *Anales Univ. Chile*, xix, Octubre, 1861, pp. 501–510, 3 figs.
"*Tulica*" *choloropoides*, King; "*T.*" *chilensis*, Gray; "*T.*" *rufifrons*, sp. n., p. 507.—3 figs.

1861. SCLATER, P. L.   On the Island-hen of Tristan d'Acunha [Gallinula nesiotis, sp. n.]   < *P. Z. S.*, xxix, 1861, pp. 260–263, pl. xxx.

1861. SCLATER, P. L.   On the Island-hen of Tristan d'Acunha [Gallinula nesiotis].   < *Ann. Mag. Nat. Hist.*, 3d ser., viii, 1861, pp. 498–501, figg. 4.
From *P. Z. S.*, June 11, 1861, pp. 260-263.

1862. COUPER, W.   Occurrence of the Yellow Rail (Porzana noveboracensis) in the vicinity of Quebec.   < *Canad. Nat. and Geol.*, vii, 1862, p. 320.

1862. LANDBECK, L.   Ueber die chilenischen Wasserhühner aus der Gattung Fulica Linn.   < *Arch. f. Naturg.*, 1862, (1), pp. 215–228.
Drei Arten—*F. chloropoides, F. chilensis, F. rufifrons*, Ph. and Landb.; nebst Kennzeichen. Uebersetzt aus d. *Anales Univ. Chile*, xix, Oct., 1861, pp. 501–510.

1863. BELAMY, [J. C.]   Observations sur les habitudes d'une poule d'eau apprivoisée.   < *Compt. Rend. de l'Acad. Sci.*, lvi, 1863, pp. 1104–1106.

1863. BELAMY, [J. C.]   Observations sur les habitudes d'une poule d'eau apprivoisée.   < *Rev. et Mag. de Zool.*, xv, 1863, pp. 239, 240.
Extrait d'une lettre lue à l'Acad. de Paris, séance du 8 juin 1863.

1863. DUTTON, J.   The Little Crake (Gallinula pusilla [Porzana minuta]) in Pevensey Marshes.   < *Zoologist*, xxi, 1863, p. 8330.

1863. DUTTON, J.   The Spotted Crake (Gallinula porzana [Porzana maruetta]) in Pevensey Marshes.   < *Zoologist*, xxi, 1863, p. 8330.

1863. HUCKETT, T.   Spotted Crakes [Porzana maruetta] in the Hackney Marshes.   < *Zoologist*, xxi, 1863, p. 8847.

1863. LAWRENCE, G. N.   Descriptions of New Species of Birds of the Families Vireonidæ and Rallidæ.   < *Proc. Acad. Nat. Sci. Phila.*, xv, 1863, pp. 106, 107.
Two new Rails here described are *Corethrura guatemalensis*, p. 106, Guatemala (cf. *Ibis*, 186? p. 238); and *Aramides axillaris*, p. 107, New Granada.

1863. MATTHEWS, M. A.   Spotted Crake (Crex porzana [Porzana maruetta]) near Taunton.   < *Zoologist*, xxi, 1863, p. 8446.

1863. SAVILLE, S. P.   Occurrence of the Spotted Crake [Porzana maruetta] near Cambridge.   < *Zoologist*, xxi, 1863, p. 8330.

1863. SAXBY, H. L.   Moorhen (Gallinula chloropus) in Shetland.   < *Zoologist*, xxi, 1863, p. 8494.

1864. ARMISTEAD, J. J.   Spotted Crake [Porzana maruetta] in Hampshire.   < *Zoologist*, xxii, 1864, p. 8890.

1864. BLAKE-KNOX, H.   Spotted Crake [Porzana maruetta] in County Antrim and Storm Petrel in Dublin Bay.   < *Zoologist*, xxii, 1864, p. 8890.

1864. BOULTON, W. W.   Spotted Crake [Porzana maruetta] near Beverley.   < *Zoologist*, xxii, 1864, p. 8890.

1864. BOULTON, W. W.   Spotted Rail [Porzana maruetta] near Beverley.   < *Zoologist*, xxii, 1864, p. 8961.

1864. BOULTON, W. W.   Sternum of Little Crake [Porzana minuta] shot in Cambridgeshire.   < *Zoologist*, xxii, 1864, pp. 9285–9289.

1864. GUNN, T. E.   Spotted Crake [Porzana maruetta] in Norfolk.   < *Zoologist*, xxii, 1864, p. 9118.

1864. MORTIMER, T.   Abundance of the Corn Crake [Crex pratensis].   < *Zoologist*. xxii, 1864, pp. 8889, 8890.

1864. SCHMIDT, MAX.   [Section einer Sultanshühn (Porphyrio).]   < *Zool. Gart.*, v, 1864, p. 224.

1864. NEWMAN, E.   The Purple Gallinule [Porphyrio hyacinthinus] in Scotland.   < *Zoologist*, xxii, 1864, p. 8961.

1864. NOLL, C. F.   Zur Nahrung der Fulica atra (L.).   < *J.f. O.*, xii, 1864, pp. 393, 394.   Aus d. *Zeitsch. d. zool. Gart. zu Frankf.*, v, S. 27.

1864. NOLL, C. F.   Das Wasserhuhn [Fulica atra] auf dem Main.   < *Zool. Gart.*, v, 1864, p. 27.

1864. SAVILLE, S. P.   Little Crake [Porzana minuta] in Cambridgeshire.   < *Zoologist*, xxii, 1864, pp. 9118, 9119.

1865. ARMISTEAD, J. J.   Moorhen [Gallinula chloropus] perching in Trees.   < *Zoologist*, xxiii, 1865, p. 9540.

1865. EYRE, H. S.   Carolina Crake [Porzana carolina] near Newbury.   < *Zoologist*, xxiii, 1865, p. 9540.

1865. HARVIE-BROWN, J. A.   Water Rail [Rallus aquaticus] in Stirlingshire.   < *Zoologist*, xxiii, 1865, p. 9468.

1865. KUTTER, --.   Ein Beitrag zur Fortpflanzungsgeschichte von Gallinula pusilla [Porzana minuta].   < *J.f. O.*, xiii, 1865, pp. 334–341.

1865. [NEWTON, A.]   [On the identity of Corethrura guatemalensis Lawr. with C. rubra, P. Z. S., 1860, p. 300.]   < *Ibis*, 2d ser., i, 1865, p. 238.

1865. NEWTON, A.   [Exhibition of a specimen of Porzana carolina shot Oct., 1864, on the Kennett, near Newbury, England.   < *P. Z. S.*, xxxiii, 1865, p. 196.

1865–66. SCHLEGEL, H.   Ralli   < *Mus. Hist. Nat. Pays-Bas*, 7ᵉ livr., avril 1865, pp. 1–76; 8ᵉ livr., 1866, pp. 77–80.
   This memoir includes representatives of several families of other authors. *Gruidæ*, 12 spp. in the single genus *Grus; Aramus*, 1 spp.; *Rallus*, 11 spp.; *Aramides*, 5; *Rallina*, 10; *Hypotænidia*, 4; *Crex*, 6; *Himantornis*, 1; *Porzana*, 14; *Gallinula*, 14; *Porphyrio*, 8; *Fulica*, 5; *Parra!*, 8; *Palamedea!*, 3; *Ocydromus*, 2; *Eurypyga!*, 1.

1865. STARES, W.   Purple Gallinule [Porphyrio hyacinthinus] in Hampshire.   < *Zoologist*, xxiii, 1865, p. 9418.

1866. LEGGE, W. V.   Moorhens [Gallinula chloropus] perching in Trees.   < *Zoologist*, 2d ser., i, 1866, p. 145.

1866. OVEREND, J.   Eggs of Baillon's Crake [Porzana bailloni] at Great Yarmouth.   < *Zoologist*, 2d ser., i, 1866, p. 389.

1866. REEKS, H.   Purple Waterhen [Porphyrio hyacinthinus] near Southampton.
    < *Zoologist*, 2d ser., i, 1866, p. 229.

1866. SHORTO, J.   Moorhens [Gallinula chloropus] perching in Trees and feeding on
    Pears.   < *Zoologist*, 2d ser., i, 1866, pp. 33, 34.

1867. FEILDEN, H. W.   Spotted Crake [Porzana maruetta] on Longridge.   < *Zoolo-
    gist*, 2d ser., ii, 1867, p. 1017.

1867. HARRISON, J. W. D.   Landrail in January [Crex pratensis, in Gloucestershire].
    < *Zoologist*, 2d ser., ii, 1867, p. 636.
    From the "Field," Jan. 19.

1867. HAWKER, F. A.   Purple Gallinule [Porphyrio hyacinthinus] in Hampshire.
    < *Zoologist*, 2d ser., ii, 1867, p. 829.

1867. MACKAY, D.   [Letter on Notornis, and other New Zealand Birds.]   < *Ibis*, 2d
    ser., iii, 1867, pp. 144, 145.

1867. MILNE-EDWARDS, A.   Mémoire sur une espèce éteinte du genre Fulica [new-
    tonii], qui habitait autrefois l'Île Maurice.   < *Ann. des Sci. Nat.*, 5e sér., viii,
    1867, pp. 195–220, pll. 10–13.
    Pl. 10, *F. newtonii*; 11, *F. atra*; 12, *Porphyrio madagascarensis*; 13, *Ocydromus australis.*
    Cf. *Zool. Rec.*, iv, 1867, pp. 117, 118; *Ibis*, 1868, p. 482, note.

1867. SCLATER, P. L.   Note on the Species of the Genus Tribonyx.   < *Ann. Mag. Nat.
    Hist.*, 3d ser., xx, 1867, pp. 122, 123.

1867. SCLATER, P. L.   [Gallinula pumila = G. minor = G. angulata.]   < *Ibis*, 2d ser.,
    iii, 1867, p. 254.

1868. BINNIE, F. G.   Scarcity of the Corn Crake [Crex pratensis, in Tadcastor].
    < *Zoologist*, 2d ser., iii, 1868, p. 1459.

1868. BLAKE-KNOX, H.   Spotted Crake [Porzana maruetta] in the County Dublin.
    < *Zoologist*, 2d ser., iii, 1868, p. 1458.

1868. FRAUENFELD, G. v.   Auffindung einer bisher unbekannten Abbildung des
    Dronte und eines zweiten kurzflügeligen wahrscheinlich von den Maskare-
    nen stammenden Vogels.   < *J. f. O.*, xvi, 1868, pp. 138–140.
    Aphanapteryx imperialis, g. sp. n.

1868. FRAUENFELD, G. v.   Herr Georg Ritter von Frauenfeld berichtete über die Auf-
    findung einer bisher unbekannten Abbildung des Dronte und eines zweiten
    bisher unbeschriebenen flügellosen Vogels, wahrscheinlich von den Maska-
    renen.   < *Verh. k.-k. zool.-bot. Ges. Wien*, xviii, 1868, p. 24.
    Aphanapteryx imperialis.—The above is all there is of it.

1868. FRAUENFELD, G. v.   Neu aufgefundene Abbildung des Dronte und eines zwei-
    ten kurzflügeligen Vogels, wahrscheinlich des Poule rouge au bec de Bécasse
    der Maskarenen in der Privatbibliothek S. M. des verstorbenen Kaisers Franz.
    Erläutert von George Ritter von Frauenfeld. Mit 4 Tafeln.   Wien: 1868.
    imp. fol.   pp. 17.
    Cf. especially *Ibis*, 1868, pp. 480–482; F. C. Noll, *Zool. Gart.*, 1868, p. 282; A. Milne-Edwards,
    Ann. Sci. Nat. Zool., 5e sér., x, pp. 325–346; *Ibis*, 1869, pp. 256–275; A. Newton, *Zool. Rec.*, v,
    p. 103. Contains full list of Dodo literature since Strickland's account. Not seen by me.—
    Cf. the original paper on *Aphanapteryx*, *J. f. O.*, 1868, pp. 138–140.

1868. MILNE-EDWARDS, A.   Mémoire sur une espèce éteinte du genre Fulica [new-
    tonii], qui habitait autrefois l'île Maurice.   < *Compt. Rend. de l'Acad. Sci.*, lxvi,
    30 mars 1868, pp. 646–650.
    Tiré des *Ann. Sci. Nat.*, 5e sér, viii, 1867, pp. 195–220, pll. 10–13, q. v.

1868. MILNE-EDWARDS, A.   Mémoire sur une espèce éteinte du genre Fulica [new-
    toni], . . .   < *Revue Zoologique*, 1868, pp. 147–152.
    Pas vu moi-même.—Abrégé du mémoire inseré dans les *Comptes Rendus*, 1868, pp. 646, 650.

1868. SCLATER, P. L., *and* SALVIN, O.   Synopsis of the American Rails (Rallidæ).
    < *P. Z. S.*, xxxvi, June 25, 1868, pp. 442–470, pl. xxxv, woodcc. figg. 1–11.
    A very complete memoir, treating of 48 spp. of 10 genera of 3 subfamilies, with synonymy
    diagnosis, geographical distribution, and criticism.   To *Rallinæ* are assigned *Rallus* with

1868. SCLATER, P. L., *and* SALVIN, O.—Continued.

spp., *Aramides* with 7, *Porzana* with 18 (under the 7 subgenera *Porzana, Rufirallus, Laterirallus, Crybastus, Creciscus, Coturnicops,* and *Neocrex* (subg. n., p. 450)), *Crex* and *Thyrorhina* (g. n., p. 458) with 1 each. The *Fulicinæ* embrace 4 genera, *Porphyrio* and *Porphyriops* with 2 spp. each, *Gallinula* with 1, and *Fulica* with 7. *Heliornithinæ* are also included, with 1 sp.—*Porzana levraudi,* p. 452, pl. xxxv; *P. castaneiceps,* p. 453; *P. hauxwelli,* p. 453, spp. nn. (p. 105, pl. 53 of *Exot. Ornith.* quoted for the last named). The heads of several species (*Thyrorhina,* the *Gallinules,* and the *Coots*) are figured on the woodcuts.

1869. ANON. Creamcoloured Moor Hen [Gallinula chloropus]. < *Zoologist,* 2d ser., iv, 1869, p. 1601.

1869. BENNETT, G. [Letter on Birds of Lord Howe's Island.] < *P. Z. S.,* Nov. 11, 1869, pp. 471, 472, pl. xxxv.

Among those mentioned, one (*Ocydromus sylvestris,* Scl., p. 472, pl. xxxv) is new.

1869. FRAUENFELD, G. v. Ueber den Artnamen von Aphanapteryx. < *Verh. (Abh.) d. k.-k. zool.-bot. Gesellsch. Wien,* 1869, pp. 761–764.

Not seen—title from *Zool. Rec.*
The author objects to the substitution of the name *A. broeckii* for *A. imperialis.*

1869. GUNN, T. E. Piebald Waterhen [Gallinula chloropus]. < *Zoologist,* 2d ser., iv, 1869, p. 1848.

1869. GUNN, T. E. Abundance of Landrails [Crex pratensis]. < *Zoologist,* 2d ser.. iv, 1869, p. 1920.

1869. GURNEY, J. H. [On a mode of capturing Ocydromus australis.] < *Ibis,* 2d ser., v, 1869, p. 463.

By displaying a red cloth, which would attract the bird so that it might be taken by hand—an account singularly coincident with that given by Hoffmann in the case of the *Aphanapteryx,* which Milne-Edwards determined to be near *Ocydromus.*

1869. HADFIELD, H. Nest and Eggs of the Corn Crake [Crex pratensis]. < *Zoologist,* 2d ser., iv, 1869. pp. 1920, 1921.

1869. HAMMOND, W. O. Extraordinary Flight of Landrails [Crex pratensis]. < *Zoologist,* 2d ser., iv, 1869, p. 1951.

1869. MILNE-EDWARDS, A. Observations sur les affinités zoologiques de l'Aphanapteryx espèce éteinte qui vivait encore à l'île Maurice au xviie siècle. < *Ann. Sci. Nat.,* 5e ser., x, 1869, pp. 325–346, pll. 15–18.

Not seen—title from *Zool. Rec.*

1869. MILNE-EDWARDS, A. Researches into the Zoological Affinities of the Bird recently described by Herr von Frauenfeld under the name of Aphanapteryx imperialis. < *Ibis,* 2d ser., v, 1869, pp. 256–275, pl. vii, woodcc. figg. 1–8.

Places it among *Rallidæ.* Identifies it with the bird figured by Pieter van den Broeck (*Voy. Mauritius,* 1617, fig. 1), which is *Didus broeckii* Schleg.
"This paper is distinct from another published in (*Ann. Sc. Nat.,* 5e sér., x, pp. 325–346, pls. 15–18) though, being written about the same time and the same materials, their similarity is at first sight obvious, and the plate is the same in both after the facsimile in Ritter von Frauenfeld's work (*Zool. Rec.,* v, p. 103); but this paper contains woodcuts, from Strickland's 'Dodo and its Kindred,' of Van den Broecke's and Herbert's figures of the bird. By means of the bones found in Mauritius by Mr. Edward Newton, the author makes out the affinities of this extinct form, which, he says, should bear the name of *A. broeckii* (Schlegel), and holds the place by the side of *Ocydromus* which that does to the more normal *Rallidæ.*"—*Zool. Rec.*

1869. SCLATER, P. L. [Characters of a new Species of Ocydromus (sylvestris), p. 472, pl. xxxv.] < *P. Z. S.,* xxxvii, 1869, pp. 472, 473, pl. xxxv.

1869. WALKER, T. C. Curious position of Nest of Water Hen [Gallinula chloropus]. < *Zoologist,* 2d ser., iv, 1869, p. 1723.

1870. COUES, E. The Clapper Rail [Rallus longirostris (crepitans)]. < *Am. Nat.,* iii, 1870, pp. 600–607.

Account of the breeding and other habits, from original observations at Fort Macon, N. C.

1870. REEKS, H. Land Rail [Crex pratensis] found alive in a Pea-rick in January. < *Zoologist,* 2d ser., v, 1870, pp. 2063, 2064.

1870. SMITH, C. Little Crake [Porzana minuta] in Somersetshire. < *Zoologist*, 2d ser., v, 1870, p. 2386.

1871. BOYES, F. Waterhen [Gallinula chloropus] submerging itself. < *Zoologist*, 2d ser., vi, 1871, pp. 2522, 2523.

1871. BOYES, F. Is the Corn Crake [Crex pratensis] Polygamous? <*Zoologist*, 2d ser., vi, 1871, p. 2869.

1871. BREHM, A. E. Zur Fortpflanzungsgeschichte des Purpurhuhus [Porphyrio smaragnotus, Temm.] < *J. f. O.*, xix, 1871, pp. 34–39.
    In the Berlin Aquarium.

1871. JESSE, W. Early Nest of the Moorhen [Gallinula chloropus]. < *Zoologist*, 2d ser., vi, 1871, p. 2771.

1871. LAWRENCE, G. N. Descriptions of New Species of Birds from Mexico, Central America, and South America, with a Note on Rallus longirostris. <*Ann. Lyc. Nat. Hist. N. Y.*, x, 1871, pp. 1–21.
    The note on *Rallus longirostris* states that with this species *R. crassirostris* Lawr. from Bahia agrees; it being apparently different from *R. crepitans* Gm.

1871. LAWRENCE, G. N. [Maintains the validity of Porzana guatemalensis.] < *Ibis*, 3d ser., i, 1871, p. 370.
    The editor maintains the contrary in a note appended.

1872. LEACH, H. R. The Landrail [Crex pratensis, near Harrow]. < *Zoologist*, 2d ser., vii, 1872, p. 3112.

1872. HADFIELD, H. Baillon's Crake [Porzana bailloni, in Isle of Man]. < *Zoologist*, 2d ser., vii, 1872, pp. 3272, 3273.

1872. MATHEW, M. A. Landrail [Crex pratensis] taking to Water. <*Zoologist*, 2d ser., vii, 1872, p. 3316.

1872. POTTS, T. H. Notes on a New Species of Rail, Rallus pictus, Painted Rail. < *Trans. and Proc. New Zealand Inst. for* 1871, iv, 1872, p. 202, 203.

1872. OWEN, R. [Letter on the Remains of Aptornis found in Glenmark Swamp, New Zealand.] < *P. Z. S.*, xl, 1872, p. 24.

1872. RICKARDS, M. S. C. Spotted Crake [Porzana maruetta] near Clifton. <*Zoologist*, 2d ser., vii, 1872, pp. 2945, 2946.

1872. WALDEN, *Lord.* Description of a new Species of Porzana [bicolor] from the Himalayas. < *Ann. Mag. Nat. Hist.*, 4th ser., ix, 1872, p. 47.

1872. WHITAKER, J., JR. Spotted Crake [Porzana maruetta] near Nottingham. < *Zoologist*, 2d ser., vii, 1872, p. 2946.

1873. ANON. Schlauheit einer Wasserhühns. <*Aus der Natur*, lxii, oder n. F., l, 1873, pp. 267, 268.

1873. ANON. The Notornis a rara avis. < *Forest and Stream*, i, Sept. 25, 1873, p. 103.

1873. ANON. [EDITORIAL.] [Abundance of Coots (Fulica americana) on the Massachusetts coast.] < *Am. Sportsman*, iii, 1873, p. 57.

1873. FINSCH, O. Bemerkungen zu dem vorstehenden [d. h., Hutton über die Ocydromus-Arten Neuseeland's] Aufsatze über die Ocydromus Arten. < *J. f. O.*, xxi, 1873, pp. 401–404.

1873. GURNEY, J. H. Note on the [habits of the] Waterhen [Gallinula chloropus]. < *Zoologist*, 2d ser., viii, 1873, p. 3580.

1873. GURNEY, J. H. Waterhens [Gallinula chloropus] nesting in Trees. < *Zoologist*, 2d ser., viii, 1873, p. 3652.

1873. HUTTON, F. W. On Rallus modestus of New Zealand. < *Ibis*, 3d ser., iii, 1873, pp. 349–352, woodcc.
    Maintaining its specific validity.

1873. HUTTON, F. W. [Note on Tribonyx mortieri.] < *Ibis*, 3d ser., iii, 1873, pp. 427, 428.

1873. HUTTON, F. W.   Ueber die Arten der Gattung Ocydromus in Neuseeland. $<$ *J. f. O.*, xxi, 1873, pp. 398–401.

> 6 spp.—*O. hectori*, p. 399, *O. finschii*, spp. nn.   Cf. *op. cit.*, 1872, pp. 174–181.

1873. NEWTON, A.   [Remarks on exhibition of an old engraving of a bird resembling the 'Géant' of Leguat.] $<$ *P. Z. S.*, xli, 1873, pp. 194, 195.

1873. SALVIN, O.   Note on the Fulica alba of White. $<$ *Ibis*, iii, 3d ser., 1873, p. 295, pl. x.

> Referred to genus *Notornis;* cf. *tom. cit.*, pp. 44, 45.

1873. TATTON, T. E.   Waterhens [Gallinula chloropus] Nesting in Trees. $<$ *Zoologist*, 2d ser., viii, 1873, p. 3692.

1874. ANON.   A strange circumstance. $<$ *Am. Sportsman*, iii, 1874, p. 316.   See also p. 364.

> Note of finding a "rail" [*Porzana carolina?*] in southern New Jersey on Nov. 20th.

1874. BREWER, T. M.   Breeding Grounds of the Sora Rail [Porzana carolina]. $<$ *Am. Sportsman*, iv, 1874, p. 339.

> Correcting errors of "Homo" (*ibid.*, July 18), defining breeding range of *Porzana carolina*, and describing nest and eggs.

1874. "C. B."   Rail [Porzana carolina] in Winter. $<$ *Am. Sportsman*, iv, 1874, p. 28.

> At Whitehall, N. Y., in February.

1874. CLARK-KENNEDY, A. J.   Baillon's Crake [Porzana bailloni] near Eastbourne. $<$ *Zoologist*, 2d ser., ix, 1874, p. 4159.

1874. CORBIN, G. B.   [Note on the habits of the] Corn Crake [Crex pratensis]. $<$ *Zoologist*, 2d ser., ix, 1874, p. 3881.

1874. COUES, E.   The Rails—Family Rallidæ. $<$ *Am. Sportsman*, v, Oct. 31, 1874, p. 65.

> From his 'Birds of the Northwest.'

1874. DURNFORD, H.   Note on the habits of the Water Rail [Rallus aquaticus]. $<$ *Zoologist*, 2d ser., ix, 1874, pp. 3881, 3882.

1874. "FRIEND OF DOG AND GUN." [JUSTUS VON LENGERKE.]   Least Water Rail [Porzana jamaicensis]. $<$ *Am. Sportsman*, v, Dec. 12, 1874, p. 171.

> Occurrence at West Hoboken, N. J.

1874. GURNEY, J. H.   Water Rail [Rallus aquaticus, captured by hand]. $<$ *Zoologist*, 2d ser., ix, 1874, p. 4036.

1874. "HOMO." [C. S. WESTCOTT.]   Rail [Porzana carolina] Shooting on the Delaware River. $<$ *Am. Sportsman*, iv, 1874, p. 166.

1874. HUTTON, F. W.   On a New Genus [Cabalus] of Rallidæ. $<$ *Trans. and Proc. New Zealand Inst. for* 1873, vi, 1874, pp. 108–110, pl. xx.

> *Cabalus*, g. n., p. 108, proposed for *Rallus modestus*, *Ibis*, July, 1872, and *op. cit.*, v, 1873, p. 223. See especially *tom. cit.*, p. 124.

1874. HUTTON, F. W.   Notes on the New Zealand Wood-hens (Ocydromus). $<$ *Trans. and Proc. New Zealand Inst. for* 1873, vi, 1874, pp. 110–112.

> Read before Wellington Philos. Soc., 22 Sept., 1873.   *O. troglodytes*, *O. hectori*, sp. n., p. 110, *O. australis*, *O. fuscus*, *O. finschi*, sp. n., p. 111, *O. earli;* diagnosis of, and remarks on.

1874. "JACOBSTAFF."   Sora [Porzana carolina] in May [in Central New York]. $<$ *Forest and Stream*, ii, May 21, 1874, p. 230.   See p. 261.

1874. KRIDER, J.   Rail [Porzana carolina] out of Season. $<$ *Am. Sportsman*, iii, 1873–74, p. 364.

> Reply to note on p. 316. *ibid.*, concerning late stay of *Porzana carolina*.

1874. O[USTALET], E.   Les anciens oiseaux des iles Mascareignes   I   La poule d'eau de l'ile Maurice. $<$ *La Nature*, 2e année, N°. 34, 24 janvier 1874, pp. 113–116, dessin.

1874. PALMER, J. E.   Baillon's Crake [Porzana bailloni] near Huddersfield. $<$ *Zoologist*, 2d ser., ix, 1874, p. 4159.

1874. PILLEY, J. B.   Landrail [Crex pratensis] in January [in Great Britain].   < *Zoologist*, 2d ser., ix, 1874, p. 3953.

1874. SCHOMBURGK, R.   [Communication from, containing an account of the nesting-habits of Fulica australis].   < *P. Z. S.*, xlii, 1874, p. 129.

1874. SUCKER, A.   [*pseudon.*]   [Occurrence of Porzana noveboracensis at Centralia, Ill.]   < *Am. Sportsman*, iv, 1874, p. 45.

> "Sucker" is a local vulgarism for a native of Illinois, said to have originated from some necessity early settlers were under of finding water in holes in the prairie so deep that they were obliged, as it were, to suck it up in drinking. However apt or otherwise eligible the slang pseudonyms of sporting writers may seem to them at the time when they "write for the newspapers," such nonsense wears a very unbecoming air when it comes to be set forth formally in Bibliography.

1875. BULLER, W. L.   [On Rallus modestus.]   < *Trans. and Proc. New Zealand Inst. for* 1874, vii, 1875, *Proc. Wellington Phil. Soc.*, p. 511.

> Prof. Newton's determination of the validity of the species.

1875. CORBIN, G. B.   Coot [Fulica atra] near Ringwood.   < *Zoologist*, 2d ser., x, May, 1875, pp. 4458, 4459.

1875. "R."   Singular Freak of a Coot [Fulica americana].   < *Forest and Stream*, v, Oct. 7, 1875, p. 131.

1875. RAMSAY, E. P.   Description of the Eggs and Young of Rallina tricolor, from Rockingham Bay.   < *P. Z. S.*, Nov. 16, 1875, pp. 603, 604.

1875. WHITMAN, G. P.   The Purple Gallinule [Porphyrio martinica, in Eastern Massachusetts].   < *Forest and Stream*, iv, Apr. 22, 1875, p. 167.

1875. WHITMAN, G. P.   The Purple Gallinule [Porphyrio martinica, in Massachusetts].   < *Am. Nat.*, ix, No. 10, Oct., 1875, p. 573.

1876. BOYES, F.   Is the Common Waterhen [Gallinula chloropus] Migratory or not?   < *Zoologist*, 2d ser., xi, Mar., 1876, pp. 4845, 4846.

1876. GARROD, A. H.   On the Anatomy of Aramus scolopaceus.   < *P. Z. S.*, Mar. 7, 1876, pp. 275–277, figg. 1–3.

> Important; with special reference to the systematic position of the genus, which is considered to be most intimately related to *Grus*, in view of many of its anatomical characters. The skull is figured in three views.

1876. [GERVAIS, P.]   (A. H.) Garrod: Sur l'anatomie de l'Aramus scolopaceus.   (Proc zool. Soc. London, 1876, p. 275).   < *Gerr. Journ. de Zool.*, v, 1876, pp. 439, 440.

> See last title.

1876. [GRINNELL, G. B.]   A Word or two about some of our Rails [North American Rallidæ].   < *Forest and Stream*, vii, Nov. 9, 1876, p. 212.

1876. GURNEY, J. H., JR.   Little Crake [Porzana minuta] at Hastings.   < *Zoologist*, 2d ser., xi, Oct., 1876, p. 5126.

1876. GURNEY, J. H., JR.   Little Crake [Porzana minuta] at Hastings.   < *Zoologist*, 2d ser., xi, Nov., 1876, p. 5167.

1876. HUDSON, W. H.   Notes on the Rails [Rallidæ] of the Argentine Republic   < *P. Z. S.*, Jan. 18, 1876, pp. 102–109.

> Very interesting, and including many notes on other birds of the same region, as *Aramus, Parra, Ibis, Milvago*, and some *Passeres*.

1876. JEFFREY, W.   The Common Waterhen [Gallinula chloropus] Migratory.   < *Zoologist*, 2d ser., xi, Apr., 1876, pp. 4882, 4883.

1876. MATHEW, G. F.   Baillon's Crake [Porzana bailloni] at Braunton Burrows   < *Zoologist*, 2d ser., xi, Mar., 1876, pp. 4844, 4845.

1876. NEWMAN, E.   White Spotted Crake [Porzana maruetta].   < *Zoologist*, 2d ser., xi, Mar., 1876, p. 4845.

1876. NICHOLLS, R. P.   Spotted Gallinule [Porzana maruetta] near Kingsbridge   < *Zoologist*, 2d ser., xi, Jan., 1876, p. 4763.

1876. PRIOR, C. M. Thirteen Eggs in a Moorhen's [Gallinula chloropus] Nest. < *Zoologist*, 2d ser., xi, July, 1876, p. 5006.

1876. PRIOR, C. M. Change of Plumage in the Moorhen [Gallinula chloropus]. < *Zoologist*, 2d ser., xi, Sept., 1876, p. 5084.

1876. "RECAPPER." [THOS. C. ABBOTT.] To Dr. Coues. < *Rod and Gun*, viii, June 24, 1876, p. 203.
Notes on *Fulica americana* observed at Trenton, N. J.

1876. [SCLATER, P. L.] [Addition of Porzana notata to the Society's Menagerie.] < *P. Z. S.*, Feb. 15, 1876, p. 255.

1876. SWINHOE, R. [Letter on Porzana exquisita, claiming the name.] < *Ibis*, 3d ser., vi, Oct., 1876, pp. 507, 508.
See *P. erythrothorax*, *J. f. O.*, 1873, p. 107; *P. undulata*, *J. f. O.*, 1874, p, 333; *Ann. Mag. N. H.*, 4th ser., xii, Nov., 1873, p. 376; *Ibis*, 1876, p. —.

1877. BROWNE, F. C. Occurrence of the Black Rail [Porzana jamaïcensis] in Massachusetts [at Plymouth, in August, 1869]. < *Forest and Stream*, viii, Feb. 22, 1877, p. 33. See p. 129.

1877. [COUES, E.] Birds. < *The Mirror* (Baltimore, Md.), Sept. 1, 1877.
Editorial extract from *Birds of the Northwest*, relating to *Rallus virginianus*.

1877. [COUES, E.] Communion with Birds. < *The Temperance Vedette* (Terrill, Texas), Aug. 11, 1877.
Editorial extract from *Birds of the Northwest*, relating to *Rallus virginianus*.

1877. CURTIS, T. D. The Occurrence of the Black Rail [Porzana jamaïcensis] in Massachusetts [in Boston]. < *Forest and Stream*, viii, Apr. 5, 1877, p. 129. See p. 33.

1877. STREETS, T. H. Description of a new Moorhen [Gallinula sandvicensis] from the Hawaiian Islands. < *Ibis*, 4th ser., i, Jan., 1877, pp. 25–27, fig.

1878. EVANS, R. D. [Porzana carolina] Caught at Sea. < *Forest and Stream*, x, Aug. 1, 1878, p. 503.
An individual captured 350 miles off the coast of Virginia.

1878. SCLATER, [P. L.] [Exhibition of the probable type of Fulica gallinuloides King, Zool. Journ., iv, p. 96 = F. leucoptera V., nec F. armillata (cf. P. Z. S., 1868, p. 465; Exot. Orn., p. 115).] < *P. Z. S.*, Mar. 5, 1878, p. 291.

1879. "AIX SPONSA." The Mud-hen of the West [Fulica americana]. < *Forest and Stream*, xii, July 10, 1879, p. 444.
Habits of young of this species.

1879. "BYRNE." The "Mud Hen" of the West [Fulica americana]. < *Forest and Stream*, xii, Apr. 24, 1879, p. 226.

1879. CHUBB, H. E. Whose Mistake? < *Forest and Stream*, xiii, Oct. 9, 1879, p. 705.
Refers to *Porzana noveboracensis* in Ohio.

1879. COUES, E. Letters on Ornithology. No. 23.—The American Coot.—(Fulica Americana, Gm.) < *The Chicago Field*, June 9, 1879.
From the "Birds of the Northwest."

1879. DEANE, R. The Florida Gallinule [Gallinula galeata] in New England. < *Forest and Stream*, xiii, Nov. 6, 1879, p. 785.

.87-. ELLIOT, D. G. The Genus Porphyrio and its Species. < *Stray Feathers*, —, 187-, pp. — – —, 1 pl.

1879. [FITCH, E. H.] The American Coot [Fulica americana]. < *The Journ. of Sci.* (Toledo, Ohio), 2d ser., ii, No. 1, Apr., 1879, cut.

1879. [GRINNELL, G. B.] A Rare Rail [Porzana noveboracensis]. < *Forest and Stream*, xiii, Sept. 18, 1879, p. 645.
Captured in New Jersey.

1879. [GRINNELL, G. B.] The Florida Gallinule [Gallinula galeata] in Connecticut. < *Forest and Stream*, xiii, Oct. 2, 1879, p. 684.

1879. HOLBERTON, W.   The Yellow-breasted Rail [Porzana noveboracensis].   < *Forest and Stream*, xii, June 26, 1879, p. 405.

    Capture of a specimen in Hackensack (N. J.) Meadows in Apr., 1879.

1879. LINDEN, C.   Note on Porzana noveboracensis.   < *Forest and Stream*, xiii, Nov. 6, 1879, p. 785.

    Capture of this species at Clinton, Iowa.

1879. MERRILL, H. W.   Rail [Porzana carolina] in Wisconsin.   < *Forest and Stream*, xiii, Nov. 20, 1879, p. 827.

    Mentions also the "King rail" (? *Rallus elegans*) and some game birds.

1879. "PERDIX."   The Common Gallinule [Gallinula galeata] in Illinois.   < *Forest and Stream*, xii, July 10, 1879, p. 444.

1879. ROBINSON, R. E.   [Gallinula galeata] Unusual in Vermont.   < *Forest and Stream*, xii, May 15, 1879, p. 285.

    Notice of capture of Florida Gallinule in Vermont, with extraordinary and no doubt incorrect statement that the "Purple Gallinule" is common there.

Gruidæ.

1701. DUVERNEY, G. J.   De Physicis & Chemicis experimentis & historia animalium. < *Reg. Scient. Acad. Hist. Paris*, Duhamel ed., i, 1701, pp. 251–255.

Gruis Africanæ dissectio, Ann. 1684.

1733. DUVERNEY, G. J.   Observation sur la trachée-artère de la grue d'Afrique. < *Mém. de l'Acad. Roy. des Sci.* depuis 1666 jusq. 1699, ii, 1733, p. 6.

1733. MÉRY, J.   Observation anatomique sur le coeur de l'Oiseau royal [Balearica pavonina].   < *Mém. de l'Acad. Roy. des Sci.* depuis 1666 jusq. 1699, i, 1733, p. 430.

1733. PERRAULT, C.   Description anatomique de six Oiseaux appellez Demoiselles de Numidie [Anthropoïdes virgo].   < *Mém. de l'Acad. Roy. des Sci.* depuis 1666 jusq. 1699, iii, pt. ii, 1733, pp. 1–14, pll. 35, 36.

1734. PERRAULT, C.   Description anatomique de deux Oiseaux royaux [Balearica pavonina].   < *Mém. de l'Acad. Roy. des Sci.* depuis 1666 jusq. 1699, iii, pt. iii, 1734, pp. 199–206, pll. 28, 29.

1757. PERRAULT, C.   Anatomische Beschreibung . . . [Anthropoïdes virgo].   < *Abhandl. Konigl. Französisch. Akad.*, ii, 1757, pp. — — —.

Not seen. German transl. from *Mém. de l'Acad. Paris*, iii, pt. ii, 1733, p. 1.

1757. PERRAULT, C.   Anatomische Beschreibung zweier Königsvögel [Balearica pavonina].   < *Abhandl. Konigl. Französisch. Akad.*, ii, 1757, pp. 355– —.

Not seen—title from Giebel. Germ. trans. from *Mém. de l'Acad. Paris*, iii, pt. iii, 1734, p. 199.

1803. FRORIEP, [L. F. V.]   Beschreibung und Abbildung des Riesen-Kranichs (Grus gigantea [leucogeranus]).   < *Voigt's Mag.*, vi, 1803, pp. 261–264, pl.

Nicht mir selbst zugänglich.

1818. THUNBERG, C. P.   Tetrapteryx capensis, ett nytt Fogelslägte.   < *Kongl. Vetensk. Acad. Handl.*, 1818, pp. 242–245, pl. viii.

This g. sp. n. is *Anthropoïdes paradiseus* (Licht.).

1824. SEYFFERTITZ, [A.] V.   Merkwürdige Beobachtungen über den grauen Kranich, Grus cinerea, Bechst. von Herrn Freiherrn v. Seyffertitz, aus dessen Briefen mit Beibehaltung seiner eigenen Worte.   < *Ornis*, Heft i, 1824, pp. 79–110.

1825. VIGORS, N. A.   Descriptions of some rare, interesting, or hitherto uncharacterized subjects of Zoology.   < *Zool. Journ.*, ii, No. 6, July, 1825, pp. 234–241, pl. 8.

This is the third article of a series with above major title; it is devoted, so far as ornithology is concerned, to *Anthropoïdes stanleyanus*, sp. n., p. 234, pl. 8 [= *paradiseus*].

1826. LESS[ON, R. P.].   Description de quelques objets de zoologie, rares, interessans, et jusqu'à présent mal caractérisés; par N. A. Vigors; . . .   < *Féruss. Bull.*, 2ᵉ sect., vii, 1826, p. 376.

Anthropoïdes stanleyanus [= *paradiseus*].

1826–27. SEYFFERTITZ, A. V.   Merkwürdige Beobachtungen des Herrn Freiherrn Anton von Seyffertitz über den grauen Kranich, Grus cinerea, Bechst.   < *Ornis*, Heft ii, 1826, pp. 64–80 ; Heft iii, 1827, pp. 42–54.

1833. [ANON.]   Om en tam Trana [Grus cinerea].   < *Tidsk. f. Jägare och Naturf.*, ii, 1833, pp. 569–571, 700.

Not seen.

1833. [BENNETT, E. T.]   [Characters of two Species of Crowned Cranes from Africa.]   < *P. Z. S.*, pt. i, 1833, pp. 118, 119.   (*Oken's Isis*, 1835, col. 549–550.)

Two species of "*Anthropoïdes*" (i. e., *Balearica*) are distinguished : *A. pavonina* from N. and W. Africa, and *A. regulorum*, of S. Africa ; the latter being *Grus regulorum* Licht.

1833. GRAY, [J. E.]   [On the Crowned and Demoiselle Cranes.]   < *P. Z. S.*, i, 1833, p. 119.

Restricting *Balearica*, Briss., to the former, and *Anthropoïdes*, V., to the latter.

1835. YARRELL, W. [Note on the trachea of the Stanley Crane (Anthropoïdes paradiseus.] < *P. Z. S.*, iii, 1835, p. 132.

1839. READE, T. [Notice of forwarding of Anthropoïdes virgo to the Society.] < *P. Z. S.*, vii, 1839, p. 169.

1844. COUPER, J. H. [Note on the doubted specific character of Grus canadensis.] < *Proc. Acad. Nat. Sci. Phila.*, ii, 1844, p. 24.

1845. SUNDEVALL, [C. J.] Samtidige Observationer [om Tranans (Grus cinerea) flyttning]. < *Öfvers. Kongl. Vetensk.-Akad. Förhandl. för år* 1844, 1845, pp. 79, 80.

  The date given for this and the next article is that of the made-up vol.—may be actually 1844.

1845. SUNDEVALL, [C. J.] Om Tranans [Grus cinerea] flyttning. < *Öfvers. Kongl. Vetensk.-Akad. Förhandl. för år* 1844, 1845, pp. 167–171.

1849–55. ANDREWS, W. On the occurrence of the Crane (Grus cinerea) in Ireland. < *Dublin Nat. Hist. Soc. Proc.*, i, 1849–55, pp. 71–73.

  Not seen—title from *Roy. Soc. Cat.* Actual date not ascertained.

1849. WOLLEY, J. Occurrence of the Common Crane [Grus cinerea] in Shetland. < *Zoologist*, vii, 1849, pp. 2352, 2353.

1850. GURNEY, J. H. Occurrence of the Crane (Grus cinerea) in Norfolk. < *Zoologist*, viii, 1850, p. 2771.

1850. [JARDINE, W.] Grus antigone. < *Jard. Contrib. Orn.*, 1850, pp. 19–26 and 153, pl. xlii.

  Observations on its eggs, habits, etc., chiefly from E. Blyth.

1851. ELLMAN, J. B. Occurrence of the Crane [Grus cinerea] at Pevensey, Sussex. < *Zoologist*, ix, 1851, p. 3234.

1851. TYZENHAUZ, [C. V.] Rectification du double emploi de la Grue à nuque blanche, Grus leucauchen, Temm. < *Rev. et Mag. de Zool.*, iii, 1851, pp. 577–579.

1852. BONSDORFF, E. J. Symbolæ ad Anatomiam Comparatam Nervorum Animalium Vertebratorum, . . . II. Nervi cerebrales Gruis cinereæ Linn. < *Acta Soc. Scient. Fennicæ*, iii, 1852, pp. 591–624, pll. x, xa.

1853. BRYANT, H. [On the Sand-hill Crane (Grus canadensis).] < *Proc. Boston Soc. Nat. Hist.*, iv, 1853, pp. 303–307.

  Maintaining the distinctness of *Grus canadensis* from *G. americana*, and giving an account of its habits as observed in Florida.

1854. BORRER, W., JR. Occurrence of the Crane (Grus cinerea) in Sussex. < *Zoologist*, xii, 1854, p. 4512.

1854. DUDLEY, W. Description of a species of Crane [Grus hoyianus] found in Wisconsin, presumed to be new. < *Proc. Acad. Nat. Sci. Phila.*, vii, 1854, p. 64.

  Cf. Hartl., *J. f. O.*, iii, 1855, pp. 336, 337.

1855. HARTLAUB, G. Ueber Grus hoyianus Dudl. < *J. f. O.*, iii, 1855, pp. 336, 337.

1856. GLOGER, C. W. L. Sollten die Kraniche [Grus cinerea] wohl eine besondere Sommertracht haben? < *J. f. O.*, iv, 1856, pp. 392–394.

  Aus *Nilsson's Skand. Fn.* Cf. *J. f. O.*, 1857, p. 168.

1857. HOMEYER, E. F. v. Zur Naturgeschichte des gemeinen Kranichs, Grus cinerea. < *J. f. O.*, v, 1857, pp. 168, 169.

  Cf. *op. cit.*, iv, 1856, p. 392.

1859. COTTLE, T. J. Grus americana and Grus canadensis: are they the same bird in different stages of growth? < *Canad. Journ.*, iv, 1859, pp. 266–268.

  Their distinctness maintained.

1859. SCLATER, P. L. [Exhibition of the eggs of Grus montignesia, Grus virgo, Grus cinerea, laid by birds in the Society's Gardens.] < *P. Z. S.*, xxvii, 1859, p. 353.

1860. MEVES, W. [Is there a paper by, on plumage of Grus cinerea?] < *Oefr. K. Vetensk.-Akad. Förh.*, xvii, 1860, p. 218.

1861. BARTLETT, A. D. Notes on the Breeding and Rearing of the Chinese Crane (Grus montignesia) in the Society's Gardens. < *P. Z. S.*, xxix, 1861, pp. 369, 370, pl. xxxv.

1862. BARTLETT, A. D. Notes on the Breeding and Rearing of the Chinese Crane (Grus montignesia) in the Society's Gardens. < *Ann. Mag. Nat. Hist.*, 3d ser., ix, 1862, pp. 324–326.
>   From *P. Z. S.*, Nov. 26, 1861, p. 369.

1862. CABANIS, J. Aufforderung zu Beobachtungen über die Wanderungen der Kraniche [Grus cinerea]. (Auszug aus einem Briefe des Prof. C. Sundevall in Stockholm an Prof. W. Peters in Berlin.) < *J. f. O.*, x, 1862, p. 134.
>   Mit Anmerkungen des Herausgebers.

1862. GLOGER, C. W. L. Die rostig-braunen Rückenfedern des Kranichs [Grus cinerea] im Sommer. < *J. f. O.*, x, 1862, pp. 132, 133.
>   Aus Meves, *Oefv. K. Vet.-Akad. Förh.*, *Årg.* xvii, Nr. 4, S. 218.

1862. NEWMAN, E. Occurrence of the Crane [Grus cinerea] at Hartlepool. < *Zoologist*, xx, 1862, p. 8005.

1863. ANON. The Numidian Crane [Anthropoïdes virgo] in Orkney. < *Zoologist*, xxi, 1863, p. 8692.

1863. GONZENBACH, J. G. v. Einige Notizen über Grus cinerea. < *J. f. O.*, x, 1863, pp. 68–72.
>   Zur Lebensweise, mit besonderer Rücksicht an dessen Zug.

1863. SACC, *Dr.* Sur les Grues [Gruidæ]. < *Bull. Soc. Acclim.*, x, 1863, pp. 736–738.
>   Traitant de cinq espèces apprivoisées.

1864. HOMEYER, E. v. Ueber die Rückenfärbung des brütenden Kranichs [Grus cinerea]. < *J. f. O.*, xii, 1864, pp. 337–339.
>   Bemerkungen über Meve's Artikel, *Oefv. K. Vet.-Akad. Förh.*, 1860, pp. 218—; *J. f. O.*, 1862, pp. 132, 133.

1865. SMITH, CECIL. Crane [Grus cinerea] at Stallford. < *Zoologist*, xxiii, 1865, p. 9848.

1866. JERDON, T. C. The Common Crane [Grus cinerea] in India. < *Zoologist*, 2d ser., i, 1866, pp. 346, 347.
>   From 'Birds of India,' ii, p. 665.

1866. JERDON, T. C. The-Demoiselle Crane [Anthropoïdes virgo] in India. < *Zoologist*, 2d ser., i, 1866, p. 347.
>   From 'Birds of India,' ii, p. 667.

1868. SCLATER, P. L. [Notices of recent additions to the Society's Menagerie.] < *P. Z. S.*, xxxvi, 1868, pp. 566, 567.
>   *Grus americana*, with list of 12 spp. of *Gruidæ*.

1869. ANON. Crane [Grus cinerea] at Lynn. < *Zoologist*, 2d ser., iv, 1869, p. 1803.

1869. GOEBEL, H. Einige Beobachtungen über den Kranich [Grus cinerea]zug. < *J. f. O.*, xvii, 1869, pp. 193, 194.

1869. GURNEY, J. H., JR. Crane [Grus cinerea] at Tewkesbury. < *Zoologist*, 2d ser., iv, 1869, p. 1803.

1869. GURNEY, J. H., JR. Occurrences of the Crane [Grus cinerea] in 1869. < *Zoologist*, 2d ser., iv, 1869, pp. 1841, 1842.

1869. HART, W. Crane [Grus cinerea] at Wareham. < *Zoologist*, 2d ser., iv, 1869, p. 1803.

1869. NICHOLLS, H., JR. Crane [Grus cinerea] on the Devon Coast. < *Zoologist*, 2d ser., iv, 1869, p. 1866.

1869. STEVENSON, H. Cranes [Grus cinerea] in Norfolk. < *Zoologist*, 2d ser., iv, 1869, p. 1803.

1870. D[ELONDRE], A. A. Des Grues [Gruidæ]. < *Bull. Soc. Acclim.*, 2e sér., vii, 1870, pp. 93, 94.
>   "Land and Water," 27 nov. 1869, p. 347.

1870. SOUBIRAN, J. L.   [Note sur les Grues (Gruidæ) de Japon et de Chine.]   < *Bull.*
        Soc. Acclim., 2ᵉ sér., vii, 1870, p. 250.

1871. GURNEY, J. H.   A Crane [Grus cinerea] seen in South Devon in 1869.   < *Zoolo-*
        gist, 2d ser., vi, 1871, pp. 2683, 2684.

1872. [F. W.]   Den fireogtrediveaarige Trane [Grus cinerea].   < *Tidssk. for popu-*
        lære Fremst. af Naturvidensk., iv ser., iv, 1872, p. 324.
        Efter F. W., i ,,Svenska Jägerförbundets Nya Tidsskrift," 1867.

1872. GRAY, R[OBERT].   [Occurrence of Grus (Balearica) pavonina in Ayreshire, Scot-
        land, Sept. 17, 1871.]   < *Ibis*, 3d ser., ii, 1872, pp. 201, 202.

1872. SCHLEGEL, H.   De Witte Kraanvogel, Grus leucogeranus.   < *Jaarboekje van het*
        Kon. Zool. Genootsch. Nat. Art. Mag., 1872, pp. 173–175, pl.
        Not seen?

1874. COUES, E.   The Cranes [Gruidæ] of America.   < *Forest and Stream*, iii, Aug. 20,
        1874, p. 20.
        Popular sketch of the two then recognized North American species, *Grus americana* and
        G. canadensis.

1875. "B."   Sandhill Cranes [Grus canadensis].   < *Forest and Stream*, iv, Mar. 25,
        1875, p. 101.

1875. "SOUTHERN CALIFORNIAN."   A Feathered Hunter [Grus canadensis?].   < *Oölo-*
        gist, i, 1875, p. 61.

1876. GURNEY, J. H., JR.   Notes on Cranes [Grus cinerea].   < *Zoologist*, 2d ser., xi,
        Mar., 1876, p. 4843.

1876. HERRIDGE, W.   The Demoiselle Crane [Anthropoïdes virgo, as a British Bird].
        < *Zoologist*, 2d ser., xi, May, 1876, p. 4928.

1876. HILLS, R. S.   Cranes [Grus cinerea] near Inverness.   < *Zoologist*, 2d ser., xi,
        Jan., 1876, pp. 4763, 4764.

1880. ALLEN, J. A.   Roberts on the Convolution of the Trachea in the Sandhill and
        Whooping Cranes [Grus canadensis and G. americana].   < *Bull. Nutt. Ornith.*
        Club, v, No. 3, July, 1880, pp. 179, 180.
        Short notice of the paper in *Am. Nat.*, xiv, 1880, pp. 108–114.

1880. COUES, E.   Note on Grus fraterculus of Cassin.   < *Bull. Nutt. Ornith. Club*, v,
        No. 3, July, 1880, p. 188.
        Stating that if the "Sand-bill" Crane of *Arctic* America be *G. fraterculus*, this is a synonym
        of *G. canadensis* L. (Edw., pl. 133), and that another name, perhaps *G. pratensis* Bartr., should
        be used for the common U. S. bird.

1880. RIDGWAY, R.   The LIttle [sic] Brown Crane (Grus fraterculus, Cassin).   < *Bull.*
        Nutt. Ornith. Club, v, No. 3, July, 1880, pp. 187, 188.
        Maintaining its distinctness from *G. canadensis*, and stating it to be the common Crane of
        Arctic America, the writer gives the diagnoses and synonymy of the two supposed species.
        See COUES, *ibid.*

1880. ROBERTS, T. S.   The Convolution of the Trachea in the Sandhill and Whooping
        Cranes [Grus canadensis and G. americana].   < *Am. Nat.*, xiv, No. 2, Feb.,
        1880, pp. 108–114, figg. 1, 2.
        Trachea of *G. canadensis*, before supposed simple, described as convoluted within the
        sternum, as in *G. americana*, though to less extent (eight inches as against twenty-seven).
        Figures of the parts in both species. Cf. *Bull. Nutt. Ornith. Club*, July, 1880, p. 179.

Psophiidæ.

1768. VOSMAER, A.   Description | du | Trompette Americain [Psophia crepitans], | Oiseau | très-peu connu, doué d'une propriété singulière; | Apporté de | Surinam; | et | Se trouvant dans la Ménagerie, & dans le Cabinet de | Son Altesse Sérénissime | Monseigneur le Prince d' Orange et de Nassau, | Stadhouder He'-re'ditaire, Gouverneur, Capi- | tain Ge'ne'ral et Amiral des Provinces-Unies | des Pais-Bas, &c. &c. &c. | Par | A. Vosmaer, | Directeur des Cabinets d'Histoire Naturelle & de Curiosités de S. A. S., Membre de | l'Académie Impériale, & Correspondant de l'Académie Royale des Sciences de Paris. | A Amsterdam, | Chez Pierre Meijer, | MDCCLXVIII.   4to.   pp. 8, pl. 1.

1824. EDITORIAL.   The Trumpeter-Bird [Psophia crepitans], a true Ventriloquist. < *Edinb. Philos. Journ.*, xi, 1824, p. 417.

1825. BLAINVILLE, H. [M. D.] DE.   Note sur l'appareil sternal de l'Agami [Psophia crepitans]. < *Nouv. Bull. Sc. Soc. Philom.*, i, ii, Août 1825, pp. 126, 127.   (*Froriep's Notizen*, xii, No. 244, 1825, pp. 17, 18.)
Not seen.

1825. BLAINVILLE, H. M. D. DE.   Note sur l'appareil sternal de l'Agami (Psophia Agami [crepitans]).   < *Féruss. Bull.*, 2e sect., vi, 1825, pp. 405, 406.
Extrait du *Bull. de la Soc. Philom.*, août 1825, p. 126.

1826. TRAIL[L], T. S.   Observations on the Habits, Appearance, and Anatomical Structure of the Bird named The Trumpeter, Psophia crepitans of Linnæus, Agami of Cuvier.   < *Mem. Wernerian Nat. Hist. Soc.*, v, pt. ii, 1826, pp. 523–532, pl. xvii.
Read Nov., 1825.   The plate shows the thorax, trachea, and bronchi.

1827. TRAILL, T. S.   [Ueber Psophia crepitans.]   < *Froriep's Notizen*, xix, No. 397, 1827, pp. 1–8.
Not seen.   From *Mem. Wern. Soc.*, v, 1826, pp. 523–532.

1838. HANCOCK, J.   Notes on the Trumpeter Bird, or Waracobi of th [sic] Arowahs of Guiana; Psophia crepitans of Linnæus.   < *Charlesw. Mag. Nat. Hist.*, ii, 1838, pp. 490–492.
Voice, habits, &c.

1838. HANCOCK, J.   [Notizen über Psophia crepitans.]   < *Froriep's Neue Notizen*, xiii, No. 160, 1838, pp. 85, 86.
Not seen: see the original, *Charlesw. Mag. Nat. Hist.*, ii, 1838, pp. 490–492.

1862. BATAILLE, —.   Observations sur l'Agami [Psophia crepitans].   < *Bull. Soc. Acclim.*, ix, 1862, pp. 210, 211.

1862. TARADE, E. DE.   Sur l'Agami [Psophia crepitans].   Lettre adressée a M. le président de la Société impériale d'Acclimatation.   < *Bull. Soc. Acclim.*, ix, 1862, pp. 293, 294.

1872. VOISIN, P.   Les Agamis (Psophia [crepitans]).   < *Bull. Soc. Acclim.*, 2e sér., ix, 1872, pp. 692, 693.
Mœurs et habitudes.

Cariamidæ.

1809. GEOFFROY SAINT-HILAIRE, É.   Description Du Cariama de Marcgrawe, micro-
dactylus Marcgravii [Dicholophus cristatus].   < *Ann. du Mus. d'Hist. Nat.*,
xiii, 1809, pp. 362–370, pl. 26.
    Avec les caractères des genres *Palamedea* et *Psophia*, et sur les habitudes du *Cariama*.
    On the strength of the above, G. R. Gray quotes *Microdactylus marcgravii*, g. sp. n., Geoffr.,
    1809.

1823. MAXIMILIAN, —.   Beiträge zur Naturgeschichte des Sariama oder Seriama
[Dicholophus cristatus].   < *Nov. Act. Acad. Leop. Carol. Nat. Cur.*, xi, pt. ii,
1823, pp. 341–350, pl. 45.
    Mir nicht zugänglich.

1836. MARTIN, W.   [Notes on the visceral and osteological Anatomy of the Cariama
(Dicholophus cristatus Ill.)]   < *P. Z. S.*, iv, 1836, pp. 29–32.

1838. MARTIN, [W.]   Zerlegung des Sariama (Dicholophus cristatus).   < *Oken's Isis*,
Bd. xxxi, 1838, p. 181.
    Aus d. *P. Z. S.*, iv, 1836, pp. 29–32.

1853. BURMEISTER, H.   Beiträge zur Naturgeschichte des Seriema [Dicholophus cris-
tatus].   < *Abhandl. d. Naturf. Gesellsch. zu Halle*, Bd. i, Quart. i, 1853, pp. 11–52,
2 Tafln.   (Auch besonders gedruckt, Halle, Schmidt, 1854.   4to.)
    Nicht mir zugänglich.—Titel aus Carus & Engelmann.   Cf. *J f. O.*, 1854, pp. 67, 68.

1853. NITZSCH, C. L.   Vergleichung des Skelets von Dicholophus cristatus mit dem
Skelettypus der Raubvögel, Trappen, Hühner und Wasserhühner.   < *Abhandl.
d. Naturf. Gesellsch. zu Halle*, Bd. i, Quart. i, 1853, pp. 53–58.
    Nicht mir selbst zugänglich.—Vergl. Sund., *Tént.*, 1873, p. 111; Parker, *M. Micr. Journ.*,
    1873, p. 45.

1854. CABINIS, J.   Abhandlungen der Naturforschenden Gesellschaft zu Halle; I.
Band, I. Quartal.   < *J. f. O.*, ii, 1854, pp. 67, 68.
    Grösstentheils eine Notiz über Burmeister's ,, Beiträge zur Naturgeschichte des Seriema.''

1857. BARRON, C.   Note on the Osteology of Cariama [Dicholophus cristatus].
< *Zoologist*, xv, 1857, p. 5428.

1860. HARTLAUB, G.   On a New Form of Grallatorial Bird nearly allied to the Cariama (Dicholophus cristatus).   < *P. Z. S.*, xxviii, 1860, pp. 334–336.
    Dicholophus burmeisteri.   See Burm., *Reise*, 1861, p. 66.

1860. HARTLAUB, G.   On a [lately] New Form of Grallatorial Bird nearly allied to
the Cariama (Dicholophus cristatus).   < *Ann. Mag. Nat. Hist.*, 3d ser., vi, 1860,
pp. 451, 452.
    D. burmeisteri.   From *P. Z. S.*, June 26, 1860, pp. 334–336.

1872. GÜNTHER, A.   Note on a Deformed Example of Cariama [Dicholophus] cristata.
< *Ann. Mag. Nat. Hist.*, 4th ser., x, 1872, pp. 67, 68.

Palameideidæ.

1797. GEOFFROY ST.-HILAIRE, É.   Sur les genres Psoplvia et Palamedea de Linné.
< *Millin, Magas. Encycl.*, iii, iv, 1797, pp. 10–12; *Bull. Sc. Soc. Philom.*, i, ii, 1797,
pp. 50, 51.
Pas vu moi-même—le titre tiré de la *Bibl.* de Carus et Engelmann.

1842. MARTIN, W.   [Notes on the Habits of the Horned Screamer (Palamedea cornuta,
Linn.)]   < *P. Z. S.*, x, 1842, pp. 15, 16.

1843. MARTIN, W.   [Zur Lebensweise von Palamedea cornuta.]   < *Froriep's Neue Notizen*, xxv, No. 545, 1843, pp. 259–261.
Not seen.   From *P. Z. S.*, 1842, pp. 15, 16.

1845. GRAY, G. R.   [Chauna derbiana, sp. n.]   < *Gray & Mitch. Gen. B.*, Jan., 1845, pl.
160.

1863. PARKER, W. K.   On the Systematic Position of the Crested Screamer (Palamedea
chavaria).   < *P. Z. S.*, xxxi, 1863, pp. 511–518.
"Probably one of the nearest relatives of the marvellous *Archæopteryx.*"

1863. SCLATER, P. L.   [On Chauna "chavaria" from New Grenada, afterward C.
nigricollis.]   < *P. Z. S.*, 1863, pp. 377, 378.
Not a separate paper.   See *P. Z. S.*, 1864, p. 74.

1863. SCLATER, P. L.   [On Chauna "derbiana", afterward C. nigricollis.]   < *Illustrated London News*, Oct. 3, 1863, fig.
Not seen.   The bird called *C. chavaria* in *P. Z. S.*, 1863, p. 377, and here figured as *C. derbiana*, afterward became type of *C. nigricollis*, *P. Z. S.*, 1864, p. 75.

1864. CRISP, E.   On the Visceral Anatomy of the Screamer (Chauna chavaria [nigri-
collis]).   < *P. Z. S.*, Jan. 12, 1864, pp. 14–16.
Also on the history and habits of the species.   The bird here described is said to be that
afterward named *C. nigricollis* by Sclater, *tom. cit.*, p. 75, pl. xi, = *derbiana*.

1864. PARKER, W. K.   On the Systematic Position of the Crested Screamer [Pala-
medea chavaria].   < *Ann. Mag. Nat. Hist.*, 3d ser., xiv, 1864, pp. 144–150.
From *P. Z. S.*, Dec. 8, 1863, pp. 511–518.

1864. SCLATER, P. L.   On the Species of the Genus Chauna.   < *P. Z. S.*, xxxii, 1864,
pp. 74–76, pl. xi.
The writer here distinguishes three spp. of the genus—*CC. chavaria, derbiana*, and *nigricollis*, sp. n., p. 75, pl. xi; the latter being that called *C. derbiana* in *Illust. Lond. News*, Oct.
3. 1863, and *C. chavaria* in *P. Z. S.*, 1863, p. 377, and 1864, p. 14.   See *P. Z. S.*, 1866, p. 369.

1866. MOORE, T. J.   On the Habitat of the Derbyan Crested Screamer (Chauna derbiana, G. R. Gray).   < *P. Z. S.*, xxxiv, 1866, pp. 368, 369.
Probably the "low and swampy parts of New Granada."

1866. SCLATER, P. L.   Note on Chauna nigricollis.   < *P. Z. S.*, xxxiv, 1866, pp. 369, 370.
Here finally identified with *C. derbiana.*

1866. SCLATER, P. L.   [Remarks upon exhibition of a specimen of Chauna derbiana
from Trinidad.]   < *P. Z. S.*, xxxiv, 1866, p. 417.
The "Palamedea cornuta" of Léotaud, *Ois. Trin.*, p. 488, suspected to be this species.

1876. GARROD, A. H.   On the Anatomy of Chauna derbiana, and on the Systematic
Position of the Screamers (Palamedeidæ).   < *P. Z. S.*, Feb. 1, 1876, pp. 189–200,
pll. xii–xv, figg. 1–4.
A very important paper, in which the structure of the genus, here largely detailed, is taken
as the guide to its classification.   The author concludes that the family cannot be kept among
the Anserine birds, where Flower had placed it.   "In the windpipe and the form of the
angle of the jaw, they no doubt closely approach them.   In their alimentary canal they are
much nearer to *Struthio* and *Rhea* (not *Dromœus* and *Casuarius*) than to any other birds.   There
is a Ciconine tendency in their myology, whilst their osteology points in no special direction.
It seems, therefore, to me that, summing these results, the Screamers must have sprung
from the primary avian stock as an independent offshoot at much the same time as did most
of the other important families."   On the species treated, cf. *P. Z. S.*, 1863, p. 511; 1867, p.
415; 1874, p. 117.

Opisthocomidæ.

1785. SONNINI DE MANONCOUR, C. N. S.   Du Sasa [Opisthocomus cristatus], Oiseau de la Guyane.   < *Journ. de Physique,* xxvii, 1785, pp. 222–224.
Pas vu moi-même: le titre tiré de la *Bibl.* de Carus et Engelmann.

1787. SONNINI DE MANONCOUR, C. N. S.   Ueber den Sasa [Opisthocomus cristatus], einen Vogel aus Guiana.   < *Licht. u. Voigt's Magaz.,* 3d ser., iv, 1787, pp. 45–50.
Nicht mir selbst zugänglich: Titel aus Carus und Engelmann, *Bibl.*

1852. DEVILLE, É.   Observations faites en Amérique sur les mœurs de différentes espèces d'Oiseaux-Mouches, suivies de quelques notes anatomiques et de mœurs sur l'Hoazin [Opisthocomus cristatus], le Caurale, et le Savacou.   < *Rev. et Mag. de Zool.,* iv, 1852, pp. 208–226, pl. 9.
Sur l'organisation et les mœurs de l'Hoazin, pp. 217-222, pl. 9.

1852. DEVILLE, É.   Observations faites en Amérique sur les mœurs de différentes espèces d'Oiseaux-Mouches, suivies de quelques Notes sur l'organisation et les mœurs du Caurale, de Savacou et de l'Hoazin [Opisthocomus cristatus].   < *Compt. Rend. de l'Acad. Sci.,* xxxiv, 1852, pp. 652–654.
Extraites par l'auteur.   Ici la quatrième et principale partie de ses "Observations," sur l'anatomie de l'Hoazin.

1870. CABANIS, J.   [Eier des Opisthocomus cristatus.]   < *J. f. O.,* xviii, 1870, pp. 318, 319, pl. i, fig. 3.

1873. PERRIN, J. B.   Note on the Myology of Opisthocomus cristatus.   < *P. Z. S.,* 1873, p. 685.

1879. GARROD, A. H.   Notes on Points in the Anatomy of the Hoatzin (Opisthocomus cristatus).   < *P. Z. S.,* Feb. 4, 1879, pp. 109–114, figg. 1, 2, and diagram.
Important.   *Opisthocomus* must be either considered Gallinaceous or form a group by itself; hardly possible to include it with *Gallinæ,* though it resembles them closely, as it also does *Cuculidæ,* and is not far removed from *Musophagidæ.*

Eurypygidæ.

1781. [PALLAS, P. S.] Beschreibung der sogenannten surinamischen Sonnen-reygers [Ardea (Eurypyga) helias, sp. n.]. < *Neue Nord. Beitr.*, ii, 1781, pp. 48–54, pl.
Nicht mir selbst zugänglich.

1844. DES MURS, O. Notice et considérations oologiques sur le genre ornithologique Caurale, Ardea [Eurypyga] helias (L.) < *Guér. Mag. de Zool.*, 2ᵉ sér., année 1844, Oiseaux, pp. 1–6, pl. 49.
Pl. 49, f. 1, Oeuf de l'*Eurypyga helias*; f. 2, Oeuf de *Rallus variegatus*.

1852. DEVILLE, É. [Quelques notes anatomiques et de mœurs sur le Caurale (Eurypyga helias).] < *Rev. et Mag. de Zool.*, iv, 1852, pp. 222 et suiv.
Formants une partie d'un article plus étendu sur l'Hoazin, etc.

Bull. v, 4——25

Ciconiidæ.

[Including *Ibis, Tantalus, Platalea*, etc.]

1630. SCHWALBACH, J. G.   Dissertatio de Ciconiis, Gruibus et Hirundinibus, quo exeunte aestate abvolent et ubi hyement. Spirae. 1630. 4to. pp. 28.
Haud mihi obvia.

1661. SCHOOCK, M.   De Ciconiis tractatus. Ed. 2da. Amstelædami. 1661. 12mo. pp. 82.
Mihi incognitus.

1672. PRAETORIUS, J., *præs.*, *resp.* BRUNO, F. R.   Disputatio de CrotaLJustrJa tepJ DJ teMporJs hospJta oder von des Storchs [Ciconia] Winterquartier. Lipsiæ, recusa 1672. 4to. 6 folia. (Ibid. 1702. 4to. pp. 48.)
Haud mihi obvia.

1679. LETTAW, EOBALD A.   Dissertatio de Ciconiis earumque proprietatibus. Freyb. 1679. 4to. 1½ folia.
Haud mihi obvia.

1679. STRAUSS, L., *præs.*, *resp.* STRAUSS, J. D.   Dissertatio de Ciconia. Giessæ. Karger. 1679. 4to. pp. 19.
Haud mihi obvia.

1680. JACOBÆUS, O.   Anatome Ciconiæ. < *Bartholini Acta Hafn.*, v, 1680, pp. 247–249.
Haud mihi obvium.

1683. PEYER, J. C.   De Ciconiæ ventre et affinitate quadam cum ruminantibus. < *Ephem. Acad. Nat. Cur.*, Dec. ii, Ann. 2, 1683, 1698, pp. 245–247, pl.
Haud mihi obvius.

1687. SCHELHAMMER, G. C.   Ciconiæ Anatome. < *Ephem. Acad. Nat. Cur.*, Dec. ii, Ann. 6, 1687, 1688, pp. 206–208.
Haud mihi obvium.

1688. SCHULTZE, S.   De Ciconiæ Vindicta. < *Ephem. Acad. Nat. Cur.*, Dec. i, Ann. 6, 7, 1675–76, 1688, pp. 227, 228.
Haud mihi obvius.

1689. SVEDERUS, M.   Ciconia seu Diss. acad. de Jure Antipelargiæ ; Præs. M. Svederus, Resp. L. A. Lechander, W. Gotho. Aboae. 1689. 4to. pp. 8, 20.
Haud mihi obvia.

1692. FOGIUS, D.   Dissertatio de Ciconiarum hibernaculis. Praes. Dav. Fogius, resp. Chr. Litzow. Hafneæ. 1692. 4to. pp. 12.
Haud mihi obvia.

1717. LIMPRECHT, J. A.   Ciconiæ Anatome. < *Ephem. Acad. Nat. Cur.*, Cent. 5 et 6, 1717, pp. 209–212.
Haud mihi obvia.

1733. ———.   [Observation sur l'Ibis blanc, oyseau singulier d'Égypte.] < *Hist. de l'Acad. Roy. des Sci.* pour l'année 1683, i, 1733, pp. 363, 364.

1734. PERRAULT, C.   Description anatomique de quatre Pallettes [Platalea]. < *Mém. de l'Acad. Roy. des Sci.* depuis 1666 jusq. 1699, iii, pt. iii, 1734, pp. 22–30, pll. 5, 6.

1734. PERRAULT, C.   Description anatomique d'un Ibis blanc et de deux Cicognes. < *Mém. de l'Acad. Roy. des Sci.* depuis 1666 jusq. 1699, iii, pt. iii, 1734, pp. 58–72, pll. 13, 14.

1752. MÜLLER, JOACH. FRIEDR.   Bemerkungen vom Storch [Ciconia]. < *Physikal. Belustiggn.*, ii, 1752, pp. 538, 539.
Mir nicht zugänglich.

1757. Perrault, C. Anatomische Beschreibung von vier Löffel- oder Spatelgänsen [Platalea]. < *Abhandl. Königl. Französisch. Akad.*, ii, 1757, pp. 193——.

> Not seen—title from Giebel. German transl. from *Mém. de l'Acad. Roy. des Sci.*, iii, pt. iii, 1734, p. 22.

1757. Perrault, C. Anatomische Beschreibung eines Ibis und zweener Störche. < *Abhandl. Königl. Französisch. Akad.*, ii, 1757, pp. 257——.

> Not seen—title from Giebel. German transl. from *Mém. de l'Acad. Roy. Paris*, iii, pt. iii, 1734, p. 58.

1798. Vahl, M. Om Tantalus Pavoninus, Spalowsky. < *Skrivt. Naturh. Selsk. Kiφbenh.*, iv, Heft ii, 1798, pp. 122–125.

> Not seen.

1798. Vahl, M. Om Mycteria orientalis. < *Skrivt. Naturh. Selsk. Kiφbenh.*, iv, Heft ii, 1798, pp. 126–132.

> Not seen.

1799. Duméril, G. Mémoire sur une espèce d'articulation dans laquelle le mouvement des os s'exécute à l'aide d'un ressort, observé sur les pattes d'un Cicogne· [Ciconia alba]. < *Bull. Sci. Soc. Philom.*, ii, An. VII (1799), pp. 4, 5.

> Pas vu moi-même.

1800. Cuvier, G. Sur l'Ibis des anciens Égyptiens. <*Bull. Sci. Soc. Philom.*, ii, An. VIII (1800), pp. 119——.

> Pas vu moi-même : le titre tiré de la *Bibl.* de Carus et Engelmann.

1800. Cuvier, G. Mémoire sur l'Ibis des anciens Égyptiens. <*Journ. de Phys. Chim. Hist. Nat.*, li, 1800, pp. 184–192, pl.

> Parmi les résultats du mémoire, il est constaté par l'auteur que l'Ibis des anciens n'est point l'Ibis de Perrault et de Buffon, qui est un *Tantalus*, ni l'Ibis de Hasselquist, qui est un *Ardea*, ni l'Ibis de Maillet, qui est un Vauteur; mais c'est un *Numenius* ou Courlis qui n'a point encore été nommé, et que Bruce a figuré sous le nom d'abou-hannès. L'auteur le nomme *Numenius ibis* (sp. n., p. 192), albus, capite et collo nudis, remigibus, pennis uropygii elongatis, rostro et pedibus nigris.
>
> Mais on doit ajouter, que l'oiseau ici décrit par l'auteur n'est néanmoins point une espece du genre *Numenius* des auteurs modernes, de la famille des Scolopacidés, mais véritablement un Ibis.

1800. Cuvier, " C." [*i. e.*, G.] Memoir on the Ibis of the Antient Egyptians. < *Tilloch's Philos. Mag.*, viii, 1800, pp. 61–70, pl. iii.

> From *Journ. de Physique*, Fructidor, An. VIII. Determined to be a *Numenius*, and called, on p. 70, *Numenius ibis*; description, p. 64. The article is chiefly occupied in bibliographical research, and concludes with the statement that the *Tantalus ibis* of Linnæus comprehended four different species of three genera. The bird is the *Ibis æthiopicus*.

1800. Shaw, G. Description of a new Species of Mycteria [senegalensis]. < *Trans. Linn. Soc.*, v, 1800, pp. 32–35, pl. iii.

> *M. senegalensis*, p. 35, pl. 3 : with characters, also, of *M. americana* and *M. australis*.

1801. Cuvier, G. Sur l'Ibis des anciens Égyptiens. < *Millin, Magas. Encycl.*, vi, pt. i, 1801, pp. 527, 528.

> Pas vu moi-même : le titre tiré de Carus et Engelmann.

1802. Cavanilles, A. J. De la Ciguëna blanca [Ciconia alba]. < *Anal. Hist. Nat.*, v, No. 15, 1802, pp. 234–244.

> Not seen.

1803. Sartorius, —. Beobachtungen über die schwarzen Störche [Ciconia nigra]. < *Voigt's Mag.*, vi, 1803, pp. 227–233.

> Nicht mir selbst zugänglich : Titel aus Carus und Engelmann.

1804. Cuvier, G. Mémoire Sur l'Ibis des Anciens Egyptiens. < *Ann. du Mus. d'Hist. Nat.*, iv, 1804, pp. 116–135, pll. lii, liii (Ibis, pll. i–iii).

> Méprises des auteurs modernes—Momies de l'ancien ibis—Description du squelette faite d'après les momies de Thèbes—Determination du véritable Ibis—Comparaison de cet oiseau avec ceux qu'on a confondus avec lui—Description qu' Hérodote a faite—Examen de plusieurs monumens antiques sur lesquels on voit la figure de l'ibis—Origine des erreurs—Preuve offerte par les momies que les ibis mangoient des serpens—Comparaison des plumes trouvées dans les momies avec celle de l'oiseau qu'on a preuvé être l'ibis—Résultat du mémoire.

1804. CUVIER, G.—Continued.

"3° L'*ibis* des anciens n'est point l'ibis de Perrault et de Buffon, qui est un tantalus, ni l'ibis de Hasselquist, qui est un ardea, ni l'ibis de Maillet, qui est un *vauteur* ; mais cèst un numenius ou courlis qui n'a été décrit et figuré au plus que par Bruce sous le nom *d'abou-hannès.* Je le nomme numenius ibis" (p. 134).

Pl. i, squelette de l'Ibis, tiré d'une momie de Thèbes ; pl. ii, L'oiseau, *Numenius ibis,* Cuv. ; pl. iii, Figure copiée sur l'un des Temples de la haute Égypte, et bec d'une momie.

Pour son premier mémoire, et pour une traduction Anglaise, voir 1800, CUVIER, G.

1805. PEARSON, J.   Some Account of two Mummies of the Egyptian Ibis [æthiopicus], one of which was in a remarkably perfect State.   < *Philos. Trans.*, xcv, pt. ii, 1805, pp. 264–271, pl. viii.

Taken by Major Hayes, in 1802–3, from catacombs at Thebes, and described with particularity. The plate, of natural size, shows the position given to the body by the embalmer.

1805. SAVIGNY, J. C.   Histoire | Naturelle et Mythologique | de l'Ibis [religiosa]; | Par Jules-César Savigny, | Membre de l'Institut d'Égypte ; | Ornée de six planches gravées par Bouquet, | d'après les dessins de H. J. Redouté et | Barraband. | [Dessin.] | Libycisque vescens ipsa scorpionibus . . . | Phile. | Paris, | Allais, Libraire, quai des Augustins, n°. 39. | — | M. DCCC. V.   1 vol. sm. 8vo. pp. i–xiv, 1–224, pll. i–vi.

This is a celebrated treatise on a very celebrated bird, replete with curious learning upon the natural, mythological, and philological history of the Ibis, gathered by the author as a part of his researches in Egypt. The bird excited much attention about that time ; the Baron Cuvier gave his views on the same subject ; and quite a literature was soon formed, both as regards the ornithological and the archæological aspects of the case. The present memoir became the occasion of much discussion, and the information it contains is found in various other writings, under different guises.

1805. VOSMAER, A.   Histoire Naturelle | du | Courli | Africain [   ]. | Ayant été conservé dans le Museum | De son Altesse Sérenissime Monseigneur le Prince | D'Orange-Nassau. | Par Feu Mr. | A. Vosmaer, | De sa vie Conseiller de S. A. S., Directeur de son Cabinet d'Histoire | Naturelle & des Curiosités, Membre de l'Académie Impériale, | Correspondant de l'Académie Royale des Sciences de Paris, | Membre de celle de Madrid & des Sociétés Litterai- | res de Flessingue & de Harlem &c. | — | A Amsterdam, chez | J. B. Elwe, | MDCCCV. 4to. pp. 8, pl.

1806. JOMARD, —.   Observations sur l'Histoire Naturelle et Mythologique de l'Ibis, Ouvrage de J. C. Savigny, Membre de l'Institut d'Égypte. [Par M. Jomard.] n. d. n. p. [Paris. Delance. 1806.] 1 vol. 8vo. pp. 27.

Extraites du Magasin Encyclopédique, numéro de Février 1806.

18—. ROZIÈRE, —.   De l'Ibis Égyptien. [Par Rozière.] 8vo. pp. 22.

Extrait du ———? À propos de l'ouvrage de M. J. C. Savigny, intitule : *Hist. Nat. et Mythol. de l'Ibis :* donnant les principaux résultats du travail de M. Savigny, en y joignant quelques observations.

1817. MONTAGU, G.   Some Remarks on the Natural History of the Black Stork [Ciconia nigra], for the first time captured in Great Britain. < *Trans. Linn. Soc.*, xii, pt. i, 1817, pp. 19–23.

1817. ORD, G.   An Account of an American Species of the Genus Tantalus or Ibis. < *Journ. Acad. Nat. Sci. Phila.*, i, 1817, pp. 53–57.

Identified, with a query, with *T. mexicanus* Gm. This is probably the earliest special notice of the Glossy Ibis (*Plegadis falcinellus*) in North America.

1822. "L'UN DE VOS AUDITEURS À L'ATHÉNÉE." Au rédacteur du Journal de Physique. < *Journ. de Phys. Chim. Hist. Nat.*, xciv, 1822, p. 320.

Quelques faits concernants les mœurs des Cicognes.

1823. MONTAGU, G.   Einige Bemerkungen über die Naturgeschichte des schwarzen Storchs, Ardea [Ciconia] nigra Linn., den man vor kurzem zum erstenmal in England angetroffen hat. < *Oken's Isis*, Jahrg. vii, 1823, (*Litter. Anzeig.*), pp. 539–543.

Aus d. *Trans. Linn. Soc. Lond.*, xii, pt. i, 1817, pp. 19–23.

1825. ADAM, J. A description of the Ciconia Argala or Adjutant Bird of Bengal. < *Trans. Med. Phys. Soc. Calcutta*, i, 1825, pp. 240–248.

Not seen—title from *Roy. Soc. Cat.* It is reprinted in several places. See below.

1826. ADAM, J. Description of the Ciconia Ardgala [sic], or Adjutant Bird. < *Edinb. New Philos. Journ.*, i, 1826, pp. 327–332.

From *Trans. Med. and Phys. Soc. Calcutta*, i, 1825, pp. 240–248. Description followed by extended account of habits. Also in *Froriep's Notizen*, xv, No. 328, 1826, pp. 307–309, and *Isis*, 1832, p. 685.

1826. [TEMMINCK, C. J., *and* LAUGIER, M.] Notice sur les Cigognes, et particulièrement sur les trois grandes espèces qui fournissent à la toilette des dames les plumes déliées dites Marabou. < *Ann. des Sci. Nat.*, vii, 1826, pp. 91–96.

Réproduite de la 64e livraison des *Planches Coloriées*.

1826. ————. Ibis noir d'Islande. < *Féruss. Bull.*, 2e sect., viii, 1826, p. 115.

Reinhardt, *Tidssk. for Naturv.*, cah. 10, p. 133.

1829. "G. H." The Storks [Ciconia] in Germany. < *Loudon's Mag. Nat. Hist.*, ii, 1829, p. 484.

1826. PAYRAUDEAU, B. C. Notice sur les Cigognes, . . . < *Féruss. Bull.*, 2e sect., viii, 1826, p. 274.

Extraite des *Ann. des Sc. Nat.*, janv. 1826, pp. 91–96 (de la 64e livraison des *Planches Coloriées*, par MM. Temminck et Laugier).

1828. L[UROTH], S. G. Description de l'oiseau adjutant (Ciconia Argala); par M. J. Adam. . . . < *Féruss. Bull.*, 2e sect., xv, 1828, p. 392.

Extraite des *Trans. Med. and Phys. Soc. Calcutta*, i, 1825, pp. 240–248; *Edinb. New Philos. Journ.*, i, 1826, pp. 327–332.

1829. ————. Cicognes avec des écussons metalliques. < *Féruss. Bull.*, 2e sect., xvi, 1829, p. 285.

Froriep's Notizen, xxi, n° 21, August, 1828, p. 329.

1829. [PRIOU, —]. Ibis noirs tués dans le département de la Loire-Inférieure le 18 mai 1828. . . . < *Féruss. Bull.*, 2e sect., xvii, 1829, pp. 292, 293.

Extrait du *Lycée armoricain*, livr. lxxi, nov. 1828, p. 383.

1829. RICHTER, M. G. Etwas über den schwarzen Storch, Ciconia nigra Bechst. < *Oken's Isis*, Bd. xxii, 1829, pp. 871–875.

Zur Lebensweise.

1832. ADAM, J. Beschreibung der Ciconia argala oder des Adjutanten-Vogels (aus Transactions of the medical and physical Society of Calcutta I). < *Oken's Isis*, Bd. xxv, 1832, pp. 685, 686.

Auszug aus dem *Edinb. New Philos. Journ.*, Bd. i, Heft ii, 1826, pp. 327–332.

1832. ANKARCRONA, T. W. Strödda underättelser. < *Tidssk. f. Jägare och Naturf.*, i, 1832, p. 191.

Uppgift om Storkens (Ciconia) ankomst till Skåne 1832.

1832. TEMMINCK, C. J., *and* LAUGIER, [M.] Note über die Ciconiae, insbesondere über drey grossen Gattungen, die die sogenannten Marabufedern liefern. < *Oken's Isis*, Bd. xxv, 1832, pp. 184–186.

Temminck und Laugier, *Planches Coloriées*, livrais. 64. Auszug aus d. *Annal. des Scienc. Nat.*, vii, 1826, pp. 91–96.

1833. BROOKES, J. On the remarkable Formation of the Trachea in the Egyptian Tantalus [ibis]. < *Trans. Linn. Soc.*, xvi, pt. iii, 1833, pp. 499–503.

Followed with general observations on the vagaries of the organ in various birds.

1833. LEES, E. The Spoonbill (Platalea leucorodia L.) [occurring in Great Britain]. < *Loudon's Mag. Nat. Hist.*, vi, 1833, p. 454.

1833. TELFAIR, C. [Exhibition of an Ibis.] < *P. Z. S.*, i, 1833, p. 133.

1834. GRAY, J. E. [Note on the New Holland Ibis of Dr. Latham.] < *P. Z. S.*, ii, 1834, p. 135.

1835. JAMESON, R. [Ibis spinicollis.] < *L'Institut*, iii, No. 125, 1835, p. 316.

Pas vu moi-même.

1836. LAFRESNAYE, F. DE. Ibis. Ibis. Cuvier. I. a cou lamelleux. I. lamellicollis. Lafresnaye. < *Guér. Mag. de Zool.*, 6e année, 1836, classe i, notice lvii, pp. 1, 2, pl. lvii.

1837. DUBUS DE GHISIGNIES, V. B. Note sur l'Ibis olivacea. < *Bull. Acad. Brux.*, iv, 1837, pp. 105, 106. (*L'Inst.*, v, No. 218, 1837, p. 259.)

Pas vu moi-même: le titre tiré de la *Bibl.* de Carus et Engelmann.

1838. DUBUS [DE GHISIGNIES, V. B.] Note sur l'Ibis olivacea. < *Revue Zoologique*, i, 1838, pp. 141, 142.

Extr. du *Bull. Acad. Roy. Bruxelles*, iv, 1837, p. 105. (Cf. *Esq. Orn.*, pl. 5.)

1840. SCHOMBURGK, R. Ueber den Jabiru, Mycteria americana. < *Froriep's Neue Notizen*, xv, 1840, pp. 136, 137.

Nicht mir selbst zugänglich.

1841. MORTON, S. G. [Remarks on exhibition of the embalmed body of an Egyptian Ibis, Ibis religiosa.] < *Proc. Acad. Nat. Sci. Phila.*, i, 1841, pp. 15, 16.

1842. ALESSANDRINI, A. Intorno una singolare disposizione dell' arteria brachiale osservata nella Cicogna bianca [Ciconia alba]. < *Nuov. Annal. delle Sci. Nat. Bologna*, vii, 1842, pp. 257–261.

1843. RODD, E. H. Note on the occurrence of the Spoonbill [Platalea leucorodia] in Cornwall. < *Zoologist*, i, 1843, p. 364.

1844. BURLINGHAM, D. C. Note on the occurrence of the Spoonbill [Platalea leucorodia] at Lynn. < *Zoologist*, ii, 1844, p. 455.

1844. GUYON, —. Sur la nature de l'alimentation des Ibis. < *Compt. Rend. de l'Acad. Sci.*, xviii, 1844, pp. 834, 835.

Sur la faculté de détruire les serpents.

1844. GUYON, —. Sur l'alimentation de l'Ibis. < *L'Institut*, xii, No. 540, 1844, p. 152.

Extr. des *Compt. Rend.*, xviii, 1844, pp. 834, 835.—Pas vu moi-même: le titre tiré de Carus et Engelmann.

1845. LEWCOCK, J. Occurrence of the Spoonbill [Platalea leucorodia] at Frensham Pond [England]. < *Zoologist*, iii, 1845, p. 878.

1845. RODD, E. H. Occurrence of the Spoonbill [Platalea leucorodia] in Cornwall. < *Zoologist*, iii, 1845, pp. 1193, 1194.

1846. HARVEY, J. R. Ciconia alba [in Ireland]. < *Ann. Mag. Nat. Hist.*, xviii, 1846, p. 70.

1846. MORRIS, F. O. Occurrence of the White Stork [Ciconia alba] near Driffield, Yorkshire. < *Zoologist*, iv, 1846, p. 1501.

1846. WOLLEY, J. The Spoonbill [Platalea leucorodia] in Andalucia. < *Zoologist*, iv, 1846, pp. 1213, 1214.

1848. BORRER, W., JR. Occurrence of the White Spoonbill (Platalea leucorodia) in Sussex. < *Zoologist*, vi, 1848, p. 2066.

1848. HIGGINS, E. T. Occurrence of the White Stork (Ciconia alba) near York. < *Zoologist*, vi, 1848, p. 2229.

1848. JOHNSON, F. W. Occurrence of the White Spoonbill (Platalea leucorodia) at Aldborough. < *Zoologist*, vi, 1848, pp. 2229, 2230.

1848. MILNER, W. M. E. Occurrence of the White Stork (Ciconia alba) near York. < *Zoologist*, vi, 1848, p. 2191.

1848. RODD, E. H. Occurrence of the White Stork (Ciconia alba) at the Land's End. < *Zoologist*, vi, 1848, p. 2147.

1849. DÉSMAREST, E. Note sur des tubercles observés dans un Jabiru (Mycteria americana Linné). < *Rev. et Mag. de Zool.*, i, 1849, p. 54.

1849. GURNEY, J. H. Occurrence of the Spoonbill [Platalea leucorodia], &c., near Yarmouth. < *Zoologist*, vii, 1849, p. 2499.

1850. BAKER, W. On the Capture, Habits and Change of Plumage in the Black Stork (Ciconia nigra). < *Zoologist*, viii, 1850, pp. 2700–2703.

     A communication by Mr. Baker of a correspondence on the above subject between R. Anstice and G. Montagu.

1850. CABOT, S., [JR.] [Observations upon the recent appearance in New England of Ibis guarauna.] < *Proc. Boston Soc. Nat. Hist.*, iii, 1850, pp. 313, 314, 332, 333.

     Not the western species now commonly called *guarauna*, but the Glossy Ibis, *Ibis falcinellus*, or *Falcinellus igneus*, or *Plegadis falcinellus* of authors.

1850. ELLMAN, J. B. Occurrence of the Glossy Ibis (Ibis falcinellus) at Piddinghoe, Sussex. < *Zoologist*, viii, 1850, pp. 2953, 2954.

     Cf. *Zool.*, p. 2967.

1850. GLIDDON, G. R. [Remarks upon the scarcity of the Ibis religiosa in Egypt.] < *Proc. Acad. Nat. Sci. Phila.*, v, 1850, p. 84.

1850. GURNEY, J. H. Occurrence of the Glossy Ibis (Ibis falcinellus) near Lowestoft. < *Zoologist*, viii, 1850, p. 2879.

1850. HARRIS, A. C. [Extract from a letter in relation to the present existence of Ibis religiosa in Egypt.] < *Proc. Acad. Nat. Sci. Phila.*, v, 1850, pp. 83, 84.

1850. HULKE, J. W. Occurrence of the Spoonbill (Platalea leucorodia) at Sandwich. < *Zoologist*, viii, 1850, p. 2853.

1850. [KIRTLAND, J. P.] The Glossy Ibis. < *The Family Visitor*, i, No. 21, 1850, p. 164.

     Quotation of occurrence of *Ibis falcinellus* sive *Plegadis igneus* in Massachusetts and Connecticut, and statement of other occurrence of the same in Ohio.

1850. NELSON, J. Occurrence of the Spoonbill (Platalea leucorodia) in East Lothian. < *Zoologist*, viii, 1850, p. 2924.

1850. RODD, E. H. Occurrence of the Spoonbill [Platalea leucorodia] at St. Mary's, Scilly. < *Zoologist*, viii, 1850, p. 2853 or thereabouts.

1851. ANON. [Anecdote of the Adjutant Stork.] < *Harper's New Monthly Mag.*, iii, 1851, p. 853.

1851. CABOT, S., JR. Ibis guarauna [i. e., falcinellus] in New England. < *Am. Journ. Sci.*, xi, 1851, pp. 435, 436.

     From *Proc. Bost. Soc. Nat. Hist.*, iii, 1850, pp. 313, 314, 332, 333, *q. v.*

1851. ELLMAN, J. B. Occurrence of the Spoonbill [Platalea leucorodia] at Hailsham, Sussex. < *Zoologist*, ix, 1851, pp. 3278, 3279.

1851. MILNER, W. M. E. Occurrence of the Spoonbill (Platalea leucorodia) in Yorkshire. < *Zoologist*, ix, 1851, p. 3278.

1851. SMITH, J. Occurrence of the White Stork (Ciconia alba) in Scotland. < *Zoologist*, ix, 1851, p. 3035.

1852. IRBY, L. H. Occurrence of the White Stork [Ciconia alba] near Yarmouth. < *Zoologist*, x, 1852, pp. 3476, 3477.

1852. POWYS, T. L. Occurrence of the Glossy Ibis [Ibis falcinellus] in Ireland. < *Zoologist*, x, 1852, p. 3477.

1852. VIERTHALER, R. Ueber Ibis religiosa. < *Naumannia*, ii, Heft ii, 1852, pp. 58–63.

     Zur Lebensweise.

1852. VIERTHALER, R. [Ueber Leptoptilos ruepellii.] < *Naumannia*, ii, Heft ii, 1852, p. 57.

     Not a separate article—notice occurs in a paper of much wider scope. On this supposed species, cf. *Naumannia*, vi, 1856, pp. 191 and 267.

1852. VIERTHALER, R. Leptoptilos argala. < *Foriep. Tagsber.*, No. 566 (*Zool.*, Bd. iii), 1852, p. 71.

     Not seen: title from Carus and Engelmann. Cf. *Naumannia*, ii, 1852, p. 56; vi, 1856, pp. 191, 267.

1853. ANON. Ibis-shooting in Louisiana. < *Harper's New Monthly Mag.*, vii, 1853, pp. 768–772, fig.

1853. BREHM, A. E.   Einige Beobachtungen über Ibis religiosa Cuv., Tantalus aethiopicus Lath.   < *J. f. O.*, i, 1853, pp. 141–144.

1854. GLOGER, C. W. L.   Nisten weisser Störche [Ciconia alba] im Spätherbste [d. 30 Novemb.].   < *J. f. O.*, ii, 1854, pp. 94, 95.
    Cf. *tom. cit.*, pp. 191, 192.

1854. GLOGER, C. W. L.   Das ,, Nisten weisser Störche [Ciconia alba] im Spätherbste,'' [u. s. w.]   < *J. f. O.*, ii, 1854, pp. 191, 192.
    Cf. *tom. cit.*, pp. 94, 95.

1854. RODD, E. H.   Occurrence of the Glossy Ibis [Ibis falcinellus] at Scilly.   < *Zoologist*, xii, 1854, p. 4478.

1854. FRANKLIN, W.   Occurrence of the Glossy Ibis [Ibis falcinellus] near Shrewsbury.   < *Zoologist*, xii, 1854, pp. 4164, 4165.

1856. BREWER, T. M.   [Occurrence of Tantalus loculator in Illinois.]   < *Proc. Boston Soc. Nat. Hist.*, v, 1856, p. 391.

1856. DENNIS, R. N.   Occurrence of the Black Stork [Ciconia nigra] in Kent.   < *Zoologist*, xiv, 1856, p. 5160.

1856. HARTLAUB, [G.]   [Leptoptilos rüppellii Vierth.=L. crumenifera ♀ .]   < *Naumannia*, vi, 1856, p. 191.

1856. HARTLAUB, G.   Leptoptilos Rüppelli eine gute Art.   < *Naumannia*, vi, 1856, pp. 267, 268.

1856. WOODROFFE, A.   A young Spoonbill [Platalea leucorodia] shot at Shoreham.   < *Zoologist*, xiv, 1856, p. 5321.

1857. GADAMER, [H.]   Ciconia alba. L.   < *Naumannia*, vii, Heft i, 1857, p. 83.

1857. MARTIN, L.   In welchen Gegenden hat es d. J. vorzugsweise an weissen Störchen [Ciconia alba] gefehlt?   < *J. f. O.*, v, 1857, pp. 69, 70.

1858. BALDAMUS, E.   [Storchneste.]   < *Naumannia*, viii, 1858, p. 509.

1858. HALL, T.   Occurrence of the Glossy Ibis [Ibis falcinellus] in South Wales.   < *Zoologist*, xvi, 1858, p. 6096.

1858. HOMEYER, E. V.   Das seltene Erscheinen der weissen Störche [Ciconia alba] im Frühling 1856.   < *J. f. O.*, vi, 1858, pp. 410, 411.

1858. NEAVE, E.   Occurrence of the Spoonbill [Platalea leucorodia] near Aldborough.   < *Zoologist*, xvi, 1858, p. 6266. .

1858. THOMPSON, W.   Occurrence of the Glossy Ibis [Ibis falcinellus] in Dorsetshire.   < *Zoologist*, xvi, 1858, pp. 6266, 6267.

1859. BAYER, J.   Herr J. Bayer übergibt folgende Notizen über Störche.   < *Verh. k.-k. zool.-bot. Ges. Wien*, ix, 1859, pp. 94, 95.

1859. BENNETT, G.   Notes on the Habits of the Mycteria australis or New Holland Jabiru (Gigantic Crane of the Colonists).   < *P. Z. S.*, xxvii, 1859, pp. 47–49.

1859. BENNETT, G.   Notes on the Habits of the Mycteria australis or New Holland Jabiru (Gigantic Crane of the Colonists).   < *Ann. Mag. Nat. Hist.*, 3d ser., iv 1859, pp. 458–461.
    From *P. Z. S.*, Jan. 25, 1859, pp. 47–49.

1860. BENNETT, G.   Note on the Habits of the Jabiru [Mycteria australis, in captivity].   < *Zoologist*, xviii, 1860, pp. 6880–6883.
    From *P. Z. S.*, 1859, pp. 47–49.

1860. BOLLE, C.   Der Storch [Ciconia alba] in Spanien.   Aus dem Spanischen de Cavanilles bearbeitet.   < *J. f. O.*, viii, 1860, pp. 53–58.
    Vergl. CAVANILLES, 1802, anteà.

1860. BUCKLAND, F. T.   [Exhibition of an embalmed Egyptian Ibis.]   < *P. Z. S* xxviii, 1860, p. 184.

1860. GLOGER, C. W. L.   Das Verunglücken der weissen Störche.[Ciconia alba] i. J. 1856, [u. s. w.]   < *J. f. O.*, viii, 1860, p. 301.

1860. MARTNER, —.   Sur les moeurs de la Cicogne.   Lettre adressée a M. le Président de la Société impériale d'Acclimatation.   < *Bull. Soc. d'Acclim.*, vii, 1860, pp. 151–153.

1861. ————?   The Calcutta Adjutant [Leptoptilus argala], or Hurghila of the natives of Bengal.   < *Chambers' Journal*, 1861, p. 40.
    Not seen.—Cf. *Ibis*, 1861, p. 268.

1861. BLYTH, E.   Note on the Calcutta 'Adjutant' (Leptoptilus argala).   < *Ibis*, iii, 1864, pp. 268–270.
    Criticizes and corrects alleged nonsense contained in *Chambers' Journal*, 1861, p. 40.

1861. HOFFMANN, —.   [Letter from Calcutta relating in part to the Adjutant (Leptoptilus argala).]   < *Zool. Gart.*, ii, 1861, pp. 208, 209.

1862. HORSFALL, W. C.   Occurrence of the Black Stork [Ciconia nigra] near Hartlepool.   < *Zoologist*, xx, 1862, p. 8196.

1863. GATCOMBE, J.   The White Spoonbill (Platalea leucorodia) near Plymouth. < *Zoologist*, xxi, 1863, p. 8330.

1863. SAXBY, H. L.   The Glossy Ibis [Ibis falcinellus] in Shetland.   < *Zoologist*, xxi, 1863, p. 8448.

1863. SCHLEGEL, H.   Ibis   < *Mus. Hist. Nat. Pays-Bas*, 4e livr., Juill. 1863, pp. 1–16.
    Treating 19 spp., all referred to the single genus *Ibis*, together with *Scopus umbretta*; represented by 114 specimens in the collection at Leyden.

1863. STEVENSON, H.   Occurrence of Spoonbills [Platalea leucorodia] on the Suffolk Coast.   < *Zoologist*, xxi, 1863, p. 8691.

1863. WAGNER, CH.   [Mittel gegen Knochenbrüchigkeit bei Vögeln.]   < *Zool. Gart.*, iv, 1863, pp. 42, 43.
    Illustrated in case of *Ciconia nigra*.

1863. WEINLAND, D. F.   Marabu [Ciconia marabu] und Schlange [Tropidonotus natrix].   < *Zool. Gart.*, iv, 1863, pp. 90, 91.

1864. BLAKE-KNOX, H.   Occurrence of the Spoonbill [Platalea leucorodia] in Dublin Bay.   < *Zoologist*, xxii, 1864, p. 9211.

1864. HARTLAUB, G.   Note on Ciconia pruyssenaëri.   < *Ibis*, vi, 1864, p. 430.

1864. MEYER, R.   Junger und alter Storch [Ciconia alba].   (Mit einer lithographirten Tafel.)   < *Zool. Gart.*, v, 1864, pp. 399–403.
    Der Tafel stellt dessen Dunenkleid dar.

1864. SCHWAITZER, F.   Ein Eingeweidewurm am Herzen einer Ciconia nigra.   < *J. f. O.*, xii, 1864, pp. 398, 399.

1865. BLAKE-KNOX, H.   Glossy Ibis [Ibis falcinellus] in Dublin Bay.   < *Zoologist*, xxiii, 1865, p. 9453.

1865. GUNN, T. E.   Spoonbill [Platalea leucorodia] on the Coast of Norfolk.   < *Zoologist*, xxiii, 1865, pp. 9418, 9419.

1865. GURNEY, J. H.   Anecdote of a Pair of Storks [Ciconia alba].   < *Zoologist*, xxiii, 1865, pp. 9453, 9454.

1865. JÄCKEL, A. J.   Die Begattung der Störche [Ciconia alba] vor ihrem Wegzuge von uns.   < *Zool. Gart.*, vi, 1865, pp. 378, 379.

1865. RODD, E. H.   Spoonbill [Platalea leucorodia] near Helston.   < *Zoologist*, xxiii, 1865, p. 9564.

1865. SCHLEGEL, H.   Ciconiae   < *Mus. Hist. Nat. Pays-Bas*, 7e livr., Déc., 1864, pp. 1–26.   (Pub. 1865.)
    Though ostensibly dating Dec., 1864, this article cannot have been published before 1865, for the end of it is a part of the same sheet of paper (signature 29) that begins the next article, dated May, 1865.
    The article treats of *Ciconia* (7 spp.), *Mycteria* (4 spp.), *Anastomus* (2 spp.), *Tantalus* (4 spp.), and *Platalea* (6 spp.), represented in the Leyden Museum by 152 specimens.

1865. SCHMIDT, MAX. [Ein junger schwarze Storch (Ciconia nigra).] < *Zool. Gart.*, vi, 1865, p. 343.

1866. HACKETT, W. A. The Stork [Ciconia alba] at Cork. < *Zoologist*, 2d ser., ı, 1866, p. 524.

1866. HARTING, J. E. On the Occurrence of the Spoonbill [Platalea leucorodia] in Middlesex. < *Zoologist*, 2d ser., i, 1866, pp. 35–37.

1866. MATHEW, M. A. Glossy Ibis [Ibis falcinellus] at Budleigh Salterton. < *Zoologist*, 2d ser., i, 1866, p. 524.

1866. RODD, E. H. Glossy Ibis [Ibis falcinellus] at Scilly. < *Zoologist*, 2d ser., i, 1866, p. 524.

1866. SCHMIDT, MAX. Zwei rothe Ibis (Ibis rubra). < *Zool. Gart.*, vii, 1866, p. 421.

1867. HAMOND, A. [Ciconia nigra in Norfolk, England.] < *Ibis*, 2d ser., iii, 1867, p. 382.

1867. JERDON, T. C. The Gigantic Stork or Adjutant (Leptoptilos argala). < *Zoologist*, 2d ser., ii, 1867, p. 834.
      From 'Birds of India', p. 731

1867. JERDON, T. C. The Shell Ibis (Anastomus oscitans). < *Zoologist*, 2d ser., ii, 1867, pp. 834, 835.
      From 'Birds of India', i, p. 766.

1867. KAWALL, J. H. Biologisches vom Storch (Ciconia alba Bris.) Aus Kurland. < *Bull. Soc. Imp. Nat. Moscou*, xl, pt. 2, 1867, pp. 486–497.

1867. MEYER, R. Ueber das Herabfallen der jungen Storche [Ciconia alba] aus dem Neste. < *Zool. Gart.*, viii, 1867, pp. 482–484.

1857. SCHMIDT, MAX. Ein senegambischer Jabirustorch (Mycteria senegalensis). < *Zool. Gart.*, viii, 1867, p. 29.

1868. CLARK-KENNEDY, A. Spoonbill [Platalea leucorodia] in the North of Yorkshire. < *Zoologist*, 2d ser., iii, 1868, p. 1135.

1868. GUNN, T. E. Glossy Ibis [Ibis falcinellus] in Norfolk. < *Zoologist*, 2d ser., iii, 1868, p. 1423.

1868. GUNN, T. E. Spoonbill [Platalea leucorodia] on the Norfolk Coast. < *Zoologist*, 2d ser., iii, 1868, p. 1295.

1868. KRAUSS, *Dr.* Aus dem Freileben des weissen Storchs [Ciconia alba]. < *Zool. Gart.*, ix, 1868, pp. 127–136.

1868. SCHMIDT, MAX. Fortpflanzung des weissen Storches [Ciconia alba] in Gefangenschaft. < *Zool. Gart.*, ix, 1868, pp. 10–23, 41–51.

1869. ANON. Spoonbill [Platalea leucorodia] at Scilly. < *Zoologist*, 2d ser., iv, 1869, p. 1848.

1869. GUNN, T. E. Glossy Ibis [Ibis falcinellus] in Norfolk. < *Zoologist*, 2d ser., iv, 1869, p. 1517.

1869. HART, W., *and* SON. Spoonbill [Platalea leucorodia] at Benacre. < *Zoologist*, 2d ser., iv, 1869, p. 1562.

1870. ANON. Der Storch als Bigamist. < *Aus der Natur.*, liii, oder n. F., xli, 1870, p 592.

1870. HORNE, C. [Letter on the nest and eggs of Mycteria australis.] < *Ibis*, 2 ser., vi, 1870, pp. 294, 295.

1871. GURNEY, J. H. Note on the Indian Adjutant [Leptoptilus argala]. < *Zoologist* 2d ser., vi, 1871, pp. 2871, 2872.

1871. GURNEY, J. H., JR. White Storks [Ciconia alba] near Lydd. < *Zoologist*, 2 ser., vi, 1871, p. 2643.

1871. GURNEY, J. H., JR. Spoonbill [Platalea leucorodia] near Yarmouth. < *Zool. gist*, 2d ser., vi, 1871, p. 2871.

1871. LEACH, H. R.   Spoonbill [Platalea leucorodia] near Aldeburgh.   < *Zoologist,* 2d ser., vi, 1871, p. 2871.

1871. HORNE, C.   [Notes on the nesting of Mycteria australis.]   < *Ibis,* 3d ser., i, 1871, pp. 110–112.

1871. RODD, E. H.   Spoonbill [Platalea leucorodia] at Scilly.   < *Zoologist,* 2d ser., vi, 1871, p. 2522.

1871. RODD, E. H.   Spoonbill [Platalea leucorodia] at the Lizard.   < *Zoologist,* 2d ser., vi, 1871, p. 2851.

1872. OUSTALET, E.   Remarques sur l'Ibis Sinensis de M. l'Abbé A. David.   < *Nouv. Arch. du Mus. d'Hist. Nat.*, viii, 1872, *Bull.*, pp. 129–137, pl. vi.
= *Ibis nippon,* var. *sinensis.*

1873. ALTUM, B.   Nochmals: ,,Störche und Mäusenahrung."   < *Zool. Gart.*, xiv, 1873, pp. 474–476.

1873. ALTUM, B.   Störche als Vertilger von Feldmäusen.   < *Zool. Gart.*, xiv, 1873, pp. 24, 25.

1873. DROSTE-HÜLSHOFF, [F.] v.   [Störche als Vertiliger von Feldmäusen.]   < *Zool. Gart.*, xiv, 1873, pp. 153, 154.

1873. DROSTE-HÜLSHOFF, F. v.   (Störche als Vertiliger von Feldmäusen und Verzehrer von Vögeln.)   < *Zool. Gart.*, xiv, 1873, pp. 394–396.

1873. JÄCKEL, [A. J.]   Die Störche als Vertiliger der Feldmäuse.   < *Zool. Gart.*, xiv, 1873, pp. 312–314.

1873. OLFERS, E. v.   (Die bewachsenen Storchnester).   < *Zool. Gart.*, xiv, 1874, p. 476.

1873. ROPE, G. T.   White Stork [Ciconia alba] in Suffolk.   < *Zoologist,* 2d ser., viii, 1873, p. 3580.

1873. SWINHOE, R.   On the Rosy Ibis of China and Japan (Ibis nippon).   < *Ibis,* 3d ser., iii, 1873, pp. 249–253.
Biographical, descriptive, and anatomical notes.

1873. SWINHOE, R.   On the White Stork of Japan.   < *P. Z. S.*, 1873, pp. 512–514.
Ciconia boyciana, sp. n., p. 513.

1874. ANON.   White Stork [Ciconia alba] near Berwick-on-Tweed.   < *Zoologist,* 2d ser., ix, 1874, p. 4199.

1874. ANON.   Eine neue weisse Storchenart [von Japan von Savuchon beschrieben].
< *Aus der Natur.*, lxiv, oder n. F., lii, 1874, p. 204.

1874. BROUGHTON, H. T.   Spoonbill [Platalea leucorodia] in Guernsey.   < *Zoologist,* 2d ser., ix, 1874, pp. 3835, 3836.

1874. COUES, E.   Shooting Wood Ibises [Tantalus loculator].   < *Am. Sportsman,* iv, 1874, p. 225.
Popular account of his experiences with these birds at Fort Yuma, California.

1874. SCLATER, P. L.   [Report on addition of Ciconia boyciana to the Society's Menagerie.]   < *P. Z. S.*, xlii, 1874, pp. 1, 2, pl. 1.
Cf. *P. Z. S.*, 1873, p. 513.

1874. SCLATER, P. L.   [Remarks upon exhibition of a skin of Ciconia boyciana.]
< *P. Z. S.*, xlii, 1874, pp. 306, 307.
Cf. *P. Z. S.*, 1873, p. 513; 1874, p. 2.

1875. GARROD, A. H.   On the Form of the Trachea in certain Species of Storks and Spoonbills.   < *P. Z. S.*, Apr. 6, 1875, pp. 297–301, figg. 1, 2.
Fig. 1, singularly complicated trachea of *Tantalus ibis;* f. 2, bifurcation of bronchi in neck of *Platalea ajaja.* Important conclusions, on anatomical grounds, of the relationships of *Ibis, Platalea, Tantalus* and *Ciconia*—the two former well distinguished from the two latter.

1876. ALLEN, J. A.   Occurrence of the Wood Ibis [Tantalus loculator] in Pennsylvania and New York.   < *Bull. Nutt. Ornith. Club*, i, No. iv, Nov., 1876, p. 96.

1876. ANON.   [EDITORIAL.]   [Wood Ibis (Tantalus loculator) in Rensselaer County, New York.]   < *Rod and Gun,* viii, July 29, 1876, p. 280.

1876. COUES, E.   Range of the Bay Ibis [Ibis falcinellus, in Oregon].   < *Am. Nat.*, x, No. 1, Jan., 1876, p. 48.

1876. GURNEY, J. H., JR.   Black Stork [Ciconia nigra] at Lydd, in Kent.   < *Zoologist*, 2d ser., xi, Jan., 1876, p. 4764.

1876. GURNEY, J. H., JR.   Glossy Ibis [Ibis falcinellus].   < *Zoologist*, 2d ser., xi, Mar., 1876, p. 4844.

1876. HUDSON, W. H.   Note on the Spoonbill [Platalea sp.] of the Argentine Republic.   < *P. Z. S.*, Jan. 4, 1876, p. 15.
   Probably distinct from *P. ajaja;* not named.

1876. WEBSTER, F. S.   The Wood Ibis [Tantalus loculator] at Troy [N. Y.].   < *Forest and Stream*, vi, July 20, 1876, p. 387.

1877. ELLIOT, D. G.   A Review of the Ibidinæ, or Subfamily of the Ibises.   < *P. Z. S.*, June 5, 1877, pp. 477–510, pl. li.

   An important memoir, not to be overlooked even by those who may disagree with many of the author's conclusions. It is based upon the material in the Paris Museum and in the Salvin-Godman and Shelley collection. It gives the leading literature of the subfamily, the systematic position, the geographical distribution, with more or less descriptive and critical matter under each species, with a very copious synonymy.

   The author recognizes 25 spp. of Ibises, which he disposes in 19 genera, three of which are new. Most of these genera were founded by Wagler in 1832 or by Reichenbach in 1851 (or thereabouts—Gray gives 1853), as appears from the following chronological enumeration, in which the 19 adopted by Elliot are asterisked:—

   1800. *Numenius*, Cuv.   Type, *Tantalus æthiopicus*, Lath.   [Preoccupied.]
   *1803. *Falcinellus*, Bechst., *Gem. Nat.*   Type, *Tantalus falcinellus*, L.   [Not so.]
   *1810. *Ibis*, Savigny. *Ois. Égypt.*, p. 392.   Type, *Tantalus æthiopicus*, Lath.
   [1829. *Plegadis*, Kaup, *Sk. Ent. Eur.*. Theirw., p. 82.]
   1832. *Tantalides*, Wagl., *Isis*, p. 1231.   Type, *Tantalus falcinellus*, L.
   *1832. *Theristicus*, Wagl., *Isis*, p. 1231.   Type, *Scolopax caudatus*, Bodd.
   *1832. *Geronticus*, Wagl., *Isis*, p. 1231.   Type, *Tantalus calvus*, Bodd.
   *1832. *Harpiprion*, Wagl., *Isis*, p. 1232.   Type, *Tantalus cayennensis*, Gm.
   *1832. *Eudocimus*, Wagl., *Isis*, p. 1232.   Type, *Tantalus ruber*, L.
   *1832. *Cercibis*, Wagl., *Isis*, p. 1232.   Type, *Ibis oxycerca*, Spix.
   *1832. *Phimosis*, Wagl., *Isis*, p. 1233.   Type, *Ibis infuscata*, Licht.
   1842. *Threskiornis*, Gray, *App. List G. of B.*, p. 13.   Type, *Tantalus æthiopicus*, **Lath.**
   [1844. *Pseudibis*, Hodgs.]
   *1851. *Comatibis*, Reich., *Nov. Syn. Av.*, figg. 2383, 2384.   Type, *Ibis comata*, Rüpp.
   *1851. *Nipponia*, Reich., *ibid.*, fig. 538.   Type, *Ibis nippon*, Temm.
   *1851. *Molybdophanes*, Reich., *ibid.*, fig. 524.   Type, *Ibis cærulescens*, Vieill.
   *1851. *Lophotibis*, Reich., *ibid.*, fig. 637.   Type, *Tantalus cristatus*, Bodd.
   *1851. *Inocotis*, Reich., *ibid.*, fig. 533.   Type, *Ibis papillosa*, Temm.
   *1851. *Carphibis*, Reich., *ibid.*, figg. 1009, 1010.   Type, *Ibis spinicollis*, Jam.
   1851. *Guara*, Reich., *ibid.*, figg. 525, 526, 527.   Type, *Tantalus ruber*, L.
   1851. *Leucibis*, Reich., *ibid.*, figg. 2385, 2825, 2826.   Type, *Tantalus albus*, L.
   *1851. *Bostrychia*, Reich., *ibid.*, figg. 1011.   Type, *Ibis carunculata*, Rüpp.
   *1855. *Hagedashia*, Bp., *Consp. Av.*, p. 152.   Type, *Tantalus hagedash*, Lath.
   *1877. *Graptocephalus*, Elliot, *P. Z. S.*, p. 483.   Type, *Geronticus davisoni*, Hume.
   *1877. *Thaumatibis*, Elliot, *P. Z. S.*, p. 483.   Type, *Ibis gigantea*, Oustalet.
   *1877. *Lampribis*, Elliot, *P. Z. S.*, p. 483.   Type, *Ibis olivacea*, Du Bus.

   His species are as follows:—

   1. *Ibis æthiopicus.* 2. *Ibis bernieri.* 3. *Ibis melanocephala.* 4. *Thaumatibis gigantea.* 5. *Graptocephalus davisoni.* 6. *Carphibis spinicollis.* 7. *Inocotis papillosus.* 8. *Comatibus comata.* 9. *Geronticus calvus.* 10. *Phimosus infuscatus.* 11. *Nipponia nippon.* 12. *Cercibis oxycerca.* 13. *Theristicus caudatus.* 14. *Lophotibis cristata.* 15. *Hagedashia chalcoptera.* 16. *Bostrychia carunculata.* 17. *Harpiprion cayanensis.* 18. *Molybdophanes cærulescens.* 19. *Falcinellus igneus.* 20. *F. guarauna.* 21. *F. ridgwayi.* 22. *F. thalassinus*, Ridgway [N. B.—This is the young of No. 20]. 23. *Lampribis olivacea* (plate li). 24. *Eudocimus albus.* 25. *E. ruber.*

   Several writers hastened to show that "*Falcinellus* Bechst." is not available, and that the name *Plegadis* Kaup, 1829, must be used for this genus.

1877. GARROD, A. H.   Note on an Anatomical Peculiarity in certain Storks [Ciconiidæ].   < *P. Z. S.*, Nov. 6, 1877, pp. 711–712.
   Storks differ in the ambiens muscle.

1877. LENTE, W. K.   A visit to a nesting place [Lake Harney, Florida] of the wood ibis—Tantalus Loculator.   < *Forest and Stream*, Nov. 29, 1877, p. 327.

1877. REICHENOW, A.   Systematische Uebersicht der Schreitvögel (Gressores), einer natürlichen, die Ibidae, Ciconidae, Phoenicopteridae, Scopidae, Balaenicipidae und Ardeidae umfassenden Ordnung.   < *J. f. O.*, Apr., 1877, pp. 113–171; July, 1877, pp. 225–277.

   Dieses Buch befindet sich beim Buchbinder und ist mir deshalb nicht zugänglich.

1877. SCLATER, P. L., *and* FORBES, A. W.   On the Nesting of the Spoonbill [Platalea leucorodia] in Holland.   < *Ibis*, 4th ser., i, Oct., 1877, pp. 412–416.

   Interesting narrative of observations.

1877. [SCLATER, P. L., *and* SALVIN, O.]   Oustalet on new Species of Ibis [gigantea, harmandi].   < *Ibis*, 4th ser., i, Oct., 1877, pp. 486, 487.

   Notices of papers in *Bull. Soc. Philom.*, 7ᵉ sér., i, 1877, pp. 25–30.

1878. ALLEN, J. A.   The Glossy Ibis [Ibis falcinellus] in Massachusetts.   < *Bull. Nutt. Ornith. Club*, iii, No. 3, July, 1878, p. 152.

1878. A[LLEN], J. A.   Elliot's Review of the Ibidinæ, or Ibises.   < *Bull. Nutt. Ornith. Club*, iii, No. 4, Oct., 1878, p. 182.

   Short notice of the paper in *P. Z. S.*, 1877, pp. 477–510.

1878. CORY, C. B.   The Glossy Ibis [Ibis falcinellus] in Massachusetts.   < *Bull. Nutt. Ornith. Club*, iii, No. 3, July, 1878, p. 152.

   Note by J. A. Allen on the occurrence of two other individuals on Cape Cod at about the same time.   Foot-note by the same on the correct generic name of the bird, which is stated to be *Plegadis*, Kaup.   (*Ibis*, 4th ser., ii, Jan., 1878, p. 112.)

1878. GARROD, A. H.   On the Trachea of Tantalus loculator and of Vanellus cayennensis.   < *P. Z. S.*, May 21, 1878, pp. 625–629, figg. 1, 2.

   The parts named of each of these species are figured on the woodcuts in the text.

1878. RIDGWAY, R.   Synopsis of the American Sub-families and Genera of Ciconiidæ.   < *Bull. U. S. Geol. and Geogr. Surv. Terr.*, iv, No. 1, Feb. 5, 1878, pp. 248–251, fig.

   A subhead of a much more extensive paper, "Studies of the American Herodiones," &c., *ibid.*, pp. 219–251.   The American *Ciconiidæ* are divided into two subfamilies, *Ciconinæ* and *Tantalinæ*, of the former of which are given two genera, *Mycteria* and *Euxenura*, g. n., p. 249 (= *Dissoura* Cab., 1850).   For the full paper, see under ARDEIDÆ.

1878. SCLATER, P. L.   Note on the Breeding of the Sacred Ibis [æthiopica] in the Zoological Society's Gardens.   < *Ibis*, 4th ser., ii, Oct., 1878, pp. 449–451, pl. xii.

   The plate shows the young and the egg.

1878. SCLATER, [P. L.]   [Remarks on living examples of Ciconia maguari and C. episcopus.]   < *P. Z. S.*, June 4, 1878, p. 633.

   On the validity of the genus *Euxenura* Ridgway, showing that Cabanis had proposed *Dissoura* in 1850 for the same group, and calling the species *Dissura maguari* and *D. episcopus*.

1878. [SCLATER, P. L., *and* SALVIN, O.]   D. G. Elliot and A. Reichenow on the Ibises [Ibidinæ].   < *Ibis*, 4th ser., ii, Jan., 1878, pp. 111–113.

   Review of Elliot, *P. Z. S.*, 1877, p. 477, *seqq.*, and Reichenow, *J. f. O.*, 1877, pp. 113. *seqq.*   The reviewers criticize the classification and nomenclature of both authors very freely.   As regards the much be-named Glossy Ibis, they show that there is no such genus as *Falcinellus* Bechst., so often employed; and that *Plegadis* Kaup, 1829, seems available for *Ibis falcinellus*. other synonyms of which are *Tringa! autumnalis* of Hasselq.. *Scolopax! rufa* of Scopoli, and *Numenius! igneus* of Gm., 1771 and 1778.

1879. COUES, E.   Letters on Ornithology.   No. 24.—The Wood Ibis.   [Tantalus loculator.]   < *The Chicago Field*, June 14, 1879.

   From the "American Sportsman", iv, 1854, p. 225, *q. v.*

1879. MERRILL, J. C.   A Nesting Place of the White-faced Glossy Ibis (Plegadis guarauna).   < *The Oölogist*, v, No. 2, Aug., 1879, p. 11.

   Quoted from p. 163 of his paper in *Proc. U. S. Nat. Mus.*, i, 1878, pp. 118–173.

Ardeidæ.

1673. JACOBAEUS, O. [Canalis alimentorum Ardeae cum duplici ductu pancreatico.] < *Bartholini Acta Hafn.*, ii, 1673, p. 242.
Non nobis obvius: titulus e Caro et Engelmanno.

1683. MURALT, J. DE. Ardeae [Botauri] stellaris examinatio. < *Ephem. Acad. Nat. Cur.*, Dec. ii, Cent. Ann. ii, 1683, (1698), pp. 60, 61.
Haud mihi obvia: titulus e Caro et Engelmanno.

1727. VALENTINI, M. B. Ardeae [Botauri] stellaris anatome. < *Act. Acad. Cæs. Leop. Car. Nat. Cur.*, i, 1727, pp. 283, 284.
Non mihi obvium: titulus e Caro et Engelmanno.

1776. OTTO, B. C. Anmärkningar om Rötdrommen, Ardea Stellaris. < *Physiogr. Sällsk. Handl.*, i, 1776, pp. 305–310.
Not seen.

1781. [WURMB, F. VAN.] De kleine witte Reiger van 't Eiland Java. < *Verh. Batav. Genootsch.*, iii, 1781, p. 376.
This is the original date: there is a reissue of the same *Verhandlungen* much later (1824); I have only seen the latter.

1782. MATTUSCHKA, H. G., *Graf von*. Ueber die Fischreiher [Ardea cinerea]. < *Schrift. d. Berlin. Ges. nat. Fr.*, iii, 1782, pp. 411–414.
Nicht mir selbst zugänglich: Titel aus Carus und Engelmann.

1792. BOSC, L. Ardea gularis. < *Actes de la Soc. d'Hist. Nat. de Paris*, i, pte. i, 1792, p. 4, pl. 2.
Pas vue moi-même.

1804. AFZELIUS, A. Ardea atricapilla En ny Fogel ifrån Sierra Leone, dår funnen och beskrifven, . . . < *Kongl. Vetens. Acad. Nya Handl.*, xxv, 1804, pp. 264–268.

1824. [WURMB, F. VAN] De Kleine witte Reiger van het eiland Java. < *Verhandl. Batav. Genootsch. Kunsb. en Wetens.*, Tweede Druk, iii, 1824, pp. 239–242.
Orig. ed. of these *Verhandlungen*, this vol., 1781.

1829. ANON. The Great American Bittern. < *Loudon's Mag. Nat. Hist.*, ii, 1829, p. 64.
Botaurus leutiginosus—or Nyctiardea gardeni? Note of a supposed power of emitting light from its breast.

1829. RENNIE, J. [On the Heather-bluiter (Ardea [Botaurus] stellaris, Linn.) of the Scotch.] < *Loudon's Mag. Nat. Hist.*, i, 1829, p. 495.

1829. "R. A." Feet and Legs of the common Heron [Ardea cinerea]. < *Loudon's Mag. Nat. Hist.*, ii, 1829, p. 206.
With note on the probably luminous powder-down feathers of the breast, and their purpose.

1831. BLAND, M. Habits of the Bittern [Botaurus stellaris]. < *Loudon's Mag. Nat. Hist.*, iv, 1831, pp. 464, 465.

1831. BREHM, C. L. Eine naturgeschichtliche Anfrage. < *Oken's Isis*, Bd. xxiv, 1831, p. 273.
Funken aus Reiherfedern.

1831. YARRELL, W. [On the Identity of Ardea gardeni and A. nycticorax.] < *P. Z. S.*, i, 1831, p. 27.

1833. CHALMERS, M. Acts of the Heron and of the Peahen. < *Loudon's Mag. Nat. Hist.*, vi, 1833, pp. 515, 516.

1834. "J. G." A common Heron [Ardea cinerea]. < *Loudon's Mag. Nat. Hist.*, vii, 1834, pp. 513, 514.
On disgorging of the contents of the stomach when disturbed.

1835. "O." The Night Heron (A'rdea Nycticorax L.). < *Loudon's Mag. Nat. Hist.*, viii, 1835, pp. 509, 510.

1835. WATERTON, C. Notes on the Habits of the Heron [Ardea cinerea]. < *Loudon's Mag. Nat. Hist.*, viii, 1835, pp. 453–457 ; editorial note, pp. 457, 458.

1835. WATERTON, C. Bemerkungen über die Lebensweise des Reihers [Ardea cinerea]. < *Froriep's Notizen*, xlvi, No. 992, 1835, pp. 17–20.
Nicht mir selbst zugänglich: Titel aus Carus und Engelmann. Auszug aus *Loudon's Mag.*, viii, 1835, p. 453.

1836. CHRISTY, W., JR. Egret [Ardea garzetta, in Britain]. < *Loudon's Mag. Nat. Hist.*, ix, 1836, p. 647.

1836. VENTRIS, E. Should the Egret (Ardea Garzetta) be classed among British Species of Birds ? < *Loudon's Mag. Nat. Hist.*, ix, 1836, pp. 319–322.

1837. DU BUS DE GHISIGNIES, V. B. Description d'une nouvelle espèce de Héron [Ardea calceolata]. < *Bull. Acad. Brux.*, iv, 1837, pp. 39–41, pl. (*L'Institut*, v, No. 217, 1837, pp. 227, 228.)
Pas vue moi-même.

1837. DU BUS [DE GHISIGNIES, V. B.] Neuer Reiher [Ardea calceolata] aus Guinea: < *Oken's Isis*, Bd. xxx, 1837, p. 842.
Aus *L'Institut*, 1837, No. 217, pp. 227, 228.

1838. DU BUS [DE GHISIGNIES, V. B.] Description d'une nouvelle espèce de **Héron** [Ardea calceolata]. < *Revue Zoologique*, i, 1838, p. 142.
Extraite du *Bull. Acad. Roy. Sc. Bruxelles*, iv, 1837, pp. 39–41.

1839. STRICKLAND, A. Upon the claims of the Ardea alba—Great Egret, or White Hearn, to be considered a British bird. < *Charlesw. Mag. Nat. Hist.*, iii, 1839, pp. 30–32.
Affirmative.

1839. STRICKLAND, A. On the Ardea Alba [as a British Bird]. < *Rep. Brit. Assoc. Adv. Sci. for* 1838, vii, 1839, (*Misc. Comm.*), pp. 106, 107.

1842. LANDBE[C]K, C. L. Die Reiher-Insel bey Adony in Ungarn. < *Oken's Isis*, Bd. xxxv, 1842, pp. 267–283.
pp. 279–283, kurze Beschreibung der Nester und Eyer der erwähnten Vögel—*Ardea cinerea, A. purpurea, A. nycticorax, A. garzetta*, sowie *Carbo cormoranus*.

1843. DOWELL, E. W. Note on the occurrence of the Cassian Heron, (Ardea [Buphus] comata) [in Norfolk]. < *Zoologist*, i, 1843, pp. 78, 79.

1843. GOULD, J. [Description of Ardea rectirostris, sp. n.] < *P. Z. S.*, xi, 1843, p. 22.

1843. GREENWOOD, A. Note on the occurrence of the Squacco Heron [Buphus comatus] near Penzance. < *Zoologist*, i, 1843, pp. 143, 144.

1843. RODD, E. H. Note on the occurrence of the Squacco Heron [Buphus comatus] near Penzance. < *Zoologist*, i, 1843, pp. 189, 190.

1844. DUNCAN, R. D. Correction of a previous [Zool. 384] error in describing the colour of the Heron's Egg. < *Zoologist*, ii, 1844, p. 575.

1844. GOULD, J. [Ardea rectirostris.] < *Ann. Mag. Nat. Hist.*, xiii, 1844, p. 70.
From *P. Z. S.*, Feb. 28, 1843, p. 22.

1844. HORE, W. S. Note on the occurrence of the Night Heron [Nyctiardea europæus] in Cornwall. < *Zoologist*, ii, 1844, p. 575.

1846. CASSIN, J. Note on an Instinct probably possessed by the Herons, (Ardea, Linn.) < *Proc. Acad. Nat. Sci. Phila.*, iii, 1846, p. 137.
Instinctive knowledge of refraction, enabling them to spear their prey in the water.

1846. COOPER, J. Occurrence of the American Bittern [Botaurus lentiginosus] near Fleetwood. < *Zoologist*, iv, 1846, p. 1248.

1846. FRERE, H. T. Anecdote of Herons fighting. < *Zoologist*, iv, 1846, pp. 1212, 1213.

1846. RODD, E. H. Occurrence of the Purple Heron [Ardea purpurea] near Penzance. < *Zoologist*, iv, 1846, p. 1331.

1846. THOMPSON, W. Notice of an American Bittern, Botaurus lentiginosus, Mont. (sp.), obtained in Ireland. < *Ann. Mag. Nat. Hist.*, xvii, 1846, pp. 91–94.

1847. PLOMLEY, F. Occurrence of the Purple Heron [Ardea purpurea] near Lydd. *< Zoologist,* v, 1847, p. 1777.

1848. BOLD, T. J. Occurrence of the Common Bittern (Ardea [Botaurus] stellaris) at Prestwick Car and Blagdon, Northumberland. *< Zoologist,* vi, 1848, p. 2066.

1848. BOND, F. Occurrence of the young of the Little Bittern [Ardetta minuta] near Enfield. *< Zoologist,* vi, 1848, p. 1969.

1848. ELLMAN, J. B. Occurrence of the Bittern (Botaurus stellaris) at Battel. *< Zoologist,* vi, 1848, p. 2023.

1848. ELLMAN, J. B. Occurrence of the Little Bittern (Ardea [Ardetta] minuta) at Ewhurst and Ledlescomb, Sussex. *< Zoologist,* vi, 1848, p. 2147.

1848. GOULD, J. Description of a new Heron [Ardea leucophæa]. *< P. Z. S.,* xvi, 1848, pp. 58, 59.

1848. JOHNSON, F. W. Occurrence of the Common Bittern [Botaurus stellaris] at Ipswich. *< Zoologist,* vi, 1848, p. 2066.

1848. MONTGOMERY, R. J. Occurrence of the Night Heron (Nycticorax Gardeni) in the county Louth. *< Zoologist,* vi, 1848, p. 2147.

1849. BIRD, W. F. W. Occurrence of the Common Bittern (Ardea [Botaurus] stellaris) in Norfolk. *< Zoologist,* vii, 1849, p. 2421.

1849. BULTEEL, C. J. C. Occurrence of eight Night Herons (Nycticorax ardeola) in Devonshire. *< Zoologist,* vii, 1849, p. 2528.

1849. ELLMAN, J. B. Occurrence of the Great White Heron ([Herodias alba]?) in Romney Marsh. *< Zoologist,* vii, 1849, p. 2419.

1849. FRERE, H. T. Occurrence of the Little Bittern (Ardea [Ardetta] minuta) at South Walsham. *< Zoologist,* vii, 1849, pp. 2498, 2499.

1849. GOULD, J. Description of a new Heron [Ardea leucophæa]. *< Ann. Mag. Nat. Hist.,* 2d ser., iii, 1849, pp. 306, 307.
    From *P. Z. S.,* May 9, 1848, p. 58.

1849. HEWETT, W. The Heronry in Coley Park, Berks. *< Zoologist,* vii, 1849, pp. 2420, 2421.

1849. MORRIS, F. O. Occurrence of the Purple Heron (Ardea purpurea) near Driffield. *< Zoologist,* vii, 1849, p. 2591.

1849. MORRIS, B. R. Note on the Heron (Ardea cinerea) as an article of Food. *< Zoologist,* vii, 1849, p. 2353.

1849. RODD, E. H. Occurrence of the Night Heron [Nyctiardea grisea] at Scilly. *< Zoologist,* vii, 1849, p. 2498.

1849. RODD, E. H. Occurrence of the Squacco Heron (Ardea [Buphus] comata) near Penzance. *< Zoologist,* vii, 1849, p. 2498.

1849. SMITH, JAMES, *Rev.* Occurrence of the Purple Heron (Ardea purpurea) in Aberdeenshire. *< Zoologist,* vii, 1849, pp. 2497, 2498.

1849. SMITH, JAMES, *Rev.* Occurrence of the Little Bittern (Ardea [Ardetta] minuta) at Yarmouth. *< Zoologist,* vii, 1849, p. 2528.

1849. WEBSTER, T. Occurrence of the Little Bittern [Ardetta minuta] near Manchester. *< Zoologist,* vii, 1849, p. 2499.

1849. WEDDERBURN, J. N. Colour of the Eyes in the Night Heron (Ardea Nycticorax [Nyctiardea grisea]). *< Zoologist,* vii, 1849, p. 2591.

1849. WRIGHT, J. Occurrence of the Bittern (Ardea [Botaurus] stellaris) at Lymington. *< Zoologist,* vii, 1849, p. 2392.

1850. BARCLAY, H. Occurrence of the Bittern (Ardea [Botaurus] stellaris) at Walthamstow. *< Zoologist,* viii, 1850, p. 2771.

1850. PEACOCK, E., JR.   Habits of the Heron (Ardea cinerea).   < *Zoologist,* viii, 1850, pp. 2879.

1850. PEARSON, W.   The Fisherman: a Character.   < *Zoologist,* viii, 1850, pp. 2842–2848.
   Popular notice of the habits, etc., of *Ardea* sp.

1850. RODD, E. H.   Occurrence of the Purple Heron (Ardea purpurea) near Land's End.   < *Zoologist,* viii, 1850, p. 2800.

1850. RODD, E. H.   Occurrence of the Night Heron (Ardea nycticorax [Nyctiardea grisea]) near Helston.   < *Zoologist,* viii, 1850, p. 2825.

1851. CLEVLAND, A.   Occurrence of the Little White Heron (Ardea russata [Herodias garzetta]) in South Devon.   < *Zoologist,* ix, 1851, p. 3116.

1851. HARPER, J. O.   Occurrence of the Little Bittern (Ardea [Ardetta] minuta) in Norfolk.   < *Zoologist,* ix, 1851, p. 2989.

1852. ANON.   The Biter bit.   < *Zoologist,* x, 1852, pp. 3710, 3711.
   From the 'Sussex Express', Oct. 30, 1852.   Heron killed by an eel it tried to swallow.

1852. BALDAMUS, E.   [Ardea nycticorax (Nyctiardea grisea) in der Nähe von Halle.]   < *Naumannia,* ii, Heft i, 1852, p. 104.

1852. ELLMAN, J. B.   Occurrence of the Purple Heron (Ardea purpurea) at Catsfield, Sussex.   < *Zoologist,* x, 1852, p. 3330.

1852. GURNEY, J. H.   Note on the Little Bittern [Ardetta minuta].   < *Zoologist,* x, 1852, pp. 3503, 3504.

1852. REIL, W.   [Ardea nycticorax (Nyctiardea grisea) bei Halle.]   < *Naumannia,* ii, Heft i, 1852, p. 104.

1852. SCHNEIDER, M.   [Ardea nycticorax (Nyctiardea grisea) in der Nähe von Halle.]   < *Naumannia,* ii, Heft i, 1852, p. 104.

1852. WODZICKI, C.   Ueber Ard. [Botaurus] stellaris.   < *Naumannia,* ii, Heft ii, 1852, pp. 48–50.
   Zur Lebensweise.—Beilage Nr. 6 zum Protok. d. sechsten Vers. d. deutsch. Orn.-Ges.

1853. GLOGER, C. W. L.   Das höchst gewandte Klettern der Rohrdommeln [u. s. w.].   < *J. f. O.,* i, 1853, pp. 379–381.
   Botaurus stellaris, Ardetta minuta.

1854. COOKE, N.   Occurrence of the Common Bittern (Botaurus stellaris) near Warrington.   < *Zoologist,* xii, 1854, p. 4254.

1854. DUTTON, J.   Occurrence of the Common Bittern (Ardea [Botaurus] stellaris) at Chiswick.   < *Zoologist,* xii, 1854, p. 4254.

1854. MARTIN, L.   Zur Ernährungsweise des grossen Rohrdommels, Ardea [Botaurus] stellaris.   < *J. f. O.,* ii, 1854, pp. 371, 372.

1854. RIMROD, —.   Die kleine Rohrdommel [Ardetta minuta] betreffend.   < *J. f. O.,* ii, 1854, pp. 370, 371.
   Cf. op. cit., 1853, p. 379.

1854. WALLENGREN, [H. D. J.]   Ardea purpurea, skjuten i Skåne.   < *Öfvers. Kongl. Vetensk.-Akad. Forhandl. för år* 1853, 1854, pp. 123, 124.

1855. RIMROD, —.   Der Zweck der schwammigen Haut und deren Dunenbekleidung, an Brust und Schenkeln der Reiher [Ardeidæ].   < *J. f. O.,* iii, 1855, pp. 190, 191.

1855. RODD, E. H.   Note on the Common Night Heron [occipital plumes of Nyctiardea grisea].   < *Zoologist,* xiii, 1855, p. 4913.

1856. ANON.   Occurrence of the Bittern [Botaurus stellaris] in Bedfordshire.   < *Zoologist,* xiv, 1856, p. 5064.

1856. BOUVÉ, T. T.   [Observations on the Nest of Ardea nycticorax.]   < *Proc. Bost. Soc. Nat. Hist.,* vi, 1856, p. 20.
   I. e., of the American variety, *Nyctiardea gardeni* Baird, or *N. grisea nævia* (Bodd.), Allen.

1856. D'URBAN, W. S. M.   Note on the Bittern (Ardea [Botaurus] stellaris) in Devonshire.   < *Zoologist*, xiv, 1856, p. 5064.

1856. GRANTHAM, G.   Occurrence of the Bittern [Botaurus stellaris] at Lewes.   < *Zoologist*, xiv, 1856, p. 4996.

1857. BALDAMUS, [E.]   [Ueber Ardea nycticorax.]   < *Naumannia*, vii, 1857, pp. 335, 336.

1857. BRIGGS, J. J.   Occurrence of the Bittern [Botaurus stellaris] in Derbyshire.   < *Zoologist*, xv, 1857, pp. 5594, 5595.

1857. RIMROD, —.   Nachträgliche Berichtigung über das Nisten von A[rdea]. nycticorax [Nyctiardea grisea] im nördlichen Deutschland.   < *Naumannia*, vii, 1857, p. 335.

1859. DRANE, R.   Occurrence of the Little Bittern [Ardetta minuta] near Cardiff.   < *Zoologist*, xvii, 1859, pp. 6562, 6563.

1860. DEWEY, W. T.   Occurrence of the Little Bittern [Ardetta minuta] near Taunton.   < *Zoologist*, xviii, 1860, p. 7274.

1861. HOMEYER, A. v.   Fliegen die Reiher [Ardea cinerea] auch in Ordnung ?   < *J. f. O.*, ix, 1861, p. 305.

1862. BODINUS, *Dr.*   Ein Fischreiher [Ardea cinerea] als Pflegevater von Wanderfalken.   < *Zool. Gart.*, iii, 1862, pp. 31, 32.

1862. RODD, E. H.   Occurrence of the Squacco Heron [Buphus comatus] near Redruth.   < *Zoologist*, xx, 1862, p. 8035.

1862. STEVENSON, H.   The Common Bittern [Botaurus stellaris] in Norfolk.   < *Zoologist*, xx, 1862, pp. 8035, 8036.

1863. BOULTON, W. W.   Occurrence of the Little Bittern [Ardetta minuta] in Yorkshire.   < *Zoologist*, xxi, 1863, p. 8770.

1863. DUTTON, J.   The Bittern (Ardea [Botaurus] stellaris) at Eastbourne.   < *Zoologist*, xxi, 1863, p. 8446.

1863. SCHLEGEL, H.   Ardeae   < *Mus. Hist. Nat. Pays-Bas*, 3ᵉ livr., avril 1863, pp. 1–64.
    Treating sixty species of *Ardeidæ*, all referred to the single genus *Ardea*, together with *Cancroma cochlearia*, which is allowed to be generically distinct. These are represented by 527 specimens in the Leyden Museum.   *A. minuta australis*, p. 39; *A. stellaris capensis*, p. 48, subspp. nn. ?

1863. SCHMIDT, MAX.   Ein Fischreiher [Ardea cinerea, brütend in Gefangenschaft].   < *Zool. Gart* , iv, 1863, pp. 132, 133.

1863. STEVENSON, H.   The Purple Heron (Ardea purpurea) in Norfolk.   < *Zoologist*, xxi, 1863, pp. 8329, 8330.

1863. STEVENSON, H.   The Squacco Heron (Ardea [Buphus] comata) in Norfolk   < *Zoologist*, xxi, 1863, p. 8725.

1864. BOULTON, W. W.   The Bittern [Botaurus stellaris] shot near Beverley.   < *Zoologist*, xxii, 1864, pp. 8959–8961.

1864. BOULTON, W. W.   Bittern [Botaurus stellaris] near Beverley.   < *Zoologist*, xxii, 1864, p. 9046.

1864. DUTTON, J.   Bittern [Botaurus stellaris] at Eastbourne.   < *Zoologist*, xxii, 1864, p. 9046.

1864. GUNN, T. E.   Abundance of the Bittern [Botaurus stellaris] in Norfolk.   < *Zoologist*, xxii, 1864, p. 9024.

1864. HOMEYER, A. v.   Ardea [Herodias] egretta Temm. als Brutvogel Deutschland   < *J. f. O.*, xi, 1863, pp. 440–447.   [Pub. April, 1864.]

1864. JEFFREY, W., JR.   Bitterns [Botaurus stellaris] near Chichester.   < *Zoologist*, xxii, 1864, p. 8961.

1864. NEWMAN, E.   Bittern [Botaurus stellaris] in Kent.   < *Zoologist*, xxii, 1864, 8961.

1864. SEAMAN, C. E. Bittern [Botaurus stellaris] in the Isle of Wight. < *Zoologist,* xxii, 1864, p. 9290.

1864. SHORTT, J. Account of a Heronry and Breeding-place of other Water-birds in Southern India. < *Proc. Linn. Soc.*, viii, 1864, p. 94.
Not seen.—Cf. *Ibis,* 1865, pp. 221; *Zool. Rec.* for 1864, p. 51.

1864. WICKE, B. Mittheilung über eine Colonie von Ardea nycticorax [Nyctiardea grisea] am Seeburger. See in Hannover. < *J. f. O.*, xii, 1864, pp. 77–80.

1865. GATCOMBE, J. Little Bittern [Ardetta minuta] near Plymouth. < *Zoologist,* xxiii, 1865, p. 9628.

1865. HUDSON, S. Bittern [Botaurus stellaris] near Epworth, Bawtry. < *Zoologist,* xxiii, 1865, p. 9419.

1865. MATHEWS, M. A. Little Bittern [Ardetta minuta] near Weston-super-Mare. < *Zoologist,* xxiii, 1865, p. 9454.

1865. MATHEWS, M. A. Little Bittern [Ardetta minuta] near Weston-super-Mare. < *Zoologist,* xxiii, 1865, p. 9457.

1865. ROCKE, J. Squacco Heron [Buphus comatus] near Yarmouth. < *Zoologist,* xxiii, 1865, p. 9419.

1865. RODD, E. H. Occurrence of the Squacco Heron [Buphus comatus] near Carhayes Castle, Cornwall. < *Zoologist,* xxiii, 1865, p. 9617.

1865. VENNOR, H. G. A few notes on the Night-heron [Nyctiardea grisea nævia]. < *Canad. Nat. and Geol.*, n. s., ii, Feb., 1865, pp. 53–56.
Habits, and comparison with *N. grisea.*

1866. BREE, C. R. Little Bittern [Ardetta minuta] at Colchester. < *Zoologist,* 2d ser., i, 1866, p. 517.

1866. GURNEY, J. H. American Bittern [Botaurus lentiginosus] in Kent. < *Zoologist,* 2d ser., i, 1866, p. 145.
Also in the 'Field' newspaper.

1866. JOYCE, R. Night Heron [Nyctiardea grisea] at Belfast. < *Zoologist,* 2d ser., i, 1866, p. 457.

1866. RODD, E. H. Little Bittern [Ardetta minuta] at Scilly. < *Zoologist,* 2d ser., i, 1866, p. 311.

1867. ANON. Bittern [Botaurus stellaris] in Yorkshire. < *Zoologist,* 2d ser., ii, 1867, pp. 635, 636.
From the 'Field,' Feb. 2.

1867. ASHMEAD, G. B. Little Bittern [Ardetta minuta] near Henley. < *Zoologist,* 2d ser., ii, 1867, p. 829.

1867. ENDICOTT, W. E. The Encampment of the Herons [Nyctiardea grisea nævia]. < *Am. Nat.*, i, 1867, pp. 343–345.
Notes of observation of a colony in Norfolk County, Mass., wantonly destroyed, and of habits of an individual kept in confinement.

1867. ENDICOTT, W. E. Habits of the Bittern [Botaurus minor]. < *Am. Nat.*, i, 1867, p. 325.
Short note, criticizing E. A. Samuels's account.

1867. GREET, T. Y. Food of the Heron. < *The Intellectual Observer*, x, 1867, p. 79.
Extract of letter, with editorial note.

1867. RODD, E. H. Little Bittern [Ardetta minuta] near the Lizzard. < *Zoologist,* 2d ser., ii, 1867, p. 829.

1867. RODD, E. H. The Purple Crested Heron [Ardea purpurea] near the Lizzard, Cornwall. < *Zoologist,* 2d ser., ii, 1867, pp. 829, 830.

1867. RODD, E. H. Squacco Heron [Buphus comatus, at Land's End]. < *Zoologist,* 2d ser., ii, 1867, p. 830.

1867. RODD, E. H.   Little Bittern [Ardetta minuta] in Cornwall.   < *Zoologist*, 2d ser., ii, 1867, p. 759.

1867. SAMUELS, E. A.   The Bittern [Botaurus minor].   < *Am. Nat.*, i, 1867, pp. 434, 435.
Reply to W. E. Endicott's strictures, *ibid.*, p. 325.

1867. SHORTO, J., JR.   Bitterns [Botaurus stellaris] near Dorchester.   < *Zoologist*, 2d ser., ii, 1867, p. 708.

1867. THOMPSON, W.   Squacco Heron [Buphus comatus] at Weymouth.   < *Zoologist*, 2d ser., ii, 1867, p. 915.

1868. ANGUS, W. C.   Common Bittern [Botaurus stellaris] in Aberdeenshire.   < *Zoologist*, 2d ser., iii, 1868, p. 1134.

1868. CLARK-KENNEDY, A.   Bittern [Botaurus stellaris] near Pontefract.   < *Zoologist*, 2d ser., iii, 1868, pp. 1134, 1135.

1868. CLARK-KENNEDY, A.   Bittern [Botaurus stellaris] in Berkshire.   < *Zoologist*, 2d ser., iii, 1868, p. 1135.

1868. BLAKE-KNOX, H.   Bitterns [Botaurus stellaris] in Ireland.   < *Zoologist*, 2d ser., iii, 1868, p. 1378.

1868. CLARK-KENNEDY, A.   Note on the Breeding of the Bittern [Botaurus stellaris] in Buckinghamshire.   < *Zoologist*, 2d ser., iii, 1868, pp. 1255, 1256.

1868. DUTTON, J.   American Bittern [Botaurus lentiginosus] in Pevensey Marshes.   < *Zoologist*, 2d ser., iii, 1868, p. 1098.

1868. GUNN, T. E.   Bittern [Botaurus stellaris] breeding in Norfolk.   < *Zoologist*, 2d ser., iii, 1868, pp. 1220, 1221.

1868. MATHEW, G. F.   Bittern (Ardea [Botaurus] stellaris) [at Slapton Lea].   < *Zoologist*, 2d ser., iii, 1868, p. 1098.

1868. MATHEW, M. A.   Little Bittern [Ardetta minuta] at Braunton, North Devon.   < *Zoologist*, 2d ser., iii, 1868, p. 1295.

1868. RODD, E. H.   Flight of Bitterns [Botaurus stellaris].   < *Zoologist*, 2d ser., iii, 1868, p. 1059.

1868. WHITE, H. J.   Bittern [Botaurus stellaris] at Steyning, Sussex.   < *Zoologist*, 2d ser., iii, 1868, p. 1178.

1869. CLERMONT, *Lord.*   American Bittern [Botaurus lentiginosus] in Ireland.   < *Zoologist*, 2d ser., iv, 1869, p. 1517.

1869. CLOGG, S.   Bittern [Botaurus lentiginosus] at Looe.   < *Zoologist*, 2d ser., iv, 1869, p. 1562.

1869. ENDICOTT, W. E.   Bitterns.   < *Am. Nat.*, iii, 1869, pp. 169–179, fig. 36.
Biographical notes on species of *Botaurus* and allied genera, especially *B. lentiginosus.*

1869. GRAVIL, J. T. [?], JR.   Bittern [Botaurus stellaris] near Epworth.   < *Zoologist*, 2d ser., iv, 1869, p. 1562.

1869. HUME, A. [O.]   [On the breeding of certain Indian Ardeidæ.]   < *Ibis*, 2d ser., v, 1869, p. 238.

1869. MATHEWS, G. F.   Night Heron [Nyctiardea grisea] in Devonshire.   < *Zoologist*, 2d ser., iv, 1869, pp. 1802, 1803.

1869. RODD, E. H.   Night Herons [Nyctiardea grisea] in Cornwall.   < *Zoologist*, 2d ser., iv, 1869, p. 1802.

1869. ROWLEY, G. D.   Contents of a Heron's Crop.   < *Zoologist*, 2d ser., iv, 1869, p. 1722.

1870. ABBOTT, C. C.   Night Herons [Nyctiardea grisea nævia].   < *Am. Nat.*, iv, 1870, p. 377.
Brief observations, made at Trenton, New Jersey.

1870. BLAKE-KNOX, H.   American Bittern [Botaurus lentiginosus] at Cahir, Ireland.   < *Zoologist*, 2d ser., v, 1870, p. 2408.

1870. BOYES, F.   Little Bittern [Ardetta minuta] in Nottinghamshire.   < *Zoologist,* 2d ser., v, 1870, p. 2308.

1870. GATCOMBE, J.   Little Egret [Herodias garzetta] in Devonshire.   < *Zoologist,* 2d ser., v, 1870, p. 2308.

1870. GURNEY, J. H.   [On certain Ardeidæ.]   < *Ibis,* 2d ser., vi, 1870, pp. 150, 151.

1870. LAYARD, E. L.   [On the occurrence of Calherodius cucullatus in South Africa.]   < *Ibis,* 2d ser., vi, 1870, p. 443.

1870. RODD, E. H.   Little Bittern [Ardetta minuta] at the Land's End.   < *Zoologist,* 2d ser., v, 1870, p. 2224.

1870. POWER, J. T.   Little Bittern [Ardetta minuta] in Ireland.   < *Zoologist,* 2d ser., v, 1870, pp. 2224, 2225.

1870. STEVENSON, H.   Curious Anecdote of a Heron [preying on a Waterhen].   < *Zoologist,* 2d ser., v, 1870, p. 2068.

1870. STIEDA, L.   Ueber den Bau der Puderdunen der Rohrdommel [Botaurus stellaris].   < *Reich. u. Bois-Reym. Arch.,* 1870, pp. 104–111, pl. ii.

1871. ANDERSON, A.   Night Heron [Nyctiardea grisea] breeding in Immature Plumage, &c.   < *Zoologist,* 2d ser., vi, 1871, p. 2807.

1871. BLAKE-KNOX, H.   American Bittern [Botaurus lentiginosus] in Ireland.   < *Zoologist,* 2d ser., vi, 1871, pp. 2642, 2643.

1871. BOYES, F.   Bittern [Botaurus lentiginosus] in East Yorkshire.   < *Zoologist,* 2d ser., vi, 1871, pp. 2484, 2485.

1871. NEHRKORN, A.   Notiz über Ardeola [Ardetta] minuta Lin.   < *J. f. O.,* xix, 1871, pp. 458, 459.
  Zur Lebensweise.

1871. PARDIE, A. C.   On a (supposed) New Species of Bittern, from the Lake District [Ardeola novæ zealandiæ].   < *Trans. and Proc. N. Z. Inst. for* 1870, iii, 1871, *Proc. Otago Inst.,* pp. 99, 100.

1871. RODD, E. H.   Squacco Heron [Buphus comatus] at the Lizard.   < *Zoologist,* 2d ser., vi, 1871, p. 2684.

1871. SMITH, CECIL.   Bittern [Botaurus stellaris] in Somersetshire.   < *Zoologist,* 2d ser., vi, 1871, p. 2522.

1871. SMITH, CECIL.   American Bittern [Botaurus lentiginosus] in Guernsey.   < *Zoologist,* 2d ser., vi, 1871, p. 2642.

1872. BELING, F.   Der Fischreiher [Ardeidæ] und die Sternschnuppen.   < *Zool. Gart.,* xiii, 1872, pp. 141–148; also, p. 284.
  Relates to the alvine discharges of Herons after feeding upon frogs. Cf. *tom. cit.,* p. 222.

1872. BETHELL, W.   British Heronries.   < *Zoologist,* 2d ser., vii, 1872, p. 3338.

1872. BOYES, F.   Bittern [Botaurus lentiginosus] in East Yorkshire.   < *Zoologist,* 2d ser., vii, 1872, p. 2994.

1872. CLOGG, S.   Heronry in Cornwall.   < *Zoologist,* 2d ser., vii, 1872, p. 3316.

1872. DURNFORD, H.   Heronry in Suffolk   < *Zoologist,* 2d ser., vii, 1872, p. 3315.

1872. GURNEY, J. H., JR.   Purple Heron [Ardea purpurea], Squacco Heron [Buphus comatus] and Night Heron [Nyctiardea grisea] in Norfolk.   < *Zoologist,* 2d ser., vii, 1872, p. 3023.

1872. GURNEY, J. H.   Notes on the Heronries of Norfolk and Suffolk.   < *Zoologist,* 2d ser., vii, 1872, pp. 3314, 3315.

1872. HARTING, J. E.   British Heronries.   < *Zoologist,* 2d ser., vii, 1872, pp. 3261–3272
  Alphabetical inventory of those that are or lately were in existence in the British Islands.

1872. MÜLLER, K.   Aufsatz des Forstmeisters Beling uber ,, Fischreiher und Sternschnuppen.''   < *Zool. Gart.,* xiii, 1872, p. 222.
  Cf. *tom. cit.,* p. 141.

1872. WHITAKER, J., JR.   Little Bittern [Ardetta minuta] in Nottinghamshire.
    < *Zoologist*, 2d ser., vii, 1872, p. 3316.

1872. ZORN, J.   Die Fischreiher.   < *Westerm. illustr. deutsche Monatshefte*, Sept., 1872.
    Mir nicht zugänglich.

1873. ANON.   [EDITORIAL.]   The Herons.   <*Forest and Stream*, i, Sept. 25, 1873, p. 105.
    Characteristics in brief, and scientific names, of the North American *Ardeidæ*.

1873. ANON.   Night Heron [Nyctiardea grisea] in Jersey.   < *Zoologist*, 2d ser., viii,
    1873, p. 3616.

1873. AUBREY, H. W. W.   Heronry near Salisbury.   < *Zoologist*, 2d ser., viii, 1873, p.
    3369.

1873. BAILEY, H. F.   British Heronries.   < *Zoologist*, 2d ser., viii, 1873, p. 3369.

1873. BOYES, F.   Heronries in East Yorkshire.   < *Zoologist*, 2d ser., viii, 1873, pp.
    3369–3371.

1873. BURNEY, H.   British Heronries.   < *Zoologist*, 2d ser., viii, 1873, p. 3651.

1873. GATCOMBE, J.   A New Heronry in Cornwall.   < *Zoologist*, 2d ser., viii, 1873, p.
    3693.

1873. HARTING, J. E.   British Heronries.   < *Zoologist*, 2d ser., viii, 1873, pp. 3404-
    3407.

1873. HART, W. E.   Heronries in Ulster.   < *Zoologist*, 2d ser., viii, 1873, p. 3454.

1873. HEATON, W. H.   Heronries: Errata [literal].   < *Zoologist*, 2d ser., viii, 1873,
    p. 3454.

1873. KERR, W. J.   Heronries in Denbighshire and Merionethshire.   < *Zoologist*, 2
    ser., viii, 1873, p. 3369.

1873. LOVETT, C. W.   [On the supposed death of a Night Heron (Nyctiardea grise
    nævia) from fright.]   < *Proc. Boston Soc. Nat. Hist.*, xv, 1873, pp. 242, 243.

1873. SWINHOE, R.   On a new Species of Little Bittern [Ardetta eurhythma] fro
    China.   <·*Ibis*, 3d ser., iii, 1873, pp. 73, 74, pl. ii.

1874. ANON.   A Fine Specimen [of Ardea herodias].   < *Am. Sportsman*, iv, 1874, p. 12
    Occurrence at Providence, R. I.

1874. ANON.   Herons in Richmond Park.   < *Zoologist*, 2d ser., ix, 1874, p. 3835.
    From the London 'Field', Dec. 6, 1873.

1874. BOYES, F.   Little Bittern [Ardetta minuta] in East Yorkshire.   < *Zoologi
    2d ser., ix, 1874, p. 4118.

1874. BULLER, W. L.   Notes on the Little Bittern of New Zealand (Ardetta mac
    lata).   < *Trans. and Proc. New Zealand Inst. for* 1873, vi, 1874, pp. 119–121.
    xxi.

1874. COUES, E.   Powder-down.   < *Forest and Stream*, ii, Apr. 9, 1874, p. 134.
    On the luminosity of these feathers in the *Ardeidæ*.

1874. DOUBLEDAY, H.   Little Bittern [Ardetta minuta] near Epping.   < *Zoolog
    2d ser., ix, 1874, p. 4199.

1874. GURNEY, J. H.   [Herodias garzetta of Ibis, 1874, p. 104 = H. intermedia.]   < *I
    3d ser., iv, 1874, p. 463.

1874. LECHEVALLIER, A.   Les Herronnieres de la Florida.   < *Naturaliste Canad.*,
    1874, pp. 179–183.

1874. L'ESTRANGE, — .   Heronry in Sussex.   < *Zoologist*, 2d ser., ix, 1874, p. 3953.
    From 'Thames to the Tamar,' 1873.

1874. "PISECO."   [L. A. BEARDSLEE.]   The Herons and their lanterns.   < *Forest
    Stream*, ii, Feb. 26, 1874, p. 54.
    On the alleged luminosity of Heron's feathers.

1874. STEPHENS, C. A.   The Heronry [Nyctiardea grisea nævia] among the gna
    Pines.   < *St. Nicholas Mag.*, i, 1874, pp. 445–447, fig.
    Sketch of encampment of Night Herons in Maine.

1874. WAGENFÜHR, —. [Hochzeitkleid der Ardea goliath.] < *J. f. O.*, 1874, p. 348.

1874. WYMAN, L. The "heron's torch". < *Forest and Stream*, ii, Mar. 26, 1874, p. 103.
Phosphorescence on breast of Herons, with reference to L. A. Beardslee's remarks on p. 54.

1875. ANON. The Green Heron [Butorides virescens]. < *Oölogist*, i, 1875, p. 14, *fig.*

1875. BREWER, T. M. [Note on the specific identity of Ardea pealii and A. rufescens]. < *Proc. Bost. Soc. Nat. Hist.*, xvii, 1875, pp. 205, 206.

1875. CLARK-KENNEDY, A. J. The Heron preying on Birds. < *Zoologist*, 2d ser., x, Feb., 1875, pp. 4340, 4341.

1875. CORBIN, G. B. Bitterns [Botaurus stellaris] in South-Western Hampshire during the Winter of 1874-5. < *Zoologist*, 2d ser., x, July, 1875, pp. 4540, 4541.

1875. "DOCK." A Rare Bird [Herodias egretta, at St. Charles, Missouri.] < *Rod and Gun*, vi, May 8, 1875, p. 91.

1875. GUNN, T. E. Bitterns [Botaurus stellaris] in Norfolk. < *Zoologist*, 2d ser., x, Feb., 1875, p. 4341.

1875. HUDSON, W. H. On the Herons of the Argentine Republic, with a Notice of a curious Instinct of Ardetta involucris. < *P. Z. S.*, Nov. 16, 1875, pp. 623-631.
The writer here gives one of the very best pieces of writing we have ever received on the nature and habits of Herons,—to be particularly recommended alike to those contemplating biographies of these birds, and to those who are fond of graphic delineations of bird-life.

1875. NEWMAN, E. Bitterns [Botaurus stellaris] in England, Ireland and Wales. < *Zoologist*, 2d ser., x, Feb., 1875, p. 4341.

1875. RIDGWAY, R. A Heronry [Ardea herodias] in the Wabash Bottoms. < *Am. Sportsman*, v, Feb. 13, 1875, p. 312.

1875. "TEAL." [R. L. NEWCOMB.] Another specimen [of Botaurus lentiginosus, at Salem, Mass.]. < *Forest and Stream*, iii, Jan. 14, 1875, p. 357.

1875. WHITAKER, J. Bitterns [Botaurus stellaris] in Nottinghamshire. < *Zoologist*, 2d ser., x, Feb., 1875, p. 4341.

1875. "W. H. C." The Sensitive Sight and Hearing of the Great Blue Heron [Ardea herodias]. < *Oölogist*, i, 1875, p. 52.

1876. ABBOTT, C. C. The Occurrence of White Egrets [Garzetta candidissima] at Trenton, New Jersey. < *Am. Nat.*, x, No. 8, 1876, pp. 473-476.
Full account of the occurrence there of these and other Herons, with much reflection on the subject.

1876. AUDUBON, J. J. The Great Blue Heron. Ardea herodias,—Linn. < *Oölogist*, i, 1875, pp. 76-78, fig. (to be cont.)
Extract from his *Ornith. Biogr.*

1876. BREWSTER, W. Singular food of the Least Bittern [Ardetta exilis]. < *Bull. Nutt. Ornith. Club*, i, No. 3, Sept., 1876, p. 76.
Stomach "fairly crammed with clean white *cotton wool.*"

1876. FISK, W. H. A Fight with a Heron. < *Forest and Stream*, vii, Nov. 16, 1876, p. 230.
Combat between a dog and a Heron, copied from the London (England) "Field"; with editorial remarks upon a similar occurrence witnessed in Minnesota, U. S.

1876. GURNEY, J. H., JR. American Bittern [Botaurus lentiginosus] in Dumfriesshire. < *Zoologist*, 2d ser., xi, May, 1876, p. 4929.

1876. HERSEY, J. C. The Little White Egret [Garzetta candidissima] in Colorado. *Am. Nat.*, x, 1876, p. 430.

1876. [HUDSON, H.] Notes on a South-American Heron [Ardetta involucris]. < *Zoologist*, 2d ser., xi, May, 1876, pp. 4928, 4929.
From *P. Z. S.*, 1875, pp. 623-631.

1876. [LOWELL, J. R.] Night Herons [Nyctiardea grisea nævia, at Boston in the winter.] < *Forest and Stream*, vi, Mar. 9, 1876, p. 68.

1876. LUMSDEN, J.   American Bittern [Botaurus lentiginosus] in Islay.   < *Zoologist*, 2d ser., ii, Feb., 1876, p. 4801.
   From the London 'Field' of Jan. 22, 1876.

1876. MATHEW, M. A.   Herons at Bishop's Lydeard.   < *Zoologist*, 2d ser., xi, Aug., 1876, p. 5046.

1876. MATHEW, M. A.   Little Bittern [Ardetta minuta] at Plymouth.   < *Zoologist*, 2d ser., xi, Aug., 1876, p. 5046.

1876. NICHOLLS, H., JR.   Night Heron [Nyctiardea grisea] near Kingsbridge.   < *Zoologist*, 2d ser., xi, Mar., 1876, pp. 4843, 4844.

1876. STEVENSON, H.   Purple Heron [Ardea purpurea] in Norfolk.   < *Zoologist*, 2d ser., xi, Mar., 1876, p. 4843.

1877. NELSON, E. W.   The Louisiana Heron [Demiegretta ludoviciana] in Indiana.   < *Bull. Nutt. Ornith. Club*, ii, No. 2, Apr., 1877, p. 51.

1877. REICHENOW, A.   Systematische Uebersicht der Schreitvögel (Gressores), einer natürlichen, die Ibidae, Ciconidae, Phoenicopteridae, Scopidae, Balaenicipidae und Ardeidae umfassenden Ordnung.   < *J. f. O.*, Apr., 1877, pp. 113–171, pll. i, ii; July, 1877, pp. 225–277.
   Da dieser Jahrgang gerade gebunden wurde, war es mir nicht möglich denselben einzusehen.

1877. [SCOTT, W. E. D.]   Notes on the Habits of the Least Bittern (Ardetta exilis).   < *The Country*, 1, 1877, pp. 91, 103.

1878. A[LLEN], J. A.   Ridgway's Studies of the American Herodiones.   < *Bull. Nutt. Ornith. Club*, iii, No. 4, Oct., 1878, pp. 182, 183.
   Review of the paper in *Bull. U. S. Geol. Surv. Terr.*, iv, pp. 219–251, Feb. 5, 1878.

1878. A[LLEN], J. A.   Reichenow's Review of the Herons and their Allies.   < *Bull. Nutt. Ornith. Club*, iii, No. 4, Oct., 1878, pp. 183–185.
   Extended review of the ,, Systematische Uebersicht der Schreitvogel," in: *Cab. Journ. für Ornith. Jahrg.*, xxv, Apr.-July, 1877, pp. 113–171, 225–278.

1878. [GARLICK, T.]   A Large Heronry [of Ardea herodias].   < *Forest and Stream*, ix, Jan. 17, 1878, p. 451.

1878. "H. W. T. E."   Booming of the Bittern [Botaurus lentiginosus].   < *Forest and Stream*, x, April 25, 1878, p. 216.

1878. LOCKWOOD, S.   The Night Herons [Nyctiardea grisea nævia], and their Exodus.   < *Am. Nat.*, xii, No. 1, 1878, pp. 27–35.
   Vivacious and interesting account of the habits.

1878. RIDGWAY, R.   Studies of the American Herodiones.—Part I.—Synopsis of the American Genera of Ardeidæ and Ciconiidæ; including Descriptions of three New Genera, and a Monograph of the American Species of the Genus Ardea, Linn.   < *Bull. U. S. Geol. and Geogr. Surv. Terr.*, iv, No. 1, Feb. 5, 1878, pp. 219–251, fig.
   No second Part of the "Studies" has appeared.
   Synonymy and diagnosis of the "order" *Herodiones*—Altricial Grallatores, p. 219.—Synopsis of the American Herodionine families, p. 220; there are five: *Cancromidæ, Ardeidæ, Ciconiidæ, Ibididæ, Plataleidæ.*—Synopsis of the American genera of *Ardeidæ*, p. 223; these sixteen: *Ardea, Herodias, Garzetta, Dichromanassa* (g. n., p. 224), *Hydranassa* (Bd., 1858), *Florida, Butorides, Syrigma* (g. n., p. 224), *Pilherodius, Nyctiardea, Nyctherodius, Agamia, Tigrisoma, Zebrilus, Botaurus, Ardetta.*—Monograph of the American species of the genus *Ardea*, p. 226; four species: *A. occidentalis* Aud. (to which *A. wurdemanni* Bd. is referred), *A. herodias, A. cinerea* (of Europe), *A. cocoi;* very full accounts of which, with copious synonymy, are given.—Description of two new American genera of *Ardeidæ*, p. 246, being *Dichromanassa* and *Syrigma*, as above given.—Synopsis of the American subfamilies and genera of *Ciconiidæ*, p. 248; the family being divided into *Ciconiinæ* and *Tantalinæ*, with *Euxenura* (g. n., p. 249 = *Dissoura* Cab., 1850) and *Mycteria* as genera.   (See *P. Z. S.*, 1878, p. 633, and *Ibis*, 1878, pp. 475–477.)

1878. ROWLEY, G. D.   On Sussex Heronries.   < *Rowl. Orn. Misc.*, iii, pt. xii, Jan., 1878, pp. 65–74, pll. lxxxix, xc.

1878. "SAWBONES." A Bittern [Botaurus lentiginosus] Bit. < *Forest and Stream*, xi, Nov. 14, 1878, p. 301.

Choked to death by a fish.

1878. [SCLATER, P. L., *and* SALVIN, O.] Ridgway's Studies of the American Herodiones. < *Ibis*, 4th ser., ii, Oct., 1878, pp. 475–477.

Review of the paper in *Bull. U. S. Geol. Surv. Terr.*, iv, No. 1, Feb., 1878, pp. 219–251.

1879. BREWSTER, W. A Second Specimen of the Yellow-crowned Night Heron (Nyctiardea violacea) in Massachusetts. < *Bull. Nutt. Ornith. Club*, iv, No. 2, Apr., 1879, pp. 124, 125.

1879. CORY, A. B. Description of a New Species of the Family Ardeidae [cyanirostris], from the Bahama Islands.= *A loose half-sheet*, dated Boston, Oct. 8, 1879.

This irregular mode of publication is highly objectionable, and scarcely admissible. The supposed new species is apparently not distinct from the common Louisiana Heron, *Ardea ludoviciana* of Wilson, *Demiegretta ludoviciana* Baird, or *Hydranassa tricolor*, Ridgw. The specific name is apparently to be taken for *cyaneirostris*.

1879. COUES, E. Letters on Ornithology. No. 20.—The American Bittern. Botaurus Minor. (Gm.) < *The Chicago Field*, May 10, 1879.

From the "Birds of the Northwest."

1879. COUES, E. Letters on Ornithology. No. 30.—The Great White Egret. Ardea Egretta (Gm.) Gray. < *The Chicago Field*, July 26, 1879.

1879. COUES, E. Nesting of the Great Blue Heron [Ardea herodias] in the West. < *The Chicago Field*, Aug. 2, 1879.

Extract from "Birds of the Northwest."

1879. DEANE, R. The Great White Egret [Herodias egretta] in New Brunswick. < *Bull. Nutt. Ornith. Club*, iv, No. 1, Jan., 1879, p. 63.

1879. EATON, D. H. Nest and Eggs of the American Bittern (Botaurus minor [lentiginosus]). < *The Oölogist*, iv, No. 10, May, 1879, pp. 73, 74, pl., fig. 1.

Original observations made in Illinois.

Phœnicopteridæ.

1716. DOUGLASS, J. The Natural History and Description of the Phœnicopterus or Flamingo; with two Views of the Head, and three of the Tongue, of that beautiful and uncommon Bird. $<$ *Philos. Trans.*, xxix, 1716, pp. 523–541, tab. ii, figg. 1–6.

> Very full—name and its etymology, genus, geographical distribution, food, nesting, flight, uses made of the bird, and extended description; the plate shows the head, and several views of the tongue and os hyoides.

1734. PERRAULT, C. Description anatomique d'un Becharu [Phœnicopterus]. $<$ *Mém. de l'Acad. Roy. des Sci.* depuis 1666 jusq. 1699, iii, pt. iii, 1734, pp. 42–49, pll. 9, 10.

1757. PERRAULT, C. Anatomische Beschreibung eines Flamingo [Phœnicopterus]. $<$ *Abhandl. Königl. Französich. Akad.*, ii, 1757, pp. 217–—.

> Not seen—title from Giebel. Germ. transl. from *Mém. de l'Acad. Paris*, iii, pt. iii, 1734, p. 42.

1797. GEOFFROY ST. HILAIRE, ÉT. Sur une nouvelle espèce de Phoenicopterus [minor]. $<$ *Millin Magas. Encycl.*, iii, 1797, pp. 433–436.

> Pas vu moi-même.

1798. GEOFFROY ST. HILAIRE, ÉT. Sur une nouvelle espèce de Phoenicopterus [minor]. $<$ *Bull. Sci. Soc. Philom.*, i, 1798, pp. 97, 98.

> Pas vu moi-même.

180–. GIORNA, M. E. Description du Phoenicopterus tué en Piémont le 31. Mai 1806, etc. $<$ *Mém. Acad. Turin* pour less années 1805–8, 18—, pp. 318–327.

> Pas vue moi-même.

1829. D'ORBIGNY, [A.] D., *and* GEOFFROY ST. HILAIRE, Is. Sur une nouvelle espèce de Phénicoptère ou Flammant (Phœnicopterus ignipalliatus). $<$ *Ann. des Sci. Nat.*, xvii, 1829, pp. 454–457.

> Les auteurs présentent quatre espèces—*PP. antiquorum, ruber, minor, ignipalliatus*, sp. n.

1829. [D'ORBIGNY, A. D., *and* GEOFFROY ST. HILAIRE, Is.] Sur une nouvelle espèce de Phénicoptère ou Flammant (Phœnicopterus ignipalliatus); . . . $<$ *Féruss. Bull.*, 2e sect., xix, 1829, pp. 111–113.

> Extrait des *Ann. des Sci. Nat.*, xvii, 1829, pp. 454–457.

1832. [GEOFFROY ST. HILAIRE, Is.] Phenicoptère. Phoenicopterus. Lin. $<$ *Guér. Mag. de Zool.*, 2e année, 1832, classe ii, Ois., notice ii, pl. ii.

> *Phœnicopterus ignipalliatus*, d'Orb. et Is. Geoffr., *Ann. Sci. Nat.*, xvii, 1829, p. 454. Traite aussi de *P. antiquorum, P. ruber* et *P. minor*.

1832. OWEN, R. [Notes on the Anatomy of the Flamingo, Phœnicopterus ruber.] $<$ *P. Z. S.*, ii, 1832, pp. 141–144.

1834. D'ORBIGNY, A. D., *and* GEOFFROY ST. HILAIRE, Is. [Phœnicopterus ignipalliatus.] $<$ *Oken's Isis*, 1834, p. 1094.

> Mir nicht zugänglich. Aus d. *Ann. Sci. Nat.*, xvii, 1829, p. 454 u. folgg.

1835. HUNTER, W. P. On the geographical Range of the Flamingo (Phœnicópterus rùber L.). $<$ *Loudon's Mag. Nat. Hist.*, viii, 1835, pp. 571, 572.

> I. e., *Phœnicopterus antiquorum*, of the Old World.

1835. OWEN, R. Anatomie von Phoenicopterus ruber mas. $<$ *Oken's Isis*, Bd. xxviii, 1835, pp. 433, 434.

> Aus d. *P. Z. S.*, 1832, p. 141.

1844. DES MURS, O. Notice et Considérations Oologiques sur la place à assigner au Genre Ornithologique Flamant (Phœnicopterus, L.) $<$ *Revue Zoologique*, vii, 1844, pp. 241–246.

> L'auteur n'hésite pas à en faire un véritable Palmipède.

1850. HULKE, J. W.   Enquiry respecting the Nest of the Flamingo [Phœnicopterus antiquorum].   < *Zoologist*, viii, 1850, pp. 2801, 2802.

1857. GUYON, —.   [Extrait d'une Note concernant les Flamants du lac de Tunis.]   < *Rev. et Mag. de Zool.*, ix, 1857, pp. 415, 416.

1864. TRISTRAM, H. B.   [Note on breeding of] The Flamingo.   < *Zoologist*, xxii, 1864, pp. 9119, 9120.
From his 'Great Sahara,' p. 62.

1865. ANDERSSON, C. J.   Note on the two Flamingoes of South Africa.   < *Ibis*, 2d ser., i, 1865, pp. 64–67.
P. erythrœus and *P. minor ;* descriptive and biographical.

1868. FEILDEN, H. W.   [Description of Phœnicopterus rubidus, sp. n.]   < *Ibis*, 2d ser, iv, 1868, pp. 495, 496.

1869. GRAY, G. R.   Notes on the Bills of the species of Flamingo (Phœnicopterus.)   < *Ibis*, 2d ser., v, 1869, pp. 438–443, pls. xiii–xv.
Commentary on the forms of the bills.   Synonymatic and geographical synopsis of 8 spp., under several subgenera: *Phœniconais*, p. 440; *Phœnicorodias*, p. 441, subgg. nn.   *Phœnicopterus glyphorhynchus*, sp. n., from the Galopagoes, p. 442, pl. xiv, f. 5.   The bills of all the other spp. are also figured.

1869. JERDON, T. C.   [On the Phœnicopterus rubidus et aff.]   < *Ibis*, 2d ser., v, 1869, pp. 230–232.

1869. SAUNDERS, H.   [Exhibition of eggs of the Flamingo (Phœnicopterus antiquorum).]   < *P. Z. S.*, xxxvii, 1869, p. 432.

1870. CLARK, J. W.   [Nidification and breeding habits of Phœnicopterus antiquorum in France.]   < *Ibis*, 2d ser., vi, 1870, pp. 439–442.

1873. JACKSON, A. J.   Flamingo in the Isle of Sheppey.   < *Zoologist*, 2d ser., viii, 1873, p. 3693.
From the London 'Field,' Aug. 16.

1873. "M. H."   The Flamingo.   < *Appleton's Journ.*, x, July, 1873, p. 85.

1873. NEWMAN, E.   The Flamingo Killed in the Isle of Sheppey.   < *Zoologist*, 2d ser., viii, 1873, p. 3737.

1875. LEIDY, J.   On a Fungus in a Flamingo [Phœnicopterus ruber].   < *Proc. Acad. Nat. Sci. Phila.*, 1875, pp. 11, 12, fig. i.
Suspected to be the same as *Aspergillus nigrescens* Robin, found in a phthisical Pheasant.

1879. ANON.   The Flamingo [Phœnicopterus ruber].   < *The Oölogist*, iv, No. 9, Apr., 1879, p. 72.
Burlesque verses, quoted from the *Toronto Globe.*

Anatidæ.

1650. BARTHOLINUS, T.   Cygni Anatome ejusque Cantus.   Resp. Joh. Jac. Bewerlin. Hafniæ.   1650.   4to.   4 folia.   1 Tab.

> Haud mihi obvius.—Edit. alteram notis auctiorem edidit Casparus Thomæ filius, Hafniæ, 1668, q. v., infrà.

1658. LELANDUS, J.   Cygnea Cantio cum commentario.   Londini.   1658.   8vo.

> Haud mihi obvius.

1660. FELLER, J., and GERHARD, G.   Cygnorum cantum defendere conabuntur.   Lipsiæ.   1660.   4to.   2 folia.

> Haud mihi obvius.

1666. MAJOR, J. D.   Progr. de Cygni Anatome.   Kiloniæ.   1666.   4to.

> Haud mihi obvius.

1668. BARTHOLINUS, T.   (Ed. Bartholinus, C.)   Thomæ Bartholini | Dissertatio | de | Cygni | Anatome ejusq; | Cantu | à | Johanne Jacobo Bewerlino | in Academia Hafniensi | olim subjecta, | nunc Notulis qvibusdam auctior edi- | ta ex schedis Paternis | à | Casparo Bartholino | Thomæ Filio. | 16[monogramma]68 | — | Apud Danielem Paulli | Regium Bibliopolam. | Literis Henrici Godiani Reg. & Acade- | miæ Typographi.   1 vol.   16mo.   pp. 96, figg. on p. 6.

> Ed. alt.—Ed. princ., Hafniæ, 1650.

1670. GLATTHORN, G. L.   Diss. de Cygno.   Resp. Rücker.   Wittebergæ.   1670.   4to. 2 folia.

> Haud mihi obvia.

1678. MORAY, R.   A Relation concerning Barnacles.   < Philos. Trans., xii, 1678, pp. 925–927, fig. 3 on pl.

> Description of these cirrhipeds: "The Bird in every shell that I opened, as well the least as the biggest, I found so curiously and compleatly formed, that there appeared to be nothing wanting, as to the external parts, for making up a perfect Sea-Fowl."

1685. ROBINSON, T.   Some observations on the French Macreuse, and the Scotch Bernacle; together with a continuation of the Account of Boyling, and other Fountains.   < Philos. Trans., xv, 1685, pp. 1036–1040.

> "The French eat it upon Fish-days, and all Lent, thinking it to be a sort of fish . . . whereas the Bernacle (as also the Macreuse itself,) is Oviparous, and of the Goos-kind; and the shells [i. e., cirripeds] themselves contain a testaceous animal of their own species, as the Oyster, Cockle and Muscle doth."   After noticing Sir R. Moray's error, Phil. Tr., No. 137, and other equally absurd mistakes, the writer speaks of the Bernacle as a Goose, and identifies the Macreuse with the Anas niger of Willughby, p. 336 or 366.   Cf. Philos. Trans., 1685, pp. 1041–1044.

1685. RAY, J.   A Letter from Mr. Ray, Fellow of the R. S. to Dr. Robinson; concerning the French Macreuse.   < Philos. Trans., xv, 1685, pp. 1041–1044.

> Acknowledges the point, and continues the subject with various further particulars; cf. Philos. Trans., 1685, pp. 1036–1040.

1688. LACHMUND, F.   De Cygni Lingua Ossea.   <Ephem. Acad. Nat. Cur., Dec. i, Cent 4 et 5, 1673–74, 1668, p. 225.

> Haud mihi obvius.

1688. WEDEL, G. W.   Cygni Sterni Anatome.   < Ephem. Acad. Nat. Cur., Dec. i, Ann. 2, 1671, 1688, pp. 30, 31, pl.

> Haud mihi obvium.

1694. TREUTZEL, D.   Berniclas sen Anseres Scoticos communiter sic dictos.   Præs. D. Treutzel, Nycop., Resp. P. Raam, Nycop. Strengnesiae.   1694.   4to.   pp. 134.

> Not seen.

1697. HAHN, P.   Disp. phil. de Cygno ejusque Cantione.   Præes. P. Hahn, Resp. M. Weckelman, Wex. Smol.   Aboæ.   1697.   8vo.   pp. 8, 36.

> Haud mihi obvia.

1698. WINTER, D. De Cantu Cygneo. Cygneæ. 1698. 4to.
Haud mihi obvius.

1703. RUDEEN, T. Exercitium acad. de Cantu Cygnorum. Præs. Th. Rudeen, Resp.
B. Granroot, Ost-Both. Aboae. 1703. 8vo. pp. 6, 30, 2.
Haud mihi obvium.

1721. VALENTINI, M. B. Anatome Clangulae. < *Ephem. Acad. Nat. Cur.*, Cent. 9, 10,
1721, pp. 431, 432, 1 pl.
Not seen: title from Carus and Engelmann.

1722. EDZARDUS, E. H. Diss. de Cygno ante mortem non canente. Resp. Martini.
Wittebergæ. 1722. 4to. 2 folia.
Haud mihi obvia.

1723. DETHARDING, G. Progr. de fabuloso Olorum Cantu. Rostock. 1723. 4to.
Haud mihi obvius.

1725. TÖRNER, F. Diss. philol. de Avibus Apollinis Cygno et Corvo. Resp. N. O.
Rabeniüs. Upsaliæ. 1725. 8vo. pp. 22.
Haud mihi obvia.

1729. MORIN, H. Question naturelle et critique, sçavoir, pourquoy les Cygnes qui
chantoient autrefois si bien, chantent aujourdhui si mal. < *Mém. Acad. In-
script. Paris*, v, 1729, pp. 207–218.
Pas vue moi-même.

1749. ILSTRÖM, J. Beskrifning om Körfogelens [Mergus merganser] nytta, när fiske-
hus blifva bygde för konom uti salt-eller insjö-vikar. < *Kongl. Vetensk.-Akad.
Handl.*, 1749, pp. 190–196. (Uebersetzung 1749, pp. 197–203.)
Not seen.

1761. TIBERTIUS, [T.] [Huru Ander kunna med fordel göras hemtamde.] < *Kongl.
Svensk. Vetensk.-Akad. Handl.*, xxii, 1761, pp. 321, 322.

1763. BRÜNNICH, M. T. Eder Fuglens [Somateria mollissima] beskrivelse. Kjøbenhavn. 1763. 8vo. pp. 60. 3 pll.

1763. BRÜNNICH, M. T. Tilltoeg til Ederfuglens [Somateria mollissima] beskrivelse.
Kjøbenhavn. 1763. 8vo. pp. 36.
I have seen neither of these tracts in the original Danish, but have handled the German
version of same date. See next title.

1763. BRÜNNICH, M. T. Die | natürliche Historie | des | Eider-Vogels [Somateria mol-
lissima] | beschrieben | von | Morten Thrane Brünniche | aus dem dänischen
übersetzt. | [Abbildung.] | mit Kupfern. | — | Kopenhagen, | bey Johann
Gottlob Rothen | 1763. 1 vol. sm. 8vo. 4 p. ll., pp. 1–70, 1 l., 3 pll.

1770. GUELDENSTAEDT, A. J. Anas nyroca. < *Novi Comment. Acad. Scient. Imp. Petrop. ad ann.* 1769, xiv, pt. i, 1770, p. 37.

1770. GUELDENSTAEDT, A. J. Anas nyroca. < *Novi Comment. Acad. Scient. Imp. Petrop. ad ann.* 1769, xiv, pt. i, 1770, pp. 403–408.

1775. BECKMANN, J. Kleiner Beitrag zur Naturgeschichte des Meerrochen, Mergus
serrator, L. < *Beschäfft. d. Berlin. Gesell. Naturf. Freunde*, i, 1775, pp. 170–176.
Nicht mir selbst zugänglich.

1775. TITIUS, J. D. Von Nutzen und Unschädlichkeit der Schwäne [Cygnus sp.].
< *Berlin. Sammlgn.*, vii, 1775, pp. 583–592.
Mir nicht zugänglich.

1776. PALLAS, P. S. Erinnerung wegen des Linneischen Mergus serrator. . . . .
< *Beschäfft. d. Berlin. Gesell. Naturf. Freunde*, ii, 1776, pp. 551–558.
Nicht mir selbst zugänglich.

1777. ————. Von dem Schwanengesange. < *Neu. Hamburg. Magaz.*, St. cvi,
1777, pp. 371–379.
Mir nicht zugänglich.

1777. CHEMNITZ, J. H.   Vom Gesang der Isländischen Schwanen.   < *Beschftgn. d.*
Berlin. Ges. Nat. Fr., iii, 1777, pp. 460, 461.   (Anmerk. dazu, von O. F. Mül-
ler, *Schrift. d. Berl. Ges. Nat. Fr.*, ii, 1781, p. 132.)
Mir nicht zugänglich.

1779. PALLAS, P. S.   Den skrockande Anden (Anas glocitans), en rar Fogel, som en-
dast blifvit funnen i Östra Siberien, beskrifven och afritad af P. S. Pallas.
< *Kongl. Svensk. Vetensk.-Akad. Handl.*, xl, 1779, pp. 26–34, pl. i.
"I de inledande anmärkningarne om Andslägtet i allmanhet säger förf., at *Merg. albellus*
är hona till *M. merganser.*"   (v. Friesen.)

1779. PALLAS, P. S.   Anas glocitans, ein seltner Vogel, nur im östlichen Sibirien zu
finden.   < *Abhandl. Schwed. Akad.*, xli, f. 1779, pp. 22–28.
Nicht mir selbst zugänglich.

1780. FAILLE, C. DE LA.   Mémoire dans lequel on examine le sentiment des anciens et
des modernes sur l'origine des Macreuses.   < *Mém. étrang. Acad. Roy. des Sci. de
Paris*, ix, 1780, pp. 331–344.
Pas vu moi-même.

1780. ÖDMAN, S.   Zoologisk Anmårkning om Mergus albellus.   < *Kongl. Vetensk. Acad.
Nya Handl.*, i, 1780, pp. 237–240.
"Här rättas Pallas' uppgift, *op. cit.*, 1779, p. 27, at *Mergus merganser* och *M. albellus*
skulle vara samma art."

1781. ————.   Over den kleinen witkoppigen Zaager [Mergellus albellus?]
< *Geneesk. Jaarbook*, v, 1781, pp. 205–209.
Not seen.

1781. OTTO, B. C.   Beschreibung der Säge-Schnäbler [Mergus serrator].   < *Oekon.
Nachricht. d. Gesell. in Schlesien*, vii, 1781, pp. 81, 90, 97.
Not seen: title from Carus and Engelmann.

1783. MONGEZ, A.   Sur les Cignes qui chantent.   < *Journ. de Phys.*, xxiii, 1783, pp.
304–314.
Not seen—see the separate memoir, same date.

1783. MONGEZ, A.   Mémoire | sur | des Cygnes | qui chantent; | Par M. A. Mongez
Garde des Antiques & du | Cabinet d'Histoire Naturelle de Sainte-Geneviève
| de plusieurs Académies. | [Dessin.] | A Paris, | Rue et Hôtel Serpente. | —
1783. 1 vol. 8vo. 1 p. l., pp. 39.
The Royal Academy considered that Abbe Mongez treated the subject carefully and elab-
rately, and the recommendation that his Mémoire be printed among those of foreign savans
has the distinguished signatures of Daubenton, Brisson and Vicq d'Azyr.

1783. ÖDMANN, S.   Ornithologiske Anmårkningar om Al-Foglen.   (Anas Hiemali
[Harelda glacialis].)   < *Kongl. Vetensk. Acad. Nya Handl.*, iv, 1783, pp. 313–32:

1785. ÖDMANN, S.   Svårtan, Anas [Œdemia] Fusca Linn. beskrifven til des Sed
och Hushållning.   < *Kongl. Vetensk. Acad. Nya Handl.*, vi, 1785, pp. 191–195.

1785. ÖDMANN, S.   Skråckans, (Mergi Merganseris) hushållning och lefnadssåt
jåmte någre anmårkningar öfver detta slågte i allmånhet.   < *Kongl. Vetens.
Acad. Nya Handl.*, vi, 1785, pp. 307–316.
"Uti den allmänna öfversigten sammanslås Linné's 6 (Svenska) arter tiel 3: ne. Dessut
anföras 1 säker och 2 osäkra exotiscka arter."   (*v. Friesen*, p. 42.) Beskrifning om *M. m
ganser, serrator, cucullatus*, og *albellus.*

1786. WALBAUM, J. J.   Beschreibung der Taucher-Gans [Mergus merganser] weib
chen Geschlechts.   < *Schrift. d. Berlin. Gesell. Naturf. Freunde*, Bd. vii, St
1786, pp. 119–130.
Nicht mir selbst zugänglich: Titel aus Carus u. Engelmann.

1788. WALBAUM, J. J.   Beschreibung der lachenden Gans [Anser erythropus] mä
lichen Geschlechts.   < *Schrift. d. Berlin. Gesell. Naturf. Freunde*, Bd. viii. 17
pp. 75b–91b.
Not seen—title from Carus and Engelmann.

1792. THILLAYE, —.   Description d'une singularité du Cygne [Cygnus sp.]. $<$ *Journ.*
d'Hist. Nat., 1792, pp. 463–467.

Pas vue moi-même.

1793. FABRICIUS, O.   Om den pukkelnabbede Edderfugl, Anas [Somateria] spectabilis, og Grönlandernes Edderfuglefangst. $<$ *Skrifter Naturh. Selsk. Kjø-*
benh., Bd. ii, Heft ii, pp. 56–83, 1 pl.

Not seen—title from Carus and Engelmann.

1794. [MEYER, F. A. A.]   Herrn Professor Thillayes Nachricht einer seltenen Abart
des Schwans. $<$ *Meyer's Zool. Annalen*, i, 1794, pp. 304–308.

Auszug aus d. *Journ. d'Hist. Nat.*, 1793.

1797. VICQ D'AZYR, F.   Observations sur les organes de la génération des Canards
[Anatidæ]. $<$ *Bull. Sci. Soc. Philom.*, i, (1), 1797, pp. 57', 58'.

Pas vues moi-même : le titre tiré de Carus et Engelmann.

1800. M[ITCHILL], S. L.   Domestication of the Wild-Goose (Anas [Bernicla] Canadensis). $<$ *Mitchill and Miller's Medical Repository*, iv, No. 2, 1800, pp. 198, 199.

1802. [MITCHILL, S. L.]   The white-back or canvas-back duck [Fuligula vallisneria].
$<$ *Mitchill and Miller's Medical Repository*, v, No. 3, 1802, pp. 342, 343.

One of the very earliest notices of this bird as a distinct species.   It is not named.

1802. SEWASTIANOFF, [A.]   Description d'une nouvelle espèce de Canard [Anas
canagica] et d'une variété de l'huitrier, qui se trouvent dans le cabinet d'histoire naturelle de l'Academie Imperiale des Sciences. $<$ *Nova Acta Acad.*
Scient. Imp. Petrop. for 1800, xiii, 1802, pp. 346–351, pl. x.

Descr. du canard, p. 349, pl. x: c'est une oye, l'*Anser canagicus*, *Chloëphaga c.* Eyton, *Phi-*
lacte c. Bann.   L'auteur décrit l'huitrier comme une variété de *Hæmatopus ostralegus*, sans le
nommer: c'est devenu plus tard le *Hæmatopus niger* Pall.

1803. LORDAT, —, (*ainé*).   Mémoire Sur la structure de l'articulation du genou dans la
macreuse [Œdemia nigra], et sur la progression de cet oiseau. $<$ *Journ. de*
Phys. Chim. Hist. Nat., lvii, 1803, pp. 32–35.

Lu à la Soc. Méd. de Montpellier, le 30 nivôse an 11 (1803).

1805. BARTON, M.   [Occurrence of the Canvas-back Duck (Fuligula vallisneria) on
the Susquehanna.] $<$ *Barton's Med. and Phys. Journ.*, part i, vol. ii, 1805,
pp. 161, 162.

With a note by the editor, identifying it as "*Anas ferina* Linn."   This notice is nine years
prior to the original description of the species as *Anas vallisneria* by Wilson, 1814, and the
bird is spoken of as if then well-known under its vernacular name.

1806. GEOFFROY ST.-HILAIRE, É.   Description D'un mulet provenant du canard
morillon, anas [Clangula] glaucion, et de la sarcelle de la Caroline, anas
querquedula [Querquedula carolinensis]. $<$ *Ann. du Mus. d'Hist. Nat.*, vii,
1806, pp. 222–226.

1806. GEOFFROY ST.-HILAIRE, É.   Mouvemens de la Ménagerie.   Notes sur le zèbre
et le canard à bec courbe. $<$ *Ann. du Mus. d'Hist. Nat.*, vii, 1806, pp. 245–248.

2° Du canard à bec courbé (*Anas curvirostra*), p. 246.

1808. CUVIER, FRÉD.   Observations Sur l'accouplement d'un cigne chanteur mâle et
d'une oie domestique femelle.   Description du mulet qui en est provenu.
$<$ *Ann. du Mus. d'Hist. Nat.*, xii, 1808, pp. 119–125.

Avec des observations générales sur l'accouplement des oiseaux de différente espèce.

1823. COOKE, T.   A | Letter | to | Mark Milbank, Esq. M. P. | of | Thorp Hall, and
Barningham, in the county of York, | with two plates, | descriptive of the
character | of | The Whistling Swan, | and of | the peculiar structure | of its
trachea. | [By Thomas Cooke.] | — | Amico minusculum levidense. | Cic. Ep.
Fam. L. ix. 12. | — | London : | printed for, and published by Rodwell and
Martin, Bond Street ; | Wood, Strand ; | Hailes, Piccadilly ; | Tucker, Christ-
church ; and Bell, Richmond ; | — | 1823. folio. cover-title, pp. 12, pll. 2.

The cover-title is different : A | Description | of | the character | of | the Whistling Swan, |
and of | the peculiar structure | of its | Trachea. | —|

The work is technically anonymous, but the author signs his name at the end.   The plates
represent the exterior of the bird, and its windpipe.

1823. WILSON, J.   Observations on some Species of the Genus Mergus.   < *Mem. Wernerian Nat. Hist. Soc.*, iv, pt. ii, 1823, pp. 475–484.

On the specific identity of *Mergus castor* and *M. merganser*, and on the differences between the females of this species and of *M. serrator.*

1824. BONAPARTE, C. [L.]   On a new species of Duck [Anas rufitorques] described by Wilson as the same with the Anas fuligula of Europe.   < *Journ. Acad. Nat. Sci. Phila.*, iii, 1824, pp. 381–389.

1824. [BREHM, C. L.]   Leislers Eidertauchente.   Platypus Leisleri, Brehm.   < *Ornis,* Heft i, 1824, pp. 28–39.

1824. [BREHM, C. L.]   [Das Sommerkleid der männlichen Eidertauchenten, Somateria mollissima.]   < *Ornis,* Heft i, 1824, pp. 40–42.

1825. BRUCH, C. F.   [Ueber die Eidertauchente (Somateria mollissima).]   < *Vereinsblatt d. Ver. f. Kunst u Lit. zu Mainz,* 26. Aug. 1825.

Nicht mir selbst zugänglich.

1825. DESM ... ST, [A. G.]   Sur une nouvelle espèce de Canard [Anas rufitorques] déscrite par Wilson, comme étant la même que l'Anas fuligula (ou le Morillon) d'Europe ; par M. Charles Bonaparte. . . .   < *Féruss. Bull.*, 2e sect., iv, 1825, pp. 128, 129.

Extrait du *Journ. Phila. Acad.*, iii, No. 13, mai 1824, pp. 381–389.

1825. "F."   Anas Rufitorques.   < *Edinb. Journ. Sci.*, ii, 1825, p. 186.

Merely a reference to the species as established by Bp., *Journ. Acad. Phila.*, iii, 1824, p. 381.

1826. ANON.   Oies de Toulouse.   < *Féruss. Bull.*, 4e sect., v, 1826, p. 107.

Acad. des Sci. de Dijon, séance du 20 août 1825, p. 31.

1826. LESSON, [R.] P.   Observations sur quelques espèces du genre Mergus, . . . ; par James Wilson . . .   < *Féruss. Bull.*, 2e sect., vii, 1826, pp. 113, 114.

Extraites des *Mem. Wern. Soc.*, iv, pt. ii, 1823, pp. 475–484, *q. v.*

1826. LESTIBOUDOIS, T.   Note sur le Cygne sauvage et le Cygne domestique (Anas Cygnus et A. olor, Temm.).   < *Recueil de la Soc. d'Amat. des Sci. de Lille,* 1826, p. 270.

Not seen—title from *Féruss. Bull.*

1826. YARRELL, W.   Notice of the occurrence of a species of Duck [Fuligula rufina] new to the British Fauna.   < *Zool. Journ.*, ii, 1826, pp. 492, 493.

1827. ————.   Der Schwan.   < *Abhandl. d. Naturf. Ges. in Görlitz,* i, 1, 1827, pp. 32–40.

1827. ————.   Education des Canards.   < *Féruss. Bull.*, 4e sect., viii, 1827, p. 260.

Asiatic Journal, juillet 1826, p. 61.

1827. CUVIER, [G.]   Du Canard Pie, a pieds demi palmés, de la Nouvelle-Hollande. (Anas [Anseranas] melanoleuca. Lath.)   < *Mém. du Mus. d'Hist. Nat..* xiv, 1827, pp. 345–347, pl. 19.

1828. [CUVIER, G.]   Du Canard Pie a pieds demi-palmés, de la Nouv.-Hollande (Anas [Anseranas] melanoleuca Lath.), . . .; par M. le baron Cuvier. . . .   < *Féruss. Bull.*, 2e sect., xiii, 1828, p. 436.

Extrait des *Mém. du Mus.*, xiv, 1827, p. 345.

1828. LAFRESNAYE, F. DE.   Extrait d'une lettre de M. Frédéric de Lafresnaye, naturaliste, à Falaise (Calvados), relatif à la Sarcelle de Chine, dont un undividu vient d'être tué en Normandie.   < *Féruss. Bull.*, 2e sect., xiv, 1828, p. 118.

Avec une note de M. Lesson.

1828. LOTZ, G.   Ornithologische Beobachtungen von Gideon Lotz ; mit Anmerkungen von Gloger.   < *Oken's Isis,* Bd. xxi, 1828, pp. 1233–1240.

Ueber die weissäugige Ente, *Anas leucophthalmus* Borckh., *A. nyroca* Gmel.

1829. "A. B."   Desertion of Geese.   < *Loudon's Mag. Nat. Hist.*, ii, 1829, p. 65.

1829. BREW, C. A.   Presentiment in a Goose.   < *Loudon's Mag. Nat. Hist.*, ii, 1829, p. 65.

1829. EIMBECK, —.   [Eine merkwürdige Mittelform zwischen Anas clangula und Mergus albellus.]   < *Oken's Isis*, Bd. xxii, 1829, pp. 400, 401.
> Vergl. *Isis*, Bd. xxiii, 1830, p. 568.

1829. [EIMBECK, —.] Beschreibung | eines | bisher nicht bekannten sehr auffallend | gebildeten | Deutschen Wasservogels | nebst einer | verhältnissmässigen Abbildung | in halber Lebensgrösse. | — | Braunschweig, 1829.   4to.   Titelbl., 2 unpaginirte Blätter = 4 Seiten, 1 Taf.
> Anonym, doch von unzweifelhafter Autorschaft. Der Vogel wird *Mergus anatarius* genannt, und für einen Bastard von *Mergus albellus* ♂ und *Anas clangula* ♀ gehalten. Vergl. *Isis*, 1829, p. 400; 1831, p. 299.

1829. HILL, W. H.   The Small Dover.   < *Loudon's Mag. Nat. Hist.*, ii, 1829, pp. 403, 404.

1829. HILL, W. H.   The Dark-looking Water Bird.   [Answer to query on p. 101.]   < *Loudon's Mag. Nat. Hist.*, ii, 1829, p. 403.

1829. L——s, J.   A dark-looking Water Bird.   < *Loudon's Mag. Nat. Hist.*, ii, 1829, p. 101, fig. 21.
> Cf. *tom. cit.*, p. 403, where supposed to be *Anas [Œdemia] nigra.*

1829. LENGERTE, A. DE.   Manière d'élever les Oies dans le Holstein . . .   < *Féruss. Bull.*, 4e sect., xii, 1829, pp. 133, 134.
> *Land- und Hauswirth*, 1825, p. 269.

1829? POHL, W. L.   Der Schwan.   < *Abhand. Naturf. Gesell. zu Görlitz*, i, pt. 1.
> Not seen.—Poem, set to music by J. Schneider, preceded by an anonymous notice of the natural history of this emblem of the Görlitz Society.

1829. SCHLEEP, [B. C.]   Anser medius.   < *Oken's Isis*, Bd. xxii, 1829, pp. 1054, 1055.

1829. "T. F."   Flying Geese.   < *Loudon's Mag. Nat. Hist.*, ii, 1829, p. 65.

1830. BLACKWALL, J.   Observations on a newly-described Species of Swan [Cygnus bewickii].   < *Zool. Journ.*, v, 1830, pp. 189–191.

1830. "CORRESPONDENT."   [T. C. HEYSHAM?]   Statement respecting the Discovery of the new Species of Swan, named Cygnus Bewickii by Mr. Yarrell.   < *Philos. Mag.*, viii, Aug., 1830, pp. 128–130.
> Original specimen shot by R. R. Wingate, Feb., 1829, near Haydon Bridge in Northumberland. Mr. Wingate's notice was read to the Nat. Hist. Soc. of Newcastle-upon-Tyne, Oct. 20, 1829; P. J. Selby's description on 16 Feb., 1830; but neither of these papers was published till after June, 1830.

1830. EIMBECK, —.   Cross of the Anas clangula [Clangula glaucium] and Mergus albellus.   < *Edinb. New Philos. Journ.*, viii, 1830, p. 202.
> See same author at 1829 and 1831.

1830. HAHN, E.   Commentatio de arteriis Anatis. Accedunt tabulæ æneæ. Hannoveræ, in Bibliopoleo aulico Hahniano. 1830.   4to.   pp. vi, 60, pll. 2.
> Haud mihi obvia.

1830. WINGATE, R. R.   Notice of a [lately] new species of Swan [Cygnus bewickii].   < *Trans. Nat. Hist. Soc. Northumb. and Durh.*, i, 1830, pp. 1, 2.   Observations by P. J. Selby, pp. 17–25.
> Not seen.

1830. YARRELL, W.   On a new Species of Wild Swan [Cygnus bewickii], taken in England, and hitherto confounded with the Hooper.   < *Trans. Linn. Soc.*, xvi, pt. ii, 1830, pp. 445–454, pll. xxiv, xxv.   (Read Jan. 19, 1830; whole vol. dated 1833.)
> *C. bewickii*, p. 453; sternum and trachea figured.
> This paper, like others in the same vol. of the *Trans.*, is often cited as of 1833, date of the completed Vol. XVI; but it was read and in full discussion and reprint in 1830.

1830. [YARRELL, W.]   [Notice of his paper on a new species of Wild Swan (Cygnus bewickii).]   < *Philos. Mag.*, vii, Feb., 1830, p. 146.
> Read before Linn. Soc., Jan. 19, 1830.

1830. YARRELL, W.   Specific Characters of Cygnus Bewickii and C. Ferus.   < *Philos. Mag.*, vii, Mar., 1830, p. 194.

Bull. v, 4——27

1830. YARRELL, W.   Reply to the Statement respecting the Discovery of Cygnus
Bewickii, published in the Phil. Mag. and Annals for August.   < *Philos. Mag.*,
viii, Sept., 1830, pp. 167–169.
Personal and controversial, in self-defense against *tom. cit.*, pp. 128–130.

1830. [YARRELL, W.]   Sur une nouvelle espèce de Cygne [bewickii] prise en Angleterre et confondue jusqu'a présent avec le cygne sauvage (Anas cygnus,
Gm.); par W. Yarrel[l].   . . .   < *Féruss. Bull.*, 2ᵉ sect., xxii, 1830, pp. 127,
128.
From *Linn. Trans.*, xvi, pt. ii, p. 445, pl.

1830. YARRELL, W.   Eine für die britische Fauna neue Ente [Fuligula rufina].
< *Oken's Isis*, Bd. xxiii, 1830, pp. 1065, 1066.
Aus d. *Zool. Journ.*, iii, 1826.

1831. BENNETT, E. T.   [On the History and Synonymy of Cereopsis novæ-hollandiæ.]
< *P. Z. S.*, i, 1831, pp. 26, 27.

1831. EIMBECK, —.   Beschreibung eines bisher nicht bekannten, sehr auffallend ge-
bildeten deutschen Wasservogels, nebst einer verhältnissmassigen Abbildung
in halber Lebensgrösse.   < *Oken's Isis*, Bd. xxiv, 1831, pp. 299–301, pl. iii.
Mergus anatarius = A. clangula ♂ × ♀ *Mergus albellus.* See same author at 1829.

1831. FIENNES, T.   [Exhibition of a hybrid Duck—Anas acuta ♂ × ♀ A. boschas.]
< *P. Z. S.*, i, 1831, p. 158.

1831. FISCHER, G.   Sur une nouvelle espèce de Canard du Kamtschatka [Anas cucul-
lata].   < *Bull. Soc. Imp. Nat. Moscou*, iii, 1831, pp. 278–280.
Le Canard à Capuchin, *Anas cucullata*, p. 279.   Voyez 1834, FISCHER, G.

1831. LESS[ON, R. P.]   Sur le Mergus cucullatus, Selby.   . . .   < *Féruss. Bull.*, 2ᵉ
sect., xxvii, 1831, p. 190.
Edinb. Journ. Nat. and Geogr. Sci., n. s., No. 4, Apr., 1831, p. 238.

1831. LESS[ON, R. P.]   Note sur une nouvelle espèce de Cygne [Cygnus bewickii];
par M. R.-R. Wingate: lu le 29 Octobre 1829.   . . .   < *Féruss. Bull.*, 2ᵉ sect.,
xxvi, 1831, pp. 297, 298.
Trans. Nat. Hist. Soc. Northumb. and Durh., i, 1830, p. 1.

1831. LESS[ON, R. P.]   Observations sur la nouvelle espèce de Cygne [C. bewickii],
découverte par M. R. Wingate; par P.-J. Selby.   . . .   < *Féruss. Bull.*, 2ᵉ
sect., xxvi, 1831, pp. 297, 298.
Trans. Nat. Hist. Soc. Northumb. and Durh., i, 1830, p. 17.

1831. SWAINSON, W.   The Habits of the long-legged whistling Ducks [Dendrocygna]
of the West India Islands, and the Habits of the Sheldrake [Tadorna cornuta].
< *Loudon's Mag. Nat. Hist.*, iv, 1831, p. 474.
Merely a query. Cf. *op. cit.*, v, 1832, p. 203.

1831. YARRELL, W.   [On the Anatomy of Cereopsis novæ-hollandiæ, and on the relations between Natatores and Grallatores.]   < *P. Z. S.*, i, 1831, pp. 25, 26.

1831. YARRELL, W.   [Remarks on the structure of Cereopsis novæ-hollandiæ.]
< *Philos. Mag.*, ix, 1831, pp. 222, 223.
From *P. Z. S.*, Jan. 25, 1831, pp. 25, 26.

1832. ALLIS, T.   The Food of the Scoter Duck (Anas nigra Linn., Oidemia nigra
Flem.; and the Food of the Eider Duck (Anas mollissima Lin., Somateria
mollissima Flem.).   < *Loudon's Mag. Nat. Hist.*, v, 1832, p. 733.

1832. ALLIS, T.   Reply to T. K.'s Queries ([tom. cit.] p. 397,) on the Windpipe, Plumage, and Weight of the Dun Diver [Mergus castor].   < *Loudon's Mag. Nat.
Hist.*, v, 1832, pp. 766, 767, figg. 126–128.

1832. ANON.   A Flock of Egyptian Geese [Chenalopex ægyptiacus] seen besids the
Tweed at Carham.   < *Loudon's Mag. Nat. Hist.*, v, 1832, pp. 565, 566.

1832. ANON.   Teal [Querquedula carolinensis].   < *Loudon's Mag. Nat. Hist.*, v, 1832,
p. 473.

1832. "A SUBSCRIBER." Habits of the long-legged whistling Ducks [Dendrocygna], and of the Sheldrake [Tadorna cornuta]. < *Loudon's Mag. Nat. Hist.*, v, 1832, p. 203.

Cf. *op. cit.*, iv, 1831, p. 474.

1832. BECKFRIIS, C. Skånska Svanjagten [Cygnus sp.]. < *Tidsk. f. Jägare och Naturf.*, i, 1832, pp. 78–83.

Not seen.

1832. BLACKWALL, J. Bemerkungen über eine kürzlich beschriebene Gattung Schwan [Cygnus bewickii]. < *Oken's Isis*, Bd. xxv, 1832, p. 661.

Auszug aus d. *Zool. Journ.*, Tom. v, No. xviii, 1830, p. 189.

1832. G[OATLEY], T. Notes on the Scoter (Anas nigra Lin., Oidemia nigra Flem.). < *Loudon's Mag. Nat. Hist.*, v, 1832, p. 82.

1832. HILL, W. H. A rare Variety of the Goose Family. < *Loudon's Mag. Nat. Hist.*, v, 1832, pp. 79, 80, fig. 33.

1832. K[NOX], T. Information and Queries on the Trachea, or Windpipe, of the Dun Diver (Mergus Castor). < *Loudon's Mag. Nat. Hist.*, v, 1832, p. 397.

1832. SELLS, W. Wild Ducks [in Chesapeake Bay]. < *Loudon's Mag. Nat. Hist.*, v, 1832, p. 452.

1832. SHARPLESS, J. T. Description of the American Wild Swan [Cygnus americanus], proving it to be a new species. < *Sillim. Am. Journ. Sci.*, xxii, 1832, pp. 83–90, pll. (figs. of sternum and trachea).

1832. SWAINSON, W. On those Birds which exhibit the typical perfection of the family of Anatidæ. < *Journ. Roy. Inst. London*, ii, 1832, pp. 11–29.

Not seen: title from Carus and Engelmann.—It seems to have passed for more than it was worth in 1832, when some queer quinarian quips, arrayed in learned ingenuity, were often mistaken for science.

1832. WATERTON, C. A Wigeon's [Mareca penelope] Nest in England. < *Loudon's Mag. Nat. Hist.*, v, 1832, p. 590.

1832. YARRELL, W. [On a hybrid between Anas (Cairina) moschata ♂ and A. domestica ♀.] < *P. Z. S.*, ii, 1832, p. 100.

1833. BLOXHAM, A. Geese from the Netherlands shot on the Trent. < *Loudon's Mag. Nat. Hist.*, vi, 1833, p. 450.

1833. BYERLEY, J. The Pride of Colour in Swans. < *Loudon's Mag. Nat. Hist.*, vi, 1833, pp. 139, 140.

1833. D[ENSON], J. A Duck that had strayed from Denmark (?) shot in Sussex. < *Loudon's Mag. Nat. Hist.*, vi, 1833, p. 450.

1833. FENNELL, J. Pride of Colour in the Black Swan [Cygnus atratus]. < *Loudon's Mag. Nat. Hist*, vi, 1833, p. 278.

1833. FENNELL, J. Enmity between the White Swan [Cygnus sp.] and the Black Swan [Cygnus atratus]. < *Loudon's Mag. Nat. Hist.*, vi, 1833, p. 514.

1833. HUNTER, P. A Pair of Ferruginous Ducks (Anas [Tadorna] rutila L.). < *Loudon's Mag. Nat. Hist.*, vi, 1833, pp. 141, 142.

Occurrence near Oxford.

1833. "J. C." The Question of the Wigeon's [Mareca penelope] breeding in England. < *Loudon's Mag. Nat. Hist.*, vi, 1833, p. 384.

1833. SCOULER, J. The Egyptian Goose (Anas [Chenalopex] ægyptiaca). < *Loudon's Mag. Nat. Hist.*, vi, 1833, p. 514.

Near Glasgow, Nov., 1832.

1833. SWAINSON, [W.] Swainson über die typischen Vögel der Anatidae, Fig. < *Oken's Isis*, Jahrg. 1833, pp. 944, 945.

Auszug aus d. *Journ. Roy. Inst.*, xxx, oder n. F., ii, Heft 4, Aug., 1832, p. 11.

1833. VIGORS, N. A. [On a New Species of Barnacle Goose (Bernicla sandvicensis) from the Sandwich Islands, presented by Lady Glengall.] < *P. Z. S.*, i, 1833, p. 65.

1833. "W. L." [Habits of] Cygnus Bewickii. < *Loudon's Mag. Nat. Hist.*, vi, 1833, pp. 449, 450.

1833. WRIGHT, M. V. Iakttagelser öfver Gräsandhannens [Anas boschas] färgför-ändringar i första året. < *Tidsk. f. Jägare o. Naturf.*, ii, 1833, pp. 473, 474.
Not seen.

1833. WRIGHT, W. V. Gräsandens (Anas boschas) sommardrägt. < *Tidsk. f. Jägare o. Naturf.*, ii, 1833, pp. 674–676.
Not seen.

1833. YARRELL, W. [On the trachea of Anas [Chloephaga] magellanica.] < *P. Z. S.*, i, 1833, pp. 3, 4.

1834. ANON. Ducks with the Toes not connected by a Web or Membrane, and the Up-per Mandible imperfect: presumed to have proceeded from a Union between the Domestic Duck [Anas boschas] and Domestic Fowl. < *Loudon's Mag. Nat. Hist.*, vii, 1834, pp. 516, 517.

1834. BRETON, —. [On the Habits of the Musk Duck of New Holland (Hydrobates [Biziura] lobatus, Temm.).] < *P. Z. S.*, ii, 1834, p. 19.

1834. EKSTRÖM, C. U. Bidrag till Ejder-fogelns [Somateria mollissima] historia. < *Tidsk. f. Jägare o. Naturf.*, iii, 1834, pp. 1043–1045.
Not seen.

1834. EKSTRÖM, C. U. Knipans (Anas Clangula Lin. [Clangula glaucium] färgförän-dring. < *Tidsk. f. Jägare o. Naturf.*, iii, 1834, pp. 1048–1051.
Not seen.

1834. FISCHER, G. Anas cucullata nova species Camtschatica. < *Nouv. Mém. Soc. Imp. Nat. Moscou*, iii, 1834, pp. 109–112, pl. ix.
Descr. orig. *Bull. Soc. Imp. Nat. Mosc.*, iii, 1831, pp. 278–280.

1834. FRIES, B. F. Al-fogelns [Harelda glacialis] ruggning om våren. < *Tidsk. f. Jägare o. Naturf.*, iii, 1834, pp. 1045–1048.
Not seen.

1834. LAFRESNAYE, F. DE. Oie. Anas. Linné. O. de Gambie. A. Gambensis, Linn., Lath. < *Guér. Mag. de Zool.*, 4e année, 1834, classe ii, notices xxix, xxx, pll. xxix, xxx.

1834. LANGMAN, A. Försök attuppföda och tämja en Ejderunge [Somateria mollis-sima]. < *Tidsk. f. Jägare o. Naturf.*, iii, 1834, pp. 883–885.
Not seen.

1834. LÖFFLER, H. Ueber die wilden Schwäne. Mit Nachwort von K. E. v. Baer. < *Preuss. Provinzialbl.*, xi, 1834, pp. 131–142.
Mir nicht zugänglich.

1834. MARSHALL, J. D. On the Green-winged Teals of America and Britain [Quer-quedula carolinensis and Q. crecca]. < *Loudon's Mag. Nat. Hist.*, vii, 1834, pp. 7–9, figg. 1, 2.

1834. STANLEY, Lord. [Letter on the Breeding of the Sandwich Island Goose (Ber-nicla sandvicensis, Vig.).] < *P. Z. S.*, ii, 1834, pp. 41–43.

1834. STANLEY, Lord. [Note on a specimen of the Bernicla sandvicensis, Vig., hatched at Knowsley.] < *Lond. and Edinb. Philos. Mag.*, v, 1834, pp. 233–235.
From *P. Z. S.*, May 27, 1834, pp. 41–43.

1834. "W. B. C." A Ferruginous Duck or Ruddy Goose (Anas [Tadorna] rutila). < *Loudon's Mag. Nat. Hist.*, vii, 1834, p. 151.
Shot on the coast of Suffolk.

1834. YARRELL, [W.] Charactere von Cygnus bewickii einer [kürzlich] neuen Gat-tung. < *Oken's Isis*, Bd. xxvii, 1834, p. 803.
Auszug aus d. *Philos. Mag.*, Bd. vii, 1830, p. 194.

1834. YARRELL, [W.] Der Leib von Cereopsis novae Hollandiae [u. s. w.]. < *Oken's Isis*, Bd. xxvii, 1834, p. 817.
Auszug aus d. *Philos. Mag.*, Bd. ix, 1831, p. 222.

1835. ANON.   Length of the Life of a Gander.   < *Loudon's Mag. Nat. Hist.*, viii, 1835, p. 509.

  From the *Morning Chronicle*, Apr. 16, 1835. 37 yrs. 9 mos. 6 days.

1835. BREHM, C. L.   Etwas über das Sommerkleid der Enten-Männchen.   < *Oken's Isis*, Bd. xxviii, 1835, pp. 238–240.

1835. BREHM, C. L.   Das Sommerkleid des weissen Sägermännchens, Mergus albellus Linn.   < *Oken's Isis*, Bd. xxviii, 1835, pp. 239, 240.

1835. HERON, R.   [Note on the History of a Black Swan, Cygnus atratus.]   •<*P. Z. S.*, iii, 1835, pp. 106, 107.

1835. JARDINE, W.   The Wigeon [Mareca penelope] has been found breeding, wild, in the North of Scotland.   < *Loudon's Mag. Nat. Hist.*, viii, 1835, p. 509.

1835. LAFRESNAYE, F. DE.   Canard. Anas. Linné. Anas tadornoïdes. William Jardine, pl. 62.—New-Holland Shildrack. Lat., gen. hist., vol. 10, p. 306.—Le Canard kasarka, Anas rutila, Pallas, Temm., man. 832.—Anas kasarka, Gmel. Lat. (Dans une livrée jusqu'alors non décrite).   < *Guér. Mag. de Zool.*, 5e sér., année 1835, classe ii, notice xxxvi, pl. xxxvi.

1835. "S. D. W."   Remarks on the Habits of the Canada Goose (A'nser canadénsis Willughby).   < *Loudon's Mag. Nat. Hist.*, viii, 1835, pp. 255–258.

1835. STANLEY, *Lord.*   Ueber Bernicla sandvicensis.   < *Oken's Isis*, Bd. xxviii, 1835, p. 1028.

  P. Z. S., ii, 1834, pp. 41–43.

1835. TREVELYAN, W. C.   A wild Bird of the Family Anátidæ deemed a hybrid one.   < *London's Mag. Nat. Hist.*, viii, 1835, p. 509.

1835. WATERTON, C.   Notes on the Habits of the Wigeon [Mareca penelope].   < *Loudon's Mag. Nat. Hist.*, viii, 1835, pp. 361–364.

1835. WATERTON, C.   Notes on the Habits of the Mallard [Anas boschas].   < *Loudon's Mag. Nat. Hist.*, viii, 1835, pp. 541–545.

1835. YARRELL, W.   Ueber die Geschlechtstheile eines Bastard-Männchens von dem Bisam-Enterich und der gemeinen Ente.   < *Oken's Isis*, Bd. xxviii, 1835, p. 428.

  P. Z. S., pt. ii, 1832, p. 100.   (*Cairina moschata* ♂ × ♀ *Anas boschas.*)

1836. BRANDT, J. F.   Note sur l'Anser canadensis et l'Anser pictus de la "Zoographie" de Pallas.   < *St. Pétersb. Acad. Sci. Bull.*, i, 1836, p. 37.

  Pas vue moi-même: le titre tiré du *Roy. Soc. Cat.*

1836. MORRIS, F. O.   A kind of Duck, deemed a wild Hybrid, between the Pintail Duck [Dafila acuta] and the Common Wild Duck [Anas boschas].   <*Loudon's Mag. Nat. Hist.*, ix, 1836, p. 107.

1837. [ANON.]   The tongues of Ducks [as dainties of Chinese epicures].   < *Sillim. Am. Journ. Sci.*, xxxi, 1837, p. 193.

1837. HERON, R.   [Ueber Cygnus australis.]   <*Oken's Isis*, Bd. xxx, 1837, p. 143.

  P. Z. S., 1835, p. 106.

1837. LAFRESNAYE, [F. DE.]   Ueber eine neue Abtheilung unter den Enten.   <*Oken's Isis*, Bd. xxx, 1837, pp. 726, 727.

  L'Institut, iv, 1836, No. 151.

1837. WEISSENBORN, W.   Wildgeese in Germany.   <*Charlesw. Mag. Nat. Hist.*, i, 1837, pp. 644, 645.

1837. YARRELL, W.   Description of the Organ of Voice in a [lately] new Species of Wild Swan (Cygnus Buccinator, Richardson).   < *Trans. Linn. Soc.*, xvii, pt. iv, 1837, pp. 1–4, pl. i.

  Very full, with excellent figures.

1838. BAILLON, —.   Observations sur le cygne de Bewick [Cygnus bewickii].—Lettre de M. Baillon à M. de Blainville.   (Abbeville, octobre 1838.)   < *Compt. Rend. de l'Acad. Sci. Paris*, vii, 1838, pp. 1021, 1022.

1838. BARTLETT, A. D. Plumage of the Smew [Mergellus albellus]. < *Charlesw. Mag. Nat. Hist.*, ii, 1838, p. 398.

1838. BLAINVILLE, [M. H. D.] DE. Remarques de M. de Blainville à l'occasion de la lettre précédente [par M. Baillon, sur le cygne de Bewick (Cygnus bewickii)]. < *Compt. Rend. de l'Acad. Sci. Paris*, vii, 1838, p. 1022–1026.

1838. BLAINVILLE, [M. H. D.] DE. [Sur quelques points intéressans de l'histoire des Cygnes.] < *Revue Zoologique*, i, 1838, pp. 307, 308.

1838. BLYTH, E. Adult plumage of the female Smew [Mergellus albellus]. < *Charlesw. Mag. Nat. Hist.*, ii, 1838, pp. 395, 396.

1838. BLYTH, E. Plumage of the Smew Merganser [Mergellus albellus]. < *Charlesw. Mag. Nat. Hist.*, ii, 1838, p. 451.

1838. EYTON, T. C. A Monograph of the Anatidæ or Duck-tribe, . . . London. Longmann & Co. 1838. 4to. pll. 24, many cuts.
    Not seen.

1838. LESSON, R. P. Description faite sur la nature du Grand Harle ou du Merganser [Mergus merganser]. < *Revue Zoologique*, i, 1838, pp. 8–10.

1838. NAUMANN, J. F. Zwei Arten Singschwäne in Deutschland. < *Arch. f. Naturg.*, 1838, (1), pp. 361–371, Taf. viii, ix.
    Nebst Zusätzen vom Herausg., pp. 367–371. *Cygnus musicus*, pl. viii, figg. a–d; *C. islandicus*, pl. viii, figg. 2 e–h; *C. bewickii*, pl. ix.

1838. YARRELL, W. [On a New Species of Swan (Cygnus immutabilis).] < *P. Z. S.*, vi, 1838, p. 19.

1838. YARRELL, W. Beschreibung des Stimmorgans eines [kürzlich] neuen Schwans, Cygnus buccinator Richardson. < *Oken's Isis*, Bd. xxxi, 1838, p. 404.
    Aus d. *Linn. Trans.*, xvii, pt. iv, 1837, pp. 1–4.

1839. BAILLON, —. [Ueber Cygnus bewickii.] < *Oken's Isis*, Bd. xxxii, 1839, pp. 394, 395.
    L'Institut, Nr. 260, p. 420.

1839. BARTLETT, A. D. On a new British species of the genus Anser [phœnicopus], with remarks on the nearly-allied species. < *P. Z. S.*, vii, 1839, pp. 2–4.
    Treating of *A. segetum, A. cinereus, A. albifrons, A. phœnicopus*, sp. n., p. 3.

1839. BLAINVILLE, [M. H. D.] DE. [Ueber die Arten der Sippe Cygnus.] < *Oken's Isis*, Bd. xxxii, 1839, p. 395.
    L'Institut, Nr. 260.

1839. LESSON, R. P. Note sur le genre Cygne. < *Revue Zoologique*, ii, 1839, pp. 321–324.
    Synopsis de 8 espèces.

1839. PELERIN, W. G.* On the Structural differences observable in the Crania of the four British Species of the Genus Cygnus. < *Charlesw. Mag. Nat. Hist.*, iii, 1839, pp. 178–180, fig. 29.

1839. PROCTOR, W. Clangula barrovii [islandica], a Native of Iceland. < *Ann. Nat. Hist.*, iv, 1839, pp. 140, 141.

1839. REINHARDT, J. Om den islandske Svane [Cygnus islandicus]. < *Krøyer's Naturhist. Tidsk.*, ii, 1839, pp. 527–532.

1839. RÜPPELL, E. Ornithologische Miscellen. . . . < *Mus. Senckenb.*, iii, Heft i, 1839, pp. 1–44.
    Mir nicht zugänglich. Monographieen der Gattung *Cygnus*, u. s. w.

1839. RÜPPELL, [E.] Allgemeine Bemerkungen über die Gattungen der Schwäne und eine besondere Beschreibung von Anas gambensis. < *Oken's Isis*, Bd. xxxii, 1839, p. 713.
    Auszug aus *Mus. Senkenb.*, iii, Heft i, 1839, p. 1.

1840. DERBY, *Earl of.* [Note on certain hybrid Anatidæ.] < *P. Z. S.*, viii, 1840, p. 33.

1840. EYTON, T. C. Remarks on the Skeletons of the common tame Goose, the Chinese Goose, and the Hybrid between the two. < *Charlesw. Mag. Nat. Hist.*, iv, 1840, pp. 90–92.

1840. JOLY, —. Passage accidental d'un oiseau de la mer Glaciale [Harelda glacialis] dans le midi de la France. < *Compt. Rend. de l'Acad. Sci.*, x, 1840, p. 250.
Extrait d'une lettre à M. Flourens.

1840. LEIB, G. C. Description of a New Species of Fuligula [grisea]. < *Journ. Acad. Nat. Sci. Phila.*, viii, "1839", not pub. till 1840, pp. 170, 171.
Printed slip accompanying states it is *F. labradora* juv. [*Camptolœmus.*]

1840. NILSSON, [S.] Professor Nilsson förevisade en fårglagd teckning af en tam Anka [Anas boschas], som antagit den vilda Andrakens fårg och utseende. < *Förhandl. Skandin. Naturf. och Läkere i Götheborg*, år 1839, 1840, p. 133.

1841. DESLONGCHAMPS, E. Cryptogames développées, pendant la vie, à la surface interne des poches aériennes d'un Canard eider, Anas [Somateria] mollissima, Latham. < *Compt. Rend. de l'Acad. Sci.*, xii, 1841, pp. 1110–1117.

1841. DESLONGCHAMPS, E. Note sur les mœurs du Canard Eider (Anas [Somateria] mollissima Latham), et sur des moisissures developpées, pendant la vie, à la surface interne des poches aériennes d'un de ces animaux. < *Ann. des Sci. Nat.*, 2ᵉ sér., xv, 1841, pp. 371–379, pl. ii B.

1841. [DESLONGCHAMPS, E.] On Parasites, Animal and Vegetable, occurring in Living Beings; and especially of a Cryptogamous Plant growing in the Air-Cells of an Eider-Duck [Somateria mollissima], and destroying it. < *Edinb. New Philos. Journ.*, xxxi, 1841, pp. 371–376.
Confer *Compt. Rend.*, 1841, pp. 1110–1117.

1841. GOULD, J. [Description and Exhibition of Nettapus pulchellus, sp. n.] < *P. Z. S.*, ix, 1841, p. 89.

1841. GOULD, J. [Characters of a New Genus and Species of Anatidæ (Merganetta armata).] < *P. Z. S.*, ix, 1841, pp. 95, 96.

1841. LAFRESNAYE, [F.] DE. Sur des Métis provenus d'une Oie de Guinée et d'une Oie à cravate. < *Revue Zoologique*, iv, 1841, pp. 141–143.

1841. LEIB, G. C. [On the Nest and Eggs of Fulica americana and Anas discors.] < *Proc. Acad. Nat. Sci. Phila.*, i, 1841, pp. 124, 125.

1841. REINHARDT, J. Ueber den isländischen Schwan [Cygnus islandicus]. < *Oken's Isis*, Bd. xxxiv, 1841, pp. 417–421.
Kröyer's Naturh. Zeitsch., Bd. ii, Heft 5, pp. 527–532.

1841. YARRELL, W. [On the Trachea of a Male Spur-winged Goose, Anser Gambensis and Chenalopex Gambensis of authors (Plectropterus gambensis).] < *P. Z. S.*, ix, 1841, pp. 70, 71.

1842. ABBOTT, S. L. [On the supposed poisoning of two Swans by Nerium oleander.] < *Proc. Boston Soc. Nat. Hist.*, i, 1842, p. 62.

1842. BABINGTON, C. C. Cygnus guineensis [near Cambridge]. < *Ann. Mag. Nat. Hist.*, ix, 1842, p. 79.

1842. BELL, J. G. [On the specific validity of Fuligula minor.] < *Proc. Acad. Nat. Sci. Phila.*, i, 1842, pp. 141, 142.

1842. LAFRESNAYE, [F.] DE. Sur les mœurs de quelques Palmipèdes [Anatidæ]. < *Revue Zoologique*, v, 1842, pp. 71–73.

1842. LANDSBOROUGH, D. Longevity of Geese. < *Ann. Mag. Nat. Hist.*, viii, 1842, p. 474.
Sixty-four years.

1842. YARRELL, W. [On the Trachea of Plectropterus gambensis.] < *Ann. Mag. Nat. Hist.*, ix, 1842, p. 147.
From *P. Z. S.*, Sept. 14, 1841.

1843. BONAPARTE, C. [L.] Ueber Querquedula angustirostris. < *Oken's Isis*, Bd. xxxvi, 1843, pp. 403, 404.
Atti. Riun. Sci. Ital. Firenze, 1841, p. 317.

1844. ANON. Note on a prolific Duck [180 eggs in one season]. < *Zoologist*, ii, 1844, p. 727.

1844. ANON. Note on the Nidification of Swans [Cygnus sp.]. < *Zoologist*, ii, 1844, p. 669.

1844. FISHER, W. R. Notes on Ducks nesting in Trees. < *Zoologist*, ii, 1844, pp. 767, 768.

1844. G[ERBE], Z. [L'Oie d'Egypte (Anser [Chenalopex] ægyptiacus), une espèce définitivement acquise à l'ornithologie européenne.] < *Revue Zoologique*, vii, 1844, pp. 441, 442.

1844. GURNEY, J. H. Note on the occurrence of the Red-crested Whistling Duck [Fuligula rufina] in Norfolk. < *Zoologist*, ii, 1844, p. 576.

1844. HARDY, J. Enquiry respecting the manner in which the newly-hatched Wild Duck is conveyed to the Water. < *Zoologist*, ii, 1844, pp. 669-671.

1844. MANSELL, T. Note on the occurrence of the Scoter [Œdemia nigra] near Farnham. < *Zoologist*, ii, 1844, p. 455.

1845. BARTLETT, J. P. Occurrence of the Gadwall [Chaulelasmus streperus] in Kent. < *Zoologist*, iii, 1845, pp. 1025, 1026.

1845. DASHWOOD, J. M. Description of an Egg of the Common Duck [Anas boschas]. < *Zoologist*, iii, 1845, p. 1077.

1845. FISHER, W. R. Description of a New Duck. < *Zoologist*, iii, 1845, pp. 1137, 1138.
Apparently a hybrid between the Common and White-eyed Pochard, *Fuligula ferina* and *F. nyroca*. This is "Paget's Pochard," which later became *Fuligula ferinoides*, Bartl., *P. Z. S.*, 1847, p. 48.

1845. FRERE, H. T. Occurrence of Bewick's Swan [Cygnus bewickii] near Somersham and Godmanchester. < *Zoologist*, iii, 1845, pp. 942, 943.

1845. GERBE, Z. Note sur le Cygne Bewick. (Cignus [sic] Bewickii). < *Revue Zoologique*, viii, 1845, pp. 244-247.
Comparaison avec le Cygne sauvage.

1845. HEWGILL, J. Enquiry respecting a species of Duck. < *Zoologist*, iii, 1845, p. 943.

1845. NEWMAN, E. Note on Ducks &c. nestling in Trees. < *Zoologist*, iii, 1845, pp. 878, 879.

1845. NEWNHAM, W. O. Remarkable Duck's Egg. < *Zoologist*, iii, 1845, p. 1077.
Egg in egg.

1845. SCLATER, P. L. Occurrence of Aquatic Birds [3 spp. Anatidæ] near Odiham. < *Zoologist*, iii, 1845, p. 1077.

1845. SELYS-LONGCHAMPS, E. DE. Récapitulation des hybrides observées dans la famille des Anatidées. < *Bull. Acad. Bruxelles*, xii, 1845, pp. 335-355.
Pas vue moi-même: le titre tiré de Carus et Engelmann.

1846. ANON. Occurrence of the Black Swan (Cygnus atratus, Bennett), in Scotland. < *Zoologist*, iv, 1846, pp. 1501, 1502.

1846. BARTLETT, A. D. Eine für England neue Gans [Anser phœnicopus] verglichen mit andern. < *Oken's Isis*, Bd. xxxix, 1846, pp. 559-560.
P. Z. S., vii, 1839, p. 2.

1846. BELL, R. J. Occurrence of Steller's Western Duck [Fuligula dispar] at Filby in Yorkshire. < *Zoologist*, iv, 1846, p. 1249.

1846. CABOT, S., JR. [Remarks on exhibition of Fuligula vallisneria from Massachusetts.] < *Proc. Boston Soc. Nat. Hist.,* ii, 1846, p. 89.

1846. CABOT, S , JR. [On the anatomy of Fuligula (Somateria) spectabilis.] < *Proc. Boston Soc. Nat. Hist.,* ii, 1846, pp. 93, 94.

1846. CABOT, S., JR. [Remarks on the supposed identity of Anas (Mareca) penelope and A. (M.) americana.] < *Proc. Boston Soc. Nat. Hist.,* ii, 1846, pp. 118–120. Anatomical comparison.

1846. FRERE, H. T. Remarks on the Tracheæ of Wild Geese. < *Zoologist,* iv, 1846, pp. 1249, 1250.

1846. FRERE, H. T. Norfolk Swan-fatting. < *Zoologist,* iv, 1846, p. 1250.

1846. FRERE, H. T. On the Rusty Tinge of the Plumage of Wild Swans [Cygnus bewickii]. < *Zoologist,* iv, 1846, p. 1300.

1846. KING, R. L. Singing of Swans. < *Zoologist,* iv, 1846, p. 1214.
Contends for the fact, in case of *Cygnus atratus!*

1846? LAWRENCE, G. N. Description of a New Species of Anser [nigricans]. < *Ann. Lyc. Nat. Hist. New York,* iv, 1846?, pp. 171, 172, pl. xii. (Read Mar. 16, 1846. Whole vol. pub. 1848.)
The article probably appeared in 1846, as it is copied into periodicals of 1847. The bird is a *Bernicla,* closely related to *B. brenta.*

1846. MORRIS, F. O. Extraordinary [non-palmate] Feet in a Duck. < *Zoologist,* iv, 1846, p. 1214.

1846. PLOMLEY, F. Occurrence of the Egyptian Goose [Chenalopex ægyptiacus] in Kent. < *Zoologist,* iv, 1846, p. 1501.

1846. SCLATER, P. L. Early appearance of the Tufted Duck [Fuligula cristata]. < *Zoologist,* iv, 1846, p. 1214.

1846. THOMPSON, W. Notice of a Surf Scoter, Oidemia perspicillata, Linn. (sp.), obtained on the coast of Ireland. < *Ann. Mag. Nat. Hist.,* xviii, 1846, pp. 368–371.

1846. TOMES, [R. F.] [Exhibition of a Female Specimen of the Bimaculated Duck (Anas glocitans).] < *P. Z. S.,* xiv, 1846, p. 121.

1846. WOLLASTON, T. V. Note on Cygnus atratus. < *Zoologist,* iv, 1846, pp. 1327–1331.
With reference to its alleged musical ability.

1846. WOLLEY, J. Note on the occurrence of the Black Swan [Cygnus atratus] in Britain. < *Zoologist,* iv, 1846, p. 1554.

1847. BAIRD, S. F. [Notice of a Hybrid between the Canvass-back Duck (Fuligula vallisneria) and the Common Duck (Anas boschas).] *Proc. Acad. Nat. Sci. Phila.,* iii, 1847, p. 209.

1847. BARTLETT, A. D. Description of a New Species of Fuligula [ferinoides]. < *P. Z. S.,* xv, 1847, pp. 48–50.
F. ferinoides, p. 48. The article includes a discussion of hybrid *Anatidæ.*

1847. BARTLETT, A. D. Description of a [lately] new species of Fuligula [ferinoides]. < *Ann. Mag. Nat. Hist.,* xix, 1847, pp. 422–424.
From *P. Z. S.,* Mar. 23, 1847, pp. 48–50.

1847. BIRD, W. F. W. The Pochard [Fuligula ferina] breeding in Norfolk. < *Zoologist,* v, 1847, p. 1782.

1847. CABOT, S., JR. [Remarks on exhibition of the sternum and trachea of Cygnus americanus.] < *Proc. Boston Soc. Nat. Hist.,* ii, 1847, p. 213.

1847. CABOT, S., JR. [Remarks on exhibition of Anas discors from Massachusetts.] < *Proc. Boston Soc. Nat. Hist,* ii, 1847, p. 226.

1847. FALCK, V. Description d'une livrée inconnue de l'Anas [Somateria] stelleri, supposé dans sa deuxième année, d'après des individus tués aux environs d'Helsingfors le 29 Mai 1841. < *Acta Soc. Scient. Fennicæ,* ii, 1847, pp. 61–64, pl. enlum.

1847. FEATHERSTONHAUGH, —. Ducks [Aix sponsa] hatched in Trees. < *Zoologist*, v, 1847, p. 1642.

1847. FEATHERSTONHAUGH, —. Swans on Lake Pepin. < *Zoologist*, v, 1847, p. 1698.

1847. FISHER, W. R. Description of and Notes respecting Paget's Pochard ('Fuligula ferinoides,') a New Species of the Duck Tribe. < *Zoologist*, v, 1847, pp. 1778–1782, figg.
    See FISHER, *Zool.*, iii, 1845, p. 1137, and BARTLETT, *P. Z. S.*, xv, 1847, p. 48.

1847. GLENCON, M. Account of a Black and White Mottled Swan, on the water in the demesne of the Earl of Shannon, Castle Martyr, County Cork. < *P. Z. S.*, xv, 1847, p. 97.

1847. GLENCON, M. Account of a Black and White Mottled Swan, on the water in the demesne of the Earl of Shannon, Castle Martyr, County Cork. < *Ann. Mag. Nat. Hist.*, xx, 1847, pp. 214, 215.
    From *P. Z. S.*, June 22, 1847, p. 97.

1847. LAWRENCE, G. N. Description of a [lately] new species of Anser [nigricans]. < *Am. Journ. Sci.*, iii, 1847, pp. 435, 436.
    From *Ann. Lyc. Nat. Hist. N. Y.*, iv, 1846?, p. 171, *q. v.*

1847. LAWRENCE, G. N. Description of a [lately] new species of Anser [nigricans]. < *Ann. Mag. Nat. Hist.*, xx, 1847, p. 214.
    From *Am. Journ, Sci.*, iii, May, 1847, p. 435.

1847. SPICER, W. W. Occurrence of the Scaup Duck [Fuligula marila] near Godalming. < *Zoologist*, v, 1847, pp. 1641, 1642.

1847. THOMPSON, W. Occurrence of the Ruddy Shieldrake (Tadorna rutila) in Ireland. < *Zoologist*, v, 1847, p. 1877.
    From *Ann. Mag. Nat. Hist.*, xx, p. 171.

1847. TOMES, R. F. Occurrence of the Bimaculated Duck [Anas glocitans, at Yarmouth]. < *Zoologist*, v, 1847, p. 1698.

1847. TYZENHAUZ, [C.] Notice sur la coloration accidentelle rose des Canards sauvages. < *Revue Zoologique*, x, 1847, pp. 273–275.

1847. WRIGHT, M. v. Bidrag till Prakt-Eiderns (Fuligula [Somateria] spectabilis, Bonap.) Natural-Historia. < *Acta Soc. Scient. Fennicæ*, ii, pt. ii, 1847, pp. 751–759, pl. xiii.

1848. BORRER, W., JR. Occurrence of the Egyptian Goose (Anser [Chenalopex] Egyptiacus) in Sussex. < *Zoologist*, vi, 1848, p. 2067.

1848. CLIBBORN, J. Occurrence of the White-fronted Goose (Anser albifrons) at Waterford. < *Zoologist*, vi, 1848, p. 2024.

1848. CURTLER, M. Occurrence of the Summer or Tree Duck [Aix sponsa] at Tenbury. < *Zoologist*, vi, 1848, p. 2067.

1848. DUNN, R. Occurrence of the Surf Scoter (Anas [Œdemia] perspicillata) in Shetland. < *Zoologist*, vi, 1848, p. 2067.

1848. FISHER, W. R. Note on the Bimaculated Duck (Anas glocitans). < *Zoologist* vi, 1848, p. 2026, fig.

1848. GOUGH, T. Capture of the Velvet and Common Scoters (Anas [Œdemia] fusca and A. [Œ.] nigra) on Windermere. < *Zoologist*, vi, 1848, p. 2230.

1848. JOHNSON, F. W. Occurrence of the Velvet Scoter (Anas [Œdemia] fusca) and Common Scoter (Anas [Œ.] nigra) in Suffolk. < *Zoologist*, vi, 1848, p. 2067

1848. JOHNSON, F. W. Occurrence of the Ferruginous Duck (Fuligula nyroca) in Suffolk. < *Zoologist*, vi, 1848, p. 2230.

1848. LAWSON, G. Occurrence of the Hooper or Wild Swan (Cygnus ferus) on the Tay. < *Zoologist*, vi, 1848, p. 2148.

1848. PARRY, ELLEN W. Account of a Hooper or Wild Swan (Cygnus ferus), nearly Seven Years in the possession of Rear-Admiral Webley Parry. < *Zoologist* vi, 1848, pp. 2024–2026.

1848. POOLE, J.   Occurrence of Bewick's Swan (Cygnus Bewickii) in Wexford Harbour.   < *Zoologist*, vi, 1848, p. 2026.

1848. SELYS-LONGCHAMPS, E. V.   Aufzählung der bekannten Bastarde in der Sippschaft der Anatiden.   < *Oken's Isis*, Bd. xli, 1848, pp. 226, 227.
    Bull. Acad. Roy. Sci. et Bel. Let. Bruxel., tom. xii, pt. 2, 1845, p. 335.   26 Bastarde.

1848. TYZENHAUS, [C.]   Coloration accidentelle rose des canards sauvages.   < *Arch. des Sc. Phys. et Nat. Genève*, vii, 1848, p. 338.
    Revue Zoologique, No. 9, 1847, pp. 273–275.

1849. BRANDT, J. F.   Fuligulam (Lampronettam) Fischeri novam avium rossicarum speciem praemissis observationibus ad Fuligularum generis sectionum et subgenerum quorundam characteres et affinitates spectantibus descripsit J. F. Brandt.   < *Mém. de l'Acad. St.-Pétersb.*, vi sér., *Sci. Nat.*, vi, 1849, pp. 1–15, pl.
    I. De *Fuligularum* generis divisionibus.   II. De *Thalassonettinis* nova *Fulig.* gen. sudivisione.   III. *Thalasson.* subdivisionis subgenera illustrata; *Lampronetta*, g. n., p. 5; *F. (L.) fischeri*, sp. n., p. 6, pl.; *Phylaconetta*, g. n., p. 9, typo *A. histrionica* L.   IV. *Fuligulæ (Lampronettæ) fischeri* maris adulti descriptio.   V. De ejusdem affinitatibus animadversiones quædam.

1849. BURROUGHES, T. H.   Occurrence of the Tufted Duck [Fuligula cristata] in Norfolk.   < *Zoologist*, vii, 1849, p. 2456.

1849. CASSIN, J.   [Remarks on a specimen of Anas rafflesii (Querquedula cyanoptera) from Louisiana.]   < *Proc. Acad. Nat. Sci. Phila.*, iv, 1849, p. 195.

1849. DAVY, J.   Notice of a peculiarity of structure observed in the Aorta of the Wild Swan [Cygnus ferus].   < *P. Z. S.*, xvii, 1849, pp. 28, 29.

1849. GURNEY, J. H.   Inquiry respecting the Gray-legged Goose [Anser cinereus].   < *Zoologist*, vii, 1849, p. 2622.
    Cf. *op. cit.*, viii, 1850, p. 2740.

1849. GURNEY, J. H.   Occurrence of the Gray-legged Goose (Anser palustris [cinereus]) in Norfolk.   < *Zoologist*, vii, 1849, p. 2456.

1849. HANSELL, P. E.   Remarkable Colour of the Yelk in the Eggs of the Common Duck [Anas boschas].   < *Zoologist*, vii, 1849, p. 2353.

1849. HULKE, J. W.   The Summer Duck (Anas [Aix] sponsa) a British Bird.   < *Zoologist*, vii, 1849, p. 2421.

1849. HULKE, J. W.   Occurrence of the Summer Duck (Anas [Aix] sponsa) near Deal.   < *Zoologist*, vii, 1849, p. 2353.

1849. KENNAWAY, G. G.   Curious Anecdote of a Duck.   < *Zoologist*, vii, 1849, p. 2456.

1849. LAFRESNAYE, F. DE.   Sur une femelle de Canard sauvage à plumage de mâle et sur une Métis de Canard pilet et de Canne sauvage.   < *Rev. et Mag. de Zool.*, i, 1849, pp. 177–179.

1849. NEWTON, A.   Inquiry respecting the Spur-winged Goose [Plectropterus gambensis].   < *Zoologist*, vii, 1849, p. 2421.

1849. NEWTON, A.   The Summer Duck [Aix sponsa] a British Bird.   < *Zoologist*, vii, 1849, p. 2529.

1849. SCHEEL, C.   Om Platypus [Fuligula] ferinus.   < *Krøyer's Naturh. Tidssk.*, n. Reihe, ii, 1849, p. 526.
    Not seen.

1849. WILLIAMS, J.   Occurrence of the Garganey (Anas querquedula [Querquedula circia]) near Tring.   < *Zoologist*, vii, 1849, p. 2421.

1849. WILLIAMS, J.   Occurrence of the Golden-eye (Anas clangula [Clangula glaucium]) at Tring.   < *Zoologist*, vii, 1849, p. 2421.

1850. AMHERST, F. H.   Sailing of the Swan.   < *Zoologist*, viii, 1850, p. 2802.

1850. BALDAMUS, E.   [Eier von Mergus merganser.]   < *Naumannia*, i, Heft ii, 1850, p. 100.

1850. BELL, T. Remarkable Act in a Duck [Cairina moschata]. < *Zoologist*, viii, 1850, pp. 2652, 2653.

1850. CASSIN, J. Notice of an American species of Duck [O. velvetina n. sp.] hitherto regarded as identical with the Oidemia fusca, (Linn.) < *Proc. Acad. Nat. Sci. Phila.*, v, Dec., 1850, pp. 126, 127.

1850. COOKE, R. B. Tufted Duck (Anas fuligula [Fuligula cristata]) breeding in Malham Waters. < *Zoologist*, viii, 1850, pp. 2879, 2880.

1850. DAVY, J. Notice of a peculiarity of Structure observed in the Aorta of the Wild Swan [Cygnus ferus]. < *Ann. Mag. Nat. Hist.*, v, 1850, pp. 139, 140.
    From *P. Z. S.*, Mar. 13, 1849, pp. 28, 29.

1850. DUFF, J. Occurrence of Rare Anatidæ, &c., near Bishop Auckland. < *Zoologist*, viii, 1850, p. 2773.

1850. ELLMAN, J. B. Occurrence of the Egyptian Goose [Chenalopex ægyptiacus] at Pevensey, Sussex. < *Zoologist*, viii, 1850, p. 2773.

1850. ELLMAN, J. B. Occurrence of Rare Anatidæ in Sussex. < *Zoologist*, viii, 1850, p. 2773.

1850. FOSTER, T. W. Occurrence of the Pink-footed Goose (Anser brachyrhynchus) and Brent Goose (Anser [Bernicla] Brenta) near Wisbeach. < *Zoologist*, viii, 1850, pp. 2772, 2773.

1850. FOSTER, T. W. Occurrence of the Wild Swan (Cygnus ferus) and Bewick's Swan (C. Bewickii) near Wisbeach. < *Zoologist*, viii, 1850, p. 2773.

1850. FOSTER, T. W. Occurrence of the Goosander (Mergus Merganser), Red-breasted Merganser (M. Serrator), and Smew (M. albellus) [in England]. < *Zoologist*, viii, 1850, pp. 2774, 2775.

1850. GRANTHAM, G. Occurrence of the Egyptian Goose (Anser [Chenalopex] Ægyptiacus) in Sussex. < *Zoologist*, viii, 1850, pp. 2772, 2773.

1850. GURNEY, J. H. A Hybrid between a Cravat Canada Gander [Bernicla canadensis] and a Bernicle Goose [Bernicla leucopsis]. < *Zoologist*, viii, 1850, p. 2969.

1850. HALL, T. Occurrence of the Red-breasted Merganser (Mergus Serrator) in the Thames. < *Zoologist*, viii, 1850, p. 2775.

1850. HIGGINS, E. T. Description of a Duck shot near Dunbar. < *Zoologist*, viii, 1850, pp. 2773, 2774.

1850. HOPE, W. J. Occurrence of the Goosander (Mergus merganser) on the Severn. < *Zoologist*, viii, 1850, p. 2853.

1850. [JARDINE, W.] Casarca leucoptera, Blyth [n. sp.]. < *Jard. Contrib. Orn.*, 1850, p. 141, pl. lxiv.

1850. JONES, J. M. Occurrence of the Merganser (Merganser [Mergus] serrator) near Montgomery. < *Zoologist*, viii, 1850, pp. 2705, 2706.

1850. K[IRTLAND], J. P. Editorial Correspondence. < *The Family Visitor*, i, No. 9, 1850, p. 72.
    Relating to domestication of *Aix sponsa*.

1850. MATTHEWS, A., *and* MATTHEWS, H. Reply to Mr. Gurney's Inquiry [Zool., p. 2622] respecting the Gray-legged Goose [Anser cinereus]. < *Zoologist*, viii, 1850, pp. 2740, 2741.

1850. MILNER, W. M. E. Occurrence of the Pink-footed Goose (Anser branchyrhynchus [sic]) near York. < *Zoologist*, viii, 1850, p. 2705.

1850. NEWMAN, E. Occurrence of the Bimaculated Duck (Anas glocitans) in the Fens of Lincolnshire. < *Zoologist*, viii, 1850, p. 2652.

1850. NEWMAN, E. Occurrence of the Swan Goose (Anser [Cygnopsis] Cygnoides) in Norfolk. < *Zoologist*, viii, 1850, p. 2705.

1850. NEWTON, A.   Variety of the Pink-footed Goose (Anser brachyrhynchus). <*Zoologist*, viii, 1850, p. 2802.

1850. NORMAN, G.   Occurrence of Wild Swans [Cygnus ferus] near Hull. <*Zoologist*, viii, 1850, p. 2773.

1850. PEACOCK, E.   Ducks Nesting in Trees. <*Zoologist*, viii, 1850, p. 2774.

1850. POWYS, T. L.   Occurrence of the Smew (Mergus albellus) in Northamptonshire. <*Zoologist*, viii, 1850, p. 2775.

1850. RISING, R.   Occurrence of the Ferruginous Duck (Anas ferruginea [Fuligula nyroca]) near Great Yarmouth. <*Zoologist*, viii, 1850, p. 2803.

1850. RUDD, T. S.   Occurrence of the Ferruginous Duck (Anas ferruginea [Fuligula nyroca]) near Redcar. <*Zoologist*, viii, 1850, p. 2773.

1850. TOBIAS, R.   [Mergus merganser hat im Jahre 1844 an der Oder gebrütet.] <*Naumannia*, i, Heft ii, 1850, pp. 99, 100.

1851. [BALDAMUS, E.]   [Fuligula homeyeri (Baed. n. sp.).]   <*Naumannia*, i, Heft iv, 1851, p. 90.
    Original-Notiz, ohne Beschreibung. Cf. *op. cit.*, ii, Heft i, 1852, pp. 12–15, pl.

1851. EVANS, J.   The Domestic or Mute Swan [Cygnus olor] in the Leamington Gardens. <*Zoologist*, ix, 1851, pp. 3208, 3209.

1851. GREEN, J.   Occurrence of the Egyptian Goose [Chenalopex ægyptiacus] at Yarmouth, and the Pink-footed Goose [Anser brachyrhynchus] at Ely. <*Zoologist*, ix, 1851, p. 3175.

1851. GURNEY, J. H.   Note on the Changes of Plumage which occur periodically in the Male Birds of several different Species of Ducks [Anatidæ]. <*Zoologist*, ix, 1851, p. 3116.

1851. GURNEY, J. H.   Longevity of the Nyroca Duck [Fuligula nyroca]. <*Zoologist*, ix, 1851, pp. 3116, 3117.

1851. GURNEY, S., JR.   Remarks on the Swan. <*Zoologist*, ix, 1851, p. 3234.

1851. GURNEY, S., JR.   Remarks on the Egyptian Goose [Chenalopex ægyptiacus.] <*Zoologist*, ix, 1851, p. 3234.

1851. HARRISON, J.   Occurrence of the Egyptian Goose [Chenalopex ægyptiacus] on Derwent Lake. <*Zoologist*, ix, 1851, p. 3175.

1851. LAFRESNAYE, [F.] DE.   Sur une espèce de Canard presumée être une variété mélanienne de l'Anas boschas. <*Rev. et Mag. de Zool.*, iii, 1851, pp. 580–583.
    Cf. *Anas purpureo-viridis* de Schinz.

1851. NORMAN, A. M.   Hybrid between the Common Mallard [Anas boschas] and the Pintail Duck [Dafila acuta]. <*Zoologist*, ix, 1851, p. 3175.

1851. OSWALD, —   [Communication of some remarks by Mr. Mack on the fact of black eggs being laid by a white Duck of the ordinary domestic breed.] <*P. Z. S.*, xix, 1851, p. 192.

1852. BÄDEKER, [—.]   Fuligula homeyeri. <*Naumannia*, ii, Heft i, 1852, pp. 12–15, (hierzu eine Tafel als Titelkupfer des 2ten Heftes dieses Bandes.)
    Beschreibung.

1852. BELL, J. [G.]   Description of a New Species of the genus Fuligula [viola]. <*Ann. Lyc. Nat. Hist. New York*, v, 1852, pp. 219, 220.   (Read Aug. 30, 1851.)

1852. BOND, F.   Occurrence of the Egyptian Goose (Chenalopex Egyptiacus, Gould) in Cambridgeshire. <*Zoologist*, x, 1852, p. 3712.

1852. GURNEY, S., JR.   Swans breeding at the age of Two Years. <*Zoologist*, x, 1852, p. 3536.

1852. GURNEY, J. H.   Note on an unusual occurrence of the Red-breasted Merganser [Mergus serrator, at Lowestoft, in July]. <*Zoologist*, x, 1852, p. 3599.

1852. HUGHES, E. I. R.   Curious want of Instinct in young Ducks. <*Zoologist*, x, 1852, p. 3579.

1852. NEWTON, E. Occurrence of the Harlequin Duck [Histrionicus torquatus] in Banffshire. < *Zoologist*, x, 1852, p. 3331.

1852. THOMPSON, W. Anas [Harelda] glacialis [in Britain]. < *Ann. Mag. Nat. Hist.*, 2d ser., ix, 1852, p. 156.

1852. TOBIAS, L. [Mergus merganser bei Grüneberg in Schlesien brütend.] < *Naumannia*, ii, Heft i, 1852, p. 102.

1852. TOBIAS, L. [Cygnus musicus bei Grüneberg in Schlesien.] < *Naumannia*, ii, Heft i, 1852, p. 102.

1853. ANON. How Eider [Somateria mollissima] Down is Gathered. < *Harper's New Monthly Mag.*, vi, 1853, pp. 784–786.
> Process and perils of procuring down on the European arctic coast.

1853. BALDAMUS, E. [Platypus marilus (Fuligula marila) in der Nähe von Braunschweig brütend; u. s. w.] < *Naumannia*, iii, 1853, pp. 337–339.

1853. BÖCK, —. Die Pracht-Eiderente [Somateria spectabilis] vorgekommen an der preussischen Kuste. < *J.f. O.*, i, 1853, p. 371.

1853. DYHR, —. [Anas falcaria Pall., funnen i Sverige.] < *Öfvers. Kongl. Vetensk.- Akad. Förh.*, 1853, pp. 227, 228.

1853. GLOGER, C. W. L. Das Fortschwimmen der Enten [Anatidæ spp.] unter dem Wasser. < *J.f. O.*, i, 1853, pp. 381–383.

1853. GLOGER, C. W. L. Die Neigung der Enten-Arten [Anatidæ] zur Vermischung durch Begattung mit einander. < *J.f. O.*, i, 1853, pp. 409–418.

1853. KJÄRBÖLLING, N. Ueber Clangula mergoides, n. sp.? (Beil. 4. zum Protok. d. siebenten Ornithol.-Versam. zu Halberstadt.) < *Naumannia*, iii, 1853, pp. 327–332.
> Cf. *J.f, O.*, i, 1853, Extrah., (1854), pp. 29–32.

1853. MACK, —. [Black eggs laid by white domestic Duck (Anas boschas).] < *Ann. Mag. Nat. Hist.*, 2d ser., xii, 1853, p. 213.
> From *P. Z. S.*, May 27, 1851, p. 192.

1853. MARTIN, L. Anas [Aix] sponsa Lin. in der Nähe von Berlin geschossen. < *J. f. O.*, i, 1853, pp. 156–158.
> Mit Bemerkungen des Herausgebers und von C. W. L. Gloger.

1853. MARTIN, L. Zur Verfärbung des Gefieders, namentlich bei Anas [Œdemia] nigra. < *J.f. O.*, i, 1853, pp. 208–212.

1853. MOGGRIDGE, M. On the Habits of the Wigeon [Mareca penelope]. < *Ann. Mag. Nat. Hist.*, 2d ser., xi, 1853, p. 158.
> Nothing beyond the fact of observing it "last summer."

1853. MÜNTER, —. Anas [Somateria] spectabilis Lin. an der pommerschen Küste erlegt. < *J.f. O.*, i, 1853, p. 207.

1853. MÜNTER, —. Anas Tadorna [Tadorna cornuta] Lin. als Hausthier. < *J.f. O.*, i, 1853, p. 302.

1853. NAUMANN, J. F. Zur Erklärung des Titelkupfers. < *Naumannia*, iii, 1853, pp 5–8.
> *Anserinæ;* fig. A, B, C, *Anser arvensis;* fig. D, E, F, *Anser segetum.*

1853. SCHLEGEL, H. Verfärbung des Gefieders. < *J.f. O.*, i, 1853, p. 67.
> *Anas carolinensis, Aix galericulata.*

1853. SMITH, A. C. Young Ducks nursed by a Cat. < *Zoologist*, xi, 1853, p. 3946.

1853. STEVENSON, H. Note on the late appearance of the Common Scoter (Anas [Œdemia] nigra) in Norfolk. < *Zoologist*, xi, 1853, p. 3989.

1854. ALTUM, B. Ueber eine neue(?) Kleine Schwanenart. < *Naumannia*, iv, 1854, pp. 145–149, nebst Taf. i, u. ii, figg. 1–4; auch p. 398 (Druckfehler).
> Cf. *tom. cit.*, p. 327.

1854. ANDREWS, [W.]   [On the Irish specimen of Malacorhynchus membranaceus.]
< *Nat. Hist. Rev.*, i, 1854, p. 25.

1854. BÖCK, —.   Die Mauser von Platypus [Œdemia] niger.   < *J. f. O.*, ii, 1854, pp. 309–312.
Zusätze d. Herausg.

1854. CABOT, S. [JR.]   [On a specimen of a hybrid Duck, a cross between the Golden-
eye (Clangula americana) and the Hooded Merganser (Mergus cucullatus).]
< *Proc. Boston Soc. Nat. Hist.*, v, 1854, pp. 57, 118–120.
From Scarborough, Maine; full description; proposed to be named *Clangula mergiformis.*

1854. GOULD, J.   [Exhibition of male and female specimens of a very rare English
Duck (Fuligula ferinoïdes).]   < *P. Z. S.*, xxii, 1854, p. 95.

1854. HARTLAUB, G.   Vorläufiges über die von B. Altum beschriebene kleine Schwanenart.   < *Naumannia*, iv, 1854, pp. 327–329.
Cf. *tom. cit.*, p. 145.—Dass die von Altum beschriebene Art keine andere als der 1831 von
Sharpless in den 22sten Bande von Silliman's *Amer. Journ. Sci.* auf S. 83 beschriebene *Cygnus americanus* sein kann. (Vergl. *op. cit.* v, pp. 101, 258.)

1854. KJÄRBÖLLING, N.   Ueber Clangula mergoïdes Kjärb., als wahre, unverkennbare
Tauchente.   (Anhang IV. zu Berichte über die VII. Jahresversammlung der
deutschen Ornithologen-Gesellschaft.)   < *J. f. O.*, i, 1853, Extrah., (1854), pp.
29–32.
Cf. *Naum.*, iii, 1853, pp. 327–332.

1854. LE PRESTRE, —.   Observations sur le Cygne noir [Cygnus atratus, en domes-
ticité].   < *Bull. Soc. Acclim.*, i, 1854, pp. 409–414.

1854. MARTIN, L.   Wie zahme Gänse [Anser] begierige Fleischfresser wurden.   < *J.
f. O.*, ii, 1854, pp. 179, 180.

1854. MILNER, W. M. E.   Tufted Duck [Fuligula cristata] breeding at Osberton.
< *Zoologist*, xii, 1854, pp. 4440, 4441.

1854. RODD, E. H.   Occurrence of the Goosander (Mergus Merganser) at Scilly.   < *Zoologist*, xii, 1854, p. 4179.

1854. ROUTILLET, F.   Nouvel art d'élever, de multiplier, d'engraisser et de chasser
les Canards [Anatidæ].   Moyen de se faire un revenu annuel de 1400 à 2000
Fr.   2e édition, augmentée.   Avec gravures.   Paris.   Tissot.   1854.   8vo.
pp. 36.
Pas vu moi-même: le titre tiré de Carus et Engelmann.

1854. STEVENSON, H.   Note on the late appearance of the Common Scoter (Anas
[Œdemia] nigra) in Norfolk.   < *Zoologist*, xii, 1854, p. 4408.

1854. [SUNDEVALL, C. J.]   Anas falcaria, funnen i Sverige.   < *Öfvers. Kongl. Vetensk.-
Acad. Förhandl. för år* 1853, 1854, pp. 227, 228.

1854. THOMPSON, W.   Occurrence of the Turf [sc. Surf] Scoter (Oidemia perspicillata, Flem.) at Weymouth.   < *Zoologist*, xii, 1854, p. 4255.

1854. WAKEFIELD, R.   Singular Hatch of Ducklings.   < *Zoologist*, xii, 1854, p. 4441.

1855. ALTUM, B.   Nachtrag zu den im II. Quartale 1854 beschriebenen und im III.
desselben Jahres abgebildeten deutschen Schwänen.   Cygnus Bewickii. (?)
< *Naumannia*, v, 1855, pp. 101–103.

1855. ANDREWS, W.   On an Addition [Malacorhynchus membranaceus] to the Ornithology of Great Britain.   < *Nat. Hist. Rev.*, (*Pr. Soc.*), ii, 1855, pp. 8, 9, 10.
Other additions to the same fauna are also noted.

1855. BERESFORD, G.   Occurrence of the Smew [Mergellus albellus] near London.
< *Zoologist*, xiii, 1855, p. 4704.

1855. BOLD, T. J.   Occurrence of the Egyptian Goose (Anser [Chenalopex] Ægyptiacus) near Newcastle.   < *Zoologist*, xiii, 1855, p. 4560.

1855. BRYANT, H.   [Remarks on exhibition of North American specimens of Mareca penelope and Querquedula crecca.]   < *Proc. Boston Soc. Nat. Hist.*, v, 1855, p. 195.

1855. FREDERICK, G. S.   Occurrence of the Polish Swan [Cygnus immutabilis] at Hornsey Mere.   < *Zoologist*, xiii, 1855, p. 4661.

1855. GADAMER, [H.]   1. Zur Naturgeschichte der Oidemia fusca, Flem.   Platypus fuscus, Brehm.   Melanita fusca, Boje.   Anas fusca, Linné.   Fuligula fusca, Bonap.   < *Naumannia*, v, 1855,.pp. 89–92.

1855. GLOGER, C. W. L.   Ein Höckerschwan [Cygnus olor], einen Fisch verzehrend.   < *J. f. O.*, iii, 1855, pp. 181, 182.

1855. GRAY, G. R.   On a new Species of Somateria [v-nigra], and the Female of Lampronetta Fischeri, Brandt.   < *P. Z. S.*, xxiii, 1855, pp. 211, 212, pll. (Aves) cvii, cviii.

    Pl. cvii, *Somateria v-nigra*, p. 212, sp. n.; pl. cviii, *Arctonetta* (n. g.) *fischeri.*

1855. GURNEY, S., JR.   Black Swans [Cygnus atratus] Breeding in Confinement.   < *Zoologist*, xiii, 1855, p. 4661.

1855. HECKEL, J.   Ueber verrirte wilde Schwäne [Cygnus musicus].   < *Verh. zool.- bot. Ver. Wien*, v, 1855, pp. 14, 15.

1855. HOMEYER, E. v.   Einige Worte über Art, Bestand und klimatische Ausartung mit besonderer Rücksicht auf Fuligula Homeyeri.   < *J. f. O.*, ii, 1854, Extrah. (1855), pp. lxvi–lxix.

1855. MÜLLER, — v.   [Ueber Anseres spp. in der Umgegend von Sternberg.]   < *Nau mannia*, 1855, pp. 104, 105.

1855. NEWMAN, E.   Curious Act of Auto-surgery in a Teal [Zool., p. 4661].   < *Zoolo gist*, xiii, 1855, p. 4704.

1855. PRESTON, T. A.   Curious act of Autosurgery in a Teal [plugging a wound with feathers].   < *Zoologist*, xiii, 1855, p. 4661.   [Cf. p. 4704.]

1855. SCHLEGEL, H.   [Ein Wort über den von Altum beschriebenen Singschwan mi ganz schwarzer Schnabelfirste.   < *Naumannia*, v, 1855, p. 258, taf. iv, f. 1–4.

1855. SCHLEGEL, H.   [Ueber die Saat- und weisstirnigen Gänse.]   < *Naumanni v*, 1855, pp. 254–257.

    15 allgemeine Bemerkungen.   5 spp.

1855. SELYS-LONGCHAMPS, E.   Bemerkungen über die wahren Gänse (Anser) Eur pas.   < *Naumannia*, v, 1855, pp. 261–265, pl. iv, f. 6, 7.

    8 spp.   *Anser pallipes*, sp. n.

1855. SELYS-LONGCHAMPS, E.   Zusätze zu den Bemerkungen über die wahren Gän [Anser] Europas.   < *Naumannia*, v, 1855, pp. 397, 398.

1855. WYMAN, J.   [Remarks on exhibition of a preparation of the wing of t] "Winter" or Pin-tailed Duck (Dafila acuta).]   < *Proc. Boston Soc. Nat. His v*, 1855, p. 169.

    Showing mechanism of flexion and extension, contributing to fixity of the limb, indeper ently of muscular action.

1856. ALTUM, [B.]   [Ueber die Schwäne.]   < *Naumannia*, vi, 1856, pp. 363–367.

1856. [BILLINGS, E.]   On Black Duck, (Anas obscura.)   < *Canad. Nat. and Geol.*, Apr., 1856, pp. 146–149.

    Compiled descriptive sketch of habits.

1856. [BILLINGS, E.]   On the Wood Duck, (Anas [Aix] sponsa.)   < *Canad. Nat. a Geol.*, i, Apr., 1856, pp. 149–152.

    Compiled description and sketch of habits.

1856. [BILLINGS, E.]   On the Green-winged Teal, (Anas [Querquedula] Carolinensi < *Canad. Nat. and Geol.*, i, Apr., 1856, pp. 153, 154.

    Mainly quotations.

1856. [BILLINGS, E.]   On the Blue-winged Teal, (Anas [Querquedula] discors.)
 < *Canad. Nat. and Geol.*, i, Apr., 1856, pp. 154-156.
  Chiefly quoted.

1856. [BILLINGS, E.]   On the Mallard [Anas boschas].   < *Cand. Nat. and Geol.*, i,
 Apr., 1856, pp. 156-159.

1856. FINGER, J.   Der Entenfang bei Holitsch.   < *Naumannia*, vi, 1856, pp. 262-267.

1856. GLOGER, C. W. L.   „Fuligula Homeyeri" Bäd. ist wirklich nur eine klimatische
 Abänderung der gewöhnlichen F. ferina.   < *Naumannia*, vi, 1856, pp. 252-257.

1856. GLOGER, C. W. L.   Schwarze Eier von Haus-Enten, Anas boschas.   < *J. f. O.*,
 iv, 1856, pp. 309-313.

1856. GURNEY, S.   Black Swans [Cygnus atratus] breeding in Confinement.   <*Zoologist*, xiv, 1856, pp. 5280, 5281.

1856. JÄCKEL, J.   Anas [Fuligula] rufina im Sommer in Bayern.   < *Naumannia*, vi,
 1856, p. 425.

1856. MARTIN, L.   Anser ruficollis Pall. in der Gefangenschaft.   < *J. f. O.*, iv, 1856,
 pp. 94, 95.

1856. MONTGOMERY, R. J.   [On the occurrence of Chenalopex ægyptiacus in Ireland;
 with remarks by R. J. Kinahan.]   < *Nat. Hist. Rev.*, (*Pr. Soc.*), iii, 1856, pp.
 53-55.

1856. NEWMAN, E.   Question respecting the American Scaup said to have been taken
 at Scarborough.   < *Zoologist*, xiv, 1856, p. 4947.

1856. PEASE, J.   Inquiry respecting the Sexes of Geese.   < *Zoologist*, xiv, 1856, p. 5280.

1856. PREEN,— v.   Die Graugänse in Mecklenburg.   < *Naumannia*, vi, 1856, p. 191.

1856. RODD, E. H.   Occurrence of the Velvet Scoter [Œdemia fusca] at the Land's
 End.   < *Zoologist*, xiv, 1856, p. 4946.

1856. SELYS-LONGCHAMPS, E. DE.   Revue der „Récapitulation des Hybrides, observés
 dans la Famille des Anatidées".   < *Naumannia*, vi, 1856, pp. 395-397.
  „ Fast alle Arten der Familie der *Anatidæ* können Hybriden erzeugen, von denen einige
 fruchtbar, aber die Mehrzahl unfruchtbar ist."

1856. SELYS-LONGCHAMPS, E. DE.   Additions à la récapitulation des hybrides observées dans la famille des Anatidées.   < *Bull. Acad. Belg.*, xxiii, pt. ii, 1856,
 pp. 6-22.
  Pas vues moi-même: le titre tiré de Carus et Engelmann.

1856. SLANEY, W. H.   Savage Conduct of a Tame Drake [Anas boschas].   < *Zoologist*, xiv, 1856, pp. 4996, 4997.

1856. SMITH, J. A.   Notice of the Ferruginous Duck [Fuligula nyroca], or White-
 Eyed Duck (Nyroca leucophthalmos, Flem.,) recently shot near Musselburgh.
 < *Edinb. New Philos. Journ.*, new ser., iii, 1856, p. 350.

1856. STEVENSON, H.   Note on the late Appearance of the Common Scoter [Œdemia
 nigra] and the Scaup Duck [Fuligula marila] in Norfolk.   < *Zoologist*, xiv,
 1856, p. 5123.

1856. STEVENSON, H.   Late Appearance of the Longtailed Duck [Harelda glacialis]
 and Common Scoter [Œdemia nigra].   < *Zoologist*, xiv, 1856, p. 5160.

1856. WILMOT, J. P.   An Egg Prodigy.   < *Zoologist*, xiv, 1856, p. 5123.
  Double egg of Goose, weighing 1¼ lbs.; larger than egg of *Alca impennis*.

1856. WILSON, *Dr.* J.   Letter from Dr. Jos. Wilson to Dr. L. J. Williams, U. S. N.
 describing the manner of hatching Ducks in China.   < *Perry's Japan Expedition*, ii, 1856, pp. 249-252, woodcuts.

1857. BRIGGS, J. J.   Occurrence of the Pinkfooted Goose (Anser brachyrhynchus) in
 Derbyshire.   < *Zoologist*, xv, 1857, p. 5595.

1857. BROCKHOLES, J. F.   Double Egg of Young Goose.   <*Zoologist*, xv, 1857, p. 5365.

Bull. v, 4——28

1857. BROCKHOLES, J. F. The Teal (Anas [Querquedula] crecca) breeding in Cheshire. <*Zoologist*, xv, 1857, p. 5365.

1857. W., CLARA, (*Frl.*) Junge Enten als Pfleglinge einer Hühnerhündin. <*Naumannia*, vii, 1857, pp. 438, 439.

1857. CLERMONT, *Lord.* Mute Swans [Cygnus olor] in Dundalk Bay. <*Zoologist*,
xv, 1857, p. 5595.

1857. FITZAU, F. [Gattentreue eines Männchen von Anser segetum.] <*Naumannia*,
vii, 1857, Heft ii, pp. 86, 87.

1857. OLPH-GALLIARD, L. Noch ein Wort über Fuligula Homeyeri. <*Naumannia*,
vi, 1857, Heft i, pp. 66–74.
    Nebst Nachschrift von C. W. L. Gloger.

1857. SCLATER, P. L. Note on the Upland Goose [Chloephaga magellanica]. <*P.
Z. S.*, xxv, 1857, p. 128.

1857. SCLATER, P. L. Note on the Upland Goose [Chloephaga magellanica]. <*Ann.
Mag. Nat. Hist.*, 2d ser., xx, 1857, p. 461.
    From *P. Z. S.*, June 9, 1857, p. 128.

1857. SMITH, R. B. Breeding of Teal in Dorset. <*Zoologist*, xv, 1857, p. 5792.

1857. SMITH, R. B. Wild Duck. <*Zoologist*, xv, 1857, p. 5792.

1857. THOMPSON, W. Occurrence of the Canada Goose (Anser [Bernicla] canadensis) at Weymouth. <*Zoologist*, xv, 1857, p. 5428.

1857. THOMPSON, W. Occurrence of the Egyptian Goose (Anser [Chenalopex] ægyptiacus) at Weymouth. <*Zoologist*, xv, 1857, p. 5429.

1857. THOMPSON, W. Occurrence of the Longtailed Duck (Anas [Harelda] glacialis)
at Weymouth. <*Zoologist*, xv, 1857, pp. 5595, 5596.

1857. THOMPSON, W. The Shoveller (Anas [Spatula] clypeata) breeding in Dorsetshire. <*Zoologist*, xv, 1857, p. 5757.

1858. BALDAMUS, [E.] [Hausente, Anas boschas, die sich mit einem Gänserich ge-
paart hatte.] <*Naumannia*, viii, 1858, p. 506.

1858. BOLLE, C. Anas Tadorna [Tadorna cornuta] kein Hausthier in Neu-Vorpom-
mern und Rügen. <*J. f. O.*, vi, 1858, pp. 489, 490.

1858. BREWER, T. M. [Note of the occurrence of Mareca penelope on Long Island,
in North America.] <*Proc. Boston Soc. Nat. Hist.*, vi, 1858, pp. 419, 420.

1858. CABOT, S. [JR.] [Occurrence of the Ruddy Duck (Erismatura dominica) on
Lake Champlain.] <*Proc. Boston Soc. Nat. Hist.*, vi, 1858, p. 343.

1858. CABOT, S. [JR.] [Remarks on exhibition of certain Anatidæ, rare in North
America.] <*Proc. Boston Soc. Nat. Hist.*, vi, 1858, pp. 375, 376.
    Erismatura dominica, Mareca penelope.

1858. CLERMONT, *Lord.* Notes on the capture of a Mute Swan (Cygnus olor) in Dundalk Bay. <*Nat. Hist. Rev.*, (*Pr. Soc.*), v, 1858, pp. 90, 91. See also p. 87.

1858. GURNEY, S. Black Swans [Cygnus atratus] nesting at Carshalton. <*Zoologist*,
xvi, 1858, p. 5988.

1858. GOULD, J. [Remarks on three specimens of Steller's Duck (Somateria stelleri)
exhibited by Mr. Stevens.] <*P. Z. S.*, xxvi, 1858, p. 78.

1858. HUSSEY, A. Domestic Ducks [Anas boschas] Nesting in a Church Tower.
<*Zoologist*, xvi, 1858, p. 6144.
    From the 'Sussex Express,' June 5, 1858. Communicated by the Rev. A. Hussey.

1858. LANGMAN, A. Till Hålskräckans [Mergus merganser] Naturhistoria. <*Öfvers.
k. Vet.-Akad. Förh.*, 1858, p. 347.
    "Utdrag ur bref till Sundevall fr. Rådm. A. Langman, hvilken varit ögonvittne till Skra-
ken transporterande af ungarne i näbbet ned i hafvet."—v. FRIESEN.

1858. MATHER, T. Occurrence of the Barheaded Goose (Anser Indica) near Chester.
<*Zoologist*, xvi, 1858, p. 5988.

1858. ROGERS, F. Occurrence of Wild Geese in the Isle of Wight. < *Zoologist*, XVI, 1858, p. 6097.

1858. SCLATER, P. L. Additional Note on the Upland Goose (Chloephaga magellanica). < *P. Z. S.*, xxvi, 1858, pp. 289, 290.

1858. STEVENSON, H. Biautiful [sic] Variety of the Garganey Teal [Querquedula circia]. < *Zoologist*, xvi, 1858, p. 6210.

1858. WILLIAMS, R. P. [Remarks on presentation of an Irish specimen of Cygnus olor.] < *Nat. Hist. Rev.*, (*Pr. Soc.*), v, 1858, p. 87. See also pp. 90, 91.
With remarks by J. B. Doyle and R. J. Montgomery.

1859. BLAKISTON, T. Showers of Feathers. < *Zoologist*, xvii, 1859, pp. 6675, 6676.

1859. CLARK, T. Occurrence of the Black Swan (Cygnus atratus) in Somersetshire. < *Zoologist*, xvii, 1859, p. 6379.

1859. ELLIOT, D. G. [Exhibition of three specimens of Hybrid Ducks from the South Shore of Long Island, U. S. A.] < *P. Z. S.*, xxvii, 1859, p. 437.

1859. GOULD, J. [Extract from a letter addressed to him by Dr. George Bennett, of Sidney, respecting the Semipalmated Goose (Anseranas melanoleuca).] < *P. Z. S.*, xxvii, 1859, pp. 39, 40.

1859. GREENE, T. W. Showers of Feathers. < *Zoologist*, xvii, 1859, pp. 6442, 6443.

1859. GREENE, T. W. Showers of Feathers. < *Zoologist*, xvii, 1859, p. 6763.
Cf. *tom. cit.*, pp. 6442, 6675. Here the editor told them both to stop.

1859. GURNEY, S. Black Swans [Cygnus atratus] Breeding at Carshalton. < *Zoologist*, xvii, 1859, p. 6330.

1859. LAFRESNAYE, [F.] DE. [Quelques détails sur des faits relatifs aux Anatidés.] < *Bull. Soc. Acclim.*, vi, 1859, pp. 226, 227.

1859. LAGERGREN, J. F. Till Hålskräckens [Mergus merganser] naturhistoria. < *Öfvers. k. Vet.-Akad. Förh.*, 1859, p. 394.
"Om storkrakens sätt att transportera sina ungar i näbbet till vatnet."

1859. NEWTON, A. Remarks on the Harlequin Duck (Histrionicus torquatus, Bp.). < *Ibis*, i, 1859, pp. 162–166, woodc. p. 162, trachea ♂, ♀.
Anatomical, geographical.

1859. NEWTON, A. Correction of a previous Error [Zool., p. 3331] respecting the Harlequin Duck (Anas histrionica [Histrionicus torquatus]). < *Zoologist*, xvii, 1859, p. 6536.

1859. ROGET, L. Notice sur un vieux mâle de Canard siffleur [Mareca penelope] à plumage de femelle. < *Rev. et Mag. de Zool.*, xi, 1859, pp. 145–148, pl. 6.

1859. ROWLEY, G. D. Occurrence of the Black Swan [Cygnus atratus] on the South Coast. < *Zoologist*, xvii, 1859, p. 6447.

1859. SCLATER, P. L. Note on the Spur-winged Geese (Plectropterus) now living in the Society's Gardens. < *P. Z. S.*, xxvii, 1859, pp. 131, 132, pl. (Aves) cliii.
P. rüppellii, sp. n.

1859. SCLATER, P. L. On some Hybrid Ducks [Tadorna vulpanser ♂ × ♀ Casarca cana] bred in the Society's Gardens. < *P. Z. S.*, xxvii, 1859, p. 442, pl. clviii.

1859. STEVENSON, H. Occurrence of the Longtailed Duck [Harelda glacialis] on the Norfolk Coast. < *Zoologist*, xvii, 1859, p. 6447.

1859. STEVENSON, H. Occurrence of Paget's Pochard (Anas [Fuligula] ferinoides), for the second time, in Norfolk. < *Zoologist*, xvii, 1859, pp. 6536, 6537.

1859. STRICKLAND, A. On the British Wild Geese. < *Rep. Brit. Assoc. Adv. Sci. for 1858*, 1859, (*Misc. Comm.*), pp. 131, 132.
Recognizing 4 species, characters of which conclude a general criticism of the subject

1859. STRICKLAND, A. On the British Wild Geese. < *Ann. Mag. Nat. Hist.*, 3d ser., iii, 1859, pp. 121–124, pl. iv, fig. 1–3.
Critical discrimination of 4 spp.

1859. WOLLEY, J., JR.   On the Breeding of the Smew, Mergus albellus. L.   < Ibis, i, 1859, pp. 69–76.

Detailed narrative of his long and successful search for the eggs of this species in Lapland.

1860. BARNSTON, G.   Recollections of the Swans and Geese [Anatidæ] of Hudson's Bay.   < Ibis, ii, 1860, pp. 253–259.

Running commentary on the species, with tabular estimates of the number annually killed at various points (some 60,000 in all). Cf. Canad. Nat., vi, Oct., 1861, pp. 337–344.

1860. BARTLETT, A. D.   [Exhibition of the head of a variety of the Common Goose, with the feathers of the back of the head reversed.]   < P. Z. S., xxviii, 1860, p. 99.

1860. BELL, A. S.   Occurrence of the Surf Scoter [Œdemia perspicillata] near Scarborough.   < Zoologist, xviii, 1860, p. 7274.

1860. BUXTON, E. C.   Great Flocks of Scoters [Œdemia nigra] in July [at the mouth of the Ribble].   < Zoologist, xviii, 1860, p. 7172.

1860. GLOGER, C. W. L.   Wie schaffen die Stockenten, Baumenten und Sägetaucher [Mergus serrator] ihre Jungen aus Nestern auf Bäumen herunter?   < J. f. O., viii, 1860, pp. 222–224.

1860. GLOGER, C. W. L.   Das Gelbliche und Röthliche an dem Gefieder der Schwäne [Cygnus].   < J. f. O., viii, 1860, pp. 308, 309.

Nilsson, Sk. Fn. Fog., ii, p. 382.

1860. HUSSEY, H.   'The Wild-fowler.'   < Zoologist, xviii, 1860, p. 6923.

Above is the title of a book by Mr. Folkard, a passage of which, relating to certain Anatidæ, is here criticised.

1860. NEWTON, A.   On some Hybrid Ducks.   < P. Z. S., xxviii, 1860, pp. 336–339, pll. (Aves) clxvii, clxviii.

Pl. clxvii, Fuligula collaris × F. americana.   Pl. clxviii, Anas boschas × Dafila acuta.

1860. NEWTON, A.   Remarks on the Anas (Anser) erythropus of Linnæus.   < P. Z. S., xxviii, 1860. pp. 339–341.

Identifies it with minutus, Naum. = temminckii, Boié = finmarchicus, Gunner.

1860. NEWTON, A.   Remarks on the Anas (Anser) erythropus of Linnæus.   < Ann. Mag. Nat. Hist., 3d ser., vi, 1860, pp. 452–454.

From P. Z. S., June 26, 1860, pp. 339–341.

1860. NEWTON, A.   Remarks on the Anas (Anser) erythropus of Linnæus.   < Ibis, ii, 1860, pp. 404–406.

Reprinted from P. Z. S., June 26, 1860, pp. 339–341.

1860. SCLATER, P. L.   Further Evidence of the Distinctness of the Gambian and Rüppell's Spur-winged Geese (Plectropterus gambensis and P. rüppellii).   < P. Z. S., xxviii, 1860, pp. 38–42, woodcc.

Anatomical characters; synonymy.

1860. SCLATER, P. L.   [Exhibition of a male example of the Bimaculated Duck (Anas glocitans) of Yarrell.]   < P. Z. S., xxviii, 1860, p. 303.

1860. SCLATER, P. L.   Further Evidence of the Distinctness of the Gambian and Rüppell's Spur-winged Geese (Plectropterus gambensis and P. Rüppellii).   < Ann. Mag. Nat. Hist., 3d ser., vi, 1860, pp. 69–73, figg. 6.

From P. Z. S., Jan. 11, 1860, pp. 38–42.

1860. SCLATER, P. L.   Note on the Spur-winged Geese (Plectropterus) now living in the Society's Gardens.   < Ann. Mag. Nat. Hist., 3d ser., v, 1860, pp. 146, 147.

From P. Z. S., Apr. 12, 1859, pp. 131, 132.

1860. SWINHOE, R.   Wild Swans on the Coast of China.   < Zoologist, xviii, 1860, pp. 6923, 6924.

1860. TURREL, —.   Notice sur le Canard du Labrador [en domesticité].   < Bull. Soc. Acclim., vii, 1860, pp. 540–544.

1861. ALTUM, B.   Anas clangula [Clangula glaucium], altes Männchen im Uebergangskleide.   < J. f. O., ix, 1861, pp. 74–76.

1861. BARNSTON, G.   Recollections of the Swans and Geese [Anatidæ] of Hudson's
Bay.   < *Canadian Naturalist,* vi, Oct., 1861, pp. 337–344.
An important and original essay. Cf. *Ibis,* ii, 1860, pp. 253-259.

1861. BARTLETT, A. D.   Notice of the Occurrence of the Pink-footed Goose, Anser
phœnicopus [brachyrhynchus, in Great Britain].   < *P. Z. S.,* xxix, 1861, p. 19.

1861. BARTLETT, A. D.   [Exhibition of two living specimens of Hybrid Ducks.]
< *P. Z. S.,* xxix, 1861, p. 44.
Aix sponsa × *Fuligula ferina, Aix sponsa* × *F. nyroca.*

1861. BARTLETT, A. D.   Notice of the Occurrence of the Pink-footed Goose, Anser
phœnicopus [brachyrhynchus, in Great Britain].   < *Ann. Mag. Nat. Hist.,* 3d
ser., vii, 1861, p. 419.
From *P. Z. S.,* Jan. 8, 1861, p. 19.

1861. bENNETT, G.   [Extract from his letter respecting the Semipalmated Goose
(Anseranas melanoleuca).]   < *P. Z. S.,* xxix, 1861, pp. 266, 267.

1861. CASSIN, J.   [On a new species of Goose (Anser rossii Baird) from Arctic America.]
< *Proc. Acad. Nat. Sci. Phila.,* xiii, 1861, pp. 72, 73.
This is the somewhat noted "Horned Wavey" of Hearne (*Journ.,* 1795, p. 442), here first
identified and named binomially. It afterward became the type of the genus *Exanthemops*
Elliot.

1861. CRISP, E.   On some Points relating to the Habits and Anatomy of the Oceanic
and of the Freshwater Ducks [Anatidæ], and also of the Hare (Lepus timidus)
and of the Rabbit (L. cuniculus), in relation to the Question of Hybridism.
< *P. Z. S.,* xxix, 1861, pp. 82–87.

1861. CRISP, E.   On some Points relating to the Habits and Anatomy of the Oceanic
and of the Freshwater Ducks [Anatidæ], and also of the Hare (Lepus timidus) and of the Rabbit (L. cuniculus), in relation to the Question of Hybridism.   < *Ann. Mag. Nat. Hist.,* 3d ser., viii, 1861, pp. 72–77.
From *P. Z, S.,* Feb. 26, 1861, pp. 82-87.

1861. FINGER, J.   Ueber den Singschwan, Cygnus musicus.   < *Verh. (Abh.) k.-k. zool.-
bot. Ges. Wien,* xi, 1861, pp. 229–234, holzschnitt.

1861. JÄCKEL, A. J.   Zur Frage über Altum's Schwan und den Cygnus melanorhinus
Naumann's.   < *J. f. O.,* ix, 1861, pp. 66–71.
„Ich halte Altums Schwäne (Naum. 1854, 145) für sehr alte Männchen und Weibchen des
Cygnus melanorhinus (minor, bewickii, und den meinigen für Uebergang zum Schwan mit
ganz schwarzer Schnabelfirste."—(*l. c.*)

1861. LAURENCE, M. A., JR.   Ueber die Zucht der Mandarin-Ente (Anas [Aix] galericulata).   < *Zool. Gart.,* ii, 1861, pp. 95–98.

1861. NEWTON, A.   On a Hybrid Duck.   < *P. Z. S.,* xxix, 1861, pp. 392, 393.
Mareca penelope × *Anas boschas (fera* × *domestica).*

1861. NEWTON, A.   On some Hybrid Ducks.   < *Ann. Mag. Nat. Hist.,* 3d ser., vii, 1861,
pp. 138–141.
From *P. Z. S.,* June 26, 1860, pp. 336–339, *q. v.*

1861. WYMAN, J.   [Remarks on exhibition of a preparation of the bones of a super-
numerary leg from a Goose.]   < *Proc. Boston Soc. Nat. Hist.,* viii, 1861, pp. 256,
257.

1862. ADAMS, A.   How they fatten Ducks in China.   < *Zoologist,* xx, 1862, pp. 8196–
8198.

1862. ATKINSON, J. C.   Note on the Goosander [Mergus merganser].   < *Zoologist,* xx,
1862, p. 7848.

1862. BARNSTON, G.   Recollections of the Swans and Geese [Anatidæ] of Hudson's
Bay.   < *Zoologist,* xx, 1862, pp. 7831–7837.
Reprinted from the *Canadian Naturalist,* vi, Oct., 1861, pp. 337-344.

1862. BENNETT, G.   [On Anseranas melanoleuca.]   < *Ann. Mag. Nat. Hist.,* 3d ser.,
ix, 1862, pp. 63, 64.
From *P. Z. S.,* June 25, 1861, pp. 266-267.

1862. BLAKE-KNOX, H.   Occurrence of the Egyptian Goose [Chenalopex ægyptiacus] near Dublin.   < *Zoologist*, xx, 1862, p. 7939.

1862. BODINUS, *Dr.*   Einiges über Anas tadorna [Tadorna cornuta, in Gefangenschaft].   < *Zool. Gart.*, iii, 1862, pp. 188–192.

1862. CROWLEY, P.   Occurrence of the Egyptian Goose [Chenalopex ægyptiacus] at Alton.   < *Zoologist*, xx, 1862, p. 7883.

1862. CROWLEY, P.   Occurrence of the Egyptian Goose [Chenalopex ægyptiacus] at Alton.   < *Zoologist*, xx, 1862, p. 8005.

1862. ELLIOT, D. G.   On the Occurrence, within the Limits of the United States, of Barrow's Golden Eye, Bucephala [Clangula] Islandica (Gmel.) Baird.   < *Ann. Lyc. Nat. Hist. New York*, vii, 1862, pp. 449–454.

1862. GOSSE, P. H.   A clever Duck.   < *Zoologist*, xx, 1862, p. 7883.
Caught a mouse and drowned it.

1862. HUSSEY, H.   Pochards [Fuligula ferina] in the Serpentine.   < *Zoologist*, xx, 1862, p. 7930.

1862. LEADBEATER, —.   [Exhibition of a Hybrid Duck (Dafila acuta × Querquedula crecca).]   < *P. Z. S.*, xxx, 1862, p. 84.

1862. MARCHAND, A.   [Observations sur la domestication de l'Anas [Fuligula] ferina.]   < *Rev. et Mag. de Zool.*, xiv, 1862, pp. 78, 79.

1862. NEWTON, A.   On a Hybrid Duck.   < *Ann. Mag. Nat. Hist.*, 3d ser., ix, 1862, pp. 339, 340.
From *P. Z. S.*, Dec. 10, 1861, pp. 392, 393, q. v.

1862. NEWTON, A.   On a hybrid Duck.   < *Canad. Journ.*, vii, 1862, pp. 226–227.
From *P. Z. S.*, Dec. 10, 1861, pp. 392, 393, q. v.

1862. PELZELN, A. v.   Notiz über Cygnus immutabilis Yarrell.   < *Verh. (Abh.) k.-k. zool.-bot. Ges. Wien*, xii, 1862, Abth. ii, pp. 785, 786.
Zum Schlusse die einstweilige Diagnose der Arten.

1862. PHILIPPI, R. A., *and* LANDBECK, L.   Sobre los gansos [Anatidæ] chilenos.   < *Anal. Univ. de Chile*, xxi, No. 5, Nov., 1862, pp. 427–439.
1. *B. melanoptera*, Eyton. 2. *B. dispar*, Ph. & L., p. 431, sp. n. 3. *B. leucoptera*, Gm. 4. *B. chiloensis*, Ph., p. 434, sp. n. 5. *B. inornata*, King. 6. *B. antarctica*, Steph. Cf. *Ibis*, 1864, p. 121.

1862. PHILIPPI, R. A., *and* LANDBECK, L.   Descripcion de una nueva especie de pato del Perú [Querquedula angustirostris, p. 439].   < *Anal. Univ. Chile*, xxi, No. 5, Nov., 1862, pp. 439, 440.

1862. RODD, E. H.   Occurrence of the Wild Goose near Penzance.   < *Zoologist*, xx, 1862, p. 8002.

1862. SCLATER, P. L.   [Exhibition of a Red-crested Duck (Fuligula rufina).]   < *P. Z. S.*, xxx, 1862, p. 163.

1862. SMITH, J. A.   Note of the Capture of the Red-Crested Whistling Duck (Fuligula rufina, Selby) in Argylshire.   < *Edinb. New Philos. Journ.*, new ser., xvi, 1862, p. 156.

1862. WAGNER, CHRIST.   [Einfangen der Sägetaucher (Mergus spp.).]   < *Zool. Gart.*, iii, 1862, pp. 84, 85.

1862. WEINLAND, D. F.   Gehäubte Schwäne [Cygnus olor].   < *Zool. Gart.*, iii, 1862, p. 43.

1863. BOULTON, W. W.   Notice of a singular Duck shot near Beverley.   < *Zoologist*, xxi, 1863, pp. 8831, 8832.

1863. BOULTON, W. W.   Capture of the Black Swan [Cygnus atratus] near Beverley.   < *Zoologist*, xxi, 1863, pp. 8725, 8726.

1863. DUTTON, J.   The Egyptian Goose (Anser [Chenalopex] ægyptiacus) in Pevensey Marshes.   < *Zoologist*, xxi, 1863, p. 8448.

1863. GLOGAN, H. Eidergans [Somateria mollissima]. < *Zool. Gart.*, iv, 1863, p. 21.

1863. PHILIPPI, R. A., *and* LANDBECK, L. Beschreibung einer neuen Ente und einer neuen Seechwalbe. < *Arch. f. Naturg.*, —, 1863, pp. 202 - —.
Mir nicht zugänglich.—*Querquedula angustirostris, Sterna atrofasciata*, aus Südamerika. *Vergl. Anal. Univ. Chile*, xxi, 1862, p. 439.

1863. SAVILLE, S. P. The Egyptian Goose (Anser [Chenalopex] ægyptiacus) in the Cambridgeshire Fens. < *Zoologist*, xxi, 1863, p. 8331.

1863. SAXBY, H. L. Pintail Duck (Anas [Dafila] acuta) in Shetland. < *Zoologist*, xxi, 1863, p. 8494.

1863. WALKER, R. On the Skeleton of a Seal (Phoca Grœnlandica?), and the Cranium of a Duck, from the Pliocene Beds, Fifeshire. < *Ann. Mag. Nat. Hist.*, 3d ser., xii, 1863, pp. 382–388.
The duck, unnamed, is described as near *Œdemia* and *Somateria.*

1864. ANON. Der Singschwan. < *Aus der Natur*, xxx, oder n. F., xviii, 1864, p. 688.

1864. BLACKMORE, H. P. Remains of Birds' Eggs found at Fisherton, near Salisbury. < *Edinb. New Philos. Journ.*, new ser., xix, 1864, pp. 74, 75.
Supposed to be those of certain *Anatidæ.*

1864. BLACKMORE, H. Tufted Duck [Fuligula cristata] near Salisbury. < *Zoologist*, xxii, 1864, p. 9047.

1864. BOULTON, W. W. Smews [Mergellus albellus] shot in Yorkshire. < *Zoologist*, xxii, 1864, p. 8962.

1864. BOULTON, W. W. Bewick's Swan [Cygnus bewickii] on the Humber, near Patrington. < *Zoologist*, xxii, 1864, p. 8962.

1864. BOULTON, W. W. Goosanders [Mergus merganser] on the River Hull, near Beverley. < *Zoologist*, xxii, 1864, p. 8963.

1864. BOULTON, W. W. Gargany Teal [Querquedula circia] at Flamborough. <*Zoologist*, xxii, 1864, p. 9048.

1864. BOULTON, W. W. Bernicle Goose [Bernicla leucopsis] at Bempton, near Flalborough. < *Zoologist*, xxii, 1864, p. 9048.

1864. BOULTON, W. W. Shoveller [Spatula clypeata] near Beverley. < *Zoologist*, xxii, 1864, pp. 9120, 9121.

1864. BOULTON, W. W. Black Swan [Cygnus atratus] near Beverley. < *Zoologist*, xxii, 1864, p. 9251.

1864. BOULTON, W. W. Eider Duck [Somateria mollissima] at Filey. < *Zoologist*, xxii, 1864, p. 9364.

1864. BRYDGES, H. J. J. Ferruginous Duck [Fuligula nyroca] in Radnorshire. <*Zoologist*, xxii, 1864, p. 9047.

1864. CARTER, S. H. American Wigeon [Mareca americana] in Essex. < *Zoologist*, xxii, 1864, p. 8962.

1864. CLARK, T. Note on the occurrence of the Egyptian Goose [Chenalopex ægyptiacus] near Glastonbury. <*Zoologist*, xxii, 1864, p. near 9047.

1864. CORDEAUX, J. Variety of the Common Wild Duck [Anas boschas]. < *Zoologist*, xxii, 1864, p. 9047.

1864. CREWE, H. H. [Cygnus bewickii, ♂, ad., Jan. 18, 1864, on the Trent, at Newton-Folney.] < *Ibis*, vi, 1864, p. 229.

1864. CREWE, H. H. Bewick's Swan [Cygnus bewickii] in Derbyshire. < *Zoologist*, xxii, 1864, pp. 8961, 8962.

1864. DUTTON, J. Pintail [Dafila acuta], Longtailed [Harelda glacialis], and Scaup Duck [Fuligula marila] at Eastbourne. < *Zoologist*, xxii, 1864, pp. 9046, 9047.

1864. DUTTON, J. Smew [Mergellus albellus] near Eastbourne. < *Zoologist*, xxii, 1864, p. 9047.

1864. Gould, J. Description of a New Species of the Genus Mergus [squamatus] < P. Z. S., xxxii, 1864, pp. 184, 185.

1864. Grill, J. W. Om en sångsvan [Ċynus musicus] i fångenskap. < Öfvers. Kongl. Vetensk.-Akad. Förh., xx, för år 1863, 1864, pp. 27–29.

1864. Hill, R. Note on the Muscovy Duck [Cairina moschata]. < Am. Journ. Sci., xxxviii, 1864, p. 294.

1864. Jeffrey, W., Jr. The Velvet Scoter [Œdemia fusca] off the Sussex Coast. < Zoologist, xxii, 1864, p. 8962.

1864. Maurice, C. J. The Tufted Duck [Fuligula cristata] near Romsey. < Zoologist, xxii, 1864, p. 8962.

1864. Millegan, W. J. The Goosander [Mergus merganser] near Richmond, Yorkshire. < Zoologist, xxii, 1864, p. 8963.

1864. Newman, E. Barrow's Goldeneye [Clangula islandica; cf. Zool., p. 9039]. < Zoologist, xxii, 1864, p. 9122.

1864. Newton, A. The Ruddy Shieldrake [Tadorna rutila] at Epworth. < Zoologist, xxii, 1864, p. 9363.

1864. Rodd, E. H. Graylegged Goose [Anser cinereus] near Penzance. < Zoologist, xxii, 1864, p. 8891.

1864. Rodd, E. H. Gadwall Duck [Chaulelasmus streperus] near St. Austell, Cornwall. < Zoologist, xxii, 1864, p. 8962.

1864. Rodd, E. H. Goosander [Mergus merganser] near the Lizard. < Zoologist, xxii, 1864, p. 8963.

1864. Rodd, E. H. Longtailed Duck [Harelda glacialis] at Scilly. < Zoologist, xxii, 1864, p. 9364.

1864. "S." Anhänglichkeit einer Ganz. < Zool. Gart., v, 1864, p. 307.

1864. Sacc, Dr. Note Sur le Canard musqué [Cairina moschata]. < Bull. Soc. Acclim., 2e sér., i, 1864, pp. 256–260.

1864. Sclater, P. L. Note on the Geographical Distribution of the Ducks of the Genus Dendrocygna. < P. Z. S., June 28, 1864, pp. 299–301.

  Synonymatic list of 8 spp. known to the author, with the habitat of each, and critical commentary; with 2 others not seen by him. DD. autumnalis, viduata, arborea, guttulata, areuata, major, vagans, eytoni; with fulva and virgata. See P. Z. S., 1866, pp. 148–150, 417, 418.

1864. Sclater, P. L. Notes on the Species of Tadorna living in the Society's Menagerie. < P. Z. S., xxxii, 1864, pp. 189–192, pll. xviii, xix.

  6 spp. T. tadornoides, pl. xviii; T. variegata, pl. xix.

1864. Sclater, P. L. Description of a New Species of Duck [Anas melleri] from Madagascar. < P. Z. S., xxxii, 1864, pp. 487, 488, pl. xxxiv.

1864. Sclater, P. L. [Notice of the addition to the Society's Menagerie of two males and a female of the Maned Goose of Australia (Bernicla jubata).] < P. Z. S., xxxii, 1864, p. 587.

1864. Smith, C. H. Bewick's Swan [Cygnus bewicki] near Woburn. < Zoologist, xxii, 1864, p. 8962.

1864. Smith, Cecil. Egyptian Goose [Chenalopex ægyptiacus] and Great Gray Shrike in Somersetshire. < Zoologist, xxii, 1864, p. 9048.

1864. Stevenson, H. Gray Lag Geese [Anser cinereus] in Norfolk. < Zoologist, xxii, 1864, p. 9119.

1865. Blackmore, II. Tufted Duck [Fuligula cristata] near Salisbury. < Zoologist, xxiii, 1865, p. 9540.

1865. Briggs, J. J. Extraordinary Death of five Swans. < Zoologist, xxiii, 1865, p. 9469.

1865. B[ruch, C.] Norddeutsche Entenzucht. < Zool. Gart., vi, 1865, pp. 155, 156.

1865. GOULD, J.   Description of a New Species of the Genus Mergus [squamatus].
  < *Ann. Mag. Nat. Hist.*, 3d ser., xv, 1865, p. 71.
  From *P. Z. S.*, Apr. 26, 1864, p. 184.

1865. HINCKS, W.   On Cygnus Passmorii, a supposed new American Swan.   < *Proc.
  Linn. Soc.*, viii, 1865, pp. 1–8, figg.
  Not seen—cf. *Zool. Rec.* for 1865, p. 134.   "The sternum and trachea figured and described
  by Yarrell (*Trans. Linn. Soc.*, xvii. pp. 1–4, tab. i.) as belonging to *C. buccinator* are referred
  to the new species."

1865. MATHEW, M. A.   Egyptian Goose [Chenalopex ægyptiacus] at Barnstaple.
  < *Zoologist*, xxiii, 1865, p. 9734.

1865. MAWSON, G.   Bernicle Goose [Bernicla leucopsis] near Cockermouth.   < *Zoologist*, xxiii, 1865, pp. 9733, 9734.

1865. PARKER, W. K.   Preliminary Notes on some Fossil Birds [Anatidæ] from the
  Zebbug Cave, Malta.   < *P. Z. S.*, xxxiii, 1865, pp. 752, 753.
  Cygnus falconeri, n. sp. foss., *C. olor?*, *C. bewicki?* and a *Bernicla* or large *Anas*.

1865. REINHARDT, J.   Notits om Canada-Gaasens (Bernicla canadensis) Forekomst i
  Grönland.   < *Vidensk. Meddel. Naturhist. Foren. Kjöbenhavn for Aaret* 1864, 1865,
  pp. 246, 247.
  Specimen from Disco; first instance of the discovery of the species in that country.

1865. RODD, E. H.   Surf Scoter [Œdemia perspicillata] at Scilly.   < *Zoologist*, xxiii,
  1865, p. 9794.

1865. WILSON, J.   Incubation artificielle des Canards en Chine.   < *Bull. Soc. Acclim.*,
  2e sér., ii, 1865, pp. 138, 139.

1866. BENNETT, G.   [Extract from a letter respecting Dendrocygna eytoni.]   < *P. Z.
  S.*, xxxiv, 1866, pp. 417, 418.
  D. vagans, *P. Z. S.*, 1866, p. 149, is *D.* (*Leptotarsis*) *eytoni*.

1866. "F."   Zur Thierseelenkunde [Gans].   < *Zool. Gart.*, vii, 1866, pp. 238, 239.

1866. HINCKS, W.   [On Cygnus passmorii.]   < *Canad. Journ.*, xi, 1866, p. 72.
  Not seen?

1866. MEYER, R.   Fang einer Nilgans (Chenalopex ægyptiacus) am Main.   < *Zool.
  Gart.*, vii, 1866, pp. 195, 196.

1866. POLLEN, F.   "Un mot sur l'acclimation du Canard à Bosse, Sarkidionis afri-
  cana, Eyton."   < *N. T. D.*, iii, 1866, pp. 322, 324; *Bull. Soc. d'Accl. et d'Hist.
  Nat. de la Réunion, Mém. Scient.*, pp. 6–11.
  Not seen.—The species is recommended for acclimatization in Réunion.

1866–67. SCHLEGEL, H.   Anseres   < *Mus. Hist. Nat. Pays-Bas*, 8e livr., 1866, pp. 1–108;
  9e livr., 1867, pp. 109–122.
  The *Anseres* of this article are equivalent to the *Anatidæ* + *Phœnicopteridæ* of authors.   Of
  the former family are described 5 spp. of *Mergus*, 9 of *Biziura*, 27 of *Fuligula*, 50 of *Anas*, 4 of
  Nettapus, 8 of *Cygnus*, 8 of *Dendrocygna*, 1 *Anseranas*, 1 *Plectropterus*, 26 of *Anser*, and 1
  Cereopsis = 132 *Anatidæ*.   Of the Flamingoes 4 species of *Phœnicopterus* are recognized.

1866. SCLATER, P. L.   Additional Notes on the Anatidæ of the Genera Dendrocygna
  and Tadorna.   < *P. Z. S.*, Mar. 13, 1866, pp. 148–150.
  Cf. *P. Z. S.*, 1864, pp. 299–301.   Further notes on *DD. major, vagans*, and *fulva*, with remarks
  on *Tadorna variegata*.   Cf. *P. Z. S.*, 1866, p. 417.

1866. SCHRÖDER, E.   Das treue Gänse-Paar.   < *Zool. Gart.*, vii, 1866, pp. 376–378.

1866. ST. GERLACH, C. DE.   Beobachtungen über die Cereopsis-Gans.   (Cereopsis
  Novae Hollandiae.)   < *Zool. Gart.*, vii, 1866, pp. 170–173.
  In Gefangenschaft.

1866. TRISTRAM, H. B.   Egyptian Geese [Chenalopex ægyptiacus] at Stockton-on-
  Tees.   < *Zoologist*, 2d ser., i, 1866, p. 525.

1866. VIAN, J.   Causeries Ornithologiques.   < *Rev. et Mag. de Zool.*, 1866, pp. 401–410.
  Not seen.   These relate to several species of *Anatidæ*.

1867. BLACKMORE, H.   Canada Goose [Bernicla canadensis] at Coombe Bissett.   < *Zoologist*, 2d ser., ii, 1867, pp. 708, 709.

1867. BOUILLOD, —.   Reproduction en domesticité du Canard Tadorne et du Canard Souchet avec la femelle de la Caroline.   < *Bull. Soc. Acclim.*, 2ᵉ sér., iv, 1867, pp. 396, 397.

1867. CLARK-KENNEDY, A.   Goosander [Mergus merganser] in Wiltshire.   < *Zoologist*, 2d ser., ii, 1867, p. 709.

1867. CLARK-KENNEDY, A.   Instinct in the Swan.   < *Zoologist*, 2d ser., ii, 1867, p. 916.

1867. CLIFTON, *Lord.*   Redheaded Pochard [Fuligula ferina] in Kent.   < *Zoologist*, 2d ser., ii, 1867, p. 636.

1867. DOBRÉE, N. F.   Smews [Mergellus albellus] from Holland.   < *Zoologist*, 2d ser., ii, 1867, p. 636.

1867. DROSTE, F. V.   Der Entenstrich.   < *J. f. O.*, xv, 1867, pp. 64–70.

1867. DROSTE, F. V.   Beobachtungen auf einer Rattgansjagd [Bernicla brenta].   < *J. f. O.*, xv, 1867, pp. 89–94.

1867. GUNN, T. E.   Ferruginous Duck [Fuligula nyroca] in Norfolk.   < *Zoologist*, 2d ser., ii, 1867, p. 709.

1867. GURNEY, J. H.   Unusual Occurrence of the Smew [Mergellus albellus].   < *Zoologist*, 2d ser., ii, 1867, p. 608.

1867. HACKETT, W. A.   Redbreasted Merganser [Mergus serrator] on the Bandon River.   < *Zoologist*, 2d ser., ii, 1867, p. 636.
From the London 'Field,' Jan. 26.

1867. HACKETT, W. A.   Goosander [Mergus merganser] and Shoveller Duck [Spatula clypeata] in the South of Ireland.   < *Zoologist*, 2d ser., ii, 1867, p. 709.
From the London 'Field.'

1867. HARTMANN, W.   Ueber 2 Bastarde vom schwarzen Schwan [Cygnus atratus] und Höckerschwan [Cygnus olor].   < *Zool. Gart.*, viii, 1867, p. 441.

1867. HARVIE-BROWN, J. A.   Scaup Duck [Fuligula marila] breeding in Britain.   < *Zoologist*, 2d ser., ii, 1867, p. 878.

1867. HARVIE-BROWN, J. A.   Gadwall [Chaulelasmus streperus] shot on the Tay.   < *Zoologist*, 2d ser., ii, 1867, p. 562.

1867. HENSMAN, H. P.   Egyptian Goose [Chenalopex ægyptiacus] near Northampton.   < *Zoologist*, 2d ser., ii, 1867, p. 831.

1867. HOOPER, W. T.   Tufted Pochard [Fuligula cristata] on the River Lea.   < *Zoologist*, 2d ser., ii, 1867, p. 709.

1867. MATHEW, M. A.   Egyptian Goose [Chenalopex ægyptiacus] at Barnstaple.   < *Zoologist*, 2d ser., ii, 1867, p. 831.

1867. MURIE, J.   On Cygnus buccinator, Richardson, and Cygnus passmori, Hincks.   < *P. Z. S.*, xxxv, 1867, pp. 8–13, figg. 2.
Maintaining their identity on anatomical grounds. The subject is discussed at length; the sternums of the two are figured.

1867. PARKER, W. K.   On some Fossil Birds from the Zebbug Cave, Malta.   < *Trans. Zool. Soc.*, vi, pt. iii, 1867, pp. 119–124, pl. xxx, figg. 1–23.
This is the memoir in full, preliminary notice of the material, with description of *Cygnus falconeri*, having been previously made in *P. Z. S.*, 1865, pp. 752, 753.

1867. SCHNETZ, H.   [Zur Fortpflanzungsgeschichte der schwarzen Schwäne (Cygnus atratus) in Gefangenschaft.]   < *Zool. Gart.*, viii, 1867, p. 276.

1867. STEPHENSON, W.   Egyptian Goose [Chenalopex ægyptiacus] in Yorkshire.   < *Zoologist*, 2d ser., ii, 1867, p. 636.
From the London "Field," Jan. 26.

1868. BAIRD, S. F.   Occurrence of the Barnacle Goose [Bernicla leucopsis, at Hudson's Bay] in North America.   < *Am. Nat.*, ii, 1868, p. 49.

1868. BOUILLOD, —. Reproduction du Canard Tadorne (deuxième année), de la Sarcelle et de la Poule d'eau. *< Bull. Soc. Acclim.*, 2e sér., v, 1868, pp. 648, 649.

1868. BREE, [C. R.] Eider Duck [Somateria mollissima] on the Essex Coast. *< Zoologist*, 2d ser., iii, 1868, p. 1221.
From the London 'Field.'

1868. CORDEAUX, J. The Ashby Decoy. *< Zoologist*, 2d ser., iii, 1868, pp. 1378, 1379.
The numbers of six species of *Anatidæ* (*Anas boschas*, *Nettion crecca*, *Mareca penelope*, *Spatula clypeata*, *Dafila acuta*, and *Ohaulelasmus streperus*) taken during thirty-five seasons (Sept., 1833 to Apr., 1868) at this celebrated Lincolnshire decoy.

1868. CRICHTON, A. W. Eider Duck [Somateria mollissima] on the Thames. *< Zoologist*, 2d ser., iii, 1868, p. 1135.

1868. HINCKS, W. [Letter on the differences between Cygnus passmori and C. buccinator.] *< P/Z. S.*, xxxvi, 1868, pp. 211–213.

1868. HOMEYER, A. v. Wie gelangen junge Enten, die in der Höhe ausgebrütet worden, auf das Wasser? *< J. f. O.*, xvi, 1868, pp. 356, 357.

1868. MATHEW, G. F. Redcrested Whistling Duck [Fuligula rufina] near Braunton. *< Zoologist*, 2d ser., iii, 1868, p. 1098.

1868. MATHEW, G. F. Mute Swan [Cygnus olor] on Northam Burrows. *< Zoologist*, 2d ser., iii, 1868, p. 1135.

1868. NOLL, C. F. Bastarde von dem schwarzen [Cygnus atratus] und dem Höcker-Schwan [Cygnus olor]. *< Zool. Gart.*, ix, 1868, pp. 189, 190.

1868. PISSOT, —. Note sur les produits obtenus de l'accouplement d'un Cygne noir [Cygnus atratus] mâle avec un Cygne blanc [Cygnus ——] femelle. *< Bull. Soc. Acclim.*, 2e sér., v, 1868, pp. 11, 12.

1868. ROGER, E. Reproductions de Céréopses (Cereopsis Novæ Hollandiæ). *< Bull. Soc. Acclim.*, 2e sér., v, 1868, pp. 501–503.

1868. SCHLEGEL, F. Die Schwäne. *< Zool. Gart.*, ix, 1868, pp. 60–62.
Bemerkungen über 8 Arten, deren 4 der alten Welt und ebensoviele der neuen Welt angehören.

1868. SCHMIDT, [MAX.] [Bastarde von dem schwarzen Schwan (Cygnus atratus), und dem Höcker-Schwan (C. olor).] *< Zool. Gart.*, ix, 1868, p. 77.

1868. SCLATER, P. L. [Note on Plectropterus gambensis.] *< Ibis*, 2d ser., iv, 1868, p. 502.

1868. SMITH, CECIL. Longtailed Duck [Harelda glacialis] at Exmouth. *< Zoologist*, 2d ser., iii, 1868, p. 1059.

1868. TIEMANN, F. [Beitrag zur Thierseelenkunde (Schwan).] *< Zool. Gart.*, ix, 1868, p. 79.

1868. WALKER, J. F. On the Occurrence of the Genus Anser in the Peat and Gravel Deposits in Cambridgeshire. *< Ann. Mag. Nat. Hist.*, 4th ser., ii, 1868, p. 388.

1868. WATERSTON, R. C. [Note on the condition of Geese's feathers after long use as bedding.] *< Proc. Boston Soc. Nat. Hist.*, xi, 1868, p. 278.
"The feathers were stripped of their plumules and the filaments formed a plush-like nap of remarkable uniformity, which adhered firmly to the whole interior of the case."

1868. WICKEVOORT-CROMMELIN, J. P. VAN. Notes sur des hybrides d'Anser et de Cygnus et de diverses espèces de Canards. *< Bull. Soc. Acclim.*, 2e sér., v, 1868, pp. 781–786.
C. olor × Anser domesticus—Anas boschas × Dafila acuta—Dafila acuta × Ohaulelasmus streperus. Cf. op. cit., vi, 1869, pp. 140, 141.

1869. BOARDMAN, G. A. Labrador Duck [Camptolæmus labradorius]. *< Am. Nat.*, iii, 1869, pp. 383, 384.
Note on the disappearance of the species from Maine.

1869. BRYDGES, H. J. J. Summer Duck [Aix sponsa] at Boultibrook. *< Zoologist*, 2d ser., iv, 1869, p. 1563.

1869. Droste, F. v. Die Gansjagd am Dollart. Aus dem Holländischen: De Doll
door Stratingh en Venema. < *J. f. O.*, xvii, 1869, pp. 283–285.

1869. Forel, F. A. Faux albinisme de trois jeunes Cygnes de Morges en 1868. < *B
Soc. Vaudoise Sci. Nat.*, x, no. 61, 1869. (*Rev. et Mag. de Zool.*, 1869, pp. 334, 3:
Pas vue moi-même.

1869. Eyton, T. C. A | Synopsis | of the Anatidæ, | or Duck Tribe. | By | T. C. 1
ton, Esq., F. G. S., F. Z. S., | And Corresponding Member of the Natu
History Society of | Philadelphia. | — | Wellington, Salop : | printed by
Hobson, Market Square. | — | MDCCCLXIX. 1 vol. 16mo. 3 p. ll., pp. 1–1
May be taken as a second ed. of his monograph of the *Anatidæ* (1838), with additions, br
ing the subject up to date. It is printed in this small form for convenience of portabil
It gives, first, a diagnostic and synonymatic synopsis of the genera and subfamilies of
Anatidæ, according to the author's views; after which the species of the family receive a
ilar treatment.

1869. Giglioli, H. H. [Bernicla ruficollis in Italy (and other matters).] < *Ibis*,
ser., v, 1869, pp. 241, 242.

1869. Gunn, T. E. Parasitical Worms in the Stomach of a Redbreasted Mergan
[Mergus serrator]. < *Zoologist*, 2d ser., iv, 1869, p. 1603.

1869. Gunn, T. E. Velvet Scoter [Œdemia fusca] in Norfolk. < *Zoologist*, 2d s
iv, 1869, pp. 1722, 1723.

1869. Gunn, T. E. Canada Geese [Bernicla canadensis] at Yarmouth. <*Zoolog
2d ser., iv, 1869, p. 1848.

1869. Gunn, T. E. Redbreasted Merganser [Mergus serrator]. < *Zoologist*, 2d s
iv, 1869, p. 1848.

1869. Gunn, T. E. Black Swan [Cygnus atratus] on the Suffolk Coast. <*Zoolog
2d ser., iv, 1869, p. 1867.

1869. Gurney, J. H. Longtailed Duck [Harelda glacialis] near Lynn. <*Zoolog
2d ser., iv, 1869, p. 1563.

1869. Gurney, J. H. The Longtailed Duck [Harelda glacialis]. < *Zoologist*, 2d s
iv, 1869, p. 1563.

1869. Gurney, J. H. Goosander [Mergus merganser] near Bedale. < *Zoologist*,
ser., iv, 1869, p. 1563.

1869. Gurney, J. H., Jr. Nyroca Duck [Fuligula nyroca] in Leadenhall Mark
< *Zoologist*, 2d ser., iv, 1869, p. 1563.

1869. Gurney, J. H., Jr. Bewick's Swan [Cygnus bewicki] at Flamboroug
< *Zoologist*, 2d ser., iv, 1869, p. 1645.

1869. Malmgren, A. J. Anteckningar om Finlands och Skandinaviska halföns A
seridæ. < *Notis. Sällsk. pro Faun. et Flor. Fennica Förh.*, x, 1869, pp. 389–401.
Not seen. "Of *Anser* proper 5 speces are included, and of *Bernicla* 3, very full bibliogra
ical references being given." Cf. *Ibis*, 1870, p. 132.

1869. Malmgren, A. J. Anteckningar om Finlands och Skandinaviska halföns A
seridæ. Helsingfors. 1869.
Not seen.—Separately printed from *Notis. Sällsk. pro Fn. et Fl. Fenn. Förh.*, x, 1869,
389–401.

1869. Skinner, A. Pintailed Duck [Dafila acuta] near Faversham. < *Zoologist*,
ser., iv, 1869, p. 1563.

1869. Smee, A. H. Redcrested Merganser [Mergus serrator] on the Thames. < *.*
ologist, 2d ser., iv, 1869, p. 1684.

1869. Watson, J. Scoter [Œdemia nigra] breeding in Strathmore. < *Zoologist*,
ser., iv, 1869, p. 1867.

1869. Wickevoort-Crommelin, J. P. van. [Cygnus olor × Anser domesticus, l
brid.] < *Ibis*, 2d ser., v, 1869, p. 127.

1869. WRIGHT, J.   Summer Duck [Aix sponsa] at Lymington.   < *Zoologist,* 2d ser., iv, 1869, p. 1563.

1869. WRIGHT, J.   Black Swan [Cygnus atratus], &c., on the Solent.   < *Zoologist,* 2d ser., iv, 1869, p. 1602.

1870. ***.   A Rare Duck [Dendrocygna fulva, at New Orleans, Louisiana].   < *Am. Nat.,* iv, 1870, p. 126.

1870. ANON.   Notes on the Ducks [Anatinæ] found on the Coast of Massachusetts in Winter.   < *Am. Nat.,* iv, 1870, pp. 49, 50.

> An anonymous sportsman's criticism of a part of E. Coues's *List of the Birds of New England,* relating to eight species which the writer seldom or never saw there in winter.

1870. ANON.   Hooper [Cygnus musicus] at St. Asaph, North Wales.   < *Zoologist,* 2d ser., v, 1870, p. 2069.

> From the London 'Field,' Jan. 22, 1870.

1870. BALDAMUS, E.   Eine Brutstelle von Branta rufina in Mitteldeutschland.   < *J. f. O.,* xviii, 1870, pp. 278-281.

1870. BANNISTER, B. H.   A Sketch of the Classification of the American Anserinæ.   < *Proc. Acad. Nat. Sci. Phila.,* xxii, 1870, pp. 130-132.

> 7 genera adopted and characterized for the 18 species treated. *Oressochen,* type *Anser melanopterus,* Gay; *Chloetrophus,* type *Bernicla poliocephala,* Gray; *Philacte,* type *Anas canagica,* Sewast, p. 131, genn. nn. The writer also uses *Branta* Scop., for the Geese commonly referred to *Bernicla* Steph.

1870. BLAKE-KNOX, H.   Eider Duck [Somateria mollissima] in Dublin Bay.   < *Zoologist,* 2d ser., v, 1870, p. 2064.

1870. BLAKE-KNOX, H.   Ruddy Shieldrake [Tadorna rutila] near Tralee, County Kerry.   < *Zoologist,* 2d ser., v, 1870, pp. 2105, 2106.

1870. BLAKE-KNOX, H.   Shoveller [Spatula clypeata] in Dublin Bay.   < *Zoologist,* 2d ser., v, 1870, p. 2225.

1870. BLAKE-KNOX, H.   Plumage of the Adult Male Merganser [Mergus merganser].   < *Zoologist,* 2d ser., v, 1870, pp. 2183, 2184.

1870. CANTO, J. DE.   [Sur les éducations de Céréopses (Cereopsis novæ-hollandiæ).]   < *Bull. Soc. Acclim.,* 2d ser., vii, 1870, p. 305.

1870. GUNN, T. E.   Smew [Mergellus albellus] at Yarmouth.   < *Zoologist,* 2d ser., v, 1870, p. 2106.

1870. GURNEY, J. H., JR.   Spurwinged Goose [Plectropterus gambensis, in Great Britain].   < *Zoologist,* 2d ser., v, 1870, pp. 2346, 2347.

1870. HOCKER, J.   Ueber die wilde Jagd [Anatidæ].   < *J. f. O.,* xviii, 1870, p. 234.

1870. HÜGEL, A. DE.   Scarce Ducks in Torquay.   < *Zoologist,* 2d ser., v, 1870, pp. 1981, 1982.

1870. JONES, J. M.   Early Arrival of Geese.   < *Am. Nat.,* iv, 1870, p. 374.

> *Anser canadensis,* Nova Scotia, 23 Feb., 1870.

1870. MALMGREN, A. J.   Anzeichnungen über die Anseridæ Finlands und der skandinavischen Halbinsel.   < *J. f. O.,* xviii, 1870, pp. 287-305.

> Notiser ur Sällsk. pro Fn. et Fl. Fenn. Förh., x, 1869, pp. 389-401.

1870. MALMGREN, A. J.   Zwei ornithologische Aufsätze. I. [Vide Palæarctic.] II. Anzeichnungen über die Anseridæ Finlands und der skandinavischen Halbinsel.   < *J. f. O.,* xviii, 1870, pp. 287-305.

> Translated from *Œfv. Tidsk. Vetensk. Soc. Förh.,* 1869, p. 6, and *Notiser ur Sällsk. pro Fn. et Fl. Fenn. Forh.,* 1869, p. 389. Cf. *Ibis,* 1870, p. 132.

1870. MATHEW, M. A.   American Wigeon [Mareca americana] and Garganey [Querquedula circia] on the Taw.   < *Zoologist,* 2d ser., v, 1870, p. 2182.

1870. MONK, T. J.   Garganey [Querquedula circia] near Lewes.   < *Zoologist,* 2d ser., v, 1870, p. 2141.

1870. MOSES, H.   Spurwinged Goose [Plectropterus gambensis] in Wiltshire. $<$ *Zoologist*, 2d ser., v, 1870, p. 2105.

1870. [NEWTON, A.]   [Mr. Skeat's interpretation of the term 'lag' in connection with Anser ferus.] $<$ *Ibis*, 2d ser., vi, 1870, p. 301.

1870. PARDOE, G. O.   Redbreasted Merganser [Mergus serrator] near Oxford. $<$ *Zoologist*, 2d ser., v, 1870, p. 2142.

1870. POTTER, T. H.   Egyptian Goose [Chenalopex ægyptiacus] in Leicestershire. $<$ *Zoologist*, 2d ser., v, 1870, p. 2225.

1870. RICKARDS, M. S. C.   Pintail Duck [Dafila acuta] on the Severn. $<$ *Zoologist*, 2d ser., v, 1870, pp. 2025, 2026.

1870. RODD, E. H.   Garganey or Summer Teal [Querquedula circia] at the Land's End. $<$ *Zoologist*, 2d ser., v, 1870, p. 2141.

1870. RODD, E. H.   Redbreasted Merganser [Mergus serrator] in Adult Plumage in Winter. $<$ *Zoologist*, 2d ser., v, 1870, pp. 2141, 2142.

1870. SUTTON, R.   Black Swans [Cygnus atratus] in Lincolnshire. $<$ *Zoologist*, 2d ser., v, 1870, p. 2410.

1871. ANDERSON, A.   Weight of Graylags [Anser cinereus]. $<$ *Zoologist*, 2d ser., vi, 1871, p. 2810.

1871. BLAKE-KNOX, H.   Ferruginous Duck [Fuligula nyroca] on the Coast of Ireland. $<$ *Zoologist*, 2d ser., vi, 1871, p. 2645.

1871. BLAKE-KNOX, H.   Gadwall [Chaulelasmus streperus] in Dublin Bay. $<$ *Zoologist*, 2d ser., vi, 1871, p. 2644.

1871. BLAKE-KNOX, H.   Swans in Ireland in the Winter of 1870–71. $<$ *Zoologist*, 2d ser., vi, 1871, p. 2644.

1871. BOARDMAN, G. A.   [On the breeding of Fuligula collaris at Calais, Maine.] $<$ *Am. Nat.*, v, 1871, p. 121.

1871. BOYES, F.   Hoopers [Cygnus musicus] in East Yorkshire. $<$ *Zoologist*, 2d ser., vi, 1871, pp. 2486, 2487.

1871. BOYES, F.   Smews [Mergellus albellus] in East Yorkshire. $<$ *Zoologist*, 2d ser., vi, 1871, pp. 2487, 2488.

1871. BOYES, F.   Anatomical Peculiarity of the Hooper's Beak [Cygnus musicus]. $<$ *Zoologist*, 2d ser., vi, 1871, pp. 2504–2506, fig.

1871. BOYES, F.   Gadwall [Chaulelasmus streperus] in East Yorkshire. $<$ *Zoologist*, 2d ser., vi, 1871, pp. 2525, 2526.

1871. BOYES, F.   Goosander [Mergus merganser] in East Yorkshire. $<$ *Zoologist*, 2d ser., vi, 1871, p. 2526.

1871. BOYES, F.   Common Scoter [Œdemia nigra] Inland. $<$ *Zoologist*, 2d ser., vi, 1871, p. 2526.

1871. BOYES, F.   Brent Geese [Bernicla brenta] Inland. $<$ *Zoologist*, 2d ser., vi, 1871, p. 2643.

1871. BOYES, F.   Scoter [Œdemia nigra] near Beverley. $<$ *Zoologist*, 2d ser., vi, 1871, p. 2644.

1871. BOYES, F.   Garganey Teal [Querquedula circia] in East Yorkshire. $<$ *Zoologist*, 2d ser., vi, 1871, p. 2644.

1871. BOYES, F.   Bewick's Swan [Cygnus bewicki] near Beverley. $<$ *Zoologist*, 2d ser., vi, 1871, p. 2644.

1871. BOYES, F.   Hoopers [Cygnus musicus] in East Yorkshire. $<$ *Zoologist*, 2d ser., vi, 1871, pp. 2643, 2644.

1871. BOYNTON, T.   Hoopers [Cygnus musicus] at Hull. $<$ *Zoologist*, 2d ser., vi, 1871, p. 2487.

1871. BRADBY, A. S.   Whitefronted Goose [Anser albifrons] at Cliddesden. $<$ *Zoologist*, 2d ser., vi, 1871, p. 2486.

1871. CLOGG, S.   Egyptian Geese [Chenalopex ægyptiacus] in Cornwall.   < *Zoologist*, 2d ser., vi, 1871, p. 2523.

1871. CUNNINGHAM, R. O.   [Notice of a Memoir on the Anatomy of the Steamer Duck (Micropterus cinereus).]   < *P. Z. S.*, xxxix, 1871, p. 262.

1871. EDITORS.   A South American Bird [Erismatura dominica, in Wisconsin] in the United States.   < *Am. Nat.*, v, 1871, p. 441.
   See 1872, BREWER, T. M.

1871. ENDER, J. G.   [Doppelei einer Gans.]   < *Zool. Gart.*, xii, 1871, pp. 190, 191.
   Mit Zusatz des Herausgebers.

1871. GOATLEY, T. H.   Wild-fowl in the Southampton Waters.   < *Zoologist*, 2d ser., vi, 1871, p. 2528.

1871. GUNN, T. E.   Goosanders [Mergus merganser] and Smews [Mergellus albellus] in Norfolk.   < *Zoologist*, 2d ser., vi, 1871, p. 2527.

1871. GURNEY, J. H., JR.   King Duck [Somateria spectabilis] in Leadenhall Market.   < *Zoologist*, 2d ser., vi, 1871, p. 2443.

1871. GURNEY, J. H.   Late Occurrence of the Tufted Duck [Fuligula cristata] in Devonshire.   < *Zoologist*, 2d ser., vi, 1871, p. 2645.

1871. GURNEY, J. H.   Number of Young produced by the White Swan [Cygnus].   < *Zoologist*, 2d ser., vi, 1871, p. 2810.

1871. HADFIELD, H.   Swan laying nine Eggs.   < *Zoologist*, 2d ser., vi, 1871, pp. 2771, 2772.

1871. HARDING, H. J.   Black Swan [Cygnus atratus] and Hooper [Cygnus musicus] near Deal.   < *Zoologist*, 2d ser., vi, 1871, p. 2563.

1871. HARTING, J. E.   On the recent Occurrence of the Redbreasted Goose (Anser ruficollis, Pallas) in Essex.   < *Zoologist*, 2d ser., vi, 1871, pp. 2513, 2514.

1871. HARTING, J. E.   [Exhibition of a specimen of Anser ruficollis from Maldon, Essex.]   < *P. Z. S.*, xxxix, 1871, p. 102.

1871. HERBERT, W. H.   Velvet Scoter [Œdemia fusca] near Newbury.   < *Zoologist*, 2d ser., vi, 1871, p. 2526.

1871. LAWRENCE, G. N.   The Barnacle Goose [Bernicla leucopsis].   < *Am. Nat.*, v, 1871, pp. 10, 11.
   Occurrence of this European species at Currituck Sound, North Carolina.

1871. NEWTON, A.   On certain species of Falconidæ, Tetraonidæ, and Anatidæ. (Communicated by Mr. Coues.)   < *Proc. Acad. Nat. Sci. Phila.*, July 4, 1871, pp. 94–100.
   The *Anatidæ* here critically considered are certain European species of *Anser*.

1871. NEWTON, A.   On a remarkable Sexual Peculiarity in an Australian Species of Duck.   < *P. Z. S.*, xxxix, 1871, pp. 649–651, woodcc.
   "*Anas punctata* Cuv." Sternum and trachea. *Virago*, n. g., p. 651.

1871. NORDVI, A. G.   Anas [Somateria] stelleri, in Europa brütend.   < *J. f. O.*, xix, 1871, pp. 208, 209.
   Am nördischen Küsten der rüssischen Finmark, im Juni.

1871. PURDIE, A. C.   On the Skeleton of a Bird (supposed to be a Swan), found in Dunedin.   < *Trans. and Proc. N. Z. Inst. for* 1870, iii, 1871, *Proc. Otago Inst.*, p. 100.

1871. RICKARDS, M. S. C.   Canada Goose [Bernicla canadensis] at Glastonbury.   < *Zoologist*, 2d ser., vi, 1871, p. 2486.

1871. RODD, E. H.   Canada Goose [Bernicla canadensis] at Enys, near Penryn.   < *Zoologist*, 2d ser., vi, 1871, p. 2486.

1871. RODD, E. H.   The Redbreasted Merganser [Mergus serrator] in Cornwall.   < *Zoologist*, 2d ser., vi, 1871, pp. 2562, 2563.

1871. SHARPE, R. B. On the American Eider Duck [Somateria dresseri, n. sp.].
  < *Ann. Mag. Nat. Hist.*, 4th ser., viii, 1871, pp. 51–53, figg. 1, 2.
    The writer undertakes to specifically distinguish the American from the European Eider
    Duck, describing and figuring the supposed differences.

1871. SMEE, A. H. Wild Swan in Leadenhall Market. < *Zoologist*, 2d ser., vi, 1871,
  p. 2487.

1871. SMEE, A. H. Smew [Mergellus albellus] on the Wandle. < *Zoologist*, 2d ser.,
  vi, 1871, p. 2487.

1871. SMEE, A. H. Wild Swans on the Thames. < *Zoologist*, 2d ser., vi, 1871, p. 2525.

1871. SMEE, A. H. Goosander [Mergus merganser] in Oxfordshire. < *Zoologist*, 2d
  ser., vi, 1871, p. 2810.

1871. SMITH, CECIL. Canada Goose [Bernicla canadensis. Remarks on its occurrence
  near Glastonbury.] < *Zoologist*, 2d ser., vi, 1871, pp. 2523, 2524.

1871. STUBBS, C. E. Tufted Duck [Fuligula cristata] at Henley-on-Thames. < *Zoologist*, 2d ser., vi, 1871, p. 2526.

1871. TAYLOR, W. Wild-fowl on the Gironde. < *Zoologist*, 2d ser., vi, 1871, p. 2528.

1872. ANON. The Wild Goose [Bernicla canadensis]. < *Am. Sportsman*, ii, 1872, pp. 11,
  24; also iii, p. 75.

1872. ANON. [EDITORIAL.] Wild Fowl in England. < *Am. Sportsman*, ii, 1872, p. 8.
    Names of wild fowl of England identified with those of the United States.

1872. BEAUFFORT, L., *Comte de.* Le Cygne noir acclimaté en Europe—Note sur la
  fécondité extraordinaire d'une femelle de Cygne noir (Chenopsis atrata, Wagler) vivant a l'état domestique en Angleterre Par John Gould, Esq. J. [sic] R.
  S., etc. Suivie de quelques renseignements sur la reproduction de cet oiseau
  dans le parc du château de Bouchout, près de Bruxelles (Belgique), 1867–1872.
  < *Bull. Soc. Acclim.*, 2e sér., ix, 1872, pp. 156–163.

1872. BREWER, T. M. [On the occurrence of Erismatura dominica at Rock River,
  Busseyville, Wisconsin, November, 1870.] < *Proc. Bost. Soc. Nat. Hist.*, xiv,
  1872, p. 205.

1872. BURMEISTER, H. Synopsis of the Lamellirostres of the Argentine Republic.
  < *P. Z. S.*, 1872, pp. 364–370.
    Remarks on 24 spp. (incl. 2 spp. of *Phœnicopterus*): chiefly with reference to their habits
    and geographical distribution, and on the number of tail-feathers of several of them.

1872. DRESSER, H. E. [Exhibition of Eggs of the Marbled Duck (Querquedula marmorata).] < *P. Z. S.*, 1872, p. 605.

1872. DURNFORD, H. Peculiarities of Whitefronted Goose [Anser albifrons]. < *Zoologist*, 2d ser., vii, 1872, p. 3339.

1872. DURNFORD, H. Polish Swan [Cygnus immutabilis, from Scotland]. < *Zoologist*, 2d ser., vii, 1872, p. 3339.

1872. DURNFORD, H. Scaup Ducks [Fuligula marila, on the Mersey] in September.
  < *Zoologist*, 2d ser., vii, 1872, p. 3339.

1872. "GADWALL." Anas [Aix] Sponsa. < *Am. Sportsman*, ii, 1872, p. 8. See *ibid.*,
  iii, p. 49. •
    Observations on habits in Eastern Nebraska.

1872. GURNEY, J. H., JR. Plumage of the Whitefronted Goose [Anser albifrons].
  < *Zoologist*, 2d ser., vii, 1872, p. 3023.

1872. HOCKER, J. Schwarze Eier von Hausenten, Anas boschas. < *J. f. O.*, xx, 1872,
  pp. 232, 233.

1872. HORNBY, H. P. Tufted Ducks [Fuligula cristata] near Garstang in July: Red-
  breasted Goose [Bernicla ruficollis]. < *Zoologist*, 2d ser., vii, 1872, p. 3236.

1872. HUTTON, F. W. [On the habits of the Blue Duck of New Zealand.] < *Trans.
  and Proc. N. Z. Inst. for* 1871, iv, 1872, *Proc. Wellington Phil. Soc.*, p. 372.

1872. JÄCKEL, [A. J.]   Eiderente (Somateria mollissima) in Bayern erlegt.   *< Zool. Gart.*, xiii, 1872, p. 123.

1872. MEYER, R.   Eine junge Eiderente (Somateria mollissima) bei Assenheim in Oberhessen erlegt.   *< Zool. Gart.*, xiii, 1872, pp. 56, 57.

1872. MEYER, R.   Eine Saatgans (Anser segetum) in Gefangenschaft.   *< Zool. Gart.*, xiii, 1872, pp. 89, 90.

1872. PURDIE, A. C.   On a Supposed New Species of Duck.   *< Trans. and Proc. New Zealand Inst. for* 1871, iv, 1872, p. 213.
    An editorial note makes it out to be *Dendrocygna eytoni* Gould.   (No. 95 of *Cat. N. Z. Birds*, 1871.)   See also *tom. cit.*, p. 415.

1872. SAUNDERS, H.   On the Introduction of Anser [Chen] albatus of Cassin into the British Avifauna.   *< P. Z. S.*, 1872, pp. 519–521.
    Two specimens shot at Wexford, Ireland.

1872. SCHLEGEL, G.   Sinico-Aryaca ou Recherches sur les Racines primitives dans les langues Chinoises et Aryennes.   *< Verhandl. Bataviaasch Genoots. Kunst. en Wetens.*, xxxvi, 1872, pp. xvi, 1–181.
    Also separate.—At pp. 26, 27 are treated the roots of the words for Goose and Swan.

1872. SCHMIDT, JACOB.   Eine alte männliche Trauerente [Œdemia nigra] in Hochzeitskleid bei Frankfurt a. M. geschossen.   *< Zool. Gart.*, xiii, 1872, pp. 253, 254.

1872. SMEE, A. H.   Singular [red] Mark on the Head of a Tame Swan.   *< Zoologist*, 2d ser., vii, 1872, pp. 3112, 3113, fig.

1872. SMITH, CECIL.   Notes on the Breeding in Confinement of the Pochard [Fuligula ferina], Pinkfooted Goose [Anser brachyrhynchus], and Wigeon [Mareca penelope].   *< Zoologist*, 2d ser., vii, 1872, pp. 3243–3245.

1872. WHITAKER, J., JR.   Ducks in Nottingham Market.   *< Zoologist*, 2d ser., vii, 1872, p. 3066.

1873. ANON.   The American Widgeon [Mareca americana].   *< Am. Sportsman*, iii, 1873, p. 70.   See also p. 116.

1873. ANON.   Canvas-back Duck [Fuligula vallisneria] Shooting.   *< Am. Sportsman*, iii, 1873, p. 116.   See also p. 218.

1873. BLASIUS, W., (*und andere.*)   [Über die Artselbständigkeit von Anser minutus Naum., u. s. w.]   *< Ber. über d. xx. Versamml. d. deutschen Orn.-Ges.*, 1873, pp. 11–15.

1873. BOYES, F.   Wild Geese.   *< Zoologist*, 2d ser., viii, 1873, p. 3371.

1873. BREE, C. R.   Black Swans [Cygnus atratus, in England].   *< Zoologist*, 2d ser., viii, 1873, p. 3492.

1873. BRIGHTWELL, L.   Bravery of a Muscovy [Cairina moschata].   *< Zoologist*, 2d ser., viii, 1873, p. 3413.

1873. BREWER, T. M.   [Remarks on exhibition of a specimen of Anser frontalis from North Carolina.]   *< Proc. Boston Soc. Nat. Hist.*, xv, 1873, p. 262.

1873. BROOKE, A. B.   Gadwall [Chaulelasmus streperus] in Ireland.   *< Zoologist*, 2d ser., viii, 1873, p. 3493.

1873. CONKLIN, W. A.   Queer Conduct of a Wild Goose [Bernicla canadensis].   *< Am. Sportsman*, iii, 1873, p. 187.
    Adoption of a Cygnet in Central Park, New York City.

1873. CORBIN, G. B.   Wild Duck and Leech [which sucked it to death].   *< Zoologist*, 2d ser., viii, 1873, p. 3652.

1873. DURNFORD, H.   Ferruginous Ducks [Fuligula nyroca] and Gadwalls [Chaulelasmus streperus] in Leadenhall Market.   *< Zoologist*, 2d ser., viii, pp. 3492, 3493.

1873. "F. B."   The Eider Duck [Somateria mollissima].   *< Forest and Stream*, i, Oct. 23, 1873, p. 166.

1873–74. FOULKS, O. D. The Ducks of Chesapeake Bay and its Tributaries. <*Am. Sportsman*, iii, 1873–74, pp. 196, 212, 266.
> Descriptions of *Anas boschas, A. obscura*, and *Dafila acuta.*

1873. HECTOR, J. On Cnemiornis calcitrans, showing its Affinity to the Natatores. < *P. Z. S.*, 1873, pp. 763–771, pll. lxv–lxviii, and woodc.

1873. HÜGEL, A. v. Eider Duck [Somateria mollissima] at Christchurch. < *Zoologist*, 2d ser., viii, 1873, p. 3371.

1873. [MCCLELLAN, J.] [Wild Swan (Cygnus americanus) Shooting in Virginia.] < *Forest and Stream*, i, Dec. 4, 1873, p. 268.

1873. OTTO, H. "Erismatura leucocephala, L.—A Magyar ornisban. < *Az Eggenberger-féle Akad. Könyvkereskedés, Hoffmann és Molnár*, 1873."
> Not seen.

1873. ROWLEY, G. D. [Remarks on exhibition of a malformed variety of the Domestic Duck (Anas boschas).] < *P. Z. S.*, 1873, p. 686.

1873. SMITH, CECIL. Pinkfooted Goose [Anser brachyrhynchus]. < *Zoologist*, 2d ser., viii, 1873, pp. 3412, 3413.

1873. STEVENSON, H. Polish Swan [Cygnus immutabilis]. < *Zoologist*, 2d ser., viii, p. 1873, 3372.

1873. SWINHOE, R. On a Scaup Duck found in China. < *P. Z. S.*, 1873, pp. 411–413.
> *Fuligula mariloides* Rich.; and supposed to be distinct from *F. affinis.*

1873. "T." The Blue-winged Teal [Querquedula discors]. < *Am. Sportsman*, iii, 1873, p. 116.

1874. ANON. [EDITORIAL.] A Goose question. < *Forest and Stream*, ii, Apr. 2, 1874, p. 123.
> Brief account of the "Wild Geese" of North America; hints upon their treatment in captivity.

1874. ANON. [Enmity between Swans and Geese.] < *Am. Sportsman*, v, Nov. 7, 1874, p. 85.
> From *Chambers's Journal.*

1874. ANON. The Largest Goose [Branta canadensis] on Record. < *Am. Sportsman*, iv, 1874, p. 139.

1874. CORBIN, G. B. The Mute Swan [Cygnus olor] and its Food. < *Zoologist*, 2d ser., ix, 1874, pp. 3915, 3916.

1874. "COSMOPOLITAN." [YARROW, H. C.] On the use of Tame Ducks as Decoys. < *Am. Sportsman*, iv, 1874, p. 36. See also p. 154.

1874. COUCH, J. Mute Swan [Cygnus olor] in Guernsey. < *Zoologist*, 2d ser., ix, 1874, p. 4239.

1874. COUES, E. Hybrid Ducks [Anas boschas × Dafila acuta]. < *Forest and Stream*, ii, Feb. 26, 1874, p. 54. Also, pp. 78, 103.
> With remarks upon cross-fertilization.

1874. DEANE, R. The Ruddy Duck [Erismatura rubida, field note on.] < *Am. Nat.*, viii, 1874, pp. 433, 434.

1874. FOULKS, O. D. Tame Ducks as Decoys. < *Am. Sportsman*, iv, 1874, p. 154.
> Reply to article by "Cosmopolitan," *ibid.* p. 36.

1874. GURNEY, J. H. Note on the Voracity of a Tame Duck [Anas boschas]. < *Zoologist*, 2d ser., ix, 1874, p. 4078.

1874. GOLDSMITH, M. Wild Ducks in a city [Bremen, Germany]. < *Am. Sportsman*, iv, 1874, p. 155.
> Nineteen species of Swans, Geese, and Ducks, living at large in the parks.

1874. [HALLOCK, C.] [How the Eider Duck (Somateria mollissima) takes its young to the water.] < *Forest and Stream*, ii, Apr. 9, 1874, p. 139.

1874. HECTOR, J.   On Cnemiornis calcitrans, Owen, showing its Affinity to the Lamellirostrate Natatores.   < *Trans. and Proc. New Zealand Inst. for* 1873, vi, 1874, pp. 76–84, pll. x–xiv A.
   The plates illustrate nearly the whole skeleton in one view, with the skull, sternum, pelvis, and other bones on a larger scale.

1874. "HOMO." [WESTCOTT, C. S.]   Strange Ducks.   < *Forest and Stream,* Jan. 8, 1874, p. 342.
   Description of a nondescript captured near Philadelphia, supposed to be a hybrid between male *Anas boschas* and some female *Anser.*

1874. "J. A. C."   Unusual Migration [of wild-fowl].   <*Am. Sportsman,* iii, 1874, p. 268.

1874. KERR, W. J.   Shieldrakes [Tadorna cornuta] breeding in Merionethshire.   < *Zoologist,* 2d ser., ix, 1874, p. 4159.

1874. LINCECUM, G.   Talk of Little Things.   The White Swan [Cygnus americanus ?].   < *Am. Sportsman,* iii, 1874, p. 405.
   Habits of the species, as observed in Texas.

1874. LINCECUM, G.   [Ducks frequenting the oak woodlands of Texas.]   <*Am. Sportsman,* v, Oct. 17, 1874, p. 40.

1874. "MORTIMER KERRY."   The Anserinæ and Cygninæ [of the Northwest].   <*Forest and Stream,* iii, Oct. 8, 1874, p. 129.

1874. RIDGWAY, R.   Story of a Wild Goose [Bernicla canadensis, var. hutchinsii].   < *Am. Sportsman,* iv, 1874, p. 258.
   Habits of a domesticated bird.   Synopsis of American Wild Geese.

1874. RIDGWAY, R.   The Snow Goose [Chen hyperboreus].   <*Am. Nat.,* viii, 1874, pp. 636, 637.
   Note on this species in semi-domestication.

1874. RODD, E. H.   Gargany Teal [Querquedula circia] at the Land's End.   < *Zoologist,* 2d ser., ix, 1874, pp. 3953, 3954.

1874. ROPE, G. T.   Nesting of the Garganey [Querquedula circia] and Wild Duck [Anas boschas].   < *Zoologist,* 2d ser., ix, 1874, p. 4036.

1874. VERRALL, J. H.   Hybrid Ducks Breeding.   <*Zoologist,* 2d ser., ix, 1874, p. 3836.
   From the London 'Field', Oct. 18, 1873.

1874. WHITAKER, J., JR.   Egyptian Geese [Chenalopex ægyptiacus] in Nottinghamshire.   < *Zoologist,* 2d ser., ix, 1874, p. 3882.

1874. WHITAKER, J.   Ducks Breeding in the Rainworth Water.   < *Zoologist,* 2d ser., ix, 1874, pp. 4159, 4160.

1875. ANON.   Great Flock of Wild Geese in California.   < *Rod and Gun,* vii, Nov. 27, 1875, p. 139.

1875. ANON.   [EDITORIAL.]   Hybrid Wild Ducks.   < *Forest and Stream,* iv, Aug. 5, 1875, p. 410.

1875. ANON.   Der Eiderente [Somateria mollissima].   < *Aus der Natur,* lxvi, oder n. F., liv, 1875, pp. 277–280.
   Nach Zinkel und Preyer's Reise nach Island im Sommer 1860 mitgetheilt.

1875. BAILEY, J. S.   The Canada Goose—(Anser [Bernicla] canadensis).   <*Forest and Stream,* iv, May 20, 1875, p. 230.

1875. BOARDMAN, G. A.   Hybrid Ducks.   < *Forest and Stream,* Dec. 9, 1875, p. 276.
   Reply to Prof. Le Conte's question (p. 260).

1875. BROOKE, A. B.   [On the breeding of Fuligula cristata in Great Britain.]   <*Ibis,* v, 3d ser., 1875, pp. 514, 515.

1875. CORBIN, G. B.   Nesting of the Teal [Querquedula crecca] in Hampshire.   < *Zoologist,* 2d ser., x, May, 1875, pp. 4457, 4458.

1875. CORBIN, G. B.   Shieldrake [Tadorna cornuta] near Ringwood.   < *Zoologist,* 2d ser., x, June, 1875, p. 4500.

1875. COUES, E.   Duck shooting a cheval [on northwestern plains].   <*Rod and Gu*
vi, Apr. 24, 1875, p. 49.

1875. CROSIER, E. S.   The Whistling Swan [Cygnus americanus, in Kentucky]
<*Am. Nat.*, ix, No. 5, May, 1875, p. 313.

1875. DALGLEISH, J. J.   Shieldrake [Tadorna cornuta] in the Færoe Islands.   <*Z*
ologist, 2d ser., x, Mar., 1875, p. 4383.

1875. "FRED."   Habits of the Wood Duck—Aix Sponsa.   <*Forest and Stream*, i
July 22, 1875, p. 374.

1875. GARROD, A. H.   On the Form of the Lower Larynx in certain Species of Duck
<*P. Z. S.*, Mar. 2, 1875, pp. 151–156, figg. 1–7.
   Conditions of the larynx in some rare *Anatidæ* not referred to by either Eyton or Yarrel
   There are figured the parts of *Sarcidiornis melanota* (f. 1 ♂, 2 ♀), *Rhodonessa caryoph*
   lacea (f. 3 ♀, 4, 5 ♂), and *Metopiana peposarca* (f. 6, 7 ♂).

1875. GURNEY, J. H.   Longevity of a Wild Duck [Anas boschas, æt. 22].   <*Zool*
gist, 2d ser., x, July, 1875, p. 4541.

1875. HAPGOOD, W.   Brant Geese; (Anser bernicla—Linn.)   Their habits—migr
tion—breeding-places.   <*Forest and Stream*, v, Sept. 2, 1875, p. 49.

1875. LAMBERTON, A. B.   Canvas-back duck, (Anas [Fuligula] Vallisneria—Wilson
<*Rod and Gun*, vi, Apr. 17, 1875, pp. 34, 35.
   With special reference to Chesapeake Bay.

1875. LE CONTE, J. L.   Is hybridity in ducks increasing?   <*Forest and Stream*,
Dec. 2, 1875, p. 260.
   Information asked, with comments on the bearings of the case, if it be so; with editor
   remarks appended.   The answers received failed to confirm Prof. Le Conte's supposition.

1875. LEIDY, [J.]   On Psorosperms in a Mallard Duck [Anas boschas].   <*Proc. Aca*
Nat. Sci. Phila., 1875, p. 125.

1875. NEWMAN, E.   Food of Wild Duck.   <*Zoologist*, 2d ser., x, Dec., 1875, p. 4732.

1875. NICHOLLS, R. P.   Longtailed Duck [Harelda glacialis] in Kingsbridge Estuar
<*Zoologist*, 2d ser., x, Nov., 1875, p. 4697.

1875. RODD, E. H.   Graylag Goose [Anser cinereus] near Penzance.   <*Zoologist*,
ser., x, May, 1875, p. 4459.

1875. [SCLATER, P. L.]   [Breeding of Anas pœcilorhyncha in the Society's Menag
rie.]   <*P. Z. S.*, Nov. 2, 1875, p. 528.

1875. SMITH, GREENE.   [Habitat of Bernicla brenta,] Brant.   <*Rod and Gun*, vi
Dec. 18, 1875, p. 185.   See also pp. 200, 211, 232, 242, 306, 312.

1875. STERLING, E.   Brant [Bernicla brenta].   <*Rod and Gun*, vii, Dec. 25, 187
p. 200.
   Do not occur in Lake Erie.

1875. SHARPE, R. B.   Description of an apparently new Species of Teal [Querquedu
eatoni] from Kerguelen's Island.   <*Ibis*, 3d ser., v, 1875, pp. 328, 329.

1875. "TEAL." [R. L. NEWCOMB.]   [Response to Prof. Le Conte's question, p. 26
as to hybridity in Ducks.]   <*Forest and Stream*, v, Dec. 9, 1875, p. 276.

1875. "TOM TRAMP."   Wild Goose [Bernicla canadensis] shooting on the Wester
Prairies.   <*Rod and Gun*, vi, Apr. 24, 1875, p. 54.

1875. VAN BENEDEN, P. J.   Un oiseau fossile nouveau des cavernes de la Nouvell
Zélande.   <*Gerv. Journ. de Zool.*, iv, 1875, pp. 267–272.
   Anas finschi, p. 271.—Extrait des *Ann. de la Soc. Géol. de Belgique*, t. ii, p. 123.

1876. ALLEN, J. A.   Breeding of the Canada Goose [Bernicla canadensis] in tree
<*Bull. Nutt. Ornith. Club*, i, No. 2, July, 1876, p. 50.

1876. ALLEN, J. A.   Anser [Chen] rossii in Oregon.   <*Bull. Nutt. Ornith. Club*, i, N
2, July, 1876, p. 52.

1876. ANON. [Attachment of a domestic Goose to its keeper.] < *Rod and Gun*, viii, Apr. 1, 1876, p. 7.

1876. ANON. [Habits of Fuligula vallisneria.] < *Rod and Gun*, vii, Feb. 12, 1876, p. 313. From "Philadelphia Times."

1876. ANON. [Enormous abundance of] Wild Geese [Bernicla canadensis] in L[ouisian]a. < *Rod and Gun*, ix, Dec. 30, 1876, p. 202.

1876. "ARROW." Brant [Bernicla brenta, in Illinois]. < *Rod and Gun*. viii, May 13, 1876, p. 99.

1876. BAGOT, C. F. A. Longtailed Duck [Harelda glacialis] at Hunstanton. < *Zoologist*, 2d ser., xi, Jan., 1876, p. 4766.

1876. BAIRD, S. F. [Information wanted concerning Camptolæmus labradorius.] < *Forest and Stream*, vi, Apr. 6, 1876, p. 133. See pp. 181, 197.

1876. BAILEY, J. H. [Hybridity in Ducks.] < *Forest and Stream*, v, Jan. 27, 1876, p. 388.
Refers to and criticizes statement (see p. 339) that hybrid Ducks were fertile at Mt. Auburn; an editorial [Ingersoll, E.] note appended reaffirms the truth of the fact questioned.

1876. BOARDMAN, G. A. The Labrador duck [Camptolæmus labradorius]. < *Forest and Stream*, vi, Apr. 27, 1876, p. 181.
Formerly common in Bay of Fundy. See pp. 133, 197.

1876. BOYES, F. Rust-colour on the Breast of Teal [Querquedula crecca]. < *Zoologist*, 2d ser., xi, Nov., 1876, pp. 5168, 5169.

1876. COUES, E. Coues to "Boone." < *Rod and Gun*, vi, Jan. 15, 1876, p. 248. See also pp. 232, 242.
Sustains truth of "Boone's" assertion that he shot *Bernicla brenta* inland.

1876. COUES, E. Dr. Coues on Brant, etc. < *Rod and Gun*, viii, Apr. 1, 1876, p. 8.
Reply to Greene Smith's remarks, vol. vii, p. 312.

1876. COUES, E. The Labrador Duck [Camptolæmus labradorius]. < *Am. Nat.*, x, 1876, p. 303.
Offer of £40 for a good pair of *Camptolæmus labradorius*, on the part of H. E. Dresser.

1876. COVERT, A. B. The Labrador duck [Camptolæmus labradorius]. < *Forest and Stream*, vi, May 4, 1876, p. 197. See pp. 133 and 181.
Specimen taken at Delhi, Mich., Apr., 1872.

1876. DALGLEISH, J. J. Velvet Scoter [Œdemia fusca]. < *Zoologist*, 2d ser., xi, Oct., 1876, p. 5126.

1876. DARRAGH, T. Edible Qualities of the Shoveller Duck [Spatula clypeata]. < *Zoologist*, 2d ser., xi, May, 1876, p. 4930.

1876. ESTEY, T. H. [Change of plumage by male of Anas boschas in summer.] < *Forest and Stream*, v, Jan. 13, 1876, p. 356.

1876. ESTEY, T. H. Hybrid Ducks. < *Forest and Stream*, v, Jan. 27, 1876, p. 388.
Rare in California; cases noted.

1876. "F. J. C. S." Crippled Birds. < *Rod and Gun*, vii, Mar. 18, 1876, p. 387.
Example of knitting of wing-bone of a mallard, and argument that wounded Ducks often recover from injuries.

1876. FOULKS, O. D. Ducks—The Idea. < *Rod and Gun*, vii, Feb. 26, 1876, p. 339.
Regarding *Bucephala albeola* and other edible species.

1876. [GERVAIS, P.] Owen (Richard): Restauration du squelette du Cnemiornis calcitrans et remarques sur les affinités de cet Oiseau avec les Lamellirostres (Trans. zool. Soc. London, t. IX, p. 253, pl. xxxv–xxxix, 1875). < *Gerv. Journ. de Zool.*, v, 1876, pp. 75, 76.

1876. [GERVAIS, P.] Hector (J.): Sur le Cnemiornis calcitrans, Owen, Oiseau fossile de la Nouvelle-Zélande; pour montrer ses affinités avec les Palmipèdes (Trans. and Proceed. New-Zealand Institut, t. IV, p. 76, pl. x à xv, 1874.—Proceed. zool. Soc. London, 1873, p. 763). < *Gerv. Journ. de Zool.*, v, 1876, pp. ———.

1876. GURNEY, J. H. [Remarks on the breeding of the Polish Swan (Cygnus immutabilis) in captivity.] < P. Z. S., June 6, 1876, p. 466.

1876. GURNEY, J. H. Curious Capture of Scoter Duck [Œdemia nigra]. < Zoologist, 2d ser., xi, Jan., 1876, p. 4764.

1876. GURNEY, J. H., JR. [Remarks on Exhibition of Anser erythropus from Egypt.] < P. Z. S., May 2, 1876, p. 414.

1876. GURNEY, J. H., JR. The Edible Qualities of the Shoveller Duck [Spatula clypeata]. < Zoologist, 2d ser., xi, Feb., 1876, pp. 4802, 4803.

1876. GURNEY, J. H., JR. Goosander [Mergus merganser] at Slapton Ley. < Zoologist, 2d ser., xi, Feb., 1876, p. 4803.

1876. GURNEY, J. H., JR. Wigeon [Mareca penelope]. < Zoologist, 2d ser., xi, Feb., 1876, p. 4803.

1876. GURNEY, J. H., JR. The Original and correct Spelling of Shielduck. < Zoologist, 2d ser., xi, Mar., 1876, p. 4846.
    "Sheld" = particoloured.

1876. GURNEY, J. H., JR. Hooded Merganser [Lophodytes cucullatus]. < Zoologist, 2d ser., xi, Mar., 1876, p. 4847.

1876. GURNEY, J. H., JR. King Duck [Somateria spectabilis] in Leadenhall Market. < Zoologist, 2d ser., xi, Feb., 1876, p. 4863.

1876. GURNEY, J. H., JR. The Labrador Duck [Camptolæmus labradorius]. < Zoologist, 2d ser., xi, May, 1876, pp. 4929, 4930.

1876. GURNEY, J. H., JR. Lesser Whitefronted Goose [Anser minutus]. < Zoologist, 2d ser., xi, May, 1876, p. 4930.

1876. GURNEY, J. H., JR. Lesser Whitefronted Goose [Anser minutus]. < Zoologist, 2d ser., xi, July, 1876, p. 5006.

1876. GURNEY, J. H., JR. Varieties of the Teal [Querquedula crecca]. < Zoologist, 2d ser., xi, Aug., 1876, p. 5047.

1876. GURNEY, J. H., JR. The Polish Swan [Cygnus immutabilis]. < Zoologist, 2d ser., xi, Aug., 1876, p. 5047.

1876. GURNEY, J. H., JR. Food of the Redbreasted Merganser [Mergus serrator]. < Zoologist, 2d ser., xi, Sept., 1876, p. 5085.

1876. HARVIE-BROWN, J. A. Varieties of the Teal [Querquedula crecca]. < Zoologist, 2d ser., xi, Sept., 1876, p. 5085.

1876. HAYMOND, R. Note on the Blue Goose [Anser cœrulescens, in Indiana]. < Am. Nat., x, No. 6, June, 1876, p. 374.

1876. HOWELL, T. H. The Barnacle Goose [Bernicla leucopsis, in La Salle County, Illinois]. < Forest and Stream, vii, Nov. 23, 1876, p. 245.

1876. "J. H. D." "Butter-Balls." < Rod and Gun, vii, Mar. 4, 1876, p. 355.
    Defense of edible qualities of Bucephala albeola.

1876. [INGERSOLL, E.] Cultivating wild rice to attract [wild] fowl. < Forest and Stream, vii, Sept. 7, 1876, p. 72. See p. 137.

1876. [INGERSOLL, E.] Hybrid Duck[s in Mt. Auburn cemetery]. < Forest and Stream, v, Jan. 6, 1876, p. 339. Also p. 388.

1876. KENDALL, C. G. The Barnacle Goose [Bernicla leucopsis]. < Forest and Stream, vii, Oct. 26, 1876, p. 181.
    Notice of capture of an individual on Long Island, N. Y.

1876. KENDALL, J. R. More about the Barnacle Goose [Bernicla leucopsis]. < Forest and Stream, vii, Dec. 7, 1876, p. 276. See p. 245.
    Further details regarding the specimen referred to in the preceding title.

1876. LONG, J. W. Brant [Bernicla brenta, in the interior]. < Rod and Gun, vii, July 22, 1876, p. 260.

1876. MACHEN, W. H.   Brant [Bernicla brenta, in Lake Erie].   < *Rod and Gun*, vii, Jan. 15, 1876, p. 242.   See also pp. 185, 200.

1876. MATHEW, G. F.   Hooded Merganser [Lophodytes cucullatus].   < *Zoologist*, 2d ser., xi, June, 1876, p. 4958.

1876. NICHOLLS, R. P.   Smew [Mergellus albellus] at Slapton Ley.   < *Zoologist*, 2d ser., xi, Feb., 1876, p. 4803.

1876. PEACOCK, A.   Variation of Colour in the Teal [Querquedula crecca].   <*Zoologist*, 2d ser., xi, Dec., 1876, p. 5180.

1876. POOLE, R.   Reported Occurrence of the King Duck [Somateria spectabilis] at Maldon.   < *Zoologist*, 2d ser., xi, Jan., 1876, p. 4766.

1876. PRINCE, H. R.   Smew [Mergellus albellus] at Taunton.   < *Zoologist*, 2d ser., xi, Mar., 1876, p. 4847.

1876. [PRINCE, H. R.]   Smew [Mergellus albellus] near Old Malton.   < *Zoologist*, 2d ser., xi, Mar., 1876, p. 4847.

1876. PRIOR, C. M.   Duck nesting in a Pollard Willow.   < *Zoologist*, 2d ser., xi, July, 1876, pp. 5006, 5007.

1876. RICE, F. L.   The True Brant [Bernicla brenta] in Wisconsin.   < *Rod and Gun*, viii, Aug. 5, 1876, p. 293.

1876. RODD, E. H.   Longtailed Duck [Harelda glacialis] near Padstow, Cornwall.   < *Zoologist*, 2d ser., xi, Dec., 1876, p. 5180.

1876. ROWLEY, G. D.   Chen albatus.   (Cassin's Snow-Goose.)   < *Rowl. Orn. Misc.*, ii, pt. v, Oct., 1876, pp. 93–100, pl. xlvii.

> An extended article on Snow Geese in general, with special reference to the capture of *O. albatus* in Ireland, Nov., 1871.

1876. SCLATER, P. L., *and* SALVIN, O.   A Revision of the Neotropical Anatidæ.   < *P. Z. S.*, Apr. 4, 1876, pp. 358–412, pl. xxxiv.

> Introduction, p. 358; Preliminary remarks, p. 358; Synopsis of the species, p. 369; Table of geographical distribution, p. 409.—*Anatidæ* divided into seven subfamilies.   *Anser* (3), *Bernicla* (7 or 8), *Chenalopex* (1), *Cygnus* (2), *Dendrocygna* (5), *Sarcidiornis* (1), *Cairina* (1), *Anas* (5), *Heteronetta* (1), *Querquedula* (10), (*Q. andium*, pl. 34), *Dafila* (3), *Mareca* (2), *Spatula* (2), *Aix* (1), *Metopiana* (1), *Fuligula* (5), *Clangula* (2), *Œdemia* (1), *Tachyeres* (Owen, *Tr. Z. S.*, ix, 1875, 254) (1), *Erismatura* (3), *Merganetta* (3), *Mergus* (2).   These spp. are worked out in a masterly manner, with copious synonymy, diagnosis, habitat, and criticism; forming by far the most satisfactory presentation of Neotropical *Anatidæ* extant.

1876. [SCLATER, P. L.]   [On the species of Sarcidiornis.]   < *P. Z. S.*, Nov. 7, 1876, pp. 694, 695, pll. lxvii, lxviii.

> Pl. 67, *S. melanonota;* pl. 68, *S. carunculata.*

1876. SMITH, GREENE.   Brant [Bernicla brenta].   < *Rod and Gun*, vii, Feb. 12, 1876, p. 312.

> Replies to criticisms of his statement (p. 185, Dec. 18, 1875) that *Bernicla brenta* was never found inland, confessing his mistake.   Also comments and inquiries upon the different forms of American *Anseres.*

1876. SOUTHWELL, T.   The Polish Swan [Cygnus immutabilis].   < *Zoologist*, 2d ser., xi, Sept., 1876, pp. 5084, 5085.

1876. STANSELL, F.   Common Scoter [Œdemia nigra] at Minehead.   < *Zoologist*, 2d ser., xi, Apr., 1876, p. 4883.

1876. STANSELL, F.   Female Smew [Mergellus albellus] near Curry Rivel.   < *Zoologist*, 2d ser., xi, May, 1876, p. 4930.

1876. STEVENSON, H.   [Letter on the rusty coloring matter of the heads of Swans.]   < *Ibis*, 3d ser., vi, Apr., 1876, pp. 276, 277.

> Determined by F. Kitton to be peroxide of iron, Fe_2O_3.   The rusty tinge probably produced by contact with ferruginous sand.

1876. STREETS, T. H.   Description of a New Duck from Washington Island [Chaulelasmus couesi].   < *Bull. Nutt. Ornith. Club*, i, No. 2, July, 1876, pp. 46, 47.

1876. "UPPER DES MOINES." Brant and Geese. < *Rod and Gun*, vii, Feb. 12, 1876, p. 306.
Habits, nesting, etc., in Iowa.

1877. ABBOTT, C. C. Leaves from my Note-Book. The Wood Duck [Aix sponsa] and Her Young. < *The Country*, i, Dec. 29, 1877, p. 115.
Fledglings carried down from nest to water on shoulders of the mother.

1877. AKHURST, J. Capture of the Egyptian Goose [Chenalopex ægyptiacus] on Long Island. < *Bull. Nutt. Ornith. Club*, ii, No. 2, Apr., 1877, p. 52.

1877. ANON. The Canada Goose [Bernicla canadensis]. < *Forest and Stream*, viii, Feb. 15, 1877, p. 17.

1877. ANON. A Proof of Instinct. < *Forest and Stream*, viii, Mar. 22, 1877, p. 96.
Wild Geese supporting a wounded one in the air.

1877. ANON. Tame Wild Geese. < *Forest and Stream*, viii, June 7, 1877, p. 280.
Reprinted from St. Louis "Republican."

1877. ANON. Shells in red head duck's [Fuligula americana] craw. < *Forest and Stream*, ix, Dec. 20, 1877, p. 380. See pp. 266, 285, 327.

1877. ANON. What our Ducks Eat [on North Atlantic coast]. < *Forest and Stream*, ix, Nov. 29, 1877, p. 327. See p. 380.

1877. ANON. What Red Head Ducks [Fuligula americana] Eat [Ruppia maritima, etc.]. < *Forest and Stream*, ix, pp. 266, 285. See pp. 327, 380.

1877. "AUDUBON." Domesticated Wild Geese [Bernicla canadensis]. < *Forest and Stream*, viii, Mar. 1, 1877, p. 50. See pp. 96, 177.

1877. COUES, E. Note on the Cinnamon Teal (Querquedula cyanoptera [in Colorado]). < *Bull. Nutt. Ornith. Club*, ii, No. 2, Apr., 1877, p. 51.

1877. [COUES, E.] Birds. < *The Mirror* (Baltimore, Md.), Dec., 1877.
Notices of certain North American *Anatidæ*, from "Birds of the Northwest."

1877. "G. P." Habits of Domesticated Wild Geese [Bernicla canadensis]. < *Forest and Stream*, viii, March 22, 1877, p. 96. See pp. 50, 177.

1877. GURNEY, J. H. Note on the Polish Swan [Cygnus immutabilis]. < *P. Z. S.* June 19, 1877, pp. 579, 580.

1877. GURNEY, J. H., JR. [Letter on the Tracheæ of certain Anatidæ.] < *Ibis*, 4t ser., i, July, 1877, pp. 395, 396.

1877. "H. H." Domestication of the Canada Goose [Bernicla canadensis]. < *Fore and Stream*, viii, April 26, 1877, p. 177. See pp. 50, 96.

1877. LAWRENCE, G. N. Occurrence of the Barnacle Goose (Bernicla leucopsis) o Long Island, N. Y. < *Bull. Nutt. Ornith. Club*, ii, No. 1, Jan., 1877, p. 18.
Covering a letter from J. R. Kendall. Including note by R. Deane.

1877. LE BARON, J. F. Habits of the Whistler [Bucephala americana]. < *Am. Na* xi, No. 1, Jan., 1877, p. 44, 45.

1877. "P." Brant [Bernicla brenta] in Texas. < *Forest and Stream*, ix, Dec. 27, 18 p. 397.

1877. "RECAPPER." [T. S. ABBOTT.] The Dusky Duck [Anas obscura]. < *T Country*, i, Dec. 8, 1877, p. 74.

1877. "R. H." Domesticated Wild Geese [Bernicla canadensis] Breeding. < *For and Stream*, viii, July 5, 1877, p. 360.

1877. ROWLEY, G. D. Somateria [Camptolæmus] labradoria (J. F. Gmelin). (T Pied Duck.) < *Rowl. Orn. Misc.*, ii, pt. vi, Jan., 1877, pp. 205–224, pl. lv, a five others, not numbered.
A very complete monograph of this rare and apparently moribund species, including a of 33 known specimens. Pl. 55 figures the bird, both sexes, in colors. The other five pl show sternums, heads, and feet of various Eiders.

1877. SCLATER, P. L. Notice of an apperently new Species of Spur-winged Goose of the Genus Plectropterus [niger]. < *P. Z. S.*, Feb. 5, 1877, pp. 47, 48, pl. vii.

1877. "SEMI-OCCASIONAL." The Habits of Wild Geese [Bernicla canadensis]. How to Capture the Birds. < *Forest and Stream*, vii, Feb. 1, 1877, p. 412.

1877. SMITH, GREENE. Brant [Bernicla brenta; habitat of, investigated]. < *Forest and Stream*, Nov. 15, 1877, p. 285.

1877. TRIMEN, R. [Letter on Sarcidiornis, with reference to P. Z. S., 1876, pp. 694, 695.] < *P. Z. S.*, Nov. 6, 1877, p. 683.

1877. VIBERT, P. Breeding of the Wild Goose [Bernicla canadensis] in Confinement. < *Forest and Stream*, vii, Jan. 18, 1877, p. 373. See p. 405.

1877. YARROW, H. C. The Black Duck [Anas obscura] in the Rocky Mountains. < *Forest and Stream*, viii, Feb. 8, 1877, p. 4.

> Correcting previous remark by editor that *Anas obscura* had not been found West previous to record on p. 404 of Vol. VII.

1878. A[LLEN], J. A. Rowley's "The Pied Duck [Camptolæmus labradorius]." < *Bull. Nutt. Ornith. Club*, iii, No. 2, Apr., 1878, p. 79, 80.

> Review of this monographic essay.

1878. ALLEN, J. A. Occurrence of three Species of Sea-Ducks [Œdemia americana, Œ. fusca, Œ. perspicillata] at St. Louis, Missouri. < *Bull. Nutt. Ornith. Club*, iii, No. 3, July, 1878, pp. 148, 149.

1878. BREWSTER, W. Occurrence of the Whistling Swan (Cygnus americanus) in Massachusetts. < *Bull. Nutt. Ornith. Club*, iii, No. 4, Oct., 1878, pp. 198, 199.

> With full particulars of the capture.

1878. BREWSTER, W. Breeding of the Hooded Merganser (Mergus cucullatus) in Florida. < *Bull. Nutt. Ornith. Club*, iii, No. 1, Jan., 1878, p. 40.

1878. B[OISEAU], R. F. Our Washington Letter [concerning Ducks on the Potomac]. < *Forest and Stream*, ix, Jan. 17, 1878, p. 458.

1878. COUES, E. Peculiar Feathers of the young Ruddy Duck [Erismatura rubida]. < *Am. Nat.*, xii, No. 2, 1878, p. 123, 124, fig. 1.

1878. GOSS, N. S. The true Brant [Bernicla brenta] in Kansas. < *Forest and Stream*, ix, Jan. 10, 1878, p. 430.

1878. "H. G." A Domesticated Teal [Querquedula discors]. < *Forest and Stream*, x, March 14, 1878, p. 95.

1878. "HOMO." [C. S. WESTCOTT.] The Brant of the United States. < *Chicago Field*, Feb., 1878, p. 4, fig.

> Discussing these Geese, with special reference to *Bernicla nigricans*, which is figured.

1878. JONES, J. M. The Mollusca of Nova Scotia. < *Forest and Stream*, x, March 7, 1878, p. 75.

> Note of contents of craw of *Clangula islandica*.

1878. LAWRENCE, N. T. The European Widgeon (Mareca penelope) in the United States. < *Bull. Nutt. Ornith. Club*, iii, No. 2, Apr., 1878, p. 98.

1878. McCARTY, P. Swan [Cygnus americanus] Shooting on the Potomac. < *Forest and Stream*, x, Mar. 14, 1878, p. 93.

1878. PACKARD, A. S., JR. Wild Geese [Bernicla canadensis] Nesting in Trees. < *Am. Nat.*, xii, No. 1, Jan., 1878, p. 54.

1878. ROWLEY, G. D. On the Breeding-places of two Members of the British Anatidæ. < *Rowl. Orn. Misc.*, iii, pt. xiv, May, 1878, pp. 229–232, pl. cx.

> *Anas fuligula, Anas ferina.*

1878. SCLATER, P. L. Further Remarks on Fuligula nationi. < *P. Z. S.*, May 7, 1878, pp. 477–479, figg. 1, 2, pl. xxxii.

> See *P. Z. S.*, 1877. p. 522. The species is here recharacterized, with figg. of trachea, and pl. of ♂ ♀.

1878. [SCOTT, W. E. D.] Snow Geese [Chen hyperboreus and var. albatus, at Curri-
  tuck]. < *The Country*, i, Feb. 16, 1878, p. 229.

1878. [SCOTT, W. E. D.] A Remarkable Bird. < *The Country*, i, Jan. 26, 1878, p. 180.
  See p. 213.
  Hybrid, supposed to be between Mallard and Muscovy.

1878. SMITH, EVERETT. Eider Ducks [Somateria mollissima]. < *The Country*, ii,
  May 11, 1878, p. 42.

1878. [STACY, D. F.] Brant [Bernicla brenta] in Minnesota. < *Forest and Stream*, x,
  Feb. 28, 1878, p. 55.

1878. "TONIC." Domesticated Wood Ducks [Aix sponsa]. < *Forest and Stream*, x,
  April 18, 1878, p. 196.

1878. WITMER, J. M. Domestication of the Mallard Duck [Anas boschas]. < *Forest
  and Stream*, xi, Nov. 14, 1878, p. 300.

1879. ARNY, H. W. Killed by Telegraph [Wires]. < *Forest and Stream*, xii, May 8,
  1879, p. 265.
  Cygnus americanus killed by flying against the wires.

1879. BERIER, L. Capture of the European Widgeon [Mareca penelope] in North
  Carolina. < *Bull. Nutt. Ornith. Club*, iv, No. 3, July, 1879, p. 190.

1879. BREWER, T. M. The Rocky Mountain Golden-Eye (Bucephala [Clangula]
  islandica). < *Bull. Nutt. Ornith. Club*, iv, No. 3, July, 1879, pp. 148–152.
  Chiefly respecting its geographical distribution; with description of its eggs. The writer
  contends that it is not the boreal species it is commonly supposed to be; very curiously adduc-
  ing its alpine range in the United States in support of his position.

1879. BREWSTER, W. Additional Notes on the Whistling Swan (Cygnus americanus)
  in New England. < *Bull. Nutt. Ornith. Club*, iv, No. 2, Apr., 1879, pp. 125, 126.

1876. CONKLIN, W. A. Animals at Central Park. Eider Duck [Somateria mollissima].
  < *Rod and Gun*, ix, Nov. 4, 1876, p. 73.

1879. COUES, E. Letters on Ornithology. No. 21.—History of the Red-breasted, or
  Cinnamon Teal.—(Querquedula cyanoptera, Cass.) < *The Chicago Field*, May
  17, 1879.
  From the "Birds of the Northwest."

1879. COUES, E. Letters on Ornithology. No. 22.—The Snow Goose, or White Brant.
  —Anser [Chen] hyperboreus, Pall. < *The Chicago Field*, May 24, 1879.
  From the "Birds of the Northwest."

1879. COUES, E. Note on Bucephala [Clangula] islandica. < *Bull. Nutt. Ornith.
  Club*, iv, No. 2, Apr., 1879, pp. 126, 127.
  J. B. Gilpin's observations on the trachea of this and *Clangula glaucium*.

1879. DEXTER, N. Capture of a Swan [Cygnus americanus] in Rhode Island. < *Forest and Stream*, xiii, Nov. 27, 1879, p. 848.

1879. EDITOR. [? HALLOCK, C.] A Hybrid Duck. < *Forest and Stream*, xii, Apr. 24,
  1879, p. 226.
  Supposed hybrid between *Aix sponsa* and *Fuligula ferina americana*.
  "I did not see skin and know nothing of it." [G. B. Grinnell *in lit.* to E. C.]

1879. GREGG, W. H. Camptolæmus labradorius. < *Am. Nat.*, xiii, No. 2, Feb., 1879,
  pp. 128, 129.
  Interesting note of the occurrence of this now very rare bird near Elmira, Chemung County,
  New York, Dec. 12, 1878.

1879. [GRINNELL, G. B.] On the Golden Eyes or Garrots in Nova Scotia. < *Forest
  and Stream*, xi, Jan. 23, 1879, p. 502.
  Notice of J. Bernard Gilpin's paper with this title.

1879. HENSHALL, J. A. What are English Ducks. < *Forest and Stream*, xiii, Dec. 4,
  1879, p. 867.
  Refers to popular name of *Anas boschas* in Florida.

1879. HENSHAW, H. W.   Occurrence of Ross's Goose (Anser [Chen] rossii) on the Pacific Coast [of the United States] and Inland.   < *Bull. Nutt. Ornith. Club*, iv, No. 2, Apr., 1879, p. 126.

1879. [INGERSOLL, E.]   [Occurrence of Anser hyperboreus (var. albatus ?) in Ireland.]   < *Science News*, i, No. 5, Jan. 1, 1879, p. 76.

  Referring to the captures before announced by J. E. Harting, in ———.

1879. "J. P. H."   Ducks Attracted by Light.   < *Forest and Stream*, xiii, Nov. 6, 1879, p. 785.

  "Coots," *Œdemia*, killed by flying against the windows of a light-house.

1879. NEILSON, J.   Another Rare Bird.   < *Newspaper* of Quebec, Canada, name unknown, date late in May (about the 21st), 1879.

  Description indicates *Aix sponsa*, and a colored drawing of the head sent to the Smithsonian by J. M. Le Moine of Quebec confirms this diagnosis.   The specimen was albinotic to a degree.

1879. TRIMEN, R.   [Letter relating to the habitat of Plectropterus niger (Zanzibar).]   < *P. Z. S.*, Jan. 14, 1879, p. 5.

Sulidæ.

1757. HÉRISSANT, F. D.   [Observation sur la structure de l'estomac de l'Anser (Sula) bassanus.]   < *Hist. de l'Acad. Roy. des Sci.* pour l'année 1753, 1757, pp. 142, 143.

1773. VINCENT, —.   Lettre sur le grand Fou [Sula bassana].   < *Observ. sur la Phys.*, i, 1773, pp. 470–473.
Pas vue moi-même.

1786. ÖDMANN, S.   Undersökning om de gamle Auctorers Catarrhactes.   < *Kongl. Vet.-Akad. Nga Handl.*, vii, 1786, pp. 73–78.

1811. MONTAGU, G.   Observations on some Peculiarities observable in the structure of the Gannet, Pelecanus [Sula] Bassanus.   And an account of a new and curious Insect, discovered to inhabit the Cellular Membrane of that Bird.   < *Mem. Wernerian Nat. Hist. Soc.*, i, 1811, pp. 176–193, pl. vii, figs. 1–3.
Read July, 1808. Introduced by notice of habits, etc. The account relates chiefly to the various air-receptacles of the body, the remarkable pneumaticity of the bird being dwelt upon. The parasite, *Cellularia bassani*, is figured, and some external parasites are noticed.

1821. FLEISCHER, E. G.   Einige Beobachtungen über den Gannet (Sula alba Meyeri, [Sula bassana]) und seine Oeconomie auf der schottischen Insel Bass.   < *Oken's Isis*, Jahrg. v, 1821, *Lit. Anz.*, pp. 330–334.

1826. BLAINVILLE, M. H. D. DE.   Sur le fou de Bassan (Sula alba de Meyer, Pelecanus de Linné [Sula bassana]).   < *Bull. Soc. Philom.*, 1826, p. 16.
Pas vu moi-même.

1826. FABER, F.   Beyträge zur arctischen Zoologie.   < *Oken's Isis*, Jahrg. x, 1826, pp. 702–714.
Vierte Lieferung.—Ueber die isländischen Schwimmvögel mit Ruderfüssigen (*Steganopodes*).—*Sula alba*, p. 706. Vergl. *Isis*, 1824, S. 967.

1826. FERRARY, —.   Sur le Fou de Bassan [Sula bassana].   < *Nouv. Bull. Sci. Soc. Philom.*, 1826, pp. 14, 15.   (*Féruss. Bull.*, 2e sect., x, 1827, p. 154.)
Pas vu moi-même.

1827. DESM[AREST], A. [G.]   Sur le Fou de Bassan (Sula alba Meyer; Pelecanus Bassanus Linn.); par Ferrary. . . .   < *Féruss. Bull.*, 2e sect., x, 1827, p. 154.
Bull. Soc. Philom., janv. 1826.

1827. DESM[AREST], A. [G.]   Sur le même oiseau [i. e. Sula bassana]; par M. de Blainville. . . .   < *Féruss. Bull.*, 2e sect., x, 1827, p. 155.
Bull. Soc. Philom., janv. 1826.

1831. OWEN, R.   [On the Anatomy of Sula bassana.]   < *P. Z. S.*, i, 1831, pp. 90–92.

1831. OWEN, R.   [Notes on the examination of the body of a Gannet (Sula bassana).]   < *Philos. Mag.*, x, 1831, pp. 231, 232.
From *P. Z. S.*, June 14, 1831, spp. 90, 92.

1834. "A SUBSCRIBER."   The Bird called "Booby" by Sailors.   < *Loudon's Mag. Nat. Hist.*, vii, 1834, p. 74.

1834. FENNELL, J.   The Booby is not a Name, even among Sailors, for the Albatross.   < *Loudon's Mag. Nat. Hist.*, vii, 1834, pp. 74, 75. Note by "J. D.", p. 75.

1834. OWEN, R.   Anatomie von Sula bassana (Gannet).   < *Oken's Isis*, Bd. xxvii, 1834, pp. 827, 828.
Auszug aus *Philos. Mag.*, Bd. x, 1831, pp. 231, 232.

1840. SCHLEGEL, H.   Ueber die Naslöcher der Sula.   < *Oken's Isis*, Bd. xxxiii, 1840, pp. 397, 398.
Tydschrift for natuurlyke Geschiedenis, Amsterdam, Bd. vi, 1839, p. 169. Cf. *Isis*, 1823, Heft xii, *Lit. Anz.*, p. 514.

1843. WILSON, J.   Sula melanura.   < *Ann. Mag. Nat. Hist.*, xi, 1843, p. 238.
Occurrence in Britain. From *Voy. round West. Isles*, ii, p. 113, note.

1844. BONNECHOSE, A. DE. Du Fou de Bassan [Sula bassana], et de la variation de son plumage. < *Mém. Soc. d'Agric. Sci. Arts et Belle Lettres de Bay.*, ii, 1844, pp. 291–300.

1847. WHITE, R. O. Occurrence of the Gannet [Sula bassana] near Dartford. Kent. < *Zoologist*, v, 1847, p. 1701.

1849. FOSTER, T. W. Occurrence of the Gannet or Solan Goose (Sula bassana) near Wisbeach. < *Zoologist*, vii, 1849, p. 2499.

1850. ANON. Great Strength and Courage in a Gannet [Sula bassana]. < *Zoologist*, viii, 1850, p. 2653.

1850. COOPER, W. W. Occurrence of the Gannet (Sula Bassana) near Great Grimsby. < *Zoologist*, viii, 1850, p. 2853.

1850. NEWTON, A. Occurrence of the Gannet (Sula Bassana) near Bury St. Edmunds. < *Zoologist*, viii, 1850, p. 2825.

1851. LEFÈVRE, A. Notice sur le [sic] Fous (Sula) d'Europe. < *Naumanni* i, Heft iv, 1851, pp. 37, 38.

Trois espèces—*S. bassana*, *S. melanura* Temm., et u   u   ets tués en Europe sont décrits; la dernière sous le nom de Fou intermédiare; c'est *ula Lefevri*, Bald., *l. c.*

1852. BOND, F. Occurrence of the Gannet (Sula Bassana) in Cambridgeshire. < *Zoologist*, x, 1852, p. 3712.

1852. NEWMAN, H. W. Habits and Instincts of Birds [i. e., of Sula bassana]. < *Zoologist*, x, 1852, pp. 3327, 3328.

1862. HINCKS, W. Observations accompanying the Exhibition of a specimen of "Sula bassana," (the Solan Goose or Gannett), lately obtained at Oshawa, C. W., and belonging to the Museum of the University of Toronto. < *Canad. Journ.*, vii, 1862, pp. 239–—.

1864. BOULTON, W. W. Gannet [Sula bassana] at Filey. < *Zoologist*, xxii, 1864, p. 9364.

1866. BOUVÉ, T. T. [Exhibition of a Gannet (Sula bassana) in its transition stage of plumage.] < *Proc. Boston Soc. Nat. Hist.*, x, 1866, p. 102.

1866. CUNNINGHAM, R. O. On the Solan Goose, or Gannet (Sula bassana, Linn.). < *Ibis*, 2d ser., ii, 1866, pp. 1–23, pl. i.

A very full history, especially of the bibliography and biography. The pl. reps. *pullus*.

1868. HUNTER, J. Gannet [Sula bassana] on the Kentish Coast. < *Zoologist*, 2d ser., iii, 1868, p. 1060.

1871. MINNIGERODE, —, V. Sula bassana in Hannover gefangen. < *J.f. O.*, xix, 1871, p. 73.

1874. SMITH, CECIL. The Black Gannet [Zool., s. s., p. 4199]. < *Zoologist*, 2d ser., ix, 1874, p. 4239.

1874. TAYLOR, W. Black Gannet [off Sidmouth]. < *Zoologist*, 2d ser., ix, 1874, pp. 4199, 4200.

1875. CHAMBERS, R. The Gannet (Sula Bassana). < *Zoologist*, 2d ser., x, Feb., 1875, p. 4343.

On its habits and actions in feeding.

1876. GURNEY, J. H., JR. The Materials of Gannets' [Sula bassana] Nests. < *Zoologist*, 2d ser., xi, Aug., 1876, p. 5048.

1879. BREWER, T. M. The Booby Gannet (Sula fiber) in Massachusetts. < *Bull. Nutt. Ornith. Club*, iv, No. 3, July, 1879, p. 191.

1879. MAYNARD, C. J. Wanderings of a Naturalist. < *Town and Country* (newspaper of Boston, Mass.), i, No. 5, May, 1879.

The second instalment of the series, being Chap. iii, describing the habits of *Sula bassana*, as observed at Bird Rock in the Gulf of St. Lawrence.

Pelecanidæ.

1730. MÉRY, J. Sur la Peau du Pelican. *< Mém. de l'Acad. Roy. des Sci.* depuis 1666 jusq. 1699, x, 1730, pp. 433–438. (Dec. 31, 1693.)

1733. MÉRY, J. Sur la peau du Pelican. *< Hist. de l'Acad. Roy. des Sci.* pour l'année 1692, ii, 1733, pp. 144–146.

1734. PERRAULT, C. Description anatomique de deux Pelicans. *< Mém. de l'Acad. Roy. des Sci.* depuis 1666 jusq. 1699, iii, pt. iii, 1734, pp. 186–198, pll. 26, 27.

1757. PERRAULT, C. Anatomische Beschreibung zweener Pelikane. *< Abhandl. Königl. Französich. Akad.*, ii, 1757, pp. 341––.
    Not seen—title from Giebel. Germ. transl. from *Mém. de l'Acad. Paris,* iii, pt. iii, 1734, pp. 186–198.

1826. PAYRAUDEAUX, B. C. Note sur le vol et les allures du Pélican; par M. Roulin, . . . *< Féruss. Bull.*, 2ᵉ sect., viii, 1826, pp. 275, 276.
    Extrait du *Journ. de Phys. Expérim. et Pathol.*, juin 1826, p. 14.

1829. SCOT, D. On the Kath of the Ancient Hebrews, considered as the Pelican of the Moderns. *< Loudon's Mag. Nat. Hist.*, ii, 1829, pp. 137–142.

1834. BENNETT, G. [On a wound inflicted by a Pelican (Pelecanus onocrotalus) on its own breast.] *< P. Z. S.*, ii, 1834, p. 49.

1835. MARTIN, W. [Notes of the Dissection of a red-backed Pelican (Pelecanus rufescens, Gmel.).] *< P. Z. S.*, iii, 1835, pp. 16–18.
    Cf. *tom. cit.*, p. 9.

1835. MARTIN, W. [Abstract of Notes of the dissection of a red-backed Pelican, Pelecanus rufescens.] *< Lond. and Edinb. Philos. Mag.*, vii, 1835, p. 223.
    From *P. Z. S.*, Feb. 10, 1835, pp. 16–18.

1835. OWEN, R. [Notes on the Anatomy of the red-backed Pelican (Pelecanus rufescens, Gmel.).] *< P. Z. S.*, iii, 1835, pp. 9–12.
    Cf. *tom. cit.*, p. 16.

1835. OWEN, R. [Abstract of Notes on the Anatomy of the red-backed Pelican, Pelecanus rufescens.] *< Lond. and Edinb. Philos. Mag.*, vii, 1835, pp. 154–156.
    From *P. Z. S.*, Jan. 27, 1835, pp. 9–12.

1837. MARTIN, W. Pelecanus rufescens m. *< Oken's Isis*, Bd. xxx, 1837, p. 121.
    Proc. Zool. Soc. London, 1835, pp. 16–18.

1837. OWEN, R. Anatomie von Pelecanus rufescens. *< Oken's Isis,* Bd. xxx, 1837, p. 120.
    Proc. Zool. Soc. London, 1835, pp. 9–12.

1839. LICHTENSTEIN, H. Beitrag zur ornithologischen Fauna von Californien nebst Bemerkungen über die Artkennzeichen der Pelikane und über einige Vögel von den Sandwich-Inseln. *< Abhand. Königl. Akad. Wissensch. Berlin aus d. Jahre* 1838, 1839, pp. 417–451, pll. 1–5. (Gelesen Juni 1837.)
    P. trachyrynchus, p. 433, pl. 2, und p. 440, pl. 3, f. 5. *P. mitratus,* p. 436, pl. 3, f. 2, sp. n. *P. onocrotalus,* p. 436, pl. 3, f. 1. *P. crispus,* p. 437, pl. 3, f. 4. *P. rufescens,* p. 439, pl. 3, f. 3. *P. fuscus,* p. 441, pl. 3, f. 6. *P. conspicillatus,* p. 444, sp. n.—Noch eine spätere in der *Isis* 184. erschienene Ausgabe dieses Artikels geben wir.

1844. LICHTENSTEIN, H. Beytrag zur ornithologischen Fauna von Californien, nebst Bemerkungen über die Artkennzeichen der Pelikane und über einige Vöge. von den Sandwichinseln. *< Oken's Isis,* Bd. xxxvii, 1844, p. 851.
    Aus d. *Abh. Berlin. Akad.*, Jahrg. 1838, erschienen 1839, pp. 417–451, *q. v.*

1849. COUCH, —. Occurrence of the Pelican [Pelicanus onocrotalus] in France *< Zoologist,* vii, 1849, p. 2592.

1851. [SUNDEVALL, C. J.]   Pelikan [Pelecanus onocrotalus] i Sverige. < *Öfvers.*
Kongl. Vetensk.-Akad. Förh. för år 1850, 1851, pp. 184, 185.

1855. BREHM, A. E.   Der grosse Pelikan des inneren Nordost-Afrika's, [u. s. w.]
< *J. f. O.*, iii, 1855, pp. 92–94.
P. *giganteus*, sp. n., p. 94, attempted to be distinguished from P. *rufescens*.

1856. TRISTRAM, H. B.   Pelican [Pelecanus onocrotalus] found dead on the Coast of
Durham. < *Zoologist*, xiv, 1856, p. 5321.

1863. SCHLEGEL, H.   Pelecani < *Mus. Nat. Hist. Pays-Bas*, 4e livr., Juillet 1863, pp.
pp. 1–44.
The "Pelecani" of this author consist of the six genera oftenest now divided into as
many families, as follows:
Fregata, 2 spp.—*Graculus*, 22 spp.—*Plotus*, 3 spp.—*Pelecanus*, 6 spp.—*Sula*, 6 spp.—*Phaeton*,
3 spp.   Total of 294 specimens.

1865. GIEBEL, C. [G.]   Zur Charakteristik der Pelekane. < *Zeitsch. für die gesammten*
Naturwiss., 1865, pp. 250–257.
Mir nicht zugänglich.

1865. SWINHOE, R.   [On Pelecanus philippensis.] < *Ibis*, 2d ser., i, 1865, pp. 111, 112.

1867. BEAL, W. J.   The Pelican [Pelecanus erythrorhynchus] in Cayuga Co., N. Y.
< *Am. Nat.*, i, 1867, pp. 323, 324.
Note of the occurrence, with extracts from other authors on habits, etc.

1867. MILNE-EDWARDS, A.   Note sur l'existence d'un Pélican de grande taille dans
les tourbières d'Angleterre. < *Ann. des Sci. Nat.*, 5e sér., viii, 1867, pp. 285–
293, pl. 14.

1867. NAUMAN, C. H.   Breeding Place of the Pelican [Pelecanus trachyrhynchus].
< *Am. Nat.*, i, 1867, pp. 436, 437.
Indian River, Florida—with reference to statements of W. J. Beal, *ibid.*, p. 323.

1868. MILNE-EDWARDS, A.   On the former Existence of a Pelican in the English
Fens. < *Ibis*, 2d ser., iv, 1868, pp. 363–370.
Translated from *Ann. Sci. Nat.*, 5me sér., viii, pp. 285-293 (*q. v.*), with editorial notes.

1868. MILNE-EDWARDS, A.   Note sur l'existence d'un Pélican de grande taille dans les
tourbières d'Angleterre. < *Compt. Rend. de l'Acad. Sci.*, lxvi, 1868, pp. 1242–
1244.
Précis de ses observations.

1868. MILNE-EDWARDS, A.   Note on the Existence of a large Pelican in the Turbar-
ies of England. < *Ann. Mag. Nat. Hist.*, 4th ser., ii, 1868, pp. 165, 166.
From *Comptes Rendus*, June 22, 1868, pp. 1242-1244.

1868. [MILNE-EDWARDS, A.]   Vorkommen eines grossen Pelikans in den Torfmooren
Englands. < *Aus der Natur*, xlvi, oder n. F., xxxiv, 1868, pp. 670, 671.

1868. NEWTON, A.   [Exhibition of humerus of a species of Pelican from the Cambridgeshire Fens.] < *P. Z. S.*, xxxvi, 1868, p. 2.
This is the same specimen treated by A. Milne-Edwards in several communications: a
bone from a young individual of a large species of *Pelecanus*, doubtfully distinct from *P.*
onocrotalus.

1868. SCLATER, P. L.   Notes on the Pelicans living in the Society's Gardens. < *P.*
Z. S., xxxvi, 1868, pp. 264–269, pll. xxv, xxvi, and woodcc.
Six or possibly 7 species are named as living as above. These are *Pelecanus onocrotalus*,
P. *mitratus*, P. *crispus*, P. *rufescens*, P. *conspicillatus*, and P. *fuscus*, of which the fourth (pl.
xxvi) and last (pl. xxv) are figured, together with portions of the head of the first, second,
and fourth. A figure is also given of what Mr. Blyth regards as P. *javanicus*, Horsf., from
a Syrian example. Notes on all these as well as on three others not exhibited in the Zoological Gardens are given, and a diagnostic list of the 10 species which seem to the author
to be well founded.

1869. BAIRD, S. F.   [On R. Ridgway's discovery of the deciduous nature of the horny
process on the bill of Pelecanus trachyrhynchus.] < *Ibis*, 2d ser., v, 1869, p.
350.

1869. ELLIOT, D. G.   A Monograph of the Genus Pelecanus. $<$ *P. Z. S.*, xxxvii, 1869, pp. 571–591, pl. xliv.

> Review of the literature.—Characters of the subfamily.—Description, with an extended synonymy and critical annotation, of 9 spp. The pl. represents *P. molinæ.*

1869. GURNEY, J. H.   [Occurrence of Pelecanus onocrotalus near Courrière, Pas de Calais.] $<$ *Ibis*, 2d ser., v, 1869, p. 463.

1870. ALLEN, J. A.   Occurrence of the Brown Pelican [Pelecanus fuscus] in Massachusetts. $<$ *Am. Nat.*, iv, 1870, p. 58.

1870. BARBOZA DU BOCAGE, J. V.   Note sur une nouvelle espèce de Pélican [Pelecanus sharpei]. $<$ *P. Z. S.*, xxxviii, 1870, p. 173.

1870. BARBOZA DU BOCAGE, J. V.   Note sur le jeune de l'année du Pelecanus sharpei. $<$ *P. Z. S.*, xxxviii, 1870, p. 409.

1870. MARTIN, L.   Aus dem Leben der grauen Pelekane [Pelecanus fuscus] und verwandten Vögel auf der westlichen Erdhälfte. $<$ *Zool. Gart.*, xi, 1870, pp. 37–42.

1871. BARBOZA DU BOCAGE, J. V.   Mélanges Ornithologiques.   I. Description d'un Pélican apparemment nouveau d'Afrique occidentale et observations sur quelques espèces du même genre. $<$ *Jorn. Sc. Math. Phys. e Nat.*, No. xi, 1871, pp. 166 seq.

> In this first part of a paper under the above major head, *P. sharpii* is redescribed (*P. Z. S.*, 1870, pp. 173, 409), with notes on other spp. of the genus, under the special subtitle quoted.

1871. CLARKE, S. C.   Pelicans. $<$ *Am. Nat.*, v, 1871, pp. 252, 253.

> Biographical notes on *P. trachyrhynchus*, Lake Michigan, and *P. fuscus*, Florida.

1871. GILLMAN, H.   The Rough-billed Pelican [Pelecanus trachyrhynchus] on Lake Huron. $<$ *Am. Nat.*, iv, 1871, pp. 758, 759.

1871. NEWTON, A.   [Remarks on Exhibition of the Humerus of a Pelican from the Cambridgeshire Fens.] $<$ *P. Z. S.*, xxxix, 1871, pp. 702, 703.

1871. SCLATER, P. L.   Additional [P. Z. S., 1868, p. 264] Remarks on certain Species of Pelicans. $<$ *P. Z. S.*, xxxix, 1871, pp. 631–634, pl. li, woodcc.

> 3 spp. treated, with list of 10. The pl. is *P. sharpii*, the head of which, as well as that of *P. philippensis*, is also figured.

1872. BEMMELEN, A. A. VAN.   Fortpflanzung des gemeinen Pelikans (Pelecanus onocrotalus) in Gefangenschaft [zu Rotterdam]. $<$ *Zool. Gart.*, xiii, 1872, pp. 264, 265.

1873. B[AIRD], S. F.   Does the Pelican feed its young with its own Blood? $<$ *Am. Nat.*, vii, 1873, p. 170.

> Note on substances vomited by various birds, as possible basis in fact for the fable alluded to in the title.

1873. HODEK, E.   Ueber Verbreitung und Verhalten der Gattung Pelecanus im europäischen Osten. $<$ *Verh. (Abh.) k.-k. zool.-bot. Ges. Wien*, xxiii, 1873, pp. 73–88.

1874. ANON.   An aged Pelican. $<$ *Pop. Sci. Monthly*, June, 1874, p. 254.

> From 'Land and Water.'—The specimen was upward of 40 years in the Dublin Zoological Gardens.

1874. ANON.   An escaped Pelican killed at Faversham. $<$ *Zoologist*, 2d ser., ix, 1874, p. 4262.

1874. HOLDER, J. B.   The Brown Pelican [Pelecanus fuscus] and its Home. $<$ *Am. Sportsman*, iii, 1874, p. 390.

1874. MAYNARD, C. J.   More about the White Pelican [Pelecanus trachyrhynchus]. $<$ *Am. Sportsman*, iv, 1874, p. 331.

> Characteristics of the species in domestication.

1874. MAYNARD, C. J.   Supposed New Species of Pelican [Pelecanus albicollis]. $<$ *Am. Sportsman*, iii, Mar. 14, 1874, p. 379.

> The specimen described from Cedar Keys, Florida. [It is doubtless identical with *P. fuscu*

1874. RIDGWAY, R.   Breeding Ground of White Pelicans [Pelecanus trachyrhynchus] at Pyramid Lake, Nevada.   < *Am. Sportsman*, iv, 1874, p. 289, figg. 1–3.

1875. ANON.   Eggs and Nest of the White Pelican [Pelecanus trachyrhynchus].   < *Oölogist*, i, 1875, p. 57.

1875. BREWER, T. M.   Female White Pelicans [Pelecanus trachyrhynchus] with center-boards.   < *Rod and Gun*, vi, June 26, 1875, p. 193.   See also p. 167.

1875. [GOSS, N. S.]   A female White Pelican [Pelecanus trachyrhynchus] with a "centre-board."   < *Rod and Gun*, vi, June 12, 1875, p. 167.

1875. INGERSOLL, E.   Habits of the White Pelican [Pelecanus trachyrhynchus].   < *Forest and Stream*, v, Dec. 2, 1875, p. 260.
Observations of **T. H.** Estey in California.

1875. SNOW, F. H.   Horny Crest on the Mandible of the Female White Pelican [Pelecanus trachyrhynchus] as well as the Male.   <*Am. Nat.*, ix, No. 12, 1875, p. 665.

1876. STEARNS, R. E. C.   Pelicans [Pelecanus fuscus, P. trachyrhynchus] in San Francisco Bay.   < *Am. Nat.*, x, No. 3, 1876, p. 177.

1876. TOMPKINS, M.   [On Pelecanus trachyrhynchus ♀, with the "centre-board."]   < *Am. Nat.*, x, No. 5, 1876, p. 313.

1877. JACKSON, J. B. S.   [Pelecanus trachyrhynchus in Massachusetts.]   < *Proc. Bost. Soc. Nat. Hist. for* 1876, xix, 1877, p. 26.
With remarks by T. M. Brewer and J. A. Allen.

1877. MIVART, [ST. G.]   [Notice of a memoir on the axial skeleton of the Pelecanidæ.]   < *P. Z. S.*, May 1, 1877, p. 368.
To be pub. in the Society's 'Transactions'.   See same author at 1878.

1877. [SCLATER, P. L.]   [Addition of Pelicanus fuscus to the Society's menagerie.]   < *P. Z. S.*, Dec. 4, 1877, p. 805.

1878. LEIDY, J.   A Louse of the Pelican [Pelecanus trachyrhynchus].   < *Proc. Acad. Nat. Sci. Phila.*, 1878, pp. 100, 101.
A Mallophagous species, named *Menopon perale.*

1878. MIVART, ST. G.   On the Axial Skeleton of the Pelecanidæ.   < *Trans. Zool. Soc. Lond.*, x, pt. 7, Aug. 1, 1878, Art viii, pp. 315–378, pll. lv–lxi.
The term *Pelecanidæ* here covers the genera *Pelecanus, Sula,* and *Phalacrocorax,* the former being taken as the type and standard of comparison, its axial skeleton being compared with that of *Struthionidæ;* then the other *Steganopodes* mentioned being compared with it and with each other.   The axial skeletons of the forms in mention are elaborately described and figured.

    Bull. v, 4——30

Phalacrocoracidæ.

1733. ————. Anatomie. < *Hist. de l'Acad. Roy. des Sci.* pour l'année 1674, i, 1733, pp. 179, 180.

De la structure du pied d'un Cormoran, p. 180.

1733. PERRAULT, C. Description anatomique d'un Cormoran [Phalacrocorax]. < *Mém. de l'Acad. Roy. des Sci.* depuis 1666 jusq. 1699, iii, pt. i, 1733, pp. 211–220, pll. 31, 32.

1757. PERRAULT, C. Anatomische Beschreibung eines Cormoranes [Phalacrocorax]. < *Abhandl. Königl. Französich. Akad.*, i, 1757, pp. 247–—.

Not seen—title from Giebel. Germ. transl. from *Mém. de l'Acad. Paris*, iii, pt. i, 1733, p. 211.

1767. GUNNERUS, J. E. Von dem Pelecano [Phalacrocorace] cristato, norwegisch Topskarven. < *Dronth. Gesellsch. Schrift*, iii, 1767, pp. 121–123.

Nicht mir selbst zugänglich.

1781. GOLDSMITH, —. Naturgeschichte des Wasserrabens [Phalacrocorax cristatus]. < *Lichtenb. Mag.*, i, St. 2, 1781, pp. 11–15.

Nicht mir selbst zugänglich.

1787. WALBAUM, J. J. Naturgeschichte des Seerabens [Phalacrocorax carbo] vom männlichen Geschlechte. < *Schriften Berlin. Gesell. Naturf. Freunde*, vii, 1787, pp. 430–445.

1800. PULTENEY, R. On the Ascarides discovered in Pelecanus [Phalacrocorax] Carbo and P. cristatus. < *Trans. Linn. Soc.*, v, 1800, pp. 24–27.

1824. [BREHM, C. L.] Die kleine Kormoranscharbe. Carbo subcormoranus, Brehm. (Carbo cormoranus, Meyer et Temminck.) < *Ornis*, Heft i, 1824, pp. 42–54.

1824. Q[UO]Y, —. Note sur le Grand Cormoran (Carbo Cormoranus [Phalacrocorax carbo]), lue à la Société canton. des Sc. natur. de Lausanne, par M. Chavannes. . . . < *Féruss. Bull.*, 2ᵉ sect., i, 1824, p. 279.

Feuille du Canton de Vaud, nᵒ 130, p. 304.

18—. RUDOLPHI, K. A. Ueber die Knochen am Hinterhaupte des Seeraben, Pelecanus [Phalacrocorax] Carbo L. < *Abhandl. Berlin. Akad. aus d. Jahr.* 1816–17, 18—, *Phys. Kl.*, pp. 111–115, pl.

Mir nicht zugänglich.

1825. [RUDOLPHI, K. A.] Sur un os surajouté à la partie postérieure de la tête du Pelecanus [Phalacrocorax] Carbo; par M. Rudolphi. . . . < *Féruss. Bull.*, 2ᵉ sect., iv, 1825, pp. 129, 130.

Extrait des *Abhand. Königl. Acad. Wiss. Berlin* pour les années 1816–17.

1826. FABER, F. Beytråge zur arctischen Zoologie. < *Oken's Isis*, Jahrg. x, 1826, pp. 791–807.

Fünfte Lieferung. Ueber die Gattung *Carbo. C. craculus* (sic), p. 792; *C. cormoranus*, p. 799.

1826. PAYRAUDEAU, B. C. [Carbo desmarestii, Larus audouinii, spp. nn.] < *Nouv. Bull. Soc. Philom.*, 1826, pp. 122, 123. (*Isis*, 1834, pp. 894, 895.)

Not seen in either of these publications. See next title.

1826. PAYRAUDEAU, [B. C.] Description de deux espèces nouvelles d'oiseaux, appartenant aux genres Mouette et Cormoran. < *Ann des Sci. Nat.*, viii, 1826, pp. 460–465.

Larus audouinii, p. 462; Carbo desmarestii, p. 464.

1827. L[UROTH], S. G. Description de deux espèces nouvelles d'oiseaux appartenant aux Genres Mouette et Cormoran; par M. Payraudeau. . . . < *Féruss. Bull.*, 2ᵉ sect., xi, 1827, p. 302.

Larus audouinii, Carbo desmarestii, Ann. Sci. Nat., août 1826, p. 460.

1828. YARRELL, W. On the use of the xiphoid bone [ossification of ligamentum nu-chæ] and its muscles in the Corvorant, (Pelecanus [Phalacrocorax] carbo, Linn.) < *Zool. Journ.*, iv, 1828, pp. 234–237, pl. 7, figs. 5, 6.

1829. K[UHN], —. Sur l'usage de l'os cervical du Cormoran [Phalacrocorax carbo] et sur le muscle qui s'y attache; par W. Yarrel[1]. . . . < *Féruss. Bull.*, 2° sect., xix, 1829, p. 357.
    Extrait du *Zool. Journ.*, No. 14, 1828, p. 234.

1832. K[NOX], T. A Crested Cormorant [Phalacrocorax cristatus, taken near Dublin, Ireland]. < *Loudon's Mag. Nat. Hist.*, v, 1832, p. 397.

1835. WATERTON, C. Notes of a Visit to the Haunts of the Cormorant [Phalacroco-rax carbo], and Facts on its Habits. < *Loudon's Mag. Nat. Hist.*, viii, 1835, pp. 166–171.

1837. GOULD, J. [Phalacrocorax brevirostris, sp. n.] < *P. Z. S.*, v, 1837, p. 26.

1838. BRANDT, J. F. Observations sur plusieurs espèces nouvelles du genre Carbo ou Phalacrocorax qui se trouvent dans le Muséum de l'Académie des Sciences de St. Pétersburg. [1837.] < *St.-Pétersb. Acad. Sci. Bull.*, iii, 1838, cols. 53–57.
    Pas vues moi-même—le titre tiré du *Cat. de la Soc. Roy. Lond.*

1839. BRANDT, J. F. Neue Gattungen von Carbo. < *Oken's Isis*, Bd. xxxii, 1839, p. 635.
    Aus *Bull. Sci. Acad. Imp. St.-Pétersb.*, iii, 1838, p. 53.

1840. BRANDT, J. F. Notice sur une nouvelle espèce du genre des Cormorans (Carbo nudigula). < *Bull. Scientif. Acad. Imp. Sci. St.-Pétersb.*, vi, 1840, pp. 290, 291.

1848. FULLER, H. Occurrence of the Common Cormorant (Phalacrocorax carbo) in the Thames. < *Zoologist*, vi, 1848, p. 2149.

1849. CURTLER, M. Occurrence of the Cormorant (Phalacrocorax carbo) in Worces-tershire. < *Zoologist*, vii, 1849, p. 2456.

1851. NORMAN, A. W. Occurrence of the Shag or Green Cormorant (Phalacrocorax graculus) at Oxford. < *Zoologist*, ix, 1851, p. 3118.

1852. ANON. Sporting by Steam. [With Note by G. Gordon.] < *Zoologist*, x, 1852, p. 3712.
    Phalacrocorax carbo killed by a locomotive.

1854. [BALDAMUS, E.] [Carbo cormoranus bei Waldenberg in Sachsen.] < *Nau-mannia*, iv, 1854, p. 395.

1855. DEHNE, A. Halieus carbo Illig. (Phalacrocorax Carbo, etc.) < *Allgem. Deutsche Naturh. Zeit.*, n. F., i, 1855, p. 441.
    Mir nicht zugänglich.

1857. GLOGER, C. W. L. Die 4te und 5te europäische Scharben-Art: Halieus desma-restii und H. leucogaster. < *J. f. O.*, v, 1857, pp. 4–23.

1857. GLOGER, C. W. L. Halieus Desmarestii ein gute Species. < *Naumannia*, vii, Heft i, 1857, p. 77.

1857. GLOGER, C. W. L. [Carbo leucogaster Cara's wahrscheinlich eine gute Art.] < *Naumannia*, vii, Heft i, 1857, p. 78.

1858. HOMEYER, E. v. Carbo Desmarestii. < *J. f. O.*, vi, 1858, p. 237.
    Selbstandigkeit der Art; geogr. Verbreitung; Zahl der Steuerfedern.

1858. PHILIPPI, R. A. Beschreibung neuer Wirbelthiere aus Chile. < *Arch. f. Na-turg.*, 1858, (1), pp. 303–311.
    Graculus elegans, p. 305.

1860. KINAHAN, G. H. [Field] Notes on the Cormorants in the neighbourhood of Castleconnell. < *Nat. Hist. Rev.*, (*Pr. Soc.*), vii, 1860, pp. 400, 401.

1860. KRÜPER, T. Carbo spec ? in Griechenland beobachtet. < *J. f. O.*, viii, 1860, pp. 369, 370.

1865. COOPER, J. G.   On a new Cormorant from the Farallone Islands, California.
< *Proc. Acad. Nat. Sci. Phila.*, xvii, 1865, pp. 5, 6.
Graculus bairdii, Gruber, MSS., p. 5.   A further note by J. Hepburn, *loc. cit.*

1866. BLAKE-KNOX, H.   A Natural History of the Shag or Green Cormorant [Phala-
crocorax cristatus], with an Account of all its Plumages and Transformations
from the Nestling to the Adult Bird.   < *Zoologist*, 2d ser., i, 1866, pp. 243–257.
The first of a series with major title "Letters on Ornithology."

1866. BLAKE-KNOX, H.   Being a detailed Account of the Summer Plumage of the
Shag [Phalacrocorax cristatus]; also an Account of its Habits in Confinement.   < *Zoologist*, 2d ser., i, 1866, pp. 328–333.
The second letter of a series with major title "Letters on Ornithology."   The Shag is here
very fully treated.

1869. GUNN, T. E.   The Cormorant [Phalacracorax carbo] inland.   < *Zoologist*, 2d
ser., iv, 1869, p. 1921.

1870. GUNN, T. E.   Cormorant [Phalacrocorax carbo] inland [Kimberley].   < *Zoologist*, 2d ser., v, 1870, p. 2386.

1870. HÜGEL, A. DE.   Voracity of the Cormorant [Phalacrocorax carbo].   < *Zoologist*,
2d ser., v, 1870, p. 1982.

1870. SCHMIDT, MAX.   Fortpflanzung des gemeinen Cormorans (Phalacrocorax carbo)
in Gefangenschaft.   < *Zool. Gart.*, xi, 1870, pp. 12–18.

1870. VOELKEL, P.   Reproduction du Cormoran [Phalacrocorax carbo] au Jardin
Zoologique de Francfort-sur-le-Mein.   < *Bull. Soc. Acclim.*, 2ᵉ sér., vii, 1870, p.
323.
Der Zoologische Garten, janvier 1870.

1871. HARVIE-BROWN, J. A.   Cormorant [Phalacrocorax carbo] breeding Inland.
< *Zoologist*, 2d ser., vi, 1871, p. 2852.

1871. SMITH, CECIL.   Cormorant [Phalacrocorax carbo] inland in Somersetshire.
< *Zoologist*, 2d ser., vi, 1871, pp. 2810, 2811.

1872. HANSMANN, A.   Unter den Cormoranen [Phalacrocorax carbo].   < *J. f. O.*,
xx, 1872, pp. 310–314.
Account of a visit to a breeding place of this bird in the vicinity of Stettin.

1873. BULLER, W. L.   Description of a new Species of Cormorant [Phalacrocorax
featherstoni] from the Chatham Islands.   < *Ibis*, 3d ser., iii, 1873, pp. 90, 91.

1873. DOOLITTLE, J.   Fishing with Cormorants.   < *Am. Sportsman*, iii, 1873, p. 108.
Extracted from Rev. Justus Doolittle's "Social Life of the Chinese."

1873. GURNEY, J. H.   [On the existence of Graculus lucidus in Damaraland.]   < *Ibis*,
3d ser., iii, 1873, p. 232.

1873. SALVIN, F. H.   Cormorant Fishing.   < *Zoologist*, 2d ser., viii, 1873, p. 3696.
From the London 'Field.'

1875. ANON.   Birds trained to fish [Cormorants of France].   < *Rod and Gun*, vii, Oct.
2, 1875, p. 11.

1878. [GRINNELL, G. B.]   Cormorants [Phalacrocorax dilophus] in Central New York.
< *Forest and Stream*, x, Apr. 4, 1878, p. 156.

Plotidæ.

1806. [BARTON, B. S.] [Occurrence of Plotus anhinga as far north in the United States as latitude 39°.] < *First Suppl. to Barton's Med. and Phys. Journ.*, Mar., 1806, pp. 67, 68.

1852. GURNEY, J. H. Note on the American and Indian Darters in Captivity; and on the known Species of the Genus Plotus. < *Zoologist*, x, 1852, p. 3711.

1852. SMITH, A. C. Supposed Capture in England of the American Black-bellied Darter (Plotus Anhinga). < *Zoologist*, x, 1852, pp. 3601-3605, fig.

1852. SMITH, A. C. Supplemental Note on the Black-bellied Darter, (Plotus Anhinga). < *Zoologist*, x, 1852, pp. 3654-3657.

1856. BREWER, T. M. [Occurrence of Plotus anhinga in Illinois.] < *Proc. Bost. Soc. Nat. Hist.*, v, 1856, p. 391.

1868. WYMAN, J. On a Thread Worm (Filaria anhingæ) infesting the Brain of the Snake-bird, (Plotus anhinga Linn.). < *Proc. Bost. Soc. Nat. Hist.*, xii, Oct., 1868, pp. 100-104, figg. 1-7.

1869. [WYMAN, J.] Parasitic Worms in the Brain of a Bird [Plotus anhinga]. < *Am. Nat.*, iii, 1869, pp. 41-43, figs. 1-7.
    Abstract of Prof. J. Wyman's article "On a Thread Worm infesting the Brain of the Snakebird," *Proc. Bost. Soc. Nat. Hist.*, Oct., 1868, pp. 100-104.

1872. WYMAN, J. Note on the Thread Worm (Filaria anhingæ) Found in the Brain of the Snake Bird [Plotus anhinga]. < *Am. Nat.*, vi, 1872, pp. 560, 561.
    Additional to *Proc. Bost. Soc. Nat. Hist.*, Oct., 1868, pp. 100-104.

1873. DÖNITZ, W. Ueber die Halswirbelsäule der Vögel aus der Gattung Plotus. < *Reich. u. Bois-Reym. Arch.*, 1873, pp. 357-360, pl. ix A.

1873. SCLATER, P. L. [Report on Additions to the Society's Menagerie in December, 1872.] < *P. Z. S.*, 1873, pp. 1-3, fig.
    Chiefly occupied with *Plotus anhinga*, which is figured.

1875. BULLER, W. L. On the Occurrence of Plotus novæ-hollandiæ in New Zealand. < *Trans. and Proc. New Zealand Inst. for* 1874, vii, 1875, pp. 217, 218.

1875. "ROAMER." Water Turkeys [Plotus anhinga]. < *Forest and Stream*, iii, Jan. 28, 1875, p. 389.

1876. ALIX, A. Garrod (A. H.): Notes sur l'anatomie de l'Anhinga (Plotus Anhinga). (Proceed. zool. Soc Lond., 1876, p. 335.) < *Gerv. Journ. de Zool.*, v, 1876, pp. 440-442.

1876. GARROD, A. H. Notes on the Anatomy of the Plotus anhinga. < *P. Z. S.*, Apr. 4, 1876, pp. 335-345, pll. xxvi-xxviii.
    Pterylosis, muscles and viscera; peculiarity of the articulations of the cervical vertebræ and their muscles; peculiarity of the gizzard. The parts in special question figured.

1878. COUES, E. Meaning of the word "Anhinga". < *Bull. Nutt. Ornith. Club*, iii, No. 2, Apr., 1878, p. 101.
    Portuguese anhina, related to Latin anguina (anguis, a snake).

1878. GARROD, A. H. Note on Points in the Anatomy of Levaillant's Darter (Plotus levaillanti). < *P. Z. S.*, June 18, 1878, pp. 679-681, fig.
    On the alimentary canal; figure of the stomach, showing peculiar structure of glandular areas, U-shaped ridge, and pyloric infundibuliform plug.

1878. [SCLATER, P. L.] [Addition of Plotus levaillanti to the Society's Menagerie in March, 1878.] < *P. Z. S.*, Apr. 2, 1878, p. 378.

Tachypetidæ.

1773. ————. Die Fregatte [Tachypetes aquilus]. < *Berlin. Sammlgn.*, v, 1773, pp. 520–524.
Mir nicht zugänglich.

1821. BURTON, E. Observations on the Natural History and Anatomy of the Pelecanus [Tachypetes] Aquilus of Linnæus. < *Trans. Linn. Soc.*, xiii, pt. i, 1821, pp. 1–11.
Placed next to *Phaëthon.*

1831. VIGORS, N. A. [On the Habits and Economy of the Frigate-bird, Tachypetes aquilus.] < *P. Z. S.*, i, 1831, pp. 62, 63.

1831. VIGORS, N. A. [Notes on the structure of the Frigate Bird (Tachypetes aquilus).] < *Philos. Mag.*, x, 1831, pp. 57, 58.
From *P. Z. S.*, Apr. 26, 1831.

1858. TAYLOR, E. C. Note on the Eggs of the Frigate Bird [Tachypetes aquilus] and Crocodile of Jamaica. < *P. Z. S.*, xxvi, 1858, pp. 318, 319.

1859. TAYLOR, E. C. Note on the Eggs of the Frigate Bird [Tachypetes aquilus] and Crocodile of Jamaica. < *Ann. Mag. Nat. Hist.*, 3d ser., iii, 1859, p. 150.
From *P. Z. S.*, June 8, 1858.

1859. TAYLOR, G. C. Account of a Visit to a Nesting-place [near Tigre Isl., Fonseca Bay, Honduras] of the Frigate-bird (Fregata [Tachypetes] aquila, L.). < *Ibis*, i, 1859, pp. 150–152.

1860. TAYLOR, G. C. Account of a Visit to a Nesting-place of the Frigate-bird (Fregata [Tachypetes] Aquila, L.). < *Zoologist*, xviii, 1860, pp. 6981, 6982.
From the 'Ibis,' i, 1859, p. 150.

1871. NEWMAN, E. Frigate Birds [Tachypetes aquilus] in the Zoological Gardens. < *Zoologist*, 2d ser., vi, 1871, p. 2811.

1874. HOLDER, J. B. The Frigate-Bird [Tachypetes aquilus]—its remarkable powers of Soaring. < *Am. Sportsman*, iii, 1874, p. 276.

1874. MATHEW, G. F. A Visit to the Breeding Haunts of the Frigate Bird [Tachypetes aquilus]. < *Zoologist*, 2d ser., ix, 1874, pp. 3991–3994.

1879. DEANE, R. The Frigate Pelican [Tachypetes aquilus] in Nova Scotia. < *Bull. Nutt. Ornith. Club*, iv, No. 1, Jan., 1879, p. 64.
Cf. *Am. Nat.*, ix, Aug., 1875, p. 470.

Phaëthontidæ.

1837. BRANDT, J. F.   Note sur les caractères des espèces du genre Phaëthon.   < *St.-Pétersb. Acad. Sci. Bull.*, ii, 1837, col. 349, 350.

Pas vue moi-même—le titre tiré du *Cat. de la Soc. Roy.*

1838. BRANDT, J. F.   Avium natantium, imprimis Steganopodum, novarum velminus rite cognitarum descriptiones et icones.   Tractatus 1.   Tentamen monographiæ generis Paëthon.   < *St.-Pétersb. Acad. Sci. Bull.*, iv, 1838, col. 97–99.

Pas vues moi-même—le titre tiré du *Cat. de la Soc. Roy.*

1839. BRANDT, J. F.   Spicilegia | Ornithologica Exotica | auctore | Joanne Frederico Brandt, | [etc., 5 lineæ.] | — | Fasciculus I | ex Actorum (Mémoires VI. Série sciences nat. Tom. V. P. II.) | separatim impressus. | Petropoli | apud Graeff, Lipsiae apud Leop. Voss. | MDCCCXXXIX.   4to.   Title, preface, each backed blank, pp. 1(239)–37(275), pll. i–v.

This is merely his monograph of *Phaëthon*, issued with new pagination and the old pagination preserved, and with new full page title and new preface—the latter explaining the reissuing of certain memoirs under the title of Spec. Ornith. Exot., as above given—this present Tentamen monographiæ zoologicæ generis Phaëthon being fasciculus I, or the first of the proposed series.

1840. BRANDT, J. F.   Tentamen monographiae zoologicae generis Phaëthon.   < *Mém. de l'Acad. St.-Pétersb.*, vi sér., v vol., ii pte., (*Sci. Nat.*, iii), 1840, pp. 239–275, pll. i–v.

Introductio—Character naturalis generis—Anatome—De vita et patria Phaëthontum, eorumque usus—Specierum descriptiones: *Ph. phœnicurus* Gm., p. 252, pl. 1, f. 1, 2; *Ph. œthereus*, pl. 2; *Ph. flavirostris* Brandt, p. 263, pl. 3, f. 1, 2, pl. 4.—Spp. dubiae, *PP. fulvus? catesbyi? edwardsii? melanorhynchos?*—Pl. 5, rostrum, pes, palatum, lingua, os hyoides et larynx Phaëthontis phœnicuri.

1852. [JARDINE, W.]   Phaëthon.   < *Jard. Contrib. Orn.*, 1852, pp. 35–39, pl. lxxxiv.

On the eggs (pl.) and the habits of species of this genus.

1860. LAWRENCE, G. N.   Description of a New Species of Bird of the Genus Phaeton, also of a New Species of Humming Bird of the genus Heliopaedica.   < *Ann. Lyc. Nat. Hist. N. Y.*, vii, Apr., 1860, pp. 142–145.

The new *Phaëthon*, from an unknown locality, is named *P. flavo aurantius*, p. 142.

1872. PEMBROKE, *Earl of*.   Habits of Tropic Birds [Phaëthon sp.].   < *Ann. Mag. Nat. Hist.*, 4th ser., ix, 1872, pp. 242, 243.

Extract from 'South Sea Bubbles', p. 143.

1872. PEMBROKE, *Earl of*.   Habits of Tropic Birds [Phaëthon sp.].   < *Am. Nat.*, vi, 1872, pp. 557–559.

Editorial reproduction of passages from the author's 'South Sea Bubbles', p. 143.

1876. BREE, C. R.   Tropic Bird [Phaëthon sp.].   < *Zoologist*, 2d ser., xi, Feb., 1876, p. 4803.

1876. GURNEY, J. H., JR.   Information Wanted about the Worcestershire Tropic-bird [Phaëthon sp.]   < *Zoologist*, 2d ser., xi, Jan., 1876, p. 4766.

1876. GURNEY, J. H., JR.   Tropic Bird [Phaëthon sp.]   < *Zoologist*, 2d ser., xi, Aug., 1876, p. 5048.

Questionable as a European bird: see *Zool.*, s. s., p. 4803.

1876. HEATON, W. H.   The Worcestershire Tropic-Bird [**Phaëthon sp.**]   < *Zoologist*, 2d ser., xi, Sept., 1876, pp. 5086, 5087.

Laridæ.

1753. GISSLER, N.   Anmärkningar om Labben, Sterna, rectricibus maximis nigris [Stercorarius parasiticus].   Faun. Svev. 129.   < *Kongl. Svensk. Vetensk.-Acad. Handl.*, xiv, 1753, pp. 291–293.

175-. GISSLER, N.   Anmerkungen von den Labben, Sterna [Stercorarius parasiticus]. < *Abhandl. d. Schwed. Akad.*, Bd. xv, aus d. J. 1753, pp. 296, 297.
Nicht mir selbst zugänglich: Titel aus Carus u. Engelm. Uebersetzung von d. Original-ausgabe.

1762. LYSONS, D.   A Description of the Cepphus.   < *Philos. Trans. for* 1761, lii, pt. i, 1762, pp. 135–139.
Called Aldrovandus's *Cepphus*.   It is one of the smaller *Stercorarii*.

1764. LIDBECK, E. G.   Beskrifning På en Fiskmås [Larus glaucus] ifrån Lappland. < *Kongl. Svensk. Vetensk.-Acad. Handl.*, xxv, 1764, pp. 149–153.

176-. LIDBECK, E. G.   Beschreibung einer lappländischen Fischmoeve [Larus glaucus].   < *Abhandl. d. Schwed. Akad. für* 1764, Bd. xxvi, 176-, pp. 155–158.
Nicht mir selbst zugänglich: Titel aus Carus u. Engelm.

1767. GUNNERUS, J. E.   Vom diebischen Joen (Larus [Stercorarius] parasiticus L.) männlichen, und der Skua [Stercorarius skua] Hojeri weiblichen Geschlechts. < *Drontheim. Gesell. Schrift.*, iii, 1767, pp. 88–101.

1767. GUNNERUS, J. E.   Von dem Krykkie (Larus [Rissa] tridactylus).   < *Drontheim. Gesell. Schrift.*, iii, 1767, pp. 101–106.
I have seen neither of the two foregoing papers.

1782. ÖDMANN, S.   Anmärkningar om Skrån-Måsen, (Sterna Caspia,).   < *Kongl. Vetensk.-Acad. Nya. Handl.*, iii, 1782, pp. 228–231.

1783. ÖDMANN, S.   Utkast til Mäse-Slågtets [Larus] Historia.   < *Kongl. Vetensk.-Acad. Nya Handl.*, iv, 1783, pp. 89–122.
10 Arter anföras, med beskrifn., synon. och historia: 1, *L. glaucus;* 2, *L. niveus*, p. 100 (= *eburneus);* 3, *L. marinus;* 4, *L. fuscus;* 5, *L. canus;* 6, *L. tridactylus;* 7, *L. ichthyætus;* 8, *L. atricilla.*

1786. ÖDMANN, S.   Undersökning om de gamle Auctorers Catarrhactes.   < *Kongl. Vetensk.-Acad. Nyt. Handl.*, vii, 1786, pp. 73–78.
The various applications of the word, by Aristotle, Oppian, Linnæus, and others.

1787. WALBAUM, J. J.   Beschreibung der bunten Sturm-Mewe ♂ u. ♀ [Larus marinus L.] und der weissgrauen [L. cinereus].   < *Schriften d. Berlin. Gesell. Naturf. Freunde*, viii, St. ii, 1787, pp. 92–116.
Not seen: title from Carus and Engelmann; others cite the title in very different words, and as of date 1788.

1791. KÄSTNER, A. G.   Hat Linné mit Recht den Teufel tumm genannt [Sterna]? < *Voigt's Magas.*, vii, St. ii, 1791, pp. 1–5.
Not seen.

1793. ÖDMANN, S.   Anmärkning rörande Larus cinerarius.   Linn.   < *Kongl. Vetensk.-Acad. Nya Handl.*, xiv, 1793, pp. 307–311.

1808. CUVIER, F.   Observations sur quelques espèces de Goélands [Lari].   < *Ann. du Mus. d'Hist. Nat.*, xi, 1808, pp. 283–292.
Sur les difficultés qu' offre l'étude de ces oiseaux—Observations générales—Du goéland à manteau voir—Du grisard et du goéland à manteau gris—De la mouette tachetée—cendrée—rieuse—Les différences que les goélands d'une même espèce présentent—Examen des ces différences et des caractères qui distinguent les espèces.

1818. RICHMANN, —.   Etwas an Kotzebue.   < *Isis*, Jahrg. ii, 1818, pp. 2130–2136.
Inhalt: Mewe, die man Kutgegehf nennet; Struntjäger; der Ibis und der Struntjäger (Gedichte, mit Abbild.).

1818. SABINE, J.   An Account of a new Species of Gull [Larus sabini] lately discovered on the West Coast of Greenland.   < *Trans. Linn. Soc.*, xii, pt. ii, 1818, pp. 520–523, pl. xxix.

> *Larus sabini*, p. 522, pl. xxix.

1819. FLEMING, J.   Observations on the Arctic [Cataractes parasiticus] and Skua [C. vulgaris] Gulls of British Ornithologists.   < *Edinb. Philos. Journ.*, i, 1819, pp. 97–104.

> Historical, descriptive, and critical, with synonymy and comparison.

1820. SABINE, J.   Ueber eine neue, kürzlich an der Westkuste von Grönland entdeckte Möven-Gattung [Larus sabini].   < *Oken's Isis*, Jahrg. iv, 1820, (*Lit. Anz.*), pp. 138, 139.

> Uebers. aus d. *Trans. Linn. Soc.*, xii, pt. ii, 1818, pp. 520–523.

1821. EDMONSTON, A.   Observations on the Natural History of some species of the Genus Larus, or Gull Tribe.   < *Edinb. Philos. Journ.*, v, 1821, pp. 168–173.

> This article, marked Part I, treats only of *Stercorarius parasiticus*, giving its characters, habits, &c.

1822. EDMONSTON, L.   Account of a New Species of Larus, shot in Zetland.   < *Mem. Wernerian Nat. Hist. Soc.*, iv, pt. i, 1822, pp. 176–181.

> Read Mar., 1821. Description and account of distribution and habits. The species is not technically named, but in a succeeding article it is called *L. islandicus*.

1822. EDMONSTON, L.   Additional Account of the Iceland Gull [Larus islandicus].   < *Mem. Wernerian Nat. Hist. Soc.*, iv, pt. i, 1822, pp. 182–185.

> Here named *L. islandicus*.   Said to have been first described in 1814.

1822. EDMONSTON, L.   Remarks on the Larus [Stercorarius] Parasiticus or Arctic Gull; and on the Larus Rissa [tridactyla] or Kittiwake; with an Account of the Greenland Kittiwake;—and on Colymbus Grylle.   < *Edinb. Philos. Journ.*, vii, 1822, pp. 90–105.

> Chiefly on the habits of these birds.

1823. EDMONSTON, L.   Notice of a Specimen of the Larus [Pagophila] eburneus, or Ivory Gull, shot in Zetland; and further Remarks on the Iceland Gull [Larus islandicus].   < *Mem. Wernerian Nat. Hist. Soc.*, iv, pt. ii, 1823, pp. 501–507.

> The *Larus islandicus* of Edmonston of 1822 proving to be *L. glaucus*, the name *islandicus* is very improperly "transferred" to another species (the *L. leucopterus* of Faber).

1823. .TRAILL, T. S.   Description of a New Species of Larus [scoresbii].   < *Mem. Wernerian Nat. Hist. Soc.*, iv, pt. ii, 1823, pp. 514–516, pl. xvi, fig. 1.

1824. KAUP, [J. J.]   Beschreibung einer neuen Seeschwalbe [Sterna nitzschii].   < *Oken's Isis*, Jahrg. viii, 1824, p. 153, 154.

> Description of *S. nitzschii*, sp. n., p. 153, giving also the specific characters of *S. hirundo* L.

1824. MACGILLIVRAY, W.   Descriptions, Characters, and Synonyms of the different Species of the Genus Larus, with Critical and Explanatory Remarks.   < *Mem. Wernerian Nat. Hist. Soc.*, v, pt. i, 1824, pp. 247–276.

> After a circumstantial account of the genus considered individually, the species are taken up in order. *L. roseus*, p. 249; *L. bathyrinchus* [sic —*lege bathyrhynchus*], p. 253; *L. argenteus*, p. 264 (renamed from *argentatus*); *L. arcticus*, p. 268 (= *argentatus* Sabine); *L. glacialis*, p. 270 (= *glaucus* Temm.), spp. nn. These and some other species are very elaborately treated, monographically, excepting the first, which is only named "provisionally" (the name *roseus*, by the way, afterward excited some acrimonious personality, as anticipating *rossii* of Richardson). The paper looks as if it were but a part of the article, but it is not marked to be continued, and no more has been found. It is one of the soundest papers ever written on Gulls.

1825. LESSON, [R.] P.   Description d'une espèce inédite de Goeland (Larus [scoresbii]); par Th. Stewart Traill . . .   < *Féruss. Bull.*, 2ᵉ sect., vi, 1825, p. 94.

> *Larus scoresbii*, Traill, *Mem. Wern. Soc.*, iv, pt. ii, 1823, pp. 514–516.

1825. LESSON, [R.] P.   Descriptions, Charactères et Synonymie de diverses espèces du genre Goeland ou Mouette [Larus], avec des Remarques critiques et explicatives; par W. Macgilivray.   < *Féruss. Bull.*, 2ᵉ sect., vi, 1825, pp. 94–96.

> Extrait des *Mém. Wern. Soc.*, v, pt. i, 1824, pp. 247–276, *q. v.*

1826. GARNOT, P.   Histoire d'une nouvelle espèce de Goeland [Larus islandicus] tuée
in Shetland; par L. Edmonston. . . .   < *Féruss. Bull.*, 2e sect., vii, 1826, pp.
112, 113.
      Mem. Wern. Soc., iv, 1822, pp. 176–181.

1826. LESSON, [R.] P.   Note sur un individu de l'espèce du Larus [Pagophila] eburneus, tué dans l'une des îles Shetland; et quelques remarques sur la Mouette
d'Islande (Larus glaucus [islandicus]); par Laurence Edmonston. . . .
< *Féruss. Bull.*, 2e sect., vii, 1826, p. 113.
      Mem. Wern. Soc., iv, pt. ii, 1823, p. 501–507.

1826. S. S.   [STRAUS, —.]   Mémoire sur une nouvelle espèce d'Hirondelle de mer.
Sterna Nitzschii; par M. Kaup . . .   < *Féruss. Bull.*, 2e sect., vii, 1826, p. 251.
      Isis, 1824, p. 153.

1826. PAYRAUDEAU, [B. C.]   Description de deux espèces nouvelles d'oiseaux, appartenant aux genres Mouette et Cormoran.   < *Ann. des Sci. Nat.*, viii, 1826, pp.
460–465.
      Larus audouinii, p. 462: *Carbo desmarestii*, p. 464.

1827. L[UROTH], S. G.   Description de deux espèces nouvelles d'oiseaux appartenant
aux genres Mouette et Cormoran; par M. Payraudeau. . . .   < *Féruss. Bull.*,
2e sect., xi, 1827, p. 302.
      Larus audouinii, Carbo desmarestii, Ann. Sc. Nat., août 1826, p. 460.

1829. FABER, F.   Ornithologischen Notizen.   < *Oken's Isis*, Bd. xxii, 1829, pp. 897–900.
      Ueber d. *Laridæ*.   Nebst Nachschrift von Brehm, pp. 899–900.

1829. MICHAHELLES, C.   Ueber das Winterkleid von Larus atricilla Temm. (plumbiceps Brehm), nebst einigen Bemerkungen über die im Haven von Triest
bemerkten Mövenarten.   < *Oken's Isis*, Bd. xxii, 1829, pp. 1269, 1270.

1830. ANON.   Sur la livrée d'hiver de la mouette a tête grise (Larus atricilla Pall.);
par M. Michahelles.   < *Féruss. Bull.*, 2e sect., xxii, 1830, p. 128.
      Tiré de l'*Isis*, 1829, p. 1269.

1831. YARRELL, W.   [On the characters of Larus capistratus, Temm.]   < *P. Z. S.*, i,
1831, p. 151.

1832. FLEMING, J.   Ueber Larus parasiticus (arctic) et catarrhactes (skua Gull.).
< *Oken's Isis*, Bd. xxv, 1832, p. 587.
      Auszug aus *The Edinb. philos. Journ.*, i, 1819, pp. 97–104.

1833. CLARKE, W. B.   Common Sea-Gull.   < *Loudon's Mag. Nat. Hist.*, vi, 1833, pp.
147, 148.
      Habits.

1833. "E. N. D."   The Kittiwake [Rissa tridactyla] in the Isle of Wight, as mentioned by Rusticus of Godalming.   < *Loudon's Mag. Nat. Hist.*, vi, 1833, p. 279.

1833. HILL, W. H.   Notes on, and a Description of, the Black-headed Gull (Larus ridibundus), as the same has been observed near Southminster, on the Coast of
Essex; also a List of the Birds seen, in the Course of Twelve Months, in the
Neighbourhood of Southminster.   < *Loudon's Mag. Nat. Hist.*, vi, 1833, pp. 450–
452.

1833. LEES, E.   [On a specimen of Larus marinus shot near Worcester, January,
1833.]   < *Loudon's Mag. Nat. Hist.*, vi, 1833, p. 453.

1833. "PHILO-RUSTICUS."   The Mention, by Rusticus of Godalming, of "the Great
Grey Seamews, or Gulls" [Larus glaucus].   < *Loudon's Mag. Nat. Hist.*, vi,
1833, p. 171.

1833. "RUSTICUS."   [NEWMAN, E.]   The Great Grey Seamews, or Gulls [Larus glau-
cus].   < *Loudon's Mag. Nat. Hist.*, vi, 1833, pp. 278, 279.

1833. SEYFFERTITZ, —, and BREHM, [C. L.]   Eine neue Gattung weissschwingige Was-
serschwalben [Hydrochelidon leucopnrus].   < *Oken's Isis*, Jahrg. 1833, pp. 985–
987.

1833. THOMPSON, W. [On the Occurrence of the Young of the Arctic Tern (Sterna Arctica, Temm.) in the North of Ireland.] < *P. Z. S.*, i, 1833, p. 33.

1833. THOMPSON, W. [On the Occurrence of the Black-headed Gull (Larus capistratus, Temm.) and Sterna cantiaca in the North of Ireland.] < *P. Z. S.*, i, 1833, p. 33.

1834. MORRIS, B. R. An Attack of a large Sea Gull [Larus sp.], in the Manner of a Species of rapacious Bird, upon a Kittiwake Gull [Rissa tridactyla]. < *Loudon's Mag. Nat. Hist.*, vii, 1834, pp. 512, 513.
    Followed by a list of some rare Birds met with in the Neighbourhood of Charmouth, Dorsetshire.

1834. "S. K." Some of the Habits of the Lesser Black-backed Gull (Larus fuscus); as shown by an Individual of this Species in partial Confinement. < *Loudon's Mag. Nat. Hist.*, vii, 1834, pp. 511, 512.

1834. "A SUBSCRIBER." The Noddy (Sterna [Anous] stolida). < *Loudon's Mag. Nat. Hist.*, vii, 1834, p. 74.

1835. THOMPSON, W. [On the Herring Gull of the North of Ireland.] < *P. Z. S.*, iii, 1835, p. 83.
    Identifies it with *Larus argentatoïdes* Sw. and Rich.

1835. THOMPSON, W. [Sterna stolida, Linn., in Ireland.] < *P. Z. S.*, iii, 1835, p. 84.

1835. THOMPSON, W. [Laridæ an der Nordostküste Irlands.] < *Oken's Isis*, Bd. xxviii, 1835, p. 523.
    P. Z. S., 1833, p. 33.

1836. DENNES, G. Singular Habit of a Gull. < *Loudon's Mag. Nat. Hist.*, ix, 1836, p. 642.

1837. GOULD, J. [Sterna poliocerca, S. macrotarsa, spp. nn., from Van Dieman's Land.] < *P. Z. S.*, v, 1837, p. 26.

1837. HANCOCK, A. Larus minutus [on the Tyne]. < *Mag. of Zool. and Bot.*, i, 1837, p. 491.

1838. EYTON, T. C. Mr. Eyton's Arrangement of the Gulls [Larinæ]. < *Charlesw. Mag. Nat. Hist.*, ii, 1838, p. 567.
    Merely a note referring to *tom. cit.*, p. 487.

1838. HANCOCK, J. Lestris parasiticus [in Durham]. < *Annals of Nat. Hist.*, ii, 1838, p. 159.

1838. Mc. 'COY, F. Remarks on Mr. Eyton's Arrangement of the Gulls [Larinæ]. < *Charlesw. Mag. Nat. Hist.*, ii, 1838, pp. 487–490.

1838. S[ELBY], P. J. Larus minutus. < *Annals of Nat. Hist.*, i, 1838, p. 238.
    Note of its first recorded appearance on the Northumbrian coast.

1839. BACKHOUSE, E. Notice of the Annual Appearance on the Durham Coast of some of the Lestris tribe. < *Rep. Brit. Assoc. Adv. Sci. for* 1838, vii, 1839, (*Misc. Comm.*), p. 108.

1839. BREME, *Le marquis* DE. Nouvelle espèce européene du genre Larus [L. geneï]. < *Revue Zoologique*, ii, 1839, p. 320.

1839. [EDITORIAL.] Larus Jacksonii, Jackson's Gull. < *Annals of Nat. Hist.*, ii, 1839, pp. 381, 382.
    Comment on Couch's *Fauna of Cornwall*, p. 28.

1839. THOMPSON, W. Zoological Notes on a few Species obtained from the South West of Scotland. < *Charlesw. Mag. Nat. Hist.*, iii, 1839, pp. 585–587.
    Stercorarius pomatorhinus the only bird.

1840. BRANDT, J. F. Ueber den Skeletbau der Scherenschnäbel (Rhynchops) im Vergleich mit den Möven (Larus), den Raubmöven (Lestris) und den Seeschwalben (Sterna). < *Mém. de l'Acad. St.-Pétersb.*, vi sér., v tom., ii pte., *Sc. Nat.*, iii, 1840, pp. 218–229, pll. xvii, xviii.
    A subtitle, being the sixth and last part of his *Beiträge zur Kentniss der Naturg. Vögel*, u. s. w.

1840. RÜPPELL, [E.] Habits of the different Species of Sterna and Larus. < *Charlesv. Mag. Nat. Hist.*, iv, 1840, pp. 47, 48.
　　　　Note of these birds breeding at Mareat; from *Trav. in Abyssinia.*

1841. MUMMERY, S. Larus glaucus;—Larus capistratus [in England]. < *Ann. Mag. Nat. Hist.*, vi, 1841, p. 526.

1842. ANON. [On a remarkable flight of Arctic Terns (Sterna arctica).] < *Ann. Mag. Nat. Hist.*, ix, 1842, pp. 352, 353.
　　　　From "Bristol Mirror."

1842. AUSTIN, T. Arctic Tern [Sterna arctica]. < *Ann. Mag. Nat. Hist.*, x, 1842, p. 75.
　　　　Cf. *op. cit.*, ix, p. 518.

1842. AUSTIN, T. Sterna arctica. < *Ann. Mag. Nat. Hist.*, ix, 1842, pp. 434, 435.
　　　　Habits, &c.

1842. LAFRESNAYE, [F.] DE. G. Sterne. Sterna Lin. S.-G. Procelsterna? (De Lafr.) Hirondelle de mer a bec cylindrique. S. tereticollis. Nob. < *Guér. Mag. de Zool.*, 2e ser., 1842, Oiseaux pp. 1, 2, pl. 29.
　　　　Rev. Zool., 1841, p. 242.

1842. STRICKLAND, H. E. Sterna arctica [in England]. < *Ann. Mag. Nat. Hist.*, ix, 1842, pp. 351, 352.

1842. STRICKLAND, H. E. Sterna arctica. < *Ann. Mag. Nat. Hist.*, ix, 1842, pp. 518, 519.
　　　　Cf. *tom. cit.*, p. 434.

1843. FISHER, W. R. Note on the voracity of the Gull Tribe [Larinæ]. < *Zoologist*, i, 1843, p. 248.

1843. GOUGH, T. Notes on the Habits of a Masked Gull [Larus capistratus] in confinement. < *Zoologist*, i, 1843, pp. 242–245, fig.

1843. JERDON, A. Note on the Habits of the Black-headed Gull [Larus ridibundus]. < *Zoologist*, i, 1843, pp. 245, 246, fig.

1843. REECE, G. Note on the occurrence of the Herring Gull [Larus argentatus] at Worcester. < *Zoologist*, i, 1843, p. 104.

1843. WILLOUGHBY, S. Notes on the occurrence of the Arctic Tern [Sterna macrura], young and adult, in Lincolnshire. < *Zoologist*, i, 1843, p. 365.

1844. BLADON, J. Note on the capture of a Kittiwake [Rissa tridactyla] near Pontypool. < *Zoologist*, ii, 1844, p. 727.

1844. BANISTER, J. D. Note on [the habits of] the Black-headed Gull [Larus ridibundus]. < *Zoologist*, ii, 1844, pp. 577, 578.
　　　　Cf. *Zool.*, p. 245.

1844. BROWN, W. Note on [the insectivorous habits of] the Black headed Gull [Larus ridibundus]. < *Zoologist*, ii, 1844, p. 455.

1844. CHANT, J. Anecdote of annual change of Plumage in a Gull. < *Zoologist*, ii, 1844, p. 768.

1844. FISHER, W. R. Note on the occurrence of the Iceland Gull [Larus leucopterus ?] at Yarmouth. < *Zoologist*, ii, 1844, p. 502.

1844. FISHER, W. R. Note on the occurrence of Richardson's Skua [Stercorarius parasiticus] at Great Yarmouth. < *Zoologist*, ii, 1844, p. 795.

1844. GILBERT, —. [Letter on the Habits of some Mammalia and Aves of Western Australia.] < *P. Z. S.*, xii, 1844, pp. 33–37.
　　　　The ornithological portion relates to species of *Anous.*

1845. BANISTER, J. D. A few Notes on the recent Change of the Herbage on Pilling Moss. < *Zoologist*, iii, 1845, pp. 881–884.
　　　　As caused by the ordure of certain *Laridæ.*

1845. BARCLAY, J G. Domesticated Herring Gulls [Larus argentatus] breeding in a garden. < *Zoologist*, iii, 1845, p. 1138.

1845. FRASER, L. [Larus bridgesii, sp. n.] < *P. Z. S.*, xiii, Feb. 25, 1845, p. 16.
Described from Valparaiso, Chili, in an untitled paper, with two new species of Parrots.

1845. GOULD, J. On the genus Anous, Leach (Megalopterus, Boie). < *P. Z. S.*, xiii, 1845, pp. 103, 104.
Descriptive synopsis of 6 spp.: *A. leucocapillus, A. melanops,* p. 103; *A. cinereus, A. parvulus,* p. 104, spp. nn.

1845. GOULD, J. [Description of a new Tern (Sterna gracilis).] < *P. Z. S.*, xiii, 1845, p. 76.

1845. GOULD, J. [Sterna gracilis.] < *Ann. Mag. Nat. Hist.*, xvi, 1845, p. 346.
From *P. Z. S.*, June 10, 1845, p. 76.

1845. HUSSEY, A. Note on the occurrence of the Pomerine Skua [Stercorarius pomatorhinus] in Sussex. < *Zoologist*, iii, 1845, p. 880.

1845. RODD, E. H. Occurrence of the Little Gull [Larus minutus] in Cornwall. < *Zoologist*, iii, 1845, p. 880.

1845. THOMPSON, W. [On the identity of Larus capistratus of Temminck with L. ridibundus.] < *P. Z. S.*, xiii, 1845, pp. 68, 69.

1845. THOMPSON, W. On the Larus capistratus, Temm. < *Ann. Mag. Nat. Hist.*, xvi, 1845, pp. 357, 358.
From *P. Z. S.*, 1845, pp. 68, 69.

1846. BLADON, J. Occurrence of the Tern [Sterna hirundo] at Ponty-Pool. < *Zoologist*, iv, 1846, p. 1555.

1846. CABOT, S., JR. [On the breeding of Sterna paradisea and S. macrura in Massachusetts.] < *Proc. Bost. Soc. Nat. Hist.*, ii, 1846, pp. 179, 248.

1846. GOULD, J. On the genus Anous, Leach (Megalopterus, Boie). < *Ann. Mag. Nat. Hist.*, xvii, 1846, pp. 285–287.
From *P. Z. S.*, Oct. 14, 1845, pp. 103, 104, *q. v.*

1847. CABOT, S., JR. A Comparison between Sterna Cantiaca, Gm. of Europe, and Sterna acuflavida, Nobis, hitherto considered identical with S. Cantiaca. < *Proc. Bost. Soc. Nat. Hist.*, ii, 1847, pp. 257, 258.

1847. CHARLESWORTH, E. Occurrence of a Specimen of Larus Rossii [Rhodostethia rosea] near Tadcaster. < *Zoologist*, v, 1847, pp. 1782–1785.
With synonymy and description, &c. From *Proc. Yorkshire Philos. Soc.*

1847. EDITORIAL. Larus eburneus [Pagophila eburnea, at Penzance]. < *Ann. Mag. Nat. Hist.*, xix, 1847, p. 213.
From *Cornwall Royal Gazette.*

1847. FALCK, V. Description d'un examplaire du Larus leucopterus de Faber, tué près de la Ville d'Helsingfors en hiver 1836. < *Acta Soc. Sci. Fennicæ*, ii, 1847, pp. 529–531. Fig. 1 of pl. facing p. 532.

1847. FALCK, V. Notices sur le Larus glaucus rencontré dans le Golfe de Finlande. < *Acta Soc. Sci. Fennicæ*, ii, 1847, pp. 655–659. Fig. 2 of pl. facing p. 532.

1847. FRY, D. H. Occurrence of the Glaucous Gull [Larus glaucus] at Ramsgate. < *Zoologist*, v, 1847, p. 1642.

1847. RODD, E. H. Occurrence of the Ivory Gull [Pagophila eburnea] at Penzance. < *Zoologist*, v, 1847, p. 1699.

1847. SMITH, *Rev.* JAMES. Occurrence of the Ivory Gull [Pagophila eburnea] in Aberdeenshire. < *Zoologist*, v, 1847, pp. 1700, 1701.

1847. [ST. JOHN, C.] Habits of the Tern [Sterna sp.] < *Zoologist*, v, 1847, p. 1879.
From his "Wild Sports in the Highlands."

1847. THOMPSON, W. Occurrence of the Whiskered Tern (Sterna leucopareia) in Ireland. < *Zoologist*, v, 1847, pp. 1877, 1878.
From *Ann. Mag. Nat. Hist.*, xx, p. 170.

1847. THOMPSON, W. Occurrence of Sterna velox in Ireland. < *Zoologist*, v, 1847, p. 1878.
From *Ann. Mag. Nat. Hist.*, xx.

1848. BURLINGHAM, D. C.   Enquiry respecting the Characters which distinguish the Young of the Black-backed Gull (Larus fuscus) from the Young of the Glaucous Gull (L. glaucus).   < *Zoologist*, vi, 1848, p. 2027.

1848. CABOT, S., JR.   A comparison between Sterna Cantiaca, Gm., of Europe, and Sterna acuflavida, Nobis, hitherto considered identical with S. Cantiaca, and a description of a new species of Wren.   < *Am. Journ. Sci.*, vi, 1848, pp. 136, 137.
  From *Proc. Bost. Soc. Nat. Hist.*, ii, 1847, pp. 257-259.

1848. CABOT, S. JR.   A Comparison between Sterna Cantiaca, Gm., of Europe, and Sterna acuflavida, nobis, hitherto considered identical with S. Cantiaca, and a description of a new species of Wren.   < *Ann. Mag. Nat. Hist.*, 2d ser., ii, 1848, pp. 364, 365.
  From *Proc. Bost. Soc. Nat. Hist.*, ii, Nov. 17, 1847, pp. 257-259.

1848. COOKSON, J.   Habits of Sea Gulls (Larus ———— ?).   < *Zoologist*, vi, 1848, p. 2149.

1848. DUNN, R.   Occurrence of the Glaucous Gull (Larus glaucus) and Iceland Gull (Larus leucopterus) in Shetland.   < *Zoologist*, vi, 1848, p. 2070.

1848. ELLMAN, J. B.   Occurrence of the Ivory Gull (Larus [Pagophila] eburneus) at Hastings.   < *Zoologist*, vi, 1848, p. 2304.

1848. FISHER, W. R.   Young of the Glaucous Gull (Larus glaucus).   < *Zoologist*, vi, 1848, p. 2070.

1848. GORDON, G.   Answer [Zool., p. 2071] respecting Larus maximus.   < *Zoologist*, vi, 1848, p. 2304.

1848. JOHNSON, F. W.   Occurrence of the Masked Gull (Larus capistratus) at Aldborough.   < *Zoologist*, vi, 1848, p. 2231.

1848. MORRIS, B. R.   Note on the Black-backed [Larus fuscus] and Glaucous Gulls [L. glaucus].   < *Zoologist*, vi, 1848, pp. 2070, 2071.

1848. MORRIS, B. R.   Inquiry respecting Larus maximus.   < *Zoologist*, vi, 1848, p. 2071.
  Cf. *tom. cit.*, p. 2304.

1848. NEWMAN, E.   Occurrence of the Little Gull (Larus minutus) at Belfast.   < *Zoologist*, vi, 1848, p. 2069.

1848. NEWMAN, E.   Occurrence of Bonaparte's Gull (Larus Bonaparti) at Belfast.   < *Zoologist*, vi, 1848, pp. 2069, 2070.

1848. NEWTON, A.   Occurrence of Buffon's Skua (Lestris parasiticus) near Thetford.   < *Zoologist*, vi, 1848, p. 2149.

1848. PRATER, T.   Occurrence of the Roseate Tern (Sterna Dougallii) near Bicester.   < *Zoologist*, vi, 1848, pp. 2230, 2231.

1848. ROUNDELL, H.   Occurrence of the Black Tern (Sterna nigra), &c., near Oxford.   < *Zoologist*, vi, 1848, p. 2191.

1848. THOMPSON, W.   Note on the Occurrence of the Bonapartian Gull (Larus Bonapartii, Rich. and Swains.) for the first time in Europe.   < *Ann. Mag. Nat. Hist.*, 2d ser., i, 1848, pp. 192-197.
  With note also on the occurrence of *L. sabinii* and *L. minutus.*

1849. BIRD, W. F. W.   Capture of the Black Tern (Sterna nigra) at Chertsey.   < *Zoologist*, vii, 1849, p. 2500.

1849. BURTON, W. D.   Occurrence of the Caspian Tern (Sterna Caspia) near Great Yarmouth.   < *Zoologist*, vii, 1849, pp. 2499, 2500.

1849. BURY, C. A.   The Masked Gull (Larus capistratus).   < *Zoologist*, vii, 1849, p 2457.

1849. ELLMAN, J. B.   Note on [flight of] Sea Gulls.   < *Zoologist*, vii, 1849, pp. 2456 2457.

1849. GURNEY, J. H. Occurrence of the Gull-billed Tern (Sterna anglica) at Yarmouth. <*Zoologist*, vii, 1849, p. 2569.

1849. GURNEY, J. H. Occurrence of the Gull-billed Tern (Sterna anglica) near Yarmouth. < *Zoologist*, vii, 1849, p. 2592.

1849. HIGGINS, E. T. Occurrence of Buffon's Skua (Lestris parasitica) near Redcar. < *Zoologist*, vii, 1849, p. 2592.

1849. JOHNSON, H. Occurrence of Rare Gulls [Lestris "arcticus," Larus glaucus] near Liverpool. < *Zoologist*, vii, 1849, p. 2422.

1849. SMITH, *Rev.* JAMES. Occurrence of the Caspian Tern (Sterna Caspia) at Yarmouth. < *Zoologist*, vii, 1849, p. 2529.

1849. SMITH, *Rev.* JAMES. Occurrence of the Little Gull (Larus minutus) at Yarmouth. < *Zoologist*, vii, 1849, p. 2529.

1849. THOMPSON, W. Note sur l'apparition en Europe du Larus Bonapartei, Richardson et Swainson, par M. W. Thompson (Ann. Nat. Hist. Mars, 1848); traduite par M. Edm. Fairmaire. < *Rev. et Mag. Zool.*, i, 1849, pp. 264–266.

1849. WOLLEY, J. Occurrence of Buffon's Skua (Lestris Buffonii) in Huntingdonshire. < *Zoologist*, vii, 1849, p. 2392.

1850. BAIKIE, W. B. The Masked Gull (Larus capistratus) in the Mediterranean. < *Zoologist*, viii, 1850, pp. 2653, 2654.

1850. BAIKIE, W. B. Masked Gull (Larus capistratus) in the Mediterranean. <*Zoologist*, viii, 1850, pp. 2880, 2881.

1850. BURY, C. The Masked Gull (Larus capistratus) in the Mediterranean. <*Zoologist*, viii, 1850, pp. 2776, 2777.

1850. CURTLER, M. Occurrence of the Arctic Gull (Lestris parasiticus) near Worcester. < *Zoologist*, viii, 1850, p. 2706.

1850. CURTLER, M. Occurrence of the Black Tern (Sterna nigra) near Worcester. < *Zoologist*, viii, 1850, p. 2706.

1850. FOSTER, T. W. Occurrence of the Black Tern (Sterna nigra), Lesser Tern (S. minuta) and Common Tern (S. hirundo) at March. < *Zoologist*, viii, 1850, p. 2854.

1850. GURNEY, J. H. Occurrence of the Glaucous Gull (Larus glaucus) in Norfolk. < *Zoologist*, viii, 1850, pp. 2777, 2778.

1850. GURNEY, J. H. Occurrence of the Gull-billed Tern (Sterna anglica) at Yarmouth. < *Zoologist*, viii, 1850, pp. 2853, 2854.

1850. GURNEY, J. H. Occurrence of the Caspian Tern (Sterna caspia) near Yarmouth. < *Zoologist*, viii, 1850, p. 2915.

1850. [JARDINE, W.] Remarks on the Sterna inca, Lesson. < *Jard. Contrib. Orn.*, 1850, pp. 32–34, woodc. col'd.
    Named *Inca mysticalis*, g. sp. n.

1850. MORRIS, B. R. Occurrence of the Little Gull (Larus minutus) at Bridlington Quay. < *Zoologist*, viii, 1850, p. 2653.

1850. MORRIS, F. O. Occurrence of the Little Gull [Larus minutus] near Bridlington Quay. < *Zoologist*, viii, 1850, p. 2653.

1850. NEWTON, A. Occurrence of the Masked Gull (Larus capistratus) on the Dart. < *Zoologist*, viii, 1850, p. 2825.

1850. PLANT, J. Occurrence of the Common Skua (Lestris parasiticus) at Fleetwood. < *Zoologist*, viii, 1850, p. 2925.

1850. POTTER, C. Occurrence of the Black Tern (Sterna fissipes) at Balmer. < *Zoologist*, viii, 1850, p. 2803.

1850. RODD, E. H. Occurrence of the Black Tern (Sterna fissipes) in Adult Summer Plumage in Mount's Bay. < *Zoologist*, viii, 1850, p. 2803.

1850. RUDD, T. S. Occurrence of the Little Gull (Larus minutus) at Redcar, and some Particulars of its Plumage. < Zoologist, viii, 1850, p. 2706.

1850. SMITH, Rev. JAMES. Occurrence of the Gull-billed Tern (Sterna Anglica) in Norfolk. < Zoologist, viii, 1850, p. 2653.

1851. BRIGGS, J. J. The Little Gull (Larus minutus) in Derbyshire. < Zoologist, ix, 1851, p. 3118.

1851. DUCK, J. N. Occurrence of the Little Gull (Larus minutus) at Weston-super-Mare. < Zoologist, ix, 1851, p. 3056.

1851. ELLMAN, J. B. Occurrence of the Little Gull (Larus minutus) at Lewes. < Zoologist, ix, 1851, p. 3036.

1851. GURNEY, J. H. Note on the Gull-billed Tern [Sterna anglica]. < Zoologist, ix, 1851, p. 3235.

1851. GURNEY, J. H. Occurrence of the Caspian Tern [Sterna caspia] at Yarmouth. < Zoologist, ix, 1851, p. 3235.

1851. LEITH, G. H. Occurrence of Bonaparte's Gull (Larus Bonaparti) in Scotland. < Zoologist, ix, 1851, p. 3117.

1851. MOGGRIDGE, M. Larus [Rissa] tridactylus [in Britain]. < Ann. Mag. Nat. Hist., 2d ser., vii, 1851, pp. 235, 236.

1851. POTTER, C. Occurrence of the Little Gull [Larus minutus] at Lewes. < Zoologist, ix, 1851, p. 3036.

1851. POWYS, T. W. Occurrence of the Caspian Tern (Sterna Caspia) near Lausanne. < Zoologist, ix, 1851, pp. 3209, 3210.

1851. RODD, E. H. Occurrence of the Whiskered Tern [Sterna leucoparia] at Scilly. < Zoologist, ix, 1851, p. 3280.

1851. RODD, E. H. Occurrence of the Pomarine Skua [Stercorarius pomatorhinus] in Adult Plumage near Penzance. < Zoologist, ix, 1851, p. 3280.

1851. THORNCROFT, T. Occurrence of Richardson's Skua (Lestris Richardsonii) at Brighton. < Zoologist, ix, 1851, p. 3054.

1851. WOOD, C. Occurrence of the Kittiwake Gull (Larus [Rissa] tridactylus) on Wandsworth Common. < Zoologist, ix, 1851, p. 3117.

1852. ELLMAN, J. B. Occurrence of Ross's Rosy Gull (Larus Rossii [Rhodostethia rosea]) at Pevensey, Sussex. < Zoologist, x, 1852, p. 3388.

1852. ELLMAN, J. B. Occurrence of the Pomerine Skua (Lestris pomerinus [sic—lege pomatorhinus]) at Hastings. < Zoologist, x, 1852, pp. 3331, 3332.

1852. IRBY, L. H. Food of the Black-headed Gull, (Larus ridibundus). < Zoologist, x, 1852, p. 3711.

1852. [JARDINE, W.] Habits of Larus canus. < Jard. Contrib. Orn., 1852, p. 40.

1852. LAWRENCE, G. N. On the occurrence of the Caspian Tern (Sylochelidon Caspius) in North America. < Ann. Lyc. Nat. Hist. New York, v, 1852, pp. 37, 38 (Read May 6, 1850.)

1852. RODD, E. H. Occurrence of the Lesser Tern [Sterna minuta] near Mount's Bay. < Zoologist, x, 1852, p. 3453.

1852. RODD, E. H. Occurrence of the Gull-billed Tern (Sterna Anglica) at Scilly < Zoologist, x, 1852, p. 3536.

1852. RODD, E. H. Occurrence of the Iceland Gull (Larus Islandicus) at Scilly < Zoologist, x, 1852, p. 3536.

1852. SCHACH, F. [Das Vorkommen von Lestris pomarina bei Krimnitzschau. < Naumannia, ii, Heft ii, 1852, p. 123.

1852. SMITH, J. A. Notice of the Occurrence of the Black Tern, Sterna nigra, Linn. near Coldstream. < Ann. Mag. Nat. Hist., 2d ser., ix, 1852, pp. 73, 74.

1852. THOMPSON, W.   Larus glaucus [in Britain].   < *Ann. Mag. Nat. Hist.*, 2d ser., ix, 1852, p. 244.

1853. BORRER, W., JR.   Occurrence of the Masked Gull (Larus capistratus) in Sussex.   < *Zoologist*, xi, 1853, p. 3912.

1853. BROWN, E.   Occurrence of the Sooty Tern (Sterna fuliginosa) in England.   < *Zoologist*, xi, 1853, pp. 3755, 3756.

1853. BRUCH, [P.]   Monographische Uebersicht der Gattung Larus Lin.   < *J. f. O.*, i, 1853, pp. 96–108, pll. ii, iii.

> Sketch of the subject; characters and habitat of 62 spp. *Larinæ*, under 12 genn., and of 5 spp. *Lestridinæ* under 3 genn. The large folded plates, uncolored, illustrate the heads of 24 spp. *Larinæ* of natural size. The article has been spoken of with some reserve, and is generally considered to have been superseded by the author's subsequent paper on the same subject, *op. cit.*, 1855, p. 273, *seq.* (See what is said at 1854, BONAPARTE, C. L.)

1853. DUNN, R.   Occurrence of the Little Gull (Larus minutus) in Shetland.   < *Zoologist*, xi, 1853, pp. 3911, 3912.

1853. FREDERICK, G.   Occurrence of the White-winged Black Tern (Sterna leucoptera) near Yarmouth.   < *Zoologist*, xi, 1853, p. 3911.

1853. FOOTTIT, W. F.   Occurrence of the Caspian Tern (Sterna Caspia) in Lincolnshire.   < *Zoologist*, xi, 1853, p. 3946.

1853. GURNEY, J. H.   Note on a White Variety of the Common Tern [Sterna hirundo].   < *Zoologist*, xi, 1853, p. 4124.

1853. HOMEYER, E. F. v.   Larus Heinei.   Heine's Möve.   < *Naumannia*, iii, 1853, pp. 129, 130.

1853. LAWRENCE, G. N.   Descriptions of New Species of Birds of the Genera Ortyx Stephens, Sterna Linn., and Icteria Vieillot.   < *Ann. Lyc. Nat. Hist. N. Y.*, vi, 1853, pp. 1–4.

> *Sterna pikei*, p. 3.

1853. LENK, *Dr.* —.   Eine briefliche Mittheilung des Hrn. Dr. Lenk.   < *Verh. zool.-bot. Ver. Wien*, iii, am 7 Dec., 1853, pp. 195–197.

> Ueber *Larus capistratus* in Böhmen.

1853. LOWENHJELM, C. G.   Myoxus avellanarius; Sterna arctica.   < *Öfvers. Kongl. Vetensk.-Akad. Förhandl. för år* 1852, 1853, pp. 234, 235.

> *Sterna arctica* häckar i mangd vid en insjö, 2 mil norr om Gellivare.

1853. NEWTON, A.   Correction of a previous Error [Zool., p. 2825] respecting the Masked Gull, (Larus capistratus).   < *Zoologist*, xi, 1853, p. 4074.

1854. BONAPARTE, C. L.   Notes sur les Larides   < *Naumannia*, iv, 1854, pp. 209–219.

> La famille entière des *Larides* (c'est à dire les subfam. *Lestridinæ* et *Larinæ*) ayant été passée en revue synoptique, l'auteur s'occupe d'une critique de M. Bruch (*J. f. O.*, 1853, pp. 96–108). *Lestridinæ*, 4 genn., 4. spp. (avec (5) *Cimoliornis diomedeus* Owen, sp. foss.); *Larinæ*, 18 genn., 73 spp. À cause des rapports qui semblent d'avoir existés entre l'auteur et M. Bruch, il devient difficile d'indiquer avec précision les noms qui sont véritablement nouveaux; surtout lorsqu'on reconnait le fait que ces auteurs tous deux ont presque toujours manqué de donner les renseignements nécessaires. Les genres qui suivant semblent être nouvellement proposés: *Procellarus* sive *Epitelarus*, p. 213; *Creagrus, Atricilla*, p. 214; *Melagavia*, p. 217; *Cirrocephalus*, p. 218.—*Atricilla catesbaei, minor, macroptera*, p. 212; *Procellarus neglectus*, p. 213; *Larus verreauxi*, p. 215; *Gavia kamtschatchensis*, p. 215; *G. bruchii*, p. 216; *Gelastes corallinus*, p. 216; *Rissa kotzebui*, p. 217, spp. nn.
>
> It may be remarked, in fine, of this article, that it is worse than worthless, being pernicious. It is ostensibly a review of Bruch's paper of 1853; this being itself a very incompetent performance, confusion is here worse confounded by Bonaparte's criticisms and "rectifications." It seems to have had, among other undesirable results, the effect of setting Bruch at the business anew, as appears by the latter's paper of 1855. The two authors together made as complete a muddle as can be found in ornithology; woe to the confiding student who trusts either of them—*crede experto!* Bruch and Bonaparte are Scylla and Charybdis of Gull literature.

1854. BORRER, W., JR.   Occurrence of Larus [Xema] Sabinei, Leach, in Sussex.   < *Zoologist*, xii, 1854, p. 4408.

Bull. v, 4——31

1854. BREHM, [C.] L.   Verfärbung und Federwechsel der europäischen Seeschwalben.   < *J. f. O.*, ii, 1854, pp. 317–321.

1854. BRIGGS, J. J.   Occurrence of the Pomarine Skua (Catarractes [Stercorarius] pomarinus) in Derbyshire.   < *Zoologist*, xii, 1854, p. 4513.

1854. GLOGER, C. W. L.   Audubon als der erste Bekenner der Ansicht von „Umfärbung ohne Mauser.‟   < *J. f. O.*, ii, 1854, pp. 328–334.
> The author's reading of Audubon furnished him with frequent occasion for writing: in this instance, he translates and comments upon what that writer has to say respecting the changes of plumage in *Laridæ*.

1854. GLOGER, C. W. L.   Das Abändern der weissen Zeichnung an den Schwingen der Möven [Laridæ].   < *J.f. O.*, ii, 1854, p. 383.
> Translation from Audubon on this subject, in the case of *L. argentatus*.

1854. GOLOWATSCHOW, A.   Larus columbinus.   (Mouette Colombine.)   Espèce nouvelle, habitant les parages de la mer Caspienne.   < *Bull. Soc. Imp. Nat. Moscou*, xxvii, pt. i, 1854, pp. 435–441, pl. iv.

1854. HARDY, J.   Description d'une espèce inédite de Lestris [spinicaudus] de l'Océan méridional.   < *Rev. et Mag. de Zool.*, vi, 1854, pp. 657, 658.

1854. KING, E. L.   Occurrence of Richardson's Skua (Lestris Richardsonii) at Lynn.   < *Zoologist*, xii, 1854, pp. 4512, 4513.

1854. LAWRENCE, G. N.   Description of a New Species of Bird of the Genus Larus [californicus] Linn.   < *Ann. Lyc. Nat. Hist. N. Y.*, vi, 1854, pp. 79, 80.

1855. BONAPARTE, C. L.   Notes sur les Larides.   < *Rev. Mag. Zool.*, vii, 1855, pp. 12–21.
> Not seen.

1855. BRUCH, [P.]   Revision der Gattung Larus Lin.   < *J.f. O.*, iii, 1855, pp. 273–293, pll. iv, v.
> Cf. *op. cit.*, 1853, pp. 96–108.   65 spp.   The present article retraces the ground of the first one; the discrepancies between the two are numerous and irreconcilable, leaving both open to suspicion.   In fact, having ourselves suffered for our indiscretion in venturing upon these papers of Bruch's, as well as those of Bonaparte's on the same subject, it is a duty we owe to posterity, and one we willingly here discharge, to warn all persons off these premises.

1855. DEGLAND, C. D.   [Fang einer für Frankreich, wenn nicht überhaupt für Europa, neuen Seeschwalbe (Sterna fuliginosa).]   < *Naumannia*, v, 1855, p. 412.
> „*S. fuliginosa* wurde bekanntlich vor mehren Jahren an der Elbe, gleichfalls lebendig gefangen.‟—Baldamus.

1855. GLOGER, C. W. L.   Auch Möven werfen lebende Schalthiere aus der Höhe auf kahle Felsen [u. s. w.].   < *J.f. O.*, iii, 1855, p. 447.
> Quotations from Audubon on the habits of *Larus argentatus*.

1855. GLOGER, C. W. L.   Auch die grösseren Möven brüten zum Theil schon im noch unvollendeten Kleide.   < *J. f. O.*, iii, 1855, pp. 521, 522.
> Quotation from Audubon, again, respecting *Larus argentatus*.   It would have simplified matters, if the writer had once copied from Audubon all he desired on the subject, and had done with it.

1855. HUSSEY, A.   Occurrence of Richardson's Skua (Lestris Richardsoni) in Sussex.   < *Zoologist*, xiii, 1855, p. 4560.

1855. MURRAY, A.   [Extract of letter from W. Jardine, on capture of Pagophila eburnea in Caithness-shire.]   < *Edinb. New Philos. Journ.*, new ser., i, 1855, p. 365.

1855. POWYS, T. L.   Occurrence of Buonaparte's Gull (Larus Buonapartii) on the Irish Coast.   < *Zoologist*, xiii, 1855, p. 4762.

1855. POWYS, T. L.   Occurrence of Buonaparte's Gull (Larus Buonapartii) on the Irish Coast.   < *Zoologist*, xiii, 1855, pp. 4809, 4810.

1855. ROBERTS, A.   Occurrence of the Lesser White-winged Gull (Larus islandicus) near Scarborough.   < *Zoologist*, xiii, 1855, p. 4560.

1855. WATTERS, [J. J.]   On the Habits and on the Varieties of some of the [Irish Laridæ.   < *Nat. Hist. Rev.*, ii, 1855, pp. 100–103.

1856. [BILLINGS, E.]   On a Sea-Gull [Larus argentatus] shot at Ottawa.   < *Canad. Nat. and Geol.*, i, 1856, pp. 159, 160.

1856. DESSAUVILLE, P. A.   Notice of the Arctic Skua (Lestris Parasitica, Tem.), shot in Skye in the Summer of 1855.   < *Edinb. New Philos. Journ.*, iii, 1856, pp. 350, 351.

1856. D'URBAN, W. S. M.   Occurrence of the Little Gull [Larus minutus] and Common Skua on the Exe.   < *Zoologist*, xiv, 1856, p. 5065.

1856. FARRAN, [C.]   On the Genus Skua.   (Lestridæ.)   < *Nat. Hist. Rev.*, (*Pr. Soc.*), iii, 1856, pp. 48–51.
Characters and habits of several species.

1857. BRUCH, [P.]   Nachtrag zur Revision der Gattung Larus.   < *J. f. O.*, v, 1857, pp. 23–25.
Cf. *J. f. O.*, 1853, pp. 96–108; 1855, pp. 273–293.   Treats further of 3 or 4 species.

1857. BRUCH, [P.]   Zweiter Nachtrag zur Revision der Gattung Larus.   < *J. f. O.*, v, 1857, pp. 113, 114, pl. i, f. 1–3.
Cf. *J. f. O.*, 1853, pp. 96–108; 1855, pp. 273–293; 1857, pp. 23–25.   *L. poiocephalus, L. lambruschini, L. fuscescens.*

1857. RODD, E. H.   Note on the British Skuas, genus Lestris.   < *Zoologist*, xv, 1857, p. 5596.

1857. SAVILLE, S. P.   Occurrence of rare Sea Birds [Laridæ, 4 spp.] near Cambridge.   < *Zoologist*, xv, 1857, p. 5834.

1858. BLASIUS, J. H.   Ein Wort über die Möven der Zoographia Rosso-asiatica von Pallas.   < *Naumannia*, viii, 1858, pp. 316–320.
Demnach würden sich die von Pallas in der Zoographia aufgefuhrten Namen und Beschreibungen auf folgende Arten beziehen: 1. *Larus marinus* L.   2. *L. argentatus* Brünn. = *L. cachinnans* Pall.   3. *L. glaucus* Brünn.   *L. canus* L. = *L. niveus* Pall.   *L. tridactylus* L. = *LL. rissa, gavia, canus, torquatus* Pall.   6. *L. ichthyaëtus* Pall.   7. *L. ridibundus* L. = *LL. atricilla, cinerarius, nœvius* Pall.   8. *L. minutus* Pall.

1858. LAWRENCE, G. N.   Descriptions of two New Species of Gulls in the Museum of the Smithsonian Institute at Washington.   < *Ann. Lyc. Nat. Hist. New York*, vi, 1858, pp. 264–266.   (Read June 29, 1857.)
Larus suckleyi, p. 264; *Rissa septentrionalis*, p. 266.   [Both = *L. brachyrhynchus* Rich.]

1858. MATHEWS, M. A.   Occurrence of the Little Gull [Larus minutus] near Barnstable.   < *Zoologist*, xvi, 1858, pp. 6245, 6246.

1858. RODD, E. H.   Occurrence of the Pomarine Skua (Lestris pomarina [Stercorarius pomatorhinus]) at the Land's End.   < *Zoologist*, xvi, 1858, p. 6267.

1858. STEVENSON, H.   Appearance of Skuas off the Coast of Yarmouth.   < *Zoologist*, xvi, 1858, pp. 6309, 6310.

1859. ANON.   Pomarine Skua (Lestris pomarina [Stercorarius pomatorhinus]) near Brighton.   < *Zoologist*, xvii, 1859, p. 6331.

1859. ANON.   Occurrence of Sabine's Gull (Larus [Xema] Sabini) at Brighton.   < *Zoologist*, xvii, 1859, p. 6331.

1859. BARTLETT, A. D.   Remarks on the Habits of a Herring Gull (Larus argentatus).   < *P. Z. S.*, xxvii, 1859, pp. 467, 468.
Voluntary semidomestication.

1859. DUNN, R.   Occurrence of the Adult Glaucous Gull [Larus glaucus] in Orkney.   < *Zoologist*, xvii, 1859, p. 6448.

1859. DUTTON, J.   Occurrence of the Pomarine Skua (Lestris pomarina [Stercorarius pomatorhinus]) at Birting Gap.   < *Zoologist*, xvii, 1859, pp. 6378, 6379.

1859. HOMEYER, E. [F.] v.   Ueber Larus Heinei.   < *J. f. O.*, vii, 1859, pp. 155, 156.
Especially on its relationships with *L. canus*.

1859. ROSS, F. W. L.   Notice of a Black-headed Gull [Larus ichthyaëtus] found recently in Devonshire.   < *Ann. Mag. Nat. Hist.*, 3d ser., iv, 1859, p. 467.

1860. ALBRECHT, —.   Verhalten einer aufgezogenen Möve [Larus argentatus]; längere Aufbewahrung frischer Eier. < *J. f. O.*, viii, 1860, pp. 367–369.
    Translated from Bartlett, *Ann. Mag. N. H.*, No. 30, June, 1860.

1860. BARTLETT, A. D.   Remarks on the Habits of a Herring Gull (Larus argentatus). < *Ann. Mag. Nat. Hist.*, 3d ser., v, 1860, pp. 498, 499.
    From *P. Z. S.*, Nov. 22, 1859.

1860. DUNN, J.   Occurrence of the Glaucous Gull [Larus glaucus] in Orkney. < *Zoologist*, xviii, 1860, p. 6813.

1860. DUTTON, J.   Occurrence of Richardson's Skua (Lestris Richardsonii) at Eastbourne. < *Zoologist*, xviii, 1860, p. 7106.

1860. GOULD, J.   Description of a new Species of Gull (Gavia roseiventris) from the Falkland Islands. < *Ann. Mag. Nat. Hist.*, 3d ser., v, 1860, p. 232.
    From *P. Z. S.*, Feb. 8, 1859, p. 97; from a paper of wider scope.

1860. GURNEY, J. H.   Note on the Carnivorous propensities of the Blackheaded Gull (Larus ridibundus). < *Zoologist*, xviii, 1860, pp. 7106, 7107.

1860. JÄCKEL, J.   Sterna leucoptera Meissn. und Schinz in Bayern brütend. < *J. f. O.*, viii, 1860, pp. 300, 301.

1860. LEADBEATER, —.   [Exhibition of Lestris cepphus from Ireland.] < *P. Z. S.*, xxviii, 1860, p. 322.

1860. MORE, A. G.   The Arctic Tern (Sterna arctica) nesting on Fresh Water. < *Zoologist*, xviii, 1860, pp. 6891, 6892.

1860. NICHOLLS, H., JR.   Occurrence of Richardson's Skua [Stercorarius parasiticus] at Kingsbridge. < *Zoologist*, xviii, 1860, p. 7106.

1860. QUISTORP, [G.]   Larus leucopterus in Pommern beobachtet. < *J. f. O.*, viii, 1860, p. 369.

1860. ROSS, F. W. L.   Occurrence of Larus icthyaëtus [sic], a new British Gull, in Devonshire. < *Zoologist*, xviii, 1860, pp. 6860, 6861.

1860. SAVILLE, S. P.   A Kittiwake Gull (Larus [Rissa] tridactylus) driven Inland [Cambridge] by the late Terrific Gales. < *Zoologist*, xviii, 1860, p. 6982.

1860. SAVILLE, S. P.   Common Tern (Sterna hirundo) shot during the late gale [in Northamptonshire]. < *Zoologist*, xviii, 1860, p. 7106.

1861. TREMBLY, J. B.   Ornithological Inquiries. < *Field Notes*, i, No. 17, Apr. 27, 1861, p. 129.
    Respecting occurrence of certain *Laridæ* in Ohio.

1861. W[HEATON], J. M.   The Gulls. < *Field Notes*, i, No. 20, May 18, 1861, p. 153.
    Alleged *Larus "occidentalis"* in Ohio is not that species.

1862. BLAKE-KNOX, H.   Occurrence of Sabine's Gull [Xema sabinii] in Dublin Bay. < *Zoologist*, xx, 1862, pp. 8093, 8094.

1862. BOND, T.   The Little Gull [Larus minutus]. < *Zoologist*, xx, 1862, pp. 7939, 7940.

1862. COUES, E.   Revision of the Gulls [Larinæ] of North America; based upon specimens in the Museum of the Smithsonian Institution. < *Proc. Acad. Nat. Sci. Phila.*, xiv, 1862, pp. 291–312.
    Stated to be "an abstract of a more extended Monograph on the Gulls on North America, prepared for publication in a Government Report." The "Monograph" here in mention appeared in 1874, as a part of the "Birds of the Northwest" (pp. 589–717), *q. v.*

    The present paper divides the *Laridæ* into 4 subfamilies, *Lestridinæ, Larinæ, Sterninæ* and *Rhynchopinæ*, and gives an outline of the North American genera and species of the second of these, which is divided into the following 8 genera: *Larus, Blasipus, Rissa, Pagophila;* and *Chroicocephalus, Rhodostethia, Xema, Creagrus.* The species recognized are as follow:—

    1, *Larus hutchinsii* (later determined to be the young of *L. glaucus*). 2, *L. glaucus.* 3, *L. leucopterus.* 4, *L. glaucescens.* 5, *L. chalcopterus* (later referred to *glaucescens*). 6, *L. marinus.* 7, *L. occidentalis.* 8, *L. smithsonianus*, sp. n., p. 296, being the *L. argentatus* of American

1862. COUES, E.—Continued.

writers; later reduced to a race of the latter. 9, *Larus californicus.* 10, *L. delawarensis.* 11, *L. brachyrhynchus* Rich., being the N. Am. representative of *L. canus ;* to it are referred *L. suckleyi* and *Rissa septentrionalis* of Lawrence. 12, *Blasipus heermanni.* 13, *Rissa tridactyla.* 14, *R. kotzebui,* the N. Pacific analogue of *R. tridactyla.* 15, *R. brachyrhyncha* Gould, or *brevirostris* Brandt. 16, *Pagophila eburnea.* 17, *P. brachytarsus* (since admitted to be same as 16). 18, *Chroicocephalus atricilla.* 19, *C. cucullatus* (afterward referred to 20). 20, *C. franklini.* 21, *C. philadelphia.* 22, *C. minutus* (given as questionably North American). 23, *Rhodostethia rosea.* 24, *Xema sabinii.* 25, *Creagrus furcatus.*

Taking from these 25 species the following 5, viz: *L. hutchinsii, L. chalcopterus, Rissa kotzebui, Pagophila brachytarsus, Chroicocephalus cucullatus,* as not valid, and *C. minutus* as extralimital, we have a residuum of 19 good species, most of which are carefully described in this paper, with brief synonymy, and extended criticism. The paper is handicapped by the author's reliance to greater extent than the facts warrant upon Bonaparte's and Bruch's misguiding and perplexing lead. It is otherwise a very fair exhibit of the knowledge we possessed at the time the paper was written.

Cf. *Ibis,* 1863, pp. 108, 109.

1862. COUES, E.   A Review of the Terns [Sterninæ] of North America.   < *Proc. Acad. Nat. Sci. Phila.,* xiv, 1862, pp. 535–559.

The genera and species critically reviewed in this paper are the following:—

1, *Gelochelidon anglica.* 2, *Thalasseus caspius ;* the N. Am. bird tentatively named *Th. imperator,* sp. n., p. 538. 3, *T. regius.* 4, *T. elegans.* 5, *T. acuflavidus* (afterward reunited with *T. cantiaca*). 6, *Sterna trudeaui.* 7, *S.* "*havelli*", considered as the winter plumage of *S. forsteri.* 8, *S. forsteri.* 9, *S. hirundo.* 10, *S. macroura.* 11, *S. pikei* Lawr. 12, *S. paradisea.* 13, *S. antillarum.* 14, *Hydrochelidon fissipes.* 15, *Haliplana fuliginosa.* 16, *Anous stolidus,* with *A. frater,* sp. n. prob., p. 558. Neither of the two new names has proven to represent much value. The identification of *S. havelli,* here first made, has been confirmed. *S. pikei* is not a good species. *T. acuflavidus* is not distinct from *T. cantiacus.* The other species hold, though some of them require other names, and several species have since been added to the North American Fauna. See same author at 1874, *Birds of the Northwest.*

Cf. *Ibis,* 1863, pp. 471, 472.

1862. GATCOMBE, J.   Occurrence of the Little Gull [Larus minutus] at Plymouth.   < *Zoologist,* xx, 1862, p. 7940.

1862. GATCOMBE, J.   Occurrence of the Iceland Gull [Larus leucopterus] at Plymouth.   < *Zoologist,* xx, 1862, p. 8036.

1862. HAMMOND, W.   Occurrence of the Little Gull [Larus minutus] in Kent.   < *Zoologist,* xx, 1862, p. 8003.

1862. PHILIPPI, R. A., *and* LANDBECK, L.   Descripcion de una nueva golondrina de mar [Sterna atrofasciata].   < *Anal. Univ. Chile,* xxi, Nov., 1862, p. 440.

1862. PREYER, W., *and* ZIRKEL, F.   Reise nach Island im Sommer 1860.   Mit wissenschaftlichen Anhangen.   Leipsig.   Brockhaus.   1862.   8vo.

Anhang C. Systematische Uebersicht der Rückgratthiere Islands. Von Wm. Preyer. pp. 377–434 Gives lists of the species, with notes on the eggs of many. *Lestris thuliaca,* Preyer, p. 418, sp. n.

1862. RODD, E. H.   Occurrence of the Common Skua [Lestris catarractes] near the Land's End.   < *Zoologist,* xx, 1862, p. 8237.

1862. ROGERS, H.   Occurrence of the Pomarine Skua [Stercorarius pomatorhinus] in the Isle of Wight.   < *Zoologist,* xx, 1862, p. 8288.

1862. SAXBY, H. L.   Variety of the Common Gull [Larus canus].   < *Zoologist,* xx, 1862, p. 7883.

1862. WILSON, W.   Occurrence of the Little Gull [Larus minutus] and Little Auk [Alca alle] near Lynn.   < *Zoologist,* xx, 1862, p. 7939.

1863. ANON.   Die Mövenkolonie auf Rottum.   < *Aus der Natur,* xxiii, oder n. F., xi, Jan. März, 1863, pp. ——.

Not seen.

1863. BLAKE-KNOX, H.   Skuas [Stercorarius skua] on the Coast of Dublin.   < *Zoologist,* xxi, 1863, pp. 8332, 8333.

1863. CLERMONT, *Lord.* The Arctic Skua [Stercorarius parasiticus] feeding on Worms near Newry. < *Zoologist*, xxi, 1863, p. 8692.

1863. COUES, E. On the Lestris richardsoni of Swainson; with a Critical Review of the Subfamily Lestridinæ. < *Proc. Acad. Nat. Sci. Phila.*, xv, 1863, pp. 121–138.

From his discussion of the claims of *Lestris richardsoni* to be considered a good species, the author passes to review the entire subfamily, recognizing the following genera and species:—

    I. BUPHAGUS, Moehr. 1, *B. skua* (Brünn.). 2, *B. antarcticus* (Less.).

    II. STERCORARIUS, Briss. 3, *S. pomarinus* (Temm.) (lege *pomatorhinus*). 4, *S. parasiticus* Brünn. 5, *S. richardsoni* (Sw.). *S. hardyi* (Bp.). 7, *S. spinicauda* (Bp.). 8, *S. buffoni* (Boie).

The nomenclature of this paper is eccentric, the author having apparently imbibed some untenable views of G. R. Gray's on this subject. *S. richardsoni* has not proved valid. The four unquestionable Jägers of the Northern Hemisphere are carefully distinguished and adequately described, with copious synonymy. See same author at 1874, *Birds of the Northwest.*

    Cf. *Ibis*, 1864, pp. 127, 128.

1863. COUES, E. [On the specific validity of Larus smithsonianus.] < *Ibis*, v, 1863, p. 367.

1863. DUNN, J. H. Pomarine Skuas [Stercorarius pomatorhinus] in the Orkneys. < *Zoologist*, xxi, 1863, p. 8332.

1863. DUTTON, J. The Pomarine Skua [Stercorarius pomatorhinus] off Beachy Head. < *Zoologist*, xxi, 1863, p. 8333.

1863. MATHEWS, M. A. Sabine's Gull (Larus [Xema] Sabini) in Devonshire. < *Zoologist*, xxi, 1863, p. 8448.

1863. MATHEWS, M. A. Buffon's Skua (Lestris parasiticus) near Wellington. < *Zoologist*, xxi, 1863, p. 8448.

1863. MATHEWS, M. A. The Little Gull [Larus minutus] and Sabine's Gull [Xema sabinii] at Weston-super-Mare. < *Zoologist*, xxi, 1863, p. 8692.

1863. NEWMAN, E. Pomarine Skuas [Stercorarius pomatorhinus] on the English Coast. < *Zoologist*, xxi, 1863, p. 8333.

1863. ROGERS, H. The Pomarine Skua [Stercorarius pomatorhinus] in the Isle of Wight. < *Zoologist*, xxi, 1863, p. 8332.

1863. SAXBY, H. L. Pomarine Skua (Lestris pomarinus) in Shetland. < *Zoologist*, xxi, 1863, p. 8494.

1863. SCHLEGEL, H. Lari < *Mus. Hist. Nat. Pays-Bas*, 4ᵉ livr., août 1863, pp. 1–50.

This group consists of the genera *Larus* and *Stercorarius* of the author, the Terns and Skimmers not being here treated.

L. ichthyaëtus minor, subsp. n., p. 34.

1863. STEVENSON, H. Sandwich Tern (Sterna Boysii [cantiaca]) in Norfolk. < *Zoologist*, xxi, 1863, p. 8332.

1863. YOUNG, E. Richardson's Skua [Stercorarius richardsoni] in Kent. < *Zoologist*, xxi, 1863, p. 8726.

1864. BOULTON, W. W. Sandwich Tern [Sterna cantiaca] Shot at Flamborough. < *Zoologist*, xxii, 1864, p. 9291.

1864. BOULTON, W. W. Little Gulls [Larus minutus] off Bridlington Quay. < *Zoologist*, xxii, 1864, p. 9365.

1864. BOULTON, W. W. Black Tern [Hydrochelidon nigra] at Filey. < *Zoologist*, xxii, 1864, p. 9365.

1864. BOULTON, W. W. Common Skua [Stercorarius skua] at Flamborough Head. < *Zoologist*, xxii, 1864, p. 9365.

1864. BOULTON, W. W. Richardson's Skuas [Stercorarius richardsoni] off Bridlington Quay. < *Zoologist*, xxii, 1864, p. 9365.

1864. BOULTON, W. W. Buffon's Skua [Stercorarius buffoni] at Flamborough Head. < *Zoologist*, xxii, 1864, p. 9365.

1864. COUES, E.   Notes on certain Central-American Laridæ collected by Mr. Osbert Salvin and Mr. F. Godman. $<$ *Ibis*, vi, 1864, pp. 387–393.
  15 or 16 spp. Critical notes. First mention of *Haliplana discolor*, n. s., subsequently described. Field notes by O. S.

1864. FISCHER, J. C. H.   Larus rossii [Rhodostethia rosea] paa Færøerne. $<$ *Krøyer's* (*Schiødte's*) *Naturhist. Tidsskr.*, iii, 1864, pp. 8–10.
  Cf. *Ibis*, 1865, pp. 103, 238.

1864. GOULD, J.   Description of a New Species of Gull [Chroicocephalus tibetanus] from Tibet. $<$ *P. Z. S.*, xxxii, 1864, pp. 54, 55.

1864. GOULD, J.   Description of a New Species of Gull from Tibet [Chroicocephalus tibetanus]. $<$ *Ann. Mag. Nat. Hist.*, 3d ser., xiv, 1864, pp. 279, 280.
  From *P. Z. S.*, Feb. 9, 1864, pp. 54, 55.

1864. SCHLEGEL, H.   Sternae $<$ *Mus. Hist. Nat. Pays-Bas*, 5e livr., 1864, pp. 1–44.
  The *Sternæ* of this author include the three genera *Sterna* (37 spp.), *Rhynchops* (3 spp.), and *Dromas* (1 sp.)!, represented by 371 specimens in the Leyden Museum. *Sterna bernsteini*, p. 9. The monograph is dated Sept., 1863, but livr. 5 did not appear until 1864.

1865. ALSTON, E. R.   [On J. Sabine's specimen of Larus rossi (Rhodostethia rosea). Cf. Ibis, 1865, p. 238.] $<$ *Ibis*, 2d ser., i, 1865, pp. 547, 548.

1865. ALSTON, E. R.   Kittiwake [Rissa tridactyla] in Ayrshire in Winter. $<$ *Zoologist*, xxiii, 1865, p. 9470.

1865. BLAKE-KNOX, H.   Iceland Gull [Larus leucopterus] in Dublin Bay. $<$ *Zoologist*, xxiii, 1865, p. 9470.

1865. GATCOMBE, J.   Whiskered Tern [Hydrochelidon leucoparia] on the Coast of Devon. $<$ *Zoologist*, xxiii, 1865, p. 9629.

1865. HARTING, J. E.   Pure White Gull [species not named]. $<$ *Zoologist*, xxiii, 1865, p. 9784.

1865. MATHEW, M. A.   Sabine's Gull [Xema sabinii] and the Ivory Gull [Pagophila eburnea] at Weston-super-Mare. $<$ *Zoologist*, xxiii, 1865, p. 9470.

1865. MATHEW, M. A.   Ivory Gull ["Pagophila eburnea"] at Weston-super-Mare. $<$ *Zoologist*, xxiii, 1865, p. 9566.
  Cf. *Zool.*, p. 9734.

1865. MATHEW, G. F.   Carnivorous Propensity of the Great Blackbacked Gull [Larus marinus]. $<$ *Zoologist*, xxiii, 1865, p. 9619.

1865. MATHEW, M. A.   The Ivory Gull [Pagophila eburnea]: Correction of an Error [Zool., p. 9566]. $<$ *Zoologist*, xxiii, 1865, p. 9734.

1865. [NEWTON, A.]   [On the known specimens (5 in number) of Rhodostethia rosea. Cf. Fn. Bor.-Am., ii, p. xii; Naturh. Tidssk., 3d ser., iii, 1864, p. 8; J. f. O., 1855, p. 278; Naum., 1858, p. 307; Zool., pp. 1694, 1785, 3388.] $<$ *Ibis*, 2d ser., i, 1865, pp. 103, 104; also p. 238; see also p. 547.

1865. RODD, E. H.   Bonaparte's Gull [Larus bonapartii] in Falmouth Harbour. $<$ *Zoologist*, xxiii, 1865, p. 9501.

1865. ANGUS, W. C.   The Black Tern [Hydrochelidon nigra] near Aberdeen. $<$ *Zoologist*, 2d ser., i, 1866, pp. 525, 526.

1866. ARMITAGE, G. D.   Little Gull [Larus minutus] at Bridlington Quay. $<$ *Zoologist*, 2d ser., i, 1866, p. 526.

1866. BLAKE-KNOX, H.   A Natural History of the Brownhooded or Blackheaded Gull [Larus ridibundus], with an Account of all its Plumages and Transformations from the Nestling to the Adult Bird; also some Questions about the Masked Gull. $<$ *Zoologist*, 2d ser., i, 1866, pp. 361–372.
  The third of a series with major title "Letters on Ornithology."

1866-67. BLAKE-KNOX, H. A Natural History of the Kittiwake Gull [Rissa tridactyla], with an Account of all its Plumages and Transformations, from the Nestling to the Adult Bird. < *Zoologist*, 2d ser., i, 1866, pp. 518-522; ii, 1867, pp. 548-553.

The fourth of a series with major title "Letters on Ornithology."

1866. BLAKE-KNOX, H. Occurrence of Sabine's Gull [Xema sabinii] in Dublin Bay. < *Zoologist*, 2d ser., i, 1866, p. 526.

1866. BLASIUS, J. H. Kritische Bemerkungen über Lariden. < *J. f. O.*, xiii, 1865, (pub. 1866), pp. 369-384; xiv, 1866, pp. 73-88.

The first article treats of *Larinæ* (36 spp.) and *Lestridinæ* (4 spp.), the second of *Sterninæ* (40) and *Rhynchopinæ* (3). Tabular view of geographical distribution follows. *Sterna macrodactyla*, p. 75; *S. macroptera*, p. 76, spp. nn. Diagnostic synopsis of 12 spp. of *Sterna* proper. This is one of the important critiques on *Laridæ*, though not infallible.

1866. LANGMAN, A. Iagttagelse af et gjensidigt Forhold i mellem Svartbag-Maagen (Larus marinus) og Sælhunden. < *Tidsek. Pop. Fremst. af Naturf.*, 3e række, iii, 1866, pp. 173, 174.

Svenska Jägarförbundets Nya Tidskrift, 2. årgången, 1864.

1866. LAYARD, E. L. [On the swimming of Stercorarius parasiticus; cf. Ibis, 1865, p. 526; 1866, p. 127.] < *Ibis*, 2d ser., ii, 1866, p. 220.

1866. LEGGE, W. V. Gulls breaking Mussel-shells. < *Zoologist*, 2d ser., i, 1866, p. 190.

1866. MATHEW, M. A. Lesser Tern [Sterna minuta] and Black Tern [Hydrochelidon nigra] at Weston-super-Mare. < *Zoologist*, 2d ser., i, 1866, p. 272.

1866. RODD, E. H. Sabine's Gull [Xema sabinii] in Mount's Bay. < *Zoologist*, 2d ser., i, 1866, p. 501.

1866. SMITH, CECIL. Black Tern [Hydrochelidon nigra] in Somersetshire. < *Zoologist*, 2d ser., i, 1866, p. 272.

1866. SMITH, H. E. Nesting of the Little Tern [Sterna minuta]. < *Zoologist*, 2d ser., i, 1866, p. 100.

1866. WHITELY, H. [Stercorarius parasiticus, swimming.] < *Ibis*, 2d ser., ii, 1866, p. 127.

1866. WRIGHT, E. P. [Letter relating to the first discovered egg of Pagophila eburnea, brought home by Sir L. McClintock from Polynia Isl., lat. 77° 25'. Cf. Carte, Journ. Roy. Dublin Soc., i, 1856, pp. 57-60, pls. 1, 2.] < *Ibis*, 2d ser., ii, 1866, pp. 216-218.

1867. ALSTON, E. R. "The Wide-awake Tern" [Zool., s. s., p. 979]. < *Zoologist*, 2d ser., ii, 1867, p. 1018.

1867. BLAKE-KNOX, H. A Natural History of the Common Gull [Larus canus], being an Account of its Habits, Food, Nidification, Cry, Flight, &c. < *Zoologist*, 2d ser., ii, 1867,pp. 625-631.

The fifth of a series with major title "Letters on Ornithology."

1867. CLIFTON, Lord. Query respecting Gulls in Kent. < *Zoologist*, 2d ser., ii, 1867, p. 637.

1867. DUTTON, J. Kittiwake [Rissa tridactyla] at Eastbourne. < *Zoologist*, 2d ser., ii, 1867, p. 793.

1867. F[AY, Miss] M. D. The history of a Sea-swallow [Sterna hirundo]. < *Our Young Folks* [juvenile magazine], Feb., 1867, pp. 92-98.

Popular account of an individual hatched and reared in confinement.

1867. FEILDEN, H. W. Breeding of the Blackheaded Gull [Larus ridibundus] at Pilling Moss, Lancashire. < *Zoologist*, 2d ser., ii, 1867, pp. 832, 833.

1867. FURNEAUX, A. Sabine's Gull [Xema sabinii] in Cornwall. < *Zoologist*, 2d ser., ii, 1867, p. 608.

1867. GREENWOOD, H. Gulls vomiting their Food. < *Zoologist*, 2d ser., ii, 1867, p. 711.

1867. GUNN, T. E. Piebald Variety of the Common Skua [Stercorarius skua]. *< Zoologist*, 2d ser., ii, 1867, p. 992.

1867. GUNN, T. E. Buffon's Skua [Stercorarius buffoni] on the Norfolk Coast. *< Zoologist*, 2d ser., ii, 1867, p. 992.

1867. GURNEY, J. H. Little Gull [Larus minutus] at Flamborough Head, Iceland Gull [Larus leucopterus] in Orkney and Tithys Redstart at Minehead. *< Zoologist*, 2d ser., ii, 1867, p. 1018.

1867. KNIGHT, J. Masked, Iceland and Glaucus Gulls [Larus capistratus, leucopterus, glaucus] near Scarborough. *< Zoologist*, 2d ser., ii, 1867, p. 637.
From the London 'Field,' Jan. 26.

1867. MATHEW, M. A. Sabine's Gull [Xema sabinii] at Weston-super-Mare. *< Zoologist*, 2d ser., ii, 1867, p. 992.

1867. MORRIS, F. O. Sabine's Gull [Xema sabinii] in Cornwall. *< Zoologist*, 2d ser., ii, 1867, p. 710.

1867. SCLATER, P. L. [Remarks on Gulls (Larinæ, three spp.) living in the Society's Menagerie.] *< P. Z. S.*, xxxv, 1867, pp. 315, 316.

1867. POWER, W. H. Gulls in Kent. *< Zoologist*, 2d ser., ii, 1867, pp. 710, 711.

1867. SMEE, A. H. Arctic Tern [Sterna macrura] near Gravesend. *< Zoologist*, 2d ser., ii, 1867, p. 1017.

1867. SMEE, A. H. Skua [Stercorarius skua] on the Thames. *< Zoologist*, 2d ser., ii, 1867, pp. 1017, 1018.

1867. SMEE, A. H. Sandwich Tern [Sterna cantiaca] at Whitby. *< Zoologist*, 2d ser., ii, 1867, p. 1018.

1867. STEVENSON, H. Occurrence of the Whitewinged Black Tern [Hydrochelidon leucoptera] in Norfolk. *< Zoologist*, 2d ser., ii, 1867, p. 951.

1868. ASHMEAD, G. B. Little Gull [Larus minutus] in the Thames. *< Zoologist*, 2d ser., iii, 1868, p. 1462.

1868. BLAKE-KNOX, H. Part II.—Being an Account of its [Larus canus] Plumages and Transformations from the Nestling to the Adult Bird. *< Zoologist*, 2d ser., iii, 1868, pp. 1075–1088.
The sixth of a series with major title "Letters on Ornithology."

1868. BLAKE-KNOX, H. Sabine's Gull [Xema sabinii] in Dublin Bay. *< Zoologist*, 2d ser., iii, 1868, p. 1099.

1868. BLAKE-KNOX, H. Sabine's Gull [Xema sabinii] in the County Down. *< Zoologist*, 2d ser., iii, 1868, p. 1099.

1868. BLAKE-KNOX, H. Iceland and Glaucous Gulls [Larus leucopterus, glaucus] off the Dublin Coast. *< Zoologist*, 2d ser., iii, 1868, p. 1463.

1868. DUTTON, J. Pomarine Skua [Stercorarius pomatorhinus] at Eastbourne. *< Zoologist*, 2d ser., iii, 1868, p. 1099.

1868. GURNEY, J. H. Iceland Gull [Larus leucopterus] off Brixham. *< Zoologist*, 2d ser., iii, 1868, p. 1222.

1868. GURNEY, J. H., JR. Little Gull [Larus minutus] at Flamborough. *< Zoologist*, 2d ser., iii, 1868, p. 1379.

1868. GURNEY, J. H., JR. Little Gull [Larus minutus] near Bridlington. *< Zoologist*, 2d ser., iii, 1868, p. 1424.

1868. GURNEY, J. H., JR. Common Skua [Stercorarius skua] on the Dogger Bank. *< Zoologist*, 2d ser., iii, 1868, p. 1462.

1868. GURNEY, J. H., JR. Richardson's Skua [Stercorarius richardsoni] near Flamborough. *< Zoologist*, 2d ser., iii, 1868, p. 1462.

1868. GURNEY, J. H., JR. Pomarine Skua [Stercorarius pomatorhinus] near Bridlington. *< Zoologist*, 2d ser., iii, 1868, p. 1462.

1868. GURNEY, J. H., JR.   Little Gull [Larus minutus] at Flamborough.   <*Zoologist*, 2d ser., iii, 1868, p. 1462.

1868. GURNEY, J. H., JR.   Little Gull [Larus minutus] near Bridlington.   <*Zoologist*, 2d ser., iii, 1868, p. 1462.

1868. GURNEY, J. H., JR.   Little Gull [Larus minutus] near Filey.   <*Zoologist*, 2d ser., iii, 1868, p. 1462.

1868. GURNEY, J. H., JR.   Little Gulls [Larus minutus] on the Yorkshire Coast.   <*Zoologist*, 2d ser., iii, 1868, p. 1482.

1868. GURNEY, J. H., JR.   Pomarine Skua [Stercorarius pomatorhinus] at Flamborough.   <*Zoologist*, 2d ser., iii, 1868, p. 1482.

1868. GUNN, T. E.   Pomarine Skua [Stercorarius pomatorhinus] on the Norfolk Coast.   <*Zoologist*, 2d ser., iii, 1868, p. 1483.

1868. HARVIE-BROWN, J. A.   Wide-awake Terns [Sterna fuliginosa?].   <*Zoologist*, 2d ser., iii, 1868, pp. 1098, 1099.

1868. SMITH, CECIL.   Black Tern [Hydrochelidon nigra] in Somersetshire.   <*Zoologist*, 2d ser., iii, 1868, p. 1378.

1868. SMITH, CECIL.   Lesser Tern [Sterna minuta] in Devonshire.   <*Zoologist*, 2d ser., iii, 1868, p. 1378.

1868. WALKER, T. C.   Kittiwake [Rissa tridactyla]: Correction of an Error [Zool., s. s., p. 1367].   <*Zoologist*, 2d ser., iii, 1868, p. 1424.

1869. BLAKE-KNOX, H.   Glaucous and Iceland Gulls [Larus glaucus, leucopterus] in Kingstown Harbour, County Dublin.   <*Zoologist*, 2d ser., iv, 1869, pp. 1517, 1518.

1869. BLAKE-KNOX, H.   Iceland Gull [Larus leucopterus] in Kingstown Harbour, County Dublin.   <*Zoologist*, 2d ser., iv, 1869, p. 1564.

1869. CLOGG, S.   Little Gull [Larus minutus] at Looe.   <*Zoologist*, 2d ser., iv, 1869, pp. 1563, 1564.

1869. DRESSER, H. E.   [Exhibition of, and remarks on, the eggs of Larus minutus.]   <*P. Z. S.*, xxxvii, 1869, pp. 530, 531.

1869. GUNN, T. E.   Little Gull [Larus minutus] near Yarmouth.   <*Zoologist*, 2d ser., iv, 1869, p. 1518.

1869. GUNN, T. E.   Sandwich Tern [Sterna cantiaca] on the Norfolk Coast.   <*Zoologist*, 2d ser., iv, 1869, p. 1517.

1869. GUNN, T. E.   Voracity of the Common Gull [Larus canus].   <*Zoologist*, 2d ser., iv, 1869, p. 1603.

1869. GUNN, T. E.   Black Tern's [Hydrochelidon nigra] Egg in Norfolk.   <*Zoologist*, 2d ser., iv, 1869, p. 1868.

1869. HARTING, J. E.   Sooty Tern [Sterna fuliginosa] at Wallingford.   <*Zoologist*, 2d ser., iv, 1869, pp. 1867, 1868.

1869. HUNTER, J.   Kittiwake Gull [Rissa tridactyla] near Faversham.   <*Zoologist*, 2d ser., iv, 1869, p. 1518.

1869. KÖNIG-WARTHAUSEN, *Baron* R.   Revue der Sterna-Eier.   <*Bericht über d. xvii. Versamml. d. Deutsch. Ornith. Gesellsch.*, 1869, pp. 36–39.
    Not seen.—The oological characters, so far as known to the author, of all the species of *Sterninæ* are briefly given.

1869. MATHEW, G. F.   Little Gull [Larus minutus, at Braunton].   <*Zoologist*, 2d ser., iv, 1869, p. 1803.

1869. NEWMAN, E.   Curious Malformation in a Gull's Leg.   <*Zoologist*, 2d ser., iv, 1869, p. 1685, fig.

1869. RICKARDS, M. S. C.   Pomarine Skua [Stercorarius pomatorhinus] at Exmouth.   <*Zoologist*, 2d ser., iv, 1869, p. 1518.

1869. SKINNER, A.   Kittiwake Gull [Rissa tridactyla] in Faversham Creek. < *Zoologist*, 2d ser., iv, 1869, p. 1564.

1869. SMEE, A. H.   Kittiwake Gulls [Rissa tridactyla] on the Thames. < *Zoologist*, 2d ser., iv, 1869, pp. 1645, 1646.

1869. WALLIS, H. M.   Pomerine Skua [Steroorarius pomatorhinus] at Aldeburgh. < *Zoologist*, 2d ser., iv, 1869, p. 1868.

1869. WONFOR, T. W.   Little Gull [Larus minutus] at Brighton. < *Zoologist*, 2d ser., iv, 1869, p. 1563.

1869. WONFOR, T. W.   Little Gulls [Larus minutus] in Sussex. < *Zoologist*, 2d ser., iv, 1869, p. 1603.

1870. ALSTON, E. R.   Kittiwake Gull [Rissa tridactyla]. < *Zoologist*, 2d ser., v, 1870, p. 2108.

1870. ANON.   A Rare Visitor [Stercorarius pomatorhinus, in Pennsylvania]. < *Am. Nat.*, iv, 1870, p. 57.

1870. BELL, A. S.   Little Gulls [Larus minutus] on the Yorkshire Coast. < *Zoologist*, 2d ser., v, 1870, p. 2107.

1870. BLAKE-KNOX, H.   About the Kittiwake's [Rissa tridactyla] First Winter Plumage, &c. < *Zoologist*, 2d ser., v, 1870, pp. 2119–2124.
    Cf. *Zool.*, s. s., p. 2184.

1870. BOND, F.   Little Gulls [Larus minutus] in Leadenhall Market. < *Zoologist*, 2d ser., v, 1870, p. 2066.

1870. BOND, F.   Little Gull [Larus minutus] in the City. < *Zoologist*, 2d ser., v, 1870, p. 2108.

1870. BOYES, F.   Common and Sandwich Terns [Sterna hirundo, S. cantiaca] at Spurn. < *Zoologist*, 2d ser., v, 1870, p. 2026.

1870. BOYNTON, T.   Little Gulls [Larus minutus] at Bridlington Bay. < *Zoologist*, 2d ser., v, 1870, p. 2107.
    From the London 'Field,' Feb. 26.

1870. CORDEAUX, J.   Common and Sandwich Terns [Sterna hirundo, S. cantiaca] at Spurn. < *Zoologist*, 2d ser., v, 1870, pp. 2065, 2066.

1870. CORNISH, T.   Blackheaded Gulls [Larus ridibundns] in Penzance. < *Zoologist*, 2d ser., v, 1870, p. 2143.

1870. GUNN, T. E.   Little Gull [Larus minutus] on the Norfolk Coast. < *Zoologist*, 2d ser., v, 1870, p. 1982.

1870. GUNN, T. E.   Abundance of the Little Gull [Larus minutus] on the Norfolk Coast. < *Zoologist*, 2d ser., v, 1870, pp. 2107, 2108.

1870. GURNEY, J. H., JR.   Pied Head in the Common Skua [Stercorarius skua]. < *Zoologist*, 2d ser., v, 1870, p. 2386.

1870. JONES, J. M.   On the Laridæ of the Nova Scotian Coast. < *Trans. Nov. Scot. Inst. Nat. Sci.*, ii, pt. iv, 1870, pp. 52–57.
    Field-notes on 7 spp.

1870. MATHEW, M. A.   Glaucous Gull [Larus glaucus] at Weston-super-Mare. < *Zoologist*, 2d ser., v, 1870, p. 2066.

1870. MÖBIUS, K.   Absonderliche Nahrung einer jungen Möve [Larus argentatus]. < *J. f. O.*, xviii, 1870, p. 118.

1870. RAMSEY, R. G. W.   Little Gull [Larus minutus] at Coldingham. < *Zoologist*, 2d ser., v, 1870, p. 2026.

1870. SMEE, A. H.   Common Tern [Sterna hirundo] in Oxfordshire. < *Zoologist*, 2d ser., v, 1870, p. 2308.

1870. STUBBS, C. E.   Terns at Henley-on-Thames. < *Zoologist*, 2d ser., v, 1870, p. 2347.

1871. BLAKE-KNOX, H. Little Gull [Larus minutus] in Dublin Bay and in London-
derry. < *Zoologist*, 2d ser., vi, 1871, p. 2646.

1871. BOYES, F. Iceland Gull [Larus leucopterus] in East Yorkshire. < *Zoologist*,
2d ser., vi, 1871, p. 2488.

1871. BOYES, F. Glaucous Gulls [Larus glaucus] in East Yorkshire. < *Zoologist*, 2d
ser., vi, 1871, p. 2488.

1871. BOYES, F. Little Gull [Larus minutus] in East Yorkshire. < *Zoologist*, 2d ser.,
vi, 1871, p. 2528.

1871. HAMMOND, W. O. Terns at St. Alban's Court. < *Zoologist*, 2d ser., vi, 1871, pp.
2684, 2685.

1871. JONES, J. M. On the Gulls [Laridæ] of the Nova Scotian Coast. < *Canad.
Nat. and Quart. Journ.*, v, 1871, pp. 231, 232.
10 spp.

1871. MÖBIUS, K. Ein Besuch der Insel Sylt in Mai 1870. < *Zool. Gart.*, 1871, p. 193.
Account of a visit to a nesting-place of *Sterna caspia;* 17 nests, where in 1819 300 were reck-
oned by Naumann, and subsequently 200 by F. Boie.

1871. SCLATER, P. L., *and* SALVIN, O. A Revised List of the Neotropical Laridæ.
< *P. Z. S.*, xxxix, 1871, pp. 564–580, woodcc.
Treating of 32 species, belonging to the subfamilies *Rhynchopinæ, Sterninæ, Larinæ,* and
Lestridinæ, which are divided into four categories:—Tropical (15), Antarctic (4), Arctic (9),
and Tropicopolitan (4), according to their range. Their synonymy is worked out with care,
and many rectifications are made. No new species are described; but the heads of *Sterna
maxima, S. galericulata, Larus heermanni, L. belcheri,* and *Leucophæus scoresbii* are figured.
The name *Chroicocephalus* is spelled *Chroocephalus.*
It may be observed that the authors' use of *Sterna maxima* Bodd. for what American
ornithologists had mostly called *S. regia* Gamb. is doubtless correct; but it has been since
shown that their reference of *S. elegans* Gamb. to *S. galericulata* Licht. is erroneous. The
paper on the whole is of a high degree of reliability.

1871. SMITH, CECIL. Iceland Gull [Larus leucopterus] in Somersetshire. < *Zoologist*,
2d ser., vi, 1871, p. 2488.

1871. STEVENSON, H. On the Abundance of Little Gulls [Larus minutus] on the Norfolk Coast in the Winter of 1869–70. < *Zoologist*, 2d ser., vi, 1870, pp. 2499–2504.

1871. STUBBS, C. E. Black Tern [Hydrochelidon nigra] at Henley-on-Thames.
< *Zoologist*, 2d ser., vi, 1871, p. 2684.

1871. SWINHOE, R. On a New Chinese Gull [Chroicocephalus saundersi]. < *P. Z. S.*,
xxxix, 1871, pp. 273–275, pl. xxii.

1871. WHARTON, C. B. Black Tern [Hydrochelidon nigra] at Elstree Reservoir.
< *Zoologist*, 2d ser., vi, 1871, p. 2810.

1872. ANDERSON, A. [On the nidification of Sterna leucoparia in Oudh.] < *Ibis*,
3d ser., ii, 1872, pp. 81–83.

1872. DURNFORD, H. Dark Variety of Richardson's Skua [Stercorarius richardsoni].
< *Zoologist*, 2d ser., vii, 1872, p. 3339.

1872. GOULD, J. [Remarks on exhibition of a specimen of Larus rossi (Rhodostethia
rosea) in adult summer plumage.] < *P. Z. S.*, 1872, p. 1.

1872. GURNEY, J. H. Pomarine Skuas [Stercorarius pomatorhinus] in Torbay.
< *Zoologist*, 2d ser., vii, 1872, pp. 2946, 2947.

1872. GURNEY, J. H. Pomarine Skuas [Stercorarius pomatorhinus] in Torbay.
< *Zoologist*, 2d ser., vii, 1872, p. 2995.

1872. HADFIELD, H. Common Tern [Sterna hirundo, near Dunnose]. < *Zoologist*, 2d
ser., vii, 1872, p. 2906.

1872. HÜGEL, A. v. Gullbilled Tern [Sterna anglica] in Hampshire. < *Zoologist*, 2d
ser., vii, 1872, pp. 3149, 3150.

1872. GURNEY, J. H., JR.   Sabine's Gull [Xema sabinii] at Bridlington.   < *Zoologist*, 2d ser., vii, 1872, p. 3316.

1872. MÖBIUS, K.   Norderoog, ein Brutplatz der Brand-Seeschwalbe, Sterna cantiaca, im Schleswigschen Waltenmeere.   < *Zool. Gart.*, xiii, 1872, pp. 202–204.
Colony estimated at 20,000.

1872. NEWTON, A.   [Remarks on exhibition of a specimen of Larus rossi (Rhodostethia rosea) in winter plumage.]   < *P. Z. S.*, 1872, p. 1.

1872. POTTS, T. H.   Notes on a New Species of Gull, Larus (Bruchigavia) Bulleri, Potts.   < *Trans. and Proc. New Zealand Inst. for* 1871, iv, 1872, pp. 203, 204.

1872. RODD, E. H., *and* YARRELL, W.   [Critical notes on] The British Skuas (Lestris).   < *Zoologist*, 2d ser., vii, 1872, pp. 2933–2935.

1872. RODD, E. H.   Glaucous and Iceland Gulls [Larus glaucus, L. leucopterus] in Mount's Bay.   < *Zoologist*, 2d ser., vii, 1872, p. 3065.

1872. RODD, E. H.   Gullbilled Tern [Sterna anglica] at St. Just, near Penzance.   < *Zoologist*, 2d ser., vii, 1872, p. 3188.

1872. SAUNDERS, H.   [Letter on Larus melanocephalus, shot near Barking Creek in January, 1866.]   < *Ibis*, 3d ser., ii, 1872, pp. 79, 80.

1872. SMEE, A. H.   Blackheaded Gulls [Larus ridibundus] in Oxfordshird.   < *Zoologist*, 2d ser., vii, 1872, p. 3316.

1872. TUCK, J. G.   Richardson's Skua [Stercorarius richardsoni] at Rye.   < *Zoologist*, 2d ser., vii, 1872, p. 2907.

1873. BREE, C. R.   [Distinctness of Larus leucophæus and] Larus cachinnans.   < *Zoologist*, 2d ser., viii, 1873, pp. 3695, 3696.

1873. DURNFORD, H.   Glaucous Gull [Larus glaucus] at Southwold, Suffolk.   < *Zoologist*, 2d ser., viii, 1873, p. 3413.

1873. DURNFORD, H.   Nesting of the Sandwich Tern [Sterna cantiaca] on Walney Island.   < *Zoologist*, 2d ser., viii, 1873, p. 3773.

1873. GRAY, ROBERT.   [On an unprecedented influx of Laridæ in the Firth of Forth, attracted by shoals of sprats.]   < *Ibis*, 3d ser., iii, 1873, pp. 332, 333.

1873. GRAY, ROBERT.   On some of the Sea Gulls [Laridæ] frequenting the Estuary of the Forth during the Winter of 1872–3.   < *Proc. Nat. Hist. Soc. Glasgow*, Jan. 7, 1873, pp. 198– —.
Not seen—title from J. A. Harvie-Brown.
Also separately reprinted, with a paper on the Iceland Gull by J. A. Harvie-Brown, read Jan. 28, 1873, 8vo, pp. 198–212.

1873. HARVIE-BROWN, J. A.   On the occurrence of The Iceland Gull [Larus islandicus] in the Estuary of the Forth during the Winter of 1872–3.   < *Proc. Nat. Hist. Soc. Glasgow*, Jan. 28, 1873, pp. — –212.
Not seen—title from author.
Also separately printed, with a paper on the Gulls of that locality by Robert Gray, read Jan. 7, 1873, 8vo, pp. 198–212.

1873. HUTTON, F. W.   On the Flight of the Black-backed Gull (Larus dominicanus).   < *Trans. and Proc. New Zealand Inst. for* 1872, v, 1873, pp. 140–144.

1873. MATHEW, G. F.   [Note on habits of] Gulls off Valparaiso.   < *Zoologist*, 2d ser., viii, 1873, pp. 3493, 3494.

1873. RODD, E. H.   Iceland Gull [Larus leucopterus] at Mount's Bay.   < *Zoologist*, 2d ser., viii, 1873, p. 3455.

1873. WHITAKER, J., JR.   Glaucous Gull [Larus glaucus] in Nottinghamshire.   < *Zoologist*, 2d ser., viii, 1873, p. 3493.

1874. BALL, R.   Affection of the Sea Gull for its Young.   < *Zoologist*, 2d ser., ix, 1874, p. 4201.

1014   BULLETIN UNITED STATES GEOLOGICAL SURVEY.   [*Vol.*V.

1874. BATTY, J. H.   Pugnacity of the Great Black-back Gull [Larus marinus]
     < *Forest and Stream*, ii, Mar. 12, 1874, p. 70.

1874. BREWER, T. M.   A New North American Bird [Hydrochelidon leucoptera, in
     Wisconsin].   < *Am. Nat.*, viii, 1874, pp. 188, 189.

1874. BREWSTER, W.   A new Bird to Massachusetts [Sterna regia].   < *Am. Sports-*
     man, iv, 1874, p. 257.

1874. BOYES, F.   Glaucous Gulls [Larus glaucus] in East Yorkshire.   < *Zoologist*, 2d
     ser., ix, 1874, pp. 3836, 3837.

1874. CLARK-KENNEDY, A. J.   Iceland Gull [a peculiarity of Larus leucopterus].
     < *Zoologist*, 2d ser., ix, 1874, pp. 4078, 4079.

1874. COUES, E.   Monograph of the North American Laridæ.   < *Birds of the North-*
     west, 1874, pp. 589–717.

The auther had paid special attention to the subject, and published three preliminary
papers in *Pr. Phila. Acad.*, 1862–'3 (*q. v.*), when the ordering of the *Birds of the Northwest* by
the Government gave him an opportunity of reviewing the case, and of presenting much
additional matter which had long lain in MSS. The subject was reworked for appearance in the present connection, to include full descriptions of the genera and species, full
synonymy, extensive criticism, and some considerable anatomical matter. A large number
of colored illustrations had been prepared, but it was not found practicable to use them.
(N. B. Many of these will probably appear in the last volume of Baird, Brewer, and Ridgway's *History of North American Birds*, now (Aug., 1880) said to be about to go to press.

The genera and species recognized by the author are as follows:

I. LESTRIDINÆ.—1. *Buphagus skua;* a, *skua;* b, *antarcticus.*   2. *Stercorarius pomatorhinus.*
3. *S. parasiticus* (Brünn.).   4. *S. buffoni* (Boie).

II. LARINÆ.—1. *Larus glaucus.*   2. *L. leucopterus.*   3. *L. glaucescens.*   4. *L. marinus.*   5.
L. argentatus; a, *argentatus;* b, *smithsonianus;* c, *occidentalis;* d, *borealis;* e? *leucophæus.*
6. *L. californicus.*   7. *L. delawarensis,*   8. *L. canus;* a, *canus;* b, *niveus;* c, *brachyrhynchus.*
9. *L. (Blasipus) heermanni.*   10. *L. (Rissa) tridactylus;* a, *tridactylus;* b, *kotzebui.*   11. *L. (R.)
brevirostris* Brandt.   12. *L. (Pagophila) eburneus.*   13. *L. (Chrœcocephalus) atricilla.*   14. *L.
(C.) franklini.*   15. *L. (C.) philadelphia.*   16. *Rhodostethia rosea.*   17. *Xema sabinei.*   18. *Xema
furcatum.*

III. STERNINÆ.—1. *Sterna (Gelochelidon) anglica.*   2. *S. (Thalasseus) caspia.*   3. *S. (T.)
regia.*   4. *S. (T.) galericulata (=elegans).*   5. *S. (T.) cantiaca.*   6. *S. trudeaui.*   7. *S. forsteri.*
8. *S. hirundo.*   9. *S. macrura.*   10. *S. dougalli.*   11. *S. portlandica* Ridg. (since abolished.)
12. *S. superciliaris* var. *antillarum.*   13. *S. aleutica.*   14. *S. (Haliplana) fuliginosa.*   15. *S.
(H.) anæstheta.*   16. *Hydrochelidon lariformis* (L., 1758).   17. *H. nigra* (=*leucoptera* Meisn.
& Schinz).   18. *Anous stolidus.*

IV. RHYNCHOPINÆ.—1. *Rhynchops nigra.*

Various extralimital species are incidentally treated in addition to those recognized as
North American.

1874. EVANS, J.   Arctic Skua [Stercorarius buffoni] in Lincolnshire.   < *Zoologist*, 2d
     ser., ix, 1874, p. 3837.

1874. HARVIE-BROWN, J. A.   Glaucous Gull [Larus glaucus: cf. Zool., s. s., p. 4078].
     < *Zoologist*, 2d ser., ix, 1874, p. 4120.

1874. HERRICK, H.   A Sea Bird [Stercorarius parasiticus] away from Home.   < *Am.
     Sportsman*, v, Dec. 12, 1874, p. 167.

Occurrence of this species at Chatham, N. J.

1874. KIRTLAND, J. P.   A rare Bird [Stercorarius richardsoni, in Ohio].   < *Proc.
     Cleveland Acad. Nat. Sci.*, 1874, p. 133.   [Read 1857.]

1874. MAYNARD, C. J.   A Naturalist on the National [Sportsmen's Association].
     < *Am. Sportsman*, iv, 1874, p. 329.

Statements as to slaughter of Gulls and Terns (*Laridæ*), etc., along the New England
coast; causes of decrease of birds.

1874. RANDALL, W. S.   The Common Gull (Larus canus) in Captivity.   < *Zoologist*,
     2d ser., ix, 1874, pp. 4129–4131.

1874. RICKARDS, M. S. C.   Pomarine Skua [Stercorarius pomatorhinus] in North
     Devon.   < *Zoologist*, 2d ser., ix, 1874, pp. 4240, 4241.

1874. RICKARDS, M. S. C.   Richardson's Skua [Stercorarius richardsoni] near Clevedon and at Instow.   < *Zoologist*, 2d ser., ix, 1874, p. 4241.

1874. RIDGWAY, R.   Notice of a Species of Tern [Sterna portlandica, sp. n.] new to
the Atlantic Coast of North America.   < *Am. Nat.*, viii, 1874, p. 433.
    This alleged new species occasioned considerable writing before it was finally identified
    with *S. macrura.*

1874. RODD, E. H.   Buffon's Skua [Stercorarius buffoni] near Falmouth.   < *Zoologist*,
2d ser., ix, 1874, pp. 4239, 4240.

1874. SAUNDERS, H.   Remarks on the Grey-capped Gulls [Cirrhocephalus Bp.] and
on the Species with which they have been confounded.   < *P. Z. S.*, 1874, pp.
291–295.

1874. SCLATER, P. L.   The Yellow-legged Herring-Gull [Larus leucophæus].   < *Ibis*,
3d ser., iv, 1874, p. 100.
    A note on its geographical distribution.

1874. SHAW, J.   Little Gull [Larus minutus] near Shrewsbury.   < *Zoologist*, 2d ser.,
ix, 1874, p. 4262.

1874. TAYLOR, W.   Caspian Tern [Sterna caspia] at Birmingham.   < *Zoologist*, 2d
ser., ix, 1874, pp. 4036, 4037.

1874. "W. M. S."   A Domesticated Gull.   < *Am. Sportsman*, iv, 1874, p. 171.

1875. ANON.   [Mode of catching Sea Gulls alive at Mt. Desert, Maine.]   < *Forest and
Stream*, v, Dec. 23, 1875, p. 308.

1875. BENNER, F.   Sterna portlandica.   < *Rod and Gun*, vi, Apr. 3, 1875, p. 7.   See
also p. 56.

1875. BREWSTER, W.   Some notes on a new species of North American Tern [Sterna
portlandica].   < *Am. Sportsman*, v, Jan. 16, 1875, p. 249.
    Notice of *Sterna portlandica*, Ridg., collected on Muskeget Island, Mass., July 1, 1870.

1875. BREWSTER, W.   A New Bird [Sterna regia] to Massachusetts.   < *Am. Sportsman*, v, Jan. 16, 1875, p. 249.
    Capture of ♂ and ♀ on Nantucket Island, July 1, 1874; the female bore marks of breeding.

1875. BREWSTER, W.   Occurrence of the Fork-tailed Gull [Xema sabinii] in Mass[a-
chusetts].   < *Am. Sportsman*, v, Mar. 13, 1875, p. 370.
    Read before Nuttall Ornithological Club, 1875.

1875. BULLER, W. L.   Notes on an alleged new Species of Tern (Sterna alba, Potts).
< *Trans. and Proc. New Zealand Inst. for* 1874, vii, 1875, pp. 214, 215.

1875. COPE, W. J.   Blackheaded Gulls [Larus ridibundus] at South Kirkby.   < *Zoologist*, 2d ser., x, July, 1875, p. 4541.

1875. "F. W. S."   Sterna portlandica.   < *Am. Sportsman*, v, Feb. 13, 1875, p. 314.
    Its nesting in numbers on an island off the coast of Maine.   (= *S. macrura*.)

1875. GURNEY, J. H., JR.   Herring Gulls [Larus argentatus] carrying off wounded
Dunlins.   < *Zoologist*, 2d ser., x, Oct., 1875, pp. 4666, 4667.

1875. GURNEY, J. H., JR.   Audacity of a Common Skua (Stercorarius catarrhactes
(Linn.).   < *Zoologist*, 2d ser., x, Nov., 1875, pp. 4698, 4699.

1875. LEGG, W. H.   Little Gull [Larus minutus] in Summer Plumage in February.
< *Zoologist*, 2d ser., x, May, 1875, p. 4459.

1875. MATHEW, M. A.   Pomatorrhine Skua [Stercorarius pomatorhinus] at Instow.
< *Zoologist*, 2d ser., x, Jan., 1875, p. 4300.

1875. MAYNARD, C. J.   Bird murder—Sterna portlandica.   < *Rod and Gun*, vi, Apr.
24, 1875, p. 56.   See also p. 7.

1875. NEWTON, [A.]   [Exhibition of two specimens of Rhodostethia rosea from Greenland.]   < *P. Z. S.*, May 4, 1875, p. 349.

1875. NICHOLLS, H., JR.   Singular Freak of a Herring Gull [Larus argentatus].
< *Zoologist*, 2d ser., x, Nov., 1875, p. 4698.

1875. RIDGWAY, R.   Note on Sterna longipennis Nordmann. $<$ *Am. Nat.*, ix, No. 1, Jan., 1875, pp. 54, 55.

   Critical comparison of *SS. hirundo, longipennis, portlandica*, and *pikei.*

1875. ROCKE, J.   Correction of an Error [Zoöl., s. s., p. 4262, respecting Xema sabinii]. $<$ *Zoologist*, 2d ser., x, Jan., 1875, pp. 4299, 4300.

1875. SAUNDERS, H.   [Remarks on a Gull from Lower California, referable to Larus fuscus.] $<$ *P. Z. S.*, Mar. 16, 1875, p. 158.

1875. SAUNDERS, H.   On the Immature Plumage of Rhodostethia rosea. $<$ *Ibis*, 3d ser., v, 1875, pp. 484–487.

   With enumeration of 11, perhaps 12, known specimens of this species.

1875. WARREN, R., JR.   Notes on the Autumnal Migration of Lestris Richardsonii and L. pomarinus in Killala Bay and the Moy Estuary $<$ *Zoologist*, 2d ser., x, Nov., 1875, pp. 4699–4703.

1876. A[LLEN], J. A.   The Portland Tern [Sterna portlandica]. $<$ *Bull. Nutt. Ornith. Club*, i, No. 3, Sept., 1876, pp. 71, 72.

   Notice of W. Brewster's paper, *Ann. Lyc. Nat. Hist. N. Y.*, xi, p. 200, where *Sterna portlandica* is referred to *S. macrura.*

1876. BREWSTER, W.   Some Additional Light on the so-called Sterna portlandica, Ridgway. $<$ *Ann. Lyc. Nat. Hist. N. Y.*, xi, Nov., 1875, pub. Feb., 1876, pp. 200–207.

   Critical examination of the supposed species, which is identified with *S. macrura.*

1876. BREWSTER, W.   Sterna portlandica, Ridgway. $<$ *Rod and Gun*, viii, Apr. 15, 1876, p. 37.

   Reprinted from *Ann. Lyc. Nat. Hist. N. Y.*, xi, Nov., 1875, pub. Feb., 1876, p. 200.

1876. DARRAGH, T.   Audacity of the Common Skua [Stercorarius skua]. $<$ *Zoologist*, 2d ser., xi, Apr., 1876, p. 4883.

1876. GURNEY, J. H., JR.   Black Tern [Hydrochelidon nigra] in Durham. $<$ *Zoologist*, 2d ser., xi, Jan., 1876, pp. 4766, 4767.

1876. GURNEY, J. H., JR.   Second Instance of the Audacity of the Skua [Stercorarius skua]. $<$ *Zoologist*, 2d ser., xi, Feb., 1876, p. 4804.

1876. GURNEY, J. H., JR.   Sabine's Gull [Xema sabinii] at Bridlington Quay. $<$ *Zoologist*, 2d ser., xi, Apr., 1876, p. 4883.

1876. GURNEY, J. H., JR.   Kittiwake [Rissa tridactyla] in Winter. $<$ *Zoologist*, 2d ser., xi, Aug., 1876, .p. 5048.

1876. HADFIELD, H.   Common Gull [Larus canus]. $<$ *Zoologist*, 2d ser., xi, June, 1876, pp. 4959, 4960.

1876. HARVIE-BROWN, J. A.   "Kittiwake [Rissa tridactyla] in Winter" (Zool. S. S. 5048). $<$ *Zoologist*, 2d ser., xi, Sept., 1876, p. 5086.

1876. HEATON, W. H.   Does the Common Gull [Larus canus] breed in the Scilly Isles? $<$ *Zoologist*, 2d ser., xi, Oct., 1876, p. 5126.

1876. [INGERSOLL, E.]   Sterna Portlandica. $<$ *Forest and Stream*, vi, Mar. 23, 1876, p. 100.

   Review of paper (*Ann. Lyc. Nat. Hist. N. Y.*, xi, Nov., 1875, p. 200) on *Sterna portlandica.*

1876. JOUY, P. L.   Notes on Forster's Tern.   Sterna forsteri, Nutt. $<$ *Field and Forest*, ii, No. 2, Aug., 1876, pp. 29–31.

   As observed in the District of Columbia, U. S.

1876. KERRY, F.   Iceland Gull [Larus leucopterus] at Aldeburgh. $<$ *Zoologist*, 2d ser., xi, 1876, p. 4848.

1876. LE BARON, J. F.   Short-Tailed Tern [Hydrochelidon nigra] in Massachusetts. $<$ *Forest and Stream*, v, Jan. 20, 1876, p. 372.

1876. MATHEW, M. A.   Herring Gulls [Larus argentatus] at Tintagel. $<$ *Zoologist*, 2d ser., xi, Oct., 1876, pp. 5126, 5127.

1876. SAUNDERS, H.   On the Stercorariinæ or Skua Gulls.   < *P. Z. S.*, Mar. 21, 1876, pp. 317–332, pl. xxiv.

Monographic; copious synonymy, description and criticism. The author recognizes one genus and 6 spp. *Stercorarius catarrhactes, S. antarcticus, S. chilensis* (figured pl. 24), *S. pomatorhinus, S. crepidatus* (=*parasiticus* auct.), and *S. parasiticus* L. (=*buffoni* auct.). Of the smaller species the same three spp. as given by Coues are recognized, but the synonymy is much better worked out.

1876. SAUNDERS, H.   On the Sterninæ, or Terns, with Descriptions of three new Species.   < *P. Z. S.*, June 20, 1876, pp. 638–672, figg. 1–5, pl. lxi.

The second of three papers in which the Jägers, Terns, and Gulls are respectively monographed. The author studied the family diligently, and enjoyed exceptional facilities for examining type-specimens; his results, therefore, being entitled to much consideration. After some general remarks, the following species are treated with synonymy, criticism, geographical distribution, and in some cases with description:—

1, *Hydrochelidon hybrida ;* 2, *H. leucopteræ ;* 3, *H. nigra.* 4, *Sterna magnirostris ;* 5, *S. anglica ;* 6, *S. seena ;* 7, *S. melanogastra ;* 8, *S. antarctica ;* 9, *S. virgata ;* 10, *S. vittata ;* 11, *S. hirundinacea ;* 12, *S. albigena ;* 13, *S. fluviatilis ;* 14, *S. tibetana,* sp. n., p. 649 ; 15, *S. longipennis ;* 16, *S. macrura ;* 17, *S. forsteri ;* 18, *S. dougalli ;* 19, *S. cantiaca ;* 20, *S. elegans ;* 21, *S. eurygnatha,* sp. n., p. 654, fig. 1 ; 22, *S. media ;* 23, *S. maxima ;* 24, *S. caspia ;* 25, *S. bernsteini ;* 26, *S. bergii ;* 27, *S. frontalis ;* 28, *S. trudeauii ;* 29, *S. melanauchen ;* 30, *S. minuta ;* 31, *S. antillarum ;* 32, *S. superciliaris ;* 33, *S. sinensis ;* 34, *S. sumatrana ;* 35, *S. nereis ;* 36, *S. exilis ;* 37, *S. balœnarum ;* 38, *S. aleutica ;* 39, *S. anæstheta,* fig. 3 ; 40, *S. lunata ;* 41, *S. fuliginosa,* fig. 2. 42, *Nœnia inca.* 43, *Gygis candida,* fig. 4 ; 44, *G. microrhyncha,* sp. n., p. 668, fig. 5. 45, *Anous stolidus ;* 46, *A. tenuirostris,* pl. lxi, fig. 1 ; 47, *A. melanogenys,* pl. lxi, fig. 2 ; 48, *A. leueocapillus,* pl. lxi, fig. 3 ; 49, *A. cœruleus* (cf. *P. Z. S.*, 1878, p. 271, *seq.*).

See Coues, *Bull. Nutt. Ornith. Club*, iii, 1878, pp. 140–142.

1876. TUCK, J. G.   Little Gulls [Larus minutus] off Flamborough Head.   < *Zoologist*, 2d ser., xi, Feb., 1876, p. 4804.

1876. TUCK, J. G.   Glaucous Gull [Larus glaucus] at Flamborough.   < *Zoologist*, 2d ser., xi, Feb., 1876, p. 4804.

1876. TUCK, J. G.   Sandwich Tern [Sterna cantiaca] on Filey Brigg.   < *Zoologist*, 2d ser., xi, Feb., 1876, p. 4804.

1876. TUCK, J. G.   Ivory Gull [Pagophila eburnea], &c.   < *Zoologist*, 2d ser., xi, June, 1876, p. 4960.

1876. WALDEN, *Lord.*   [Letter on Sterna albigena Rüpp. on the Bombay Coast.] < *Ibis*, 3d ser., vi, July, 1876, pp. 384, 385.

1876. WHITAKER, J.   Common Skua [Stercorarius skua] near Mansfield.   < *Zoologist*, 2d ser., xi, Apr., 1876, p. 4883.

1877. ANDERSON, A.   [Remarks on exhibition of young examples of Rhynchops albicollis and Seena aurantia.]   < *P. Z. S.*, Dec. 4, 1877, p. 807.

No difference in the bills on first hatching, so that the extraordinary shape of that of *Rhynchops* must be later developed.

1877. DEANE, R.   Occurrence of the Sooty Tern [Sterna fuliginosa] in Massachusetts. < *Bull. Nutt. Ornith. Club*, ii, No. 1, Jan., 1877, p. 27.

1877. GURNEY, J. H., JR.   [On a peculiar white stage of plumage of Larus glaucus.] < *Ibis*, 4th ser., i, Oct., 1877, p. 492.

This seems to be what Coues called *Larus hutchinsii* (after Rich., *F. B. A.*, ii, 1831, p. 419) in *Pr. Phila. Acad.*, 1862, p. 294. See Coues, *B. Northwest*, 1874, p. 621.

1877. HUME, A. O.   [Letter on the distinctness of species of Anous, with reference to P. Z. S., 1876, p. 638, pl. lxi.]   < *P. Z. S.*, Nov. 6, 1877, p. 683.

1877. ROBERTS, T. S.   Notes on the Breeding of the Black Tern (Hydrochelidon lariformis) in Minnesota.   < *Bull. Nutt. Ornith. Club*, ii, No. 2, Apr., 1877, pp. 34–36.

1877. ROWLEY, G. D.   On Scoulton Mere, Norfolk, and the Black-headed Gull (Larus ridibundus).   < *Rowl. Orn. Misc.*, ii, pt. x, Oct., 1877, pp. 407–416, pll. lxxvi-lxxviii.

Very interesting. The handsome plates represent scenery, filled with the birds.

Bull. v, 4——32

1877. SAUNDERS, H. [On the Occurrence of the Panay Sooty Tern, Sterna anæstheta, in Great Britain.] < *P. Z. S.*, Feb. 6, 1877, p. 43.

1877. SAUNDERS, H. [Remarks on Exhibition of a Specimen of Sterna aleutica from Alaska.] < *P. Z. S.*, Nov. 20, 1877, p. 754.

1877. SAUNDERS, H. Reports on the Collections of Birds made during the Voyage of H. M. S. 'Challenger.'—No. V. On the Laridæ collected during the Expedition. < *P. Z. S.*, Nov. 20, 1877, pp. 794–800.

    Remarks on 17 spp., with special reference to geographical distribution. "On the whole this collection of *Laridæ*, although small in numbers, is one of the most productive of knowledge which has yet been made by any of our national expeditions."

1877. [SCOTT, W. E. D.] Terns. < *The Country*, i, Dec. 1, 1877, p. 67.

    Observations and data concerning the *Sterninæ* of the U. S. Atlantic Coast.

1878. ALLEN, J. A. Sabine's Gull [Xema sabinii] in Maine. < *Bull. Nutt. Ornith. Club*, iii, No. 4, Oct., 1878, p. 195.

    Only other New England record for this species is found in *Am. Sportsman*, v, 1875, p. 370; *Proc. Bost. Soc. Nat. Hist.*, xvii, 1875, p. 449.

1878. BALLOU, W. H. Additions to the Avi-fauna of Illinois. < *The Oölogist*, iv, No. 4, June, 1878, p. 32.

    Stercorarius buffoni.

1878. BENNER, F. The gulls of New York Bay. < *The Country*, i, Jan. 5, 1878, p. 133.

1878. B[REWER], T. M. Saunders on the Larinæ. < *Bull. Nutt. Ornith. Club*, iii, No. 4, Oct., 1878, pp. 185–187.

    Review of the paper in *P. Z. S.*, Feb. 5, 1878, pp. 155–212.

1878. BREWER, T. M. The Skua Gull (Stercorarius catarractes) on the Coast of Massachusetts. < *Bull. Nutt. Ornith. Club*, iii, No. 4, Oct., 1878, p. 188.

    A suspicious statement that this is the first recorded instance of its occurrence in "any part of North America other than Greenland". (*Cf.* Lawr. in *Baird's B. N. A.*, 1858, p. 838; "California".)

1878. BREWSTER, W. The Short-tailed Tern (Hydrochelidon fissipes) in Massachusetts. < *Bull. Nutt. Ornith. Club*, iii, No. 4, Oct., 1878, p. 190.

    Its common occurrence, where it had been considered a rare visitor.

1878. COLLINS, W. H. Notes on the Nesting of the Black Tern [Hydrochelidon lariformis], at St. Clair Flats, Mich[igan]., June 7, 1878. < *The Oölogist*, iv, No. 4, June, 1878, p. 26.

1878. COUES, E. Mr. H. Saunders on the Sterninæ. < *Bull. Nutt. Ornith. Club*, iii, No. 3, 1878, pp. 140–142.

    Favorable review of the paper in *P. Z. S.*, 1876, pp. 638–672; presenting also a synonymatic synopsis of the 17 North American species, according to the author reviewed.

1878. DEANE, R. The Sooty Tern [Sterna fuliginosa] in New Hampshire. < *Bull. Nutt. Ornith. Club*, iii, No. 4, Oct., 1878, p. 195.

    Its first recorded occurrence in that State, though well known as a bird of Massachusetts, Connecticut, and Rhode Island.

1878. [EDITORIAL.] Instinct in Birds. < *The Country*, ii, July 6, 1878, p. 168.

    Remarks upon an anecdote of "instinct" in a Gull.

1878. FEILDEN, H. W. [Letter on the occurrence of Rhodostethia rosea in the Novaya Zemlya Sea.] < *Ibis*, 4th ser., ii, Apr., 1878, pp. 200, 201.

    Shot by Julius Payer, summer of 1873; *Cf.* English ed. of *New Lands within Arctic Circle*, ii, p. 91.

1878. GAETKE, H. [Letter on the occurrence of Larus affinis in Heligoland.] < *Ibis*, 4th ser., ii, Oct., 1878, p. 489.

1878. ROWLEY, G. D. Larus tridactylus. (The Kittiwake Gull.) < *Rowl. Orn. Misc.*, iii, pt. xiv, May, 1878, pp. 233–236, pl. cxi.

1878. SAUNDERS, H. On the Larinæ or Gulls. < *P. Z. S.*, Feb. 5, 1878, pp. 155–212, figg. 16.

Th's is an admirâble memoir, which was immediately accepted as the leading authority upon the subject. The principal previous Laridists were Boie, Brehm, Bruch, Bonaparte, Schlegel, Blasius, Coues, and Sclater and Salvin.

"The literature of this group has been rendered specially intricate through the perverted ingenuity of two systematists who have undertaken its revision. Boie and Brehm are not guiltless. . . . But when Bonaparte and Bruch undertook the revision of the *Larinæ* of the whole world, they speedily enveloped the question in a perfect fog of synonymy; . . . and to the work of the declining days of both these authors we owe at least half of the synonymy which encumbers these pages. It was their intention to perform a similar office for the Terns; but death cut their plans short, . . ."

In Bonaparte's last completed list (for that in *Consp. Av.* was never finished) in *Comptes Rendus*, xlii, 1856, p. 770, he makes 68 spp. and 22 genn. of *Larinæ*, besides 5 doubtful species. Schlegel's *Mus. Pays-Bas* is said by Blasius to be the foundation of all true Gull-knowledge. Blasius reduces the species to 35. Saunders here gives 49 spp. under the 5 genera *Pagophila*, *Rissa*, *Larus*, *Rhodostethia*, and *Xema*. These are carefully treated, with copious synonymy, habitat, description in some cases, and the important critical remarks which Mr. Saunders's general familiarity with the subject and especially his examination of many type specimens enabled him to offer. Much of the "fog" is lifted from the subject, and many of the spectres of Bonaparte's and Bruch's distorting mediumship are laid, it is to be hoped, forever. The figures illustrate the pattern of the primaries of many of the species. The paper closes with correction of an error, *P. Z. S.*, 1876, p. 671, where two species are united under name of *Anous cæruleus*.

Saunders recognizes the following species:—1, *Pagophila eburnea*. 2, *Rissa tridactyla*; 3, *brevirostris*. 4, *Larus glaucus*; 5, *leucopterus*; 6, *glaucescens*; 7, *argentatus*; 8, *cachinnans*; 9, *affinis*; 10, *occidentalis*; 11, *fuscus*; 12, *californicus*; 13, *delawarensis*; 14, *canus*; 15, *brachyrhynchus*; 16, *auduboni*; 17, *marinus*; 18, *dominicanus*; 19, *pacificus*; 20, *belcheri*; 21, *heermanni*; 22, *crassirostris*; 23, *modestus*; 24, *fuliginosus*; 25, *scoresbii*; 26, *novæ hollandiæ* (figg. 1–3); 27, *scopulinus* (f. 4); 28, *hartlaubi* (f. 5); 29, *bulleri* (figg. 6, 7); 30, *gelastes* (f. 8); 31, *leucophthalmus*; 32, *hemprichi*; 33, *atricilla* , 34, *franklini*; 35, *serranus* (f. 9); 36, *brunneicephalus* (f. 10); 37, *ichthyaetus*; 38, *melanocephalus* (f. 11); 39, *ridibundus* (f. 12); 40, *maculipennis* (f. 13); 41, *glaucodes* (f. 14); 42, *cirrocephalus*; 43, *phæocephalus*; 44, *saundersi* (f. 15); 45, *minutus*; 46, *philadelphia* (f. 16). 47, *Rhodostethia rosea*. 48, *Xema sabinii*; 49, *X. furcatum*.

The following dates of introduction of generic names may be found useful:—

1766. *Larus*, Linn., *S. N.*, p. 224; for all Gulls. 1819. *Xema*, Leach, *App. Ross's Voy.*, p. lvii; *X. sabinii*. 1822. *Xema*, Boie, *Isis*, p. 563; for European hooded Gulls. 1844. *Xema*, Boie, *Isis*, p. 192; for various spp. (N. B. *Gavia*, Moehring, 1752, out of date; *Gavia*, Briss., 1760, indefinite.) 1822. *Gavia*, Boie, *Isis*, p. 563; *L. eburneus* and *L. tridactylus*. 1826. *Gavia*, Boie, *Isis*, p. 980; *L. eburneus*. 1844. *Gavia*, Boie, *Isis*, p. 191; various spp. 1829. *Gavia*, Kaup, *Sk. Ent. Eur. Thierw.*, pp. 99, 196; *L. ridibundus* and *L. capistratus*. 1842. *Gavia*, Macg., *Man. Brit. Orn.*, p. 239; for all hooded Gulls. 1853. *Gavia*, Bruch., *J. f. O.*, p. 106; for small grey-mantled hoodless Gulls. 1825. *Rissa*, Steph., *Shaw's Gen. Zool.*, xiii, pt. i, p. 180; *L. tridactylus*. 1829. *Cheimonea*, Kaup, *Sk. Ent. Eur. Thierw.*, pp. 84, 196; *L. tridactyla*. 1829. *Pagophila*, Kaup, *op. cit.*, pp. 69, 186; *L. eburneus*. 1829. *Lencus*, misprint for *Leucus*, Kaup, *op. cit.*, pp. 86, 196; for *L. marinus, glaucus, fuscus*. 1857. *Leucus*, Bp., *O. A.*, ii, p. 215; *L. glaucus*, etc. 1829. *Hydrocolœus*, Kaup, *op. cit.*, pp. 113, 196; *L. minutus*, etc. 1829. *Ichthyætus*, Kaup, *op. cit.*, pp. 102, 196; *L. ichthyætus*. 1831. *Laroides*, Brehm, *V. D.*, 738; for most European hoodless Gulls. 1836. *Chroicocephalus*, Eyton, *Brit. B.*, p. 53; for the hooded Gulls (emend *Kroicocephalus*, Jameson, 1839; *Chroiocephalus*, Reich., *Chrœcocephalus*, Strickl., 1841; *Chroocephalus*, S. & S., 1871). 1838. *Rossia*, Bp., *Comp. List*, p. 62; no descr.; preoccupied. 1842. *Rhodostethia*, Macg., *op. cit.*, pt. ii, p. 251; *L. roseus*. 1842. *Cetosparactes*, Macg., *tom. cit.*, p. 251; *L. eburneus*. (*Catosparactes*, Gray, *G. of B.*, iii, 1845, p. 655, note.) 1852. *Plautus*, Reich., *Nat. Syst. Vög. Longip.*, p. 5 (after Klein, 1750; out of date). 1853. *Glaucus*, Bruch, *J. f. O.*, p. 101; for large and medium gray-mantled spp. 1853. *Gabianus* "Bp.", Bruch, *J. f. O.*, p. 100; Bp., *Naum.*, 1854, pp. 211, 215; *L. pacificus*. 1854. *Gavina*, Bp., *Naum.*, p. 212; for *L. canus*, etc. 1857. *Gavina*, Bp., *O. A.*, ii, p. 222; *L. audouini*. 1853. *Dominicanus*, Bruch, *J. f. O.*, p. 100; for large dark-mantled Gulls. 1853. *Leucophœus* "Bp.", Bruch, *J. f. O.*, p. 108; *L. scoresbii*. 1854. *Leucophœus*, Bp., *Naum.*, p. 211; also includes *L. heermanni*. 1857. *Leucophœus*, Bp., *O. A.*, ii, p. 231; *L. fuliginosus* and *L. belcheri*. 1853. *Blasipus* "Bp.", Bruch, *J. f. O.*, p. 108; *L. modestus*. 1854. *Blasipus*, Bp., *Naum.*, p. 211, includes *crassirostris*. 1853. *Adelarus* "Bp.", Bruch, *J. f. O.*, p. 106; for dark-mantled hooded spp. 1854. *Gelastes*, Bp., *Naum.*, p. 212; for *L. gelastes*, etc. 1854. *Atricilla*, Bp., *Naum.*, p. 212; for *L. atricilla*. 1854. *Creagrus*, Bp., *Naum.*, p. 213; for *L. furcatus*. 1854.

1878. SAUNDERS, H.—Continued.

Gavia, subgg. *Melagavia, Cirrhocephala*, Bp., *Naum.*, 1854, pp. 212, 213. (*Cirrhocephalus*, Bruch.) 1857. *Bruchigavia*, Bp., *C. A.*, ii, p. 228: a joke. 1854. *Procellarus* sive *Epitelarus*, Bp., *Naum.*, pp. 211, 213; type *neglectus=scoresbii*, juv. (done to "chaff" Cabanis). 1857. *Olupeilarus*, Bp., *C. A.*, ii, p. 220; *L. fuscus*, and so forth.

1878. SHARPE, R. B.   On a small Collection of Birds from the Ellice Islands. . . . With a Note on the other Birds found there, by the Rev. S. J. Whitmee. < *P. Z. S.*, Feb. 19, 1878, pp. 271–274.

The collection consists almost entirely of Terns, 5 spp. of which are given, with an *Ardea·* The synonymy of the two Grey Pacific Noddies, alleged to be wrongly given by Saunders (*P. Z. S.*, 1876, p. 671) is worked out, *Anous cinereus* and *Anous cœruleus* being differentiated.

1879. BREWER, T. M.   The Black Skimmer [Rhynchops nigra] in Massachusetts. < *Bull. Nutt. Ornith. Club*, iv, No. 4, Oct., 1879, p. 243.

1879. BOARDMAN, G. A.   Rhynchops nigra in the Bay of Fundy. < *The Oölogist*, v, No. 2, Aug., 1879, pp. 13, 14.

An account of the remarkable flight of these birds, northward from the Middle and Southern States, which occurred this year.

1879. BREWSTER, W.   The Terns [Sterninæ] of the New England Coast. < *Bull. Nutt. Ornith. Club*, iv, No. 1, Jan., 1879, pp. 13–22.

A well-written popular account of habits, &c.

1879. "C. E. P." *and* "R. H."   The Black Skimmer [Rhynchops nigra] in New Jersey. < *Forest and Stream*, xiii, Oct. 2, 1879, p. 684.

Note of capture.

1879. DEANE, R.   The Black Skimmer (Rhynchops nigra) in New England. < *Bull. Nutt. Ornith. Club*, iv, No. 4, Oct., 1879, pp. 242, 243.

1879. "F. M."   The Gull's Flight. < *Science News*, i, No. 15, June 1, 1879, p. 240.

On the mechanics of the case.

1879. GOSS, N. S.   Bonaparte's Gull [Larus bonapartii] in Kansas. < *Bull. Nutt. Ornith. Club*, iv, No. 3, July, 1879, pp. 190, 191.

1879. HENSHAW, H. W.   Occurrence of the Caspian Tern (Sterna caspia) upon the Coast of Virginia. < *Bull. Nutt. Ornith. Club*, iv, No. 4, Oct., 1879, pp. 243, 244.

1879. MAYNARD, C. J.   The Kittiwake Gull.   (Rissa tridactyla.) < *Town and Country* (newspaper of Boston, Mass.) for August, 1879.

Being Chap. VI of his *Wanderings of a Naturalist.*

1879. RICHMOND, C. A.   A Tame Gull [Larus marinus]. < *Forest and Stream*, xii, June 12, 1879, p. 365.

Notice of a specimen kept in captivity for twenty years.

1879. "R. H. R. M."   [R. H. ROBERTSON *and* G. B. GRINNELL.]   Northern Range of the Black Skimmer [Rhynchops nigra]. < *Forest and Stream*, xiii, Nov. 6, 1879, pp. 784, 785.

Notice of capture of this species at Martha's Vineyard, Mass., by Mr. Robertson, in Aug., 1879, with introduction by G. B. Grinnell, noting the occurrence of the species in New England during the same summer.

Procellariidæ.

1674. LACHMUND, F.   De ave Diomedea [Procellaria æquinoctialis]. Diss. cum vera ejus effigie aeri incisa. Amstelodami. Andr. Fris. 1674. 12mo. pp. 52, pl.
   Haud mihi obvius: titulus e Caro et Engelm.

1745. LINNÆUS, C.   Storm-våders-fogelen Beskrifven af Carl Linnæus. < *Kongl. Swensk. Wetens. Acad. Handl.*, vi, 1745, pp. 93–96, pl. vi.
   Procellaria pelagica, L., posteà. ("Procellaria est avis Passerini ordinis"!)

1745. LINNÆUS, C.   Beschreibung des Ungewittervogels, Procellaria. < *Abh. d. Schwed. Akad. für* 1745, pp. 93–96, 1 Taf.
   This German version of the title taken from Carus and Engelmann.

1759. MARTIN, A. R.   Beskrifning på en Procellaria [glacialis], som finnes vid Norrpolen. < *Kongl. Svensk. Vetens. Acad. Handl.*, xx, 1759, pp. 94–99, pl. iii.

1759. MARTIN, A. R.   Beschreibung einer Procellaria [glacialis] die sich um den Nordpol findet. < *Abhandl. d. Schwed. Acad. für* 1759, pp. 94–98, 1 Taf.
   This German version of the original title extracted from Carus and Engelmann.

1765. GUNNERUS, J, E.   Vom Havhest oder Seepferd, einem Seevogel (Procellaria groenlandica). < *Der Drontheim Gesellsch. Schrift.*, Th. i, 1765, pp. 154–170, pl.
   Nicht mir selbst zugänglich: Titel aus Carus & Engelm.

1785. FORSTER, —.   Mémoire sur les Albatros [Diomedea]. < *Mém. de Math. et Phys. prés. à l'Acad.*, x, 1785, pp. 563–572, pll, 3.
   Pas vu moi-même: le titre tiré de Carus et Engelmann.

1788. ÖDMANN, S.   Beskrifning på Hofhästen [Procellaria glacialis]. < *Uppfostr.-Sällsk. allm. Tid.*, 1788, D. i., nro. 38.
   Not seen.

1820. KUHL, H.   Beiträge zur Kenntniss der Procellarien. < *Beiträge zur Zool. und Vergl. Anat.*, 1820, pp. 135–149, pll. x, xi, figg. 1–13.
   This important contribution to our knowledge of the *Procellariidæ* forms one of a very miscellaneous collection of zoological and anatomical papers by Kuhl, and by Hassell and Kuhl, published in a sm. 4to volume in 1820. I cite the whole volume elsewhere; but take this paper out for special notice here under *Procellariidæ*.
   The paper on the *Procellariidæ* treats of 28 spp., most of which are described, with synonymy, and the heads of many of which are figured on two folding plates, as follows:
   A. Naribus tubo unico coalitis: 1. *P. furcata* L., p. 136, pl. ; 2. *P. oceanica* Banks, p. 136, pl. x, f. 1; 3. *P. marina* Lath., p. 137, pl. x, f. 2; 4. *P. leachi* Temm., p. 137 ; 5. *P. fregatta* Banks, p. 138, pl. x, f. 3 ; 6. *P. pelagina*, p. 139; 7. *P. glacialis*, p. 139, pl. x, f. 4 ; 8. *P. capensis*, L., p. 140; 9. *P. gigantea* L., p. 140 ; *P. aequinoctialis*, p. 141, pl. x, f. 5; 11. *P. hasitata* Forst., p. 142 ; 12. *P. fuliginosa* (Banks, tab. 19), p. 142, pl. x, f. 6 ; 13. *P. desolata* (ex definitione), p. 143, pl. xi. f. 7 ; 14. *P. turtur* Banks, p. 143, pl. xi, f. 8; 15. *P. grisea* L., p. 144, pl. xi, f. 9 ; 16. *P. coerulea* Forst., p. 145. 17. *P. urinatrix* Forst., p. 145; 18. *P. nivea*, p. 145; 19. *P. antarctica* Forst., p. 145; 20. *P. lugens* Forst., p. 145; 21. *P.* ——— (Forst., pl. 20), p. 145.—B. Naribus aperturis duabus separatis, etc.: 22. *P. puffinus*, p. 146, pl. xi, f. 10; 23. *P. anglorum*, p. 146; 24. *P. obscura*, p. 147, pl. xi, f. 11; 25. *P. cinerea* L., p. 148, pl. xi, f. 12; 26. *P. munda* (Banks, tab. 24), p. 148; 27. *P. fuliginosa* (Banks, tab. 23), p. 148.—C. Naribus subbasalibus, discretis, etc.: 28. *P. vittata* Forst., p. 149, pl. xi, f. 13.

1822. EDITORIAL.   M. Kuhl's Zoological Observations. < *Edinb. Philos. Journ.*, vii, 1822, pp. 187, 188.
   Relating to absence of air-cells in bones of *Daption capensis*.

1824. BONAPARTE, C. [L.]   An Account of Four Species of Stormy Petrels. < *Journ. Acad. Nat. Sci. Phila.*, iii, 1824, pp. 227–233, pll. viii, ix.
   Procellaria pelagica, pl. 8; *P. leachii*, pl. ix, upper fig. ; *P. wilsonii*, n. sp., p. 231, pl. 9, lower fig. ; *P. oceanica*.

1824. [BREHM, C. L.]   Der Wintersturmvogel. Procellaria hyemalis, Brehm. < *Ornis*, Heft i, 1824, pp. 20–28.

1824. FABER, F. Beyträge zur arctischen Zoologie. < *Oken's Isis*, Jahrg. viii, 1824, pp. 779–795.

Zweyte Lieferung. Ueber die isländischen Schwimmvögel mit Rohrennasen (Tubinares). Gattung *Puffinus:* 1) *P. arcticus* Faber, p. 782; 2) *P. major*, n. s.? p. 785. Gattung *Procellaria: P. glacialis*, p. 786; *P. pelagica*, p. 791.—Nachtrag zum 'Prodromus,' pp. 792–795.

1824. V[IGORS, N. A.] New Species of Procellariæ. < *Zool. Journ.*, i, 1824, pp. 425, 426.

Reproduction in part of Bonaparte's article, *Journ. Phila. Acad.*, iii, 1824, pp. 227–233, q. v.

1825. DESM . . . ST. [DESMAREST, A. G.] Description de quatre espèces de Pétrels ou Oiseaux de tempêtes ; par M. Charles Bonaparte. . . . < *Féruss. Bull.*, 2ᵉ sect., iv, 1825, pp. 126–128.

Extraite du *Journ. Acad. Phila.*, iii, No. 8, 1824, pp. 227–233, q. v.

1826. LESSON, R. P. Remarques sur quelques Oiseaux pélagiens, et particulièrement sur les Albatrosses ; par M. Marion de Procé. . . . < *Féruss. Bull.*, 2ᵉ sect., viii, 1826, pp. 277–279.

Extraite des *Ann. des Sci. Nat.*, viii, mai 1826, pp. 90–96.

1826. PROCÉ, MARION DE. Remarques sur quelques Oiseaux pélagiens, et particulière-ment sur les Albatros. < *Ann. des Sci. Nat.*, viii, 1826, pp. 90–96.

1827. ACERBI, G. Intorno ad una specie di Procellaria [yelkouan] osservata nell' Ellesponto, nella Propontide, e nel Bosforo Tracio. < *Bibl. Ital.*, xlvii, 1827, pp. 294–298.

Not seen : title from *Roy. Soc. Cat.*

1827. BONAPARTE, C. L. Supplement to "an Account of four Species of Stormy Pe-trel," (Thalassidroma, Vigors). < *Zool. Journ.*, iii, 1827, pp. 89, 90.

Cf. *Journ. Phila. Acad.*, iii, 1824, pp. 227–233 ; *Zool. Journ.*, i, 1824, pp. 425, 426.

1829. ACERBI, G. Sur une espèce nouvelle de Procellaria [yelkouan] observée dans l'Hellespont, la mer de Marmora et le détroit de Constantinople ; par G. Acerbi. . . . < *Féruss. Bull.*, 2ᵉ sect., xvi, 1829, pp. 463, 464.

Voici la description de cette espèce, telle que l'auteur la donne lui même, extraite de la *Biblioteca ital.*, nᵒ cxl, août 1827, pp. 294–297.

1830. BONAPARTE, C. L. [Ueber Procellaria wilsoni, u. s. w.] < *Oken's Isis*, Bd. xxiii, 1830, pp. 423, 424.

From *Journ. Acad. Phila.*, iii, 1824, pp. 227–233, q. v.

1830. BONAPARTE, C. L. Nachtrag zu den Sturmvögeln (Thalassidroma Vigors). < *Oken's Isis*, Bd. xxiii, 1830, p. 1151.

Cf. *tom. cit.*, pp. 423, 424. Aus d. *Zool. Journ.*, Nr. ix, Vol. iii, 1827, pp. 89, 90.

1831. BENNETT, G. Observations on the Albatross [Diomedea]. < *London Medical Gazette*, viii, 1831, pp. 848– —.

Not seen.

1831. LOWE, R. T. Note on Procellaria Anginho, Hein., and Proc. Bulverii, Selby and Jard. < *Zool. Journ.*, v, 1831, p. 384.

Their identity with each other and with *P. fuliginosa* Gm.

1831. RENNIE, S. Zur Naturgeschichte der Procellaria [pelagica]. < *Froriep's Notizen*, xxxii, No. 691, 1831, pp. 133, 134.

Not seen.

1832. ALLIS, T. Inland [in England] Specimens of the Forked-tail Petrel [Cymochorea leucorrhoa]. < *Loudon's Mag. Nat. Hist.*, v, 1832, p. 589.

1832. "ARISTOPHILUS." The British Species of Petrel. < *Loudon's Mag. Nat. Hist.*, v, 1832, pp. 589, 590.

1832. BREE, W. T. Stormy Petrels [Procellaria pelagica] taken in the Interior o the Island [England]. < *Loudon's Mag. Nat. Hist.*, v, 1832, pp. 588, 589.

1832. BREE, W. T. The Fork-tailed Petrel [Cymochorea leucorrhoa] taken at Birmingham. < *Loudon's Mag. Nat. Hist.*, v, 1832, p. 733.

1832. "C." Two Stormy Petrels [Procellaria pelagica] taken at Birmingham. < *Loudon's Mag. Nat. Hist.*, v, 1832. p. 283.

1832. EARLE, —. Ueber das Eierlagen und Aufwachsen der Jungen der Diomedea
exulans. < *Froriep's Notizen*, xxxiv, No. 738, 1832, pp. 177, 178.
Not seen: title from Carus and Engelmann.

1832. MORRIS, F. O. The Fork-tailed Petrel (Procellaria Leachii [Cymochorea leucorrhoa, in England]). < *Loudon's Mag. Nat. Hist.*, v, 1832, p. 733.

1832. STRICKLAND, A. [On the occurrence of Puffinus fuliginosus, n. sp., in Yorkshire, England.] < *P. Z. S.*, ii, 1832, pp. 128, 129.

1833. BENNETT, F. D. [On the Larynx of the Albatross (Diomedea exulans, Linn.).]
< *P. Z. S.*, i, 1833, pp. 78, 79.

1833. D[ENSON?], J. The Wandering Albatross (Diomedea exulans L.). < *Loudon's
Mag. Nat. Hist.*, vi, 1833, pp. 372–374.
Its flight, etc.

1833. STRICKLAND, A. Observations on a species of Procellaria [fuliginosa], new to
the British Fauna, which was shot at the mouth of the Tees, in Yorkshire, in
August 1828. < *Rep. Brit. Assoc. Adv. Sci. for* 1832, 1833, p. 598.
An abstract of the paper in *P. Z. S.* for July 12, 1832, pp. 128, 129.

1834. BENNETT, G. [On the Nasal Gland of the wandering Albatross (Diomedea exulans, Linn.).] < *P. Z. S.*, ii, 1834, p. 151.

1834. GAIRDNER, M. Observations during a voyage from England to Fort Vancou-
ver, on the Northwest Coast of America. < *Edinb. New Philos. Journ.*, xvi,
1834, pp. 290–302.
Contains some remarks on Albatrosses, and an allusion to *Chionis*.

1834. KING, P. P. [Observations on Oceanic Birds, particularly those of the Genus
Diomedea, Linn.] < *P. Z. S.*, ii, 1834, pp. 128, 129.

1834. PROCÉ, MARION DE. Ueber einige Meervögel, insbesondere über die Albatros
(Diomedea). < *Oken's Isis*, Bd. xxvii, 1834, p. 862.
Auszug aus d. *Annales des Sci. nat.*, Tom. viii, 1826, pp. 90–96.

1834. "A SUBSCRIBER." The Wandering Albatross (Diomedea exulans L.). < *Loudon's Mag. Nat. Hist.*, vii, 1834, p. 74.

1835. BENNETT, F. D. Oberer Kehlkopf von Diomedea exulans, habe einen Kehl-
deckel. < *Oken's Isis*, Bd. xxviii, 1835, p. 537.
From *P. Z. S.*, 1833, pp. 78, 79.

1835. STRICKLAND, [A.] [Puffinus fuliginosus.] < *Oken's Isis*, Bd. xxviii, 1835, pp.
431, 432.
From *P. Z. S.*, 1832, pp. 128, 129.

1835. TULK, A. The Storm Petrel (Procellària pelàgica L.). < *Loudon's Mag. Nat.
Hist.*, viii, 1835, pp. 513, 514.
On the River Thames, in England.

1835. KING, P. P. [Letter respecting certain Procellariidæ observed during a voyage
from Europe to New South Wales.] < *Lond. and Edinb. Philos. Mag.*, vi, 1835,
pp. 387, 388.
From *P. Z. S.*, Nov. 11, 1834.

1835. KING, [P. P.] Brief aus Neuholland. < *Oken's Isis*, Bd. xxviii, 1835, p. 1051.
Procellariidæ betreffend. *P. Z. S.*, 1834, p. 128.

1836. HENNING, —. [Note on the capture of an Albatross with a hook.] < *P. Z. S.*,
iv, 1836, p. 63.

1837. SKAIFE, J. A Fork-tailed Stormy Petrel (Thalassidroma Leachii [Cymochorea
leucorrhoa, in Lancashire]). < *Charlesw. Mag. Nat. Hist.*, i, 1837, pp. 555, 556.

1838. BERTOLONI, A. Annunzi di nuovi Libri < *Nuovi Ann. Sci. Nat. Bologna*, ii,
1838, pp. 156–159.
Under subhead of G. Gasparrini's Descrizione delle isole di Tremiti, etc., occurs matter relating to several *Procellariidæ*.

1838. Couch, J.   A Letter on the Occurrence of Procellaria wilsoni [Oceanites oceanicus] on the British Coast.   < *Proc. Linn. Soc.*, i, No. 1, 1838, pp. 2, 3.
    Not seen.

1840. Goatley, T.   On a specimen of the Shearwater Petrel, Kite, &c. [in England.]   < *Ann. Mag. Nat. Hist.*, vi, 1840, pp. 73, 74.

1841. Abbott, S. L. '[On the habits of the Albatross, Diomedea exulans.]   < *Proc. Bost. Soc. Nat. Hist.*, i, 1841, p. 8.

1841. "J. M."   A strange News-Carrier.   < *Ann. Mag. Nat. Hist.*, vi, 1841, pp. 526, 527.
    Diomedea exulans.   From *Essex* (Mass.) *Register*, Feb., 1840.

1842. Thompson, W.   Note on Puffinus major, Faber.   Greater Shearwater.   < *Ann. Mag. Nat. Hist.*, ix, 1842, pp. 433, 434.

1843. Gould, J.   [Diomedea culminata, sp. n.]   < *P. Z. S.*, xi, 1843, pp. 107, 108.

1843. Yarrell, W.   [On a specimen of Puffinus obscurus, from the Dardanelles.]   < *P. Z. S.*, xi, 1843, p. 70.

1844. Cliffe, H. F.   Note on [the habits of] the Cape Pigeon [Daption capensis].   < *Zoologist*, ii, 1844, p. 579.

1844. Fisher, W. R.   [On the capture of] Two Fulmar Petrels [Procellaria glacialis, off Great Yarmouth], . . .   < *Zoologist*, ii, 1844, p. 456.

1844. Gould, J.   On the Family Procellaridæ, with descriptions of Ten new Species.   < *Ann. Mag. Nat. Hist.*, xiii, 1844, pp. 360–368.
    Diomedea gibbosa, D. olivaceorhyncha, p. 361; *Procellaria atlantica,* p. 362; *P. mollis,* p. 363; *P. flavirostris, Puffinus brevicaudus* (descr. nulla!), *P. sphenurus,* p. 365; *Thalassidroma tropica,* p. 366; *T. melanogaster, T. leucogaster,* p. 367; with short notices of many other species of the family.

1844. Hombron, —., *and* Jacquinot, [H.]   Remarques sur quelques points de l'anatomie et de la physiologie des Procellaridées, et essai d'une nouvelle classification de ces oiseaux.   < *Compt. Rend. de l'Acad. Sci.*, xviii, 1844, pp. 353–358.
    Priofinus, p. 355; *Ossifraga,* p. 356; *Priocella,* p. 357, genn. nn.; *P. garnotii,* "nob", p. 357, descr. nulla.

1844. Jacquinot, —.   Remarques sur quelques points de l'anatomie et de la physiologie des Procellaridées, et essai d'une nouvelle classification de ces Oiseaux.   < *Revue Zoologique*, vii, 1844, pp. 118, 119.

1844. Strickland, H. E.   On Thalassidroma melitensis, Schembri, a supposed new species of Stormy Petrel.   < *Ann. Mag. Nat. Hist.*, xiv, 1844, pp. 348, 349.
    = *T. pelagica.*   The paper also makes a few corrections of *Drummond's Birds of Ionian Islands and Crete.*

1844. Yarrell, W.   [On a specimen of Puffinus obscurus from the Dardanelles.]   < *Ann. Mag. Nat. Hist.*, xiii, 1844, pp. 305, 306.
    From *P. Z. S.*, May 19, 1843, p. 70.

1845. "A. P."   [Sur le vol de l'albatros.]   < *Revue Zoologique*, viii, 1845, p. 60.
    Extr. du Voyage autour du monde sur la Frégate la Vénus.

1846. Hall, T.   Stormy Petrel [Procellaria. pelagica] in London in 1824.   < *Zoologist*, iv, 1846, p. 1502.

1847. "Anon."   Occurrence of the Stormy Petrel [Procellaria pelagica] at Halifax.   < *Zoologist*, v, 1847, p. 1643.

1847. Garth, J. C.   Occurrence of the Stormy Petrel [Procellaria pelagica] near Knaresborough.   < *Zoologist*, v, 1847, p. 1643.

1847. Goatley, T.   Occurrence of the Stormy Petrel (Procellaria pelagica) near Chipping Norton.   < *Zoologist*, v, 1847, p. 1643.

1847. Lawrence, G. N.   A new species of Procellaria [brevirostris, afterward called P. meridionalis] from Florida.   < *Am. Journ. Sci.*, iii, 1847, p. 436.
    From the preliminary notice in *Ann. Lyc. Nat. Hist. N. Y.*, Feb. 18, 1847.

1847. LAWRENCE, G. N.   A new species of Procellaria [brevirostris, later P. meridionalis] from Florida.   < *Ann. Mag. Nat. Hist.*, xx, 1847, p. 21.
  From *Am. Journ. Sci.*, May, 1847, p. 436, *q. v.*

1848. ELLMAN, J. B.   Occurrence of the Stormy Petrel (Thalassidroma [Procellaria] pelagica) at Hailsham.   < *Zoologist*, vi, 1848, p. 2073.

1848. LAWRENCE, G. N.   Description of a new Species of Procellaria [meridionalis].   < *Ann. Lyc. Nat. Hist. N. Y.*, iv, 1848, pp. 475, 476.   (Read Feb. 18, 1847.)
  Same as that called *P. brevirostris* on covers of Nos. 8 and 9 of Vol. IV of the *Annals*, and elsewhere published as such in 1847.

1848. MILNER, W. M. E.   Occurrence of the Great Shearwater (Puffinus Anglorum) near Robin Hood's Bay.   < *Zoologist*, vi, 1848, p. 2027.

1849. BORRER, W., JR.   Occurrence of the Fork-tail Petrel (Thalassidroma Leachii [Cymochorea leucorrhoa]) near Brighton.   < *Zoologist*, vii, 1849, p. 2392.

1849. GURNEY, J. H.   Occurrence of the Fork-tailed Petrel (Thalassidroma Leachii [Cymochorea leucorrhoa]) near Yarmouth.   < *Zoologist*, vii, 1849, p. 2622.

1849. MORRIS, F. O.   Occurrence of the Fulmar Petrel (Procellaria [Fulmarus] glacialis) near Bridlington.   < *Zoologist*, vii, 1849, p. 2592.

1850. BOND, F.   Occurrence of the Fork-tailed Petrel (Thalassidroma Leachii [Cymochorea leucorrhoa]) near London.   < *Zoologist*, viii, 1850, p. 2803.

1850. CURTLER, M.   Occurrence of the Fork-tailed Petrel (Thalassidroma Leachii [Cymochorea leucorrhoa]) near Worcester.   < *Zoologist*, viii, 1850, p. 2706.

1850. ELLMAN, J. B.   Occurrence of the Fork-tailed Petrel (Thalassidroma Leachii [Cymochorea leucorrhoa]) at Brighton.   < *Zoologist*, viii, 1850, pp. 2969, 2970.

1850. GURNEY, J. H.   Occurrence of the Fork-tailed Petrel (Thalassidroma Leachii [Cymochorea leucorrhoa]) in Norfolk.   < *Zoologist*, viii, 1850, p. 2654.

1850. NEWTON, A.   Occurrence of the Fork-tail Petrel (Thalassidroma Leachii [Cymochorea leucorrhoa]) near Torquay.   < *Zoologist*, viii, 1850, p. 2778.

1850. SAXBY, S., JR.   Occurrence of the fork-tailed Petrel (Thalassidroma Leachii [Cymochorea leucorrhoa]) in the Isle of Wight.   < *Zoologist*, viii, 1850, p. 2969.

1850. TOMES, R. F.   Occurrence of the Fork-tailed Petrel (Thalassidroma Leachii [Cymochorea leucorrhoa]) in Warwickshire.   < *Zoologist*, viii, 1850, pp. 2706, 2707.

1851. BREWER, T. M.   [Notice of a paper by, on the eggs of Cymochorea leucorrhoa and other Procellariidæ.]   < *Proc. Bost. Soc. Nat. Hist.*, iv, 1851, p. 7.

1851. HARPER, J. O.   Occurrence of the Fork-tailed Petrel (Thalassidroma Leachii [Cymochorea leucorrhoa]) at Lowestoft.   < *Zoologist*, ix, 1851, pp. 2990, 2991.

1851. KING, E. L.   Occurrence of the Greater Shearwater (Puffinus cinereus) at Lynn.   < *Zoologist*, ix, 1851, pp. 3234, 3235.

1851. NORMAN, A. W.   Occurrence of the Fork-tailed Petrel (Thalassidroma Leachii [Cymochorea leucorrhoa]) at Blenheim Park.   < *Zoologist*, ix, 1851, p. 3118.

1852. BREWER, T. M.   Notice of the Egg of Thalassidroma leachii [Cymochorea leucorrhoa], with descriptions of the Eggs of Procellaria bulwerii, Procellaria obscura, and Puffinus major.   Read before the Boston Society of Natural History.   < *Journ. Bost. Soc. Nat. Hist.*, vi, pt. iii, 1852, pp. 308–312.

1852. NEWTON, A.   Some Account of a Petrel [Œstrelata hæsitata], killed at Southacre, Norfolk; with a Description and Synonymy.   < *Zoologist*, x, 1852, pp. 3691–3698, figg. 2.

1853. BONAPARTE, C. L.   Zoological Notices.   < *Rep. Brit. Assoc. Adv. Sci. for* 1852, 1853, (*Misc. Comm.*), p. 72.
  Ornithological in relating to certain *Procellaridæ.*

1853. GRAY, G. R.   On a New Species of Thalassidroma [hornbyi].   < *P. Z. S.*, xxi, 1853, p. 62.

1853. RODD, E. H.   Occurrence of the Fork-tailed Petrel (Procellaria Leachii [Cymochorea leucorrhoa]) near Penzance.   < *Zoologist*, xi, 1853, p. 3756.

1853. YARRELL, W.   Occurrence of a Petrel [Puffinus obscurus] new to Britain on the West Coast of Ireland.   < *Zoologist*, xi, 1853, pp. 3947–3950.

1855. GOULD, J.   On a New Species of the Genus Prion [brevirostris].   < *P. Z. S.*, xxiii, 1855, pp. 87, 88, pl. xciii.

1855. GRAY, G. R.   On a New Species of Thalassidroma [hornbyi].   < *Ann. Mag. Nat. Hist.*, 2d ser., xvi, 1855, p. 78.
    From *P. Z. S.*, May 10, 1853, p. 62.

1855. KJÆRBÖLLING, M.   Om en ny Art, Procellaria minor, fra Groenland.   < *Förhandl. Skandin. Naturf. i Stockholm, Sjette Möte, år* 1851, 1855, pp. 254, 255.

1856. FULLER, A.   Occurrence of the Storm Petrel (Thalassidroma [Procellaria] pelagica) at Newmarket and near Cambridge.   < *Zoologist*, xiv, 1856, p. 5065.

1856. GOULD, J.   On a new Species of the Genus Prion [brevirostris].   < *Ann. Mag. Nat. Hist.*, 2d ser., xviii, 1856, pp. 56, 57.
    From *P. Z. S.*, June 12, 1855, p. 87.

1856. RETZIUS, [A.]   On the peculiar development of the Vermis Cerebelli in the Albatros (Diomedea exulans).   < *Rep. Brit. Assoc. Adv. Sci. for* 1855, 1856, (*Misc. Comm.*), p. 133.
    Upon which depends, it is believed, the strong, continuous, and tranquil flight of the bird.

1857. BLOOMFIELD, E. N.   Explanation of supposed Phenomenon.   < *Zoologist*, xv, 1857, pp. 5365, 5366.
    Of Swallows emerging from the water: the birds being *Procellaria* sp.

1857. COCKS, W. P.   Rare British Birds.   < *Ann. Mag. Nat. Hist.*, 2d ser., xix, 1857, p. 107.
    Only one sp., *Cymochorea leucorrhoa.*

1857. HADFIELD, H. W.   Occurrence of the Forktailed Petrel [Cymochorea leucorrhoa] near Tunbridge.   < *Zoologist*, xv, 1857, pp. 5429, 5430.

1857. M'LACHLAN, R.   Food of the Storm Petrel [Oceanites oceanicus].   < *Zoologist*, xv, 1857, p. 5833.

1857. RODD, E. H.   Occurrence of the Forktailed Petrel (Thalassidroma Leachii [Cymochorea leucorrhoa]) near Helston.   < *Zoologist*, xv, 1857, p. 5429.

1857. THOMPSON, W.   Occurrence of the Forktailed Petrel (Thalassidroma Leachii [Cymochorea leucorrhoa]) at Weymouth.   < *Zoologist*, xv, 1857, p. 5429.

1858. BORRER, W., JR.   Occurrence of the Fulmar Petrel (Procellaria [Fulmarus] glacialis) at Brighton.   < *Zoologist*, xvi, 1858, pp. 5988, 5989.

1858. STEVENSON, H.   Occurrence of the Dusky Petrel (Puffinus obscurus) in Norfolk.   < *Zoologist*, xvi, 1858, pp. 6096, 6097.

1859. ELWES, R.   Note on the Breeding and Mode of Capture of the Short-tailed Petrel, or Mutton Bird (Puffinus obscurus [?]) in the islands in Bass's Straits.   < *Ibis*, i, 1859, pp. 397–399.

1859. HATTON [*i. e.*, HUTTON], F. W.   Remarks on the Southern Petrels.   < *Zoologist*, xvii, 1859, pp. 6331, 6332.

1859. HUTTON, F. W.   Remarks on the [habits of the] Southern Petrels.   < *Zoologist*, xvii, 1859, pp. 6379, 6380.

1859. MARSH, G. S.   Sea Birds [Procellariidæ] found Inland [in England].   < *Zoologist*, xvii, 1859, p. 6492.

1859. MATHEWS, M. A.   Occurrence of the Fulmar Petrel [Fulmarus glacialis] in Barnstaple.   < *Zoologist*, xvii, 1859, pp. 6447, 6448.

1860. HORTON, E.   Use of the Albatross [Diomedea exulans].   < *Zoologist*, xviii, 1860, p. 6981.
    Radius of this bird as a pipe-stem: poetry on the subject.

1860. MACGILLIVRAY, J.   Zoological Notes from Aneitum, New Hebrides.   < *Zoologist,* xviii, 1860, pp. 7133-7142.

> *Procellaria torquata,* n. sp., p. 7133: the only ornithological item.

1860. PENNEY, W.   Occurrence of the Forktailed Petrel (Thalassidroma Leachii [Cymochorea leucorrhoa]) at Poole.   < *Zoologist,* xviii, 1860, p. 6892.

1861. PHILIPPI, R. A., *and* LANDBECK, L.   Descripcion de una nueva especie de pájaros del jénero Thalassidroma [segethi, p. 27].   < *Anal. Univ. Chile,* xviii, enero 1861, pp. 29, 30.

> ". . . i famosos entre los marineros i otros, que los llaman Mother Carrey's Kitchen" (lege Mother Carey's Chickens!).

1861. PITTARD, S. R.   [Notice of a letter from, containing remarks relative to the flight of Albatrosses (Diomedea) and other oceanic Birds.]   < *P. Z. S.,* xxix, 1861, p. 135.

1862. BENNETT, G.   [Explanation of his diagram (in "Gatherings of a Naturalist in Australasia") of the flight of the Albatross (Diomedea).]   < *Ibis,* iv, 1862, p. 90.

1862. BENNETT, G.   [On an albino Ossifraga gigantea.]   < *Ibis,* iv, 1862, p. 193.

1862. GOULD, J.   [Exhibition and Description of Prion magnirostris sp. n.]   < *P. Z. S.,* Apr., 8, 1862, p. 125.

1862. GOULD, J.   [On Prion magnirostris.]   < *Ann. Mag. Nat. Hist.,* 3d ser., x, 1862, p. 317.

> From *P. Z. S.,* Apr. 8, 1862, p. 125.

1862. LAYARD, E. L.   Notes on the Sea-birds [chiefly Procellariidæ] observed during a Voyage in the Antarctic Ocean.   < *Ibis,* iv, 1862, pp. 97-100.

1862. SAVILLE, S. P.   Breeding Habits of the Petrel [not named; Nova Scotia].   < *Zoologist,* xx, 1862, pp. 7940, 7941.

1862. SAXBY, H. L.   Occurrence of the Manx Shearwater [Puffinus anglorum] at Sheerness.   < *Zoologist,* xx, 1862, p. 8287.

1863. SCHLEGEL, H.   Procellariae   < *Mus. Hist. Nat. Pays-Bas,* 4ᵉ livr., Juillet 1863, pp. 1-40.

> The group here treated is equivalent to the family *Procellariidæ* of authors, and the three genera which the author adopts, viz, *Procellaria, Diomedea* and *Halodroma,* represent the three subfamilies into which it is divisible. It is represented in the Leyden Museum by 209 specimens, which the author refers to 43 spp. of *Procellaria,* 8 spp. of *Diomedea,* and 3 spp. of *Halodroma.* Two species, *Proc. incerta,* p. 9, and *P. neglecta,* p. 10, are described as new.

1863. SMITH, *Rev.* JAMES.   The Fulmar Petrel (Procellaria [Fulmarus] glacialis) near Birmingham.   < *Zoologist,* xxi, 1863, p. 8449.

1863. STEVENSON, H.   The Forktailed Petrel (Thalassidroma Leachii [Cymochorea leucorrhoa]) in Norfolk.   < *Zoologist,* xxi, 1863, p. 8449.

1863. STEVENSON, H.   [Occurrence of Cymochorea leucorrhoa at Salthouse, near Cromer, England.]   < *Ibis,* v, 1863, pp. 235, 236.

1864? ————.   Some account of the Storm Petrel, Sea Serpent, Albicore, &c., as observed at St. Margaret's Bay, Nova Scotia.   < *Trans. Nova Scotia Inst.,* i, pt. ii, 1864?, pp. 34- —.

1864. BOULTON, W. W.   Manx Shearwater [Puffinus anglorum] Shot at Flamborough.   < *Zoologist,* xxii, 1864, pp. 9291, 9292.

1864. BOULTON, W. W.   Manx Shearwater [Puffinus anglorum] at Flamborough and Filey.   < *Zoologist,* xxii, 1864, pp. 9330, 9331.

1864. BOULTON, W. W.   Fulmar Petrel [Fulmarus glacialis] near Flamborough Head.   < *Zoologist,* xxii, 1864, p. 9365.

1864. Coues, E. A critical Review of the Family Procellaridæ; Part I., embracing the Procellarieæ, or Stormy Petrels. < *Proc. Acad. Nat. Sci. Phila.*, xvi, 1864, pp. 72-91.

This is the first of a series of five papers in which the whole family *Procellariidæ* are critically reviewed. The Petrels are divided into three subfamilies, *Procellariinæ, Diomedeinæ,* and *Halodrominæ,* the first of these into the sections *Procellarieæ, Puffineæ, Fulmareæ, Æstrelateæ,* and *Prioneæ.* Of the mode in which the genera and species are handled it may be remarked that those actually known by specimens to the author are carefully and satisfactorily described, and that the synonymy and criticism presented in such cases is in the main correct; but that the writer is not so fortunate in the instances in which he attempted to supplement his own knowledge by compilation from the writings of others, he having suffered not a little from imprudence in believing Bonaparte. The following 8 genera and 21 species of *Procellarieæ* or "Stormy Petrels" are treated:— 1. *Oceanodroma furcata.* 2. *O. hornbyi.* 3. *Cymochorea* (g. n., p. 73) *leucorrhoa.* 4. *C. melania.* 5. *C. homochroa,* sp. n., p. 77. 6. *Halocyptena* (g. n., p. 78) *microsoma,* sp. n., p. 79. 7. *Procellaria pelagica.* 8? *P. tethys.* 9? *P. lugubris.* 10. *P. melitensis.* 11. *P. nereis.* 12. *P. fasciolata.* 13. *Oceanites oceanica.* 14. *O. lineata.* 15. *O. segethi.* 16. *O. gracilis.* 17. *Fregetta tropica.* 18. *F. grallaria.* 19. *F. melanogastra.* 20. *F. lawrencii.* 21, *Pelagodroma fregata.* The paper concludes with an analytical and diagnostic synopsis of these genera and species. For Part II, see next title; for Parts III-V, see 1866.

1864. Coues, E. A Critical Review of the Family Procellaridæ:—Part II.; Embracing the Puffineæ. < *Proc. Acad. Nat. Sci. Phila.*, xvi, 1864, pp. 116-144.

For Part I, see last title; for Parts III-V, see 1866. The "Shearwaters" are treated in this paper, under 5 genera and 21 spp., as follows:— 1. *Majaqueus æquinoctialis.* 2, *M. conspicillatus.* 3. *Adamastor cinereus.* 4. *A. gelidus.* 5. *A. sericeus.* 6. *Thiellus sphenurus.* 7. *T. chlororhynchus.* 8. *Nectris fuliginosus.* 9. *N. amaurosoma,* sp. n., p. 124. 10. *N. carneipes.* 11. *N. tenuirostris.* 12. *N. brevicaudus.* 13. *Puffinus kuhlii.* 14. *P. leucomelas.* 15. *P. creatopus* Cooper, MS., sp. n., p. 131. 16. *P. major.* 17. *P. anglorum.* 18. *P. yelcuanus.* 19. *P. obscurus.* 20. *P. opisthomelas,* sp. n., p. 139. 21. *P. nugax.*

1864. Meyer, R. Verschlagene Sturmvögel [Thalassidroma sp.]. < *Zool. Gart.*, v, 1864, pp. 24-26.

1864. Jeittelles, L. H. [Verschlagene Sturmvögel.] < *Zool. Gart.*, v, 1864, p. 88.

1864. Radcliffe, C. D. Wilson's Petrel [Oceanites oceanicus] in the Isle of Wight. < *Zoologist,* xxii, 1864, p. 8892.

1865. Gurney, J. H. Leach's Stormy Petrel [Cymochorea leucorrhoa] at Worthing. < *Zoologist,* xxiii, 1865, p. 9419.

1866. Andersson, C. J. [On the mode of alimentation of Young Diomedeæ; cf. Ibis, 1865, p. 279, seq.] < *Ibis,* 2d ser., ii, 1866, p. 324.

1866. Blackmore, H. Forktailed Petrel [Cymochorea leucorrhoa] near Salisbury. < *Zoologist,* 2d ser., i, 1866, p. 101.

1866. Brooking-Rowe, J. Forktailed Petrel [Cymochorea leucorrhoa] at Plymouth. < *Zoologist,* 2d ser., i, 1866, p. 102.

1866. Carte, A. On an Undescribed Species of Petrel [Pterodroma caribbea] from the Blue Mountains of Jamaica. < *P. Z. S.*, xxxiv, 1866, pp. 93-95, pl. x.

This is the Blue-Mountain Duck of Gosse, *B. Jam.*, p. 437, now first described and named.

1866. Coues, E. A Critical Review of the Family Procellariidæ:—Part III; embracing the Fulmareæ. < *Proc. Acad. Nat. Sci. Phila.*, xviii, 1866, pp. 25-33.

For Parts I and II see 1864. This 3d part treats of the 3 genera *Fulmarus, Thalassoica,* and *Ossifraga,* of which are given the following species: *F. glacialis, F. pacificus, F. rodgersi, Th. glacialoides, Th. antarctica,* and *O. gigantea.*

1866. Coues, E. Critical Review of the Family Procellariidæ:—Part IV; Embracing the Æstrelateæ and Prioneæ. < *Proc. Acad. Nat. Sci. Phila.*, xviii, 1866, pp. 134-172.

For Parts I, II, see 1864; for Parts III and V, see preceding and following titles.

This Part opens with a criticism of Bonaparte, whom the writer seems to have just begun to find out, and continues with a discussion of 20 spp. of 3 genn. of *Œstrelateæ,* and 5 spp. of 2 genn. of *Prioneæ;* concluding with an analytical diagnostic synopsis of these two groups. The genus *Œstrelata* (οἰστρήλατος) is misspelled *Æstrelata,* as was the fashion then.

1866. COUES, E.—Continued.

    I. ŒSTRELATEÆ.—1. *Æstrelata hæsitata.* 2. *Æ. lessoni.* 3. *Æ. rostrata.* 4. *Æ. parvirostris.* 5. *Æ. incerta.* 6. *Æ. neglecta.* 7. *Æ. solandri.* 8. *Æ. grisea.* 9. *Æ. mollis.* 10. *Æ. cookii.* 11. *Æ. gavia.* 12. *Æ. desolata.* 13. *Æ. macroptera.* 14. *Æ. fuliginosa.* 15. *Æ. aterrima.* 16. *Æ. bulweri.* 17. *Æ. macgillivrayi.* 18. *Æ. carribæi.* 19. *Pagodroma nivea.* 20. *Daption capensis.*

    II. PRIONEÆ.—1. *Halobæna cærulea.* 2. *Pseudoprion* (g. n., p. 164) *banksii.* 3. *Ps. turtur.* 4. *Ps. ariel.* 5. *Prion vittatus.*

1866. COUES, E. Critical Review of the Family Procellariidæ;—Part V; embracing the Diomedeinæ and the Halodrominæ. With a General Supplement. < *Proc. Acad. Nat. Sci. Phila.*, xviii, 1866, pp. 172–197.

    For Parts III, IV, see preceding titles; for Parts I, II, see 1864.

    This concluding paper of the series presents 12 spp. of Albatrosses under 2 genera, and 3 spp. of *Halodrominæ*, as follows:

    I. DIOMEDEINÆ.—1. *Diomedea exulans.* 2. *D. brachyura.* 3. *D. leptorhyncha*, sp. n., p. 178. 4. *D. nigripes.* 5. *D. gibbosa.* 6. *D. melanophrys.* 7. *D. gilliana*, sp. n., p. 181. 8. *D. cauta.* 9. *D. culminata.* 10. *D. chlororhyncha.* 11. *D. olivaceirostris.* 12. *Phœbetria fuliginosa.*

    II. HALODROMINÆ.—1. *Pelecanoides garnoti.* 2. *P. urinatrix.* 3. *P. berardii.*

    The general supplement gives some additions to, and corrections of, all the five papers, and a bibliographical appendix identifies the Petrels treated by Linnæus, Gmelin, Latham, Vieillot, Kuhl, Stephens, and Forster.

    A recapitulation of the genera and species treated in all five papers gives the following result:

Subfamilies and sections.	Genera.	Species.	Doubtful species.
Procellariinæ :			
Fulmareæ	3	6	
Œstrelateæ	3	23	6
Prioneæ	3	6	1
Procellarieæ	7	21	5
Puffineæ	5	21	1
Diomedeinæ	2	12	2
Halodrominæ	1	3	2
Total	24	92	17

1866. DOUBLEDAY, H. Shearwater [Puffinus anglorum] at Epping. < *Zoologist,* 2d ser., i, 1866, p. 526.

1866. GOULD, J. Habits of the Shorttailed Petrel (Nectris brevicaudus). < *Zoologist,* 2d ser., i, 1866, pp. 208–211.

    Extracted from Gould's 'Handbook of the Birds of Australia,' ii, p. 464.

1866. GUISE, M. V. Forktailed Petrel [Cymochorea leucorrhoa] at Elmore. < *Zoologist,* 2d ser., i, 1866, p. 229.

1866. LOWNE, B. T. Notes on a Voyage round the World. < *Zoologist,* 2d ser., i, 1866, pp. 114–118.

    Cursory remarks on a few *Procellariidæ.*

1866. RODD, E. H. Forktailed Petrel [Cymochorea leucorrhoa] at Penzance. < *Zoologist,* 2d ser., i, 1866, pp. 101, 102.

1866. SAUNDERS, H. [Letter relating to various Procellariidæ.] < *Ibis,* 2d ser., ii, 1866, pp. 124–126.

1866. SMEE, A. H. Leach's Petrel [Cymochorea leucorrhoa] at Shoreham. < *Zoologist,* 2d ser., i, 1866, p. 190.

1867. BUXTON, T. F. Storm Petrel [Procellaria pelagica] at Cromer. < *Zoologist,* 2d ser., ii, 1867, p. 992.

1867. GUNN, T. E. Storm Petrel [Procellaria pelagica] in Norfolk. < *Zoologist,* 2d ser., ii, 1867, p. 992.

1867. HUTTON, F. W.   Notes on the Birds seen during a Voyage from London to New Zealand in 1866.   < *Ibis*, 2d ser., iii, 1867, pp. 185–193.

About 20 species (all but one belonging to *Procellariidæ*) are noticed.

1867. MOOR, E. C.   Storm Petrel [Procellaria pelagica] at Aldeborough.   < *Zoologist*, 2d ser., ii, 1867, p. 992.

1867. OVEREND, J. G.   Forktailed Petrel [Cymochorea leucorrhoa] at Yarmouth.   < *Zoologist*, 2d ser., ii, 1867, p. 916.

1868. BLAKE-KNOX, H.   Leach's Petrel [Cymochorea leucorrhoa] in Dublin Bay.   < *Zoologist*, 2d ser., iii, 1868, p. 1424.

1868. BREE, C. R.   Forktailed Petrel [Cymochorea leucorrhoa] at Colchester.   < *Zoologist*, 2d ser., iii, 1868, pp. 1060, 1061.

1868. CLARK-KENNEDY, A.   Storm Petrel [Procellaria pelagica] at Bridlington Quay.   < *Zoologist*, 2d ser., iii, 1868, p. 1060.

1868. CLARK-KENNEDY, A.   Storm Petrel [Procellaria pelagica] in Yorkshire.   < *Zoologist*, 2d ser., iii, 1868, p. 1135.

1868. CLARK-KENNEDY, A.   Storm Petrel [Procellaria pelagica] in Buckinghamshire.   < *Zoologist*, 2d ser., iii, 1868, pp. 1178, 1179.

1868. GURNEY, J. H., JR.   Fulmar Petrel [Fulmarus glacialis] at Flamborough.   < *Zoologist*, 2d ser., iii, 1868, pp. 1461, 1462.

1868. GURNEY, J. H., JR.   Fulmar Petrel [Fulmarus glacialis] near Sutherland.   < *Zoologist*, 2d ser., iii, 1868, p. 1462.

1868. GURNEY, J. H., JR.   Fulmar Petrel [Fulmarus glacialis] near Filey.   < *Zoologist*, 2d ser., iii, 1868, p. 1483.

1868. GURNEY, J. H., JR.   Fulmar Petrel [Fulmarus glacialis] at Flamborough.   < *Zoologist*, 2d ser., iii, 1868, p. 1483.

1868. HARRISON, J. W.   Forktailed Petrel [Cymochorea leucorrhoa] near Spalding.   < *Zoologist*, 2d ser., iii, 1868, p. 1061.

1868. STEVENSON, H.   Five Forktailed Petrels [Cymochorea leucorrhoa] near Lynn, Norfolk.   < *Zoologist*, 2d ser., iii, 1868, p. 1099.

1869. GIGLIOLI, H. H., *and* SALVADORI, T.   Nuove specie di Procellaridi raccolte durante il viaggio fatto intorno al mondo negli anni 1865. 6. 7. 8. dalla pirocorvetta italiana Magenta.   < *Atti della Soc. Ital. Sci. Nat.*, xi, fasc. iii, Sept. 16, 1868, pp. 450–458.   (Not pub. till 1869.)

Not seen. This is the ostensible original of the paper, but it is said not to have appeared until after the English version in the *Ibis*, 1869, pp. 61–68, which see for the new species.

1869. GIGLIOLI, H. H., *and* SALVADORI, T.   On some new Procellariidæ collected during a Voyage round the World in 1865–68 by H. I. M.'s S. 'Magenta'.   < *Ibis*, 2d ser., v, 1869, pp. 61–68.

This is an English version of the paper in *Atti Soc. Ital. Sci. Nat.*, xi, fasc. iii, "16 Sept. 1868"; said to have actually appeared before the ostensible original in Italian.   Five species are named and described as new : *Æstrelata magentæ*, p. 61; *Æ. arminjoniana*, p. 62; *Æ. defilippiana*, p. 63; *Æ. trinitatis*, p. 65; and *Puffinus elegans*, p. 67, from the S. Atlantic, lat. 43°, long. 9° E.   The descriptions are complemented with critical observations.

1869. GURNEY, J. H., JR.   Fulmar Petrels [Fulmarus glacialis] at Scarborough.   < *Zoologist*, 2d ser., iv, 1869, p. 1518.

1869. GURNEY, J. H., JR.   Fulmar Petrel [Fulmarus glacialis] at Whitby.   < *Zoologist*, 2d ser., iv, 1869, pp. 1518, 1519.

1869. GURNEY, J. H., JR.   Food of the Fulmar [Fulmarus glacialis].   < *Zoologist*, 2d ser., iv, 1869, p. 1603.

1869. GURNEY, J. H., JR.   Fulmar Petrel [Fulmarus glacialis] at Saltburn.   < *Zoologist*, 2d ser., ii, 1869, p. 1868.

1869. HUTTON, F. W. On the Mechanical Principles involved in the Flight of the Albatross. < *Trans. and Proc. N. Z. Inst. for* 1868, i, 1869, (2d ed., 1875), pp. 465–467.

> Abstract only here; paper deferred for want of algebraic type to second vol. of the same publication, 1870, pp. 227–232, where in full.

1869. HUTTON, F. W. On the Mechanical Principles involved in the Sailing-Flight of the Albatros. < *Philos. Mag.*, Aug., 1869, pp. 130–136.

> Not seen. Cf. *Ibis*, 1870, p. 122; *Zool. Rec.*, iv, pp. 45, 46, 50.

1869. HUTTON, F. W. [Letter relating to certain Procellariidæ.] < *Ibis*, 2d ser., v, 1869, pp. 351–353.

> *Æstrelata gouldi*, sp. n., p. —. Description of *Majaqueus parkinsoni*, Gray. Criticism of E. Coues's review of the *Procellariidæ* in *Proc. Phila. Acad.*, 1864–66.

1870. GUNN, T. E. Abundance of the Storm Petrel [Procellaria pelagica] in Norfolk. < *Zoologist*, 2d ser., v, 1870, p. 1983.

1870. GUNN, T. E. Fulmar Petrel [Fulmarus glacialis] on the Norfolk Coast. < *Zoologist*, 2d ser., v, 1870, p. 1983.

1870. HUTTON, F. W. Description of two Birds [Procellariidæ] new to the Fauna of New Zealand. < *Trans. N. Z. Inst.*, ii, 1870, pp. 78–80.

> Not seen.

1870. HUTTON, F. W. On the Mechanical Principles involved in the Flight of the Albatros. < *Trans. and Proc. New Zealand Inst. for* 1869, ii, 1870, pp. 227–232.

> In full; abstract in *op. cit.*, vol. i, 1869, pp. 465–467. Also pub. in *Philos. Mag.*, Aug., 1869, pp. 130–136. Read before Auckland Inst. June 1, 1868.—A notable paper, which occasioned considerable comment and criticism. Cf. *Ibis*, 1870, p. 122; *Zool. Rec.*, iv, pp. 45, 46, 50.

1870. WEBB, J. S. On the Mechanical Principles involved in the Sailing Flight of the Albatros. < *Trans. and Proc. New Zealand Inst. for* 1869, ii, 1870, pp. 233–236, with 1 diagram.

> It seems to the author, who commends Capt. Hutton's "ably written and very interesting paper," that the latter has "not been happy in the mathematical treatment of the subject," "having made a mistake at the outset of his calculations."

1871. ANON. Albatross in Derbyshire. < *Zoologist*, 2d ser., vi, 1871, p. 2527.

> From the London 'Field', Nov. 26.

1871. GURNEY, J. H. Forktailed Petrel [Cymochorea leucorrhoa] in South Devon. < *Zoologist*, 2d ser., vi, 1871, p. 2443.

1871. GURNEY, J. H. Albatross in Derbyshire. < *Zoologist*, 2d ser., vi, 1871, p. 2563.

1871. GURNEY, J. H., JR. Wholesale Destruction of Manx Shearwaters [Puffinus anglorum]. < *Zoologist*, 2d ser., vi, 1871, p. 2646.

1871. HERBERT, W. H. Storm Petrel [Procellaria pelagica] near Wantage. < *Zoologist*, 2d ser., vi, 1871, p. 2563.

1871. ROWLEY, G. D. Forkedtailed Petrel [Cymochorea leucorrhoa] at Brighton. < *Zoologist*, 2d ser., vi, 1871, p. 2443.

1871. WEST, C. Albatross in Derbyshire. < *Zoologist*, 2d ser., vi, 1871, p. 2527.

> From the London 'Field,' Dec. 4, 1870.

1872. HUTTON, F. W. On the Sailing Flight of the Albatros; a Reply to Mr. J. S. Webb. < *Trans. and Proc. New Zealand Inst. for* 1871, iv, 1872, pp. 347–350.

> For Webb's article, see *op. cit.* for 1869, ii, 1870, pp. 233–236. For Hutton's previous papers, see *op. cit.*, i, pp. 465–467; ii, pp. 227–232; *Philos. Mag.*, Aug., 1869, pp. 130–136. Cf. *Ibis*, 1870, p. 122; *Zool. Rec.*, iv, pp. 45, 46, 50.

1872. HUTTON, F. W. [On the synonymy of certain Procellariidæ, &c.] < *Ibis*, 3d ser., ii, 1872, pp. 83, 84.

1872. SPERLING, R. M. [Letter on certain Procellariidæ, and various South American Birds.] < *Ibis*, 3d ser., ii, 1872, pp. 74–79.

1873. ANON. Mother Carey's Chickens. < *Am. Sportsman*, iii, 1873, p. 183.

> Account of *Procellaria pelagica*, "from English magazine."

1873. POTTS, T. H. Notes on a supposed new Species of Prion [australis]. < *Ibis*, 3d ser., iii, 1873, pp. 85, 86.

1873. SWINHOE, R. On a Black Albatross [Diomedea derogata, sp. n.] of the China Seas. < *P. Z. S.*, 1873, pp. 784–786.

1874. ANON. [Capture of Fulmars (Fulmarus glacialis) at St. Kilda.] < *Am. Sportsman*, iv, 1874, p. 19.

1874. BENNER, F. Our Petrels. < *Forest and Stream*, ii, Apr. 9, 1874, p. 133.
Nesting habits of three species on the coast of Maine.

1874. GATCOMBE, J. Greater Shearwater [Puffinus major] on the Coasts of Devon and Cornwall. < *Zoologist*, 2d ser., ix, 1874, p. 4262.

1874. GURNEY, J. H. Note on the Occurrence of the Greater Shearwater [Puffinus major] in Bridlington Bay. < *Zoologist*, 2d ser., ix, 1874, pp. 3882, 3883.

1874? REINHARDT, J. Sur la structure anatomique des ailes dans la famille des Pétrels (Procellaridæ, s. Tubinares). < *Vidensk. Meddel. Naturhist. Foren. Kjøbenhavn for aaret* 1873, 1874? pp. 38–41.
Résumé français.

1874? REINHARDT, J. Om Vingens anatomiske Bygning hos Stormfugle-Familien (Procellaridæ s. Tubinares). < *Vidensk. Meddel. Naturhist. Foren. Kjøbenhavn for aaret* 1873, 1874? pp. 123–138, figg. in text.
The actual date of the paper is in question; but it probably appeared in 1873.
The wing-structure of *Procellariidæ* is treated with reference to the presence of one or two ossicles at the elbow-joint, developed in connection with the apophysial hooklet of the humerus, and the origin of the extensor metacarpi longus and extensor plicæ alaris. These ossicles are found in 6 genera and not in 8, but the 6 are enough richer in species to indicate that they occur in about two-thirds of the species of the family. Being peculiar to *Procellariidæ*, it is proposed to divide the group primarily upon this character.
Cf. Coues, *Am. Nat.*, viii, 1874, p. 546; *Zool. Rec.*, x, pp. 71, 72.

1874. REINHARDT, J. Sur la Structure anatomique des ailes dans la famille des Pétrels (Procellaridæ seu Tubinares). < *Gerv. Journ. de Zool.*, iii, 1874, pp. 139–144, figg. 2.
Résumé fait par l'auteur de son Mémoire inséré dans le *Vidensk. Meddel. Foren. Kjøb.* 1873, pp. 123–128.

1874. RODD, E. H. Greater Shearwater [Puffinus major] on the Cornish Coast. < *Zoologist*, 2d ser., ix, 1874, pp. 4261, 4262.

1875. BULLER, W. L. Description of a new Species of Petrel (Procellaria affinis). < *Trans. and Proc. New Zealand Inst. for* 1874, vii, 1875, p. 215, 216.
Compared with *P. cookii*.

1875. GATCOMBE, J. Large Number of the Greater Shearwater [Puffinus major] off the Coasts of Devon and Cornwall. < *Zoologist*, 2d ser., x, Jan., 1875, p. 4300.

1875. RODD, E. H. Fulmar Petrel [Fulmarus glacialis] in Mount's Bay. < *Zoologist*, 2d ser., x, May, 1875, pp. 4459, 4460.

1875. SALVIN, O. Critical Notes on Procellariidæ. < *Rowl. Ornith. Misc.*, pt. iv, May, 1876, pp. 223–238, 249–257, pll. xxx–xxxiv.
A specially important and trustworthy paper, clearing up many obscure moot points in this difficult group. It consists of two separately titled and paged parts. Part I: Banks's unpublished Drawings. This is an attempt to identify these drawings, which figure so prominently in the literature of *Procellariidæ*, yet are really little understood, and accessible to few. The 16 spp. drawn by Parkinson, being Nos. 12–27, are nearly all satisfactorily accounted for. Part II is: *The new species of Petrels obtained during the Voyage of the Italian Corvette 'Magenta' round the World.* These are described, and all are figured in colors, as follows: Pl. xxx, *Œstralata magentæ*, p. 251; Pl. xxxi, *Œ. arminjoniana*, p. 252; Pl. xxxii, *Œ. trinitatis*, p. 253; Pl. xxxiii, *Œ. defilippiana*, p. 255; Pl. xxxiv, *Puffinus elegans*, p. 256.

1876. CORDEAUX, J. Manx Shearwater (Puffinus anglorum, Temminck) on the North-East Coast. < *Zoologist*, 2d ser., xi, Dec., 1876, p. 5169.

1876. GATCOMBE, J. Greater Shearwater [Puffinus major] in Devon. < *Zoologist*, 2d ser., xi, Oct., 1876, p. 5127.

1876. GURNEY, J. H., JR.   Fulmar Petrel [Fulmarus glacialis] of Martin.   < *Zoologist,* 2d ser., xi, May, 1876, p. 4931.

The picture in 'Voy. St. Kilda,' 1698, was drawn by James Monroe: cf. Edwards, *Nat. Hist.*, p. 289.

1876. GURNEY, J. H., JR.   Yellow-nosed Albatross [Diomedea chlororhyncha] in Derbyshire.   < *Zoologist,* 2d ser., xi, Apr., 1876, pp. 4883, 4884.

With quotation from the *Analyst,* vi, Apr., 1837, p. 160, as copied in Wood's *Naturalist,* ii, p. 104 and p. 294.

1876. GURNEY, J. H., JR.   Manx Shearwater [Puffinus anglorum].   < *Zoologist,* 2d ser., xi, July, 1876, pp. 5007, 5008.

1876. ROWLEY, G. D.   Thalassidroma bullockii, Fleming.   [Cymochorea leucorrhoa, Coues.]   (Bullock's Petrel.)   < *Rowl. Orn. Misc.,* ii, pt. v, Oct., 1876, pp. 101-111, pll. xlviii, xlix.

Pl. 48, portrait of Wm. Bullock, F. L. S.; pl. 49, "Mother Carey and her Chickens"—very spirited.   It is a pleasant gossipy article, rich in historical flavor.

1877. B[REWER], T. M.   Salvin on the Procellariidæ.   < *Bull. Nutt. Ornith. Club,* ii, No. 3, July, 1877, pp. 69, 70.

Review of Salvin's paper in the 4th part of *Rowley's Ornithological Miscellany.*

1877. BREWER, T. M.   Breeding of Leach's Petrel [Cymochorea leucorrhoa] on the Coast of Maine.   < *Bull. Nutt. Ornith. Club,* ii, No. 3, July, 1877, pp. 80, 81.

1877. FINSCH, O.   On a New Species of Petrel [Procellaria albigularis] from the Feejee Islands.   < *P. Z. S.,* Nov. 6, 1877, p. 722.

1878. ANON.   Stormy Petrel.   < *The Country,* i, Mar. 2, 1878, p. 260.

Account of habits quoted from "Science Gossip." (Jan., 1878), with editorial remarks.

1878. [FITCH, E. H.]   Wandering Albatross [Diomedea exulans].   < *The Journ. of Sci.* (Toledo, Ohio), 2d ser., i, No. 5, Aug., 1878, cut.

Popular notice, with a figure.

1878. SALVIN, O.   Reports on the Collections of Birds made during the Voyage of H. M. S. 'Challenger.'—No. XII.   The Procellariidæ.   < *P. Z. S.,* June 18, 1878, pp. 735–740.

Eighty specc. of 22 spp. of 13 genn.   "None of the species present any difficulty as regards their nomenclature."   *Œstrelata* "*sericea* Less." identified with *lessoni* Garn., or *kidderi* Coues, referred to *brevirostris* Less.

1879. "UBIQUE."   Cape Pigeons [Daption capensis] and how to capture them.   < *Forest and Stream,* xi, Jan. 9, 1879, p. 462.

1879. BREWER, T. M.   Fulmarus glacialis on the Massachusetts Coast.   < *Bull. Nutt. Ornith. Club,* iv, No. 1, Jan., 1879, p. 64.

Bull. v, 4——33

Colymbidæ.

1765. GUNNERUS, J. E.   Von einigen Lom- oder Lummenartigen Vögel [Colymbus].
  < Dronth. Gesellsch. Schriften, i, 1765, pp. 201 -—, 4 pll.
  Nicht mir selbst zugänglich—Titel aus Giebel.

1767. GUNNERUS, J. E.   Von dem Meer-Hymber [Colymbus maximus].   *< Dronth.
  Gesellsch. Schriften*, iii, 1767, pp. 107–113.
  Nicht mir selbst zugänglich—Titel aus Carus und Engelmann.

1814. EDMONSTON, "A."   Observations on the Natural History of the Colymbus Immer.   *< Mem. Wernerian Nat. Hist. Soc.*, ii, pt. i, 1814, pp. 232–237.
  Read Apr., 1811. Habits and description of a specimen.

1822. EDMONSTON, L.   Observations on the Immer Goose [Colymbus glacialis] of
  Zetland.   *< Mem. Wernerian Nat. Hist. Soc.*, iv, pt. i, 1822, pp. 207–212.
  Determined to be the young of *Colymbus glacialis*, and its habits, &c., treated at length.

1824. KNOX, —.   [Note on the dark color of the periosteum of Colymbus septentrionalis.]   *< Edinb. Journ. Sci.*, i, 1824, p. 177.

1826. FABER, F.   Beyträge zur arctischen Zoologie.   *< Oken's Isis*, Jahrg. x, 1826, pp.
  909–927.
  Sechste Lieferung. Ueber die isländischen Schwimmvögel mit vierzehigen ungespaltenen
  Steissfussen. Gattung *Colymbus*. *C. glacialis*, p. 913; *C. septentrionalis*, p. 921.

1830. BREHM, C. L.   Ueber die doppelte Mauser der zur Sippe Taucher, Colymbus
  gehörigen Vögel.   *< Oken's Isis*, Bd. xxiii, 1830, pp. 979–984.
  C. glacialis (maximus, hiemalis Br.); *C. arcticus (macrorhynchus* Br., *balthicus* Hornsch. und
  Schill.); *C. septentrionalis (lumme* Brünn. u. Br., *borealis* Brünn. u. Br.).

1832. JORDAN, W. R.   The Imber (Colymbus Immer Lin.).   *< Loudon's Mag. Nat.
  Hist.*, v, 1832, p. 284.
  Its occurrence in Great Britain.

1833. FALK, V.   Anteckningar om Colymbus Arcticus.   *< Tiddsk. f. Jägare och. Naturf.*,
  Årg. ii, 1833, pp. 673, 674.

1836. MARTIN, T. S.   The Northern Diver [Colymbus torquatus, in England].   *< Loudon's Mag. Nat. Hist.*, ix, 1836, p. 480.

1838. MOORE, E.   Northern Diver [Colymbus torquatus, in Devonshire].   *< Charlesw.
  Mag. Nat. Hist.*, ii, 1838, p. 634.

1840. BRANDT, J. F.   Ueber Podiceps und Eudytes als zwei besondere Typen in der
  Ordnung der Schwimmvögel.   *< Mém. de l'Acad. St.-Pétersb.*, vi sér., v, pte. ii,
  Sc. Nat., iii, 1840, pp. 203–212, pll. xi, figg. 5–8, xiv–xvi.
  A subtitle, being the fourth part of his series, *Beiträge zur Kenntniss der Naturg. Vögel*,
  u. s. w.

1843. EDMONSTON, T., JR.   Note on the Northern Diver [Colymbus torquatus].
  < Zoologist, i, 1843, p. 365.

1843. ROBINSON, J. B.   [Notice of presentation of Colymbus torquatus.]   *< P. Z. S.*,
  xi, 1843, p. 123.

1844. GREENWOOD, A.   Note on the change of Plumage in the Northern Diver [Co-
  lymbus torquatus].   *< Zoologist*, ii, 1844, pp. 455, 456.

1844. RODD, E. H.   Note on the Great Northern Diver [Colymbus torquatus].   *< Zoologist*, ii, 1844, p. 795.

1848. BOLD, T. J.   Occurrence of the Black-throated Diver (Colymbus arcticus) at
  Cullercoats, Northumberland.   *< Zoologist*, vi, 1848, pp. 2067, 2068.

1848. COOPER, W. W.   Occurrence of the Speckled Diver at Worcester.   *< Zoologist*,
  vi, 1848, p. 1969.

1848. COOPER, W. W. Occurrence of the Red-throated Diver (Colymbus septentrionalis) at Worcester. < *Zoologist*, vi, 1848, p. 2027.

1848. SALMON, J. D. Occurrence of the Red-throated Diver (Colymbus septentrionalis) near Guilford. < *Zoologist*, vi, 1848, p. 2304.

1849. HOMEYER, E. v. Ueber den Federwechsel der Seetaucher [Colymbidæ]. < *Naumannia*, i, Heft i, 1849, pp. 14–17.

1849. RODD, E. H. Occurrence of the Great Northern Diver [Colymbus torquatus] at Penzance. < *Zoologist*, vii, 1849, p. 2621.

1850. BOND, F. Occurrence of the Black-throated Diver (Colymbus arcticus) at Chesterfield. < *Zoologist*, viii, 1850, p. 2775.

1850. BURROUGHES, T. H. Occurrence of the Black-throated Diver [Colymbus arcticus] on Barton Pond. < *Zoologist*, viii, 1850, p. 2775.

1850. GURNEY, J. H. Note on the Changes of Plumage periodically incident to the Great Northern, Black-throated and Red-throated Divers [Colymbus torquatus, C. arcticus, C. septentrionalis]. < *Zoologist*, viii, 1850, pp. 2775, 2776.

1850. MATTHEWS, H. Occurrence of the Black-throated Diver (Colymbus septentrionalis) in Lincolnshire. < *Zoologist*, viii, 1850, p. 2803.

1850. NELSON, C. Curious Capture of the Red-throated Diver (Colymbus septentrionalis). < *Zoologist*, viii, 1850, p. 2706.

1850. NEWMAN, E. Occurrence of the Black-throated Diver (Colymbus arcticus) in the Thames. < *Zoologist*, viii, 1850, p. 2706.

1850. NEWTON, A. Occurrence of the Great Northern Diver (Colymbus gracialis [sic]) in Torbay. < *Zoologist*, viii, 1850, p. 2776.

1851. ELLMAN, J. B. Occurrence of the Black-throated Diver (Colymbus arcticus) at Pevensey. < *Zoologist*, ix, 1851, p. 3036.

1851. GURNEY, J. H. Note on the Autumnal Moult of the Red-throated Diver [Colymbus septentrionalis]. < *Zoologist*, ix, 1851, p. 3301.

1851. NICHOLLS, H. Occurrence of the Great Northern Diver (Colymbus glacialis [torquatus]) in Devonshire. < *Zoologist*, ix, 1851, p. 3035.

1851. POTTER, C. Occurrence of the Great Northern Diver (Colymbus glacialis [torquatus, at Lewes]). < *Zoologist*, ix, 1851, pp. 3035, 3036.

1852. MOGGRIDGE, M. Colymbus septentrionalis [in Britain]. < *Ann. Mag. Nat. Hist.*, 2d ser., x, 1852, p. 398.

1854. SMITH, A. C. Occurrence of the Great Northern Diver [Colymbus torquatus] in Wilts. < *Zoologist*, xii, 1854, pp. 4165, 4166.

1855. MORE, A. G. On the [habits of the] three Species of Divers or Loons [Colymbidæ]. < *Zoologist*, xiii, 1855, pp. 4628, 4629.

1857. PELZELN, A. v. [Ueber das Vorkommen von Colymbus arcticus und C. glacialis.] < *Verh. d. k.-k. zool.-bot. Ges. zu Wien*, vii, 1857, *Sitzungsber.*, p. 85.
Not seen.

1859. GRAY, G. R. Description of a New Species of Diver (Colymbus [adamsii]). < *P. Z. S.*, xxvii, 1859, p. 167.

1859. SCLATER, P. L. Remarks on exhibiting specimens of Two Species of Divers (Colymbus), from Mr. Gurney's Collection. < *P. Z. S.*, xxvii, 1859, pp. 206, 207.

1860. GRAY, G. R. Description of a New Species of Diver (Colymbus [adamsii]). < *Ann. Mag. Nat. Hist.*, 3d ser., v, 1860, p. 331.
From *P. Z. S.*, May 10, 1859, p. 167.

1862. BELL, A. S. Occurrence of the Blackthroated Diver [Colymbus arcticus] near Scarborough. < *Zoologist*, xx, 1862, p. 8005.

1862. Coues, E. Synopsis of the North American Forms of the Colymbidæ and Podicipidæ. < *Proc. Acad. Nat. Sci. Phila.*, xiv, 1862, pp. 226–233.
Abstract of a monograph revised and published in 1874 in the author's 'Birds of the Northwest,' *q. v.* Of *Colymbidæ* are recognized 1 genus, *Colymbus*, with 5 spp.—*torquatus, adamsii, arcticus, pacificus,* and *septentrionalis.*
Cf. *Ibis*, 1863, pp. 107, 108.

1863. Grill, J. W. Om Stor-Lommen, Colymbus arcticus. < *Öfvers. Kongl. Vetensk.-Akad. Förhandl. för år* 1862, xix, 1863, pp. 361, 362.

1863. Stevenson, H. The Redthroated Diver (Colymbus septentrionalis) in Norfolk. < *Zoologist*, xxi, 1863, p. 8331.

1864. Blake-Knox, H. Scarcity of the Redthroated Diver [Colymbus septentrionalis] and plenty of the Great Northern Diver [C. torquatus] in Dublin Bay. < *Zoologist*, xxii, 1864, p. 8963.

1864. Boulton, W. W. Redthroated Diver [Colymbus septentrionalis] near Beverley. < *Zoologist*, xxii, 1864, p. 9048.

1864. Bruch, C. Polar taucher [Colymbus arcticus] in Ungarn. < *Zool. Gart.*, v, 1864, pp. 26, 27.

1864. Coues, E. The Crania of Colymbus torquatus and C. adamsii compared. < *Proc. Acad. Nat. Sci. Phila.*, xvi, 1864, pp. 21, 22.

1864. Hintz I., W. Ueber den Nestbau von Colymbus arcticus [u. s. w.]. (Anlage I. zum Protocoll der vierten Versamml. der Ornithologen Mecklenburgs, 1. u. 2. October, 1863). < *J. f. O.*, xii, 1864, pp. 66–68.
Inhalt sowie *a)* merkwürdiger Nestbau einiger Vögel, *b)* Ueber *Nucifraga caryocatactes, c) Syrrhaptes paradoxus.*

1865. Böck, —. Die Mauser des Eudytes arcticus [u. s. w.]. < *J. f. O.*, xiii, 1865, pp. 367, 368.

1865. Bree, C. R. Note on the Great Northern Diver (Colymbus septentrionalis). < *Zoologist*, xxiii, 1865, p. 9629.
Cf. *tom. cit.*, p. 9697.

1865. Bree, C. R. Correction of an Error [Zool., p. 9629]. < *Zoologist*, xxiii, 1865, p. 9697.

1865. Hodgson, C. B. Note on the Blackthroated Diver [Colymbus arcticus]. < *Zoologist*, xxiii, 1865, p.9566.

1865. Jeffrey, W., Jr. Great Northern Diver [Colymbus torquatus] on the Sussex Coast. < *Zoologist*, xxiii, 1865, p. 9419.

1866. Clogg, S. Change of Plumage in Great Northern Diver [Colymbus torquatus]. < *Zoologist*, 2d ser., i, 1866, pp. 99, 100.

1866. Coues, E. The Osteology of Colymbus torquatus; with Notes on its Myology. < *Mem. Boston Soc. Nat. Hist.*, i, pt. ii, art. i, Apr., 1866 (read Sept., 1863), pp. 131–172, woodcc. 1, 2, pl. 5, figg. 1–4. (Issued separately, 4to, paper.)
A detailed purely descriptive account of the skeleton, with less elaborate description of all the principal muscles; including some notice of the mechanism involved. The woodcc. show the sternum and scapular arch (2 views); the pl. shows the skull (3 views) and profile of the pelvis and posterior extremity. (Cf. *Ibis*, 1868, p. 229.)

1866. Fulford, J. L. L. Great Northern Diver [Colymbus torquatus] near Bridport. < *Zoologist*, 2d ser., i, 1866, p. 145.

1866. Harvie-Brown, J. A. Nesting of the Blackthroated Diver [Colymbus arcticus]. < *Zoologist*, 2d ser., i, 1866, p. 525.

1866. Rodd, E. H. The Great Northern Diver [Colymbus torquatus]: Summer and Winter Plumage. < *Zoologist*, 2d ser., i, 1866, p. 99.

1867. Clogg, S. Great Northern Diver [Colymbus torquatus] at Looe. < *Zoologist*, 2d ser., ii, 1867, p. 951.

1867. Cornish, T. Redthroated Diver [Colymbus septentrionalis] netted at Penzance. < *Zoologist*, 2d ser., ii, 1867, p. 992.

1867. CRICHTON, A. W.   Blackthroated Diver [Colymbus arcticus] at Wickham, Hants.   < *Zoologist*, 2d ser., ii, 1867, p. 608.

1867. FEILDEN, H. W.   Nesting of the Blackthroated Diver [Colymbus arcticus]. < *Zoologist*, 2d ser., ii, 1867, p. 710.

1868. BLAKE-KNOX, H.   [Prone] Position of the Divers (Colymbidæ) when on Land. < *Zoologist*, 2d ser., iii, 1868, pp. 1379, 1380.
    Cf. *tom. cit.*, p. 1424.

1868. BLAKE-KNOX, H.   Divers [Colymbidæ] on Land.   < *Zoologist*, 2d ser., iii, 1868, pp. 1423, 1424.

1868. BLAKE-KNOX, H.   Blackthroated Diver [Colymbus arcticus] off the Dublin Coast.   < *Zoologist*, 2d ser., iii, 1868, p. 1424.

1868. CLARK-KENNEDY, A.   Great Northern Diver [Colymbus torquatus] near Birkenhead.   < *Zoologist*, 2d ser., iii, 1868, p. 1221.

1868. GUNN, T, E.   Blackthroated Diver [Colymbus arcticus] at Lowestoft.   < *Zoologist*, 2d ser., iii, 1868, pp. 1221, 1222.

1868. HARVIE-BROWN, J. A.   Note and Query regarding [natural attitudes of] the Blackthroated Diver [Colymbus arcticus].   < *Zoologist*, 2d ser., iii, 1868, pp. 1320, 1321.

1868. HARVIE-BROWN, J. A.   Great Northern Diver [Colymbus torquatus] breeding in Scotland.   < *Zoologist*, 2d ser., iii, 1868, p. 1424.

1868. MATHEW, G. F.   Great Northern Diver [Colymbus torquatus] on the River Taw. < *Zoologist*, 2d ser., iii, 1868, p. 1098.

1868. WALKER, T. C.   [Attitudes, etc., of the] Blackthroated Diver [Colymbus arcticus].   < *Zoologist*, 2d ser., iii, 1868, p. 1380.

1869. BISSENDEN, J.   Blackthroated Diver [Colymbus arcticus] at St. Leonard's. < *Zoologist*, 2d ser., iv, 1869, p. 1684.

1869. GUNN, T. E.   Contents of the Stomach of a Redthroated Diver [Colymbus septentrionalis].   < *Zoologist*, 2d ser., iv, 1869, p. 1848.

1869. HUNTER, J.   Redthroated Diver [Colymbus septentrionalis] in Faversham Creek.   < *Zoologist*, 2d ser., iv, 1869, p. 1517.

1869. RODD, E. H.   The Seasonal Plumage of the Divers (Colymbidæ).   < *Zoologist*, 2d ser., iv, 1869, p. 1723.

1869. WONFOR, T. W.   Redthroated Diver [Colymbus septentrionalis].   < *Zoologist*, 2d ser., iv, 1869, p. 1684.

1870. BROWNE, A. M.   Great Northern Diver [Colymbus torquatus] in the Midland Counties.   < *Zoologist*, 2d ser., v, 1870, pp. 2064, 2065.

1870. GATCOMBE, J.   Redthroated Diver [Colymbus septentrionalis] on the Devonshire Coast.   < *Zoologist*, 2d ser., v, 1870, pp. 2106, 2107.

1870. MOSLEY, O.   Great Northern Diver [Colymbus torquatus] at Burton-on-Trent. < *Zoologist*, 2d ser., v, 1870, p. 1982.

1870. SCLATER, P. L.   [On addition to the Society's Menagerie of Colymbus torquatus.]   < *P. Z. S.*, xxxviii, 1870, p. 86.

1871. GORDON, C.   Blackthroated Diver [Colymbus arcticus] at Folkestone.   < *Zoologist*, 2d ser., vi, 1871, p. 2528.

1871. WHARTON, C. B.   Divers at Elstree Reservoir.   < *Zoologist*, 2d ser., vi, 1871, pp. 2645, 2646.

1873. DURNFORD, H.   Blackthroated Diver [Colymbus arcticus] in Suffolk.   < *Zoologist*, 2d ser., viii, 1873, p. 3413.

1873. "L. W. L."   Loons [Colymbus torquatus] under water.   < *Forest and Stream*, i, Dec. 4, 1873, p. 258.

1874. N[EWCOMB], R. L. [Colymbus septentrionalis at Salem, Mass.] < *Forest and Stream*, iii, Nov. 29, 1874, p. 245.

1875. CLARKE, W. E. Great Northern Diver [Colymbus torquatus] in Bridlington Bay. < *Zoologist*, 2d ser., x, Jan., 1875, p. 4299.

1875. GUNN, T. E. Blackthroated Diver [Colymbus arcticus] in Norfolk. < *Zoologist*, 2d ser., x, Apr., 1875, p. 4422.

1875. GURNEY, J. H., JR. Redthroated Diver [Colymbus septentrionalis]. < *Zoologist*, 2d ser., x, Nov., 1875, p. 4698.

1876. GURNEY, J. H., JR. On Adams' Diver (Colymbus Adamsi) in England. < *Zoologist*, 2d ser., xi, Jan., 1876, p. 4767.

1876. GURNEY, J. H., JR. The Divers. < *Zoologist*, 2d ser., xi, June, 1876, p. 4958.

1876. SMEE, A. H. Great Northern Diver [Colymbus torquatus] off Erith. < *Zoologist*, 2d ser., xi, May, 1876, p. 4930.

1876. SMITH, CECIL. Blackthroated Diver [Colymbus arcticus] in Somersetshire. < *Zoologist*, 2d ser., xi, Feb., 1876, p. 4804.

1876. TUCK, J. G. Blackthroated Diver [Colymbus arcticus] in Filey Bay. < *Zoologist*, 2d ser., xi, Feb., 1876, p. 4804.

Podicipedidæ.

[N. B.—Hujusce familiæ nomen "*Podicipedidæ*" nec *Podicipidæ* rite scribendum, generis nomino a podice et pede derivato; unde *Podicipes*, scilicet "rump-foot."]

1794. TENGMALM, PEHR GUST.   Slågtet Podiceps och de Svenska Arterna dåraf.
< *Kongl. Vetensk. Acad. Nya Handl.*, xv, 1794, pp. 300–315.
Characteren på detta Slägte, p. 301.—1. *P. cristatus.*   2. *P. rubricollis.*   3. *P. auritus.*   4. *P. cornutus.*   5. *P. obscurus.*   6. *P. minor.*

1805. MEWES, —.   Bemerkungen über die Nahrungmittel von Podiceps subcristatus.
< *Wiedem. Arch. f. Zool. u. Zoot.*, Bd. iv, St. ii, 1805, pp. 178–180.
Not seen.

1832. ALLIS, T.   The Food of the larger Grebes (species of Latham's genus Podiceps).
< *Loudon's Mag. Nat. Hist.*, v, 1832, p. 733.

1833. FENNELL, J.   A Dabchick [Podiceps minor] choked by a Bullhead Fish.
< *Loudon's Mag. Nat. Hist.*, vi, 1833, p. 520.

1833. K[NOX], T.   Instances of Feathers found in the Stomach in the larger Species of Grebe.   What End in the Economy of Digestion do these Feathers subserve?
< *Loudon's Mag. Nat. Hist.*, vi, 1833, pp. 519, 520.

1836. GUILDING, L.   The Dabchick [Podiceps minor], Remarks on.   < *Loudon's Mag. Nat. Hist.*, ix, 1836, p. 326.

1836. K[NOX], T.   Feathers in the Gizzard of the Larger Species of Grebe, and why?
< *Loudon's Mag. Nat. Hist.*, ix, 1836, p. 202.

1836. WOOD, C. T.   The Blackchin Grebe.   < *Loudon's Mag. Nat. Hist.*, ix, 1836, p. 647.

1836. WOOD, N.   Feathers in the Gizzard of the larger Species of Grebe, and why?
< *Loudon's Mag. Nat. Hist.*, ix, 1836, p. 326.

1836. WOOD, N.   Feathers in the Gizzard of the Grebe.   < *Loudon's Mag. Nat. Hist.*, ix, 1836, p. 597.

1843. HOLME, F.   Note on the occurrence of the Eared Grebe [Podiceps auritus] at Oxford.   < *Zoologist*, i, 1843, p. 223.

1843. PARSONS, C.   Note on the Habits of the Dabchick [Tachybaptes minor].   < *Zoologist*, i, 1843, pp. 364, 365.

1844. ATKINSON, J. C.   Notes on the Dabchick [habits of Tachybaptes minor].
< *Zoologist*, ii, 1844, pp. 499–502.

1844. GOULD, J.   [Description of Podiceps australis, sp. n.]   < *P. Z. S.*, xii, 1844, p. 135.

1844. CHENNELL, F. A.   Note on the occurrence of the Crested Grebe [Podiceps cristatus] in Middlesex.   < *Zoologist*, ii, 1844, p. 502.

1845. BURY, C. A.   Enquiry relative to the Staining of the Eggs of the Dabchick [Tachybaptes minor].   < *Zoologist*, iii, 1845, pp. 863–865.

1845. GOULD, J.   Description of a new species of Australian Bird [Podiceps australis].
< *Ann. Mag. Nat. Hist.*, xv, 1845, p. 142.

1848. ELLMAN, J. B.   Occurrence of the Great Crested Grebe (Podiceps cristatus) at Battel.   < *Zoologist*, vi, 1848, p. 2148.

1849. BIRD, W. F. W.   Occurrence of the Red-necked Grebe (Podiceps rubricollis) in the Medway.   < *Zoologist*, vii, 1849, p. 2422.

1849. CHENNELL, F. A.   Occurrence of the Great Crested Grebe (Podiceps cristatus) near Reigate.   < *Zoologist*, vii, 1849, pp. 2421, 2422.

1849. FOSTER, J. W.   Occurrence of the Eared Grebe (Podiceps auritus) at Wisbeach.
< *Zoologist*, vii, 1849, p. 2569.

1849. **Gurney, J. H.**   Occurrence of the Eared Grebe (Podiceps auritus) in Norfolk.
< *Zoologist*, vii, 1849, p. 2456.

1850. **Ellman, J. B.**   Occurrence of the Sclavonian Grebe (Podiceps cornutus) at Piddinghoe, Sussex.   < *Zoologist*, viii, 1850, p. 2775.

1850. **Foster, T. W.**   Occurrence of the Eared Grebe (Podiceps auritus) on Whittlesea Wash.   < *Zoologist*, viii, 1850, p. 2775.

1850. **Garth, J. C.**   Occurrence of the Red-necked Grebe (Podiceps rubicollis [sic]) near Burton-on-Trent.   < *Zoologist*, viii, 1850, p. 2706.

1850. **Plant, J.**   Occurrence of the Horned Grebe (Podiceps cornutus) at Manchester.
< *Zoologist*, viii, 1850, p. 2924.

1850. **Rodd, E. H.**   Occurrence of the Red-necked Grebe (Podiceps ruficollis) near Penzance.   < *Zoologist*, viii, 1850, p. 2803.

1850. **Sundevall, C. J.**   Podiceps arcticus, cornutus, auritus.   < *Öfvers. Kongl. Vetensk.-Akad. Förhandl. för år* 1849, 1850, pp. 206–210.
P. auritus L. = *P. cornutus* Luth. + *P. arcticus*. *P. nigricollis*, n. sp. = *P. auritus* auct.
Cf. *Vet.-Akad. Arsb. i Zool.*, 1845–50, p. 299; *Arch. f. Naturg.*, xvi, 1850, p. 44.

1850. **Sundevall, C. J.**   Ueber Podicipes arcticus, cornutus, auritus.   < *Arch. f. Naturg.*, 1850, (1), pp. 44–48.
Aus *Öfv. K. Vet.-Akad. Förh.*, aus d. Jahr 1849, SS. 206–210, *q. v.*

1851. **Green, J.**   Occurrence of the Eared Grebe (Podiceps auritus) at Yarmouth.
< *Zoologist*, ix, 1851, p. 3175.

1851. **Irby, L. H.**   Occurrence of the Red-necked Grebe (Podiceps rubricollis) in Devonshire.   < *Zoologist*, ix, 1851, p. 3035.

1851. **Joshua, W.**   Occurrence of the Rednecked Grebe (Podiceps rubicollis [sic]) in Gloucestershire.   < *Zoologist*, ix, 1851, p. 3056.

1851. **Strangewayes, R.**   Occurrence of the Eared Grebe (Podiceps auritus) at Yarmouth.   < *Zoologist*, ix, 1851, p. 3117.

1851. **Strangewayes, R.**   The Great Crested Grebe (Podiceps cristatus) in Norfolk.
< *Zoologist*, ix, 1851, p. 3209.

1851. [**Sundevall, C. J.**]   Podiceps nigricollis.   < *Öfvers. Kongl. Vetensk.-Akad. Förhandl. för år* 1850, 1851, pp. 291, 292.

1852. **Irby, L. H.**   Curious Death of a Dab-chick, or Little Grebe, (Podiceps minor).
< *Zoologist*, x, 1852, p. 3711.

1852. **Newman, E.**   Occurrence of the Eared Grebe [Podiceps auritus] at Yarmouth.
< *Zoologist*, x, 1852, p. 3477.

1854. **Gloger, C. W. L.**   Der Schwanz der Steissfüsse [u. s. w.].   *J. f. O.*, ii, 1854, p. 480.
An extract from Audubon's *Ornith. Biogr.*, iii, p. 598, on the structure of the tail of *Podiceps cristatus*.

1855. **Davis, R.**   [On the breeding of Podiceps auritus in Ireland.]   < *Nat. Hist. Rev.*, ii, 1855, p. 20.

1856. **D'Urban, W. S. M.**   Occurrence of the Sclavonian Grebe (Podiceps cornutus) in Devonshire.   < *Zoologist*, xiv, 1856, p. 5065.

1856. **Walker, A. O.**   Occurrence of the Eared Grebe [Podiceps auritus] in Flintshire.
< *Zoologist*, xiv, 1856, p. 5321.

1857. **Clermont,** *Lord.*   On the occurrence of the Eared Grebe [Podiceps auritus, in Ireland].   < *Nat. Hist. Rev. (Pr. Soc.)*, iv, 1857, p. 72.

1857. **Schlüter, W.**   Schwarze Eier von Podiceps cristatus.   < *J. f. O.*, v, 1857, pp. 302, 303.

1862. **Coues, E.**   Synopsis of the North American Forms of the Colymbidæ and Podicipidæ.   < *Proc. Acad. Nat. Sci. Phila.*, xiv, 1862, pp. 226–233.
Abstract of a monograph, published in 1874 in the author's 'Birds of the Northwest,' *q. v.*
The Grebes are considered as a family apart from *Colymbidæ*, with two subfamilies, *Podi-*

1862. COUES, E.—Continued.
  cipinæ and *Podilymbinæ*, and the following North American genera and species:—*Æchmophorus* (g. n., p. 229) *occidentalis; Æ. clarkii; Podiceps cristatus; P. cooperi; P. (Dytes) cornutus; P. (Proctopus) californicus; P. (Pedetaithya) holbölli; Sylbeocyclus dominicus; Podilymbus podiceps.* Cf. *Ibis*, 1863, pp. 107, 108.

1862. COUES, E. Supplementary note to a "Synopsis of the North American Forms of the Colymbidæ and Podicepidæ [sic]." < *Proc. Acad. Nat. Sci. Phila.*, xiv, 1862, p. 404.
  Breeding plumage of *Æchmophorus clarkii*, not before known.

1862. EDITORIAL. [Podiceps auritus breeding in Algeria and Epirus.] < *Ibis*, iv, 1862, p. 195.

1862. PARKE, G. H. Occurrence of the Sclavonian Grebe [Podiceps cornutus] at Halifax. < *Zoologist*, xx, 1862, p. 8005.

1862. STEVENSON, H. Occurrence of the Sclavonian and Eared Grebes [Podiceps cornutus, P. auritus] in Norfolk in full Summer Plumage. < *Zoologist*, xx, 1862, pp. 8092, 8093.

1864. BLACKMORE, H. Sclavonian or Dusky Grebe [Podiceps cornutus] near Salisbury. < *Zoologist*, xxii, 1864, p. 9048.

1864. BOULTON, W. W. Sclavonian or Dusky Grebe [Podiceps cornutus] near Beverley. < *Zoologist*, xxii, 1864, p. 8891.

1864. BOULTON, W. W. Eared Grebe [Podiceps auritus] on the Humber, near Hull. < *Zoologist*, xxii, 1864, p. 9048.

1864. BOULTON, W. W. Dusky or Sclavonian Grebe [Podiceps cornutus] near Selby, Yorkshire. < *Zoologist*, xxii, 1864, pp. 9047, 9048.

1864. NORMAN, G. Crested Grebe [Podiceps cristatus] in the Humber. < *Zoologist*, xxii, 1864, p. 9121.

1864. REYNOLDS, R. Habits, &c., of the Little Grebe [Podiceps minor]. < *Zoologist*, xxii, 1864, p. 8891.

1865. CORDEAUX, J. Rednecked Grebe [Podiceps griseigena] in Lincolnshire. < *Zoologist*, xxiii, 1865, p. 9469.

1865. DEVIS, C. W. Note on the Great Crested Grebe [Podiceps cristatus]. < *Zoologist*, xxiii, 1865, pp. 9565, 9566.

1865. GURNEY, J. H. Sclavonian Grebe [Podiceps cornutus] at Worthing. < *Zoologist*, xxiii, 1865, pp. 9540, 9541.

1865. HODGSON, C. B. Sclavonian Grebe [Podiceps cornutus] at Fern Island, Northumberland. < *Zoologist*, xxiii, 1865, p. 9500.

1865. HODGSON, C. B. Great Crested Grebe [Podiceps cristatus] in Warwickshire. < *Zoologist*, xxiii, 1865, p. 9565.

1865. HODGSON, C. B. Note on the Rednecked Grebe [Podiceps griseigena, in England]. < *Zoologist*, xxiii, 1865, p. 9565.

1865. HORSFALL, W. C. Rednecked Grebe [Podiceps griseigena] near Leeds. < *Zoologist*, xxiii, 1865, p. 9500.

1865. MATHEW, G. F. Eared Grebe [Podiceps auritus] near Barnstaple. < *Zoologist*, xxiii, 1865, pp. 9618, 9619.

1865. MORRES, A. P. Sclavonian Grebe [Podiceps cornutus] near Salisbury. < *Zoologist*, xxiii, 1865, p. 9565.

1866. GLOGER, [C. W. L.] Der grosse gehäubte Steissfuss, (Colymbus [Podiceps] cristatus,) in Weiss ausgeartet. < *J. f. O.*, xiv, 1866, pp. 285, 286.

1866. JEPHCOTT, T., JR. Great Crested Grebe [Podiceps cristatus] near Birmingham. < *Zoologist*, 2d ser., i, 1866, p. 100.

1867. BRIGGS, J. J. Little Grebe [Podiceps minor] affected by the Cold. < *Zoologist*, 2d ser., ii, 1867, pp. 636, 637.
  From the London 'Field,' Jan. 19.

1867. GUNN, T. E.   Rednecked and Sclavonian Grebes [Podiceps griseigena, P. cornutus] and Great Northern Diver [Colymbus torquatus] in Norfolk.   < Zoologist, 2d ser., ii, 1867, pp. 709, 710.

1868. BLAKE-KNOX, H.   Eared Grebe [Podiceps auritus] in County Dublin and County Antrim, Ireland.   < Zoologist, 2d ser., iii, 1868, p. 1424.

1868. HEDDERLY, J. S.   Rednecked Grebe [Podiceps griseigena] near Nottingham.   < Zoologist, 2d ser., iii, 1868, p. 1060.

1868. STEPHENSON, J. W.   Abundance of the Little Grebe [Podiceps minor] in Sussex.   < Zoologist, 2d ser., iii, 1868, p. 1482.

1869. GURNEY, J. H., JR.   Great Crested Grebe [Podiceps cristatus] at Hempstead.   < Zoologist, 2d ser., iv, 1869, p. 1603.

1869. SKINNER, A.   Sclavonian Grebe [Podiceps cornutus] near Faversham.   < Zoologist, 2d ser., iv, 1869, p. 1563.

1869. SOUTHWELL, T.   Note on the Nest of Podiceps minor.   < Zoologist, 2d ser., iv, 1869, pp. 1803, 1804.

1870. BLAKE-KNOX, H.   Sclavonian Grebe [Podiceps cornutus] in County Dublin.   < Zoologist, 2d ser., v, 1870, p. 2182.

1870. CHALK, W. J.   Rednecked Grebe [Podiceps griseigena] in Bedfordshire.   < Zoologist, 2d ser., v, 1870, p. 2064.

1870. CHALK, W. J.   Sclavonian Grebe [Podiceps cornutus] at Taunton.   < Zoologist, 2d ser., v, 1870, p. 2106.

1870. CREWE, H. H.   Great Crested Grebe [Podiceps cristatus] feeding its Adult Young.   < Zoologist, 2d ser., v, 1870, p. 2386.

1870. GATCOMBE, J.   Rare Grebes in Devonshire.   < Zoologist, 2d ser., v, 1870, p. 2106.

1870. GATCOMBE, J.   Grebes on the Coast of Devon.   < Zoologist, 2d ser., v, 1870, pp. 2142, 2143.

1870. GURNEY, J. H., JR.   Dabchicks [Podiceps minor] in Kensington Gardens.   < Zoologist, 2d ser., v, 1870, p. 2347.

1870. GOEBEL, H.   Ueber Podiceps Widhalmi nov. spec.   < J. f. O., xviii, 1870, pp. 312–315.
    Nachtrag von E. F. von Homeyer, p. 315.

1870. GUNN, T. E.   Sclavonian Grebes [Podiceps cornutus] in Norfolk.   < Zoologist, 2d ser., v, 1870, p. 2225.

1870. RODD, E. H.   Horned Grebe [Podiceps cornutus] in Cornwall.   < Zoologist, 2d ser., v, 1870, p. 2142.

1870. SMEE, A. H.   Sclavonian Grebe [Podiceps cornutus] on the Wandle.   < Zoologist, 2d ser., v, 1870, p. 2106.

1870. SMITH, CECIL.   Rednecked Grebe [Podiceps griseigena] at Teignmouth.   < Zoologist, 2d ser., v, 1870, p. 2106.

1871. BOYES, F.   Rednecked Grebe [Podiceps griseigena] in East Yorkshire.   < Zoologist, 2d ser., vi, 1871, p. 2527.

1871. GATCOMBE, J.   Eared Grebe [Podiceps auritus] in Devonshire.   < Zoologist, 2d ser., vi, 1871, p. 2646.

1871. GUNN, T. E.   Rednecked Grebe [Podiceps griseigena] in Norfolk.   < Zoologist, 2d ser., vi, 1871, p. 2872.

1871. TRAVERS, W. T. L.   Notes on the Habits of Podiceps cristatus.   < Trans. and Proc. New Zealand Inst. for 1870, iii, 1871, pp. 113–116.
    See also proceedings for the same year, separately paged, p. 25, where, under slightly modified title, an abstract appears.

1873. BOYES, F.   Eared and Rednecked Grebes [Podiceps auritus, P. griseigena] in East Yorkshire.   < Zoologist, 2d ser., viii, 1873, p. 3413.

1873. COUES, E. Range of the Eared Grebe [Podiceps auritus var. californicus, in Dakota, U. S.]. < *Am. Nat.*, vii, 1873, p. 745.

1873. THURN, E. F. IM. Sea Woodcock [Podiceps minor]. <*Zoologist*, 2d ser., viii, 1873, pp. 3371, 3372.

1874. CANE, T. Great Crested Grebe [Podiceps cristatus] at Luton. < *Zoologist*, 2d ser., ix, 1874, p. 3836.

1874. SCLATER, P. L. Note on the correct name of Podiceps minor. < *Ibis*, 3d ser., iv, 1874, pp. 98, 99.

　　　Tachybaptes Reich., stands, since *Sylbeocyclus* Bp. = *Podilymbus* Less.

1875. BOYES, F. Sclavonian Grebe [Podiceps cornutus] in East Yorkshire. < *Zoologist*, 2d ser., x, Jan., 1875, p. 4299.

1876. BOYES, F. Summer Plumage of the Little Grebe [Podiceps minor]. < *Zoologist*, 2d ser., xi, Nov., 1876, p. 5169.

1876. GURNEY, J. H., JR. Summer Plumage of the Little Grebe [Podiceps minor]. < *Zoologist*, 2d ser., xi, Aug., 1876, pp. 5047, 5048.

1876. GURNEY, J. H., JR. Retention of Summer Plumage by Grebes. < *Zoologist*, 2d ser., xi, Mar., 1876, p. 4847.

1876. NICHOLLS, R. P. Great Crested Grebe [Podiceps cristatus] near Kingsbridge. < *Zoologist*, 2d ser., xi, Feb., 1876, p. 4804.

1877. ANDERSON, A. [Remarks on exhibition of skins of Podiceps cristatus.] < *P. Z. S.*, Dec. 4, 1877, p. 807.

1877. COUES, E. Note on [the occurrence in the United States of] Podiceps dominicus. < *Bull. Nutt. Ornith. Club*, ii, No. 1, Jan., 1877, p. 26.

1878. MERRIAM, C. H. Correction. < *Bull. Nutt. Ornith. Club*, iii, No. 1, Jan., 1878, p. 47.

　　　Of his *Review of Connecticut Birds*, where *Podiceps cristatus* should read *P. griseigena* var. *holbölli*.

Alcidæ.

1767. GUNNERUS, J. E.   Vom Langviren und Martens Lumba [Uria troile].   <Dron-
   theim Gesellsch. Schriften, iii, 1767, pp. 114–120.
   Nicht mir selbst zugänglich—Titel aus Carus und Engelmann.

1781. ÖDMANN, S.   Uria grylle, Gryssla, beskrifven.   < Kongl. Vetensk.-Acad. Nya
   Handl., ii, 1781, pp. 225–235.
   Cf. v. Friesen, Öfv. Sver. Orn. Litt., 1860, p. 43.

1781. WILCKE, J. C.   Betänkande om flera upgifna sått at hålla månniskor flytande
   uti vattnet, och at således förekomma deras drunknande.   <Kongl. Vetensk.-
   Acad. Nya Handl., ii, 1781, pp. 319–328.
   Om Uria grylle, p. 325.

1788. ÖDMANN, S.   Tordmulens (Alcæ Tordæ Linn.) Hushållning, jämte några Anmärkningar öfver Alkslågtet i allmänhet.   < Kongl. Vetensk.-Acad. Nyt Handl.,
   ix, 1788, pp. 205–218.
   Slågtets Kånnetecken—Arternas Skiljetecken—Boställe—Ägg låggning och Kläckning—
   Flyttning—Föda—Fangst—Nytta—Tordmulens Synonyma och Historia.

1789. WALLBAUM, J. J.   Beschreibung des Scheerschnabels [Alca torda].   <Schriften
   Berlin. Gesell. Naturf. Freunde, ix, 1789, pp. 75–87.

1801. LEPECHIN, J.   Alca camtschatica proposita.   < Nova Acta Acad. Scient. Imp.
   Petrop. for 1798, xii, 1801. pp. 369–371.

1819. LEACH, W. E.   Descriptions Des nouvelles espèces d'Animaux découvertes par
   le vaisseau Isabelle dans un voyage au pôle boréal.   < Journ. de Phys. Chim.
   et Hist. Nat., lxxxviii, 1819, pp. 462–467.
   Pour les oiseaux, seulement la description d'Uria francsii, p. 463.   (Voir Linn. Trans.,
   xii, 1818, p. 588.)

1821. NAUMANN, J. F.   Ornithologische Neuigkeiten.   < Oken's Isis, Jahrg. v, 1821,
   pp. 779–787, pl. 7.
   This vaguely-titled article consists chiefly of a monographic sketch of the genus Mormon,
   four species of which are treated. Here occurs the original description of M. corniculata,
   sp. n., p. 782, pl. 7, figg. 3, 4. Bills of other species are figured on the same plate.
   Also, Sylvia cariceti, sp. n., p. 785.

1824. EDMONSTON, L.   Observations on the Lesser Guillemot and Black-billed Auk,
   the Columbus Minor and the Alca Pica of Linnæus.   < Mem. Wernerian Nat.
   Hist. Soc., v, pt. i, 1824, pp. 8–25.
   Read Apr., 1823. A critical and descriptive article (though longer than necessary) to show
   that the two supposed species are not separable from, respectively, Columbus [i. e., Uria]
   troille and Alca torda.

1824. FABER, F.   Beyträge zur arctischen Zoologie.   < Oken's Isis, Jahrg. viii, 1824,
   pp. 967–982.
   Dritte Lieferung (1te Lief., cf. Isis, 1824, p. 779). Ueber die drey Arctischen Lummen,
   welche unter Uria troile auctorum sind inbegriffen gewesen.   Uria brünnichii, p. 972; U.
   troile, p. 976; U. ringvia, p. 978; U. grylle, U. mandtii, p. 980; U. alle, U. unicolor (n. s.), p. 981.

1826. LESS[ON, R. P.]   Observations sur le Columbus minor et sur l'Alca Pica de
   Linnæus ; par M. Edmonston. . . .   <Féruss. Bull., 2e sect., vii, 1826, pp.
   376, 377.
   Trans. Wernerian Soc., v, pt. i, 1824, pp. 8–25.

1827. FABER, F.   Beyträge zur arctischen Zoologie.   <Oken's Isis, Bd. xx, 1827, pp.
   633–685.
   Achte Lieferung.—Ueber die isländischen Schwimmvögel mit dreyzehigen Steissfüssen.
   Uria grylle, p. 635; U. alle, p. 647; Mormon fratercula, p. 658; Alca torda, p. 669; A. impennis,
   p. 678 (Critik—Geschichte).—Seereise nach dem Vogelscheeren, pp. 685–688.

1829. LEES, E.   Puffins [Fratercula arctica, in Worcester].   < Loudon's Mag. Nat.
   Hist., i, 1829, p. 394.

1833. MICHAHELLES, *Dr.* Zur Geschichte der Alca impennis. < *Oken's Isis*, Jahrg. 1833, pp. 648–651.

1835. MORRIS, F. O. The Guillemot's [Uria troile] Habits. < *Loudon's Mag. Nat. Hist.*, viii, 1835, p. 617.

1835. WATERTON, C. Notes of a Visit to the Haunts of the Guillemot [Uria troile], and Facts on its Habits. < *Loudon's Mag. Nat. Hist.*, viii, 1835, pp. 162–165.

1837. BLYTH, E. [On the Osteology of the Great Auk (Alca impennis) in comparison with that of Sphenisci.] < *P. Z. S.*, v, 1837, pp. 122, 123.

1837. BRANDT, J. F. Rapport sur une monographie de la famille des Alcadées. < *St.-Pétersb. Acad. Sci. Bull.*, ii, 1837, col. 344–349.
    Pas vu moi-même—le titre tiré du *Cat. de la Soc. Roy. Londres*.

1837. BRANDT, J. F. [Ueberbleck von einer Monographie, welche er über die Alcaden bearbeitet.] < *Oken's Isis*, Bd. xxx, 1837, pp. 937–940.
    Aus *Bull. Sci. Acad. St.-Pétersb.*, i, 1837, Nr. 24.

1837. MOORE, E. Change of Plumage in the Guillemot [Uria troile]. < *Charlesw. Mag. Nat. Hist.*, i, 1837, pp. 607, 608.

1838? ————. Gejrfuglen [Alca impennis] ved Jydland? < *Krøyer's Naturh. Tidsk.*, ii, 1838?, p. 207.

1838. BURNELL, E. H. [Occurrence of Mergulus alle at Witham, England.] < *Charlesw. Mag. Nat. Hist.*, ii, 1838, p. 53.

1839. REINHARDT, J. Gejerfuglens [Alca impennis] Forekomst paa Island. < *Krøyer's Naturh. Tidsk.*, ii, 1839, pp. 533–535.

1841. BLYTH, [E.] [Zeigt einen Theil vom Skelett der Alca impennis und zeigt der Unterschiede mit Aptenodytes.] < *Oken's Isis*, Bd. xxxiv, 1841, pp. 939, 940.
    Aus d. *P. Z. S.*, Nov. 14, 1837, pp. 122, 123.

1841. REINHARDT, J. Ueber das Vorkommen des grossen Alks (Alca impennis) auf Island. < *Oken's Isis*, Bd. xxxiv, 1841, pp. 421, 422.
    Aus *Krøyer's Naturh. Tidsk.*, Bd. ii, Heft 5, pp. 533–535.

1841. TOWNSEND, C. T. Little Auk [Mergulus alle, in Suffolk]. < *Ann. Mag. Nat. Hist.*, viii, 1841, p. 317.

1842. STRICKLAND, H. E. Little Auk [Mergulus alle, in England]. < *Ann. Mag. Nat. Hist.*, viii, 1842, pp. 394, 395.

1846. HUNTER, C. B. Occurrence of the Little Auk [Mergulus alle] near Downham, in Norfolk. < *Zoologist*, iv, 1846, p. 1502.

1847. ANON. Occurrence of the Little Auk [Mergulus alle] in the Moray Firth. < *Zoologist*, v, 1847, p. 1642.
    From the "Inverness Courier," Dec. 16, 1846.

1847. ANON. Occurrence of the Little Auk [Mergulus alle] near Durham. < *Zoologist*, v, 1847, p. 1642.
    From the "Newcastle Journal," Dec. 5, 1846.

1847. FITCH, S. E. Occurrence of the Little Auk [Mergulus alle] near Cromer. < *Zoologist*, v, 1847, p. 1642.

1847. GOATLEY, T. Occurrence of the Little Auk [Mergulus alle] near Chipping Norton. < *Zoologist*, v, 1847, p. 1701.

1847. HUNTER, C. B. Occurrence of the Little Auk [Mergulus alle] near Downham. < *Zoologist*, v, 1847, p. 1642.

1848. FISHER, W. R. Egg of the Ringed Guillemot (Uria lacrymans). < *Zoologist*, vi, 1848, pp. 2148, 2149.

1848. HARTLAUB, G. Ueber Uria dubia Pall. < *Zeitung Zool. Zoot. Palæoz.*, No. 20, 1848, p. 160.
    Not seen—title from Giebel.

1850. BOND, F.   Occurrence of the Little Auk (Alca [Mergulus] Alle) at Newmarket. < *Zoologist*, viii, 1850, p. 2706.

1850. CROTCH, W. D.   Occurrence of the Little Auk (Alca [Mergulus] Alle) at Weston-super-Mare.   < *Zoologist*, viii, 1850, p. 2653.

1850. CURTLER, M.   Occurrence of the Little Auk [Mergulus alle] near Malvern. < *Zoologist*, viii, 1850, p. 2706.

1850. ELLMAN, J. B.   Occurrence of the Little Auk (Alca [Mergulus] alle) at Crawley, Sussex.   < *Zoologist*, viii, 1850, p. 2970.

1850. GAMBEL, W.   Description of a [lately] new species of Mergulus [cassinii], Ray. from the coast of California.   <*Journ. Acad. Nat. Sci. Phila.*, ii, pt. i, Nov., 1850, art. v, p. 55, pl. vi.

   Originally described in the *Proc. Acad. Phila.*, i, 1845, p. 267. [This is the *Ptycorhamphus aleuticus.*]

1851. AMHERST, F. K.   Description of a Gullemot shot on the Coast of Sligo, Ireland. < *Zoologist*, ix, 1851, p. 3117.

1851. BONAPARTE, C. L.   On the largest known species of Phaleridine Bird [Sagmatorrhina lathami, g. sp. n.].   < *P. Z. S.*, xix, 1851, pp. 201–203, pl. (Aves) xliv.

   The article concludes with a sketch of the division of birds into *Altrices* and *Præcoces.*

1851. THOMPSON, W.   Occurrence of the Puffin (Alca [Fratercula] arctica) in Winter. < *Zoologist*, ix, 1851, p. 3175.

1852. NEWTON, A.   British Species of Guillemot [Uria].   < *Zoologist*, x, 1852, pp. 3425, 3426.

1852. WOLLEY, J.   On the Specific Distinctness of the Ringed Guillemot [Uria lachrymans].   < *Zoologist*, x, 1852, pp. 3477–3479.

1853. BONAPARTE, C. L.   On the largest known species of Phaleridine Bird [Sagmatorrhina lathami].   < *Ann. Mag. Nat. Hist.*, 2d ser., xii, 1853, pp. 278, 279.

   From *P. Z. S.*, July 22, 1851, pp. 201–203.

1853. MORE, A. G.   Occurrence of the Puffin (Fratercula arctica) in Winter off the Isle of Wight.   < *Zoologist*, xi, 1853, p. 3755.

1853. TRISTRAM, H. B.   Occurrence of the Little Auk (Uria [Mergulus] Alle) in the City of Durham.   < *Zoologist*, xi, 1853, p. 3755.

1854. BALL, —.   [Remarks on exhibition of Mergulus alle shot in Ireland, 30 miles from the sea.]   < *Nat. Hist. Rev.*, (*Pr. Soc.*), i, 1854, p. 98.

1854. LLOYD, L.   The Great Auk [Alca impennis] still found in Iceland.   < *Edinb. New Philos. Journ.*, lvi, 1854, pp. 260–262.

   Extract from his "Scandinavian Adventures," ii, p. 495.

1855. BOLD, T. J.   Occurrence of the Little Auk (Alca [Mergulus] alle) in Northumberland.   < *Zoologist*, xiii, 1855, p. 4560.

1856. CARTE, [A.]   Occurrence of the Bridled Guillemot (Uria lachrymans [ringvia]) in Ireland.   < *Nat. Hist. Rev.*, (*Pr. Soc.*), iii, 1856, p. 24.

1856-57. STEENSTRUP, J. [J. S.]   Et Bidrag til Gierfuglens, Alca impennis Lin., Naturhistorie, og særligt til Kundskaben om dens tidligere Udbredningskreds. < *Vidensk. Meddel. Naturhist. Foren. Kjöbenhavn, for aaret* 1855, Nr. 3–7, 1856–57, pp. 33–116, Kartet og Tavlen.

   A. Geirfuglens Ophold ved den vestlige Side af Atlanterhavet: ved de nordlige Dele af Nordamerikas Östkyst. 1. Geirfuglen ved Grönlands Kyster. 2. Geirfuglen i St. Lawrencebugten, ved Newfoundland, o. s. v., pp. 44–71. B. Geirfuglens Forekomst ved Udöerne i den Östlige Del af Atlanterhavet. 1. Geirfuglen ved Islands Kyster. 2. Gierfuglen ved Færöerne. 3. Geirfuglen ved de vestligste Skotske Smaaöer. 4. Geirfuglens Forekomst ved Norges Kyster. C. Summen af de enkelte Undersögelser om Geirfuglens Udbredning, 1) Geirfuglen har aldrig været en egentlig arkisk Fugl, o. s. v., 2)–9). D. Benævnelsen ,, Pengwins " Be-

1856-57. STEENSTRUP, J. [J. S.]—Continued.

> tydning, Oprindelse og Historie. E. Om Geirfuglens Stilling till sine nærmeste Beslægtede. —Oplysning om Kaartet og Tavlen.—Tillægsanmærkning.
>
> *Gyralca,* g. n., p. 114.
>
> This celebrated article is also published separately, 1 vol.; 8vo., Kjöbenhavn, 1857. There are two German versions: one in *Gelehrten Anzeigen der k. Bayerischen Akad.,* 1860, pp. — - —; the other in *Bull. Acad. Imp. Sci. St.-Pétersb.,* vi, 1863, pp. 513-576, reprinted in *Mélanges Biol. Acad. Imp. Sci. St.-Pétersb.,* iv, 4e livr., 1864, pp. 399-490, by K. E. von Baer. There is also a French translation in *Bull. Soc. Ornith. Suisse,* ii, 1e pte., 1868, pp. 5-70. Cf. *Ibis,* 1865, p. 228; 1868, p. 342; *Zool. Rec.,* v, pp. 111, 112.

1857. BRIGGS, J. J.   The Little Auk (Uria [Mergulus] alle).   < *Zoologist,* xv, 1857, p. 5365.

1857. MORRIS, F. O.   On the specific distinction of the Bridled Guillemot (Uria [ring-via] lachrymans, Temminck).   < *Nat. Hist. Rev., (Pr. Soc.),* iv, 1857, pp. 253-256.

1857. RODD, E. H.   Occurrence of the Bridled or Ringed Guillemot [Uria ringvia] near Penzance.   < *Zoologist,* xv, 1857, p. 5596.

1857. STEVENSON, H.   Note on the Little Auk (Uria [Mergulus] alle) appearing on the Norfolk Coast in Summer.   < *Zoologist,* xv, 1857, p. 5758.

1857. STEENSTRUP, J. J. S.   Et Bidrag | til | Geirfuglens Naturhistorie | og særligt til Kundskaben om dens tidligere | Udbredningskreds | af | J. Jap. Sm. Steenstrup. | — | Med Kaart og en Tavle. | — | Kjöbenhavn. | Trykt i Bianca Bogtrykkeri ved F. S. Muhle. | 1857.   1 vol.   8vo.   2 p. ll., pp. 1-84, 1 map, 1 pl.

> Separate, with new title and table of contents, from *Naturh. Foren. Vidensk. Meddelelser for Aaret* 1855, Nos. 3-7, 1856-57, pp. 33-116.
>
> Inhold: Indledning, p. 1.   A. Geirfuglens Ophold ved den vestlige Side af Atlanterhavet o: ved de nordlige Dele af Nordamerikas Östkyst, p. 5.   1. Ved Grönlands Kyster, p. 6.   2. I St. Lawrencebugten, ved Newfoundland o. s. v., p. 12.   B. Geirfuglens Forekomst ved Udöerne i den Östlige Del af Atlanterhavet, p. 39.   1. Ved Islands Kyster, p. 39.   2. Ved Færöerne, p. 51.   3. Ved de vestlige Skotske Smaaöer, p. 54.   4. Ved Norges Kyster. p. 59. C. Summen af de enkelte Undersögelser over Geirfuglens Udbredning, p. 63.   D. Benævnelsen „Pengwins" Betydning, Oprindelse og Historie, p. 66.   E. Om Geirfuglens Stilling til sine nærmeste Beslægtede, p. 76.   Oplysning om Kaartet og Tavlen, p. 82.   Tillægsanmærkning, p. 83.
>
> Pl., ossa *Tetraonis urogalli* L. et *Alcæ impennis* L. varia inter Mytilos, Cardia, Ostreas, ceterasqve reliqvias cœnarum aboriginum Daniæ inventa. (*Oversigt. Kongl. Vidensk. Selsks. Förh.,* 1855.)

1858. MORRIS, F. O.   On the Specific Distinctions of Uria troile and Uria lachrymans [ringvia].   < *Rep. Brit. Assoc. Adv. Sci. for* 1857, 1858, (*Misc. Comm.*), p. 105.

1859? CHARLTON, E.   On the Great Auk [Alca impennis].   < *Trans. Tyneside Nat. Field Club,* iv, 1859 (?), pp. 113 seq.

> Not seen.—Reprinted in *Zoologist,* 1860, pp. 6883-6888.   Contains extracts from Faber's paper, *Isis,* 1827, p. 633.

1860. BRYANT, H.   [Notice of the Breeding of Uria brünnichii, and Uria marmorata on Gannet rock, Gulf of St. Lawrence.]   < *Proc. Bost. Soc. Nat. Hist.,* vii, 1860, p. 349.

> *Uria "marmorata"* should read *U. lachrymans* or *ringvia.*

1860. CHARLTON, E.   On the Great Auk (Alca impennis).   < *Zoologist,* xviii, 1860, pp. 6883-6888.

> Historical notes, reprinted from the *Trans. Tyneside Nat. Hist. Soc.,* iv, 1859? p. 113 *seq.*

1860. DUNN, J.   Occurrence of the Little Auk [Mergulus alle] in Orkney.   < *Zoologist,* xviii, 1860, pp. 6812, 6813.

1860. GLOGER, C. W. L.   Die frühere ausserordentliche Häufigkeit der grossen oder Schwimm-Alke, (Alca impennis L., Mataeoptera impennis Glog.) Nach. S. Nilsson.   < *J. f. O.,* viii, 1860, pp. 60-63.

> *Skand. Fn. Fogl.,* ii, SS. 367-372.

1860. HELLMANN, —. Notizen über Alca impennis und Podiceps rubricollis. < *J. f. O.*, viii, 1860, pp. 206, 207.
> Account of a specimen of *A. impennis.*

1860. M'CLINTOCK, F. J. The Great Auk [Alca impennis]. < *Zoologist,* xviii, 1860, p. 6981.
> Note of its alleged occurrence in South Greenland "some 25 years ago."

1860. PÄSSLER, W. Die Eier der Alca impennis in deutschen Sammlungen. < *J. f. O.*, viii, 1860, pp. 58–60.
> Mechlenburg's in Fleusburg, Schulz's in Neubaldensleben, Huhnel's in Leipzig. Thienemann's, Pässler's—5.

1860. STEENSTRUP, J. J. S. [A German Version of his Memoir on the Great Auk.] < *Gelehrten Anzeigen d. k. Bayer. Akad.*, 1860, pp. ———.
> Not seen. I learn from the *Zool. Rec.* for 1868 that there is such a version, but am unable to give the title.

1861. BRYANT, H. Monograph of the Genus Catarractes, Moehring. < *Proc. Bost. Soc. Nat. Hist.*, viii, 1861, pp. 134–144, woodcc. on p. 135.
> This memoir recognizes four species of the restricted genus "*Catarractes*"—calling them *C. troille* Linn., *C. ringvia* Brünn., *C. lomvia* Linn. (=*arra* Pall.), *C. californicus*, p. 142, sp. n. Cf. *Ibis*, 1862, pp. 185, 186.

1861. NEWTON, A. Abstract of Mr. J. Wolley's Researches in Iceland respecting the Gare-fowl or Great Auk (Alca impennis, Linn.). < *Ibis*, iii, 1861, pp. 374–399.
> Rather a summary of the history of the species in many particulars, with the copious bibliographical and historical references which this scholarly author usually gives.

1862. BELL, T. Occurrence of the Little Auk [Mergulus alle, in England] Inland. < *Zoologist*, xx, 1862, p. 7883.

1862. BOLLE, C. Notiz, Alca impennis betreffend. < *J. f. O.*, x, 1862, pp. 208, 209.

1862. HOMEYER, A. v. Notiz zu Alca impennis. < *J. f. O.*, x, 1862, p. 461.
> Specimen in Mus. Senkenb. Naturf. Gesell. zu Frankfurt a. M.

1862. KING, S. Little Auk [Mergulus alle] at Sudbury. < *Zoologist*, xx, 1862, p. 7848.

1862. NEWMAN, E. Puffins [Fratercula arctica] in Winter. < *Zoologist*, xx, 1862, pp. 8003, 8004, figg. 1, 2.

1862. NEWTON, A. Abstract of Mr. J. Wolley's Researches in Iceland respecting the Gare-fowl or Great Auk [Alca impennis]. < *Zoologist*, xx, 1862, pp. 8108–8130.
> Reprinted from 'Ibis,' Oct., 1861, pp. 374–399, *q. v.*

1862. PREYER, W. Ueber Plautus impennis Brünn. < *J. f. O.*, x, 1862, pp. 110–124, 337–356.
> Systematic position, bibliography and synonymy, geographical distribution, past and present, including much historical matter.

1862. PREYER, W. Ueber | Plautus impennis | (Alca impennis L.) | von | William Preyer. | — | Von der Philosophischen Facultät zu Heidelberg genehmigte | Doctordissertation. | — | Heidelberg, | druck von Adolph Emmerling. | 1862. 1 vol. 8vo. Titel und pp. 42.
> I. Ueber die Stellung des Brillenalks im System, pp. 3–17. II. Geographische Verbreitung, p. 17. III. Geschichte, pp. 18–42.

1862. PREYER, W. Der Brillenalk, (Plautus [Alca] impennis) in Europäischen Sammlungen. < *J. f. O.*, x, 1862, pp. 77–79.
> 19 specimens.

1863. BAER, K. E. v. Über das Aussterben der Thierarten in physiologischer und nicht physiologischer Hinsicht überhaupt u. s. w. < *Bull. Acad. Imp. Sci. St.-Pétersb.*, vi, 1863, pp. 513–576, nebst Karte.
> This article is entirely devoted to *Alca impennis*, and consists chiefly of a German version of Steenstrup's well-known memoir.

1863. BLAKE-KNOX, H. The Normal and Abnormal Puffins [Fratercula arctica]. < *Zoologist*, xxi, 1863, pp. 8331, 8332, fig.

1863. BLAKE-KNOX, H. Postscript to the preceding Paper. < *Zoologist*, xxi, 1863, p. 8332.

1863. DES MURS, O.   Notice sur l'oeuf de l'Alca impennis. < *Rev. et Mag. de Zool.*, xv, 1863, pp. 3–5, pll. 1, 2.

1863. NEWTON, A.   Remarks on the Exhibition of a Natural Mummy of Alca impennis. < *P. Z. S.*, xxxi, 1863, pp. 435–438.
> From the Funk Island, Newfoundland.   The remarks are of an historical character.   The author incidentally mentions that 63 or 64 stuffed skins of the Great Auk are at present known to exist.

1863. GATCOMBE, J.   Razorbills and Guillemots in Devonshire. < *Zoologist*, xxi, 1863, p. 8832.

1864. BAER, K. E. v.   Über das Aussterben der Thierarten in physiologischer und nicht physiologischer Hinsicht überhaupt u. s. w. < *Mélanges Biol. Acad. Imp. Sci. St.-Pétersb.*, iv, 4e livr., 1864, pp. 399–490 (nebst Karte: Ehemalige Verbreitung von Alca impennis).
> Aus dem *Bulletin*, t. vi, 1863, pp. 513–576, *q. v.*

1864. BOULTON, W. W.   The Little Auk [Mergulus alle] near Beverley. < *Zoologist*, xxii, 1864, pp. 8963, 8964.

1864. BOULTON, W. W.   Bridled Guillemot [Uria lachrymans] at Flamborough Head. < *Zoologist*, xxii, 1864, p. 9291.

1864. CHAMPLEY, R.   The Great Auk [Alca impennis]. < *Ann. Mag. Nat. Hist.*, 3d ser., xiv, 1864, pp. 235, 236.
> List of the birds (27), skeletons (7), and eggs (53) extant, with possessors or place of deposit.

1864. DUTTON, J.   Ringed Guillemot [Uria lachrymans] off Eastbourne. < *Zoologist*, xxii, 1864, p. 9122.

1864. DUTTON, J.   Puffin [Fratercula arctica] in Sussex. < *Zoologist*, xxii, 1864, p. 9122.

1864. GRAY, J. E.   Notice of a Skeleton of the Great Auk [Alca impennis] found in Guano near Newfoundland. < *Ann. Mag. Nat. Hist.*, 3d ser., xiv, 1864, p. 319.

1864. HARTING, J. E.   The Bridled Guillemot [Uria lachrymans] at Flamborough Head. < *Zoologist*, xxii, 1864, pp. 9251, 9252.

1864. JENNER, E.   Razorbill [Alca torda] at Lewes. < *Zoologist*, xxii, 1864, p. 8964.

1864. NEWTON, A.   Remarks on the Exhibition of a Natural Mummy of Alca impennis. < *Ann. Mag. Nat. Hist.*, 3d ser., xiv, 1864, pp. 138–141.
> From *P. Z. S.*, Nov. 10, 1863, pp. 435–438, *q. v.*

1864. NEWTON, A.   Remarks on the Exhibition of a Natural Mummy of Alca impennis. < *Zoologist*, xxii, 1864, pp. 9122–9124.
> From *P. Z. S.*, Nov. 10, 1863, pp. 435–438, *q. v.*

1864. NEAVE, E.   Young Puffin [Fratercula arctica] in November. < *Zoologist*, xxii, 1864, pp. 8891, 8892.

1864. PELZELN, A. v.   The Gare-Fowl, or Great Auk (Alca impennis). < *Ann. Mag. Nat. Hist.*, 3d ser., xiv, 1864, p. 393.
> Note of a specimen in the Imperial Museum at Vienna.

1864. SCLATER, P. L.   Note on the Great Auk [Alca impennis]. < *Ann. Mag. Nat. Hist.*, 3d ser., xiv, 1864, p. 320.
> Criticizes the incompleteness of R. Champley's list of specimens.

1864. SMITH, CECIL.   Little Auk [Mergulus alle] in Somersetshire. < *Zoologist*, xxii, 1864, p. 8891.

1864. OWEN, R.   [On the Skeleton of Alca impennis.] < *P. Z. S.*, 1864, p. 258.
> Merely a note announcing his forthcoming memoir.   Cf. *P. Z. S.*, 1863, p. 435.

1865. [ANON.]   Der grosse Alk (Alca impennis), ein ausgestorbener Vögel. < *Aus der Natur*, xxxi, oder n. F., xix, 1865, pp. 81–86, 97–103, 113–117.

1865. [FIELD, E.]   Letter from the Right Rev. The Bishop of Newfoundland, concerning the Mummy of the Great Auk, (Alca impennis,) found on the Funk Islands.   < *Trans. Nova Scotia Inst. Nat. Sci.*, i, pt. iii, 1865, p. 145.

> 3 specimens—one went to Prof. A. Newton, another to Prof. L. Agassiz, the other to J. M. Jones, President of the Institution.

1865. HOMEYER, A. v.   Alca impennis im Breslauer Museum.   <*J. f. O.*, xiii, 1865, pp. 151, 152.

1865. [NEWTON, A.]   [On some remains of Alca impennis.]   < *Ibis*, 2d ser., i, 1865, pp. 116, 117.

1865. NEWTON, A.   The Gare-fowl [Alca impennis] and its Historians.   < *Nat. Hist. Rev.*, Oct., 1865, pp. 467–488.

> A very complete summary of the history of the remarkable bird.

1865. OWEN, R.   Description of the Skeleton of the Great Auk, or Garfowl (Alca impennis, L.).   < *Trans. Zool. Soc. London*, v, pt. iv, 1865 [read 1864], pp. 317–335, pll. li, lii, and a map.

> A full account, with results of comparison with its allies. The specimen was that from Funk Island, mentioned in *P. Z. S.*, 1863, pp. 435–438.

1866. CLOGG, S.   Little Auk [Mergulus alle] at Liskeard.   < *Zoologist*, 2d ser., i, 1866, p. 101.

1866. COLLETT, R.   Briefliches über Alca impennis in Norwegen.   <*J. f. O.*, xiv, 1866, pp. 70, 71.

> Ein schönes Ex. von Island, in der Samml. des Herrn Nicolai Aall, Besitzer der Eisenwerke bei Twedestrand.—Ref. Rasch, *Nyt Magazin for Naturvid.*, i, 1838, p. 386; Sommerfelt, *Sv. Vet.-Akad. Förh.*, 1862.

1866. MATHEW, M. A.   The Great Auk [Alca impennis] on Lundy Island.   < *Zoologist*, 2d ser., i, 1866, pp. 100, 101.

> Strong presumptive evidence that it was alive there within 30 years.

1866. [NEWTON, A.]   [On several old or little known works which mention Alca impennis, and on the discovery of a nearly complete skeleton of that bird in the Museum of the Royal College of Surgeons, supposed to have belonged to John Hunter.]   < *Ibis*, 2d ser., ii, 1866, pp. 223, 224.

1866. NEWTON, A.   Auszug aus Herrn J. Wolley's Untersuchungen in Island betreffend den Geier-Vogel oder grossen Alk (Alca impennis L). Uebersetzt aus ,, The Ibis ''   October 1861.   < *J. f. O.*, xiv, 1866, pp. 310–338.

1866. [NEWTON, A.]   Der Geiervogel [Alca impennis] and seine Geschichtsschreiber. (Uebersetzt aus der ,, Natural History Review,'' Oct. 1865.)   < *J. f. O.*, xiv, 1866, pp. 394–419.

1867. BOARDMAN, G. A.   On the Plumage of the Black Guillemot [Uria grylle].   < *Am. Nat.*, i, 1867, p. 53.

> Asks for information on the changes of plumage, noting that the species is found in Maine in full black feather all winter.

1867. DUTTON, J.   Guillemot and Razorbill near Eastbourne.   < *Zoologist*, 2d ser., ii, 1867, pp. 759, 760.

1867. GUNN, T. E.   The Black Guillemot [Uria grylle], an Addition to the List of Norfolk Birds.   < *Zoologist*, 2d ser., ii, 1867, p. 710.

1867. GUNN, T. E.   Puffins [Fratercula arctica] on the Norfolk Coast.   < *Zoologist*, 2d ser., ii, 1867, p. 878.

1867. GUNN, T. E.   Puffin [Fratercula arctica] on the Norfolk coast.   < *Zoologist*, 2d ser., ii, 1867, p. 951.

1867. STUBBS, C. E.   Little Auk [Mergulus alle], &c., at Henley-on-Thames.   < *Zoologist*, 2d ser., ii, 1867, p. 710.

1868. BLAKE-KNOX, H.   Little Auk [Mergulus alle] in Dublin Bay.   < *Zoologist*, 2d ser., iii, 1868, p. 1424.

1868. BLAKE-KNOX, H. Occurrence of the Ringed Guillemot [Uria lachrymans] in three instances off the Dublin Coast. < *Zoologist,* 2d ser., iii, 1868, p. 1461.

1868. COUES, E. A Monograph of the Alcidæ. < *Proc. Acad. Nat. Sci. Phila.,* **xx,** 1868, pp. 2–81, figg. 1–16 (woodcc.).

> I. Review of the literature of the family. II. Of the characters of the family, and its subdivisions. III. Descriptions of genera and species. 2 subfamilies; 13 genera; 33 spp. *Simorhynchus cassini,* p. 45, fig. 10, n. sp.
> Reprinted in *Zoologist,* v, 1870, pp. 2004, *seq.*
> Cf. *Ibis,* 1868, pp. 483–485; *Zool. Rec.,* v, p. 111; *Canad. Nat. and Geol.,* n. s., iv, 1869, p. 101.

1868. COUES, E. A Monograph | of | The Alcidæ. | By | Elliott Coues, A. M., M. D. | (Ass't. Surgeon U. S. Army.) | — | Philadelphia: | Merrihew & Son, Printers, | No. 243 Arch Street, | 1868. | 8vo. pp. 81, figg. 16.

> Fifty copies, separately reprinted from *Proc. Acad. Nat. Sci. Phila.,* Jan., 1868, pp. 2–81, *q. v.*

1868. FATIO, V. Quelques Mots sur les exemplaires de l'Alca impennis, oiseaux et œufs qui se trouvent en Suisse. < *Bull. Soc. Orn. de la Suisse,* tom. ii, 1ᵉ partie, pp. 73–79.

> Three specimens of the skins and two of the eggs are described.

1868. FATIO, V. Liste des divers représentants de l'Alca impennis en Europe oiseaux, squelettes et œufs. < *Bull. Soc. Orn. de la Suisse,* tom. ii, 1ʳᵉ partie, pp. 80–85.

> The author enumerates 51 skins, 6 skeletons, and 60 eggs. Cf. *Zool. Rec.,* v, p. 112.

1868. GURNEY, J. H., JR. The Great Auk [Alca impennis]. < *Zoologist,* 2d ser., iii, 1868, pp. 1442–1453.

> Historical.

1868. KÖNIG–WARTHAUSEN, R. Zur älteren Literatur [über Alca impennis]. < *J. f. O.,* xvi, 1868, pp. 246–258.

1868. NEWMAN, E. [Corrected (Zool. s. s., p. 1354) date of the Extinction of Alca impennis,] The Great Auk. < *Zoologist,* 2d ser., iii, 1868, p. 1483.

1868. OLPH-GALLIARD, L. "Phalaris psittacula trouvé en Suède." < *Revue Zoologique,* 1868, pp. 95, 96.

> Not seen.

1868. STEENSTRUP, J. Matériaux pour servir a l'histoire de l'Alca impennis (Lin.) et recherches sur les pays qu'il habitait < *Bull. de la Soc. Orn. de la Suisse,* ii. pte. i, 1868, pp. 5–32, 32a–h, 33–70, pl.

> This article is a French version of Steenstrup's famous Memoir, which originally appeared in *Vid. Meddel. Naturh. Foren. i. Kjøbenhavn för aaret* 1855, 1856–57, pp. 33–116, *q. v.*
> There is a plate which belongs either to this article, or to V. Fatio's in the same part of the *Bulletin.*
> "The publication of this translation by the Swiss Ornithological Society is greatly to be applauded, for few were able to read the original, published as it was in Danish, though it had already appeared in German, . . ." (*Zool. Rec.*)

1868. WYMAN, J. [Note on Bones of the Great Auk (Alca impennis), found at Goose Island, Casco Bay, Maine.] < *Proc. Boston Soc. Nat. Hist.,* xi, 1868, p. 303.

1869. ANON. The Egg of the Great Auk (Alca impennis). < *Am. Nat.,* iii, 1869, p. 550.

> An anonymous reference to Dr. Baldamus's report of 22 specimens in Europe, with mention of 2 known to the writer in the United States; also, on 3 skins in the United States, 2 skeletons in England and United States, and numerous osseous fragments.

1869. CLARK, J. A. Little Auk [Mergulus alle] at Loughton. < *Zoologist,* 2d ser., iv, 1869, p. 1867.

1869. FEILDEN, H. W. [On certain specimens of Eggs of Alca impennis.] < *Ibis,* 2d ser., v, 1869, pp. 358–360.

1869. GURNEY, J. H., JR. Great Auks [Alca impennis] for Sale. < *Zoologist,* 2d ser., iv, 1869, p. 1603.

1869. GURNEY, J. H., JR. Notes on the Great Auk [Alca impennis]. < *Zoologist,* 2d ser., iv, 1869, pp. 1639–1643.

1869. GURNEY, J. H., JR. Bridled Guillemot [Uria lachrymans] at Bridlington. < *Zoologist,* 2d ser., iv, 1869, p. 1684.

1869. GURNEY, J. H., JR.   The Great Auk [Alca impennis].   < *Zoologist*, 2d ser., iv, 1869, p. 1684.

1869. HUNTER, J.   Little Auk [Mergulus alle] and Common Guillemot [Uria troile] at Faversham Creek.   < *Zoologist*, 2d ser., iv, 1869, p. 1517.

1869. ORTON, J.   The Great Auk [Alca impennis].   < *Am. Nat.*, iii, 1869, pp. 539–542, fig. 83.
> Miscellaneous observations, not entirely correct.

1869. PRESTON, T. A.   Winter Puffin [Fratercula arctica] at Marlborough.   < *Zoolo-gist*, 2d ser., iv, 1869, pp. 1951, 1952.

1869. REINHARDT, J.   [Reprint of the original description of Uria mandti.]   < *Ibis*, 2d ser., v, 1869, pp. 239–241.
> From Mandt's ' Observations,' with comment.

1869. ROWLEY, G. D.   The Skins of Alca impennis.   < *Zoologist*, 2d ser., iv, 1869, p. 1645.

1870. [BAIRD, S. F.]   Specimens extant of the Great Auk [Alca impennis].   < *Harper's New Monthly Mag.*, xli, 1870, p. 308.

1870. BLAKE-KNOX, H.   Puffin [Fratercula arctica] on the Dublin Coast in February.   < *Zoologist*, 2d ser., v, 1870, p. 2107.

1870. BOETTGER, O.   Der nordische Papageitaucher, Mormon arctica L., verirrt in Hessen.   < *Zool. Gart.*, xi, 1870, p. 163.
> Aus d. *Offenbacher Ver. Naturk.*, x, p. 64.

1870? BRANDT, J. F.   Ergänzung und Berichtigungen zur Naturgeschichte der Familie de Alciden.   < *Bull. de l'Acad. Imp. des Sci. St.-Pétersb.*, xiv, (1869–70), 1870 ?, pp. 449–497.
> The actual date of publication is in question: it is ostensibly November, 1869, but I doubt that it really appeared before 1870.
>
> Conspectus familiæ *Alcidarum*, secundum Brandt:—Subfam. I.—*Pterorhines* seu *Alcinæ*. 1, *Alca;* a, *Plautus;* 1, *A.* (*P.*) *impennis;* b, *Utamania;* 2, *A.* (*U.*) *torda*. 2, *Uria;* a, *Lomvia;* 3, *U.* (*L.*) *arra;* 4, *troile:* b, *Grylle;* 5, *U.* (*G.*) *carbo;* 6, *grylle;* 7, *columba*. 3, *Brachyramphus;* 8, *B. marmoratus;* 9, *B. kitlitzii*. 4, *Synthliboramphus;* 10, *S. antiquus;* 11, *S. temminckii;* (App. *hypoleucus, craveri*). 5, *Mergulus;* 12, *M. melanoleucus*.
>
> Subfam. II.—*Gymnorhines* seu *Phalerinæ*. 6, *Ptychoramphus;* 13, *P. aleuticus*. 7, *Simorhynchus;* a, *Tyloramphus;* 14, *S.* (*T.*) *cristatellus;* b, *Phaleris;* 15, *S.* (*P.*) *camtschaticus;* 16, *pusillus; ? cassini*. 8, *Ombria;* 17, *O. psittacula*. 9, *Ceratorhina;* 18, *C. monocerata*. 10, *Lunda;* a, *Ceratoblepharum;* 19, *L.* (*C.*) *arctica;* 20, *corniculata;* b, *Gymnoblepharum;* 21, *L.* (*G.*) *cirrata*.
>
> Anhang: Bemerkungen über die Gattung *Sagmatorrhina* Bp.—Uebersicht der Alciden.— Bemerkungen über die Classificationen, die Entwickelungsstufen und die Verbreitung der Alciden.

1870. BRANDT, J. F.   Ergänzungen und Berichtigungen zur Naturgeschichte der Familie der Alciden.   < *Melanges Biol. Acad. Imp. Sci. St.-Pétersb.*, vii, 2ᵉ livr. 1870. pp. 199–268.
> Aus dem *Bulletin*, xiv, pp. 449–497, separatabdruckt.

1870. CORNISH, T.   Puffins [Fratercula arctica] in Mackerel Nets.   < *Zoologist*, 2d ser., v, 1870, p. 2143.

1870. COUES, E.   The Great Auk [Alca impennis].   < *Am. Nat.*, iv, 1870, p. 57.
> Corrects several misstatements in *Am. Nat.*, iii, 1869, p. 539, *seq.*

1870. COUES, E.   Extracts from a Memoir intituled 'A Monograph of the Alcidæ'.   < *Zoologist*, 2d ser., v, 1870, pp. 2004–2016, 2081–2090, 2124–2132, 2155–2163, 2205–2214, 2245–2253, 2289–2296, 2327–2334, 2369–2378, 2396–2403.
> Nearly a reprint from *Pr. Phila. Acad.*, 1868: bibliographical and synonymatic matter omitted.

1870. FATIO, V.   Supplément à la liste des divers representants de l'Alca impennis en Europe.   < *Bull. Soc. Orn. Suisse*, ii, 1870, pp. 147–157.
> Pas vu moi-même.—Pour la liste, voir *tom. cit.*, 1868, pp. 80–85.

1870. GATCOMBE, J.   Bridled Guillemot [Uria lachrymans] and Little Auk [Mergulus alle, near Plymouth].   < *Zoologist*, 2d ser., v, 1870, p. 2143.

1870. GISSING, T. W. [Egg of Uria arra,] Brunnich's Guillemot. <*Zoologist*, 2d ser., v, 1870, pp. 2261, 2262.

1870. GURNEY, J. H., JR. [The Funk Island Specimen of] The Great Auk [Alca impennis]. < *Zoologist*, 2d ser., v, 1870, p. 1982.

1870. HÜGEL, A. DE. Great Auk's [Alca impennis] Eggs in Edinburgh. < *Zoologist*, 2d ser., v, 1870, p. 1982.
  2 specimens in Mus. Sci. and Art.

1870. JONES, J. M. [Disposition of] The Mummy Specimen of Alca impennis at Halifax, Nova Scotia. < *Zoologist*, 2d ser., v, 1870, p. 1982.

1870. JONES, J. M. The Great Auk [Alca impennis] from Funk Island. < *Zoologist*, 2d ser., v, 1870, pp. 2182, 2183.
  Personal—controversial—but with note on the mode of preservation of the mummy.

1870. NEWTON, A. "The Mummy Specimen of Alca impennis at Halifax, Nova Scotia." < *Zoologist*, 2d ser., v, 1870, p. 2065.

1870. NEWTON, A. On Existing Remains of the Gare-fowl (Alca impennis.) < *Ibis*, 2d ser., vi, 1870, pp. 256–261.
  Supplementary to V. Fatio's list in *Bull. Soc. Orn. Suisse*, ii, pt. i, pp. 80–85, *q. v.* 71 or 72 skins, 9 skeletons, detached bones of 38 or 41 individuals, and 65 eggs.

1871. BLAKE-KNOX, H. Brunnich's Guillemot [Uria arra] on the Dublin Coast. < *Zoologist*, 2d ser., vi, 1871, p. 2609.

1871. GURNEY, J. H., JR. Ringed Guillemot [Uria ringvia] near Flamborough. < *Zoologist*, 2d ser., vi, 1871, p. 2729.

1871. POTTS, T. H. Notes on an Egg of Alca impennis, Linn., in the Collection of the writer. < *Trans. and Proc. N. Z. Inst. for* 1870, iii, 1871, pp. 109, 110.
  Abstract in *Proc.* for same year, separately paged, p. 33, with modified title.

1871. [WHEATLAND, H.] Little Auk [Mergulus alle, occurring in New England]. < *Bull. Essex Inst.*, iii, No. 11, Nov., 1871, pp. 156, 157.

1872. ANON. Mortality amongst Razorbills [Alca torda]. < *Zoologist*, 2d ser., vii, 1872, pp. 3023, 3024.
  From the London 'Field,' Feb. 24.

1872. CUPPAGE, H. C. Mortality amongst Razorbills [Alca torda]. < *Zoologist*, 2d ser., vii, 1872, pp. 3024, 3025.
  From the London 'Field,' Mar. 2

1872. DEANE, R. Great Auk (Alca impennis). < *Am. Nat.*, vi, 1872, pp. 368, 369.
  Specimen found dead near St. Augustin, Labrador, Nov., 1870 (fide A. Lechevallier), ♂; sent to Europe ($200).

1872. DUNNING, J. W. Great Auk [Alca impennis]. < *Zoologist*, 2d ser., vii, 1872, p. 2946.
  Extract from I. I. Hayes's 'Land of Desolation.'

1872. GOODE, G. B. A Sea Bird [Mergulus alle] Inland. < *Am. Nat.*, vi, 1872, p. 49.
  At Middletown, Conn.; editorial note on same species at Middletown, Mass.

1872. GRIMSHAW, C. Mortality amongst Razorbills [Alca torda]. < *Zoologist*, 2d ser., vii, 1872, p. 3025.

1872. GURNEY, J. H., JR. Great Auk [Alca impennis] at Disco. < *Zoologist*, 2d ser., vii, 1872, pp. 3064, 3065.
  Examination of evidence on the question, etc.

1872. HALE, N. F. Mortality amongst Razorbills [Alca torda]. < *Zoologist*, 2d ser., vii, 1872, p. 3024. [Bis.]

1872. LEACH, H. R. Mortality amongst Razorbills [Alca torda]. < *Zoologist*, 2d ser., vii, 1872, p. 3024.

1872. MORCOM, G. F. Great Auk [Alca impennis]. < *Zoologist*, 2d ser., vii, 1872, p. 3338.
  Note on the Labrador specimen, from *Am. Nat.*

1872. "R. F. C." Mortality amongst Razorbills [Alca torda]. < *Zoologist*, 2d ser., vii, 1872, p. 3024.
> From the London 'Field,' Mar. 2.

1872. RICKARDS, M. S. C. Mortality amongst Razorbills [Alca torda]. < *Zoologist*, 2d ser., vii, 1872, p. 3023.

1872. SCLATER, J. Mortality amongst Razorbills [Alca torda]. < *Zoologist*, 2d ser., vii, 1872, p. 3025.

1873. PERKINS, G. H. The Thick-billed Guillemot [Uria arra, in Vermont]. < *Am. Nat.*, vii, 1873, p. 240.

1873. [SALVIN, O.] [Notice of Brandt's Memoir on Alcidæ.] < *Ibis*, 2d ser., iii, 1873, p. 104.

1873. SMITH, CECIL. Guillemot [Uria troile] moulting its Quill-feathers. < *Zoologist*, 2d ser., viii, 1873, pp. 3454, 3455.

1874. ANON. The Great Auk [Alca impennis]. < *Am. Sportsman*, iv, 1874, p. 401, fig. 1.

1874. GURNEY, J. H. Note on the Changes of Plumage in Guillemots [Uria troile] and Razorbills [Alca torda]. < *Zoologist*, 2d ser., ix, 1874, p. 3954.

1874. H[ARVEY], M. The Great Auk [Alca impennis] in New Foundland. < *Forest and Stream*, ii, May 28, 1874, p. 244.

1874. NEWMAN, E. The Guillemots at the Zoological Gardens. < *Zoologist*, 2d ser., ix, 1874, pp. 4119, 4120.

1874. WALLIS, H. M. How the Puffin [Fratercula arctica] ascends to its Nest. < *Zoologist*, 2d ser., ix, 1874, pp. 4118, 4119.

1875. ANON. Relics of the Great Auk [Alca impennis] on Funk Island. < *The London Field*, Mar. 27, Apr. 3, Apr. 10, 1875.
> Not seen: perhaps three separate articles run together.

1875. ANON. The Great Auk [Alca impennis], an Extinct English Bird. < *Rod and Gun*, vi, Sept. 18, 1875, p. 375.
> Reprinted from the "Cornhill Magazine."

1875. BOYES, F. Guillemot [Uria troile] bringing down its Young from the Cliff. < *Zoologist*, 2d ser., x, Feb., 1875, p. 4342.

1875. [ELLIOTT, H. W.] Birds that breed by millions [i. e., Alcidæ of North Pacific]. < *Rod and Gun*, vi, May 1, 1875, p. 66.

1875. GURNEY, J. H. Variety of the Razorbill [Alca torda]. < *Zoologist*, 2d ser., x, Mar., 1875, p. 4382.
> With yellow bill and feet.

1875. GURNEY, J. H., JR. Descent of the young Guillemot [Uria troile] from its Cliff. < *Zoologist*, 2d ser., x, Oct., 1875, p. 4666.

1875. GURNEY, J. H., JR. Young Razorbills [Alca torda] and Guillemots [Uria troile]. < *Zoologist*, 2d ser., x, Nov., 1875, pp. 4697, 4698.

1876. ALLEN, J. A. The Extinction of the Great Auk [Alca impennis] at the Funk Islands. < *Am. Nat.*, x, No. 1, Jan., 1876, p. 48.

1876. GURNEY, J. H., JR. Waterford Great Auk [Alca impennis]. < *Zoologist*, 2d ser., xi, Mar., 1876, pp. 4847, 4848.
> See p. 1449; respecting this specimen further information is here given.

1876. GURNEY, J. H., JR. Attitudes of the Guillemot [Uria troile]. < *Zoologist*, 2d ser., xi, June, 1876, p. 4958.

1876. GURNEY, J. H., JR. Scarcity of the Razorbill [Alca torda]. < *Zoologist*, 2d ser., xi, June, 1876, p. 4959.

1876. GURNEY, J. H., JR. Scarcity of the Razorbill [Alca torda]. < *Zoologist*, 2d ser., xi, Aug., 1876, p. 5048.

1876. GURNEY, J. H., JR. Breast-bones of Guillemots [Uria troile]. < *Zoologist*, 2d ser., xi, Sept., 1876, p. 5086.

1876. HARVEY, M.   The Great Auk [Alca impennis].   < *Forest and Stream*, vi, July 20, 1876, p. 386; 1 fig.

1876. [INGERSOLL, E.]   [Occurrence of Mergulus alle in New England.]   < *Forest and Stream*, vi, Feb. 10, 1876, p. 4.

1876. SCLATER, J.   Scarcity of the Razorbill [Alca torda].   < *Zoologist*, 2d ser., xi, July, 1876, p. 5007

1876. TUCK, J. G.   The Puffin [Fratercula arctica].   < *Zoologist*, 2d ser., xi, June, 1876, p. 4958.

1877. BARROWS, W. B.   Catalogue of the Alcidæ contained in the Museum of the Boston Society of Natural History, with a Review and proposed Classification of the Family.   < *Proc. Bost. Soc. Nat. Hist.*, xix, for Apr. 4, 1877; pub. Oct.-Nov., 1877, pp. 150–165.

The paper treats of 21 spp., being those that the author recognizes as valid, whether specimens of them be in the Museum or not.   These are ranged under the genera *Fratercula, Phaleris, Mergulus, Brachyrhamphus, Uria, Lomvia,* and *Alca;* dispensing with sub-families altogether.

1877. BUREAU, L.   De la Mue du Bec et des Ornements Palpébraux du Macareux arctique, Fratercula arctica (Lin.) Steph. après la saison des amours.   < *Bull. Soc. Zool. de France*, 1877, pp. 1–22, table, pll. iv, v.   (Aussi séparément, in-8°, Paris, 1877, pp. 1–22, table, pll. iv, v.)

I have only seen the separate, which however is identical with the *Bulletin* in which the paper originally appeared.   In 1879 it was combined with a later paper on same subject, the two together being reissued apart from the *Bulletin* under the title of the later paper alone. See 1879, same author.

This is a contribution of great originality, interest, and importance.   It establishes a be-fore unsuspected fact, that *Fratercula arctica* regularly moults portions of the horny sheath of the bill, and also the excrescences upon the eyelids.   The whole process and its results are presented in detail, according to the author's extended and novel researches.   Two horse-shoe-shaped pieces, which are saddled on the bases of the upper mandible, and two other pairs of pieces; together with a similar shoe-shaped piece, and a similar pair of slender pieces, from the under mandible, making in all nine separate portions of the horny covering of the bill, are moulted; as is the excrescence upon each eyelid.   All these deciduous pieces, as well as the permanent portions of the bill, are elaborately described, and the appearance of the bird at different seasons, conformably with these extraordinary circumstances, is also fully presented.   The history of the author's experiences—how he came to make the discovery, and how he established the facts—is an interesting part of the paper.   The conditions of the bill before, during, and after the process are figured in colors in an ingenious manner. The author was, of course, greeted with acclamation; the article was immediately translated, with editorial comment, by E. Coues, for the *Bulletin of the Nuttall Ornithological Club*, iii, Apr., 1878, pp. 87–91; and J. E. Harting gave a synopsis, with one of the plates, in the *Zoologist* of that year.   The latter I have not seen.

M. Bureau's discovery naturally directed attention to the various and curious North Pacific allies of *F. arctica*, raising the expectation, afterward justified, that a similar condition of things would be established among these forms.   The author discreetly forbore to prophecy, but entered upon the now obvious course of inquiry which resulted in 1879 in a second ad-mirable paper on the same subject.

1877. [GRINNELL, G. B.]   The Little Auk [Mergulus alle, in Connecticut].   < *Forest and Stream*, vii, Jan. 25, 1877, p. 388.

1877. NEWTON, A.   [Remarks on Exhibition of a Variety of the Guillemot, Uria troile.]   < *P. Z. S.*, Jan. 2, 1877, p. 2.

With yellow bill and feet, and white claws.   Attention called to similar conditions of *Pica rustica* and of *Colymbus torquatus*.

1877. [SCOTT, W. E. D.]   Little Auk (Mergulus alle [inland]).   < *The Country*, i, Dec. 15, 1877, p. 91.

1878. A[LLEN], J. A.   Barrow's "Catalogue of the Alcidæ."   < *Bull. Nutt. Ornith. Club*, iii, No. 2, Apr., 1878, p. 86.

Review of his paper in *Pr. Bost. Soc.*, xix, 1877, pp. 150–165.

1878. Coues, E. On the Moult of the Bill and Palpebral Ornaments in Fratercula
arctica. < *Bull. Nutt. Ornith. Club*, iii, No. 2, Apr., 1878, pp. 87–91.

An abridged translation, with notes, of L. Bureau's extraordinary paper in *Bull. de la Soc.
Zool. de France*, 1877. 8vo, pp. 1–22, pll. 4, 5. Paris, 1877.

1878. [Sclater, P. L., *and* Salvin, O.] Bureau on the Moulting of portions of the
Puffin's [Fratercula arctica] beak. < *Ibis*, 4th ser., ii, Oct., 1878, p. 475.

Notice of the remarkable paper in *Bull. Soc. Zool. de France*, 1877, pp. 1–22, *q. v.*

1878. [Scott, W. E. D.] [Utamania torda on the Coast of New Jersey, Feb. 7th.]
< *The Country*, i, Mar. 2, 1878, p. 260.

1879. Bureau, L. Recherches sur la Mue du Bec des Oiseaux de la Famille des Mormonidés. < *Bull. Soc. Zool. de France*, 1879, pp. 1–68, table, carte, pll. i–vi.
(Aussi séparément, in–8°, Paris, F. Savy, 1879 ; pp. 1–68, table, carte, pll. i–vi.)

This I have not seen as published in the Bulletin. It was immediately reproduced, combined with the author's paper of 1877 on the same subject. *See next title.*

This paper continues the author's important researches into the moult of the bill in certain *Alcidæ*, and shows that, as was expected, the same conditions obtain among the various
Pacific forms related to *Fratercula arctica*. The happy discovery, so important in itself, was
further the means of settling the status of several vexed species. The following are the main
points of this admirable study :

A family, *Mormonidæ*, is separated from *Alcidæ* to accommodate the genera *Fratercula*,
Lunda, *Ceratorhyncha*, *Ombria*, and *Simorhynchus*, in which there is a moult of portions of
the bill, and a double moult of the plumage. The whole matter of the seasonal changes.
both of the bill and of the plumage, is very elaborately presented.

Fratercula arctica is differentiated into three geographical races, shown by a colored map
to correspond with certain isothermal lines. *F. armoricana* (n. v.), of certain portions of
Europe alone, chiefly south of 60° N. lat. ; *F. islandica* (n. v.), of general dispersion on the
north coast of Europe, in Iceland, Southern Greenland, Labrador, Newfoundland, and Ko-
diak Island in the Pacific ; *F. glacialis*, of Spitzbergen, Northern Greenland, and possibly
Northern Labrador.

The moult of the bill in *Fratercula corniculata* is the same as in *F. arctica*, excepting that
one pair of the deciduous pieces is wanting. The moult of the eyelids is the same.

The moult in *Lunda cirrhata* is the same as in *F. corniculata*, as far as the bill is concerned ;
but there are no excrescences to shed from the eyelids. The *Sagmatorhina lathami* of Bonaparte is the young bird.

Chimerina cornuta (*Ceratorhina monocerata*) moults the horn and a small horny strip
below the nostrils. The *Cerorhina suckleyi* or *Sagmatorhina suckleyi* is the same bird,
young or old, without the horn.

Ombria psittacula sheds a saddle-shaped piece from the base of the upper mandible.

Simorhynchus cristatellus sheds all the red parts of the bill. in four pairs of pieces, three
from the upper mandible. *S. "dubius"* and *S. "tetraculus"* are the same bird, without these
ornaments.

Simorhynchus camtschaticus probably moults one pair of pieces from the upper mandible,
being nearest in respect to *Ombria*. *S. cassini* of Coues is the young bird.

Simorhynchus microceros moults the tubercle on the upper mandible. *S. pusillus* is the
same bird.

The author does not appear to have seen Brandt's latest paper, in which he makes a similar
reduction of the species of this group. It may be added, without detracting in the least from
the merit of M. Bureau's brilliant discovery, that his determinations of species are, without
exception, the same as those given in E. Coues "Key to North American Birds," 1872.
Neither Brandt nor Coues had any idea of the actual state of the case, so far as the moult of
the bill is concerned, but made their determinations of species upon other considerations.

1879. Bureau, L. Recherches | sur la | Mue du Bec des Oiseaux | de la | Famille des
Mormonidés | par | Le Docteur Louis Bureau [etc., 6 lignes] | — | (Extrait
du Bulletin de la Société Zoologique de France, [1877 et] 1879.) | — | Paris |
Librairie F. Savy | 77, Boulevard Saint-Germain, 77 | — | 1879 8vo. Cover-
title, half-title, title, each 1 leaf ; pp. 1–22, 1 folding table, pll. iv, v ; pp. 1–
68, 1 folding table, 1 chart. pll. i–vi.

This brochure consists of two entirely distinct articles, united under the same three titles.
The first article consists of the paper "De la Mue du Bec et des Ornements palpébraux du
Macareux arctique, *Fratercula arctica* (Lin.) Steph. après la saison des amours," pp. 1–22,
table and 2 plates, reproduced from the *Bull. Soc. Zool. de France*, 1877. The second article
is "Recherches sur la Mue du Bec des Oiseaux de la Famille des Mormonidés," pp. 1–68,

1879. BUREAU, L.—Continued.

> table, map and 6 plates, reproduced from the *Bull. Soc. Zool. de France*, 1879.   Each article is separately paged, and the two together are furnished with the cover-title, half-title, **and** regular title above given.   The numbering of the plates is the same as in the *Bulletin*.   For comment on these papers *see* each of them, 1877 and 1879, BUREAU, L.

1879. COUES, E.   Note on Alle nigricans, Link.   < *Bull. Nutt. Ornith. Club*, iv, No. 4, Oct., 1879, p. 244.

> Showing that this term, proposed by Link in 1806, has priority over any of the names usually employed for the Dovekie, *Mergulus alle* of authors.

1879. MAYNARD, C. J.   Wanderings of a Naturalist.   < *Town and Country* (newspaper of Boston), June, 1879.

> Chap. IV.   The Razor-billed Auk, *Alca torda*.   Full biography.

Spheniscidæ.

1769. PENNANT, T. Account of the different Species of the Birds, called Pinguins. < *Philos. Trans. for* 1768, lviii, 1769, pp. 91–99, pl. v.

Patagonian P., p. 91, pl. v, n. sp., not binomially named. The other two species given are the Lesser P. (= *Diomedea demersa* L.) and the Red-footed P. (=*Phaeton demersus* L.)

1774. M[URR], C. G. v. Beschreibung des Patagonischen Pinguins. Aus dem 58. Band der philosophischen Transactionen, vom Jahr 1769. übersezt von C. G. v. M[urr]. < *Der Naturforscher*, i, 1774, pp. 258–261.
Cf. op. cit., xxiii, 1788, p. 127.

1781. FORSTER, J. R. Historia Aptenodytæ, generis Avium orbi australi proprii. < *Comment. Soc. Reg. Sci. Göttingen*, iii, 1781, (*Comm. Phys.*), pp. 121–148, pll.
Seen, but title taken at second hand.

This article stands easily first among the early writings upon the subject, marking a great advance upon previous knowledge of the family, and representing the starting-point of the exact literature of *Spheniscidæ*. Forster throws all the Penguins into one genus, *Aptenodytes*, dividing them into the *Cristatæ*, with one species, *chrysocome*, and the *Alophæ*, with eight species. Of Forster's nine species, six are named for the first time; seven or eight are valid; four are valid and new. The species are: *A. chrysocome*, n. s., p. 135, pl. 1; *A. patchonica*, n. s., p. 137, pl. 2; *A. papua*, Scop., p. 140, pl. 3; *A. antarctica*, n. s., p. 141, pl. 4; *A. magellanicus*, n. s., p. 143. pl. 5; *A. demersus* Linn.; *A. catarractes*, n. s., p. 145 (= *Phaëton demersus* Linn.); *A. torquata*, n. s., p. 146; *A. minor*, n. s., p. 147.

1797. GEOFFROY ST.-HILAIRE, É. Sur les Manchots [Spheniscidæ]. < *Millin, Magas. Encycl.*, iii, vi, 1797, pp. 11, 12. (*Bull. Sc. Soc. Philom.*, i, ii, 1798, p. 81.)
Pas vu moi-même—le titre tiré de Carus et Engelmann.

1825. WEDDELL, —. Ueber die Aptenodytes und Diomedea-Arten Süd-Georgiens. < *Fror. Notizen*, Bd. xii, nr. 255, 1825, pp. 198–200.
Not seen—title from Carus and Engelmann.

1832. EARLE, —. Die Brutplätze des Pinguins. < *Fror. Notizen*, xxxiv, No. 738, 1832, pp. 178–180.
Not seen.

1832. JÄGER, G. Theilung der Luftröhre durch eine Scheidewand bei der Fettgans (Aptenodytes demersa). < *Muller's Arch. Anat. Phys.*, vi, 1832, pp. 48–54.

1833. YARRELL, W. [On the Woolly and Hairy Penguins (Aptenodytes) of Latham.] < *P. Z. S.*, i, 1833, pp. 33, 34.

1833. YARRELL, W. [On the Identity of the Woolly Penguin of Latham with the Aptenodytes patachonica, Gmel.) < *P. Z. S.*, i, 1833, p. 65.

1834. BENNETT, G. [On the Habits of the King Penguin (Aptenodytes patachonica, Gmel.).] < *P. Z. S.*, ii, 1834, p. 34.

1834. BENNETT, G. [On the Habits of the King Penguin (Aptenodytes patachonica).] < *Lond. and Edinb. Philos. Mag.*, v, 1834, p. 231.
From *P. Z. S.*, May 13, 1834.

1834. BENNETT, G. [Sur la manière de vivre du Pingouin royale, Aptenodytes patachonica.] < *L'Institut*, ii, No. 81, 1834, p. 388.
Not seen—title from Carus and Engelmann.

1834. MEYEN, F. J. F. [Spheniscus humboldtii, sp. n.] < *Nova. Acta Acad. Cæs. Leop.-Carol.*, xvi, suppl. i, 1834, p. 110, pl. 21.
This is not properly citable as a separate title, the new Penguin being described in a paper of much wider scope.

1835. BENNETT, [G.] Ueber die Lebensart des Königspinguins (Aptenodytes patachonica). < *Oken's Isis*, Bd. xxviii, 1835, p. 1027.
Auszug aus *P. Z. S.*, ii, 1834, p. 34.

1835. REID, —. [Anatomical Description of the Patagonian Penguin (Aptenodytes patachonica, Forst.).] < *P. Z. S.*, iii, 1835, pp. 132–148.
> Very full, especially on the osteology and myology.

1835. REID, —. [Anatomical Description of the Patagonian Penguin, Aptenodytes patachonica, Forst.] < *Lond. and Edinb. Philos. Mag.*, vii, 1835, pp. 519–534.
> From *P. Z. S.*, Sept. 22, 1835, pp. 132–148.

1835. YARRELL, [W.] [Beschreibt den wolligen und den haarigen Pinguin, Lath. x. p. 392.] < *Oken's Isis*, Bd. xxviii, 1835, p. 523.
> From *P. Z. S.*, 1833, p. 33.

1837. BRANDT, J. F. Note sur une nouvelle espèce du genre Catarhactes [chrysolophus] de Brisson. < *Bull. Acad. Impér. Sci. St.-Pétersb.*, ii, 1837, pp. 314, 315.
> Not seen—title from *Roy. Soc. Cat.*

1838. BRANDT, [J. F.] Note sur une nouvelle espèce du genre Catarhactes [chrysolophus] de Brisson. < *Revue Zoologique*, i, 1838, pp. 114, 115.
> Extraite du *Bull. de l'Acad. impér. de St.-Pétersb.*, 7 Juillet 1837, pp. 314, 315.

1839. COUCH, J. Disposition of the Marsupialia. < *Charlesw. Mag. Nat. Hist.*, iii, 1839, p. 312.
> Extract from Goodridge's "Narrative of a Voyage to the South Seas," etc., Exeter, 1838, p. 45, giving "a plain sailor's" account of the temporary pouch in which the eggs of Penguins are carried; believed to be the earliest intimation recorded of the singular fact.

1840. BRANDT, J. F. Ueber die Flossentaucher (Impennes seu Aptenodytidæ) als Typen einer eigenen Gruppe unter den Schwimmvögeln. < *Mém. de l'Acad. Imp. Sci. St.-Pétersb.*, vi sér., v tome, ii pte., *Sci. Nat.*, iii, 1840, pp. 213–217, pll. xii (figg. 5–7), xiii.
> A subtitle, being the fifth part of the series entitled: „ Beiträge zur Kenntinss der Naturg. Vögel," u. s. w.

1843. GRAY, G. R. Aptenodytes. < *Ann. Mag. Nat. Hist.*, xiii, 1843, p. 315.
> Discrimination of 2 spp. of "King" Penguins, hitherto confounded; one being named *A. pennantii*, the other *A. forsteri*, spp. nn.

1848. OBŒUF, —. Mœurs du pingouin de Patagonie (aptenodytes patagonica) et de deux autres espèces voisines. < *Arch. des Sci. Phys. et Nat. Genève*, vii, 1848, p. 244.
> *Revue Zoologique*, 1847, No. 8.

1855. BREWER, T.·M. [On a Fossil Egg, supposed to be of a Penguin, from the Chincha Islands. < *Proc. Boston Soc. Nat. Hist.*, v, 1855, p. 107.
> Cf. *tom. cit.*, p. 165.

1855. HAYES, A. A. Report on a Specimen of Fossilized Egg, from the Guano Islands, off the coast of Peru. < *Proc. Boston Soc. Nat. Hist.*, v, 1855, pp. 165–167.
> The body is named Oöguanolite. Cf. p. 107, where the egg is supposed to be that of a Penguin.

1856. BONAPARTE, C. L. Conspectus Ptilopterorum Systematicus. < *Compt. Rend. de l'Acad. Sci. Paris*, xlii, 1856, p. 775.
> À la fin des "Tableaux paralléliques des Pelagiens ou Gaviæ" se trouve un *Conspectus Ptilopterorum Systematicus*, dans lequel l'auteur propose le genre *Eudyptula*, et donne les noms de *Aptenodytes rex* et *A. imperator*, "auct.", sans en donner aucune description.

1860. ABBOTT, CHARLES CONRAD. The Penguins [Spheniscidæ] of the Falkland Islands. < *Ibis*, ii, 1860, pp. 336–338.
> Field-notes on four spp.

1860. [SCLATER, P. L.] [Notice of a collection, containing five species of Spheniscidæ, made by Captain Pack at the Falkland Islands.] < *The Ibis*, ii, 1860, p. 432.

1860. GOULD, J. [Exhibition of a series of five Penguins, and descriptions of two new Species.] < *P. Z. S.*, xxviii, 1860, pp. 418, 419.
> *Eudyptes nigrivestis*, p. 418; *E. diadematus*, p. 419.

1861. GOULD, J. [On two new species of Penguins.] < *Ann. Mag. Nat. Hist.*, 3d ser.,
vii, 1861, pp. 217–219.
From *P. Z. S.*, Nov. 27, 1860, pp. 418, 419.

1865. ANON. The Penguin at the Zoological Gardens [of London]. < *The Intellectual Observer*, vii, 1865, p. 321.
Note on habits in captivity.

1865. ANON. Der Pinguin oder die Fettgans. < *Aus der Natur*, xxx, oder n. F., xxi,
1865, pp. 438–442.

1865. OWEN, R. On the Morbid Appearances observed in the Dissection of the Penguin (Aptenodytes forsteri). < *P. Z. S.*, xxxiii, 1865, pp. 438, 439.
The species was afterward determined to be *A. pennanti*, not *A. forsteri*, as at first supposed.

1865. SCLATER, P. L. [Announcement of the arrival of a specimen of the King Penguin (Apterodytes pennanti).] < *P. Z. S.*, xxxiii, 1865, p. 318.

1865. TEGETMEIER, W. B. The King Penguin (Apterodytes Pennantii). < *The Intellectual Observer*, vii, 1865, pp. 403–409, 1 col'd pl., and 1 woodcut.

1867. SCHLEGEL, H. Urinatores < *Mus. Hist. Nat. Pays-Bas*, 9me livr., Avril,1867,
pp. 1–52.
The "Urinatores" of this author consist of the genera *Spheniscus, Alca, Colymbus, Podiceps*, and *Heliornis*, and they are treated in the ninth livraison of the unfinished work above
quoted, along with "Coraces," and the conclusion of "Anseres," occupying pp. 1–52 of the
third of the three paginations of which this livraison consists. (The work is issued in serial
fashion, and, until it is finished, with its parts rearranged, and furnished with title pages, it
cannot easily be cited in any usual bibliographical manner.
The genus *Spheniscus* of this author, *i. e.*, the family *Spheniscidæ*, occupies pp. 1–12 of the
pagination just indicated, and is treated in the well-known manner. The species recognized
and described at greater or less length are twelve in number, namely: *Spheniscus pennantii,
patagonicus, adeliae, papua, antarcticus, chrysocome, chrysolophus, diadematus, catarractes,
antipodes, minor*, and *demersus.*.

1868. ANON. Der Pinguin in Patagonien . . . < *Aus der Natur*, xliv, oder n. F.,
xxxii, 1868, p. 239.

1868. ANON. Pinguine. < *Aus der Natur*, xlvi, oder n. F., xxxiv, 1868, p. 800.
,,Man schätzt die im Jahre 1867 auf den Maluinischen Inseln getödteten Pinguine auf 405,000
Stück."

1869. NEWTON, A. On the Origin of the Name "Penguin." < *Ann. Mag. Nat. Hist.*,
4th ser., iv, 1869, p. 133.
Penguin or Pengwin meaning pen-wing or pin-wing; probably no relation with the Latin
pinguedo or Welsh pen gwyn.

1870. [BAIRD, S. F.] Nesting place of Penguins. < *Harper's New Monthly Mag.*, xli,
1870, p. 152.
A note on the carrying of the egg in the temporary pouch in the belly.

1870. FINSCH, O. Description of a new Species of Penguin [Dasyrhamphus herculis].
< *P. Z. S.*, xxxviii, 1870, p. 322, pl. xxv.

1871. SUNDEVALL, C. J. [Spheniscus mendiculus, sp. n.] < *P. Z. S.*, 1871, p. 129.
This is not properly citable as a separate title, for the description occurs in a paper "On
Birds from the Galapagos Islands," *l. c.*, pp. 126–130; I, however, make the reference.

1872. A[LLEN], J. A. Catalogue of the Penguins in the Museum of the Boston Society
of Natural History. < *Am. Nat.*, vi, 1872, pp. 545, 546.
A review of A. Hyatt's paper, *Proc. Bost. Soc.*, xiv, 1872, pp. 237–251. (Cf. *Am. Nat.*, vi
1872, pp. 472, 473.)

1872. C[OUES], E. The Boston Society's Ornithological Catalogue. < *Am. Nat.*, vi,
1872, pp. 472, 473.
A review of A. Hyatt's paper on the *Spheniscidæ, Proc. Bost. Soc.*, xiv, 1872, pp. 237–251,
(Cf. *Am. Nat.*, vi, 1872, pp. 545, 546.)

1872. COUES, E. Osteological Notes [on Spheniscidæ]. < *Proc. Bost. Soc. Nat. Hist.,* xiv, 1872, pp. 251–253.

A subtitle in conclusion of a preceding article, *i. e., Hyatt's Catalogue of the Ornith. Collection of the Boston Soc. Nat. Hist.,* pp. 237–251. These "notes" consist of a sketch of the leading features of the skeleton.

1872. COUES, E. Material for a Monograph of the Spheniscidæ. < *Proc. Acad. Nat. Sci. Phila.,* xxiv, 1872, pp. 170–212, pll. 4, 5.

Based chiefly on the specimens in the Museums of the Smithsonian Institution and of the Philadelphia Academy, the former being notable as containing T. R. Peale's types, and the latter including the largest collection of Penguins in America.

The copious synonymy gives nearly every name, generic or specific, which had at that time been proposed for this group of birds; and each species recognized by the author is fully described, with much critical matter. The paper is divided into parts, as follows :

I. On the Literature of the Subject, pp. 170–181. This is a list, in chronological order, of the principal writings upon Penguins, sufficiently analyzed to give the gist of each author, especially with reference to the successive establishment of new generic and specific names, and the identification thereof; it takes note not only of special papers on *Spheniscidæ,* but also of those portions of more general works which treat of birds of this family. Those who have occasion to look up the literature of *Spheniscidæ* will find this article in some respects more satisfactory than the present Bibliography.

II. On Certain Points of Cranial Structure bearing upon the Determination of the Genera, pp. 181–189. The author describes the skulls of various species in sufficient detail to show that there are three leading modifications of the cranium, upon which he would recognize three genera, *Aptenodytes, Eudyptes, Spheniscus;* he however retains for certain species a fourth genus, *Pygoscelis.* The wing and leg bones of *Aptenodytes* are also described. This part of the subject is illustrated with the two plates.

III. On the Geographical Distribution of the Family, pp. 189, 190, followed, p. 191, by a Key to the Species.

IV. Determination of the Species, pp. 192–212. The following species are recognized :

1. *Aptenodytes patagonica* Forst. (*forsteri* Gray, *imperator* Bp.).
2. *Aptenodytes longirostris* Scop. (*patachonica* Aliq., *pennantii* Gray, *rex* Bp.).
3. *Pygoscelis tæniata* Peale (*papua* Forst., *wagleri* Scl.).
4. *Pygoscelis adeliæ* H. and J. (*brevirostris* Gray, *longicauda* Peale, *herculis* Finsch).
5. *Pygoscelis antarctica* Forst.
6. *Eudyptes antipodes* H. and J. (*flavilarvata* Peale).   [*fua* Bonn.).
7. *Eudyptes catarrhactes* Forst. (*Phaëton demersus* L., *cristata* Shaw, *saltator* Steph., *gor-*
8. *Eudyptes chrysocome* Fort. (*pachyrhyncha* Gray, *nigrivestis* Gould).
9. *Eudyptes chrysolopha* Brandt.
10. *Eudyptes diadematus* Gould.
11. *Spheniscus minor* Forst. (*undina* Gould).
12. *Spheniscus demersus* Linn., with *S. magellanicus* as a variety
    Spheniscus mendiculus Sund., not treated.

Cf. *Zool. Rec.* for 1872, p. —; *Am. Nat.,* vii, 1872, pp. 38–40.

It may be useful to give here in chronological order a nearly complete **list of the names** which have been proposed for *Spheniscidæ,* beginning with Linnæus :

1766. *Diomedea demersa* Linn., *Syst. Nat.,* i, p. 214.
1766. *Phaëton demersus* Linn., *Syst. Nat.,* i, p. 219.
1777. *Aptenodytes longirostris* Scopoli.
1777. *Aptenodytes papua* Scopoli.
1777. *Aptenodytes platyrhyncha* Scopoli.
1781. *Aptenodytes chrysocome* Forst., *Conm. Reg. Soc. Sci. Gött.,* **iii, p. 135.**
1781. *Aptenodytes patachonica* Forst., *l. c.,* p. 137.
1781. *Aptenodytes antarctica* Forst., *l. c.,* p. 141.
1781. *Aptenodytes magellanicus* Forst., *l. c.,* p. 143.
1781. *Aptenodytes catarractes* Forst., *l. c.,* p. 145.
1781. *Aptenodytes torquata* Forst., *l. c.,* p. 146.
1781. *Aptenodytes minor* Forst., *l. c.,* p. 147.
1782. *Aptenodytes gorfua,* Bonnaterre, *Encyc. Méth.,* i, p. 67.
1788. *Aptenodytes chilensis* Gm., *Syst. Nat.,* i, p. 559.
1788. *Aptenodytes chiloensis* Gm., *Syst. Nat.,* i, p.559.
1790. *Aptenodytes molinæ* Lath., *Ind. Orn.,* p. 881.
17—. *Pinguinaria cristata* Shaw, *Nat. Misc.,* pl. 437.
1800. *Aptenodgtes fuscirostris* Illiger.
1816. *Eudyptes* Vieillot, *Analyse.*
1825. *Chrysocoma saltator* Steph., *Shaw's Gen. Zool.,* xiii, p. 58.

1872. COUES, E.—Continued.

1825. *Spheniscus novæ hollandiæ* Steph., *l. c*, p. 68.
1832. *Pygoscelis* Wagler, *Isis*, p. 183.
1834. *Spheniscus humboldtii* Meyen, *Nov. Act. Acad. Caes. Leop.*, xvi, supp. i, p. 110.
1837. *Catarractes chrysolopha* Brandt, *Bull. Acad. Sc. St. Pétersb.*, ii, p. 324.
1841. *Catarractes adeliæ* Homb. and Jacq., *Ann. Sc. Nat.*, p. 320.
1841. *Catarractes antipodes* Hombr. and Jacq., *l. c.*
1842. *Dypsicles* Gloger, *Handb. Natury.*
184-. *Pygoscelis brevirostris* Gray, *Voy. Ereb. & Terr.*
1841. *Eudyptes pachyrhyncha* Gray, *l. c.*
1844. *Aptenodytes palpebrata* Licht., ed. Forst. *Descr. An.*, p. 356.
1844. *Aptenodytes brasiliensis* Licht., *l. c.*, p. 355.
1844. *Aptenodytes forsteri* Gray, *Ann. Mag. N. H.*, p. 315.
1844. *Aptenodytes pennantii* Gray, *l. c.*
1844. *Aptenodytes undina* Gould, *P. Z. S.*, p. 87.
1846. *Dasyrhamphus*, Hombr. and Jacq.
1848. *Aptenodytes magnirostris* Peale, *U. S. Expl. Exped.*, p. 263.
1848. *Aptenodytes flavilarvata* Peale, *l. c.*, p. 260.
1848. *Aptenodytes longicaudata* Peale, *l. c.*, p. 261.
1848. *Aptenodytes tæniata* Peale, *l. c.*, p. 264.
1856. *Aptenodytes rex* Bp., *Compt. Rend.*, p. 775.
1856. *Aptenodytes imperator* Bp., *Compt. Rend.*, p. 775.
1859. *Palæeudyptes antarcticus* Huxley, *Journ. Geol. Soc.*, xv, p. 672.
1860. *Pygoscelis wagleri* Scl., *P. Z. S.*, p. 392.
1860. *Eudyptes nigrivestis* Gould, *P. Z. S.*, p. 418.
1860. *Eudyptes diademata* Gould, *l. c.*, p. 419.
1870. *Dasyrhamphus herculis* Finsch, *P. Z. S.*, p. 322.
1871. *Spheniscus mendiculus* Sund., *P. Z. S.*, p. 129.
1873. *Spheniscus trifasciatus* Philippi, "*Zeitschr. ges. Naturw.*, xli, 1873, p. 121."
1874. *Eudyptula albosignata* Finsch, *P. Z. S.*, p. 207.
1875. *Eudyptes vittata* Finsch, *Ibis*, p. 112.
1875. *Eudyptes atrata* (Hutton) Finsch, *Ibis*, p. 114.

1872. HECTOR, J. On the Remains of a Gigantic Penguin (Palæeudyptes antarcticus, Huxley) from the Tertiary Rocks on the West Coast of Nelson. < *Trans. and Proc. New Zealand Inst. for* 1871, iv, 1872, pp. 341–346, pll. xvii, xviii.

For a preliminary notice see *op. cit.*, ii, p. 403; paper delayed for the illustrations.

1872. HYATT, A. Catalogue of the Ornithological Collection of the Boston Society of Natural History. [Part I. Spheniscidæ.] < *Proc. Bost. Soc. Nat. Hist.*, xiv, 1872, pp. 237–251.

The author carefully treats of the nine species contained in the Society's Museum, making of the "Catalogue," in fact, a monographic sketch of the group.

1873. A[LLEN], J. A. Monograph of the Spheniscidæ. < *Am. Nat.*, vii, 1872, pp. 38–40.

Review of E. Coues's *Material for a Monograph of the Spheniscidæ, Proc. Acad. Nat. Sci. Phila.*, 1872, pp. 170–212.

1873. HECTOR, J. Further Notice of Bones of a Fossil Penguin (Palæeudyptes antarcticus, Huxley). < *Trans. and Proc. New Zealand Inst. for* 1872, v, 1873, *Proc. Wellington Phil. Soc.*, pp. 438, 439.

Additional specimens; cf. *op. cit.*, iv, 1872, pp. 341–346.

1873. [SALVIN, O.] [Reference to Bonaparte's Conspectus Ptilopterorum Systematicus, Comptes Rendus, 1856, p. 775.] < *Ibis*, 3d ser., iii, 1873, pp. 103, 104.

Where appear the names *Aptenodytes rex* and *A. imperator.*

1874. FINSCH, O. Description of a new Species of Penguin [Eudyptula albosignata] from New Zealand. < *P. Z. S.*, 1874, pp. 207, 208.

1874. HYATT, A. Note on Aptenodytes patagonica Forst. < *Proc. Bost. Soc. Nat. Hist.*, xvii, 1874, p. 94.

Its specific distinctness from *A. pennanti.*

1874. NEWMAN, E. The Penguin at the Zoo[logical Society of London]. < *Zoologist*, 2d ser., ix, 1874, pp. 4262–4264.

Interesting account of actions and appearance in confinement. Cf. *op. cit.*, p. 4848.

1875. FINSCH, O.   On two apparently new Species of Penguins from New Zealand.
    < *Ibis*, 3d ser., v, 1875, pp. 112–114.
      Eudyptes vittata, p. 112: *E. atrata* "Hutton", p. 114.

1876. NEWMAN, E.   The King Penguin at the Zoo[logical Society of London].
    < *Zoologist*, 2d ser., xi, Mar., 1876, p. 4848.
      Obituary. See *op. cit.*, p. 4262.

1877. [BULKLEY, J. M.]   A domesticated Penguin.   < *Forest and Stream*, viii, Apr. 19,
    1877, p. 160.

1878. [SCLATER, P. L.]   [Report on additions to the Society's Menagerie in January,
    1878.]   < *P. Z. S.*, Feb. 5, 1878, p. 116.
      Spheniscus humboldti the only bird.

1879. ANON.   A Group of Penguins.   < *Pacific Rural Press*, xvii, No. 18, May 3, 1879,
    p. 289; cut of 5 figg.
      A slight sketch, "written up" to the cut.

1879. BARTLETT, A. D.   Remarks upon the Habits and Change of Plumage of Hum-
    boldt's Penguin [Spheniscus humboldti].   < *P. Z. S.*, Jan. 14, 1879, pp. 6–9,
    figg. 1, 2.
      An interesting article, from observations upon an individual in captivity.

Tinamidæ.

1832. GEOFFROY ST.-HILAIRE, ISID. Eudromie. Eudromia. Isid. Geoff. <*Guér. Mag. de Zool.*, 2e année, 1832, Classe ii, Ois., Notice i, pl. i.

Eudromia elegans, D'Orb. et Is. Geoff., gen. sp. n.

1836. VIGORS, N. A. [Characters of a new and singular form among the Tinamous (Tinamotis pentlandii, g. sp. n.)] < *P. Z. S.*, iv, 1836, p. 79.

1837. VIGORS, N. A. [Note on Tinamotis pentlandii (from P. Z. S., Sept. 13, 1836.)] < *Lond. and Edinb. Philos. Mag.*, x, 1837, p. 289.

1838. VIGORS, N. A. Ueber einen neuen Vogel [Tinamotis pentlandii] zwischen Tinamu und Trappen, mitgebracht von Pentland von den hohen Anden. < *Oken's Isis*, Bd. xxxi, 1838, p. 195.

Auszug aus P. Z. S., iv, Sept., 1836, p. 79.

1863. NATTERER, J. (*Ed. Pelzeln, A. v.*) Handschriftliche Notizen [über drei Arten der Gattung Tinamus]. < *Verh. (Abh.) k.-k. zool.-bot. Ges. Wien*, xiii, 1863, pp. 1128–1130.

Als Anhang zu Pelzeln's ,,Ueber vier von Natterer in Brasilien gesammelte noch unbeschriebene Vogelarten,'' tom. cit., pp. 1124–1130.

1863. PELZELN, A. v. Ueber vier von Natterer in Brasilien gesammelte noch unbeschriebene Vögelarten. < *Verh. k.-k. zool.-bot. Gesellsch. Wein*, xiii, Oct. 10, 1863, pp. 1125–1130.

Three spp. of Tinamidæ: T. guttatus, p. 1126; T. erythropus, p. 1127; T. brevirostris, p. —.

1867. BARTLETT, A. D. [Remarks on the breeding of Rhynchotis rufescens.] < *P. Z. S.*, xxxv, 1867, p. 687.

1870. NATHUSIUS, W. v. Ueber die Eischalen von Æpyornis, Dinornis, Apteryx und einigen Crypturiden. < *Zeitschr. f. wiss. Zool.*, xxi, 1870, pp. 330–335, pll. xxv, xxvi.

Cf. Ibis, 1871, pp. 454, 455.

1874. ALIX, E. Mémoire sur l'ostéologie et la Myologie du Nothura major. < *Gerv. Journ. de Zool.*, iii, 1874, pp. 167–214, 253–285, pll. viii, xi.

"Ou peut résumer cette comparaison [du Squelette du Nothura avec celui des Vertébrés et des Oiseaux] en disant que les Tinamidés ressemblent davantage aux Struthidés par leur tête, aux Gallinacés par le thorax et les ailes, au Râles par le bassin, et qu'en même temps ils offrent quelques affinités avec les Échassiers pressirostres et longirostres de Cuvier.

"Un examen détaillé des os et des muscles du Nothura major nous amène à conclure que si les Tinamidés ont de grandes ressemblances soit avec les Autruches, soit avec les Gallinacés, on ne peut pourtant pas les confondre avec l'un ou l'autre de ces deux groupes, et qu'ils diffèrent encore plus des Rallidés, des Échassiers pressirostres, longirostres et des Palmipèdes, auxquels ils ne se rattachent que par des traits isolés. Nous sommes ainsi conduits, tout en tenant compté de ces affinités, a partager l'opinion de Lherminier, qui faisait de ces Oiseaux un groupe séparé."

1876. ALIX, E. Sur la Myologie du Rhynchotus rufescens. < *Gerv. Journ. de Zool.*, v, 1876, pp. 411, 412.

Vérification que les particularités que l'auteur signale dans les muscles du Nothura (op. cit., iii, pp. 167, 252, 1872) se retrouvent chez les autres Tinamidés.

Rheidæ.

1808. HAMMER, F. L. Observations Sur le Touyou ou Autruche d'Amérique (Struthio [Rhea] americanus. Lin.), faites à Strasbourg en janvier 1806. < *Ann. du Mus. d'Hist. Nat.*, xii, 1808, pp. 427–433, pl. 39.
Avec des observations sur ce que les naturalistes en ont dit.

1834. MARTIN, W. [Notes on Anatomy of the Rhea (R. americana, Vieill.) and Cassowary (Casuarius emeu, Lath.).] < *P. Z. S.*, ii, 1834, p. 9.

1837. DARWIN, C. [On the Habits of the American Ostriches (Rhea darwinii).] < *P. Z. S.*, v, 1837, pp. 35, 36.

1837. GOULD, J. [On a New Rhea (darwinii) from Mr. Darwin's Collection.] < *P. Z. S.*, v, 1837, p. 35.

1837. [EDITORIAL.] Notice respecting [D'Orbigny's claim of his prior name, R. pennata, for the] Rhea darwini Gould. < *Charlesw. Mag. Nat. Hist.*, i, 1837, p. 504.

1838. [EDITORIAL.] Rheà. < *Mag. of Zool. and Bot.*, ii, 1838, pp. 92, 93.
Merely a note on the existence of a second species, discovered by Darwin.

1839. GOULD, J. Eine neue Rhea [darwini] aus Patagonien von Darwin. < *Oken's Isis*, Bd. xxxii, 1839, p. 144.
P. Z. S., Marz 14, 1837, p. 35.

1841. HERON, R. [On the Breeding of Rhea americana in Confinement.] < *P. Z. S.*, ix, 1841, pp. 79, 80.

1842. DERBY, *The Earl of.* [Letter relating to the Hatching of Rhea americana in Confinement, &c.] < *P. Z. S.*, x, 1842, p. 147.

1842. HERON, R. [On the breeding of Rhea americana in Confinement.] < *Ann. Mag. Nat. Hist.*, ix, 1842, pp. 344, 345.
From *P. Z. S.*, Oct. 12, 1841, pp. 79, 80.

1856. GOSSE, L. A. Questionnaire relatif a l'autruche et au Nandou, ou autruche d'Amérique [Rhea americana]. < *Bull. Soc. d'Acclim.*, iii, 1856, pp. 290–297.

1857. WYMAN, J. [Remarks on exhibition of a skeleton of a young South American Ostrich (Rhea americana).] < *Proc. Boston Soc. Nat. Hist.*, vi, 1857, p. 127.

1858. VAVASSEUR, —. Note sur le Nandou ou Autruche d'Amérique [Rhea americana] et sur les moyens de l'amener a l'état de domesticité et de l'acclimater en France. < *Bull. Soc. Acclim.*, v, 1858, pp. 388–394.

1860. DE MOUSSY, M. Domestication du Nandou ou Autruche d'Amérique [Rhea americana]. < *Bull. Soc. Acclim.*, vii, 1860, pp. 182–186.

1860. SCLATER, P. L. On the Rheas in the Society's Menagerie, with Remarks on the known species of Struthious Birds. < *P. Z. S.*, Apr. 24, 1860, pp. 207–211, figg. 1–3.
Rhea macrorhyncha, sp. n., p. 207, fig. 1; *R. americana*, fig. 2; *R. darwini*, fig. 3. The remarks relate also to *Struthio*, 1 sp.; *Casuarius*, 5 spp.; *C. bicarunculatus*, sp. n., p. 211; and *Dromæus irroratus.* The living species of Struthious birds are supposed to be not fewer than 14 or 15 in number.

1860. SCLATER, P. L. On the Rheas in the Society's Menagerie, with Remarks on the known species of Struthious Birds. < *Ann. Mag. Nat. Hist.*, 3d ser., vi, 1860, pp. 142–146, figg. 3.
From *P. Z. S.*, Apr. 24, 1860, pp. 207–211, q. v.

1862. SCLATER, P. L. Remarks on the late Increase of our Knowledge of the Struthious Birds. < *Rep. Brit. Assoc. Adv. Sci. for* 1861, 1862, (*Misc. Comm.*), pp. 158, 159.
Concluding with a "Tabula Avium Struthionum," in which 16 spp. are enumerated.

Bull. v, 4——35

1863. BÖCKING, A.   Monographie des Nandu oder südamerikanischen Strausses [Rhea americana].   < *Troschel's Arch.*, 1863, pp. 212--—.
Mir noch nicht selbst zur Ansicht.

1863. BÖCKING, A.   De | Rhea Americana. |— | Dissertatio zoologica | qvam | svmmorvm in philosophia honorvm | avctoritate amplissimi | philosophorvm ordinis | in Vniversitate Fridericia Gvelelmia Rhenana | rite obtinendorvm cavsa | vna cvm sentensiis controversis | die XIV. Mensis Febrvarii anni MDCCCLXIII | pvblice defendet | Adolphvs Böcking | Rhenanvs. |— | . . . | Bonnae | typis Caroli Georgi. 1 vol. 8vo. 3 p. ll., pp. 32.
De quo libello scripsit Hartlaubius (Bericht, 1863, p. 29): ,,Wichtiger Beitrag zu unserer Kenntniss des Amerikanischen Strausses. Der Verfasser lebte längere Zeit in den La Plata Provinzen und scheint Lebensweise, Fortpflanzung, Verbreitung, Zähmung gut beobachtet zu haben. *Rhea Darwini* wird sehr irrthümlich als Lokalrasse von *Rh. americana* behandelt.''

1863. LEADBEATER, B.   [Exhibition of specimens of eggs of a species of Rhea.]   < *P. Z. S.*, xxxi, 1863, p. 1.

1865. CRISP, E.   On the Anatomy of the Struthionidæ, Ostriches, Rheas, and Casuaries.   < *Rep. Brit. Assoc. Adv. Sci. for* 1864, 1865, (*Misc. Comm.*), pp. 92, 93.
Relating to the important differences in the visceral anatomy of these birds *inter se*.   A note by E. Bartlett, on the characters of the eggs of *Struthionidæ*. An *Apteryx* weighing 60 ounces laid a 14-ounce egg, relatively the largest known in ornithology.

1865. SCHMIDT, MAX.   [Einen Weiblichen amerikanischen Strauss (Rhea americana).]   < *Zool. Gart.*, vi, 1865, p. 308.

1866. FITZINGER, L. J.   Ueber den plötzlich eingetretenen Tod einer südamerikanischen Rhea (Rhea Americana) und die in desselben vorgefundenen Helminthen.   < *Zool. Gart.*, vii, 1866, pp. 131–133.

1866. SCHMIDT, MAX.   Beobachtungen über den amerikanischen Strauss. (Rhea americana [in Gefangenschaft].)   < *Zool. Gart.*, vii, 1866, pp. 8–14.

1868. HAUGHTON, S.   Muscular Anatomy of the Rhea (Struthio rhea).   < *Proc. Roy. Irish Acad.*, ix, 1868, pp. 497–504.
Not seen.

1868. ANON.   Der südamerikanische Strauss [Rhea americana].   < *Aus der Natur*, xliv, oder n. F., xxxii, 1868, pp. 300–303, 315–318, 329–333.

1870. S[ENONER], A.   [Ueber Rhea americana.]   < *Zool. Gart.*, xi, 1870, pp. 34, 35.

1871. CUNNINGHAM, R. O.   Notes on some points in the Osteology of Rhea americana and Rhea darwinii.   < *P. Z. S.*, xxxix, 1871, pp. 105–110, pll. vi, viᵃ.

1874. ANON.   Der südamerikanische Strauss [Rhea americana].   < *Aus der Natur*, lxiv, oder n. F., lii, 1874, pp. 258, 259.

1877. [SCLATER, P. L.]   [On the addition of Rhea macrorhyncha? to the Society's Menagerie.]   < *P. Z. S.*, Mar. 6, 1877, p. 160.
Note of possible occurrence of a *Rhea* in Surinam: Cf. *Stedman's Narrative of an Expedition to Surinam*, London; 1806.

1878. DAVIS, F. J.   The Nandou, or South American Ostrich (Rhea americana).   < *The Oölogist*, iv, No. 1, Mar., 1878, pp. 5, 6.

1879. BEERBOHM, J.   Ostrich [Rhea americana] Hunting.   < *Chicago Field*, xi, No. 6, Mar. 22, 1879, p. 92.
From Beerbohm's *Wanderings in Patagonia*.

1879. BEERBOHM, J.   Leisure Hour Series.—No. 104 |— | Wanderings in Patagonia | or | Life among the Ostrich-hunters | by | Julius Beerbohm | [Trade-mark] | New York | Henry Holt and Company | 1879 1 vol. 16mo. frontisp., title, map, and pp. 1–294.

Note.—Index to Bibliography is unavoidably deferred.—Ed.

NATURAL SCIENCES IN AMERICA

An Arno Press Collection

Allen, J[oel] A[saph]. **The American Bisons,** Living and Extinct. 1876

Allen, Joel Asaph. **History of the North American Pinnipeds:** A Monograph of the Walruses, Sea-Lions, Sea-Bears and Seals of North America. 1880

American Natural History Studies: The Bairdian Period. 1974

American Ornithological Bibliography. 1974

Anker, Jean. **Bird Books and Bird Art.** 1938.

Audubon, John James and John Bachman. **The Quadrupeds of North America.** Three vols. 1854

Baird, Spencer F[ullerton]. **Mammals of North America.** 1859

Baird, S[pencer] F[ullerton], T[homas] M. Brewer and R[obert] Ridgway. **A History of North American Birds:** Land Birds. Three vols., 1874

Baird, Spencer F[ullerton], John Cassin and George N. Lawrence. **The Birds of North America.** 1860. Two vols. in one.

Baird, S[pencer] F[ullerton], T[homas] M. Brewer, and R[obert] Ridgway. **The Water Birds of North America.** 1884. Two vols. in one.

Barton, Benjamin Smith. **Notes on the Animals of North America.** Edited, with an Introduction by Keir B. Sterling. 1792

Bendire, Charles [Emil]. **Life Histories of North American Birds** With Special Reference to Their Breeding Habits and Eggs. 1892/1895. Two vols. in one.

Bonaparte, Charles Lucian [Jules Laurent]. **American Ornithology:** Or The Natural History of Birds Inhabiting the United States, Not Given by Wilson. 1825/1828/1833. Four vols. in one.

Cameron, Jenks. **The Bureau of Biological Survey:** Its History, Activities, and Organization. 1929

Caton, John Dean. **The Antelope and Deer of America:** A Comprehensive Scientific Treatise Upon the Natural History, Including the Characteristics, Habits, Affinities, and Capacity for Domestication of the Antilocapra and Cervidae of North America. 1877

Contributions to American Systematics. 1974

Contributions to the Bibliographical Literature of American Mammals. 1974

Contributions to the History of American Natural History. 1974

Contributions to the History of American Ornithology. 1974

Cooper, J[ames] G[raham]. **Ornithology.** Volume I, Land Birds. 1870

Cope, E[dward] D[rinker]. **The Origin of the Fittest:** Essays on Evolution and **The Primary Factors of Organic Evolution.** 1887/1896. Two vols. in one.

Coues, Elliott. **Birds of the Colorado Valley.** 1878

Coues, Elliott. **Birds of the Northwest.** 1874

Coues, Elliott. **Key To North American Birds.** Two vols. 1903

Early Nineteenth-Century Studies and Surveys. 1974

Emmons, Ebenezer. **American Geology:** Containing a Statement of the Principles of the Science. 1855. Two vols. in one.

Fauna Americana. 1825-1826

Fisher, A[lbert] K[enrick]. **The Hawks and Owls of the United States in Their Relation to Agriculture.** 1893

Godman, John D. **American Natural History:** Part I — Mastology and **Rambles of a Naturalist.** 1826-28/1833. Three vols. in one.

Gregory, William King. **Evolution Emerging:** A Survey of Changing Patterns from Primeval Life to Man. Two vols. 1951

Hay, Oliver Perry. **Bibliography and Catalogue of the Fossil Vertebrata of North America.** 1902

Heilprin, Angelo. **The Geographical and Geological Distribution of Animals.** 1887

Hitchcock, Edward. **A Report on the Sandstone of the Connecticut Valley,** Especially Its Fossil Footmarks. 1858

Hubbs, Carl L., editor. **Zoogeography.** 1958

[Kessel, Edward L., editor]. **A Century of Progress in the Natural Sciences:** 1853-1953. 1955

Leidy, Joseph. **The Extinct Mammalian Fauna of Dakota and Nebraska,** Including an Account of Some Allied Forms from Other Localities, Together with a Synopsis of the Mammalian Remains of North America. 1869

Lyon, Marcus Ward, Jr. **Mammals of Indiana.** 1936

Matthew, W[illiam] D[iller]. **Climate and Evolution.** 1915

Mayr, Ernst, editor. **The Species Problem.** 1957

Mearns, Edgar Alexander. **Mammals of the Mexican Boundary of the United States.** Part I: Families Didelphiidae to Muridae. 1907

Merriam, Clinton Hart. **The Mammals of the Adirondack Region,** Northeastern New York. 1884

Nuttall, Thomas. **A Manual of the Ornithology of the United States and of Canada.** Two vols. 1832-1834

Nuttall Ornithological Club. **Bulletin of the Nuttall Ornithological Club:** A Quarterly Journal of Ornithology. 1876-1883. Eight vols. in three.

[Pennant, Thomas]. **Arctic Zoology.** 1784-1787. Two vols. in one.

Richardson, John. **Fauna Boreali-Americana;** Or the Zoology of the Northern Parts of British America, Containing Descriptions of the Objects of Natural History Collected on the Late Northern Land Expeditions Under Command of Captain Sir John Franklin, R. N. Part I: Quadrupeds. 1829

Richardson, John and William Swainson. **Fauna Boreali-Americana:** Or the Zoology of the Northern Parts of British America, Containing Descriptions of the Objects of Natural History Collected by the Late Northern Land Expeditions Under Command of Captain Sir John Franklin, R. N. Part II: The Birds. 1831

Ridgway, Robert. **Ornithology.** 1877

Selected Works By Eighteenth-Century Naturalists and Travellers. 1974

Selected Works in Nineteenth-Century North American Paleontology. 1974

Selected Works of Clinton Hart Merriam. 1974

Selected Works of Joel Asaph Allen. 1974

Selections From the Literature of American Biogeography. 1974

Seton, Ernest Thompson. **Life-Histories of Northern Animals:** An Account of the Mammals of Manitoba. Two vols. 1909

Sterling, Keir Brooks. **Last of the Naturalists:** The Career of C. Hart Merriam. 1974

Vieillot, L. P. **Histoire Naturelle Des Oiseaux de L'Amerique Septentrionale,** Contenant Un Grand Nombre D'Especes Decrites ou Figurees Pour La Premiere Fois. 1807. Two vols. in one.

Wilson, Scott B., assisted by A. H. Evans. **Aves Hawaiienses:** The Birds of the Sandwich Islands. 1890-99

Wood, Casey A., editor. **An Introduction to the Literature of Vertebrate Zoology.** 1931

Zimmer, John Todd. **Catalogue of the Edward E. Ayer Ornithological Library.** 1926

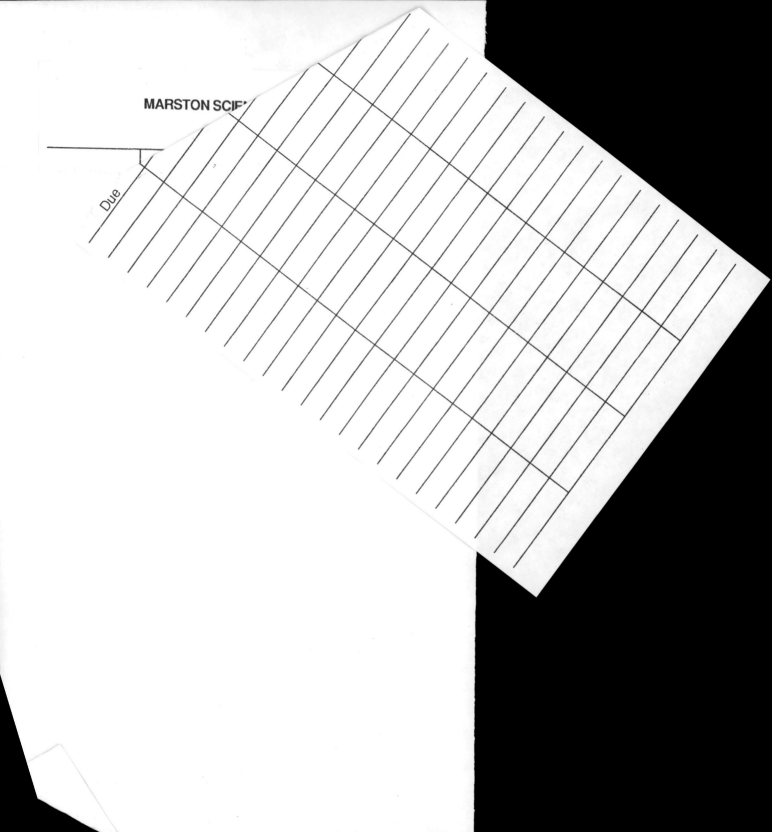

MARSTON SCIE

Due